# AN EIGHT-GENERATION GENEALOGY OF THE

# EATONS

## OF
## SALISBURY AND HAVERHILL
## MASSACHUSETTS

## William H. Eaton
and
## Philip E. Converse

HERITAGE BOOKS
2011

# HERITAGE BOOKS

### *AN IMPRINT OF HERITAGE BOOKS, INC.*

## Books, CDs, and more—Worldwide

For our listing of thousands of titles see our website
at
www.HeritageBooks.com

Published 2011 by
HERITAGE BOOKS, INC.
Publishing Division
100 Railroad Ave. #104
Westminster, Maryland 21157

International Standard Book Numbers
Paperbound: 978-0-7884-3145-6
Clothbound: 978-0-7884-8932-7

# PREFACE

The collaboration producing this volume is unusual to say the least, since the junior author writing this foreword has never met the lead author, Rev. William Hadley Eaton. Nor could he have, for the Reverend died in 1896, 32 years before the junior author was born. Yet the Reverend deserves to be first-listed for reasons that go well beyond his overwhelming chronological seniority: he is responsible for the original conception of this project and for a substantial fraction of the text itself. At the time of his death in 1896, a fair portion of this manuscript, designed to carry the descendants of John[1] and Anne Eaton of Salisbury, Mass., out to the eighth generation, had already been prepared, with segments carefully wrapped in papers labelled "Ready for Printer." It never arrived at the printer because the Reverend died too soon. But it is our good fortune that these materials soon thereafter were lodged under the superb auspices of the New England Historic Genealogical Society (NEHGS) at Boston, Mass., where the junior author, already at work on the John/Anne descendants, found them in the manuscript archives about 1986 or 1987.

Our senior author, William Hadley Eaton, was born to David and Betsey Eaton in Goffstown, N.H., on Sept. 4, 1818. Technically, he was William[7] (David[6], James[5-4], Jonathan[3], Thomas[2], John[1]/Anne). He graduated from Brown University in 1845 and from Newton Theological seminary in 1848. His first pastorate was at the Second Baptist Church, Salem, Mass., from 1849 to 1854. He then served at the First Baptist Church in Nashua, N.H., from 1856 to 1870, and finally was pastor at Keene, N.H., 1871 to 1889, before returning to Nashua for his retirement.

## THE HISTORY OF THIS MANUSCRIPT

The Reverend was always interested in his roots tracing to John[1] Eaton the immigrant, a Proprietor in Salisbury, Mass., in 1640. When an Eaton Family Association was formed about 1880 covering all of the New England branches of Eatons arriving in the New World during the Great Migration, he was an avid participant and soon became the primary expert on the Salisbury and Haverhill Eatons. Before 1890 he published a genealogy of the first four generations of this Eaton branch under the aegis of the Association. Since there were only two sons of John[1] making up the second generation, this was not as long a work as it might appear. Nonetheless, it was well done and has been the primary reference for serious students of the John/Anne clan of Eatons since its publication.

By 1890, the Reverend was already at work on the much more massive project of extending his four-generation compilation out to eight generations. This extension brought the record close to the Reverend's own times: whereas there were eighth-generation births in this Eaton line as early as 1780 and as late as 1900, the great majority of the eighth generation had been born in the decades of the 1820s, 1830s and 1840s. This meant that the vast bulk of members of this Eaton generation were still alive in the 1880s, and of an age where they had some retrospective familiarity with the two and sometimes three of their preceding generations, i.e., back to the fifth generation. And while the Reverend was experienced in courthouse and cemetery searches in the style of family historians of the day, he also organized a major effort to tap the firsthand ancestral memories of relevant Eatons all over the country. He developed a form on which Eatons addressed by mail could report in a systematic way the family situation of their own generation and their knowledge of their immediate forebears. It is not entirely clear how he targeted particular Eaton families (city directories may have helped), but he did receive returns from many relevant Eatons in the midwest and west, as well as New England. He also personally interviewed many Eaton elders in various areas in New Hampshire and Maine. In the process he harvested some testimony as to family linkages that might not have been reconstructible from documentary sources alone. This trolling for oral-history information went on for a decade or so in the latter 1880s and early 1890s.

As the summer of 1896 approached, the Reverend appeared to be coming down the home stretch with this crowning eight-generation genealogy. His death then cut the project short. The manuscript passed into the hands of a relative, General John Eaton of Washington, D.C. The General himself died in 1906, but had had the splendid sense to deposit the manuscript with the NEHGS in Boston in 1904. The deposit includes not only the bundles of text ready for the printer, but all sorts of supporting papers, including some of the returns from the Reverend's mail surveys and a large assortment of correspondence with Eaton informants.

This treasure trove was a godsend to the junior author attempting to reconstruct the lineage of his mother, Evelyn[11] (Eaton) Converse (Daniel E.[10], Daniel B[9]., Elisha[8-7], John[6], Elisha[5], Samuel[4], John[3-1]). Among other things, I was charmed to find submissions of forms with accompanying letters written a century earlier by my great grandfather Daniel Brown Eaton.

This "find" was also enthusiastically received in other quarters, but most notably in Seabrook, New Hampshire. This small township, which now makes up the southeast corner of the State of New Hampshire just over the state line from Salisbury, Mass., has had a peculiar jurisdictional history that has left many of its vital records in a fragmentary state. This history is too protean and complex to review in detail here. Suffice it to say that in the beginning the land area which is now Seabrook straddled the first town lines established by the Massachusetts Bay Colony, which at that time controlled the whole coast of northern New England. The southern part of proto-Seabrook was the northern extreme of the large Salisbury grant, extending a number of miles inland; and the northern part was the southern extreme of the Hampton grant, also large, which after a while (1680) was turned over to the newly independent royal province of New Hampshire, which meant that proto-Seabrook not only straddled town lines, but province and later state lines as well (see Maps #3-4; also Sidebars #3-4). In other words, until 1768, when Seabrook attained town status, now all within New Hampshire due to the 1741 change in the province line, the area had been a split jurisdiction, both pieces of which were always on the outskirts of somebody else's town center. This is not good for record-keeping. At the outset, for example, the villages of Salisbury and Hampton, only 10 miles apart by the "country way," kept adequate public records, especially for their villages proper. Inhabitants of the *southern* part of the proto-Seabrook area, where all our Eatons congregated in large numbers, had their records kept in Salisbury. This means that classic texts such as David W. Hoyt's *Old Families of Salisbury and Amesbury, Mass.* are good sources for the first generations here, despite the fact that these citizens of Seabrook-to-be were somewhat peripheral to civic activity in Salisbury village, and were less adequately documented as a result.

After the province lines changed and the inhabitants of the southern part of the proto-Seabrook area found themselves suddenly in New Hampshire, Salisbury record-keepers no longer had responsibility for them. They were for over 25 years an outpost of the parish of Hampton Falls, itself a southern outpost of the area's main center of activity at Hampton village. And even after Seabrook township was established in 1768, the southern (Eaton) part of the district was in some continued confusion since South Hampton, N.H., carved out as a new township to the west of Seabrook soon after the province line moved south, felt it had been guaranteed some kind of access to the sea across the southern end of Seabrook. The status of this claim, which was still in litigation well into the 19th century, mainly affected the south end of Seabrook's beach and hence access to the rich fowling and clamming grounds there.

All of these circumstances affected the keeping of the vital records in the southern neighborhoods of Seabrook, especially prior to 1768, but to some degree thereafter. In the latter regard, Stearns (1908, p. 1489) recounts a tradition that some inhabitants so resented their transfer from Massachusetts to New Hampshire that for several decades they still claimed to live in Salisbury, and refused to record their births, marriages and deaths in any New Hampshire jurisdiction, even after they were obliged to pay taxes to the new Seabrook authorities. Such determined non-report may be overstated, but particularly prior to 1768 and to some degree thereafter, vital records for Seabrook had rather feeble coverage, and some of the local micro-history can only be discerned in episodic records kept by local ministers and other interested private citizens.

This long-term jurisdictional chaos makes Seabrook in general, and southern Seabrook in particular, a sort of "black hole" for New England genealogy. If we couple this phenomenon with another fact, that the most common surname in southern Seabrook, by an unbelievable margin over nearly 300 years, has been Eaton, then it is clear why the Reverend's manuscript, based as it was on late nineteenth-century interviews and surveys, was so welcomed by historians there. The reasons for such an extraordinary Eaton density in this very spot are discussed in Sidebar #8, p. 230; but the short answer is that the enduring centroid for the Eaton population in southern Seabrook lies barely more than two miles, as a crow would fly across the tidal marshes, from the spot where John[1] Eaton the immigrant built his first dwelling in 1640 in Salisbury.

The Reverend Eaton spent many hours with South Seabrook informants trying to reconstruct this dense thicket of Eaton twigs and branches. Most centrally, perhaps, he had discussions there with "Squire" Oliver[7] Eaton (cf. Bio **#1218**, below). For much of the latter half of the nineteenth century, Oliver was arguably the Seabrook Eaton best known in the southeast part of the state. He served in the many paralegal capacities of nineteenth century practice, including estate settlement and a long term as Justice of the Peace. Locally immersed in a sea of Eaton families, he was fascinated by Eaton family history, and was reputed to have been the only Eaton in the region who had clearly in mind the prior century or two of interwoven Eaton branches. Reputedly, too, he had committed this lore to paper. According to the probate record, his papers were carefully preserved by the trustees of his estate after his death in 1892, but they have not been found in any more recent searches. However, Rev. Eaton was granted access to Oliver's genealogical papers by a trustee for the last three or four years of the Reverend's own remaining life. Thus it is fair to expect that discovery of the Reverend Eaton's manuscript gives us considerable purchase on what Oliver Eaton knew about the Salisbury/Seabrook Eaton lineages as of, say, 1890.

**Since the Rediscovery.** For obvious reasons, the junior author was concerned from the outset that this manuscript be cleaned up and made more broadly available to interested researchers. The only question was when and how. It was clear that the Reverend was a very competent and judicious genealogist for his day. At the same time, fugitive information had been unearthed in Seabrook in the interim that the Reverend had never encountered, which required a few rearrangements of his Eaton tree in the 1700-1850 period. In addition, one sturdy Seabrook branch which must have mystified the Reverend, can now be appropriately tied into the main trunk. This Seabrook spadework was only possible because of the sterling efforts of a cluster of local and family history researchers there, capped by the enthusiastic and creative help of Evelyn Fowler, an active member of the Historical Society of Seabrook and a

long-term researcher on Seabrook data and lore. Evelyn in turn has
critically assembled years of work on Seabrook family trees compiled by
Ralph C. V. Eaton, Jr., Sadie Embree (now deceased), William Fellows,
Russell C. Jones (now deceased), Donald LaPlante, Donald Small
(deceased) through his son Eric Small, Evelyn Snow (deceased) and Di-
ane Soucy. I cannot say enough about the value of these contributions
to this part of the project. Again, some of the new information assembled here contained or implied revisions and additions that needed to be
made in the Reverend's manuscript before publication.

My own time was very limited before retirement in 1994. After
that point, I had a variety of competing projects on my agenda, but I calculated that I could a get an enhanced version of the Reverend's manuscript in camera-ready form for publication with at most a year or two of
part-time work. The optimism of this estimate hinged on one crucial
short-cut that I was prepared to take. John[1] the migrant had only two
sons. In 1646 he deeded the elder, John[2], his lands and proprietorial
rights to further land divisions in Salisbury, and took the rest of the family up the Merrimac River a score of miles to assume new rights as an
Original Proprietor of the town being assembled at Haverhill. These
rights in due time he deeded to his younger son Thomas[2]. Thus this Eaton clan breaks very cleanly in the second generation into two main
branches. The Salisbury/Seabrook branch from John[2] is visibly the
larger of the two; the Haverhill branch from Thomas[2] arguably the more
venturesome and has on average more eminent descendants. Since I am
from the former branch, I had never done a stitch of fresh research on
the Haverhill branch. Nor had I, alas, even examined closely that part of
the discovered manuscript. But the Reverend was of the Haverhill
branch, so he would be the ruling expert there. Hence my shortcut was
that I would simply copy the Reverend's text verbatim and uncritically
for that whole Haverhill branch. Indeed, this plan was one reason for
putting the Reverend in as the senior author.

Eight months after retirement I was well on schedule, finding my-
self already almost halfway through my computer entry of the sixth generation. Then I came to a calamitous realization: the Reverend had not
yet sent the materials to the printer because he had chosen to do the
Salisbury branch first, and had as yet hardly begun to continue his own
Haverhill branch beyond the fourth generation, with their fifth generation child rosters. This had not been apparent to me earlier, because
there were indeed some Haverhill-branch mini-biographies out through
the eighth generation. I had not examined them, and the fact that they
were not numerous was not alarming: I knew already that it was the less
populous branch. But early in text entry for the sixth generation I began
to wonder about child rosters to be carried over to generation six in the
Haverhill branch that had not even been presented in the Reverend's
treatment of the fifth generation. Most obviously, I discovered that the
Reverend's own twig, which had removed from Haverhill to Goffstown
about 1760, had vestigial coverage even in Generation V, and nothing

about the Reverend himself was to be found.  Indeed, on closer inspection, I found that his treatments of the sixth generation broke off exactly at the point where the next biography in the logical order would have been that for his oldest uncle, Samuel[6] of Goffstown.

This was a crisis point.  Either I had to accept a delay of unforeseeable length to pursue primary research on the Haverhill branch, or cut my losses by converting this manuscript to a study of the Salisbury branch alone.  It was six years later that I returned to text entry, so it is clear which fork I took.  Some readers may be happy that I did.  I can put numbers on the difference this has made in the scope of coverage of this manuscript.  The Reverend's manuscript that was interrupted by death had biographies of only eight adult males of the Haverhill line in the fifth generation, and listed only 71 children sired by them.  My revision of the fifth generation contains 19 adult biographies, associated with lists of 157 children.  Contrasts for coverage in later Haverhill generations would be even more dramatic.  This is a great gain.  It even left me wondering whether I should continue to list the Reverend as the senior author, since I have by now written more fresh text than he provided.   I have decided to stand pat on that.  There is a distinct loss, however, that the Reverend was unable to do much with his own branch after the fourth generation.   I think at some points, easier access to far-flung information--and the Haverhill branch scattered much more widely than the Salisbury one--means that I have been able to include information he would not have found.  But there are numerous small riddles, and one large one that I call affectionately the "James of Deering Mystery" (see Appendix C), that are so close to his own time and twig that I suspect he could have resolved them off the top of his head.  For these we probably shall never have clear resolution.

For text where the Reverend had already laid down firm biographical material not needing any factual revision, I have tended to reproduce his text largely verbatim, although on many of them I have added material, often having to do with social context in which the person under discussion was operating, such as the level of his tax evaluations relative to the overall levels in his community, or details of land conveyances that were apparently pivotal in either family politics or migration decisions.

More generally it must be recognized that the style of genealogical description in the 1890s differs from what we expect now.  Odes of praise for the high character, charm and intelligence of many ancestors are no longer in fashion.  I have discarded some of the most purple of this prose; but felt it was only fair to leave some of this flavor just as the Reverend wrote it, he being the lead author.  Hopefully this will not be too jarring to the modern reader.  It is also true that research references were casual to non-existent in this period.  Since much of the Reverend's materials were based on conversations with protagonists or their near relatives, I have not cared to excise descriptions just because specific citations are missing. (I do, however, stress points at which oral recollections about certain predecessors clearly suffer some distortion, such as the common telescoping of generations and the like.)   In some few cases the Reverend mentions a written source, but so vaguely that I rarely can trace the item.   Again, I feel that preservation of these mentions has some value, even though I cannot vouch for their validity.

To define the main bounds of this genealogy, the Reverend planned to cover eight generations of this Eaton line.  We have kept to this basic design, with one amendment.  When the termination is defined by generation alone, some lines involving older children of older children may finish the eighth generation by 1820, while lines involving younger children of younger children may not finish the eighth generation before 1900.   Our rule has been to carry the serious mini-biographies of descendants through the eighth generation *or* thru 1850, whichever is later.  Thus we have some limited treatment of the ninth generation for Eatons who had largely lived their adult lives before 1850. More generally, we list children well after 1850, and consider other life events after 1850, but we do so opportunistically, when the information is at hand without a separate investment in further search.

## OTHER GENEALOGIES OF THE SALISBURY LINE

We have already mentioned the first serious treatment of the line from John and Anne of Salisbury, which is our Reverend's brief early four-generation one.  This volume encompasses and supercedes that in the obvious way.   The first four generations of the manuscript discovered at NEHGS began with a printed copy of that work, with numerous excisions, expansions and corrections that the Reverend had pencilled into the margins of that printed copy in ensuing years.   Of course we have honored all these revisions.

**The Nova Scotia Branch.**  David[5] Eaton from the Goffstown line out of Haverhill in 1761 took advantage of British encouragement for New England settlers to come and occupy Nova Scotia soon after British armies had driven out the French Acadian population.   This branch prospered greatly there, being joined as well by a cousin or two from elsewhere in the Haverhill line.  A great, great grandson of the Nova Scotia plantation founder David[5], Rev. Arthur[9] Wentworth Hamilton Eaton (William[8], Ward[7], John[6], David[5], James[4], Jonathan[3], Thomas[2], John[1]), a writer of some skill, became the genealogist of the Nova Scotia Eatons. Like our Reverend, he completed a short work on that branch in 1885, and continued to update and amplify the text until the late 1920s, near the time of his death.  In the early period, he was in touch with our Reverend and was aware of the progress he was making on this eight-generation genealogy.   There is correspondence to suggest that the younger A. W. H. Eaton wanted to present his material in the older William Hadley Eaton's genealogy, but as a separate and independent section, while the older author was not too happy with that idea, in part because the Nova Scotia treatments of descendants tended to be more extensive, decorated with poems, and the like. Our Reverend's death before the manuscript was completed ended the discussion, although later A. W. H. did append a postscript in his hand to the Introduction our Reverend had written for his volume, explaining why the Nova Scotia branch would be taken up as a separate section in the genealogy. Of course as we have seen, the manuscript never went to the printer, probably to the great chagrin of the younger author.

A. W. H. Eaton did continue to develop his Nova Scotia account, and had it privately printed in 1929 (cf. Bibliography). He had suffered another indignity, however, when in 1911 Molyneux included a considerable portion of his work on the Nova Scotia Eatons in her volume purporting to cover all of the ancient Eaton lines arriving in New England in the Great Migration. Indeed, she made the Nova Scotia branch more or less the centerpiece of her treatment of the Eaton line from John[1] and Anne, despite the fact that this branch was a limited minority even of the Haverhill Eatons and, of course, a much smaller fraction of the legion of John/Anne descendants as a whole. The popularity of her opus left Molyneux the reigning authority on the Nova Scotia Eatons, undoubtedly to the further chagrin of A. W. H. Eaton.

Under these circumstances, difficult decisions have faced us with regard to the treatment of Nova Scotia Eatons. Initially it seemed that it would be a great benefit to students of this Eaton line if we were to fold the Nova Scotia materials into their logical place(s) in this volume. This solution began to pale on us as we tried paring back Rev. Arthur Eaton's extended and flowery biographical treatments to some reasonable parity with our more functional treatments for the rest of this line. The problem was that we were setting aside a great deal of material that would undoubtedly be of interest to Nova Scotia Eaton descendants. Of course we could continually point out that more detail, including rhapsodic poetry, was offered in A. W. H. Eaton (1929). But this meant that our ideal of a presentation of this line "all under one cover" was rather hollow anyway. Since Nova Scotia by itself is a single integral subject, it also seemed awkward to scatter short segments of Nova Scotia across a unified treatment of Generations V-VIII. This led us to consider briefly reprinting the 1929 treatise as a separate Appendix of this volume, just as Rev. Arthur originally wanted. But our volume without Nova Scotia is already of substantial length, and we could imagine strong publisher resistance to tacking on extended material from a book already available as a publication elsewhere. Our final solution then became as follows. We would include the skeleton of the Nova Scotia line without further detail in the structure of this volume, assigning descendant numbers accordingly, and including the names of all Nova Scotia descendants in our Eaton index, so that lines exiting to Nova Scotia can easily be located, although with detail only provided elsewhere. (This general policy has not kept us from making annotations in our skeletal listing showing some of the places that members of the Nova Scotia branch emigrated to in later years, including numerous returns to the United States.)

At the risk of confusing the reader, we do give primary coverage to one cognate Eaton line in Nova Scotia. A nephew of the Nova Scotia pioneer David[5] visited him at one point and decided to settle there as well. The Rev. Arthur did not, apparently, choose to add this line (much of which retreated to the United States in due time anyway) to his genealogy of lineal descendants of David, so it is appropriate for us to provide this coverage in our standard form here.

**Molyneux (1911).** In the earliest days of my personal researches on this Eaton line, I learned of the work signed by Nellie Zada Rice Molyneux, and picked it up with high anticipation. I found some parts of it to be credible genealogy; but these were interspersed with an incredible number of pages littered with striking inconsistencies and assaults on the simplest logic, such as parents born after their children were, or who lived in three different centuries; cross-references that did not work; geographic references to town names that were often badly misspelled and lacking in state locations even for town names that most New England states have in common. Her treatment of the descendants of John[1] Eaton before picking up the Nova Scotia history after 1760 was well done up through Generation IV but after that dissolved into a fragment or two, including an absolutely bizarre assignment of the Revolutionary pensioner David[6] in Seabrook around 1830 and 1840 to a birthplace in Connecticut within a totally different Eaton clan. Furthermore it was hard to believe that any human mind had looked at the page proofs with a critical eye. I rapidly concluded that anything in the volume that might be correct about the John/Anne line I already knew; and that anything new could easily be garbage. I set the book aside.

Eighteen years later, as I neared the completion of my research on the Haverhill branch, I decided that I must as a last act of contrition review the thousands of family group sheets for the Eaton surname lodged at the Mormon Family History Archive in Salt Lake City. These sheets are unreviewed submissions from informants who are, for the most part, novice researchers prone to all the elementary errors of this trade. I assumed that most of what I would encounter I already knew; and any surprises would have to be put through the ordeal of more primary research validation. But I undertook this mind-numbing expedition on the off chance that (e.g.) I might learn of a fugitive family Bible somewhere that had never reached the public domain, that might fill in an important chink or two.

I did catch two or three glints of this sort, although nothing very earth-shaking. But in the process I learned something about Molyneux (1911). A saving grace of this family group sheet collection, accumulating apparently since the early 1930s, is that donors are asked to provide documentation for their submissions. And Molyneux absolutely dominates these citations: even now, she is the reigning authority for the Eaton lines of old New England. This led me to feel that as another act of contrition, I must return to Molyneux and go over her work with a fine-tooth comb, comparing it with mine, not only for the Salisbury Eatons, but for the Reading, Dedham and Plymouth lines as well, which I had also researched for reasons to be introduced momentarily.

This return to Molyneux was greatly illuminating on two absolutely central points. The first was a sudden understanding as to the hodge-podge mixture of credible genealogy with wild and self-impeaching inferences. This revelation began as I was reading early in the John/Anne module, and began to encounter passages five or ten lines long that were exceedingly familiar to me. Not only did I know they were Reverend William's writing directly copied from his four-generation publication; but they were passages that I had, with perhaps a light editing here or there, simply transferred into the text of this genealogy. These copyings were without quotation marks; and while citation styles in 1911 were much less precise than they are today, Rev. William's name is never mentioned in the bibliography; and there is no item there which could conceivably refer to his four-generation publication.

This discovery brought two moments of panic. First, I wondered if I could be sued for plagiarizing from Molyneux (1911), because we would have verbatim copy without my acknowledging that she had "authored" it!   I relaxed on this matter because after all, I was making the Reverend the lead author of this new genealogy, and he would surely be legally free to use work that he had published in his four-generation Eaton genealogy decades before Molyneux copied it without attribution for her 1911 volume. But then I had a new panic: had Molyneux discovered the Reverend's eight-generation manuscript and copied from that as well, thereby getting into actual publication first?   A quick assay showed that this was not true, either. Indeed, some of her copying from the four-generation publication ignored pencilled corrections the Reverend had made in the manuscript I had found; and of course her complete collapse into incoherence and error once beyond Generation IV for the Salisbury branch was the final guarantee.   In short, Nellie did credible work when she was merely copying others verbatim (for the Nova Scotia twig as well as the more basic work of Reverend William); but in the sporadic solo flights, she seemed to have only a limited idea of what she was doing with our particular Eaton line.

The second great illumination about Molyneux is in some senses more charitable. Nobody can review her book without being impressed by the sheer volume of  raw materials that have been assembled for the publication.  This is especially true if we keep in mind the glacial pace at which data-ferreting still had to proceed  in 1900.  The materials from England alone either must have required some residence abroad or the wealth to hire stringers there under conditions of what we now call snail mail. The total corpus assembled seems likely to have occupied a part-time researcher for at least three decades. Now it turns out that while Nellie herself declines to reveal her own birthdate, she could not have been much over 50 when she deposited the manuscript with the printer, and correspondingly younger if the publication was a slow process. While she may have been involved as an accessory in the later stages of data collection, it is extremely unlikely that, being a woman who married and had her own children young, she organized the whole work. Who then launched it? An obvious candidate would be her mother, born Ellen Amy Eaton and the keeper of the Eaton flame in the Rice family where Nellie was reared. Mother Ellen also appears to have had rather advanced formal education for a woman of her era (a female seminary with "Polytechnic" overtones as well). Indeed, it is quite possible that her educational attainments were well beyond those of her daughter. This mother died in 1903, when Nellie was probably not yet 45. And it is easy to imagine deathbed scenes in which Nellie, who as eldest child may well have helped in the later stages of the assembly, is exhorted to preserve this life's work at all cost, by publication if possible, along with instructions as to what remained to be done before a publisher could be approached. As we have said, this can put a more charitable light on the enterprise, because Nellie may well have been little more than a naive bystander in the operation, without much feel for genealogy or any way of knowing that lengthy passages in her mother's hand had been simply copied from other published material; and mother Ellen herself may have had every intention to document these copyings more properly for any final publication. Nellie's inexperience can also explain the total lack of proofreading for the publication, and any number of other oddities which have escaped even a quick-and-dirty editing.

This scenario does leave one matter unexplained. We have been unable to find sign of an acknowledgement from Nellie as to any contribution to this enterprise by her mother or, for that matter, anybody else. If such appears, it is not in the place where one would nowadays expect to find it. Then again, as an unschooled amateur, even this gracious touch may simply not have occurred to her.

## TWO ADDED FEATURES

Although the basic structure of this genealogy was laid down by the lead author, we have added two small features on our own. These deserve explanation here.

**The Census Project.** We could probably have completed the new primary research on the Haverhill branch of Eatons in three years rather than five or six, had we resisted one very labor-intensive addition to our agenda. In doing the Salisbury branch we had found it illuminating to challenge ourselves to account for Salisbury Eaton mentions in the manuscripts of the seven Federal Censuses, 1790-1850.

As we became immersed in reconstructing the Haverhill branch we thought it wise to do the same. Here, however, this Census effort, mainly useful in tracking Eatons who participated in the great inland migrations touched off by the fall of Quebec in 1759, took on a more urgent tone. The Salisbury branch of our Eatons, when they left the natal area in Salisbury/Seabrook, tended to move primarily northeast to Maine. A few went west of the Merrimack River, and even to Vermont, but most of those not headed for Maine stayed in eastern New Hampshire at places like Sandown, Candia, Pittsfield and Gilford. The Haverhill branch was a mirror image, headed further to the northwest. Very few families went to Maine and almost none east of the Merrimack. The main flow was to the west half of the state, to places like Goffstown, Hopkinton, Warner, Sutton and Grafton County. A smaller but noteworthy fraction crossed into Vermont. This latter flow of traffic began to cause diagnostic confusion, since the other old New England lines of Eatons--even those who had gone from Reading or Dedham to Connecticut for a generation or two-- were moving if at all, in considerable numbers to the same areas of land openings that the Haverhill branch was buying up. This was especially true in the period between 1760 and the Revolution; after the Revolution the Eaton lines around Boston and in Connecticut began serious moves westward into New York, Pennsylvania and Ohio.

Thus the river of migration of "our" Eatons from Haverhill mingled with these rivers of "other" Eaton lines. And it seemed that the only safe way, if far from perfect, was for us to get all the old New England lines of Eatons into focus at once, the better to separate migrants who are "our Eatons" for the purposes of this volume, from those with the same given names who are not. This is why we decided to take on the task of identifying genealogically *all* Eatons named in the first seven Federal Censuses for New England. This involved several stages. First, all Eatons were catalogued from these Censuses for the six New England states. Meanwhile we were getting under computer control family trees for the other Eaton clans from Reading, Dedham and Plymouth, no mean job in itself. Finally we could go to work with matching and sorting across these two data sets.

Although it was annoying to be spending enormous amounts of time on Eatons who were in majority not even ours, we decided that this long labor could be turned to some collective good by keeping close track of our work and publishing as appendix material in this volume our genealogical identifications (if any) for all Eaton Census sightings in at least the three states of Vermont, New Hampshire and Maine. (We did some work in the southern half of New England as well; but since our Salisbury line of Eatons very rarely migrated southward before 1850, the returns of use to us in the southern tier of states was seen very early to be vanishingly small.) All of this Census work was enormously time-consuming, but reasonably successful. With caveats explained at the outset of Appendix B, we felt we could identify plausibly over 87% of Eaton

<u>sightings</u> (not <u>individuals</u>, which is a somewhat different calculation) over these 60 years of the Census in northern New England, while greatly enhancing the accuracy of our distinguishing Haverhill/Salisbury migrants from the several other large Eaton lines.

The fact that we have substantial control over all of the old New England Eaton lines pays dividends for a variety of inferences, since we can always check for confounding references. This is extremely useful, and can enhance confidence in identifications on somewhat circumstantial evidence, since we do not have to worry about the spectre of large reservoirs of unknown Eatons who may share these given names and rough ages on the same turf. This is not, of course, to argue that our control is complete. After the second and third generations, a small margin of known births "disappear." The majority of these probably died in childhood; but some went on to have progeny, and thus the "percentage control" we have erodes progressively with passing generations. It is also true that a small trickle of new Eaton lines arrives in New England, although mainly not until after the Revolution. (The 1850 Census question about birthplace has been indispensable in flagging some of these. And interestingly, at least as many of these new lines are founded by Eaton natives of Scotland and Ireland as are from old England itself.) Thus caution in assignment is always required; but we are dealing with a considerably larger known Eaton population than most students of one or another of these lines have ever had available.

**Sidebars.** A second added feature is the presentation of a number of sidebars discussing aspects of the broader contexts of the lives of these Eaton ancestors of ours. We decided to add these in part for fun, despite our recognition that most people in their right minds do not read a genealogy of this kind from front to back like a novel, but use it more like an encyclopedia to fish out wanted information from persons listed in the index as falling on page 43 or 179. Nonetheless, the point of these sidebars is to provide contextual information that is hard to insert when we are discussing individual life histories, generation by generation.

It is not easy to characterize all of these sidebars, for they vary widely in type. This just means, not surprisingly, that what we call the "context" of these Eaton lives is enormously diverse. One type, for example, helps us keep in mind the main challenges faced by all members of some of these generations, which were invisible in other generations. These are less the most general conditions impacting the lives of American colonists, which readers tend to understand, but rather conditions and events that were pivotal in the micro-region in which these Eatons lived. Examples here are summaries of the ebb and flow of fear about Indian raids in the colonial days along the Merrimac River; or the devastating effects on certain cohorts of outbreaks of disease; or collective Eaton participation in various military operations. Sidebars can also be used to cut across time within ancestral lines. This type allows us to summarize the long-term history of certain concentrations of our Eatons, such as in

Seabrook, N.H., or Deer Isle, Me., or to present the history of some few pieces of property which were held as homesteads by various of our lineages for a half-dozen generations or more. The constantly-evolving traffic flows of our Eatons along particular migration routes is another of this kind. Collective preferences for certain occupations or religious preferences can also be worth a sidebar. Needless to say, it is easy to position the synchronic sidebars (our first type above) within the cohorts or generations where they were most relevant. The diachronic ones, stretching across generations, are harder to know where to locate; so we have put these few together after the main text is complete (Appendix A).

## OUR POSTURES ON METHODS

All serious research requires careful attention to methods of inference. Proper discussion of these matters cannot be carried out briefly, but we can summarize a few of our postures on the issues involved.

**Error.** I once suggested to a friend who had collaborated with me on a set of genealogical reconstructions that we should write the work up for publication. To my surprise, my collaborator declined on grounds that there might be errors in our work, and that would be too embarrassing. This is, as it seems to me, exactly the wrong view.

I can fearlessly announce that there will be errors in this volume. I do not say this with pride: obviously any serious research, which we have tried to conduct here, is one long battle to minimize error. But no information of this complexity, based often on sources that are distressingly fragmentary, can hope to be processed to an error-free state. This is in the obvious sense "too bad!". But there are at least two reasons why it is in no way alarming.

The less important reason is a conditional one. That is, errors in genealogical work, as in all other types of inference, vary greatly in their size and hence their gravity. Take calendar dates for birth, marriage and death as an example. With great frequency, the fine details of these dates used in this volume, such as the day within a month, are not exactly the same in different public records. Certain offsets have likely interpretations: "birth dates" from credible sources that are a week or two apart usually (but not always) mean the date of actual birth vs. a date of baptism, and the user is likely to choose the earlier of the options. Marriage discrepancies are similar, being the date of published intentions vs. the actual marriage, and here we usually go for the later date. But some discrepancies have no such rules of thumb. However, it is rare in the extreme that choosing the wrong date of two different days within the same month, for example, will ever damage any other genealogical inferences one is likely to make. Many people die at night in their sleep; but observers have no practical way of knowing whether it was before or after midnight. But does it matter genealogically? Almost never. Nor if faced with slightly conflicting dates is it usually even worth the time to cast about to find some third account of the actual date, on grounds that two tries out three will be more trustworthy, since most of the time the third estimate C will not be independent: it will be a casual copy of either A or B in a way that says nothing about which of them is "right."

In short, some types of error vary in magnitude in obvious ways. And where the degree is trifling, it is a waste of time to pursue a "certainty" which is usually impossible in any event. John Tukey, dean of American statisticians in the latter half of the 20th century, once wrote (but did not publish) a list of what he called "Badmandments" for inference, meaning rules you should not follow, being the opposite of Good Commandments for proper inference. One of these speaks to our case above: "Be exactly wrong, rather than approximately right."

There is however a vastly more important reason for publishing highly plausible inferences, even though fuller information may some day produce minor corrections here and there, along with the occasional but inevitable huge correction that may turn an earlier conjecture totally upside down. This is the simple fact that the efficient pursuit of knowledge is both progressive and collective across researchers. It is only when erroneous facts or inferences are publicized that other parts of the interested community with conflicting or incongruent information in hand can descend upon component parts and make public what is wrong with them. If nobody proposes anything, all manner of private but conflicting views can blithely co-exist without the saving grace of correction in the marketplace of ideas. Who would know that somebody else has arrived at a notably different conclusion, if nobody publishes anything? So the same old errors persist, in conflicting pockets across the landscape. Indeed, this whole process of "collectivized inference" is exactly how scientific communication produces steady progress to more and more precise approximations of proper interpretation of reality. When Newton observed that if he had seen farther than most men, it was because he had been able to stand on the shoulders of giants, he meant just this: he was able to review the conclusions of earlier extremely thoughtful observers, and with them in hand, he could see how to improve upon them. Absent their "shoulders," his views would have had to start back where the ancients started and could not have carried as much further as he achieved. To be sure, in genealogy, some erroneous inferences will never be correctible because the historical record is permanently inadequate. But in that case reality is simply unknowable in any event.

**Uncertainty.** It is first useful for us to abandon the concept of total certainty about much of anything in genealogical inference. Even the most strict-constructionist doctrines of what is necessary to "prove" relationships fall well short of total certainty. As one example, the unvarnished statistics on extramarital conceptions, while they vary by time and culture, are always sobering to anybody who thinks of such conventional "proofs" (often in legal documents) as infallible. In this particular regard, the advance of DNA matching in the past decade has raised the bar much closer to total certainty than even the strictest constructions genealogical experts have placed on past practice. And yet while such matches may raise probabilities extremely close to certainty under ideal conditions, such that there are a lot of 9s after the decimal point, the probability still does not mount all the way to 1.00. (Think tainted samples, or record-keeping glitches in the lab.) If total certainty is required, no meaningful genealogical reconstruction can be written at all. In fact, if even extremely high probabilities of correct inference are required, there would not be enough certainty to build much of a chain of begats that would pass muster under the record-keeping regimes typically available to us from the deeper past.

So uncertainty is entirely a matter of degree, and genealogy, like most inference, reduces necessarily to a game of probabilities. Hence the only issue worth discussing is how one assesses these probabilities and how one communicates them in published genealogical research. For much inference where records are reasonably good and robustly interlocking, such as when multiple assessments from different points of view or independent data bases lead to the same conclusion (as is true of many of the relationships chronicled in this volume) it is probably valid to imagine that we have something like at least nineteen chances out of twenty of being right, and perhaps more like 99 of 100. And under such circumstances it is not customary to apologize for the fact than an assertion could possibly be wrong. No serious person needs to be told that.

As evidence becomes muddier and more circumstantial, it is not useful to refrain from making assertions; but it is important to flag them with at least some warning as to their weaker probability. Most genealogists turn under these circumstances to hedging adverbs like "probably," "perhaps," "possibly," and the like, and so shall we. As inferences get down into these less certain registers, it is often useful in addition to inform the reader in more detail as to how specific pros and cons stack up, so that if the reader has some relevant information bearing on the case, it will be clear whether or not it has already been taken account of in making that published inference which is hesitant, but worth suggesting as a well-informed observer's best guess. It also permits the reader to judge the case differently even with the same information. These additional discussions cannot always be done in total detail, especially in the kind of "extensive" genealogy represented in this volume, because of the complexity of some judgments. But we shall engage in this discussion of alternatives in quite a number of instances where the evidence we have unearthed is somewhat confusing at the margin, but where the stakes for the shape of the family tree are large.

One problem in communicating uncertainty is what we think of as the "weak-link" problem. That is, suppose we have normally high levels of certainty that A begat B, B begat C, and C begat D. Then we find the odds substantial (e.g., three chances in four) that D begat E, but for one reason or another the evidence is much more circumstantial. Then we are back on firm ground again in knowing that E begat F and F begat G. The case for D begetting E requires discussion and defense. But even if we underscore the weakness of such a particular link in the chain by discussing it, it subsequently is often easy for the reader to lose sight of. Therefore we have adopted a convention that in the classic genealogical form of identification with a chain of ancestors, any weak but probably serviceable links are kept flagged by writing them in italics thusly:

James[7] (Ezekiel[6], *James[5]*, *William[4]*, Jacob[3], John[2], William[1])

Here the weak link involves the supposition that this William[4] begat this James[5]. The odds seem to be much better than 50-50 that he did; but a substantial margin of doubt remains. The point of our convention is, of course, to confront the naive reader with the yellow warning flag of weaker-than-usual inference at every turn. This said, we hasten to add that we stoop to this uncertainty in print in only a handful of links over the whole volume, and even then, only in later generations. We are scarcely brazen enough ever to deal here with two successive weak links!

**Documentation**. We have already mentioned that because we want to use copy left by our lead author, who wrote in times when explicit documentation for assertions was less in style, this volume may seem at some points to be underdocumented. We must live with this, because we cannot always know what prompted all of his assertions; and we know that in many cases he is presenting information from oral or written interviews with individuals who had personal experience with the famlies involved.

However, there are other practical limitations on documentation in what we have just labelled as "extensive" genealogies such as this. By extensive genealogies we mean ones that literally cover thousands of descendants in the same treatise. An "intensive" genealogical contribution is typically of article length worrying some very narrow problem which is at issue in the literature, with the kind of title such as "What was Henry Jones's Wife's Maiden Name?" For intensive genealogical contributions on such narrow and usually contentious points, documentation is appropriately intensive as well: almost any assertion must be explicitly related to one or ideally several sources. This is less practical for an extensive genealogy, and in truth, for the most part, less necessary.

This is so for several reasons. One is the fact that much of the time we are working with genealogical linkages which have been unchallenged in published material for a century or more. Another reason has to do with the complexity of some of the information we use. For example, in those areas where multiples of our Eaton families have lived for extended periods, such as in Salisbury, Haverhill, Seabrook, Deer Isle, as well as Candia, Pittsfield, N.H. and elsewhere, we have assembled what we call "continuity guides" melding Census, taxation, land deed and mentions in all other available public records in time lines for each Eaton male. Some of our assertions, such as approximate death dates to within a year or so for people without death or probate records, float on the interlocking testimony of all or several of these serial records at once. Where dense contextual data of these kinds are available, it would be possible, although self-defeating for an extensive genealogy, to cite a dozen or two pieces of these record series, since it is the combined pattern that mightily bolsters the probabilies, not any single record.

Instead of such intensive documentation, we try to pursue a more selective strategy. We do not give elaborate citations for information from the most obvious sources, such as the manuscript Censuses, published town vital records and the like, except upon occasion when the information is "fugitive," meaning that it turns up only in some source that would not be obvious, such as a birth unexpectedly registered in a church in a neighboring town. We also are less likely to document intensively when there seems to be long-term consensus on a genealogical fact or inference than when a conclusion we reach diverges in one degree or another from past assumptions or is otherwise obscure or controversial.

One issue involving documentation warrants special comment. Because of the centuries-long concentration of the Eaton surname in the Seabrook, N.H., area, more vital dates (births, marriages and deaths) in this volume come from Seabrook than from any other single community. We have already noted the problems surrounding vital records here. This problem is especially acute for the "proto-Seabrook" period before the area was set off with its own town government in 1768. But it persists in some degree well into the 19th century. In 1998, William Haslett Jones published a compendium of vital statistics of Seabrook for the period, 1768-1903, "collected from all known sources." This is a considerable help in centralizing a lot of records which have survived in scattered documents. Nonetheless, for whatever reasons, the Jones net missed a surprising number of valid Seabrook vital records, especially for the period before 1850. I do not know how to account for this; but in comparing our vital dates in this volume with the Jones catalogue, the numerous dates we have that do not appear in Jones are usually annotated in my working notes as "Seabrook VR at Concord," which refers to the large trove of these records deposited by Seabrook authorities to be copied by the state government many years ago, and which now are accessible to researchers at the New Hampshire State Library in Concord.

----Philip E. Converse
Ann Arbor, Mich.
Apr. 4, 2003

# ACKNOWLEDGEMENTS

This genealogy being the product of two incarnations, one in the 1890s and the other starting in the 1990s, two sets of acknowledgements are appropriate.

Our senior author, Rev. William Hadley Eaton, wrote no formal section of acknowledgements before he died. However, he often graciously noted how helpful the subject of a sketch just completed had been in providing crucial information on a larger set of twigs covering that immediate family. He would certainly want to celebrate the more general contribution made by Oliver Eaton (#1218) in reconstructing the Eatons of southeastern N.H. And of course without the wisdom of Gen. John Eaton (#2967), then of Washington, D.C., in depositing his cousin's genealogy manuscript with the New England Historic Genealogical Society (NEHGS) in Boston in 1904, this genealogy would not have appeared at all. In this regard, of course, the diligence of NEHGS in preserving and cataloguing the materials has been equally pivotal.

Moving to the reincarnation, we want to recognize first and foremost the tireless help, over nearly twenty years, of Evelyn Fowler of Seabrook with local materials. She is quick to note the degree to which her own Seabrook materials have been assembled from the labors of many of her local colleagues, already listed in the Preface above. She also wishes to acknowledge the present and former staff of both the Seabrook, N.H. and Salisbury, Mass. Town Offices, as well as the staff and volunteers of the Archival Room in the Newburyport, Mass., Library.

Since almost all of our fresh research was carried out before the marvels of the Internet for genealogy, we acknowledge the many informative hours we have spent not only at NEHGS in Boston, but at the library of the N.H. Historical Society and the N.H. State Library in Concord; at the LDS Family History Archive in Salt Lake City, Utah.; with less intensive assists from the Allen Co. Public Library in Ft. Wayne, Ind., the Burton Historical Collection in Detroit, Mich., and the Newberry Library in Chicago. Among a large number of other reference libraries and public records archives visited, we would like to mention the enormous help provided over one "emergency" weekend by Sally Malone, genealogist in the Morley Library in Painesville, Ohio.

Finally we are thankful for the considerable help provided on our Maine Eatons over dozens of interchanges by Beth Wescott of Bucksport, Me., recently deceased; and by Paul Eaton of Greensboro, N.C., with regard the likely roots of his Eatons of Harrington, Me.

# Table of Contents

# Sidebars

# MAPS

## Map 2. Detail (East side only) from 1639-40 Map of First House Lots in Salisbury, Mass.
(John[1] Eaton's unused house lot highlighted, upper left)

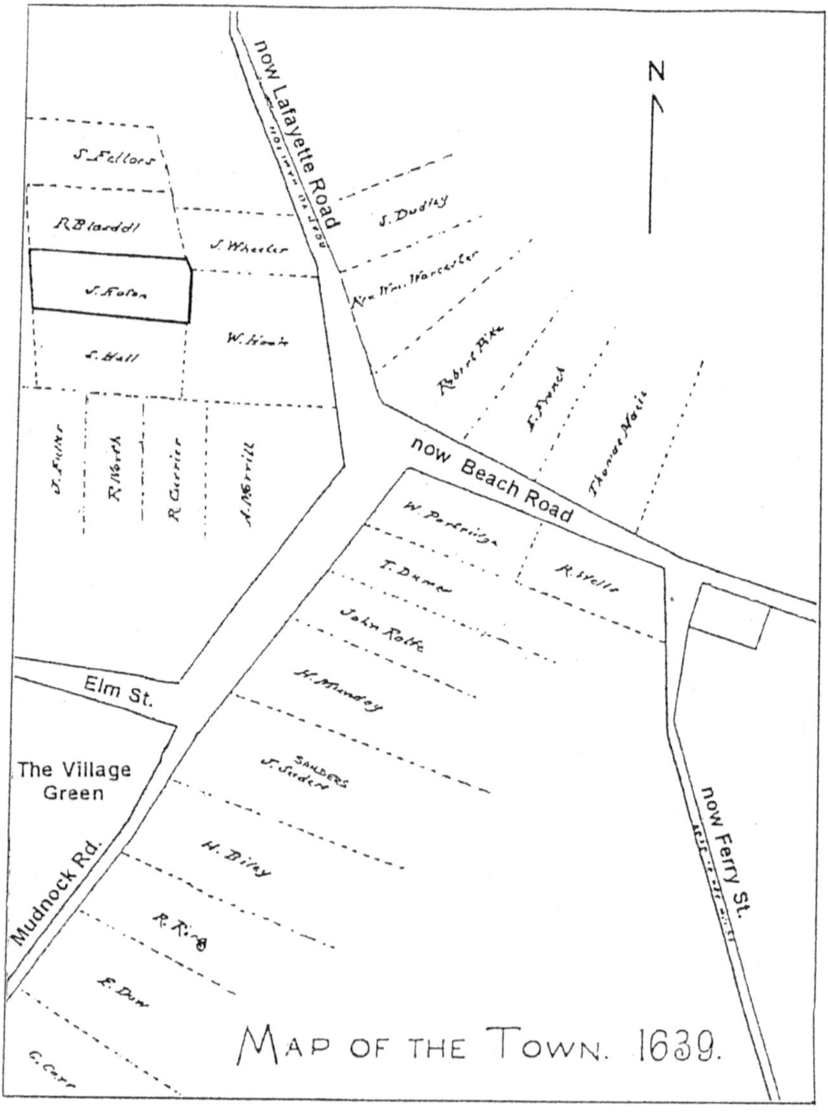

MAP OF THE TOWN. 1639.

**Map 3. Evolution of old Norfolk County, 1643-1742**
(showing the continuing subdivision of the original large Hampton
grant into six townships by 1742; and the land that went over from
Mass. to N.H. (shaded area) in the colony line adjustment, 1741.)

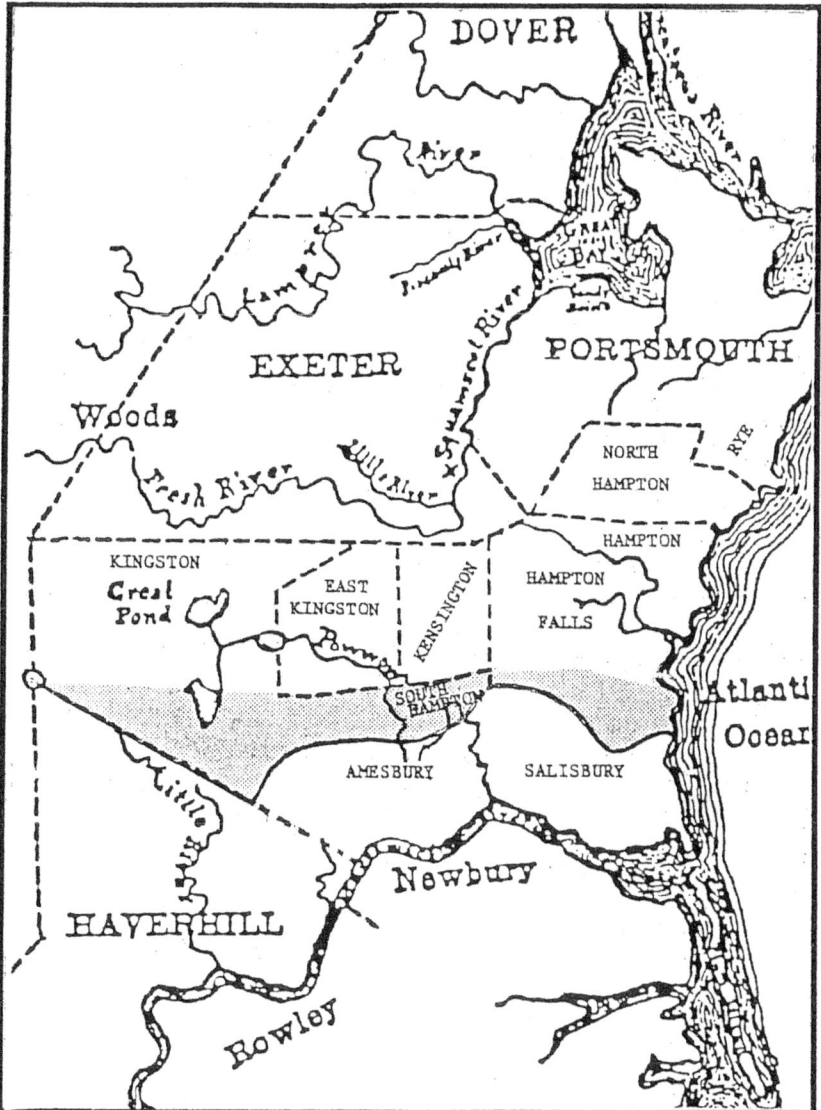

## Map 4. The Emergence of Seabrook, N.H., 1768

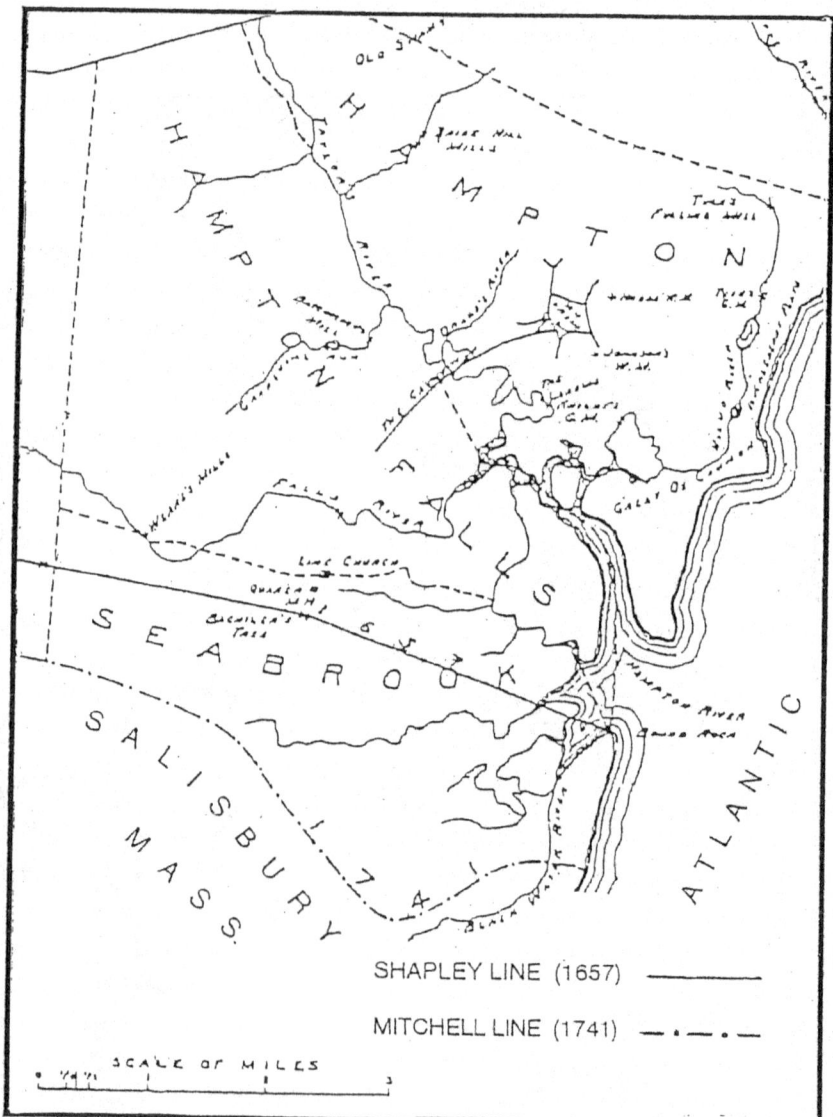

SHAPLEY LINE (1657) ———

MITCHELL LINE (1741) —·——·—

SCALE OF MILES

## Map 7. Southern Seabrook Residences, 1857

(Given a map of residences in Seabrook in 1857, we zoom in here on southern portion of the town, where all Eatons lived. For important further explanatory details, see Sidebar #10.)

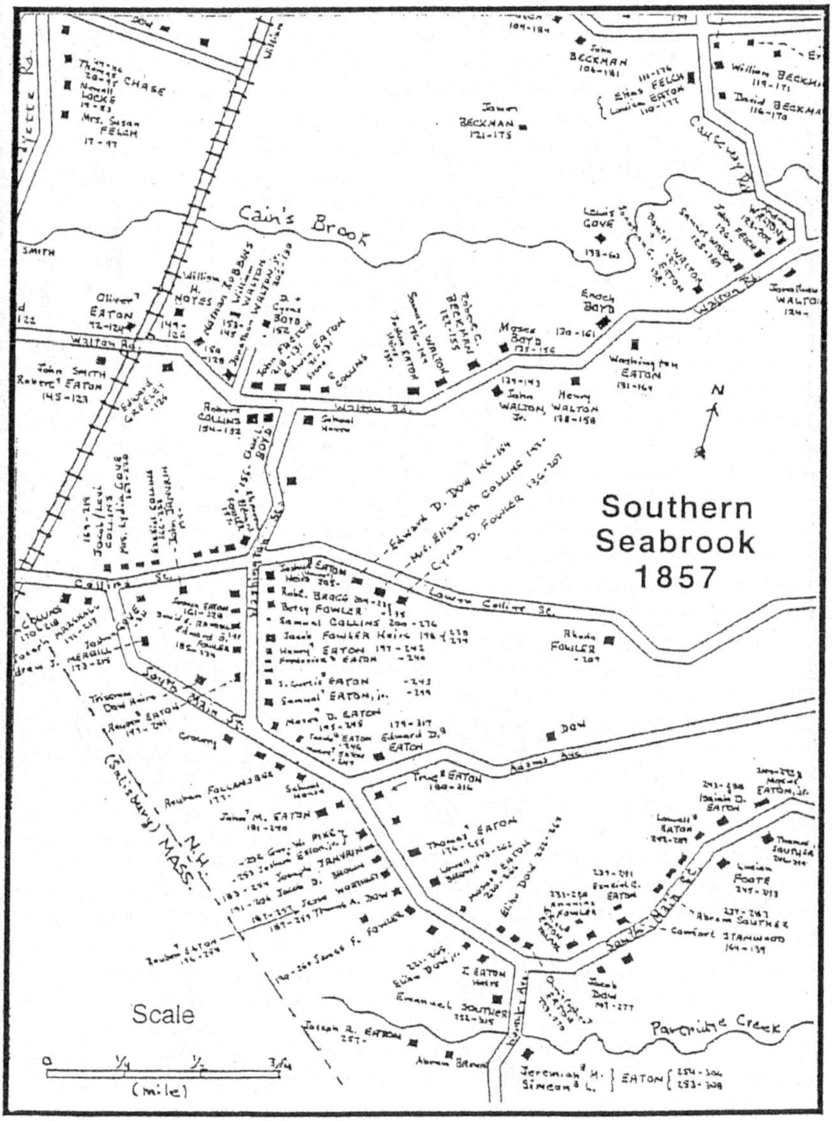

xxx

**Map 8. Eaton Households, Salisbury vs. Seabrook, 1884-92.**
(For further discussion, see Sidebar #8, p. 230.)

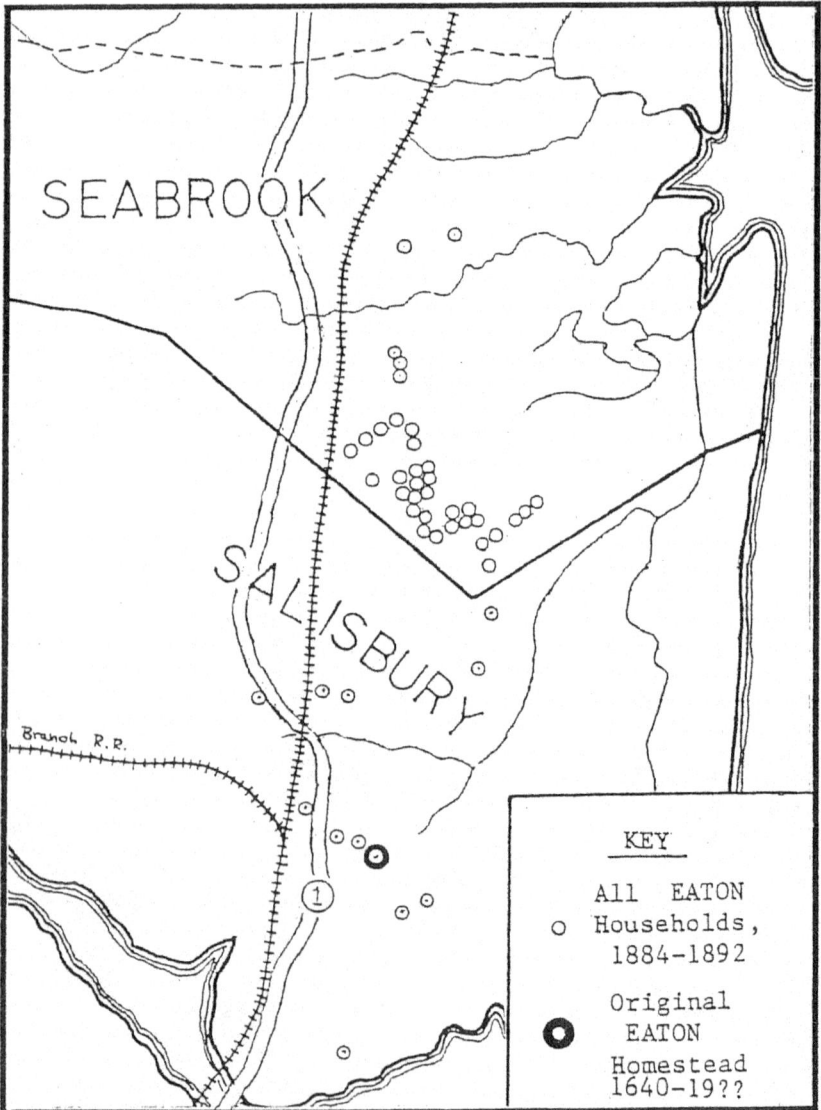

# INTRODUCTION

## The Eatons in Old England

According to the best authority, the surname "Eaton" stems from the Old English words *eá* for water or riverside, and *tún* for village or farmstead (Harrison, 1967). A place of origin which is a "town on a river" is not particularly distinctive; and we might therefore expect that the Eaton surname, while certainly not among the hundred most common English surnames in the past 500 years, nonetheless could have originated independently in various parts of Merry England.

The senior author of this volume, in his original 1896 manuscript, included a brief Introduction which took a "wide-angle" view of Eatons in England. By this we mean that he took stock of all of the several Eaton tribes who arrived in New England during the Great Migration in the generation after 1620, rather than limiting his view to the old-world origins of that John Eaton of Salisbury, Mass. who was the sire of all the Eatons in his manuscript. He began this Introduction as follows:

"The six notable Eaton families of New England are descended, respectively, from:

Francis Eaton on the Mayflower, settling in Plymouth, 1620
John Eaton of Watertown, 1635, and later Dedham
John Eaton of Salisbury, circa 1640, later Haverhill
Jonas Eaton of Reading, circa 1640
Theophilus Eaton, first Governor of the New Haven Colony,
    with his brothers the Reverends Nathaniel and Samuel,
    [pausing first at] Boston, 1637
William Eaton of Watertown, then Reading, circa 1636

Of these founders of the New England Eatons, the immediate ancestry and somewhat earlier history of Governor Theophilus and his brothers is known and has long been in print. We also have information concerning the English towns or shires where some of the other Eatons seem to have originated. Thus John Eaton of Dedham was from Dover, and William Eaton was from Staple, both in the County of Kent."

The old manuscript went on to note that the origin of the John Eaton establishing himself in Salisbury and Haverhill had never been determined, despite decades of search through old parish records in England. It was then argued that he was probably from Wiltshire, since he had arrived in close association with a number of migrants from that county, a fact which led to the choice of "Salisbury," the shire town of Wilts, as a name for the new plantation in Massachusetts.

A first compelling case for this John's town of origin has just been presented in the past few years, and as we shall see it is not in Wiltshire. This, along with other conjectures in the original version of this Introduction are obsolete. Therefore we shall not reprint more of the prior text here. We shall, however, proceed with new text which is very much in the spirit of the old Introduction, but based on newer information.

Let us start with a brief review of the geographical distribution of the Eaton surname in England. A special virtue of this wide-angle approach is that it encourages us to ask whether any subsets of the six main founders of the Eaton name in New England, as listed above, may have come from the same Eaton branches in the Old World.

## THE DISTRIBUTION OF EATONS IN ENGLAND

The International Genealogical Index (IGI) contains for England many million records of births and marriages mainly from parish registers since the sixteenth century, although some few vital records from earlier times are present as well. One way of deriving a crude estimate of the distribution of Eatons across the shires of England is to count the number of Eaton events in each shire, dividing this number by the total number of events for all surnames recorded for the shire. (The latter total can be efficiently estimated by multiplying the number of fiches needed for each shire by the average number of events on each fiche.) This ratio expresses the relative concentration of Eaton events from one shire to the next.

This estimate remains crude for several reasons, including the fact that in the current period not all extant registers have yet been logged into the IGI system, so that this data base remains incomplete. Despite such defects, we find that for names like Eaton there are ten to 100 times greater incidence of Eaton events in some shires than in others; and differences of this magnitude across shires are very unlikey to disappear or shift around dramatically as the remaining data are added.

Moreover, if we map the differences in Eaton concentrations found in the 1992 update of the IGI, we find the coherent picture shown in Figure 1. The picture is coherent in the sense that shires with unusual Eaton concentrations largely make up a contiguous stripe running from the Midlands in the northwest to Kent in the southeast. The only exception of any note is Glamorgan in Wales, and this shire had the next weakest concentration of any to receive shading. (The other apparent exception to the contiguity rule--the gap between London and Hertford--may

Figure 1. The Historical Distribution of Eatons in England
(based on the 1992 International Genealogical Index)

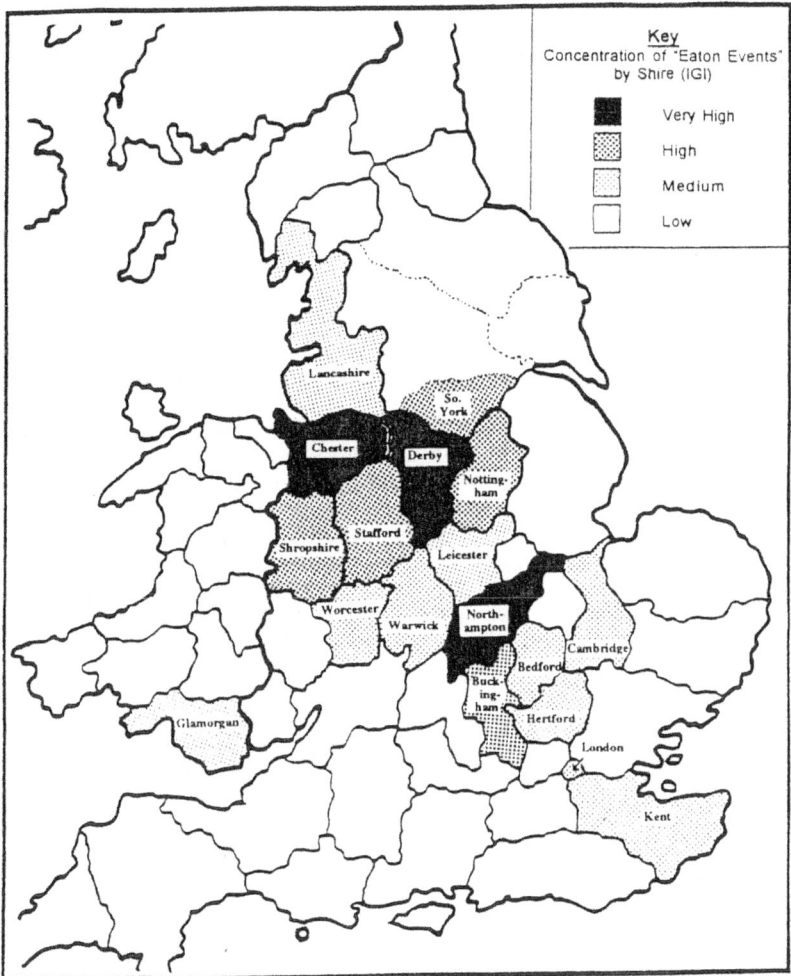

not be real, since the intervening shire of Middlesex is the only one in England for which no data have been processed, and it is unshaded for this reason rather than because of any documented absence of Eatons within its bounds). In addition, the picture is satisfying in that Cheshire, the shire usually singled out by Eaton historians as the ancient center of the family, joins with neighboring Derbyshire to form the point of greatest Eaton concentration, with Northamptonshire a somewhat distant third. Finally, the map shows that the core areas in black are for the most part neatly ringed with shades of lighter gray. This is just what one would expect if a clan originating in some narrow area continues to multiply there but also, over the centuries, disperses itself to some degree over a wider and wider domain.

Thus despite its crude base in the IGI, our map shows features that are very reasonable and dovetail well with other things we know about Eaton history. Given this demonstrated validity, we feel that we can venture to learn things from the map that are new. Here is one good example. It has sometimes been suggested (cf. Molyneux, 1911) that Eaton was originally a Welsh name as well as a Saxon one, since in Welsh the name had the meaning "the hill by the water." Our distribution map, however, implies that any Eaton origin in Wales has been negligible. The small concentration registered in Glamorgan is minor, disengaged from any main mass of Eatons and, as we shall see shortly, of relatively recent origin. There where we would expect some significant dispersion of the ancient Eatons westward into Wales from a point of origin "next door" in Cheshire, there is no sign of concentration at all. Indeed, the Welsh boundary alongside Cheshire and Shropshire is the only one of any extent where a heavily shaded area is not abutted by more lightly shaded ones. The Welsh border was clearly a barrier of some sort to Eaton dispersion: thus the report of joint Welsh origins of the name are dubious.

The main shortfall of this map for our purposes is that it reflects several centuries of Eaton presence added together, and wipes out any evidence of change in Eaton concentrations that may have occurred in the past five centuries or so. After all, we are interested in the origins of Eatons who left England before 1650 in the Great Migration, so that factoring Eaton clusters of 1850 into our estimates as well as those of earlier times could be a source of confusion. We can make a limited correction on the map in order to get a firmer fix on where Eatons were concentrated in the earliest period of these records. We do so by counting the Eaton events in each shire that occurred before 1700. Ideally, we would also compute the total of events recorded in each shire before 1700 as well, to use as a divisor. This is, alas, quite impractical, as it would require working through millions of IGI events to purify them to the pre-1700 ones, unlike the case with Eaton-events, where at most a thousand or two Eaton events must be reviewed to isolate the truly early ones. But a count of the pre-1700 Eaton events by itself, especially if compared to the total of Eaton events for the whole period, gives us some sense as to what a defensible pre-1700 map comparable to the one in Figure 1 might have looked like.

We have carried out this kind of review, with both expected and unexpected results. The most expected result is that the intense concentration of Eatons in Cheshire is of ancient origins. This is moderately true for Derbyshire as well, although much less clearly. At the same time, the intense concentration of Eatons that appears for Northamptonshire in Figure 1 is in a certain sense spurious: it occurs mainly because the data include many events after 1700. Before 1700, there was probably no unusual concentration of Eatons there at all. We did not find this result entirely unexpected, but very worthy of mention, since if we mentally correct Figure 1 by lightening the shading of Northhamptonshire considerably, the primacy of Cheshire as the ancestral home of the Eatons comes into much sharper relief.

What is most unexpected when we limit our data to the earliest period is the implication that pre-1700, there was quite an intense concentration of Eatons in County Kent, with secondary concentrations beyond what Figure 1 already suggests in the contiguous shires of Hertford, Cambridge and Bedford, as well as in London, the hub that links these shires with Kent. (The other shire that appears to have had a signicant early Eaton concentration is Shropshire, which of course is a satellite of the Cheshire epicenter.) This Eaton center in Kent immediately reminds us of the data above suggesting that several Eatons in the Great Migration came from Kent.

In the broad view, it is possible that the distribution of Eatons in the England of 1600 was distinctly bipolar, with one pole in Cheshire in the northwest corner of southern England, and the other in Kent in the southeast corner. This bipolarity does not rule out the possibility that some Cheshire Eatons might in truth have migrated to Kent and multiplied extravagantly over the next six or seven generations. But it is more plausible to think that these two Eaton clusters were originally unrelated. They may even reflect the differences between a Saxon strain of Eatons in Cheshire (although a thin Norman aristocracy was there as well), and a Norman strain in Kent, as suggested by names like "Peter de Eton."

Before turning directly to the question of how the Eaton families who moved from Old England to New England during the Great Migration may have formed subclusters of kinsmen and friends before the voyage, we should summarize a final product from our analysis of Eaton events in the IGI before 1700. Just as Eatons are not distributed evenly over the face of England, but turn up heavily in some shires and hardly at all in others, they also cluster in limited parts of the shires where they are concentrated, and are largely absent from other parts of those same shires.

Much of this clumpiness within shires stems from the accidents of life history of particular migrant Eatons at particular times. But a significant portion is easy to understand in terms of the same simple spillover model of migration we have already mentioned in connection with the fact that most shires where Eatons have congregated in special numbers are contiguous with one another. Because people migrate much more frequently in short hops than long ones (an effect still more marked in an earlier period of limited transportation and communication than it is today!), it follows that when Eatons spilled out of a core shire like Cheshire into neighboring shires, they were more likely to come to rest near the Cheshire border than in the farther corners of the same shire.

We encountered many examples of this effect in our map-making. One of the most dramatic turned up in the massive county of Yorkshire, covering an area roughly twice as large as the next largest counties of England, and one which could encompass eight or nine of the smaller shires of the land. In our first version of the map in Figure 1, we were surprised to discover that Yorkshire should be shaded black, along with Cheshire, Derby and Northhampton. Closer examination showed that this was true but misleading, for two reasons. One was that since the IGI lumps in the same barrel similar-sounding surnames, the "Eaton" entries include events involving persons of the Heaton name as well. And Heatons were very numerous in Yorkshire, adding enormously to the impression of "Eaton" concentration. When we tried discarding them for the purpose of the revised map of Figure 1, we not only got a more coherent picture over the English shires as a whole, but Yorkshire no longer deserved the rating of solid black. With pure "Eatons" alone, the area rated only the faint stippling of a "medium" concentration (cf. Fig. 1).

But even this adjustment was inadequate for the actual situation. True Eatons were not evenly sprinkled over Yorkshire. While there were a few interesting clusters of Eatons in the old East Riding of that County, including some on the North Sea coast, most of the Yorkshire Eatons were compressed in a small fraction of the county, centering on the area around the city of Sheffield. It is no surprise that this South Yorkshire area hugs the border of Derbyshire, a core Eaton province, just as the spill-over model would predict. Taken alone as a small part of Yorkshire, it rates as having a "high" concentration of Eatons, and we have tried to represent this on our map, although this is our only effort to convey concentrations in subregions of shires. Had we done the same thing for Lancashire, for example, the result would have been much the same as well, for most Lancashire Eaton events took place within ten or fifteen miles of the Cheshire border; and such events are rare over the more northerly three-quarters of that county. In the same vein, it is interesting to note that the pre-1700 Eatons in Kent are largely clustered in the north and east of that shire, most heavily near the road that mounted northwest from Dover through Canterbury to London.

## THE EATON MIGRANTS TO NEW ENGLAND

The above distributional information is useful context as we review the main bearers of the Eaton surname into New England in the general period of the Great Migration. The bare list of those migrants remains essentially as our senior author originally listed them (above), but we can do a certain amount of updating and correction on the basis of an intervening century of research.

We shall take these migrants in the apparent order of their arrivals in New England. In most cases, there is a good deal more detail known about the migrants themselves than warrants repetition here, and readers interested in particular lineages are encouraged to read more broadly in sources cited. Our focus here is restricted mainly to information about likely points of origin for these migrants in old England, which may be fruitfully laid against the distributional background for Eatons in the Old Country; and to their immediate geographical destinations in the New England colonies.

**Francis Eaton of the Mayflower**, arriving in 1620, is one of the more poorly documented of passengers on that famous vessel. He does not have a high profile even in the Plymouth colony; and his life before embarking for the New World has been hard to establish. We do know that he was accompanied on that voyage by his wife Sarah and a son Samuel, then a babe in arms, which gives some glimpse as to his life in England. We also know that he was by trade a carpenter, and was thus possessed of skills that were in high demand as the small band of Pilgrims tried to build the settlement at Plymouth, Mass. Presumably he had plied that trade in the old country.

Banks (1929) noted a record from Bristol, England, apprenticing a young man to a Francis Eaton, carpenter of that city, and his wife Dorothy, "the M[aste]r at New England." This raised hopes that Francis's origin had at last been discovered in the far west of England. One careful review of this case, however, published as Volume 9 (Francis Eaton) in the series called the "Five Generations Project" of the General Society of Mayflower Descendants (van Antwerp, 1996), raised serious issues about this solution. Most notably, the Bristol apprenticeship record is dated in December, 1626. The Mayflower Frances on the other hand had sailed with a wife named Sarah in 1620. This Sarah did not survive the "sickness" of the first winter at Plymouth. Francis then married "Mrs. Carver's maid," unnamed, who died in fairly rapid succession, without bearing him any children. Then at some later time, perhaps as early as 1624 or 1625, he married as his third wife a Christian Penn, who had arrived at the new colony in 1623, and who in due time presented him with three children in addition to the son brought over as a baby from England. This account does not seem to leave much room for a wife Dorothy in either Plymouth or Bristol.

These doubts about the Bristol origin have in turn been challenged by a carefully-argued case by Thompson (1997), ratified with further information by Greene (1997). To simplify somewhat, if the name of the second wife was Dorothy, and if the date of 1625 estimated on somewhat loose information for the birth of Christian's first child Rachel was not until 1626, as is very conceivable, then the emissary assigned to finding an apprentice for Francis Eaton may have set sail back to England before Dorothy's death, and hence used her name on the papers mistakenly. The case is strengthened a great deal by the marginal note on the papers indicating that Francis the carpenter was at that time in New England, along with another notation on the document offering the apprentice a grant of land in New England after his seven-year term was over. There were precious few other Englishmen in New England at that moment expecting to remain there for any extended time; and any that might have had such expectations were members of business operations which, unlike the Plymouth colony, were not granting any of their chartered lands to their settlers. Thus this carpenter Francis Eaton, still a legal resident at Bristol, almost has to be the Francis Eaton, carpenter, at Plymouth.

While further information may turn up to push the balance of the evidence one way or the other, we shall provisionally accept the shipping center of Bristol in the southwest of England as the likely point of origin for Francis Eaton.

**John Eaton, ultimately of Dedham, Mass.**, is believed to have embarked from England, 30 Apr 1635, on the ship The Elizabeth & Ann. He first is registered as residing at Watertown, on the north bank of the Charles River just west of Cambridge. By 1636, however, he had already established himself in the new town of Dedham, a dozen miles or so southwest of downtown Boston. He is generally presumed to have been the John Eaton who was baptized at Dover in the shire of Kent on 21 Aug 1611, son of Nicholas Eaton, a prominent Dover merchant, and his wife Katherine (Master). As Molyneux (1911), a descendant of this branch, has documented, this Eaton family had already resided in the Dover area for at least a number of decades, so that we can rule out the common and justifiable concern that perhaps John had come from elsewhere in England and was simply waiting in Dover to find transportation to America.

**William Eaton, ultimately of Reading, Mass.**, originally a husbandman of Staple in the shire of Kent, embarked for New England in the latter part of 1636 or early 1637 with his wife Martha, three children and one servant on the "Hercules & Sandwich." (Molyneux, 1911). This family resided first at Watertown, like John of Dedham, but remained there for a longer period. William was a proprietor of Watertown in 1642, but subsequently settled on the east side of the Great Pond in Reading, Mass., a new town about a dozen miles almost due north of downtown Boston. At this point we should introduce **Jonas Eaton**, who probably did not arrive in the Bay Colony until after William's party (although some have hypothesized that Jonas was the unnamed servant), and possibly as late as 1640, yet who stopped first at Watertown, and then quite quickly after William Eaton's removal to Reading, followed suit and settled in his neighborhood on the east side of the Great Pond there. Although our senior author treats Jonas as a separate sixth Eaton migrant to America (which he indeed may have been from the point of view of arrival time) few have doubted that he was very immediate kin of William Eaton. Some (Molyneux, 1911) have seen William as Jonas's father; but circumstantial evidence, such as the estimate that he was only eleven or so years younger than William, favors the hypothesis that he was instead a younger brother (see Little, 1909). In an important sense, then, William and Jonas did not represent a separate Eaton lineage; and so we can provisionally reduce these Eaton clans arriving in the Great Migration from six down to no more than five. It follows as well, of course, that Jonas like William was out of the area of Staple town in Kent.

**Theophilus Eaton** arrived in Boston in 1637 with his younger brothers, **Nathaniel** and **Rev. Samuel**. These gentlemen were sons of the Rev. Richard Eaton, an Oxford graduate who was vicar of the church of the Holy Trinity in Coventry during the period when his older children were growing up; and who later succeeded his own father as vicar of the large parish at Great Budworth in the heart of old Eaton territory in Cheshire (cf. Figure 1). Theophilus had early in his career become a leading London merchant, and an investor in the Massachusetts Bay Company. His brother Samuel had graduated from Cambridge and become a supporter of the Puritan movement. In 1632 Rev. Samuel was committed to Newgate Prison as a dangerous schismatic by Archbishop Laud, the powerful leader of the established Church whose oppression did much to spur the Great Migration of Puritans to America. Brother Theophilus supplied bail, but Samuel's freedom was endangered. In 1635, a patent granting Archbishop Laud and others broad authority over the American colonies produced an indictment effectively requiring the Massachusetts Bay investors to vacate their roles, thereby losing much of their investment. It was under these pressures that the brothers decided to visit New England.

Upon their arrival, they were of course the three most consequential Eatons in New England. Theophilus, looking for business opportunities in international trade, removed rapidly to New Haven, Conn., and soon became the first Governor of the New Haven Colony, a venerated leader to his death in 1658. Brother Nathaniel was pressed into service as the first "president" (actually, professor) of the newly opened Harvard College. This turned out to be a horrible choice, as Nathaniel was the black sheep of the family and was soon fired for a long list of misconducts involving drunkenness, fiscal fraud and other unbecoming acts. Chased out of New England, he retreated to Virginia and in no time was enmeshed in a whole new round of scandals there. His wife and all but one of his children, trying to join him in Virginia, took passage on a boat that was never again heard from.

Although consequential Eatons in a status sense, this Eaton branch was of very little consequence genealogically in New England. Rev. Samuel, who had accompanied Theophilus to New Haven, returned to England in 1640. Nathaniel also retreated to old England, leaving one remaining son, Benoni, being raised by a guardian in Cambridge, Mass. Theophilus, remaining in Connecticut, had a viable son who married but was childless and also returned to England after his father's death. The sole remaining trace of this branch in New England, Benoni, did marry in the 1660s and had two well documented sons at Cambridge, Mass., at least one of whom died unmarried early in adulthood, and the other may have as well. A further but unrecorded son Samuel has been imputed to Benoni on grounds that have some plausiblity; but one grandson by this Samuel left New England early, and the second has left no known adult record at all (Papers of the New Haven Colony Historical Society, Vol. IV, pp. 185-192). All told, this particular Eaton clan has vanished from our field of view.

**John Eaton of Salisbury and Haverhill, Mass.**, the progenitor of the eight generations of Eatons covered by this genealogy, first appears in the public record at Salisbury in 1640. After many decades of confusion as to the native area in which this John grew up in Old England, Douglas Richardson (1993) has finally provided a very satisfying answer, and with it, information about three generations of this John's forebears. We strongly recommend that interested readers consult this source for a rich array of details that we shall not reproduce here. For our immediate purposes, we report that John Eaton's family for these generations had lived in the northern reaches of Warwickshire, near the border of Staffordshire, a few miles northwest of the shire town of Warwick, which in turn is only a dozen miles or so up the Avon River above Stratford, Shakespeare's birthplace. One can draw a circle less than 2 1/2 miles in radius, just outside Warwick, which encloses more than a half-dozen hamlets mentioned in small legacies to road upkeep or churches in wills of John[1] Eaton's father, grandfather and great grandfather. The larger parish is that of Hatton; the main residences of this lineage were at Rowington early and Beausale ("Bewsall") late, the latter being the village where this migrant John Eaton actually grew up. His family lacked any high pretensions in the English social structure; but they owned land and during the 1500s had sufficient legacies to warrant the drawing up of wills. John himself was a skilled artisan, a cooper, a trade which would turn out to be in high demand on the sea-faring coast of New England.

* * * * *

We saw earlier that the six Eaton patriarchs listed by our senior author a century ago as arriving in New England during the Great Migration actually reduce at most to five distinct lineages, since two of them at Reading, Mass., were close kin, probably brothers. We can close this section on English origins with a suggestion or two which could lead to further reductions. At the very least, they help to simplify the geography we have covered; and in the degree that migrations tend to enlist clusters of relatives and neighbors, they may mean more.

The Eaton brothers who ended up in Reading and John Eaton who settled in Dedham all originated in the County of Kent, England. William and Jonas were at the village of Staple; and John of Dedham came from Dover. We cannot fail to mention that Staple and Dover are only about ten miles apart. As we have seen, there was a fair concentration of Eaton households in Kent in the decades before the Great Migration, so that there is no *prima facie* supposition that these two sets of Eatons were related or coordinated their migrations in any way. They did, after all, come on at least two and probably three separate ships, in differing years. But if we add to the proximity of Staple and Dover the fact that William, trailing John by a year or two, followed John's lead in lying over for a while at Watertown while getting his own bearings in the New World, then we can well imagine other Old-World connections between the two. Perhaps William decided to migrate after receiving attractive descriptions by letter from John. And perhaps the two were more than acquaintances, having a cousinly relation of one degree or another. More research in Kent might illuminate such possibilities.

There is another geographic simplification which probably has less cousinly significance, yet which is tantalizing nonetheless. We have noted that Theophilus Eaton, later New Haven governor, and his two brothers, were sons of Rev. Richard Eaton, who had spent his own childhood before going to Oxford at the parish of Great Budworth in Cheshire, the heart of the original Eaton country in our distribution maps. This Richard was a parish clergyman at Stony Stratford in Buckinghamshire, not far from Oxford, when eldest son Theophilus was born in 1590. The next year, however, he became vicar at Coventry, roughly twice as far to the northwest of London, and the other two brothers were born there. In 1604, Rev. Richard moved on another leg farther to the northwest to Great Budworth; but Theophilus, by then about 14, did not accompany the family there. Instead, he was sent to continue his studies at Oxford. In short, Theophilus spent his childhood from age one to 14 at Coventry.

Now Theophilus and the John[1] Eaton who is the patriarch of this genealogy were almost exact agemates, as best one can tell, both having putatively been born in 1590. And it turns out that Beausale, where we at last know that John[1] grew up, is a mere 8 miles from downtown Coventry, which thus was only slightly farther away from Beausale than the shire town of Warwick to the other side.

There are several reasons not to make too much of this sheer physical and temporal proximity between these two Eaton youngsters. In terms of the rigid English class system, they undoubtedly lived in vastly different social worlds. Moreover, while the clerical Eatons had originated in the Eaton bastion of Cheshire in the preceding generation, John's line, which may have originated there also, had been in Warwickshire for more than two generations. At the same time, Rev. Richard Eaton's position at Coventry was a highly visible one, and it is beyond belief that John's family in the near hinterland would have been unaware of his local presence. If there were kin ties at all, there might have been interaction. If not, the rural Eatons may at least have heard him preach on some high holy days, since Coventry was a more impressive ecclesiastic site than Warwick. Again, we cannot carry this too far: it is clear that young John[1] was not exposed to the heresy of Separatism in Rev. Richard's sermons, since even the Reverend's sons Theophilus and Rev. Samuel were apparently not drawn into the dissident orbit until much later times and more distant places. None of these reasons for caution, however, can rule out the likelihood that the Rev. Richard's family was salient for our John[1]; and especially if he had taken on Separatist leanings himself in his early adult years, he was likely to have known of the departure of the three Eaton brothers for the New World before he made his own decision to embark. This awareness may have helped that decision along.

More generally, it is of interest that all of these migrants save the first (Francis) originated in the two regions of England (Kent and the northwest Midlands) that our distribution maps show to have had the strongest Eaton concentrations entering the era of the Great Migration.

## THE NEW ENGLAND EATON LINEAGES COMPARED

Before we take leave of the several Eaton lineages arriving in New England during the Great Migration, it is of interest to compare their fates in the New World in a few basic particulars. This is possible for us because, for reasons outlined in Appendix A ("Eatons in New England Censuses,") we have invested significant time in tracing all of these branches in America. over subsequent years. (For reasons mentioned above, we shall not pursue the line of Theophilus[1], which was not a permanent migration.) Here we shall compare these four branches with respect to (a) their subsequent demographic increase from their founding patriarchs; and (b) the general trends in their subsequent migrations within the colonies or the United States. There are marked contrasts in both regards.

**Population Increase**. These four lines vary sharply in their rates of population increase. For opportunistic reasons of data availability, we shall consider how many children are recorded for Eaton patriarchs of the fifth generation from the boat in each of these lines. We shall count all births we have, including recorded infant deaths, for this sixth generation, lineage by lineage. This means we count both sons and daughters in this sixth generation, although otherwise we are proceeding patrilineally, i.e., we are not including offspring of earlier Eaton daughters whose husbands are not themselves also Eatons. This more or less halves the calculation of natural increase out of the founding father; but is a restriction forced by the data readily available to us, which are in most lines--save the Mayflower Francis line--limited patrilineally as well.

Table 1. Numbers of Children in Generation V,
by Eaton Lineages

| EATON LINEAGES | Child[6] N | Child[6] per Father[5] | Ave. Birth Year, Fathers[5] |
|---|---|---|---|
| FRANCIS[1] (Mayflower) | 66 | 6.0 | 1740 |
| JOHN[1] (Dedham) | 300 | 7.5 | 1745 |
| WILLIAM[1] (Reading) | 166 | 6.9 | 1742 |
| JONAS[1] (Reading) | 396 | 6.7 | 1757 |
| JOHN[1] by John[2] (Salisbury) | (229) | (7.2) | (1732) |
| " " Thos[2] (Haverhill) | (158) | (7.9) | (1741) |
| JOHN[1] (Salisbury): TOTAL | 387 | 7.4 | 1735 |

In assembling this table we subdivide two lineages. The Reading lineage is naturally subdivided because there were two founders of Generation I, contrary to the case elsewhere. But there is no point totalling these two lines, because all other founders are single persons. We also subdivide the line of John of Salisbury, the subject of this volume, because his history lends itself to this partition. He arrived first at Salisbury, and received proprietorial rights to land divisions there. After a few years he deeded all those rights to his elder son John[2], and removed some 18 miles up the Merrimack River to become a proprietor at Haverhill, Mass. Before he died at Haverhill, he deeded all his rights there to his other younger son Thomas. We separate these two branches of this lineage as we do throughout this volume, but put the entries between parentheses, and then provide a sum relevant to the single founder John[1] since that row is more comparable to the other table entries.

Finally, we add a column indicating the average age of the Generation V patriarchs who had any children at all. This is because the sixth generation can cover slightly different periods of New England history as we move from one lineage to the next. While the differences in this column are not for the most part very large, it is useful to know about them in evaluating entries in both Figures 1 and 2. This is because birth rates were beginning to decline in the later period covered by the sixth generation. On the other hand, rates of internal migration in the northeastern region of the colonies began to rise rapidly after 1759, and saw another spurt after the Revolution. Knowing how early or late in the 18th century the fifth and sixth generations occur for different lineages is therefore helpful, especially in the couple of instances where the differences in "real" chronology are largest.

As we see in Table 1, there are huge contrasts in the amount of natural increase in these Eaton lines by the time of the sixth generation in New England. Before placing too much weight on these contrasts, it is worth considering what artifacts may afflict our totals. Most obviously, any totals of children in a generation are likely to be underestimates in one degree or another, because some ancestors have dropped from sight, and the effect of these losses cumulates through the passing generations. With generations held constant, as we do here, the size of the shortfall can still vitally depend on the amount of diligent search lavished on a particular lineage. In this regard, the most shocking number in the table-- the tiny size of the sixth generation out of Francis--seems real for the simple reason that because of the historical prominence of the Mayflower, it seems likely that more diligent search by a larger array of well-trained genealogists has been carried out in the case of Francis than any other of these Eaton lines. Hence we cannot dismiss the small observed increase as merely due to inadequate detective work.

We do know that the Francis line had more than its share of sickness early; and as late as the third generation there were only three Eaton sons who married and passed the surname onward. This is quite a bottleneck. It is also true that more Eaton daughters married than sons in the early going, and their contribution to natural increase is hidden in our patrilineal data. In short, the contrast between the Francis lineage and the others appears to have a good deal of reality.

While there are other differences present in Table 1, they are much smaller and within the range that might be explained by factors like diligence of coverage, and so on. The joint Reading increase is awesome (559 children in Generation VI), but two founders are represented here, so that the average number of children per founder is only a bit under 300, and not greatly out of line with the two Johns. The fact that brother Jonas of Reading so greatly outproduces brother William traces in no small part to the luck of the draw whereby Jonas had five prolific Eaton sons to constitute the second generation, whereas William, along with John of Salisbury, had but two, and John of Dedham had only one. Differences of this degree in the early going simply multiply in later generations.

**Migration Destinations.** It is interesting to note that our four or five major early plantations of Eatons in New England array themselves in something like a semi-circle around Boston. If due north from downtown Boston is taken to be 12 o'clock on the face of a clock, then Francis Eaton at Plymouth is at 4:45; John at Dedham is about 7:15; the Eaton brothers at Reading (and John of Salisbury after removing to Haverhill) are a few minutes short of 12 o'clock; and John when at Salisbury is about at 12:35. If Boston is a hub, the spokes of which run into the hinterland north, west and south, then the most probable lines of migration of our Eaton lines radiate outward from Boston along these spokes. This is not an ironclad rule, of course. A major exception, for example, is the Samuel Eaton descending from Francis who came to Cambridge from Plymouth County to get his theological training; and who then settled for his lifetime in a pastorate at Harpswell, Me., directly contrary to the outward radiation prediction. Exceptions can easily occur, but the radiation model governs the bulk of migration flows in this period.

There is a simple story line to account for the likelihood of such radiating migration. In the conditions pertaining at the time, young men considering migration to greener pastures from their native places tended to learn about those pastures from travellers whom they encountered in local inns or public houses, the latter busy following the local artery radiating out of Boston. One such artery went through Salisbury to Portsmouth, N.H. and on to Maine; and Salisbury locals will be disproportionately enticed further outward on it. Similar arteries mount into southern New Hampshire through Reading and Haverhill; or southwest into Connecticut through the main artery that passed through Dedham. Of course cross-artery movement took place as well. For example, a substantial branch of Jonas Eaton's descendants removed cross-artery from Reading to Framingham, Mass., in the third generation, and thus had Boston to their northeast, instead of to their south. This was near the Dedham artery; and further descendants of Jonas who became refugees from Framingham moved outward to the northeastern counties of Connecticut, just as the refugees from Dedham did. It is also true that as spokes are followed farther and farther away from Boston, natural features of the landscape deflect those flows this way and that. For example, the Connecticut River runs north-south, as does the Merrimack above Lowell, Mass., where it enters into New Hampshire. These river "highways" are somewhat athwart the radiation lines from the Boston hub, so that when migrants radiating outward along their spokes encountered these natural highways, they often turned to the right to follow them.

The case of Plymouth is of particular interest to this model, since unlike the other Eaton plantations, the spoke out of Boston through Plymouth soon goes into the ocean. There just is not much "there" there. But by the same token, Eatons in the Plymouth area are not getting much in the way of enticing pictures of "outward" travel from passersby. One might then predict that absent word of such attractions, the Plymouth contingent would be much less likely to engage in migration at all. We shall soon find out.

For Table 1 we added up the sixth-generation children of each Eaton lineage. For Table 2 below we shall simply examine where the sets of children of each line were born. For each lineage we have a "ground zero" which is the county in which the old family homestead was located, converted to the county structure as of 1850 to provide further resolution; and we shall chart outward movement from this county of origin to other counties in the same state, as well as to other states. The figures for sixth-generation children in the native county are emboldened.

As we see in Table 2, each lineage has a more or less distinctive "signature" or fingerprint in the geography of its subsequent migrations. The most distinctive of all is that for the line of the Mayflower Francis, which has hardly migrated at all. Actually, using counties as our units conceals one fact about this line. Whereas all the other Eaton tribes still have sixth-generation births in the specific town where the migrant forebear made first permanent settlement, none of the Francis descendants represented here were born in Plymouth. At a much earlier point, the small and struggling family had removed from Plymouth to the town of Middleboro, Mass., some 17 miles inland from Plymouth. And 88% of their sixth-generation offspring were born right there in Middleboro. Only one other of these births occurred in Massachusetts, and this was at Dartmouth, in Bristol Co. next door. Four other births were in Maine, associated with the preacher already mentioned. And the final three were in the western part of N.Y. State.

This almost total lack of migration for Francis Eaton descendants is presumed to stem in part from the fact, already noted, that the route radiating from Boston into Plymouth County, unlike the other great lines of radiation, led to a small *cul de sac*: travellers' tales of greener pastures further away from Boston were hardly encountered. It is also true, however, that the pressure of natural increase, which sent some sons, often the younger ones, looking for land stakes elsewhere, must have been weak within the Francis tribe. That is, while we see from Table 1 that fifth-generation patriarchs out of Francis had sixth-generation broods that were nearly as large as in the other lines, they cannot have had such large families in the earlier generations; and this means that the big land divisions commanded by the earlier generations were not being as finely subdivided across their sons.

In any event, the 88% of sixth-generation births out of Francis who still remain 150 years later in their line's original county is unique among these Eaton lines. For the Haverhill line out of John the same figure is 43%, and 42% for Jonas of Reading. The line from William of Reading and that from John of Salisbury are both at 26%; and the line out of John of Dedham shows a mere 13% of its sixth-generation births still in the family"s original Norfolk County. In short, the scions of Francis were stay-at-homes; those of John of Dedham went west in droves.

Table 2. Native Counties for Generation VI Children,
by Eaton Lineages

| County | Francis[1] (Plymouth) | John[1] (Dedham) | Wm.[1] (Reading) | Jonas[1] (Reading) | John[1] Salisb. | Haver. |
|---|---|---|---|---|---|---|
| **Massachusetts** | | | | | | |
| Essex | | | 1 | 12 | **59** | **68** |
| Suffolk | | | 1 | 26 | | |
| Plymouth | **58** | | | | | |
| Bristol | 1 | | | | | |
| Norfolk | | **40** | | | | |
| Middlesex | | 8 | **43** | **165** | | |
| Worcester | | 20 | 4 | 100 | | |
| Hampden | | 6 | 1 | | | |
| Hampshire | | 13 | | | | |
| Franklin | | 1 | | | | |
| Berkshire | | 4 | | | | |
| | | | | | | |
| **New Hampshire** | | | | | | |
| Rockingham | | | 47 | | 89 | 25 |
| Merrimac | | | 6 | | 2 | 12 |
| Belknap | | | 8 | | | |
| Hillsborough | | 11 | 9 | 14 | | 29 |
| Cheshire | | 2 | | 19 | | 2 |
| Grafton | | 6 | | | | 4 |
| | | | | | | |
| **Maine** | | | | | | |
| York | | | | | 27 | |
| Cumberland | | | | | 8 | 1 |
| Oxford | | | 8 | 3 | | |
| Lincoln | 4 | | | | 34 | |
| Hancock | | | | | 10 | |
| | | | | | | |
| **Vermont** | | | | | | |
| Windham | | 6 | | | | |
| Windsor | | | | 16 | | |
| Lamoille | | 4 | 4 | | | |
| Chittenden | | 10 | | | | |
| | | | | | | |
| **Connecticut** | | | | | | |
| Windham | | 83 | | 41 | | |
| Tolland | | 23 | 20 | | | 6 |
| Hartford | | | 12 | | | |
| Litchfield | | 26 | | | | |

Table 2. Native Counties for Generation VI Children (cont.)

| | Francis[1] | John[1] | Wm.[1] | Jonas[1] | John[1] Salis. | Haver |
|---|---|---|---|---|---|---|
| **New York** | | | | | | |
| Albany | | 4 | | | | |
| Columbia | | 3 | | | | |
| Suffolk | | 12 | | | | |
| Schoharie | | 3 | | | | |
| Herkimer | | 15 | | | | |
| Genessee | 2 | | | | | |
| Monroe | | | | 1 | | |
| Allegany | 1 | | | | | |
| **CANADA** | | | | | | |
| Nova Scotia | | | | | | 9 |
| New Brunswick | | | | | | 2 |
| Quebec | | | | 1 | | |

(NOTE: Numerical entries in bold face are native counties for each lineage.]

Turning to destinations, the restless Dedham line spread almost everywhere save to Maine and eastern New Hampshire. Many descendants here sprinkled themselves across central and western Massachusetts, and a substantial branch removed early to colonize Windham, Tolland and Litchfield counties in Connecticut. This line also figures more centrally than any of the others in the settlement of upper New York state, a move which was just getting underway after the Revolution, with the beginnings apparent in the sixth generation.

The Reading Eatons tended to migrate northwest into the southern tier of New Hampshire counties. The larger line descending from brother Jonas also went heavily west into Worcester Co. in Massachusetts, and one branch of considerable size mingled with the Dedham line in the settlement of Windham and Tolland counties in Connecticut. Descendants of Jonas also established some Eaton presence in Boston.

We shall largely postpone discussion of the migrations of the Salisbury and Haverhill lines out of John[1] until the main text. However, it is of keen interest to note in Table 2 that while both of these lines had their origins in Massachusetts, they tended not to stay within that state if they moved at all. Instead, conforming nicely to our "radiation" model, they tended to move northward out of that state, to Maine from Salisbury or to eastern New Hampshire (Rockingham County) from both Salisbury and Haverhill. The bulk of the Haverhill emigrants, however, moved up

the Merrimac River into New Hampshire to settle in the central and western half of that state (Hillsboro, Cheshire and Grafton counties), and later
into Vermont as well.

It is important to emphasize, however, that Table 2 merely cap-
tures the geographic distribution of a single generation of Eaton lines--
the sixth.  Not only are there strays in all these lines who were exceptions
to the main trends of migration characteristic of their lineages; there were
many movements in later generations which depart from the time frame
frozen here in the sixth generation.  Thus, for example, while the line of
John of Dedham led the charge into New York State, and would continue
to dominate the Eaton migrants in that state as of 1850 and beyond, all
of these lineages in due time had representatives in upstate New York as
well as in New York City.

The reader should also be reminded that our focus here has been
upon the Eaton lines which arrived in New England during the Great Migration.  Although immigration fell off radically in subsequent decades,
there was always some; and occasional new Eaton lines turn up in it.  Indeed, there are a significant number of Eatons in the New York Census of
1850 who report having been born in England, Ireland or Scotland; and
at least a handful of similar new arrivals in New England as well.  Thus
even by 1850 the probability that an Eaton turning up west of New England is a member of the Eaton families of the great Migration has declined substantially.

# Generation One

## John¹ and Anne EATON, Immigrants

**1. John¹ Eaton** (Thomas[A-B], John[C]), called the "eldest son" of father Thomas, was baptized 26 Dec. 1590 at Hatton, county Warwick, England, and presumably had been born shortly before. He appears to have grown up at Beausale in Hatton parish, a village about five miles northwest of Warwick, the county seat of Warwickshire (see map on front cover). He mar. 1st, **Anne __?__ \*** about 1620. Over the next two decades they had eleven children born to them, all but two of them baptized at Hatton. The final baptism of the series, for a son Job, is dated 29 Sep 1639, an event which probably lays to rest theories that John and Anne might have been in New England for some years before surfacing in the new grant at Salisbury, Mass. (Richardson, 1993).

In any event, they and six surviving children must have departed for the New World soon after the 1639 baptism, at a point when John was nearing 50 years of age. There is no known record of the vessel which brought them across the sea. It is reasonable to think that they passed through both Ipswich and Newbury, Massachusetts, in connection with other families with whom they afterward appear to have been closely associated. But John¹'s name first appears in the New World on the proprietors' books for Salisbury in the winter of 1639/40, essentially when the settlement was launched, although it is likely that his name was a retrospective addition. He probably had arrived in Salisbury by the "26th of ye 6th mo. 1640" (August 26, 1640, N.S.), since on that date "John Eaton, Senior" received from the "ffreemen" of Salisbury the first of a series of land divisions that continued until his departure from Salisbury in 1646. This first grant involved "two acres, more or less, for his house lotte, lying between the house lotts of Mr. Samuel Hall and Ralfe Blesdale." This lot is visible on the ancient but still preserved map of house lots ringing the village green (see Map 2, p. xxiv), and lay "about a stone's cast" from where the East Salisbury town office stood in 1890.

It is not believed that John¹ ever placed a house upon this lot. On

---

\* NOTE. Molyneux (1911) and others note that Anne was probably a Crossman. This guess springs from a marriage recorded for a John Eaton and a Mrs. Anne Crossman in London, Dec. 26, 1621. This is not out of the question, but no collateral information has been developed to make this identification compelling. It is humbling that there are at least two other marriages between a John Eaton and an Anne in the London area in this general period. Moreover, the Warwickshire records that would logically have covered the marriage of our John Eaton are missing.

the contrary, it is thought that he lived upon his "planting lott" granted on "the 7th of the 9th mo. 1640...containing pr estimation six acres more or less, lying uppon ye great necke," having his house near the "great neck bridge" on "the beach road." This homestead, on what is still called "Beach Road" in East Salisbury, remained in the Eaton family for over 250 years (see the history of this property, Sidebar #13), and the "neck bridge" may survive as a visible culvert on that road a few rods west of the point where Dock Lane forks south off Beach Road.

Although John[1] Eaton farmed like everyone else, he was by trade a "cooper." He also must be the "John Eaton" of Salisbury who was "commissioned Captain of the Provincial Militia," from August 1643 to 1647 (General Society of Colonial Wars, 1941), since his son John[2] would have been too young for such a role. In the Spring of 1646 John[1] Eaton was chosen "grand juror" and also one of five "Prudential men," to manage the affairs of Salisbury town.

Still, before the year 1646 was out, John[1] at age 56 had transferred his homestead on "the great neck" together with all his rights and privileges as one of the proprietors-in-common to his son John[2] Eaton, (by this time about age 35), and had taken the rest of his family some 15 miles up the Merrimack River to participate in a new settlement at Haverhill, Massachusetts. The reasons for this move are not entirely clear. However, the Haverhill plantation drew its founders disproportionately from the town of Newbury, just across the Merrimac from Salisbury, and from Ipswich, the next major settlement to the south. The Rev. Nathaniel Ward of Ipswich, who sold John[1] Eaton his first land in Haverhill in Nov. 1646, was a prime mover (and largest landholder) in the development of Haverhill. That John[1] was in close touch with the Ipswich/Newbury settlers is exemplified by the fact that his son John[2] found his 1644 bride in a prominent Ipswich family. Thus father John[1] was abreast of Haverhill developments.

Although John[1] was slightly tardy in joining the Haverhill move, he arrived in time to qualify as a "proprietor" with rights to subsequent divisions of land in this large new tract. As noted, he already had enjoyed this status in Salisbury, deeding these rights over to elder son John[2] upon his departure. Haverhill was a new start in provisioning his younger son, Thomas[2], with a similarly large land stake; and parallel types of land grants there tended to be larger than in Salisbury. Proprietors in Haverhill, as in many other grants, had different levels of entitlement to land in each new division of commons. John[1], as a mere artisan, did not compete with the large allotments to magistrates, ministers and other higher professions, but nonetheless ranked in the upper half of the Haverhill settlers for size of entitlements, a status also reflected in the fact that he was elected a Selectman for Haverhill in 1648. By 1659, his own eight tracts of land (house lot, meadow and planting land), were approaching 100 acres in sum, despite the fact that he had by this time hived off a half of his proprietorial claim to his son Thomas[2], who already had accumulated another 35 acres in his own right. While land accumulation may not have been father John's main purpose in the

Haverhill move, the eleven grandsons produced by his own two sons
surely profitted handsomely from the double proprietorship.

We do not know whether John[1] built on his eight-acre house lot
in the nascent village of Haverhill, or once again made the uncommon
decision to reside on a planting lot as he had in Salisbury. But it is clear
that before his death he lived on a homestead some three miles northwest
of the town center, in what later became Haverhill's West Parish. This
location was exposed to the Indian raid of 1697, and lay within a short
distance of the Dustin farm that figured so prominently in that episode
(see Sidebar #1, p. 36). Subsequent Haverhill Eaton progeny scattered
their residences in other neighborhoods; but this West Parish area was the
center of gravity of the Eaton family for a couple more centuries.

John[1] spent the last 22 years of his life in Haverhill, manufactur-
ing barrel staves and keeping a farm. His wife Anne died at Haverhill 5
Feb 1660. He mar. 2d, **Mrs. Phebe Dow**, widow of Thomas[1] Dow of
Haverhill, on 20 Nov 1661. She lived until 3 Nov 1672. John[1] died at
Haverhill 29 Oct 1668. His will, written 6 Aug 1668,
reads:

In ye name of god Amen: ye 6th day of August in ye year of our Lord God
1668___ I John Eaton of Haverhill in ye county of Norfolk in New england being
of whole mind and in good and perfect remembrance doe make and ordeine this tto
be my last will and testament concerning my outward estate in Manner and forme
following: viz: first I will all such debts and duties as I owe of right, or of con-
science to any person or persons & my funerall expenses bee pay'd by my Executors hereafter named without any Contradiction or delay:

I give unto my present wyfe the use of my now dwelling house and oarch-
yard duering her Naturall life & such other things according as is exprest in writing
comitted to ye keeping of Henry Palmer & whereas ye said writing mentions a Cow
which shee is to have after my decease, In case I have not a cow att my death I will
that my Sone Tho: Eaton shall pay unto her five pounds, or secure her a good cow.
I give her also six bushels of corne, & one of my best swine. I give her more also
the Remainder of what is due to mee from Jno. Todd being about eighteen shillings.

I bequeath unto my Sone John Eaton my bigest sylver spoone & brass
candlestick & my bible. I give my Sone John also all my liveing in Salisbury,
provided that hee never clayme anything for what hee pay'd for mee to any person or
persons upon any account whatsoever. I give him also my 2d division of upland &
all my share of meadow in ye west meadow which meadow and upland lieth in ye
towne of Haverhill in Norfolke.

I give unto my Sone Thomas my home Lott after my decease & my now
dwelling house & Orchyard after ye decease of my present wyfe. I give him also all
my share upon ye Iland lying against Haverhill & all my share of meadow in ye
Hawkes meadow & my meadow att ye pond meadow after ye death of my wyfe. I
give him also my shop tools with beetle & wedges long saw & grindiestone & my
part of ye plough & cart with their present furniture. I give to my son Thomas ye
use of my tyllage land that is now up in my Ox common lott duering the life of my
wyfe paying to my wife ye sum of twelve shillings per annum. I give him also ye
use of ye said Ox common lott for ye Sowing and gathering in of two cropps after
ye death of my wyfe; wheras there is mention made of a cowe to bee given to my

wyfe at my death my will is that in case I have no cow then in being my son Thomas upon consideration of what I give him shall make good the said Cowe, or five
pounds as aforesaid; otherwise he shall pay as followeth: to my daughter Brown
forty shillings, to my daughter Davis forty shillings, & to my daughter Ingalls forty
shillings, which summs shall be payd within two years after my death. I give my
son Thomas also my other sylver spoone & my Spitt.

I give and bequeath unto Tho: Eaton ye Son of my son John Eaton all ye
land that is in my possession in ye great playn & four acres lying without ye said
playn fence & my East meadow, & I give him also my Ox common Lott which hee
shall have delivered up to him by my son Thomas two years after ye death of my
wyfe & he ye said Thomas my grandchild shall in consideration of my playn lot pay
six shillings yearly to my wyfe so long as shee shall live.

I give unto my grand children Jno. Davis & John Ingalls all my 3d division of upland to bee equally divided betwixt them. I give to the sd. Jno. Davis my
grandchilde all my Share of meadow lying upon my son James Davis's meadow
being my 3d division of meadow. I give to the sd. Jno. Ingalls my grandchilde my
2d division of meadow lying upon a branch of Spickett meadow joining to meadow
of my son Thomas. I give to my grandchilde Tho: Eaton my musquet, Sword &
bandaleeros. I give to my son Thomas Eaton's son Thomas my little gunne.

I give to my son John Eaton ye priviledge and rights of two Cow commons. I give to my grand child John Davis rights of one Cow common. I give to
my grand child John Davis rights of one Cow common & I give to my grand child
John Ingalls ye rights of one Cow common.

I give that calfe that my son James Davis hath of mine to keep to Hester
Davis.

I will that ye five pounds worth in corne that is in ye hands of my son
Brown be disposed of as followeth: to my Daughter Brown three pounds: to my
Daughter Davis twenty shillings & to my Daughter Ingalls twenty shillings.

I give to my son Thomas ye halfe of an ox that is between him and mee.

I give my brass, pewter, bedding & household stuff that is not formerly
disposed of, to my three daughters, Ann, Elizabeth & Ruth to bee equally divided
among them.

I will that my Executors shall pay twenty shillings to my daughter Ruth
Ingalls more than what is above mentioned.

I give to my son John Eaton my fourth division of upland when it shalbe
layd out in consideration of what charge soever he hath bin att upon any occasion of
mine.

I constitute & appoint my sons Tho: Eaton & Georg Brown to be Executors of this my last will and testament.

In witness to this writing as my last will & testament I have herunto sett
my hand and Seale ye day month & yeare first mentioned.

Signed & sealed in ye presence of          The mark  "E"  of Jno. Eaton
      Nathaniel Saltingstall                       with a seale to it
      James Davis  Sen.
         his   ∧  mark Palmer                       Tho: Eaton who is
one nominated in this will to be one of the Executors doth in the presence of  ye
Court held att Salisbury ye 13th 2d m:  69 accept of the same.
                                                   Tho: Bradbury   rec.

Mr. Nathaniel Saltingstall attested to
this will upon oath before the Court
held at Salisbury ye 13, 2d mo. 69.

\*\*\*\*\*\*\*

An Inventorie of the estate of John Eaton of Haverhill who deceased October ye 29th, 1668, taken and apprized by James Davis, Sen. and Henry Palmer the 2d day of November 1668.

| | |
|---|---|
| Wareing clothes | 06=00=00 |
| Bedding | 01=00=00 |
| Brass | 01=07=00 |
| Pewter | 01=02=00 |
| a pott skillet spitt & morter | 01=10=00 |
| Trammels & Iron Ware | 00=10=00 |
| A bedstead & chayer | 01=10=00 |
| a warming pan | 00=07=00 |
| A chest, 2 tables, a trunk & a box | 02=04=00 |
| Lumber about ye house | 01=14=00 |
| in Millitary armes | 02=05=00 |
| 2 sylver spoones | 00=12=00 |
| in axes, scythe, how & pitch fork | 01=00=00 |
| in books | 00=14=00 |
| in tooles | 02=10=00 |
| A share, plough yrons, cart & yrons | 01=02=00 |
| Indian corne (60) bushels | 08=00=00 |
| Oates 15 bushels | 01=07=00 |
| Wheat fower bushels | 01=00=00 |
| Ric six bushels | 01=04=00 |
| Halfe an Oxe | 03=10=00 |
| a steere | 03=00=00 |
| a calfe | 01=00=00 |
| 4 Swine | 04=10=00 |
| a grinstone | 00=12=00 |
| in  Debts | 07=10=00 |
| house & house lott | 05=00=00 |
| Ox common | 03=00=00 |
| 8 acres of land in the upper & lower plaine | 28=00=00 |
| 25 acres of 2d Division of upland | 25=00=00 |
| 3d division of upland | 05=00=00 |
| 5 cow commonages | 15=00=00 |
| 2 acres of meadow at ye hart meadow | 10=00=00 |
| 1 1/4 acre at ye pond meadow | 06=00=00 |
| 1 3/4 acre of meadow in two places | 08=00=00 |
| 5 acres of 2d & 3d division meadow | 20=00=00 |
| 3/4 of an acre of upland upon ye Iland | 01=00=00 |
| the right of ye 4th division of upland | 08=00=00 |

Tho: Eaton ye Executor doth testifie unto this Court now held att Salisbury 13th:2d mo:69 upon his oath that this is a true Inventory of ye Estate of John Eaton of Haverhill late deceased according to his best knowledg
as attests Tho: Bradbury recsse

* * * * * * *

Known children of John[1] Eaton and Anne were:

+ **2**   i. John[2] Eaton, b. ca. 1621, prob. at Hatton, England; mar. Martha Rowlandson of Ipswich, Mass.; resided at Salisbury.

  **3**   ii. Anne[2] Eaton, bp. 14 Sep 1623 at Hatton; mar. Lt. George Brown 25 June 1645 at Salisbury; resided in Haverhill. She died 16 Dec 1683, leaving no children. Lt. George Brown mar. 2d, wid. Hannah Hazen of Rowley, Mass., 17 Mar 1684.

+ **4**   iii. Thomas[2] Eaton, bp. 19 Feb 1625/26 at Hatton, England; mar. 1st, Martha Kent, 14 Aug 1656; 2d Eunice Singletery, 6 Jan 1658/59 at Andover, Mass.; resided at Haverhill.

     iv. Richard[2] Eaton, bp. 12 Oct 1628; bur. Hatton 27 Mar 1630.

  **5**   v. Elizabeth[2] Eaton, bp. 31 Jan 1629/30, Hatton; mar. James Davis of Haverhill, 1 Dec 1648; lived on a farm in Haverhill. They had ten children: Hannah Davis, b. 19 Jun 1650. Hester Davis, b. 8 Oct 1651. Elizabeth Davis, b. 11 Mar 1654. Ann Davis, b. 13 Feb 1655. Sarah Davis, b. 5 Aug 1658. James Davis, b. 3 Oct 1660. John Davis, b. 30 Jun 1664, killed in Canada, 1690. Daniel, b. 19 Sep 1666. Elisha, b. 30 Aug 1670. Constance, b. 9 Mar 1674. Elizabeth[2], wife of James Davis, died 21 Jan 1683, and Mr. Davis mar. 2d, Mary __?__. He himself d. 18 Jul 1694.

     vi. Sarah[2] Eaton, bp. not found; bur. Hatton, 4 Aug 1633.

     vii. Daniel[2] Eaton, bp. 8 Dec 1633 at Hatton; died young.

     viii. Daniel[2A] Eaton, bp. 26 Feb 1634/35 at Hatton; bur. Hatton 13 Aug 1635.

  **6**   ix. Ruth[2] Eaton, bp. 12 Feb 1636/37; mar. Samuel Ingalls, 9 Dec 1656 in Ipswich, Mass., where their children were born: Ruth Ingalls, b. 19 Nov 1657. Samuel Ingalls, b. 24 Jan 1659. Edmund Ingalls, b. 23 Jul 1662. John Ingalls, b. 26 Aug 1664. Joseph Ingalls, b. 23 Dec 1666. Mary Ingalls, b. 13 Mar 1688. Anna Ingalls, b. 8 Mar 1671. Elizabeth Ingalls, b 27 Sep 1673.

  **7**   x. Hester[2] Eaton, bp. 6 May 1638 at Hatton; d. early, unmarried.

     xi. Job[2] Eaton, bp. 29 Sep 1639 at Hatton; not in father's will.

NOTE. For the rest of this volume, all known children will be assigned consecutive Arabic numerals. This principle is apparently violated above, where all 11 children are given Roman numerals, but five are left out of the Arabic-numeral sequence. None of these five children is, however, known to have seen the New World (Job being the only one not surely buried before the voyage). Therefore leaving these five out of the main sequence is appropriate.

*******

Of the two sons in New England, John[2] and Thomas[2], John[2] settled in Salisbury and became the head of a numerous tribe which, for
convenience, we shall call the **Salisbury Branch**.    Thomas[2] settled in
Haverhill, so we shall call his line the the **Haverhill Branch**.    In this volume the chapters covering each generation are subdivided into two parts
for these two branches.

# Generation Two

## A.  *The Salisbury Branch*

**2.  John[2] Eaton** (John[1]) was born about 1621, presumably in England, and came to Salisbury, Mass., with his parents in the winter of 1639-40.  About 1644 he mar. **Martha Rowlandson**, a dau. of Thomas Rowlandson, Sr., of Ipswich, Mass., and sister of Rev. Joseph Rowlandson, who was graduated from Harvard University in 1652, the only member of his class.  When father John removed from Salisbury to Haverhill in Nov 1646, he made over his homestead on "the great neck," along with other real estate and proprietorial claims to subsequent divisions of Salisbury land to his son John[2], who lived out his life on the original homestead.  His father also bequeathed him both upland and meadow tracts in Haverhill.  While John[2] was possessed of much real estate, he did not turn it over with the frequency shown by Eatons in subsequent generations.  In land conveyances he is sometimes called "cooper" and at other times, "planter," or just the same mix as found for his father.

John[2] frequently served the town as one of the surveyors of highways, and was a member of the Salisbury church.  Hoyt (1899) suggests that John[2] may have returned to London in March, 1664-5, since John[2] Hall (John[1]) wrote his mother that he had encountered John Eaton there: "I can discerne the face of a N: E: man though he forgot mine."

John[2] died 1 Nov. 1682.  The first paragraph of his Sept 1682 will says "I commend my soul to Almighty God, my Creator, assuredly believing that I shall receive full pardon and a free remission of my sins, and be saved by the precious death and merits of my blessed Saviour and Redeemer, Christ Jesus."  He bequeaths each son save Thomas (see **#10**) major pieces of land, to be described as we focus on each child in the next chapter.  But he mentions his son John[3] first in the will, leaving him his "north lot of upland" (in proto-Seabrook?), with marsh and grazing lots.  Hence we put the latter's name first among the male children below, although it does not appear in the records of Salisbury with those of the other children.  His wife Martha survived him by three decades, dying in July, 1712, "a woman of great age, and of great excellence of character."

Children at Salisbury, Mass.:

   **8**    i.   Hester[3] Eaton, b. August, 1645; died 1649.
+  **9**    ii.  John[3] Eaton, b. ca. 1646; mar. Mary __?__ ; res. Salisbury.
+ **10**   iii.  Thomas[3] Eaton, b. 17 Jan 1646/47; mar. Hannah Hubbard.
  **11**   iv.  Martha[3] Eaton, b 12 Aug 1648; mar. 1st, Benjamin Collins
               of Salisbury, 9 Jul 1668, by whom she had at least six

children: Mary Collins, b. 8 Jan 1669. John Collins, b. ca.
1673. Samuel Collins, b 18 Jan 1676. Anna Collins, b. 1
Feb 1679. Benjamin Collins, b. 29 May 1681. Ephraim
Collins, b. 30 Sep 1683. Martha's husband Benjamin
Collins died 10 Dec 1683, and she mar. 2d, Philip Flanders
of Salisbury, 4 Nov 1686.

**12**   v. Elizabeth[3] Eaton, b. 12 Dec 1650; mar. John Groth, M.D. of
Salisbury, 7 Jan 1673/74. He was admitted to practice medicine at Hampton in 1679.

**13**  vi. Ann[3] Eaton, b. 17 Dec 1652; died 12 Jun 1658.

**14** vii. Sarah[3] Eaton, b. 28 Feb 1655; mar. Robert[2] Downer of Salisbury, 6 May 1675; had children at Salisbury: Robert Dow-
ner, b. 23 Jul 1676. Martha Downer, b. 1 Oct 1678. John
Downer, b. 1 Apr 1681. Andrew Downer, b. 7 Sep 1683.
Samuel Downer, b 5 Apr 1686. Joseph Downer, b. 4 Mar
1687/88. Sarah Downer, b. 6 Oct 1690. Mary Downer, b.
22 Feb 1695/6. Joseph Downer, b. 15 May 1699.

**15** viii. Mary[3] Eaton, b. 9 Dec 1656; died 1 Jan 1656/7.

+ **16**  ix. Samuel[3] Eaton, b. 14 Feb 1659. A seaman, died young.

+ **17**   x. Joseph[3] Eaton, b. 6 Mar 1661; mar. Mary French.

+ **18**  xi. Ephraim[3] Eaton, b. 12 Apr 1663; mar. Mary True.

*******

## B. *The Haverhill Branch*

    **4. Thomas[2]** (John[1]) was bpt. 19 Feb 1625/26 at Hatton, England.
He was with his parents in Salisbury, and went with them to Haverhill,
Mass., in November, 1646. Here he mar. 1st, **Martha Kent**, on 14 Aug
1656. She died 9 Mar 1657, leaving a daughter about 10 days old.
Thomas[2] mar. 2d **Eunice Singletery**, 6 Jan 1659 at Andover, Mass. She
was the dau. of Richard and Susannah Singletery of Salisbury, born 7 Jan
1641. They lived on a farm in Haverhill where all of their children were
born. If this was the homestead that Thomas's son Ebenezer[3] took over
at his father's death, it was located not in the West Parish, where most of
the rest of the family resided, but on the Merrimack River "below the
buttonwoods," about a mile east of the village center at the junction of
Groveland and Water Streets. This imposing dwelling remained in the
family for over a century.

    In 1652 Thomas[2] Eaton was one of 37 signers of a petition to the
General Court to revoke the sentence of disfranchisement against Robert
Pike for freedom of speech. In 1675 he was one of the Selectmen of the
town. On 12 Oct 1681 he was made Ensign of the Foot Company in
Haverhill, in place of James Pecker, thereby becoming the "eldest sargent
to the foot." In 1692 Thomas[2], now was named first Selectman. In 1697
he was one of a committee on the location of the meeting house. Obviously a well-to-do farmer, he was much interested in church and town

affairs, and was highly esteemed by his fellow citizens. After his decease 15 Dec 1708, the inventory of his estate amounted to £404/5sh. His wife "Unes", as he wrote it in his will, died 5 Oct 1715.

Child with Martha at Haverhill, Mass.:

**19**  i. Martha³ Eaton, b. 27 Feb 1657; died young.

Children with Eunice, also at Haverhill:

+ **20**  ii. Thomas³ Eaton, b 18 Mar 1660; mar. Hannah Webster.
  **21**  iii. Lydia³ Eaton, b. 23 Jul 1662; mar. Jacob Hardy. She d. 24 Jun 1737.
+ **22**  iv. John³ Eaton, b. 6 Mar 1664; mar. Mary Singletery, 1700.
+ **23**  v. Jonathan³ Eaton, b. 23 Apr 1668; mar. 1st, Sarah Sanders.
+ **24**  vi. Job³ Eaton, b. 22 Apr 1671; mar. Mary Simons, 1698.
+ **25**  vii. Timothy³ Eaton, b. 19 May 1674; mar. Ruth Chapman.
  **26**  viii. Ebenezer³ Eaton, b. 5 Apr 1677. He was a rich bachelor farmer, who occupied the homestead of his father, and died there in Haverhill, 14 May 1737. The inventory of his estate, returned 25 Jul 1737, amounted to the large sum of £1757/13sh, much of it in choice properties. It was divided into seven shares, and distributed to his siblings or their heirs. Essex Co. Deeds 87-61/63/64 are of greatest interest in tracing the division across the family.
  **27**  ix. Martha³ᴬ Eaton, b. 16 Mar 1680; mar. Thomas Roby.
  **28**  x. Ruth³ Eaton, b. 23 Nov. 1684. She mar. 1st, Ebenezer Kimball of Haverhill, by whom she had three children: Jemima Kimball, b. 22 Oct 1709. Abner Kimball, b. 20 Apr 1712. Abraham Kimball, b. 3 Jan 1714. Ruth mar. 2d, 30 Dec 1716 in Haverhill, Stephen Johnson, a son of the John Johnson to whom a house and land were given so that he would settle in Haverhill as a blacksmith as of 1656. Ruth died 6 Apr 1750.

# Generation Three

## A. _The Salisbury Branch_

      **9. John**[3] **Eaton** (John[2.1]) was born ca. 1646 in Salisbury; and married **Mary __?__** about 1684. In 1682 his father's will gave him the "north lot of up land and...salt marsh lott" in Salisbury, which may well have been in the Cow Common Division northeast of East Salisbury village center. He may, however, have continued to reside at the family homestead on what is now Beach Road: he surely came to possess that property after the death of his mother Martha in 1712.

      Like his father and grandfather, he was a cooper by trade. His earliest appearance on the public record occurred in Mar 1667/68, when he confessed to the town selectmen that he had felled two trees on the town common, and was fined 20 shillings, to be paid by 400 barrel staves of red oak (_Salisbury Town Records_, p. 151). About 1670, according to one deposition, he went to York, Maine, to help Mr. William Hooke of Salisbury with a harvest of hay. He added little or nothing to the major land holdings he inherited from his father in Salisbury, but his familiarity with the Maine frontier helped him with extensive land purchases he made in later years, particularly at Winnegant's Cove, on the coast 25 miles beyond Portland at Kennebec. These investments provided land stakes for his sons William and Thomas. In the early 1690s, John was paid by the town for his services as church sexton and bell-ringer for the town meeting. He also added to his income with numerous sales of property that he had inherited. His will is dated 15 Jan 1718.

      When his death approached, John[3] had already provided a land stake for his three eldest sons, to be described in their turn in the next chapter. The eldest of the three younger sons still at home, Jonathan[4], then age 19, was bequeathed the old homestead, with land in Maine going to Thomas[4] and a smaller Salisbury stake for Daniel[4A], still only seven years old. Father John[3] died 17 Jan 1717/18.

      Children at Salisbury:

   **29**   i. Mary[4] Eaton, b. 13 Dec 1685. Not mentioned in will.
+ **30**   ii. John[4] Eaton, b. ca. Jun 1687; mar. Esther Swett, 1708.
+ **31**  iii. William[4] Eaton, b. ca. Nov 1689; mar. Mary Littlefield, 1709.
   **32**   iv. James[4] Eaton, b. 27 Apr 1691. Not cited in father's will.
+ **33**   v. Samuel[4] Eaton, b. 25 Nov 1692; mar. 1st, Hannah Worthen,
               ca. 1713; 2d Huldah Stanyan, 1745; resided Salisbury.
   **34**  vi. Martha[4] Eaton, b. 5 Sep 1695; mar. Isaac[4] Buswell of Salis-
               bury, 16 Jan 1719 at Hampton Falls.

+ **35** vii. Jonathan[4] Eaton, b. 2 Oct 1698; mar. Judith Ash, 1720.
+ **36** viii. Thomas[4] Eaton, b. 21 Mar 1701; mar. Mehitable Cilley, 1727.
  **37** ix. Daniel[4] Eaton, b. 13 Jul 1704; died young.
+ **38** x. Daniel[4A] Eaton, b. 11 Mar 1710; mar. Nancy Pike, 1730.

    **10. Thomas**[3] **Eaton** (John[2-1]) was born 17 Jan 1646/47 at Salisbury; mar. **Hannah Hubbard,** 14 Nov 1679, at Salisbury. She was probably a descendant of William Hubbard, "eminent inhabitant" of Ipswich, Mass. Thomas and his wife settled on a farm in Salisbury "laid out to him in the peak division, so called, 9th lot," where their children were born. In 1680 he joined his brother John and father John in signing a Norfolk County petition. In his father's will of 1682, Thomas is given no land and only "five pounds of merchantable provisions," perhaps because he had already bought Thomas his lot in Salisbury, or for other reasons. Before 1687 he moved his family to Boston, Mass., where he died 9 Jul 1699. It appears that he was not survived by any sons reaching maturity.

    Children at Salisbury:

  **39** i. Thomas[4] Eaton, b. 15 Sep 1680; died in Boston, 1699.
  **40** ii. Hannah[4] Eaton, b. 23 Jun 1682; died 8 Jul 1683, Salisbury.
  **41** iii. Hannah[4A] Eaton, b. 10 Mar 1684; of Boston 1711, a single
      woman.

    NOTE. Molyneux (1911, p. 373) lists two other children for Thomas & Hannah: a Joseph and a John, both born 1686. We have hunted diligently in the Salisbury area, Boston, and points between for such records without success. We see no reason to add them here.

    **16. Samuel**[3] **Eaton** (John[2-1]) was born 14 Feb 1659 at Salisbury. The senior author could not find any subsequent record for this son, but presumed that he must have been the father of a later Samuel (see **#107**). This is almost certainly incorrect, as a different paternity for the later Samuel has now been reconstructed. This Samuel[3] was a seaman who appears on the list for the oath of allegiance and loyalty at Salisbury in 1678. As the oldest son not yet "up and out," his dying father bequeathed him the family homestead in 1682, to be possessed after the death of his mother Martha. His personal record soon vanishes, however, and his mother lived until 1712, when ownership of the homestead passed to his older brother John[3]. It therefore seems likely that Samuel[3] was lost at sea soon after the will took effect in 1682.

    This conjecture gained force later when we discovered a power of attorney (Essex Co. Deed 15-172) which this Samuel[3] had granted to his "loving and well beloved" younger brother Ephraim, signed on 12 Dec 1683. Ephraim is deputized to act in Samuel's behalf with regard to collection of all moneys owed him, including his share "in this voyage I

am bound out upon, whether it be Gold, Silver, amber grease...or whatsoever..." Samuel goes on to declare "that if it should so fall out that I
should depart this life before making my Return from the voyage I am
now Bound out upon", then brother Ephraim shall receive his whole estate. One of the witnesses to his 1683 signature, an Elizabeth Rawlings,
later appeared in court to testify under oath as to the its validity. This
appearance occurred in 1690, two weeks short of seven years later. Presumably this interval was the one legally required for a terminal judgment involving a missing person.

From this more extended record, it seems extremely unlikely that
Samuel³ survived his twenty-sixth year; and there is no record of his marriage. Even had he been married before his disappearance, siring a Samuel, Jr., as our senior author posited, this conjectured son could not very
plausibly have both stayed out of sight of the public record for over 60
years, and then emerged as a sexagenarian to marry Huldah Stanyan in
1745, as the earlier account averred. Fortunately, the records make amply clear that a different Samuel⁴ was Huldah's bridegroom (see **#33**).

**17. (Capt.) Joseph³ Eaton** (John²⁻¹) was born 6 Mar. 1661 at
Salisbury; mar. 1st, **Mary French** of Salisbury, 14 Dec 1683, daughter of
John and Mary French, and the granddaughter of Edward French, the
Salisbury pioneer. They resided at Salisbury, perhaps on "the three acres
of land at Sandy Hill, be it more or less," left him by his father. He was
also established by the will as co-owner with brother John of any new
town land divisions, so he benefitted from the several Salisbury land divisions in the 1702-05 period. It is not sure where he lived, but in 1717
Capt. Joseph's homestead was a 35-acre lot on the west side of the road to
Hampton, just north of the parsonage of the time. It is possible that this
land was an extension of the house lot his grandfather John¹ Eaton had
received from the town in 1640 but never used for that purpose, which
was in the same area.

Capt. Joseph was a house carpenter by trade, but also dealt heavily in real estate. He figures in three dozen land conveyances between
1683 and 1737, and clearly turned over property, often improved, in all
sections of the town. Late in life, for example, he appears to have controlled almost two dozen of the small (2 1/2 acre) lots in the Great Neck
Division where the ancestral homestead was. He also served the town in a
great variety of capacities. He rose to the rank of captain in the local militia by about 1710, and served in Queen Anne's War the next year. He
was Town Constable, Juror, Tithing Man and Select Man before he was
forty, and later served as representative to the General Court; conducted
negotiations on behalf of the town with its neighbors or officials in Boston; was perennially engaged in planning for the maintenance of the old
meeting house or the building of a new one; on the school committee,
and so on. He was by far the most visible Eaton of his generation in the
area.

He was fond of hunting and trapping, and at the right season of
the year he would go with others as far east as Brunswick, Maine. On his

return he would entertain his family with many pleasing and exciting incidents of his excursion.  By those stories three of his sons, Samuel, Moses and Jacob, were fired with an adventurous spirit to seek their fortune in the forests of Maine.  Mary, his wife, died 12 Jul 1726.  Capt. Joseph mar. 2d, **Mrs. Mary (Cheyny) Worcester** of Bradford, Mass., 18 Dec 1726.  She had been mar. to Francis Worcester 29 Jan 1691, and died 2 Sep 1759.  Capt. Joseph joined the East Parish church at Salisbury 18 Feb 1727.  He died testate on 13 Jan 1743.  As he had already set up three sons in Maine and two others--John[4A] and Benjamin[4]--with "tenements" or homesteads in Salisbury, he left these sons only tokens in his will and gave son Nicholas[4] all of his remaining real estate not reserved for his mother.  Nicholas was also sole executor of his will.

Children with Mary (French) at Salisbury:

**42**   i. John[4] Eaton, b. 23 Aug 1684; died 12 Dec 1684.
+ **43**  ii. John[4A] Eaton, b 18 Oct 1685; mar. 1st, Esther Johnson.
+ **44**  iii. Samuel[4] Eaton, b. 7 Dec 1687; mar. Mary Malcolm; resided Brunswick, Maine.
+ **45**  iv. Joseph[4] Eaton, b. 14 Aug 1690; mar. Mary French; resided Newbury, Mass.
+ **46**  v. Benjamin[4] Eaton, b. 14 Feb 1693; mar. Sarah Morrill, 1718.
  **47**  vi. Moses[4] Eaton, b. 18 May 1695.  Killed by the Indians at Pleasant Point near Brunswick, Maine, in June, 1722.
  **48**  vii. Mary[4] Eaton, b. 9 Apr 1697; mar. Benjamin[3] True of Salisbury 4 Jan 1715.  Children: Mary True, b. 6 Feb 1717, d. young. Ruth True, b. 1 Apr 1719.  Mary True, b. 1 Feb 1720/21, prob. d. young.  Hannah True, b. 5 Jun 1722.  Twins Keturah & Sarah, b. 14 Feb 1723/24.  Joseph True, d. before 1750.  Moses True, living 1750.
+ **49** viii. Nicholas[4] Eaton, b. 12 Sep 1699; mar. Mercy Walton, 1756.
  **50**  ix. Sarah[4] Eaton, b. 20 May 1701; mar. Daniel Buswell of Bradford, Mass., 30 Jun 1726.
+ **51**   x. Jacob[4] Eaton, b. 16 Apr 1703; mar. 1st, Sarah Plumer; and 2d, Sarah Malcolm; resided Topsham, Maine.


**18. Ephraim[3] Eaton** (John[2-1]) was born 12 Apr 1663 in Salisbury; mar. **Mary[3] True** (she born 30 May 1668 to Henry[2]/Jane (Bradbury) True, out of Henry[1]), also of Salisbury, 5 Feb 1688/9; resided in Salisbury.  In addition to Ephraim's father's bequest to him of "90 acres above the mill," his mother gave him "all my upland meadow and common right in said town [Salisbury] given me by my sister Wells, after my natural life is ended."  The latter bequest appears to have included half-lots in at least six of the Salisbury land divisions as well as the Wells homestead at the southwest corner of Beach and Ferry roads in Salisbury. He also owned land in Haverhill.  In part because of his receipt of his brother Samuel's estate (see **#16**, above), along with his own land wealth, Ephraim[3]'s line in the longer run was the most affluent of the three brothers left in Salisbury (i.e., John[3] and Joseph[3] ). In part as well, it was because of his marriage into the True family, which had been, or was becoming, quite wealthy. Wife Mary received some True property, and the two principle surviving sons of Ephraim/Mary both married True girls in the next generation.

Like so many other early Eatons, Ephraim[3] was both a cooper and a farmer. Given his numerous land parcels, it is not entirely certain where he lived. We do know that his homestead late in life was a 10-acre lot, although he owned a half-dozen tracts fitting that description. Several of his land deeds as early as 1706 hint of a near-Hampton location to the north of Salisbury. It is quite likely that his homestead was at Lot #20 in the newly subdivided Gravelly Ridge Division (now the southern part of Seabrook), bounded to the north by Walton Road and to the south by lower Collins St. Nine months after his death in 1723 a note in the Town Records talks of a fence to be placed across the "Boiling Spring Way" "below Ephraim Eaton's house." It is not sure whether the reference was to the just-deceased father Ephraim[3] or to his eldest son Ephraim[4], but the house would have been the same in any event. Despite his relative affluence, Ephraim[3] was somewhat less active in town affairs than his brother Capt. Joseph, possibly for the simple reason that he lived on the remote margins of town, three or four times farther away from the village center. However this may be, it seems likely that Ephraim[3] was one of the two main pioneers for the large Eaton implantation in what would later become southern Seabrook (see Sidebar #10, p. 368).

In a storied if somewhat murky episode, the record shows that an Ephraim Eaton, presumably this patriarch rather than his eldest son, was carried prisoner from proto-Seabrook to Portsmouth in 1720 by Hampton constable Longfellow for failure to pay his Province tax. However this may be, Ephraim[3] the father died testate, 8 Jun 1723, leaving his eldest son Ephraim and youngest son Jabez all his property and rights in common in Salisbury; while leaving the two middle sons Samuel and Henry all his property and rights in Haverhill. Wife Mary died about 1748.

Children at Salisbury:

**52**  i. Mary[4] Eaton, b. 11 Dec 1689; mar. Jacob Green of Hampton, N.H., 8 Oct 1713; admitted to 1st Church, Salisbury, 20 May 1713.
**53**  ii. Ephraim[4] Eaton, b. 24 May 1692; "published to Mary Bartlett of Newbury, 12 January 1722 and forbid." He never did marry, and probably lived on the family homestead in the Gravelly Ridge Divison. This neighborhood became part of Hampton Falls, N.H. in 1741 (and Seabrook, 1768) so Ephraim[4] became a regular on the Hampton Falls tax lists until his death, being assessed less than his brother Jabez[4A], but more than any other of the growing tide of neighboring Eatons. Like his father, he was a cooper. He died in 176?.
**54**  iii. Jane[4] Eaton, b. 13 Sep 1694; admitted to 1st Church in Salis-

bury, 10 May 1713; mar. John Stevens, 16 Dec 1718.

**55**  iv. Samuel[4] Eaton, b. 6 Aug 1697; no mention of wife or children: presumed unmarried. Shared with brother Henry the land and common rights in Haverhill willed them by their father; also shared with Henry five parcels of land in the Gravelly Ridge and Cow Common Divisions bequeathed by his grandfather Henry[2] True for use after the death of his daughter Mary, their mother. Samuel[4] joined his brother Jabez[4A] in buying the 73-acre homestead of Edward Browne in 1735 on the north side of lower Walton Road. He may have lived there with Jabez: he was on all of the Hampton Falls tax lists thru 1754, being assessed only about half the rate of Jabez. "Administration of the estate of Samuel[4] Eaton of Hampton, N.H., was granted to his brother Jabez, 18 May 1756." Samuel[4]'s three parcels of real estate on the south side of Hampton Falls were evaluated at £635 in the inventory.

**56**  v. Jemima[4] Eaton, b. 15 Apr 1701; died 13 Oct 1709.

+ **57**  vi. Henry[4] Eaton, b. 22 Jan 1704; mar. Mary True, 1727.

**58**  vii. Jabez[4] Eaton, b. 11 Aug 1705; died in infancy.

+ **59**  viii. Jabez[4A] Eaton, b. 9 Aug 1708; mar. Sarah True; 1732.

\* \* \* \* \* \* \*

## B. *The Haverhill Branch*

**20. Thomas[3] Eaton** (Thomas[2], John[1]) was born 18 Mar 1660 in Haverhill, the first male Eaton born in that town. He mar. **Hannah Webster** of Haverhill 5 May 1684, and probably lived on the farm deeded him by his father in consideration of "natural love and affection." This farm the father had purchased of Henry Kimball 6 Dec 1682. It consisted of two lots, "one of four acres of upland," and "another lot adjacent thereto on the west of 12 acres, laid out in commons land." Thomas[3] Eaton, Jr., was killed by the Indians 15 Mar. 1697, in the same raid that Mrs. Hannah Dustin was taken prisoner (see Sidebar #1, p. 36). His widow, Hannah, died 14 Aug. 1747. The Eaton neighborhood for a hundred years and more was in plain sight of the famous Dustin homestead.

Children with Hannah at Haverhill:

**60**  i. Stephen[4] Eaton, b. 21 Mar 1685; died 29 Nov 1685.

+ **61**  ii. Thomas[4] Eaton, b. 7 Aug 1686; mar. Lydia Kimball, 1729.

**62**  iii. Hannah[4] Eaton, b. 30 Sep 1688; mar. Caleb Allen of Enfield, Mass., 4 Apr 1721. She d. 8 Jan 1786.

**63**  iv. Judith[4] Eaton, b. 5 Mar 1691; mar. Joseph Hazeltine, 28 Nov 1717, and had five daughters and a son. The son and three girls died young.

**64**  v. Joseph[4] Eaton, b. 18 Feb 1693; died ca. 1715, an unmarried weaver.

## #1. The Indian Wars

Few concerns were as prevalent for early English settlers in New England as those surrounding relationships with the native Indian population. In the decade or two before the arrival of the Mayflower in 1620, New England Indians had been laid waste by their lack of immunity to infectious European diseases like smallpox. Thus they were a thinned-out population, and one with which the first arrivals were able to establish reasonably friendly relations, by purchases of land and the like. As the Great Migration reached its climax in the 1630s, however, the "visitors" began to encroach more and more upon the Indians' hunting areas, and conflict became more intense.

Out of fear of the Indians, the English had first settled most intensively in coastal New England. But the natural increase of settlers, along with a large and steady flow of new migrants, assured that population pressure soon forced settlers further inland, straining relationships further. By the same token, of course, the Indian population near the coast was becoming a smaller and smaller minority of the whole. Sporadic conflict finally came to a head in King Philip's War in 1675-76. A coalition of tribes under the leadership of King Philip increased attacks on border communities until white settlers responded with an assault on the stronghold of the Narragansett leaders near Kingston, Rhode Island.

After this defeat, the Indian menace began to follow a different pattern. There was little organized resistance from local Indians, who were progressively disappearing in any case. But a number of strong Indian tribes in the province of Quebec were mobilized by the French colonial government there to carry out raids on the New England settlements some 300 miles to the southeast, as a simple extension of French-English hostilities in Europe. The royal road southeast was down Lake Champlain, across Vermont and then south again down the Connecticut or Merrimac River valleys.

By 1690, the Eaton population in the Salisbury area on the coast was somewhat buffered from these raids by new English settlements to the north and west. But Haverhill, 18 miles westward up the Merrimac, was very much exposed. And on the ill-fated 15th of March, 1697, Thomas Dustin and Jonathan Eaton (**#23**), who lived on adjacent tracts in the West Parish nearly three miles northwest of Haverhill village, were the first to spot the ad-

vancing Indians. The wives of both men had borne children six
days before, and were "lying in" at their homes. Jonathan Eaton
raced home and took wife and baby into a nearby swamp for con-
cealment. Thomas Dustin also warned his wife, but did not linger.
A troop of neighborhood children, some his own, were playing
nearby, so he mounted his horse to herd the children pell-mell
a half-mile or so to the safety of a town garrison.

The Indians behind him fell upon the Dustin house first.
They captured wife Hannah, knocking her baby Martha's brains
out against a tree in Jonathan Eaton's orchard. Then they split
into smaller parties to attack other houses in the area. In a very
short time they had plundered and torched nine houses, killing
all of their owners, including Thomas Eaton (**#20**), Jonathan's
older brother. In all, 27 settlers were killed (15 were children).
At this point, worried that the alarm had reached the village,
they retreated with Hannah Dustin and 12 other captives.

The denoument was a most celebrated story in the annals of
colonial New England. Hannah and her nurse Mary a few days
later were being held on an island in the Merrimac River near the
present Concord, N.H. by a family group of 13 Indians. Aided by
a prior captive white boy, age 14, whom they had discovered in the
group, the women rose in the night to slay their tormentors, then
returned downriver to great welcome in Haverhill (Chase, 1861).

Eatons in Maine also suffered casualties from the Indians in
this general period. As population pressure pushed the settlers
further and further inland, the threat of Indian attack at the frontier was ever present. Over the next half-century, sporadic attacks
continued and were met from time to time by British expeditions
nothward to strategic targets in Canada. The climax was reached
in the more formal hostilities of the French and Indian War begun
in 1756. The fall of Quebec to the British in September, 1759,
soon put all of Canada in English hands.

Just as suddenly, the New England colonies were liberated
from the longstanding Indian menace. A new Great Migration
broke out, bringing pioneers from coastal areas into western
Massachusetts, northward into New Hampshire, and surging into
the territory now Vermont, but then hotly disputed between the
New Hampshire and New York colonial governments. Warfare
with the Indians went on famously to the westward for another
century and a half; but the preoccupations of New Englanders
turned from Indian foes to discontent with British rule.

**65**  vi. Lydia[4] Eaton, b. 18 Oct 1694; mar. Joseph Harriman of Hav-
        erhill, 23 May 1723, and had four daughters and three sons;
        one of each died young.
**66**  vii. Nathaniel[4] Eaton, b. 14 Aug 1696; died 10 Jan 1698.

NOTE. In 1714, "several women petititioned for leave to build a women's
pew in the meeting house; among them were Hannah and Judith Eaton."

**22.  John[3] Eaton** (Thomas[2], John[1]) was born 6 Mar. 1664 in
Haverhill, Mass. He married **Mary Singletery** of Haverhill, 25 Jun 1700,
and settled on a five-acre farm deeded him by his father in Haverhill's
"Great Plain" to the east of the village. He added acreage over time, and
all of his children were born there. The main problem of the location
was its distance from the Haverhill Meeting House, and John[3] was active
in movements to establish a separate East Parish meeting house. He also
had a memorable term of service as Haverhill Town Clerk from 1717
until near his death, whereupon he was succeeded by his elder son John
(see **#69**). Wife Mary died 26 Jan 1729. He died in 1736, with conflicting dates of 10 Feb or 10 July. Since his son John was busy collecting quitclaims on his father's estate from his sisters in the June 1-July 10
period, the earlier date is preferable.

Children at Haverhill:

   **67**   i. Mary[4] Eaton, b. 10 Apr 1701; mar. Thomas Whittier of
              Methuen, Mass., 21 Aug 1729.
   **68**  ii. Sarah[4] Eaton, b. 4 Jun 1703; died unmarried.
 + **69** iii. John[4] Eaton, b. 5 Feb 1705; mar. Judith Hale of Newbury.
   **70**  iv. Anne[4] Eaton, b. 19 Apr 1708; spinster; died 26 Nov 1766
              in Haverhill, with her estate valued at £66.
 + **71**   v. Moses[4] Eaton, b. 6 Sep 1710; mar. Susanna Lecount, 1768.
   **72**  vi. Nathaniel[4] Eaton, b. 28 Apr 1714; died young.
   **73** vii. Thomas[4] Eaton, b. 25 May 1717; died young.
   **74** viii. Eunice[4] Eaton, b. 6 May 1720; died young.

NOTE. When father John's estate was settled, daughters Mary and Anne
sold portions to their brother John, who took the homestead and paid all the debts.

**23. Jonathan[3] Eaton** (Thomas[2], John[1]) was born 23 Apr 1668 in
Haverhill, Mass. He mar. 1st, **Sarah Sanders** of Haverhill, 17 Mar 1695.
His eldest son James was born 9 Mar 1697, the same day as Mrs. Dustin's
child nearby. The Dustin infant's brains were dashed out six days later
by Indians against an apple tree on Jonathan[3]'s land. That his wife might
escape the attack, Jonathan concealed her in a swamp nearby, and with
this exposure took cold, leading to her death, although she survived until
23 Apr 1698. Jonathan[3] mar. 2d, **Ruth Page** of Haverhill, 23 Jan. 1699.
He was a farmer and lived on the original Eaton homestead deeded him

"from love" by his father Thomas², who says that it "was formerly my father John Eaton's." The inventory of Jonathan³'s estate, "appraised 6 May 1724 amounting to £743/2sh/6d.," quite a large real estate, mentions "homestead 38 acres with old house, with new house with boards, nails and bricks and all other materials ready to finish it." The cellar, where this new house had stood, was all that marked the site in 1888. It was found in the West Parish, a little south of the old grave yard. Of Jonathan³'s six children, only three lived to be married. He died 20 Jan 1723, and wife Ruth died 2 Apr 1743.

Child by Sarah at Haverhill:

+ **75**   i. James⁴ Eaton, b. 9 Mar 1697; mar. 1st, Mrs. Rachel (Kimball) Ayer, 13 Jun 1728.

Children by Ruth at Haverhill:

**76**   ii. Nathaniel⁴ Eaton, b. 5 Mar 1701; died early in life.
**77**   iii. Sarah⁴ Eaton, b. 7 Mar 1702; died young.
+ **78**   iv. Jonathan⁴ Eaton, b. 30 Mar 1705; mar. Jane Page, 1733.
**79**   v. David⁴ Eaton, b. 14 Feb 1707; died young.
**80**   vi. Ruth⁴ Eaton, b. 17 Apr 1712; mar. Samuel Merrill of Haverhill, 2 May 1732; had two daughters and two sons.

**24. Job³ Eaton** (Thomas², John¹) was born 22 Apr 1671 in Haverhill; mar. **Mary Simons** of Haverhill, 10 Jan 1698. He occupied a small farm in the West Parish, where his children were born. Like most of his brothers, he was a member of the Haverhill contingent of the "snowshoe regiment" organized in the bleak winter of 1710 as one protection against the Indians. He died 17 Sep 1717. His widow Mary mar. 2d, John Marsh, also of Haverhill, 8 Feb 1721.

Children with Mary at Haverhill:

+ **81**   i. Samuel⁴ Eaton, b. 5 Oct 1699; mar. Mehitable Harriman, 1721.
+ **82**   ii. Thomas⁴ Eaton, b. 20 Feb 1701; mar. Mehitable Carter, 1730.
**83**   iii. Abigail⁴ Eaton, b. 14 Feb 1703; died young.
**84**   iv. Mary⁴ Eaton, b. 9 Jun 1707; mar. Isaac Dalton, cordwainer of Haverhill, 28 Dec 1727 and had four sons and six daughters. Husband Isaac died at Cape Breton. Wife Mary died 6 Jul 1758 at Haverhill.

**25. Timothy³ Eaton** (Thomas², John¹) was born 19 May 1674 in Haverhill; mar. **Ruth Chapman** 1 Mar 1721 at Greenland, N.H.; and lived on a farm provided by his father on Kenoza Lake (then, the "Great Pond") in Haverhill. This put him some distance east of the village, and he like his brother John frequently agitated for a separate East Parish. He was the most active Haverhill Eaton in real estate. In 1752, with the town facing a smallpox epidemic, his dwelling was declared a "pest house." In his will, probated 5 Jul 1763, from which it is evident that he left no children nor grandchildren, he divided his real estate among 14 legatees, among which was "Rev. Benjamin Parker, Congregational minister of the East Parish in Haverhill, all my homestead lying between Moses Hazen and the present parsonage land, after my wife's decease." He appointed Benjamin Parker executor and made him residuary legatee. This "homestead" given to Mr. Parker, according to the *History of Haverhill* (Chase, 1861) "was occupied in 1860 by Henry Davis, next north of Joshua Lake."

# Generation Four

## A. *The Salisbury Branch*

**30. John[4] Eaton** (John[3-1]) was born ca. Jun 1687 in Salisbury, Mass.; mar. **Esther Swett**, 18 Nov. 1708.    She had been born 10 June 1690 to Joseph Swett of Hampton, N.H.    John[4] was a housewright, and appears to have made some of his living by improving property and re-selling it.    Soon after his marriage, his wife's father gave Esther the 20-acre Lot #137 in the 2d (West) Division in Hampton, on the southeast side of the Hampton-Exeter road (Rockingham County deed 7:362).    Al-though no house is mentioned in this 1709 deed, the couple seem to have lived there, and 18 months later, in Sep 1711, they sold this lot *with house* to Jacob Green (Deed 10: 328).    Soon thereafter, in March 1711-2, John[4] bought Lot #8 of the Cain's Brook Division back in what was still his na-tive Salisbury, Mass. (now in   central Seabrook, N.H.) (Essex County Deed 56:91).    Although the lot seemed unimproved when purchased, it not only had a house on it when John[4] sold it in early 1718 to John Gove (Rockingham Deed 12:26), but was described as the second homestead of John[4]'s family at the time.    The family then moved to a lot in Salisbury's Gravelly Ridge Division (once again, now in Seabrook, probably not far south or north of the corner of Washington and Collins in South Seabrook) owned by father John[3] Eaton.    The father died immediately thereafter, officially bequeathing John[4] this property, although he and his family were already residing there before the will was drawn up.

It is very likely that they remained at this third homestead in proto-Seabrook thereafter.    The tax lists for Hampton Falls are available continuously beginning with 1747, and for each of the 21 years 1747-67, there are separate entries for a John Eaton and a John Eaton, Jr.    The tem-poral stability of the relative tax levels for these two Johns helps to rule out the possibility that an eldest John died in a given year and a younger John came onto the tax stream in the same year, such that "John, Jr." is not the same person throughout.    It is also beyond much doubt that these two John Eatons are this John[4] and his oldest son John[5].    In fact, their re-spective tax liabilities are interdependent over time: the senior John's de-clines in the period when he is 62-67 years old, and John Jr.'s increases correspondingly: this is a common timing pattern that reflects *de facto* transfer of real and personal property to the next generation, especially, as in this case, to the eldest son.    The general tax level for this succession of John households was average for Hampton Falls or slightly better.    It does not compare with the high levels of the Walton Road Eatons out of Eph-raim[3], but is generally higher than that for other Eatons living south of Walton Road in proto-Seabrook.

After Seabrook was established as a separate jurisdiction in 1768, the two John Eatons continue on Seabrook tax lists. Father John[4] lived into his mid-nineties, dying most probably in 1782. He is said to have died testate, but no will seems to have survived. The record of the children of John[4]/Esther is somewhat incomplete at all three of their residences, but has been reconstructed (with possible gaps) from miscellaneous sources.

Children:

+ **85**   i. John[5] Eaton, b. ca. Sep 1709 at Hampton; mar. Hannah Fowler.
  **86**  ii. Joseph[5] Eaton, b. 30 Aug 1711 at Hampton; died young.
+ **87**  iii. Benjamin[5] Eaton, b. ca. 1718; mar. Jane Hutchins, 1747.
+ **88**  iv. William[5] Eaton, b. ca. 1720; mar. Meribah Wardwell. He was
           the first white man to settle permanently on Deer Isle, Maine.
+ **89**   v. Thomas[5] Eaton, b. 17 Mar 1722; mar. Jane Wheeler, 1743.
+ **90**  vi. Wyman[5] Eaton, b. 24 Jul 1725; mar. Ruth Merrill, 1745.
+ **91** vii. Joseph[5A] Eaton, b. 9 May 1728; mar. Sarah Burnell ca. 1751.
  **92** viii. Rachel[5] Eaton, b. 2 May 1731. A Rachel Eaton, otherwise
           unidentified, mar. Samuel Colby on 5 Oct 1766 at South
           Hampton, N.H. (So. Hampton church records).

**31. William[4] Eaton** (John[3-1]) was born ca. Nov 1689 at Salisbury Mass. His father gave him by his 1718 will "one half of my land and righ in the Winnegant's Cove, so called, at Kennebeck." Mrs. Rebecca King o Essex Co., Mass., sold "marsh land in Wells, to William Eaton of Wells" (Deed dated 29 Oct 1718). Records of Wells, Me., state that William Eator and **Mary Littlefield** were joined in marriage 19 Jan 1709. The records o the 1st Congregational Church in Wells show that William Eaton unitec with the church 10 Feb. 1722, and that Mary Eaton joined 23 Dec 1722 Their first four children were baptized there 10 Feb 1723. Thus it seem: that seven children were born to William and Mary Eaton of Wells. In the will of William[4] Eaton of Wells dated 31 Mar. 1741, he mentions but fou children: Joshua Eaton, Mary "Credifer," Ruth Eaton and Joseph Eaton from which we suppose that the other three children died in childhood o youth. He speaks of Ruth and Joseph as under age, and provides "fo education, learning and bringing up of my son Joseph until he arrives a 21, and Ruth until she arrives to the age of 18." We thus see that William at the age of 21 set up a branch house of the Eaton Family, from which ha: gone forth a long line of descendants.

Children at Wells, Me.:

  **93**   i. Mary[5] Eaton, b. 4 Jul 1710; mar. Josiah Crediford, int. 3 Apr
           1734; resided Wells, Me.
  **94**  ii. Sarah[5] Eaton, b. 21 Apr 1713; died young.
+ **95**  iii. Joshua[5] Eaton, b. 9 Mar 1714; after possible other brief marri-

ages, he mar. Anna Delzell, 1745; resided at Wells.
**96**   iv. William[5] Eaton, b. 1 Apr 1717; died 1723.
**97**   v. Martha[5] Eaton, b. ca. 1720; died young.
**98**   vi. Ruth[5] Eaton, b. ca. 1725; mar. Joshua Adams, resided at Wells.
+ **99**  vii. Joseph[5] Eaton, b. ca. 1727; mar. Lydia Moulton; res. at Wells.


**33. Samuel[4] Eaton** (John[3-1]) was born 25 Nov 1692 in Salisbury, Mass.  He married 1st, **Hannah[3] Worthen** then of Amesbury, in 1713 (intentions 3 Oct. 1713).   Hannah was the eldest daughter of John[2] Worthen (Ezekiel[1]) and had been born 10 Oct 1690 at Amesbury.  Samuel[4] and Hannah probably lived out their lives on a lot in the upland portion of the old Salisbury Cow Commons Division, inherited from his father, on the east side of the corner made when Forest Rd. turns from heading east to heading north alongside the marshes.  Their homestead burned at some time before Nov. 1728, when Samuel was obliged to reconstruct deeds lost in the fire (cf. Essex Co. deed 63:236).  He and wife Hannah attended Quaker meeting, requesting in 1732 that they might be under the care of the Hampton Meeting of Friends.
In the winter of 1742-3 events occurred which were to shape the future of Samuel[4]'s line vitally.  Hannah's father John Worthen died intestate, and Samuel[4] was asked by probate court to administer the estate (N.H. Probate 15:227), probably because the surviving Worthen children were all daughters, and Samuel was the husband of the eldest daughter.  The estate in question was a farm that John Worthen had bought in 1728 from James Toppan of Salisbury, centered on a ten-acre lot at the "Long Pines", later "Worthen's Point", in old Salisbury's Gravelly Ridge Division, yet which had just become part of Hampton Falls, because of the change in colony boundaries.  This Lot #49 (original right of Enoch Greenleaf) lay at the tip of the point of land running east into the marshes on which South Main St. in what is now South Seabrook then terminated.  Administration of this estate turned out to be slow and controversial.  Samuel[4] was obliged in May 1743 to swear he had shown those appointed to inventory the estate all of the property.  At some time, probably late 1744, Samuel's wife Hannah died in her turn.  Just before or just after her death, Samuel[4] petitioned the court in Nov. 1744 to settle the whole estate on the deceased John's eldest daughter, who was his wife, on grounds that dividing the homestead among all seven daughters "would be prejudicial to the whole" (N.H. Probate, 12:417).  This petition was apparently denied, and the estate was finally settled in March 1744-5, divided into seven thin strips.  One of these went to the heirs of Hannah (Worthen), and formed the base of the homestead of her son David[5].  Two other strips were purchased by son Elisha[5] Eaton in 1747 from the Select Men of Hampton Falls, who needed the proceeds to cover town losses in paying for the keep and care of two of the seven Worthen daughters, Rebecca and Abigail, who had inherited one strip each but were *non compos mentis*.
Samuel[4] mar. 2d, **Huldah (Stanyan) Kenney**, 17 Oct 1745, at Hampton.  Huldah was also a member of the Hampton Quaker Meeting, daughter of James Stanyan of that town.  She had mar. 1st, John Kenney of

Dover, N.H., son of Joseph Kenney, in a Quaker wedding 3 Oct 1729, and
they had had two daughters.  Samuel[4] and Huldah continued as active
Quakers, living on the Cow Commons homestead in Salisbury but participating in the Hampton meeting of Friends.  Throughout this period Samuel[4] is taxed for possession of Hampton Falls property, although on the
separate list of "Salisbury men."  He died 7 May 1765 at Salisbury, and his
Hampton Falls taxation ends appropriately in that year.

        Children with Hannah:

   **100**   i. Jemima[5] Eaton, b. 2 Oct 1717; int. mar. with Jacob Satterle, Jr.,
                17 Nov 1739; mar. Samuel Maxfield of Salisbury, 31 Jan
                1741/42.
 + **101**   ii. Elisha[5] Eaton, b. 3 Feb 1723; mar. Elizabeth Blake, 1747.
   **102**  iii. Sarah[5] Eaton, b. 23 July 1726; mar. Christopher Toppan of
                Hampton, N.H., 14 Dec 1748.  "Sally" died in 1807, a year
                after her husband, and is buried in the Baptist Cemetery at
                Center Sandwich, N.H. [LDS Film #015575].
 + **103**   iv. David[5] Eaton, b. 15 Nov 1728; mar. Lydia Fowler, 1756.
   **104**   v. Martha[5] Eaton, b. 22 Jan 1730; mar. Abraham Drake, 5 Mar
                1752 at Hampton.
   **105**   vi. Lydia[5] Eaton, b. 8 Aug 1737.  A Lydia Eaton of Salisbury
                mar. Benjamin Lovering of Fairfield or Ipswich, Mass.,
                26 Jan 1775.


        Likely children with Huldah at Salisbury:

 + **106**  vii. Jonathan[5] Eaton, b. late 1745 or early 1746; mar. Nancy
                Towle (?) in 1768; resided Chester, then Pittsfield, N.H.
 + **107** viii. Samuel[5] Eaton, b. 28 Aug. 1747; mar. Rachel Greeley.


        NOTE. The reconstruction of this family is radically revised over the original
Rev. Eaton manuscript, and copied by Molyneux (1911).  Rev. Eaton gave Samuel's
wife as "Huldah Worthen", thereby telescoping the two wives into one.  This left him
with a need to explain the 1745 marriage of a Samuel Eaton with a Huldah Stanyan.
With no other recorded Samuels available at that place and time, but signs of an
affinity between the Samuel[4] family and the later Samuel/Huldah, it was decided that
Samuel[4] must have had an unrecorded child Samuel[5] who could become the missing
bridegroom.  The problem was that in order to qualify, such a Samuel[5] had to be born
before 1730, whereas the recorded Samuel/Hannah birth order as first reconstructed by
the Reverend for the Eaton Family Association publication of 1891 was essentially
"full" from 1717 through 1730.  To cope with this inconvenience, the son Jonathan[5],
putatively of Samuel/Hannah, with an unrecorded birth that Rev. Eaton had used in the
1891 publication to plug an earlier hole as "ca. 1720", was postponed until the next
available hole as "ca. 1733," to accomodate a speculative Samuel[5] birth as "ca. 1720."
In one sense this postponement seemed plausible, as there is no clear sign of the
Jonathan involved until a 1768 marriage, already late by normal standards even for a
1733 birth, much less a 1720 one.  But it is repeatedly clear that Samuel[4] was first

married to a Hannah (Worthen); that she died about 1744; and that his wife was Huldah at the time of his death in 1765. Therefore there is not much doubt but that the 1745 marriage with Huldah Stanyan gave him a second wife, and that there is no need to concoct a son Samuel born ca. 1720 to serve as this bridegroom. It is worth note that this solution is exactly the one used by Hoyt in his *Old Families of Salisbury and Amesbury* which only began to appear in print the year after Rev. Eaton's death in 1896. It is also true that a typescript of deaths in Pittsfield, N.H., shows that Jonathan, son of Samuel[4], died there June 18, 1809, *at age 63*. If this account is accurate, then this Jonathan was born more than a decade later than even the Rev. Eaton's second assignment for him. This means in turn that his 1768 marriage was at a more conventional age than had earlier appeared to be the case. But it also means that this Jonathan[5] was born too late to have been a son of Hannah [Worthen]; and in the time of transition to the new wife, Huldah [Stanyan]. Of course the age at death may have been underestimated, and thus Jonathan may indeed have been a son of Hannah's. On the other hand, this Jonathan has always had a peculiar role in Samuel's family, and may have actually been instead a stepchild of Samuel[4]. See discussion under **#106** below.

**35. Jonathan[4] Eaton** (John[3-1]) was born 2 Oct 1698 in Salisbury, Mass.; mar. **Judith Ash** of Salisbury, 24 Nov 1720. He was a farmer of some means in Salisbury, where all of his children were born. In the will of his father John[3], Jonathan had received all of his father's land and rights in the "Little Neck", so-called; the half-lot his father had held on the Great Neck in common with his uncle Capt. Joseph; and one-quarter of his meadow and marshland after the death of his mother. Most of this land was east of East Salisbury village, in the general area of Beach Road where the original Eaton family homestead was. Jonathan's own homestead was described as 30 acres "near the Neck bridge," which presumably passed over the small stream a few rods west of the fork to Dock Road. Jonathan's few other ventures into real estate seem to have been focussed on embellishing his inherited core of land. Although his family was large, a fortnight before he died intestate at a relatively young age, Jonathan[4] took pains to deed away his possessions across his family (Essex Co. deed 89:185). After the death of their mother, eldest son Theophilus[5], then age 24, was to receive two-thirds of all of his real and personal estate, while third son Thomas[5], then 16, would receive the other third (second son Abel[5] was by this time established in Maine). His two surviving daughters and four other sons received cash bequests. He died 7 July 1745.

There was a great dispersal of the Jonathan/Judith children from their point of origin on Beach Road, Salisbury. Of the six males surviving till adulthood, three went to Maine; one to Sandown, N.H.; and two to Newbury, Mass.

Children born at Salisbury, Mass.:

+ **108**    i. Theophilus[5] Eaton, b. 3 Jul 1721; mar. Abigail Fellows; resided Sandown, N.H., Brunswick and Deer Isle, Maine.

## #2. The "Throat Distemper" of 1735-36

In May, 1835, Farmer Clough of Kingston, N.H. was distressed at the sudden death of his hog, and examined its inflamed throat. Within a day his own throat was badly swollen, and a few days later he was dead. His family was infected and soon their neighbors as well, with what we would now call a transgenic disease. Thus began the raging epidemic of "throat distemper" that swept away a large number of children and some adults in the lower Merrimack Valley in the 1735-36 period. In Kingston alone, 114 deaths occurred over 14 months, and the impact was even more lethal in the Hampton Falls area, with 210 people-- one-sixth of the total population dying, 160 of them children under ten. Twenty families there lost all of their children (Brown, 1900, p. 301).

For our Eaton clan, the records of fourth-generation parents are laden with these child deaths. Many members of the Salisbury branch of the family were drifting northward from Salisbury toward the Hampton grant, of which Hampton Falls was the southernmost township, and hence they were close to the center of the storm. But Haverhill, only 12 miles south of Kingston, lost more than half of its children under 15, and a smaller spike of child deaths registered in Salisbury, Mass.

We can define the Eaton children at greatest risk as those born from 1724 to 1736, who were residing in the Salisbury or Haverhill areas (i.e., excluding Eatons who had emigrated to more distant places like Maine). There were 30 such children in Salisbury and proto-Seabrook, of whom 13 died, all in 1736 or early 1737. The distribution of these children across families was, as we would expect with this kind of contagion, quite uneven. Out of the 10 Eaton households with children at risk, four with a sum of 9 children had no deaths. Of the other six households, one had a single death, three had two, and two families had three deaths. This is 13 deaths across 21 children at the ages of risk in infected households. Most desolated of the parents were Jabez[4A] and Sarah Eaton, who lost all three of their first children. The toll was lighter but still visible in the smaller population of Eatons at Haverhill. There, with 17 Eaton children at risk, 3 died in 1736.

The epidemic rolled on in every direction from the Kingston epicenter. It took two years, but it reached the Hudson River in New York State (Chase, 1861).

**109** ii. Nancy[5] ("Nanna") Eaton, b. 15 Nov 1723.
**110** iii. Patience[5] Eaton, b. 6 Apr 1725. Either Nancy[5] or Patience mar.
    a Pritchard of Newburyport: descendants still there, 1891.
+ **111** iv. Abel[5] Eaton, b. 1 Mar 1727; mar. 1st, Mrs. Dorcas Coombs at
    Brunswick, Me.
+ **112** v. Thomas[5] Eaton, b. 8 Feb 1729; mar. Eunice Moulton of New-
    bury, Mass.
+ **113** vi. Ezekiel[5] Eaton, b. 7 Dec 1730; mar. Mary Campbell; resided
    at Sandown, N.H.
**114** vii. James[5] Eaton, b. 11 Feb 1733; died 21 Jul 1748.
**115** viii. Joseph[5] Eaton, b. Jan 1735; died 5 May 1736.
**116** ix. Mary[5] Eaton, b. 17 Aug 1737; died 1 Nov 1737.
**117** x. Judith[5] Eaton, b. 14 Oct 1738; died 6 May 1740.
+ **118** xi. Joseph[5A] Eaton, b. 7 Mar 1741; probably mar. Sarah Webster;
    resided Newbury, Mass.
**119** xii. Judith[5A] Eaton, bp. 18 Sep 1743 at Salisbury.
+ **120** xiii. Jonathan[5] Eaton, b. 6 Sep 1745; rem. to Maine; mar. Diana
    Dow and settled on Deer Isle, Maine.

**36. Thomas[4] Eaton** (John[3-1]) was born 21 Mar 1701 at Salisbury;
mar. on 6 Jan 1727 at Salisbury, **Mehitable Cilley**, daughter of
Benoni/Elenor who had been born 15 Feb 1704 at Salisbury. He received,
along with his brother William, a half-share in his father's land and rights in
Winnegant's Cove, Maine. But he could not capitalize on this bequest,
because he must have died very soon after the marriage, for Salisbury
records say that "widow Mehitable Eaton was married to Elihu Dow of
Salisbury, 6 May 1728." No known children.

**38. Daniel[4A] Eaton** (John[3-1]) was born 11 Mar. 1710, and baptized
23 Apr 1710; mar. **Nancy Pike** of Salisbury 24 Nov 1730 (Newbury,
Mass. Church Records). Daniel[4A] lived nearly the last 50 years of his life
on the original Eaton homestead on Beach Road, and this property remained in the possession of his ancestors for another century. It is not
perfectly clear who occupied this homestead between the death of father
John[3] in 1718, and 1750 when Daniel[4A] moved back to reside on the homestead. Rev. Eaton read the record as saying that Daniel's older brother
Jonathan[4] resided there in the intervening period. It is true that Jonathan[4]
received in his father's will a "half-lot" on the Great Neck which by other
clues was in the immediate vicinity of the old homestead, along with other
outlying parcels. But nothing is mentioned about a homestead or any
"tenement" on the lot; and later in the same will the youngest son, Daniel[4A],
then a mere seven years old, is bequeathed "all my homestead," along with
other outlying parcels, to be enjoyed upon the death of his mother. One
interpretation is that the bequests were designed to divide the original
homestead lot into two halves for the two surviving younger sons, although
Daniel[4A] was due to get the half with the dwelling unit on it when his
mother died. In 1745, as we have just seen, Jonathan[4] died and left his

estate and homestead to his elder sons Theophilus[5] (two-thirds) and Thomas[5] (one-third).  In Dec 1749, Theophilus and his mother Judith sold th
deceased Jonathan's 30-acre homestead, or at least their share of it, t
brother Thomas for £160 (Essex Co. Deed 95:228).   Two months late
however, Theophilus bought out Thomas's interest in father Jonathan'
homestead for £12 (99:118).  A month later, in Mar 1750, Theophilus, wh
was residing in Sandown, N.H., with an eye on removing to Maine, sold hi
cousin Daniel[4A] for £80 two parcels of land, one of which was of 20 acre
with buildings "near the Neck Bridge" (also 99:118).  A day later Daniel[4]
sold the 2-acre "homestead" where he had been living more or less sinc
marriage to other cousins Nicholas[4] (Capt. Joseph[3]) and Abraham[5]
(Benjamin[4], Capt. Joseph[3]), presumably because he no longer needed i
(99:120).   What underlies all these maneuvers is less than clear, althoug
they obviously bear on how Daniel[4A] came to live in the old homestea
already bequeathed him over 30 years earlier.  The most likely construc
tion is that Daniel's mother died about 1750, making the original home
stead available to him; and that the dealings with Theophilus referred to
restoration of more of the original estate by incorporating back into it th
half-lot, now improved, that had gone to Jonathan[4].  By this construction
John[3]'s widow probably lived there most of the time between 1718 an
1750, although son Jonathan was living in his own house close by.

It might be thought that acquisition of the old homestead provide
Daniel[4A] with a substantial base of operations.  It was not, however, an im
pressive piece of real estate in this period, in part due to progressive parti
tion over two generations.  In the Massachusetts Tax Valuation of 1771
carried out when Daniel[4A] was 61, he had less than ten acres in agricultura
production, and the total value of the homestead was about one-fifth that o
his cousin Capt. Henry[4] Eaton's, and less than half of the value of hi
nephew Samuel[5] Eaton's on Forest Road, and only about half the averag
for all estate holders in the town.

Daniel[4A] was a "yeoman" and did little in real estate beyond the fev
dealings mentioned.  He engaged in civic affairs, but also only in a mino
way.  He was a tithing-man once in 1746, and frequently served the town a
one of their hog reeves.  In 1794 he deeded his son James[5] the Salisbury
homestead and supplementary parcels.  Daniel[4A] died 20 Sep 1798.

Children born at Salisbury, Mass.:

121    i. William[5] Eaton, b. 12 Jun 1731; may have mar. an Anna, there-
          by accounting for the birth of a Hannah to a William & Ann
          Eaton on 2 Jun 1769 at Salisbury, who apparently died there
          5 Feb 1777 at age 8.  An Anna, wife of William, died at Salis-
          bury on 21 Dec 1804.  It is also possible that this Anna was
          the widow Anna Arnold, who was in the area in this period,
          although she is as likely to have married Jonathan[5] Eaton (cf.
          #106).  This William[5] is also said to have died without issue a
          Salisbury, 1814.
122   ii. Abigail[5] Eaton, b. 21 May 1733; died 22 May 1736.
123  iii. Mary[5] Eaton, b. 23 Jul 1735; died 13 Dec 1736.

**124** iv. Moses[5] Eaton, b. 3 Aug 1737; a mariner; died at sea unmar.
**125** v. Abigail[5A] Eaton, b. 31 May 1739; mar. Jonathan Ealot (Elliot?), 22 Sep 1769; resided in Salisbury.
**126** vi. Joshua[5] Eaton, b. 9 Mar 1741; a mariner, never married.
**127** vii. Mary[5A] Eaton, b. 27 May 1743; remained unmarried, living on the family homestead until she died 15 Jul 1834.
+ **128** viii. Daniel[5] Eaton, b. 19 May 1745; mar. Hannah Walton, 1771.
+ **129** ix. Benjamin[5] Eaton, b. 4 Aug 1747; mar. Mary Manning, 1778.
**130** x. Nancy[5] "Nanne" Eaton, b. 5 Sep 1749; mar. John Hinkson of Salisbury; resided in Epping, N.H.
**131** xi. Martha[5] Eaton, b. 30 Aug 1751; mar. Abel[6] Eaton (cf. **#279**).
**132** xii. Bette[5] Eaton, b. 1753; mar. Caleb Pike, 7 Mar 1776; res. Salisbury. Caleb died 8 Mar 1824; Bette died 13 Feb 1830.
**133** xiii. Sarah[5] Eaton, b. ca. 1756; mar. William Pike of Salisbury, 9 Feb 1783. No issue.
+ **134** xiv. James[5] Eaton, b. ca. 1759; mar. Sarah[6] Eaton (**#280**), daughter of Wyman[5], 1780.

**43. John[4A] Eaton** (Capt. Joseph[3], John[2-1]) was born 18 Oct 1685 in Salisbury, Mass.; mar. 1st, **Esther Johnson** of Kingston, N.H. ca. 1713, and lived in Salisbury. He was a housewright. Wife Esther died 22 Jan. 1728, having had at least eight children. John[4A] Eaton mar. 2d, **Elizabeth Hook**, 2 July 1728, by whom he had two children.

In 1731 he bought from his father Capt. Joseph[3] a 48-acre "tenement" in Salisbury, including a dwelling-house, barn and orchard (Essex Deeds, 65:22). When his own son Joseph[5] was 25 in 1736, John[4A] deeded the east half (25 acres) of the homestead to his son Joseph[5] "for love and affection" (72:118). John[4A] died intestate 1 Mar. 1746. "Administration granted to his son Joseph[5], cordwainer of Salisbury, his mother Elizabeth having declined the appointment." The inventory showed a significant estate valued at £307, two-thirds of it represented by the remaining homestead of 30 acres. Wife Elizabeth mar. 2d, Abner Lowell, 28 Dec. 1752.

Children with Esther at Salisbury, Mass.:

**135** i. John[5] Eaton, b. 13 May 1714; died 9 June 1736.
+ **136** ii. Joseph[5] Eaton, b. 30 Aug 1715; mar. Jane True, 1737.
**137** iii. Abigail[5] Eaton, b. 27 Sep 1716; mar. Jacob Bradbury of Salisbury, 18 Dec 1733, at Salisbury.
**138** iv. Benjamin[5] Eaton, b. ca. Oct 1718; may have died 14 Mar 1737, although this may represent a confusion with the certified death date of his uncle Benjamin[4] (cf. **#46**).
**139** v. Hannah[5] Eaton, b. 7 Sep 1721.
**140** vi. Mary[5] Eaton, b. 27 Mar 1723; mar. Benjamin Kimball of Haverhill, Mass. and Hampstead, N.H., 22 Dec 1742. Had seven sons and one daughter. Mary[5] died 29 Aug 1757.
**141** vii. Moses[5] Eaton, b. 28 Dec 1724; died 8 June 1736.

**142** viii. Esther⁵ Eaton, b. 16 Jan 1728; died 5 Jun 1736.

Children with Elizabeth, at Salisbury, Mass.:

**143**  ix. Elizabeth⁵ Eaton, b. 21 Oct 1730; died 6 June 1736.
**144**  x. John⁵ᴬ Eaton, b. 22 Sep 1732; mar. Mary Merrill of Salisbury, 25 Jan 1770.  Perhaps this boy's name was changed to John after the death of his half-brother John⁵ on 9 Jun 1736, altho his record of baptism 1 Oct 1732 also reads "John." He resided in Seabrook and was a yeoman. Administration of his estate granted in 1819. Wife Mary died 15 Jul 1834.

**44. Samuel⁴ Eaton** (Capt. Joseph³, John²⁻¹) was born 7 Dec 1687 in Salisbury.  He inherited a love of exploration.  To gratify it he plunged into the forests of Maine, and finally settled in what is now Brunswick, Me. The following quotation from Wheeler (1878) is presumably true with exceptions noted in brackets: "Samuel Eaton, the ancestor of the Brunswick family of this name, came to Brunswick from Salisbury, Mass., early in the last century, and built a house on what is now the southern corner of Bank and Main streets, where the billiard saloon stands (1878).  He had two children and perhaps more.  One of his children, Samuel, was a soldier at Fort George in 1722." [The soldier must have been the father, who was probably not married until about 1715.]  "He was the one sent to George-town with a letter to Captains Harmon and Moody.  The letter was tied in his hair.  When it was not safe by land, he took to the water and swam.  The other son, Moses" [actually, brother Moses⁴ (**#47**), born 18 May 1695], was taken prisoner in June, 1722, cruelly mutilated and carried to Pleasant Point where the Indians killed him."

Samuel⁴ mar. **Mary Malcolm**, daughter of John Malcolm of Brunswick, formerly of Salisbury, Mass. about 1715. Martin Eaton, a great grandson born 1796, described their two sons, including Daniel⁵, men-tioned as grandsons in the will of John Malcolm.

Children (order of birth speculative):

**145**   ?. Enoch⁵ Eaton, drowned in boyhood.
+ **146**   ?. Daniel⁵ Eaton, b. ca. 1722; mar. Jane Dunlap; through them has descended the Eaton family of Brunswick, Me.
**147**   ?. Mary⁵ Eaton, mar. intentions with Thomas Stoddard of Bruns-wick, 1747?

**45. Joseph⁴ Eaton** (Capt. Joseph³, John²⁻¹) was born 14 Aug. 1690; mar. **Mary French**, also of Salisbury, 25 Mar 1724.  They probably re-sided in Newbury, Mass.  Joseph⁴ died a few years after the marriage, for "Administration of Joseph Eaton of Newbury was granted to his widow Mary, 4 Apr 1727."  Essex Co. Probate)  In the will of his father, Capt. Joseph³, dated 14 Mar, 1742, bequest is made to "two daughters, Mary and

Sarah, of my son Joseph deceased." His widow, Mary, mar. 2d, Ensign Andrew Downer of Salisbury, 24 Jan 1740.

Children:

**148**    i. Mary[5] Eaton, b. 9 Jan 1725.
**149**   ii. Sarah[5] Eaton, b. May 1727; mar. Joshua Pike of Salisbury,
              25 Feb 1749/50.

**46. Benjamin[4] Eaton** (Capt. Joseph[3], John[2-1]) was born 14 Feb 1693 in Salisbury, Mass.; mar. **Sarah[3] Morrill** (Abraham[2-1]) of Salisbury, 3 Feb. 1718/19. Sarah had been born 18 Dec. 1696, and before her marriage had declared herself the only child and heir of her father Abraham. Benjamin[4] was admitted to the First Church of Salisbury in Jan. 1728, and his wife was admitted a month later, both having been baptized in infancy. Benjamin was given a tenement next to the village green by his father in 1719 (Essex Deed 37:120), and as a carpenter and housewright appears to have had a cooper's shop there as well. He was more active in real estate than his oldest brother John[4A], and dealt in numerous lots of the Cow Common Division. He died early, 16 Mar 1737. Wife Sarah died 9 Apr 1743.

Children at Salisbury:

**150**    i. Abraham[5] Eaton, b. 9 Feb 1720; died 25 Mar 1720.
+ **151**  ii. Abraham[5A] Eaton, b. 13 May 1721; mar. 1st, Martha True,
              19 Dec 1742; 2d, Thankful Hubbard; res. Salisbury.
**152**  iii. Sarah[5] Eaton, b. 1 Mar 1722/23; mar. Jabez True, Jr., of Salis-
              bury, 10 Feb 1741.
**153**  iv. Anna[5] Eaton, b. 30 Mar 1725; mar. Thomas Arnold, a black-
              smith of Newbury, 10 Nov 1747. They resided first at New-
              bury, and then at Salisbury, where Thomas died in 1763,
              leaving Anna with two sons and two or three daughters. It
              is possible that she married her second cousin Jonathan[5]
              Eaton in 1769 (see discussion of **#106** below).
**154**   v. Rhoda[5] Eaton, b. 15 Mar 1727; bapt 19 Mar 1727; mar. Joseph
              Dow of Salisbury, son of Jonathan Dow, 9 Dec 1747.
**155**  vi. Elizabeth[5] Eaton, b. 19 Oct 1729; mar. Simon Noyes of New-
              bury, Mass., 9 Nov 1754, his 2d wife. Issue, 3 children.
**156** vii. Benjamin[5] Eaton, b. 29 Dec. 1731; died 22 Oct 1737.
**157** viii. Rachel[5] Eaton, b. 1 Apr 1735; died 20 Oct 1737.

**49. Nicholas[4] Eaton** (Capt. Joseph[3], John[2-1]) was born 12 Sep 1699 at Salisbury. He was admitted to the 1st Church 7 Apr 1728. The will of his father Capt. Joseph[3] Eaton, dated 2 Feb 1735 but not implemented until 1743, made Nicholas sole executor and residuary legatee to receive the homestead, household goods, livestock, etc. Having this home, he desired a companion, so he mar., although late in life, **Mercy Walton**, of South Hampton, 29 Jul 1756.

Unlike his brothers, Nicholas[4] was not a carpenter, and is referred to in deeds, 1750-70, as a "yeoman." His own estate, counted in the 1771 Tax Valuation, was not worth much more than half the average for estates in town as he entered his 70's, perhaps in some degree because of some latter-day selling off. He had been very active in trading Salisbury real estate in the period from 1748 to 1774. He also was fairly active in village affairs, holding one or another minor town office in almost every one of the 30 years of his middle age, including three terms as tithingman. He was still living in Mar 1781, but probably died soon thereafter.

Child at Salisbury:

**158**    i. Rebecca[5] Eaton, b. 24 Dec 1757; died 2 Sep 1759.

NOTE. Molyneux (1911, p. 385) states that after marrying "Mercie Walton," Nicholas settled in New Hampshire. She goes on to cite one child, a son Joseph, as the issue of this couple. We are unable to find truth in either claim. Apparently Molyneux, learning of a Joseph Eaton who was near Thomaston, Maine, a generation later, and who had come there from New Hampshire with a wife "Mercie Nicholas," decided from the odd similarity of names to assign this Joseph to the above Nicholas/Mercie Eaton. We cannot identify the Thomaston Joseph. But despite long search we find no record of such a birth to this couple at Salisbury, Mass., or any other likely place. Moreover, there is no reason in the record to imagine that this Nicholas ever lived in New Hampshire. On the contrary, he has a very continuous record of land deeds and civic positions at Salisbury, Mass. And starting in 1776, when he was age 76, he took over the care of the East Salisbury Meeting House, a role he played continuously until the town had to replace him with his brother William Eaton in March, 1782, because of either his incapacitation or death (cf. Salisbury *Town Records*).

**51. Jacob[4] Eaton** (Capt. Joseph[3], John[2-1]) was born 16 Apr 1703 in Salisbury; published to 1st, **Sarah Plumer** 16 Apr 1726, and married her soon thereafter. We do not know when she died, but they had two children in Newbury, and she may have died soon thereafter. The same spirit of adventure animated Jacob[4] that inspired his brother Samuel, and he had gone to Topsham, Me., as early as 1730, possibly as a widower. By 1740 if not earlier he had mar. 2d, **Sarah Malcolm**, undoubtedly a close relative of his brother Samuel's wife. They had at least four sons born to them, probably in Topsham, where Jacob[4] remained until October 1744, when he was to be found in York, Me. In 1748 he returned to Topsham, remaining there until 1761 and perhaps later. By May of 1763 he had moved to a part of Bristol, Me. It is uncertain whether he died in Bristol or Topsham. He was a blacksmith and husbandman by trade, and served as Deputy Sheriff during his stay in York.

Children with Sarah Plumer, recorded in Newbury:

**159**   i. Sarah⁵ Eaton, b. 17 May 1727.
**160**   ii. Hannah⁵ Eaton, b. 5 Nov 1728.

Some sons with Sarah Malcolm, born in Maine:

+ **161**   iii. Jacob⁵ Eaton, b. 8 Apr 1741; mar. Elizabeth Thorn, 1764.
+ **162**   iv. Joseph⁵ Eaton, b. ca. Nov 1742; mar. Jane McGlathery, 1769.
+ **163**   v. Benjamin⁵ Eaton, twin b. 30 May 1744; mar. Tabitha Whalen.
  **164**   vi. ___?___⁵ Eaton, twin b. 30 May 1744; drowned in the Androscoggin River about 1757.

**57. (Capt.) Henry⁴ Eaton** (Ephraim³, John²⁻¹) was born 22 Jan. 1703/04, and baptized 11 Jun 1704; mar. **Mary⁴ True**, daughter of Ensign Henry³ True of Salisbury, 10 Aug 1727.   Before his marriage, Henry⁴ Eaton had been a beneficiary of several parcels of land that his grandfather Henry² True had deeded to his daughter Mary (Henry⁴'s mother) as an intermediary, that the grandfather wished Henry⁴ and his brother Samuel to share (1723: Essex Deed 35:452).  This was in addition to the bequest, also shared with brother Samuel, from their own father, Ephraim³, to all of the latter's land holdings in Haverhill, Mass. Thus before age 20, Henry⁴ stood to possess an impressive amount of real estate.  After he married a few years later, he set to buying quitclaims in 1728 and 1729 from his widowed mother-in-law Abigail True and his wife's siblings, such that he took over sole control of the homestead of his wife's father Ensign Henry³ True who had died in 1722.  They were undoubtedly already living at this homestead at the time, and were clearly living there in 1766: presumably they died there as well.  This place was in Salisbury on what was later Lafayette Road north of the Little River and Gerrish St., probably on the west side of that road.

Capt. Henry⁴ was by some margin the most active dealer in real estate among Eatons in the Salisbury/Seabrook area over the latter half of the 18th century.  He appears on Hampton Falls tax lists assessed as a Salisbury resident for his properties there.  He bought and sold land not only locally, but in some townships that were opening up as he achieved maturity, such as Kingston and Chester, N.H.  In the earlier deeds he is described either as a yeoman or a cordwainer.  After 1770 he was usually referred to as "a Gentleman of Salisbury."  The colony-wide Massachusetts Tax Valuation of 1771 gives some sense of his real estate situation, at least in Salisbury, at a time when he was 67 and just beginning to deed property to children or sell off some of his holdings.  At that time he had a homestead, and was credited with possession of a mill, probably on the Little River.  In addition, he had 18 acres of pasture, 4 acres in tillage, 12 acres in producing saltmarsh, and another 6 acres producing fresh hay, for a total of 40 acres in agricultural production.  He also had enough orchard to produce five barrels of cider a year.  He had two oxen, two cows, eight goats or sheep, and a pig.  The total estate was taxed for £14/16sh, a sum which was almost as great as the taxation for the five

# 54 GENERATION IV

other Eaton estates in Salisbury added together. This level of taxation locates Captain Henry at the bottom edge of the top 10% of all estate holders listed for Salisbury in that valuation.

He was also very active in village affairs, and there are dozens of references to him in the Salisbury town records over a span of 45 years. We can trace the vague outlines of his military career in his succession of titles in this period. He appears to have been commissioned an Ensign, presumably in the local militia, at an early stage of the French & Indian war (by Mar 1757), and was a Captain by Mar 1759 for the last four years of that conflict. Subsequently he is listed again as a Lieutenant or Ensign, although he is rapidly elevated again to Captain at the outset of the Revolutionary War. Since he was already over 70 before the latter war began, there is no reason to believe that he saw any strenuous duty. He was, however, prominent as early as 1773 and 1774 in regional cooperation among townships to stand fast against "British incursions on liberty," and continued this kind of activity during the early years of the war.

Capt. Henry served the town in an endless stream of offices after being chosen one of the "surveyors of highways" in 1739. By 1749 he was a town constable, responsible among other things for the collections of taxes. In 1753 the town limited itself to three Selectmen for the first time, and he was one chosen, repeating in that office for nearly a decade. By 1760 he began to be chosen almost routinely as Moderator of the town meeting when it was held in the East parish, and served several times as town treasurer, grand juryman, and attorney to represent the town in various internal and external disputes. He was active in these roles until he was nearly eighty. He died in his 87th year, on 20 Dec 1790.

Children:

**165**    i. Mary[5] Eaton, b. 20 Jun 1728; mar. Nathan Green of Hampton, 3 Jun 1756.
**166**    ii. Jemima[5] Eaton, b. 31 Jul 1730; died 4 May 1736.
**167**    iii. True[5] Eaton, b. 1 Mar 1733; died 30 Apr 1752.
**168**    iv. Henry[5] Eaton, b. 5 Aug 1735; died unmarried, 22 Oct 1758.
**169**    v. Sarah[5] Eaton, b. 4 Dec 1737; perhaps mar. Henry Maxfield.
**170**    vi. Abigail[5] Eaton, b. 10 May 1740; died 31 May 1746.
**171**    vii. Johannah[5] Eaton, b. 5 Sep 1742; died unmar., August 1768.
+ **172**    viii. Ephraim[5] Eaton, b. 1 Feb 1745; mar. 1st, Abigail Perkins.
**173**    ix. Peter[5] Eaton, b. 23 Mar 1747; died in infancy.
+ **174**    x. Peter[5A] Eaton, b. 25 Mar 1748; mar. Abigail Greeley, 1770.
+ **175**    xi. Timothy[5] Eaton, b. 11 Mar 1750; mar. Abigail Meeder, 1785.

**59.**    (Lt.) **Jabez[4A] Eaton** (Ephraim[3], John[2-1]) was born 9 Aug 1708 in Salisbury; mar. **Sarah[4] True**, daughter of Ens. Henry[3] True, 16 Jan 1732. Jabez[4A] was only 14 when his father Ephraim died, and he picked as his guardian his oldest brother Ephraim. Therefore he continued to grow up in the family homestead in the Gravelly Ridge division of proto-Seabrook. After marriage, however, he lived briefly in Salisbury on a 10-acre piece of land he inherited with brother Ephraim from their grandfather, Ens. Henry[3] True, and the births of Jabez and Sarah's children are recorded in Salisbury. He shortly sold this lot to his brother Henry and moved back to the Gravelly Ridge homestead now run by Ephraim[4] (Essex Co.Deeds, 65:80). Soon thereafter, in May, 1735, he joined with his brother Samuel to buy Edward Browne's homestead, consisting of 63 acres of upland and 10 acres of marsh. The house itself was on the north side of lower Walton Road, although most of the land was on the south side.

Once this large spread was in hand, Jabez[4A] only occasionally traded in real estate. He is referred to consistently as a yeoman, being basically a farmer. At the young age of 39 he was a Selectman for the town of Hampton Falls and also served as Constable. He was called a "Lieutenant," apparently within the local militia. Otherwise, however, he was not extremely active in civic affairs. From the start of extant records until his death (1747-1759), he was routinely on the Hampton Falls tax lists. Throughout this period his assessments were the highest of Eatons in the neighborhood, and toward the end they were more than double that of the next most highly-rated Eaton. He died of smallpox, 28 Jan 1760.

Children:

**176**   i. Sarah[5] Eaton, b. 3 May 1733; died 3 Oct 1736.
**177**   ii. Paul[5] Eaton, b. 19 Jan 1735; died 7 Oct 1736.
**178**   iii. Jemima[5] Eaton, b. early 1736; died 3 Oct 1736.
+ **179**   iv. Samuel[5] Eaton, b. 20 Apr 1737; mar. 1st, Molly Merrill.
+ **180**   v. Paul[5A] Eaton, b. 29 Aug 1739; mar. 1st, Mary Tilton.
**181**   vi. Sarah[5A] Eaton, b. 3 Jul 1743; of Seabrook when she married Robert Smith 18 Oct 1768; resided Salisbury, N.H.
**182**   vii. Jabez[5] Eaton, b. 17 Sep 1746. Presumably the Cpl. Jabez who served in Capt. Hobbs Co., reinforcing Pierce's Island off Portsmough against the British, Nov 1775, serving with Levi[6] Eaton and William Eaton. He died unmarried but testate, 6 Jun 1819.
+ **183** viii. Joshua[5] Eaton, b. 19 Jul 1749; mar. Anna Smith, 1773.
**184**   ix. Abigail[5] Eaton, b. 30 Apr 1752; mar. John Smith, 10 Dec 1772. He died 6 Dec. 1828; she died 1 Apr 1839.
**185**   x. Mary[5] Eaton, b. 22 Apr 1755; died unmarried, 1 Oct 1800.

\* \* \* \* \* \* \*

## B. *The Haverhill Branch*

**61. Thomas[4] Eaton** (Thomas[3-2], John[1]) was born 7 Aug 1686 in Haverhill, Mass.; mar. **Lydia Kimball**, 22 May 1729, in Bradford, Mass. They lived in Haverhill. In his will (proved 17 Apr 1767), he provides

for his wife's support during her widowhood, makes legacies to his surviving children, and constitutes his eldest son his executor, giving him the
balance of the estate after the legacies were paid.   As son Joseph[5] lived
and died opposite the old Garrison House, it is supposed that he received
that farm from his father.

Children at Haverhill:

+ **186**    i. Joseph[5] Eaton, b. 27 Feb 1730; mar. Sarah Webster, 1754.
  **187**   ii. Thomas[5] Eaton, b. 18 Sep 1731; died 10 Jan 1740.
+ **188**  iii. Moses[5] Eaton, b. 29 Jan 1734; mar. Anna Webster, 1760.
  **189**   iv. Lydia[5] Eaton, b. 13 Apr 1736; mar. Stephen Noyes of Plais-
                tow, 2 Mar 1757; had three sons and two daughters.  Re-
                sided at Atkinson, N.H.
  **190**    v. Nathaniel[5] Eaton, b. 5 Mar 1738; died 29 Mar. 1739.
  **191**   vi. Mehitable[5] Eaton, b. 17 Aug 1741; mar. Eben Bagley 21
                Oct 1762.
+ **192**  vii. Thomas[5A] Eaton, b. 3 Feb 1744; mar. Mary Swaine ca. 1768.
  **193** viii. Hannah[5] Eaton, b. 17 Mar 1747; mar. Abraham Emerson of
                Haverhill, 16 Jul 1767; had four sons and four daughters.
                She died 30 Mar 1819.

**69. John[4] Eaton** (John[3], Thomas[2], John[1]) was born 5 Feb 1705 at
Haverhill; and mar. **Judith Hale** of Newbury 21 Oct 1741.  *The History
of Haverhill* (Chase, 1861) says: "In 1774, John Eaton, after faithfully
serving as Town Clerk  and Treasurer for the long period of 57 years,
retired from office...That he was well fitted for the responsible post, and
commanded the respect and confidence of his fellow townsmen, is abundantly demonstrated by his 56 annual re-elections to the office."   A
plaque commemorating this marathon performance was affixed to the
onetime residence of John[4] at the time of Haverhill's 250th birthday
celebration in 1890.   We can see, however, that there is a problem with
this account, since it implies that John[4] was first elected Clerk at age 12.
The oddity is quickly dispelled: a John Eaton was indeed Town Clerk for
57 consecutive years, but it was a father-son sequence.   At some time
between 1717 and 1736, when John[3] (**#22**) died, his son took over the
role.   Perhaps in the father's waning years they prepared reports jointly.
Probably it was in connection with this role that John[4] was listed, in 1757,
as one of 40 local leaders of Haverhill on the "Alarm List," exempt
from more broad-ranging military duty, but available to serve locally.
        John[4] presumably grew up at his father's homestead on the Great
Plain well east of the village.   But his residence for most of his adult life--
and the one receiving the abovementioned plaque--was a structure built
in 1721 and still intact in 1890, located "under the buttonwoods" at the
junction of Groveland and Water Streets a mile east of the village center.
At this point a small bluff, dominated by sycamores, looks out splendidly
on the Merrimac River.   This site has more general Eaton importance
because the previous owner was Ebenezer[3] (**#26**), the well-to-do bachelor

uncle of John[4] who died early in 1737, distributing his estate in seven shares across his siblings and their heirs. And the site had once contained the main homestead of patriarch Thomas[2], who unlike his own father and much of the rest of the family, had chosen not to reside out in the West Parish. John[4] spent the period from 1737 to 1741 collecting quitclaims from uncles and cousins to put this main estate back together again under his control.

In his own will, signed 23 Jan 1788 and proved in August, 1788, John[4] makes liberal bequests to his two daughters, and gives his son Moses[5] all the balance, both real and personal, of the remaining estate. Moses was appointed executor, but was finally dismissed from this office, with the estated settled instead by Samuel Walker. The fact that some few years later (1795) nephews Moses[5] (**#199**) and Ebenezer[5] (**#201**) are joining to sell parts of John[4]'s Estate, lends weight to the impression below that John[4]'s paternal line did not continue to the sixth generation.

Children at Haverhill:

**194**    i. John[5] Eaton, b. 12 Jan 1743. He was killed at Bunker Hill, 17 Jun 1775, apparently unmarried.

**195**    ii. Mary[5] Eaton, b. 1 Jun 1745; unmar. when her father's will was written (1788), she may later have mar. Isaac Pearson as a "payment on legacy" made to him before 7 Aug 1792.

**196**    iii. Timothy[5] Eaton, b. 8 Apr 1748. Unmentioned, father's will.

**197**    iv. Moses[5] Eaton, b 20 Jan 1751. "In the settlement of his father's estate he seemed like a crotchety old bachelor." [Rev. Eaton's original text] Later life unknown.

**198**    v. Sarah[5] Eaton, b. 11 May 1754; mar. Moses Parker of Bradford, Mass., 24 May 1781. She died 11 Dec 1847. Had descendants in Salem, Mass.

**71. Moses[4] Eaton** (John[3], Thomas[2], John[1]) was born 6 Sept. 1710 at Haverhill; mar. **Susanna Lecount** of Haverhill, 21 June 1768, quite late in life. In the years before his marriage he had acquired a number of parcels of real estate scattered around the town. He apparently was a favorite of his uncle Timothy[3]. In 1741 they both signed a petition requesting that the town meeting-house be moved eastward closer to their own residences. In 1745 he received of Timothy a 70-acre lot on the road to Amesbury "for love and affection." Although he had issue, his late marriage was a relatively brief one, as he died 31 May 1774. His widow probably mar. again, as her son Ebenezer gives her surname as "Malcomb."

Children at Haverhill:

**+ 199**    i. Moses[5] Eaton, b. 11 Oct 1768; mar. Betsy Plummer, and may have removed to Maine after 1797.

**200**    ii. Nathaniel[5] Eaton, b. 6 Nov 1770. Altho Rev. Eaton's four-generation publication had this Nathaniel marrying Sarah

Emerson in 1797 (an attribution repeated by Molyneux),
he had hand-corrected the entry for the new publication
to say that this Nathaniel died unmarried.  Sarah Emerson's
actual groom  was a different Nathaniel[6] (see **#535**).

+ **201**   iii. Ebenezer[5] Eaton, b. 6 Aug 1773; mar. Susannah Coburn.


**75. James[4] Eaton** (Jonathan[3], Thomas[2], John[1]) was born 9 Mar
1697 in Haverhill, Mass.  When six days old he was concealed with his
mother in a neighboring swamp, and thus escaped the fate of Hannah
Dustin's infant of the same age, whom the Indians killed in the famous
raid.  The mother finally died from the exposure about 13 months afterward.  James himself was very feeble for many years, but finally attained
"good powers of body and mind."  He mar. widow **Rachel (Kimball)
Ayer** 13 June 1728.  She had had one son Samuel with Samuel Ayer, Jr.,
in 1727 before his early death.

As James[4] was the older of two surviving sons, it seemed very
suitable that at marriage he should take possession of the "new house"
which his father at death four years earlier had left unfinished.  Here on
the old site purchased of Rev. Nathaniel Ward of Ipswich by John[1] Eaton,
James[4] and Rachel Eaton lived and brought up their children.  He was
active in real estate with his brother Thomas[4] in Methuen, Mass. just west
of Haverhill, (where the latter had settled at marriage), as well as in
Haverhill itself.  He died 18 Mar 1773, according to the inscription on an
old stone, inclined with age as of the 1880s, in a yard a little north of his
living residence, in the West Parish.

Children at Haverhill:

+ **202**   i. David[5] Eaton, b. 1 Apr 1729; mar. Deborah White of Ando-
            ver, Conn., and removed to Nova Scotia to sire the impor-
            tant line of Eatons in that area.
+ **203**   ii. Timothy[5] Eaton, b. 31 Jul 1731; mar. Abigail Massey, 1755.
  **204**   iii. Sarah[5] Eaton, b. 13 Aug 1733; died 17 Oct 1736.
  **205**   iv. Rachel[5] Eaton, b. 3 Mar 1736; mar. Daniel Griffing of
            Haverhill, 12 Dec 1751, and had four Griffing children:
            Timothy, Ebenezer, Daniel and Bettee.
+ **206**   v. James[5] Eaton, b. 23 May 1738; mar. Abigail Emerson, 1758;
            was the grandfather of the senior author of this genealogy.
  **207**   vi. Susannah[5] Eaton, b. 14 Sep 1740; mar. Benjamin Richards;
            settled in Goffstown, N.H.  She was the great grandmother
            of Emily Chubbuck, the third wife of famed missionary
            Adoniram Judson.
+ **208**  vii. Nathaniel[5] Eaton, b. 5 May 1743; m. Rebecca Dodge, 1766.
+ **209**  viii. Ebenezer[5] Eaton, b. 10 Aug 1745; mar. Abigail Folsom.
+ **210**   ix. Enoch[5] Eaton, b. 6 Nov 1748; mar. Esther Williams, 1769.

### #3. BORDER DISPUTES, 1720-41

The original charter of the Massachusetts Bay Colony set its
north boundary as being "three miles north of the Merrimack...
River". This specification would be fine if that river always flowed
to the sea on an east-west course, as it roughly did in its final 15
miles. But working upstream, even before Haverhill it began to
angle southwest; and then at Lowell it turned almost due north for
the final 70 miles to its headwaters. As a northern boundary, this
left much to the imagination. Massachusetts, which got there first,
preferred to set a straight east-west line from the northernmost point
of River before it turned uncontestably north. But this definition
cut rather deeply into land that the later New Hampshire grant felt
had been awarded to it.

Near the ocean, an authoritative line had been set to divide the
Hampton grant in the N.H. Colony, from the Salisbury grant in
Massachusetts as early as 1657 (cf. Map 3, xxv). But this line did not
proceed westward beyond the east edge of the Haverhill grant, and
the Proprietors there claimed a triangle of land to the north, the
apex of which was called "the Peak". This was the most remote extension of Haverhill land, and was held in common until distributed
among the Proprietors as the "Fifth Division" in 1721. In the same
micro-period, a group of 120 Scottish Presbyterian families had
come to form Londonderry, N.H., named after their city in Ulster Co.,
Ireland. And a portion of the land they were distributing in Londonderry overlapped with the new lots in the Peak that Haverhill citizens
were just beginning to develop.

Territorial conflicts are rancorous enough in themselves. But
adding ethnic/religious divisions to them is a combustible mixture
in the extreme. Actually, the migrants from Ireland were neither
Irish nor Catholic: indeed, they had fled Scotland for Ireland to escape the persecution of Protestants by King James in the early 1600s.
Still feeling oppressed by the intensely Catholic environment in Ireland, they had been delighted to learn of land available in fiercely
Protestant New England. But enraged Haverhill citizens doggedly
referred to them as "the Irish Party"; and since everyone knew that
the Irish were Catholic, reviled them as "papists" and "Romans."

Tensions in the disputed territory went on for nearly 20 years,
with more or less serious vandalism and skirmishes by vigilante
groups on both sides. They became most inflamed around 1730,
culminating in an episode which left four Londonderry citizens
wounded by gunfire. Colony authorities in Boston and Portsmouth
increasingly begged London to provide a more definitive account

of the colony line, to forestall more serious bloodshed. The mother
country moved glacially; but finally encouraged serious surveying
which produced, as of Feb 1741, a new line that paralleled the main
undulations of the lower Merrimack but three miles north; and then
a bit short of Lowell where the River turned north, extended a line
straight westward to New York.

The Massachusetts authorities were aghast at the outcome, because the new line gave New Hampshire "a territory of about 50 miles
by 14 more than she had ever asked for!" (Chase, 1861). Two of the
subpopulations most vitally affected were those originally in Salisbury and Haverhill, or exactly the home bases of our Eatons out of
John[1]/Anne. To the east, Eatons who thought they were Massachu-
sett citizens discovered that they lived in Hampton Falls, New Hampshire instead. And to the west, Eatons who had equally migrated into
the northern territories of Haverhill found they were in New Hampshire at towns like Atkinson, Plaistow and Hampstead. There was a
good deal of bitterness about the change; and litigation of one kind
or another went on for many years. [For more detailed accounts, see
sources such as Chase (1861); and Wallace (1994)].

**78. Jonathan[4] Eaton** (Jonathan[3], Thomas[2], John[1]) was born 30
Mar 1705 in Haverhill, Mass. He mar. **Jane Page** of Haverhill 27 Nov
1733, and lived on a farm in the northwest of Haverhill which after the
state line adjustment of 1741 lay partly in Atkinson, N.H. (see Sidebar
**#3**). One of his smaller distinctions came during the late stages of per-
sistent strife within the Haverhill community over the fact that a limited
set of heirs of the town's original proprietors were still eligible, many
decades after the town founding, for new divisions of common land,
whereas later comers were not. This controversy boiled from at least
1720 onward. At a climax in the spring of 1748, all four of Jonathan's
surviving brothers signed a petition defending the primal rights of proprietor heirs. Although he was also such an heir, Jonathan did not join
them, such an extension of privilege being against his principles. He died
early in 1772, testate. His estate was appraised at a fairly prosperous
£943. His sons Jonathan and Amos joined to settle the estate.

Children at Haverhill:

**211**   i. Ruth[5] Eaton, b. 1 May 1734; died 8 Aug 1736.
+ **212**  ii. Jonathan[5] Eaton, b. 27 Jul 1736; m. Mary Stone of Plaistow.
**213**  iii. Benjamin[5] Eaton, b. 21 Sep 1738; died unmar., 17 Jun 1762.
**214**  iv. Sarah[5] Eaton, b. 13 Dec 1740; mar. Stephen Page of Haver-
        hill, 10 Apr 1764; had two sons, David and Jonathan Page.
**215**  v. Eunice[5] Eaton, b. 1 Jan 1743; mar. Pearse Gage of Pelham,

N.H., 17 Sep 1782.
**216**  vi. Hannah[5] Eaton, b. 27 Jun 1745; mar. Samuel Cross of
        Methuen, 14 Apr 1774.
**217**  vii. David[5] Eaton, b. 10 Dec 1747; died 10 Feb 1756.
+ **218**  viii. Amos[5] Eaton, b. 18 Oct 1751; mar. 1st, Mary Gage, ca. 1774.
**219**  ix. Abiah[5] Eaton, b. 9 May 1754; died 23 Jun 1762.
**220**  x. Ebenezer[5] Eaton, b. 18 Apr 1756; died 1762.


**81. Samuel[4] Eaton** (Job[3], Thomas[2], John[1]) was born 5 Oct. 1699
in Haverhill, Mass.; mar. **Mehitable Harriman** of Haverhill, 11 Jun 1721.
Early in life he had a 10-acre farm in the western part of Haverhill which
abutted land of his brother James. When the new West Parish was set off,
the first parish meeting of the West Parish was held 1 May 1734. At this
meeting it was "voted to build and set the meeting house on the south-
easterly corner of Samuel Eatton's pasture," with Samuel being recom-
pensed for the quarter-acre used. This location was a few rods from the
house occupied in 1860 by Timothy J. Goodrich. In March, 1736/37,
Samuel[4] was the yeoman who bought a farm from the Harrimans on the
Kingston Road north of Haverhill [NH deeds 45-362, 364]. Soon thereafter his wife Mehitable died, 14 Feb 1739. On 5 Nov 1741, Samuel
mar. 2d, **Hannah Emerson** of Haverhill. A few weeks later he sold his
first farm, moving the family a few miles northeast to the Kingston Road
site, which because of the state line shift had just become part of Plaistow,
N.H., where he began his second round of children with Hannah. He
apparently died before Jun 1761, when son Samuel sold a quitclaim on
his estate.

Children with Mehitable at Haverhill:

+ **221**  i. Job[5] Eaton, b. 14 Mar 1725; mar. Hannah Stevens, ca. 1753.
**222**  ii. Mehitable[5] Eaton, a twin b. 14 Jun 1726; died 24 Jun 1726.
**223**  iii. Abigail[5] Eaton, a twin b. 14 Jun 1726; died 16 Jun 1726.
**224**  iv. Mary[5] Eaton, b. 31 May 1727; mar. Nehemiah Heath of
        Plaistow early in 1745. Issue: two sons and two daughters.
**225**  v. Samuel[5] Eaton, b. 29 Sep 1729; mar. Edna Hunkins, 26 Mar
        1761 at Hampstead, N.H. This couple sold property at
        Hampstead three months after their marriage and removed
        to parts unknown, possibly including Weare and Piermont,
        N.H., but left little trail that we have located.
**226**  vi. Mehitable[5A] Eaton, b. 14 May 1731; died 14 Sep 1736.
+ **227**  vii. Ebenezer[5] Eaton, b. 10 May 1734; m. Phebe Shepard, 1762.
**228**  viii. Abigail[5A] Eaton, b. 8 Aug 1736; mar. Samuel Merrill, 25 Oct
        1759. Was residing in Haverhill as of 1804.

Children with Hannah at Plaistow:

+ **229**  ix. Ithamar[5] Eaton, b. 13 Mar 1743; mar. 1st, Mary Ordway.
**230**  x. Mehitable[5B] Eaton, b. 12 Feb 1744; mar. Ebenezer Bailey 21

Oct 1762 and settled in Weare, N.H. Had eight sons and
two daughters. She died April, 1818; he died Sept 1807.
+ **231**   xi. Obadiah[5] Eaton, b. 22 Apr 1747; mar. Betsey Paige, 1775.
  **232**  xii. Betsey[5] Eaton, b. 14 Dec 1749.
  **233** xiii. Peter[5] Eaton, b. 21 Jun 1753.


**82. Thomas[4] Eaton** (Job[3], Thomas[2], John[1]) was born 20 Feb 1701
in Haverhill, Mass.; mar. to **Mehitable Carter** 24 Dec 1730 by Rev.
Christopher Sargent of Methuen, Mass. The couple settled in the north
parish of Methuen. In the first parish meeting here held on 15 Jan 1736,
"Thomas Eaton was chosen parish treasurer." When the church was organized, 16 Jan 1740, "Thomas Eaton was chosen deacon." The north
parish received a town charter in 1750 as Salem, N.H., some years after
the final settlement of the colony line. Rev. Abner Bailey was the pastor
of the Congregational Church of this parish. In the will of Timothy[3]
Eaton of the East Parish of Haverhill, dated 19 Feb 1755, one bequest is
"To cousin Thomas Eaton, Deacon of Mr. Bailey's church in Salem, N.H.,
my great bible." The births of his children are all recorded in the old
town book of Methuen, Mass.

Children at Methuen:

  **234**   i. Ebenezer[5] Eaton, b. 22 Sep 1731; died 23 May 1738.
+ **235**  ii. John[5] Eaton, b. 18 Jun 1733; m. 1st, Abigail Peaslee, c. 1775.
+ **236** iii. Timothy[5] Eaton, b. 28 Jul 1735; mar. Mary Dalton, 1776.
  **237**  iv. Mehitable[5] Eaton, b. 28 Aug 1737; died 15 May 1738.
  **238**   v. Mehitable[5A] Eaton, b. 27 Feb 1739; died 6 Oct 1754.
  **239**  vi. Susanna[5] Eaton, b. 7 Jan 1741.
  **240** vii. Hannah[5] Eaton, b. 21 Jul 1745; mar. Edward Pattee, 1766.
  **241** viii. Lydia[5] Eaton, b. 22 Apr 1747; mar. Moors Bailey, 5 May
      1772.
  **242**  ix. Sarah[5] Eaton, b. 8 Mar 1749; mar. Oliver Emerson 15 May
      1777.

# Generation Five

## A. *The Salisbury Branch*

**85. John⁵ Eaton** (John⁴⁻¹), was born ca. Sept. 1709 when his parents lived near the center of current Hampton Falls; mar. **Hannah Fowler** 13 Jan. 1734/35 ("both of Salisbury": Newbury Church Records). After his earliest years, he grew up in proto-Seabrook, and later appears to have run the family homestead near the current corner of Washington and Collins in South Seabrook.  He and Hannah attended church in Salisbury in the early days, where they owned the covenant at the First Church in 1742.  Like his father, John⁵ is represented on the sequence of annual tax lists of Hampton Falls, N.H., from 1747 through 1767, but is distinguished from him as "John Eaton, Jr."  As his father aged and turned property over to him, his tax liability grew, permanently surpassing that of his father in 1752, when he was 42 and his father 65.  Once established on his own, his taxable wealth was about average for household heads in Hampton Falls, although his next younger brother Benjamin⁵ surpassed him by a considerable margin after 1761.

John⁵ was moderately active in real estate trading for over 45 years.  In his prime he is referred to both as a blacksmith and a yeoman in these deeds. He also is identified as living variously in Hampton Falls and South Hampton before the creation of Seabrook in 1768, although in context these amounted to the same thing; and he probably never moved from the family homestead.  In the first town meeting of Seabrook in that year he was named Town Constable, and appears consecutively on later Seabrook tax lists.  We lack a death date for him, but he appears like his father to have lived well into his nineties.  In 1792, when he was 82, he "appeared personally" to ratify a deed (Rockingham County Deed 165-310) whereby for £260 assembled by his second, third and fourth sons Benjamin⁶, Silvanus⁶ and John⁶, he turned over to them 50 acres of land and marsh he possessed in Seabrook and Salisbury, along with 100 acres in Weare, N.H., his farm implements, etc.  Thus this was a kind of will, despite the sons' payment, and probably reflected the fact that the eldest son Ebenezer⁶ had already been given the family homestead on Washington St. near Collins in South Seabrook. John⁵ lived past 1800, and probably died late 1803 or early 1804, as on 2 May 1804 the same three younger sons pledge to pay their "honoured mother Hannah" (Fowler) and six of their sisters £90, as well as all household goods to those sisters upon Hannah's death (Deed 165-309).

### #4. Seabrook, N.H., Eaton Bastion (I)

The small township of Seabrook, N.H., forming the southeast corner of the State of New Hampshire and abutted to the south by Salisbury, Mass. (see Map 4, p. xxvi), deserves beyond question to be called the "chief bastion" of those New England Eatons who descend from John[1] and Anne Eaton, 1640 settlers at Salisbury. Why is this status so abundantly clear? The short answer is because more of these Eaton descendants have lived in Seabrook than in any other town in the New World, and by an extremely large margin.

Here are some numbers. In the first U.S. Census of 1790, the tiny village of Seabrook registered some 22 households headed by these Eatons, whereas Salisbury, Mass., the point of origin for this tribe, only registered nine; and Haverhill, Mass., origin for the other branch of the John[1]/Anne tree, had a mere six. Moreover, this Seabrook margin widened dramatically in subsequent Censuses, with the the number of Eaton households there rising to about 60 in the latter part of the 19th Century. And the 2001 telephone book lists 73 Eaton subscribers. This, it should be recalled, is for a village of only 820 souls in 1820, and still under 8,000 souls in 2000.

Of course the initial Eaton migration to what we call "proto-Seabrook," or the land area which was to become incorporated under that name in 1768, is not hard to understand. Given three generations of growth, much of the habitable "upland" and productive salt marsh in the east end of Salisbury was owned and exploited. The Eaton homestead itself stood well out on a long peninsula (or "the Great Neck") in marshy land eastward from the village, so there was no immediately-adjacent land for expansion south, east or north; and land to the west was filled by other families. With the grandsons of the original Proprietors thickly settled and the fourth generation in the offing, the town began subdividing and assigning lots to its last frontier northward. In 1682 it laid out the "Cain's Brook Division" made up of 58 25-acre lots. This land ran west from the "country way" (now Lafayette Rd.) to the foot of Titcomb and Grape Hills, with Cain's Brook roughly to the south, and the New Hampshire line to the north. Of course all of this land was at the time a part of Salisbury (see Map 4). Two decades later the town laid out a "Gravelly Ridge Division," a more complex set of ranges bounded west by the by the country way and southward from Cain's Brook. It was this division, the central spine of which was Worthen's Point, the next peninsula poking into the eastern marshes to the north of John[1] Eaton's Great Neck homestead, where his great grandsons began to congrein very serious numbers.

Ephraim[3] Eaton (**#18**) was an early purchaser of land on the northern side of the Gravelly Ridge Division, between what is now Walton Rd. and Collins St. east of Washington St., and may have lived there as early as 1706. However, he was well-to-do and owned many parcels of land in the region; and most of his sons, including notably Capt. Henry[4], lived back in Salisbury. The most central pioneer for proto-Seabrook among the Eatons was John[4] (#30), who settled on the south side of the Gravelly Ridge Division, probably ca. 1719, with five of his six sons (John[5], Benjamin[5], Thomas[5], Wyman[5] and Joseph[5]). These sons had about 44 children between them; and this prolific John[4] twig produced 17 of the 22 Eaton families in 1790 Seabrook.

All Eatons in proto-Seabrook resided in Salisbury, Mass., until 1741, when the boundary change put them in New Hampshire (cf. Map 4). For the next 25 years they were in the Hampton Falls parish. In 1765, 56 proto-Seabrook males petitioned N.H. authorities to have their own parish, because they preferred the pastoral teaching of Rev. Samuel Perley, a Presbyterian preaching in the neighborhood, to that of Rev. Payne Wingate of the established Congregational Church in Hampton Falls, and could not suffer being taxed for Wingate's support. Eight Eatons signed, including John[4] (#30) and his five sons, one of whom had just named a new son Samuel Perley Eaton a month before. Hampton Falls notables questioned how many of these signers had heard a Wingate sermon more than once if at all; or would be able to tell a Congregational doctrine from a Presbyterian one. Nonetheless, the N.H. government authorized the creation of Seabrook as of 3 Jun 1768. At last there was local administration and enhanced record-keeping in the area.

Although Eaton rapidly became the most common surname in Seabrook, the first extant tax list for the new Seabrook (1770), shows 16 Dows and only 14 Eatons, reflecting another source of religious diversity. An active Quaker meeting had been established in Hampton in the preceding century, but Quakers had suffered sporadic persecution from both Massachusetts and New Hampshire. In 1683, a young Joseph Dow at Hampton, seeking an isolated spot away from close civil authority and preferably near a colony line, led a group of Friends to settle in proto-Seabrook, ideal for these purposes. This produced other religious cross-currents, along with lots of Dows. In general, Friends' relations with other persuasions in Seabrook seem to have been entirely cordial. In fact, Samuel[4] Eaton (#33) took a Quaker wife and became a convert, as did a few other Eatons over time. But there were occasional frictions: Quakers would not sign the Loyalty Oath of 1776 for religious scruples; and other townsmen complained to authorities that tax and muster quotas to support the Revolutionary War effort, based merely on town size, lay heavy on Seabrook non-Quakers, since local Quakers did not participate, due to their pacifism. For more extended discussion of the Seabrook context in these and several other regards, see Dow (1929).

Children born to John[5]/Hannah (Fowler) in proto-Seabrook (i.e., Salisbury, Mass. to 1741; then Hampton Falls, N.H.):

**243**    i. Elizabeth[6] (Betsey) Eaton, b. Mar 1734/35; mar. a Lowell.
+ **244**    ii. Ebenezer[6] Eaton, b. 10 Apr 1738; mar. Mrs. Nancy Brown.
**245**    iii. Molly[6] Eaton, b. 22 Jun 1740; mar. Ezekiel Carr, 10 Nov 1762.
**246**    iv. Thomas[6] Eaton, b. May 1742? Probably a ghost entry, admittedly inserted in an uncommonly large hole in the birth roster of John[5]/Hannah by the senior author of this volume without any direct documentary support whatever to address "testimony of a grandson, or more probably a great grandson," collected in the late 19th century, concerning a Thomas Eaton forebear whose son Thomas had married a Rhoda Eaton just before 1819. The junior author has concluded that the Thomas, Sr., who seemed to require invention was in fact the better-documented if still somewhat shadowy Thomas[7] Eaton, *son* of Ebenezer[6] rather than this hypothetical younger *brother*, as assumed here (see **#627**, below). Nonetheless, we reproduce the entry here and allot a unique Eaton-number as a place-holder, in order to signal a point of controversy.
**247**    v. Jemimah[6] Eaton, b. 6 Apr 1747; of Hampton Falls when she mar. Christopher Cross of Amesbury, 19 Nov 1766.
+ **248**    vi. Benjamin[6] Eaton, b. 18 Jul 1749; mar. Grace Beckman.
**249**    vii. Lydia[6] Eaton, b. 18 Jan 1751; mar. a Wright; died 26 Dec 1813.
**250** viii. Rachel[6] Eaton, b. 10 Dec 1754. In 1822 she applied to the town for assistance. She died unmarried, Jan. 1832.
+ **251**    ix. Silvanus[6] Eaton, b. 18 Jun 1756; mar. Abigail Jackman.
**252**    x. Miriam[6] Eaton, b. 19 Oct 1760; mar. Benjamin Brown, son of widow Nancy Brown, 15 Jul 1776. Miriam died 10 Sep 1846 at Newburyport after 11 children.
+ **253**    xi. John[6] Eaton, b. 8 Jul 1762; mar 1st, Sarah Colby, 1786.

**87. Benjamin[5] Eaton** (John[4-1]), was born ca. 1718, probably in the proto-Seabrook area of the old Hampton, N.H. grant; mar. **Jane Hutchins** of Kittery, Me. at Hampton Falls, 18 Jun 1747 (*History of Hampton Falls,* W. Brown, 1900, p. 138), and settled in proto-Seabrook. He was said to have been at the capture of Louisburg in 1745, and is probably the Benjamin Eaton listed with first cousin David[5] Eaton (Samuel[4], John[3-1]) in Capt. John Goffe's Co. at Dover in Dec 1746 (*N.H. State Papers,* XVI, p. 913). It is also said that the "Louisburg Benjamin Eaton" dwelt where Richard and Eben Fowler were living about 1860, on the northwest corner of Washington & Collins St. Thus he probably spent his life a few rods from his father's homestead.

He dealt in modest degree in real estate, where he was described as a "husbandman" or "yeoman." Tracts were mainly local ones of salt marsh and upland, the latter including Lot #17 in the Gravelly Ridge Division, embracing his Seabrook neighborhood.   Like his father and older brother John[3], he appears on 21 consecutive tax lists of Hampton Falls (1747-1767) just before Seabrook was established as a separate town.   Over this period, his tax rates reflect a major surge in taxable wealth after 1752, and he arrived at well above average prosperity by the 1760s, matching that of the Walton Rd. line of Eatons out of Ephraim[3] and outdistancing all of his male siblings and closer cousins by a wide margin.   He succeeded his brother John as Constable in Seabrook's second year, and occupied a few other minor town posts.   We lack a death record for Benjamin[5], but he left a will in Dec 1784 distributing his lands and chattels across four sons, with the homestead going to the youngest (Samuel) "Perley," then 18, not to be possessed until he was 21.

Children in proto-Seabrook:

+ **254**    i. Ephraim[6] Eaton, b. 20 Mar 1748; mar. Sarah Moody, 1770.
+ **255**    ii. Winthrop[6] Eaton, b. 18 May 1751; mar. Phebe Green.
   **256**    iii. Sarah[6] Eaton, b. 14 Dec 1754; mar. Josiah French, Jr., 20 Feb 1777 and moved to Salisbury, Mass.
+ **257**    iv. Levi[6] Eaton, b. 6 Nov 1757; mar. 1st, Ruth Eaton; 2d, Phebe Walton.
+ **258**    v. Samuel Perley[6] Eaton, b. 30 Oct 1765; never married.


**88. William[5] Eaton** (John[4-1]), was born ca. 1720, probably in the proto-Seabrook area of the Salisbury, Mass. grant.   On arriving at his majority he went to York, Me., next town south of Wells, where his uncle William[4] Eaton (John[3-1]) had lived for about thirty years.   In York William[5] entered his intention of marriage with 1st, **Meribah Wardwell** 20 Nov 1742.   Meribah was nominally the fifth child of Eliakim and Ruth (Bragdon) Wardwell, born 25 Dec 1720.   But local lore suggests that mother Ruth had been captured by the Indians and that Meribah was the product of a forced union with an Indian chief, who later returned mother and daughter to her original husband, as described by Hosmer (1905, pp. 39-40), and Noyes (1942, p. 50).   It is known by church records in Salisbury, Mass., and in York, Me., that William[5] and Meribah remained in the old town of York till after 7 Jul 1762, for on that day their last child Samuel Wardwell Eaton received infant baptism.   Other records show that York was their home for twenty years after their marriage, where probably all their children were born.   In 1762, this family moved to Deer Isle, Me., where they made the first permanent settlement of the island as squatters at the north tip of Great Deer Isle (see Map 6, p. 176), on the shore facing Eggemoggin Reach (Noyes, 1942).   This site by 1890 was called the "Scott Farm," near the steamboat landing (Hosmer, 1905).   In this eastern island home five of their six children married and settled in comfortable homes.   The youngest, Samuel[6] Wardwell Eaton, however, settled first in Seabrook, N.H., and later in Chesterville, Me.

William[5] was chosen first major by the legislature and accepted in Council 2 May 1776, and placed with the Lincoln Regt. of Col. Jonathan

Buck. In 1779, after the British had taken possession of Deer Isle, Maj. Eaton left home to escape the necessity of taking the oath of allegiance or neutrality. It is not clear exactly where he went first, but perhaps to York; and possibly wife Meribah died there shortly thereafter. In any event, by the spring of 1781 William[5] is described as a yeoman of Seabrook when with his brother Benjamin he sells Jacob Dow five acres of land (Rockingham Co. deed 124-179). A York, Me., record later in 1781 (15 Dec) indicates that "William Eaton of Seabrook and Olive Lord of York entered their intentions of marriage." This potential marriage has often been credited to Maj. William, presumably because of the Seabrook/York venue. It seems likely, however, that these intentions were associated with the much more junior William[6] Eaton of Seabrook (see **#318**) who is reported to have married a "Molly Lord," 26 Jun 1782 (Seabrook Vital Records in Concord, N.H.). It is unlikely that Maj. William was involved with the Lord lady, since previous to 6 Feb 1784 he had more certainly been married (2d?) to **Mrs. Jane (Page) Felch**, widow of Daniel Felch of Seabrook, as is evident from a deed of that date made and executed by William[5], Jane Eaton and John Felch, a son of the said Jane by a former husband. Later in 1784 and 1785, there are five other Seabrook land transfers by William[5], now described as a "Gentleman," and on 10 Dec 1784 a Maine court decides in his favor against one Peter Hardy, who tried to occupy 200 acres of the Major's land at the north end of Deer Isle (Wiscasset Co. records, Bk. 17, Pg. 207). This seems to be the same land that he sold Nathaniel Scott of Worcester, Mass. on 16 Mar 1786. In Mar 1787 he is under threat of jail in Seabrook for failure to fulfill a court decision to repay Samuel Fowler nearly £48. On 27 Oct 1789, Maj. William, still of Seabrook, was married (3d?) to **Mrs. Mary (Stickney) Gove**, widow of Eleazer Gove of Seabrook. The Major appears as a household head in the 1790 Census at Seabrook; but a Jane Eaton, presumably his estranged wife, appears in a separate household.

It is reported on good authority that Maj. William, for some cause unknown, abandoned his latest wife and went to what is now Chesterville, Me., where his son Samuel[6] Wardwell Eaton had already established a home for his family in the autumn of 1794. Later he returned to Deer Isle despite having disposed of his property there earlier, and in due time died at the home of his daughter, Mrs. Benjamin Weed, on Little Deer Isle. The names of those six of his children who survived to accompany their parents on the first settlement of Deer Isle, are known, but for 14 years after their 1742 marriage, the church records at York are missing. Therefore the birth dates are not known, although baptism records for the two youngest are available. We give the probable order and dates of birth, although we shall stand corrected by discovery of any more certain information.

Children with Meribah:

+ **259**    i. Eliakim[6] Wardwell Eaton, b. ca. 1745; mar. Mary Bunker.
   **260**    ii. Hephzibah[6] Eaton, b. ca. 1747; in 1767, mar. Jonathan
       Torrey, who came to Deer Isle from Falmouth, Me., in

1763. They had five sons and three daughters with descendants still on Deer Isle at least until 1890. Wife Hephzibah died 2 Nov 1785.

+ **261**    iii. Jeremiah[6] Eaton, b. ca. 1749; mar. Abigail Haskell, 1770.
  **262**    iv. Hannah[6] Eaton, b. ca. 1751; mar. Benjamin Weed ca. 1768,
who resided first at Little Deer Island, but afterward moved
near Campbell's Neck, where he died. They had four sons
and three daughters who prospered in life.
+ **263**    v. William[6] Eaton, infant baptized 10 Feb 1756; mar. Hannah
Haskell, 1781.
+ **264**    vi. Samuel[6] Wardwell Eaton, infant bapt. 7 Jul 1762; mar.
Hannah Lowell, 1782.

NOTE. The above account, apart from the correction of the Lord marriage
and a documentary addition or two, is what the senior author composed in the light
of both documentary research and his discussions with Deer Isle relatives in the
1880s. It may fruitfully be compared with the account of Noyes (1942), which differs in some particulars. Noyes begins by inferring that Maj. William and first wife
Meribah must have died by the 1780s because they have disappeared from Deer Isle
records by that period. Later in the same account he finds some of the Seabrook
traces above and decides that a better account of the Major's later life might be assembled with a more thorough working of the Seabrook data. The chief mistake
which he leaves in his account is a failure to identify properly the youngest son,
Samuel. He does not appear to know Samuel's diagnostic middle name, "Wardwell," which the latter commonly included in his name for identification purposes.
And he searched the Maine Census for Samuel Eatons in 1790s, thereby being
forced to decide between Samuel Eatons at Harpswell and Brunswick to carry on
Maj. William's line. However, both of these Maine Samuels have well-known origins with other fathers than Maj. William. The Major's youngest son had already
long since removed from Maine to Seabrook (see **#264**), and is on view there in the
1790 Census as "Samuel W. Eaton." Thus Noyes also missed the fact that Maj.
William in his aging years followed Samuel Wardwell to new lands in Chesterville,
Maine, before a final return to his daughter's on Little Deer Isle.

**89. Thomas**[5] **Eaton** (John[4-1]) was born 17 Mar 1722 in the proto-
Seabrook area of the Salisbury, Mass., grant; mar. **Jane Wheeler** of
Salisbury 8 Dec 1743 and settled near the family homestead, probably
not far from the corner of what is now Washington St. and South Main in
Seabrook. He appears with his father and brothers on 20 of the 21 of the
Hampton Falls tax lists, 1747-67, missing only 1760. He married early
and his estate accumulation was slow, although he must have had his own
household from an early age to be taxed in his own right. By his mid-
40s however he began to move upward in relative tax levels to about the
average levels for householders in Hampton Falls more generally. He
does not appear to have bought any land on his own account until he was
almost 50 (in 1769), but then bought three more local parcels in fairly

brisk succession. He is always identified as a yeoman on these deeds. In addition to producing a large number of children of their own, Thomas and Jane took in three or four young grandchildren in the late 1770s, when they were orphaned by the deaths of son Josiah[6] and his wife Miriam in No. Yarmouth, Me. Thomas[5] died testate on 8 Mar 1798. His real estate inventoried in 1798 amounted to almost 50 acres in 10 pieces of marsh, meadow and upland, and was valued at nearly $2,000, a fairly conse-quential amount at the time.

Children (all births recorded at Hampton Falls):

+ **265**   i. Josiah[6] Eaton, b. 28 Sep 1744; mar. Miriam True and re-moved to Maine.
  **266**   ii. Jedidah[6] Eaton, b. 26 Apr 1746; mar. David Osgood, 2 Dec 1779; she died 16 Jan 1823.
  **267**   iii. Martha[6] Eaton, b. 1 Jan 1749; mar. Ephraim True 23 May 1776 and res. in Seabrook. He absconded in 1790, leav-ing his wife dependent on his parents. He went to Marietta, Ohio, and never returned.
  **268**   iv. Olive[6] Eaton, b. 25 Mar 1752; mar. Jacob Green and lived in Seabrook. When she died, he mar. 2d, Abigail French. He died 7 Apr 1826, aged 84 and 2 days.
  **269**   v. Rhoda[6] Eaton, b. 27 Aug 1754; mar. 1st, Samuel Brown, 16 Mar 1777. He died in Northwood, N.H., 7 Dec 1781; and she mar. 2d, Mr. Waldron, remaining in Northwood. She died before 1798.
+ **270**   vi. William[6] Eaton, b. 28 Dec 1756; mar. Betsey[7] Eaton (**#621**) and moved to Sanbornton, N.H.
+ **271**   vii. Bryant[6] Eaton, b. 28 May 1760; mar. 1st, Elizabeth Collins.
+ **272**   viii. Wheeler[6] Eaton, b. 12 Feb 1763; mar. Judith Goodwin, 1788.
  **273**   ix. Meribah[6] Eaton, b. 28 Feb 1766; mar. Simeon[6] Eaton, son of Wyman, 22 May 1777 (cf. **#284**).
+ **274**   x. Aaron[6] Eaton, b. 31 Jan 1769; mar. 1st, Betty Chandler.


**90. Wyman[5] Eaton** (John[4-1]), was born 24 Jul 1725 in the proto-Seabrook area of Salisbury, Mass; mar. **Ruth Merrill**, 17 Dec 1745, in Salisbury. They settled on a farm on current Worthley Avenue where it crosses Partridge Creek off South Main St., and their home-lot property ran along the Massachusetts line at the southernmost point of South Seabrook. This homestead was in the family for many generations, al-though it has been replaced for some time now. The Rev. Eaton, writing in the 1890s, remarks of the dwelling itself: "The stone door step, the thickness of the natural layer, more remarkable for its size than for its beauty, is still preserved on the place. On this place, that is now one of the ancestral landmarks, Wyman Eaton and his wife Ruth spent their en-tire married life, and here their ten children were born. It is sacred in the memory of a large number of descendants." Wyman was on all 21 Hampton Falls tax lists from 1747 to 1767, and then like his brothers and father, shifts off to the new Seabrook lists thereafter. His tax assessments were lower than those of his brothers for most of this period, but some of this stems from the fact that he was the youngest. Late in in the period he began to show higher assessments that were, like brothers John and Thomas, about average for Hampton Falls taxpayers. Nevertheless, he does not appear to have been prosperous: he died late in 1802 or early 1803, leaving a will that gave the homestead and much of his property to his youngest son Simeon[6]. The inventory of his estate in 1803 showed about one-third the total valuation given his next older brother Thomas's estate five years earlier.

Their ten children produced eight marriages, six with either Eatons or Merrills, the two parental surnames. All children born in proto-South Seabrook:

+ **275**     i. Humphrey[6] Eaton, b. 6 Apr 1746; mar. Judith Cilley.
+ **276**    ii. John[6] Eaton, b. 2 Apr 1748; mar. Jemima Green.
  **277**    iii. Tristram[6] Eaton, b. 11 Feb 1750. A mariner, unmarried when lost at sea after the 1776 Association Test, which he signed, but before his father's will in 1802. In Nov. 1775 he had been a private in Capt. Henry Elkins's Company raised for the defense of Portsmouth harbor, with his older cousins Ephraim[6] and Levi[6], sons of his uncle Benjamin.
  **278**    iv. Anna[6] Eaton, b. 7 Feb 1752; mar. Samuel Merrill of Buxton, Me., 5 Nov 1776, by whom she had 3 sons, 4 daughters.
+ **279**    v. Abel[6] Eaton, b. 28 Mar 1755; mar. Martha[5] Eaton (**#131**), daughter of Daniel[4A] and Nancy Eaton, 20 Mar 1777.
  **280**    vi. Sarah[6] Eaton, b. 19 Sep 1759; mar. James[5] Eaton (#134), son of Daniel[4A] and Nancy Eaton, 1 Jun 1780.
  **281**    vii. Jane[6] Eaton, b. 9 Mar 1761; mar. John Merrill, Jr., 26 Jun 1780. She died 1 Jan 1837.
  **282**    viii. Ruth[6] Eaton, b. 27 Jan 1765; mar. Samuel Merrill, 24 Aug 1788. They resided in Salisbury, and had one daughter, Nancy Merrill, b. 7 Feb 1789.
  **283**    ix. Zilpha[6] Eaton, b. 8 Jul 1767; she died before her father's will in 1802.
+ **284**    x. Simeon[6] Eaton, b. 9 Sep 1768; mar. Meribah[6] Eaton (**#273**), daughter of Thomas[5] and Jane Eaton, 22 May 1787.

**91. Joseph**[5A] **Eaton** (John[4.1]), was born 9 May 1728. Tradition says that he was one of the 304 men from New Hampshire who joined with Massachusetts forces in 1745 for the reduction of the famous French fortress of Louisburg; that he was a drummer boy under the command of Gen. Pepperell; and that here he beat the reveille on his 17th birthday; and that he was one who shouted for joy when the French capitulated June 17, 1745. After this exciting adolescence he took to the sea, becoming a successful shore seaman in the deep sea fishing in the Provincial waters of Great Britain. On 9 Sep 1751 and stationed at Falmouth, Me., he entered intentions of marriage with **Sarah Burnell**, also of Falmouth. After marriage he returned to settle in Seabrook, near the

Massachusetts line by his brother Wyman. This was apparently about
1755, for after one appearance in the Hampton Falls tax list at age 22 in
1750, he does not appear again until 1756, but repeats annually until
1768, when Seabrook was created. He appears to have been of very
modest means, as his taxes are throughout the period very significantly
lower than those of his four older brothers (and lower than they were at
comparable age), and even when compared with Seabrook peers in 1770,
rather than the more affluent citizens of Hampton Falls, his rates are well
below average. He is listed in *Seabrook* for the 1790 Census, but in
*Salisbury* Censuses thereafter. The reason seems to be an indenture of 13
Dec 1794, wherein the aging parents settled £200 on youngest son Caleb,
who had recently removed to Salisbury himself, for a guarantee that he
would find and provide for them "a comfortable house or room" for the
rest of their lives, as well as provide space for his two unmarried sisters
until they did marry. Joseph[5A] died 18 Feb 1815, and his wife the next
year, 21 Dec 1816.

Children in the Seabrook area:

**285**  i. Betsey[6] Eaton, b. ca. 1754; mar. Ezekiel Collins, son of Robert Collins. Ezekiel died 15 Jun 1848, a very old man.

**286**  ii. Martha[6] Eaton, b. ca. 1757; mar. Reuben[7] Eaton (**#620**), son
of Ebenezer, in 1786; removed to Sanbornton, N.H. in
1800.

+ **287**  iii. Josiah[6] Eaton, b. ca. 1760; mar. Eunice Ricker, 1794.

+ **288**  iv. Jonathan[6] Eaton, b. ca. 1762-3; mar. Sarah Merrill, 1787.

**289**  v. Sarah[6] Eaton, b. ca. 1767; mar. Thomas[7] Eaton (**#627**), son
Ebenezer[6], 4 May 1798.

+ **290**  vi. Caleb[6] Eaton, b. 8 Jan 1773; mar. 1st, Lucy Dalton; 2d, Mrs.
Elsie Drown.

**291**  vii. Mary[6] Eaton, born ca. 1775; mar. Samuel Collins 24 Sep
1803 (Salisbury *VR*).


**95. Joshua[5] Eaton** (William[4], John[3-1]), was born 9 Mar 1714 in
Wells, Me. He entered his intentions of marriage with **Mary Boston**, 23
March 1737, according to Wells records. A Joshua Eaton and **Hannah
Wardwell**, the former of Wells and the latter of York, were mar. by Jere-
miah Moulton, Esq., 12 Oct 1741, according to York records. A Joshua
Eaton and **Anna Delzell** were mar. 23 Jan 1744, according to Wells rec-
ords. If these three Joshuas were one and the same person, as it appears
they are, then Anna Delzell was Joshua's second or third wife; and other
Wells records confirm this idea. Joshua and Anna resided on a farm in
Wells and had a large family.

Children with Anna at Wells:

+ **292**  i. Joshua[6] Eaton, b. 17 Oct 1745; mar. Lucy Maxwell, 1770.

**293**  ii. Elizabeth[6] Eaton, b. 20 May 1747; mar. Benjamin Hatch.

+ **294**  iii. Joseph[6] Eaton, b. 11 Jan 1749; mar. Hannah Maxwell, 1772.
  **295**  iv. Anna[6] Eaton, b. 22 Jun 1750; mar. Joseph Littlefield.  She
          died 10 Nov 1838; he died 27 Apr 1826.
  **296**  v. Sarah[6] Eaton, b. 4 Sep 1753; mar. Peltiah Littlefield.
  **297**  vi. Mary[6] Eaton, b. 24 Nov 1755; never married.
  **298**  vii. Abigail[6] Eaton, b. 15 Jan 1758; died 18 Mar 1758.
  **299**  viii. James[6] Eaton, b. 1 Apr 1759; died 11 Sep 1780.
  **300**  ix. Esther[6] Eaton, b. 26 Jul 1761; mar. James Littlefield.
  **301**  x. Forrest[6] Eaton, b. 4 Mar 1763; died 3 Apr 1764.
  **302**  xi. Susanna[6] Eaton, b. 4 Feb 1767; mar. Samuel Hill.

**99. Joseph[5] Eaton** (William[4], John[3-1]) was born ca. 1727 in Wells, Me.; mar. 1st, **Lydia Moulton** of York 6 Dec 1750 in York.  They resided in Wells, although he spent most of his life on the water, as he was the master of a vessel.  There were six children born to them, after which Lydia died.  Capt. Eaton then mar. 2d, **Edith Cole**, by whom he had four more children.

Children by Lydia at Wells, Me.:

+ **303**  i. Jeremiah[6] Moulton Eaton, b. ca. 1751; mar Mary Emery.
+ **304**  ii. Daniel[6] Eaton, b. ca. 1752; m. Hannah Sherif in Portsmouth.
  **305**  iii. Lydia[6] Eaton, b. ca. 1754.
  **306**  iv. Betsey[6] Eaton, b. ca. 1755.
+ **307**  v. William[6] Eaton, b. 17 Dec 1756; mar. Abigail Littlefield.
+ **308**  vi. Jacob[6] Eaton, b. 28 Feb 1765; mar. Abigail Bourne, 1794.

Children by Edith at Wells, Me.:

  **309**  i. Martha[6] Eaton, b. ca. 1767.
  **310**  ii. Mary[6] Eaton, b. ca. 1769; died 26 Feb 1832.
+ **311**  xi. John[6] Eaton, b. 21 Oct 1771; mar. Sarah Cole ca. 1795.
  **312**  xii. Jonathan[6] Eaton, b. ca. 1773; died 25 Jun 1827.

**101. Elisha[5] Eaton** (Samuel[4], John[3-1]) was born 3 Feb 1723 in Salisbury.  In June, 1744, he was one of 20 men sent under the command of Capt. Jeremiah Clough to quell Indian activity in the Upper Merrimack Valley at Contoocook and Canterbury (N.H. Adjutant General's Report, p. 54).  This was the period in which father Samuel[4] was trying to establish control over the estate of his father-in-law, John Worthen, at Worthen's Point (So. Main St.) in proto-Seabrook (see **#33**).  He failed, but nonetheless two of his sons, David[5] and Elisha[5] profited from this family connection.  The court had divided the Worthen estate into 7 equal parts for the seven Worthen daughters.  One of the daughters, Samuel's wife Hannah, had died before the settlement, and this part-- taken at the tip of the point itself --went to Samuel[4] as her heir.  Two of the other Worthen daughters--Rebecca and Abigail--had been declared *non compos mentis,* and were wards of the town. To help pay for their care, their land shares were sold, presumably at attractive prices, and Elisha[5], then listed as a "Salisbury yeoman" since his father lived on current Forest Rd. in E. Salisbury, was able to purchase Rebecca's parcel in Mar 1746 (Rockingham Co. Deeds, 35-315). Shortly thereafter on 17 Nov 1747, Elisha[5] mar. **Elizabeth Blake** of Hampton at Hampton Falls (Brown, 1900, p. 138). Presumably the couple began their family near the end of So. Main St. on the southeast edge of Seabrook, since Elisha paid taxes on this land as a Hampton Falls citizen in 1748 and 1751.

Disaster soon struck this family when young Elisha[5] died near his 30th birthday. We do not know how, although possibly he was lost at sea as no record of his death or cemetery marker is known. In any event, wife Elizabeth is listed as "Widow of Elisha Eaton" in Hampton Falls tax lists referring to the Worthen Point property beginning in 1753 and continuing for consecutive years through 1757. She is not listed among the Hampton Falls taxpayers, as Elisha[5] had been earlier, but is on the list of "Salisbury men" rated for property they owned in Hampton Falls. This means that having decided to leave Worthen's Point, she chose to retreat in the direction of her husband's family on Forest Rd., Salisbury, rather than to her own family in Hampton, N.H. When Samuel[4] died in 1765, he made a special bequest to grandson Elisha[6] of his "gun or fire-lock," as though perhaps he and the 12-year-old had gone fowling together. Widow Elizabeth finally resettled in Pittsfield, N.H., with her eldest son John[6] (see **#314**). A typescript of Pittsfield Vital Records notes that "Old widow Eaton died at her son John Eaton's, aged 84, 6 Oct 1807."

Children, all of whom were baptized together at the First Church in East Salisbury on 7 Dec 1755, when mother Elizabeth owned the covenant there (Salisbury Church Records):

> **313**    i.   Hannah[6] Eaton, b. 3 Feb 1747; may have mar. Enoch Boyd, 1767, in proto-Seabrook.
> + **314**   ii.  John[6] Eaton, b. 1 Oct 1749 at Salisbury or proto-Seabrook; mar. Sarah "Sally" French on 1 Feb 1773 at Seabrook.
> **315**   iii.  Molly[6] Eaton, b. ca. Sept. 1751 at proto-Seabrook; probably mar. Abither Merrill, 5 Jun 1771, at Salisbury.
> + **316**   iv.  Elisha[6] Eaton, b. 13 Mar 1753 at proto-Seabrook; mar. Hannah Sleeper, 8 Nov 1774, at Hampton.

**103. David[5] Eaton** (Samuel[4], John[3-1]) was born 15 Nov 1728 at Salisbury, Mass; mar. **Lydia Fowler** on 11 Mar. 1756 at the West Parish Congregational Church in Salisbury. In Dec 1746, David was listed in the muster roll of Capt. John Goffe's Co. at Dover, with his first cousin Benjamin[5] (*New Hampshire State Papers*, Vol. XVI, p. 913). In 1753 he was received as an adult into the First Church at E. Salisbury (Church Records). In 1755 he was a corporal in Stephen Sergents' Co., Bagley's Regt. on the Crown Point Expedition (*Mass. Officers in the French and Indian Wars*, p. 61).

In addition to his soldiering, he was listed in deeds as a yeoman. His father Samuel was anxious to settle him on a piece of the Worthen estate in proto-Seabrook, as he had already done for his brother Elisha[5]. The piece available was the one at the tip of the point, given to Samuel[4] as his right after his wife Hannah (Worthen) had died. It is clear that David[5] was invited to settle here. David appears first on the Hampton Falls tax rolls in 1752, suggesting that he was then a Hampton Falls citizen. But in the next three years (1753-55), he paid Hampton Falls taxes on property he owned there, despite being by residence a "Salisbury man." Once married, however, he moved permanently to the Worthen estate in proto-Seabrook, and from 1756 onward is taxed as a local citizen by Hampton Falls until Seabrook was created in 1768. For much of this 1756-1767 period he had rather little tax liability, partly because as a young man he had accumulated little. When his father died in 1765, he deeded him the property at the tip of Worthen's point that David[5] already occupied. In this period, too, he was able to buy another tract of equal size in the proto-Seabrook area, and by the late 1760s he ranks as about average in wealth in the new Seabrook town.

In 1789, a David Eaton, "Seabrook yeoman," was declared *non compos mentis*, and William 3d Eaton was named as his guardian. It is likely that this was our David[5], rather than his son David[6], the Revolutionary War veteran (#320), as some have thought. The William 3d Eaton at this time in Seabrook would have been David[5]'s own son. According to tradition, David[5] went from Seabrook to Weare, N.H. on horseback to see his son at some time in 1795, and on his way home was suddenly taken sick and died, perhaps at Chester. Administration of the estate was granted to three persons, one being the son David[6], thereby assuring us again that it was not the son who had six years earlier been declared *non compos mentis*. His children were poorly registered at birth; most of what we know about the child roster comes from the estate administration papers of 1795.

Children (dates and even ordering are partially guesswork):

+ **317**    i. David[6] Eaton, b. ca. 1755 at proto-Seabrook; mar. Polly Rogers. A Revolutionary War pensioner.
+ **318**    ii. William[6] Eaton, b. 26 May 1757; mar. Molly Lord, 1782.
  **319**    iii. Hannah[6] Eaton, b. ca. 1759; mar. John Davis of Gloucester, Mass., on 16 Nov 1780. Residing Seabrook in 1796.
  **320**    iv. Sarah[6] Eaton, b. 4 Aug 1773; prob. mar. Henry[7] Eaton (**#622**, q.v. for children), 4 Aug 1791 at Seabrook.
+ **321**    v. Samuel[6] Eaton, b. ca. 1765. Probably the Samuel Eaton who mar. Polly[7] Eaton (**#625**), daughter of Ebenezer[6], and removed to Weare, N.H., before 1800.
+ **322**    vi. True[6] Eaton, b. 17 Dec 1770; mar. Abigail Knowles, 1796.
  **323**    vii. Lydia[6] Eaton, b. ca. 1773; mar. Pelatiah Hoyt of Amesbury, Mass., about 1793; res. Amesbury.

**106. Jonathan**[5] **Eaton** (Samuel[4], John[3-1]) lacks a birth record, and has been variously estimated as having been born in 1720 or 1733 (see extended Note under sketch for his father (**#33**)). That such a person existed and had a vital relationship to Samuel[4]'s family cannot be questioned, since among other things he is listed as an heir in Samuel[4]'s 1765 will, along with other known children of Samuel. Moreover, he is known to have removed to Pittsfield, N.H. for the latter part of his life. More recently, a typescript copying of Pittsfield Vital Records has come to view with the entry, "Jonathan Eaton died, age 63, June 18, 1809." Strictly construed, this means that Jonathan was not born until the latter half of 1745 or early 1746. This unexpectedly late date solves some peculiarities surrounding Jonathan. Most obviously, it explains why he did not marry until the end of the 1760s: instead of marrying at 35 or 48 he married at a conventional age indeed.

At the same time, it creates a new puzzle. By the strict construction, this Jonathan was born at a time when supposed father Samuel[4] was just taking on a second wife, Huldah. This pair was married 17 Oct 1745; it is implied that Jonathan was born between June 1745 and June 1746. Of course, statements of ages at death were quite approximate in this period. Possibly the age at death of 63 was an underestimate: then Jonathan might well have been first wife Hannah's final child. Or perhaps Jonathan was Huldah's first child with Samuel[4], a possibility underscored by the fact that years later, Jonathan[5]'s firstborn was named Huldah. In any event, the situation may relate to the peculiar treatment of Jonathan in father Samuel[4]'s 1765 will. He is mentioned fifth among seven children. He is, however, the only name in that list not introduced as (e.g.) "my son David Eaton," or "my daughter Lydia Eaton." Instead, the bequest is made "to Jonathan Eaton" *tout court*. And the bequest of five shillings is tiny, worth vastly less than the lands granted two brothers, and only one-third the cash awarded to each sister save one given "five shillings together with all she hath already had of me towards her portion," a further qualification not made for Jonathan. Thus the will gives Jonathan short shrift, and has been construed as a near disinheritance, an interpretation furthered by the pointed note that by the 1765 will, Samuel was revoking "all prior wills." All of this raises the possibility that Jonathan was not in fact a normal biological child of Samuel[4], but was perhaps a stepchild coming from new wife Huldah's earlier 1729 marriage to John Kenney, one granted the Eaton surname at the time of marriage, but with whom relationships had soured considerably in late adolescence; or that he was an illegitimate biological child sired by Samuel[4] between marriages. With this caution in mind, we can only review what the public record says of this Jonathan.

As best we can see, his name surfaces first in 1769, when a Jonathan Eaton marries an **Anna Arnold**, "both of Salisbury," on 13 Apr 1769 (from Rev. Samuel Perley's list of marriages in Seabrook). There is no guarantee that this Jonathan is our quarry, and at least one piece of evidence speaks against the hypothesis. On the other hand, in our extensive files of Eatons there are no competing Jonathans, since others given this name are off to Maine with other wives; and the homestead of putative father Samuel[4] (deceased less than four years earlier) was being run by another son Samuel[5]. (The only obvious Anna Arnold in Salisbury at this time was Anna[5] (Eaton) Arnold, widowed six years earlier, and the second cousin of this Jonathan[5], although she would have been twenty years his senior.)

A Jonathan is also listed in Salisbury two years later as part of the 1771 Massachusetts Tax Valuation. It is clear this Jonathan had no taxable property, and is rated for a poll tax alone, a situation utterly common for males still in their mid-20s. Suggestive, too, is his position in the listing. There are vague streaks of alphabetizing over the 349 polls on the list, but essentially any surname initial can appear anywhere in the list. For example, of nine Eatons on the total list, four occur in the first 15 names--all E.'s--with one singleton and eight lines later an adjacent threesome of Eatons. Near the end of the list, in another internally alphabetized segment, a new round of "E.'s" begins with two adjacent Eatons, then passes through four non-Eatons before an adjacent threesome of Eatons again. The main fact of interest is that the clustering seems to reflect common micro-neighborhood residence (and usually but not always, nuclear-family membership), as though each alphabetic stretch was the work of a different assessor given a district of the township to canvass. It is therefore interesting that Jonathan is the last of a threesome begun by John Eaton and John, Jr. Of these three, only the middle entry is listed as having a house in Salisbury, This is very likely to be John[6] (Elisha[5], Samuel[4]), or this Jonathan's putative nephew, who was very junior in the sense of having just attained his majority a year or two before, but who as elder son of his mother widowed fifteen years earlier, had long been "man of the house" (see **#101** and **#314**). Within a couple of years after the Tax Valuation, this Jonathan (**#106**) surfaces to buy a tract in the new lands opening up in Pittsfield, N.H., and soon thereafter the nephew John[6], newly married, has moved his family there as well. It is in the ensuing Pittsfield decades that the family relationship between Uncle Jonathan[5] and Nephew John[6] is most clearly confirmed.

Of course the proximity of Jonathan and John, Jr. on the Tax Valuation does little to raise the probability that this was the Jonathan marrying Anna Arnold, beyond certifying that he was likely to have been in Salisbury at the time. The negative evidence about the Anna Arnold marriage arises because this Jonathan's wife in Pittsfield was clearly a Nancy; and an aged informant about the Pittsfield Eatons, a Rosa Eaton, reported about 1890 that this Jonathan had married, (2d?) a **Nancy Towle** in "about" 1768, before his arrival in Pittsfield, a matter which if true would pre-empt a 1769 marriage to Anna Arnold. At the same time, the 1768 date is obviously vague, and there could have been a brief Anna Arnold marriage in 1769 in Salisbury, with a second marriage to Nancy Towle more or less soon thereafter.

This Jonathan, identified as a yeoman, bought 50 acres of land in the "Upper City" north of Pittsfield town (then still part of the Chichester grant) on 13 Aug 1773, altho he probably had arrived in Pittsfield somewhat earlier. He added at least 70 more acres to this initial stake in ensuing years. He was one of the Selectmen of Pittsfield in 1784, and in

1785 he boarded the school master for five shillings per week. In 1792 he joined the Baptist Society in Gilmanton. In 1794 he deeded half of his primary lot to his son Thomas. His will was proved 20 Sep 1809 (nicely fitting the reported death date of June 18, 1809), and mentions his widow "Anna" (an equivalent to Nancy, or a hint that the Anna marriage still obtained?) and the two children whose births were recorded at Salisbury.

Children (the third is speculative):

**324**   i. Huldah[6] Eaton, b. 10 Nov 1770; mar. Benjamin Sias on 17 Nov 1791. She died 7 Apr 1793, leaving a daughter Huldah Sias b. 5 Mar 1793.
+ **325**   ii. Thomas[6] Eaton, b. 6 Aug 1772; mar. Mrs. Sally Ackerman on 13 Nov 1794 in Pittsfield, N.H.
**326**   iii. Jonathan[6] Eaton, b. ? . An aging Rosa Eaton, long-time Pittsfield resident, sent the senior author of this volume a letter, undated but written between 1885 and 1895, opining that there was this second son of Nancy and Jonathan[5], who later married a Huldah Eaton of Seabrook. We have failed to find any confirmation of the possibility, but leave a place-holder here in the event confirmation is found.

**107. Samuel[5] Eaton** (Samuel[4], John[3-1]) was born 28 Aug 1747 to Samuel[4] and his 2d wife Huldah (Stanyan); mar. **Rachel Greeley** of Salisbury 19 Jun 1769 at Salisbury. Samuel[5]'s father died when he was 17 years old and willed him the family homestead on Forest Rd. in Salisbury along with all other Salisbury property such as salt marsh. We get a view of the value of this estate in the 1771 Tax Valuation for Massachusetts, where the tax rate is £7. Compared with other Salisbury Eatons visible in this valuation, the rate is about half of that for the farm of Capt. Henry[4] Eaton (**#57**) over in the True family neighborhood on the Country road; but it is more than double that of any other Eaton homestead in Salisbury, including the old ancestral home on Beach Rd. now in the possession of Daniel[4A] Eaton, rated only at £3/2sh. Hence this Samuel[5] was rather well endowed at an early age.

He was in considerable active service in the Revolutionary War. At the outset he was a private in Capt. Jonathan Evans's Co. of Minute Men, responding to the alarm of 19 Apr 1775, and stayed on for a while at the encampment at Cambridge. He did a second tour of duty in May-July 1777 as a corporal with Capt. Moses Nowell's Co. at Providence. Then he served for 3 months in the fall of 1778 with Capt. Oliver Titcomb's Co. guarding and fortifying posts in and around Boston (*Massachusetts Soldiers & Sailors*, p. 182). He maintained some kind of commission in the postwar period: he appears every year on Salisbury tax lists from 1777 thru 1828, the year of his death, and from 1786 to 1795 he is usually listed as "Lt. Samuel"; from 1797 thru 1811 he is listed as "Capt. Samuel." Perhaps the War of 1812 led to some retirements of older men from their commissions.

He dealt very little in real estate, perhaps because he had received before marriage a farm that was coherent as well as capacious for its time. Early in public records he was identified as a yeoman, but later is called a "Gentleman of Salisbury." After the death of Capt. Henry[4] Eaton in 1790, Capt. Samuel[5] soon became the most prosperous Eaton head of household in Salisbury for the first quarter of the 19th century, with tax valuations on his estate in the lower reaches of the top quartile of Salisbury householders. His farm in this period boasted 4 acres of "good land" (for planting), 10 acres of highly productive salt marsh, 15 acres of woodland, and over 40 acres of pasture land to feed his normal complement of two pigs, a horse, a pair of oxen, and five to ten cows and calves.

His wife Rachel died in April 1813 in Salisbury. Capt. Samuel[5] died intestate on 12 Sep 1827 or within a few months thereof. Although he had passed off some of his land to children in the later years of his life, his inventory reported in Mar. 1829 showed real estate of 60+ acres evaluated at $1,582 (Essex Co. Probate, Book 67, p. 64). Samuel and Rachel had numerous children, several of whom migrated to Maine and several of whom remained to populate the family homestead for a period after their father's death.

Children born at Salisbury (order usually, but not always, clear):

+ **327**    i. Richard[6] Eaton, b. 22 Oct 1769; mar. Rhoda Hook, 1802.
+ **328**   ii. Joseph[6] Eaton, b. 14 Aug 1771; mar. Hannah Stockman.
  **329**  iii. Elisha[6] Eaton, b. 10 Oct 1773; never married, lived on the homestead. Probably a sailor, who died 18 Dec 1833.
  **330**   iv. Rachel[6] Eaton, b. ca. 1775. Never married, lived on the homestead. Died 28 Dec 1849.
+ **331**    v. Samuel[6] Eaton, b. 10 May 1778; mar. Sally French, 1811.
  **332**   vi. Moses[6] Eaton, b. 27 Feb 1781; mar. Lydia Sawyer of So. Hampton in Feb. 1822 and removed to Solon, Me. following his older brother Samuel. They lived on a farm, but there were no issue. He died 27 Jun 1853; she died 30 May 1855.
  **333**  vii. Benjamin[6] Eaton, b. ca. 1783; died in infancy.
  **334** viii. Jonathan[6] Eaton, b. ca. 1785; died at sea with a fever before he was 18 years old.
  **335**   ix. Jane[6] Eaton, b. ca. 1787; mar. Josiah French of Salisbury, 1 Jan 1806 at Salisbury. They removed to Solon, Me., with her brother Samuel, and resided there.

**108. Theophilus[5] Eaton** (Jonathan[4], John[3-1]) was born 3 July 1721 in Salisbury, and mar. **Abigail Fellows** of Kingston, N.H., 23 Feb 1743. According to land conveyances, he resided at Haverhill, Mass. in 1746, probably the first male Eaton of the Salisbury branch to take up residence in Haverhill since John[1] the Migrant moved his family there a

century before.  By 1751 he had removed to the western end of the large
Kingston, N.H. division of the original Hampton grant, which before the
changing of the state line abutted the Haverhill grant to the north.  In
1753 he bought land in this neighborhood on the west side of Punch
Pond [N.H. Deeds 57-4, 6].  In 1755 he was registered as an innkeeper
there.  In 1756, he was a principal agent in obtaining the charter to set
this west part of the Kingston grant off as a separate parish named Sandown.  Once this was accomplished, he became Selectman in Sandown in
1756-57 and 1759, where his younger brother Ezekiel[5] had joined him.

By Aug 1759, however, he began to sell his Kingston/Sandown
holdings [NH Deed 89-228], and shortly he left Ezekiel behind, removing his family to Maine, in the "New Meadows" (later, West Bath, just beyond Brunswick, Me.).  Although the precise reasons for this move are
not known, Theophilus's younger brother, Abel[5], had in 1750 mar. at
Brunswick, Me., and taken up residence in the area (see #111 below).  By
1765, Theophilus is recorded in the Registry of Deeds as being of Harpswell, Me.  According to Hosmer (1983), about this time the husband of
his eldest daughter Judith, Edward Howard of Brunswick, moved to Deer
Isle, Me., to start a settlement.  Judith was taken sick there, and her
mother Abigail came to take care of her.  Judith died, however, in 1767
at the North West Harbor, and father Theophilus[5] came by boat to bring
his wife home.  Mr. Howard gave his mother-in-law all his rights to land
at the Harbor as a compensation for her services.  It is said that Theophilus was pleased with the location, and the next spring (1768), moved
his family to Deer Isle, settling on a lot of land on the Harbor shore adjoining that of Mr. Dow to the southeast, in an area later known as "Dow
Town."  The fact that Theophilus was a cousin of Major William[5] Eaton
(#88) was an additional motive for the move to Deer Isle.

Theophilus was the same enterprising man here that he had been
in Sandown and other places.  He built the first saw and grist mill in
Sedgwick just across "the Reach" from Deer Isle.  He was a very valuable
man in town and church affairs until his death 7 Feb 1793.  At that time,
with his three elder sons long established with families elsewhere, his Deer
Isle estate passed to his youngest son, James[6A] (cf. Noyes, 1942, for further details).  James later sold the Deer Isle estate and removed across the
reach to Prospect, Me. about 1813.  His mother, widow Abigail, had a
remarkable constitution, and lived to be some 103 years and 9 months,
according to local records  She died at the Prospect, Me., residence of her
son James,  17 Oct 1823.

Eight children were recorded for them in Kingston, but the place
of birth is not always clear:

336      i. Judith[6] Eaton, b. 29 Feb 1744; bpt. 22 Apr 1744 at Haver-
            hill; mar. Edward Howard  7 Mar 1764 and moved to Deer
            Isle, where she died in 1767.  Mr. Howard occupied the
            little island known as "Saddle Back," although he died with
            his children in Brooksville.
+ 337     ii. Moses[6] Eaton, b. 8 Feb 1746; mar. Patience Bridges, 1768.

**338** iii. Elizabeth[6] Eaton, b. 20 Jul 1749, probably proto-Sandown; mar. Josiah Harding of Sedgwick where they settled, had eight children, and where she died 25 Feb 1826.

+ **339** iv. Jonathan[6] Eaton, b. 24 Feb 1752, proto-Sandown; mar. Sally Emerton of Sedgwick.

**340** v. James[6] Eaton, b. ca. 1754; died ca. 1760.

+ **341** vi. Ebenezer[6] Fellows Eaton, b. 22 Aug 1756, Sandown; mar. Abigail Herrick of Sedgwick.

**342** vii. Sarah[6] Eaton, b. 28 Apr 1759, Sandown; mar. John Raynes (son born in 1753 to Master Mariner John/Sarah Raynes) at Deer Isle, 25 Dec 1777. He died 25 Dec 1837, age 84, on their 60th anniversary; she died 5 Feb 1850, age 90.

**343** viii. Abigail[6] Eaton, b. July 1763, near Brunswick, Me.; mar. Solomon Billings (son of early settlers John/Hannah Billings who had come to Deer Isle from Lincoln, Mass. in 1763); and the couple lived on the northwest side of Walker's Pond in Brooksville, Me.

+ **344** ix. James[6A] Eaton, b. 27 Jan 1769, Deer Isle; m. Hannah Jordan.

**111. Abel[5] Eaton** (Jonathan[4], John[3-1]) was born 1 Mar 1727 in Salisbury, Mass. He removed to Maine at an early age: while he is usually treated as following his elder brother Theophilus to that state, the record shows that he married, 1st, Mrs. **Dorcas Coombs**, int. 22 Oct 1750 at Brunswick, Me. This is ten years before his brother Theophilus sold his land in Sandown and brought his family to the town of Brunswick. The likely magnet that brought Abel to Brunswick was his first cousin once removed, Samuel[4] (**#44**) who had settled in Brunswick before Abel's birth. Abel later married, 2d, **Sarah Brown**, 26 Jan 1763; and 3d, **Ruth Marriner** (?), 5 Mar 1778, at Bath, Me. He was at Bath, Me. for the 1790 and 1800 Censuses.

Given Abel's three wives, it is ironic that we have a very sparse record of any offspring. If Abel himself was fertile, we assume that the paucity of children reflects less a reality than the fact that Abel was something of a rolling stone in what is now Sagadahoc Co., Maine. He lived several places in that district, most notably at Bath, but also at nearby Georgetown. There is no reason to believe that he ever followed his elder brother Theophilus northeastward to Deer Isle (although his children, if any, had reason to have extended family ties to Deer Isle and Hancock County). Indeed, Abel[5] died in 1806 and is buried at Harpswell, Me., some few miles south of Brunswick (and Bath). Nonetheless, Eatons who by death or Census ages were born in this small region of Maine in the 1752-75 period but whose lineage is not otherwise known may well be progeny of this Abel[5].

Probable children with Dorcas (with siblings, if any, unknown):

**345** ?. Judith[6] Eaton, b. 29 Apr 1756; mar. Moses Staples of Swan's

Island, Me., ca. 1776.  She died there, 4 Jan 1843.
346    ?. Dorcas[6] Eaton, b.   ?     ; mar. Robert Purrington, 17 Jul 1777
       at Litchfield, Me.


**112. Thomas[5] Eaton** (Jonathan[4], John[3-1]) was born 8 Feb 1729 in
Salisbury, Mass. in the supplementary house built on the ancestral Eaton
homestead land on Beach Rd. near the "Great Neck Bridge."   He published to marry **Eunice Moulton** 26 Aug 1749 (Newbury Records).  On
18 Dec 1749 he traded with his widowed mother and brother Theophilus,
for the homestead of his late father.  He lived there about two years.  But
as he was a mariner the farm upkeep was doubtless a burden to him.  So
on 15 Feb 1751 he sold the family farm back to brother Theophilus[5],
and bought a household lot in Newbury on 25 Dec 1751.  It is likely that
he resided there the rest of his life.  His widow Eunice died 10 Aug 1797
at Newburyport.

Children:

347    i. Stephen[6] Eaton, b. 28 Jun 1750 in Salisbury.  Prob. died in
          1776 in Newburyport.
348    ii. Eunice[6] Eaton, b. 8 Sep 1753 in Newbury; mar. int. with
          Hugh Pritchard, 18 Apr 1772, Newburyport.
349    iii. Thomas[6] Eaton, b. 9 Feb. 1756 in Newbury; mar. Elizabeth
          Cilley, 29 Jun 1779.
350    iv. Mary[6] Eaton, bpt. 23 Aug 1759, Newbury.


**113. Ezekiel[5] Eaton** (Jonathan[4], John[3-1]) was born 7 Dec 1730 in
Salisbury, Mass.; mar. **Mary Campbell** of Danville, N.H., 11 Dec 1752 at
Kingston, N.H.  They resided on a farm in Sandown, N.H. and he held
town offices there in the period from 1756 to 1778.  At the time of his
death his will, proved 19 Dec 1810, showed him owning several lots of
land in Sandown and Kingston, N.H., which he distributed among his
four children and a grandson.

Children, all born in Sandown:

+ 351    i. Joseph[6] H. Eaton, b. 17 Aug 1757; mar. Elizabeth George.
  352    ii. Ezekiel[6] Eaton, bpt. 9 Dec 1759 (Sandown Church Records,
            LDS Film #015575).  This son not mentioned in father's
            1810 will, and thus not included in usual lists of his child-
            ren.  Yet the Sandown records say "Ezekiel, son of Ezekiel"
            for this baptism.  No further trail; may have died young.
+ 353    iii. James[6] Eaton, b. ca. 1761; mar. Jemima George ca. 1778.
  354    iv. Jonathan[6] Eaton, b. ca. 1763; unmarried; said to have resi-
            ded in Vermont, altho we have no unidentified Jonathans
            in Censuses there thru 1850.  May have passed westward.
  355    v. Jane[6] Eaton, b. ca. 1767; died unmar., 12 May 1849.

**118. Joseph⁵ Eaton** (Jonathan⁴, John³⁻¹) was born 7 Mar 1741; mar. perhaps **Sarah Webster** (not to be confused with the Haverhill Branch's Capt. Joseph⁵ Eaton, **#186**, who unquestionably married a Sarah Webster, the latter being a very common name in the Merrimack Valley of this period). This couple resided in Newbury. Joseph⁵ was a sailor who apparently died young, perhaps soon after their first child.

Child:

+ **356**   i. Joseph⁶ Eaton, b. Sep 1772 in Newbury "Old Town." Moved to Beverly, Mass., and mar. Sally Mack, 1798.

**120. Jonathan⁵ Eaton** (Jonathan⁴, John³⁻¹) was born 6 Sep 1745 in Salisbury, Mass., two months after the death of his father. His oldest brother Theophilus (**#108**), already 24 years old when Jonathan was born, was the closest thing to a father that he ever knew. Thus he accompanied Theophilus⁵ first to Sandown and then to New Meadows, Me., in the vicinity of Brunswick. In the latter place he mar. **Diana Dow** (called "Dina"), daughter of Nathan and Mary (Flanders) Dow, in the spring of 1767. He thereupon removed with his father-in-law to Deer Isle, and settled upon the lot of land adjoining that of Mr. Thomas Saunders whose wife was from Salisbury, Mass., thus bringing former townspeople to be neighbors in the distant East. This 100-acre lot was between Pressey Village and Dunham's Point. Jonathan⁵ was an enterprising man. Hosmer (1905, pp. 16-17) describes the desperate need for salt in the pioneer days, among other things for the preservation of meat and fish. He singles out this Jonathan as one of those on Deer Isle who boiled down seawater in large kettles on the beach for the 2% residue of salt it would yield, selling the precious product as far away as the Merrimack Valley of his youth, with large profits. He came to own substantial real estate. The house he built well before 1800, after a major renovation in 1883, was still standing in 1890. His wife Diana died first, on 19 Mar 1803. He died on 27 Feb 1805, age 59. His will gave his oldest son Joseph a proprietor's right in Sedgwick, and left the substantial homestead to his youngest sons, Nathan and James.

Children at Deer Isle:

+ **357**   i. Joseph⁶ Eaton, b. 17 Nov 1767; mar. Patty Morgan of Sedgwick, (int.) 12 Sep 1804.
  **358**   ii. Molly⁶ Eaton, b. 24 Oct 1769; mar. William Weed, son of Benjamin/Hannah (Eaton) Weed, and resided on Deer Isle, or in the later days at Stonington. They had three sons and one daughter.
  **359**   iii. Judith⁶ Eaton, b. 14 Dec 1771; mar. Joseph Weed, the brother of her sister's husband, in Dec 1794, and resided on Deer Isle. They had four sons and six daughters.

+ **360**    iv. Jonathan[6] Eaton, b. 24 Mar 1774; mar. Esther Torrey.
+ **361**    v. John[6] Eaton, b. 25 Mar 1776; mar. Polly Webb, 1797.
  **362**    vi. Hannah[6] Eaton, b. 14 Dec 1778; mar. Samuel Webb, son of
             Seth/Hannah (Winship) Webb (int.) 22 Mar 1798, and
             resided on Deer Isle. They had five sons and six daugh-
             ters. She died at Webb's Cove (Oceanville) in 1837.
+ **363**    vii. Nathan[6] Eaton. b. 17 Mar 1781; mar. Dorothy Pressey, 12
             Aug 1806.
+ **364**    viii. James[6] Eaton, b. 15 Mar. 1784; mar. Betsey Howard, 1808.
  **365**    ix. Betty[6] Eaton, b. 15 Dec 1787; died 10 Sep 1792.

**128. Daniel[5] Eaton** (Daniel[4A], John[3-1]) was born 19 May 1745 at
Salisbury, Mass.; mar. **Hannah Walton**, 16 May 1771. According to a
great grandson in 1882, he had followed the sea for over a decade before
his marriage. For a brief time after his marriage he was in Seabrook;
then he bought land in Pittsfield, N.H., in 1773 and removed there. He
soon tripled his holdings there to 150 acres (1776). In 1797 he sold one
of his lots to his son Daniel[6], Jr. He lived most of his married life in
Pittsfield, and appears there in four Censuses from 1790 to 1820. About
1807 he became a Free Will Baptist and joined the Calvin Baptist Church
(*Morning Star* obituary). At some time after 1825 he moved north to
Sandwich, N.H., where he died in Dec 1841.

Children (compiled from reports of descendants):

+ **366**    i. Daniel[6] Eaton, b. ca. 1771; mar. 1st, Sarah __?__ : 2d,
             Hannah Marshall of Portsmouth, N.H.
+ **367**    ii. Joshua[6] Eaton, b. 23 Feb 1772; mar. Hannah Chase, 1794.
  **368**    iii. Hannah[6] Eaton, b. ca. 1775; mar. John Avery. She died in
             Pittsfield, N.H.
  **369**    iv. Benjamin[6] Eaton, b. ca. 1778; died unmar. in Concord, N.H.

**129. Benjamin[5] Eaton** (Daniel[4A], John[3-1]) was born 4 Aug 1747;
perhaps mar. 1st, **Ruth __?__** , the wife of a Benjamin Eaton who died 5
Dec. 1775 at Newburyport (*Newburyport VR*); more surely mar. **Mary
Manning** of Newburyport 26 Nov 1778. He was quite probably the
Benjamin who enlisted from Salisbury, perhaps between marriages, to
serve as a private in Capt. Joshua French's Co. in Albany, N.Y. (*Mass.
Soldiers & Sailors*, p. 165); and the private in Capt. Samuel Huse's Co. at
Winter Hill and Cambridge in Apr-Jul 1778 (*Soldiers & Sailors*, p. 187).
Benjamin was the only son of Daniel[4A] not mentioned in his father's will
of 1794.

No known issue.

**134. James⁵ Eaton** (Daniel⁴ᴬ, John³⁻ⁱ) was born ca. 1759; mar. **Sarah⁶ Eaton**, daughter of Wyman⁵, 1 Jun 1780 (Salisbury *VR*). The old ancestral homestead on Beach Road in Salisbury was deeded to him by his father on 10 Sep 1794, the consideration being "£10 and five years labor" (Essex Co. Deeds 174-199). He appears on the Salisbury tax lists for 41 consecutive years, 1785 through 1825, and typically was a bit below average for Salisbury citizens in tax liability. He also figures in Censuses from 1790 to 1820. He died 18 Aug 1825. In a series of 1826 deeds, the estate sold his sons James⁶ and Jonathan⁶ four parcels of supplementary wood, tillage and marsh land totalling about 31 acres to be held in common. His widow, Sarah, died 8 Mar 1834 at Salisbury.

Children at Salisbury:

+ **370**   i. Tristram⁶ Eaton, b. 26 Dec 1780; mar. Jemima Brown, 1801.
+ **371**   ii. Benjamin⁶ Eaton, b. 6 Apr 1784; mar. Betsey French, 1805.
   **372**   iii. Zilpha⁶ Eaton, b. 3 Mar 1786; mar. Robert Bragg, son of Peter, 28 Feb 1804. They moved to Chichester, N.H. in 1804, and thence in 1807 when he was 40 years old, to Thetford, Vt. Later they moved again to Strafford, Vt., but returned to Salisbury in 1847, where he died 29 July 1851. She died 4 Jan 1863.
   **373**   iv. William⁶ Eaton, b. 3 Apr 1788; was a mariner early in life. He never married. He was taken prisoner by a British cruiser in the War of 1812, from which he escaped and went to Savannah, Ga. He purchased a vessel there and freighted cotton on the Savannah River for large profits. He died in Savannah and Mr. Lewis Greenleaf of Salisbury went south to settle his estate.
   **374**   v. Polly⁶ Eaton, b. 7 Jun 1790; mar. Philip Greenleaf, son of Samuel, 26 May 1811. They moved to Newburyport that year but returned to Salisbury the next. Philip was a soldier in the War of 1812. He enlisted at Haverhill in Capt. Smiley's Co. in 1813, and was last heard from at Greenbush, N.Y. He had been by trade a blacksmith. Polly died 16 Apr 1854, leaving a son, Lewis Greenleaf, b. 20 Oct 1811, long a distinguished citizen of Salisbury.
   **375**   vi. Sally⁶ Eaton, b. 5 Apr 1794; mar. Alexander Bragg, son of Peter, about 1814, and moved to Thetford, Vt. the same year, where their children were born. She died early and he remarried.
   **376**   vii. Nancy⁶ Eaton, b. 17 Sep 1796; mar. Levi Dow of Seabrook, 4 Feb 1821. They res. Salisbury, rearing two sons and three daughters. He died 15 May 1842; she 15 Apr 1874.
+ **377**   viii. James⁶ Eaton, b. 22 May 1799; mar. Hannah Greeley, 1821.
+ **378**   ix. Jonathan⁶ Eaton, b. 16 Jun 1801; mar. Betsy Morrill, 1822.

**136. Joseph**[5A] **Eaton** (John[4A], Joseph[3], John[2-1]) was born 30 Aug 1715 in Salisbury, Mass., and mar. **Jane True** of Salisbury, 11 Jan 1737. They settled on a farm of 25 acres, part of father John[4A]'s estate (Essex Co. Deed 72-118), and stayed there about 10 years, through the births of their first five children.  Starting in 1746 he administered his father's estate, after his mother declined to do so.  As of 1747, he was a cordwainer.  Some time between May 1746 and Nov 1749 this family removed to Hawke, N.H. (now Danville).  They had a comfortable home on a farm there to the day of the father's death, which occurred very suddenly 15 Jan 1776.

Children (first five born Salisbury; last five born in Hawke (now "Danville"), although several were baptized at Newbury, Mass., 1749-58:

| | | |
|---|---|---|
| **379** | i. | Esther[6] Eaton, b. 23 Aug 1737; unmar. early in 1776. |
| **380** | ii. | Elizabeth[6] Eaton, b. 1 May 1739; mar. Taylor Little. |
| **381** | iii. | Sarah[6] Eaton, b. 23 Sep 1740; died 12 Jun 1746. |
| **382** | iv. | Moses[6] Eaton, b. 22 Nov 1743; not mentioned, father's will. |
| + **383** | v. | John[6] Eaton, b. 13 May 1746; prob. mar. Mary Sawyer; removed to Maine. |
| **384** | vi. | Sarah[6A] Eaton, b. 12 Nov 1749; mar. Stephen Emerson. |
| + **385** | vii. | Jabez[6] Eaton, b. 22 Feb 1752; mar. Susanna Colcord, 1792. |
| **386** | viii. | Abigail[6] Eaton, b. 23 Apr 1755; unmar. early in 1776. |
| **387** | ix. | Hannah[6] Eaton, b. 13 Dec 1756; unmar. early 1776. |
| + **388** | x. | Joseph[6] True Eaton, b. 3 Apr 1758; mar. Mehitable Eastman. |

**146. Daniel**[5] **Eaton** (Samuel[4], Joseph[3], John[2-1]) was born in 1722, probably in Brunswick, Me.  He entered his intentions of marriage with **Jane Dunlap** of Topsham, Me. on 27 May 1752.  Through him has descended the Eaton family of Brunswick.  According to the "Pejepscot Papers," it was in the summer of 1757, as John Malcolm and Daniel Eaton were gathering salt hay, "that they were waylaid by Indians.  Malcolm escaped, but Eaton received a bullet in his wrist, was captured and carried to Canada, where he remained about a year.  He was captured by the famous chief Sabattis who sold him for $4.  Years after, about 1800, Sabattis passed through Brunswick.  Quite a number collected to see the old chief, and Eaton was sent for.  He was at once recognized by Sabattis, who seemed really glad to see him.  At the request of some present, Eaton drew up his sleeve to show the shot scar in his arm.  Sabattis looked with reluctance, saying 'That long time ago, war time too.'  After a friendly chat, he departed."  Martin Eaton of Durham, Me., when over eighty, remembered that his grandfather, Daniel Eaton, according to family tradition, was with the Indians and afterwards with the French, to whom he was sold, about four years in all.  If so, it would change the birth dates of the last five children.  We have followed the Pejepscot Papers as to the time of his captivity in Canada, as the more probable.

Children:

389    i. Jane[6] Eaton, b. ca. 1753; mar. David Sparks. No issue.
+ 390    ii. Samuel[6] Eaton, b. ca. 1755; mar. Dolly Danforth, 1780.
391    iii. Christina[6] Eaton, b. ca. 1757; mar. Abner Danforth and had
            six children.
+ 392    iv. Daniel[6] Eaton, b. ca. 1760; mar. Annie Millet in 1789.
393    v. Betsey[6] Eaton, b. ca. 1762; unmarried.
+ 394    vi. Moses[6] Eaton, b. 1763; mar. Mary Dunlap, 20 Apr 1796.
+ 395    vii. John[6] Eaton, b. ca. 1767; mar. Jane Grant, 27 Jan 1789.
396    viii. Abigail[6] Eaton, b. ca. 1770; unmarried.


**151. Abraham**[5A] **Eaton** (Benjamin[4], Joseph[3], John[2-1]) was born 13
May 1721 in Salisbury, Mass.; mar. 1st, **Martha True**, 19 Dec 1742 at
Salisbury, where they resided.  As an only son he inherited his father's
full estate in 1745, including the homestead on the training green in East
Salisbury village, and another 10-acre lot on the east side of the ferry,
along with various tracts of orchard and meadow land.  He was a ship-
wright, and over the next decade served the town in various minor offices.  In 1751, when Daniel[4A] Eaton was moving from his own home
near the parsonage west of the Country Road to Hampton, Abraham
joined with his uncle Nicholas[4] to buy that place and may have moved
there.  In the 1750-55 period he was selling off  parts of his inherited
land, and in 1755 sold a half-acre quadrant from the land he owned with
Nicholas.  In 1758 he joined with Daniel Moody to buy another lot with
a dwelling unit on it, now probably on the east side of the Country Road.
His first wife had died 19 Apr 1754, and on 6 Dec 1758, a few weeks after the purchase with Moody, he mar. 2d, **Thankful Hubbard**.  He soon
died prematurely on 4 Mar 1763, and the inventory of his estate that
October showed him to be insolvent.  His wife Thankful remarried to
Thomas Barnard of  Amesbury in 1780.

Four children were recorded to Abraham[5A] and Martha, about
whom little is known:

397    i. Benjamin[6] Eaton, b. 13 Sep 1743.
398    ii. Nicholas[6] Eaton, b. 4 Sep 1748.
399    iii. Sarah[6] Eaton, b. 8 Feb 1749.
400    iv. Elizabeth[6] Eaton, b. 6 Apr 1754.

A further child with Thankful:

401    v. Eleazer[6] Hubbard Eaton, b. 30 Oct 1759, Salisbury. Despite
            some accounts, this is not the Eleazar who appears later in
            Connecticut, and who has been given this exact birth date,
            but supposedly at Salisbury, *Conn.*, instead. Indeed, ex-
            cept for the "Elizur" who prompted this birth assignment

by his single appearance in the 1840 Census at Stafford, Conn., and who is more than a generation younger than our Eleazer here, no other household head with any recognizable spelling of this name appears in any Census index in any New England state for the whole 1790-1850 period. A serious candidate for this Eleazer[6], however, is the household head of this name listed at Duanesburgh, N.Y. in 1790, who prob. pushed on to Onondaga Co. in 1800 and then 1820. Ages for this Eleazer had little precision until the 1820 sighting, when Eleazer is 45+.

**161. Jacob[5] Eaton** (Jacob[4], Joseph[3], John[2-1]) was born 8 Apr 1741 at Pemaquid, now Bristol, Me.; mar. **Elizabeth Thorn** on 27 Nov 1764. She was daughter of William Thorn of Topsham, Me. and born 29 Dec 1740. The *History of Farmington, Me.* (Butler, 1885) recounts the following story:

"Among the pioneer settlers who first came to the valley of the Sandy River, there is no one whose character stands out in bolder outline, nor whose name is surrounded with more of personal history, than Jacob Eaton. He was by occupation a ship carpenter, and during his residence in Bristol he spent his time in the shipyard, or in the coasting trade. Prof. Johnson, in his history of Bristol, says, 'Jacob Eaton, Jr., was elected one of the selectmen, and afterward filled several important trusts, and his name is mentioned in the act of incorporation.'

"Jacob Eaton, at the very beginning of the Revolutionary War, was captured by the enemy, and taken to England with Joseph Berry of Topsham. All that is known of his capture and escape is contained in the following joint petition (Mass. *Archives*, Vol. 180, No. 281) of Eaton and Berry for aid, addressed to the Massachusetts Legislature then in session, and dated 8 Jan 1776. In it they affirm 'they were taken by men-of-war belonging to Britain, viz,; the said Eaton and the said Berry, in Aug. 1775, and brought into the Port of Boston; afterward they were put on board the Boyne man-of-war, to help work her home to England: and they say they arrived safely in Plymouth, and from thence your petitioners ran away and got to France, where they entered on board a continental vessel bound for America; that they were taken off the capes of Philadelphia, and carried into New York. From New York they got to New Haven, and there obtained a pass home. And your petitioners, being now two hundred miles from home, without money or clothing, and being now in their own State, from which they were taken, and having lived upon charity ever since they left New York, humbly pray your Honors would be pleased to take their distressed case into your compassionate consideration, and grant them a supply of money and clothing to get home to their families, or to relieve them in such other way as your Honors in your known wisdom shall see fit.' What answer was returned to this petition is not stated."

The *History of Farmington* furnishes another interesting passage. "In 1783 Jacob Eaton, with his brother Joseph, first came to Sandy River township. They purchased the gristmill and sawmill, together with the privilege, which had been erected on the mill-lot by Colburn and Pullen, and put in operation in Nov 1781. They at once built a new dam, and put the mills with their appurtenances in good order for milling purposes. The settlers assisted very generously by their labor in the furtherance of the enterprise; for, as before they had frequently been obliged to go to Winthrop to have their grain ground, they hailed the erection of a gristmill as the harbinger of better days. Mr. Eaton seemed very prosperous in his undertaking. He saw his broad acres teeming with luxuriant crops, and his flocks and herds increasing from year to year, while plenty smiled around him. The township was settling rapidly, and his mills were liberally patronized; but amidst all this prosperity he was restive and discontented: he seemed to sigh for the sea, upon and around which he had spent so large a portion of his life. So with a view to gratifying this desire, he conceived the plan of building a vessel, and in the autumn and early winter of 1790-91 he laid the keel of a small vessel at what is now Farmington Falls, a point following the course of rivers, some 50 miles from navigable waters. In the early summer of 1791 the vessel was completed and ready to launch. This little craft was christened the Lark. Tradition says the sails were made from duck" [cloth], "spun and woven by Mrs. Eaton from flax grown upon the mill-lot, and that the rigging was made from flax by Jesse Bartlesfield. On the 14th of June, 1791, everything being in readiness, Mr. Eaton, as master, with a crew of three, probably partners, cast off from the shore, and the little Lark, impelled by the current, glided down the river like a thing of life, destined for the port of St. John, New Brunswick.

"During the voyage Mr. Eaton kept a daily journal, of which the following is an extract: 'voyage begun on the 14th of June, 1791. Left Sandy River, our crew consisting of four persons, viz: Hugh Cox, Jacob Eaton, William Gower, and Ebenezer Jones: left Tuft's Mills, our wives crying upon the bank, strange unwillingness, willing and not willing to part with their husbands. However, we proceeded down the river; we got down to Jones rips, where we had a hard spell getting down the rips. We got that night to Mr. Young's: he was gone from home. We found four children, but they were almost naked. There was a sled walled into the house, that the children had for a bedstead. A little straw was laid between the side for their lodging. He had on a leather jacket, and Mrs. Young was ordinarily clad; they lodged on straw. When Mr. Young came to strip himself to go to bed, we found he had little shirt on, and his wife less. The next day we proceeded down the rips.'

"It seems they landed at St. John, N.B. early in July, and commenced trading and freighting between St. John and the numerous islands which dot the Bay of Fundy, occasionally making a trip up the river. Their business was attended with varying success until Friday, the 18th of Nov. 1791, when in passing the Falls of St. John, and taking the tide at the wrong time, the little Lark went to the bottom of the Bay, and Mr. Eaton to a watery grave.

"While a resident of Sandy River, Mr. Eaton did much to develop its resources. The new settlers were always greeted with a smile at his house, with the latch string upon the outside, and a cordial welcome waiting at the far side." (Butler, 1885).

Mrs. Elizabeth (Thorn) Eaton survived her husband many years. She died 15 Mar 1804.

Children, all born at Bristol, Me.:

402    i. Sarah[6] Eaton, b. 6 Sep 1765; mar. Ezekiel Lancaster of New Sharon, Me. in 1788; died 4 Oct 1839. Mr. Lancaster was born in Rowley, Mass., in 1758; died 16 Oct 1836. Seven children were born to them.

403    ii. Martha[6] Eaton, b. 11 Apr 1770; mar. Joseph Fairbanks, 15 Mar 1796. She died 17 Sep 1842.

404    iii. Hannah[6] Eaton, b. 8 Apr 1772; mar. Joshua Perley, 4 May 1797. She died 17 Sep 1802, in Ohio.

405    iv. Elizabeth[6] Eaton, b. 6 Apr 1774; mar. Thomas Wendell, 6 Feb 1793. She died 17 Jun 1843, after bearing 11 children.

+ 406    v. Robert[6] Eaton, b. 16 Feb 1776; mar. Rachel, dau. of Moses Starling, 1 Apr 1800; removed to northeastern Ohio.

407    vi. Rachel[6] Eaton, b. 10 Oct 1778; mar. Jabez Gay, 21 Nov 1799. She died 13 Nov 1857.

+ 408    vii. Isaac[6] Eaton, b. 10 Nov 1780; mar. Mary Lyon, 2 Jun 1808.

+ 409    viii. Jacob[6] Eaton, b. 12 Jul 1784; mar. Abigail Bradford, 1805.

NOTE: The above five daughters are mentioned by Rev. Paul Coffin in his jounal of his missionary tour as "remarkable for beauty and intelligence. They all married most favorably. Their husbands took a foremost rank in the early history of Farmington and surrounding towns."

**162. Joseph[5] Eaton** (Jacob[4], Joseph[3], John[2-1]) was born ca. Nov 1742, probably in Topsham, Me., although it is said by some that he was born in Bristol, Me.; mar. **Jane McGlathery** 25 Feb 1769, probably in New Harbor, Me., an outpost of Bristol, Me. (She had been born in Londonderry, Ireland, ca. 1746, and came to this country when an infant.) They settled in New Harbor on a farm. There they remained until 1783, after their children had been born. Then they removed to Sandy River, and afterward (between 1786 and 1789) on to Camden, Me., where he became postmaster in 1794. He seems to have been highly esteemed for his integrity and capability. He died in Camden 30 Jul 1828. Mrs. Jane Eaton died there 12 Aug 1834.

Children at New Harbor and Bristol:

410    i. Polly[6] Eaton, b. ca. Mar 1770; mar. Bela Jacobs: no issue. She was buried, Camden. Very intelligent, great memory.

411    ii. Jacob[6] Eaton, b. 26 May 1771.

+ 412    iii. Joseph[6] Eaton, b. 21 Feb 1773; mar. Deborah Waterman.

+ 413    iv. William[6] Eaton, b. 7 Feb 1775; mar. Lucy White, 1797.

**414**    v. Nancy[6] Eaton, b. ca. Mar 1777; mar. Asa Hosmer. She died
                  7 Dec 1860.
**415**    vi. Jane[6] Eaton, b. in 1799; mar. Benjamin Cushing. She died
                  Aug 1846, after having had a large family.


**163. Benjamin[5] Eaton** (Jacob[4], Joseph[3], John[2-1]) was born 30 May
1744, probably in Topsham, Me. He was a twin whose mate was drowned
when a boy of 13 years in the Androscoggin river. Benjamin[5] mar 1st,
**Tabitha Whalen** of Topsham, certificate granted 24 Jan 1773, by whom
he had four sons. After her death he mar. 2d, **Lucy Moody** (b. 11 Apr
1766), with intentions entered 27 Dec 1784. She was the mother of 12
sons and two daughters who lived to mature years. Mr. Eaton was the
father of 23 children. Five of these died at birth, and we have no record
for them. Benjamin was a farmer on whose broad acres his children
were reared. For some unknown reason he was commonly called "Dr.
Eaton," possibly because of his skill in training so large a family. He
died in Topsham, 12 Jan 1827, aged 82. His second wife Lucy died
there also, 16 Jan 1846, in her 80th year.

Children with Tabitha, all born at Topsham:

**416**    i. John[6] Eaton, b. 12 Nov 1773; never married. Was a sea cap-
                  tain. He died in Virginia when about age 50.
**417**    ii. Benjamin[6] Eaton, b. 20 Jan 1776; never married. A sailor, he
                  sailed from Bath, Me., one day at noon. There was a
                  terrible storm that night, after which the vessel was never
                  heard from.
**418**    iii. James[6] Eaton, b. 26 Jun 1779; never married. He was a shoe-
                  maker in Topsham. He died before he was 30.
**419**    iv. Jotham[6] Eaton, b. 24 Nov 1783; died young.

Children with Lucy, all born in Topsham:

**420**    v. Mary[6] Eaton, b. 4 Jun 1785; mar. David Work of Topsham,
                  7 Jul 1810, and had seven each, daughters and sons.
+ **421**    vi. Isaac[6] Eaton, b. 24 Nov 1787; mar. Hannah Wilson, 1814.
+ **422**    vii. William[6] Eaton, b. 2 Jul 1789; mar Rachel Parsons, 1817.
+ **423**    viii. Charles[6] Eaton, b. 17 Mar 1790; mar. Catharine Nichols.
**424**    ix. Joseph[6] Eaton, b. 14 Apr 1792; died at sea, unmarried.
**425**    x. Susan[6] Eaton, b. 19 Mar 1794; mar. John Haley, 21 May
                  1820 (his second wife).
**426**    xi. Abel[6] Eaton, b. 17 Mar 1796; went West and married, but
                  never reported himself to his relatives.
+ **427**    xii. Jotham[6A] Eaton, b. 8 Jan 1798; mar. Mehitable True, 1821.
+ **428**    xiii. Humphrey[6] Eaton, b. 13 Dec 1800; mar. Melissa White.
+ **429**    xiv. Stephen[6] Eaton, b. 3 Jan 1802; mar. Caroline Nye, 1835.
+ **430**    xv. Stockbridge[6] Eaton, b. 30 Nov 1805; m. Ruth Wales of Bath.
+ **431**    xvi. James[6] Eaton, b. 28 Nov 1807; mar. Esther Wilson, 1831.

+ **432** xvii. Hiram[6] Moody Eaton, b. 14 Jul 1810, one of twins; mar.
            Nancy Morrison and resided at New Limerick.
+ **433** xviii. Horace[6] Malcolm Eaton, b. 14 Jul 1810, the other twin; mar.
            Hannah D. Wilson, 11 Feb 1841.


      **172. Ephraim[5] Eaton** (Henry[4], Ephraim[3], John[2-1]) was born 1 Feb
1745 in Salisbury, Mass.; mar. 1st,, **Abigail Perkins** of Seabrook, N.H.,
15 Nov 1768.  They lived on or near his father Henry[4]'s homestead in
Salisbury.  Abigail died soon after the birth of their first child about
1769.  Ephraim[5] mar. 2d, **Sarah Stevens** of Salisbury, 9 Jan 1772.  Late
in 1772, Ephraim was given a 93-acre farm on South Road in the Candia
part of Chester, N.H. "for affection" by his father, and the couple moved
there soon after.  Their lot adjoined one settled three years earlier by
Ephraim's first cousin Paul[5] Eaton (**#180**), and lay near the Candia Post
Office.  (These two lots were but one lot north beyond another pair of
Candia lots settled in the same period by sons of the Rev. Benjamin[4] Eaton, including (Capt.) Jesse, Ebenezer and William.  This line of Eatons
stemmed from William[1]/Mary of Reading, who had come from Kent,
England with no obvious connection to our John[1] of Salisbury/Haverhill.
However, these two Eaton lineages were important in Candia affairs for
several generations, and in at least one instance, intermarried.)
      Ephraim was a farmer, and appears at Candia for the first four
Federal Censuses, 1790-1820.  The *History of Candia* (Moore, 1893)
notes that he "was an active man, often employed in town affairs, ready in
the support of religious institutions, of good judgment and strong common sense, and of a rather taciturn disposition."  His wife died at Candia
in 1822; he died there Nov. 22, 1826.

      Child with Abigail, born Salisbury:

**434**    i. Abigail[6] "Nabby" Eaton, bp. 20 Aug 1769; mar. Hezekiah
        Blake of Andover, N.H. and had one son.

      Children with Sarah (ii at Salisbury; iii-vi at Candia):

**435**    ii. Molly[6] Eaton, b. ca. 1772; mar. Dr. Jacob Bayley Moore of
        Andover, N.H., son of Dr. Coffin Moore, the first physician
        in Candia.  They had four children: Jacob Bayler Moore,
        Jr., who mar. a sister of Gov. Isaac Hill and collaborated
        with him in publishing the "New Hampshire Patriot" and
        with John Farmer, the early genealogist, in publishing a
        Gazeteer of New Hampshire.  Mary Moore, who mar. Dr.
        Thomas Brown.  John W. Moore who mar. Emily Jane
        Eastman.  Henry Eaton Moore, a celebrated musician who
        m. Susan Farnum.
**436**    iii. Sally[6] Eaton, b. 27 Jul 1775; died unmarried, 1836.
+ **437**    iv. Henry[6] Eaton, b. 24 Apr 1777; mar. Hannah Eaton, dau. of
        Jesse Eaton of the William[1]/Martha line of Reading Eatons,

on 24 Apr 1804.
**438**    v. Hannah[6] Eaton, b. 4 Nov 1782; mar. Moses Patten of Candia,
son of Thomas. Had a daughter and two sons, one of
whom was Rev. Moses Patten of Greensborough, Vt.
+ **439**   vi. Peter[6] Eaton, b. 17 Apr 1788; mar. Hannah Kelley of Chester.


**174. (Lt.) Peter[5A] Eaton** (Henry[4], Ephraim[3], John[2-1]) was born 25
Mar 1748 in Salisbury, Mass.; mar. **Abigail Greeley**, 5 Dec 1770 at
Salisbury. They resided on a farm in the northwest corner of the junction of the "Country Road" from Salisbury to Portsmouth, and the "Little
River", then near a gristmill called the "Huckleberry Mill", and still near
the railroad overpass at what is now Lafayette Road. Peter marched as a
private in Capt. Stephen Merrill's Co., Col. Caleb Cushing's Regt., in re-
sponse to the alarm of 19 Apr 1775, putting in 3 1/2 days' service. By
1782 he is referred to as Lt. Peter in the Town Records, although we have
no evidence of other spells of active service. In the 1778-82 period he
served the town in various capacities, including Grand Jury Man for
Salisbury. He was primarily a farmer, and was on the Salisbury tax lists,
1777-1784. He died very prematurely, 30 July 1784, predeceasing his
own father, Capt. Henry. His widow Abigail died 9 Mar 1801.

Children, all born Salisbury:

**440**    i. Joanna[6] Eaton, b. 9 Nov 1771; died unmar. 26 Oct 1805.
**441**   ii. Jemima[6] Eaton, b. 28 Jun 1773; mar. Levi Jackman, 16 Jan
1807; had two sons and three daughters.
+ **442**  iii. Henry[6] Eaton, b. 12 Jun 1775; mar. Sally Stevens, 1799.
+ **443**  iv. Stephen[6] Eaton, b. 10 Jun 1777; mar. Susan Currier, 1800.
+ **444**   v. Peter[6] Eaton, b. 16 Jun 1779; mar. Sally Hook, 1800.
**445**   vi. Abigail[6] "Nabby," Eaton, b. 8 May 1781; d. 30 Dec 1816.
+ **446**  vii. Samuel[6] Eaton, b. 3 Oct 1783; mar. Ruth French, 1803.


**175. Timothy[5] Eaton** (Henry[4], Ephraim[3], John[2-1]) was born 11
Mar 1750; mar. **Abigail Meeder** 31 Dec 1785 (Friends Records); resided
in Hampton Falls, N.H., and Hampton. This was probably the Pvt.
Timothy Eaton who with his Seabrook cousins Cpl. Levi[6], Pvt. Benjamin[6]
and Pvt. David[6], served with Capt. Moses Leavitt's Co., Col. Abraham
Drake's Regt., to reinforce the northern Continental Army at Stillwater
near Albany, N.Y. in the fall of 1777. In the same year as his marriage,
1788, Timothy requests the care of the Friends' Hampton/Amesbury
Meeting, and is received into membership. His inventory rendered 10
Mar 1791, with his daughter the only heir mentioned.

Child:

**447**    i. Rachel[6] Eaton, b. 1789 or 1790.

**179. Samuel[5] Eaton** (Jabez[4A], Ephraim[3], John[2-1]) was born 20 Apr 1737 in Salisbury, Mass., but at a very young age his family moved back to the Gravelly Ridge homestead of his father shared with his brother Ephraim[4], so he grew up there. He is very likely to have been the Sam Eaton who on 28 Mar 1759 enlisted in Capt. Samuel Leavitt's Co., Weare's Regt., for the Canadian Expedition of that year, because no other Samuel Eatons in the area at the time were of even vaguely appropriate age for such a role, while his age was ideal (N.H. *State Papers*, Vol. XIV, p. 23). He also served as a corporal in Vermont in the Revolution. His father died in Jan 1760, and Samuel[5], the eldest surviving son, came into a major share of his father's estate. No doubt as a result, in 1760 although still unmarried and only 23, he comes onto the Hampton Falls tax-paying stream and remains there until Seabrook splits off in 1768, and then turns up on Seabrook tax lists, as well as the Association Test of 1776. In 1765 he had signed a petition for exemption from the minister's tax favoring the Congregational Rev. Paine Wingate, because he, along with numerous of the other proto-Seabrook Eatons, was already contributing to the support of the Presbyterian Rev. Samuel Perley.

When he was 45 he finally married 1st, **Mary "Molly" Merrill**, daughter of Eliphalet of Hampton Falls, and presumably continued residence at the family place in the Gravelly Ridge Division in Seabrook. We do not have records of births of their children, but from later events we know the couple had at least two sons before Molly died. Samuel then married 2d, **Abiah Marston** of Hampton at some time before Oct. 1789, when she is listed as his wife on a Seabrook land deed. When he was approaching 60, Samuel decided to move "up country" to Chichester, N.H. In 1796, he sold Winthrop[6] Eaton, a younger cousin once removed, five parcels of land in Seabrook totalling 25 acres, with "all my buildings thereon." (Rockingham Co. Deeds, 142-351). This sounds like an exit, although there is no record of Samuel buying any land in Chichester until May 1798, and he continues to be described as a yeoman of Seabrook in two deeds of 1800, after which in 1801, comparable deeds finally identify him as being of Chichester. Nonetheless, wife Abial is recorded as having died in Chichester 9 Apr 1798.

In 1805 when he was almost 70, Samuel[5] sold out his land in Chichester, and proceeded to St. Johnsbury, Vt., to rejoin his son Samuel who had moved there about 1804. In a letter from St. Johnsbury dated Wed 8 May 1811, son Samuel[6] wrote to his father's brother Paul[5] Eaton at Candia (see **#180**, below) that his father had been taken ill on 8 Mar 1811 [a Friday] and had "died on Monday at 10 of the clock in the forenoon," thus departing either 11 Mar or 6 May of 1811.

Child birth records sparse, but at least two with Molly:

+ **448**  i. Samuel[6] Eaton, b. 11 May 1782, Seabrook; m. Betsey Moore.
  **449**  ii. Benjamin[6] Eaton, b. 178?; was a mariner who was lost at sea leaving a wife and three children.

NOTE. Making *this* Samuel the husband for Molly Merrill and Abiah Marston has not been commonly done in the past. More frequently he has been seen as the 1769 bridegroom of Rachel Greeley, instead of the Samuel (**#107**) whom we choose. Indeed, the senior author of this genealogy possessed a letter from a Mrs. Merrill, a granddaughter of Samuel and Rachel (Greeley) Eaton, testifying that her grandfather Samuel was the son of Jabez/Sarah Eaton. However, Oliver[7] Eaton, the 19th-century authority on the Seabrook Eatons and himself a direct descendant from Jabez/Sarah, was certain that the Jabez/Sarah son Samuel had not in fact married Rachel Greeley, and for at least two reasons. One was that the Samuel out of Jabez/Sarah had later died in St. Johnsbury, Vt. in the home of his own son Samuel, Jr., whereas the only emigrants among the Samuel/Rachel (Greeley) offspring had gone instead to Solon, Me. The second reason he offered was that he knew which other Samuel Eaton was actually Rachel's bridegroom. Unfortunately--shades of Fermat's last theorem--his memorandum does not mention which Samuel this was. However, the junior author has developed considerable evidence for Samuel (**#107**) as Rachel Greeley's groom, including among other things the fact that the Samuel/Rachel homestead site is almost certainly one which was earlier owned by Samuel[4], the father of the (**#107**) Samuel.

**180. Paul[5] Eaton** (Jabez[4A], Ephraim[3], John[2-1]) was born 29 Aug 1739 in proto-Seabrook, and thereby lived in four towns without changing his residence: (1) Salisbury, Mass.; (2) So. Hampton, N.H.; (3) Hampton Falls, N.H.; and (4) Seabrook. He mar. 1st, **Mary "Molly" Tilton**, ca. 1764. From 1762 he was on six consecutive Hampton Falls tax lists before Seabrook was set off. He was taxed in Seabrook in 1770, but had already sold out his inheritance of part of his father's estate there in Mar 1769, and removed from Seabrook to Candia, N.H., in the spring of 1770, to a 50-acre plot he had purchased in 1765 [see NH Deed 89-168]. He would spend the rest of his life in that town, accumulating more land in the process. He bought of Isaiah Rowe a place at No. 114, 2d P., 2d D., still occupied a century later by his grandchildren, and was soon joined on lot No. 113, next to the south, by his first cousin, Ephraim[5] (see **#172**). His wife Mary died about 1775, after she had borne five children. He then mar. 2d, **Hannah Emerson** of Haverhill, Mass., date unknown. Paul served in the Revolutionary War, and was by tradition an amazingly strong man. The *History of Candia* (Moore, 1893) recounts "on good authority, that once he moved, by means of a chain and lever placed across his thighs, a log which a smart yoke of steers could not start." Wife Hannah predeceased him, dying 5 Oct 1819. He died 29 Apr 1830 at age 91 in Candia.

Children with Mary at Seabrook and Candia:

    450   i. Mary[6] "Molly" Eaton, b. ca. 1764; mar. Timothy Morse.
    451   ii. Anna[6] Eaton, b. ca. 1766; mar. Stephen Clay.
+   452   iii. Henry[6] True Eaton, b. 29 May 1768; m. Elizabeth Emerson.

**453** iv. Sarah[6] Eaton, b. ca. 1770; died in infancy.
**454** v. John[6] T. Eaton, b. in 1774; never married.

Children with Hannah at Candia:

**455** vi. Lydia[6] Eaton, b. ca. 1792; mar. Josiah French.
**456** vii. Luke[6] Eaton, b. ca. 1794; mar. a Pennsylvania native; she died 1864; he died 1868.


**183. Joshua[5] Eaton** (Jabez[4A], Ephraim[3], John[2-1]) was born 19 Jul 1749 in the proto-Seabrook part of Hampton Falls, N.H.; mar. **Anna Smith**, daughter of Jacob and Mercy (Gill) Smith, 24 Oct 1773, and lived on a farm on the north side of lower Walton Road in Seabrook, a part of his father's estate. He also must have inherited a number of other parcels from his father, since there are no land purchases in his name, but after his death 17 Oct 1831, he had left nearly 70 acres of land in 12 different parcels to his two legitimate sons. He appeared in 5 consecutive Censuses at Seabrook, 1790-1830. His wife Anna had died 29 Oct 1819 (Mrs. Locke's List).

Child, mother unknown:

+ **457** i. "Azel[6]" (Asahel?) Eaton, b. ca. 1774; mar. Polly Foster of Connecticut.

Children with Anne at Seabrook:

**458** ii. Mercy[6] Eaton, b. 5 Apr 1776; mar. Robert Collins on 24 Feb 1796. He died 27 Nov 1842, aged ca. 75; she died 11 Aug 1835.
+ **459** iii. Jabez[6] Eaton, b. 9 Nov 1777; mar. Susan Beckman, 1802.
+ **460** iv. Joshua[6] Eaton, b. 14 Feb 1780; mar. Ruth Merrill, 1801.
**461** v. Nancy[6] Eaton, b. 16 Mar 1782; mar. William Beckman, son of John R. Beckman, 10 Jan 1804. She died 6 Nov 1855.
**462** vi. Rhoda[6] Eaton, b. 2 Sep 1790; mar. John Brown, son of Benjamin. He died 26 Jun 1838; she died 27 Apr 1849.

\* \* \* \* \* \*

## B. *The Haverhill Branch*

**186. (Capt.) Joseph[5] Eaton** (Thomas[4-2], John[1]) was born 27 Feb 1730, in Haverhill, Mass.; mar. **Sarah Webster** of Haverhill 24 Jan 1754. She was doubtless of the same stock as Daniel Webster, the great statesman. Mr. Eaton was a husbandman whose farm was near the celebrated Dustin estate in the West Parish, and whose residence was nearly opposite the "old garrison house." As a Company captain in Col. Johnson's Regt. of militia he marched on the alarm of 19 Apr 1775 from the town of Haverhill to Cambridge. He served seven days. On 3 Apr 1776 he was commissioned Captain of Co. 14 in the 4th Regt. of militia in Essex Co. His company went with Col. Samuel Johnson's Regt. in an expedition to the northward from 15 Aug to 30 Nov 1777. On 20 Sep 1779, he was commissioned Adjutant to the 5th Regt. of Essex County. (All from the Massachusetts *Archives*.)

Joseph[5] Eaton was chosen Deacon of the West Parish Church in 1785. About this time there were only two chaises owned in this part of town, one by Joseph and the other by his associate Deac. Moses Webster. He died 20 Feb 1805; his wife Sarah died 31 Jan 1809.

Children at Haverhill:

**463**   i. Abigail[6] Eaton, b. 9 Dec 1754; mar. Jesse Webster.
**464**   ii. Sarah[6] Eaton, b. 2 Oct 1756; m. Rev. Isaac Smith of Gilmanton, N.H., 10 Nov 1791. He died in 1817 at 72, in the 43rd year of his ministry. She is mentioned in her father's will.
**465**   iii. Samuel[6] Eaton, a twin b. 22 Aug 1758; died the same day.
**466**   iv. Lydia[6] Eaton, a twin b. 22 Aug 1758; mar. Joseph How.
+ **467**   v. Samuel[6A] Eaton, b. 15 Jul 1760; m. Lois Swain of Lynnfield, Mass., 21 Jun 1808.
**468**   vi. Elizabeth[6] Eaton, b. 5 Jul 1762; died before June 1792.
+ **469**   vii. Peter[6] Eaton, b. 15 Mar 1765; mar. Sarah Stone of Reading.
**470**   viii. Betsey[6] Eaton, b. 24 Feb 1767.
**471**   ix. Judith[6] Eaton, b. 5 Jun 1771. A single woman in 1823, at Haverhill.
**472**   x. Mary[6] Eaton, b. 14 Sep 1773; d. 23 Feb. 1805.

**188. Moses[5] Eaton** (Thomas[4-2], John[1]), was born 29 Jan 1734 in Haverhill, Mass.; mar. **Anna Webster** 5 Feb 1760. She had been born in Plaistow, N.H. in 1742. Between purchasing a farm on the Chester Road in Hampstead, N.H. [NH Deed 85-132] in May 1764 and selling their property in Haverhill in 1766, they removed to Hampstead, N.H. After a few years there, they went on to Pelham, N.H. According to the *History of Francestown, N.H.* (Cochrane & Wood, 1895) in about 1779 they moved again to a farm on Bible Hill Road in the northeast quadrant of Francestown, known in the later 19th century as the George and Henry Richardson place. There they spent the remainder of their days. Ac-

cording to their gravestones, plainly visible from the road, Moses died 1
Mar 1813 at age 79; his widow Anna died 5 Sep 1831 at age 90.

Children:

**473**    i. Hannah⁶ Eaton, b. 26 Apr 1761 in Haverhill, Mass; mar.
Robert Bradford of Francestown and resided there until
her death, 9 Oct 1840.
**474**   ii. Lydia⁶ Eaton, b. 18 Aug 1763 in Haverhill; died 21 Apr
1767, probably in Hampstead, N.H.
**475**  iii. Mary⁶ Eaton, b. 22 Nov 1765 in Haverhill; mar. 1st, James
Wilson of Windham, N.H., and later Francestown, 24 Nov
1785; mar. 2d, Eliphalet Webster of Gilsum, who died at
Francestown, 25 Apr 1857. Mrs. Wilson was mother of
six sons and four daughters.
+ **476**  iv. Thomas⁶ Eaton, b. 6 Feb 1769, Hampstead, N.H. After his
parents moved to Francestown he mar. Betsey⁶ Eaton
(**#602**), dau. of Obadiah⁵ of Weare, N.H., 20 Feb 1798.
**477**   v. Sarah⁶ Eaton, b. 9 Mar 1772 in Pelham, N.H.; mar. Rev.
Moses Bradford of Francestown as his second wife, and
became mother of seven sons and three daughters. Three
of the sons became ministers and one a physician. The
eldest daughter died at 13 and the next at 11, both at
Francestown; the youngest mar. Francis Boardman
and res. in Newport, N.H. Rev. Bradford was pastor in
Francestown for 37 years.
**478**  vi. Moses⁶ Eaton, b. 22 Jul 1775 in Pelham; d. there in Oct
1778.

**192. Thomas⁵ᴬ Eaton** (Thomas⁴⁻², John¹) was born 3 Feb 1744 in
Haverhill, Mass. He bought 90 acres in Bow, N.H. in Dec 1764 [NH
Deed 76-443] and was residing in that township by 16 Oct 1765. On 6
Oct 1768 he bought 154 acres of land in Concord, the next township
north, from his cousin Nathaniel⁵ (**#208**), who was retreating to his native
Haverhill after a two-year experiment in New Hampshire. About this
time Thomas mar. **Molly Swaine** and settled on his farm on Beech Hill
by the Concord-Hopkinton town line, where he stayed the rest of his life.
He was the patriarch for most of the Eatons in Hopkinton, N.H. He died
in Concord 17 Apr 1799; wife Molly died 9 Jan 1825 in Boscawen, aged
about 80 years.

Children:

**479**    i. Polly⁶ Eaton, b. 10 Aug 1769; mar. Ezra Eastman in 1787
and settled on a farm on Putney Hill in Hopkinton, N.H.,
where they had eight children surviving infancy. Ezra died
there 14 June 1816. Polly died 11 Jan 1825.
+ **480**   ii. Thomas⁶ Eaton, b. 21 Jul 1771; mar. Sarah Eastman, 1790.

+ **481**    iii. Moses[6] Eaton, b. 19 Jan 1775; mar. Lucy Hazeltine, 1794.
+ **482**    iv. Joseph[6] Eaton, b.18 Dec 1776; mar. Hannah French, 1809.
  **483**    v. Sarah[6] Eaton, b. 23 Jan 1779; mar. a Samuel Eaton "of Con-
             cord, N.H.," quite likely her cousin (see **#599**), 18 Dec
             1797; resided in Dunbarton and Weare, raising three
             sons and two daughters. If her husband was the Weare
             Samuel Eaton, she died in 1818, and he later mar. a
             Betsey Edmunds.
  **484**    vi. Hannah[6] Eaton, b. ca. 1780; mar. 1st, David Blanchard of
             Concord, 4 Oct 1796; and 2d, Samuel Cilley, resided in
             Weare, N.H. Had one son Samuel Cilley, Jr., who was
             drowned in Washington, N.H. about 1850, without issue.
  **485**    vii. Ruth[6] Eaton, b. ca. 1782; mar. Amos Webster of Hopkinton,
             18 May 1804, and had eight children.
  **486**    viii. Nancy[6] Eaton, b. ca. 1783; mar. Thomas Abbot of Concord,
             N.H., 14 Apr 1801, and had seven children.
+ **487**    ix. Peter[6] Eaton, b. ca. 1784; mar. Clarissa Kimball, 1804.


**199. Moses[5] Eaton** (Moses[4], John[3], Thomas[2], John[1]) was born 11
Oct 1768 in Haverhill, Mass; mar. **Betsey Plummer**, dau. of Nathaniel
and Hannah (Walker) Plummer of Bradford, Mass., 29 Dec 1795. This
young couple sold their capacious 45-acre homestead in Haverhill for
$900 (Essex Co. deed 272-127) on 7 Apr 1797 and a week later joined
with youngest brother Ebenezer[5] in selling another six acres from their
parental estate. Six weeks later Moses ("a yeoman of Haverhill") bought
a tract of land in Canaan, N.H. The brothers then removed to Grafton
Co. N.H. While their land stakes there were probably no more than two
miles apart, Moses's tract was in Canaan township, and Ebenezer's was just
west of the Canaan town line in Hanover township. And we find them
both in the 1800 Census, Moses in Canaan and Ebenezer in Hanover.
The Moses household was comprised just of Moses and apparently Betsy:
this couple seems childless at the time. While Ebenezer lived out his life
in the area, moving himself in due time into Canaan (see **#201**), Moses
shortly after the 1800 Census sold his tract to brother Ebenezer and he
and wife disappeared from the scene (Grafton Co. deeds 37-170/1.)
         We feel the odds are better than 50-50 that this Moses and Betsey
explain a couple (otherwise a mystery, fitting none of the Moses Eatons
known to us in any of the major branches of Eatons in New England)
who turn up, with children, in Harrington, Me. (Washington County) in
1830 and ensuing Censuses. The ages of the parents are appropriate.
Furthermore, a plausible story as to their itinerary after Canaan is near at
hand. Wife Betsey was a Plummer, and the Plummer clan, with its original New World home in Newbury and Rowley, Mass., had begun extensive colonization of southern Maine (York and Cumberland counties) as
early as the 1720s. We know also that the Harrington Moses family of
1830 had had children around 1810 in the Portland area, before removing to Harrington by 1830. Betsey had a particularly large and vigorous
set of cousins who had settled a generation or two earlier in Portland and

its environs (most notably, the Scarboro/Gorham area). It was out of this seedbed that a Jeremiah Plummer left the Scarboro area for better prospects at Addison, next door to Harrington in Washington Co., Me., before 1770. So it is not hard to imagine that Moses and Betsey, disillusioned by the bleak wilderness they had bought into at Canaan, might have left for the Portland/Scarboro area as a more forgiving frontier. And with that package, a move a decade or two later northeast to Harrington in Washington County, following other Plummer cousins, makes sense as well.

Despite this plausible scenario, there are are rough edges which leave doubt. It is not even certain that the wife of the Moses Eaton of Harrington was named Elizabeth/ Betsy, altho the woman who appears to be his relict, of a roughly appropriate advanced age and living in 1850 in a daughter's household, is called "Eliza A. Eaton." It is even possible, however, that this is a second wife after the first produced no issue. Most frustrating of all is our inability to find any sign of this Moses in the Censuses of 1810 or 1820 in Maine or, for that matter, anywhere else in New England. Of course, when newcomers joined old relatives in long migrations, they often cadged lodging until they got on their own feet in the new environment, thereby remaining hidden from Censuses limited to naming just one head of household. This "excuse" might cover the Moses/Betsey absence for the 1810 Portland area Census, despite independent evidence that they were there. But as we have seen, Moses had been financially comfortable for his age, and it is hard to believe that he would not have been on his feet for a decade or more. Again, we can find excuses why this couple might have escaped the 1820 Census as well: there is murky evidence that the Harrington Eaton children born in after 1810 later considered their birthplace to have been in New Brunswick, although barely so, such as at Campobello Island across the narrows from Lubec, Maine, only 50 miles from the final destination at Harrington. A sojourn there would have taken this family out of the view of the Census also. And of course, it is true that our inability to find in two earlier Censuses the Moses who emerges at Harrington in 1830 at about age 60 with children nearly up and out, does not in itself logically reduce the possibility that this is our Haverhill Moses. That is, the fact is clear that *some* Moses Eaton materializes in this fashion at Harrington in 1830, when all other known Moses Eatons in his cohort in New England (or, for that matter, Nova Scotia) are otherwise occupied save this Haverhill-Canaan refugee. In short, the case is likely, but is of the circumstantial kind that many types of new information could quickly disconfirm.

Children (may be incomplete):

+ **488**   i. Moses[6] Eaton, b. 7 Aug 1809, probably around Portland, Me.;
            mar. Sarah Mitchell, 1830.
+ **489**   ii. Asa[6] Eaton, b. ca. 1815, possibly Portland or Campobello Island, New Brunswick; mar. Lydia Mitchell, 1835.
  **490**   iii. Patience[6] Eaton, b. ca. 1816, perhaps New Brunswick, Can.;
            mar. James Morrison 25 Dec 1837 in Harrington, Me.

Later resided in Milbridge, Me.

**201. Ebenezer**[5] **Eaton** (Moses[4], John[3], Thomas[2], John[1]) was born 6 Aug 1773 in Haverhill, Mass.; mar. **Susannah Coburn** about 1798. She had been born 14 Sep 1775, supposedly at Sutton, N.H. They settled on a farm in the wilderness on the east side of the mountain in Hanover, N.H., where they began their married life in a log hut, overlooking Canaan, N.H., where his brother Moses[5] resided for a few years (see **#199**). They brought their children up to adulthood there. Then in August, 1820, Ebenezer bought a large farm on Sawyer Hill in Canaan, N.H. moving his family there, where he became a wealthy farmer for that period. He died on this farm, where he was living with his son Nathaniel, 26 Dec 1851. After his death, widow Susannah lived with her daughter Polly Huntoon in Enfield, N.H., and died there 28 Dec 1853. Both Ebenezer and Susannah were buried in the yard on Sawyer Hill, Canaan.

Children born Hanover:

491    i. Polly[6] Eaton, b. 7 Jan 1799; mar. Philip Huntoon of Hanover and settled in Enfield, N.H., where they had two sons. She died 4 Oct 1872 at Enfield.

492    ii. Sally[6] Eaton, b. 15 May 1802; mar. Moses Morse and settled on a farm in Hanover, where they had six children. She d. there 30 Jul 1854. Later the family went to Wisconsin.

+ 493    iii. Nathaniel[6] Eaton, b. 28 Jan 1806; mar. Lucinda Paddleford.

**202. David**[5] **Eaton** (James[4], Jonathan[3], Thomas[2], John[1]) was born 1 Apr 1729 in Haverhill, Mass. He moved to Tolland, Conn. as a young man, and mar. 1st, **Deborah White** of Andover, Conn., 10 Oct 1751. She was the second daughter and fourth child of Thomas and Sarah (Miller) White, b. 19 May 1732. Their first six children were born in Tolland. In 1760, however, David became part of a growing enthusiasm in eastern Connecticut sparked by British encouragements to New England colonists to take individual possession of the valuable lands that had been developed by French farmers in "Acadia", or "Nova Scotia" as the British had renamed it upon driving out the French residents in 1755. About the spring of 1761, David and his family embarked from New London, Conn., for Nova Scotia, where the last eight of their children would be born. His original grant was for 750 acres in the Cornwallis area of King's County near the southeast shore of the Bay of Fundy and the Minas Basin. Between Apr 1761 and Feb 1768 he made more than a half-dozen further purchases and thus quickly became an extensive landowner. The first house he built burned, but was soon replaced with a larger well-appointed one.

David's wife Deborah died on 20 May 1790 in Cornwallis. He mar. 2d, **Mrs. Alice (English) Willoughby**, b. 2 Oct 1738, and the widow of Dr. Samuel Willoughby, M.P.P. of Cornwallis. Alice's death date is unknown, but David[5] spent his last years as a widower. He died 17 Jul 1803, leaving a large estate. His will was recorded in Kentville, the county seat.

Children by Deborah:

494   i. Susannah[6] Eaton, b. 26 Sep 1752 in Tolland, Conn.; died 18 Oct 1761 in Cornwallis, Nova Scotia.

+ 495   ii. Stephen[6] Eaton, b. 29 Jan 1754 in Tolland; mar. Elizabeth Woodworth, 23 Nov 1775, in Cornwallis.

496   iii. Timothy[6] Eaton, b. 17 Jul 1755 in Tolland; died early.

+ 497   iv. Elisha[6] Eaton, b. 8 Jan 1757 in Tolland; mar. Irene Bliss, 31 May 1779.

+ 498   v. Timothy[6A] Eaton, b. 27 Aug 1758 in Tolland; mar. Huldah Woodworth, 25 Oct 1781.

499   vi. Elijah[6] Eaton, b. 29 May 1760 in Tolland; died 15 Aug 1761 in Cornwallis.

500   vii. Sarah[6] Eaton, b. 13 Feb 1762 in Cornwallis, Nova Scotia; mar. Abel Strong, 28 Sep 1784.

+ 501   viii. Elijah[6A] Eaton, b. 16 Oct 1763 in Cornwallis; mar. Elizabeth Rand, 2 May 1785.

+ 502   ix. David[6] Eaton, b. 13 Jul 1765 in Cornwallis; mar. Eunice Wells, 17 Jan 1785.

+ 503   x. James[6] Eaton, b. 14 Aug 1767 in Cornwallis; mar. 1st, Nancy Manning, probably summer, 1793; and 2d Lucy Farnsworth, Jun 1799.

504   xi. Susannah[6A] Eaton, b 24 Jun 1769 in Conrwallis; mar. Capt. Harry Cox. 19 Dec 1793.

505   xii. Deborah[6] Eaton, b. 6 Jan 1771 in Cornwallis; mar. John Manning of Falmouth, N.S., 17 May 1792.

+ 506   xiii. John[6] Eaton, b. 29 May 1773 in Cornwallis; mar. 1st, Tabitha Rand, 29 May 1794, who died 26 Oct 1807; and 2d, her sister, Abigail Rand, 28 Jan 1808.

507   xiv. Prudence[6] Eaton, b. 13 Oct 1774 in Cornwallis; mar. John Wells, M.P.P., 31 Oct 1793.

508   xv. Amos[6] Eaton, b. 9 Sep 1778 in Cornwallis; died by an accident, Apr 1784.

NOTE: The above David[5] Eaton (#202) was founder of the Nova Scotia branch of Eatons out of John and Anne of Salisbury. This is the line to which Molyneux (1911) gives central billing as the "Elmwood" branch from Salisbury. Although the founder David had a healthy crew of seven sons who helped swell the progeny, this line is only a twig on the Haverhill branch of the Salisbury, Mass. founders. Nonetheless, it is a twig which has been well covered in the literature; and as announced in the Preface, we shall not duplicate this detailed coverage for this volume. We shall list the dramatis personae in our numbering system, but our treatment will intentionally be no more than skeletal. We strongly encourage interested readers to consult the 1929 treatise by Arthur Wentworth Hamilton Eaton (see Bibliography), a member of this line who spent decades organizing the definitive genealogy, richly embroidered with detail, for the Nova Scotia branch.  This source is vastly preferable to Molyneux (1911), who did little more than copy the first version of the A.W.H. Eaton compilation, privately printed in 1885.  Between 1885 and 1929, A.W.H. Eaton made many corrections and further explorations which of course do not appear in Molyneux.  It is of historical interest that A.W.H. Eaton was in negotiation with the lead author of this volume in the early 1890s, hoping that his work might be added, but as a separate section, to the publication that the older Rev. Eaton had in preparation.  He was clearly disappointed when Rev. Eaton died in 1896 short of completion of this work.

     **203. (Capt.) Timothy⁵ Eaton** (James⁴, Jonathan³, Thomas², John¹) was born 31 Jul 1731 in Haverhill, Mass.; mar. **Abigail Massey** of Salem, N.H. in 1755.  She was born 25 Aug 1736 to Daniel and Abigail Massey. They resided in Haverhill, where he was a founder by trade, and owned real estate in Haverhill and other towns.  He first lived in the East Parish, but rather early on he established his homestead, embracing 63 acres, with a handsome "mansion house" situated on the Londonderry Road in the West Parish.  He played a very active part in the revolutionary cause. Before 1770 he led a group confronting the powerful local tory "loyalist", Col. Richard Saltonstall, and embodied the pressures which fairly soon led Saltonstall to retreat to England (see Chase, 1861, pp. 377ff.)  In 1774, he was appointed to serve on the first Committee of Correspondence for Haverhill to maintain contact with the Boston "patriots," a role he continued to play throughout the war.  Militarily, he was first a Sergeant in Capt. James Jones's Co. marching on the alarm to Lexington 19 Apr 1775.  He was commissioned Captain on 3 Feb 1776, and became one of the officers who reinforced the army under Col. Huntingdon (Mass. Archives).  When not away in the army he was working for it at home, helping with the mustering of troops and the mobilization of local funds to contribute to the war effort, including finding subsidies for Haverhill families suffering special hardships because their menfolk were away fighting the war.

     In the period after the war subsided in New England, Timothy, by now a man of very considerable wealth due in part to successful land speculation in western New Hampshire which had come to fruit with the abatement of the Indian menace after the fall of Quebec in 1759, began to settle his four eldest sons on some of these properties.  His wife Abigail died 31 May 1797; and Capt. Timothy mar. 2d, **Widow Mary Coburn** of Dracut, 28 Nov 1797.  He died 14 Oct 1811, in his 81st year.

     Children with Abigail in Haverhill:

**509**    i. Sarah⁶ Eaton, b. 28 May 1756; mar. 1st, Moses Haseltine, 8 Sep 1777; and 2d, Jesse Smith.  She died 8 Sep 1835.

+ **510**    ii. Isaiah⁶ Eaton, b. 15 Oct 1757; mar. 1st, Priscilla West; 2d, Azubah Grout.

+ **511** iii. Abijah⁶ Eaton, b. 16 Aug 1759; mar. Elizabeth Poor, 1790.
+ **512** iv. Timothy⁶ Eaton, b. 20 Jul 1761; mar. 1st, Betty Frye; 2d, Sarah Clark.
+ **513** v. James⁶ Eaton, b. 6 Aug 1763; mar. Polly Noyes, 1787.
   **514** vi. Abigail⁶ Eaton, b. 23 May 1765; mar. Peter Ayer. She died 19 Dec 1815.
   **515** vii. Phebe⁶ Eaton, b. 7 Sep 1767; mar. Rev. Ebenezer Dutch as his 2d wife, 15 Feb 1798. He was pastor of the Congregational Church in Groveland, Mass. He died 4 Aug 1813. She mar. 2d, a Mr. Clapp, int. 29 Mar 1830, Woodstock, Conn.
+ **516** viii. Daniel⁶ Eaton, b. 18 Apr 1769; mar. Mrs. Esther Cater, 1791, in Nova Scotia, where he had gone to visit his uncle David.
   **517** ix. Polly⁶ Eaton, b. 18 Apr 1771. She was declared *non compos mentis*, and her father provided for support in his will.
+ **518** x. Phineas⁶ Eaton, b. 8 Jun 1773; mar. Elizabeth Emerson.
+ **519** xi. Ward⁶ Eaton, b. 25 May 1775; mar. 1st, Judith Ingalls, 1800.
   **520** xii. Betsey⁶ Eaton, b. 30 Sep 1788; mar. Caleb Morse of Salem, N.H., 13 Aug 1795.

**206. James⁵ Eaton** (James⁴, Jonathan³, Thomas², John¹) was born 23 May 1738; mar. **Abigail Emerson**, 7 Sep 1758 at Haverhill. She was the daughter of Micah and Catherine (Morrill) Emerson. In Feb 1761, James purchased 60 acres in Goffstown (Provincial Deed 72-254), and soon removed there, after a likely way station at Hampstead, N.H., where his eldest daughter was baptized after her parents had become "of Goffstown." They lived in the south end of the township, near the Bedford town line. In fact their final home was later part of the campus of St. Anselm's College. Ironically, although James⁵ Eaton was the grandfather of the lead author of this volume, neither he nor his descendants had yet been mentioned in the manuscript that the Rev. Eaton left at his death. Our author did not, however, know this grandfather personally, since James⁵ was killed while sitting in his home when lightning struck a nearby tree on 29 Jun 1809, about nine years before our author's birth. His widow Abigail died in 1826, aged 94.

Children, as retrieved from the family's Bible:

+ **521** i. Samuel⁶ Eaton, b. 15 Jul 1759 in Haverhill, Mass; mar. Alice Hadley.
+ **522** ii. James⁶ Eaton, b. 17 Dec 1760, in Haverhill; said to have died 1 Jul 1785.
   **523** iii. Abigail⁶ Eaton, b. 6 Mar 1763, Goffstown; mar. Matthew Richardson of Goffstown.
   **524** iv. Lydia⁶ Eaton, b. 15 Jul 1765; mar. 1st, Nathaniel Davidson; 2d, Timothy Worthley.
+ **525** v. David⁶ Eaton, b. 15 Jul 1767; mar. Betsey Hadley of Goffstown, 1796. They were the parents of Rev. Dr. William Hadley Eaton, the lead author of this genealogy.

**526**    vi. Jesse[6] Eaton, b. 9 Aug 1769; died 4 Oct 1776.
**527**    vii. True[6] Eaton, b. 29 Oct 1771; died 26 Sep 1776.
**528**   viii. Sarah[6] Eaton, b. 24 Aug 1774; died 27 Sep 1776.
+ **529**    ix. Cotton[6] Eaton, b. 6 Sep 1777; mar. Sally Gordon and re-
         moved to Maine.
**530**     x. Philadelphia[6] Eaton, probably b. after 1785; otherwise
         unknown and presumably died young.

       **208. (Lt.) Nathaniel[5] Eaton** (James[4], Jonathan[3], Thomas[2], John[1])
was born 5 May 1743; mar. **Rebecca Dodge** of Lunenburg, Mass., 8
May 1766. Seven months later Nathaniel bought 154 acres in Rumford,
N.H. (now Concord) and the young couple removed to this "Penacook"
area and had their first child there. In 1768 Nathaniel was licensed as an
innkeeper in Concord. In Oct 1768, however, Nathaniel sold his farm to
his cousin Thomas[5A] **(#192)** who was then at Bow, and returned to
Haverhill in order to care for Nathaniel's father James. Just why this was
so, given that James was not widowed and had at least a son and a
daughter still in Haverhill for support, is unclear. But all the other four
sons excepting Timothy had gone to distant parts, and the return undoubtedly left Nathaniel and Rebecca with the oldest family homestead
in Haverhill's West Parish after James[4]'s death in Mar 1773. Early in
1775 Nathaniel trained with the Haverhill Minute Men, and he, his brother Enoch[5], his nephew Isaiah[6] and his cousin John[5] were all among the
105 Haverhill men who responded to the alarm of Apr. 19 and marched
to the Boston area. Nathaniel was also at Bunker Hill two months later,
receiving his commission as second lieutenant there in Capt. James Sawyer's Co. In the absence of the captain, Nathaniel led the company into
the battle itself. His cousin John **(#194)** was killed in this action.
       In later land deeds Nathaniel was referred to as a "Gentleman" of
Haverhill. He died somewhat prematurely, 29 Dec 1796 at Haverhill.
His wife Rebecca then removed to Sutton and married a Mr. Gile.

       Children (all but first at Haverhill):

+ **531**    i. John[6] Eaton, b. 21 Feb 1767; mar. Mary Kimball, 1792.
**532**    ii. Elizabeth[6] Eaton, b. 15 Mar 1769; mar. Jeremiah Hutchins
         of Fryeburg, Me., 15 Mar 1795.
+ **533**   iii. Elijah[6] Eaton, b. 12 Jan 1771; mar. Betsey Vose, 1797.
+ **534**   iv. Ebenezer[6] Eaton, b. 5 Feb 1773; mar 1st, Deborah Vose.
+ **535**    v. Nathaniel[6] Eaton, b. 4 May 1775; mar. Sarah Emerson.
**536**    vi. Rebecah[6] Eaton, b 11 Apr 1777; mar. Stilson Hutchins of
         Fryeburg, Me.
+ **537**   vii. Ichabod[6] Eaton, b. 3 Jun 1779; mar. Rebekah Haseltine.
**538**   viii. Priscilla[6] Eaton, b. 12 Dec 1781; mar. her first cousin,
         Enoch[6] Eaton **(#549)** of Goffstown, 21 Feb 1797.
**539**    ix. Matilda[6] Eaton, b. 1783; died 22 Aug 1795, Haverhill.
**540**     x. Pamelia[6] (or Pamila) Eaton, b. 17 Oct 1785; mar. James
         Messer, b. 1782 to a family which had recently removed

from Methuen, Mass. to Sutton, N.H. (then "Perrystown").
She taught in district schools of Warner and Sutton, and
bore three Messer daughters before her death 9 Apr 1828.

**209. Ebenezer**[5] **Eaton** (James[4], Jonathan[3], Thomas[2], John[1]) was
born 10 Aug 1745; mar. 1st, **Abigail Folsom**, 10 Jan 1769 at Haverhill.
They began their family in Haverhill, Mass., but after about five years
they removed to Walpole in Cheshire Co., N.H., where records thin out.
Ebenezer's family was joined in Walpole in about 1788 by his nephew
Isaiah[6] (**#510**) and his new family. These two Eaton heads of households
are present in Walpole for the Censuses of 1790 and 1800. Ebenezer
apparently lost his wife Abigail around 1790, since Walpole records show
that an Ebenezer Eaton mar., 2d, **Comfort Emerson** there on 10 Nov
1793, and later deeds surrounding the settlement of this Ebenezer's estate
by his son Calvin[6] refers to his "Widow Comfort" and her dower require-
ments. Molyneux (1911, p. 416) calls Ebenezer[5] "the ancestor of the
Albany (N.Y.) branch of Eatons." At least one son, Josiah, did remove to
Albany, but father Ebenezer died testate in Walpole in 1805. It is due to
his will, signed 20 Mar 1805 and proved 28 Sep 1805, that we have information about his children not formally recorded in Walpole.

Children with Abigail (i-iii, Haverhill: iv and prob. rest, Walpole):

+ **541**　　i. Eliphalet[6] Eaton, b. 27 Aug 1769; mar. Elizabeth Goodridge.
　**542**　　ii. Elizabeth[6] Eaton, b. 17 Nov 1771.
　**543**　　iii. James[6] Eaton, b. 4 Mar 1774. The only apparent child not
　　　　　　　mentioned in his father's will, he prob. died young.
+ **544**　　iv. Josiah[6] Eaton, b. ca. 1779, Walpole; mar. Zerviah Robinson.
　**545**　　v. Abigail[6], b. ca. 1782. Still alive, 1805.
　**546**　　vi. Calvin[6] Eaton, b. ca. 1786. He was the residual legatee and
　　　　　　　co-executor (with the widow) of his father's estate in 1805.
　　　　　　　He died 4 Mar 1809 in Walpole, probably unmarried.

**210. Enoch**[5] **Eaton** (James[4], Jonathan[3], Thomas[2], John[1]) was born
6 Nov 1748 at Haverhill West Parish; mar. **Esther Williams** of Ipswich,
Mass., 20 Dec 1769. Given the revolutionary activism of his brother
Timothy[5] (**#203**), older by 17 years, it is not surprising that Enoch was a
busy participant as well. In Mar 1775, Enoch at age 26 is listed as a Corporal in the Haverhill militia, and he soon received pay as a "Minute
Man" at Cambridge, 26 Apr 1775. He also enlisted as a private in Capt.
Samuel McConnell's Co. 19 July 1777, and thus served under Gen. John
Stark at the Battle of Bennington, Vt. on 16 Aug 1777. At some time
between 1775 and 12 Jun 1779 (cf. Hillsborough Deed 35-282), Enoch
and Esther removed their young family to Goffstown, according to one
account from a way station in Londonderry, N.H. The move was undoubtedly influenced by brother Timothy[5], who was investing in Goffstown land, and brother James[5] who had moved there over a decade ear-

lier. The young couple retained some emotional roots in Haverhill, as all of their childbirths from 1770 to 1788, save one, were somewhat exceptionally recorded both in Goffstown and in Haverhill.

In 1795, with the older of his children up and out, Enoch sold his Goffstown farm for $900 and removed to Cavendish, Windsor Co., Vermont, where the family appears in the Censuses of 1800 and 1810. In 1810 the nest is empty: the household is a man and woman both over 44 years of age. Enoch himself was "warned out" of Cavendish (no mention of Esther, who may have died) on 5 Mar 1814, and clearly retreated to Haverhill late in life, appearing there as an aging man living alone in both the Censuses of 1810 (a double count with Cavendish, Vt.?) and 1820. But we lack death records for either Enoch or Esther.

Children:

547    i. Lucy[6] Eaton, b. 22 Nov 1770, Haverhill; mar. John Kezar Gile, 17 Jul 1991 at Haverhill.

+ 548    ii. Kimball[6] Eaton, b. 14 Jun 1772, Haverhill; mar. 1st, Polly Page; 2d Sarah Cram.

+ 549    iii. Enoch[6] Eaton, b. 17 Mar 1774, Haverhill; mar. cousin Priscilla[6] Eaton (#538).

+ 550    iv. Jonathan[6] Eaton, b. 22 Mar 1776, Haverhill or Goffstown; mar. a Susanna of Deering, N.H.

+ 551    v. Warren[6] Eaton, b. 15 Jan 1778, at Haverhill or Goffstown; mar. Jane Woodside; removed to Cumberland Co., Maine.

+ 552    vi. Frazier[6] Eaton, b. 23 Jan 1780, at Goffstown; mar. Lucinda Blakesley.

553    vii. Dolly[6] Eaton, b. 5 Feb 1785, Goffstown; mar. Eliphalet Chapman, prob. at Cavendish, Vt. She died 2 Jan 1845.

554    viii. Debby[6] Eaton, b. 10 Feb 1788, Goffstown.

**212. Jonathan[5] Eaton** (Jonathan[4-3], Thomas[2] John[1]) was born 27 Jul 1736 at Haverhill, Mass.; mar. **Mary Stone** of Plaistow, N.H., 13 Sep 1759. In 1757 he and five other young Eatons were listed in the 2d "Foot Company" in Haverhill. In 1763 and 1764, soon after marriage, he bought tracts of land in Plaistow, and in 1769, while a "husbandman of Atkinson," he received 26 acres in Atkinson from his father. He later is upon occasion designated as a Plaistow resident, and of the couple's eight children, the births of five are registered in both Plaistow and Atkinson, with two in Plaistow only and one in Atkinson, in no very decipherable sequence. Jonathan's farm probably straddled the town line between the two communities. Death dates are not in evidence for either parent.

Children:

555    i. Ruth[6] Eaton, b. 9 Mar 1760; died 25 Jun 1762, Plaistow.

556    ii. Molley[6] Eaton, b. 3 May, 1761.

+ 557    iii. Benjamin[6] Eaton, b. 12 Jul 1762.

**558**  iv. Betty[6] Eaton, b. 25 Jan 1764.
**559**  v. Jean[6] Eaton, a twin b. 17 May 1766.
**560**  vi. Jesse[6] Eaton, a twin b. 17 May 1766.  The twins are registered
        as such in Atkinson, but Jesse is not mentioned in the Plais-
        tow record and probably died soon after birth.
+ **561**  vii. Jonathan[6] Eaton, b. 7 May 1768.  "Reputedly" was sired by
        Jonathan[5] with Mehitable Whittaker.
**562**  viii. Lucy[6] Eaton, b. 29 Oct 1771.


**218. Amos[5] Eaton** (Jonathan[4-3], Thomas[2], John[1]) was born 18 Oct
1751 at Haverhill Mass.; mar. 1st, **Mary Gage** of Pelham, N.H., ca. 1774.
Amos, like his brother Jonathan, received eight acres in Atkinson, N.H.
from his father's estate, and later bought other land there, but he is listed
throughout as a "yeoman of Haverhill," and appears in the Censuses for
Haverhill until his death (i.e., in 1790, 1800 and 1810).  His wife Mary
died 3 May 1795 in Haverhill, and he mar. 2d, **Anna Ordway** of Haverhill, 29 Mar 1796.  Amos died 11 Sep 1811 at Haverhill.

Children with Mary at Haverhill:

**563**  i. Sarah[6] Eaton, b. 6 Apr 1775; mar. 1st, James Gutterson of
        Atkinson, 15 Oct 1795, at Haverhill; resided Methuen,
        Mass.  Mar. 2d, Jonathan Parker of Dracut, Mass., 6 Dec
        1821, and res. at Dracut.
**564**  ii. Joseph[6] Eaton, b. 7 Aug 1777; died 12 Aug 1777.
**565**  iii. Daniel[6] Eaton, b. 28 Mar 1779.  No other sign of him; may
        have died young.
**566**  iv. Ruth[6] Eaton, b. 24 May 1781; mar. Simon Colburn of Salem,
        N. H., 25 Nov 1802.  They later removed to Cornish, N.H.
**567**  v. Mary[6] Eaton, b. 15 Sep 1783.  Not listed as Amos[5] heir after
        his death, 1811.
+ **568**  vi. Amos[6] Eaton, b. 30 Oct 1785; mar. Alice Emerson, 1820.
**569**  vii. Eunice[6] Eaton, b. 16 Jan 1785; mar. Warren Webster of
        Salem, N.H., 14 Apr 1808, Haverhill.
+ **570**  viii. Jonathan[6] Eaton, b. 21 Feb 1790; mar. Susan Saunders, 1815.
+ **571**  ix. David[6] Eaton, b. 27 Feb 1792; mar. Ruth Little, 1811.

Further children with Anna, from a list of Amos heirs convened
to discuss his estate on 4 Oct 1831 (cf. Essex Deed 265-167):

**572**  x. Lucy[6] Eaton, b. >1795; mar. Isaiah Kelley of Salem, N.H.
**573**  xi. Anna[6] (Ann) Eaton, b. ca. 1806; mar. Jesse Eaton of
        Haverhill, whom we cannot otherwise identify.


**221. Job[5] Eaton** (Samuel[4], Job[3], Thomas[2], John[1]) was born 14
Mar 1725 at Haverhill, and was about 16 when his father Samuel moved
the family to Plaistow.  Job mar. 1st, **Hannah Stevens**, about 1753 at

Plaistow. He spent his life farming there, and had accumulated considerable acreage in the township by 1767, mostly in the neighborhood of
the mill of Abram Harriman, probably his maternal grandfather. There
is also reason to believe that he, like many of his friends and relatives in
the Haverhill area, speculated in new land developments in northern New
Hampshire; and of his five sons, three removed "up country" into northern N.H. The other two for the most part remained in Plaistow. The
death of Job's first wife is unrecorded, but at the time of his own death in
the early 1790s, his wife was 2d, **Sarah** ___?___ .

Children, by Hannah at Plaistow:

574   i. Susannah[6] Eaton, b. 8 Nov 1754; mar. Jonathan __?__.
+ 575   ii. Samuel[6] Eaton, b. 31 Dec 1756; mar. Lydia Ladd, 1780.
576   iii. Mehitable[6] Eaton, b. 10 Sep 1759; died young.
+ 577   iv. Job[6] Eaton, b. 29 May 1762; mar. Mrs. Sarah Kimball, 1783.
+ 578   v. Jesse[6] Eaton, b. 20 Aug 1765; mar. Hannah Smith, ca. 1788.
579   vi. Hannah[6] Eaton, b. 8 Sep 1768; mar. Daniel Chase.
580   vii. Mehitable[6A] Eaton, twin b. 7 Nov 1770; mar. Oliver Noyes.
+ 581   viii. Moses[6] Eaton, twin, b. 7 Nov 1770; mar. 1st, Hannah Currier.
+ 582   ix. James[6] Eaton, b. 29 Dec 1772; mar. 1st, Sally Bradley,1794.

**227. Ebenezer[5] Eaton** (Samuel[4], Job[3], Thomas[2], John[1]) was born
10 May 1734 at Haverhill, Mass.; mar. **Phebe Shepard** in 1762 at Plaistow, N.H. Like his brothers and cousins, he began immediately to specu-
late in lands opening up to the north in the Connecticut River valley, and
in 1763 became an original proprietor of the new grant in Newbury, Vt.
But unlike many of his peers he chose not to migrate himself. (The
Ebenezer/Phebe parents  not far up the road in Candia  N.H.,  in exactly
the same child-rearing period of their lives, are from the line of William
Eaton of Reading, and not to be confused with this Plaistow couple.) We
have no death records for either Ebenezer[5] or Phebe, but he seems to
have died sometime before 1789.

Children, at Plaistow:

+ 583   i. Samuel[6] Eaton, b. 6 Jun 1763; mar. 1st, Susanna Noyes; re-
          moved to Landaff, N.H.
+ 584   ii. Ebenezer[6] Eaton, b. 10 Jul 1765; mar. Ruth Hutchins; re-
          moved to Landaff, N.H.
+ 585   iii. David[6] Eaton, b. Feb 1768; mar. Esther Sanborn; removed to
          Landaff, N.H.
586   iv. Lydia[6] Eaton, b. 8 May 1770; mar. Samuel Marshall of
          Hampstead, N.H.; removed to Landaff, N.H.
587   v. Phebe[6] Eaton, b. Oct 1772.
588   vi. Hannah[6] Eaton, b. 17 Jan 1779.

### #5. Our Eatons in the Revolution

War lays its hand on a population in characteristic ways, particularly where age cohorts, defined by year of birth, are concerned. The American Revolution was no exception. In the conditions of the time, armies were made up of very large numbers of foot soldiers, a small number of non-commissioned officers, and a tiny sprinkling of senior officers. The senior officers were usually older men. The foot soldiers were young bucks, males finishing adolescence or in their early twenties, most often not-yet-married. The NCOs were a varied lot, but usually of ages in between. Given these patterns, and if we take heed of the fact that the Revolution broke out in 1775 and military activity had largely disappeared from New England by 1778, we can assert with some confidence that top officers would be gentlemen born 1715-35; and that the bulk of fighting would be done by males born, say, from 1755 on to kids lying about their age in 1778.

Birth years for our Eatons of the Generation V stretch from 1709 to 1759; and for Generation VI from 1738 to 1815. So most combatants are Generation V, although some of the youngsters will come from the early ranks of Generation VI. Our Eaton Revolutionary activity fits these prescriptions neatly:

| Born... | Rev. | Total | % | Born... | Rev. | Total | % |
|---------|------|-------|-----|---------|------|-------|-----|
| 1720-24 | 1 | 6 | 17% | 1745-49 | 5 | 15 | 33% |
| 1725-29 | 0 | 8 | 0 | 1750-54 | 3 | 9 | 33 |
| 1730-34 | 3 | 6 | 50 | 1755-59 | 13 | 18 | 72 |
| 1735-39 | 3 | 5 | 60 | 1760-63 | 8 | 14 | 57 |
| 1740-44 | 4 | 8 | 50 | | | | |

Note that there remains substantial service here among those born 1730-44, or males aged 31-45 in 1775. This drops off in the next two cohorts, or males 21-33 in the 1775-78 period. These are the peak years for marriage and families full of small children, when a household head would be least able to get away.

Over all, about 40 of the Eaton males listed in this genealogy fought in the Revolution. The number is imprecise because some cases fall in the gray. One Eaton in Maine was informed against by a neighboring Tory sympathizer and had to escape from a posse of British solders (#339). Another Maine Eaton (#161) was captured with a buddy and shipped to England, but escaped there and got back to America on a French ship. There is no sign that either of these Eatons enlisted: they were probably civilians. Perhaps they did not "serve" in the Revolution, but they certainly had rancorous interactions with British forces. Or again, in perhaps three cases of the 40, family lore alone reports such Revolutionary service, which we have been unable to confirm with other documents. Thus perhaps half a dozen of the cases should not count. On the other hand, there is reason to suppose that we do not know about the service of some few of these males. So 40 is a reasonable estimate for participants.

The oldest Eaton to serve, born in 1720, was also the highest in rank during the actual Revolution. (There are other Eatons called "Major" in their later years, but none in the Revolution at that rank: either the title was imaginary, or was achieved after the Revolution in local militias, a rather common occurrence, especially during the War of 1812). Major William (#88) received that commission from Maine authorities early in the war. A decade younger were Eatons (#186) and (#203), both of them bona fide Captains leading companies into into action. One or two others of the mid-age cohort seem to have had actual commissions as captains or lieutenants during the war. Several of the more seasoned Eaton youngsters became non-commissioned officers, including a battlefield promotion or two. One, a Samuel Eaton (#583) was a quartermaster sergeant in a regiment raised to defend the upper Connecticut River valley in northern New Hampshire and Vermont; but since he was not born until June 1763, it seems unlikely that he played this role until after the war.

Geography also affected what Eatons did war service. Among the many Eatons by then in Maine, those along the coast encountered British forces frequently. But those farming 20 miles or more in the Maine interior were far from the action and their service rates were very low. Indeed, while about 45% of our available Eaton males served, the figure was well over 50% when Eatons resided closer to to the action.

Eatons took part in all of the more celebrated military actions of the New England and Hudson River parts of the War. Eight Eaton "Minute Men" marched to the Boston area responding to the alarm of 19 Apr 1775. Five of them, including two Company Captains (Timothy[5] #203 who was the most active Son of Liberty throughout the Revolutionary period, and his second cousin Joseph[5] #186) with their sons, were from Haverhill; three others were from Salisbury and Seabrook. At least five Eatons fought at Bunker Hill (with Haverhill's John[5] #194 killed there), and probably more, since other Eatons were at the Cambridge encampment at the time. Four Eaton cousins from Seabrook helped defend Fort Ticonderoga for five months in 1777. That same summer a Haverhill Eaton and his two nephews from Goffstown, N.H. marched to fight under Gen. Stark in the pivotal Battle of Bennington, Vt. Special honors for action beyond New England go to William[7] Eaton of Seabrook (#619, q.v.), who runs Seabrook's Sylvanus[6] Eaton (#251) a close race for longest active service as well. At least five Eatons survived long enough to draw war pensions in 1818 or 1832. Seven others made applications, and it is likely that many of these were successful as well.

**229.** (**Col.**) **Ithamar**[5] **Eaton** (Samuel[4], Job[3], Thomas[2], John[1]) was
born 13 Mar 1743 at Plaistow to his father's second wife Mehitable Harriman.  He was a soldier in the French and Indian War, and then established himself as a cooper at Kingston, N.H., where he mar. 1st, **Mary
Ordway** of Kingston, 23 Feb 1769.  In 1767 he had purchased the 120-
acre Lot #92 in the North Range at Weare, N.H. in the vicinity of Sugar
Hill.  This was in the northeast corner of Weare close to the Hopkinton
and Dunbarton town lines.  It was on this property that the new couple
settled before the birth of their first child, and would spend the rest of
their lives.  Ithamar developed a large farm there.  He did further military
service in the Revolution, advancing to lieutenant, and later became a
colonel in the state militia.  He also was active in town affairs, serving as a
town Selectman for eight years and as a representative to the State Legislature as well (Little, 1888, p. 830).  Wife Mary died 25 Oct 1802, and
Ithamar mar. 2d, Mrs. Hannah Low, 31 Dec 1805 (record at Haverhill,
Mass.).  He died 11 Nov 1817; widow Hannah died at age 86, 6 May
1845.  All of these principals and related Eatons are buried in the Sugar
Hill cemetery, Weare.

Children with Mary at Weare:

+ **589**    i. Peter[6] Eaton, b. 3 Mar 1770; mar. Elizabeth Brackenbury.
  **590**    ii. Nathan[6] Eaton, b. 25 Nov 1771; died apparently unmar. at
         Weare, 29 Sep 1796.
+ **591**  iii. Samuel[6] Eaton, b. 10 Feb 1773; wife's name unknown.
+ **592**  iv. Jacob[6] Ordway Eaton, b. 23 Jul 1776; mar. Sally Cleaves.
+ **593**   v. Ithamar[6] Eaton, b. 28 Aug 1778; mar. Jane Prince, 1805.
  **594**   vi. Abigail[6] Eaton, b. 18 Jan 1781;  died 28 Jan 1781.
  **595** vii. Joseph[6] Eaton, b. 23 Jul 1782. He was "of Weare" when he
         mar. Patty Farrington, 12 May 1803 at Hopkinton.  It was
         presumably he who was in the Weare Census, 1810, and in
         Hopkinton, 1820.  There are apparently children, not lo-
         cally recorded.  It also is likely that it was this Joseph who
         died 4 Jul 1826 at Hopkinton.
  **596** viii. Mary[6] Eaton, b. 18 Jul 1785; died 21 May 1812.
+ **597**  ix. George[6] Washington Eaton, b. 7 Jan 1788; mar. Hannah Low.
  **598**   x. Hannah[6] Eaton, b. 1 Oct 1793; mar. Edward Greeley at Weare,
         10 May 1814.

**231. Obadiah**[5] **Eaton** (Samuel[4], Job[3], Thomas[2], John[1]) was born
22 Apr 1747 in Plaistow, N.H., where his father had moved a few years
earlier after taking his second wife.  In 1769 Obadiah was listed as a cooper of Kingston when he bought a lot in Weare, N.H.  He had the same
listing when in Dec 1771 he bought a half lot in Deerfield, N.H.  He presumably moved there, as he is described as a Deerfield cooper when in
June, 1773, he bought still another tract of 22 acres, this time in East
Kingston, N.H.  After these travels he mar. **Elizabeth "Betsey" Paige** of

Plaistow, dau. of Benjamin Paige, on 9 Jan 1775. At some later time this couple removed to join brother Ithamar[5] in the Sugar Hill neighborhood in Weare (see #229 just above.). Obadiah followed his brother's model in many particulars: he had a large farm, was described as "an active and energetic businessman; did a large amount of town business, and represented Weare in the legislature from 1792 to 1795" (*History of Hillsborough*, Browne, p. 830). Obadiah died 22 Apr 1800, and is buried in Sugar Hill cemetery, Weare, with numerous of his kin.

Children (probably all born at Weare, several with somewhat indeterminate birth dates, so that birth order is not always clear):

+ **599**　i. Samuel[6] Eaton, b. ca. 1776, prob. at Plaistow; mar. 1st, Sarah.
+ **600**　ii. Benjamin[6] Eaton; b. ca. 1778; mar. Phebe Chandler, 1800.
+ **601**　iii. Obadiah[6] Paige, b. late 1779; mar. Abigail Woodbury.
　**602**　iv. Betsey[6] Eaton, b. ca. 1781; mar. Dr Thomas[6] Eaton (**#476**) 20 Feb 1798 at Weare. They resided Francestown, N.H. She died 14 Oct 1840.
　**603**　v. Mary[6] ("Polly") Eaton, b. ca. 1785; mar. Samuel Wilson of Henniker, N.H. She died 31 Mar 1858.
+ **604**　vi. Paige[6] Eaton, b. 19 Jul 1790; mar. Roxanna Bradford, 1817.

**235. John[5] Eaton** (Thomas[4], Job[3], Thomas[2], John[1]) was born 18 Jun 1733 at Methuen, Mass.; mar. 1st, **Abigail Peaslee** of Methuen, ca. 1755. Abigail died, however, 23 Feb 1772, at Salem, N.H. Then John[5] mar. 2d, **Sarah Clarke**, int. 4 Jul 1772, at Methuen, and soon removed the family northward. They stopped at the new settlement in Bradford, N.H.; and John was of Bradford when he joined a group of men from Hopkinton, Hillsborough and Warner to help form a 7th Company in John Stark's Brigade mustered for the Battle of Bunker Hill on 17 Jun 1775. Later, this couple established a much longer residence at Hopkinton, N.H., appearing there for three Censuses, 1790-1810. Wife Sarah died 2 Mar 1814, and soon thereafter the now aged John[5] joined several of his children at Bradford, N.H. He died 10 Jan 1823, age 89.

Children with Abigail at Methuen:

+ **605**　i. Ebenezer[6] Eaton, b. 1 Apr 1757; mar. Hannah French, 1780.
　**606**　ii. Mehitable[6] Eaton, b. 3 Apr 1759.
+ **607**　iii. Nathaniel[6] Eaton, b. 26 Mar 1761; mar. Elizabeth Bowan.
+ **608**　iv. Daniel[6] Eaton, b. 28 Feb 1763; mar. Lydia __?__.
+ **609**　v. John[6] Eaton, b. 14 Jul 1765; mar. Phebe Brockway, 1788.
+ **610**　vi. Joshua[6] Eaton, b. 25 Feb 1768; mar. 1st, Sarah Hoyt, 1792.

Children with Sarah:

+ **611**　vii. Thomas[6] Eaton, b. 1 Sep 1773 at Methuen; mar. Sally Young.

**612** viii. Abigail[6] Eaton, b. 9 Mar 1775, at Methuen or Hopkinton.


**236. Timothy[5] Eaton** (Thomas[4], Job[3], Thomas[2], John[1]) was born 28 Jul 1735 in Salem, N.H., formerly the North Parish of Methuen; mar. **Mary Dalton** of Plaistow, N.H., intentions published 4 Oct 1765. They settled on a farm in Methuen, which he worked in the normal way but was a hatter by trade. His will is dated 4 Apr 1803; proved 5 Dec 1803.

Children at Methuen, Mass.:

**613**    i. Hannah[6] Eaton, b. 16 Dec 1768; mar. William Batchelder of Haverhill, Mass., 30 Oct 1794.
**614**    ii. Betty[6] Eaton, b. 26 Jan 1770; never mar.; still alive, 1837 and probably 1850.
+ **615**  iii. Moses[6] Dalton Eaton, b. 16 Jun 1772; mar. Jane Hilton, 1802.
+ **616**  iv. Samuel[6] Eaton, b. prob. 15 June 1776; mar. 1st, Ruth Bailey.
**617**    v. Abigail[6] Eaton, b. 3 Aug 1779; mar. Woodbridge Cottle of Windham, N.H., published 24 Jan 1813.
**618**    vi. Timothy[6] Eaton, b. 6 Aug 1781; died 12 Mar 1828. Never married.

# Generation Six

## A. *The Salisbury Branch*

**244. Ebenezer[6] Eaton** (John[5-1]) was born 10 Apr 1738 in then-Hampton Falls, or proto-Seabrook; mar. in 1759 **Mrs. Nancy (Merrill) Brown**, whose first husband had been lost at sea soon after their marriage, a union which had produced one son, Benjamin Brown, who would later (in 1776) marry Ebenezer[6]'s youngest sister Meriam. Ebenezer was a mariner, at least early in life. He is present on the Hampton Falls tax lists in 1760 and 1761, but then disappears until 1766, perhaps because of absences at sea. At one time he may have contemplated moving "up country" with a number of his kin and neighbors, as at age 28 he bought two lots totalling 220 acres in Weare, N.H. (Rockingham Deed 92-403). He rapidly sold a half-lot to his father John[5] (111-554), but this is the end of information about these properties. The purchase of the tracts in Weare reflects something of a high point in his prosperity: by his tax ratings in Seabrook after 1768, he had less of a taxable estate than most Seabrook citizens or Seabrook Eatons.

It is not clear just where his residence was, since he had been "up and out" of his family of origin years before his parents left the family homestead to his younger brothers. However, he clearly lived in South Seabrook, and probably in the general area near the intersection of Washington St. and South Main, perhaps on a smaller tract carved out of his father's original stake. According to Mrs. Locke's list of Seabrook deaths, "Eben Eaton, son of John, died Mar. 5, 1811."

Children, born at Seabrook:

+ **619**   i. William[7] Eaton, b. ca. 1756-60; mar. Betsey Swain, 1777. They removed to Sanbornton, N.H.
+ **620**   ii. (Capt.) Reuben[7] Eaton, b. 1762; mar. Martha[6] Eaton (**#286**), Nov. 1786. Removed to Sanbornton, N. H.
  **621**   iii. Betsey[7] Eaton, b. 1764; mar. William[6] Eaton (**#270**), son of Thomas[5] (**#89**). This couple also removed to Sanbornton, N.H., with the two elder brothers.
+ **622**   iv. Henry[7] Eaton, b. 29 Aug 1766; prob. mar. Sarah[6] Eaton (**#320**), dau. of David[5]/Lydia, 3 or 4 Aug 1791.
  **623**   v. Hannah[7] Eaton, b. 1768; mar. 1st, Zophar Dow, 7 May 1790, by whom she had one son, Reuben Dow; mar. 2d, Charles Stevens, whom she accompanied to Sanbornton, N.H., where she ultimately died.
+ **624**   vi. Moses[7] Eaton, b. 1769; mar. a Rhoda Eaton, 5 Dec 1795 at

Seabrook (Seabrook *VR* at Concord, N..H.) The bride is said to have been the dau. of William/Hannah Eaton, but we have been unable to find a record of this couple.

625   vii.   Mary[7] "Polly" Eaton, b. 1771; mar. a Samuel Eaton, 2 Oct 1788 (So. Hampton, N.H. *VR*), presumably Samuel[6] Eaton (David[5], Samuel[4], John[3-1]), or (**#321**). In any event, this couple removed to Weare, N.H.

626   viii.  Joshua[7] Eaton, b. 1773; was lost at sea on the Grand Banks, unmarried.

+ 627   ix.   Thomas[7] Eaton, b. 1775; mar. Sarah[6] "Sally" Eaton (**#289**), 4 May 1798.


**248. Benjamin[6] Eaton** (John[5-1]), born 18 Jul 1749 at Hampton Falls or proto-Seabrook (Hampton Falls *VR* at Concord); mar. **Grace Beckman**, daughter of Israel/Mary Beckman of Gosport, probably after 1790. This is probably the Benjamin[6] who, with Seabrook cousins Levi[6] and Elisha[6], appears on the roll of Capt. Samuel Nye's Co. in the Northern Army in Continental Service; having enlisted 10 Jul 1776, probably serving about 5 months at Ticonderoga (*N.H. State Papers*, Vol. XIV, p. 350). Also, probably the Pvt. Benjamin who marched with Capt. Stephen Dearborn's Co. from Chester, N.H., to serve 2 months, 8 days (*idem*, Vol. XV, p. 159). And probably the Benjamin who with Seabrook cousins Cpl. Levi[6] and Pvts. David[6] and Timothy[5] Eaton, joined Capt. Moses Leavitt's Co. raised out of Col. Jonathan Moulton's Regt., to reinforce the Northern Continental Army at Stillwater, N.Y., serving from 8 Sep to 15 Dec 1777 (*idem*, Vol. XV, p. 321).

Benjamin's only recorded real estate venture, in 1792, joined him with his younger brothers Silvanus[6] and John[6] in buying from their father for £260, all of his land in Seabrook, Salisbury and Weare (ca. 150 acres total), with all buildings thereon, and farm tools for possession as long as their mother Hannah remained their father's widow. In short, this was a conveyance serving as a will, although eldest brother Ebenezer[6] is left out, most probably because Father John[5] had already helped him with his own homestead. In the Seabrook tax list for 1800 these three younger brothers are relatively impoverished, perhaps because they are subdividing an estate that was not large to begin with.

On 15 Mar 1805, Benjamin was declared *non compos mentis*, and placed under the guardianship of John Smith of Seabrook. Nonetheless, under this tutelage he purchased of his two younger brothers two pieces of land in 1807; and John Smith sold off pieces of property in his behalf, presumably to provide his support in later years. Benjamin appears to have died by 1821. His wife Grace appears in the 1830 and 1840 Censuses for Seabrook, and survived until 16 Jun 1849. Although some accounts have said that Benjamin/Grace had no issue, it is quite clear that they had at least one son, and that Grace at least, and probably the couple, had a daughter referred to in a rare document or two, and visible in a number of later Seabrook Censuses.

Children born at Seabrook:

**628**    i. Elizabeth[7] S. Eaton, b. ca. 1802; prob. never mar.  She is
living alone, 1850, on Farm Lane, Seabrook; is a pauper in
the 1860 and 1870 Censuses, in the household of Isaiah
Dow on Farm Lane.

+ **629**   ii. Israel[7] Eaton, b. 8 Jul 1804; mar. 1st, Elizabeth Fowler, 2 May
1822 at Seabrook.

**251. Silvanus[6] Eaton** (John[5.1]) was born 18 Jun 1756 in Hampton
Falls, proto-Seabrook; mar. **Abigail Jackman** of Salisbury, Mass., 13
May 1777.  Silvanus, or "Venus" as he often appears in written records,
was born into the cohort serving in great proportions as the common
troops in the Revolutionary War.  He cites four different spells of mili-
tary service in his 1832 application for the veteran's pension granted in
January, 1833.  Official records list five, one inconsequential.  He was a
"Minute Man," marching with Capt. Jonathan Evans Co. to Lexington
on 19 Apr 1775, and then retiring to the encampment at Cambridge with
his regiment until Jan. 1, 1776 (*N.H. State Papers*, Vol. XV, p. 747).  In
Apr 1776 he served four days as a private in Capt. Nathaniel Wood's Co.
In Aug 1776 he enlisted at Seabrook under Capt. Prescott and Col. Tash,
and served to the end of the year, being discharged at New York (*idem*,
XIV-243).  He interrupted his service for marriage in 1777, but soon was
bearing arms again, enlisting in Aug 1778 at Newburyport in the Massachusetts militia under Capt. Stephen Jenkins, and being discharged at
Greenbush in November.  He enlisted again at Newburyport in Oct 1779
under Capt. Samuel Huse, and was discharged with his company at Winter Hill, Mass. at the end of April, 1780.  His pension application is
signed with an "X." All told, Silvanus served longer in the Revolutionary
cause than any other of the Eatons we consider here.
    He was not a prosperous man by his tax ratings.  He does appear
in land conveyances, joining his brothers Benjamin and John in buying
his father's estate in 1792, supporting his mother and sisters in 1804,
and buying and selling small tracts of land and marsh among his brothers.  In 1815-1817, Silvanus's family was struck by tragedy: three of his
sons sailed on a ship captained by Joshua Janvrin of Seabrook bringing
fish down the coast to Baltimore.  They never returned.    In 1818 Silvanus sold his surviving son Christopher a half-acre with a dwelling
thereon, and in 1837 sold him what appears to be most of the rest of his
property.  Silvanus is visible as a head of household in Seabrook Censuses from 1790 through 1830, altho the spelling of  his name is various
(even, as best can be told, "Enos" Eaton in 1810).  In 1840, he and Abigail are visible living in the household of their son Christopher in
Seabrook, a residence on the north side of South Main Street at the head
of Worthley Avenue that had been their own, or next to it.  Silvanus died
5 Oct 1842.  Wife Abigail remained a "Revolutionary pensioner" until
her own death 22 Apr 1848.

Children born at Seabrook:

**630**    i. Daniel[7] Eaton, b. 22 Oct 1777 at Seabrook; said to have mar.
"Mrs. Olive Eaton," which at that place and time is likely to
describe the widow of William[6] Eaton (**#318**), where the
precise death date of the latter is unknown, but occurred in
the decade of the 1790s. Daniel/Olive probably produced
no issue, presumably from some combination of Olive's
advancing age and the fact that husband Daniel died
prematurely in the Baltimore tragedy.

**631**   ii. Abigail[7] Eaton, b. Oct 1778; died young.

**632**  iii. Elsie[7] Eaton, b. 20 May 1780; called a "queer one."

+ **633**  iv. Abel[7] Eaton, b. Oct 1788 at Seabrook; the second son to have
died at sea on the Baltimore run. Had mar. Polly Collins.

**634**   v. Eleanor[7] "Nettie" Eaton, b. 12 Nov 1791; mar. Henry Brown.
She died, 1859.

+ **635**  vi. Christopher[7] Eaton, b. 2 Jul 1794; mar. Lydia[8] Eaton, granddaughter of Ebenezer[6] through Henry[7], in 1813. One
source posits that Christopher was the third son of Silvanus
to die on the Baltimore run, but he lived until 1880.

**636** viii. Andrew[7] Eaton, b. 2 Mar 1797; the third son, unmarried, to
lose his life on the sail to Baltimore.

**637**  ix. Susan(nah)[7] L. Eaton, b. 4 Feb 1800; mar. William E. Davis.

**638**   x. Polly[7] Eaton, b. 5 Sep 1802; mar. James F. Fowler of Salisbury, Mass., 16 Jun 1822. She died 25 Jun 1858.

**253.   John[6] Eaton** (John[5-1]) was born 8 Jul 1762 at Hampton
Falls, or proto-Seabrook; was listed as "John 3d of Seabrook" when he
mar. 1st, **Sarah Colby**, 21 Jul 1786 (South Hampton, N.H. Church Record). By the 1790 Census, after the death of his Seabrook grandfather
John[4], he is listed as "John, Jr.," with an apparent wife and two children.
In the period from 1791-1807 he appears on a number of deeds, usually
buying tiny lots of less than an acre from relatives such as his father-in-
law or other local Eatons, as well as joining with his older brothers Benjamin[6] and Silvanus[6] in the 1792 purchase of his father's homestead and
lands. On the Seabrook tax list of 1800 he is well below average in his
tax rating, although with significantly more resources than those brothers. Both John and wife Sarah make their "marks" rather than leaving
signatures on their land deeds.

The 1896 version of this genealogy listed John[6]/Sarah as without
issue. Actually, they had eight children before Sarah died 22 Jul 1807
(see Mrs. Locke's list of deaths under " ------ Eaton, wife of John"). Un-
fortunately, the parents were not diligent about getting these births recorded, which is why thay have passed unnoticed. There is also no record of a John[6] remarriage, but he did mar. 2d, a **Hannah __?__**, since
she figures prominently as his wife in his 1817 will. It is this will
(Rockingham Co. Probate #9493), with a settlement process that due in
part to the untimely death of the first administrator, son Samuel[7], was not

completed until 1832, which illuminates the structure of this hitherto obscure family and accounts genealogically for a number of Eaton families in Seabrook in the mid-19th century.   The will also implies that a major center of gravity of John[6]'s land holdings, including perhaps his homestead, lay on the southwest corner of the intersection of South Main St. and Worthley Avenue, north of the Wyman[5] Eaton place and across the street from the homestead of brother Silvanus.

Children with Sarah, probably all born at Seabrook, as reconstructed from probate material and later Census ages:

+ **639**      i. Samuel[7] Eaton, b. ca. 1787; mar. Polly Dow, 1808; died 28 Jan 1820 while responsible for settling father's estate.
  **640**     ii. Hannah[7] Eaton, b. 15 Nov 1789; mar. Henry[8] Eaton, Jr., grandson of Ebenezer[6] by Henry[7] (see **#1693**), 3 Jan 1811.
  **641**    iii. Mary[7] Eaton, b. ca. 1792; mar. Moses[7] Eaton of Weare, N.H., (see **#868**), 22 Nov 1818; res. Weare; died there in 1844.
+ **642**     iv. Jacob[7] Eaton, b. ca. 1794; mar. Martha[7] Eaton (**#772**), 10 May 1818 and resided Seabrook.
  **643**      v. Rachel[7] Eaton, b. ca. 1797; mar. David Brown, 12 Jan 1820, and resided Seabrook. She died Jul 1849 of consumption.
+ **644**     vi. John[7] Eaton, b. ca. 1800; mar. Lucy Morrill of Salisbury, 19 Nov 1823; resided at Salisbury, Mass.
  **645**    vii. Jemima[7] Eaton, b. ca. 1802; mar. Gamaliel Rowe, 4 Sep 1825 and resided at Seabrook. She died ca. Spring, 1872.
  **646**   viii. Miriam[7] Eaton, b. 180?; mar. Chase[8] Eaton (grandson of Ebenezer[6] by Thomas[7] Eaton: see **#1713**) on 28 Nov 1825; resided Seabrook.

Children with Hannah:

  **647**     ix. David[7] Eaton, b. ca. 1809; still alive at 1832 estate settlement.
  **648**      x. Abigail[7] Eaton, b. ca. 1815; mar. Edward Randall, 3 Apr 1833, with the couple selling her land two days later. She died 17/18 Sep 1884.
  **649**     xi. Sally[7] Eaton, b. ca. 181?.

**254. Ephraim[6] Eaton** (Benjamin[5], John[4-1]) was born 20 Mar 1748 in Hampton Falls or proto-Seabrook; mar. **Sarah Moody** of Salisbury, Mass., intentions entered 29 Sep 1770. They settled for life on a farm in Seabrook.   In 1775 he served the Revolutionary cause at least briefly as an ensign with Capt. Henry Elkins Co. working to fortify Portsmouth harbor.   As the elder son of one of the most affluent Eatons of the preceding generation in Seabrook, he was always comfortably situated.   He dealt a good deal in real estate, and his conveyances begin to call him "Gentleman" of Seabrook by the time he is age 32.   He was for much if not all of his career the most affluent of the many Eaton patriarchs in Seabrook, and active in public life.   He is later also called "Lt. Ephraim" in various records, although the timing of such a commission is unclear. Because none of his conveyances refers directly to a family homestead or, for that matter, much in the way of improved properties, it is as hard to localize his residence as it was for that of his father (probably the same place). Nonetheless, much of his property seems to lie on the south side of Walton Road east of Washington Street.

Ephraim died 24 Jun 1822, age 74. His will, written much earlier (in 1805), made only small cash bequests to his numerous daughters and his eldest surviving son, Henry Moody Eaton, who had migrated to Maine. Son Ephraim[7] received half of the buildings and livestock, and two-thirds of the substantial accumulation of real estate, with wife Sarah receiving the remainder. Sarah was thus well-to-do, and died testate on 6 Apr 1828. Her will, also dated 1805, is a replica of her husband's, with all of the property now passing to son Ephraim[7] and only small cash settlements to the other heirs.

Children:

650    i. Jenny[7] Eaton, b. 24 Aug 1771; died in infancy.
651    ii. Hannah[7] Eaton, b. 7 Aug 1772; died young.
652    iii. Benjamin[7] Eaton, b. 30 Jul 1775; died in infancy.
653    iv. (Henry) Moody[7] Eaton, b. 30 Jan 1778; died young.
654    v. Hannah[7A] Eaton, b. ca. 1781; mar. Abraham Brown and resided in Salisbury, Mass. No children.
+ 655  vi. (Henry) Moody[7A] Eaton, b. ca. 1783; mar. Sarah Philbrick, 1800 and removed early to Maine.
+ 656  vii. Ephraim[7] Eaton, b. 24 Mar 1785; mar. Sarah ("Sally") Tilton, 1814.
657    viii. (Sarah) Sally[7] Eaton, b. 19 Aug 1787; mar. Edmund Barnard. She died in Salisbury, Mass., 20 Mar 1843. He died testate 10 Sep 1856.
658    ix. Jemima[7] Eaton, b. 20 Aug. 1790; mar. Robert Tilton and resided in Salisbury, Mass. She died there 31 Oct 1867.
659    x. Abigail[7] "Nabby" Eaton, b. ca. 1792; mar. Jonathan[7] Eaton (#663, q.v. for children), her first cousin.
660    xi. Betty[7] Eaton, b. 1796; she died unmarried, 12 Nov 1825.

**255. Winthrop[6] Eaton** (Benjamin[5], John[4-1]), born 18 May 1751 in Hampton Falls, or proto-Seabrook; mar. **Phebe Green** 1 Nov 1772 (Rev. Perley's list of marriages). They settled in South Seabrook, supposedly where "Richard and Eben Fowler" lived in the third quarter of the 19th century, on the northwest corner of the intersection of Washington and Collins St., although father Benjamin[5] is known to have owned significant property on the east side of Washington St. as well, between Walton Rd. and Collins. Winthrop[6] is described as a yeoman in many land deeds spread across the years from 1775 to 1838. He was not as prosperous as his brother Lt. Ephraim[6], but still was above the mean for Seabrook and the other local Eaton families.  He is registered on all Census lists for Seabrook from 1790 thru 1840.

His family strategies in his late years were deeply affected when first his wife Phebe died 13 May 1825, and then the younger of his two sons, Winthrop[7], predeceased him in 1831.  After the second death he hastily made three large and complex transactions, all on 26 Jan 1832, aimed at distributing much of his real estate to his sole remaining son Jonathan, his unmarried daughter Phebe (then age 44), and even, in smaller quantities, his six grandchildren.  He himself died 9 Oct 1840.

Children:

**661**    i. Abigail[7] Eaton, b. 5 Sep 1773; mar. Amos Buswell of Salisbury, Mass., 13 Jul 1800 and had four daughters, three of whom married and lived in Salisbury.

**662**    ii. Olive[7] Eaton, b. 8 Jun 1776; prob. the Olive Eaton who 9 Dec 1840 is declared "a distracted person" (Rockingham Co. Vol. 66-436), and put under the guardianship of a Phebe Eaton, likely to refer to her unmarried younger sister Phebe (**#666**) below.

+ **663**    iii. Jonathan[7] Eaton, b. 24 Apr 1779; mar. Nabby Eaton (**#659**).

+ **664**    iv. Winthrop[7] Eaton, b. 19 Aug 1781; mar. Mehitable Dow.

**665**    v. Jane[7] "Jenny" Eaton, b. 4 Jun 1784; mar. Jeremiah Dow, 4 Feb 1808.

**666**    vi. Phebe[7] Eaton, b. 24 Jan 1788; served as guardian for sisters Olive and Sally; died unmar. 31 Aug 1878, at age 90.

**667**    vii. Polly[7] Eaton, one of twins b. 14 Mar 1791.  In 1850 she lives with her sister Phebe as a Seabrook household under the same roof as her brother Jonathan's household.  She has disappeared from view, however, by 1860.

**668**    viii. Sally[7] Eaton, twin b. 14 Mar 1791; may have died unmar. in early 1840s.

**257. Levi[6] Eaton** (Benjamin[5], John[4-1]) was born 6 Nov 1757 in Hampton Falls or proto-Seabrook.  He was also a young bachelor at the outset of the Revolutionary War, and was swept into service at age 17.  Local lore recounted that he served seven years in the War; was under Gen. Washington's command, and made 2d Lieutenant before his final discharge.  Much of this is gilded, as was so often the case, by comparison with his formal 1832 deposition in search of a pension.  Very many were in some sense under Gen. Washington's command, and undoubtedly he was too; but he claimed only 18 months of service, albeit in four tours of duty: (1) he enlisted at Portsmouth, N.H. as a 17-year-old under Capt. Elkins with Eaton cousins (see above), partly to defend Portsmouth but also in the encampment at Cambridge, Mass., serving four months; (2) he enlisted again in 1776 at Seabrook to serve five months at Ticonderoga under Capt. Samuel Nye; (3) he enlisted at Seabrook in 1777 under Capt. Leavitt for a tour of three months, serving at Albany; and (4) he enlisted in the Massachusetts militia in 1778 under Capt. Jonathan Evans, serving six months in Rhode Island.

Presumably just after this service he mar. 1st, a **Ruth Eaton** whom we have been unable to trace. She and a first child died very rapidly. Levi then mar. 2d, **Phebe Walton**, intentions entered 19 Apr 1783 at Salisbury, Mass., and in due time had 13 children with her. He was, however, of a "migratory character." He moved to Boston, where his next child was born in 1784. He then tried Maine briefly in 1786, while continuing to be taxed as a Salisbury resident. He soon went back to Boston, where another child was born in 1788. Then he returned to Salisbury, but removed to Chelsea, Vt., by 1790. He stayed put there for about 20 years, while another 11 children were being born. In 1810, however, when well over 50, he moved the family, now including eight surviving children (two sons and six daughters), to Franklinton, Ohio, now Columbus. Rather soon after the family was installed there, Levi abandoned them, accusing his wife of witchcraft, and returned to familiar haunts in So. Hampton, N.H. Wife Phebe mounted a strong effort to have her husband return to Ohio. She first sent their son Levi[7] on horseback to find out why her husband had not returned, but the son discovered upon arrival in So. Hampton that his father had already married, 3d, to **Mrs. Mary (Bagley) Jones** of Salisbury, on Dec. 8 1814 at Kensington, N.H. Therefore he rested but one night in So. Hampton and rode back to Ohio. Wife Phebe was, however, not to be put off lightly, and when she found son Levi empty-handed, she hitched up a small one-horse wagon in the fall of 1815, and took her youngest daughter Lorana, then at most seven years old, on the trip east to confront her errant husband and bring him back alive. She found the new wife Mary in a late stage of pregnancy, but managed to induce Levi to return to Ohio to rejoin his abandoned family. He did remain with the family in Ohio until 1818, when he again left them to see his new son in New Hampshire, and to sire a second son with alternate wife Mary. He never returned.

[Upon writing up this sketch, the senior author of this volume, in proper 1895 Victorian dudgeon, wrote in the margins that "The record above needs to be revised. The 3d marriage was not legal. Less should be said about the man."]

From 1825 thru 1835, Levi[6] is listed in Salisbury, Mass. tax valuations as a So. Hampton resident owning land in Salisbury; his heirs were so taxed at least through 1847. He himself died 13 May 1834 (date from memo in the Revolutionary War Pensions Office). His "main" wife Phebe, after a checkered life of more than four score years, died 25 Aug 1850 in Parkman Twp., Geauga Co., Ohio. Alternate wife Mary died 17 Nov 1853 at So. Hampton, N.H.

Child by Ruth:

**669**    i. Infant lived two weeks.

Children by Phebe, surviving at least to 1810:

+ **670**  ii. Stephen[7] Eaton, b. 21 May 1784; mar. Olive Davis, 1810.
  **671**  iii. Ruth[7] Eaton, b. 4 Jul 1788 in Boston; mar. William Hills,
          12 Oct 1811; had seven children and died 7 June 1869.
  **672**  iv. Fannie[7] Eaton, b. 22 Jul 179? in Chelsea, Vt.; mar. Aaron
          Drande.
  **673**  v. Phebe[7] Eaton, b. 14 Mar 1800 in Chelsea, Vt.; mar. Truman
          Case.
+ **674**  vi. Levi[7] Eaton, b. 10 Apr 1802 in Chelsea, Vt.; mar. Jeannette
          Stocking.
  **675**  vii. Ariel[7] Eaton, b. 2 Aug 180? in Chelsea, Vt.; mar. Isaac
          Patten, 27 Nov 1826; she died 5 Oct 1872.
  **676**  viii. Philanda[7] Eaton, b. 9 Aug 180? in Chelsea, Vt.; mar., 1st,
          Luther Walton; 2d, Jason Clarke.
  **677**  ix. Lorana[7] Eaton, b. 31 Aug 1808 in Chelsea, Vt.; mar. Guy
          Sabine and had six children surviving infancy. They
          resided in Alliance and New Philadelphia, Ohio.

Children by Mary, at South Hampton, N.H.:

+ **678**  x. Stephen[7] Jones Eaton, b. 24 Dec 1815; mar. Hannah Rowe.
+ **679**  xi. Samuel[7] Perley Eaton, b. 22 Dec 1819; mar. Louisa M.
          Dennett, 1847.

**258. Samuel[6] Perley Eaton** (Benjamin[5], John[4-1]) was born 30 Oct 1765 in Hampton Falls or proto-Seabrook, and named after the local Presbyterian minister, the Rev. Samuel Perley, whose parishioners in 1765 signed a petition requesting relief from taxation in support of the Congregational minister in the same parish. "Perley," as he was usually called, never married. When his father Benjamin[5] died in 1784, he succeeded him in the ownership and occupancy of the family homestead, apparently on the east side of Washington St. just south of Walton Rd. His older brother Winthrop was a close neighbor, and the two collaborated in various ventures including land purchases. In the 1800 Seabrook tax list, yeoman Perley and Winthrop had similar tax ratings, both quite affluent. In 1811, Perley sold the South Seabrook School District Committee a 12-rod enclave carved from his property on the southeast corner of Walton Rd. and Washington St. for a school lot, apparently that now used as a museum by the Seabrook Historical Society, in a frame structure built later. About 1828, when he was in his early 60s, Perley began to sell off much of his property lot by lot, several pieces going to his neighbor Thomas Boyd. In 1829 he split off a piece of his "home lot" and gave it to his nephew Winthrop[7], Jr. (**#664**, above) for a bargain price, along with occupancy of the east half of his dwelling. In Feb 1832 the Seabrook Selectmen dismissed a petition to place S. P. Eaton under some form of guardianship, on grounds that his "state" did not come within the description of persons to be so sequestered. Perley died 11 Nov 1839. In ensuing years his unmarried niece Phebe (**#666**) lived where he had lived, and exercised guardianship of her sister Olive.

**259. Eliakim⁶ Wardwell Eaton** (William⁵, John⁴⁻¹) was born ca. 1744, probably in York, Maine. He appears to have been an eldest son from parents married about 1 Dec 1742, and was named for his maternal grandfather (Noyes, 1942). In 1762 he came with his father to Deer Isle, where he mar. **Mary Bunker** of Big Duck Island, whose father, tradition says, lived to the extraordinary age of 110 years. Eliakim and Mary were married about 1768 and settled for life on the southeast end of Little Deer Island on that part known in the 19th century as Stave Island, then occupied by Eliakim's grandson, Mr. Benjamin H. Eaton. Eliakim died there about 1800. In 1801 his widow Mary became the 3d wife of Charles Stewart, who was well known in Sedgwick and Brooksville. She died in the early 1840s, when about 100 years old.

Children (perhaps incomplete, and order estimated):

680    i. Abigail⁷ Eaton, b. ca. 1771; mar. Jacob Johnson, 23 Mar 1794, Deer Isle. The Johnsons had a background in Harpswell, Me.
+ 681    ii. Solomon⁷ Eaton, b. ca. 1773; mar. 1st, Catherine Howard.
+ 682    iii. Isaac⁷ Eaton, b. ca. 1775; mar. Lucy Hardy, 25 Feb 1802.
683    iv. Eliakim⁷ Eaton, b. ca. 1777; a sailor, he died at sea unmar.
684    v. Polly⁷ Eaton, b. ca. 1784; mar. Ezekiel Alexander of Harpswell, Me., his 2d wife, 10 Oct 1817. They were very poor, living in "little huts" on Deer Isle (see Noyes, 1942), and were at times public charges. Polly had had a child or two before marriage, and another one or two afterward.
685    vi. Phebe⁷ Eaton, b. ca. 1786; had two children before marriage, a Rufus b. 23 May 1814 who went by the name of "Rufus Benson," and a Henry "Foster," b. 16 Dec 1818, both at Deer Isle. She later mar. 1st, Charles Smith, int. 3 Jul 1825; and 2d, Christopher Gray of Pickering's Island, 31 May 1840, as his second wife (Noyes, 1942).
686    vii. Betsey⁷ Eaton, b. ca. 1790.
+ 687    viii. Peter⁷ Hardy Eaton, b. 8 Nov 1793; m. Catherine, 1821.
688    ix. Rachel⁷ Eaton, b. ca. 1795; mar. 1st, Jeremiah⁷ Eaton (#695), who was drowned Aug 1833; 2d, John Gray of Brookville.

**261. Jeremiah⁶ Eaton** (William⁵, John⁴⁻¹) was born ca. 1749, prob. in York, Me. He came with his parents to Deer Isle in 1762. There, about 1770, he mar. **Abigail Haskell**, b. at Gloucester, Mass. ca. 1755, and daughter of that Mark who migrated to Deer Isle as a native of Rockport, Mass. They settled on the western shore of the same north tip of Deer Isle where his father's homestead faces east, south of the place where the tidal road exits from the main island to Little Deer Isle. They had no children, but Mr. Eaton decided to adopt two brothers, the children of Eleanor Bray, who took the name of Eaton and were called Edward B. Eaton, b. 5 Feb 1790; and Asa B. Eaton, b. 2 Mar 1792. A

scandal developed in the local church in 1792 due to a public perception
that Jeremiah had fathered both children himself. He bequeathed his
property to them, but they never received it, for legal reasons unclear.
Jeremiah[6] Eaton died 8 Oct 1801. His widow mar. for her second husband, John Howard, who had been the next-door neighbor to the southwest for many years, blessed with a large family from his first wife.

Two children of Eleanor Bray who were surely adopted and perhaps fathered by Jeremiah[6] as well (their surnames were "Bray" before
their adoption):

+ **689**   i. Edward[7] Bray Eaton, b. 5 Feb 1790; mar. Polly Pressey.
+ **690**   ii. Asa[7] Bray Eaton, b. 2 May 1792; mar. Mercy Raynes, 1816.


**263. William[6] Eaton** (William[5], John[4-1]), was born early in 1756,
given his baptism 10 Feb 1756 in York, Me. Early in 1781 he mar.
**Hannah Haskell** of Deer Isle, whose father, Deacon Francis, had arrived
to settle in 1770 from Gloucester and Newburyport, Mass. The young
couple first built a log cabin on their 100-acre lot at North Deer Isle, on
the road about halfway between Carmans rock and the North Deer Isle
ferry landing. When lumber could be sawed at the mill, they built a
house about halfway up the hill from the shore to the present highway.
A third house was built after the children were grown. This lot was later
owned and occupied by William E. Powers and Frances M. Holdren.
Wife Hannah died 12 Jun 1838. William[6] died 6 Sep 1842.

Children:

**691**   i. Elizabeth[7] Eaton, b. 23 Oct 1781; mar. Moody Powers 2 Mar
          1801, both of Deer Isle. He was the youngest son of Rev.
          Peter Powers, and practiced as a physician on Deer Isle for
          many years. They had a large family.
+ **692**   ii. William[7] Eaton, b. 3 Jul 1783; mar. Abigail Howard, 19 Apr
          1807.
**693**   iii. Abigail[7] "Nabby" Eaton, b. 3 Aug 1784; mar. Amasa Holden
          of Deer Isle or Mendon, Mass., (int.) 16 Oct 1802. He was
          a Deer Isle school teacher for many years. They had at
          least 11 children.
**694**   iv. Hannah[7] Eaton, b. 5 Nov 1786; mar. John Short of New-
          port. Mass, 25 Dec 1810. He was a lumber surveyor.
          They first went to Castine, Me., and afterward to Bangor
          for many years. Three children were recorded for them
          on Deer Isle.
+ **695**   v. Jeremiah[7] Eaton, b. 3 Feb 1789; mar. Rachel[7] Eaton (#688).
**696**   vi. Sarah[7] "Sally" Haskell Eaton, b. 22 Jul 1791; mar. Ignatius
          Haskell, Jr., 9 Dec 1813, both of Deer Isle. He was a
          house carpenter and in command of a militia company in
          1812.

**697**　vii. Lucy David Eaton, b. 4 Jan 1794; mar. James Knight of
　　　　　　Deer Isle, 6 May 1813. He was a carpenter from Newbury-
　　　　　　port, Mass., and the couple returned there to have their
　　　　　　family.
**698**　viii. Esther[7] Eaton, b. 18 Apr 1796; died unmar., 15 Oct 1840.
**699**　ix. Samuel[7] Eaton, b. 10 Mar 1800; while young and still single
　　　　　　he was lost at sea.
**700**　x. Elcy[7] Eaton, b. 1 May 1803; mar. 1st, Avery Small (both of
　　　　　　Deer Isle), int. 12 Dec 1829. Their one son was lost at sea.
　　　　　　She mar. 2d, William Greenlaw, Jr., 24 Mar 1835, as his
　　　　　　second wife, and had three more children.


　　　**264. Samuel[6] Wardwell Eaton** (William[5], John[4-1]) was born ca.
Mar 1762 in York, Me. and baptized 7 Jul 1762 in the old Congregational Church there. That same year his family moved to Deer Isle and
made the first permanent settlement on that island. In his late teens Samuel W. became a sailor and rose to master mariner, in which capacity he
navigated the shore soundings of the Provincial Waters of Great Britain
and Maine during the summer and fall for several years. As a part of this
business he visited the home of his ancestors on the New Hampshire
shore, and before he was 21 he chose Seabrook as his place of residence.
A major reason for the choice is indicated by the fact that he married
**Hannah Lowell** at Hampton 5 Dec 1782. She was the daughter of Barnard and Comfort Lowell and was born 28 Oct 1758, residing in or near
Seabrook. In 1785 he is listed as a yeoman when he buys of father William two lots in Seabrook which the latter had just purchased of Charles
Chase, Seabrook "Gentleman." This house lot of 8+ acres seems to have
been on the west side of "the Great Country Road" (now Lafayette high-
way) just north of the Quaker Meeting House.
　　　This couple lived in Seabrook for about 12 years, and four of
their six children were born there. On 17 Jul 1794 Samuel W. was of
Seabrook as he began to sell some of his Seabrook property; but two
weeks later he bought property at "Wyman's Plantation" in Lincoln Co.,
Mass., later Chesterville, Me., and is identified as a resident yeoman there
by Feb 1795 in a further sale of land back at Seabrook. According to
Sewall (1875), while he occupied the farm he spent most of his time for
15 years or more before 1827 at sea. He made no foreign voyages apart
from one to the West Indies, and mainly was occupied with "coasting"
and fishing. Although he had no formal training in navigation he was so
thoroughly familiar with Maine rivers and harbors that he was sought
after as a pilot. He became well-to-do and set up each of four sons at
marriage with large farms on the east side of Sandy Pond, near the parental home, which incidentally the noted Chesterfield Ridge passed
through. Samuel W. died in So. Chesterville, Me., 28 Nov 1831. Wife
Hannah died there as well 5 Mar 1842. The parents and their six children all rest in a family graveyard near the original homestead.

　　　Children:

+ **701**    i. Jeremiah[7] Eaton, b. 8 Mar 1783 at Seabrook; mar. Sally
             Warren of Monmouth, Me.
  **702**   ii. Abigail[7] Eaton, b. 12 Oct 1785 at Seabrook; mar. Moses
             Walton of Chesterville and had four children. She died
             19 Oct 1828.
+ **703**  iii. Isaac[7] Eaton, b. 24 Jul 1789 at Seabrook; mar. Almira
             Sewall of Chesterville.
+ **704**   iv. Lowell[7] Eaton, b. 8 Oct 1792 at Seabrook; mar. 1st, Sabina
             Warren of Monmouth, Me.; 2d, Sarah Dexter.
  **705**    v. John[7] Eaton, b. 13 Dec 1795 at Chesterville; mar. Betsey
             Crowell in 1843 and resided in Chesterville, where he died
             without issue in Mar 1874.
  **706**   vi. Hannah[7] Eaton, b. 19 Jun 1798; died unmar. Sep 1870.

**265. Josiah[6] Eaton** (Thomas[5], John[4-1]) was born 28 Sep 1744 in
Hampton Falls, N.H. (proto-Seabrook); mar. **Miriam True** 15 May 1769
(Rev. Perley's list of marriages) and remoyed to No. Yarmouth, Me.,
where bride Miriam's father John True had purchased land, and where
she had siblings and cousins already located. Here four children were
born to them. The original manuscript narrative about this family says
that father Josiah died prematurely in 1777 one month before the last
child was born; and wife Miriam died as well about a month after the
birth, orphaning the children. However, conveyances in No. Yarmouth
do not fit this tale. Miriam is already widowed on a deed signed 1 Feb
1775, when kinsman Abner True sells her for the bargain price of £12 a
20-acre lot on the west side of the Royal River in No. Yarmouth as a haven for her "and their surviving children" [Cumberland Deed 8-349].
Moreover, widow Miriam appears to have survived for some years to
mother her four children. Among other things, her estate is not being
settled by John True of nearby Falmouth, with the 20-acre lot sold, until
November, 1785. In any event, the children were indeed orphaned while
still minors; and at that time were taken to their grandparents, Thomas[5]
and Jane Eaton (#89) in Seabrook, who acted as their guardians until
each was of age. In the later 1790s the two daughters, Miriam[7] and
Jenny[7], get the aid of their brother Thomas[7], then residing in Wells, Me.,
in selling quitclaims on one-ninth portions of their grandfather John
True's land stake in No. Yarmouth [Deeds 31-134/5 and 32-311].

Children:

+ **707**    i. Thomas[7] Eaton, b. 27 Apr 1769; mar. Phebe Young, 1793.
+ **708**   ii. Bradbury[7] Eaton, b. 10 Jan 1774; mar. Rebecca True, 1799.
  **709**  iii. Miriam[7] Eaton, b. 17 Jan 1775; mar. Reuben Derby of York,
             Me., 9 Sep 1802. She had one son and two daughters, and
             died 9 May 1853.
  **710**   iv. Jenny[7] Eaton, b. ca. 1777, leaving obvious questions about

her paternity, if Deed 8-349 above is correctly dated; mar.
Daniel Felch of Seabrook, 18 Mar 1793. He farmed and
was a seaman in the schooner fishery who died 30 Jun
1839; she died 6 Jun 1840 (Felch, 1881).

**270. William**[6] **Eaton** (Thomas[5], John[4-1]) was born 28 Dec 1756 in
Hampton Falls (proto-Seabrook).   His 1832 application for a Revolutionary War pension speaks of a first enlistment at Salisbury, Mass. in
1776, when he served under Capt. Huse at Winter Hill, Mass.  He enlisted
again in 1777 at Newburyport, and served under Capt. Jenkins at North
River, near Albany, N.Y. (For these two stints he was awarded a pension
of $23.33 a year). After his second discharge he took up residence in
Salisbury, Mass., although he was courting a Seabrook cousin.   In Jan
1780 he mar. **Betsey**[7] **Eaton** (see **#621**), dau. of Ebenezer[6] (Hampton
Falls *VR* at Concord).   At some time in the later 1780s he teamed up
with his wife's older brother, William[7] (of Ebenezer[6]: see **#619**), who had
already removed to Sanbornton, to buy a farm lot (#33, in the 2d Division) straddling Salmon Brook on the southwest side of the Sanbornton
township.   By one account, the William[6] of this notice did not actually
move his family to Sanbornton until Mar 1800, but it is clear that both
Williams are there in time for the 1800 Census.   More generally, the fact
that his brother-in-law William[7] was also married to a Betsey and that
both men were born in Seabrook, served in the Revolution (although not
together), removed to Sanbornton and shared land there, has produced
several points of confusion as to which William/Betsey is which in later
deeds, wills and other Sanbornton references (for more details, see **#619**).
However, our final account here has the William[6] of this notice dying at
Sanbornton on 11 Oct 1837.  Widow Betsey died 14 Dec 1839, after an
1838 application for continuation of her husband's small pension which
was apparently rejected in part because of confusion of this widow with
another widow Betsey Eaton.

Children of William[6] and Betsey (Eaton) Eaton, with places of
birth often uncertain, but probably deducible from the pension application account of family moves (note, however, that young couples taking
up residence in newly settled parts sometimes register their children in
their prior native districts, and this may be true here, where at least some
children's births are recorded in Salisbury, Mass., at times when the family has probably already removed to Sanbornton):

711    i. Josiah[7] Eaton, b. Sep 1780.  He appears to have lived with
          his parents until their deaths in Sanbornton. He died there
          also, still unmarried, 12 Apr 1861.
712    ii. Nancy[7] Eaton, b. Oct 1782; mar. Joshua Dow of Seabrook
          27 Jul 1799, and died in Seabrook 9 Jan 1875, age 92.
713    iii. Dorothy[7] Eaton, b. in 1785; mar. 1st, Samuel Dow of Sea-
          brook; 2d, S. Palmer. She resided and died in Seabrook.
+ 714    iv. Wheeler[7] Eaton, b. 2 Sep 1787; mar. 1st, Abigail Perkins,

5 Mar 1811; and 2d, Mrs. Nancy Sleeper, 19 Oct 1840.

**715**  v. Judith[7] Eaton, b. 13 Sep 1788; mar. Reuben[7] Eaton of Weare (see **#867**) 2 Apr 1813; they settled in Weare, having children discussed under her husband's name.

**716**  vi. Miriam[7] Eaton, b. ca. 1790; mar. Aaron Dow of Alexandria, N.H., 8 Sep 1811, and had seven children.

**717**  vii. Jane[7] Eaton, b. 22 Jan 1792; mar. Josiah Swain of New Chester (now Hill), N.H., on 12 Jul 1812, and they lived first at Hill. Later they removed to Warren, N.H., and settled on a hill north of the village. They had nine children and scores of grandchildren, many of whom populated the same hill at the end of the 19th century. Jane died on this hill 18 Jan 1862; Josiah died there 11 May 1875, age 84.

**718**  viii. Ruth[7] Eaton, b. 1 May 1795; mar. 1st, David Flood, who soon died; 2d, Jesse Wiggin, 10 Nov 1816, a farmer who died 9 Feb 1860, age 53; wife Ruth died 3 Mar 1863.

**+ 719**  ix. Thomas[7] Eaton, b. 9 May 1797; mar. Betsey Blake, 1819.

**720**  x. Susan[7] Eaton, b. 1799; died 23 Dec 1801.

**+ 721**  xi. Joshua[7] Eaton, b. 4 Jul 1801; mar. his first cousin Dorcas[7] Eaton (see **#726**).

**722**  xii. Betsey[7] Eaton, b. ca. 1803; mar. Seth Noble Marshall of Weare, N.H., 23 Feb 1831 and had three children.

**723**  xiii. Martha[7] Eaton, b. ca. 1805; mar. William Marshall of Weare, N.H. (brother of Seth above), 2 Mar 1825 at Weare.


**271. Bryant[6] Eaton** (Thomas[5], John[4-1]) was born 28 May 1760 in Hampton Falls (proto-Seabrook); mar. 1st, **Betsey Collins**, 13 Oct 1788, at South Hampton, N.H., by whom he had two children. They resided on the old Samuel Collins homestead of some five acres on the south edge of Seabrook. He mar. 2d, **Sarah** (or **Elizabeth**) **Bagley**, 25 Mar 1799. Although like many young males in Seabrook he was briefly a mariner, he is described as a yeoman in all but one of his ten land conveyances-- almost all purchases--between 1784 and 1811. In the 1795 exception, he is called "Esquire". And indeed he was a very prosperous farmer: in the 1800 Seabrook tax list he falls just into the top 20% of Seabrook house-holders in general, with tax ratings that are half again higher than any other Eaton listed. One oddity about Bryant has survived in family lore: he was distinguished for a striking dissimilarity in the color of his eyes, one being black and the other blue.

Bryant died intestate, 6 Aug 1829, but he had a rather large estate that had to be divided among heirs. The inventory of his estate, dated 14 Oct 1829, estimates the estate as worth almost $4,800, quite substantial for the period. Over 90% of the value lay in 11 tracts of real estate, half of them marsh acreage. The most valuable of these tracts by far--5 times the value of the improved homestead lot, and half of the total estate--was a huge tract of 70 acres in the "Cove Marsh", presumably lying along the south side of Worthen's Point, just north of the state line. This estate was divided by a committee between two surviving sons, Nathaniel[7] and Sam-

uel[7], and two daughters, Dorcas[7] (married to Bryant's nephew, Joshua
Eaton of Sanbornton) and Elizabeth[7], unmarried. Second wife
Sarah/Elizabeth died 7 Jan 1838.

Children with Betsey at Seabrook:

724    i. Samuel[7] Eaton, b. 4 Jan 1790; drowned 23 Mar 1810.
725    ii. Esther[7] Eaton, b. 17 Apr 1791.

Children with Sarah/Elizabeth at Seabrook:

726    iii. Dorcas[7] Eaton, b. ca. 1800; mar. Joshua[7] Eaton (#721), son
           of William[6] of Sanbornton. She died 8 Dec 1871.
727    iv. Bryant[7] Eaton, b. ca. 1802. It is not clear why he did not
           share in the 1832 division of his father's copious estate, but
           he goes unmentioned, and died himself, apparently unmar.
           and certainly intestate, Oct 1836.
728    v. Elizabeth[7] Eaton, b. ca. 1804; mar. Franklin Gerrish, 6 Apr
           1843 and had one son and daughter. She d. 29 Jan 1881.
729    vi. Nathaniel[7] Eaton, b. ca. 1806; a son "Nathan" is recognized
           in his father's estate in the 1832 division, and presumably
           this is he; but he died at sea, in parts unknown.
+ 730  vii. Samuel[7A] Eaton, b. 16 Feb 1814; mar. Judith Palmer, 1842.


**272. Wheeler[6] Eaton** (Thomas[5], John[4-1]) was born 12 Feb 1763 in
Hampton Falls (proto-Seabrook); mar. **Judith Goodwin** at Salisbury, 10
Sep 1788, and settled in Amesbury, Mass. after 1808. Before the end of
1809, a Wheeler Eaton, called a "Salisbury laborer" and presumably our
subject here, was declared *non compos mentis* and put under the care of
Jacob Brown of Salisbury. He was registered in Salisbury in the 1820
Census, but died 17 Nov 1820.

Only recorded child:

731    i. Hannah[7] Eaton, b. 1 Nov 1799 at Salisbury, Mass.; died un-
           mar. 9 Jun 1870 (Salisbury *Vital Records*).


**274. Aaron[6] Eaton** (Thomas[5], John[4-1]) was born in the newly
chartered town of Seabrook 31 Jan 1769; mar. 1st, **Elizabeth "Betty"
Chandler** on 28 Sep 1790. He was a farmer, and above average for
Seabrook in taxable estate even at the young age of 30. He and brother
William[6] had inherited the bulk of their father's estate at his death in
1798, and as William was based in Sanbornton or Rhode Island in this
general period, Aaron had found the resources to buy out William's
share. The couple settled first in Seabrook, probably in the So. Main St.
area, where their children were born. For about 15 years Aaron was quite
active in buying up Seabrook real estate. In Feb 1808 he bought Tho-

mas Sawyer's 76-acre farm in neighboring South Hampton, and took his family to that town in May 1808. Over the next ten or 15 years he slowly disposed of his various Seabrook properties. His wife Betty died 11 Feb 1843, and later in that year Aaron mar. 2d, **Mrs. Sarah (Perkins) Jones.** He died testate, 5 Nov 1863 in South Hampton.

Children with Betsey, born at Seabrook:

+ **732**    i. Moses[7] Chandler Eaton, b. 2 Jan 1791; mar. Betsey Jones.
  **733**   ii. Susannah[7] Eaton, b. in 1792; died 17 Nov 1796.
  **734**  iii. Susannah[7A] Eaton, b. ca. Dec. 1796 and died Sep 1797.
  **735**   iv. Olive[7] Eaton, b. 25 Mar 1798; mar. Parker Merrill, 13 Nov 1815. They had two sons and four daughters. Olive died 13 Aug 1846.
  **736**    v. Maria[7] Eaton, b. 8 Mar 1802; mar. Tappan Sargent, 22 Oct 1818. They had three sons and four daughters. Maria died 11 Mar 1867.
+ **737**   vi. Aaron[7] Thomas Eaton, b. 5 Apr 1803; mar. Sarah Collins.
+ **738**  vii. Darius[7] Eaton, b. 17 Jan 1807; mar. Sarah Taylor, 1833.
  **739** viii. Jeremiah[7] Wilson Eaton, b. 1810; died 27 Oct 1821.

**275. Humphrey[6] Eaton** (Wyman[5], John[4-1]) was born 6 Apr 1746 in Hampton Falls (proto-Seabrook); mar. **Judith Cilley** of Seabrook, 29 Mar 1770 (Rev. Perley's List of Marriages). They lived in Seabrook for nearly twenty years, and had four of their five children there. He was a farmer. In Sep 1785 he bought of William[5] Eaton (#88) a farm of 8+ acres on the west side of the "Great Country Road" (later, Route 1 or the Lafayette Highway) just north of the Quaker Meeting House at the northern edge of Seabrook. It is not clear that Humphrey's family ever moved there, however, because four months later Humphrey bought 90 acres of land in Weare, N.H. and fairly soon transferred his family there, appearing on the 1790 Census list in that town. He did not sell the farm he had just purchased in Seabrook until 1800, and then he sold it to Samuel[6] Wardwell Eaton (#264), son of prior owner William[5], despite the fact that Samuel Wardwell had some years before removed permanently to Maine. Perhaps both owners were renting out this small Seabrook farm. In any event, Humphrey's family resided on the Weare farm at least until his death 4 Feb 1834.

Children:

  **740**    i. Jeremiah[7] Eaton, b. ca. 1773 at Seabrook; unmar. when lost at sea.
+ **741**   ii. Jacob[7] Eaton, b. 28 Nov 1775 at Seabrook; mar. Jane Goodwin of Weare in 1800.
  **742**  iii. Lydia[7] Eaton, b. 30 May 1780 at Seabrook; mar. Jonathan Cilley of Weare in 1801, and resided there as ten Cilley children were born to them.

+ **743**   iv. Tristram[7] Eaton, b. 30 May 1782 at Seabrook; mar. Abigail
         Murray of Dunbarton, 1808.
  **744**   v. Ruth[7] Eaton, b. 3 Sep 1791 at Weare; mar. Ambrose C.
         Cilley of Weare, 29 Nov 1823. She had two children and
         died at Manchester, N.H. in Nov 1861.

**276. John[6] Eaton** (Wyman[5], John[4-1]) was born 2 Apr 1748 in
Seabrook. Apparently he had moved at a young age to Buxton, Me.,
because in Rev. Perley's list of marriages he was of that town when he
mar. **Jemima Green** of Seabrook, 20 Jan 1774. The plot thickens because it was not until 1 Apr 1774 that John[6]'s father Wyman actually
bought a plot of land for them in Buxton. Furthermore, father Wyman
failed to give him a deed to this Buxton property until 28 Oct 1790, by
which time most of his own family was underway. This leaves fair uncertainty as to where his own children were born, but this was probably in
Buxton, Me., since this was John's home for many years. He died in
Buxton in 1813.

Children:

+ **745**   i. John[7] Eaton, Jr., b. 19 Nov 1774; m. Keziah Dearborn 1792.
  **746**   ii. Betsey[7] Eaton, b. 19 Apr 1777; mar. Benjamin Bradbury of
         Boston, 10 Nov 1795; she died in Buxton, 23 Nov 1814,
         after two sons and four daughters.
  **747**   iii. Ruth[7] Eaton, b. 10 Sep 1779; mar. Jeremiah Trueworthy of
         Boston, 25 Sep 1800. After two sons and three daughters,
         she died at Rockland, Me., 30 May 1834.
+ **748**   iv. Tristram[7] Eaton, b. 16 Dec 1781; mar. Betsey Woodman.
+ **749**   v. Nathan[7] Eaton, b. 24 Jan 1785; mar. Mary Tarbox, 1823.
+ **750**   vi. Abel[7] Eaton, b. 8 Jun 1786; mar. Mary Smith, 1809.
  **751**   vii. Acel[7] (Asahel?), b. 22 Oct 1788.
+ **752**   viii. Humphrey[7] W. Eaton, b. 26 Jul 1793; mar. Mary Brewster.
  **753**   ix. Ann[7] Eaton, b. 29 Feb 1798; mar. George Jewett of Pitts-
         ton, Me., 23 Oct 1828. She died 30 Jan 1830. No issue.

**279. Abel[6] Eaton** (Wyman[5], John[4-1]) was born 28 Mar 1755 in
Hampton Falls (proto-Seabrook); mar. **Martha[5] Eaton** (#131), daughter
of Daniel[4A] of Salisbury, Mass., 20 Mar 1777. They lived on a farm on
the north side of Beach Road in Salisbury, near the original family
homestead and perhaps on a part of that property, then occupied by
Abel's father-in-law. Abel is listed in Salisbury tax lists for 50 consecutive years, from 1777 through 1826, a farmer of rather modest means.
He died 23 Jan 1827; wife Martha died 1 Oct 1839, aged 86, also in
Salisbury.

Children born at Salisbury:

**754**    i. Hannah[7] Eaton, b. 6 Jan 1782; died 19 Oct 1800.
+ **755**    ii. Daniel[7] Eaton, b. 3 Aug 1786; mar. Sally Brown, 1804.
**756**    iii. John[7] Eaton, b. 13 Sep 1788; died unmarried.

**284. Simeon[6] Eaton** (Wyman[5], John[4-1]) was born 9 Sep 1768 in Seabrook, N.H.; mar. **Meribah[6] Eaton** (see **#273**), daughter of Thomas[5] and Jane, 22 May 1787. They resided on the south edge of Seabrook a few rods from the paternal homestead on Worthley Ave. by Partridge Brook. He was the residuary legatee to the estate of his father, who was quite well-to-do, and tax lists show Simeon as above average in estate size as well. He was as active in real estate as any Eaton of his period in Seabrook or Salisbury, participating in some three dozen conveyances over the time span from 1790 to 1850. He is almost always described as a yeoman, although in one 1834 deed he is a called a "Gentleman" of Seabrook. Toward the end of his life he began to sell off his property, often to sons and grandsons. In 1845 he sold his 60-acre homestead to his eldest son Wyman[7] for $2500, and later requested that his estate be settled during his lifetime by his distant cousin Oliver[7] Eaton (**#1218**). Wife Meribah died 8 May 1849. Simeon was visible in all preserved Seabrook Censuses from 1790 on, and appears for a last time in the 1850 Census, in his own dwelling unit, but under the same roof as his grandchildren by deceased son Jeremiah. He died 28 Mar 1851 at Seabrook.

Children, all born at Seabrook:

+ **757**    i. Wyman[7] Eaton, b. 1 Oct 1787; mar. Miriam Fowler, ca. 1807.
**758**    ii. Rhoda[7] Eaton, b. 10 Apr 1792; mar. David Rossiter, 14 Feb 1819, and had one son, Benjamin Rossiter, who died in infancy, 1824. Rhoda died 11 Sep 1831.
**759**    iii. Ruth[7] Eaton, b. 11 May 1796; mar. Tristram Collins, 7 Apr 1817, and had a daughter. Wife Ruth died 19 Dec 1838.
**760**    iv. Hannah[7] Eaton, b. 7 Apr 1800; mar. John E. Browne and res. Salisbury. They had four sons and two daughters.
**761**    v. Belinda[7] Eaton, b. 5 Aug 1802; died unmar., 20 Dec 1826.
+ **762**    vi. Jeremiah[7] P. Eaton, b. 3 Sep 1804; mar. Phebe[8] K. Eaton (see **#1698**), granddaughter of Ebenezer[6] through Henry[7], 26 Sep 1824.
**763**    vii. Sarah[7] Jane Eaton, b. 3 Sep 1806; mar. Jacob Fowler 3d of Salisbury 10 Oct 1830 and had a daughter, Belinda Fowler, who was to marry Jacob[8] Eaton (see **#1747**) in 1848. Sarah Jane died 22 Oct 1834. Our senior author reported that her husband Jacob Fowler mar. 2d, Rebecca[8] Eaton, (**#1715**) but the basis for this conjecture is unclear. Jacob Fowler soon drowned while shore fishing near the "Sandy Cove Ledges," 14 Aug 1854.

**287. Josiah⁶ Eaton** (Joseph⁵, John⁴⁻¹), was born ca. 1760 in Hampton Falls (proto-Seabrook); mar. **Eunice (Westcott) Ricker** of Eastport, Me., ca. 1794. His family may have resided in Seabrook while he was a share fisherman in the deep sea and Labrador fishery, a situation he later abandoned for the more ready and constant employment in the merchant marine. He is, nonetheless, almost certainly that Josiah who is the first Eaton in a Washington Co., Maine, Federal Census, listed in 1800 at Eastport, where his wife had lived before their marriage. He was also on the Seabrook tax list for 1800 (the 1800 USC returns for Seabrook were lost), reminding us that persons in the coastal trades were often found at several places in different seasons. At some time soon after 1800 he moved his primary residence from his natal Seabrook to neighboring Salisbury, presumably because that village was a shorter commute to his maritime activities. He thus appears in the 1810 USC in Salisbury, where all of his known children are recorded. In two related land deeds of May, 1808, Josiah appears to have sold his 6-acre Salisbury homestead to his equally sea-faring but more prosperous younger brother Caleb⁶ (see **#290**). Josiah cannot be found in Salisbury, Seabrook or Maine in the 1820 Census, presumably because of extended absence in parts unknown. However, the fact that two of his daughters who were in their late teens in the period after 1815 found their husbands and came to reside in Milltown, Washington Co., Maine suggests that their family may have been centered in that area for some of this later period. Josiah died 20 Dec 1828, according to our original manuscript, but the place is not specified.

Children, recorded in Salisbury (there is a possibility of later children elsewhere):

**764**    i. Elizabeth⁷ "Betsey" Eaton, b. 27 Feb 1796; mar. a Hopkins and lived in Exeter, N.H. They had a daughter, Elizabeth.
**765**   ii. William⁷ Eaton, b. 7 Feb 1798; died 27 Nov 1808.
**766**  iii. Aurelia⁷ Eaton, b. 25 Aug 1801; mar. Isaac T. Lane and lived in Milltown, Me. Had three daughters and a son.
**767**   iv. Reuben⁷ Eaton, b. 20 Apr 1804.
**768**    v. Josiah⁷ Eaton, b. 8 Feb 1806; he was a mariner, unmar., and from one voyage never returned.
**769**   vi. Elias⁷ Maybe Eaton, b. 4 Feb 1808; also an unmar. mariner. Where he died is unknown, but he left a silver medal given him by the British government for bravery in the marine service. Perhaps he had removed to Canada's Maritime Provinces.
**770**  vii. Frances⁷ M. Garrison Eaton, b. 11 Feb 1810; mar. 1st, Moses Rhines and lived in Milltown, Me. They had one daughter. She mar. 2d a Webster and had another girl.

**288. Jonathan[6] Eaton** (Joseph[5], John[4-1]) was born ca. 1762-3 in Hampton Falls (proto-Seabrook). He was too young for participation with his cousins in the early stages of the Revolution; but by Mar 1778, if not as early as Apr 1777, he enlisted as a private from Hampton Falls for two years or three (N.H. *State Papers* XV, pp. 456, 730; and XVI, p. 17). He enlisted again in Capt. Frye's Co. in Dec 1779, this time from Seabrook and for the duration of the war. He appears on the rolls for Continental service as late as May 1781, and his deposition for a pension in 1818 speaks of still being in service when peace was achieved, presumably after the Yorktown surrender in Oct 1781. (The pension claim was allowed in Nov 1818.)

On 11 Oct 1787 he mar. **Sarah Merrill**, daughter of Capt. John Merrill and Sarah (Adams) of Salisbury. After his military service he was primarily a seaman in the merchant marine. In 1820 he is put under the guardianship of two Seabrook notables, who describe him as an erstwhile fisherman but one become "decrepit," in connection with continuation of his pension. In June 1828 when he was was 65 he also applied for bounty land due him as a "during the war man," and received a grant for 100 acres. According to an 1838 petition by widow Sarah to continue his pension further, he had died 15 Sep 1832.

Children with Sarah:

+ **771**   i. Archelaus[7] Eaton, b. 20 Mar 1789; mar. 1st, Betsey Hackett.
  **772**   ii. Martha[7] Eaton, b. ca. 1794; mar. Jacob Eaton (**#642**), son of John[6], 10 May 1818.
  **773**   iii. Sarah[7] Eaton, b. ca. 1796; mar. William Dow of Seabrook, 28 Oct 1818. She died 12 Nov 1882, age 86.
+ **774**   iv. Jabez[7] Eaton, b. ca. 1799; mar. Sally Dow, 17 Jan 1822.
  **775**   v. Eliza[7] Eaton, b. ca. 1803; mar. Jacob Collins of Seabrook, son of Ezekiel, on 9 Apr 1824. She died 23 Jul 1875.
+ **776**   vi. Samuel[7] Eaton, b. 10 Jul 1810; mar. Susan Collins, 1833.
+ **777**   vii. John[7] M. Eaton, b. ca. 1813; mar. Martha Brown, 1831.

**290. (Capt.) Caleb[6] Eaton** (Joseph[5], John[4-1]) was born 8 Jan 1773 in Seabrook, N.H.; mar. 1st, **Lucy Dalton**, the daughter of Samuel, on 3 Jun 1798. He was a ship captain and master mariner in the lanes along the northern coast of North America. He bought homestead land of his father as a Seabrook yeoman in late 1794, but sold it immediately and removed to Salisbury, Mass., where he is visible in the four Censuses from 1800 thru 1830. He was well-to-do and traded a fair amount of Salisbury real estate, including homesteads. He seems to have lived in different houses himself at various times, generally on the north side of town and near Cushing Corner. Wife Lucy, by whom he had seven children, died 7 Jan 1827. He mar. 2d, **Elsie Wadleigh (Davis) Drown**, widow of Peter, 20 Jun 1830, and they had three more children. In Sep 1836 Caleb died on board his vessel off Labrador, and was buried on a nearby shore. He left a daughter a ring with the inscription, "C. Eaton obt. Aug. 31st, 1836." Wife Elsie survived in Salisbury until 3 Dec 1874.

Children with Lucy:

778    i. Rebecca[7] Eaton, b. 26 Apr 1799; mar. John Webb Coffin and resided in Salisbury. They had one daughter and two sons, both of whom were in the Civil War.

+ 779  ii. Jonathan[7] D. Eaton, b. 13 Aug 1803; mar. 1st, Lucy Fellows.

780  iii. Hannah[7] D. Eaton, b. 26 Apr 1809; mar. Eben Hoyt of Newburyport, Mass. and lived in Boston, having two sons and one daughter.

781  iv. Susannah[7] Eaton, b. 10 Jan 1811; mar. William Pecker of Amesbury, Mass. and had one son. The senior author of this volume once visited Mrs. Pecker in her pleasant home.

782  v. Edward[7] Dorr Eaton, b. 22 Oct 1813. He was a trader who went to California and died unmar. in Oregon.

783  vi. John[7] Webb Eaton, b. 14 Oct 1816. When he was 22 he went to North Carolina, where he died unmarried.

784  vii. Caleb[7] Eaton, b. 15 Jul 1820. Became a grocer and a ship chandler in Boston and was unmarried.

Children with Elsie:

785  viii. Lucretia[7] Harriet Eaton, b. 26 Sep 1831; mar. 1st, Henry C. Nash of Sweden, Me., 1 Sep 1852. He died at Lee Center, Ill., 3 Nov 1858, age 29. She mar. 2d, Lyman Curtis Wheat of Putney, Vt., 23 Aug 1863., res. in Amboy, Ill.

786  ix. Adeline[7] Sarah Eaton, b. 13 Nov 1833; mar. 1st, Mr. Drowne, with whom she had one daughter and two sons; and 2d, William Swift Pierce of Salisbury, 3 Dec 1874. They resided in Weymouth, Mass., and had one son.

787  x. Charles[7] Edwin Eaton, b. 15 Aug 1836. No known record.


**292. Joshua[6] Eaton** (Joshua[5], William[4], John[3-1]) was born 17 Oct 1745 in Wells, Me.; mar. **Lucy Maxwell** (she b. 19 Dec 1743) on 2 Aug 1770, and lived on a farm in Wells. Joshua died 10 Mar 1833; wife Lucy died 29 Sep 1837, at the age of 88.

Children:

788  i. Mehitable[7] Eaton, b. 19 Feb 1771; mar. a Mr. Penney; died 15 Apr 1804.

789  ii. Phebe[7] Eaton, b. 3 Apr 1773; mar. John Tenney; resided in Shapleigh, Me.

790  iii. John[7] Eaton, b. 6 Mar 1775; mar. _?_ and died 3 Mar 1801, leaving one daughter.

791  iv. James[7] Eaton, b. 16 Mar 1777; died 1 Oct 1801.

+ **792**    v. Forrest[7] Eaton, b. 22 May 1779; mar. Louise Goodwin.
+ **793**    vi. Joshua[7] Eaton, b. 3 Aug 1781; mar. Mehitable Bickford.
  **794**    vii. Abigail[7] Eaton, b. 30 Mar 1784; died 19 Oct 1786.
+ **795**    viii. Jabez[7] Eaton, b. 18 Apr 1787; mar. 1st, Sally Chick, 1810.
+ **796**    ix. Noah[7] Eaton, b. 5 Feb 1790; mar. Aphia Furbush, 1812.

**294. Joseph[6] Eaton** (Joshua[5], William[4], John[3-1]) was born 11 Jan 1749 in Wells, Me.; was married three times, although all of his children were born of his second wife. He married 1st, **Adah Wells**, 1 Feb 1769; 2d, **Hannah Maxwell** in 1772; and 3d, **Sarah Weeks**, who outlived her husband and died in Wells, 14 Jul 1848. Joseph began adult life as a farmer in his native town, and continued to farm in some degree throughout his life, but his occupation in due time took a religious turn. He was a Baptist, and for a time in his younger days was a member of the Baptist Church in No. Berwick, since that option was not available in Wells itself. On 10 Oct 1780, however, he was one of 14 persons who constituted the first Baptist Church in Wells. He was chosen a deacon of that church on 2 Dec 1780; and became licensed to preach on 4 Dec 1793. Then on 28 Feb 1798 he was ordained as pastor of the Wells Baptist Church, with Rev. William Hooper making the ordination sermon. He continued in this pastorate until his connection with the church was dissolved 24 Jun 1822. Joseph died on 27 Dec 1831. The house in which he lived was still standing and in good repair near the end of the 19th century.

Children with Hannah:

  **797**    i. Anna[7] Eaton, b. 12 Mar 1776; mar. Evat Willard, Alfred, Me.
  **798**    ii. Orpha[7] Eaton, b. 11 Dec 1777; mar. Aaron Ricker, of
              Limerick, Me.
+ **799**    iii. Joseph[7] Eaton, b. 26 Jun 1782; mar. Sarah Hatch, 1805.
  **800**    iv. Sarah[7] Eaton, b. 20 Jul 1785; lived and died unmar., Wells.
  **801**    v. Hannah[7] Eaton, b. 6 Sep 1787; mar. Edward Edes and res.
              near her parents' home.
  **802**    vi. Grace[7] Eaton, b. 20 Dec 1789; mar. James Hatch in 1812;
              lived and died in Wells.

**303. Jeremiah[6] Moulton Eaton** (Joseph[5], William[4], John[3-1]) was born ca. 1751 in Wells, Me.; mar. 1st, **Mary Emery**, 4 Jan 1776 in Wells, and had two children. He was a mariner, and made his home in Wells. He later mar. 2d, **Mary Davis**, 26 Nov 1781 in Wells; and 3d, **Alice Wheelwright**, 19 Oct 1794, although these later marriages were childless.

Children with Mary (Emery):

+ **803**    i. John[7] Emery Eaton, b. ca. 1778; mar. Dorcas Hatch, 1802.
+ **804**    ii. Samuel[7] Eaton, b. ca 1780; mar. Betsey Hatch, ca. 1807.

### #6. Our Eaton Migrations up to 1820

The history of migration within early New England is sharply divided into two periods: before and after 1759. Originally, because of the Indian menace, the growing population of European settlers clung to the ocean shoreline, where there was safety in numbers. Expansion of the population, however, required more and more land, so that by 1700 some had dared to inch into the interior, occasionally to their regret. By early in the 1700s or so, the native Indian population had thinned out considerably, and the main fear was of the raiding parties of Indians that the French in Quebec would encourage to descend on mainly English colonists to their southeast (see the case of Haverhill, Sidebar #1). In 1759, however, Quebec City fell to the English, and in very short order many young bucks born in the late stages of Gen. V of our Eatons, and all of Gen. VI, surged to establish selves on new land in the interior.

Here we summarize their main streams of migration out of Salisbury, Seabrook and Haverhill in the period ending in 1820. Of course it is hard to summarize migrations that took place to many destinations, often with progressive stops, over nearly a century. Therefore we focus on the largest of the Eaton "plantations" formed by our Eaton emigrants, and take a "snapshot" of where they had arrived by 1820, thanks to the Census of that year. (Eatons of the other main new England lineages were also spreading out in this period, in some cases into New Hampshire; but our display in Map #5 is limited to Eatons out of John[1]/Anne of Salisbury.)

Much of Map #5 is self-explanatory. But a few further annotations may help. Shown are town locations harboring over 20 of our Eaton individuals in 1820. The size of the circle is chosen to reflect relative numbers of Eatons by town. Clear winner is Deer Isle, especially if we add in (appropriately) the Eatons spilling over to the mainland at Sedgwick from the Isle itself. This accounts for some 135 Eatons as of 1820 (but still only 18 families, and far behind Seabrook). The circles also differentiate between the Salisbury and Haverhill lines of our Eatons. At Weare, for example, 7 families are from the former and 3 from the latter. At Hopkinton, next door, all Eatons are from Haverhill. The fact that so few destination towns show Haverhill migrants reflects several facts: the Haverhill line is roughly half the size of the Salisbury one in this period; and tended to spread out more as well. Thus, for example, Haverhill Eaton clusters at East Kingston, Hillsborough and Sutton, N.H. just fall short of inclusion.

The map fails to show the timing of moves, although in general, the further into the interior from the home base, the later the arrival. The earliest was at Wells, where William[4] (#31) married a Wells girl in 1709 and stayed to found a colony which would rival in size the one at Deer Isle, had we not included the Sedgwick spillover in the count.

**Map 5.  Our Eaton Migrations to 1820**
(for further notes, see Sidebar #6)

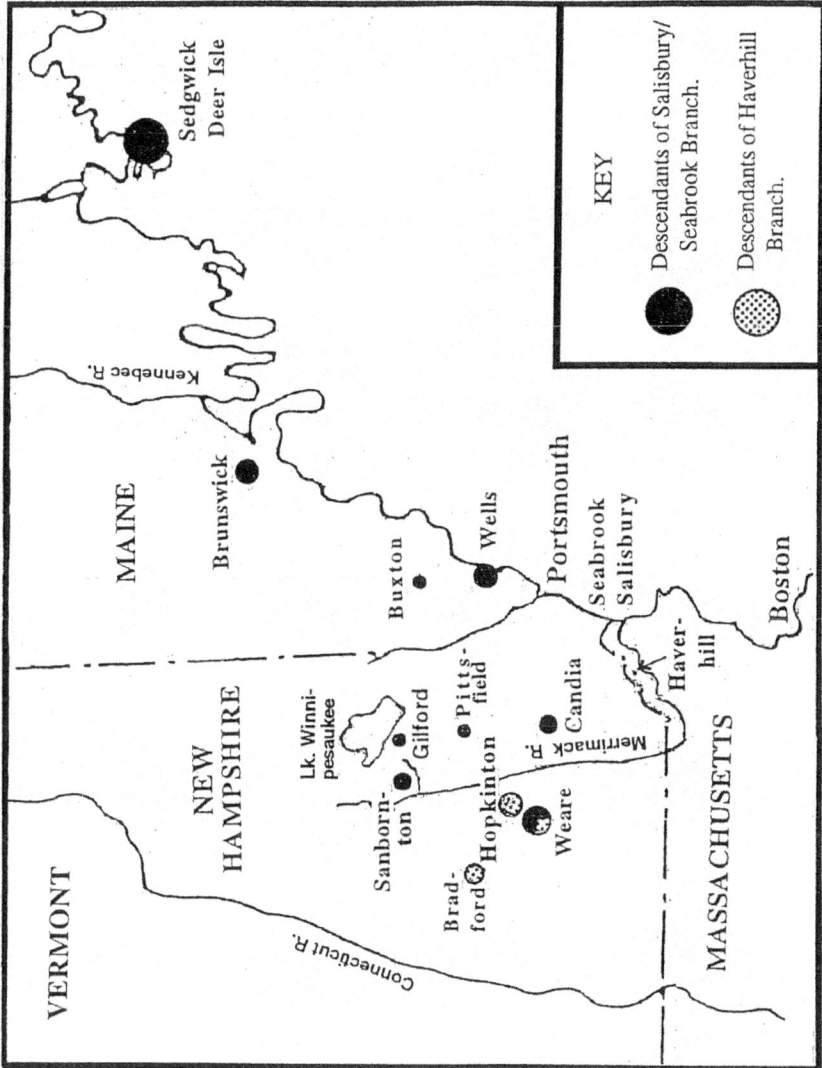

**304. Daniel⁶ Eaton** (Joseph⁵, William⁴, John³⁻¹) was born ca. 1752 in Wells, Me.; mar. **Hannah Sherif** and lived in Portsmouth, N.H., where he was visible in the 1800 and 1810 Censuses and engaged in mercantile pursuits for many years. No record of children.

**307. William⁶ Eaton** (Joseph⁵, William⁴, John³⁻¹) was born 17 Dec 1756 in Wells, Me. He served in the Revolution in both the Continental and Mass. Lines. He mar. **Abigail Littlefield** 9 Dec 1781, she having been born 27 Jul 1760. He was a master mariner and kept his homestead in Wells. He applied for a Revolutionary War pension in 1818, and also was given a Revolutionary War bounty land grant of 200 acres in Wells in 1835. He died 30 Nov 1841; she died 3 Oct 1852.

Children:

+ **805**   i. Rufus⁷ Eaton, b. 27 Jun 1785; mar. Sarah E. Lombard.
  **806**   ii. Lydia⁷ Eaton, b. 6 May 1787; no further report.
  **807**   iii. Jeremiah⁷ Eaton, b. 22 Apr 1789; died 19 May 1811.
+ **808**   iv. William⁷ Eaton, b. 22 Aug 1791; mar. Abigail Jacobs.
  **809**   v. Elizabeth⁷ Eaton, b. 23 Nov 1793; no further report.
  **810**   vi. Andrew⁷ Eaton, b. 3 Oct 1797; no further report.
  **811**   vii. Nancy⁷ Eaton, b. 16 Nov 1799; died 4 Nov 1801.
  **812**   viii. Nancy⁷ᴬ Eaton, b. 1 Feb 1802; no further report.

**308. Jacob⁶ Eaton** (Joseph⁵, William⁴, John³⁻¹) was born 28 Feb 1765 in Wells, Me.; mar. **Abigail Bourne**, 4 Jun 1794. She had been born 24 Oct 1776. He was a master mariner. Wife Abigail died in 1841; he died 17 Nov 1850.

Children:

  **813**   i. Olive⁷ Eaton, b. 22 Jan 1795; died Aug. 1828.
  **814**   ii. Nancy⁷ Eaton, b. 13 Sep 1797; mar. 1st, Abner Bragdon. They had at least one daughter, Abbie B. Bragdon, before father Abner died. She mar. 2d, Capt Joshua Winn of York, Me., and had two children, Temperance and Nathaniel Eaton Winn.
+ **815**   iii. Nathaniel⁷ Eaton, b. 14 Dec 1800; was a planter in Cuba.
  **816**   iv. Lydia⁷ Eaton, b. 3 Jan 1803; mar. James Donnell, a sea captain; she died 27 Jan 1866.
+ **817**   v. Daniel⁷ Eaton, b. 31 Jul 1807; mar. Sarah A. Bragdon.
  **818**   vi. Jacob⁷ Eaton, b. 3 Aug 1809; died 28 Oct 1817 in Wells.
+ **819**   vii. Hophni⁷ Eaton, b. 11 Dec 1812; mar. Clara Small, 1849.

**311. John**[6] **Eaton** (Joseph[5], William[4], John[3-1]) was born 21 Oct 1771 in Wells, Me.; mar. 1st, **Sarah Cole**, ca. 1795. They resided on a farm in Wells, although a daughter later testified that her father was a master mariner. Wife Sarah died 21 Jan 1827, and John mar. 2d, **Hannah Hill**, daughter of Comfort.

Children with Sarah:

| | | |
|---|---|---|
| 820 | i. | Abigail[7] Eaton, b. 18 Mar 1796; died unmar. 7 Jul 1822. |
| 821 | ii. | Sarah[7] Eaton, b. 20 May 1798; mar. Samuel Gordon of Biddeford, Me. |
| + 822 | iii. | John[7] Cole Eaton, b. 15 Aug 1800; mar. Dorcas Jacobs. |
| 823 | iv. | Jonathan[7] Eaton, b. 30 Sep 1802; died young. |
| 824 | v. | Louisa[7] Eaton, b. 18 Aug 1805; mar. John Hayes and res. in Portland, Me. They had one son and three daughters. |
| 825 | vi. | Harriet[7] Eaton, b. 22 Jul 1807; died young. |
| 826 | vii. | Eliza[7] Eaton, b. 6 Jan 1811; died in childhood. |
| 827 | viii. | Julia[7] Ann Eaton, b. 18 Jan 1816; mar. 1st, John Cooper, in 1842. He had been born in Dubuque, Iowa, but at the time of marriage was a mason in Boston, Mass. They resided in Boston, where he died in 1855 after at least two sons. She mar., 2d, Joseph Cheney and resided in Nashua, N.H. |
| 828 | ix. | Jeremiah[7] Eaton, b. 3 May 1818; died 29 Jul 1822. |

**314. John**[6] **Eaton** (Elisha[5], Samuel[4], John[3-1]), was born 1 Oct 1749 at Salisbury, Mass. or in the proto-Seabrook area of Hampton Falls, N.H. He almost certainly began childhood living on part of the old John Worthen estate at the tip of Worthen's Point in proto-Seabrook. He lost his father, however, before he was four, and his widowed mother Elizabeth took John and her three other little children back into Salisbury by the end of 1753, probably on or near the paternal grandfather's homestead in the Cow Commons section of East Salisbury. Apart from a mention in Grandfather Samuel's 1765 will, nothing more is known of John until his marriage to **Sarah**[6] **"Sally" French** of Seabrook on 1 Feb 1773, conducted by the Rev. Samuel Perley. Even the record of this marriage has, however, been somewhat fugitive, since the Rev. Perley listing gives the bridegroom as a "John Eaton Taylor," and one has to encounter other land conveyances in which John[6] is listed in his early years as "John Eaton, tailor," to understand the cryptic recording. Bride Sally was the daughter of Jacob[5] French of Seabrook.

Some months before the marriage John[6], then of Salisbury, had sold cousin Thomas[5] Eaton of Seabrook (**#89**) 2+ acres at Worthen's Point, probably his father's stake there; and not long after the marriage John[6] removed to Pittsfield, N.H., undoubtedly following the lead of his Uncle Jonathan. He bought several pieces of land sooner or later in Pittsfield, but it is likely that the main farm he worked for nearly forty years lay by Eaton pond on the southeast flank of Catamount Mountain, just off modern route #107. It was here that John and Sally raised their large family. One episode in family lore presumably occurred in this Pittsfield period. John[6] was having trouble with an Indian. He made an effigy of himself and hid in the bushes nearby. When the Indian took a shot at the effigy, he shot and killed the Indian. The gun taken from the Indian in this episode was in the possession of a great grandson, Joseph[10] Smith Eaton (#5091) of Taunton, Mass. in 1950. Similarly, a grand-daughter, Mrs. James B. Taylor (#2124), had the tailor's shears of John[6] at the turn of the 20th century.

As he approached 70 years of age, John[6] and Sally decided to move one more stage northward. In Dec. 1817, John bought a 200-acre Lot #7 in the second Masonian range in Gilford [Belknap Deed 112-285], on the east flank of Mt. Gunstock overlooking Alton Bay in Lake Winnipesaukee. This site was a few score yards from a lot developed by the third son of John and Sally, Joseph[7], who had removed to the area (then still Gilmanton) around 1801. Nearby on the same road to Alton, a niece and Pittsfield native, Hannah (Eaton) Chesley, had resided for some time. Moreover, their own daughter Betsey, who had married Andrew Flanders in 1811, was also close by in Alton. Finally, John[6] and Sally brought with them from Pittsfield the two last children they were raising, their own son Samuel[7] Sherburne Eaton (then age 19), and their grand-son Elisha[8] (then age 23), whose own father, Elisha[7] had died leaving him an infant of four months, to be brought up by the grandparents.

Thus the neighborhood was full of Eaton families. John and Sally set off sublots for the two young men, both of whom had married within a year or two of arrival. The original family homestead, later owned by grandson Elisha[8], on the south side of Route 11A, was still in good repair in 1990. John[6] Eaton died there on 27 May 1829. His wife Sally died in Feb 1833.

Children, all but possibly the first at Pittsfield:

+ **829**   i. Elisha[7] Eaton, b. 9 May 1774; mar. Betsey Sherburne, 1794.
+ **830**   ii. John[7] Eaton, b. 3 May 1776; mar. 1st, Sarah Prescott; 2d, Mrs. Abigail Towle.
  **831**   iii. Mary[7] Eaton, b. 23 Mar 1778; mar. James Staniels ca. 1800.
+ **832**   iv. Joseph[7] Eaton, b. 3 Jul 1780; mar. Abigail Meader, 1804.
  **833**   v. Sarah[7] Eaton, b. 5 Sep 1782; mar. Theodore Clark of Pitts-field 19 May 1800. He was b. in Haverhill, Mass., but set-tled in Pittsfield, building one of the first mills in the Sun-cook River valley. He was a man of much enterprise, but lost his life in an accident at age 57. They had nine children. She died 27 May 1856.
+ **834**   vi. Jonathan[7] Eaton, b. 29 Sep 1784; mar. Elizabeth Locke.
  **835**   vii. Nancy[7] Eaton, b. 15 Aug 1786; mar. John Mathews, 26 Dec 1804. They lived in Loudon, N.H. and had three children.
  **836**   viii. Elizabeth[7] Eaton, b. 14 May 1790; mar. Andrew Flanders, 5 May 1811, and lived in Alton, N.H., having eight children.
  **837**   ix. Amasa[7] Eaton, b. 10 Sep 1792; mar. Sally Page, 13 Jan

1814. Relatives recount that Amasa was killed by a truck cart in Boston about 1820. There is no record of children.

+ **838**    x. Jacob[7] Eaton, b. 13 Aug 1794; mar. Judith Rollins in 1818.
+ **839**   xi. Samuel[7] Sherburne Eaton, b. 16 Jun 1798; m. Hope Gilman.


**316. Elisha[6] Eaton** (Elisha[5], Samuel[4], John[3-1]) was born 13 Mar 1753 in Salisbury, Mass., or proto-Seabrook, N.H., perhaps after his father had already died; mar. **Hannah Sleeper**, 8 Nov 1774 at Hampton. When a young man Elisha served in the Revolution, and perhaps in the Battle of Bunker Hill, as family lore would have it. He is almost certainly the Elisha Eaton of Seabrook, N.H. listed as a private in Capt. Jonathan Evans's Co., Col. Frye's (1st) Regt. at the Cambridge encampment from at least mid-May to mid-November, 1775 (*Mass. Soldiers & Sailors*, p. 169). Similarly, he must be the Elisha who was a private in Capt. Samuel Nye's Co. in the Continental service with his cousins Levi[6] (**#257**) and Benjamin[6] (**#248**) for about 5 months at Fort Ticonderoga (N.H. *State Papers*, XIV, p. 350).

It is not clear where Elisha and Hannah first settled, but in due time they followed brother John[6] to Pittsfield, N.H. and raised their family there. On a torn page of the Pittsfield typescript of vital events in that community, it is noted that on 8 Feb 1794, "Mr. Elisha Eat[on] hanged himself with a not of yarn in his barn." A widow Hannah Eaton, presumably his wife, is listed as dying on 10 Dec 1810. From the conveyances of his real estate, which Hannah had finally been asked to administer on 10 Mar 1809, we learn of eight children.

Children, all or most at Pittsfield (order at points speculative):

**840**     i. Elisha[7] Eaton, b. ca. 1780; removed unmar. to Barnston, Stanstead Co., Lower Canada about 1810. Listed as a husbandman of that town, in Nov 1811 he sold his title to his father's real estate in Pittsfield.
**841**    ii. Deborah[7] Eaton, b. ca. 1782; remained unmarried.
**842**   iii. Hannah[7] Eaton, b. ca. 1784; mar. Aaron Chesley, 23 Sep 1804. They removed to Gilford, N.H., and at her death left two sons, Levi and Amos Chesley.
**843**   iv. Sally[7] Eaton, b. ca. 1786; mar. Joseph Bunker, 13 Nov 1806 and settled in Kennebec, Me.
**844**    v. Nancy[7] Eaton, b. ca. 1788; not married in 1812.
+ **845**   vi. Stephen[7] Eaton, b. 26 Feb 1790; mar. Mary Underwood.
**846**  vii. Elizabeth[7] Eaton, b. ca. 1792; remained unmar. in 1827.
**847** viii. Ruth[7] Eaton, b. ca. 1794; not married in 1812.


**317. David[6] Eaton** (David[5], Samuel[4], John[3-1]), was born in proto-Seabrook at a time which seems slightly indefinite, despite a Hampton Falls birth record dated Dec. 9, 1756. This date follows nicely after his parents' marriage, said to have occurred 11 Mar 1756. But it is less than six months before the date given for their next child William (below), and David's 1832 Revolutionary pension request and age at death imply an earlier birth in 1755. In any event, he mar. **Polly Rogers** of Newburyport ca. 1772, she being apparently the daughter of William Rogers, given a 1797 quitclaim to his estate signed by the couple. Apart from his service time, he lived out his days in Seabrook at the tip of Worthen's Point where he had grown up. His pension application reports that he first enlisted in Aug 1776, serving as a private for three months with Capt. Prescott's Co. in the N.H. Militia, being discharged at New York at the end of November. He served again for three months in the latter part of 1777, this time at Ticonderoga with Capt. Leavitt's Co., along with his cousins Levi[6], Benjamin[6] and Timothy[5] Eaton. Levi[6] and Sylvanus[6] appeared in order to testify as to his war service. Later he was locally known as "Major Eaton", although there were no signs that he ever had a commission. He appears in Seabrook Censuses from 1790 through 1830, and probably was the octogenarian in son Joseph R.'s household in the 1840 Census. His pension dossier indicates that he died 13 Nov 1848 at Seabrook.

Children at Seabrook:

**848**    i. Elisha[7] Eaton, b. 1772.
**849**    ii. Hannah[7] Eaton, b. 1774; mar. a Samuel Eaton.
**850**   iii. Charity[7] Eaton, b. 1776; mar. a Flanders.
**851**    iv. Rebecca[7] Eaton, b. 1777.
**852**    v. Abigail[7] Eaton, b. 1780.
**853**    vi. Polly[7] Eaton, b. 1782; mar. John Odum.
**854**   vii. David[7] Eaton, b. 1784; died at sea, unmar.
+ **855** viii. Abraham[7] Eaton, b. 1786; mar. Phebe Norton.
**856**    ix. __?__[7] Eaton, b. 1788; mar. James Jackman.
**857**    x. Joseph[7] R. Eaton, b. 1790; mar. Olive Eaton, prob. widow
             of Daniel[7] Eaton (**#630**). She would have been in her
             40s or 50s at this time, and there is no reason to believe
             that this marriage (or Joseph R.) had any issue.
+ **858**    xi. Daniel[7] Eaton, b. 1792; mar. Belinda Knowles.
**859**   xii. Rhoda[7] Eaton, b. 1795; mar. Robert Messer, or "Missier", a
             native of Labrador, 30 Sep 1824 (Salisbury, Mass. *VR*).
             She was a widow by 1850. In 1855 she petitioned on
             behalf of herself and her siblings for any residual Revolu-
             tionary War pension owed her father David.
**860** xiii. Mahala[7] Eaton, b. 1800; became the second wife of Jonathan
             Worthley about 1835, and removed to join him in Weare,
             N.H., where she had children in 1837 and 1840.
**861** xiv. Catherine[7] Eaton, b. 1804 and taken at an early age by her
             sister Polly Odum to Boston, where she was brought up.
             She mar. a foreigner, Angus Robinson, 11 Nov 1827.

NOTE: None of the above births come from public records, and the Rev. Eaton's original manuscript gives no source for this roster. Indeed, this is the one biographical sketch which he left without placement of the subject in the family tree. The current author does not find his own assignment--as a son of David⁵-- at all problematic. Furthermore, various pieces of independent evidence are at least consistent with the birth order as originally presented, and we have therefore kept this intact. However, the approximate dates of birth have required major revision. Apparently without specific evidence to the contrary, Rev. Eaton decided to put these fourteen children on a lockstep two-year birth schedule, with the first child born in 1765 and the fourteenth in 1791, with the sole exception of Rebecca, who came a year early. While the two-year stairstep pattern is entirely familiar from this place and period, the spacing usually tends to increase beyond two years near the end of the birthing, particularly when the series is as long as this. More disconcerting still is the moment Rev. Eaton chose to begin the series: there is ambiguity as to when father David⁶ was born, although most evidence suggest either 1755 or 1756. But this means that David's firstborn came when he was nine or ten! Clearly there is something amiss here. Fortunately, we have in later Census materials independent estimates, usually multiple, of the ages of five of these children (viii and x-xiii). In the middle of the series these estimated ages are running seven years later than in the Reverend's original account; and for the last children the lag is greater still, since Rhoda was probably not born before 1795, instead of the original 1787; and Mahala was almost certainly not born before the year 1800, instead of 1789. Therefore we have revised the birthdate sequence to fit this independent evidence. The corrected series still finds David with a firstborn by age 16 or 17, which is very precocious for the period, but not out of the question.

**318. William⁶ Eaton** (David⁵, Samuel⁴, John³⁻¹) was born 26 May 1757 in proto-Seabrook; and mar. **"Molly" Lord** (probably **Olive Lord** born in Maine), 26 Jun 1782 (Seabrook *VR* at Concord). William was the youngest of three Seabrook William Eatons in his early adulthood, and he is referred to as "William 3d" when in 1789 he is named guardian of his *non compos mentis* father. However, at some time no later than 1796 he prematurely died, and two of his children came under the care of the town, despite the fact that their mother, referred to only as Widow Eaton, is still on the scene. Discussion of these children's care continues sporadically in town meetings for the next six years at least, although we find no identification of them by given name. Therefore:

Children at Seabrook (perhaps partial, and order not always clear):

**862** i. Jeremiah⁷ Eaton?. This would account for a Jeremiah Eaton, b. late in 1784 at Seabrook, recorded as the son of a William Eaton, but not associable with other Williams on that scene at the time. This Jeremiah mar. a Sarah __?__ b. ca. 1786, who died of consumption 19 Nov 1844 (Salisbury VR). This couple had a daughter Eunice M. who also died of consumption at 18 and is buried with her parents at Mt. Prospect in Amesbury, Mass.

**863** ii. Mary[7] Eaton, prob. born later 1780s. In Jan 1818, she and
her younger sister Eunice, described as "spinsters of North
Hampton," sell off three parcels of land totalling about two
acres, which they received from the estates of their father
William and grandfather David Eaton (Rockingham Co.
Deed 237-410).

**864** iii. Son[7] Eaton. Perhaps a William?

**865** iv. Eunice[7] Eaton, b. after the 1790 Census; as a daughter of
William Eaton, late of Seabrook, but still a minor (under
14), she received a guardian, Jacob Moulton of Hampton
Falls, 9 May 1803 (Rockingham Co. Probate #7061).

**321. Samuel[6] Eaton** (David[5], Samuel[4], John[3-1]), was born ca. 1765
in proto-Seabrook; probably mar. **Mary[7] "Polly" Eaton** (**#625**), daughter of Ebenezer[6], 2 Oct 1788 (South Hampton *VR*). In 1796 he is listed
as receiving his share of the estate of father David, just deceased. About
1800 the couple removed to Weare, N.H. and settled on Barnard Hill on
the east edge of that township. Samuel died in Weare 9 Feb 1817. His
wife Mary died 20 Feb 1844.

Children (listed in the following order in the *History of Weare*
(Little, 1888), but without birthdates or places, some of which we can
supply from other sources):

**866** i. Huldah[7] Eaton, b. ca. 1789; mar. Reuben Barnard and resided
in Weare, but later removed just east into Dunbarton.

+ **867** ii. Reuben[7] Eaton, b. 8 Sep 1790; mar. Judith[7] Eaton (**#715**),
daughter of William[6] of Sanbornton, 2 Apr 1813.

+ **868** iii. Moses[7] Eaton, b. ca. 1792; mar. 1st, Mary Eaton (**#641**).

**869** iv. Mary[7] Eaton, b. ca. 1793; mar. James Worthley.

**870** v. Edmund[7] Eaton, b. ca. 1795; died young.

**871** vi. Polly[7] Eaton, b. ca. 1796; mar. Nathan George.

+ **872** vii. Samuel[7] Eaton, b. ca. 1800; mar. Betsey Dow of Seabrook,
24 Apr 1825, and resided in Seabrook.

+ **873** viii. William[7] Eaton, b. 6 Sep 1802; mar. Julia Ann Haynes.

+ **874** ix. David[7] Eaton, b. 26 Jun 1804; mar. Mary Worthley, 1830.

**875** x. Sarah[7] Eaton, b. ca. 1805; mar. Josiah Swain.

**876** xi. Lydia[7] H. Eaton, b. 1807; mar. Marden Emerson, a farmer
in Weare, where she died 20 Feb 1876; he d. 5 Nov 1880.

**322. True[6] Eaton** (David[5], Samuel[4], John[3-1]) was born 17 Dec
1770 at Seabrook, N.H.; mar. **Abigail Knowles** of Seabrook, 17 Nov
1796. He was a yeoman residing in Seabrook. Earlier in the year of his
marriage he received his share of his father David's estate, and bought up
further shares of his sisters Lydia Hoit and Hannah Davis at that time. He

died suddenly, however, less than a year into his marriage.    His widow Abigail was granted administration of his estate 23 Oct 1797.

Child with Abigail in Seabrook, N.H.:

**877**    i. Rhoda[7] Eaton, b. 15 Aug 1797; mar. Jacob Rowe 6 Dec 1818 but she died 4 Sep 1825 (Mrs. Locke's List).

**325. Thomas[6] Eaton** (Jonathan[5], Samuel[4], John[3-1]), was born 6 Aug 1772 at Salisbury; mar. **Mrs. Sally Ackerman** (born 29 Mar 1772, Portsmouth, N.H.) on  13 Nov 1794, probably at Pittsfield, N.H.  Seven months before his marriage, Thomas had bought of his father Jonathan a half of the Pittsfield homestead lot, and probably received the whole lot upon his father's death in 1809.  He remained farming at Pittsfield, at least through 1820, when his name appears on a local tax list.  By about 1832, however, he returned to Seabrook to reside, and appeared there as a household head in the 1840 Census.  Wife Sally had died 4 Aug 1835. Thomas died, apparently as the result of a hernia, 12 Feb 1847.   He and Sally are buried in Seabrook's Methodist Cemetery.

Children, based on a record of the family found in an attic:

+ **878**    i. Jonathan[7] L. Eaton, b. 26 Apr 1796; mar. Nancy P.
  **879**   ii. Nancy[7] Eaton, b. 22 Jun 1797; died in 1808.
  **880**  iii. Sally[7] Eaton, b. 17 Apr 1799 at Pittsfield, N.H.; mar. Jacob Dow, Jr., of Seabrook, 17 Jan 1822. She died 8 Mar 1878.
  **881**   iv. Mary[7] "Polly" Eaton, b. 4 Jan 1801; mar. Lowell Brown of Seabrook, 27 Nov 1827. She died 12 Apr 1891.
  **882**    v. Huldah[7] Eaton, b. 30 Sep 1802; died 1815.
  **883**   vi. Thomas[7] L. Eaton, b. 1 Jan 1805.
  **884**  vii. Charlotte[7] A. Eaton, b. 17 Feb 1807; mar. Elihu Dow of Seabrook, 26 Dec 1824 (Dow, 1929).  She died 16 Oct 1842, leaving two daughters and a son.
  **885** viii. Nancy[7A] A. Eaton, b. 1 Dec 1811; mar. John Peel. She died 30 Aug 1901.

**327. Richard[6] Eaton** (Samuel[5-4], John[3-1]), was born 22 Oct 1769 in Salisbury, Mass; mar. **Rhoda Hook** of Seabrook, 17 Apr 1802 (Salisbury, Mass. *VR*). This union produced a daughter Rhoda in 1804, but her mother died 2 Sep 1804, probably due to complications of child-birth.  Richard never remarried, and lived out his life with a surprising number of his siblings, also unmarried, at their father Samuel's home-stead facing the fork where Seabrook Rd. heads north and Forest Rd. continues eastward in northeast Salisbury. He may have been a sailor by occupation.  Richard was taxed at Salisbury in consecutive years from 1792 through 1823, although it is unclear why his town taxation ended at that point.  His father Samuel died in 1827, leaving a homestead of some

value, but also a large array of debts. These debts were largely liquidated
by May 1829, when Aaron Boyd, then a Salisbury mariner and perhaps a
sailing mate of Richard's, bought the 37-acre homestead for $1,050
[Essex Co. Deed 267-14].   A few weeks later, presumably by prior design, Richard (with $100), his brother Elisha (with $146), and his unmarried sister Rachel (with $279), put up the exact funds to buy back one
undivided half of the homestead where they all were still living [258-89].
In his final Census in 1850, Richard at 81 was the sole Eaton survivor of
this arrangement, in a household of younger Boyds.   He shortly died, on
2 Mar 1852.

        Child, at Salisbury:

**886**    i. Rhoda[7] Eaton, b. before the last quarter of 1804; she mar.
            John Pike, Jr. and apparently removed to Jay, Me., where
            she had a son Amasa, who returned to see his grandfather
            Richard. She died 12 Nov 1878.


        **328. Joseph[6] Eaton** (Samuel[5-4], John[3-1]) was born 14 Aug 1771,
Salisbury, Mass.; mar. **Hannah Stockman** of Newburyport 30 Oct 1800.
He was a ship's carpenter, combining the ancestral woodworking with the
maritime setting.  He was taxed in Salisbury the year he was 21, but after
that appears to have resided in Newburyport. He died there 9 Mar 1840.

        Children:

**887**    i. Maria[7] Eaton, b. 24 Sep 1801; mar. Ira Tarbell, 3 May 1825
            and removed to Solon and then Smyrna, Maine. They had
            three sons and daughters.
**888**   ii. Joseph[7] Eaton, b. 19 Oct 1802.  About 1830 he removed to
            Florida, where he purchased land but died unmar. ca.
            1845.
**889**  iii. Harriet[7] Eaton, b. 3 Jul 1805; mar. Aaron Boyd of Seabrook,
            of the same family buying half of her grandfather's home-
            stead (see **#327**), on 9 Jan 1825 in Salisbury.  He was a
            shoemaker and mariner, residing in Salisbury.  Harriet
            died 21 Nov 1872, Salisbury.
**890**   iv. Mary[7] Jane Eaton, b. 3 Aug 1806; went to New Jersey with
            Rev. Proudfit, marrying Francis Howard there and res. in
            New Brunswick, N.J., having two daughters.
**891**    v. Elizabeth[7] Eaton, b. 19 Jul 1809; mar. a mariner, John Bailey
            3d, 28 Sep 1843 at Newburyport; no issue.
**892**   vi. Charles[7] Eaton, b. 10 Feb 1811; mar. 1st, Lavinia Glines, on 1
            Jan 1836; and 2d, Susan Glines, 5 Jun 1838.  He drowned
            in the Merrimac River, 13 Aug 1838, leaving one son.
**893**  vii. John[7] Eaton, b. ca. 1813; never married.  He removed first to
            New Jersey, later to Maine.
**894** viii. Hannah[7] Eaton, b. ca. 1815; mar. George Austin of New-

buryport, 1 Nov 1835, and bore 10 children; died in
Feb 1858.


**331. Samuel⁶ Eaton** (Samuel⁵⁻⁴, John³⁻¹) was born 10 May 1778
at Salisbury, Mass.; mar. **Sally French**, 21 Feb 1811. He began his married life in Salisbury, being taxed there from 1797 through 1808. But
then he removed to Solon, Me., where he appears with his younger
brother Moses in the 1810 Census. At Solon he was a prosperous farmer
with a spread of 1,400 acres. He died 3 Sep 1843. Four acres of land on
the edge of the marsh in Salisbury were sold in 1845 as part of his estate.

Children (the first recorded in Salisbury, perhaps retrospectively,
the rest at Solon, Me.):

+ **895**  i. Benjamin⁷ F. Eaton, b. 4 Dec 1811; m. Betsey Durgin, 1840.
  **896**  ii. Jane⁷ Eaton, b. 21 Apr 1816; a teacher in the public schools;
          died unmar. 8 Sep 1903 at Salisbury, Mass.
  **897**  iii. Jonathan⁷ Eaton, b. 31 Aug 1819; never married. He resided
          at the family homestead in Solon till he died, 10 Mar 1889.
  **898**  iv. Samuel⁷ Eaton, b. 1 Mar 1821; never married. He was a
          lumber dealer, residing at the family homestead in Solon
          until death, 20 Nov 1893.
  **899**  v. Sarah⁷ Eaton, b. 8 Jul 1823; died 12 Apr 1831.
  **900**  vi. Rachel⁷ G. Eaton, b. 20 Feb 1827; mar. William Merrill of
          Salisbury, Mass., 30 Sep 1854; res. Salisbury.
+ **901**  vii. Moses⁷ Eaton, b. 14 Mar 1829; mar. Louisa Hunnewell 1858.
  **902**  viii. Sarah⁷ᴬ Eaton, b. 19 Nov 1831; died at age 22 in Solon, Me.


**337. Moses⁶ Eaton** (Theophilus⁵, Jonathan⁴, John³⁻¹) was born 8
Feb 1746 at Kingston, N.H., and bapt. at Haverhill, 23 Mar 1746. He
naturally proceeded to Maine with his family as a young adolescent, and
later, although by that time of age himself, went on to Deer Isle with
them. He married **Patience Bridges** of Sedgwick township on 2 May
1768. Rather than staying on Deer Isle, this couple established themselves on the mainland across the Reach in his bride's neighborhood on
the west side of the Benjamin River. Moses took the potential mill property there which his father had acquired, and built the first mill dam on
that River at a point above the Brooklin-Sedgwick bridge. He was also
important in the organization of Sedgwick Village, sending out the call to
the first town meeting which he hosted in his own home. Over the years
he accumulated a handsome estate which, after his decease, was squan-
dered by his children. Moses died 6 June 1807; wife Patience died 24
Aug 1819.

Children:

+ **903**  i. Theophilus⁷ Eaton, b. 24 Mar 1769; m. Joanna Evans, 1790.

+ **904**   ii. John[7] Eaton, b. 24 Apr 1771; mar. Sally Pickering, 1798.
+ **905**   iii. Benjamin[7] Eaton, b. 13 Oct 1773; m. Susanna Dodge, 1798.
  **906**   iv. Judith[7] Eaton, b. 25 Apr 1777; mar. Hezekiah Dodge, 27
            Mar 1799 at Sedgwick.
+ **907**   v. Moses[7] Eaton, b. 11 Oct 1778; mar. Mary Thomas, 1810.
  **908**   vi. Patience[7] Eaton, b. 13 Oct 1779; mar. Capt. Thomas Bunker,
            30 Dec 1801. He had been b. in Scarboro, Me. in 1776.
            They removed to Charleston, Me. where he became a
            famous builder of maritime vessels. The union produced
            three children in Sedgwick and four more in Charleston.
+ **909**   vii. Jonathan[7] Eaton, 25 Mar 1781; mar. Mary Whitmore, 1807.

**339. Jonathan[6] Eaton** (Theophilus[5], Jonathan[4], John[3-1]), was born 24 Feb 1752. He went with his parents to Deer Isle, Me. He married **Sarah Emerton** of Sedgwick, Me., where he spent most of his adult life. Hosmer says "he was informed against by a Tory and was arrested by a file of soldiers in the evening who were guided by him who gave the information. They started to carry him to Castine, and on their way the road led near the top of a high bank by the shore, which was thickly covered with trees, and on their arrival there, he, being a powerful man, shook off those who were on each side of him, jumped down the bank, and in the darkness escaped. In a few minutes he returned to his house, took a few things, and went to Isle au Haut, which was then a wilderness, and remained there all the season, not returning until the danger was over." (Hosmer, 1905, pp. 27-28).

Jonathan died at his home in Sedgwick in the 1810s, and reportedly the marriage was without issue. However, Jonathan is a primary suspect in an illegitimate birth that produced a substantial twig of further Eatons in Hancock Co. On 2 Mar 1784, a boy was born to an unwed young lady who christened him "Jeremiah Eaton," and so he was known for the rest of his life. The mother was a "Lucy Emmerton," the daughter of Joseph Emmerton and Lucy (Somes), who were recent arrivals in the area, Lucy herself having been baptized 26 May 1765 in Ipswich, Mass. A first order of business here might be to discover the relationship between this Lucy and the "Sarah Emerton," whom Jonathan is said to have married, but the most obvious hypothesis does not work. While Lucy had a much older sister named Sarah (b. 1749), the latter was in a long-term marriage to a Joseph Smith. Young Jeremiah was raised and lived out his life in Blue Hill, Me., the next community of any size, six miles north of Sedgwick, where the Jonathan of this notice spent his life. His mother Lucy married a William Norris and had ten children in Blue Hill. Although locals assumed that the Jeremiah lad had been sired by one of the Eatons out of Deer Isle, there is no surviving tradition as to his more specific paternity. We have calculated that some six Deer Isle males were conceivable candidates for this role, but taking account of age, stage and apparent marital situation, two of these candidates seem far more likely than others. Both had barren marriages, although there were other suggestive factors as well. A runner-up choice would have been Jeremiah[6]

Eaton (#261), who was thought to have had other dalliances in the same period, and can be seen as a namesake. Jonathan, on the other hand, has the Emerton connection (which, like the namesake factor, can cut two ways in the context of illegitimacy); but seems to have enjoyed much more opportunity as well in terms of residential proximity. Therefore we include the Blue Hill Jeremiah here, with our usual flagging of a questionable link by italicization as a *caveat emptor*.

A possible child by Lucy Emmerton:

+ **910**    i. *Jeremiah*[7] Eaton, b. 2 Mar 1784; mar. Martha Friend, 1805.


**341. Ebenezer**[6] **Fellows Eaton** (Theophilus[5], Jonathan[4], John[3-1]) was born 22 Aug 1756 in the new Sandown parish carved from Kingston, N.H., and removed as a small boy with his family to Maine. He married **Abigail Herrick**, a native of Scituate, Mass., but then residing in Sedgwick, in 1776. He served in Capt. Fales's Co. in the Revolutionary War. He moved his family to a site at Southwest Harbor, Mt. Desert Island, about 1781, where he became the first preacher of the gospel, Congregational version, on the island. According to Noyes (1942), Ebenezer refused to be formally ordained until 1823, since he began as a lay preacher without the education normally expected of that role. After his ordination he continued to serve the church until 1832, and then sporadically for a further period until his death there, 15 Jun 1841.

Children:

+ **911**    i. Amos[7] Eaton, b. 28 Sep 1777 at Sedgwick; mar. 1st, Susanna Herrick, 1799; 2d, widow Betsey Burnham.
  **912**    ii. Mary[7] Eaton, b. 29 Sep 1779; mar Capt. Ebenezer Webster of Portland, Me., 1799.
  **913**    iii. Abigail[7] Eaton, b. 28 Jan 1781; mar. Richard Currier of Sedgwick, 20 Feb 1799.
  **914**    iv. Ebenezer[7] Eaton, b. 8 Feb 1783, prob. at Mt. Desert. He was a sea captain, residence unknown.
  **915**    v. David[7] Eaton, b. 6 Feb 1787, prob. at Mt. Desert. He was a sea captain who died in Europe, unmarried.
  **916**    vi. Joanna[7] Eaton, b. 20 Nov 1791, Mt. Desert; mar., 1st, Charles Norris of Alexandria, Me.; 2d, Capt. Thomas Bunker of Cranberry Isle, Me., 24 Oct 1832.
  **917**    vii. Joshua[7] Eaton, b. 20 Sep 1795, Mt. Desert; mar. Esther Moore, but died without issue.
  **918**    viii. Clarissa[7] Eaton, b. 29 May 1798, Mt. Desert; mar. Allen Hopkins, a teacher of Ellsworth, Me.

**344. (Deac.) James**[6A] **Eaton** (Theophilus[5], Jonathan[4], John[3-1]), was born 27 Jan 1769 at Deer Isle, Me; mar. **Hannah Jordan**, daughter of James Jordan of Jordan's Island, 28 Jan 1793 at Deer Isle. This couple settled first on a 100-acre grant of land with house and barn from father Theophilus on the shores of Deer Isle's Northwest Harbor near the family homestead; but in 1813 they sold that homestead to Jonathan Haskell and removed to that part of Prospect, Me. that would in 1845 become incorporated as Searsport, where they spent the rest of their lives. It was there that James received his mother in her waning years. He himself died 13 Mar 1825.

Children, all born at Northwest Harbor, Deer Isle:

**919**   i. Judith[7] Eaton, b. 17 Nov 1793; mar. a Mr. Houston and died 1840 in East Belfast, Me.
**920**   ii. Calvin[7] Eaton, b. 1794; died young.
**921**   iii. Mary[7] Campbell Eaton, b. 30 Oct 1796.
**922**   iv. Thomas[7] Eaton, b. 9 Oct 1798; no issue.
+ **923**   v. James[7] Eaton, b. 26 Jun 1800; mar. Elizabeth Nolan, 1839.
**924**   vi. Amos[7] Eaton, b. 30 Jun 1802; no issue.
**925**   vii. Calvin[7A] Eaton, b. 18 Feb 1804; no issue.
**926**  viii. Sylvanus[7] Eaton, b. 17 Jul 1807; died unmar. at some time after the Aroostook War, Prospect, Me.
**927**   ix. Herbert/Hubbard[7] Eaton, b. ca. 29 Sep 1810; no issue.
**928**   x. Pearl[7] Eaton, a son, b. 1 Mar 1813. The unusual given name clearly stems from a Pearl Spofford, a business associate of father James. This is obviously not, however, the Pearl Eaton who surfaces in the 1830 Census in Onondaga Co., New York, and who is of the line of John of Dedham.

**351. Joseph**[6] **H. Eaton** (Ezekiel[5], Jonathan[4], John[3-1]) was born 17 Aug 1757 at Sandown, N.H.; mar. **Elizabeth George** 13 Dec 1781 (Haverhill, Mass. *VR*). He had been a soldier in the Revolution, enlisting from Sandown. Before 1786 he had removed to the large "Society Land" grant in southwestern N.H. associated with the Proprietors of the Masonian patent, settling in the part of that area which was annexed as the northern part of Greenfield, N.H. This couple was very active in church and charitable affairs, and it is said of them that "they were always first in sickness and trouble; night or day they were always ready and willing to go to the needy." In this wild region where they had ventured, with the roads for many years being no more than paths bounded by marked trees, the young bride of the forest became the mother of twelve in addition to the first child born in Haverhill. And some of these children fully equalled their mother in the number of their offspring. Joseph is listed as a household head in the first five Federal Censuses in Greenfield. Wife Elizabeth died there 16 Sept 1840; and husband Joseph followed on 2 Dec 1844.

Children (all but the first in Greenfield, N.H.):

**929**  i. Polly[7] Eaton, b. 22 Nov 1782, at Haverhill, Mass.; mar. John Rogers. They lived on a farm in the north part of Greenfield. Polly bore 13 children. In the later years she moved into the village, where she died 5 Sept 1858.

+ **930**  ii. John[7] George Eaton, b. 1786; mar. Polly Favor ca. 1809.

**931**  iii. Sally[7] Eaton, b. 1789; mar. Samuel White, a farmer. She died in Nashua, N.H.

**932**  iv. Ezekiel[7] Eaton, b. 1791; mar. Jane Leonard, 1820. They removed to New York State, where he changed his name to Ezekiel George. He died in 1865; she in 1883.

**933**  v. Lydia[7] Eaton, b. 1793?; mar. 1st, William George, 30 Dec 1816; 2d, Adams Flint; and 3d, Joel Brown. They resided in Greenfield. She never had children; died 2 Apr 1876.

+ **934**  vi. Nathaniel[7] A. Eaton, b. 1795?; mar. Eunice Pollard, ca. 1818.

+ **935**  vii. Robert[7] Wise Eaton, b. 21 Aug 1796; mar. Helen Campbell.

**936**  viii. Betsey[7] Eaton, b. 1798; died in childhood.

**937**  ix. Sophronia[7] Eaton, b. 28 Feb 1800; mar. William Burdick and resided in Boston. She had nine children, and returned to Greenfield village for the last years of her life. She died there 9 Aug 1866.

**938**  x. Apphia[7] Eaton, b. 28 Feb 1802; mar. George Barnes, a painter; they had seven children. She died 24 Apr 1867 at New Buffalo, Mich.; he died 2 Nov 1874.

**939**  xi. Nancy[7] Jane Eaton, b. 1805; mar. William Bradford Dickey of Francestown, N.H.; resided Bennington, N.H., having 13 children there; she died 11 Aug 1882 in Bennington, but is buried in Greenfield village.

**940**  xii. Julietta[7] Eaton, b. 1807; mar. 1st, John Monahan; 2d, James Quimby. She lived on the old homestead and had seven children. She died, 28 May 1883.

**941**  xiii. Betsey[7A] E. Eaton, b. 1809; mar. Lewis Martin of Francestown, N. H.; res. Bennington, N.H., and had seven children. Husband Lewis died 6 Aug 1882; she died 14 Dec 1884.

**353. James[6] Eaton** (Ezekiel[5], Jonathan[4], John[3-1]) was born in Sandown, N.H., ca. 1761. He was a soldier in the Revolution. He mar. 1st, **Jemima George**, ca. 1778. She died 27 Oct 1803. He then mar. 2d, **Hannah Harvey.** James was a farmer in Sandown, appearing in the first five Federal Censuses there. He died 12 Dec 1834 (Sandown *VR* at Concord, N.H.). Hannah later moved to Manchester to be with her stepson James.

Children with Jemima at Sandown:

+ **942**  i. Joshua[7] Eaton, b. 22 Dec 1779; mar. Polly Edmunds, 1799.

**943**  ii. James[7] Eaton, b. 1781. Was later in Manchester, N.H.

**944**   iii. Sarah[7] "Sally" Eaton, b. 1783. mar. Joel Page and resided on
             farm in Sandown. They had no issue.


**356. Joseph[6] Eaton** (Joseph[5], Jonathan[4], John[3-1]) was born Sep
1772 in Newbury "old town," Mass., but was bereaved of his father when
quite young.   The widow of a common sailor could not give children
much of an education in the schools, but would at least seek to provide a
good home.   She farmed young Joseph out to a foster home in Beverly,
Mass.   In due time he was able to acquire an "express team" of horses
which he could use to make a comfortable livelihood.   Hence as recorded
in the *Town Records*, he married **Sally Mack**, also of Beverly, b. ca.
1768, on 28 Oct 1798.   Since Sally's father was a ship builder, further
resources were undoubtedly available to the young couple.   Joseph continued in the express business until 1812 when he moved his family to
Wolfeborough, N.H., where he spent the rest of his days on a farm.   His
wife died there, 14 Sep 1855; and he followed on 19 Jan 1861.

       Children, all born in Beverly, Mass.:

**945**    i. Sally[7] Eaton, b. 12 May 1801; mar. Obadiah Stoddard (he b.
             in Brookfield, N.H., 9 Aug 1799) on 15 Nov 1824.   They
             settled on a farm in Wolfeborough, N.H. and had eight
             children.
**946**   ii. Joseph[7] Eaton, b. 24 Dec 1802; mar. Margaret Chandler,
             9 May 1833.   They had no children; he died 17 Nov
             1883 at Wolfeborough, N.H.
+ **947**  iii. Richard[7] Eaton, b. 9 Apr 1804; mar. Lydia Ann Wheeler.
+ **948**  iv. Chandler[7] Eaton, b. 14 Nov 1805; mar. Mary J. Cottle.
  **949**   v. Lydia[7] Cobbett Eaton, b. 17 Feb 1808; mar. Richard H.
             Horne (b. Wolfeborough, 16 Oct 1800) on 10 Mar 1829.
             They settled on a farm in neighboring Tuftonborough,
             N.H., where they had four sons and one daughter.   Hus-
             band Richard died Jul 1887 at Tuftonborough.


**357. Joseph[6] Eaton** (Jonathan[5-4], John[3-1]) had the distinction of
being the first white child born on Deer Isle, Me., when he arrived in the
world 17 Nov 1767 at the Northwest Harbor.   His wife-to-be, **Martha
"Patty" Morgan** had been born in Manchester, Mass., 5 Sep 1776.   They
were joined in marriage 12 Sep 1804, and removed across the Reach to a
farm in that part of Sedgwick later called Sargentville.   They enjoyed a
large tract of land stretching from Sargentville to the shores of Walker's
Pond.   Wife Patty died 29 Sep 1825 and Joseph followed her on 8 Sep
1827, leaving eight children with ages from six to 22 years old.   All of
these children lived on the homestead until they were married; and after
marriage, all lived on the same road on which they had been born, within
a span of three miles.   All were members of the same Baptist church in

Sedgwick, and they divided and settled their father's estate by mutual agreement.

Children at Sedgwick:

+ **950**    i. Joseph[7] Eaton, b. 26 Aug 1805; mar. Hannah Roberts, 1837.
  **951**   ii. Lois[7] (or Louise) Eaton, b. 3 Mar 1807; mar. Nathan Parker of Blue Hill in Nov 1855, and resided on a farm in Sedgwick.
  **952**  iii. Betsey[7] Eaton, b. 25 Oct 1808; mar. 1st, Hezekiah Dodge, a master mariner, ca. 27 Nov 1832. He died at sea in Dec 1844, and Betsey mar. 2d, Wyer G. Sargent, 20 Oct 1861, her sister's widower. She died 21 Oct 1867, without issue.
+ **953**   iv. Daniel[7] Eaton, b. 30 Jul 1810; mar. Betsey Byard in 1836.
  **954**   v. Martha[7] Eaton, b. 4 Dec 1812; mar. Wyer G. Sargent, 22 Oct 1834. He was a successful merchant, for whom Sargentville was named. He had been b. in Gloucester, Mass., 24 June 1810. His first wife Martha died of consumption, 20 Aug 1860, after bearing three sons and four daughters; and he then mar. her widowed sister Betsey (**#952**), who had taken care of Martha in her illness. When Betsey died from consumption in her turn, he took a third wife, Maria Susan Gower of Providence, R. I., 1 Jun 1868.
+ **955**   vi. John[7] Eaton, b. 31 Jan 1815; mar. Asenath Roberts, 1841.
  **956**  vii. Harriet[7] Eaton, b. 5 Sep 1817; mar. Simeon Grant, Dec 1837. He had been b. in Penobscot, Me., Jul 1810. He was a master mariner. After five sons and four daughters, she died in Sedgwick 23 Dec 1876.
  **957**  viii. Lydia[7] Dodge Eaton, b. 7 Jan 1820; mar. Robert Byard of Sedgwick, 21 Oct 1840. He was a carpenter. They had three sons and two daughters. She died 6 Jun 1876.

**360. Jonathan**[6] **Eaton** (Jonathan[5-4], John[3-1]) was born 24 Mar 1774 at the Northwest Harbor in Deer Isle, Me. He mar. **Esther Torrey**, daughter of Jonathan Torrey, and they spent their lives on Deer Isle. Jonathan died 12 Oct 1863 at age 89; his widow Esther lived almost as long, although she suffered dementia for many years prior to her death on 16 Sep 1867.

Children (all born at Deer Isle):

  **958**   i. Diana[7] Eaton, b. 3 Jun 1801; mar. Mark Carr, a gardener of Roxbury, Mass., 4 May 1830 at Boston. They had one child before Diana died at Roxbury, 23 Oct 1835.
  **959**   ii. Daniel[7] Torrey Eaton, b. 31 Dec 1802; died 4 Nov 1822.
  **960**  iii. Levi[7] Eaton, b. ca. 1806; died in the winter of 1830 in the West Indies.
  **961**   iv. Lovina[7] Eaton, b. 4 Jan 1808 or '09; mar. Samuel Saunders,

Jr., 1 Aug 1853, in Belfast, Me. He was a farmer. Given
their advanced age at marriage, they had no children.

**962**　　v. Eliza[7] Webster Eaton, b. 29 Jan 1812; mar. 1st, Barnard
Lynch, a currier of Roxbury, Mass., 15 Apr 1850, at Roxbury. He died of consumption, 8 Jun 1865, at their home
in Roxbury. She mar. 2d, a mechanic named John Bowdeleau, 11 Oct 1868 at Jamaica Plains, Mass. He died 18
Feb 1881. Eliza returned to Deer Isle after her second
husband's death. She died 12 Feb 1897.

**963**　　vi. Joseph[7] Eaton, b. 29 June 1814; he died at sea, 7 Feb 1835.

**964**　　vii. Hephzibah[7] Haskell Eaton, b. 23 Feb 1817; mar. Enos Williams Dean, a mechanic, 27 Sep 1837, at Roxbury, Mass.
They kept a boarding house at Dedham, Mass., and
became well-to-do.

**965**　　viii. Salome[7] Eaton, b. 10 Dec 1820; mar. Abram S. Parker on
31 Dec 1844 at Roxbury, Mass., and lived on Tremont
Street. He died 2 Nov 1871.

**+ 966**　　ix. Daniel[7A] Torrey Eaton, b. 21 May 1823; mar. Mary Ann
Thompson, 1852.

**361. John[6] Eaton** (Jonathan[5-4], John[3-1]) was born at the Northwest
Harbor in Deer Isle, Me., 25 Mar 1776; he mar. **Polly Webb**, daughter
of Deer Isle pioneer Seth Webb, 23 Mar 1797, and resided in Deer Isle.
Hosmer (1905, p. 86) reports that John was drowned in 1814 while engaged with two other men in taking a cow across the bay to Vinalhaven
in a boat. Their bodies were never found, but the body of the cow
drifted ashore at Seller's Point. Wife Mary died 15 Feb 1861.

Children (all born Deer Isle):

**+ 967**　　i. Jonathan[7] Eaton, b. 11 Jul 1797; mar. Edna Jordan, 1826.

**968**　　ii. Betty[7] Eaton, b. 1799; died of whooping cough, Feb 1803.

**969**　　iii. Hannah[7] W. Eaton, b. 16 Nov 1801; mar. Moses[8] Eaton
(**#2211**, q.v.). She died 9 Feb 1882.

**970**　　iv. Betsey[7] Eaton, b. 10 Feb 1803; mar. Solon Hagar; she died
27 Aug 1854.

**971**　　v. Olivia[7] P. Eaton, b. 12 Feb 1805; mar. 1st, a Perkins; mar.
2d, a Russell; she died 21 Dec 1851.

**972**　　vi. Sally[7] Eaton, b. 10 (16?) Feb 1808; mar. John K. Fletcher
of Boston. They had one son who died as a young man.

**973**　　vii. Martha[7] "Patty" Eaton, b. 29 Nov 1810; called "queer" and
never married although she worked for a time in Boston.
She raised a girl, Lizzie, who mar. Peter Anderson, Jr.

**974**　　viii. David[7] J. Eaton, b. 1 Feb 1812. He was a sailor who never
married, and who was living with his widowed mother in
the 1850 Census. In 1860 he was an inmate at an institution, insane and a pauper.

**975**　　ix. Mary[7] Eaton, b. 18 Jul 1813; mar. William Lowe, 15 Feb

1835.

**363. Nathan**[6] **Eaton** (Jonathan[5-4], John[3-1]) was born 17 Mar 1781 at the Northwest Harbor in Deer Isle, Me. He mar. **Dorothy "Dolly" Pressey**, daughter of Chase and Sarah (Howard) Pressey of Deer Isle, 12 Aug 1806. He succeeded his father in ownership and occupancy of the family homestead at Northwest Harbor. Nathan was a very smart and industrious man, and over his lifetime extended the property by a substantial number of acres. The house itself was still standing a century later, one of the earliest frame houses on the island. Nathan died 8 Feb 1859; and wife Dorothy died 4 May 1865.

Children (all born at Deer Isle):

976    i. Maria[7] Eaton, b. 1807; mar. Ebenezer Jordan, Jr., of Deer Isle, son of Ebenezer/Olive (Sellers) Jordan, int. 24 Apr 1830. They raised eight children at Deer Isle.

977    ii. Eli[7] Eaton, b. 27 Jul 1808; a bachelor who lived much of his life with his sister Hannah. He was self-employed doing various forms of stonework, making underpinnings, digging wells and the like. He built a cabin on Isle au Haut, and was the first to erect a real bridge across to Oceanville. He died 27 Jan 1862.

+ 978    iii. Charles[7] Eaton, b. 19 Mar 1810; mar. Rebecca Doane, 1839.

979    iv. Drusilla[7] Eaton, b. 9 Mar 1813; mar. Sullivan Green, 23 Nov 1834. She bore him a son and three daughters before she died. He mar. 2d, Mrs. Elizabeth Stinson, in 1846.

+ 980    v. Eliphalet[7] C. Eaton, b. 21 Mar 1816; mar. Sally J. Doane.

+ 981    vi. Frederick[7] Eaton, b. 24 Apr 1818; mar. Barbara Haskell.

+ 982    vii. Davis[7] H. Eaton, a twin b. 26 Jun 1820; mar. Susan Greenlaw.

983    viii. Sarah[7] Eaton, also b. 26 Jun 1820; mar. Capt. Lemuel Whittemore, also of Deer Isle, 13 Aug 1853 as his second wife, and added three children to the three he already had.

984    ix. Dorothy[7] Eaton, b. 8 Feb 1823; never married; she worked in Boston for a time, returning "to keep the home together."

985    x. Hannah[7] W. Eaton, b. 12 Feb 1825; mar. Hezekiah Lufkin, son of Hezekiah & Mehitable (Saunders) Lufkin, 23 Mar 1848. She was a remarkable woman and was held in great esteem. They had no children. Hezekiah died in Sunset, 4 Jul 1903 of apoplexy. Hannah died 20 Dec 1919.

986    xi. Eliza[7] Eaton, b. 21 Dec 1828; mar. David Trundy of Rockland Me., son of John/Hannah (Small) Trundy, int. 18 Jul 1853. He went to New York City as a sailmaker, but Eliza left him after 15 years there and returned to spend the rest of her life at Sunset. They had no children. She died 11 Mar 1816.

987    xii. Ebenezer[7] Jordan, b. 25 Sep 1830; he lived unmar. on the family homestead and was called "Professor." He owned a

substantial amount of property, and bought a lot of stock in the silver mine at Dunham's which turned into quite a loss.  He died of cancer.


**364. James[6] Eaton** (Jonathan[5-4], John[3-1]) was born 15 Mar 1784 at the Northwest Harbor in Deer Isle, Me.    He mar. **Elizabeth "Betsey" Howard**, also of Deer Isle, in 1808.   It is said that this James[6] followed the example of his first cousin James[6] (see **#344**), son of Theophilus[5], who removed to the Prospect section of what later became Searsport.   We have not found his death record, although he appears in successive Federal Censuses at Prospect, 1820-40, and then after its incorporation in Searsport in 1845, he reported an age of 65 in 1850 Searsport, where he lived in the home of his son Hiram, apparently next door to the home of another son Otis.  Wife Betsey had probably died.   Their children seem only partially registered as well, with three known by name and two others likely from family compositions in the Census.

Children (may be partial):

988    i. Irene[7] Eaton, b. 11 May 1810, probably at Deer Isle.
989    ii. (Daughter, prob. b. 1811)
+ 990    iii. Otis[7] Eaton, b. ca. 1813; prob. mar. 1st, Olive S., ca. 1840.
+ 991    iv. Hiram[7] Eaton, b. 25 Dec 1814; mar. Nancy Staples, ca. 1843.
992    v. (Daughter, b. 1816-19)


**366. Daniel[6] Eaton** (Daniel[5-4A], John[3-1]) was born about 1771 in Salisbury, Mass.  As a toddler he removed with his family to Pittsfield, N.H., and grew up there.   He was a "husbandman" at Pittsfield when he bought up his father's homestead in 1797.  In this period he mar. **Sarah ___?___** , although he may have had a second wife **Polly __?__** at an early date, since her name appears as mother of his children. Daniel removed his family first to Gilmanton, but sold out there in Oct 1800 and went on to a new settlement at "Goshen" (now Vienna), Me., buying land there in Jan 1801.  Daniel had a religious conversion soon thereafter and became one of the first Free-will Baptists in Vienna.   Initially, this meant some travel to the church in Starks, but he was central in the creation of the church in Vienna and was for many years a deacon thereof.  After his death at Vienna 16 Feb 1848, an effusive but not entirely informative obituary in the Free-Will Baptist *Morning Star* notes that "his house was the home of the pilgrim, and many of our aged ministers remember with interest, the kind reception they met at his house."   Only two of his children survived him, and he had deeded half of his real estate to his eldest daughter, Mrs. Sophronia Dow in 1842.

Children (reconstructed from the Kennebec Co. IGI):

**993**   i. Sophronia$^7$ Eaton, b. 10 Dec 1799; mar. Daniel Dow, 10 Jan 1819.
**994**   ii. Daniel$^7$ Eaton, b. 8 Feb 1802.
**995**   iii. Polly$^7$ Eaton, b. 13 Sep 1806.
**996**   iv. Lovina$^7$ A. Eaton, b 29 Aug 1809; mar. Jonathan Marden, 26 Jan 1828.
**997**   v. Gideon$^7$ W. Eaton, b. 14 Aug 1812.


**367. Joshua$^6$ Eaton** (Daniel$^{5\text{-}4A}$, John$^{3\text{-}1}$) born 23 Feb 1772 in Salisbury, Mass.; mar. **Hannah Chase** of Pittsfield, N.H., 13 Nov 1794. (She had been b. 14 Apr 1770.) It appears that this couple very shortly removed to the northern part of the Gilmanton, N.H., grant, an area which by 1812 would be set off as Gilford Township.   The Census schedules for 1800 are lost, but in Nov 1804 Joshua, identified as a "Gilford yeoman," bought a 25-acre part of Lot #9, Range 1, in the Masonian lands in Gilford, from his distant cousin Joseph$^7$ Eaton (**#832**), with whom he had grown up in Pittsfield. He increased his farm size progressively in the next two decades, extending into Lot #10.   In 1826, however, Joshua$^6$ sold out his now 75-acre farm homestead in Gilford, and removed to a 100-acre farm purchased in Sandwich, N.H., where his father had already lived for a decade after emigrating from Pittsfield. He is in the Censuses from 1830 to 1850 in Sandwich, residing in the latter one in the home of his daughter, Mrs. Clarissa (Eaton) Mudgett, whose husband had bought land from Joshua in 1835.   Wife Hannah had died there 19 Aug 1849; and Joshua himself died 17 Dec 1858.

Children (all born in proto-Gilford, N.H.):

+ **998**   i. Jonathan$^7$ W. Eaton, b. 11 Dec 1795; m. Judith Straw, 1832.
  **999**   ii. Mary$^7$ Eaton, b. 28 Jan 1798; died 13 May 1881.
  **1000**  iii. Hannah$^7$ Eaton, b. 20 Feb 1801.
  **1001**  iv. Rhoda$^7$ Eaton, b. 18 Mar 1804; died 16 Oct 1813.
  **1002**  v. Clarissa$^7$ Eaton, b. 6 May 1806; mar. Moses Mudgett of Sandwich and raised a family with him.
  **1003**  vi. Sally$^7$ Eaton, b. 7 Jan 1809.


**370. Tristram$^6$ Eaton** (James$^5$, Daniel$^{4A}$, John$^{3\text{-}1}$) was born 26 Dec 1780 at Salisbury, Mass., and grew up on the original Beach Road Eaton homestead farm which his father then owned and operated.  He married **Jemima Brown** of Seabrook, 22 Oct 1801, and the couple resided in Salisbury.  In his early years Tristram did some small subsistence farming, but was principally a mariner, presumably in the coastal fishing fleet, so most of his ploughing was done on the sea, and the fruit of his labor was in the fishes thereof. However, that kind of sailing below the officer level was a young man's labor, and like most of his sailing mates, by the time that he was beyond middle age he farmed more than he sailed. He was on the Salisbury tax list for 23 consecutive years, 1802-24, and then, after a hiatus of six years, appeared again, 1831-36. This period of absence may be associated with the fact that in Oct 1825, seven weeks after his father's death, Tristram sold out all of his rights as an heir to his father's estate. Whether he went on a longer voyage or used the money to try a living somewhere else is not known. In any event, Tristram was routinely at the bottom of the tax valuation ladder among the Eaton males of Salisbury in both time spells. He appears on the Census lists for Salisbury in all six of the first Censuses, and died of palsy (usually, a loss of power to feel or control movement) 3 Aug 1845 in Salisbury.

Children (all born in Salisbury, Mass.):

**1004**  i. Jemima[7] Eaton, b. ca. 1805; mar. Henry[7] Eaton (**#1181**) of Salisbury, 17 Aug 1829. They spent a brief period in Corinth, Vt. but returned to reside in Salisbury. Widow Jemima died 4 Aug 1869 in Salisbury.

**1005**  ii. Ruth[7] Eaton, b. ca. 1808; mar. Ezra M. Jackman and had three children. She died 21 Jun 1872.

**1006**  iii. Jeremiah[7] Eaton, b. ca. 1811; died 16 Jan 1819.

**1007**  iv. Jeremiah[7A] B. Eaton, b. 22 Jan 1820; died 27 Aug 1821.

**1008**  v. Daniel[7] Eaton, b. 12 Aug 1823; died young.

**1009**  vi. John[7] A. Eaton, b. 25 Oct 1825; a cordwainer residing in Salisbury who never married; died 7 Dec 1880.

**371. Benjamin[6] Eaton** (James[5], Daniel[4A], John[3-1]) was born 6 Apr 1784 in Salisbury, Mass.; mar. **Elizabeth "Betsey" French** of Salisbury, 11 Apr 1805. Like his brother, he may have been a mariner for much of his life, as he only appears to have accumulated real estate later in life. He was, however, visibly more prosperous than his brother Tristram, climbing out of the bottom level of tax valuations about the time of his father's death in 1825, and continuing to a position where his household was about the median for Eaton males of Salisbury by the time he was fifty years old. He was on the tax lists annually from 1806 to the end of our available record in 1847. A widower in his last years, he resided with his son William, and died 12 Mar 1871.

Children in Salisbury, Mass.:

**1010**  i. Hannah[7] Eaton, b. 18 May 1806; mar. 1st, Joseph Moody of Salisbury and bore him four sons; mar. 2d, Elias Felch of Seabrook, with no issue. She died 27 Jul 1879, Salisbury.

**1011**  ii. Jane[7] Eaton, b. 28 Sep 1808; died 15 Jan 1819, Salisbury.

**1012**  iii. Mary[7] Eaton, b. 27 Aug 1810; mar. True Pike of Salisbury, 27 Dec 1836 and had one son and one daughter.

**1013**  iv. Ruth[7] French Eaton, b. 10 May 1813; died young.

**+1014**  v. William[7] Eaton, b 30 Oct 1815; m. Rhoda[8] Eaton (**#1982**).

**1015**  vi. Ruth[7A] French Eaton, b. 25 Sep 1818; mar. William M. Morrill of Salisbury, a farmer, and had two children.

She died 1889 in Salisbury.

**1016** vii. Betsey[7] Eaton, b. 9 Jul 1822; died 1 Sep 1822.

**+1017** viii. Benjamin[7] Eaton, b. 6 Sep 1823; mar. 1st, Margaret[8] Eaton (**#1985**), daughter of Wyman[7] of Seabrook, 1847; 2d, Sarah A. Baker, 1863.


**377. James[6], Jr., Eaton** (James[5], Daniel[4A], John[3-1]) was born 22 May 1799 in Salisbury, Mass., growing up on the original Beach Road Eaton homestead as his father's next-to-last child. He married **Hannah Greeley** of Salisbury, 11 Oct 1821, and it is likely that they settled initially on some part of the homestead acreage. Less than four years later, father James[5], Sr., died, and judging by changes in tax valuations in the next few years, the two youngest sons (see also **#378** below)--their two much older brothers Tristram[6] and James[6] were long since up and out--shared equally in the estate and thus became reasonably prosperous, although it appears that the James[6] of this notice actually inherited the homestead dwelling. James and Hannah had eight daughters and no sons. Only one daughter died in infancy, with the other seven all marrying and having their own families. Father James[6] died of consumption intestate 22 May 1874. His wife Hannah died 17 Sep 1883. The seven sisters then co-owned the homestead essentially for the rest of the 19th century (see Sidebar # 13 on the history of this homestead).

Children born in Salisbury, Mass.:

**1018** i. Ruth[7] Pike Eaton, b. 21 Feb 1823; mar. David Beckman of Seabrook on 19 Oct 1846, having one son and one daughter on their farm in Seabrook. David died 21 May 1891. She died 3 Feb 1905.

**1019** ii. Sarah[7] Elizabeth Eaton, b. 28 Oct 1825; mar. David Boyd of Seabrook, 8 Nov 1850, having two sons and two daughters on their farm in Seabrook. She died 10 Jan 1904.

**1020** iii. Hannah[7] Adaline Eaton, b. 8 Feb 1829; mar. William H. Noyes, a miller of Seabrook, 4 Jan 1860. They lived in Seabrook and had two daughters. Hannah died 21 Nov 1915 in Seabrook.

**1021** iv. Abby[7] March Eaton, b. 1 Nov 1831; mar. Charles[7] Eaton (see **#1224**) of Seabrook, 22 Oct 1850. They lived on a farm in Seabrook, with children as listed under Charles[7]. Abby died 23 Jan 1893, Newburyport, Mass.

**1022** v. Mary[7] Jane Eaton, b. 24 Apr 1835; died 22 Feb 1836.

**1023** vi. Mary[7A] Jane Eaton, b. 8 Feb 1837; mar. John G. Lake of Haverhill, a shoe cutter. They resided both in Haverhill and in Salisbury at the ancestral homestead. One son.

**1024** vii. Laura[7] Angeline Eaton, b. 22 Jul 1840; mar. James E. Tilton of Epping, N.H., shoe maker, on 4 May 1859. They had two sons and two daughters. Laura died in 1929.

**1025**  viii. Ellen[7] Frances Eaton, b. 12 Feb 1844; mar. George A. Dow of Salisbury 16 Oct 1866. They lived on a farm in Salisbury, and had two daughters and one son. She died 26 May 1906, Salisbury.

**378. Jonathan[6] Eaton** (James[5], Daniel[4A], John[3-1]) was born 16 Jun 1801 at Salisbury, Mass., the youngest son of James[5], who therefore also grew up on the old ancestral Eaton homestead on Beach Road. He mar. **Betsey Morrill** of Salisbury, 19 Nov 1822. It is likely that they lived in another dwelling unit on the homestead acres. When father James died in August, 1825, after the two much older sons were up and out, Jonathan[6] apparently co-owned the rest of the estate with brother James[6] (**#377**), for their separate tax valuations rose rapidly and in near-perfect lockstep in the ensuing years as the estate was settled, without any corresponding increase in the fortunes of the older brothers who were sailors. Jonathan[6] died in Salisbury, 17 Oct 1873. Wife Betsey lived on for some years, dying 25 Feb 1886 when over 90 years of age.

Children (born Salisbury, Mass.):

+**1026**  i. John[7] French Eaton, b. 3 Aug 1824; mar. Chastina Deal.
  **1027**  ii. Miriam[7] Eaton, b. 28 Jun 1833; mar. James P. Palmer in 1856 and settled in Derry, N.H., having two sons and two daughters.

**383. John[6] Eaton** (Joseph[5A], John[4A], Joseph[3], John[2-1]) was born 13 May 1746 at Salisbury, Mass., and baptized at Newbury, Mass. He was a babe in arms when his family removed to Hawke (later Danville), N.H. A few things are known about his migration history, but otherwise we have only plausible guesses as to where his record fits. He settled briefly as a young man in neighboring Hampstead, N.H. It is probably he who mar. **Mary Sawyer** there, 2 Oct 1772, and left a few traces of likely children. But after twenty years or so he removed to Maine, where the trail is lost except as he may be the John Eaton listed at Durham, Cumberland Co., Me. in the Census of 1800.

Likely children at Hampstead (undoubtedly partial):

  **1028**  i. Sarah[7] Eaton, b. 1780; a "daughter of John Eaton" who died at Hampstead, 11 Nov 1791, ae 11.
  **1029**  ii. A child of John Eaton d. young at Hampstead, 2 Sep 1787.

**385. Jabez[6] Eaton** (Joseph[5A], John[4A], Joseph[3], John[2-1]) was born in Hawke (now Danville), N.H., on 22 Feb 1752. He mar. **Susanna Colcord** 1 Jun 1792 and lived on a farm in Danville. His farm was small at first, but he purchased more and more real estate as time went on, until in

1827 he sold most of his land to his children Samuel and Susan, presumably in anticipation of death at age 75. He did not die, however, untill Jul 1837, age 85. Wife Susan had died 31 Oct 1823.

Children at Danville:

1030    i. Jane[7] Eaton, b. 24 May 1793; mar. Phineas French. She
           died young, 1 May 1826.
1031    ii. Samuel[7] Eaton, b. 30 Dec 1796; mar. Mary Eastman, 16 Jan
           1841 in Danville. He died 26 Nov 1871, leaving a will
           which mentions no other relative save his wife. His
           widow, Mary, died 8 Aug 1872, age 70.
1032   iii. Susan[7] Eaton, b. 19 Jul 1799; a single woman in 1827.


**388. Joseph[6] True Eaton** (Joseph[5A], John[4A], Joseph[3], John[2-1]) was
born 3 Apr 1758 in Hawke (now Danville), N.H. **Mehitable Eastman**,
daughter of Edward/Sarah Eastman, was also born at Hawke 30 Mar
1767. This couple was joined in marriage 29 May 1791. They lived on
a farm in Danville some 15 years where six of their children were born.
On 6 Mar 1806 they sold the farm and removed to Washington Co., Vt.,
where two or three of their last children were born, two of them before
maturity. Joseph was in that county by Mar 1807, when he sold a three-
quarter acre tract of salt marsh back in Seabrook. He seems to have been
missed in the 1810 Census but in 1820 he was at Vershire near Corinth in
Orange Co., Vt., and by 1830 he was back in Washington Co. at
Marshfield. He applied for a Revolutionary War pension from
Marshfield in 1832, was still a household head there in 1840, and died
there 23 Nov 1845.

Children (the first six born Danville, the last three in Vermont):

1033     i. Sarah[7] E. "Sally" Eaton, b. 5 Apr 1792; died unmarried in
            East Corinth, Vt., 8 May 1855.
+1034    ii. Moses[7] Eaton, b. 1794; mar. Mercy Norris of Corinth, 1815.
1035    iii. Jane[7] Eaton, b. Sep 1796; mar. Robert Sleeper 20 Aug 1816
            and had one son. Jane died in Corinth, Vt., 5 Jun 1826.
1036    iv. Betsey[7] Eaton, b. 1799; mar. Nathan Capron 5 May 1839;
            had one daughter who died young. Betsey died in
            Williamstown, Vt., 17 Oct 1883.
+1037    v. Joseph[7] Eaton, b. 1 Sep 1801; mar. Judith Gove, 1830.
1038    vi. Edward[7] Eaton, b. 1805; died unmar. in Marshfield, Vt., on
            30 Oct 1834.
+1039   vii. True[7] Eaton, b. 16 Nov 1806; mar. Abigail Cummings, 1835.
1040   viii. Child[7] Eaton, died young.
1041    ix. Child[7] Eaton, died young.

**390. Samuel⁶ Eaton** (Daniel⁵, Samuel⁴, Joseph³, John²⁻¹), was born probably in Brunswick, Me., about 1755; mar. **Dorothy "Dolly" Danforth**, 27 Sep 1780.  Neither his residence, nor his employment, nor the birth dates of his children could be supplied by the senior author's original informant, Martin Eaton of Durham, Me.  He did provide the names of five children, about whom we have been able to expand information in some degree.

Children:

+ **1042**   i. Samuel⁷ Eaton, b. ca. 1781; mar. Nancy Nason, 1805.
  **1043**   ii. Dorcas⁷ Eaton, b. ca. 1783; mar. Nathaniel Nason, 5 Nov 1810 at Brunswick.
  **1044**   iii. Enoch⁷ Eaton, b. ca. 1786.  He was unmar. when killed.
+ **1045**   iv. Abner⁷ Eaton, b. ca. 1788; mar. Hannah Douglass, 1815.
  **1046**   v. Sally⁷ Eaton, b. ca. 1795; mar. Samuel Gordon of Biddeford, Me. (he b. 1797); she died 1830, and he in 1857.


**392. Daniel⁶ Eaton** (Daniel⁵, Samuel⁴, Joseph³, John²⁻¹), was born probably in Brunswick, Me., about 1760; mar. **Annie Millet** (or **Mallot**), 5 May 1789.  Daniel is listed as a household head in the first four Censuses in Brunswick (1790-1820).  They had eight children, and he died, presumably, in the 1820s.

Children at Brunswick (after the first, dates are by Census-aided calculation):

+ **1047**   i. Daniel⁷ Eaton, b. 25 Oct 1792; mar. Margaret McIntosh.
+ **1048**   ii. John⁷ Eaton, b. ca. 1794; mar. Mary Badger, 1814.
  **1049**   iii. Isaac⁷ M. Eaton, b. ca. 1797; mar. Rosina; res. China, Me.
  **1050**   iv. William⁷ L. Eaton, b. ca. 1800; mar. and res. So. Prospect, Me.
  **1051**   v. Isabell⁷ Eaton, b. ca. 1802; mar. Moses Douglass; both died in Brunswick without isssue.
  **1052**   vi. Margaret⁷ Eaton, b. ca. 1804; marital status unknown; removed to Bangor, Me.
  **1053**   vii. Andrew⁷ Eaton, b. ca. 1806.
  **1054**   viii. Susan⁷ Eaton, b. ca. 1809.


**394. Moses⁶ Eaton** (Daniel⁵, Samuel⁴, Joseph³, John²⁻¹), was born 1763 in Brunswick, Me.; mar. 1st, **Mary Dunlap** of Topsham, 20 Apr 1791, by whom he had seven children.  He dealt in the milling of lumber, and with a colleague Joseph Dunlap had an interest in the Cutting & Noyes mill on the upper falls of the Androscoggin River in Brunswick as of 1801.  He also bought potential mill property at the outlet of Taylor's Pond in Minot/Auburn in 1802, but appears never to have developed the property.  His wife having died about 1805, he mar. 2d, **Mrs. Dorcas**

**Tracy** of Rome, Me., int. 5 Mar 1806. About this time he began to sell some of his property in Brunswick to cover a heavy indebtedness; but in May-June of 1807 he lost a whole series of judgments against him for failure to pay on notes outstanding. At some time after 1810, when he was still in the Brunswick Census, he removed to Rome, Me., where he continued his lumber-milling activities.

Children with Mary, all at Brunswick:

**1055**    i. Jane[7] Eaton, b. ca. 1791.
**1056**   ii. Polly[7] Eaton, b. ca. 1793.
**1057**  iii. Abner[7] Eaton, b. ca. 1795. Still unmar. when drowned.
**1058**   iv. Margaret[7] Eaton, b. 1798; mar. Mark Young of Brunswick.
**1059**    v. Moses[7] Eaton, b. ca. 1800.
**1060**   vi. William[7] Eaton, b. ca. 1802; mar. and res. in Biddeford, Me.
**1061**  vii. Eliza[7] Eaton, b. ca. 1804; mar. Mr. Earl and resided in Litchfield, Me.

Children with Dorcas:

**1062** viii. Dorcas[7] Eaton, b. 15 Dec 1806 in Brunswick; mar. Hartley Boyington and resided in Mercer, Me.
**1063**   ix. Rhoda[7] Eaton, b. 15 Oct 1808 in Brunswick; mar. Joseph Orr and resided in Jay, Me. They had three children. Rhoda died in Jay, Me. on 4 Apr 1843.
**+1064**   x. Asa[7] Eaton, b. 11 Mar 1811 in Brunswick; mar. Esther.
**1065**   xi. Abigail[7] Eaton, b. 6 Dec 1814; mar. William Knight and res. in Skowhegan, Me., having five children there.

**395. John[6] Eaton** (Daniel[5], Samuel[4], Joseph[3], John[2-1]) was born about 1767, probably in Brunswick, Me. He mar. **Jane Grant**, 27 Jan 1789, and resided at Brunswick until his untimely death in a bank, 31 May 1801. Widow Jane would die 3 Jul 1842, aged 74.

Children, all probably at Brunswick:

**1066**    i. Jane[7] Eaton, b. 16 Jan 1790; died 26 Jan 1869, unmarried, at Brunswick.
**1067**   ii. Abigail[7] Eaton, b. 29 Sep 1791; mar. Benjamin French; she died Jul 1868.
**1068**  iii. Lucy[7] Eaton, b. 1793, died in infancy.
**1069**   iv. Sally[7] Eaton, b. 22 Dec 1794; died 3 Apr 1816.
**+1070**    v. Martin[7] Eaton, b. 15 Aug 1796; mar. Phebe Winslow, 1834.
**+1071**   vi. John[7] Eaton, b. 14 Jul 1798; mar. Persis Joy, 1820.
**+1072**  vii. David[7] Eaton, b. 29 May 1800; mar. Lucy Dunlap, 1821.

**Map 6. Deer Isle and Sedgwick, Me.**

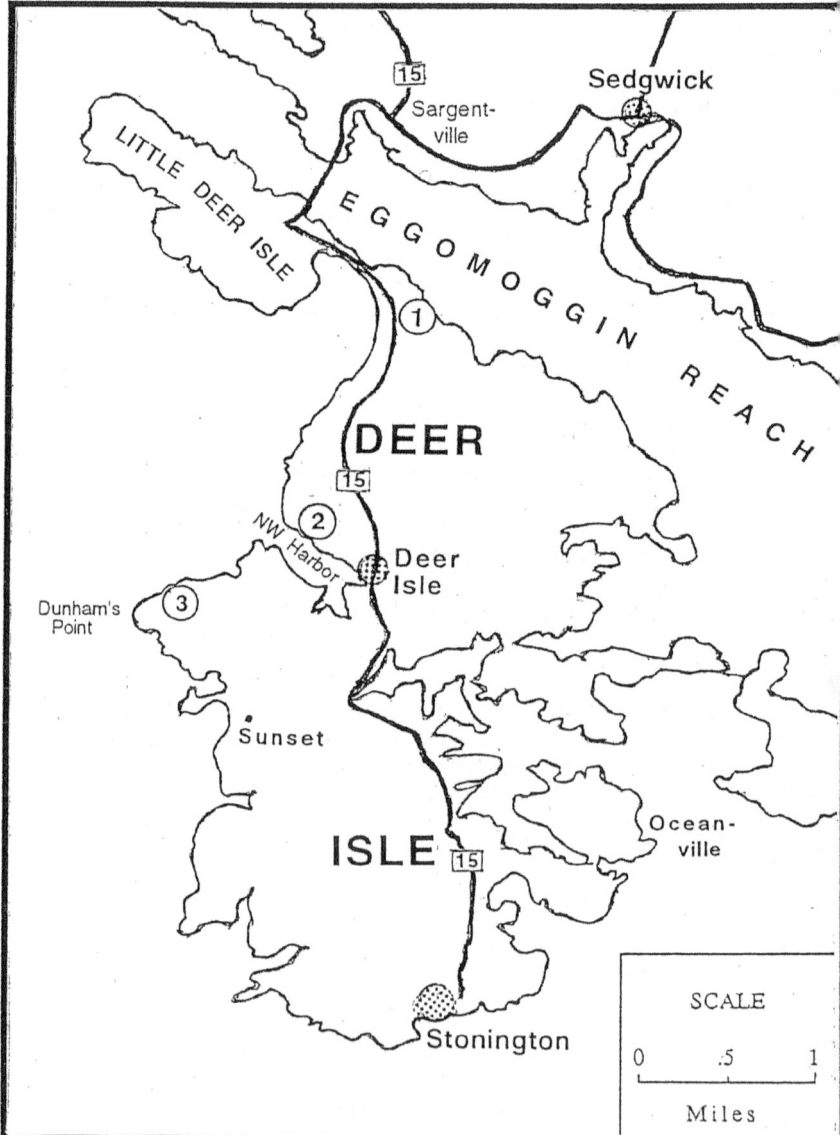

### #7. Eatons in Deer Isle and Sedgwick, Me.

Map 6 on the facing page shows Deer Isle and the surrounding area, including Sedgwick on the mainland facing the Isle, which drew a considerable spillover of our Eatons from the Isle in later years. (The map does not attempt to show the considerable population of smaller islands that surround the two Deer Isles, big and "Little", although some of our Deer Isle Eatons resided on various of them for diverse periods of time.)   The main island is roughly five miles long from the north tip to the southern "toe."   State route 15 (shown) runs up the spine of the island from Stonington, crosses to Little Deer Isle over a causeway and thence over a bridge to the mainland.  Map 5 of this volume may help the reader to see how this Deer Isle region fits into the larger New England picture.

As is evident from the map, "Deer Isle" as a locator is somewhat ambiguous.  Most broadly, it encompasses both of the main islands.  More narrowly, it can refer to the small town at the head of Northwest Harbor.  Historically the main Isle has been further partitioned into several post offices, representing such other villages as Sunset and Mountainville.

Toward the northwest of the main Isle there are encircled numbers showing the locations taken up by the main Eaton founders of this large Deer Isle congregation of Eatons.  All three were of Generation V and born in Salisbury, Mass., decades before Seabrook was created, sharing a common grandfather in John[3] Eaton; and two of them were brothers.  In order of arrival:

(1)  William[5] Eaton (John[4-1])(cf. **#88**) came in 1762 as the first permanent settler on the Isle, "squatting" in an excellent location at north tip of the island.

(2)  Theophilus[5] (Jonathan[4], John[3-1])(**#108**) came in 1768 via Sandown, N.H. and Brunswick, Me.  Having had a glimpse of the Northwest Harbor the preceding season, he was glad to settle there.

(3)  Jonathan[5] (Jonathan[4], John[3-1]) (**#120**), then only 23, came with his much older brother, but soon established himself on the north side of Dunham's Point.

The individual notices of these founders add much detail.  But these cousins had problems in common.  To be sure, an enormous bounty of the sea surrounded them (a reason for the choice!), but they needed to farm as well, and they faced a wilderness that took labors of clearing before plowing.  Nonetheless, as they settled in, all three lines burgeoned with children, assuring the growing abundance of Eatons in the area.  William's descendants populated the the Isle's north tip, and spilled over in numbers to Little Deer Isle. The other two lines expanded on the Isle as well, and also produced the strong clusters on the mainland at Sedgwick and Sargentville.

**406. Robert⁶ Eaton** (Jacob⁵⁻⁴, Joseph³, John²⁻¹) was born in Bristol, Me., 16 Feb 1776, but at the age of seven moved with his family inland to Sandy River township (later, Farmington), Me. When young Robert was 15 his father drowned in the mishap recounted under **#161** above, and as eldest son he had to shoulder unusual responsibility in keeping his family afloat. Ten years later the family was stabilized, and he mar. **Rachel Starling**, daughter of Moses, 1 Apr 1800. He had longed to go west to seek his fortune, and in the summer of 1801 he made a scouting trip to Ohio. Prospects in the "Western Reserve" or the northeast corner of Ohio, just beginning to fill with New Englanders, pleased him. His bride dreaded the prospect of a remove to the wilderness, but in the summer of 1802, a caravan made up of six large two-horse wagons carried Robert⁶ and Rachel, his two younger brothers, Isaac aged 22 and Jacob, aged 18, and his sister Hannah, then 30, and her husband, Joshua Perley, westward.

Six weeks later they found themselves admiring large tracts of flat farmland at Deerfield, Portage County, Ohio, and determined to stay. During the course of the winter and spring they found that water supplies there were inadequate, so they moved to Ravenna, the county seat. Life even here was difficult, with provisioning from Pittsburgh erratic, and a surround of pilfering Indians and dangerous wild animals. Sister Hannah sickened and died; brothers Isaac and Jacob, along with the widowed Perley, became disgusted and returned to Maine. Robert and Rachel determined to stick it out, but after seven years even they felt defeated and decided on a trip back to Maine. They were pleased to see friends and relatives, but the place had changed and they no longer felt at home.

After a year in Maine they returned to Ohio with a new plan. Robert, a good mechanic, followed his father's example in Sandy River and erected in fairly rapid succession a saw mill, and grist mill, and a house commodious enough that the county court used one room for their sessions until other quarters could be built. Settlers were flooding in from the East, and they quickly prospered. Soon after the War of 1812 broke out, the British began to encroach on Cleveland, not much more than 30 miles away, and Robert set off to fight. The threat had been overstated, and he soon returned. But as the son of a sea-faring family, he had taken survey of what he could see of Great Lakes navigation. About 1813 he went to Sandusky and commissioned the building of a small schooner for $3,000, which he named *Rachel* for his wife. At first he intended to manage his shipping company on shore. But as his initial hire for captain turned out to be both dishonest and incompetent, he determined to sail the vessel himself. Therefore in 1815 he removed from Ravenna to the Lake Erie shore, first at Fairport. The family fell ill from "lake fever" at that swampy spot, so he moved a mile or two off the shore at Painesville. He had numerous harrowing adventures in winter storms on the Lakes, and after 1819 or so hired other captains for the *Rachel*. In due time he gave up the business entirely, although in its day it had prospered handsomely and had funded an affluent homestead in Painesville.

He retired to farming, and kept an inn as well. He was "hospitable and generous to a fault; was possessed of an inexhaustible fund of anecdote; was an excellent singer...and was frequently called upon to sing at political meetings in 1840, when Harrison was a candidate for the presidency." Such is the description from his daughter, Rachel (Eaton) Ferriss, near the end of an extended 4,500-word biography of her father, from which we have extracted the summary above, and which we strongly recommend to descendants for its wealth of further vignettes about the family (Ferris, 1878). He died of lung congestion in Painesville, 7 Apr 1842, age 64. Wife Rachel survived him by over a decade, living to welcome old Maine friends at her western home. She died aged 74, on 27 Apr 1855, with her daughter Mary at Harpersfield, Ohio.

Children (perhaps incomplete, as these are ones living to survive mother Rachel):

+1073    i. Shepard[7] Starling Eaton, b. 10 Jan 1801, Farmington, Me.
 1074   ii. Mary[7] Eaton, b. ca. 1803, Ravenna, Ohio; mar. Orlando Barrett; resided Harpersfield, Ohio.
 1075  iii. Amanda[7] Eaton, b. ca. 1804, Ravenna, Ohio; mar. Arnold Mason; resided Painesville, Ohio. She died 11 Apr 1886.
 1076   iv. Rachel[7] Eaton, b. 29 Aug 1809, Ravenna, Ohio; mar. E. J. Ferriss; resided Little Mountain, Ohio. She died 14 Jan 1892; bur. at Mentor, Ohio.
 1077    v. Sophia[7] Eaton, b. 1811? Ravenna, Ohio; mar. Jacob D. Truax; resided Unionville, Ohio.
 1078   vi. Elizabeth[7] Eaton, b. 12 May 1814, Ravenna, Ohio; mar. Martin Carroll of Concord, Ohio; had five sons and two daughters, residing in Concord.
 1079  vii. Robert[7] Eaton, b. ca. 1817; mar. Caltha (or Catherine) Whitney, born Connecticut, 14 May 1845. As of 1850 Robert was a surveyor at Concord Twp., Lake Co., Ohio, living with Catherine and a girl Rosetta, age 8. Family lore has it that he later took the family westward to conduct surveying operations in Iowa and Kansas, and indeed we find the couple in the 1880 Census in Burrell, Decatur Co., Iowa. Robert at 63 is still a surveyor, and they are living with Caltha's aging mother and her younger brother, who is engaged in running a sawmill and is the household head.

**408. Isaac[6] Eaton** (Jacob[5-4], Joseph[3], John[2-1]), was born in Bristol, Me., 10 Nov 1780. **Mary Lyon** was born in Readfield, Me., 22 Dec 1787. They were mar. 2 Jun 1808. Isaac had accompanied his brother Robert and brother-in-law, Joshua Perley, to Ohio in 1801, with an eye to permanent settlement there, but he returned in 1803, leaving a sovereign state where he had found a territory. He settled on a lot in the northeast part of Farmington, Me. In 1833 he sold this farm and removed to Fairbanks Village, where he spent the rest of his life. Wife Mary died 31 Aug 1862; he died 31 Jul 1867.

Children at Farmington:

**1080**  i. Emeline[7] Eaton, b. 9 Mar 1809; mar. Nathaniel Goodridge of Industry, Me., 29 Jun 1830. They had four children. She died 25 Apr 1878; he died 1 Oct 1871.

**1081**  ii. Rachel[7] Lyon Eaton, b. 4 May 1810; mar. Joseph Fairbanks, Jr., 31 Jan 1842. She died 10 Sep 1844 without issue.

**1082**  iii. Mary[7] Ann Eaton, b. 27 Aug 1812; mar. William Reed of Strong, Me., 25 Dec 1837. They had one son, and Mary Ann died at Hennepin, Ill., 27 Dec 1867.

**1083**  iv. Greenwood[7] Eaton, b. 15 Sep 1815; died in childhood.

**+1084**  v. Eliab[7] Lyon Eaton, b. 15 Aug 1818; mar. Julia Hackett.

**1085**  vi. Susan[7] Wendell Eaton, b. 12 Jan 1821; mar. Truman A. Allen of Vineyard Haven, Mass., 13 Oct 1850. He was a retired sea captain, and they had one son.

**1086**  vii. Louisa[7] Carsley Eaton, b. 31 Dec 1822; d. 25 Aug 1825.

**+1087**  viii. Horatio[7] Greenwood Eaton, b. 25 Jun 1828; mar. Hannah Whitmore, 25 Jul 1850.

**409. Jacob[6] Eaton** (Jacob[5-4], Joseph[3], John[2-1]) was born 12 Jul 1784 in Bristol, Me. He mar. 1st, **Abigail Bradford**, daughter of Joseph Bradford, 16 Feb 1805; she died about 1813. He mar. 2d, **Mary Davis**, (she born to father Wendell Davis of New Vineyard, Me., in 1792) on 15 May 1814. They spent their married life on a farm adjoining that of his brother Isaac, in the northeast portion of Farmington. Jacob died prematurely on 10 Oct 1825. Widow Mary lived until 16 Aug 1858.

Children with Abigail, all born at Farmington:

**+1088**  i. Lyman[7] Eaton, b. 8 Mar 1808; mar. Susan Whitehouse.

**1089**  ii. Martha[7] Eaton, b. 7 Jan 1812; mar. Andrew L. Whitehouse of Topsham, Me., 17 Dec 1839, having four children. She died in the autumn of 1847.

Children with Mary, all born at Farmington:

**+1090**  iii. Wendell[7] Davis Eaton, b. 15 Aug 1815; m. Hannah Norton.

**1091**  iv. Mary[7] Smith Eaton, b. 22 Mar 1817; mar. John Bullin, 5 Nov 1839 and had two children. She died in Flushing, Long Island, 4 Jan 1892.

**1092**  v. Eliza[7] Ann Eaton, b. 28 Jun 1819; mar. Henry Beetle of Vineyard Haven, Mass. They had four children. She died 15 Jul 1872.

**1093**  vi. Abbie[7] F. Eaton, b. 10 May 1822; never married. She res. in Vineyard Haven, Mass; and later removed to Flushing, Long Island. She was a dressmaker.

**412. Joseph⁶ Eaton, Jr.** (Joseph⁵, Jacob⁴, Joseph³ John²⁻¹) was born in Bristol, Me., 21 Feb 1773.  He removed with his family first to Sandy River, Me., with his brother Jacob about 1783; and then on to Camden, Me. as an adolescent later in the decade.  He began adult life as a sailor, but later became master of a coasting vessel.  He mar. **Deborah Waterman** of Waldoborough about 1802, establishing their home first in Camden, Me., and in the adjacent area of Rockport, Me.  He died 6 Feb 1846; Deborah died at age 82, also in Camden, 21 Feb 1868.

Children (all born at Camden, Me.):

| | |
|---|---|
| **1094** | i. Julia⁷ Ann Eaton, b. 3 Oct 1803; died 6 Oct 1803. |
| **1095** | ii. Ann⁷ Maria Eaton, b. 24 Jan 1805; died 9 Jan 1808. |
| **1096** | iii. Louisa⁷ Waterman Eaton, b. 6 Aug 1807; mar. Charles Pendleton, 26 Sep 1833 and had four sons and one daughter. This daughter, Mrs. L. E. Knowlton of Belfast, Me., has furnished most of the memoranda of the Camden Eatons. Mrs. Louisa Pendleton died 4 Sep 1870. |
| +**1097** | iv. Nathaniel⁷ Thomas Eaton, b. 9 Nov 1809; mar. 1st, Lucy Hanaford, 1835; and 2d, Nancy Heald, 1854. |
| **1098** | v. Mary⁷ Elizabeth Eaton, b. 24 Dec 1812; mar. Putnam Simonton of Prospect, Me., 18 Nov 1836, and had one son and one daughter. She died 20 Oct 1841. |
| **1099** | vi. Deborah⁷ H. Eaton, b. 10 Oct 1819; mar. James Burrill of Boston, 2 Nov 1847 and had one son and one daughter. She died 19 Apr 1859. |

**413. William⁶ Eaton** (Joseph⁵, Jacob⁴, Joseph³, John²⁻¹) was born 7 Feb 1775 in that part of Bristol, Me. called New Harbor.  He then removed with his parents and Uncle Jacob's family to Sandy River, Me., when he was about age eight; and then in a few years on to Camden, Me., where the family came to rest.  He was married there to **Lucy White** on 23 Nov 1797.  He was a farmer and a millwright, and they raised eight of ten children to adulthood.  William⁶'s household is represented in the Camden Censuses from 1800 through 1840.  He died 20 Feb 1844; and Lucy died at age 93 in Hollis, Me., 30 Apr 1867.

Children (all at Camden):

| | |
|---|---|
| **1100** | i. Mary⁷ Eaton, b. 7 Sep 1798; mar. Deac. Joseph Stetson, 27 Aug 1820, and had seven daughters and two sons. She died 8 May 1882. |
| **1101** | ii. George⁷ W. Eaton, b. 14 Jul 1800; a mariner who died unmar. at sea, 1829. |
| +**1102** | iii. William⁷ Eaton, b. 26 Sep 1802; mar. Hannah Emery, 1830. |
| **1103** | iv. Horatio⁷ Cushing Eaton, b. 30 May 1805; mar. Ann Stetson 8 Oct 1826; he was lost at sea, Dec 1826; without issue. |

+**1104**   v. Joseph[7] Huse Eaton, b. 13 Mar 1807; mar. Harriet Hosmer.
 **1105**   vi. Edward[7] Eaton, b. 31 May 1809; died 20 Aug 1809.
 **1106**   vii. Edward[7A] H. Eaton, b. 1 Sep 1810; a sailor who died unmar.
             20 Sep 1834.
 **1107**   viii. Benjamin[7] F. Eaton, b. 18 Jan 1813; a sailor who died unm.
             10 May 1838.
 **1108**   ix. Lucy[7] Jane Eaton, b. 10 Jul 1815; mar. 26 Jul 1835 Thomas
             Glover of Camden, Me., who was a master mariner. They
             had one son and three daughters. She died 24 Oct 1857.
 **1109**   x. Martha[7] Ann Eaton, b. 28 Aug 1819; died 3 Oct 1819.

**421. Isaac[6] Eaton** (Benjamin[5], Jacob[4], Joseph[3], John[2-1]) was born
24 Nov 1787 in Topsham, Me. He mar. 1st, **Hannah Wilson** of Kennebunk, Me. 28 Feb 1814. They settled in Waterboro, Me., where they appear in the Censuses of 1820 and 1830, while they were having six children there. During the 1830s they moved from Waterboro in York Co.
to the area of Chandlerville and Detroit in southeastern Somerset Co.,
where they are found in the Censuses of 1840-50. Wife Hannah died
there, 11 Apr 1855, aged 68, and Isaac moved back to Kennebunk in
York Co. and mar. 2d, a **Mercy** (or **Mary**) **Edwards.** She died at Kennebunk 4 Nov 1869, and Isaac removed north again to Exeter, Me. in
Penobscot Co. He died there 18 Nov 1878. His peripatetic life can be
understood in part because he was a carpenter by trade, and therefore not
tied to a tract of farmland.

Children with Hannah at Waterboro, Me.:

+**1110**   i. Charles[7] Eaton, b. 6 Aug 1817; mar. Adaline Wing, 1846.
 **1111**   ii. Martha[7] Ann Eaton, b. 2 Mar 1819; mar. Nicholas A. Britt
             and had a son and three daughters. They moved West
             and she died there.
+**1112**   iii. Benjamin[7] Elwell Eaton, b. 19 May 1822; mar. Ethalinda
             Crosby, 1856.
 **1113**   iv. Mary[7] Eaton, b. 24 May 1824; mar. 1st, William Howard
             and had a son and a daughter; 2d, William Gardner, and
             had two more sons. They resided in Canaan, Me.
 **1114**   v. Electa[7] Eaton, b. 23 Jan 1827; mar. Joseph Smiley: had two
             daughters while residing in Vassalboro, Me.
 **1115**   vi. Hannah[7] Emily Eaton, b. 27 Jan 1831; she removed to the
             West but was unmarried.

**422. William[6] Eaton** (Benjamin[5], Jacob[4], Joseph[3], John[2-1]) was
born 2 Jul 1789 in Topsham, Me. He mar. **Rachel Parsons** of Clinton,
Me., certificate granted 20 Sep 1817; and they soon settled in Clinton
where seven children were born to them and where it is supposed William
died at some time before 1850, since his widow Rachel, b. ca. 1794, is a
head of household at Clinton in that Census.

Children at Clinton:

1116    i. Susan[7] Eaton, b. ca. 1820.
1117    ii. William[7] Moody Eaton, b. 1823; a lumberman who at some
           time after 1850 migrated to California.
1118    iii. Jane[7] Eaton. b. ca. 1825; mar. Samuel Flood of Fairfield,
           Me.
1119    iv. Louisa[7] Eaton, b. ca. 1827; mar. Mark Sibley of Vassalboro,
           Me.
1120    v. Isabell[7] Eaton, b. ca. 1829; mar. Columbus Fought of
           Lewiston, Me.
1121    vi. Margaret[7] Eaton, b. ca. 1834.
1122    vii. Esther[7] Eaton, b. ca. 1836.


423. **Charles[6] Eaton** (Benjamin[5], Jacob[4], Joseph[3], John[2-1]) was
born 17 Mar 1790 in Topsham, Me. He served in the War of 1812. On
30 Mar 1817 in Phippsburg, Me., he  mar. **Catherine Nichols** (daughter
of John/Esther Nichols, b. 9 May 1796 in Georgetown, Me.). They settled in Topsham, where Charles was a lumber merchant for some 50
years. They had ten children, seven of them girls. Two of the three boys
were twins, born under unusual conditions. In the time of a great freshet
in the Androscoggin River in 1820, when the log owners went down the
river to collect their logs, Charles proceeded to Georgetown, Me., for this
purpose. His wife decided to accompany him despite her advanced
pregnancy. While there, she welcomed her twin boys into the world. All
of the other children were born in Topsham. Charles[6] died in 1875 at
Bath, Me. His wife lived on for nearly two decades, residing with son Joseph, also a prosperous lumber merchant, at Bath. To the end she continued  receiving her husband's 1812 War pension of $12 per month.

Children (all but the twins born at Topsham, Me.):

1123    i. Mary[7] Eaton, b. 15 Feb 1817; died 28 Mar 1817.
+1124   ii. Charles[7] M. Eaton, b. 28 Apr 1818; mar. Deborah Wade.
+1125   iii. Joseph[7] Eaton, twin b. 17 Aug 1820; mar. 1st, Margaret
           Clifford.
1126    iv. Benjamin[7] Eaton, the other twin b. 17 Aug 1820; mar.
           Sarah Brown of Litchfield, Me., 19 Dec 1850. He was a
           joiner res. in Phippsburg, Me., dying there in 1855.
1127    v. Priscilla[7] Eaton, b. 25 Dec 1822; mar. Warren Hathorne, 31
           Mar 1842, and resided in Bath, Me.
1128    vi. Catherine[7] Eaton, b. 8 Jun 1827; mar. Joseph Milton Frost
           of Bath, Me., on 22 Nov 1853 and resided in Bath.
1129    vii. Mary[7A] Eaton, b. 9 Jun 1829; mar. Charles M. Parker;
           removed to California, where they res. at Eureka.
1130    viii. Augusta[7] Sophia Eaton, b. 11 Mar 1835; mar. Solon K.
           Clark, 4 May 1862; she died 1863 in Lewiston, Me.

**1131**    ix. Melissa[7] W. Eaton, b. 12 Jun 1837; mar. Alonzo Haley,
            26 Apr 1866; died in Topsham, 6 Nov 1867.
**1132**    x. Lucy[7] Emma Eaton, b. 19 May 1843; mar. Frank A.
            Furlong, 22 Dec 1861. They resided in Chelmsford or
            Lowell, Mass.


**427. Jotham[6A] Eaton** (Benjamin[5], Jacob[4], Joseph[3], John[2-1]) was
born 8 Jan 1798 at Topsham, Me. He mar. **Mehitable True** (b. 5 Aug
1801 in Litchfield, Me.) on 4 Jul 1821, and they lived on a farm in Topsham, Me. The household is listed in Censuses from 1830 at least
through 1850. He died in Topsham 4 Aug 1863; she was still living
there in 1894.

Children (all born at Topsham):

+ **1133**    i. Emery[7] W. Eaton, b. 13 Oct 1823; m. Emily H. Tarr, 1848.
  **1134**    ii. Caroline[7] Eaton, b. 4 Oct 1825; mar. S. P. Griffin, Jr., 28
              Sep 1851 and res. in Lowell, Mass.
  **1135**    iii. Lucinda[7] Eaton, b. 21 Feb 1829; mar. M. P. Reed, 17 Oct
              1853, and res. in Topsham. She had one daughter of her
              own and later adopted a daughter, Ida G. Eaton, of her
              brother James, who had been born 28 Feb 1867.
  **1136**    iv. James[7] M. Eaton, b. 2 Sep 1831; no further information.
  **1137**    v. Alpheus[7] T. Eaton, b. 15 Oct 1838; never married; died at
              Little Rock, Ark., 3 Nov 1865.
  **1138**    vi. Isaac[7] O. Eaton, b. 28 Dec 1840; lost at sea, 19 Jan 1861.
  **1139**    vii. Stephen[7] Eaton, b. ca. 1843. Died very young.
+ **1140**    viii. Jotham[7] Edwin, b. 20 Nov 1846; mar. Amelia Miller, 1873.


**428. Humphrey[6] M. Eaton** (Benjamin[5], Jacob[4], Joseph[3], John[2-1])
was born 13 Dec 1800 in Topsham, Me.; mar. 1st, **Melissa White** of Dixfield (Oxford Co.), Me. They resided in Dixfield, Me., although not
much is known of their life and times. Unless Melissa had the nickname
"Sally," which is not impossible, she died and Humphrey mar. 2d, a **Sally
__?__**, who is listed as his wife in a will he wrote in 1839. The possibility
that Melissa and Sally are the same may be enhanced by the fact that
Humphrey[6] died in the early 1840s, and a marriage is listed at Dixfield
between a "Malissa" Eaton and an Isaac Randall, 25 May 1842.

Children (the order comes from the 1839 will only):

**1141**    i. Phoebe[7] C. Eaton; b. ? ; mar. a Wheeler.
**1142**    ii. Abigail[7] D. Eaton; b. ? : mar. a Howe.
**1143**    iii. Simeon[7] Eaton, b. ? .
**1144**    iv. Emily[7] Eaton, b. ? .
**1145**    v. David[7] K. Eaton, b. ? .
**1146**    vi. Sarah[7] Eaton, b. ? .

**429. Stephen**[6] **Eaton** (Benjamin[5], Jacob[4], Joseph[3], John[2-1]), was born 3 Jan 1802 in Topsham, Me.; mar. **Caroline Nye** of Fairfield, Me., in May 1835 (she born 13 May 1810 at Clinton) and resided on a farm in Clinton, Me. He died prematurely, however, in Feb 1842. Wife Caroline mar. 2d, John Tottman, 3 Apr 1853 at Clinton, and did not die until 15 May 1883.

Children, all born at Clinton:

+**1147**   i. Benjamin[7] F. Eaton, b. 1 Mar 1836; mar. Sarah Tottman.
 **1148**   ii. Martha[7] W. Eaton, b. 3 May 1838; mar. Rev. A. W. Pottle of the Maine Conference of the Episcopal Church, 20 May 1861. She had two sons and three daughters.
+**1149**   iii. Stephen[7] P. Eaton, b. 10 Nov 1839; mar. Jennie Libby.

**430. Stockbridge**[6] **Eaton** (Benjamin[5], Jacob[4], Joseph[3], John[2-1]) was born 30 Nov 1805 in Topsham, Me. He mar. 1st, **Ruth Wales** of Bath, Me., ca. 1830. They were first at Clinton, Me., and then removed to Topsham, where they were living in 1840. They later resided at Dixfield, Me., and by 1850 Stockbridge and Ruth were found at Harpswell Neck, Me. He traded considerably in real estate, and on conveyances was called an "innkeeper of Harpswell" and a "Gentleman of Dixfield." At some time after 1850 Stockbridge mar. 2d, **Susan Curtis**, the widow of John Merriman of Harpswell, Me. He died 21 Oct 1891 in Harpswell.

Children, all by Ruth:

 **1150**   i. Ann[7] Maria Eaton, b. 12 Mar 1831 in Clinton, Me.; mar. 1st, Charles T. Chase, 18 Nov 1855, who died 10 Feb 1875 at Bryant's Pond, Me.; 2d, C. K. Pulsifer, 17 Dec 1881. She had no children, and resided at Mechanic's Falls, Me.
 **1151**   ii. George[7] Dana Eaton, b. 16 Oct 1835 in Topsham; died 17 Jul 1841.
 **1152**   iii. Humphrey[7] White, b. 16 Oct 1837. Later resided in South Minneapolis, Minn.

**431. James**[6] **Eaton** (Benjamin[5], Jacob[4], Joseph[3], John[2-1]) was born 28 Nov 1807 in Topsham, Me. He mar. **Esther E. Wilson** (b. 14 May 1807 in Topsham), on 15 Sep 1831 in Topsham. They settled on a farm in Fairfield, Me., where their children were born and where James died 13 Feb 1870, and wife Esther died 5 Dec 1884.

Children (all born at Fairfield):

**1153**     i. Marietta[7] B. Eaton, b. 24 Sep 1833; mar. Robert W. Savage, 5 Sep 1851, and went to California.
**1154**     ii. Jane[7] S. Eaton, b. 13 Jan 1837; mar. John B. Ricker, 25 Sep 1856, and died without issue.
+**1155**    iii. George[7] Collins Eaton, b. 4 Mar 1840; mar. Emily Russell.
**1156**     iv. Susan[7] A. Eaton, b. 22 Jul 1842; died 13 Jul 1845.
**1157**     v. Charles[7] A. Eaton, b. 22 Apr 1847; mar. Belle Prince (9th generation out of John[1] Prince).
**1158**     vi. Stockbridge[7] H. Eaton, b. 27 Oct 1851; in 1900 he was a grocer living with his wife Ella L. in his mother's household, with no sign of new children.

**432. Hiram[6] Moody Eaton** (Benjamin[5], Jacob[4], Joseph[3], John[2-1]) was born 14 Jul 1810 in Topsham, Me., a twin of Horace Malcolm Eaton below. In 1840 he mar. **Nancy Morrison** (she b. 1823 in Limerick, Me.), and they resided on a farm in New Limerick, where their children were born and where he died in 1877. Widow Nancy was still living with her son on the farm as of 1894.

Children (all at New Limerick, Me.):

+**1159**    i. Hiram[7] A. Eaton, a twin b. 1841; mar. 1st, Hattie Morrill.
**1160**     ii. Aprandy[7] Eaton, Hiram's twin, b. 1841; mar. 1st, Levi Berry and resided at Houlton, Me., having two sons there; mar. 2d, Henry Lamb, also at Houlton, had one daughter who died young.
**1161**     iii. Mary[7] Eaton, b. 1843; mar. Edward Hayes in 1864 and had two sons, both at Houlton.
+**1162**    iv. Charles[7] H. Eaton, b. in 1847; mar. Miranda Bragg, 1872.

**433. Horace[6] Malcolm Eaton** (Benjamin[5], Jacob[4], Joseph[3], John[2], John[1]) was born 14 Jul 1810 in Topsham, Me., the twin of Hiram Moody Eaton just above. He mar. **Hannah D. Wilson** of Lisbon, Me. (she born 10 Mar 1815) on 11 Feb 1841, and they resided in Topsham. Horace died in Topsham, 4 Jul 1891. Widow Hannah was still living in the old Topsham homestead with son Abial as of the 1900 Census.

Child, born Topsham:

+**1163**    i. Abial[7] Washburne Eaton, b. 20 Jan 1851; mar. Georgiana Knight, 1871.

**437. Henry⁶ Eaton** (Ephraim⁵, Henry⁴, Ephraim³, John²⁻¹), was born 24 Apr 1777 (Candia VR at Concord, N.H.) or 30 Jan 1778 (Seabrook VR at Concord, N.H.) at Candia, N.H.; mar. **Hannah⁶ Eaton**, daughter of "Maj." Jesse⁵/Hannah (Worthen) of Candia, and grandaughter of Rev. Benjamin⁴ (William³, John², William¹/Martha of the Reading, Mass., line of Eatons). They resided on the original Eaton homestead in Candia established by father Ephraim and raised a large family. The *History of Candia* (Moore, 1893) notes: "[Henry⁶] was a man of excellent judgment, planning all his business with precision and foresight, and prompt in the discharge of every obligation. An estimable and worthy man, a valuable citizen, an upright and conscientious Christian..." (p. 68). In 1850 he reported the value of his real estate to be $3,000, and he had already arranged other property for his remaining married sons. He died 5 Mar 1852 at Candia.

Children, all at Candia, N.H.

| | | |
|---|---|---|
| **1164** | i. | Lavinia⁷ Eaton, b. 24 Dec 1804; mar. Thomas Anderson and res. Candia. She had one daughter, and died 1878. |
| **+1165** | ii. | Henry⁷ Moore Eaton, b. 6 Jun 1806; mar. 1st, Eliza Parker. |
| **+1166** | iii. | Ephraim⁷ Eaton, b. 13 Sep 1808; mar. Mary J. Cilley, 1842. |
| **+1167** | iv. | Charles⁷ Edwin, b. 10 Dec 1811; mar. Eliza McCready. They removed to Ohio, ca. 1839. |
| **1168** | v. | Susan⁷ Eaton, b. 30 Sep 1813; mar. Freeman Parker, also of Candia, 2 Sep 1837. |
| **1169** | vi. | Sarah⁷ L."Sally" Eaton, b. 15 Oct 1817; mar. Henry Clough of Manchester, N.H. |
| **1170** | vii. | Martha⁷ Eaton, a twin b. 5 Aug 1821; mar. John T. Spofford, 9 Sep 1862 (his 3d wife). |
| **1171** | viii. | Mary⁷ Eaton, the other twin b. 5 Aug 1821; died unmar. 13 Mar 1849. |
| **1172** | ix. | Hannah⁷ Eaton, b. 7 Apr 1823; mar. John D. Patterson, 24 Sep 1846 at Candia; res. Manchester, N.H. |
| **1173** | x. | Caroline⁷ Eaton, b. 19 Jul 1825; mar. John T. Spofford, 28 Nov 1850, as his 2d wife. She had three children with him, and died 28 Nov 1861. |

**439. Peter⁶ Eaton** (Ephraim⁵, Henry⁴, Ephraim³, John²⁻¹) was born 17 Apr 1788; mar. **Hannah Hale Kelley** (born 4 Oct 1787, daughter of Deacon E. H. Kelley, a trader in Candia), int. 9 Nov 1813. Four children were born to them while Peter⁶ ran a store in Candia from about 1812 to 1835. Then he moved to Concord, N.H. for a few years, but returned to Candia by 1840. By 1850 he had moved into Manchester, N.H., where he was again a merchant. His wife died there 19 Mar 1870. We lack a death record for husband Peter.

Children, all at Candia:

+**1174**   i. Ephraim[7] Kelley Eaton, b. 1 Aug 1814; mar. Hannah.
 **1175**   ii. Mary[7] Jane Eaton, b. 28 Oct 1816; resided in Manchester,
            and died 31 Jan 1892.
 **1176**   iii. Henrietta[7] Eaton, b. 19 Jun 1820; died 21 Jun 1820.
+**1177**   iv. Francis[7] Brown Eaton, b. 26 Feb 1825; mar. Lucretia Lane.

    **442. Henry[6] Eaton** (Peter[5], Henry[4]. Ephraim[3], John[2-1]) was born
12 Jun 1775 at Salisbury, Mass. He mar. **Sally Stevens**, 6 Oct 1799, and
about 1804 removed to Corinth, Orange Co., Vt., where two of his three
younger brothers were also headed.   He purchased a farm there, on
which he built a sawmill, a classic tactic for establishing prosperity in
newly-settled lands.  However, his ambition exceeded his judgment: his
marriage was not a happy one and he was unsuccessful in business. He
sold his farm to his brother Stephen and returned to Salisbury for a season.  He was not there long enough to appear in the 1810 Census, but
was on his way to new ventures in Pennsylvania, where he died.

    Children:

 **1178**   i. Peter[7] Eaton, b. 3 Jul 1803, as recorded at Salisbury; he
            probably mar. but was not known to have had living de-
            scendants by late in the 19th century.
 **1179**   ii. Sally[7] Eaton, b. about 1805, probably at Corinth, Vt.
 **1180**   iii. Joanna[7] Eaton, b. Mar 1806, probably Corinth; she married
            a French, perhaps Moses of Salisbury, 27 Feb 1822.  She
            died a widow in Salisbury, Mass. on 4 May 1881.
+**1181**   iv. Henry[7] Eaton, b. May 1807, Corinth; mar. Jemima[7] Eaton.

    **443. Stephen[6] Eaton** (Peter[5], Henry[4], Ephraim[3], John[2-1]) was born
10 Jun 1777 at Salisbury, Mass. He mar. **Susan Currier** of Salisbury, 23
June 1800.  Soon after they removed to Corinth, Vt., and in due time
bought the farm that Stephen's older brother Henry had established there
not long before. They were accompanied in this migration by Stephen's
younger brother Peter[6]; and this pair of household heads appears in the
1810 Census at the adjacent township of Topsham, Vt., and then, 1820
thru 1850, in Corinth.   They spent the rest of their lives on the farm,
where Stephen died 22 Sep 1852.  Wife Susan died 15 Jul 1867, after a
consecrated Christian life.

    Children (all births recorded in Corinth, Vt.):

 **1182**   i. Abigail[7] Eaton, b. 31 May 1802; mar. David Dearborn
            (he born 19 Nov 1796 in Weare, N.H.) on 23 Sep 1821.
            They settled in Corinth, Vt., where ten children were born
            to them.  David died 20 Jul 1871; wife Abigail died
            22 Sep 1873.
 **1183**   ii. Mary[7] Ann Eaton, b. 9 Oct 1807; mar. Hubbard Fellows

(he born 6 May 1800 in Corinth), 13 Mar 1828. They spent their lives on a farm in Corinth, where they had 11 children. Husband Hubbard died highly esteemed, 17 Sep 1862. Wife Mary Ann was a devoted Methodist, a bright and well-informed woman of remarkable memory, still living in Nov 1893.

1184    iii. Liberty[7] Eaton, b. 27 Feb 1813; died 7 Aug 1817.
1185    iv. Susanna[7] M. Eaton, b. 2 Sep 1817; d. 25 Sep 1838, unmar.
+1186   v. Frederick[7] P. Eaton, b. 18 Oct 1822; mar. Julia Dearborn.


**444. Peter[6] Eaton** (Peter[5], Henry[4], Ephraim[3], John[2-1]) was born 16 Jun 1779 in Salisbury, Mass. He mar. **Sarah "Sally" Hook** (she b. 5 Jun 1782, also in Salisbury) on 22 Oct 1800 and they removed to a farm in Corinth, Vt., in the same general period that both of Peter's older brothers, Henry and Stephen, moved there as well. Wife Sally died there, 26 Dec 1855; Peter followed her on 4 Jan 1858.

Children, all born Corinth, Vt.:

1187    i. William[7] H. Eaton, b. 26 Sep 1803; married, and resided in Corinth as a farmer, but had no issue. He died of consumption 1 Sep 1868 at Eden, Vt.
1188    ii. Samuel[7] Eaton, b. 4 Nov 1805; married and resided Waterbury, Vt. Father, mother and children all died of consumption.
1189    iii. Stephen[7] Eaton, b. 24 Sep 1807; never married; travelled beyond the knowledge of his kindred.
1190    iv. James[7] M. Eaton, b. 29 Aug 1809; mar. Lois Olmsted, 1842.
1191    v. Eliza[7] Ann Eaton, b. 5 Mar 1812; mar. David Prescott, 28 Feb 1853; she died of consumption in Waterbury, Vt., May 1874.
1192    vi. Sarah[7] Eaton, b. 10 Jun 1814; died 15 Jan 1819.
1193    vii. Abigail[7] Eaton, b. 19 Aug 1816; mar. William Towne, 3 Jun 1844, and went to Jackson, Mich., where she died 3 Jun 1863.
+1194   viii. Peter[7] Eaton, b. 19 Feb 1819; mar. Harriet Cabot, 1844.


**446. Samuel[6] Eaton** (Peter[5], Henry[4], Ephraim[3], John[2-1]) was born 3 Oct 1783 at Salisbury, Mass. He mar. **Ruth French** of Salisbury, 14 Jun 1803, and with the older brothers all off to seek their fortunes in Vermont, Samuel took over the very prosperous homestead that his widowed mother had supervised with great success after the untimely death of his father Peter[5] when Samuel was not yet a year old. Samuel is taxed at Salisbury from 1803 through the end of the series we have reviewed in 1847. In the great majority of those years his holdings warrant the highest tax valuation in town of any Eaton household heads; and by the time he is age 53 he is repeatedly in the 93d or 94th percentile of wealth

among Salisbury townsmen more generally. Ironically, the sixth and
seventh generations of this prosperous family, in Salisbury and Vermont,
were ravaged by "consumption," or tuberculosis. Wife Ruth died 14 May
1838; Samuel himself died of consumption 24 Jan 1854.

Children (all born Salisbury, Mass.):

+ **1195**     i. Joshua[7] French Eaton, b. 16 Aug 1808; mar. 1st, Mary
               Stevens, 1844; 2d, Abby Fittz, 1859.
  **1196**    ii. Abigail[7] Greeley Eaton, b. 3 Jan 1812; died unmarried, 19
               Dec 1850.
  **1197**   iii. Clarissa[7] H. Eaton, b. 24 Jul 1814; died unmar. of consump-
               tion, 25 Apr 1851.


**448. Samuel[6] Eaton** (Samuel[5], Jabez[4A], Ephraim[3], John[2-1]) was
born 11 May 1782 in Seabrook. Early in adulthood he removed to
Chester, N.H., where he bought land. In the same period he mar. **Betsey
Moore** of Chichester, N.H. on 15 Mar. 1804. Before 1810 he had
moved onward to St. Johnsbury, Vt., where he appears in the Census of
that year with a young wife and probably three daughters of his own. At
some time in this period he was joined by his aging father Samuel[5] and in
the spring of 1811 he wrote a letter to his Uncle Paul[5A] reporting his father's death (see details, **#179**). In the years after this death, Samuel[6] appears now and again buying and selling land in St. Johnsbury. In the
1820 Census he is found at Waterford, Vt., although this is just a mile or
so from downtown St. Johnsbury. Wife Betsey died 1 Sep 1820 at St.
Johnsbury, age 39. Samuel[6] cannot be found in Censuses of 1830 or
1840. In 1833 a Samuel, Jr., Eaton is selling land in St Johnsbury. This
could possibly be Samuel[6], but as he has lost his "Jr." status in deeds after
the death of his own father, this is more likely to be an unrecorded son,
Samuel[7], Jr. And soon thereafter, in 1834, a "Samuel, Jr. Eaton," apparently 28 years old or younger, died at St. Johnsbury. In 1850, a Samuel
Eaton is recorded again at St. Johnsbury, this time as a pauper age 68.
While his birth state is reported as "Connecticut," there are not in our files
Samuel Eatons unaccounted for, from other lines, that would fit this time
or place, and given the exact age fit for Samuel[6], we are inclined to be-
lieve it is he.

Children (approximated from Census family compositions):

  **1198**     i. Daughter[7] Eaton, b. ca. 1805.
  **1199**    ii. Daughter[7] Eaton, b. ca. 1807.
  **1200**   iii. Daughter[7] Eaton, b. ca. 1809.
  **1201**    iv. Samuel[7] Jr. Eaton, b. early 1810s; died 1834, St. Johnsbury.
  **1202**     v. Son[7] Eaton, b. later 1810s.

452. (Col.) Henry[6] True Eaton (Paul[5A], Jabez[4A], Ephraim[3], John[2], John[1]) was born 29 May 1768 in Hampton Falls just before his neighborhood was set off as Seabrook. He mar. **Elizabeth Emerson** (daughter of Col. Nathaniel Emerson, and native of Candia) on 7 Jul 1796. They lived on the homestead of father Paul[5] on South Road in Candia. According to Stearns (1908, p. 1485), Henry T. "was a member of the Universalist Church, a Democrat in politics, and was selectman and representative in the New Hampshire legislature." Wife Elizabeth died in Jan 1818 after bearing ten children. Henry T. died 4 Jan 1851 at Newmarket, N.H.

Children, all born Candia:

+ 1203    i. Richard[7] Eaton, b. 12 Dec 1797; mar. Catherine Hughlett.
   1204    ii. Elizabeth[7] Eaton, b. 9 Oct 1798; died 27 Sep 1799.
   1205    iii. Eliza[7] Eaton, b. 27 Oct 1800; mar. John Sargent of Candia, a trader, and had three children.
+ 1206    iv. Henry[7] S. Eaton, b. 22 Oct 1802; mar. Lavina Woodbury.
   1207    v. Sarah[7] T. Eaton, b. 31 May 1804; never married.
   1208    vi. Jonathan[7] Eaton, b. 25 Sep 1806; died 15 Jul 1838, unmar.
+ 1209    vii. True[7] Eaton, b. 17 Oct 1809; mar. Susan York of Deerfield.
   1210    viii. Waity[7] S. Eaton, b. 5 Dec 1813; she d. unmar. 23 Oct 1865.
   1211    ix. Margery[7] L. Eaton, b. 12 Dec 1815; mar. Ingalls Bunker, 12 Dec 1841, and lived first at Newmarket, N.H., then in Manchester, N.H.; and finally back to Candia.
   1212    x. Julia[7] Ann Eaton, b. 26 Feb 1817; mar. Barron B. Bunker and resided in Hampstead, N.H., Saco, Me., Lockport, N.Y., Hudson, N.Y., and Newmarket, Manchester, and Dover, all N.H. He was the first Attorney General of Nevada under President Lincoln, and enlisted in the Civil War near its close. They also lived at Breckenridge, N.J. and Burlington, N.J., where he was in 1887. Wife Julia Ann died Oct 1889. We have no account of children.

457. "Azel[6]" (Asahel) Eaton (Joshua[5], Jabez[4], Ephraim[3], John[2-1]) was born about 1774, presumably in Seabrook, N.H., before father Joshua[5] mar. his 1st wife Anne Smith. Azel's mother's name is unknown. He was apparently bundled off to Connecticut as a child and there mar. **Polly Foster** of Connecticut, to whom five children were born. There is no sign of this couple in New England censuses, but we can plausibly trace their westward movement in the form of an "Asel" in Onondaga Co., N.Y. in 1800; an "Asahel" in Ontario, Co., N.Y. in 1810; and an "Azel" Eaton in Geauga Co., Ohio in 1820. There the trail seems to end.

Children (birthplaces unknown):

   1213    i. Harry[7] Eaton, b. 1797.

1214    ii. Rhoda[7] Eaton, b. 1799; mar. John Colwell and had eight
        children.
+1215   iii. Ira[7] Eaton, b. 1801; mar. Almira Hall, Dec 1822.
1216    iv. Polly[7] Eaton, b. 1803; mar. Orson Roth, had two children.
1217    v. Nathaniel[7] Eaton, b. 1805; mar.  ?  ; had children Nelson
        and Lydia.


**459. Jabez[6] Eaton** (Joshua[5], Jabez[4], Ephraim[3], John[2-1]) was born 9
Nov 1777 in Seabrook, N.H. He mar. **Susan Beckman**, daughter of John
R. Beckman of Seabrook, about 1802. They lived on a farm on land that
had passed down from his great grandfather Ephraim[3] near the eastern
extremities of Walton Road and lower Collins St., where further passage
to the east is blocked by the great marshes over which the tide waters
ebbed and flowed. This picturesque setting is very graphically described
by son Oliver[7], the same Oliver who was the chief genealogist of the
Seabrook Eatons in the 19th century, yet whose work appears to have
been lost, save for what the senior author of this volume used. Jabez[6]
served as a representative of Seabrook in dealings with other towns for
nine years. He died 24 Nov 1841.

Children, all born Seabrook:

+1218   i. Oliver[7] Eaton, b. 29 Sep 1803; mar. 1st, Caroline Hull, 1831.
1219    ii. Judith[7] Eaton, b. 12 Dec 1805; never married.
1220    iii. Charles[7] Eaton, b. 27 Dec 1807; died Nov 1827.
1221    iv. Clarissa[7] Eaton, b. 25 Jul 1810; died unmar., 11 Feb 1861.
+1222   v. Edwin[7] Eaton, b. 15 Jan 1813; mar. Mary George, 1839.
1223    vi. Son[7] Eaton, b. Jun 1815; died June 1815.
+1224   vii. Charles[7A] A., b. 6 Nov 1827; mar. Abby[7] M. Eaton (**#1021**)
        of Salisbury, who later was one of the seven Eaton sisters
        co-owning the original Eaton homestead on Beach Road.


**460. Joshua[6] Eaton** (Joshua[5], Jabez[4A], Ephraim[3], John[2-1]) was born
14 Feb 1780 in Seabrook, N.H. He mar. **Ruth Merrill** about 1801, and
like a number of descendants of Ephraim[3], lived among the Walton families on Walton Road east of Washington St. in Seabrook. Occupationally,
he followed a familiar Seabrook pattern, being a mariner for the first two
or three decades of his adult life, and leaving the perils of the sea for
farming once he had built sufficient capital to put together enough property. He appears as a household head in Seabrook Censuses from 1810
through 1850, when he reports his farm as worth $1500, a rather average
sum for this time and place. Wife Ruth disappears from the record before 1840. In 1850 Joshua, age 70, lives with his son Giles, the latter
long estranged from his own wife. Joshua seems to have died about
1853.

Children, all born at Seabrook:

+1225    i. Giles⁷ Eaton, b. 31 Jan 1802; mar. Waity Collins, 1824.
 1226   ii. Tabitha⁷ Eaton, a twin b. 1804; mar. Levi Collins, 18 Sep
         1829. She died 28 Apr 1859.
 1227   iii. Merrill⁷ Eaton, the other twin b. 1804; died June 1809.
 1228   iv. Elsie⁷ Eaton, b. 12 Jul 1809, mar. Samuel Walton and had
         one son, Reuben. She died 23 Jul 1885.
 1229    v. Almira⁷ Eaton, b. 14 Jul 1812; mar. Reuben D. Felch, 24
         Nov 1831, and bore two sons and two daughters. She
         died 14 Dec 1879.
 1230   vi. Arvilla⁷ Eaton, b. ca. 1815; mar. Henry Walton, 12 Jan
         1832, and had one son and one daughter.
 1231  vii. Ruth⁷ Ann Eaton, b. ca. 1818; mar. Amos Collins, 1 Sep
         1842, and had one son and three daughters.

* * * * * * *

## B. *The Haverhill Branch*

**467. Samuel⁶ᴬ Eaton** (Joseph⁵, Thomas⁴⁻² John¹) was born 15 Jul 1760 in Haverhill, Mass.; mar. **Lois Swain** of Lynnfield, Mass., 21 Jun 1808. They lived on the same West Parish farm in the general Dustin neighborhood where Samuel was born. He enlisted in the Revolution and was in the Rhode Island service a few days, leaving home 30 Jul 1780 and being discharged 7 Aug 1780. He was a war pensioner for several years before his death, receiving $45.20 a year. He was a household head in Haverhill Censuses from 1810 through 1830, and presumably was present as an octogenarian in the house of a child after that. He died 17 Jan 1852 at Haverhill.

Children at Haverhill:

 1232    i. Sarah⁷ Webster Swain Eaton, b. 24 Dec 1810; mar. a Mr.
         Chase of Hampstead, N.H.
 1233   ii. Mary⁷ Judith Eaton, b. 7 Jul 1813; also mar. a Chase from
         Hampstead, N.H.

**469. Peter⁶ Eaton** (Joseph⁵, Thomas⁴⁻² John¹) was born 15 Mar 1765 in Haverhill, Mass. He graduated from Harvard University in 1787 and took his course in theology under Rev. Phineas Adams of Haverhill. He was ordained in the Congregational church in West Boxford, Mass., on 7 Oct 1789. He then mar. 1st, **Sarah Stone** (she born 9 Aug 1766 in Reading to Rev. Eliab Stone, the local Congregational minister) on 2 Sep 1792. Rev. Peter remained as the Boxford pastor for the rest of his life,

enjoying a "quiet, happy and useful ministry" there.  His Alma Mater
Harvard appreciated his services, and in 1820 conferred upon him the
honorary degree of  Doctor of Sacred Theology.   Wife Sarah died 15
June 1824; and by 17 Aug of that year he was published 2d to widow
**Sarah Swett** of Andover, whom he soon married.   Peter died 14 Apr
1848, and his second wife survived him for many years.

Children (all born at Boxford to first wife Sarah):

**1234**    i. Sarah[7] Eaton, b. 24 Jul 1794; mar. Maj. Daniel Flint of
            Reading, Mass., 11 Dec 1821.
**1235**   ii. Mary[7] Eaton, bapt. 10 Apr 1796; died young.
+**1236**  iii. Peter[7] Sidney Eaton, b. 7 Oct 1798; mar. Elizabeth Leman.
**1237**   iv. Francis[7] Welch Eaton, b. 28 Jul 1800; d. at sea 15 Nov 1821.
**1238**    v. Mary[7A] Stone Eaton, b. 30 May 1802; mar. Moses Kimball
            of Boxford, 20 Oct 1833; and had one daughter.
**1239**   vi. Joseph[7] Webster Eaton, b. 1 May 1804; died 29 Oct 1821.
**1240**  vii. John[7] Hubbard Eaton, b. 12 Apr 1806; graduated from
            Harvard University in 1827;  He completed his theologi-
            cal studies at Yale.  He labored in city missionary work
            in New York City for a number of years, where he died
            unmarried.

**476.  (Dr.) Thomas[6] Eaton** (Moses[5], Thomas[4-2], John[1]) was born
6 Feb 1769 in Hampstead, N.H.  He mar. on 20 Feb 1798 at Weare, N.H.,
**Betsey[6] Eaton** (**#602**), a somewhat distant cousin who had been born to
Obadiah[5] Eaton, 12 Oct 1782 on Sugar Hill in Weare.  Thomas[6] graduated from the Vermont Medical School and was in the practice of medicine for eight years in Weare and Henniker, and 32 years in Francestown,
the latter town being where he had spent his adolescent years with his
family.   Thomas "succeeded his father upon the Eaton or Richardson
place, and became one of the most progressive, practical and successful
farmers in New England.  His farm was for a number of years the 'pre-
mium farm' of the town...He was moreover a large-hearted man, liberal
with those in his employ, of the prosperity of many of whom he was the
founder.  He also won a place in the history of American farming as the
introducer of the Spanish Merino sheep into this country, and he was
among the foremost to prohibit the free use of liquor upon the farm, and
was the champion of the first temperance reform in the town...antedating
some of the best men of his time by fully a quarter of a century" (*History
of Francestown*, Cochrane, 1895, p. 663).   Thomas and Betsey were
members of the Congregational church for many years.  Betsey died 14
Oct 1840; and Dr. Thomas died 23 Jan 1858, also in his home at
Francestown.

Children:

**1241**    i. Daughter[7] Eaton, died in infancy.

+1242   ii. Obadiah[7] Page Eaton, b. 13 Sep 1800 in Francestown; mar.
            Clarissa Farley, 1829.
+1243   iii. Moses[7] Webster Eaton, b. 14 Apr. 1803 in Weare; mar.
            Louisa Lawrence, 1828.
 1244   iv. Betsey[7] Eaton, b. 3 Aug 1807 in Henniker; mar. James Har-
            vey Dudley of Boston and resided there, having one son.
 1245    v. Harvey[7] Wallace Eaton, b. 22 Jun 1813, He was educated
            for the medical profession at Dartmouth, Union College
            (Schenectady) and at Boston, Mass. Immediately after
            his graduation he was appointed surgeon of the Eye and
            Ear Infirmary of Syracuse, N.Y., which position he re-
            signed and finally settled in Burlington, Iowa, where he
            died 10 Nov 1838, unmarried.
 1246   vi. Anna[7] Frances Eaton, b. 1824; mar. Levi Bartlett Gale of
            Concord, N.H., 29 Jul 1845; resided in Boston, where they
            had a son and a daughter. Husband Levi died on his way
            home from a trip to California.

    **480. Thomas[6] Eaton** (Thomas[5A--2], John[1]), was born 21 Jul 1771
in Concord, N.H., on his father's farm at Beech Hill by the Hopkinton
town line. He mar. **Sarah Eastman** (b. Aug 1770 in Hopkinton) on 5
Oct 1790. Thomas was called a "joiner" (e.g., cabinetmaker) when he
sold Hopkinton land abutting his father's Concord farm in 1799. This
couple resided variously in Concord, Warner and Hopkinton, N.H., but
mainly in the latter, where Thomas was recorded as a household head in
all five U.S. Censuses, 1800-1840. The death dates of this couple are unknown, but they disappear from the record in the 1840s.

    Children:

 1247    i. Molly[7] Eaton, b. 14 Apr 1791, Concord; died in Hopkinton,
            unmarried.
 1248   ii. Moses[7] Colby Eaton, b. 29 Dec 1792 in Warner; never mar.
 1249  iii. Stephen[7] Gould Eaton, b. 1 Jul 1795 in Warner; died without
            issue in Hopkinton, 1815 or 1816.
 1250   iv. Enoch[7] Eaton, b. 4 Mar 1797 in Warner; never married.
 1251    v. Rebecca[7] Eaton, b. 21 Mar 1799 in Warner; never married.
 1252   vi. Sarah[7] Eaton, b. 27 Feb 1801 in Warner; died in 1816-17.
 1253  vii. Thomas[7] Eaton, b. 17 Feb 1803 in Warner; died unmar.
+1254 viii. True[7] Eaton, b. 16 Feb 1805 in Hopkinton; mar. Betsey
            Marshall, 1838.
 1255   ix. Walter[7] Eaton, b. 16 Mar 1807 in Concord; never married.
 1256    x. Infant[7] Eaton, b. ca. 1808, died without name.
+1257   xi. Rufus[7] P. Eaton, b. 6 Feb 1809 in Hopkinton; mar. 1st,
            Sophalia Gibson; 2d, Marietta Bailey; 3d Rachel Hill.

**481. Moses[6] Eaton** (Thomas[5A-2], John[1]) was born 19 Jan 1775 in Concord, N.H. On 24 Nov 1794 at Concord, N.H. he mar. 1st, **Lucy Hazeltine**, who was born 13 June 1775 in Andover, Mass. This couple settled on a farm on the eastern side of Hopkinton near the Concord town line where they both spent their lives. Wife Lucy died 30 Jun 1841. This is undoubtedly the Moses of Hopkinton who mar. 2d, widow **Rachel Marshall**, then of Keene, N.H., relict of a Jonathan Marshall, on 2 Feb 1844 (Sanborn, 2002, p. 23), since in the 1850 Census at Hopkinton our Moses[6] here, age 75, is living with one other person, a Rachel Eaton who is also 75 and hard to account for as any near relative. Moses died a few weeks after the Census, 15 Aug 1850.

Children (all with Lucy at Hopkinton):

1258    i. Nicholas[7] Eaton, b. 4 Jun 1797; went to Illinois; never mar.
1259    ii. Roxana[7] Eaton, b. 2 Dec 1799; resided in Boston, where she died 21 Apr 1865; never married.
1260    iii. Mahala[7] Eaton, b. 22 Apr 1802; died 1 Jul 1817, unmarried.
+1261   iv. Jasper[7] Hazen Eaton, b 16 Sep 1811; mar. Elizabeth Tuttle.

**482. Joseph[6] Eaton** (Thomas[5A-2], John[1]) was born 18 Dec 1776 at the Beech Hill farm in Concord, N.H. On 14 May 1809 he mar. **Hannah K. French** in her home town of Plymouth, N.H. This couple began their marriage on a farm at Groton, N.H. near Plymouth. They were both members of the Baptist church in nearby Hebron, N.H. Later in life they removed to northeastern Massachusetts. They appear at Bradford, Mass., in the 1840 Census; and Joseph died there 14 Apr 1844. Wife Hannah died, 1858, in the home of her eldest daughter in Longville, Pa.

Children (probably all born Groton):

+1262   i. Moses[7] French Eaton, b. 25 Dec 1810; mar. Sarah Gregg.
1263    ii. William[7] Eaton, b. 14 Nov 1812; removed to Texas to farm; he died Dec 1850, said to have been unmarried.
1264    iii. Lucretia[7] Eaton, b. 3 Apr 1815; mar. John Lang, 18 Aug 1856 and resided in Longville, Jefferson Co., Pa.
+1265   iv. Leonard[7] H. Eaton, b. 20 Apr 1817; mar. Mary A. Berford.
1266    v. Mary[7] Hazeltine Eaton, b. 28 Jun 1819; mar. Abner W. Lane, 9 Dec 1852 and resided in Freeport, Pa.
1267    vi. Sophia[7] Abigail Eaton, b. 30 Aug 1822; mar. Ambrose C. Dresser, 16 Apr 1843 and resided in Medford, Mass.
1268    vii. Rebecca[7] Mullikin Eaton, b. 4 May 1825; mar. Thomas K. Litch 17 Feb 1848 and resided in Brookville, Pa.

**487. Peter[6] Eaton** (Thomas[5A-2], John[1]) was born about 1784 in Concord, N.H. and mar. **Clarissa H. Kimball** of Hopkinton, N.H. 8 May 1804. They settled first on a farm on Putney Hill just west of Hopkinton

Village. In the winter of 1811-12 they removed northwest to New London, N.H. We know little of their later life.

Children (perhaps partial):

1269    i. Jennette[7] Eaton, b. ca. 1807.
1270   ii. Lydia[7] Eaton, b. ca. 1810.
1271  iii. Livermore[7] Kimball, b. 20 Aug 1814 at New London; he can be found at Springfield, Vt. in the 1850 Census, age 35 but living alone.


**488. Moses[6] Eaton** (*Moses[5]*, Moses[4], John[3], Thomas[2], John[1]) was born 7 Aug 1809, most likely at Portland, Me. He married **Sarah S. Mitchell** of Harrington, Me., 13 Jan 1830. He was a sea captain by trade and resided at Harrington for much of his life. At some time in the 1850s he removed to Machiasport, Me., but appears to have returned to Harrington after 1880, as he died there, 7 Sep 1888.

Children at Harrington (may be partial):

+1272    i. Jerome[7] B. Eaton, b. May 1832; mar. Eliza Grace, 1859.
+1273   ii. William[7] A.C. Eaton, b. 1833; mar. 1st, Violetta M. Mitchell.


**489. Asa[6] Eaton** (*Moses[5]*, Moses[4], John[3], Thomas[2], John[1]) was born about 1815, perhaps at Campobello Island, New Brunswick. He mar. **Lydia L. Mitchell**, int. 10 Nov 1835, Harrington, Me. He is listed as a sailor in the 1850 Census. Asa is described as dying of "accidental poisoning" 16 Oct 1898. Wife Lydia died 11 Nov 1903, also at Harrington.

Children, all born at Harrington, Me.:

+1274    i. Moses[7] Warren Eaton, b. Oct 1836; mar. Sarah Morrison.
 1275   ii. Ruth[7] Annie Eaton, b. 18 Nov 1838; mar. George B. Dinsmore, 6 Mar 1858 in Harrington and had 11 children. She died 21 Aug 1881 in Harrington.
+1276  iii. Elijah[7] Eaton, b. Dec 1841; mar. Henrietta Whitney, 1863.
 1277   iv. Henry[7] William Eaton, b. 1844; died 17 Feb 1860 at Harrington, Me.


**493. Nathaniel[6] Eaton** (Ebenezer[5], Moses[4], John[3] Thomas[2], John[1]) was born 28 Jan 1806 in Hanover N.H. township, on Moose Mountain overlooking Goose Pond in Canaan, N.H. He mar. 1st, **Lucinda Paddleford** of Enfield, N.H. They settled on the farm in Canaan, N.H. which father Ebenezer had established as the family homestead after 1810. At some time after wife Lucinda's death, he mar. 2d, **Susanna Kimball** of

Canaan.    In 1850 Nathaniel's parents were still living with this young family.

Children with Lucinda:

1278      i. Mary[7] H. Eaton, b. 20 Jan 1829; died 9 Apr 1848.
1279     ii. Nathaniel[7] Jr., Eaton. b. ca. 1840.
1280    iii. James[7] M. Eaton, b. ca. 1842.

Child with Susanna:

1281     iv. George[7] M. Eaton, b. ca. 1845.

++++++++++++++++++++++++++++++++++++++++++++++++++++++++++++++++++

**B(1).** *The Nova Scotia Branch*

(Skeletal form: for details, see Arthur W. H. Eaton (1929)).

**495. Stephen[6] Eaton** (David[5], James[4], Jonathan[3], Thomas[2])

+1282      i. Jacob[7], b. 1776.
  1283     ii. Zerviah[7], b. 1779.
  1284    iii. Rebecca[7], b. 1781.
  1285     iv. Olive[7], b. 1782.
  1286      v. Deborah[7], b. 1783.
+1287     vi. Amos[7], b. 1785.
+1288    vii. Nathan[7], b. 1787.
  1289   viii. Elizabeth[7], b. 1789.
+1290     ix. Stephen[7], b. 1792.
  1291      x. Nancy[7], b. 1795.

**497. Elisha[6] Eaton** (David[5], James[4], Jonathan[3], Thomas[2])

+1292      i. Dan[7], b. 1780.
+1293     ii. Enoch[7], b. 1781.
+1294    iii. Elisha[7], b. 1783.
+1295     iv. William[7], b. 1786.
  1296      v. Lydia[7], b. 1788.
+1297     vi. George[7], b. 1790.
+1298    vii. David[7], b. 1792.
  1299   viii. John[7], b. 1795.
  1300     ix. Eunice[7], b. 1798.
+1301      x. James[7], b. 1802.

**498. Timothy[6A] Eaton** (David[5], James[4], Jonathan[3], Thomas[2])

1302    i. Ruth$^7$ Ann, b. 1784.
1303    ii. Alice$^7$, b. 1786.
1304    iii. Olive$^7$, b. 1788.
+1305   iv. Gideon$^7$, b. 1791.
1306    v. Sarah$^7$ S., b. 1797.
+1307   vi. Timothy$^7$, b. 1800.
1308    vii. Sophia$^7$, b. 1802.

### 501. Elijah$^{6A}$ Eaton (David$^5$, James$^4$, Jonathan$^3$, Thomas$^2$)

+1309   i. Ebenezer$^7$ Eaton, b. 1786.
+1310   ii. Caleb$^7$, b. 1787.
1311    iii. Susannah$^7$, b. 1790.
1312    iv. Deborah$^7$, b. ? .
1313    v. Prudence$^7$, b. ? .
1314    vi. Elizabeth$^7$, b. ? .
1315    vii. Charlotte$^7$, b. ? .
1316    viii. Rebecca$^7$, b. ? .
1317    ix. Melinda$^7$, b. ? .
1318    x. Mary$^7$ Ann, b. ? .
1319    xi. Elijah$^7$, Jr., b. ? .
+1320   xii. Elisha$^7$, b. 1808.
1321    xiii. Alice$^7$ Jane, b. 1809.

### 502. David$^6$ Eaton (David$^5$, James$^4$, Jonathan$^3$, Thomas$^2$)

+1322   i. Guy$^7$ Eaton, b. 1788.
1323    ii. Emily$^7$ Eaton, b. 1791.
+1324   iii. Judah$^7$ Eaton, b. 1792.
+1325   iv. David$^7$ Eaton, b. 1795.
1326    v. Eunice$^7$ Eaton, b. 1798.
1327    vi. Ann$^7$ Eaton, b. 1801.
1328    vii. Asenath$^7$ Eaton, b. 1803.
1329    viii. Prudence$^7$ Eaton, b. 1806.
1330    ix. Eliza$^7$ Eaton, b. 1810.
+1331   x. Levi$^7$ Wells Eaton, b. 1812.

### 503. James$^6$ Eaton (David$^5$, James$^4$, Jonathan$^3$, Thomas$^2$)

1332    i. Ruth$^7$ Eaton, b. 1794.
1333    ii. Mary$^7$ Ann Eaton, b. 1796.
1334    iii. Nancy$^7$ Eaton, b. 1801.
1335    iv. Harriet$^7$ Eaton, b. 1803.
+1336   v. Edward$^7$ Eaton, b. 1804.
1337    vi. Fanny$^7$ Eaton, b. ? .
1338    vii. James$^7$ Eaton, b. ? .
1339    viii. Rebecca$^7$ Eaton, b. ? .

**1340**    ix. Caroline[7] Eaton, b.  ?  .


        **506. John[6] Eaton** (David[5], James[4], Jonathan[3], Thomas[2])

   **1341**     i. Abigail[7] Eaton, b. 1796.
 **+1342**    ii. Ward[7] Eaton, b. 1797.
 **+1343**   iii. Abijah[7] A. Eaton, b. 1798.
   **1344**   iv. Sophia[7] Eaton, b. 1799.
 **+1345**    v. Charles[7] Eaton, b. 1802.
   **1346**   vi. Catherine[7] Eaton, b. 1803.
   **1347**  vii. Jane[7] Eaton, b. 1806.
   **1348** viii. Alice[7] Eaton, b, 1809.
   **1349**   ix. Olive[7] Eaton, b. 1811.
   **1350**    x. Emma[7] Eaton, b. 1813.
   **1351**   xi. Mary[7] Eaton, b. 1815.
 **+1352**  xii. John[7] White Eaton, b. 1817.


        (End Generation VI for Nova Scotia Branch)
+++++++++++++++++++++++++++++++++++++++++++++++++++++++++++++++++++++


        **510. (Maj.) Isaiah[6] Eaton** (Timothy[5], James[4], Jonathan[3], Thomas[2], John[1]) was born 15 Oct 1757 in Haverhill, Mass.  Father Timothy[5] was Captain of the Haverhill militia, and on 19 Apr 1775, the news of the Battle of Lexington reached Haverhill soon after noon.   Before night Isaiah, the oldest son but still less than 18 years old, had gone to the war under his father's command.   Later, Isaiah and his cousin John[5] Eaton (**#194**), who was killed at Bunker Hill, had enlisted in Capt. James Sawyer's Co. of Col. Frye's Regiment.  When and where the title of Major was conferred is unknown, but inflation of military rank as the Revolution receded in memory was commonplace, and the title was used routinely for Isaiah.  After the war, Isaiah mar. 1st, **Priscilla West** of Dartmouth, Mass., at Needham, Mass.  Rather promptly the new couple removed to Charlestown, N.H., on the Connecticut River, where Isaiah had bought land.  Within a few years, however, they moved south on the River to Walpole, where they are found in the Censuses of 1790 and 1800.  About 1803 they moved a few miles across the River to settle anew in Westminster, Vt.  It was there that first wife Priscilla died 5 Nov 1804, and was buried in the Old East Parish cemetery.  Isaiah mar. 2d, widow **Azuba Grout** (she born 21 Sep 1765 at Grafton, Mass.) on 27 Jan 1807.  Azuba bore him one child, but died 3 Sep 1813.  He lived on at Westminster at least through his war pension application in 1832.  He died 17 Dec 1847 at Chattanooga, Tenn., but was buried at Westminster.

Children by Priscilla:

**1353**   i. Clarissa[7] Eaton, b. 10 Aug 1784 at Charlestown, N.H.; mar.
            Nathaniel Gould 22 Feb 1807. Had ten children.
**1354**   ii. Priscilla[7] Eaton, b. 7 Dec 1786 at Charlestown; mar. John A.
            Graham on 1 Jan 1806. No issue.
**1355**   iii. Ira[7] Eaton, b. 2 Aug 1789 at Walpole, N.H.; mar. Sarah P.
            Ward of Salem, Mass. 20 Apr 1813.  She was born ca.
            1795 and died 28 Sep 1852.  He died 10 Oct 1841.
            There is no record of children, although his estate was
            administered (1841) by an I. Ward Eaton, likely a son,
            who is undoubtedly the Ira, age 15-19, who appears in the
            Westminster, Vt. Census for 1840 as a household head
            with an apparent mother and other siblings, and no sign
            of an Ira of Ira[7]'s age, who may have been away.
**1356**   iv. Isaiah[7], Jr., Eaton, b. 16 Mar 1792 in Walpole, N.H.; mar.
            Mrs. Grace Billings; he died 18 Sep 1830.
**1357**   v. Cynthia[7] Eaton, b. 9 Nov 1794 in Walpole, N.H.; mar Levi
            Powers, 11 Mar 1817. No issue.
**1358**   vi. John[7] West Eaton, b. 27 Apr 1797 in Walpole, N.H. He was
            declared insane by his sister Priscilla in Mar 1847; appears
            as a solo resident in the 1850 Census at Westminster. Vt.
**1359**   vii. Harriet[7] M. Eaton, b. 4 Nov 1799 in Walpole, N.H.; never
            mar.; died 13 Dec 1846, Westminster, Vt.

Child by Azubah at Westminster, Vt.:

**1360**   viii. William[7] Grout Eaton, b. 3 Jun 1808; died Sep 1813.


**511.   Abijah[6] Eaton** (Timothy[5], James[4], Jonathan[3], Thomas[2],
John[1]) was born 16 Aug 1759 at Haverhill, Mass.  Like his older brother
he served in the Revolution, but was too young for the first hostilities.  He
mar. **Elizabeth Poor** of Atkinson, N.H., on 8 Apr 1790.  The son of a
well-to-do Haverhill citizen, he followed his father in purchasing lands
opening up to the north in New Hampshire.  In 1783, for example, he is
described as a "trader" as he buys land in "Gunthwait," which would become Lisbon, N.H.  He is described as a "Gentleman of Haverhill" in several deeds involving Haverhill land, 1790-1809, although he is missing
from Haverhill Censuses of 1800 and 1810, being counted in 1810 at
Atkinson, and probably in 1800 as well, although those Census schedules
were lost.  It is also true that most of his children's births in this period
are recorded in Atkinson, N.H. and not Haverhill.  This Atkinson link is,
however, easily explained in view of the likelihood that Abijah's farm
straddled the town line between Haverhill and Atkinson.  This couple has,
however, returned to Haverhill for the 1820 Census, where they are in
their sixties and empty-nested.  Neither death record has been found, but
a Revolutionary War pension application was filed in Aug 1832.

Children (with inferences from above):

+ **1361**    i. Daniel[7] Poor Eaton, b. 24 Feb 1792, Haverhill: mar. Sarah.
  **1362**    ii. Betsey[7] Eaton, b. 8 Apr 1794 at Atkinson, N.H.; mar. John
              Johnson Merrill, 25 Dec 1813; she died 26 Aug 1853.
  **1363**    iii. Sally[7] Eaton, b. 10 Jul 1796 at Atkinson; mar. Samuel
              Webster, 2 May 1816; she died 21 Jul 1828.
  **1364**    iv. Abigail[7] Massey Eaton, b. 27 Sep 1798 at Atkinson; mar.
              John Pettengill, 1820.
+ **1365**    v. Edwin[7] Eaton, b. 10 Nov 1800 at Atkinson; mar. Abigail.
+ **1366**    vi. Thomas[7] Jefferson Eaton, b. 6 Feb 1805, at Atkinson.

   **512. Timothy[6] Eaton** (Timothy[5], James[4]. Jonathan[3], Thomas[2],
John[1]) was born 20 Jul 1761 in Haverhill, Mass. He mar. 1st, **Elizabeth
"Betty" Frye** of Haverhill, 23 Feb 1782, by whom he had 13 children.
This couple apparently joined Timothy's older brother Isaiah in Walpole,
N.H., for a time early in their marriage, as a Timothy who can only be
this one is a head of household there in the 1790 Census. However, in
due time they returned to Haverhill. Wife Betsy died 22 Aug 1821.
Timothy mar. 2d, **Sarah Clark** of Haverhill. From his father's metal
work as a founder, Timothy had become a silversmith, a not uncommon
trade in the Haverhill branch of Eatons. He also occasionally dealt in
real estate. After returning from Walpole, the family resided in the West
Parish. Timothy died 27 May 1848 at age 86. Given that Timothy[6] and
Betty had eight sons, seven of whom had known wives, it is remarkable
how limited our knowledge is of their susequent lines. Several disappeared to various ends of the earth where we have been unable to trace
them; but the record is thin even for those who never left Massachusetts.

   Children with Betty, all at Haverhill:

+ **1367**    i. Timothy[7] Eaton, b. 10 Jun 1782; mar. Mary Gleason.
  **1368**    ii. Thadeus[7] Eaton, b. 29 Dec 1783; mar. Abigail Deland of
              Salem, Mass. about 1812.
  **1369**    iii. Abijah[7] Eaton, b. Aug 1785; mar. Ann Brown of Boston;
              d. 1844.
+ **1370**    iv. Francis[7] Eaton, b. 7 Sep 1787; mar. Mary Hildreth, 1814.
  **1371**    v. Royal[7] Eaton, b 29 Nov 1789; died "by a fall from the
              bank near Merrimack River," 5 May 1826 (Amesbury,
              Mass. *VR*). No issue reported.
  **1372**    vi. Elizabeth[7] Eaton, b. 2 Jun 1792; mar. Joab Peaslee of
              Plaistow, N.H. and had seven children.
+ **1373**    vii. Cyrus[7] Eaton, b. 30 Aug 1794; mar. Mary Eva Kuhn.
  **1374**    viii. Cynthia[7] Eaton, b. 10 Oct 1796; mar. Sylvester Priest of
              Watertown, Mass, having several children.
  **1375**    ix. Phebe[7] Eaton, b. 4 Feb 1798; mar. Benjamin Davis of
              Haverhill; she died 27 May 1841.

**1376**  x. Lydia[7] Eaton, b. 16 Apr 1801; mar. John Richardson of
          Franklin, Mass.
**1377**  xi. James[7] Eaton, b. 11 Aug 1803; mar. Caroline Billings of
          Boston and removed to Cincinnati, Ohio
**1378**  xii. A. Caroline[7] Eaton, b. 19 Apr 1806; mar. Isaac Butterfield
          of Boston.
**1379**  xiii. Benjamin[7] Eaton, b. 3 May 1810; mar. Sarah Douglass.

    Child with Sarah:

**1380**  xiv. Mary[7] Ann Eaton, b. 21 Nov 1822; mar. David H. Priest of
          Watertown, Mass.


   **513. James[6] Eaton** (Timothy[5], James[4], Jonathan[3], Thomas[2], John[1])
was born 6 Aug 1763 in Haverhill, Mass. The senior author of this volume goes on to say of this James, "no account of his marriage," and gives
no further information about him save his death date. This general blank
is surprising because the senior author was a cousin once removed of all
dozen children of Timothy[5], and transmits substantial amounts of biographical material about the other eleven. Moreover, this James[6] had a
rather illustrious career in Hillsborough, N.H., only 17 miles from where
the senior author was growing up in Goffstown, N.H.--much closer by
than any of the other siblings--and he did not die until 1832, when the
senior author was 14 years old. Leaving this James a mystery is thus
perplexing. The mystery is compounded by the fact that another James
Eaton, equally left a mystery in the senior author's account, is easily confused with the Hillsborough one, because they are almost the same age
and the second one lived most of his life on a mountain in Deering township, barely more than four miles south as the crow flies from where the
first James lived for over three decades in Hillsborough town. Identifying the ancestry of the Hillsborough James was not difficult once we
added more information about his life and times, and he clearly is the
unsung fifth child of Timothy[5] at Haverhill. Identifying the Deering
James, who was the patriarch of a large family, has been much more difficult despite enormous amounts of information about his life and times
that we have been able to assemble. Our efforts in this regard are the
subject of an extended Appendix, designed to explain the hesitant assignment of ancestry we have finally made for the Deering James. With
this said, we proceed, summarizing our notes on the Hillsborough James.

   According to Haverhill *VR*, James Eaton published intentions to
marry **Polly Noyes** of Hampstead, N.H., 3 May 1787. This bride is a
perfect fit in every respect, including precise age, for the Mary (Polly)
Noyes who was James's wife at Hillsborough. As we have begun to see,
Capt. Timothy[5] distributed land stakes in New Hampshire to all of his
elder sons, and James[6] was no exception. Timothy was very active with
proprietorial grants in New Hampshire, where partners included an affluent Haverhill Son of Liberty, Samuel Gilman White, along with Polly

Noyes's father and grandfather. Samuel White had bought a large tract in the northwest corner of Goffstown called "White's Farm," and in Oct 1788, Timothy bought a 70-acre parcel of it explicitly for son James (Hillsborough Deed 44-203). This stake apparently was not, upon inspection, entirely to James's liking; for 8 month's later, Capt. Timothy bought two further slivers of adjacent land which would give command of a segment of Gorham brook with mill and damming privileges (23-198). This apparently still did not satisfy James, for 14 weeks later and labelled "a yeoman of Goffstown," he purchased what would be his primary residence for the rest of his life, a farm in the southeast corner of Hillsborough township straddling the main road to Hopkinton, just east of the most vibrant neighborhood in that township, Hillsborough "Lower Village" on the Contoocook River (Deed 27-158). From this base, James became very active in town affairs. In 1794 at age 31, James was elected one of the town's three Selectmen, and was re-elected for a near-record five years. He also helped the town take advantage of N.H. State legislature inducements toward free public libraries, becoming one of the four "official proprietors" of the new Hillsborough "social library" in 1797. After a decade in public life, James largely disappears from the scene, but he and his wife are there in 1810 and 1820 Censuses, and James appears on such Hillsborough tax lists as have survived, well into the 1820s. He is well-to-do, and sometimes referred to as "Capt." Eaton. There is no clear proof that James and Polly had children, despite reasonable diligence of Town Clerks, some of them James's political allies, in keeping birth records. In 1800, 1810 and 1820 their household shows a juvenile or two, but never one that is under ten years of age, and hence are likely to be household help. One tantalizing note arises because in the next generation there is a Hiram Eaton who is a long-time prominent citizen in Washington, N.H., 8 miles west of Hillsborough, who has resisted our strenuous attempts at genealogical identification. The only thing known of his background is that he was born in Hillsborough in 1804. About 1807 a John Eaton, young newly-wed son of the Deering James, arrives in Hillsborough. But in 1804, James/Polly must have been, as it were, the only Eaton show in town. Therefore it is possible that Hiram was in fact their son; but we have resisted the temptation to make this assignment. Wife Polly was buried in Hillsborough in 1825; husband James died there 29 Jan 1832.

**516. Daniel**[6] **Eaton** (Timothy[5], James[4], Jonathan[3], Thomas[2], John[1]) was born 18 Apr 1769 in Haverhill, Mass. He studied medicine, and then went to visit his uncle David's family in Nova Scotia about 1790. He was pleased with the country, and decided to tarry a while, choosing Onslow in Colchester Co. as his place of residence. There he met and married **Mrs. Esther (McLellan) Cater**, widow of William Cater, 9 Dec 1791. She was a young woman "of many attractions and well off." The couple lived in Truro, N.S., and Dr. Eaton practiced medicine in the county. At one point Dr. Daniel was a successful candidate for a seat in the Provincial Parliament. At a certain point he returned to the United States to get some money that was due him, or for medical help, stopping on the way to visit his friends in Haverhill, Mass. He then proceeded to Philadelphia, Pa. and died there in 1808. His widow was married again in 1815 to Capt. Simon Kollock, who had been in the British Army in the Revolutionary War. She died in Truro, N.S. at the home of her son Daniel, on 19 Sep 1863, alleged to be 106 years old.

Children (born at Truro, Nova Scotia):

+**1381**    i. William[7] Cater Eaton, b. 9 Oct 1792; mar. Lucy Smith, 1820.
 **1382**    ii. Phoebe[7] Eaton, b. 16 Mar 1795; mar. Judge Wheaton, New Brunswick, a member of the Supreme Court; had children.
+**1383**    iii. Daniel[7] Eaton, b. 19 Sep 1797; mar. Mary Ann Clark, 1822.
 **1384**    iv. James[7] Eaton, b. 1 Apr 1801; mar. and lived in Miramichi, N. B., but names of his wife and several children are unknown to us. He died 23 Apr 1850 at Chaleur Bay.

**518. Phineas[6] Eaton** (Timothy[5], James[4], Jonathan[3], Thomas[2], John[1]) was born 8 Jun 1773 in Haverhill, Mass. On 15 Nov 1798 he mar. **Elizabeth Emerson** (she born 29 Mar 1775 in Haverhill). Phineas was by trade a cabinetmaker and painter, according to land deeds when he was in his twenties. By 1804 and thereafter, he is referred to as "Gentleman," and he, like his younger brother Ward, clearly was well fixed in his inheritance after his father's death in 1811, for Capt. Timothy made clear in his will that the far-flung older brothers had long since received their proper share of his estate in land stakes he had given them as young adults. Phineas and Elizabeth lived on Londonderry Road in Haverhill's West Parish, near Capt. Timothy's family homestead, but not on it, for Phineas sold that 40-acre homestead for $500 in 1817. Phineas died 21 Apr 1829; wife Elizabeth survived him by many years, dying 8 Jun 1863 at age 89.

Children (all born at Haverhill):

 **1385**    i. Jeremiah[7] Eaton, b. 29 Jul 1800; died 24 Nov 1802.
+**1386**    ii. Elbridge[7] Gerry Eaton, b. 29 Mar 1802; mar. Nancy Gage.
 **1387**    iii. Clarinda[7] Eveline Eaton, b. 28 Mar 1805; mar. Benjamin Kimball and resided in Haverhill, having six children.
+**1388**    iv. Jeremiah[7A] Bodwell Eaton, b. 12 Jul 1807; mar. Martha Rollins, 1833.
+**1389**    v. James[7] Madison Eaton, b. 23 Oct 1809; mar. Hannah Pettengill, 1842.
 **1390**    vi. Mary[7] Elizabeth Whittier Eaton, b. 26 Mar 1812; mar. James Noyes, 16 Jan 1834, and resided in Haverhill, having four children.
+**1391**    vii. Daniel[7] Whittier Eaton, b. 4 Jun 1814; mar. Sarah Smith.
 **1392**    viii. Lucy[7] Ann Eaton, b. 20 Nov 1816; d. 3 Nov 1839, unmar.

**519. Ward⁶ Eaton** (Timothy⁵, James⁴, Jonathan³, Thomas², John¹) was born 25 May 1775 in Haverhill, just between the Battle of Lexington and the Battle of Bunker Hill. He mar. 1st, **Judith Ingalls** of Walpole, N.H. (whom he undoubtedly met in visits to his brother Isaiah there) about 1800. The couple lived in Haverhill, where Ward was very favorably known in the community, and his name has been borne by many of his descendants and other relatives. He was a silversmith, and traded much in silver ware for the time in which he lived. Wife Judith died 28 Dec 1821. Ward then married 2d, **Rebecca Hayward** of Dublin, N.H. about 1825. Ward died in the spring of 1842, at age 67.

Children by Judith at Haverhill:

| | | |
|---|---|---|
| **1393** | i. | Fanny⁷ Eaton, b. 9 Aug 1801; mar. William Smiley. |
| **1394** | ii. | Julia⁷ H. Eaton, b. 29 Oct 1803; mar. Edmund Kimball of Bradford, N.H. |
| **+1395** | iii. | Ward⁷ Eaton, b. 10 May 1808; mar. twice, removed to Pa. |
| **1396** | iv. | Isaiah⁷ Eaton, b. 24 Sep 1810; never married; died ca.1850. |
| **1397** | v. | Sarah⁷ Phebe Eaton, b. 3 Mar 1813; became second wife of William Smiley after sister Fanny's death. |
| **1398** | vi. | Thomas⁷ Eaton, b. 20 May 1815; as a young man went West, prob. to Wisconsin, but was rarely heard from. |
| **+1399** | vii. | James⁷ Jackson Eaton, b. 4 Feb 1819; mar. Ellen Fielding. |

Children by Rebecca at Haverhill:

| | | |
|---|---|---|
| **1400** | viii. | Minot⁷ Hayward Eaton, b. 1824; d. 1879; mar. Elizabeth Godkin and had one son, Charles who was lost at sea. |
| **1401** | ix. | Abigail⁷ Prescott Eaton, b. ca. 1826; mar. Alvah Whittier and had three daughters. |
| **1402** | x. | Charles⁷ Joseph Eaton, b. 9 Nov 1828; mar. Florence Price, Nov 1865 but there the trail ends. |

**521. Samuel⁶ Eaton** (James⁵⁻⁴, Jonathan³, Thomas², John¹) was born 15 July 1759 at Haverhill, Mass. He was brought to Goffstown, N.H. by his family when he was about two. He enlisted as a private in the military service from Goffstown, and along with his uncle Enoch (**#210**) and his brother James (**#522**) went with Capt. Samuel McConnell's Co. to join Gen. Stark's Brigade in the Battle of Bennington in August, 1777. After the war, on 19 Nov 1782 he married a Goffstown girl, **Alice Hadley**, a daughter born to Joseph/Martha (Guile) Hadley at Hampstead, N.H. They settled for some years on the south edges of Goffstown and raised their family there. As he approached age 60, Samuel moved his family to Reading in Windsor Co., Vt., where he appears in the Censuses of 1820 and 1830, and filed for a Revolutionary War pension in 1832; and then to neighboring Plymouth/Bridgewater, Vt. by 1840 to live near his son Joseph⁷. Wife Alice died at Bridgewater 13 Mar 1843; Samuel followed suit a week later, 20 Mar 1843.

Children (all at Goffstown):

1403    i. Sally[7] Eaton, b. 14 Nov 1783; m. Philip Emery of Dunbar-
           ton, N.H., 26 Dec 1805.
1404    ii. Mary[7] Eaton, b. 10 Sep 1785; mar. Ebenezer Ferrin. She
            died 11 Apr 1826.
1405    iii. Rebecca[7] Eaton, b. 29 Mar 1788; mar. John Sargent of
             Plymouth, Vt., 24 Apr 1810. She died 14 Feb 1849.
1406    iv. James[7] Eaton, b. 18 Feb 1790; and died "after reaching
            manhood".
1407    v. Alice[7] Eaton, b. 6 Dec 1794; mar. Francis Ferrin, 11 Sep
           1811; she died 10 Mar 1863.
1408    vi. Samuel[7] Eaton, b. 1797; died young.
1409    vii. Clarissa[7] Eaton, b. 22 Mar 1800; mar. Thomas Abbott; res.
             in Derby, Vt. and then Hadley, Can.
+1410   viii. Joseph[7] Eaton, b. 24 Apr 1802; mar. Elizabeth Day, 1827.
1411    ix. Abigail[7] Eaton, b. 1804; died young.
1412    x. Lydia[7] Eaton, b. 11 May 1806; mar. Vernon Bean of
           Hadley, Can.; she died 18 Jan 1894.
1413    xi. Almira[7] Eaton, b. 8 Jun 1810; mar. 1st, Horace Marsh, 23
            Jan 1840; 2d, Jared Marsh.

-------------------------------------------------------------

**Warning:** The genealogical assignment of **#522, James of Deering**,
is likely to be the most controversial in this volume.    Appendix
C is devoted to a detailed examination of this curious case.    In
a nutshell,  we have compiled an enormous amount of information about James of Deering, and except for one ugly little fact,
this assignment seems totally obvious.  However, the assignment
does rest on the chance  that a report of the death of this James[6]
in Feb 1785 is "greatly exaggerated." **Proceed with caution!**

-------------------------------------------------------------

**522.** *James[6]* Eaton (*James[5]*, James[4], Jonathan[3], Thomas[2], John[1])
was born 17 Dec 1760 at Goffstown.  A few weeks before his 16th birthday, he joined his uncle Enoch and his elder brother Samuel in Gen.
Stark's Brigade to fight at Bennington, 16 Aug 1777.   He also served
near Stillwater, N.Y. in the fall of 1777 and with Capt. Dearborn's Co. in
Rhode Island in 1778.   Soon after the War gravitated out of New England, James began to develop a 93-acre farm for himself on the south
flank of Hedgehog Mountain on the west side of Deering, N.H.   On 26
Nov 1782, James mar. 1st, **Martha McClure**.  She was described as being
"of Goffstown," but the wedding took place in Hillsborough, N.H., a few
miles north of James's new home in Deering.   She was almost surely the
daughter of David McClure, a citizen of Goffstown who had joined in the
same mobilization to Bennington as the Eaton boys, and who, like James,

was just taking up residence in Deering along with a remarkable number
of other young men who had marched together to that battle.  The couple established themselves on the mountain in Deering and began gener-
ating a large family.  About 1815, and with thirteen children in the fold,
Martha died.  In Jan 1817, James[6] signed an agreement which gave his
main still-at-home son William more control of the homestead, provided
that he guarantee to maintain his father with all necessities for life; and to
do so for his wife or widow were he to remarry.  Very soon after this
agreement James did mar. 2d, **Mrs. Sarah (George) White**, who was a
native of Antrim, the other nearby town in addition to Hillsborough that
James would have traded at frequently.  She was the widow of Silas White
of Antrim, and considerably younger than James.  She was to bear him
another four children with the first one arriving 11 Dec 1817, a bit more
than 11 months after the agreement with son William. James and Sarah's
last conveyance in Deering dated 6 Mar 1820 sells all or most of their
farm, although James continues to be taxed in Deering through the end
of Deering tax records in 1823, albeit at very deflated rates after the farm
was sold.  In Sep 1823, James is "of Antrim" when buying a small three-
acre farm straddling the line between "Society Land" (later to be named
Bennington, N.H.) and Francestown, N.H.  This farm could not have
been more than four miles as the crow flies from James's old homestead,
and could have been as close as two.  The farmhouse itself must have
been on the Bennington side of the line, as the aging James is listed in the
Censuses of 1830 and 1840 as living in "Society Land."  Father James
died 5 Jan 1849; mother Sarah outlived him by some decades, during
which she spent some time trying to establish Revolutionary pension
rights as James's widow.  She finally succeeded, as her pension rights
were terminated as of 22 Nov 1883, a date which coincides with her death
on the tombstone she shares with James in the center of Bennington, N.H.

Children with Martha at Deering (the first 11 births are found in
the town records of Deering):

1414      i. Hannah[7] Eaton, b. 10 Apr 1783; prob. mar. Josiah Newman
             ("both of Deering"), 15 Nov 1804.
+1415     ii. David[7] Eaton, b. 7 Apr 1784; mar. Susanna Roberson, 1804.
+1416    iii. John[7] Eaton, b. 30 Mar 1786; mar. Betsey Moor, 1807.
+1417     iv. James[7] Eaton, b. 7 Mar 1788; mar. Olive Wilson.
1418      v. Robert[7] Eaton, b. 20 Dec 1790; no more account.
+1419     vi. Samuel[7] Eaton, b. 13 Feb 1792; mar. Betsey White, 1817.
1420    vii. William[7] Eaton, b. 13 Apr 1794; mar. Hannah Shattuck
             ("both of Deering") on 17 Feb 1820.  This marriage was
             just in the period when William's parents were moving
             off the Mountain and turning the family homestead over
             to William, their last son in residence.  William is said to
             have lived there until his death, 28 Aug 1847, and this
             is undoubtedly true, although no Deering Census-taker
             discovered them in either 1830 or 1840.  There is no
             record of children.

**1421**  viii. Mary[7] Eaton, b. 11 Mar 1796; mar. David Bass ("both of
          Deering"), 30 Dec 1819. She died 12 Mar 1856.
**1422**   ix. Lucretia[7] Eaton, a twin b. 6 Nov 1798; no further account.
**1423**    x. Rocksey[7] Eaton, the other twin b. 6 Nov 1798; mar. Isaac
          Wilkins ("both of Deering"), 1824.
**+1424**  xi. Isaac[7] Eaton, b. 5 Mar 1801; mar. Betsey Atwood.
**1425**  xii. Child[7] Eaton, b. ? . Too late for town record listings.
**1426** xiii. Betsey[7] E. Eaton (??), b. ca. 1809; mar. Lewis Martin; she
          died 1884 at Bennington.

Children with Sarah at Deering:

**+1427** xiv. Hiram[7] Eaton, b. 11 Dec 1817; mar. Edna Sweetser, 1844.
**1428**  xv. Joseph[7] Eaton (??) (a Molyneux addition, but a second son
          is known to have been born to James/Sarah.)
**1429** xvi. Martha[7] J. Eaton, b. 1824.
**1430** xvii. Sarah[7] F. Eaton, b. 1826.


**525. David[6] Eaton** (James[5-4], Jonathan[3], Thomas[2], John[1]) was born
15 Jul 1767 in Goffstown. In 1796 he mar. **Betsey Hadley** of Goffstown (she born 11 Jul 1773). They resided in Goffstown on a farm
bought in 1793, virtually on what is now the campus of St. Anselm's
College in the southeast corner of the township. David died 23 Oct
1839; wife Betsey died 9 Apr 1856.

Children, all born Goffstown:

**1431**    i. Betsey[7] Eaton, b. 2 Nov 1796; mar. Paige Richardson; she
          died 5 Oct 1861.
**+1432**  ii. James[7] Eaton, b. 19 Mar 1798; mar. Rebecca Gould, 1826.
**1433**  iii. Lydia[7] Eaton, b. 5 Jul 1799; mar. Ebenezer French of Bed-
          ford. She died 5 Sept 1881.
**1434**  iv. Hannah[7] Eaton, b. 9 Mar 1801; mar. Nathan Wheeler of
          Lyndeborough, 8 Feb 1831. She died 15 Feb 1874.
**1435**   v. Abigail[7] Eaton, b. 21 Nov 1802; she died unmar. 15 Apr
          1834.
**+1436**  vi. David[7] Eaton, b. 26 Sep 1804; mar. Sarah __?__ of Ky.
**1437** vii. Clarissa[7] Eaton, b. 22 Jul 1806; mar. John Barr, Oct 1828.
          She died 22 Dec 1891.
**1438** viii. Albert[7] Eaton, b. 15 Apr 1808; mar. Mary Ann __?__.
          They res. Charlestown, Mass., but later removed to Went-
          worth, N.H. They had a daughter, Mary, who mar. a
          Simpkins. Albert[7] died 1 May 1882.
**1439**  ix. Mary[7] Eaton, b. 15 Nov 1809; mar. 1st, William Horne of
          Watertown, Mass., 1836; 2d, Samuel Noyes, 1866 of
          Watertown. She died 17 May 1899.
**+1440**  x. Horace[7] Eaton, b. 5 Oct 1811; mar. 1st, Sarah Chandler.
**1441**  xi. Orissa[7] Eaton, b. 30 Apr 1813; m. Daniel Bond of Water-

town, 4 Apr 1844. She died 28 Apr 1894.

**1442** xii. Sophia[7] Eaton, b. 1815; d. 1816.

+**1443** xiii. **William[7] Hadley Eaton, senior author of this volume:**
b. 4 Sep 1818; mar. Caroline Bartlett of Milford, N.H.

**529.** Cotton[6] Eaton (James[5-4], Jonathan[3], Thomas[2], John[1]) was born 6 Sep 1777 at Goffstown, N.H. Not too long before 1800 he mar. **Sally Gordon** of Bedford, N.H., the daughter born to John and Mary (Campbell) Gordon ca. 26 Aug 1777. This was in the same period as when Cotton won a license to sell "spirituous liquors" in Goffstown in 1797. Early in the marriage the couple were members of the unified Presbyterian Congregational Church there. At some time before 1810, more or less in the middle of their child-rearing, Cotton determined to remove to Maine. This migration led to something of a collapse of information about the family, in part because they became rolling stones. We have found no land deeds, for example, in Maine, and their children were as poorly recorded there as in Goffstown. Our chief trail is provided by subsequent Maine Censuses. In 1810 Cotton is quite deep in the interior of Maine at Madison, Somerset Co. By 1820 he has moved over 40 miles south to Greene, Kennebec Co. In 1830 he is found 35 miles southeast on the coast at Woolwich, Lincoln Co. In 1840 he is back some 60 miles to the north at Hermon in Penobscot Co. There the family comes to rest for 1850 as well. Wife Sally died there 12 Oct 1842; but Cotton survived until 20 Feb 1862. Both are buried at Snow's Corner Cemetery in Hermon. We do not know what trade Cotton pursued to lead such a peripatetic life; but it is unlikely to have been the usual Maine sea-faring one.

Children: several sources, probably copying from one another, mention that this couple had 12 children, but present no actual list of their names. Census family compositions suggest that roughly eight of the twelve were females. After much search, we have identified two daughters and two sons. We leave room for the other eight below, with a rough approximation of the likely birth order:

**1444** i. Son[7] Eaton, b. ca. 1800.
**1445** ii. Daughter[7] Eaton, b. 1802.
**1446** iii. Daughter[7] Eaton, b. 1804.
**1447** iv. Daughter[7] Eaton, b. 1806.
**1448** v. Daughter[7] Eaton, b. 1808.
**1449** vi. Daughter[7] Eaton, b. 1810; died young?
**1450** vii. Abigail[7] R. Eaton, a twin b. 7 Aug 1812; d. 21 Jun 6 1896.
**1451** viii. Sarah[7] Ann Eaton, the other twin b. 7 Aug 1812; mar. Capt. James Johnson of Cleveland, Ohio.
+**1452** ix. Nathaniel[7] D. Eaton, b. 1816; mar. Ann B. Clark, 1846.
**1453** x. Daughter[7] Eaton, b. 1817.
+**1454** xi. Josiah[7] G. Eaton, b. 1819; mar. 1st, Nancy B. Snow, 1848.
**1455** xii. Child[7] Eaton, b. 1823; died young.

**531. John**[6] **Eaton** (Nathaniel[5], James[4], Jonathan[3], Thomas[2], John[1])
was born 21 Feb 1767, presumably at Penacook (later, Concord, N.H.)
although equally recorded at Haverhill, Mass. He grew up in Haverhill,
Mass., but in 1791 when he was 24 he removed to Sutton, N.H., settling
on the brow of Kimball's Hill. It was there on 20 Dec 1792 that he mar.
**Mary "Polly" Kimball**, the eldest child of Caleb and Sarah (Sawyer). In
1796 he bought an 81-acre tract of land from father-in-law Caleb on that
hill and built his own house there. Like other Haverhill Eatons in this
period he was an artisan in metals, his specialty being brass-making (a
"brazier"), as well as a trader and farmer, probably in that order, because
he was not as tightly bound to a plot of land as most. He is described as
"a man of splendid physique, of a vigourous mind, but not thrifty." The
Census of 1800 found him still at Sutton; but before 1802 he had moved
to Warner Lower Village. returning to Sutton about 1806. Then in 1808
he removed to Hartley, Lower Canada. He returned after a while to Sutton again, although he missed the 1810 Census there. When death
caught up with him in Nov 1817, he was in Montreal, Canada.

Children:

1456    i. Frederick[7] Eaton, b. 16 Nov 1793 at Sutton; mar. 1st, Polly S.
        Badger, 18 Jun 1829. They settled at Warner, N.H., where
        he was for a time a clothier there. He was a religious man,
        and wanted to study for the ministry. But he turned to
        farming full-time, while serving as deacon for 28 years in
        the Congregational Church at Warner. Wife Polly died 27
        Aug 1861 without issue; and Frederick later mar. 2d,
        Abiah Heath, 26 Mar 1863. He died in Warner, 31 Jan
        1865.
1457   ii. Ruth[7] Kimball Eaton, b. 10 Feb 1795 at Sutton. She studied
        at the academies of Sutton and Pembroke. N.H. On 5 Sep
        1825 she mar. Robert H. Sherburne of Derry, N.H. at Sut-
        ton. He was a bookseller who became a publisher in Con-
        cord, N.H., Portland, Me. and Boston, Mass. This couple
        lived to celebrate their 50th wedding anniversary. He died
        25 July 1877; she died 13 Sep 1882.
1458  iii. Rebecca[7] Dodge Eaton, b. 3 Jun 1796, at Sutton. She was a
        teacher in the schools at Utica and Rochester, N. Y. She
        spent her last years with her brother John in Sutton and
        died 9 Dec 1852.
1459   iv. Sarah[7] Eaton, b. 12 Oct 1797 at Sutton; died in infancy.
+1460   v. John[7] Eaton, b. 7 Nov 1798 at Sutton; mar. Janet Andrews.
1461   vi. Sarah[7A] Sawyer Eaton, b. 27 Apr 1800 at Sutton; mar.
        Samuel Dresser, 11 Jun 1835 at Sutton. He was a promi-
        citizen of Sutton, elected seven times a town selectman
        and three times elected representative to the state legisla-
        ture. He died 18 May, 1868. She spent her last years

at the home of her son and died 14 Dec 1878.
**1462**   vii. Hiram[7] Eaton, b. 14 Jan 1802 at Warner Lower Village. He
was a silversmith and watchmaker at places like Montpelier and St. Albans, Vt., as well as at Warner and Concord,
N.H. When caught in the 1830 Census at St. Albans he
seems to have a wife and no children. We do not know
the wife's name or whether there were children later.
Hiram died 8 Aug 1876 at Warner.
**1463**  viii. Lucretia[7] Kimball Eaton, b. 12 Mar 1803 at Warner;  She
was a milliner there for some years, but died 13 Jul 1881
at Harvard, Mass. in the home of her brother Jacob.
**+1464**    ix. (Dr.) Jacob[7] Sawyer Eaton, b. 4 Jan 1805 at Warner; mar.
1st, Mrs. Harriet Kimball, 1830; 2d, Alma Tyler, 1849.
**1465**    x. Charles[7] Eaton, b. 4 Feb 1807 at Sutton; a millwright
who removed early to Pennsylvania, and thence to live in
Plaquemines, La. He was known for his skill in building
cotton-gins, presses, and sugar-mills. As a long-term
resident of the South, he was so angered by the Union
victory in the Civil War that he moved to Valparaiso,
Chile and later to Tahiti, where he died, 14 Nov 1877.
**+1466**    xi. Lucien[7] Bonaparte Eaton, b. 17 Dec 1808 at Hartley, Can.
**+1467**   xii. (Rev.) Horace[7] Eaton, b. 7 Oct 1810, Sutton; mar. Anna.


**533.  Elijah[6] Eaton** (Nathaniel[5], James[4], Jonathan[3], Thomas[2],
John[1]) was born 12 Jan 1771 in Haverhill, Mass.  He mar. **Elizabeth
"Betsey" Vose** (she born 10 Aug 1777) of Bedford, N.H., on 1 Jan 1797
at Bedford.  She was the daughter of Lt. James and Abigail (Richardson)
Vose.  Elijah and Betsey lived first at Haverhill, Mass., but soon decided
to follow Elijah's elder brother John to settle in Sutton, N.H., buying of
John an 82-acre tract of land there in Nov 1800.  This property was on
the eastern slope of Kimball's Hill on the road from Sutton to Warner.  It
became known as the Eaton Grange, and was for decades a summer reunion spot for the numerous, accomplished and far-flung descendants of
Nathaniel[5] Eaton (see Sidebar #12).  Elijah Eaton was the scholar of his
family and as a young man studied medicine, but gave it up as he came
to doubt the validity of some of its prevalent practices.  The couple
reared their children at the Eaton Grange until death stopped Elijah in
middle age, 6 Sep 1818 at Sutton.  Widow Betsey died 12 Aug 1849.

Children (the last eight all born at Sutton):

**+1468**    i. Jubal[7] Harrington Eaton, b. 1 Aug 1798 at Haverhill, Mass;
mar. 1st, Pluma  Putney; 2d, Sarah Dresser.
**1469**   ii. Nathaniel[7] Eaton, b. 1800, Haverhill, Mass.; died 1804.
**+1470**  iii. Elijah[7] Eaton, b. 24 Mar 1803 at Sutton; mar. Fanny Sawyer.
**+1471**   iv. Nathaniel[7A] Eaton, b. 27 Apr 1805;  removed to N.Y. State.
**1472**    v. James[7] Vose Eaton, b. 27 Jul 1807; removed to Pennsylva-

nia as a stone quarrier about 1831-32. He went into business later, then studied law and practiced in Philadelphia
until his health declined. He died unm.13 Nov 1843.
1473   vi.  Sumner[7] Eaton, b. 1809; died 1818.
1474   vii. Roxana[7] Eaton, b. 26 Jun 1811; taught school at Sutton,
            Warren and Bradford, N.H., and at a select school for
            young ladies in Boston. She died 11 Feb 1893.
+1475  viii. Ariel[7] Kendrick Eaton, b. 1 Dec 1813; removed to Ohio.
1476   ix.  Pelatiah[7] Chapin Eaton, b. 1815, named like his brother
            Ariel, for a Baptist minister; died 1818.
+1477  x.   Carlos[7] Smith Eaton, b. 4 May 1818; mar. Laura Dimond.


**534. Ebenezer[6] Eaton** (Nathaniel[5], James[4], Jonathan[3], Thomas[2],
John[1]) was born 5 Feb 1773 at Haverhill, Mass. He mar. 1st, **Deborah
Vose** of Bedford, N.H., int. 21 May 1794, She was born 4 Jul 1775, the
next older sister of the Betsey Vose who married Ebenezer's brother Elijah above. This couple appears to have settled for a while in the later
1790s at Hopkinton, N.H., on the north side of the Contoocook River
toward the Warner town line. The husband is possibly the Ebenezer Eaton at Warner in 1800, although the age report is excessive by nearly 20
years. By 1810, however, they have surely joined Eaton brothers Elijah
and Nathaniel at Sutton. It may well be that wife Deborah died in the
later 1810s, for Ebenezer before 1820 has left Sutton and migrated
northward to the deep White Mountains, marrying 2d, **Sarah Carlton** of
Bartlett, N.H. By 1830 Ebenezer and a somewhat younger woman are at
Bethlehem, N.H. where Ebenezer dies in the spring of 1840.

The child record is very fragmentary in the later going. Our best
reconstruction is based on Census family compositions and an assumption that two of the younger Eatons in Bethlehem, N.H.--Horatio and Jabez, known to be brothers--are more likely to be sons of Elias[6] Eaton out
of the line of William[1] of Reading, also on the scene, than out of this
Ebenezer. Then, children with Deborah:

+1478  i.   Nathaniel[7] Eaton, b. ca. 1795; mar. Susan Philbrick, 1820.
1479   ii.  Son[7] Eaton, b. ca. 1803.
1480   iii. Son[7] Eaton, b. ca. 1805.
1481   iv.  Deborah[7] (??) Eaton, b. ca. 1808.


Children with Sarah:

1482   v.   Ruth[7] (??) Eaton, b. ca. 1816-19; she is of Bethlehem when
            she mar. Jesse Fowler of Dorchester, N.H., 1838.
1483   vi.  Daughter[7] Eaton, b. ca. 1816-1819.
1484   vii. Son[7] Eaton, b. ca. 1820-25.
1485   viii. Daughter[7] Eaton, b. ca. 1820-25.
1486   ix.  Son[7] Eaton, b. ca. 1820-25.

**535. Nathaniel[6] Eaton** (Nathaniel[5], James[4], Jonathan[3], Thomas[2], John[1]) was born 4 May 1775 at Haverhill, Mass. His three older brothers had removed north to New Hampshire through places like Hopkinton, Bradford and Sutton, and found their wives along the way. Nathaniel mar. a Haverhill girl, **Sarah Emerson** (born 21 Apr 1778, daughter of Eltrimer/Sarah Emerson) on 11 Oct 1797. A few months later in Feb 1798 he bought an 80-acre lot on the north edge of Hopkinton, N.H., from his brother Ebenezer (**#534**), who was moving on to Sutton, N.H. This couple were at Hopkinton briefly, appearing in the 1800 Census there. But in 1801 they in turn sold the 80 acres, partitioned into three parcels, and bought an 80-acre farm from Josiah Cutler in Sutton to replace it, where they remained the rest of their lives. Nathaniel built a large mansion-style house on the property. He had the first chaise in the neighborhood. He was an "enterprising and thrifty farmer, of clear and strong mind, and decided convictions" (Worthen, 1890). He was an active member of the Baptist Church, first in Sutton, then later in Warner. He was devoted to his extended family, and frequently journeyed around New England to visit. He especially visited his roots in Haverhill, Mass. It was on one of these trips that wife Sarah became ill and died ca. 1855; Nathaniel lived five days past his 100th birthday, dying at Sutton 9 May 1875.

Children (all but the first at Sutton, N.H.):

+1487    i. Leonard[7] Eaton, b. 10 Jun 1800 in Haverhill, Mass.; mar. Susanna Evans, 1829.

1488    ii. Meshellum[7] Eaton, b. Oct 1803; he lived just south of Sutton on the edge of Warner, N.H., although he removed for a time to Maryland with his brother Alvin; he died 28 Jun 1864 at Sutton.

+1489    iii. Alvin[7] Eaton, b. 18 Dec 1805; mar. Hannah Hardy, 1845.

+1490    iv. Nathaniel[7] Eaton, b. 22 Jan 1808; mar. Harriet Ricketts.

1491    v. Rolinda[7] Eaton, b. 12 Jun 1810; died 1818.

+1492    vi. George[7] Clinton Eaton, b. 28 Jul 1814; m. Lorinda Rowell.

1493    vii. Cynthia[7] Eaton, b. 21 May 1821; a very esteemed teacher early in life. On 20 Dec 1860 she mar. William H. Allen, a prosperous merchant at Penacook, N.H.

**537. Ichabod[6] Eaton** (Nathaniel[5], James[4], Jonathan[3], Thomas[2], John[1]) was born 3 Jun 1779 in Haverhill, Mass. He mar. **Rebecca Haseltine**, 8 Sep 1799, also in Haverhill. They resided in Haverhill throughout the period of child-bearing, but after their final child in 1811 they removed to Hopkinton, where they appear in Censuses from 1820 to at least 1850. Ichabod died in 19 Jun 1860.

Children (all at Haverhill):

1494    i. Susannah[7] Eaton, b. 23 Feb 1799.

**1495**    ii. Matilda[7] Eaton, b. 17 Aug 1801.
+**1496**   iii. Ichabod[7], Jr., Eaton, b. 28 Aug 1803; mar. 1st, Louisa Jones.
+**1497**   iv. Nathaniel[7] Clarks Eaton, b. 1 Sep 1805; mar. Harriet.
**1498**    v. Richard[7] Haseltine Eaton, b. 5 Nov 1807; mar. Rebecca who died 13 Jul 1840, ae 28; he died 20 Dec 1848, Hopkinton.
**1499**    vi. Mary[7] Hardy Eaton, b. 6 Jan 1810.
**1500**    vii. Clarissa[7] Ann Eaton, b. 25 Mar 1811; mar 1st, Stilson Hutchins, who died 4 Jun 1838; 2d, Hiram Somerby, who died 8 Jul 1868. She died 29 Dec 1869, St. Louis, Mo.

**541. Eliphalet[6] Eaton** (Ebenezer[5], James[4], Jonathan[3], Thomas[2], John[1]) was born 27 Aug 1769 at Haverhill, Mass. He removed to Walpole, N.H., with his family, probably before he was ten years old. He mar. **Elizabeth "Betsey" Goodridge** of Rindge, N.H., 12 Sep 1792. The couple settled first at Walpole, where Eliphalet had purchased tracts of land in 1791 and 1793. In 1796 and 1797, however, he sold these parcels, whereupon the family appears to have removed to Waterford township adjoining St. Johnsbury in Caledonia Co., Vt., since an Eliphalet Eaton of appropriate age and family composition is registered there in the 1800 Census, and in our data base of thousands of Eaton males covering all the New England Eaton lineages there is only one other given name of Eliphalet (an 1816 birth in Maine). There is no further sighting of this Eliphalet in New England; but it is likely that he is the "Liflet Eaton" recorded in 1810 in Genessee Co., New York, with his apparent children now numbering ten. Here the Census trail ends.

Children (neither birth records nor given names have been found, but we leave a set of place-holders congruent with family composition data from the two Censuses covering the period of most intensive family formation by this couple, although the birth order within decades is arbitrary, and the list is probably partial):

**1501**    i. Daughter[7] Eaton, b. 1793-1799.
**1502**    ii. Son[7] Eaton, b. 1793-99.
**1503**    iii. Daughter[7] Eaton, b. 1793-99.
**1504**    iv. Son[7] Eaton, b. 1793-99.
**1505**    v. Daughter[7] Eaton, b. 180?.
**1506**    vi. Daughter[7] Eaton, b. 180?.
**1507**    vii. Son[7] Eaton, b. 180?.
**1508**    viii. Daughter[7] Eaton, b. 180?.
**1509**    ix. Daughter[7] Eaton, b. 180?.
**1510**    x. Daughter[7] Eaton, b. 180?.

**544. Josiah[6] Eaton** (Ebenezer[5], James[4], Jonathan[3], Thomas[2], John[1]) was born ca. 1779 at Walpole, N.H. where his parents had just arrived from Haverhill, Mass. In 1802 he bought land well to the north in Coos Co., N.H., but there is no reason to believe that he ever sought his fortune there.  Soon after this purchase he mar. 1st, **Zerviah Robinson**, 23 Apr 1803 at Walpole.  After his father's death in 1805, Josiah was quite active for some years in Walpole real estate.  His oldest brother Eliphalet had long since departed westward, and the next brother James had apparently died.  Early in 1809 the final brother, Calvin, died very prematurely as well, so Josiah presumably took over what was left of his father's estate.  He is present in the 1810 Census at Walpole, and his local real estate activity continues until late in December of that year.  After childbirths to 1812, however, the Walpole record goes silent.  As noted earlier (cf. **#209**), Molyneux identifies Josiah's father Ebenezer[5] as "the ancestor of the Albany (N.Y.) branch of the Eatons," but the only son who could have colonized that city was this Josiah, and he does not seem to have proceeded there by any straight line method.  In fact, it is quite possible he abandoned his Walpole family at roughly the point when his record stops there.  He next surfaces in Somerville, N.J., where he seems to have mar. 2d, **Gertrude Mae ("Gitty")** __?__, a New Jersey native, and has a small new family with her.  He is probably in New Jersey in 1820, but the Federal Census for that year in New Jersey has been lost.  Early in 1828 he buys land in Albany's Second Ward, where he and his new family reside as of the 1830 Census.  In 1833 they purchase a larger property in the Schuyler Farm District of the First Ward, and are recorded there in the Albany Censuses of 1840 and 1850.  As of the latter year, their residence is flanked by the new household of their son James W., who in the fullness of time became a very prominent Albany citizen, lending some weight to the Molyneux description.  As a final twist to the story, a "Zerva Eaton" appears in the 1840 Census back in Walpole, N.H., living with a younger woman in her twenties, after the other Eaton families of Walpole have long since left the area.  She reports her own birth in the 1780s, and thus is almost certainly Josiah's first wife Zerviah.  Her companion may well be one of her daughters.

Children with Zerviah at Walpole, N.H.:

**1511**    i. Daughter[7] Eaton, b. ca. 1809; died by drowning, 1811.
**1512**    ii. Edna[7] Eaton, b. 4 Apr 1811.
**1513**    iii. Corana[7] Eaton, b. 5 Oct 1812.

Children with Gertrude, probably all New Jersey:

**1514**    iv. Abigail[7] Eaton, b. ca. 1815.
+**1515**   v. James[7] W. Eaton, b. 22 Aug 1817 at Somerville, New Jersey; mar. Elizabeth Brenner, 1840.
**1516**    vi. Gitty[7] Ann Eaton, b. ca. 1819.  She was unmar. as of 1843, when she sells her father a quitclaim to the parental properties in Albany.

**548. Kimball[6] Eaton** (Enoch[5], James[4], Jonathan[3], Thomas[2], John[1]) was born 14 Jun 1772 at Haverhill West Parish, but grew up in Goffstown, N.H.; mar. 1st, **Mary ("Polly") Page**, 24 Mar 1796 at Dunbarton, N.H., after the parents and younger siblings had removed to Cavendish, Vt. The young couple caught up to them in Vermont by the 1800 Census if not earlier. It was in Cavendish that they reared most of their children. Wife Polly died 5 Aug 1817 at Cavendish; and Kimball mar. 2d, **Sarah Cram**, 26 Mar 1819 at Andover, Vt. The family cannot be found in the 1820 Census, but apparently continued moving westward, emerging for the 1830 Census at Crown Point (Essex Co.), N.Y., and thence on to Stockholm in St. Lawrence Co., N.Y., for 1840. There the trail ends.

Children by Polly, all but possibly the first two at Cavendish, Vt.:

| | | |
|---|---|---|
| **1517** | i. | Polly[7] Eaton, b. 2 Nov 1796. |
| **1518** | ii. | Deborah[7] Eaton, b. 2 Aug 1798. |
| **1519** | iii. | Sally[7] Eaton, b. 27 Nov 1801; mar. Isaac Cornell of Arlington, Vt. |
| **1520** | iv. | Abigail[7] Eaton, b. 28 Dec 1803. |
| **+1521** | v. | Kimball[7] Eaton, b. 16 Feb 1806; mar. Margaret. |
| **+1522** | vi. | Ryland[7] Fletcher Eaton, b. 18 Mar 1808; mar. Clarissa Clark. |
| **1523** | vii. | Saloma[7] Eaton. She was b. 24 Jun 1811. |

**549. Enoch[6] Eaton** (Enoch[5], James[4], Jonathan[3], Thomas[2], John[1]) was born 17 Mar 1774 at Haverhill, Mass.; mar. his first cousin **Priscilla[6] Eaton** (see **#538**) at Haverhill, (int.) 21 Feb 1797. There is no sign that this couple joined Enoch[6]'s family of origin at Cavendish, Vt., and we do not know where they spent their early married years. But Enoch is a "yeoman of Bowdoinham" in Lincoln Co., Me., as of Feb 1808, as he buys two plots of land in the immediate vicinity of his younger brother Warren (**#551**), bounded south by the Topsham town line, near the channel of the Cathance River. He joins Warren in the 1810 Census at Bowdoinham, and appears on several more land deeds there, ultimately listed as a "painter." He appears to be selling out, however, in Aug 1815, and then the family disappears from the Maine record. Molyneux (1911) has them removing to Chenango Co., New York, and indeed a Warren Eaton likely to be their son (see **#1523** below) is at Oxford in that county in 1840 and beyond. Information as to children is very inadequate, in part because of residential mobility, and in part perhaps because the family in its Maine period lived a fair distance from either the village at Bowdoinham or at Topsham.

Children surviving infancy, largely inferred from Census family compositions, with birth order only approximate:

| | | |
|---|---|---|
| **1524** | i. | Son[7] Eaton, b. ca. 1802-04; alive in 1820. |
| **1525** | ii. | Daughter[7] Eaton, b. ca. 1805-09; alive 1820. |

**1526**    iii. Daughter[7] Eaton, b. ca. 1805-09; alive 1820.
**1527**    iv. Daughter[7] Eaton, b. ca. 1810-12; alive 1820.
+**1528**    v. Warren[7] Eaton, b. 2 Apr 1814, prob. at Bowdoinham, Me.
**1529**    vi. Daughter[7] Eaton, b. later 1810s; alive 1820.
**1530**    vii. Son[7] Eaton, b. 1810s; alive 1820.


**550. Jonathan[6] Eaton** (Enoch[5], James[4], Jonathan[3], Thomas[2], John[1]) was born 22 Mar 1776 at Haverhill or Goffstown; mar. **Susanna __?__** of Deering, N.H.   This is another "rolling stone" son of Enoch[5], and one about which we know very little. The couple probably went with the family to Cavendish, Vt. (cf. below), but then proceeded onward to unknown parts.

A probable child:

**1531**    i. Jonathan[7] Straw Eaton, born 8 Dec 1796 at Cavendish, Vt.


**551. Warren[6] Eaton** (Enoch[5], James[4], Jonathan[3], Thomas[2], John[1]) was born 15 Jan 1778 at Haverhill or Goffstown. While the rest of his family of origin moved westward into Vermont, Warren proceeded at a rather precocious age to Bowdoinham, Lincoln County, Me., where he mar. **Jane Woodside**, 11 Oct 1798, at Brunswick. Their land in Bowdoinham, amounting in time to 85 acres, abutted the Topsham town line. They were later joined by his older brother Enoch's family in the 1808-15 period. Warren himself appears at Bowdoinham in the six consecutive Censuses from 1800 through 1850. He is usually described as a yeoman, although by 1824 a deed denotes him as "Esquire." Wife Jane died in 1823 at Topsham; but Warren did not die until 1859, also Topsham.

Children (those through 1810 from Bowdoinham Town Records, the later ones from Census inferences):

+**1532**    i. Edmund[7] Eaton, b. 6 Mar 1799 at Topsham, Me.; mar. Ann Fisher, 1834.
**1533**    ii. Warren[7] Eaton, b. 29 Apr 1802 at Topsham; mar. Margaret Mountford (she b. ca. 1804) on 11 Jul 1823 in Bowdoin ham, Me. It seems likely that Warren died early, since nobody of his description can be found in later Censuses either in New England, N.Y., Pennsylvania or the Northwest Territory states in the 1840-70 period. Furthermore, his wife Margaret M. is living with his brother Edmund's family in the 1850 Census; and a woman of her description is in that family or Warren's father's earlier, with never a sign of young children.
**1534**    iii. Clariey[7] Eaton, a dau. b. 10 Sep 1804 at Topsham.
**1535**    iv. Mary[7] Eaton,. 7 Jan 1807 at Bowdoinham.
**1536**    v. *Jthait[7] Eaton, son or dau. b. 24 Apr 1810 at Bowdoinham.

**1537** vi. Son[7] Eaton, b. 1815-19.
**1538** vii. Daughter[7] Eaton, b. 1820-24.

*NOTE. There is obviously some problem with this name, but it is not simply because the microfilm is faint, or because the record is smudged right there, or because the clerk writes with a shower of curlicues that are hard for the modern eye to decode. To the contrary, the clerk writes in bold strokes which are cursive, but so very simple and clear that they are almost bloc printing. The last five letters are totally unambiguous. The capital letter--the most inappropriate symbol here--is indeed a squiggle; but it is essentially same squiggle that precedes dates of -uly and another of -une on the same page, along with names like -ohn and -ames. None of the other capital letters--17 of 26 possible--on the page could be confused with this; and none of the unrepresented nine (F, I, K, P, Q, U, V, X and Z) save possibly the vowels gives a more plausible first initial. A period handwriting expert was stumped. (See for yourself on FHL US/Can Film #0010563.)

**552. Frazier[6] Eaton** (Enoch[5], James[4], Jonathan[3], Thomas[2], John[1]) was born 23 Jan 1780 at Haverhill or Goffstown. He removed with his parents and most of his siblings to Cavendish, Vt., and is listed there in the 1800 Census. He mar. **Lucinda Blakesley** on 19 Nov 1799 in neighboring Weathersfield, Vt. This family escapes the 1810 Census; but by 1820 they have arrived in Rushford in Allegany Co., New York. They are here or in Portage, N.Y., 18 miles or so away, through their last Census in 1850. In the latter Census Frazier, now in his early 70s, lists his current occupation as a (church) sexton, a rather common "retirement" job in this period. Since this aging couple by this time has an "empty nest," and New York State is still years from reinventing birth records, we cannot identify their children among the Eatons scattered over this general area. (At least two of the three other Eaton households in 1850 Rushford with heads of an appropriate age to be Frazier/Lucinda children are more likely to be out of the Reading, Mass., line of Eatons.) Family composition data from pre-1850 Censuses suggest a rather large roster of children, but there is also evidence of a "compound" family under the same roof, at least as of 1830, clouding the issue.

**557. Benjamin[6] Eaton** (Jonathan[5-3], Thomas[2], John[1]) was born at Atkinson/Plaistow, N.H., on 12 Jul 1762. Patches of his life are well-illuminated while others seem irretrievably lost. He saw some latter-day service in the Revolution, and then established himself briefly at Loudon, N.H. Like a number of his relatives, he began to invest in land to the north (e.g., at Landaff, Grafton Co., N.H.), calling himself a "trader" in his conveyances. By 1783 he had removed to Piermont, N.H., on the upper Connecticut River. He did not tarry long there, however, and was soon off westward in pursuit of still more virgin territory. This he found about 1787 at Painted Post, N.Y., which was then the name not only of a tiny initial settlement but also of the broader "howling wilderness" which

was later constituted as Steuben County, N.Y. He was active in the incorporation of the town and the county, and "Ben Eaton's general store," the
first such convenience in the area, gets prominent mention in Steuben
County annals (Roberts, 1891). The five-day canoe trip floating down
the Cohocton River and poling up the Susquehanna to Unadilla, N.Y., in
Delaware County (three counties to the northeast) in order to import the
initial stock for the store, is the subject of a colorful account by a participant (Erwin, 1917). Benjamin is named as a household head at Erwin
Township (Painted Post) in the 1790 Census, and was clearly there running his store well into the ensuing decade. But he is not listed there in
1800; and apart from a few land deeds through 1806, he mysteriously
disappears for nearly 40 years from any public records, Census or otherwise, that we can find in Steuben Co. or New York State or, for that matter, in neighboring Pennsylvania. This disappearance is the more perplexing in light of the fact that Benjamin's only surviving brother, Jonathan[6] (#**561** below), migrated from New England to Steuben Co. in the
first decade of the new century, presumably to join him, and is visible
there for the next half-century. We do know however that Benjamin died
28 May 1847 at his half-brother Jonathan's home in Urbana, N.Y.; and
since a second septuagenarian male lives with Jonathan's family in the
1840 Census, this is presumably Benjamin as well. His obituary mentions
that for the preceding eight years Benjamin had been a member of the
Presbyterian Church in nearby Hammondsport. About three months after Benjamin's death, an obituary from neighboring Orange Twp. (later
in Schuyler Co.) reports the death of "Mrs. Mary Eaton, aged about 45
years, consort of Benjamin Eaton." Given the dearth of other Benjamins
in the immediate area, this is likely to be a wife of our subject here, albeit
in view of the age differential, probably not a first wife. We have no clue
whatever as to Benjamin's issue, if any.

**561. Jonathan[6] Eaton** (Jonathan[5-3], Thomas[2], John[1]) was born at
Plaistow 7 May 1768 under unusual circumstances. The will of Daniel
Whitaker, an Atkinson neighbor, dated 18 May 1770 and proved 29 Aug
1770 when Jonathan was early in his third year of life, left him the whole
of Daniel's estate on grounds that this Jonathan[6] Jr., while the son of
Jonathan[5] Eaton, was (as Whitaker's will put it), "reputedly the son of my
daughter Mehitable, now deceased" (see pp. 400-401, *Probate Records of
the Province of N.H.*, LDS Film #1033745). Since the baby Jonathan
had lost not only his maternal grandfather and his mother in very short
order, he was put under the guardianship of Joseph Emerson of Haverhill
on the same date as Whitaker's will was proved. He thus presumably was
hardly if at all raised in the family of his biological father, despite his
later close attachment to the older half-brother, Benjamin[6]. The next
clear view we have of this Jonathan is in the 1810 Census at Bath, the seat
of Steuben County, N.Y., where he has obviously been drawn by the earlier exploits of brother Benjamin. In 1822 he was among the early settlers who succeeded in getting Urbana, New York, on the shores of Keuka
Lake, set off from Bath. He was at this address when, on 16 Oct 1832, he

signed an affidavit supporting Benjamin's application for a Revolutionary War pension. He only survived his half-brother by some three years, and is said to have died "on or about Nov. 9, 1850." He did leave a will (Steuben Co. Wills, 5-137) which gives us our only view of his family structure. He provides for his wife **Lucinda** __?__ for her natural life, and mentions as beneficiaries five daughters by first name only, and one son, along with a grandson, James Owen Daun. A daughter Julia Ann is the favored beneficiary, being named a co-executor and receiving all of father Jonathan's 40-acre homestead and his personal estate as well, provided she cares for widow Lucinda. Bequests of $100 are made to the other five children and the grandson, but the disbursement is staggered at two-year intervals over a period of 12 years. Hence there is no clue to birth order in the order of mention, which is dictated by financial need (i.e., the older son, long established, will wait 12 years for his $100.) The division of children by sex in the will--5 girls and one boy--does show reasonable correspondence with the evolution of the composition of this family over the Censuses, where one would guess six girls and two boys, with the boys occurring second and fifth in the birth order, but erosion by early deaths may occur as well.

Probable children:

| | | |
|---|---|---|
| **1539** | i. | Daughter[7] Eaton, b. 1790-92. |
| **+1540** | ii. | Benjamin[7] Eaton, b. 1794. |
| **1541** | iii. | Daughter[7] Eaton, b. 1795-99. |
| **1542** | iv. | Daughter[7] Eaton, b. 1800-1804. |
| **1543** | v. | Son[7] Eaton, b. 1805-09; probably died young. |
| **1544** | vi. | Daughter[7] Eaton, b. 1805-09. |
| **1545** | vii. | Julia Ann[7] Eaton, b. 1814; mar. George Warren. They probably resided at her family homestead, having two children, both of whom had died before 1880. Julia Ann died 16 Apr 1880. |
| **1546** | viii. | Daughter[7] Eaton, b. 1810s. |

Other daughters include Mary Jane, Lucinda, Hannah and Betsey.

**568. Amos[6] Eaton** (Amos[5], Jonathan[4-3], Thomas[2], John[1]) was born 30 Oct 1785 at Haverhill, Mass. to Mary, the first wife of his father Amos. He mar. somewhat late to **Alice Emerson** on 26 May 1820. We have few details of his life, although he does appear in Censuses of 1820, 1830 and 1840 at Haverhill. Contrary to Molyneux (1911, p 439), he can hardly be the Amos Eaton who married and moved to Wilton, N.H., in 1792. (The latter is out of the line of Jonas Eaton of Reading, born there in 1760.) Amos died 22 Sep 1848 in Haverhill.

Children listed as Haverhill births (possibly incomplete):

**1547**     i. Maria[7] Eaton, b. 28 Feb 1821; died 8 Oct 1829, Haverhill.
**1548**     ii. Daniel[7] Eaton, b. 10 Apr 1824; poss. mar. Elizabeth O.
             Eastman of Epsom, N.H. However, in 1860 he is at Hav-
             erhill, a shoemaker age 36, living with his mother Alice,
             age 64. He is not listed in the Mass. Census in 1870.
**1549**    iii. Mary[7] Elizabeth Eaton, b. 24 Mar 1825.

**570. Jonathan[6] Eaton** (Amos[5], Jonathan[4-3], Thomas[2], John[1]) was
born 21 Feb 1790 at Haverhill, Mass.; mar. **Susan Saunders** (b. 1794) on
3 Apr 1815. This couple may have been briefly at Newbury, Mass., with
Jonathan's younger brother David. However, they lived mainly in Plaistow, N.H., where their children were born, despite being listed as
Haverhill residents in the 1830 Census. Husband Jonathan died 22 Apr
1849, although he is buried in Plaistow; wife Susan followed him in death
on 8 Apr 1850.

Children at Plaistow:

+ **1550**     i. John[7] G. Eaton, b. 1816; mar. Mehitable Emerson, 1845.
  **1551**    ii. Daughter[7] Eaton, b. 1820-24.
+ **1552**   iii. Albert[7] W. Eaton, b. 1828; mar. Mary Burley.
  **1553**   iv. Lois[7] Eaton, b. 1833.

**571. David[6] Eaton** (Amos[5], Jonathan[4-3], Thomas[2], John[1]) was born
27 Feb 1792 at Haverhill, Mass. He removed at a young age to Newbury,
Mass., where he appears in the 1810 Census. He mar. **Ruth Little** there
on 23 Oct 1811. They remained in Newbury through 1820, but then
their trail is lost.

Children at Newbury:

**1554**     i. Judith[7] Bartlett Eaton, b. 11 Jan 1812.
**1555**    ii. Edmund[7] Little Eaton, b. 14 Feb 1814.

**575. (Capt.) Samuel[6] Eaton** (Job[5], Samuel[4], Job[3], Thomas[2],
John[1]) was born 31 Dec 1756 at Plaistow, N.H. He served in the N.H.
Line during the Revolution, although his claim to the rank of Captain was
either a militia commission well after the Revolution, or some hyperbole.
He then married **Lydia Ladd** of Kingston, N.H., 10 Oct 1780. Either in
connection with his military service or, as is more likely, because of his
father's land speculation in new settlements in northern New Hampshire,
he appears to have controlled several "wilderness" properties at rather
early age. Thus, for example, when he was a mere 23, he brings in
£1,000 from the sale of two hundred-acre tracts in Enfield (Grafton Co.),
N.H. And a decade later he sells another tract in Warren, N.H., also
Grafton Co. At some time before 1800, however, he and his wife left

Plaistow and established themselves at the less remote new town of Salisbury, N.H. (ultimately, Merrimack Co.) where they spent the rest of their lives. Samuel died there 7 Mar 1826; and wife Lydia died at Salisbury, age 80, on 29 Mar 1839.

Children, the earlier at Plaistow, the later at Salisbury, N.H.:

1556    i. Hannah[7] Eaton, b. 14 May 1781; mar. Moses Greeley, 10 Mar 1803. She died 8 Aug 1833.

1557    ii. Lydia[7] Eaton, b. 25 Apr 1783; mar. Peter Fifield, 4 Mar 1805. She died 9 Jun 1880.

1558    iii. Sarah[7] Eaton, b. 7 Jan 1785; mar. Capt. Silas Call of Boscawen, 22 Dec 1814. She died 12 Jul 1836.

1559    iv. Samuel[7] Eaton, b. 19 Feb 1787 and died 11 Aug 1792.

1560    v. Mehitable[7] Eaton, b. 2 May 1789; mar. Caleb Smith, 30 Mar 1813. She died 6 Jun 1864.

1561    vi. Abigail[7] Eaton, b. 2 Sep 1791; mar. Joseph Huntoon of Andover, N.H., 24 Dec 1815. She died 4 Dec 1825.

1562    vii. Samuel[7A] Eaton, b. 7 Dec 1793 and died 11 Apr 1808.

1563    viii. John[7] Eaton, b. 29 Mar 1796 and died 22 Sep 1797.

+1564    ix. John[7A] Eaton, b. 27 Jul 1798; mar. 1st, Mary Morgan.

1565    x. Lucy[7] Eaton, b. 5 Aug 1800; mar. 1st, William Jackman of Enfield, N.H., 25 Jun 1822. William died 2 Jul 1832, and Lucy mar. 2d, Alstead Brownell, 14 Feb 1835. She died 29 Apr 1872 at Enfield.

+1566    xi. Jesse[7] Eaton, b. 13 May 1803; mar. Susan H. Rogers.

**577. Job[6] Eaton** (Job[5], Samuel[4], Job[3], Thomas[2], John[1]) was born 29 May 1762 at Plaistow, N.H. He mar. 1st, Widow **Sarah Kimball** on 3 Jul 1783 at Haverhill, Mass. Like his elder brother, Job had acquired a tract of land in Warren township, Grafton County, N.H., probably from his father. He removed to that tract in time to be resident there in the 1790 Census, although by this time a more exact surveying showed that the property was in Wentworth, rather than Warren. Wife Sarah died in this general period, and Job mar. 2d, **Phebe ___?___**, who had been born in 1764 in Massachusetts. Job's next younger brother Jesse bought Wentworth land with the thought of joining him, but then opted to remain in Plaistow, selling his tract in 1794 on to the next younger brother Moses[6], who did go north to join Job permanently. Job established a prosperous farm north of the village center, and in the next 20 years bought up considerable further property in Wentworth and Warren. He "died instantly while threshing" on 9 Dec 1830. Wife Phebe survived at Wentworth until 28 Feb 1853.

Children with Sarah K.:

1567    i. Hannah[7] Eaton, b. ca. 1784; mar. Aaron Jewell, Wentworth.

1568    ii. Sarah[7] "Sally" Eaton, b. ca. 1786; mar. Moses Kimball of

Warren, N.H.
+ **1569** iii. Job[7], Jr. Eaton, b. ca. 1788; mar Sally Brown.

Children with Phebe:

+ **1570** iv. Moses[7] Eaton, b. ca. 1791; mar. Abigail Blood, 1816.
+ **1571** v. Jonathan[7] Merrill Eaton, b. ca. 11 Jun 1794; mar. Betsey.
  **1572** vi. Daughter[7] Eaton, b. ca. 1797.
+ **1573** vii. Ezra[7] B. Eaton, b. 24 Aug 1799; mar. 1st, Mary Currier.
+ **1574** viii. Worcester[7] Eaton, b. ca. 1803; mar. Maria.

**578. Jesse[6] Eaton** (Job[5], Samuel[4], Job[3], Thomas[2], John[1]) was born 20 Aug 1765 at Plaistow, N.H.; mar. **Hannah Smith** ca. 1788. Both of his older brothers had removed northward, and he himself bought property near his brother Job at Wentworth, N.H., but in 1794 (the period when his father died), sold it on to his younger brothers, perhaps because he had come into the family homestead. In any event, this couple ended up raising their children in Plaistow. Jesse died 8 Dec 1836, and wife Hannah died 15 May 1845, also at Plaistow.

Children at Plaistow:

  **1575** i. Lucy[7] Eaton, b. 12 Dec 1789.
  **1576** ii. Edna[7] Eaton, b. 19 Aug 1794; died the same day.
  **1577** iii. Hannah[7] Eaton, b. 11 Mar 1799.
  **1578** iv. Samuel[7] Eaton, b. 20 Jan 1801; died 6 Oct 1803.
+ **1579** v. Samuel[7A] Eaton, b. 6 Aug 1805; mar. 1st, Emeline Colby.
  **1580** vi. Mehitable[7] Eaton, b. 30 Jun 1807; died 12 Apr 1819.

**581. Moses[6] Eaton** (Job[5], Samuel[4], Job[3], Thomas[2], John[1]) was born with twin Mehitable[6A] on 7 Nov 1770 at Plaistow, N.H. He followed his elder brother Job to Wentworth, buying his first stake there from his brother Jesse in 1794. In this period he mar. 1st, **Hannah Currier**, daughter of Rev. Samuel Currier of Wentworth. By 1802 or so, Rev. Currier had died leaving a substantial estate, parts of which came to wife Hannah as an heir. Hannah herself died not too long thereafter (between 1802 and 1810), and Moses mar. 2d, **Abigail ___?___**. Moses had cleared a large farm on Atwell Hill northwest of Wentworth village, with a capacious house surrounded on three sides by a large veranda. and several separate barns and a carriage shed. He was even richer in land in Wentworth than his brother Job; and figures as a principal in more than two dozen land conveyances there in the period from 1802 to 1824. He died while still at the farm on 7 May 1839; his wife Abigail survived him there until 11 Aug 1876, dying at about age 95.

Children with Hannah at Wentworth:

**1581**    i. Son[7] Eaton, b. 1785-89.
**1582**    ii. Daughter[7] Eaton, b. 1785-89.
**1583**    iii. Son[7] Eaton, b. 1785-89.
**1584**    iv. Daniel[7] Eaton, b. 29 Apr 1795; died 9 Jun 1800.
**+1585**    v. Jesse[7] Eaton, b. 28 Aug 1796; mar. Elinor Page.
**1586**    vi. Samuel[7] Eaton, b. 1798; died Sep 1798.
**1587**    vii. Moses[7] Eaton, b. 3 Sep 1800; died ? Dec 1800.
**1588**    viii. Rowell[7] Eaton, b. 7 Nov 1801; died 7 Sep 1803.
**1589**    ix. Hannah[7] Eaton, b. ca. 1803; died 7 Sep 1805.

Children with Abigail at Wentworth:

**1590**    x. Son[7] Eaton, b. and died, 16 Dec 1811.
**1591**    xi. David[7] Eaton, b. 22 Nov 1815.

**582. James[6] Eaton** (Job[5], Samuel[4], Job[3], Thomas[2], John[1]) was born 29 Dec 1772 at Plaistow, N.H.; mar. 1st, **Sarah ("Sally") Bradley** of Plaistow, 13 Mar 1794. As a "yeoman of Plaistow," James bought a hundred-acre lot in Wentworth, N.H., where two of his older brothers had already settled, and proceeded to develop a farm there, appearing with those brothers as a resident of Wentworth in 1800. At some time in the next few years, first wife Sally died; and James mar. 2d, **Sarah ("Sally") Dow**, the daughter of Ezekiel and Sarah (Merrill) Dow of Wentworth, on 11 Jun 1806. In the next two years James sold off his accumulated property in Wentworth, and then apparently returned to his native Plaistow to resume farming there, although he does not appear as a household head there until the 1820 Census. James died 5 Mar 1848 at Plaistow; and second wife Sally died there 5 Feb 1853.

Children with Sally (Bradley) at Wentworth:

**+1592**    i. Job[7] Eaton, b. 9 Jan 1795; mar. Ruth Sawyer at Hampstead.
**1593**    ii. Betsey[7] Bradley Eaton, b. 23 Nov 1796.

Children with Sally (Dow) at Plaistow, N.H.:

**+1594**    iii. Daniel[7] Eaton, b. 27 Jan 1815; mar. Louisa Hadley.
**+1595**    iv. Alonzo[7] Willis Eaton, b. 1817; mar. Louisa Noyes.
**1596**    v. Mehitable[7] Eaton, b. 10 Jul 1818; mar. Calvin Sawyer, 27 Apr 1854 at Plaistow as his 2d wife. She died 18 Mar 1876 at Plaistow.
**1597**    vi. Philena[7] W. Eaton, b. 27 Jul 1822; mar. John B. Nichols of Haverhill.

**583. Samuel[6] Eaton** (Ebenezer[5], Samuel[4], Job[3], Thomas[2], John[1]) was born 6 Jun 1763 at Plaistow. At a tender age he became a Quartermaster Sergeant in Capt. Simon Stevens's Co., Col. Timothy Bedell's

Regt., raised "for the defense of the frontiers on and adjacent to the Connecticut River." In this role he served at Haverhill, N.H., and saw the green meadows of the floodplain there. One fruit of this service was the fact that he mar. 1st, **Susanna Noyes**, daughter of Sylvanus Noyes of Landaff, Grafton Co., N.H. and settled at Landaff in the company of his two brothers, Ebenezer and David, no later than 1788. He sired his family there with Susanna on a 60-acre homestead in Range 4, the 1st Division, abutting his brothers. Wife Susanna died 21 Apr 1837 at Landaff, and Samuel then mar. 2d, **Candace ___?___**, a woman over 30 years his junior. He died 6 Sep 1846 at Landaff; she died there in 1865.

Children with Susanna at Landaff, N.H.:

+1598    i. Timothy[7] Eaton, b. 29 Aug 1789; mar. "Patty" Northy.
+1599    ii. Ebenezer[7] Eaton, b. 9 Oct 1791; mar. Betsey Chandler.
 1600   iii. Phebe[7] Eaton, b. ca. 1794.
 1601   iv. Lydia[7] Eaton, b. ca. 1796.
 1602   v. Daughter[7] Eaton, b. ca. 1798.
 1603   vi. Samuel[7] Eaton, b. ca. 1800.
 1604  vii. Daughter[7] Eaton, b. 180?.

     **584. Ebenezer[6] Eaton** (Ebenezer[5], Samuel[4], Job[3], Thomas[2], John[1]) was born 10 Jul 1765 at Plaistow, N.H. Either through his father's efforts or his own precocity, he had removed to Landaff, Grafton Co., N.H., presumably with his brother Samuel (above) and as a resident there bought half of a Proprietor's Right in the settlement in Sep 1784. He mar. on 13 Sep 1792, **Ruth Hutchins**, daughter of Jeremiah Hutchins, the most prominent citizen of neighboring Bath, N.H. (Stearns, 1908). Between 1793 and 1825 he bought a score of other tracts of land in Landaff, many of them purchased for a song from the Tax Collector after default of tax payment. After 1804 he had graduated from the status of "yeoman" to that of Gentleman. In his waning years he moved one township north into Lisbon, N.H., and died there 22 Apr 1843. Wife Ruth died at Lisbon on 15 May 1862.

Children with Ruth at Landaff:

 1605    i. Ebenezer[7] Eaton, b. 25 Jul 1793.
 1606   ii. Stephen[7] Eaton, b. 2 Oct 1796.
+1607  iii. Ira[7] Eaton, b. 6 Jul 1798; mar. Priscilla McKean.
+1608  iv. Mitchell[7] H. Eaton, b. 19 Apr 1800; mar. Sarah Eastman.
 1609   v. Eliza[7] Eaton, b. ca. 1804; died young.
 1610   vi. Phebe[7] Eaton, b. 17 Jul 1807; mar. Elias O. Holton and
            resided at Landaff. She died 21 Aug 1854, Landaff.
 1611  vii. Hannah[7] Sheppard Eaton, b. 12 Apr 1810.

**585. David$^6$ Eaton** (Ebenezer$^5$, Samuel$^4$, Job$^3$, Thomas$^2$, John$^1$) was born ? Feb 1768 at Plaistow. He removed early to Landaff to join his elder brother, already being described as a "yeoman of Landaff" when he purchased a 100-acre lot there in the 6th Range, 2d Division, in Dec 1789. He later mar. **Esther Sanborn**, 8 Jul 1799, presumably at Landaff. He appears in the first three Censuses at Landaff, along with his brothers; but he died at a relatively early age, 17 May 1817.

Children with Esther at Landaff:

+**1612**    i. Peter$^7$ Eaton, b. 17 Apr 1800; mar. Elizabeth.
  **1613**    ii. Esther$^7$ C. Eaton, b. 16 Apr 1802.
+**1614**    iii. David$^7$ Fox Eaton, b. 21 Dec 1805; mar. 1st, Eleanor.
  **1615**    iv. Mary$^7$ H. Eaton, b. 31 Jan 1812; removed to Dover, N.H.; mar. Jabez F. Edgerly of Barnstead, 1838.
  **1616**    v. Hannah$^7$ Eaton, b. 25 Jun 1814. It is probably she who mar. Dr. J. C. Haynes of Deerfield, N.H. in Mar 1841 at Barnstead, N.H. (*N. H. Genealogical Record*, Vol. 17, No. 2 (Apr. 2000), p. 77.

**589. Peter$^6$ Eaton** (Ithamar$^5$, Samuel$^4$, Job$^3$, Thomas$^2$, John$^1$) was born at Sugar Hill in the northeast corner of Weare, N.H. on 3 Mar 1770; and mar. **Elizabeth Brackenbury** of Hopkinton on 8 Dec 1796 at Hopkinton. They lived on a farm in Weare near the Hopkinton line. Peter died there 31 Aug 1817; wife Elizabeth died 11 Feb 1835. The couple is buried in the Sugar Hill Cemetery along with Peter's parents and some of his siblings.

Children with Elizabeth at Weare:

+**1617**    i. Nathan$^7$ Eaton; b. ca. 1797; mar. Dorcas Marshall.
  **1618**    ii. Mary$^7$ Ann Eaton, b. 180?; mar. Freeman Bachelder and resided at Concord, N.H.
  **1619**    iii. Hilliard$^7$ L. Eaton, b. ?  ; resided at Concord, N.H.

**591. Samuel$^6$ Eaton** (Ithamar$^5$, Samuel$^4$, Job$^3$, Thomas$^2$, John$^1$) was born 10 Feb 1773 at Sugar Hill, Weare, N. H. He was married but his wife's name is unknown. He can largely be excluded as the Samuel Eaton, husband of Sarah (Eaton) (cf. **#483**) at Weare, since she had five children with her Weare Samuel (cf. **#599**, below) after a late Dec 1797 marriage, which would be hard to accomplish within eight years. For this Samuel$^6$ died at Weare on 21 Oct 1805. What little is known of his children comes from the will of his father Ithamar dated 8 Apr 1816.

Children with ? at Weare who survived to 1816:

  **1620**    i. Nathan$^7$ Eaton.

**1621**     ii. Jacob[7] Ordway Eaton.
**+1622**    iii. Ithamar[7] Eaton, b. 1805; mar. Anna R. Bartlett.


**592. Jacob[6] Ordway Eaton** (Ithamar[5], Samuel[4], Job[3], Thomas[2], John[1]) was born 23 Jul 1776 at Weare, N.H. He removed early to East Kingston, N.H., and mar. there **Sarah ("Sally") Cleaves** on 25 Dec 1798. This couple reared their children in East Kingston, and spent the rest of their lives there, with the family appearing in four consecutive Censuses from 1810 to 1840. Wife Sally died first, on 17 Mar 1837; Jacob followed her on 16 Feb 1848. They are, however, buried in Kensington, N.H.

Children, all born East Kingston:

**+1623**    i. Nathan[7] Ordway Eaton, b. 14 Nov 1799; mar. Ruth Martain.
**1624**     ii. Rebekah[7] Eaton, b. 7 Nov 1801; died 4 Nov 1818, East Kingston, and bur. in Kensington.
**1625**    iii. Son[7] Eaton, b. and died, 1804.
**+1626**   iv. Merchant[7] Cleaves, b. 15 Mar 1806; mar. Mary Lawrence.
**1627**     v. Mary[7] Eaton, b. 29 Sep 1808; died in infancy.
**1628**    vi. Sally[7] Cleaves Eaton, b. 27 Jul 1809; died 1 Dec 1819; bur. in Kensington.
**1629**   vii. Mary[7A] Ordway Eaton, b. 3 Apr 1812; died 8 Dec 1819; bur. in Kensington.
**1630**  viii. Hannah[7] Ordway Eaton, b. 13 Dec 1814; died 5 Dec 1819; bur. at Kensington.


**593. Ithamar[6] Eaton** (Ithamar[5], Samuel[4], Job[3], Thomas[2], John[1]) was born 28 Aug 1778 at Weare, N.H.; mar. **Jane Prince** on 21 May 1805 at Manchester, Mass., on the base of Cape Anne. The couple had their first child at Manchester, and then returned to East Weare, N.H., where Ithamar kept a public house for some years. They returned to Manchester, Mass., in due time; and Ithamar died of consumption there on 3 Jul 1835. Wife Jane died 6 Jun 1837.

Children:

**1631**     i. Mary[7] Ann Eaton, b. 20 Feb 1806 at Manchester, Mass.; died there 21 Jun 1806.
**+1632**    ii. Andrew[7] Leach Eaton, b. 9 Jun 1807 at Weare, N.H.
**1633**    iii. Harriet[7] Eaton, b. 16 Mar 1810 at Weare, N.H.; mar. Hezekiah Knowlton of Beverly, Mass., Jul 1838.
**+1634**   iv. John[7] Lee Eaton, b. 24 Jan 1813 at Weare, N.H.
**1635**     v. Elizabeth[7] C. Eaton, b. 1817; died 15 Dec 1820.

**597. George[6] Washington Eaton** (Ithamar[5], Samuel[4], Job[3], Thomas[2], John[1]) was born 7 Jan 1788 at Weare, N.H.; mar. **Hannah Low(e)**,

25 Jan 1813 at Weare. As "Washington Eaton," he is listed as the household head in Censuses from 1820 thru 1840 at Weare. He died on 2 Sep 1841 at Weare.

Children at Weare:

+1636    i. William[7] Lowe Eaton, b. 21 Mar 1814; mar. Hannah.
+1637    ii. Peter[7] Eaton, b. 9 Nov 1815; mar. Eliza Pillsbury.
 1638    iii. Otis[7] Robinson Eaton, b. 9 Apr 1818; died young.
 1639    iv. Abigail[7] Ann Eaton, b. 9 Jun 1819; mar. Rev. Joseph Foster of Brattleboro, Vt., 14 Apr 1843. They resided in Brattleboro, 1843-56, and then removed to Beverly, Mass. She died 11 Sep 1864.
 1640    v. James[7] Eaton, a twin b. 11 Dec 1821.
 1641    vi. Willis[7] Eaton, a twin b. 11 Dec 1821; died 1 Apr 1853.

**599. (Capt.) Samuel[6] Eaton** (Obadiah[5], Samuel[4], Job[3], Thomas[2], John[1]) was born ca. 1776 at Plaistow, N.H., but as a babe in arms removed with his family to Sugar Hill in Weare, N.H. He mar. 1st, a Sarah whose maiden name is unknown, but who is quite likely to have been his cousin **Sarah[6] Eaton** (see **#483**), who was raised in Hopkinton less than three miles up the road from where Capt. Samuel grew up in Weare, and who is known to have mar. a "Samuel Eaton of Concord, N.H.," the latter being the main market town for both of them. The date of Sarah's marriage with her Samuel Eaton was 18 Dec 1797; and it is known from her side that she provided her Samuel with three sons and two daughters before she died in 1818 at Weare. The three known children of our Capt. Samuel here were sons born between 1802 and 1815. At a later unknown date after he was widowed, Samuel mar. 2d, **Betsey Edmunds**, although there is no record of children for this pair. In the 1820s, Samuel moved to Barnstead, N.H., perhaps because his son Obadiah had moved there, and resided on Lot #60 in the 2d Division with him. Capt. Samuel died 1848 at Barnstead.

Children with Sarah (assuming she was the cousin who gave him three sons and two daughters, and congruent with family composition data in 1810, albeit confused somewhat by a multiple family arrangement in that year):

 1642    i. Daughter[7] Eaton, b. ca. 1799.
 1643    ii. Obadiah[7] Eaton, b. 9 Mar 1802. He was a farmer at Barnstead, probably unmarried, who died there without issue.
 1644    iii. Hasket[7] Eaton, b. 22 Mar 1804; died 31 Jan 1819.
 1645    iv. Daughter[7] Eaton, b. 1806-09.
+1646    iii. Benjamin[7] P. Eaton, b. 1815; mar. Abigail Ayers.

**600. Benjamin[6] Eaton** (Obadiah[5], Samuel[4], Job[3], Thomas[2], John[1]) was born ca. 1778 at Sugar Hill, Weare, N.H.; mar. **Phebe Chandler**, daughter of Isaac Chandler of Hopkinton, N.H. on 9 Nov 1800 at Hopkinton. "Lt." Benjamin was a saddler residing in Hopkinton, who died there 13 Oct 1807 before he was 30, and whose children were largely unrecorded and have been reconstituted from other sources.

Children with Phebe at Hopkinton (perhaps not complete):

+ **1647**    i. Thomas[7] Eaton, b. 12 Mar 1802; mar. Elizabeth Henley.
  **1648**    ii. Betsey[7] Paige Eaton, b. ca. 1805.
  **1649**    iii. Charlotte[7] Maria Eaton, b. 3 Sep 1808(?); mar. Dr. Harrison[8] Eaton (**#3197**) of Hopkinton, 25 Dec 1838, and res. with him at Merrimack, N.H. She died 21 Dec 1866.

**601. Obadiah[6] Paige Eaton** (Obadiah[5], Samuel[4], Job[3], Thomas[2], John[1]) was born late in 1779 at Sugar Hill, Weare.; mar. **Abigail Woodbury**, date unknown. He res. in Weare as a young adult, and in land deeds of 1805 is described as a trader. At some time before 1809 he removed to Montpelier, Vt., where he and his family were "warned out" of Montpelier as of Feb. 1809 (which at that time merely indicated that his family was a new arrival in town, not that they were necessarily indigent or undesirable: cf. Rollins, 1997). However, Obadiah makes his only Census appearance as a household head at Montpelier in 1820. He died intestate at Montpelier 30 Jan 1824. His widow Abigail was appointed to administer the settlement of the estate, but resigned her trust upon finding that the estate was too insolvent to cover debts. She received $651 worth of property to sustain herself (Washington Co. Probate, Vol. E-58).

Child (only one listed; while the 1820 family composition has several children, the household may include more than one parent pair):

  **1650**    i. Child[7] Eaton, b. and died, 15 Nov 1809.

**604. Paige[6] Eaton** (Obadiah[5], Samuel[4], Job[3], Thomas[2], John[1]) was born 19 Jul 1790 at Sugar Hill, Weare, N.H.; mar. **Roxanna Bradford** of Francestown, N.H. in 1817. It was in this year that Paige with others bought land in Kennebec Co., Maine. Instead of removing to Maine, however, the couple took up residence in nearby Henniker, N.H., and were registered there in the 1820 Census. And despite Paige's distinctive name, they are nowhere to be found in the 1830 and 1840 Censuses in either New England or New York State. But in 1850 Paige and "Roxy" are in Henniker, with an "empty nest," where they probably were all along, somehow out of the view of the Enumerator, since as of 1850 they have a rather prosperous farm. By 1853, however, they had removed to Woburn, Mass., where the aging "Page" heads a household in 1860, listing himself as a "Gentleman", age 69, despite the fact that he credits himself with no resources at all. His nearest agemate in the unit is a Nora styled as a "Gentlewoman," age 65. He had no sister of this name, and this person is possibly a mistaken rendering of Roxanna or more likely, a second wife. That this Woburn gentleman has indeed arrived from Henniker seems beyond question, from a conjunction of three facts in addition to the Henniker lore that he had removed to Woburn: first, of the several thousand Eaton males of the old New England branches that we have catalogued, only the Weare/Henniker one carries the given name of "Page", apart from the marginal exception in the Note below; second, at the time of the 1860 Census, the Henniker Paige Eaton was exactly 69, as reported; and he was born in New Hampshire, along with all the other members of this household save for an Irish servant girl. While Paige himself reports no resources, real estate or personal, the household includes a Robert B. Eaton who is very prosperous, with $15,000 in real estate and $6,000 in personal estate, rather princely sums for a fellow only age 42. That his occupation is as a "chemical manufacturer," lends some credibility to his report.

In part because of our dearth of information about Paige and his wife in their child-rearing period at Henniker, our list of children for them is weak. However, we have seen fit to include as a child not only Robert B. (subject to a caveat in the Note below), since his age fits him to be their first child born in late 1818 or early 1819, after their 1817 marriage, but a Thomas C. Eaton half his age as well, who is also in the Woburn household in 1860. Paige is still in Woburn in 1870 with these putative children dispersed elsewhere in the interim, and he died there 14 Jun 1872. This is a somewhat curious family that could well reward further investigation.

Children (quite probably partial), all born in N. H.:

**1651**  i. Robert[7] B. Eaton, b. 1818-19; a chemist removed to Mass.
**1652**  ii. Thomas[7] Eaton, b. ?   ; died 20 Jan 1836 in Henniker, N.H.
**1653**  iii. Thomas[7A] C. Eaton, b. ca. 1839; in 1860 a clerk at Woburn.

NOTE 1. Paige Eaton died intestate, but probate papers show that the executor of his estate was Robert B. Eaton, who had removed to Troy, N.Y. This would, of course, have been an entirely normal assignment for a son after his lone remaining parent had died. An oddity arises, however, because the court papers describe Robert B. as Paige's brother, not his son. This is next to impossible, and not merely because Robert B. was 27 years younger than Paige. Paige as it happens was the last of a rather large litter (q.v.), and his father had died when he was ten, or some 17-18 years before Robert B. was born. We do not know Paige's mother's birthdate; but since she was married in 1775 and had her first child straightway, she must have been born by 1760 at the very latest, meaning that she would have been 57 or older when Robert B. was born. So if Robert B. was a brother, it was at most some highly unusual half- or stepbrother relationship, although given the time lapse it is even hard to construct a scenario of this kind that is at all plausible. While for some hard-line genealogists, formal court documents of this kind trump any other form of evidence about long-ago relationships, it seems simpler to assume here that some clerk or judge misunderstood Robert B.'s relationship to Paige Eaton.

NOTE 2. Another likely son of this family poorly documented in Henniker, N.H., is the Page Eaton claiming birth in N.H. ca. 1827, who as a day laborer with an apparent wife Mary (b. ca. 1850, Maine) resides in Marietta, Cobb Co., Georgia (near Atlanta) in 1870, probably swept to that area earlier by service in the Civil War.

**605. Ebenezer[6] Eaton** (John[5], Thomas[4], Job[3], Thomas[2], John[1]) was born 1 Apr 1757 at Bradford, N.H., although he grew up in Methuen, Mass., after his father returned there from Bradford, and later spent time at Hopkinton, N.H. He mar. **Hannah French** (b. 12 Oct 1759) on 7 Dec 1780, and the couple had settled at Bradford, N.H., by 1782-83. This initiated the plantation of Eatons at Bradford. Ebenezer built his homestead on the West Road, and on 30 May 1787 was one of 20 settlers to sign the petition for an act of incorporation of "New Bradford" township. At the first town meeting of that year, he was designated Town Clerk and was one of three elected as a Selectman. He was the sole Eaton in Bradford in the 1790 Census, but had been joined by three of his younger brothers in the 1800 Census. Ebenezer was the Bradford representative to the General Court of N.H. in 1796. He died 5 Jan 1806; wife Hannah died 29 Jun 1823 at Bradford. Both are buried at the Bradford Center Cemetery.

Children:

| | | |
|---|---|---|
| **1654** | i. | Child[7] Eaton, stillborn 6 Oct 1781, at Hopkinton. |
| **1655** | ii. | Abigail[7] Eaton, b. 1 Apr 1783 at Bradford; died 8 Sep 1839. |
| **+1656** | iii. | Samuel[7] Eaton, b. 1 Jun 1785 at Bradford; mar. Margaret. |
| **+1657** | iv. | Elisha[7] Eaton, b. 11 Apr 1788 at Bradford; mar. Eliza. |
| **1658** | v. | Hannah[7] Eaton, b. 4 Apr 1792, Bradford; died 10 Oct 1804. |

**607. (Maj.) Nathaniel[6] Eaton** (John[5], Thomas[4], Job[3], Thomas[2], John[1]) was born 26 Mar 1761 at Methuen, Mass.; mar. **Elizabeth Bowan** about 1786. His initial purchase of land in Bradford is dated 1796. As Capt. Nathaniel he is a Selectman for Bradford in 1799. He was the only Eaton brother to "retreat" from the new settlement: about 1804 he sold his land there and returned to Hopkinton, N.H., where he had largely grown up. Wife Elizabeth died at Hopkinton on 20 Jul 1823, at age 62. Nathaniel died there on 24 Jan 1837.

Children (birthplaces not clearly recorded):

| | | |
|---|---|---|
| **+1659** | i. | Moses[7] Eaton, b. 1788; mar. Judith Merrill. |
| **1660** | ii. | Sarah[7] ("Sally") Eaton, b. ca. 1790; mar. Deacon Thomas |

White, 26 Aug 1810 at Hopkinton. She died 17 Dec
1837 at Hopkinton, age 48.

1661  iii. Susan[7] E. Eaton, b. ca. 20 Feb 1792 at Hopkinton; mar.
Henry Dodge. She died 25 Jul 1884 at Hopkinton.

1662  iv. Polly[7] Eaton, b. ca. 1795; she died 15 Aug 1817 at Hopkinton at age 21.

+1663  v. Thomas[7] Eaton, b. 1797; mar. Anna B. Cressey.

1664  vi. Betsey[7] Eaton, b. 1799; she died 1 Nov 1864.

**608. Daniel[6] Eaton** (John[5], Thomas[4], Job[3], Thomas[2], John[1]) was
born 28 Feb 1763 at Methuen, Mass. Since he plausibly proceeded both
to Hopkinton with father John and then on to Bradford with his brothers,
he must be the Daniel Eaton of Bradford, N.H., who twice purchases
tracts of land in Tunbridge, Orange Co., Vt. in 1789, and removes there
with his bride, **Lydia ___?___** in time for the 1790 Census. He is still
residing there in 1800, but then his trail disappears. However, it is likely
that the family remained at Tunbridge for some time, since both known
sons married there.

Early children, both born at Tunbridge, Vt.:

+1665  i. Timothy[7] Eaton, b. 11 Jun 1790; mar. Sarah Forest.

+1666  ii. Joshua[7] Eaton, b. 30 Apr 1792; mar. Susan Cleveland.

**609. John[6] Eaton** (John[5], Thomas[4], Job[3], Thomas[2], John[1]) was
born 14 Jul 1765 at Methuen, Mass. He moved with the family to
Hopkinton, N.H. He mar. **Phebe Brockway** in Dec 1788 at Washington,
N.H. The couple soon settled in Bradford where other Eaton brothers
were converging; and they are visible there in the Censuses of 1800 thru
1820. As the couple aged in the 1820s, they joined the household of
their eldest son John[7], who had moved a few miles north into Newbury,
N.H. It was there that father John died, 19 Jan 1844.

Children, all recorded at Bradford:

1667  i. John[7] Eaton, b. 13 Oct 1789.

1668  ii. Phebe[7] Eaton, b. 18 Dec 1791.

+1669  iii. James[7] Eaton, b. 28 May 1805; mar. Lydia.

1670  iv. Hannah[7] Eaton, b. 30 Mar 1807.

+1671  v. Ebenezer[7] Eaton, b. 7 Feb 1809; mar. Hannah Cross.

NOTE. The temporal distribution of these births is curious, with a hiatus
of 14 years after a start and a finish, both of which conform to the typical two-year,
stairstep sequence of births. Between the care with which Bradford records were kept
and the fact that family composition data in 1800-20 Census shows the same large
hole in reproduction, we assume that this hole is "real." Perhaps Phebe died early
and John remarried; or perhaps Phebe had some ailment limiting her fertility for a

while; or perhaps she had a sequence of miscarriages or infant deaths. In any event, we doubt that several children actually reaching adulthood somehow escaped the records here.

**610.** (**Maj.**) **Joshua**[6] **Eaton** (John[5], Thomas[4], Job[3], Thomas[2], John[1]) was born 25 Feb 1768 at Methuen, Mass.; when still of Hopkinton, N.H., Joshua mar. 1st, **Sarah Hoyt** of Bradford (daughter of Stephen[6]/Sarah Hoyt) on 8 Jun 1792. The couple resided initally in Hopkinton, but before 1800 they moved on to join the Eaton brothers in Bradford, N.H. Joshua's family then appears in five consecutive Censuses there, 1800 thru 1840. Wife Sarah died 17 Apr 1815, and Joshua mar. 2d, **Mrs. Anna (Blaisdell) Hill** on 23 Jan 1817 at Warner, and she added three more children to his family. Of the Eaton brothers in Bradford, Joshua was by some margin the most active on the real estate market, being a party to nearly two dozen conveyances between 1805 and 1829. In the early days he is described as a "yeoman"; but by 1810 he is usually called a "Gentleman." Joshua died 11 Apr 1850; and his wife Anna, considerably his junior, survived until 2 Sep 1892.

Children with Sarah at Hopkinton:

+ **1672**    i. Moses[7] Eaton, b. 9 Apr 1793; mar. Polly Whittemore.
  **1673**    ii. Nancy[7] Eaton, b. 4 Jun 1796; mar. a Brockway. She died 24 Nov 1870 at Hopkinton.

Children with Anna at Bradford:

+ **1674**    iii. Joshua[7] Eaton, b. 22 Dec 1817; mar. Alzina Gillingham.
+ **1675**    iv. John[7] Hill Eaton, b. 22 Nov 1819; mar. 1st, Hannah Twiss.
  **1676**    v. Roxanne[7] Eaton, b. 20 Mar 1823; d. 31 Jan 1842, Bradford.

**611. Thomas**[6] **Eaton** (John[5], Thomas[4], Job[3], Thomas[2], John[1]) was born to John[5] and his 2d wife Sarah (Clarke) on 1 Sep 1773 at Methuen, Mass. Thomas was "of Hopkinton," N.H. when he mar. **Sally Young**, 12 Jan 1797, at Hopkinton. The trail disappears largely here, although there is one likely child:

  **1677**    ?. Betsey[7] P. Eaton, b.    ?    ; mar. 1st, Stephen Sargent, 12 Nov 1829; mar. 2d; John Brockway.

**615. Moses**[6] **Dalton Eaton** (Timothy[5], Thomas[4], Job[3], Thomas[2], John[1]) was born 16 Jun 1772 at Methuen, Mass. We find him next as the "Moses D. Eaton" registered in the 1800 Census at Pownalboro, Me. The assignment can be made with some confidence since the deed whereby Moses D. establishes a place for his shop in Pownalboro identifies him as a "felt-maker" by trade, while the Moses Dalton Eaton born in Methuen had a father and brother who were both "hatters." His career in Maine was brief. He published intentions of marriage with **Jane Hilton**, also of Pownalboro, on 28 Feb 1802 at Wiscasset, Me. Then Moses died intestate at Wiscasset, Me. at some time before 9 Sep 1803, on which date his widow Jane was involved in settling his estate (Lincoln Co. Probate, 9-57). Then on 26 Jul 1807, a Mrs. Jane Eaton mar. a Capt. William Boyd (both local) at Wiscasset. There is no sign that Moses D. and Jane had any children.


      **616. Samuel⁶ Eaton** (Timothy⁵, Thomas⁴, Job³, Thomas², John¹) was born 15 Jun 1776 at Methuen, Mass. He had learned the hatter's trade from his father, and pursued it as an adult resident of Methuen. He mar. 1st, **Ruth Bailey** of Methuen on 15 Jun 1814. Ruth died 21 Mar 1831; and Samuel mar. 2d, **Mrs. Frances Berry** of neighboring Salem, N.H., int. 8 Apr 1832 at Methuen. Samuel no longer appears in the Census at Methuen as of 1840, but we have no death date for him.

      Children with Ruth at Methuen:

**1678**    i. Emily⁷ Eaton, b. 5 Aug 1817.
**1679**    ii. Aurelia⁷ Eaton, b. 3 Apr 1821.
**1680**    iii. William⁷ Boyd Eaton, b. 26 Jul 1824.

# Generation Seven

## A. *The Salisbury Branch.*

**619. William**[7] **Eaton** (Ebenezer[6], John[5-1]) was born in that southern portion of Hampton Falls, N.H., that would be set off as Seabrook,
N.H. on 3 June 1768.   His birthdate is, however in some dispute, although the later 1750s is a good guess.   Our senior author mentioned 8
Mar 1760, probably to adjust to an inferred marriage date of his parents,
located vaguely in 1759; the *History of Sanbornton* (p. 256) lists 8 Mar
1756; and the age of 75 which he reports on his Revolutionary Pension
application of 1832 would, if literally true, locate his birth in the twelve
months following mid-August, 1756.   He was very active in the Revolution.   He enlisted first in June 1775 for six months in the Massachusetts
Line under Capt. John Evans, arriving in the Boston area the day after the
Battle of Bunker Hill (17 Jun).   Then he re-enlisted under Capt. Asa Barnes for another year in the same regiment.   After marching to New London, Conn., his company was shipped to New York City.   He was stationed at Hell's Gate there until the British took the city, and then went to
White Plains, and to New Jersey and Newtown, Pa., before returning to
New Jersey where he was in the Battle of Trenton on Christmas morning,
1776.   After a few months as a civilian early in 1777, he enlisted again
for three months under Capt. Evans, and went with him to Pawlet, Vt.;
through the wilderness to Lake George, participating in the battle there;
and then on to Stillwater, N.Y..   In the battle there on 7 Oct 1777  he was
wounded with a ball in his thigh.   He was carried to Albany and fur-
loughed for the last days of his service stint.
        He probably returned home to convalesce, since *Church Records*
at Hampton, N.H. say that he mar. 1st, **Betty "Betsey" Swain** on 30 Oct
1777.   She had been born in Oct 1755 (Hampton Falls records say "29
Oct 1757") to Caleb and Anna (Fellows) Swain in Hampton Falls, 15
years before her father died and her mother Anna had taken the family
to Sanbornton to settle on the parcel adjacent to the one which the two
William and Betseys from Seabrook (see also **#270**) would later occupy
in the 2d Division.   In the early summer of 1778, William[7] left his bride
to enlist at Hampton Falls for six months under Lt. Jonathan Leavitt and
served the rest of the year in Rhode Island.   All told, while several of his
Eaton cousins from the Salisbury/Seabrook area served in the Revolution,
William[6] probably saw a wider swath of the northern campaigns by some
margin than any other.   He is said to have held a captain's commission at
the time of his death, but it is not clear whether he received it during the
Revolution or in later years.   After 1832 he began to receive the substantial pension of $80 a year for his war service.

About 1790 he and Betsey removed to Sanbornton to join his own sister Betsey[7] and her husband William[6] Eaton (**#270**) on the lot adjacent to his mother-in-law Anna Swain.  They lived there some 15 years, and then decided to remove to Rhode Island, presumably on the basis of an attraction formed during his year of service there.  By 1820, however, they had returned to Sanbornton, where they would remain for the rest of their lives.  Wife Betsey died 16 Jul 1833, and William[7] mar. 2d, widow **Betsey (Stevens?)(Calley) (Swain) Ela** at Sanbornton in early Oct 1833 "in the 79th year of their ages" (Chipman, 1993).  (It was the discovery of the fugitive record of this marriage by Evelyn Fowler that rescued us from a tortured solution to the two-William problem.)    William[7] died testate on 3 Sep 1835, mentioning eight surviving children of his eleven in the will.  His widow, by now Betsey (Stevens?)(Calley) (Swain) (Ela) Eaton survived to launch a pension application based on the Revolutionary service of her first husband, Ichabod Swain.  Being the third Betsey married to a William, and the second William wife claiming the name Betsey (Swain) Eaton, her petition troubled suspicious pension authorities of the time as much as it has baffled subsequent genealogists.

Children, all with the original Betsey (first five in Seabrook; last four or five in Sanbornton):

+**1681**    i. Caleb[8] Eaton, b. 30 Jan 1778; mar. Sarah Cass.
 **1682**    ii. Mary[8] "Polly" Eaton, b. 15 Aug 1780; m. Daniel Hilliard, 6 May 1802 and res. at Sanbornton.
+**1683**    iii. Jonathan[8] Eaton, b. 25 May 1783; mar. Molly Prescott.
+**1684**    iv. William[8] Eaton, b. 25 May 1785; mar. Judith Burleigh.
 **1685**    v. Anna[8] "Nancy" Eaton, b. 9 Dec 1787; mar. Jacob Burleigh, 25 Jun 1807.  They had four children before Jacob went to northern New York State and there died.  Wife Nancy died in Franklin, N.H. in the home of eldest daughter Mrs. Rhoda Thompson.
 **1686**    vi. Sarah[8] Eaton, b. 26 Jan 1790; mar. Stephen Bartlett in Newbury, Mass., 1816; res. Newbury.
 **1687**    vii. Betty[8] Eaton, b. 21 May 1792; died Oct 1805, Sanbornton.
+**1688**    viii. Reuben[8] Eaton, b. 4 Sep 1794; mar. Elizabeth Peckham.
 **1689**    ix. Olive[8] Eaton, b. 24 Sep 1796; mar. 1st, Thomas C. Wyatt in 1823.  He died in Northfield, N.H.; mar. 2d, Augustus Haynes.  After his death she mar. 3d, Joseph Libbey of Gilford, N.H.
+**1690**    x. Joseph[8] Eaton, b. 28 Feb 1799; mar. Abby.
 **1691**    xi. "Patty[8]" Eaton, b.  ?  ; final "daughter" listed in William[7]'s will; apparently mar. a Gage.

**620.  (Capt.) Reuben[7] Eaton** (Ebenezer[6], John[5-1]) was born in proto-Seabrook, ca. 1762; mar. **Martha[6] Eaton** (# **286**), daughter of Joseph and Sarah, Nov 1786.  The couple appears in the 1790 Census at Seabrook, but they removed to Sanbornton to catch up with brother Wil-

liam and wife Betsey there in 1800.  Reuben died at sea, 10 Sep 1821.
His wife Martha died in Sanbornton, 15 Feb 1848, age listed as 87.

Only known child:

**1692**    i. Betty[8] Eaton, b. 23 Jun 1787, Seabrook; mar. Israel
            Beckman.

**622. Henry[7] Eaton** (Ebenezer[6], John[5-1]) was born 29 Aug 1766 at
Seabrook; mar. **Sarah[6] "Sally" Eaton** (#320), dau. of David[5] and Lydia,
4 Aug 1791, at Seabrook (Seabrook *VR* at Concord).  They remained in
south Seabrook, raising a large family on a small farm in the general area
near Adams Ave. and So. Main St.  However, Henry[7] mainly chose the
sea for a livelihood over farming, and is referred to as a mariner until
well into middle age.  He died 6 May 1838.  Sally died 12 Jan 1840, and
they are buried in the Methodist Cemetery in Smithtown (Seabrook).

Children in Seabrook:

+**1693**    i. Henry[8] Eaton, b. 30 Nov 1792; mar. Hannah[7] Eaton (**#640**).
 **1694**   ii. Lydia[8] Eaton, b. 4 Aug 1794; mar. Christopher[7] Eaton
            (**#635**, q.v.).
 **1695**  iii. Rhoda[8] Eaton, b. 1797; mar. Thomas[8] Eaton (**#1709**, q.v.).
+**1696**   iv. True[8] Eaton, b. 1800; mar. Betsy Brown.
 **1697**    v. Infant[8] Eaton, b. ca. 1802.
 **1698**   vi. Phebe[8] Knight Eaton, b. 20 Oct 1804; mar. Jeremiah[7] P.
            Eaton (**#762**, q.v.).
+**1699**  vii. Edward[8] Dearborn Eaton, b. 4 Aug 1807; mar. Elizabeth[8]
            Eaton (**#1981**), daughter of Wyman[7].
+**1700** viii. Moses[8] Eaton, b. 2 Dec 1808; m. Rebecca[8] Eaton (**#1980**).
+**1701**   ix. Lowell[8] Eaton, b. ca. 1812; mar. Pauline Hunt.

**624. Moses[7] Eaton** (Ebenezer[6], John[5-1]) was born ca. 1769 at Sea-
brook; mar. **Rhoda Eaton**, 5 Dec 1795 (Seabrook *VR* at Concord).  This
Rhoda was said by the senior author to have been the daughter of some
William and Hannah Eaton.  A long search, however, fails to find these
parents in Seabrook, Salisbury or Haverhill, save as Rhoda might have
been an unrecorded daughter of the shadowy William and "Anna" at
Salisbury in this period (cf. **#121**).  Moses lived on a small farm in South
Seabrook toward the eastern end of South Main St.  Over nearly a dozen
land deeds from 1795-1849 he is usually listed as a yeoman, although he
may have done some shoemaking.  This couple apparently had a large
family, mostly daughters, since two boys and eight girls were residing
with them as of the 1820 Census.  However, birth records for these children are few.  Moses[7] is listed in Seabrook Censuses through 1850, when
he is age 80, residing with Rhoda, age 73, with some of their known children still in the nest; along with other given names that may fill in some

of the missing daughters (see below).    Moses died 10 Feb 1853; Rhoda died 28 Mar 1859.

Children at Seabrook (partial, with guesses indicated):

1702    i. Olive[8] "Olla" Eaton, b. 1 Aug 1796; died 15 Jul 1868.
1703    ii. Sarah[8] "Sally" Collins Eaton, b. ca. 1798; died Jan 1877.
1704    iii. Eben[8] Eaton, b. ca. 1804; living with parents, 1850, and died, apparently without issue, 10 Dec 1878.
1705    iv. Mary[8] Eaton?, b. ca. 1808; probably an unrecorded daughter living with parents, 1850, who may have been the 2d wife of Caleb[8] Eaton (#1710).
1706    v. Betsey[8] Eaton b. ca. 1813; another unrecorded daughter, mar. a James Wood, born England.  She died 21 Feb 1915.
1707    vi. Lydia[8] Eaton, b. ca. 1816; mar. Lucien Foote (int.) 23 Oct 1836; had at least four children.  She died 3 Apr 1886.
1708    vii. Moses[8] Eaton, b. Apr 1820; never mar.; died 10 May 1890 of heart disease at Seabrook.


627. Thomas[7] Eaton (Ebenezer[6], John[5-1]) was born ca. 1775-6 in Seabrook; mar. Sarah[6] "Sally" Eaton (#289), daughter of Joseph[5] and Sarah, on 4 May 1798 at Seabrook.  This couple raised ten children on a small farm of an acre or two near his father's in South Seabrook.   He is referred to both as a mariner and yeoman in his few land deeds.    His household in 1820 is absent a wife; and Thomas himself died 31 Mar 1825.

Children at Seabrook:

+1709    i. Thomas[8] Eaton, b. ca. 1798; mar. Rhoda[8] Eaton (#1695), daughter of Henry[7].
+1710    ii. Caleb[8] Eaton, b. 1 Aug 1800; mar. 1st, Hannah Eaton, 1824.
+1711    iii. Joshua[8] Eaton, b. 7 Sep 1802; mar. Cynthia Collins, 1825.
1712    iv. Nancy[8] Eaton, b. 9 Oct 1804; mar. John Walton, 2 May 1824.  He died 15 Jul 1879 and widow Nancy died 7 Oct 1882.
+1713    v. Chase[8] Eaton, b. ca. 1806; mar. Miriam[7] Eaton (#646), dau. of John[6] and Sarah.
+1714    vi. William[8] Eaton, b. 11 Sep 1809; mar. Nancy Brown, 1827.
1715    vii. Rebecca[8] Eaton, b. ca. 1811; mar. Jacob Fowler, 16 Dec 1838.  She died 15 Apr 1910.
+1716    viii. Reuben[8] D. Eaton, b. Jun 1813; mar. Sally Brown, 1833.
1717    ix. Joanna[8] Eaton, b. 1815; mar. Samuel Collins, 10 Oct 1834.  She died 21 Apr 1848.  Her husband survived until 21 Aug 1891.
1718    x. Abel[8] Eaton, b. 1818; "a foolish fellow from birth," never married.

### #8. Seabrook, N.H., Eaton Bastion (II)

In Sidebar #4 we documented (1)the remarkable <u>size</u> and (2) the <u>durability</u> even to present times of the Eaton "plantation" in Seabrook.  Here, picking up the thread, we add another remarkable feature of this gathering of Eatons: (3) the sheer <u>density</u> of this settle-within the narrow confines of Seabrook, one of New Hampshire's smaller townships, especially where acreage of habitable land is concerned.  Eaton dwellings were not scattered thinly across the township, but instead were for the most part packed into one small corner of it, commonly known as South Seabrook, which probably occupies less less than one-seventh of the town's land standing above the great extent of its tidal marshes.

This density of Eaton residences is shown rather dramatically by Map #8 (p. xxviii), drawn up by combining an 1884 map of residences in Salisbury, Mass., with a parallel map for Seabrook in 1892. (See also Map #7 of 1857 residents in Seabrook).  Map #8 may risk being misleading, since there appear to be only 35 Eaton residences, whereas we have mentioned 55-60 Eaton households in Seabrook in the closing decades of the 19th century.  Several reasons underlie this "undercount" in Map #8; but the most important is the fact that Map #8 shows only residential structures, including some that may be rented out but attributed to their legal owners.  The U.S. Census permits us to count households, which because of multiple occupancies are typically more numerous than dwelling structures.  Despite these definitional ambiguities, the map makes clear where in Seabrook our Eatons have tended to live in great numbers.  This again was a very durable pattern for 200 years.  At any point in time, a very few Eaton families could be found living outside South Seabrook, but rarely far from it.  For many years (but not in 1892), for example, there were two to four Eaton families living on Walton Road running just south of Cain's Brook, but this was only a few hundred yards north of South Seabrook.  In 1892 there were two Eaton households on the north side of Cain's Brook, on Farm Lane.  As population expanded, of course there was no more room in the area.  But of the 73 telephone subscribers named Eaton living in Seabrook in 1986, some 60% still lived in South Seabrook or on Walton Rd., the traditional Eaton residential area.

Another way to underscore the great density of Eatons in this corner of Seabrook is to compare it with residential patterns of the Eatons in Deer Isle and Sedgwick.  For most of the 1850-1900 period, there were nearly 60 Eaton households in Seabrook, fifty-plus of them in South Seabrook.   In 1850 there were only about half that number of Eaton households with Deer Isle and Sedgwick combined, although this population grew rapidly in subsequent decades, such that it came to rival Seabrook in sheer numbers.  But hardly so in

density.  After all, the *terra firma* in the Deer Isle/Sedgwick complex
must total upward of 20 square miles, whereas 30 of the 35 Eaton
families of Map 8 live in a South Seabrook area which fit within a
rectangle barely two-thirds of a square mile, and less than half a sq.
mile if uninhabitable marshland within this rectangle is excluded.
The numbers may be similar to Deer Isle, but the density of the Seabrook Eatons is on toward ten times as great.

This density has had various consequences in Seabrook.  One
is that Eaton youngsters quite often married their Eaton cousins.
This is not a phenomenon of note for Eaton youth on the margins of
the Eaton-dense areas.  Those who grew up on Walton Rd. for example, had ample marriage partners among their Beckman, Boyd,
Felch and Walton neighbors.  But for those who grew up in the heart
of South Seabrook, it was another story.  One of these patriarchs
Henry[7] (**#622**), had eight children who married, 1812-1838, and six
of them took Eaton mates.   More generally, if you were an Eaton
growing up in South Seabrook, 1805-30, the odds were better than
50-50 that you would marry another Eaton.  While Eatons married
Eaton cousins occasionally on Deer Isle, it was rare by comparison,
and density was clearly the root of the difference.

Both Seabrook and Deer Isle were communities "by the sea,"
so that there were many similarities in the way people made a living.
Young men went to sea in substantial number in both communities.
Among Eaton household heads reporting an occupation in 1850, almost half were seamen.  Drowning was the most common cause of
death for them, not only "lost at sea" from larger vessels, but also from
fishing accidents near shore.  Sea life attracted the young, although
many of those not officer material tried by early middle age to gain
a stake of land to which they might retire to farm.  The typical family
in both communities farmed in some degree, although local fishing
could feed a family amply much of the year, along with clamming on
the mud flats (Seabrook) and lobster trapping (Deer Isle).  "Market
gunning" for waterfowl could be remunerative in both communities.
And rich hay from Seabrook salt marshes (when one owned such a
plot) was in high demand from neighboring husbandmen.  Thus a
reasonable living could be pieced together from a whole patchwork
of activities not fully reflected in Census occupation categories.

With the post-Revolution growth of commerce, central New England and with it Seabrook developed a widespread cottage industry of
shoemaking, and in time  the proliferation of  small sheds out back
for leatherworking.  Many Seabrook Eatons, altho rarely skilled artisans otherwise, had joined this trend as a welcome source of income
before 1850.  And soon the development of water power and the new
machinery of the Industrial Revolution moved this activity from back
yards into full-fledged factories.  These began to mushroom in Seabrook in the 1860s, changing economic life there considerably.

**629. Israel[7] Eaton** (Benjamin[6], John[5-1]) was born 8 Jul 1804 at Seabrook. It is likely that he had a troubled childhood, in that his father Benjamin[6] (cf. **#248**) was declared *non compos mentis* before baby Israel was a year old. Despite the fact that father Benjamin was put under a guardianship at this time, in 1810 Benjamin's household is only three persons: Benjamin, apparently wife Grace and young Israel. In 1820 these three have been joined by two young women aged 16-26, one of whom could be their daughter Elizabeth (**#628**), along with a girl under 10 who could also be a daughter, but of whom we know nothing else.

In 1877, the aging Israel was deposed by officials of South Hampton who still claimed vague rights to a piece of ocean beach on the south edge of Seabrook. They were filing suit against folk who a half century earlier "squatted" on that strand beyond the tidal marshes and the Hampton River, who were from Seabrook town itself. Israel had been one of these, and we get a glimpse of his early adult life from this testimony. He recounts that he had taken up with 1st, **Elizabeth "Eliza" Fowler**, about a decade his senior, when he was only 14 or 15. She was the daughter of Jacob Fowler, who with his own father had built dwellings on the beach. Israel mar. her 2 May 1822. In this period the couple lived for five years or so in the beach shanty with Jacob, and then Israel built a place of their own on the beach, about 20 yards from the Massachusetts state line. They lived there some twenty years, during which time Israel occupied himself with fishing, clamming and going to sea. They are there in 1830, a two-person household, apparently childless. Near 1850, Israel had his structure hauled across the marsh to Worthen's Point, at the eastern extremity of So. Main St. in Seabrook.

On 19 Aug 1855 (prob. some symbolic choice), with wife Eliza very much alive, Israel "married" 2d, **Miriam Wright**, a daughter of James and Mary Elizabeth (Souther) Wright who was at the time about 16 years old, and removed, perhaps hastily, to Vermont. The couple was briefly at Ludlow, Vt., and then settled at Winooski Falls, Vt., where erstwhile sailor Israel became employed in the local woolen mill. At Ludlow, Israel had changed his name to "John Brown," and by Census entries there wife Miriam was known as "Martha Brown." They claimed to be Maine natives. The children also grew up as Browns in Winooski. The family is there in the Censuses of both 1860 and 1870. In the latter year John "Brown" reports his age as 67, and is employed at the mill, as are his son age 12 and two daughters then age 13 and nine.

In the later 1870s, this family returned to Seabrook, N.H., where Israel's first wife Eliza had died, 3 Aug 1864. Israel and Miriam, returning to their original identities, formalized their marriage in Seabrook, 15 Nov 1882. Israel died 1 Aug 1889 at Seabrook; wife Miriam died there 26 Sep 1898.

Children with Miriam, all but perhaps the last in Vermont:

**1719**      i. Rachel[8] Jane "Brown" Eaton, b. 30 Jun 1856; mar. 1st, John[8] C. Eaton (**#2008**), son of Samuel[7] and Susan (Collins), 21

Oct 1877 at Seabrook; mar. 2d, John Lowell Brown, son of Benjamin F. and Abigail M. Brown, 11 Oct 1905 at Seabrook. She died 22 Nov 1916, also at Seabrook.

+ **1720**  ii. John[8] A. "Brown" Eaton, b. 1858; mar. Sarah Brown, 1885.

**1721**  iii. Eliza[8] "Annie" "Brown" Eaton, b. 11 Dec 1860; mar. 1st, Thomas M. Souther, son of George and Betsey Souther, 9 Feb 1879 at Seabrook. She later mar. 2d, Nicholas[9] Tracy Eaton (#3740, his first marriage), 1 Jan 1894 at Newburyport, Mass. She died there 2 Jun 1906, but is buried at Seabrook.

**1722**  iv. Benjamin[8] F. "Brown" Eaton, b. ca. 1862; mar. widow Susan (Souther) Eaton, her 2d mar. after 1st, John[8] H. Eaton (#1994).

**1723**  v. Carrie[8] M. "Brown" Eaton, b. ca. 1865; mar. John[10] S. Eaton (#4996), son of William[9] and Lucretia (Fowler) Eaton, 17 Aug 1881 at Seabrook. She died there 9 Feb 1890.

**1724**  vi. James[8] A. "Brown" Eaton, b. ca. 1871; mar. Mary __?__, of Irish extraction. He ran "Camp Eaton" on Rte. 1A in York, Maine. James[8] is thought to have had a daughter.

**1725**  vii. Hattie[8] May "Brown" Eaton, b. ca. 1873; mar. George W. Henderson, son of Benjamin P. and Mary A. Henderson, 29 Nov 1893 at Newburyport. She died there, 1958.

**1726**  viii. Mary[8] L. "Brown" Eaton, b. 6 Jan 1875.

**1727**  ix. Frederick[8] J. "Brown" Eaton, b. 14 Aug 1878, at Seabrook; mar. Josephine Sweeney, 20 Sep 1898.

**633. Abel[7] Eaton** (Silvanus[6], John[5-1]) was born Oct 1788 at Seabrook, N.H.; mar. **Polly Collins**, presumaby the daughter of Ezekiel and Betsey (Eaton) Collins of Seabrook, 11 Oct 1812. This couple took up residence in Seabrook, but disaster soon struck, when husband Abel, along with brothers Daniel and Andrew, were lost at sea on a run to Baltimore with a load of fish in the 1815-17 period. There are no records of births to Abel and Polly, but there is strong circumstantial evidence that two Eatons on the Seabrook scene in the next generation, of otherwise unknown parentage, were in fact their children, at least conceived, and probably born, before Abel set off on his fatal trip. Our current Seabrook colleague, Evelyn Fowler, believes that Abel's "Polly" can account for the otherwise mysterious "widow Molly Eaton" who took as a second husband, David Fowler, mar. at Seabrook by Rev. Elias Hull on 10 Sep 1818, with these children of the former marriage being visible growing up in that household in subsequent years. This surmise is strengthened by evidence that the original Abel/Polly household, the subsequent David Fowler household, and even the residential center of gravity for both Abel's putative son Ezekiel[8] and later, his grandson Abel[9], were all within a few doors of each other on upper So. Main St. in South Seabrook. Moreover, two other genealogical sleuths of the area had arrived independently at the same conclusion.

Presumed children with Polly in Seabrook, N.H.:

+1728    i. Ezekiel[8] C. Eaton, b. ca. 1813 and presumed to be named for his maternal grandfather; mar. Nancy Souther, 1836.

1729    ii. Sarah[8] Eaton, b. ca. 1815; mar. Abraham Souther. (int.) 11 Apr 1840, Seabrook. This was siblings marrying siblings, since Abraham was Ezekiel's wife Nancy's brother.

**635. Christopher[7] Eaton** (Silvanus[6], John[5-1]) was born 2 July 1794 at Seabrook (Seabrook *VR* at Concord). In 1812 he was drafted for the war against Britain, and was stationed at Shapley's Island in Portsmouth Harbor for 60 days. He soon mar. his first cousin **Lydia[8] Eaton** (#1694), daughter of Henry[7] and Sally, 24 Aug 1813 at Seabrook. Christopher had a homestead in Seabrook on the north side of So. Main St. at the head of Worthley Avenue, where the couple raised their children. He did some farming, but mostly followed the sea for a living until age caught up with him and kept him ashore. Wife Lydia died in the 1870s. Christopher died at his son True's place in Salisbury, 7 Sep 1879 (the 1880 Census Mortality Schedule says he d. Mar 1880).

Children in Seabrook:

+1730    i. Cyrus[8] Eaton, b. ca. 1814; mar. Sally E. Collins, 1837.
+1731    ii. True[8] Eaton, b. 11 Jan 1819; mar. Jane Moody, 1841.
1732    iii. Sophronia[7] Eaton, b. ca. 1821 and died young.
+1733    iv. Andrew[8] Eaton, b. ca. 1823; mar. Lois Dow, 1844.
1734    v. Sarah[8] Ann Eaton, b. ca. 1828; died Aug 1842, age 14.
1735    vi. Marietta[8] Eaton, b. ca. 1832; died ca. 1842.
+1736    vii. Lowell[8] Eaton, b. ca. 1835; mar. Hannah (Brown) Eaton.
1737    viii. John[8] Eaton, b. ca. 1837; drowned when quite young.
+1738    ix. Christopher[8] Eaton, b. 5 Sep 1839; mar. 1st, Clarissa Eaton.

**639. Samuel[7] Eaton** (John[6-1]) was born ca. 1787; mar. **Polly Dow**, daughter of Winthrop Dow, 20 Nov 1808 at Seabrook. He died prematurely by drowning, 28 Jan 1820, while responsible for settling his father's estate. He left five children who were recognized in their grandfather John[6]'s will, when it finally cleared probate in Oct 1832.

Children in Seabrook:

1739    i. Lucy[8] Eaton, b. ca. 1809; mar. Moses Morrill, Jr., on 30 Nov 1843, and resided at Salisbury, Mass.
+1740    ii. Winthrop[8] Dow Eaton, b. ca. 1811; mar. Hannah Brown.
1741    iii. Samuel[8] Eaton, Jr., b. ca. 1813.
1742    iv. Sally[8] Eaton, b. ca. 1817.
1743    v. John[8] Eaton, b. ca. 1819; he became the 2d husband of widow Lovilla (Dow) Merrill, 1867. She brought a

235

son, b. ca. 1855, to the marriage, and in the 1870
Census he is listed as "Franklin M. Eaton," but he is
actually John[9]'s stepson. This couple does not appear
to have had issue.

**642. Jacob[7] Eaton** (John[6-1]) was born ca. 1794 at Seabrook. He
served in the War of 1812, and his children received a government pension for his contribution to that effort. He mar. a **Martha[7] Eaton** (see
**#772**), who was probably the daughter of Jonathan[6] and Sarah (Merrill)
Eaton, on 10 May 1818 at Seabrook. The couple settled in Seabrook,
where Jacob was, like so many of his relatives and friends, a husbandman
and a mariner, although he also worked as a carpenter. He died at a
rather young age, on 28 Feb 1840. Oliver[7] Eaton (**#1218**), administering
his estate in 1844, petitioned that he be declared insolvent; and his two
younger sons were put under the guardianship of their older brother
Emery B. Eaton (then himself barely age 21) 15 Oct 1845 (Rockingham
Co. Probate, 72-283, 73-435 and 76-47).

Children born in Seabrook:

| | | |
|---|---|---|
| **1744** | i. | Stephen[8] Eaton, b. ca. 1820. Although visible in the 1820 Census, there is no entry for a child of his age in Jacob's household in 1830. Presumably he died young. |
| **+1745** | ii. | Emery[8] B. Eaton, b. ca. Feb 1824; mar Hannah Brown. |
| **1746** | iii. | Samuel[8] Eaton, b. ca. 1825. Presumably orphaned at this point, he can be found in the 1850 Census as a "seaman" age 24, living in the household of William Dow, probably his maternal uncle. In 1860 a Samuel 3d age 35 is a "shoemaker," apparently still unmarried, living in the large household of Andrew Merrill. There the trail ends. |
| **+1747** | iv. | Jacob[8] Eaton, b. 14 Jan 1830; mar. Belinda Fowler, 1848. |
| **1748** | v. | Ardesira[8] Eaton, prob. b. 1830s. |
| **1749** | vi. | Caroline[8] A. Eaton, b. 27 Sep 1835; mar. Samuel H. Beckman, 19 Oct 1854. She died 26 Mar 1918. |

**644. John[7] Eaton** (John[6-1]) was born ca. 1800 at Seabrook; mar.
**Lucy Morrill** of Salisbury, daughter of Moses and Hannah (Hoyt) Morrill, on 19 Nov 1823. This couple lived their early years in Lucy's parent's homestead, on the north edge of Salisbury next door to Wyman[7]
Eaton, where they still resided in 1830. Later they had their own domicile in Salisbury, as John[7] mixed farming with life as a mariner. As of
1850 he was still a fisherman without any reported real estate. He died in
4 Sep 1852 in Salisbury. Widow Lucy died 29 Jul 1865.

Children born in Salisbury:

| | | |
|---|---|---|
| **+1750** | i. | Enoch[8] Hoyt Eaton, b. 9 Mar 1824; mar. 1st. Mary L. |

Eaton (#**1912**).

**1751**   ii. Eliza[8] Eaton, b. 27 Jul 1825; mar. Joseph Carr, then a "laborer", Jun 1846. She died 13 Oct 1857, age 32.

+**1752**   iii. John[8] Colby Eaton, b. 28 Jul 1827; mar. Mary[8] Jane Eaton (#**2013**).

**1753**   iv. Almira[8] Eaton, b. 12 May 1830; died 22 Mar 1847.

**1754**   v. Moses[8] Morrill Eaton, b. 4 Sep 1832; died single, 31 Aug 1852.

**1755**   vi. Hannah[8] Morrill Eaton, b. 3 Feb 1835; mar. John Stevens, 185?. She died 3 Sep 1865 in Salisbury.

**1756**   vii. Lucy[8] Emery Eaton, b. ca. 1837; mar. Daniel Martin, 1853.

**1757**   viii. Sarah[8] A. Eaton, b. ca. 1841; mar. Jacob Bartlett of Salisbury, 1866.

**1758**   ix. Albert[8] Franklin Eaton, b. 25 Oct 1844; died 26 Jun 1865.

**1759**   x. Charles[8] Edward Eaton, b. Oct 1847; died of consumption, 30 Aug 1849 at Salisbury.

**655. (Henry) Moody**[7A] **Eaton** (Ephraim[6], Benjamin[5], John[4-1]) was born ca. 1783 in Seabrook, and for much of his life used his middle name, which was his mother's maiden name, rather than his own first name. He mar. **Sarah Philbrick** of Hampton, N.H., probable daughter of Joseph and Jemima Philbrick, on 9 Mar 1800 at Hampton. This couple removed very early to Maine, settling first at East Pond Plantation (later the Smithfield/Norridgewock area in what is now Somerset Co., Me.). Soon, however, they had pressed on to the very northeast corner of the United States, at Eastport and Lubec, Me., Moody being chosen tithingman and constable at the first town meeting of the latter community in 1811 (Townsend, 1996). The couple raised their children here and remained for the rest of their lives. Moody died 28 May 1836 at Lubec.

Children:

+**1760**   i. Samuel[8] Perley Eaton, b. ca. 1801-02 in "N.H." (presumably at Seabrook); mar. Love(y) Huckins, 1833, at Lubec.

**1761**   ii. Jemima[8] Parker Eaton, b. ca. 1806; married a Morrill.

+**1762**   iii. James[8] Moody Eaton, b. 18 Jul 1808 at Eastport, Me.; mar. Eliza Ramsdell.

**1763**   iv. Elizabeth[8] "Betsey" White Eaton, b. 28 Jan 1809 at Eastport, Me.; mar. Asahel Rice, (int.) 5 Apr 1826.

**1764**   v. Sally[8] Moody Eaton, b. 21 Nov 1810 at Eastport, Me.; died 11 Oct 1811.

**1765**   vi. Hannah[8] Woodward Eaton, b. 3 Jan 1814 at Lubec, Me.; mar. Daniel Crosby, 27 Jan 1833 at Lubec.

**1766**   vii. Joseph[8] Philbrick Eaton, b. 2 Aug 1817 at Lubec. He can not be found in Maine Census indexes, 1850-70. In 1880 he was a solo Eaton boarder on the farm of John Card at Lubec. Joseph P. died 19 Mar 1883, Lubec.

**656. Ephraim[7] Eaton** (Ephraim[6], Benjamin[5], John[4-1]) was born 24 Mar 1785 at Seabrook; mar. **Sally Tilton** of Hampton Falls 10 Jul 1814. The couple resided in Seabrook all their lives on an 80-acre lot on the eastern stretches of Walton Rd., that Ephraim[7] had acquired from his father for a bargain price in 1807. His numerous land deeds describe him as a yeoman or husbandman, so his maritime life was limited by comparison to his Eaton relatives in Seabrook. Ephraim died 11 Sep 1832 at Seabrook. Wife Sally outlived him by a half-century, dying on 9 Oct 1882.

Children born in Seabrook:

**1767**  i. Maria[8] Eaton, b. 3 Jul 1815; mar. William Short, Amesbury; She was widowed when she died of paralysis, 26 Jun 1893.
**1768**  ii. Sarah[8] M. Eaton, b. 1 Jul 1817; mar. David Tilton, 1869. This couple removed to Connecticut, but in 1900 Sarah returned to Seabrook, prob. widowed, and lived in the "Jonathan Walton house" on Walton Rd. with Jonathan's widow, Eleanor. Sarah died in Seabrook 11 May 1906.
**1769**  iii. Susan[8] R. Eaton, b. 15 Oct 1822; mar. 1st, Henry A. Eaton of Malden, Mass., a Universalist minister of the Reading Eaton stock, in 1850. Their son, Charles H., b. 1852, became a Universalist minister of renown in New York City. Mother Susan R. died in 1887.
**1770**  iv. Hannah[8] Eaton, b. 11 Aug 1827; died young.

**663. Jonathan[7] Eaton** (Winthrop[6], Benjamin[5], John[4-1]) was born 24 Apr 1779 at Seabrook; mar. his first cousin, **Abigail[7] "Nabby" Eaton** (**#659**), 13 years his junior, on 7 Mar 1811 at Seabrook, where they were to raise three children. Father Jonathan[7] is a "yeoman" in a very steady series of some 22 Seabrook land deeds, mostly sales of tracts in the Walton Rd. neighborhood, that runs from early 1830 to Oct 1850, suggesting a continual presence in the Seabrook area despite rumors that he had removed either to Chelsea, Vt., or to Canterbury, N.H., and despite our inability to find any trace of the household in the 1840 Census for Seabrook. We do find him again as a farmer age 70 in Seabrook in a household now headed by his 38-year-old son Jonathan G. Eaton in 1850, although there is no sign of wife Abigail. Father Jonathan appears to have succumbed at some point to doctrines of the Shakers, and perhaps had spent time in the Canterbury, N.H., colony. Later on, he was unquestionably in a Shaker community at Enfield, N.H., and his wife Abigail is mentioned (she "of Seabrook") in Enfield vital records as well, although no dates are attached. He died 22 Feb 1865 in Enfield, and is buried in the Shaker Cemetery there.

Children born in Seabrook:

**1771**    i. Jonathan[8] G. Eaton, b. ca. 1812; no sign of marriage. He apparently resided at Seabook, although he is not present in 1840 or 1860, being possibly at sea. In 1850 he is a laborer, age 38, living with his father and two aunts.
**1772**   ii. Daughter[8] Eaton, b. ca. 1814.
**1773**  iii. Daughter[8] Eaton, b. in 1815-19 period.

**664. Winthrop[7] Eaton** (Winthrop[6], Benjamin[5], John[4-1]) was born 19 Aug 1781 at Seabrook; mar. **Mehitabel Dow**, daughter of Hubbard and Martha Dow, on 28 Jun 1821 (from Winthrop Eaton bible). The couple settled in Seabrook and raised their children there. Winthrop was close to his uncle, (Samuel[6]) Perley Eaton (**#258**), a well-to-do bachelor. The two worked together hauling lumber for pay, and in Dec 1829 Perley deeded Winthrop part of a dwelling unit and the half-acre around it for "love and affection," with a small additional sum. The land in question was almost surely east of Washington St. on Walton Rd. A year later, however, Winthrop died on Christmas Day, 1830. Widow Mehitable survived until 25 Nov 1871.

Children at Seabrook:

**1774**    i. Mary[8] Jane Eaton, b. 11 Sep 1821; died 30 Jan 1850.
**1775**   ii. Lavinia[8] B. Eaton, b. 16 Aug 1823; died 26 Jan 1847.
**+1776**  iii. Washington[8] Eaton, b. 18 Sep 1825; mar. Clarissa Boyd.
**1777**   iv. Nancy[8] S. Eaton, b. 1828; died 4 Nov 1846.
**1778**    v. Wells[8] Healy Eaton, b. ca. 11 Jun 1830; mar. Margaret A. Dow, 5 Jun 1856. Wells was a shoemaker whenever such reports were collected. No issue is visible.
**1779**   vi. Ruth[8] A. Eaton, b. 20 Jun 1831; died unmar., 24 Jan 1873.

**670. Stephen[7] Eaton** (Levi[6], Benjamin[5], John[4-1]) was born 21 May 1784 at Boston, in that period when his peripatetic family spent a brief residence there. He grew up with his family in Chelsea, Vt., and mar. **Olive Davis**, a Vermont native born ca. 1791, on 3 Feb 1810 at Bradford, Vt. This was in the period when his parents were taking the rest of the children westward to Ohio, and apparently the new couple went with them. Stephen's family can be found in the 1820 and 1830 Censuses at Orange Twp, Delaware Co., Ohio, and may have led the rest of the family, which had paused first in Geauga Co in northeastern Ohio, to continue once again deeper into Ohio. Also, at points in the early 1840s Stephen was "of Delaware County, Ohio," as he gives power of attorney to a N. H. lawyer to help settle father Levi[6]'s estate. He himself died 25 Aug 1845 and is called "late of Seabrook" as his own N.H. legacies are administered by Oliver Eaton of Seabrook (**#1218**) early in 1846 (cf. Rockingham Deed 343-247). The property involved was a 4-acre plot on the south side of South Main St. in Seabrook.

Children:

1780    i. Lucinda[8] Eaton, b. 1816, Ohio; mar. Riley Case and res. in
            Orange Twp., Delaware Co., Ohio.
1781    ii. Eliza[8] Eaton.
1782   iii. Lorenzo[8] Eaton, b. 1827 in Ohio; in 1850 he lived with a
            Mary, age 18, in Orange Twp. There the trail ends, prob.
            to the westward.

**674. Levi[7] Eaton** (Levi[6], Benjamin[5], John[4-1]) was born 10 Apr
1802 in Chelsea, Orange Co., Vt. He was about six when his parents
moved on westward, settling first at the village of Parkman in Geauga Co.
in the northeast corner of the newly developing state of Ohio. This corner was part of the "Western Reserve," seen as an extension of Connecticut prior to 1800, with the Federal government selling land there prefer-
entially to Connecticut citizens. Therefore, when Levi mar. **Jeannette
Stocking** there, probably about 1830, it is not surprising that she later
reports her birthplace as Connecticut. The bride was nearly 20 years his
junior. Levi was a farmer of modest means, and stayed on in Parkman
after his abandoned mother and several siblings moved on to Delaware
County more to the center of Ohio. But this was only into the 1850s. By
the 1860 Census the couple with remnant children has moved 40 miles or
so southeast to Smith Twp. in Mahoning Co., Ohio, where Levi is a
shoemaker; and by 1870, moved another short hitch westward to Alli-
ance, Stark Co., where the aging parents (Levi now a laborer) can watch
with pride as daughters Fanny and Clara, now living with them, are running a significantly financed millinery business.

Children (ages based on Census reports):

1783    i. Newell[8] Eaton, b. ca. 1831; later removed to Texas.
1784   ii. Fanny[8] Eaton, b. ca. 1835.
1785  iii. Clara[8] Eaton, b. ca. 1842.
1786  iv. Ruth[8] Eaton, b. ca. 1844; died in the 1850s.
1787   v. Mary[8] Eaton, b. ca. 1846.
1788  vi. Perry[8] Eaton, b. ca. 1849. No further trail found.

**678. Stephen[7] Jones Eaton** (Levi[6], Benjamin[5], John[4-1]) is the second Stephen with the same lineage who grew to adulthood, the first being
**#670** above. When the bigamist father Levi[6], back in New Hampshire
after depositing his first family in Ohio, mar. widow Mary (Bagley) Jones
in 1814, he chose to give the name Stephen to the eldest son, just as he
had with the prior marriage. This Stephen[7] J. Eaton was born 24 Dec
1815 at South Hampton, N.H. (the town just west of Seabrook where Levi
and Mary had decided to settle), and was thus 30 years younger than the
first Stephen. He mar. **Hannah Rowe** of Campton, N.H. in Dec 1835,

and after perhaps a brief sojourn in Boston, the couple resided at least into the 1860s at South Hampton, where Stephen was a carpenter and farmer. Later, however, they removed to join their son George and his large brood of children at Melrose, Iowa. Stephen J. died there, 12 Oct 1867. Wife Hannah died 2 Feb 1877.

Children:

+1789     i. George[8] Levi Eaton, b. 29 Jul 1836 at Boston, Mass.
  1790    ii. Eliza[8] Ann Eaton, b. 13 Mar 1838 at So. Hampton, N.H.
             She mar. Jared Smith, Aug 1856, and res. first in Kensing-
             ton, N.H., and later in Lowell, Mass.
  1791   iii. Mary[8] Abby Eaton, b. 25 Jan 1847, So. Hampton; mar. Ben-
             jamin D. James, 8 Aug 1865; removed to Jasper, Arkansas.
  1792    iv. Rebecca[8] Ellen Eaton, b. ca. 1850 at So. Hampton. She mar.
             __?__ in Dec 1867 and removed to Great Bend, Kansas.
  1793     v. Emma[8] Susan Eaton, b. Dec 1854. She mar. __?__ 3 Jul
             1869 and removed to Belville, Kansas.


        **679.  Samuel[7] Perley Eaton** (Levi[6], Benjamin[5], John[4-1]) was born
on 22 Dec 1819 at So. Hampton, N.H.; mar. 1st, **Louisa M. Dennett**, 16
Jun 1847. In the wake of her third childbirth, Louisa died, 14 Feb 1852
at So. Hampton. "Perley" (as he preferred to be called) then mar. 2d,
**Elizabeth Parsons**, 17 Mar 1853, a marriage which produced no issue.
Perley's primary residence throughout was at South Hampton, where he
kept a farm. He died 2 Jan 1891, and is bur. in Center Cemetery.

        Children with Louisa in South Hampton, N.H.:

  1794    i. Albert[8] Perley Eaton, b. 14 May 1848; mar. Theresa
             Josephine Anson, 5 Mar 1882; a girl was born to them
             6 Sep 1886, but prob. died young.
  1795   ii. Olive[8] Jane Eaton, b. 7 Nov 1849.
+1796   iii. Lowell[8] Dennett Eaton, b. 1 Feb 1852; mar. Wilhelmina.


        **681.  Solomon[7] Eaton** (Eliakim[6], William[5], John[4-1]) was born ca.
1773 at Little Deer Isle, Me.; mar. **Catherine "Kate" Howard**, daughter
of Benjamin Howard, of what later became Brooksville, Me., ca. 1798.
This couple settled on the southwest side of Little Deer Isle and spent
their lives there. Kate bore Solomon eight children, but died 17 Jan
1820. Solomon mar. 2d, **Mary Billings**, daughter of Daniel Billings and
over 20 years his junior, 9 Apr 1820. Mary bore another seven children
who survived infancy, but died Dec 1839. Whereupon Solomon mar. 3d,
**Mrs. Martha (Howard) Tibbetts** of Brooksville, a sister of his first wife
Kate, (int.) 13 Sep 1840. Martha died 25 Jul 1854, and Solomon soon
followed 22 Feb 1858. This couple is buried at Swain's Cove, Little Deer

Isle. The homestead of this large family soon afterward became the property of Silas L. Hardy.

Children with Kate on Little Deer Isle (largely from B. Noyes, typescript ca. 1942):

1797   i. Susan[8] Eaton, b. ca. 1799, but not recorded at Deer Isle. She was the only daughter by Solomon's first wife who remained at Deer Isle. She mar. 1st, Peter H. Haskell, son of Tristram, and had a large family with him. She mar. 2d, Thomas Howard, 5 Sep 1869.

+1798  ii. Solomon[8] Eaton, b. 27 Nov 1802; mar. Sophia Hendrick.

+1799  iii. Benjamin[8] H. Eaton, b. ca. 1803-04; mar. Maria Weed.

+1800  iv. James[8] Eaton, b. ca. 1805; mar Sarah Blake, 1829.

+1801  v. John[8] Calhoun Eaton, b. 14 Feb 1807; mar. Phebe Billings.

1802  vi. Hannah[8] Eaton, b. ca. 1809; mar. David Robbins, 7 Jun 1827 (senior author ms.); or mar. Benjamin Pederick of Marblehead, Mass. (Noyes, ca. 1942) (or both).

1803  vii. Catherine[8] Howard Eaton, b. 12 Apr 1811; mar. Joseph Robbins, 3 May 1845 (senior author ms,); or mar. Samuel Lyman Childs of Marblehead, and had nine children. She died at Lynn, 1 Feb 1907 (Noyes, ca. 1942).

+1804  viii. Mark[8] Haskell Eaton, b. 11 Dec 1814 (town rec.) or 16 Oct 1813 (family Bible); mar Lydia Benson, 11 Feb 1835.

Children with Mary on Little Deer Isle:

1805  ix. Mary[8] Eaton, b. 10 May 1821; died in infancy.

1806  x. Mary[8] Wasson Eaton, b. 29 Apr 1822; mar. 1st, Henry Foster, 20 Sep 1840, who died 5 Jun 1842; mar. 2d, William Blaster, 27 Sep 1842 (son of Samuel & Hannah (Gray) Blaster of Brooksville).

+1807  xi. Isaac[8] Billings Eaton, b. 24 Jul 1824; mar. 1st, Barbara Smith.

1808  xii. Esther[8] Carter Eaton, b. 17 Dec 1825; mar. William Roger Gray of Brooksville, 20 Apr 1845.

+1809  xiii. Daniel[8] Billings Eaton, b. 21 Jul 1827; mar. 1st, Philena.

+1810  xiv. Amos[8] Allen Eaton, b. 3 May 1831; mar. Sarah Dow, 1853.

+1811  xv. (Peter) Hardy[8] Eaton, b. 3 Jun 1835; mar. 1st, Mary Haskell.

1812  xvi. Lucy[8] Eaton, b. 13 Dec 1839; died unmarried.

**682. Isaac[7] Eaton** (Eliakim[6], William[5], John[4-1]) was born ca. 1775 on Little Deer Isle, Me.; mar. **Lucy Hardy**, daughter of Peter Hardy, Sr., and Elizabeth (Haskell) Eaton on 25 Feb. 1802. Isaac was a farmer, but died of consumption soon after the marriage, 23 Jun 1802. Wife Lucy went on to marry, 2d, Jonathan Haskell, 7 Feb 1805.

Child on Deer Isle:

+**1813**    i. Isaac[8] Eaton, b. Nov 1802; also mar. a Lucy __?__.


**687. Peter[7] Hardy Eaton** (Eliakim[6], William[5], John[4-1]) was born 8 Nov 1793 at Deer Isle; mar. **Catherine Billings**, daughter of Daniel and Catherine (Carter) Billings, (int.) 13 Mar 1821, at Deer Isle. Family lore says that Peter enlisted in the War of 1812, and served out his time with a company at Portland, Me. (Noyes, ca. 1942). Peter was a mariner by trade. This couple took up residence on Campbell's Neck on the east side of Deer Isle, where their children were born; they later removed for a period of time to Bear Island, as well as to McGlathery Island off the south coast, on the way to Isle au Haut. It was on the latter island that wife Catherine committed suicide, 18 Feb 1864. In later years Peter as widower went to live with his son Samuel in Addison, Me. He died in this household, 14 or 18 Oct 1887; at his request, his body was brought to join his wife's on McGlathery Island.

Children on Deer Isle (combining overlapping lists from Noyes (1942) and from the senior author's ms.):

**1814**      i. Jonathan[8] Haskell Eaton, b. 10 Oct 1821; infant death.
+**1815**     ii. Jonathan[8A] Haskell Eaton, b. 13 Aug 1822; mar. Martha.
**1816**     iii. Peter[8] Hardy Eaton, b. 15 Dec 1824; infant death.
+**1817**     iv. Peter[8A] Hardy Eaton, b. 25 Aug 1826; mar. Louise Harvey.
**1818**      v. Harriet[8] Billings Eaton, b. 19 Apr 1827; mar. Ebenezer
               Small, 2d, son of Ebenezer and Sally Small of Cape
               Elizabeth, 3 Nov 1844. They had 10 children.
+**1819**     vi. Samuel[8] S. Eaton, b. 19 Mar 1831; mar. Margaret Harvey.
+**1820**    vii. George[8] Washington Eaton, b. 25 Oct 1833; mar. Hannah[9]
               Eaton (#3539).
+**1821**   viii. Otis[9] Convers Eaton, b. 16 Aug 1834; mar. Zemira Billings.
**1822**      ix. Abigail[8] R. Eaton, b. 2 May 1837; mar. Levi Barker of
               Deer Isle, 2 Dec 1851.
**1823**       x. Joanna[8] H. Eaton, b. 27 Jun 1838; mar. Otis[9] L. Eaton of
               Deer Isle (#3450) on 14 Sep 1856.
**1824**      xi. Catherine[8] Eaton. b. 22 Oct 1839; mar. 1st, Joseph Robbins;
               2d, John Closson.
**1825**     xii. Charlotte[8] S. Eaton, b. 18 Jul 1844; mar. Joseph H. Harvey
               of Deer Isle, 25 Nov 1859.


**689. Edward[7] (Bray) "Eaton"** (*Jeremiah[6]*, William[5], John[4-1]) was born to Eleanor Bray of Deer Isle, 5 Feb 1790, with paternity not officially known. Edward and his younger brother were subsequently officially adopted by Jeremiah[6] Eaton (#261, q.v.), whose marriage with Abigail (Haskell) had produced no issue, and who was commonly believed to have sired these boys. Edward mar. **Polly Pressey**, (int.) 10 Apr 1812, and the couple resided on Deer Isle. Edward died in 1830.

Children on Deer Isle:

**1826**    i. Mary[8] Eaton, b. 29 Jul 1816; mar. George Howard, 2 Nov 1844.
**1827**    ii. Adaline[8] Eaton, b. 1817.
**1828**    iii. Lucy[8] Eaton, b. 1818.
**1829**    iv. Caroline[8] Eaton, b. 1820; died 2 Mar 1831.
**1830**    v. Hiram[8] Eaton, b. 8 May 1822; left Deer Isle upon arriving at his majority, and trail is lost.

**690. Asa[7] (Bray) "Eaton"** (*Jeremiah[6]*, William[5], John[4-1]) was born to Eleanor Bray of Deer Isle, 2 May 1792, with paternity not officially known. Asa and his older brother were subsequently officially adopted by Jeremiah[6] Eaton (**#261**, q.v.), whose marriage with Abigail (Haskell) had produced no issue, and who was commonly believed to have sired these boys. Asa mar. **Mercy Raynes**, 20 Aug 1816 at Deer Isle, where this couple took up residence. Asa was a mariner. He died Oct 1851 in Chelsea, Mass.; wife Mercy died 24 Jan 1865 on Deer Isle.

Children on Deer Isle:

**1831**    i. Martha[8] Eaton, b. 2 Dec 1820; mar. George Dexter of Boston, and died 30 June 1854.
**1832**    ii. Joan[8] Eaton, b. 1 Jan 1823; died 14 Dec 1823.
**1833**    iii. William[8] Eaton, b. 21 Nov 1825; died 8 Jan 1826.
**+1834**    iv. (Capt.) William[8] Eaton, b. 2 Feb 1827; mar. Ann Saunders.
**+1835**    v. Nathan[8] H. Eaton, b. 3 Apr 1829; mar. Clara Stinson, 1853.
**1836**    vi. Elizabeth[8] P. Eaton, b. ca. May 1831; died Jan 1837.
**1837**    vii. Jonathan[8] Pressey Eaton, b. 17 Nov 1833; died 4 Apr 1834.

**692. (Capt.) William[7] Eaton** (William[6-5], John[4-1]) was born 3 Jul 1783 at North Deer Isle; mar. **Abigail Howard**, a daughter of Deer Isle pioneer John and Abigail (Pressey) Howard, 19 Apr 1807. The couple always lived and raised their children at North Deer Isle. William was a master mariner. But he sailed to New York City as a pilot of the old sloop the <u>Huntress</u> of Castine, Me., under the command of Capt. John Greenlaw, Jr., in Dec 1830. On the return trip the boat was last sighted off Nantucket Shoals, and no trace was thereafter found of her, with all four crew lost. After her husband's death, widow Abigail mar. Nathan Ingalls of Corinth, Me., 7 Dec 1837. She died 3 Aug 1860 and is buried with her first husband in the old Deer Isle Cemetery.

Children in North Deer Isle:

**1838**    i. Mary[8] Eaton, b. 28 Jun 1810; mar. William Lowe, son of Maj. Nathan Lowe of Deer Isle, 9 Mar 1835. They had six children. She died 1 Oct 1872; he died 20 Feb 1888, and they both are bur. in the Forest Hill Cemetery at the "Reach."

**1839**    ii. William[8] Augustus Eaton, b. 28 Jan 1812; died 20 Mar 1813.

**+1840**   iii. William[8A] Augustus Eaton, b. 29 Apr 1814; mar. Susan W.

**1841**    iv. Abigail[8] Haskell Eaton, b. 13 Jul 1817; mar. Capt. Daniel S. Torrey, son of Daniel and Lydia (Haskell) Torrey, 17 Nov 1839. They had three sons and four daughters at Deer Isle, and are bur. at Mt. Adams Cemetery, Deer Isle.

**1842**    v. Esther[8] Eaton, b. 21 Jun 1819; mar. John Weed, Jr., 29 Apr 1838; they had six children before Esther died of typhoid fever on Little Deer Isle.

**1843**    vi. Hannah[8] Eaton, b. 16 Nov 1821; mar. Capt. Francis H. Torrey, 11 Oct 1842; res. in Deer Isle and had four sons and four daughters.

**1844**   vii. Samuel[8] Eaton, a final son lacking a birth record; drowned at sea at a young age.

**695. Jeremiah[7] Eaton** (William[6-5], John[4-1]) was born 3 Feb 1789, probably at North Deer Isle; mar. his first cousin **Rachel[7] Eaton** (#688), daughter of Eliakim[7], 18 Jul 1812. Jeremiah (called "Jay") was a farmer and a mariner; they lived at what was later known as "the William Eaton place" at Little Deer Isle, near the bar (cf. 1881 Colby Atlas of Hancock Co.) where his third son lived and died. Noyes (ca. 1942) recounts that in the haying season, 1835, he had a crew cutting grass at Stave Island, across a small strait from his home. When called to dinner, the crew took a boat to cross over, but Jeremiah decided to swim instead. He apparently suffered a cramp and drowned, although a man of great vigor who prided himself on his swimming. Wife Rachel later mar. John Gray of Brooksville, Me., but is bur. with her first husband on Little Deer Isle.

Children on Little Deer Isle:

**+1845**    i. Jeremiah[8] Eaton, b. 3 Mar 1813; mar. Angelina Blastow.

**+1846**   ii. Samuel[8] Eaton, b. ca. 1815; mar. Olive Joyce Weed, 1834.

**+1847**   iii. William[8] Eaton, b. ca. 1818; mar. Elizabeth Weed, 1844.

**+1848**   iv. Alfred[8] Eaton, b. 5 May 1820; mar. Sophia[9] Eaton.

**1849**    v. Haskell[8] Eaton, b. ca. 1822; he was lost overboard during a mackerel trip, 1835.

**1850**    vi. Mary[8] Eaton, b. ca. 1824; mar. 1st an Eaton, but they separated soon after the marriage, and their one son died young. She mar. 2d, George Howard of Brooksville, Me., 2 Nov 1844. They lived at Little Deer Isle or Brooksville.

**1851**   vii. Hannah[8] Eaton, b. 1 Oct 1826; died in infancy.

**1852**  viii. Elcy[8] E. Eaton, b. ca. 1827; mar. Ebenezer J. Weed, son of Jeremiah and Elethea (Wood) Weed, 11 Jan 1843. This couple res. on Little Deer Isle, where he was a sailor. They had eight children.

**1853**    ix. Hannah[8A] Eaton, b. 15 Dec 1828; mar. William Smith of
            Bucksport, Me. and removed to that community.
**1854**    x. Charlotte[8] H. Eaton, b. 4 Dec 1830; after her father's drown-
            ing, she was raised by an aunt, Elizabeth (Eaton) Powers,
            wife of a doctor; mar. Joseph Curtis of Frankfort, Me. on
            1 Jan 1849. They had several children at Winterport, Me.
**1855**    xi. Elizabeth[8] Eaton, b. 21 Sep 1831; probably died young.
**1856**    xii. Elizabeth[8A] Eaton, b. 14 Sep 1833; mar. 1st, Jeremiah
            "Jerry" Billings, son of Jeremiah and Rosanna Billings.
            They had four children before Jerry died, 15 Jul 1866
            at Deer Isle. She mar. 2d, Edward Collins, a sea captain in
            Rockland, Me.
**1857**  xiii. Olive[8] Eaton, b. 5 Feb 1834; died young.
**1858**   xiv. Olive[8A] Eaton, b. 20 Jan 1835; mar. Amaziah Gray of Buck-
            sport, Me., and reared a family there.


   **701. Jeremiah[7] Eaton** (Samuel[6] W., William[5], John[4-1]) was born 8
Mar 1783 at Seabrook, N.H. in the period when his father resided there
before returning to Maine to settle at Chesterville. After this return, Jeremiah mar. **Sally Warren** of Monmouth, Me., 28 May 1809. They lived
on a farm on the west side of Sandy Pond in Chesterville. Father Jeremiah died 12 Nov 1828; wife Sally mar. 2d, an Enoch Dearborn back in
Monmouth, Me.

        Children in Chesterfield, Me.:

**+1859**    i. Samuel[8] Warren Eaton, b. 14 Aug 1809; mar. Polly Hanson.
 **1860**   ii. William[8] Moore Eaton, b. 13 Apr 1812; remained unmar.,
            residence unknown.
 **1861**  iii. Livonia[8] Eaton, b. 5 Dec 1817; mar. Parker Jaquith, a Presi-
            ding Elder in the Maine Conference; had two children.
 **1862**   iv. Joseph[8] Nelson Eaton, b. 17 Dec 1820; died young.


   **703. Isaac[7] Eaton** (Samuel[6] W., William[5], John[4-1]) was born 24 Jul
1789 in Seabrook, N.H. He was a youngster when his parents returned to
Maine to settle at Chesterville. He enlisted in the War of 1812, but did not
leave the state. He mar. ca. 1810 a Chesterville native, **Almira Sewall** (b.
28 Mar 1793), and they lived on a farm on Sandy Pond in that community, where all their children were born. Wife Almira died there 23 Sep
1867; Isaac followed her 6 Nov 1868.

        Children in Chesterville, Me.:

 **1863**    i. Clar(iss)a[8] Eaton, b. 4 May 1812; died 27 Aug 1813.
**+1864**   ii. Sewall[8] Eaton, b. 8 Jul 1814; mar. Elizabeth Porter, 1845.
 **1865**  iii. Sophronia[8] Eaton, b. 14 Dec 1816; mar. 1st, Hezekiah H.
            Merrick of Pittsfield, Me. After one son, her husband

died, Feb 1841. She mar. 2d, David French of Mt. Vernon, Me. They had five children. He died 24 Sep 1877;
she died 11 Jan 1887.

**1866**    iv. Olive[8] Violette Eaton, b. 10 Jul 1819; died unm. Mar 1851.

**1867**    v. Clarissa[8A] Eaton, b. 27 Dec 1821; died 28 Feb 1822.

**+1868**    vi. Crosby[8] Eaton, b. 3 Jun 1823; mar. Ellen Woodman, 1851.

**1869**    vii. Eliza[8] Jane Eaton, b. 23 Feb 1827; mar. David Edwin Hislid
of Penn., May 1861; they res. in South Haven, Michigan,
having two children.

**1870**    viii. Abby[8] Josephine Eaton, b. 31 Jul 1829; mar. Charles H.
Wigglesworth, 1 Jan 1855. This couple res. in South
Haven, Mich. with her sister Eliza Jane. No issue.

**+1871**    ix. John[8] Calvin Eaton, b. 22 Feb 1832; mar. Lucy Sanderson.

**1872**    x. Arvilla[8] Bailey Eaton, b. 27 Dec 1834; mar. Almon B.
Gardner, a carpenter b. in Nelson, N.H., 26 Aug 1857.
They res. in Lowell, Mass. Arvilla was an important
source for the senior author's original manuscript.


**704. Lowell[7] Eaton** (Samuel[6] W., Benjamin[5], John[4-1]) was born 8
Oct 1792 at Seabrook. He was a youngster when his parents returned to
Maine to settle at Chesterville. His given name was Lowell in honor of
his mother's maiden name. He was a soldier in the War of 1812, and later
received a military pension of $8 per month. He mar. 1st. **Sabina War-
ren**, b. 9 Jan 1791 at Monmouth, Me., and probably a sister of his older
brother Jeremiah's wife, on 18 Aug 1814. They lived on a farm on the
west side of Sandy Pond in Chesterville, near his brother Jeremiah.
Sabina died 26 May 1860. Lowell then mar. 2d, **Sarah Dexter**, 5 May
1868, who in turn died 11 Nov 1875. Lowell died 24 Apr 1882.

Children with Sabina in Chesterville:

**1873**    i. Harriet[8] Parker Eaton, b. 11 Sep 1817, mar. Jacob H.
Manuell, 7 Nov 1844, and res. Presque Isle, Me. She had
three daughters.

**1874**    ii. Nancy[8] Fidelia Eaton, b. 30 Oct 1821; mar. Joseph Wads-
worth of Livermore Falls, Me. She had two sons, one of
whom was a professor at "Michigan Mining School" at
Houghton, Mich.

**1875**    iii. Matilda[8] Gould Eaton, b. 21 Aug 1824.

**1876**    iv. Clarissa[8] Ann Eaton, b. 16 Dec 1830.

**1877**    v. Rachel[8] French Eaton, b. 18 Oct 1832.

**1878**    vi. Julia[8] Angeline Augusta Eaton, b. 13 Jun 1835.

**1879**    vii. Hiram[8] Russell Wardwell Eaton, b. 8 Jan 1837.


**707. Thomas[7] Eaton** (Josiah[6], Thomas[5], John[4-1]) was born 27 Apr
1769 at No. Yarmouth, Me. His father died when Thomas was only
eight; his mother died not too many years later. Thus orphaned, he and

his siblings were put under the care of their grandparents Thomas[5] (**#89**) and Jane Eaton in Seabrook. He mar. **Phebe Young** on 14 Nov 1793 (place unknown), and this couple resided at one time on a farm in Seabrook. However, there were sojourns as well back in York Co., Me. Thus on 27 Aug 1795, Thomas was residing at Wells, Me., when he was named guardian of his younger sister Miriam Eaton of Seabrook, described as "a minor upwards of 14 years" (age 20, actually); and he appears to account for the Thomas Eaton household in Wells in the 1800 Census (although otherwise they are hard to find in Censuses). At least two of his children were also born in Kennebunk, Me. Thomas died at Newburyport, Mass., 17 Mar 1836.

Children (with help from Bernice (Eaton) Chase ms.):

**1880**  i. Sarah[8] Eaton, b. 3 Oct 1794; mar. a Trafton; died 21 Jan 1876.
+**1881**  ii. George[8] Eaton, b. 1 Apr 1797 at Kennebunk, Me.
**1882**  iii. Phebe[8] Eaton, b. 19 Jul 1799; mar. John Morse, Jr.
**1883**  iv. Thomas[8] Eaton, b. 10 May 1801; mar. Mary Barton.
+**1884**  v. John[8] Eaton, b. 19 Jul 1803; mar. Susan Emerson, 1833.
**1885**  vi. Bryant[8] Eaton, b. 23 May 1805.
**1886**  vii. Osborne[8] Eaton, b. 14 Apr 1807; mar. Charity Morse.
**1887**  viii. Miriam[8] Eaton, b. 31 May 1810; mar. Horace Fabyan, proprietor of the "Fabyan House" hostelry in the White Mountains of N.H. Seven children.
**1888**  ix. Josiah[8] Eaton, b. 24 June 1812.
**1889**  x. Caroline[8] Eaton, b. 10 Oct. 1814; mar. Stephen Hill, 12 Apr 1832.
**1890**  xi. Mary[8] Jane Eaton, b. 16 Apr 1818; mar. Joel Prince, Dec 1836. Res. Portland, Me. Three of their children resided in California.

**708. Bradbury[7] Eaton** (Josiah[6], Thomas[5], John[4-1]) was born 10 Jan 1774 in No. Yarmouth, Me. Orphaned very young, he was brought up by his grandparents, Thomas[5] (**#89**) and Jane Eaton in Seabrook, N.H. He mar. **Rebecca True**, 11 Mar 1799 in Litchfield, Me (Seabrook *VR* in Concord). The couple settled in Litchfield, then Lincoln Co., where we find them in the 1800 Census with two boys under 10, and again in 1810, now with no male youngsters, but with three girls under 10. Thus, reconstitution of a child roster is challenging. Bradbury died early, 15 Dec 1811. Wife Rebecca died 28 Aug 1832. It is worth noting that a Bradbury Eaton is found at Lee in Penobscot Co. in 1850, altho he is age seven, a solo Eaton in the household of a Bradbury Blake.

Known children (prob. partial):

**1891**  i. Miriam[8] Eaton, b. 27 Dec 1802; mar. Thomas True, Jr. She died 10 Aug 1879. Issue: three sons, one daughter.

**1892**    ii. Lavina[8] Eaton, b. 17 Nov 1806; mar. John E. Currier of
            Merrimac, Mass., 10 Nov 1845. No issue.

     **714. Wheeler**[7] **Eaton** (William[6], Thomas[5], John[4-1]) was born 2 Sep
1787 in Salisbury, Mass.; mar. 1st, **Abigail Perkins** of Raymond, N.H., 5
May 1811 in So. Hampton, N.H. This couple settled first at Weare, N.H.,
where Wheeler earned a living as a tanner and a shoemaker. About 1835,
however, he bought a substantial farm on the north side of the new community of Franklin, N.H., two miles south of the town of Hill. He was a
very successful farmer there for 36 years. After wife Abigail died, 23
Dec 1838, he mar. 2d, **Mrs. Nancy (Burley) Sleeper**, daughter of David
Burley, on 19 Oct 1840. Wheeler died 1 Sep 1871.

     Children with Abigail, all born in Weare, N.H.:

+**1893**    i. Horace[8] Perkins Eaton, b. 30 Aug 1811; m. Ismenie Merrill.
+**1894**    ii. Cyrus[8] Wheeler Eaton, b. May 1813; mar. Phebe Goodwin.
+**1895**    iii. Gorham[8] Eaton, b. 6 Jan 1816; mar. Weltha Cartwright.
 **1896**    iv. Emily[8] Wilmarth Eaton 1st, b. 27 Jul 1817; mar. John Shaw,
            son of David Shaw, 17 Feb 1841. She died 26 Nov 1845,
            having had two children.
 **1897**    v. William[8] Eaton, b. 29 Mar 1820; died unmar. Dec 1842.

     Child with Nancy in Franklin, N.H.

 **1898**    vi. Emily[8A] Wilmarth Eaton the 2d, b. 29 Jul 1847, and hence
            christened after the death of her half sister; mar. Dana
            W. Call, and had two daughters by him.

     **719. Thomas**[7] **Eaton** (William[6], Thomas[5], John[4-1]) was born 9 May
1797 at Salisbury, Mass., and was a toddler when his parent moved to
Sanbornton, N.H. about 1800. He mar. **Betsey Blake**, daughter of James
Blake, 4 Nov 1819. This couple res. for the most part on the west side of
Sanbornton on the homestead his father established upon arrival. Thomas[7] died 20 Dec 1884, age 87 and the oldest person in town at the time,
leaving a widow and six surviving children.

     Children with Betsey in Sanbornton:

+**1899**    i. Warren[8] Eaton, b. 18 Nov 1820; mar. Zilpha Hancock, 1845.
 **1900**    ii. Arvilla[8] Eaton, b. 15 Feb 1823; mar. William B. Mason, 20
            Jun 1846. She had three children and died 14 Feb 1861.
+**1901**    iii. John[8] Wiggin Eaton, b. 15 Dec 1825; mar. Climena Davis.
+**1902**    iv. Joshua[8] Eaton, b. 15 May 1829; mar. Rachel Mason, 1852.
+**1903**    v. Ira[8] Blake Eaton, b. 11 Nov 1832; mar. 1st, Elizabeth Sargent.
+**1904**    vi. Horace[8] Eaton, b. 24 Sep 1834; mar. Esther Ann Burleigh.
 **1905**    vii. James[8] W. Eaton, b. 11 Dec 1837; unmar. as of 1880.

**1906**   viii. Lavina[8] Eaton, b. 8 Nov 1839; unmar. as of 1880.
**1907**    ix. Roswell[8] Gorham Eaton, b. 21 Jul 1842; a dentist in
           Manchester, N.H.


    **719. Joshua[7] Eaton** (William[6], Thomas[5], John[4-1]) was born 4 Jul
1801, the first child of his parents to be born in Sanbornton after their
migration. At age 18, however, he decided to go to sea, a project that
brought him back to the Salisbury/Seabrook area. He mar. his first
cousin, **Dorcas[7] Eaton (#726)** of Seabrook, daughter of Bryant and
Sarah Bagley, on 17 Jun 1821 at Hampton Falls (Seabrook *VR* at Concord). In the early period this couple res. at Salisbury, Mass, near "Mills
Village," with their first three children recorded there, and Joshua taxed
as a Salisbury resident, 1824-32. In Nov 1832, they sold out in Salisbury
and removed to Seabrook. Our senior author described Joshua as a
"manufacturer" at Seabrook, but he is self-described as a "farmer" in the
Censuses there, 1850-70, with real estate in the $2-3,000 range, probably
residing on upper Washington St. He was very active in Seabrook land
conveyances, 1832-1867. Joshua died 1 Mar 1870; wife Dorcas followed 8 Dec 1871.

    Children with Dorcas:

**1908**     i. Asenath[8] G. Eaton, b. 11 Oct 1821 at Salisbury, Mass.; died
            unmarried.
+**1909**   ii. George[8] Folsom Eaton, b. 27 Jan 1824, Salisbury, Mass.
+**1910**  iii. (Manual) Bryant[8] Eaton, b. 8 Sep 1826, Salisbury, Mass.
**1911**    iv. Israel[8] B. Eaton, b. Jun 1832, Seabrook?; died 20 Feb
            1853 in Seabrook (gravestone, Methodist Cemetery).
**1912**     v. Mary[8] L. Eaton, b. ca. 1835, Seabrook; mar. Enoch[8] Hoyt
            Eaton (**#1750**, q.v.) 13 Jun 1853 at Salisbury.


    **730. Samuel[7A] Eaton** (Bryant[6], Thomas[5], John[4-1]) was born 16 Feb
1814, and named after his older brother who had drowned in 1810. He
mar. **Judith A. Palmer**, (born in Sanbornton, N.H. to Benjamin Palmer),
on 3 Apr 1842 at Seabrook. This couple lived first at Salisbury, having
their children there in the 1840s and still residents in 1850, when Samuel
is a laborer and a Jedediah Palmer, age 65 and presumably of Judith's
family, lives with them. In 1860-70 they are in Seabrook, near the head
of South Main St., and in the former year Samuel[7A] was farming; in the
latter year he and his son Benjamin are working in the shoe factory.
Samuel was known as a pugilist in his neighborhood, and participated in
the Civil War. His wife Judith died 17 Jul 1884; Samuel[7A] died 22 Jun
1911.

    Children (most or all born in Salisbury):

**1913**     i. Benjamin[8] F. Eaton, b. 11 Jul 1842; he never mar. and died

22 Jul 1914.
**1914**    ii. Child[8] Eaton, b. ca. 1844; died in infancy.
**1915**    iii. Sarah[8] Elizabeth Eaton; b. 11 Sep 1846; died 22 Sep 1862.
**1916**    iv. (Mary) Abby[8] Ann Eaton; b. 9 Aug 1848; she died unmar.
of epilepsy, 24 Oct 1893 at Seabrook.


**732. Moses[7] Chandler Eaton** (Aaron[6], Thomas[5], John[4-1]) was born
2 Jan 1791, prob. in Salisbury, Mass. (given his repeated later reports of
having been born in Mass.) and later, in 1808, moved with his parents
from Seabrook to the adjacent South Hampton, N.H.    He mar. **Betsey
Jones** in Jan 1820, and the couple soon established themselves on a farm
"down the hill" from father Aaron's homestead, 10 Apr 1826.    In 1850
and 1860, Moses appears to be a prosperous farmer, with $3-4,000 worth
of real estate and $1,000 personal estate.    He died 3 Aug 1869.

Children born in So. Hampton:

+**1917**    i. Jeremiah[8] W. Eaton, b. 29 Dec 1821; mar. Polly Currier.
+**1918**    ii. Jacob[8] Eaton, b. 21 Nov 1823; mar. Lizzie Paige, 1860.
+**1919**    iii. Thomas[8] Eaton, b. 8 Jul 1826; mar. 1st, Mary Morrill.
**1920**    iv. Mary[8] A. Eaton, b. 13 Jul 1828; taught school for 40 years;
she died 2 Aug 1890.
+**1921**    v. Moses[8] J. Eaton, b. 26 Apr 1834; mar. Mary J. Follansbee,
13 Apr 1865, South Hampton; he died 12 May 1907.
+**1922**    vi. Benjamin[8] F. Eaton, b. 16 Sep 1836; mar. H. N. Kennard.
**1923**    vii. Sarah[8] Jane Eaton, b. 6 Oct 1837; mar. Charles E. Tuck of
Kensington, N.H., 3 Jul 1858; had two sons and two
daughters.


**737. Aaron[7] Thomas Eaton** (Aaron[6], Thomas[5], John[4-1]) was born
on 5 Apr 1803 in Seabrook, N.H., and removed with his parents to So.
Hampton, N.H. in 1808.    He mar. **Sarah Collins** of Seabrook, 17 Mar
1834.    In the 1850 Census, Aaron[7]'s family is a second household under
the same roof with his father Aaron[6].    Aaron, Jr., died 23 Jan 1857; wife
Sarah died 22 Jun 1874.

Children born in So. Hampton, N.H.:

**1924**    i. Olive[8] Maria Eaton, b. 2 Aug 1834; mar. Benjamin R. Jewell
24 Dec 1863.  Mr. Jewell was distinguished as a worker
for temperance in Mass., and a liberal supporter of the
Baptist cause in N.H.  Issue: one daughter and two sons.
Benjamin died in 1891; Olive in 1914.
**1925**    ii. Abby[8] F. Eaton, b. 10 Mar 1837.  She was for many years
in the office with Mr. Jewell (above) in Boston.  While
there she aided greatly in compiling this genealogy, especially the descendants of Thomas[5] Eaton (**#89**).  She died

18 Jul 1887.

**738. Darius**[7] **Eaton** (Aaron[6], Thomas[5], John[4-1]) was born 17 Jan 1807 in Seabrook, N.H., and moved as a babe with his family to So. Hampton, N.H. in 1808. He mar. **Sarah Taylor**, 24 Sep 1833. Darius was a tanner and currier. The couple lived first in Barnstead, N.H., on a farm by Tannery Brook, a property he had received from his father in 1833, where all five of their children were born (Merrill, 1979). Later in the 1840s, the family moved to Pittsfield, N.H. Darius died 20 Jul 1851 on board the steamship <u>Georgia</u>, headed belatedly to California to join the 49ers, but he is bur. in Pittsfield, N.H. with his wife.

Children, born in Barnstead, N.H.:

1926     i. Emily[8] A. T. Eaton, b. 5 Sep 1835; mar. 1st, Jacob Bickford; 2d, Oliver Brooks.

1927    ii. Aroline[8] E. S. Eaton, b. 2 Mar 1837; died 5 Sep 1855.

1928   iii. Nancy[8] P. Eaton, b. 1 Aug 1839; died 2 Oct 1854.

1929   iv. Isabella[8] E. Eaton, b. 20 Dec 1840; mar. David F. Kaine of St. Louis, Mo., 7 Aug 1859. Had three sons and three daughters.

1930    v. Jairus[8] Lysander Eaton, b. 16 Aug 1844; was a physician in St. Louis, Mo. Died unmarrried.

**741. Jacob**[7] **Eaton** (Humphrey[6], Wyman[5], John[4-1]) was born 28 Nov 1775 at Seabrook, N.H.; presumably removed with his family to Weare, N.H., ca. 1786. He mar. **Jane Goodwin** of Weare in 1800. They settled on an East Weare farm, where all their children were born. Jacob also owned a gristmill and a carding mill. He and his sons were strong advocates of moral reform. Jacob died 24 Mar 1832 in East Weare.

Children born in E. Weare, N.H.:

1931     i. Louis[8] French Eaton, b. 24 Apr 1801; res. in Weare and mar. Cassan Dana (Cilley) Eaton, widow of his brother John[7] Q. in 1846. They had no children.

1932    ii. Lavina[8] A. Eaton, b. 4 Jan 1804; mar. Elijah Johnson of East Weare, 26 Nov 1828, and they res. in Goffstown, N.H. They had six children. Lavina died 5 Nov 1879.

1933   iii. Elvira[8] J. Eaton, b. 6 Nov 1805; mar Ezra Dow of No. Weare, 8 Aug 1830, and had five daughters.

1934   iv. John[8] Q. Eaton, b. 10 Jun 1808; mar. Cassan Dana Cilley, 15 Nov 1832. He died 4 July 1845, without issue.

+1935    v. Jeremiah[8] S. Eaton, b. 19 June 1810; mar. Harriet Bacon.

1936   vi. Helen[8] M. Eaton, b. 4 Apr 1812; mar. Thomas M. Preble of Weare. She had one daughter at Nashua, N.H. in 1838. Helen died 29 Mar 1864 at Weare.

**1937** vii. Jacob[8] F. Eaton, b. Apr 1821; died unmar. at Weare, 12 Oct 1841.

**743. Tristram[7] Eaton** (Humphrey[6], Wyman[5], John[4-1]) was born 30 May 1782 in Seabrook, N.H., and brought by his parents to a new home in East Weare, N.H., four years later. He mar. **Abigail Murray** of neighboring Dunbarton, N.H., 13 Oct 1808. Tristram was a merchant, and they res. at Weare for some time while their children were born, but after 1830, they removed to Gainesville, Ala, perhaps for his health, where he died 10 Oct 1840. The will that father Humphrey[6] had drawn up 2 Sep 1828, gave much to Tristram's older brother Jacob[7] (above), but bequeathed the actual family homestead to Tristram[7], on condition that this homestead pass directly on to the grandson Humphrey[8] F. when came of age. It does not appear that this happened because of the move South.

Children born in Weare, N.H.:

**1938** i. Julia[8] M. Eaton, b. 1812; mar. John Clark of Gainesville, Ala. and died at Enterprise, Miss., leaving two children, b. 1847 and 1849.
**+1939** ii. Humphrey[8] F. Eaton, b. 1814; mar. 1st., Elisa, ca. 1839.

**745. John[7] Eaton, Jr.** (John[6], Wyman[5], John[4-1]) was born 19 Nov 1774, about the time that his parents were removing from Seabrook, N.H. to Buxton, Me., and his actual birth could have occurred in either place. He surely grew up in Buxton, and mar. **Keziah Dearborn** of that town on 2 Dec 1792. The couple settled there, where John was a farmer until he died early, 29 Feb. 1809.

Children born in Buxton, Me.:

**+1940** i. Jacob[8] Eaton, b. 10 Apr 1793; mar. Dorcas Edgecomb.
**+1941** ii. Simeon[8] Eaton, b. 23 Aug 1795; mar. Betsey Paine, 1816.
**1942** iii. Polly[8] Eaton, b. 17 May 1797; died 8 Jul 1826.
**1943** iv. Sally[8] A. Eaton, b. 10 Jan. 1799; mar. Samuel J. Perry of Limerick, Me., 24 Feb 1827. They had 3 sons and four daughters. Sally died 8 Jun 1844 in Buxton.
**+1944** v. John[8] G. Eaton, b 10 Aug 1802; mar. Hannah Boulter, 1837.
**1945** vi. Jemima[8] G. Eaton, b. 16 Sep 1804; mar. John Drew of Scarborough, Me., 1822. The couple had six sons and one daughter, and Jemima died in Dixon, Ill., 30 Oct 1806.
**1946** vii. Eliza[8] J. Eaton, b. 16 Oct 1806; died 10 Mar 1819.

**748. Tristram[7] Eaton** (John[6], Wyman[5], John[4-1]) was born 16 Dec 1781 at Buxton; mar. **Betsey Woodman** of Buxton, 15 Jan 1801. In 1808 this couple settled on the farm in Buxton where they still were 64 years later. In the Town history, Tristram reports being present at the raising of what was the first mill (a sawmill) in the area, at what is now Bar Mills, on the Hollis side of the Saco River. The compiler of the Centennial History for Buxton reports of Tristram, "'though feeble in body,' is said to be 'sound in mind with a remarkably clear and distinct memory.' The compiler seems to have availed himself of all the assistance this ancient man could give him, which without doubt was no little, but he did not give him a single line of biographical sketch, though he devotes page after page to other men and their families." (Little, 1909, p. 223). Tristram died in 1875 at Buxton.

Children born in Buxton, Me.:

**1947**  i. James[8] W. Eaton, b. 16 Mar 1802; died 19 Oct 1841.
**1948**  ii. John[8] Eaton, b. 18 Feb 1804; mar. 1st, Nancy Eldridge, 3 Sep 1844; 2d?, Hannah Redlow, 27 Jun 1853. He was a farmer in Buxton, without issue, and died 15 Jun 1879.
**1949**  iii. Jemima[8] Eaton, b. 1 May 1805; died 6 May 1805.
**+1950**  iv. Stephen[8] Woodman Eaton, b. 2 Mar 1806; mar. Miranda.
**1951**  v. Tristram[8], Jr., Eaton, b. 4 Aug 1808; died 18 Mar 1834.
**+1952**  vi. Isaac[8] W. Eaton, b. 11 Jan 1811; mar. Phebe Haseltine, 1834.
**+1953**  vii. Humphrey[8] W. Eaton, b. 1 Nov 1812; mar. Annorill Pray.
**1954**  viii. Elizabeth[8] A. Eaton, b. 26 May 1815; died 8 Oct 1816.
**+1955**  ix. Charles[8] C. Eaton, b. 14 May 1817; mar. Esther Frost, 1851.
**1956**  x. Mary[8] A. Eaton, b. 16 Nov 1819; mar. Aaron B. Chapman of Limerick, Me., 10 Feb 1843. They had a daughter and two sons. Mary died 18 Aug 1873 at Limerick.
**1957**  xi. Eliza[8] J. Eaton, b. 7 Jan 1823; died 17 May 1886.
**1958**  xii. Harriet[8] R. Eaton, b. 18 Oct 1824; died 25 Jun 1854.

**749. Nathan[7] Eaton** (John[6], Wyman[5], John[4-1]) was born 24 Jan 1785, at Buxton, Me.; mar. **Mary Tarbox** of Buxton, 25 Mar 1823, and lived in Buxton on the original homestead which his grandfather, Wyman[5], had bought for his father John[6] in 1774. In the 1850 Census, he is a farmer there reporting real estate worth $2,500. He died 22 Mar 1857.

Children born in Buxton, Me.:

**1959**  i. Roxana[8] G. Eaton, b. 1 Mar 1825; she was unmar., but "in single blessedness, she greatly blessed others." With great painstaking and accuracy, she wrote the genealogy of Wyman[5] and Ruth Eaton and their descendants. She died 26 Dec 1894.
**+1960**  ii. Samuel[8] T. Eaton, b. 10 Nov 1826; mar. Lucy Johnston.
**1961**  iii. William[8] H. Eaton, b. 16 Oct 1828; mar. 1st, Amanda Steele of Buxton, Me., 5 Feb 1856; she died 25 Feb 1857. He mar. 2d, Eudoxy Garland of Buxton, 13 Jun 1861. He was a shoe manufacturer in Melrose, Mass. He died 11

May 1884, and left no children.

**750. Abel[7] Eaton** (John[6], Wyman[5], John[4-1]) was born 8 Jun 1786 at Buxton, Me.; mar. 1st, **Mary Smith** of neighboring Hollis, Me., on 1 Dec 1809, with whom he had four children. Mary died in the late 1810s, and he mar. 2d, **Sally Frathy** of York, Me. about 1820. His household is present at Buxton in U.S. Censuses from 1810 thru 1850 and probably beyond. He was a farmer, reporting real estate worth $2,500 in 1850. He died 1 Mar 1867.

Children with Mary in Buxton, Me.:

+ **1962**    i. Joshua[8] T. Eaton, b. 12 Feb 1811; mar. Cordelia Bean, 1843.
  **1963**   ii. Acel[8] E. Eaton, b. 3 Dec 1813; died 8 Mar 1836.
  **1964**  iii. George[8] W. Eaton, b. 20 Feb 1815; died 27 Sep 1823.
+ **1965**   iv. John[8] W. Eaton, b. 4 Mar 1817; mar. Harriet N. Noyes, 1841.

Children with Sally in Buxton, Me.:

  **1966**    v. Henry[8] F. Eaton, b. 12 Mar 1823; died 14 Nov 1844.
  **1967**   vi. George[8A] W. Eaton, b. 20 Feb 1827; died 12 Jul 1852.
  **1968**  vii. Hannah[8] L. Eaton, b. 22 Feb 1829; mar. Isaac Hutchinson of Buxton, 4 Nov 1857. They had two each, boys and girls.
  **1969** viii. Mary[8] A. Eaton, b. 10 Jun 1831; died 13 Aug 1843.
  **1970**   ix. Charlotte[8] H. Eaton, b. 10 Oct 1833; mar. Samuel H. Smith of Boston, 30 Nov 1858. They had two sons and a daughter. Charlotte died at Tryon, No. Carolina, 5 Jul 1886.
  **1971**    x. Acel[8A] Eaton, b. 21 Feb 1836.

**752. Humphrey[7] W. Eaton** (John[6], Wyman[5], John[4-1]) was b. 26 Jul 1793 at Buxton, Me.; mar. **Mary Brewster** of Buxton, 24 Nov 1819. He became a lawyer at Biddeford, Me., but suffered an untimely death there, 17 Nov 1825.

Children, prob. born in Biddeford, Me.:

  **1972**    i. Cornelia[8] A. Eaton, b. 20 Sep 1822; mar. Dr. Moses D. Van Pelt of New York City, 29 Apr 1840; she left four children when she died 4 Aug 1861.
  **1973**   ii. Humphrey[8] W. Eaton, Jr., b. June 1824. Died 21 Nov 1851 of consumption at Portland; prob. unmarried.

**755. Daniel[7] Eaton** (Abel[6], Wyman[5], John[4-1]) was born 3 Aug 1786 at Salisbury, Mass.; mar. **Sarah M. Brown** of Salisbury, 8 Nov 1804. They res. on a farm in Salisbury, probably the homestead Daniel grew up in, on the north side of Beach Road in Salisbury, near the original Eaton homestead, since Daniel was the only surviving son and in 1820 and 1830 his aging parents were part of the household. Daniel is listed as a resident on Salisbury tax lists for 44 consecutive years, from 1806 to the series end in 1849. At his peak in the years 1826-33, when he took over the family wealth from his father, his valuations are a bit above average for Salisbury household heads; but before and after they are well below. He is also a household head in all Censuses from 1810 to 1870. He died 15 Apr 1871.

Children born in Salisbury:

**1974**   i. Hannah[8] Eaton, b. 26 Sep 1805; died single, Dec 1856.
**1975**   ii. Sarah[8] Jane Eaton, b. 21 Mar 1811; died single, Jun 1898.
**1976**   iii. Mary Ann[8] Porter Eaton, b. 3 May 1819; mar. Edward D. Brown of Salisbury, Mass., 21 Jul 1844, and had one daughter, Abby Brown, b. 18 Sep 1845. She died 15 Mar 1902 at Salisbury.

**757. Wyman[7] Eaton** (Simeon[6], Wyman[5], John[4-1]) was born 1 Oct 1787 at Seabrook, N.H.; mar. **Miriam Fowler**, daughter of Thomas, ca. 1807, and lived on the old stage road (later Route 1), adjoining the estate of Samuel Eaton, on the north corner of Pine St. The house was still standing in 1895, owned by Joshua Janvrin, his nephew. On this place they raised a large family, the records of whose births must be left to calculation. Wife Miriam died 16 May 1860; Wyman[7] followed 31 May 1865.

Children born in Seabrook:

**1977**   i. Meribah[8] Eaton, b. ca. 1807; mar. John Janvrin of Seabrook, (int.) 1825, and had two children.
**+1978**   ii. Simeon[8] Eaton, b. ca. 1809; mar. Martha Jackman, 1833.
**1979**   iii. Jacob[8] Eaton, b. ca. 1811; mar. 1st, Mary Brown, 25 Dec 1839; mar. 2d, Sally (Collins) Eaton, widow of Cyrus Eaton of Salisbury (**#1730**), 17 Nov 1844. Neither wife had issue with him.
**1980**   iv. Rebecca[8] Eaton, b. ca. 1813; m. Moses[8] Eaton (**#1700**, q.v.).
**1981**   v. Elizabeth[8] Eaton, b. ca. 1815; mar. Edward[8] D. Eaton, (**#1699**, q.v. for children).
**1982**   vi. Rhoda[8] R. Eaton, b. 8 Oct 1817; mar. William[7] Eaton (**#1014**, q.v.).
**1983**   vii. Ruth[8] Eaton, b. ca. 1822; mar. Joshua Moody, but died, 25 Mar 1845.
**1984**   viii. Jane[8] Eaton, b. ca. 1824; became Joshua Moody's 2d wife after the death of her sister, Ruth (**#1983**).
**1985**   ix. Margaret[8] Eaton, b. 28 Jun 1827; mar. Benjamin[7] Eaton (**#1017**, q.v. for children).

**762. Jeremiah[7] Perry Eaton** (Simeon[6], Wyman[5], John[4-1]) was born 3 Sep 1804 at Seabrook, N.H.; mar. **Phebe[8] Knight Eaton** (#1698), daughter of Henry[7] and Sarah (Eaton), 26 Sep 1824 at Seabrook. This couple seems to have resided under the same roof Jeremiah had grown up under, the Partridge Creek homestead established by Wyman[5], still shared with his father, Simeon[6] who, as it turned out, outlived Jeremiah in any event. Jeremiah is described as a husbandman in his very few land deeds. He died 19 Jan 1846.

Children born in Seabrook, N.H.:

**1986**  i. Simeon[8] Eaton, b. 1 Mar 1826; mar. Jane M. Dow of Seabrook, 19 Sep 1846, a few months after his father's death. This couple remained in Seabrook, where Simeon was a farmer. He died without issue, 13 Jun 1886. Wife Jane died Jul 1895.

+**1987**  ii. Jeremiah[8] Eaton, b. 18 Sep 1828; mar. Georgiana Pearson.

**1988**  iii. Rhoda[8] Eaton, b. 29 Apr 1831; mar 1st, William E. Brown; mar. 2d, Philip C. Dow of Seabrook, 29 Jun 1854; had three daughters, and she died 15 Dec 1870.

**1989**  iv. Meribah[8] Eaton, b. 18 Sep 1833; mar. Thomas Boyd of Salisbury, 29 Nov 1852; res. at Smithtown (a southern Seabrook neighborhood), without issue. Meribah died 17 Jun 1909 at Seabrook.

+**1990**  v. Alvah[8] Eaton, b. 25 Apr 1836; mar. Lydia Walton, 1858.

+**1991**  vi. Henry[8] Eaton, b. 25 Jul 1838; m. Elizabeth Souther, 1861.

+**1992**  vii. Albert[8] Eaton, b. 12 Oct 1844; mar. Matilda Wright, 1861.

**771. Archelaus[7] Eaton** (Jonathan[6], Joseph[5], John[4-1]) was born 20 Mar 1789 at Salisbury, Mass., his given name apparently stemming from his maternal grandfather, Archelaus Adams. He mar. 1st, **Betsey Hackett**, 19 Jan 1814, at Salisbury. "She was a woman of beautiful countenance and a lovely character." Archelaus was a mariner, and in the early period of child-raising was of average prosperity for a Salisbury household head. The couple resided first apparently in the Gerrish Rd. area in Salisbury. After her eighth child, Betsey died 25 Apr 1834. Archelaus soon mar. 2d, **Rebecca Jones**, int. 16 Jan 1835, Salisbury. His fortunes were diminishing rapidly, perhaps because he was trying to escape seafaring. In 1840 he appears exceptionally at Seabrook, and is now a laborer. By 1860 a farm laborer at age 71, his household is back in Salisbury, probably residing out on Beach Rd. near his son Jabez. He died 18 Jun 1863.

Children at Salisbury:

**1993**  i. Elizabeth[8] Eaton, b. 13 Aug 1814; died 19 Dec 1815.

**1994**  ii. John[8] H. Eaton, b. 28 Apr 1817. He mar. once without issue; then mar. in 1868 Susan Souther and had a daughter by her.

+**1995**   iii. Azor[8] Webster, b. 25 Jan 1820; mar. Adaline Brown.

+**1996**   iv. Jabez[8] Eaton, b. 18 Jun 1823; mar. 1st, Charlotte Barker.

  **1997**   v. Elizabeth[8] Nancy Eaton, b. 11 Aug 1825; mar. 1st George Evans of Amesbury, Mass., having two sons and one daughter; mar. 2d, Benjamin Hinkson and res. at Groveland, Mass.

  **1998**   vi. Lucy[8] Dalton Eaton, b. 31 Aug 1827; mar. 1st, John Blaisdell and had two sons and two daughters; mar. 2d, Hebor Hinkson and res. at Groveland, Mass.

+**1999**   vii. Samuel[8] D. Eaton, b. Aug 1829; mar. Mary Brown of Me.

  **2000**   viii. Martha[8] Eaton, b. 19 Jul 1832; mar. Tilly Haynes and res. in Springfield, Mass, without issue. She died Mar 1876, and he removed to Boston, becoming the proprietor of the U.S. Hotel there.

**774. Jabez[7] Eaton** (Jonathan[6], Joseph[5], John[4-1]) was born ca. 1799 at Seabrook, N.H.; mar. **Sarah "Sally" Dow** of Seabrook, 17 Jan 1822. Jabez was a sea captain, and the couple settled for a time at Seabrook. At some time in the later 1840s, however, after their children were born, Jabez moved his base of operations to Newburyport, Mass., and was residing there at the time of his death, 14 Nov 1887.

Children born in Seabrook:

**2001**   i. Elizabeth[8] Eaton, b. 1822; mar. John D. Frost, mariner, 24 Nov 1846, Newburyport.

**2002**   ii. Belinda[8] K. Eaton, b. 1824; mar. William Follansbee, 22 Dec 1842. He was a ship captain who drowned on Newburyport bar 9 Mar 1855. Belinda died 5 Mar 1893 at Newburyport.

**2003**   iii. Leonard[8] Eaton, b. 1832.

+**2004**   iv. Jabez[8] Merrill Eaton, b. ca. 1835; mar. Ann Pierce, 1857.

**2005**   v. Louise[8] T. Eaton, b. 1839.

**2006**   vi. Charlotte[8] Eaton, b. 1842; mar. Samuel Pearson, 15 May 1863. She died 1910 at Newburyport.

**2007**   vii. Lavonia[8] T. Eaton, b. 22 Jun 1845; mar. Charles Landford; she died 21 Jun 1915 at Newburyport.

**776. Samuel[7] Eaton** (Jonathan[6], Joseph[5], John[4-1]) was born 10 Jul 1810 (cradle roll of C. Dow) at Seabrook, N.H.; mar. **Susan Collins**, dau. of Robert Collins, 17 Dec 1833 at Seabrook. He is usually described as being a "seaman" or a "fisherman." As of the 1850 Census, his family shared a dwelling unit with somewhat distant cousin Moses[9] D. Eaton and his family, and probably resided in the neighborhood around the intersection of Washington & Collins in So. Seabrook. The 1860 Census adds the information that Samuel[7] was illiterate. While not an uncommon adult characteristic in this era, very few other Seabrook citizens are given this indication. As of 1870, Samuel, now 59, is working at the shoe factory and reports $200 worth of real estate. He died, 6 May 1877 at Seabrook.

Children born in Seabrook, N.H.:

+2008    i. John[8] Curtis Eaton, b. 20 Dec. 1834; mar. 1st, Mary Eaton.
+2009    ii. Robert[8] Collins Eaton, b. 7 Mar 1836; mar. Mary Fowler.
+2010    iii. Samuel[8] A. Eaton, b. 5 Jul 1840; m. Abigail[9] Eaton (#3324).
 2011    iv. Susan[8] Olive Eaton, b. 12 Sep 1841; mar. Luther[9] Eaton (#2171, q.v.) She died 28 Apr 1910.
 2012    v. Augustus[8] Eaton, b. ca. 1847; died 6 Oct 1848, age 1.

**777. John[7] Merrill Eaton** (Jonathan[6], Joseph[5], John[4-1]) was born ca. 1813 at Seabrook, N.H.; mar. **Martha Brown** of Seabrook, dau. of Henry and Eleanor[7] (Eaton: #634) Brown, 3 Sep 1831 (Salisbury, Mass. VR). John M. was a seaman by trade and the couple resided at Seabrook. He died there 9 Sep 1859.

Children born in Seabrook:

 2013    i. Mary[8] Jane Eaton, b. Mar 1834; mar. John[8] Colby Eaton (#1752, q.v.) 7 Aug 1850, Salisbury. She died 12 Jan 1877.
+2014    ii. Frederick[8] A. Eaton, b. 5 Sep 1836; mar. 1st, Mary Fowler.
 2015    iii. Ardesira[8] Eaton, b. 21 Jun 1839; mar. 1 Jun 1856, Charles Knowles. She died 10 Mar 1902.
 2016    iv. Martha[8] A. Eaton, b. ca. 1843.
 2017    v. (Gilman) Frank[8] Eaton, b. ca. 1853; at age 8, in household of the widowed Martha Eaton, 1860 Census, Seabrook; apparently never married, and died 16 Oct 1896. Bur. in plot with John M. and Martha B. Eaton.

**779. Jonathan[7] Dalton Eaton** (Caleb[6], Joseph[5], John[4-1]) was born 13 Aug 1803 in Salisbury, Mass.; mar. 1st, **Lucy Fellows** of Salisbury, 12 Aug 1824 in Salisbury. After bearing one daughter, Lucy died 23 Apr 1827, and Jonathan, or "J. Dalton", mar. 2d, **Joanna Janvrin**, dau. of William and Abigail (Adams) Janvrin, int. 6 Apr 1830, also in Salisbury. This couple had two more daughters, after which Jonathan was lost at sea. Widow Joanna mar. 2d, John R. W. Mahar.

Child with Lucy in Salisbury, Mass.:

 2018    i. Hannah[8] F. Eaton, b. 1 May 1826.

Children with Joanna:

**2019** ii. Lucy[8] D. Eaton, b. ca. 1832; mar. Robert Morgan, son of William and Comfort Morgan.
**2020** iii. Abigail A. Eaton, b. ca. 1834; mar. 1st, Albert Chase, son of Capt. David Chase, mariner and businessman who was one of the richest figures in the area in the early 1800s, owner or part owner of 13 schooners in the 1815-30 period. Abigail mar. 2d, Tristram Collins, 13 Sep 1860.

**792. Forrest[7] Eaton** (Joshua[6-5], William[4], John[3-1]) was born 22 May 1779 in Wells, Me.; mar. **Louise Goodwin**, 4 Feb 1801. This couple res. in Wells on the seaward slope of Mt. Agamenticus. Forrest was a joiner by trade. He died 9 June, 1862.

Children born in Wells, Me.:

**2021** i. Susan[8] Eaton, b. 19 Jul 1801; mar. a Smith; d. 24 Oct 1857.
**+2022** ii. Forrest[8] Eaton, b. 6 Oct 1802; mar. 1st, Harriet Gordon.
**2023** iii. Joshua[8] Eaton, b. 17 Mar 1804; mar. Betsey Knight and removed to Alfred, Me., where the couple can be seen in the Censuses of 1850, '60 and '70 with no apparent issue. He is throughout a farm laborer. Joshua died 3 Apr 1876.
**2024** iv. Lucy[8] Eaton, b. 12 Jan 1806; mar. an Otis.
**+2025** v. (Rev.) Eben[8] G. Eaton, b 6 Sep 1807; mar. 1st, M. Barker.
**2026** vi. Nancy[8] Eaton, b. 4 Apr 1809; mar. James Tripp of Kennebunkport, Me.
**2027** vii. Louise[8] Eaton, b. 11 Feb 1811; died unmar., 1883.
**2028** viii. Clarissa[8] Eaton, b. 11 Nov 1812; mar. Isaac Seaver; res. in East Cambridge, Mass.
**2029** ix. Hannah[8] Eaton, b. 15 Apr 1815; mar. Alphonso Russell.
**2030** x. Mehitable[8] Eaton, b. 22 Dec 1817; no further report.
**+2031** xi. (Rev.) Rufus[8] G. Eaton, b. 20 Dec 1819; mar. Eliza Trussell.
**2032** xii. Bion[8] Eaton, b. 2 Sep 1822; died 27 Jul 1832.
**2033** xiii. Charles[8] Eaton, b. 25 Mar 1825; mar. Cynthia Ann Merrill (she b. 14 Nov 1825 in Hebron, Conn.), on 25 Nov 1852. No issue. Formerly he was in the wholesale grocery business in Boston. As of 1894, however, he was living in East Boothbay, Me.

**793. Joshua[7] Eaton** (Joshua[6-5], William[4], John[3-1]) was born 3 Aug 1781 at Wells, Me.; mar. **Mehitable Bickford** about 1805. This couple had moved by 1810 to Arundel, before it was renamed Kennebunkport, Me. All but perhaps the first three of their children were born on their farm there. They are there at least through 1850, when Joshua[7] is still a farmer, and reports $700 of real estate, although he has turned over part of his original homestead to his blacksmith son Joshua[8] and wife, now living next door.

Children, all born in Kennebunkport save perhaps the first three:

2034　　i. Erastus[8] Eaton, b. ca. 1806; died unmar. Oct 1841 at Orrington, Me.
2035　　ii. Lucy[8] Eaton, a twin of Olive[8], b. 1807; mar. Henry Richardson of Orono, Me., 4 Feb 1836.
2036　　iii. Olive[8] Eaton, a twin of Lucy, b. 1807; mar. Samuel Fabyan.
2037　　iv. Mary[8] A. Eaton, b. 1811.
2038　　v. Salome[8] Eaton, b. 1813.
2039　　vi. James[8] A. Eaton, b. 1815.
2040　　vii. George[8] M. Eaton, b. 1817.
2041　　viii. Mehitable[8] Eaton, b. 1820.
+2042　　ix. Joshua[8] Eaton, b. 1822; mar. Elizabeth.
2043　　x. Sarah[8] S. Eaton, a twin of Isaac[8], b. May 1825.
2044　　xi. Isaac[8] B. Eaton, a twin of Sarah[8], b. May 1825.

**795. Jabez[7] Eaton** (Joshua[6-5], William[4], John[3-1]) was born 18 Apr 1787 in Wells, Me.; in 1810 he mar. 1st, **Sally Chick** of Wells, who bore him nine children at Wells. He traded in large amounts of real estate. Wife Sally died 4 Nov 1848 at Wells. Jabez then mar. 2d, **Lydia Waitt** in 1862. He died 11 Jul 1870 at Wells.

Children with Sally in Wells, Me.:

2045　　i. Lydia[8] Eaton, b. 6 Aug 1811; died unmar., Jan 1847 in Wells.
+2046　　ii. Horace[8] Eaton, b. 4 Oct 1813; mar. Hannah Morrill, 1843.
2047　　iii. John[8] Eaton, b. 7 Nov 1815; died 31 Aug 1818.
+2048　　iv. John[8A] Eaton, b. 11 Aug 1819; mar. Elizabeth Kimball, 1850.
+2049　　v. Walter[8] Eaton, b. 29 Jan 1821; mar. Susannah Chadbourne.
2050　　vi. Oren[8] Eaton, b. 13 Jul 1823; d. unmar. 22 Mar 1846, Wells.
2051　　vii. Charles[8] Eaton, b. 5 Mar 1826; mar. Jennie Gunner; died Jun 1846 in Wells; no issue.
2052　　viii. Roxanna[8] Eaton, b. 20 Mar 1829; mar. 1st, a Jameson and had one daughter; mar. 2d, Eben Hatch and had a son and a daughter. She died Jun 1889.
2053　　ix. Sarah[8] Ann Eaton, b. 23 Jul 1832; mar. Oliver B. Littlefield, and died in Wells, 26 Dec 1856 without issue.

**796. Noah[7] Eaton** (Joshua[6-5], William[4], John[3-1]) was born 5 Feb 1790 in Wells, Me; mar. **Aphia Furbush** of Sanford, Me. (born 26 Jul 1793), on 7 Apr 1812. He was a farmer in Wells, and all their children were born on that farm. Noah died 15 Mar 1834; Aphia died 15 Feb 1845 in Belmont, Me.

Children born in Wells, Me.:

| | | |
|---|---|---|
| **2054** | i. | Keziah[8] Emery Eaton, b. 20 Aug 1813; died 25 Feb 1839. |
| **+2055** | ii. | Ira[8] Eaton, b. 23 Jul 1816; mar. Nancy Hatch, 1837. |
| **2056** | iii. | Phebe[8] Eaton, b. 30 Mar 1819; mar. Thomas Storrow and res. Moro Plantation, Me. |
| **+2057** | iv. | Isaac[8] Eaton, b. 10 Jan 1821; mar. Sarah J. Perkins, 1842. |
| **2058** | v. | Olive[8] F. Eaton, b. 8 Jun 1825; mar. Stephen Emery. |
| **2059** | vi. | Almira[8] Eaton, b. 10 Aug 1827; mar. a Littlefield. |
| **+2060** | vii. | Noah[8] Eaton, b. 2 Jun 1829; mar. Sarah Williams, 1852. |

**799. Joseph[7] Eaton** (Joseph[6], Joshua[5], William[4], John[3-1]) was born 26 Jun 1782 in Wells, Me.; mar. **Sarah "Sally" Hatch** (born 28 Oct 1783 in Wells), 20 Nov 1805 and resided at Wells at Joseph's old family homestead. He called himself a farmer in the 1850 Census. Wife Sally died 9 Jul 1843; Joseph lived until 22 Dec 1864.

Children born in Wells, Me.

| | | |
|---|---|---|
| **2061** | i. | Hannah[8] Eaton, b. 22 Aug 1806; mar. John Chadbourne of Wells, 9 Apr 1829. |
| **2062** | ii. | Sarah[8] Eaton, b. 28 Jul 1808; mar. Eben K. Hatch of Wells, 16 Feb 1831. She died 17 Nov 1857, at Wells. |
| **2063** | iii. | Julia[8] Ann Eaton, b. 1 Sep 1811; mar. Alvah Littlefield of Wells, 10 Nov 1830. She died 29 Oct 1849 at Wells. |
| **2064** | iv. | Mary[8] Jane Eaton, b. 6 May 1815; mar. Isaac Getchell of Wells, 20 Mar 1833. She died 11 Jan 1850. |
| **+2065** | v. | Adoniram[8] Judson Eaton, b. 16 Oct. 1817; mar. Abbie S. |
| **+2066** | vi. | Forrest[8] Eaton, b. 1 Oct 1821; mar. Betsey Hobbs, 1842. |
| **2067** | vii. | Joseph[8] Wells Eaton, b. 9 Apr 1826; d. 23 Jan 1827. |

**803. John[7] Emery Eaton** (Jeremiah[6], Joseph[5], William[4], John[3-1]) was born ca. 1778 in Wells, Me.; mar. **Dorcas Hatch**, 24 Nov 1802. They resided in Wells until his early death 21 Oct 1817.

Child born in Wells, Me.:

| | | |
|---|---|---|
| **+2068** | i. | Jeremiah[8] Moulton, b. 5 Feb 1804; mar. Nancy Donnell. |

**804. Samuel[7] Eaton** (Jeremiah[6], Joseph[5], William[4], John[3-1]) was born ca. 1780 in Wells, Me.; mar. **Betsey Hatch** about 1807, and res. in Wells. Wife Betsey died 17 May 1833; Samuel himself, unlike his older brother (**#803**), lived to an old age, dying in 1870 in Wells.

Children born in Wells, Me.:

+**2069**    i. John[8] E. Eaton, b. 7 Dec 1807; mar. Almeda Hatch.
+**2070**    ii. Stephen[8] Eaton, b. 16 Apr 1809; mar. Almira __?__.
  **2071**   iii. Mary[8] Eaton, b. 7 Aug 1819.

**805. Rufus[7] Eaton** (William[6], Joseph[5], William[4], John[3-1]) was born 27 Jun 1785 in Wells, Me.; mar. 1st, **Sarah Elizabeth Lombard** (born 11 Sep 1787 in Truro, Mass. near the tip of Cape Cod), about 1805. The circumstances of their meeting are unknown, but it would safe to bet that coastal trade, with Rufus the wanderer, had something to do with it. They took up residence in the Boston area, being in Ward 1 in 1810, and later in Newton, Mass. Rufus was a carpenter. Wife Sarah died 6 May 1826 in Boston; and Rufus mar. 2d, **Susan L. Doane** (born 1792, also Truro, Mass.), 20 May 1827 at Boston. Rufus died in 1849 at Newton, Mass. Susan died in Jan 1880 at Provinceton, Mass.

Children with Sarah:

  **2072**    i. Aphia[8] Freeman Eaton, b. 24 Sep 1806 in Provincetown, Mass.; mar. Walter Watkins of Winchester, N.H., 1 May 1825. They resided in Boston and had six children. She died 8 Oct 1874.
+**2073**    ii. William[8] Eaton, b. 23 Oct 1808; mar Augusta Patten.
+**2074**   iii. Solomon[8] Lombard Eaton, b. 23 Jun 1811; mar. Susan.
  **2075**   iv. Lydia[8] Eaton, b. ca. 1813; mar. Edward J. Newhall and resided in Boston.
  **2076**   v. Sarah[8] Elizabeth Eaton, b. 21 Nov 1814 in Boston; mar. Henry Beal, 26 Jan 1836 and res. in Boston where she died 29 Apr 1864.
  **2077**   vi. Abby[8] Story Eaton, b. 20 Oct 1817 in Boston; mar. Jedediah Kimball and res. in Boston where she died in 1879.
  **2078**  vii. Mary[8] Matilda Eaton, b. 6 Apr 1821 in Boston; died unmar. 15 May 1839.
  **2079** viii. Susan[8] L. Eaton, b. 22 Jun 1824; died 22 Aug 1824.

Children with Susan:

  **2080**   ix. Child[8] Eaton, infant death.
+**2081**   x. Cyrus[8] James Eaton, b. Jun 1830; mar. 1st, Mary Brady.

**808. (Capt.) William[7] Eaton** (William[6], Joseph[5], William[4], John[3-1]) was born 22 Aug 1791 in Wells, Me.; mar. **Abigail Jacobs** (born 1 July 1789) in Mar 1818, and res. in Wells. He was a master mariner in his prime, although as of 1850, when he is 59, he describes himself as a farmer. William died 17 Apr 1856, being killed by a bloody accident in his mill while sawing lumber. Abigail died 30 Jul 1863.

Children born in Wells:

2082    i. Elizabeth[8] Stone Eaton, b. 18 Jan 1819; mar. Alfred
           Sherwin, 4 Jul 1841, and had two children.
2083    ii. Mary[8] Merrill Eaton, b. 9 Oct 1820.
2084    iii. Abigail[8] Littlefield Eaton, b. 15 Sep 1823; mar. Edwin N.
           Cleaves, 25 Feb 1844 and had three children.
2085    iv. Hannah[8] Hubbard Eaton, b. 31 Jul 1829; mar. Nathaniel
           Barker, 19 Oct 1851. They had five children.


   **815. Nathaniel[7] Eaton** (Jacob[6], Joseph[5], William[4], John[3-1]) was
born 14 Dec 1800 in Wells, Me. He went to Cuba where he mar. 1st, a
lady of that island and became a rich planter there. He was of Trinidad
de Cuba when he later returned to Maine at least long enough to mar. 2d,
**Malvina Small** of Limington, Me., 19 Nov 1857 in Portland.

   Children in Cuba:

2086    i. Louise[8] A. Eaton, b. 20 May 1832; mar. William Fenley.
2087    ii. Olive[8] Eaton, b. 6 Jun 1833; died before age 18.


   **817. Daniel[7] Eaton** (Jacob[6], Joseph[5], William[4], John[3-1]) was born
31 Jul 1807 in Wells, Me.; mar. **Sarah A. Bragdon** (born Sep 1809 in
Wells) on 19 Nov 1833 and res. in Wells. He was a sea captain, although
by the 1850 Census he reports merely being a farmer. He died 19 Nov
1879. With deep interest and true pleasure Mrs. Sarah Eaton has contributed largely to the genealogy of the Wells Eatons.

   Children born in Wells:

2088    i. Ezra[8] Oliver Eaton, b. 17 Aug 1834; died 15 Feb 1837.
2089    ii. William[8] Henry Eaton, b. 19 Nov 1835; died 12 Apr 1850.
2090    iii. Annie[8] Sarah Eaton, b. 11 May 1838; mar. 29 Feb 1862
           and resided in New York City.
2091    iv. Daniel[8] Eaton, b. 27 Sep 1842; died at sea, 1862.
2092    v. Nathaniel[8] Eaton, b. 14 May 1843; mar. 28 Feb 1862. He
           was a machinist who was killed in the Civil War at Syca-
           more Church, 1863.
2093    vi. Abbie[8] Louisa Eaton, b. 27 Apr 1848; mar. 21 Oct 1867.
+2094   vii. Henry[8] Oliver Eaton, b. 14 Feb 1850; mar. Josephine Eaton.
2095    viii. Katharine[8] Bourne Eaton, b. 16 May 1853; d. 16 Jun 1854.


   **819. Hophni[7] Eaton** (Jacob[6], Joseph[5], William[4], John[3-1]) was born
11 Dec 1812 in Wells, Me.; mar. **Clara Cole Small** (b. 31 Jul 1826 in
Limerick, Me.), on 22 Nov 1849, and took up residence in Portland, Me.,
where Hophni was by 1850 a merchant with a significant inventory

($4,500). His mercantile activities came to focus on the wholesale West India goods trade. He died testate "of dropsy" in Portland, 2 Apr 1873.

Children born in Portland, Me.:

+2096    i. Charles⁸ Augustus Eaton, b. 14 Aug 1850; m. Annie Millett.
2097    ii. George⁸ Franklin Eaton, b. 16 Feb 1852: a commercial traveller who was as yet unmar. in 1894.
2098    iii. Hartley⁸ Coleridge Eaton, b. 21 Oct 1853; a merchant in "Glenwood Springs Col. Div." (??).
2099    iv. Leonard⁸ Percy Eaton, b. 4 Oct 1858; died 15 May 1864 in Portland.
2100    v. Clara⁸ Eaton, b. 9 Nov 1861; res. 23 Pine St, Portland, unmar.
2101    vi. Irwin⁸ Ross Eaton, b. 1 Oct 1868; a store clerk residing in Portland, unmar. as of 1894.

**822. John⁷ Cole Eaton** (John⁶, Joseph⁵, William⁴, John³⁻¹) was born 15 Aug 1800 in Wells, Me.; mar. 1st, **Dorcas Jacobs** (born 1802) on 25 Sep 1833, and res. on a farm in Wells. Wife Dorcas died in Wells in 1847. We lack details, but John⁷ C. mar., 2d, a Hannah __?__, since there is a Hannah Eaton, born in Wells and seven years his junior, registered with him in the normal wife position in the 1850 Census for Wells. John C. for some reason died in Leavenworth, Kans., 2 Aug 1858, which is presumably long before the establishment of the federal penitentiary there!

Children born in Wells, Me.:

+2102    i. Charles⁸ Eaton, b. 25 Jun 1834; mar. Mary Buzzell, 1875.
2103    ii. Sarah⁸ E. Eaton, b. 15 Mar 1836; mar. 1st, George Dykeman; 2d, C. M. Smith, 22 Aug 1885, a farmer in Wells who died 12 Aug 1890.
2104    iii. Harriet⁸ Eaton, b, 17 Jan 1838; was a dressmaker in Lynn, Mass.
+2105    iv. Christopher⁸ Eaton, b. 3 Jan 1840; mar. Helen Smith, 1884.
2106    v. Hannah⁸ A. Eaton, b. 7 Jul 1845; a stitcher in Lynn, Mass.

**829. Elisha⁷ Eaton** (John⁶, Elisha⁵, Samuel⁴ John³⁻¹) was born 9 May 1774, very probably after his parents had removed from Seabrook to settle in Pittsfield, N.H. He certainly grew up on Catamount Mtn. on Eaton Pond above Pittfield Village, and mar. **Elizabeth "Betsey" Sherburne** of neighboring Epsom, N.H. on 25 Feb 1794 (Pittfield *VR* at Concord). Not long after the first wedding anniversary, Elisha⁷, not yet age 21, fell sick and died on 27 Apr 1795, leaving a four-month-old son. Widow Betsey in rather short order decided to remarry a James Rollins and remove to Vermont, leaving the infant Elisha⁷ to be raised by grandparents John⁶ and Sally (French), who would not complete their own litter of children for another three years (in 1798). Widow Betsey Rollins died "of old age" in Greensboro (Orleans Co.), Vt., 21 Mar 1858 at age 82, her death record in that town noting her birthplace as Epsom, N.H., despite the 1850 Census report that she had been born in Vermont. We do not know if her son Elisha[7] had contact with her again.

Child born in Pittsfield, N.H.:

+**2107**    i. Elisha[8] Eaton, b. 26 Dec 1794; mar. Betsey Brown.

**830. John[7] Eaton** (John[6], Elisha[5], Samuel[4], John[3-1]) was born in Pittsfield, N.H., 3 May 1776; mar. 1st, **Sarah Prescott**, who died soon after the marriage, without issue. John[7] then mar. **Mrs. Abigail (Green) Towle**, 7 Jan 1800. He was a farmer and they resided at Pittsfield. They were both still living with an empty nest in 1850 at Pittsfield.

Children with Abigail in Pittsfield, N.H.:

**2108**    i. Sally[8] Eaton, b. 2 May 1801; mar. Levi Swain and res. in Concord, N.H. They had two daughters who married.
+**2109**   ii. Nathan[8] Eaton, b. 1 Jan 1803; mar. Mary Bowman.
**2110**   iii. Mary[8] Eaton, b. 11 Jan 1805; mar. William Lewis and took up residence in Franklin, N.H. They had two sons and two daughters, all of whom married.
+**2111**   iv. Perkins[8] T. Eaton, b. 22 Dec 1806; mar. Phebe Hilton, 1836.
**2112**    v. Abigail[8] Eaton, b. 22 Apr 1809; mar. Alfred Bailey of Dunbarton, a farmer. They res. for some years at Hooksett, N.H., but in 1845 they removed to Manchester, N.H., where she was residing as a widow in the 1890s. They had two sons and three daughters, all of them having died before 1891, save one unmar. daughter living with her mother. The household indicates comfort.
**2113**   vi. Green[8] Eaton, a son b. 2 May 1811; died 27 Jan 1816.
**2114**  vii. Eliza[8] Eaton, b. 1 Sep 1813; mar. Freeman Whitney of Maine and res. in Portland. She had only a daughter, who mar. a Millett, and lived in Gorham, N.H. Mother Eliza died at her daughter's house there, 15 Apr 1885.
**2115** viii. Green[8A] Eaton, b. 28 Nov 1815; mar. Phebe Smith, and they are said to have res. and died in Augusta, Me., having had a daughter, Addie, who mar. a Waldron of that city. About 1890 she resided at 240 State St., Portland, Me.
+**2116**   ix. John[8] Jr. Eaton, b. 18 Dec 1818; mar. Olive True, ca. 1840. They apparently had at least four children.
+**2117**    x. True(worthy)[8] Eaton, b. 9 Mar 1821; mar. Margaret Page.

**832. Joseph[7] Eaton** (John[6], Elisha[5]. Samuel[4], John[3-1]) was born 3 Jul 1780 in Pittsfield, N.H.; mar. **Abigail Meader** ca. Jan 1804. Joseph was, like his father John[6], a seeker of greener pastures in northern New Hampshire.  In 1801 before his marriage he had bought 70-acres in the northern end, or "Gunstock Parish" of the large Gilmanton grant, an area that bordered on Lake Winnipesaukee and which in 1812 would be set off as the town of Gilford, N.H.  This is where he brought his bride, Abigail, and where they almost surely had their children.  It is also the place that attracted Joseph's father John[6], then approaching 70, to pack up his large family and move from a flank of Catamount Mtn. in Pittsfield to a flank of Gunstock Mtn. in Gilford, on a site with a spectacular view of Lake Winnipesaukee.  About 1821 Joseph bought land on the opposite side of that lake and settled for a while at Wolfeborough, N.H.  He moved on again to a new stake in Moultonborough, N.H. in 1826.  Then tragedy struck: on 9 Oct 1832, a boat carrying Joseph[7], his oldest child John[8] and two family friends capsized on Lake Winnipesaukee.  Joseph drowned; son John barely escaped.  Widow Abigail later mar. a Roberts and died of cancer in Wakefield, N.H.

Children born in proto-Gilford:

+ **2118**   i. John[8] Eaton, b. 9 Nov 1804; mar. Judith Caswell.
  **2119**   ii. Nancy[8] Eaton, b. ca. 1806; mar. Isaac Smith of West Alton, N.H.; she had two sons and two daughters, and died at West Alton.
  **2120**   iii. Eliza[8] Eaton, b. ca. 1807; never married.
  **2121**   iv. Sarah[8] Eaton, b. ca. 1809; mar. Ezekiel Flanders of West Alton and resided at Moultonborough Corner.
  **2122**   v. Eleanor[8] Eaton, b. ca. 1813; died when a young lady.
  **2123**   vi. Joseph[8] Eaton, b. ca. 1818; died 1832.

**834. Jonathan[7] Eaton** (John[6], Elisha[5], Samuel[4], John[3-1]) was born 29 Sep 1784 in Pittsfield, N.H.; mar. **Elizabeth Locke** (born 1 Jan 1780 in Epsom, N.H.) about 1806.  They are said to have res. first on a farm in Epsom, and may have had their first child or two there.  However, the household appears at Pittsfield in the 1810 Census.  Then mysteriously there is no sign of Jonathan or family until the 1850 Census unambiguously finds him by himself at the poor house at Pittsfield, and he is said to have died at Pittsfield, although the date is unknown.  Our Census work has given us small rosters of unidentified Eatons sighted by the Censuses, 1790-1850, for all of northern New England, and there are two or three Jonathans household heads there, but none could even vaguely be associated with a Jonathan of this birth year.  Since the best way to hide from the Census prior to 1850 was to live in a household headed by somebody else, this is probably the solution to the mystery.  Wife Elizabeth died 15 Jan 1866 in Hamilton, Mass.

Children, prob. born in Pittsfield N.H., save for the earliest:

  **2124**   i. Mary[8] Eaton, b. 7 Apr 1807, at Epsom, N.H.; mar. James B.

Taylor, a machinist, at Meredith Bridge, N.H., 6 Oct 1833. They had three children. Husband James died in Laconia N.H., 5 Jun 1873. Wife Mary died in Laconia, N.H., 8 Sep 1890.

+ **2125** ii. William[8] B. Eaton, b. ca. 1808 in Epsom; mar. Mary Morrill.

**2126** iii. Hannah[8] Eaton, b. ca. 1810; mar. Jacob Brown and removed to Hamilton, Mass.

+ **2127** iv. Abram[8] Eaton, b. about 1811; mar. 1st, Asenath Parsons.

**2128** v. Louisa[8] Eaton, b. about 1813; mar. Romaine Smith and resided in Andover, N.H., where he died. She died in Hamilton, Mass.

+ **2129** vi. John[8] Eaton, b. ca. 1814; mar. widow Armstrong, and went to California to work on the railroad construction there.

**2130** vii. Sarah[8] Eaton, b. ca. 1816. Never married, she died at East Kingston, N.H., 10 Aug 1836.


**838. Jacob[7] Eaton** (John[6], Elisha[5], Samuel[4], John[3-1]) was born in Pittfield, N.H., 13 Aug 1794; mar. **Judith Rollins** (born Loudon, N.H., 1790) in 1818, and res. on a farm in Gilford, N.H., where Jacob's parents had just settled the year before. It appears that they returned soon to Pittsfield, where they raised their two children and where both died, Judith in 1844 and Jacob in 1858.

Children:

**2131** i. Sarah[8] A. Eaton, b. 11 Jun 1820 in Loudon, N.H.; mar. Harris Morse, a carpenter of Loudon, 16 Oct 1842, and res. on a Loudon farm where they had five children.

+ **2132** ii. John[8] M. Eaton, b. 29 Feb 1822 at Pittsfield; mar. Julia.


**839. Samuel[7] Sherburne Eaton** (John[6], Elisha[5], Samuel[4], John[3-1]) was born 16 Jun 1798 in Pittsfield, N.H. and was raised there, but proceeded on with his parents to the new home in Gilford, N.H. when he was 19. He soon found a girl there, and mar. **Hope Gilman** (born in neighboring Alton, N.H., 28 Aug 1799) in 1821. They resided most of their lives in Gilford (although they were found in Gilmanton to the south for the moment of the 1840 Census). This was probably not a prosperous household. While Samuel S. describes himself as a farmer, at one time in midlife he is called by others a "farm laborer," or hired hand; and he has no real estate of his own to report in 1850. Samuel S. died 22 Dec 1881 at Gilford; wife Hope followed there on 5 Sep 1882.

Children mostly at Gilford:

**2133** i. Hope[8] Eaton, b. 5 Nov 1822; mar. Joseph P. Davis and res. in Farmington, N.H.

**2134** ii. Betsey[8] F. Eaton, b. 22 Oct 1829; mar. Morrill J. Sanborn and resided in Warren, N.H.

**2135**   iii. Mary[8] E. Eaton, b. Apr 1831; mar. Randall O. Farrar in
             1854; res. at Lake Village. She died 16 Mar 1857.

**2136**   iv. Samuel[8] Sherburne Eaton, Jr., b. 1833, Gilmanton, N.H.;
             mar. Emma Chase, b. Conway, N.H.; later removed to
             Haverhill, Mass. They had no children.

**2137**   v. Susan[8] S. Eaton, b. Apr 1835; mar. Albert A. Pike; died
             30 Apr 1857.

**2138**   vi. Hannah[8] Eaton, b. 13 May 1841; mar. 1st, Joseph Ellinwood
             of Deering, N.H., 9 May 1857 and had two children.
             Joseph died 6 Nov 1864; Hannah mar. 2d, John A.
             Norris, 8 Jan 1866; res. Dorchester; had another child.

**+2139**  vii. John[8] L. Eaton, b. 16 Dec 1843; mar. Amanda Emerson.


**845. Stephen[7] Eaton** (Elisha[6-5], Samuel[4], John[3-1]) was born 26 Feb
1790 in Pittsfield, N.H.; mar. **Mary L. Underwood** (born 22 Sep 1787 at
Litchfield, N.H.) in Dec 1813. They settled first on a farm at Pittsfield,
but later in the decade they followed the lead of Eaton relatives in the
move to Gilford, N.H. They are there in time for the 1820 Census, and
are involved in land deeds there as well until they sell out early in 1825
and return permanently to Pittsfield. Stephen[7] died there, 14 Jul 1841.
Wife Mary died in Muscatine, Iowa, 1 Feb 1872, drawn westward by the
migration of her son Mark[8].

Children (birthplaces by inference):

**2140**   i. Almira[8] Eaton, b. 12 Dec 1814 in Pittsfield, N.H.; died there
             18 Jan 1815.

**+2141**  ii. Samuel[8] Eaton, b. 31 Aug 1816 in Pittsfield; m. Julia Chase.

**2142**   iii. Almira[8A] Eaton, b. 8 Jan 1818 in Pittsfield; mar. Abram
             Swain on 4 Jul 1836 and res. in Epsom, N.H. She died
             16 Jun 1840.

**+2143**  iv. Mark[8] Fernald Eaton, b. 8 Jun 1823 in Gilford; mar. Eliza.

**2144**   v. Olive[8] Page Eaton, b. 27 Sep 1825 in Pittsfield; died 23 Oct
             1845.


**855. Abraham[7] Eaton** (David[6-5], Samuel[4], John[3-1]) was born ca.
1786 at Seabrook; mar. **Phebe Norton** ca. 1804, and resided at Seabrook
in the Worthen's Point area on So. Main St. which his line had frequented
for two earlier generations. This was not a prosperous household: in
1850 Abraham was a "laborer" without real estate at age 64; and in 1860,
both Abraham and Phebe are listed as paupers in the Census. Their
meager roster of two children might be imagined to hide a much larger
set of offspring that went unrecorded; but a minute analysis of their
household compositions in every Census from 1810 to 1860 does not
make this number seem inappropriate, although there may have been one
or two more. Phebe died in 1856; Abraham died 3 Feb 1861.

Children born in Seabrook, N.H.:

**2145**    i. John[8] O. Eaton, b. ca. 1806; a shoemaker who appears to have been a bachelor; died 6 Jun 1864.
**2146**    ii. Phebe[8] Eaton, b. 181?.

**858. Daniel[7] Eaton** (David[6-5], Samuel[4], John[3-1]) was born ca. 1792 at Seabrook, N.H.; was one of those drafted for the war in 1812, and was stationed at Shapley's Island in Portsmouth Harbor under Capt. Josiah Dearborn for a 60-day term. Soon thereafter he mar. **Belinda Knowles** and res. at Seabrook, appearing as a household head there, 1820-50. In the latter year he was a laborer without real estate value, living with son Daniel, with wife Belinda not present. Daniel Sr. died 20 Mar 1853 at Seabrook.

Children born in Seabrook:

**2147**    i. Daniel[8] Eaton, Jr., b. ca. 1815. He was a seaman, apparently unmar., living with his father at Seabrook in 1850. From the Philbrick Journal, Dec. 18/19, 1850: "Daniel Eaton, Jr., found dead in woods---was intemperate---was the son of Daniel and the grandson of David, a Revolutionary War pensioner."
**2148**    ii. Daughter[8] Eaton, b. ca. 1820; prob. died young.
**2149**    iii. Laura[8] Eaton, b. ca. 1826; mar. Nicholas Bartlett, 19 Jan 1848 at Newburyport, Mass.
**2150**    iv. Olive[8] Eaton, b. ca. 1830; mar. William C. Colby, 30 Jan 1849 at Newburyport, Mass.
**2150a**   v. Rhoda[8] Eaton, b. 1832-33; was of Newburyport when she mar. George W. Bidwell of Lawrence, int. 10 Sep 1852.

**867. Reuben[7] Eaton** (Samuel[6], David[5], Samuel[4], John[3-1]) was born 8 Sep 1790, prob. at Seabrook, N.H., but removed with his parents to East Weare, N.H. when still a youngster, ca. 1800. On 2 Apr 1813 at Weare he mar. **Judith[7] Eaton** (#715), born 1788 to William[6] of Sanbornton, whom he may well have known from Seabrook days. The couple resided on a farm in Weare and raised their children there. Reuben died 24 Oct 1862, and wife Judith died 24 Jan 1868, both at Weare (Little, 1888).

Children born in Weare:

**2151**    i. Betsey[8] Eaton, b. ca. 1814; mar. Samuel Paige and res. at Merrimack, N.H.
**+2152**   ii. James[8] W. Eaton, b. ca. 1816; mar. Mary Williams.
**2153**    iii. Thomas[8] Eaton, b. ca. 11 May 1818 (from age at death);

mar. Katherine Dow (she b. 12 Mar 1821). The couple
resided at East Weare, but had no children. He died
5 Nov 1890; she died 25 Dec 1906.

2154    iv. Daniel[8] B. Eaton, b. ca. 1820; died young.
+2155    v. Daniel[8A] B. Eaton, b. 5 Jul 1822; mar. Lucretia Gould.
2156    vi. Ruth[8] A. Eaton, b. ca. 1823-4; mar. William H. Brown.
2157    vii. Lovilla[8] Eaton, b. ca. 1825; died 1845.
+2158    viii. Pillsbury[8] R. Eaton, b. 1832; mar. Julia A. Felch.
+2159    ix. William[8] S. Eaton, b. ca. Nov 1835; mar. Eliza Hoyt.


**868. Moses[7] Eaton** (Samuel[6], David[5], Samuel[4], John[3-1]) was born
ca. 1792, surely at Seabrook, N.H., but as a youngster removed with his
Seabrook parents to East Weare, N.H. He mar. 1st, **Mary[7] Eaton (#641)**,
born to John[6] (John[5-1]) ca. 1797, on 22 Nov 1818 in Weare. Moses appears in consecutive Weare Censuses as a moderately prosperous farmer
from 1820 through 1860. Wife Mary died in 1844; and Moses mar. 2d,
**Ruth Johnson** of Weare (born 1809), 12 Jul 1847 at Weare. Moses died
23 Mar 1868 (Weare *VR* at Concord), and is buried at the East Weare
cemetery. Wife Ruth died 24 Jan 1891.

Children with Mary born in East Weare, N.H.:

2160    i. Samuel[8] Eaton, twin of William[8], b. 1819; died 1835.
2161    ii. William[8] Eaton, twin of Samuel, b. 1819; died 1822.
2162    iii. Nancy[8] W. Eaton, b. 1823; mar. Moody Huse.
+2163    iv. William[8A] Eaton, b. Nov 1829; mar. Celestia Swett, 1852.
2164    v. Hannah[8] J. Eaton, b. ca. 1828; mar. Joseph Whipple, 27
        Dec 1848 at Manchester; resided Manchester.
2165    vi. Julia[8] Eaton, b. ca. 1830; mar. 1st, John Phelps; 2d, Fred
        Spofford; resided in Hopkinton, N.H.
2166    vii. Adeline[8] A. Eaton, b. ca. 1832; became the 2d wife of
        Moody Huse, who had mar. her sister Nancy. She
        died 10 Apr 1880 at Hopkinton.
2167    viii. Walter[8] S. Eaton, b. ca. 19 Sep 1839 (from age at death);
        mar. Zillah[9] Eaton (#3950). They res. on Sugar Hill in
        in East Weare, but had no children. He died there
        16 Dec 1894.
2168    ix. Abbie[8] Eaton, b. date unknown; mar. Augustus Parker.


**872. Samuel[7] Eaton** (Samuel[6], David[5], Samuel[4], John[3-1]) was born
ca. 1800 at Seabrook N.H., just before his parents moved the family to
Weare. N.H. The family must have maintained contact with their roots in
Seabrook some 50 miles away, because Samuel[7] was "of Weare" when he
mar. **Betsey B. Dow** of Seabrook on 24 Apr 1825 (Salisbury, Mass. *VR*).
They res. in Seabrook, and appear in Censuses there from 1830-60;
Samuel is in 1850 a laborer, in 1860 a farmer, reporting a moderate
amount of estate. Samuel died 29 Mar 1870 (Seabrook *VR* at Concord).

Children, born in Seabrook, N.H.:

2169    i. David[8] Eaton, b. ca. 1825; died 1829.
2170    ii. Adeline[8] Eaton, b. Oct 1826; mar. Hiram Beckman 2 Sep
           1858. She had 11 children, altho only one survived to
           1900. She died 16 Aug 1903.
+2171   iii. Luther[8] Eaton, b. 22 Aug 1831; mar. 1st, Julia Ann Walton.
2172    iv. Lucinda[8] J. Eaton, b. 1832; mar. a Pike of Salisbury, Mass.,
           1851.
2173    v. Sarah[8] Eaton, b. 1834; mar. Edward Barnard of Salisbury,
           Mass., 1854.
2174    vi. Robert[8] D. Eaton, born ca. 17 Apr 1841; died 11 May 1842.

**873. William[7] Eaton** (Samuel[6], David[5], Samuel[4], John[3-1]) was born
6 Sep 1802 at East Weare, N.H. The genealogy of Weare Eatons due to
Little (1888) reports that this William[7] "went to Maine" (page 831) without further detail. Our senior author established that he settled in the
town of Dexter in Penobscot Co., Me. He mar. **Julia Ann Haynes**, 29
Jan 1826 at Dexter. According to the town history, he became a clothier
there, visible in the Censuses of 1830 and 1840. In later years he operated a variety store. He died ca. 1880.

Children with Julia in Dexter, Me. are listed in the Dexter *VR*
(LDS microfilm #0 010 830):

+2175   i. William[8] Lucien Eaton, b. 11 Jun 1826; mar. 1st, Charlotte.
2176    ii. Julia[8] Ann Eaton, b. 12 Apr 1828; mar. George L. Waters
           and went with him to San Francisco, Cal.
+2177   iii. (David) Walter[9] Eaton, b. 29 Dec 1830; mar. 1st, Betsey.
2178    iv. Charles[8] Stanley Eaton, b. 10 Jul 1843.

**874. David[7] Eaton** (Samuel[6], David[5], Samuel[4], John[3-1]) was born
26 Jun 1804 at East Weare; mar. 1st, **Sarah Wilson Williams**, who apparently died early in the marriage. He then mar. 2d, **Mary "Polly"
Worthley** of Weare, 13 Oct 1830 at Weare. They settled on a rather
small farm at Weare. David died 15 Oct 1875 "of old age" at Weare
(Weare *VR* at Concord).

Child by Sarah in Weare:

2179    i. Mary[8] E. Eaton, b. Aug 1824; died unmar. 24 Apr 1891.

Children with Polly in Weare:

2180    ii. Sarah[8] Eaton, b. 1834; mar. John Martin.
+2181   iii. Perry[8] A. Eaton, b. 27 May 1837; mar. Letitia L. Williams.

**878. Jonathan[7] L. Eaton** (Thomas[6], Jonathan[5], Samuel[4], John[3-1]) was born 26 Apr 1796 at Pittsfield, N.H.; mar. a **Nancy P(erkins?)** (born ca. 13 Sep 1797) about 1820. He was a stone mason who stayed on in Pittsfield's "Upper City" after his parents, Thomas[6] and Sally, had gone back to Seabrook, N.H. to live. Wife Nancy died 24 Jun 1857, and is buried in the tiny family cemetery on Norris Rd. across from the junction of Eaton Rd. with it. Both of their sons predeceased her and are buried there as well, but Jonathan's grave is elsewhere.

Children in Pittsfield, N.H.:

2182    i. Thomas[8] P. T. Eaton, b. ca. May 1822; died 22 Dec 1845.
2183    ii. Jonathan[8] J. Eaton, b. ca. 1832; he was a shoemaker living with his parents in 1850; he died, probably unmar., 27 Feb 1855.

**895. Benjamin[7] F. Eaton** (Samuel[6-4], John[3-1]) was born 4 Dec 1811 at Salisbury, Mass. He was a babe in arms when his parents removed from Salisbury to the town of Solon, Me., in Somerset Co., only about 25 miles west of Dexter, Me. where his second cousin William[7] (#873) had settled in the same general decade. Benjamin mar. **Betsey Durgin** of Solon, Me. on 28 Aug 1840, and they res. in Solon. The development of this family was soon cut short by Benjamin's death, 3 Aug 1848 in Solon.

Children in Solon, Me,:

2184    i. Amanda[8] G. Eaton, b. 7 Jul 1841; mar. Charles Roberts, Jan 1865.
2185    ii. Oscar[8] B. Eaton, b. 17 Mar 1843; mar. Abby Woodman, 1 Jan 1867. This couple res. Skowhegan in 1870, with no children showing; and are described as "after four years of consumption, both died within three days of each other." It seems unlikely they had later children.
2186    iii. Lenora[8] Eaton, b. 22 Mar 1845; mar. Hiram Spalding of Skowhegan, Me.
2187    iv. Luella[8] Eaton, b. 25 Feb 1848; mar. George Varney of Skowhegan, Me.

**901. Moses[7] Eaton** (Samuel[6-4], John[3-1]) was born 14 Mar 1829 at Solon, Me.; mar. **Louisa Hunnewell**, daughter of Levi, and "the girl next door," 5 Feb 1858. The couple settled in a new home halfway between their natal homesteads in Solon, where Moses farmed, and died 15 May 1876.

Children born in Solon, Me.:

**2188**     i. Herbert[8] Edwin Eaton, b. 9 Apr 1859; mar. 1st, Nellie Rowell, and they had one daughter who d. in infancy. He mar. 2d, Etta M. __?__, but in 1900 no children were in sight for this couple.

**2189**     ii. Charles[8] Francis Eaton, b. 16 Sep 1861; unmar. in 1894.

**2190**     iii. Alfred[8] Selden Eaton, b. 27 Nov 1863; unmar. in 1894.

**2191**     iv. Mary[8] Maria Eaton, b. 11 May 1865; unmar. in 1894.

**2192**     v. William[8] Elden Eaton, b. 14 Apr 1867; unmar. in 1894.

**2193**     v. Nellie[8] Ella Eaton,, b. ca. 1869; died 1882.

**2194**     vii. Infant[8] Eaton, b. Apr 1870; may have died young.

**903. Theophilus[7] Eaton** (Moses[6], Theophilus[5], Jonathan[4], John[3-1] ) was born 24 Mar 1769 on Deer Isle, Me; mar. **Joanna Evans** of Sedgwick, Me. (dau. born 14 Jul 1767 to Richard and Joanna Evans of Marblehead, Mass.) in 1790. They lived on a farm in Sedgwick, where their household is registered for five consecutive Censuses, 1800-40. Theophilus died 6 Nov 1843; and Joanna followed, 14 Jan 1852.

Children at Sedgwick, Me.:

**2195**     i. Ebenezer[8] Eaton, b. 15 Aug 1792; drowned in 1815.

**2196**     ii. Charlotte[8] Eaton, b. 10 Apr 1797; mar. James[2] Eaton of Mt. Desert, Me., as his 2d wife in 1818. This James Eaton introduces into this Genealogy an entirely new race of Eatons, for he was the son of a David[1] Eaton and Anna Pray, where the father had been born near Glasgow, Scotland. He had come to this country in an English man-of-war, and deserted from the ship on her arrival at the island of Mt. Desert about 1776. His son James[2] had mar. 1st, Betsey Murch of Ellsworth, Me., 2 Jan 1814, who had been born 1 Jan 1791 and died Mar 1817. To keep these Eatons distinct from the more ancient Eaton lineages in Maine, we catalogue James's children here:

With Betsey (Murch):
(1) David[3] Eaton, b. 5 Oct 1814; died 3 Oct 1815.
(2) Betsey[3] M. Eaton, b. 13 May 1816; mar. Charles Bates of Princeton, Me. and had 6 children.

With Charlotte (Eaton):
(3) Ebenezer[3] James Eaton, b. 9 Mar 1819; mar. Harriet E. Philbrook, 1842.
(4) David[3] G. Eaton, b. 21 Mar 1821; mar. Sarah Jane Stanley, 17 Sep 1843.
(5) Hiram[3] T. Eaton, b. 15 Apr 1823.
(6) Stephen[3] T. Eaton, b. 6 Nov 1825; d. 15 Jul 1850.
(7) Mary[3] Joann Eaton, b. 24 Feb 1828.

(8) Elizabeth³ A. Eaton, b. 10 Jul 1831.
The mother Charlotte died 2 Mar 1837.

James² mar. 3d, Mehitable Jordan of Sedgwick, 31 Aug 1837. With Mehitable:
(9) Frances³ M. Eaton, b.  ?  ; mar. Edwin H. Grant
3 Mar 1863 and died 25 Aug 1863.
James² Eaton, father of these nine children,
d. 15 Feb 1873; wife Mehitable d. 11 Mar 1881.

+2197   iii. Amasa⁸ Eaton, b. 9 Nov 1799; m. Roxalina Ober, 1823.
2198   iv. Judith⁸ Eaton, b. 15 Apr 1805; mar. Nicholas Ober of
Sedgwick, 30 Oct 1826 and had two children.
2199   v. Joann⁸ Eaton, b. 2 Feb 1810; mar. Jeremiah Friend of
Sedgwick, about 1836 and had at least one son. She
died 10 May 1854 in Massachusetts.

**904. John⁷ Eaton** (Moses⁶, Theophilus⁵, Jonathan⁴, John³⁻¹) was
born 24 Apr 1771 in Sedgwick, Me.; mar. **Sally Pickering** (born 1775)
on 9 Aug 1798. "He was one of the early settlers of the region known as
Sedgwick Ridge, coming to the foot of the Ridge near the Frost Pond
about the year 1800" (Noyes, 1942). The couple resided on a farm in
Sedgwick and are there in the Censuses, 1800-20. Wife Sally died 20
Mar 1824; John himself died 1 Jul 1828, both at Sedgwick.

Children in Sedgwick, Me:

2200   i. Sally⁸ Eaton, b. 30 Nov 1798; mar. Jeremiah McIntire and
lived in No. Sedgwick.
+2201   ii. Aaron⁸ Eaton, b. 10 Apr 1800; mar. 1st, Eunice Neal.
+2202   iii. Joseph⁸ Eaton, b. 19 Dec 1801; mar. Rebecca Woods.
+2203   iv. Pickering⁸ Eaton, b. 2 Aug 1804; mar. Barbara Marks.
2204   v. Mary⁸ Eaton, b. 20 May 1806; mar. Thomas Lufkin of
Sedgwick, 6 Apr 1829; res. Sedgwick and had four
sons and two daughters. She died Feb 1882.
+2205   vi. John⁸ Eaton, Jr., b. 16 Mar 1808; mar Mary K. Doten.
+2206   vii. Moses⁸ Eaton, b. 23 Apr 1810; mar. Abigail Lufkin.
+2207   viii. David⁸ Eaton, b. 12 Nov 1812; mar. Joanna H. Doten.
+2208   ix. Ebenezer⁸ J. Eaton, b. 2 May 1816; mar. Deborah Doten.

**905. Benjamin⁷ Eaton** (Moses⁶, Theophilus⁵, Jonathan⁴, John³⁻¹)
was born 13 Oct 1773 in Sedgwick, Me.; mar. **Susanna Dodge** (born 17
Dec 1771 to Jonah (Jonas?) and Lydia (Herrick) Dodge of Beverly,
Mass.), also of Sedgwick, on 11 Dec 1798 in Sedgwick. They res. on a
farm on the east side of the Benjamin River in Sedgwick. Benjamin died
9 Jun 1838; Susanna died 11 Sep 1863.

Children born in Sedgwick, Me:

2209       i. Patience[8] Eaton, b. 25 Dec 1799; mar. Samuel Crocker, 11
              Sep 1850, both of Brooklin, Me. No issue reported.
+2210     ii. Amaziah[8] Eaton, b. 16 Oct 1801; mar. Roxanna Ober.
+2211    iii. Moses[8] Eaton, b. 11 Sep 1803; mar. Hannah Eaton (#969).
 2212     iv. Benjamin[8] Eaton, Jr., b. 3 Dec 1804; died 13 Mar 1824.
 2213      v. Nancy[8] Eaton, b. 11 Mar 1807; died 21 Mar 1824.
 2214     vi. Judith[8] Eaton, b. 22 Oct 1808; died 29 Oct 1808.
+2215    vii. Ezra[8] D. Eaton, b. 28 Oct 1809; mar. Lovinia Bakeman.
 2216   viii. Amy[8] Eaton, b. 22 Oct 1811; mar. Isaiah Ober of Sedg-
              wick, 1832.
 2217     ix. Mehitable[8] Eaton, b. 11 Sep 1813; mar. Abijah Curtis of
              Surry, Me., 19 Aug 1853.
 2218      x. Lucy[8] Eaton, b. 5 Oct 1815; mar. Ephraim Closson (prob.
              his 2d wife), ca. 16 Nov 1844, and had two sons and
              two daughters. He died 7 Aug 1864.


**907. Moses[7] Eaton** (Moses[6], Theophilus[5], Jonathan[4], John[3-1]) was
born 11 Oct 1778 in Sedgwick, Me.; mar. **Mary Thomas**, also of Sedgwick, on or soon after 6 Nov 1810. They res. in West Brooklin on the
east side of the Benjamin River. Moses died 29 Jan 1846, and Mary died
13 Sep 1866. Both are bur. at the Old Sedgwick Cemetery.

Children at West Brooklin:

+2219      i. Richard[8] Eaton, b. 15 Aug 1812; mar. Joanna Grant, 1840.
 2220     ii. Eliza[8] Eaton, b. 9 Dec 1814; mar. Jacob Seavey of Sedgwick
              (int.) 23 Dec 1838. She had a daughter in 1839.
 2221    iii. Alfred[8] Eaton, b. 8 Jan 1817; mar. Ruth B. Grant, 8 Apr
              1844. No issue reported.
+2222    iv. Jesse[8] Thomas Eaton, b. 3 Nov 1819; mar. Susan M. Grant.


**909. Jonathan[7] Eaton** (Moses[6], Theophilus[5], Jonathan[4], John[3-1])
was born 25 Mar 1781 in Sedgwick, Me.; mar. **Mary Whitmore** of Deer
Isle (she born 29 Oct 1787, dau. of Joseph and Abigail (Babbidge)
Whitmore of Oceanville, Stonington and Deer Isle), on 31 Dec 1807.
They res. in Sedgwick during the period their children were born, appearing there in the 1810 and 1820 Censuses. Much later, in 1860, father Jonathan is seen living with his seafaring and prosperous eldest son
in Searsport, Me.

Children at Sedgwick, Me.:

2223       i. Rebecca[8] Eaton, b. 27 Nov 1808; mar. David Sands of Lubec
              Me., 12 Nov 1829 at Belfast.
2224      ii. Mary[8] Eaton, b. 9 Jul 1810; mar. Capt. Samuel Whitney of

Northport, Me., 24 Sep 1832 at Belfast.
+2225    iii. Theophilus[8] Eaton, b. 23 Mar 1812; mar. Betsey Kempton.
 2226    iv. Jonathan[8] Eaton, b. 9 Jun 1813.
 2227     v. John[8] Eaton, b. 20 Feb 1815; may be he who mar. Abigail B.
             Merrow, 30 Nov 1837 at Minot, Me. (Contrary to Noyes
             (1942), he is not the John C. with Phebe at Sedgwick, who
             is clearly **#1801**).
+2228    vi. Hezekiah[8] Dodge Eaton, b. 11 Jan 1817; mar. Statira Dutch.
 2229   vii. David[8] Carleton Eaton, b. 26 Nov 1818.
 2230  viii. Thomas[8] Eaton, b. 5 May 1821.
 2231    ix. Abigail[8] Eaton, b. 28 May 1823.


**910. Jeremiah[7]** (*Jonathan[6]*, Theophilus[5], Jonathan[4], John[3-1]) was
born out of wedlock 2 Mar 1784, probably around Sedgwick. His
mother was Lucy Em(m)merton, daughter of a family recently arrived
from Ipswich, Mass. The most likely candidate for his father was Jonathan[6] Eaton of Sedgwick (**#339**, q.v. for fuller details), although another
plausible candidate would have been Jeremiah[6] Eaton of Deer Isle
(**#261**). This Jeremiah[7] was brought up by his mother at Blue Hill, Me., a
few miles north of Sedgwick; and he mar. **Martha "Patty" Friend**, 14
Nov 1805. The couple settled on a farm at Blue Hill, where all their children were born and where the parents died. The family lived in the old
Puritan faith, having no fellowship with card-playing or dancing. At the
proper seasons, Jeremiah engaged in the fishing business. Wife Martha
died 29 Apr 1859.

Children in Blue Hill (from LDS Films #0443670 and 0010608):

+2232      i. Oliver[8] Eaton, b. 15 Mar 1806; mar. Dorcas Finny, 1829.
 2233     ii. Martha[8] Eaton, b. 4 May 1808; mar. a Chatto, 6 Jan 1825.
+2234    iii. Abner[8] Eaton, b. 15 May 1810; mar. Isabel Wilson, 1834.
 2235    iv. Lucy[8] Eaton, b. 13 May 1812; mar. a Herrick.
 2236     v. Asenath[8] Eaton, b. 19 Aug 1814; mar. __?__, 24 Sep 1828.
 2237    vi. Hannah[8] Eaton, b. 31 May 1817; mar. a Mann of Surry, Me.
 2238   vii. Irena[8] Eaton, b. 20 Oct 1820; mar. O. Drew.


**911. Amos[7] Eaton** (Ebenezer[6], Theophilus[5], Jonathan[4], John[3-1])
was born 28 Sep 1777 in Sedgwick; mar. 1st, **Susanna Herrick**, also of
Sedgwick, 14 Mar 1799. They res. in Sedgwick at least during the years
they were having children, as covered by the 1800-1820 Censuses. Wife
Susanna died 21 Oct 1822, presumably still in Sedgwick. By 1826 or
so, however, Amos mar. 2d, Widow **Betsey Burnham** (born 1787) and by
the 1830 Census had removed to Mt. Desert Island, Me. The couple is
there in 1840 and 1850, where Amos is a farmer at Tremont with Betsey
in the 1850 Census. Amos died there 20 Oct 1855.

Children with Susanna in Sedgwick, Me.:

2239    i. Rebecca[8] Herrick Eaton, b. 13 Aug 1799; mar. Elisha
          Friend, 18 Nov 1818, and raised a large family.
2240    ii. Mary[8] "Polly" Webster Eaton, b. 19 Jul 1801; mar. Capt.
          John C. Tibbetts and had four sons and four daughters.
2241    iii. Abigail[8] Eaton, b. 5 Jun 1803; died 17 Sep 1819.
2242    iv. Prudence[8] Lear Eaton, b. 21 Apr 1805; mar. Joshua Grindle
          the 2d of Sedgwick about 16 Mar 1823, and had six
          sons and five daughters. Prudence died 18 Dec 1867.
2243    v. Lucy[8] Hermon Eaton, b. 12 Mar 1807; mar. Elisha Wood of
          Blue Hill, Me., in 1829 and had three children.
+2244   vi. Amos[8] Eaton, Jr., b. 21 Mar 1809; mar. Joanna Burnham.
2245    vii. Louisa[8] Eaton, b. 17 Apr 1811; died 3 Nov 1812.
+2246   viii. Herrick[8] Munson Eaton, b. 4 Sep 1813; mar. Joann Hopkins.
2247    ix. Joshua[8] Eaton, b. 13 Jan 1816; mar. Lydia Burnham. He
          was a sea captain for 30 years. No issue reported. He
          died in 1882.
2248    x. Wilford[8] Eaton, b. 19 Jan 1818. He was a sea captain who
          died and was buried at sea in 1840. Never married.
2249    xi. Solomon[8] Billings Eaton, b. 17 Nov 1821; he married in
          1846, but he and his wife died the same day in 1846.

Child with Betsey, probably at Mt. Desert, Me.

2250   xii. Daniel[8] Burnham Eaton, b. 1827; mar a Miss Babson in
          1853. He was a master ship carpenter. No issue reported.

**923. James[7] Eaton** (James[6], Theophilus[5], Jonathan[4], John[3-1]) was
born at the Northwest Harbor on Deer Isle, Me. on 26 Jun 1800, and removed with his parents first to Prospect, Me. and then to Seartsport, Me.
He went to sea early in life, and for many years after reaching manhood
he was master of a vessel sailing from New York City. He mar. **Elizabeth
Nolan** (born 24 Dec 1812 in Marblehead, Mass. to John and Elizabeth
Nolan) on 7 Nov 1839 at New York City. Wife Elizabeth died in Brooklyn, N.Y, 14 May 1879; Capt. James, who had accumulated a handsome
property, died 27 May 1887, also Brooklyn.

Children in Brooklyn, N.Y.:

2251    i. James[8] Edward Eaton, b. 24 Jul 1840; died July 1842.
2252    ii. Sarah[8] Elizabeth Eaton, b. 15 Mar 1842; mar. William T.
          De Nyse, 29 Oct 1873. They res. in Brooklyn and had
          one child.
2253    iii. Virginia[8] Eaton, b. 28 Feb 1844; mar. 1st, Edgar Chase,
          24 Sep 1868, and had one child. Capt. Chase died 30
          Sep 1872. Virginia mar. 2d, George A. Carver, 30 Oct
          1879, and had one child in Brooklyn. Virginia died in
          Searsport, Me., 6 Aug 1813, but is bur. in Brooklyn.

**2254**    iv. James[8A] Calhoun Eaton, b. 24 Mar 1846; died unmar. 15
            Feb 1899 at Brooklyn, N.Y.
**2255**    v. Thomas[8] Hubbard Eaton, b. 6 Jul 1848; died 2 Jan 1850
            in Brooklyn, N.Y.
**2256**    vi. Franklin[8] Pierce Eaton, twin of Amanda, b. 7 Apr 1853; he
            died Jul 1854 in Brooklyn, N.Y.
**2257**    vii. Amanda[8] Melvina Eaton, twin of Franklin, b. 7 Apr 1853;
            mar.William M. Sawyer, 11 Dec 1875, and had five chil-
            dren, while res. in Brooklyn, N.Y.


**930. John[7] George Eaton** (Joseph[6], Ezekiel[5], Jonathan[4], John[3-1])
was born in that part of "Society Land" which later became Bennington,
N.H., ca. 1786; mar. **Polly Favor** (born 1788 in Francestown, N.H.)
about 1809. They lived on a farm in Bennington. John G. died there in
1831; wife Polly died in Lowell, Mass., in 1870.

Children, all born in Bennington, N.H.:

**2258**     i. Susan[8] F. Eaton, b. 1810; mar. George Eastman. She died
            in Lowell, Mass.; he died in New Orleans.
**+2259**   ii. Moses[8] Favor Eaton, b. 19 Nov 1812; mar. Lydia Doane.
**+2260**  iii. John[8] George Eaton, b. 25 Dec 1814; mar. Martha Bullard.
**+2261**   iv. Joseph[8] Eaton, b. 1816; mar. Rebekah Martin; removed
            to Minnesota.
**2262**    v. Elizabeth[8] Eaton, b. 1818; mar. a Hemmenway and lived
            in Leominster, Mass.


**934. Nathaniel[7] A. Eaton** (Joseph[6], Ezekiel[5], Jonathan[4], John[3-1])
was born about 1795 in that part of "Society Land" which later became
Bennington, N.H.; mar. **Eunice Pollard** of neighboring Greenfield about
1818, and resided on a farm in Bennington. His children reported that
he was a soldier in the War of 1812, but not in any engagement with the
enemy. They had nine children, but five of them died of "consumption"
(tuberculosis). Father Nathaniel, however, lived into old age, dying in
1870 in Bennington, although he is buried in Greenfield, N.H.

Children born in Bennington (then "Society Land"), N.H.:

**2263**     i. Benjamin[8] Eaton, b. ca. 1819; died at about 30, unmar., of
            consumption.
**2264**    ii. Sophronia[8] Eaton, b. ca. 1821; mar. 1st, Andrew Currier by
            whom she had two children; and 2d, ?  , without issue.
            She died of consumption in Nashua, N.H.
**2265**   iii. Sarah[8] Eaton, b. ca. 1822; mar. Ammi Eastman and res. in
            Brookfield, Mass.
**+2266**   iv. Nathaniel[8] Eaton, b. 24 Jun 1824; mar. Clara Howe, 1846.
**+2267**    v. Amos[8] Eaton, b. 30 Aug 1826; mar. Apphia Martin, 1857.

**2268**    vi. Ezekiel[8] Eaton, b. ca. 1829; mar. a Stevens but soon died
of consumption.
**2269**   vii. Almira[8] Eaton, b. ca. 1832; died age 11 of consumption.
**2270**  viii. Caroline[8] Eaton, b. ca. 1835; died age 11 of consumption.
**2271**    ix. Child[8] Eaton, b. ca. 1837; died at birth.


**935. Robert[7] Wise Eaton** (Joseph[6], Ezekiel[5], Jonathan[4], John[3-1])
was born 21 Aug 1796 in that part of "Society Land" that later became
Bennington, N.H. In the early part of his life he worked for 17 bachelor
years in the Charlestown (Boston) Navy Yard, and among other things
aided in repairing the famed old ship the <u>Constitution</u>. Later he removed
to New York State to become an enterprising and prosperous farmer, and
mar. **Helen Campbell** (born 2 Oct 1818 in Broadalbin, Fulton Co., New
York) on 7 May 1844. He was living at Gloversville, N.Y. and later at
West Providence, N.Y. in Saratoga Co., where he died 24 May 1866.

One child in Providence with Helen in this late marriage:

+**2272**    i. John[8] George Eaton, b. 18 Apr 1845; m. Philena Hemstreet.


**942. Joshua[7] Eaton** (James[6], Ezekiel[5], Jonathan[4], John[3-1]) was
born 22 Dec 1779 in Sandown, N.H.; mar. **Polly Edmunds** (born 17 Feb
1779 in Sandown) on 16 Jul 1799. They lived on a farm in Sandown,
where Polly died, 14 Aug 1856; and Joshua followed 26 Mar 1864.

Children at Sandown, N.H.:

**2273**    i. Caleb[8] Eaton, b. Apr 1800; and died Oct 1802.
**2274**   ii. Judith[8] Eaton, b. Dec 1801; died Oct 1802.
**2275**  iii. Mary[8] Eaton, b. 16 Jul 1804; mar. Capt. Cotton and res. on
a farm in Sandown. They had four children.
**2276**   iv. George[8] Eaton, b. ca. 1806 and died young.
**2277**    v. Clarissa[8] Eaton, b. 20 Oct 1808; mar. Lyman Pillsbury on
15 Nov 1832 and lived on a farm in Sandown, where
after four children, she died 6 Jan 1849.
**2278**   vi. Nancy[8] Jane Eaton, b. 16 Apr 1811; mar. Jeremiah Swett, a
Methodist minister, and had one daughter.
+**2279**  vii. George[8A] Washington Eaton, b, 1 Oct 1813; mar. 1st, Mary P.
**2280** viii. Thomas[8] Eaton, b. 20 Nov 1816; he was still living with his
parents in 1850, and was still unmar. in 1893.
+**2281**   ix. Harrison[8] Eaton, b. 29 Dec 1818; mar. Martha Johnson.


**947. Richard[7] Eaton** (Joseph[6-5A], Jonathan[4], John[3-1]) was born 9
Apr 1804 in Beverly, Mass., but grew up in Wolfeborough, N.H. He mar.
**Lydia Ann Wheeler** (born in Pepperell Mass., 10 Feb 1810) in Jan
1830. Richard was a hotel proprietor and a R.R. station agent, and they

lived in various communities. Wife Lydia died in Roxbury, Mass., 19 Nov 1862, while Richard did not die until 22 Jul 1882 at Lowell, Mass.

Children:

+ 2282  i. William[8] Henry Eaton, b. 4 Oct 1830 at Wolfeborough, N.H.
  2283  ii. Mary[8] Caroline Eaton, twin of Martha, b. 22 Mar 1833 in West Cambridge, Mass.; mar. James Monroe Battles, a lay Episcopalian missionary in East Boston, Mass. They later lived in Goffstown, N.H., and had one son.
  2284  iii. Martha[8] Emeline Eaton, twin of Mary, b. 22 Mar 1833 in West Cambridge, Mass.; died in Sep 1833.
  2285  iv. Joseph[8] Dexter Eaton, b. 5 Oct 1835 in Lexington, Mass.; died 6 Jan 1841.
+ 2286  v. Richard[8] Eaton, b. 17 Aug 1837 in West Cambridge, Mass.
  2287  vi. Anna[8] Maria Eaton, b. 27 Aug 1839 in Lincoln, Mass.; mar. Daniel Little of Goffstown, N.H., 1868, in Dedham, Mass. They had no children.
  2288  vii. Alfred[8] Warren Eaton, b. 15 Mar 1843 in Concord, Mass.; died 30 Nov 1865 in Medina, Mich.
  2289  viii. Abby[8] Eliza Eaton, b. 18 Jul 1846 in Roxbury, Mass.; died Sep 1847 in Roxbury.

**948. Chandler[7] Eaton** (Joseph[6-5A], Jonathan[4], John[3-1]) was born 14 Nov 1805 in Beverly, Mass., but grew up in Wolfeborough, N.H. whence his parents had removed. He mar. **Mary J. Cottle** of Kittery, Me. (born Oct 1806) 21 Dec 1835. Chandler was a farmer, and early in their marriage the couple lived in Brookfield, N.H. Soon however, they returned to the homestead in Wolfeborough where Chandler was a boy, working the farm and living under the same roof as his aging parents as of 1850. By 1870, however, they were back in Brookfield with some of their children. (As Brookfield adjoins Wolfeboro to the east, the distance between these farmsteads may have been rather small.) Wife Mary died 29 Mar 1882; Chandler followed on 13 Nov 1886. Both are buried in Wolfeborough.

Children born in Wolfeborough, N.H.:

+ 2290  i. Samuel[8] S. Eaton, b. 25 Jul 1836; mar. Mary.
  2291  ii. Orin[8] J. Eaton, b. 6 Aug 1839; a farm laborer in Wolfeborough, N.H. before his death 26 Nov 1879, probably unmarried.
  2292  iii. Lucy[8] M. Eaton, b. 8 Feb 1841.
+ 2293  iv. Abial[8] Chandler Eaton, b. 23 May 1842; mar. Sarah Ann.
+ 2294  v. John[8] C. Eaton, b. 1 May 1847; mar. Lois Martin.
  2295  vi. Mary[8] Eaton, b. 1849; died young.
  2296  vii. Joseph[8] Eaton, b. 3 Jan 1851; removed young to the town of Stuart in Holt Co., northern Nebraska.

**950. Joseph**[7] **Eaton** (Joseph[6], Jonathan[5-4], John[3-1]) was born in Sedgwick, Me., 26 Aug 1805; mar. **Hannah Roberts** (born 22 Jul 1815 to John in Brooksville, Me.) on 28 Dec 1837. They settled on a medium-size farm in Sedgwick, where Hannah's sister Lydia lived with them. Wife Hannah died there 5 May 1872; Joseph died 6 Jun 1874.

Children born in Sedgwick, Me:

2297    i. Emily[8] V. Eaton, b. 7 Apr 1844; mar. 1st, Lucius B. Dority at Sedgwick, 10 Feb 1864. He was a master mariner, and was drowned off Cape Hatteras about 14 Apr 1877. They had no issue. She mar. 2d, George Osgood of Blue Hill, Me., where they resided on Pleasant Rd., Rt. 1. Emily died about 1814.

2298    ii. Eliza[8] S. Eaton, b. 13 May 1846; mar. Herbert S. Dority of Sedgwick, son of Robert, 10 Oct 1866. They lived on a farm on the Reach Rd. in Sargentville. Eliza d. ca. 1804.

2299    iii. Ella[8] G. Eaton, b. 13 Jan 1849; died engaged but not yet married, 4 Apr 1871 at Sedgwick.

2300    iv. Louise[8] Martha Eaton, b. 22 Dec 1856; mar. Grover[9] D. Eaton (**#2306**, just below) of Sargentville, her cousin. They resided on a farm on the Sargentville Reach Rd. until her death, 25 Mar 1882.

**953. Daniel**[7] **Eaton** (Joseph[6], Jonathan[5-4], John[3-1]) was born 30 Jul 1810 in Sedgwick, Me.; mar **Betsey Byard** (born 13 Feb 1817 to James Byard in Sedgwick) on 23 Feb 1836. They lived on a farm in Sargentville, and Daniel served also as ferryman, rowing passengers across the Reach to Deer Isle. The couple is buried in the old cemetery in Sargentville.

Children born in Sargentville:

2301    i. Vi(o)letta[8] L. Eaton, b. 29 Jul 1837; mar. Russell H. Sargent on 4 Dec 1855. He was a master mariner, but also did ferrying across the Reach. They had one son.

2302    ii. Elizabeth[8] Harding Eaton, b. 8 Sep 1839; died 20 Jan 1843.

2303    iii. Diantha[8] Eaton, b. 27 Sep 1841; died 24 Dec 1842 of scarlatina.

2304    iv. Elizabeth[8] "Lizzie" Eaton, b. 30 Dec 1843; mar. John E. Trafton of Waterville, Me., 11 Jun 1862. They lived in Sargentville, where she d. 12 Oct 1882, leaving two sons.

2305    v. Abbie[8] Mary Eaton, b. 25 Feb 1846; mar. Edward Alphonso Byard, son of Hezekiah D., 27 Oct 1869. They lived in Sargentville, where he was a master mariner. They had three sons and one daughter.

+2306     vi. Grover[8] Daniel Eaton, b. 9 Apr 1853; mar. his cousin,
          Louise Eaton (#2300, just above).


**955. John[7] Eaton** (Joseph[6], Jonathan[5-4], John[3-1]) was born in the
part of Sedgwick that became Sargentville, Me., on 31 Jan 1815; mar. 1st,
**Asenath Roberts** (born 5 Mar 1821 to Amaziah and Polly Roberts at
Sedgwick) on 3 Oct 1841. John was a farmer and sea captain residing in
Sargentville. He was a deacon of the Baptist church, and held in highest
esteem by all who knew him. Wife Asenath died at some unknown time,
and John mar. 2d, **Vesta A. Billings**, 18 May 1876. John himself died 13
Feb 1879.

          Children with Asenath in Sargentville, Me.:

2307      i. (Frances) Adelle[8] Eaton, b. 24 Jul 1848; mar. Groves
          Parker, 29 Dec 1868. He was a master mariner. They
          had two daughters.
2308      ii. Emma[8] Josephine Eaton, b. 10 Dec 1854; mar. Robert G.
          Gray of Blue Hill, Me., 22 Aug 1878. He was a master
          mariner who res. in Sedgwick.


**966. Daniel[7] Torrey Eaton** (Jonathan[6-4], John[3-1]) was born 21
May 1823 at Deer Isle; mar. **Mary Ann Thompson** (born 12 Nov 1833
to Adam and Lucy (Haskell) Thompson) on 24 Mar 1852 on Deer Isle.
He was a joiner by trade, at least early in life. The couple lived "on the
homestead," presumably of Daniel's parents, located on the east side of
the road between the "watering trough brook" and the Dexter place, a
half mile north of Carman's Rock. Daniel was often called "Torrey" Eaton. Wife Mary died 4 Jun 1888. Daniel lived to a ripe old age, winning
the Boston Post golden cane as the oldest man in the town of Deer Isle
before his death, 6 Nov 1909.

          Children, all born in Deer Isle:

2309      i. Eliza[8] Ann Eaton, b. 6 Sep 1852; mar. Frank B. Weed, a sea
          captain. They had five children and Eliza died in 1905.
2310      ii. Izora[8] Lerigger Eaton, b. 20 Nov 1854; mar. William Morey
          (son of Levi and Mary Ann (Barbour) Morey) on 25 Dec
          1878 in Deer Isle. They had two children. Izora died at
          Deer Isle, 15 Sep 1886. Husband William died, 1908.
+2311     iii. Charles[8] Fremont Eaton, b. 20 Oct 1856; m. Annie Johnson.
2312      iv. William[8] Wallace Eaton, b. 3 Oct 1858; drowned in Portland
          harbor, 12 Nov 1872.
2313      v. Horace[8] Dean Eaton, b. 13 Sep 1861. No further report.
2314      vi. Byron[8] Lynch Eaton, b. 7 Nov 1863.
2315      vii. Esther[8] Fraethy Eaton, b. 27 Mar 1866; died 26 Apr 1884.
2316      viii. Wallace[8] Parker Eaton, b. 15 Oct 1875.

**967. Jonathan**[7] **Eaton** (John[6], Jonathan[5-4], John[3-1]) was born in Deer Isle on 11 Jul 1797 (Fam. Records); mar. **Edna Hale Jordan** (born 14 Feb 1798 to Samuel and Abigail (Harden) Jordan), int. 15 Oct 1826. Jonathan, a mason by trade (1850), first lived in a log house, but later lived in a house on a lane off Sylvester's Cove Road. Wife Edna died 8 Jul 1869; Jonathan died 15 Feb 1881.

Children with Edna at Deer Isle:

+ **2317**    i. John[8] Eaton, b. 28 Apr 1828; mar. Caroline Perkins, 1853.
+ **2318**    ii. Samuel[8] Jordan Eaton, b. 25 Sep 1829; m.1st, Eliza Pressey.
   **2319**    iii. David[8] A. Eaton, b. 21 Jun 1831; mar. Susan Kelsey (born 1840 to Robt. and Olive (Pickering) Kelsey). This couple removed to East Boston, Mass, residing at the corner of Marion and White Sts. there. One child died young. David built a summer house in Deer Isle where his wife's parents had lived. Susan died ca. May 1916. David, who spent that summer with his brother, Jasper, died suddenly in Jul 1916, at Sunset on Deer Isle.
   **2320**    iv. Ebenezer[8] Eaton, b. 6 May 1833; mar. Clementine Pressey (b. 3 Oct 1842 at Deer Isle to Enos and Abigail (Crockett) Pressey) on 13 Jan 1864. They settled in Ebenezer's house of origin after his father died. They are remembered as having no children, although Deer Isle records show a son Goodwin born to them ca. 1865-66, who died as an infant.
+ **2321**    v. Jasper[8] Stillphen Eaton, b. 24 Jan 1835; mar. Susan C. Pressey, sister of brothers Eatons' wives Eliza and Clementine above, 23 Jun 1853.
   **2322**    vi. Angeline[8] Eaton, b. 20 Sep 1836; mar. Samuel Brown of Newburyport, Mass., as his 2d wife, 11 Mar 1869. They res. at Newburyport, and had at least two daughters.
   **2323**    vii. Helen[8] Melinda Eaton, b. 18 Nov 1841; mar. George Stimpson, but died soon thereafter, 7 Jun 1860.

**978. Charles**[7] **Eaton** (Nathan[6], Jonathan[5-4], John[3-1]) was born 19 Mar 1810 on the old Eaton homestead at Dunham's Point on Deer Isle, Me.; mar. **Rebecca Doane** (born 28 Mar 1818 at Newburgh, Me., to Nathan and Polly Doane) on 26 Nov 1839 in Deer Isle. Charles was a prosperous young trader who used the title of "Esq." when married. He also farmed, dealt in real estate, and ran a cooper's shop on the wharf he owned, where barrels were made to take his clam bait to market. About 1869, Charles erected a large hall to meet community need for theatre and dance space, which became known as "Olympic Hall." While visiting his daughter Carrie Chilcott in Bangor he failed and died, Jun 1900.

Wife Rebecca lived on for some time, but also died on a visit to her Bangor daughter, 28 Sep 1907.

Children born on Deer Isle:

+ 2324    i. Henry[8] Eaton, b. 10 Oct 1840; mar. Tryphosa Raynes, 1864.
  2325    ii. (Augustus) Parker[8] ("Parker Tuck") Eaton, b. 20 May 1842. As a young man his store ("P. T. Eaton's") at Green's Landing, served the family's mercantile and packing business under his own name. They shipped thousands of barrels of clam bait to Portugal to stock their fishing fleet. Parker was last heard from in Vineyard Haven, Me., when he sailed 14 Aug 1872 as captain of a barque bound for Copenhagen, Denmark.
  2326    iii. (Mary) Anna[8] Eaton, b. 11 Dec 1844; mar. Edwin R. Doane, 1865, in Harwichport, Mass. They were still alive in 1930.
  2327    iv. Juliette[8] "Ett" Eaton, b. 11 May 1847; mar. Ebenezer Fifield Simpson (b. West Stonington, Me., 1841). She ran a very successful millinery shop. The couple lived at Waterville, Me. and Hyde Park, Mass., before returning to settle in Stonington, Me. Ett died of cerebral apoplexy, 18 Apr 1899; Eben died suddenly as well, 27 Jan 1907.
+ 2328    v. (Charles) Fred[8] Eaton, b. 17 Mar 1850; mar. Lois Sargent.
  2329    vi. Frances[8] Ellen Eaton, b. 12 Sep 1852; mar. as 2d wife to Capt. George W. Collins of Belfast, Me. Fannie and her husband res. at Rockland, Me., and then removed to So. Boston, Mass. They were childless. Late in life she moved to Cape Cod to live with her sister at Harwichport. She died 3 Oct 1932.
  2330    vii. John[8] Doane Eaton, b. 31 Jan 1856. When a very young man he went out to Springfield, Mo., to help his eldest brother sell lightning rods. After a while he returned to Stonington to become the assistant for his brother Fred, running Eaton & Co. in Stonington. He mar. Lillian Jane Greenlaw (b. 14 Dec 1868 to Eben/Mary Greenlaw of Oceanville), 29 Apr 1896. They res. in the house left by John's parents, opening the place to transients and boarders as "Eaton's Inn." John was also partner in various business enterprises with his brother C. Fred. They were childless save for a stillbirth.
  2331    viii. Carrie[8] Lillian Eaton, b. 31 Mar. 1860; mar. Langdon S. Chilcott, a highly esteemed dentist in Bangor, Me.

**980.    Eliphalet[7] Chase Pressey Eaton** (Nathan[6], Jonathan[5-4], John[3-1]) was born 21 Mar 1816 at Deer Isle, Me; mar. **Sally J. Doane** (born 17 May 1822 at Newburgh, Me.) on 1 Mar 1840 in Newburgh. They settled in Searsport, Me., where Eliphalet was both a ship and house carpenter. Death dates are unknown.

Children, all but the first born in Searsport, Me.:

+ **2332**   i. Oscar[8] G. Eaton, b. 6 Nov 1841 at Newburgh; mar. Addie.
+ **2333**  ii. Park[8] J. Eaton, b. 22 Jul 1843; mar. Matilda M. Turner.
  **2334** iii. Zilpha[8] M. Eaton, b. 23 Apr 1848; died unmar. 3 Aug 1866.
  **2335**  iv. John[8] H. Eaton, b. 14 Nov 1852; died 17 Nov. 1852.
  **2336**   v. Cora[8] E. Eaton, b. 13 May 1860.

**981. Frederick[7] Eaton** (Nathan[6], Jonathan[5-4], John[3-1]) was born 24 Apr 1818 at Deer Isle, Me.; mar. **Barbara G. Haskell** (also of Deer Isle, born 2 Nov 1821 to Tristram Haskell and his 2d wife Betsey (Barton) Haskell) on 10 Jan 1841. The couple ultimately settled at the corner of the Dow Town Road and Shakespeare Hill (Noyes, 1942). In 1850 Frederick was a sailor. Wife Barbara died 8 Sep 1898; she is buried in the Adams Cemetery at Deer Isle with husband "Capt. Frederick," who died 5 Nov 1899.

Children born on Deer Isle:

  **2337**   i. George[8] Washington Eaton, b. 14 Dec 1841; mar. Harriet A. Pressey, dau. of Sylvanus and Harriet (Gross) Pressey, on 8 Jan 1871; they had no children.
  **2338**  ii. Davis[8] Eaton, b. 12 Nov 1843; died 21 Nov 1843.
  **2339** iii. Caroline[8] Eaton, b. 5 Oct 1844; mar. Frederic P. Weed, 10 Jul 1863, She had three children, and died 24 Jul 1932. For an obituary, see Noyes (1942).
+ **2340**  iv. John[8] Sylvanus Eaton, b. 25 Jan 1845; m. Martha Pickering.
  **2341**   v. Eliza[8] Barton Eaton, b. 16 Jan 1847; died 6 Jan 1862.
  **2342**  vi. Charles[8] E. Eaton, b. 22 Sep 1853; mar 1st, __?__; mar. 2d, Mrs. Jennie E. Brackett. He died 1910 (monument).
  **2343** vii. Mary[8] H. Eaton, b. Mar 1856; died 19 Mar 1862.
  **2344** viii. Henrietta[8] M. Eaton, b. 4 Sep 1860; mar. Everett S. Haskell, 15 May 1879, a sea captain as of 1910, living on the Dow Road. They had five children.
  **2345**  ix. Wallace[8] W. Eaton, b. 7 Jul 1861; m. Mary Frances Haskell, dau. of Tristram and Lydia (Reddy-Pressey) Haskell, on 24 Oct 1895. They had a farm on the "Reach." This was a late marriage for Mary, and they had no children of their own. They did adopt a Charles Frank Hutchinson, born 1904.

**982. Davis[7] Haskell Eaton** (Nathan[6], Jonathan[5-4], John[3-1]) was one of twins born 26 Jun 1820 at Deer Isle, who like twin Sarah, lived to be married. He mar. **Susan Robbins Greenlaw**, 1 Jan 1850 and settled in the "Sunset" neighborhood on Deer Isle, where they raised a large family, although one ravaged by diphtheria in Aug 1862.

Children born on Deer Isle:

+ **2346**   i. Herman[8] Eaton, b. 25 Sep 1850; mar. Ella Thurlow, 1883.
**2347**   ii. Dorothy[8] Ellen Eaton, b. 24 Jul 1852; died 10 Aug 1862 of diptheria.
**2348**   iii. Franklin[8] Pierce Eaton, b. 13 Nov 1853; died 21 Aug 1862.
**2349**   iv. Charles[8] Jordan Eaton, b. 18 Jan 1856; died 21 Aug 1862.
**2350**   v. Drusilla[8] Green Eaton, b. 10 Jul 1857; died 10 Aug 1862.
**2351**   vi. Effie[8] D. Eaton, b. ca. 1859; died as an infant.
**2352**   vii. Nathan[8] Marcus Eaton, b. 23 Jun 1861; died 18 Aug 1862.
**2353**   viii. George[8] McClellan Eaton, b. 3 Nov 1863; died unmar. of measles, 12 Feb 1881.
**2354**   ix. Ulysses[8] S. Grant Eaton, b. 22 Jul 1865; died young.
**2355**   x. Eliza[8] Ellen Eaton, b. 26 Jul 1867; mar. 1st, Hugh McVeigh of Londonderry, Ireland, who arrived at Deer Isle from Boston to work at the pants factory on 11 Apr 1885; they had two children. She mar. 2d, Fred William Sylvester, but had no children with him. She died Jun 1920 at Deer Isle. Cf. obituary, Noyes (1942).
+ **2356**   xi. Goodwin[8] Pressey Eaton, b. 11 Jul 1868; m. Abby[10] Eaton.
**2357**   xii. Maria[8] Jordan Eaton, b. 7 Oct 1870; mar. George Maurice Dodge 17 Nov 1888 in Sunset, Deer Isle. They res. at Sylvester's Cove and had four children.
+ **2358**   xiii. Oscar[8] Davis Eaton, b. 8 Oct 1872; mar. Laura Dow.


**990. Otis[7] Eaton** (James[6], Jonathan[5-4], John[3-1]) was born ca. 1813 at Searsport, Me.; prob. mar. **Olive S.** (b. ca. 1819) around 1840, as he is living with a female agemate of this name and a decade's worth of children, in Searsport, Me. in the 1850 Census. He was at that time a joiner, no doubt in fitting out ships. He died in the 1860s, and widow Olive mar. 2d, Henry S. Howe, a blacksmith, although they continued to live in the same home next to brother-in-law Hiram[7] (**#991**, below) in Searsport.

Children with Olive in Searsport, Me.:

**2359**   i. Franklin[8] N. Eaton, b. ca. 1842; in 1880 was a cabinetmaker in Somerville, Mass. and unmar. Trail then lost.
**2360**   ii. Joseph[8] G. Eaton, b. ca. 1844; in 1880 was a carpenter in the Trott household in Boston, not yet married. That he did marry a Merrill girl is implied by his residence in a household on Atlantic St., Boston, 1900, headed by a Mary Merrill, his "mother-in-law," altho that wife is not present. Others are his aunt, Ellen Trott, and three other aunts.
**2361**   iii. Selden[8] L. Eaton, b. ca. Mar 1849.
+ **2362**   iv. Hiram[8] O. Eaton, b. Sep 1856; mar. Clara Danforth, 1880.

**991. Hiram**[7] **Eaton** (James[6], Jonathan[5-4], John[3-1]) was born 25 Dec 1814 at Searsport, Me.; mar. **Nancy A. Staples** (b. ca. 1819, Me.), ca. 1843. They res. in Searsport, where as a young man in 1850 he was a sailor, but by 1860 and after, described himself as a farmer instead. He died 23 Jan 1884.

Children born in Searsport, Me.:

+ 2363    i. William[8] M. Eaton, b. ca. 1845; mar. Anna E. Harriman.
  2364   ii. Harriet[8] M. Eaton, b. 1847; mar. Ralph S. Ellis, a mariner.
  2365  iii. Nancy[8] E. Eaton, twin of Elizabeth, b. 1850.
  2366   iv. Elizabeth[8] N. Eaton, twin of Nancy, b. 1850. Died young.
  2367    v. Mary[8] Eaton, b. 1852.
  2368   vi. Abba[8] Amelia Eaton, b. 1858.
+ 2369  vii. James[8] S. Eaton, b. 3 Mar 1861; died 14 Mar 1939.
  2370 viii. Lester[8] Clarence Eaton, b. 28 Jun 1864; mar. Sadie G. _?_
            (b. Sep 1864) and was a farmer at Searsport on a plot of
            land next to his brother James's farm. No sign of chil-
            dren as of 1900.

**998. Jonathan**[7] **W. Eaton** (Joshua[6], Daniel[5-4A], John[3-1]) was born 11 Dec 1795 at proto-Gilford, N.H.; mar. 1st, **Nancy __?__**, ca. 1820. In 1824, Jonathan, "Gilford yeoman," bought an undivided half of his father's 85-acre Gilford homestead and settled there. Wife Nancy, after bearing one child, died 13 Jul 1829 at Gilford. His father, Joshua[6], had sold his stake in Gilford and moved on to Sandwich, N.H., on the other (northern) side of Lake Winnipesaukee, appearing there in the 1830 Census. Not too long after his wife's death Jonathan W. followed suit. About 1832 he mar. 2d, **Judith Straw** of Sandwich. Of their five sons, four served in the Civil War and two were killed. Both parents died in Sandwich, N.H.

Child with Nancy at Gilford, N.H.:

  2371    i. Child[8] Eaton, b. 1820s; died young.

Children with Judith at Sandwich, N.H.:

  2372   ii. Daniel[8] C. Eaton, b. ca. 1833, mar. Martha Kennedy. Died
            in Civil War, 2 Jul 1863.
  2373  iii. Nancy[8] L. Eaton, b. ca. 1835; mar. Charles S. Sanborn of
            Moultonborough, N.H.. They res. in Maine. As a widow,
            she removed to Colorado.
+ 2374   iv. William[8] Henry Eaton, b. 16 Jun 1837; mar. Philean Hoyt.
  2375    v. Alfred[8] Eaton, b. 5 Oct 1839; mar.  ?  .
  2376   vi. Joshua[8] Eaton, b. ca. 1841. He was committed to the New
            Hampshire State Prison in Concord, N.H., after he was

convicted of murder at age 15. His sentence was for six
years and one day in prison, but he died there on 27 Jul
1860 (*Register of Convicts Committed to State Prison in
Concord, 1812-1883*). We were unable to find more
details of the crime in the local press.

2377   vii. Charles[8] H. Eaton, b. ca. 1844; enlisted in the Civil War
as a private in the 5th N.H. Regt., and was promoted to
corporal; was killed near Petersburg, Va., 18 Jun 1864.


**1014. William[7] Eaton** (Benjamin[6], James[5], Daniel[4A], John[3-1]) was
born 30 Oct 1815 in Salisbury, Mass.; mar. **Rhoda[8] R. Eaton (#1982)**,
dau. of Wyman[7] of Seabrook, 6 Dec 1838. The couple appears to have
settled on part of the farm of William's parents on Beach Road in Salisbury east of the original homestead site, and remained there for life. In
1870 they have father Benjamin[6] as well as son William S. living with
them.

Children born in Salisbury, Mass.:

2378      i. Amelia[8] Ann Eaton, b. 1842; died 1846.
+ 2379     ii. William[8] Sherburne Eaton, b. 16 Nov 1847; mar 1st, Belinda.
2380     iii. Anna[8] Amelia Eaton, b. 25 May 1850; mar. Francis Asbury
Jackman, 1869, and had one son. She died 20 Nov 1894.


**1017. Benjamin[7] Eaton** (Benjamin[6], James[5], Daniel[4A], John[3-1]) was
born 6 Sep 1823 in Salisbury, Mass.; mar. 1st, **Margaret[8] Eaton (#1985)**,
dau. of Wyman[7] Eaton of Salisbury, on 24 Nov 1847. After a brief stay
in Seabrook, the couple lived for more than a decade in the home of her
parents in Salisbury, with Benjamin helping with the farming. Margaret
died on 29 Jan 1862, and Benjamin mar. 2d, **Sarah A. Baker** of Solon,
Me., daughter of Frank and Deborah Baker, 18 Jun 1863. Widow Sarah
survived until 5 Dec 1920.

Children with Margaret:

2381      i. Benjamin[8] Franklin Eaton, b. 7 Jan 1849, Seabrook, N.H.; he
died unmar., 10 Mar 1881.
2382     ii. Aroline[8] Almena Eaton, b. 7 Jun 1850, Salisbury, Mass.; died
7 Jun 1850.
2383    iii. Rhoda[8] Jane Eaton, b. 16 Nov 1854, Salisbury; mar. George
Bragg, 5 Apr 1872, and had two children. She died 1 Sep
1892.

Children with Sarah in Salisbury, Mass.:

2384     iv. Addie[8] Frances Eaton, b. 8 Nov 1863; mar. John J. Pike.
She died 6 Feb 1950; husband John died 1 Mar 1850.

+**2385**    v. George[8] Wilson Eaton, b. 18 Apr 1866; mar. Carrie Fernald.
**2386**    vi. Nellie[8] Florence Eaton, b. 16 Feb 1873; mar. George W.
        Colby, 29 Sep 1897.  She died 4 Feb 1940.

    **1026. John[7] French Eaton** (Jonathan[6], James[5], Daniel[4A], John[3-1])
was born 3 Aug 1824 at Salisbury, Mass.; mar. **Chastina B. Deal**, also of
Salisbury, on 5 Apr 1848.  John was a farmer, and his rather substantial
farm can be seen on the 1884 Walker atlas map of East Salisbury (p. 5).
It was on the north side of Beach Road, at a point which corresponds
rather well with the corner of Meaders Lane on modern maps.  This site
was probably within the eastern edge of Eaton ancestral lands at their
peak.  Somewhat further out and on the south side of Beach Rd. in 1884
we find depicted the home of a "Mrs. Eaton", who is almost certainly
John[7]'s 84-year-old mother, Betsey, living at or very close to the center of
the original homestead.  John F. died 23 May 1897; his widow died 30
Jan 1905, both at Salisbury.

    Children born in Salisbury, Mass.:

**2387**    i. Emma[8] Chastina Eaton, b. 4 Feb 1849; mar. John Brown
        and res. at Derry Depot, N.H..  They had one daughter.
**2388**    ii. John[8] Edward Eaton, b. 17 Jul 1856; in 1895 he was still
        unmar., and running an electric car.  He later mar. 1st,
        Mary Gould; and 2d, Ada Shaw.

    **1034. Moses[7] Eaton** (Joseph[6-5A], John[4A], Joseph[3], John[2-1]) was born
ca. 1794 in Hawke (now Danville) N.H.  When he was about 13 his parents sold their farm in Hawke and moved to Vermont, where they circu-
lated between Washington Co. (Marshfield) and Corinth in Orange Co.
When Moses[7] was "of Washington, Vt." he mar. **Mercy B. Norris** (she
born 19 May 1797 in Lyndon, Caledonia Co., Vt.) on 15 Oct 1815 in
Corinth, Vt.  This family presents a number of challenges, in part because
of its frequent geographical rotation around a limited number of Vermont villages not many miles apart from one another, but in three different counties; and also in part because Moses had a sporadic preference to
be called "Freeman Eaton."  Thus, for example, the birth of their first
child at Marshfield, Vt., was attributed to Freeman and Mercy B. (Norris)
Eaton, with no mention of a Moses.  We have tried in complicated ways
to show that perhaps Freeman Eaton was somebody other than our
Moses[7] here, but none of these efforts seem confirmed.  And in any
event, the fact that the first son was christened "Freedom" Eaton suggests a parent with strong feelings on the subject.  There are other
complications and oddities in the trail left by this family, but they do
not seem worth trying to untangle here.  The basic outline seems to be
that Moses and Mercy had all their children in a short span of time,
from 1816 to 1821, despite the fact that Moses did not die until Mar
1828 in Danville, Vt., and may well have been ill or possibly estranged

from his wife for some time. Widow Mercy for her part mar. 2d, Rev. Jonathan Woodman in Sep 1832, and she had a further son. Mercy died in Sheffield, Vt. 26 Nov 1876.

Children with Mercy:

+ 2389    i. Freedom[8] Eaton, b. 19 Jan 1816, recorded both at Marshfield and Corinth, Vt.

  2390    ii. Caroline[8] H. Eaton, b. Jul 1819 in Danville, Vt.; mar 1st, Dr. Arza Witt, Feb 1836; mar. 2d, Dr. Jerome B. Harris, Jun 1851. She had no issue, and died 18 Dec 1882 in Pelham, N.H.

  2391    iii. Sallie[8] Maria Eaton, b. 29 Oct 1821 in Danville, Vt. She mar. 1st, David F. Thompson of Danville on 6 Nov 1839; mar. 2d, William J. Stanton, 9 May 1874. No children.

**1037. Joseph[7] Eaton** (Joseph[6-5A], John[4A], Joseph[3], John[2-1]) was born 1 Sep 1801 in Hawke (now Danville), N.H. When he was about six years old, his parents took the family to settle in Vermont. He took for a wife **Judith Gove** (she born 14 Mar 1808 in Strafford, Orange Co., Vt. to a family which probably had roots in Seabrook, N.H., as well) on 25 Jan 1830. They settled on a farm in Marshfield, Washington Co., Vt. one of this Eaton family's first ports of call after their migration. Joseph died there 6 Jul 1848; his widow Judith also died in Marshfield, 30 Apr 1877.

Children born in Marshfield, Vt.:

  2392    i. John[8] Harris Eaton, b. 3 Jan 1831; mar. Catherine Capron Adams (she born in Uxbridge, Mass., 25 Aug 1846) on 27 Mar 1878. They lived on a farm in Marshfield, but had no issue.

  2393    ii. Emeline[8] Eaton, b. 23 Sep 1832; mar. Lewis Bemis, 19 Jan 1858. They removed to Chatfield, Minn., where she died, 10 Aug 1873.

  2394    iii. Samuel[8] Moses Eaton, b. 1 May 1835; he lived on a farm in Marshfield where he died unmar. 26 Aug 1876.

  2395    iv. Nathaniel[8] Joseph Eaton, b. 23 Sep 1837; lived unmar. on a farm in Marshfield.

**1039. True[7] Eaton** (Joseph[6-5A], John[4A], Joseph[3], John[2-1]) was born 16 Nov 1806, as recorded in Danville, N.H. in the period when his parents were removing the family to Vermont. He presumably grew up mainly in Marshfield, Washington Co., Vt., although the family lived sometimes in nearby Orange Co. as well. He mar. **Abigail Cummings** (she born 18 May 1811) at Calais, Vt., 3 Dec 1835. This couple settled first on a farm in Marshfield, but in the mid-1840s removed to East Corinth, Penobscot Co., Maine. Between the fact that this was a rather unusual move, and the fact that parts of this Eaton twig frequented nearby Corinth, Vt., it might be thought that the Maine destination is an error of geographical assignment. It is not: True's family is registered in Marshfield in the 1840 Census, but the Corinth, Me., area in 1850. Later on the family sold out again and removed to California. True died in Copperopolis, Cal., in the Calaveras Co. approaches to the Sierras, 13 Jun 1863.

Children:

2396  i. Delphina[8] Jane Eaton, b. 7 Jul 1836 in Marshfield; mar. 1st, William Dennis, 8 Nov 1855 at East Corinth, Me. and had three sons. When widowed she mar. 2d, William Oren Cutler, 15 Jan 1873 and res. in "Jenny Lind", Cal.

2397  ii. Fidelia[8] Noble Eaton, b. 16 Feb 1838 in Marshfield; mar. 1st, Alonzo K. Dudley, 23 Oct 1858; mar. 2d, a Pruce from Derby, England, Sep 1881.

2398  iii. Martha[8] Cummings Eaton, b. 23 Oct 1840 in Marshfield; mar. Charles Jarvis, 25 Nov 1863 and res. in California, having one child.

2399  iv. Sarah[8] M. Eaton, b. 9 Mar 1844 in Marshfield; mar. Hiram Beigle, 27 Aug 1874 and res. in Montana, with one son.

2400  v. Emery[8] T. Eaton, b. 7 Nov 1847 in E. Corinth, Me.; died in California, 2 Apr 1867.

2401  vi. Leslie[8] True Eaton, b. 23 Feb 1856 in E. Corinth, Me; in 1900 he res. in Twp. #2, Amador Co. (Malibu), Cal. with his sister, Mrs. Martha Jarvis, perhaps widowed, as the only other registrants are three boarders and three servants.


**1042. Samuel[7] Eaton** (Samuel[6], Daniel[5], Samuel[4], Joseph[3], John[2-1]) was born ca. 1781 prob. at Brunswick, Me.: mar. **Nancy Nason** of Minot, Me., 17 Mar 1805, at Minot. They res. in the part of Minot, Me., that became the town of Auburn in the 1840s, and can be seen in the Censuses at this location from 1820 at least through 1850, when Samuel farms a rather small stake with his wife Nancy and a daughter Mary.

Children in Minot, Me. (perhaps incomplete):

+2402  i. David[8] N. Eaton, b. 18 Sep 1809; mar. Hannah N. Merrow.
2403  ii. Anna[8] Eaton, b. 10 Jun 1814.
2404  iii. Mary[8] Eaton, b. 23 Apr 1818; unmar. and living with her parents as of 1850.
2405  iv. Dexter[8] Eaton, b. 20 Apr 1820.


**1045. Abner[7] Eaton** (Samuel[6], Daniel[5], Samuel[4], Joseph[3], John[2-1]) was born ca. 1788, prob. at Brunswick, Me.; mar. **Hannah Douglass**

(born after 1794) ca. 1815. This couple res. at Brunswick in 1820 and
1830, but had removed to Lisbon, Me. as of 1840. We know little further
save that Abner died 10 Sep 1844 at Lisbon, and Hannah followed almost immediately, on 8 Oct 1844.

Children in Brunswick, Me. (inferred from family compositions):

2406    i. Girl[8] Eaton, b. ca. 1817.
2407    ii. Girl[8] Eaton, b. ca. 1819.
2408    iii. Girl[8] Eaton, b. ca. 1821.
2409    iv. Girl[8] Eaton, b. ca. 1824.
2410    v. Girl[8] Eaton, b. ca. 1828.
2411    vi. Girl[8] Eaton, b. ca. 1832.
2412    vii. Boy[8] Eaton, b. ca. 1835.
2413    viii. Boy[8] Eaton, b. ca. 1838.

**1047. Daniel[7] Eaton** (Daniel[6-5], Samuel[4], Joseph[3], John[2-1]) was
born 25 Oct 1792 in Brunswick, Me.; mar. **Margaret McIntosh**, a woman
12 years his senior, about 1813. This couple spent their lives in Brunswick, where Daniel listed his occupation as "laborer" in the 1850 Census.
Wife Margaret died 14 Sep 1867; he died 12 May 1873.

Children in Brunswick, Me.:

2414     i. Richard[8] Eaton, b. 7 Jun 1814; died unmar. ca. 1851.
+2415    ii. George[8] L. Eaton, b. 20 Jun 1816; mar. Frances McDonald.
+2416    iii. Ensign[8] B. Eaton, b. 11 Sep 1823; mar. Rachel Ross, 1851.

**1048. John[7] Eaton** (Daniel[6-5], Samuel[4], Joseph[3], John[2-1]) was born
ca. 1794 in Brunswick, Me.; mar. **Mary Badger**, 30 Nov 1814. While
this couple is said to have res. for their lives in Brunswick, John never
appears as a household head in any Census there. Our supposition, supported by the brevity of the child roster, is that John may have met some
early fate, although his date of death is unknown.

Children in Brunswick, Me.:

2417    i. Mary[8] Ann Eaton, b. 3 Apr 1815.
2418    ii. Mindwell[8] Eaton, b. 3 Nov 1817.

**1064. Asa[7] Eaton** (Moses[6], Daniel[5], Samuel[4], Joseph[3], John[2-1]) was
born 11 Mar 1811 in Brunswick, Me.: mar. **Esther Farnham** (she born
15 Nov 1816 in Mercer, Me.) on 11 Nov 1835. He spent the rest of his
life on a modest farm in Rome, Me. Wife Esther died in Abbott, Me., 19
Nov 1875; he died 16 Jun 1884 in Rome.

Children, all but the eleventh born in Rome, Me.:

2419   i. John[8] B. Eaton, b. 28 Apr 1837; mar. Maria S. Lunt, 30 Jan 1862. He was a cooper in Boston, Mass, and died 6 Jun 1876 in Michigan. No sign of children, altho the family cannot be found in the 1870 Census.

2420  ii. Greenwood[8] C. Eaton, b. 1838; died in infancy.

2421  iii. Greenwood[8A] C. Eaton, b. 1839; he removed to Pennsyl- at a precocious age and died there, 1858, without issue.

2422  iv. Charlotte[8] B. Eaton, b. 1841; died 12 Sep 1841, Rome.

+2423  v. Charles[8] E. Eaton, b. 22 Mar 1845; mar. Mary Scarborough.

+2424  vi. Moses[8] W. Eaton, b. 29 Dec 1846; mar. Catherine Mullaly.

2425  vii. Harriet[8] Eaton, b. ca. Jan 1848; died when five years old.

2426  viii. Charlotte[8A] B. Eaton, b. 24 Apr 1849; mar. Nelson Chase of Searsport, Me. and res. in Lowell, Mass. She died 16 Oct 1883; husband Nelson died 3 Oct 1884.

2427  ix. Child[8] Eaton, died before naming, 1851.

2428  x. Elizabeth[8] E. Eaton, b. 5 Mar 1853; mar. Isaac D. Draper of Leeds, Me., 23 Dec 1871. They res. in E. Somerville, Mass., where he was a carpenter, and had five children.

+2429  xi. Anson[8] T. Eaton, b. 4 Oct 1855, in Shirley, Me.; m. Ella.

2430  xii. Harriet[8A] Eaton, b. ca. 1862; died in 1877.

**1070. Martin[7] Eaton** (John[6], Daniel[5], Samuel[4], Joseph[3], John[2-1]) was born 15 Aug 1796, prob. at Brunswick, Me; mar. **Phebe Winslow** (of Winslow, Me., born ca, 1805) on 27 Apr 1834. They settled first at Lisbon, Me., where apparently all of their children were born. By 1845 or so, they moved to Brunswick, Me., where the family appears in Censuses from 1850-70. After 1879, the couple moved to Durham, Me., where Martin died. He had a great memory which aided him much in furnishing the proper memoranda of the descendants of Daniel[5] (**#146**) and Jane Grant.

Children, prob. all born in Lisbon, Me.:

2431  i. Sarah[8] Jane Eaton, b. 30 May 1835; mar. George P. Day of So. Durham, Me, 17 Oct 1879; she died 8 Jun 1906.

+2432  ii. William[8] W. Eaton, b. 20 May 1836; mar. Agnes Magoun.

2433  iii. (Rebecca) Annie[8] Eaton, b. 18 Jul 1837; mar. George R. Richardson, Apr 1878.

2434  iv. Abigail[8] Stewart Eaton, b. 10 Oct 1838; died 13 Jul 1839.

2435  v. Martha[8] Eaton, b. 8 Oct 1839; mar. James Clark. She died 4 Feb 1872 in Lewiston, Me.

+2436  vi. Alonzo[8] James Eaton, twin of Lucinda, b. 10 Jan 1841.

2437  vii. Lucinda[8] M. Eaton, twin of Alonzo, b. 10 Jan 1841. She died 2 Nov 1842.

2438  viii. Edward[8] R. Eaton, b. 29 May 1843; died in the Civil War, 30 Oct 1861.

**1071. John⁷ Eaton** (John⁶, Daniel⁵, Samuel⁴, Joseph³, John²⁻¹) was born 14 Jul 1798 in Brunswick, Me.; mar. **Persis Joy** (born in Machias, Me., 21 Sep 1800) on 26 Oct 1820. They settled early on in Lisbon, Me., with brother David, and were there in 1830. But they returned to Brunswick well before the 1840 Census, and remained there the rest of their lives. John was a blacksmith. He died 1 Apr 1875; wife Persis died, 25 Dec 1876, both in Brunswick.

Children (the first four or five in born Lisbon, Me; the rest in Brunswick, Me., although all are recorded at Brunswick also):

2439  i. Sarah⁸ Eaton, b. 3 Sep 1821; mar. William Whitney of Canada. They res. in Manchester, N.H., but by 1894 had returned to Maine at Kennebunkport.

2440  ii. Abby⁸ Eaton, b. 7 Apr 1824; mar. William Miers of Boston. She died 8 Aug 1851 in Brunswick.

+2441  ii. George⁸ W. Eaton, b. 6 Nov 1826; mar. Diana Deane.

+2442  iv. Dexter⁸ W. Eaton, b. 3 Apr 1831; mar. Hannah Remick.

2443  v. Emma⁸ Eaton, b. 21 Sep 1834; mar. Lewis Joy of Durham, Me. and res. in Brunswick, bearing seven children.

+2444  vi. Alfred⁸ J. Eaton, b. 9 Oct 1837; mar. Mary F. Remick. He was a caulker residing in Brunswick. No issue.

2445  vii. Charles⁸ H. Eaton, b. 5 Dec 1841; mar. Adrannah Libby, 18 Jun 1872. He was a barber residing in Brunswick, and the parents had one daughter.

**1072. David⁷ N. Eaton** (John⁶, Daniel⁵, Samuel⁴, Joseph³, John²⁻¹) was born 29 May 1800, in Lisbon, Me.; mar. 1st, **Lucy Dunlap**, 8 Mar 1821 at Litchfield, Me. David settled the family first in Lisbon; but then, probably after the death of his wife, moved to the part of Minot, Me., which later became Auburn, where he continued as a mechanic. He mar. 2d, **Hannah Merrow**, 24 Mar 1835 at Minot. David's was a large brood of children, but they were not long-lived. David saw most of them die before he did on 27 Feb 1882, and although we are shy on other death dates, we know that all had died before 1894.

Children with Lucy in Lisbon, Me,:

+2446  i. John⁸ Eaton, b. 2 Jun 1822.

2447  ii. Sarah⁸ Eaton, b. ca. 1824.

2448  iii. Mary⁸ Jane Eaton, b. ca. 1826.

2449  iv. David⁸ Eaton, b. 29 May 1828.

2450  v. Martin⁸ Eaton, b. 10 Aug 1830.

2451  vi. Joseph⁸ Eaton, b. 15 Oct 1832.

2452  vii. Drummond⁸ Eaton, twin of Sacine (?), b. ca. 1833.

2453  viii. Sacine⁸ (?) Eaton, twin of Drummond, b. ca. 1833.

Children with Hannah in Minot, Me.:

**2454**   ix. Nathaniel⁸ Eaton, b. 25 Nov 1836.
**2455**   x. Edwin⁸ Eaton, b. ca. 1839.


**1073. Shepard⁷ Starling Eaton** (Robert⁶, Jacob⁵⁻⁴, Joseph³, John²,
John¹) was born 10 Jan 1801 at Farmington, Me. just before his parents
removed to Ravenna, Ohio, where he grew up; mar. 1st, **Anna __?__**; 2d,
**Sarah M. Evans** (she born Va.) on 11 Mar 1833. In 1850, he was a
joiner by trade, res. in Jolly Twp., Washington Co., Ohio. By 1860 he
had taken the family north into Monroe Co., also on the upper reaches of
the Ohio River, to settle in Franklin Twp., Ohio. In both 1860 and 1870
he lists himself as a hotel keeper. He seems to have died in the 1870s.

Children with Sarah (inferred from Census lists):

**+2456**   i. John⁸ W. Eaton, b. ca. 1834; mar. Emily.
**2457**   ii. Sarah⁸ Elizabeth Eaton, b. ca. 1837. Still at home with
               parents in 1870, and with her widowed mother, 1880.
**2458**   iii. Martha⁸ E. Eaton, b. ca. 1840. She was also still at home
               with parents in 1870.
**2459**   iv. Hannah⁸ J. Eaton, b. ca. 1846.
**2460**   v. James⁸ S. Eaton, b. ca. 1849; mar. Frances _?_ and res.
               in Franklin Twp., Ohio, working in a shoe shop.


**1084. Eliab⁷ Lyon Eaton** (Isaac⁶, Jacob⁵⁻⁴, Joseph³, John²⁻¹) was
born 15 Aug 1818 in Farmington, Me.; mar. **Julia Wendell Hackett** (she
born 27 Oct 1828, dau. of Leonard and Abigail (Wendell) Hackett of
New Vineyard, Me.) on 20 Feb 1851, Manchester, Me. Eliab settled his
family for a time on the homestead farm in Farmington, but about 1858
they removed to Manchester, Me.

Children (i-ii born in Farmington; iii ?; iv-v in Manchester);

**2461**   i. Louise⁸ Lyon Eaton, b. 4 Jan 1852; mar. Abner C. Jewett of
               Augusta, Me., 23 Dec 1882.
**2462**   ii. Hiram⁸ A. Eaton, b. 2 Jun 1853.
**+2463**   iii. Greenwood⁸ P. Eaton, b. 22 May 1858; mar. Ada B. Rankin.
**2464**   iv. (Mary) Abby⁸ Eaton, b. 2 Apr 1862.
**+2465**   v. Charles⁸ G. Eaton, b. 2 Feb 1866; mar. Georgie Cummings.


**1087. Horatio⁷ Greenwood Eaton** (Isaac⁶, Jacob⁵⁻⁴, Joseph³,
John²⁻¹) was born 25 June 1828 in Farmington, Me.; mar. **Hannah
Whitmore** (born 10 Jul 1828 in Strong, Me., to Benjamin and Martha
(Perley)Whitmore) on 25 Jul 1850. In his prime, H. G. owned and oper-

ated the sawmill at Fairbanks' Mills, a post office address within Farmington.

Children born in Farmington, Me.:

2466    i. Aura[8] Genevieve Eaton, b. 15 Mar 1852.
2467    ii. Clarence[8] Melvin Eaton. b. 8 Nov 1853; mar. Alice M. Chick of New Portland, Me., 11 Jun 1880. They had one child, Florence[9] G. Eaton, b. 3 Oct 1881.
2468    iii. Florence[8] Emma Eaton, b. 25 Sep 1857.
2469    iv. Stella[8] Marion Eaton. b. 15 Jul 1860; died 17 Dec 1869.
2470    v. Daughter[8] Eaton, b. and died, 31 Oct 1871.

**1088. Lyman[7] Eaton** (Jacob[6-4], Joseph[3], John[2-1]) was born 8 Mar 1808 at Fairbanks Village, near Farmington, Me.; mar. 1st?, **Susan Whitehouse** of Orono, Me., ca. 1840. Lyman was a brick mason, and the couple settled at "Oldtown" (Orono). [Ed. Molyneux (1911) has this Lyman marrying a Lucy Brown, rather than Susan (cf. p. 443), and having a son Frank with Lucy in 1851. But Lyman did live with Susan in the US Censuses through 1870, so we ignore the Molyneux account.] Lyman died 23 Jun 1885 at Orono.

Children, presumably born in Oldtown, Me.:

2471     i. Albert[8] N. Eaton, b. ca. 1840.
2472     ii. Martha[8] Eaton, twin of Lyman, Jr., b. Nov 1845; d. young.
+2473    iii. Lyman[8] Eaton, Jr., twin of Martha. b. Nov 1845; mar Kate.
2474     iv. Juliet[8] Eaton, b. 1848.

**1090. Wendell[7] Davis Eaton** (Jacob[6-4], Joseph[3], John[2-1]) was born 15 Aug 1815 in Farmington, Me.; mar. **Hannah S. Norton** (dau. of Elihu) on 29 Dec 1842. This couple settled first upon the farm homestead where Wendell grew up; and later moved to the Alexander Hillman farm, where he died 8 Jun 1867, leaving a widow and four children.

Children born in Farmington, Me.:

+2475    i. Oliver[8] Davis Eaton, b. 11 Jan 1844; m. Emily F. Bulkeley.
+2476    ii. Jacob[8] Elihu Eaton. b. 23 Jul 1845; mar. Ella M. Fales.
2477     iii. Mary[8] Fletcher Eaton, b. 15 Dec 1847; mar. E. M. Preston, 4 Mar 1875, and had one child.
2478     iv. Lizzie[8] Norton Eaton, b. 21 Apr 1854; mar. J. S. Tilton, 30 Jun 1883, with one child by 1894.

**1097. Nathaniel[7] Thomas Eaton** (Joseph[6-5], Jacob[4], Joseph[3], John[2-1]) was born 9 Nov 1809 in Camden, Me.; mar. 1st, **Lucy A. Ha-**

**naford** of Camden on 7 Dec 1835 with whom he had three children recorded at Rockport, Me. She died 6 Mar 1846. He later mar. 2d, Miss **Nancy P. Heald** of Lincolnville, Me., 13 Nov 1854. Nathaniel was a sea captain until he was 55, and then turned to farming for the rest of his life. He died 25 May 1870, and his widow Nancy mar. 2d, Joseph Allenwood, 16 Sep 1879.

Children with Lucy in Rockport, Me.:

2479     i. Adelia⁸ Frances Eaton, b. 31 Oct 1836; died 17 May 1838.
2480    ii. Edward⁸ H. Eaton, b. 27 May 1840; unmar. into his 50s,
             then living in Worcester, Mass.
2481   iii. Lucy⁸ H. Eaton, b. 27 Dec 1844; d. 22 Aug 1858, Camden.

Child with Nancy, prob. in Camden:

2482    iv. Frank⁸ C. Eaton, b. 12 Feb 1868; unmar. when nearly 30,
             and not present in the 1900 Census for Maine.


**1102. William⁷ Eaton** (William⁶, Joseph⁵, Jacob⁴, Joseph³, John²⁻¹) was born 26 Sep 1802 in Camden, Me.; mar. **Hannah Emery** of Portland, Me., 18 Sep 1830. He was a seafaring man by trade, and he died at sea or in some foreign port in 1834, before his last child was born.

Children, presumably born in Camden:

2483     i. Martha⁸ Elizabeth Eaton, b. 12 Oct 1831; died 14 Jan 1832.
2484    ii. Louise⁸ Eaton, b. 15 Oct 1832.
2485   iii. George⁸ H. Eaton, b. 16 Mar 1835; died 20 Apr 1838.


**1104. Joseph⁷ Huse Eaton** (William⁶, Joseph⁵, Jacob⁴, Joseph³, John²⁻¹) was born 13 Mar 1807 in Camden, Me.; mar. **Harriet Hosmer** of Camden, 2 Sep 1836. They res. in Camden, and in 1850 Joseph called himself a farmer, with $2,800 in real estate. He died 26 Mar 1890.

Children born in Camden, Me.:

2486     i. Georgianna⁸ T. Eaton, b. 9 Mar 1838; mar. Fred Lewis, 25
             Jan 1868; they had two sons dying young.
2487    ii. Harriet⁸ E. Eaton, b. 1 May 1840; was married.
2488   iii. William⁸ Eaton, b. 6 Jul 1842. He was the last male descen-
             dant of his grandfather William⁶, but unmar. in 1890s.
2489    iv. Ann⁸ Maria Eaton, b. 22 Jul 1844; mar. Capt. David W.
             Avery of Camden, 23 Nov 1869; had twin sons, 1870.
2490    v. Emily⁸ H. Eaton, b. 8 May 1847; unmar. "at last account."

**1110. Charles[7] Eaton** (Isaac[6], Benjamin[5], Jacob[4], Joseph[3], John[2-1]) was born 6 Aug 1817 in Waterford, Me. In 1844 he removed to establish himself on a farm at Exeter, Me. There he mar. 1st, **Adaline Wing**, 1 Jan 1846, who the next day fell into the fire and was burned to death. He mar. 2d, **Lucinda Chandler** of Exeter, 30 Mar. 1848, with whom he had his seven sons. Charles died 20 Jul 1861.

Children with Lucinda in Exeter, Me.:

2491    i. Charles[8] O. Eaton, b. 25 Mar 1849; died Aug 1863.
2492    ii. Anson[8] Marcellus Eaton, b. 8 Feb 1851; res. in Bangor, unmar. as of 1894, a dealer in "beef and sheep."
2493    iii. Edgar[8] Chandler Eaton, b. 9 Apr 1853; res. in Waltham, Mass., unmar. as of 1894, in the "meat market business."
2494    iv. Lucien[8] Arthur Eaton, b. 23 May 1855; mar. Etta Lerman, 1881.
2495    v. Elbridge[8] Augustus Eaton, b. 12 May 1857; res. Waltham, Mass., unmar., in the meat market with brother Lucien.
+2496    vi. Joseph[8] Prescott Eaton, b. 15 Nov 1859; mar. Evie __?__ (she b. May 1857).
2497    vii. Benjamin[8] Elwell Eaton, b. 3 Mar 1861; died Mar 1862.


**1112. Benjamin[7] Elwell Eaton** (Isaac[6], Benjamin[5], Jacob[4], Joseph[3], John[2-1]) was born 19 May 1822 in Waterford, Me.; mar. **Ethalinda G. Crosby** of Albion, Me., 26 Feb 1856. He was a farmer, and settled first in Detroit, Me. In 1863, however, the family moved to Exeter, Me., where Benjamin's brother Charles had lived until his recent death, possibly to take over his farm. Wife Ethalinda died 30 Mar 1885 at Exeter.

Children:

+2498    i. Isaac[8] Arthur Eaton, b. 14 May 1857 in Detroit, Me.
+2499    ii. Howard[8] A. Eaton, b. 15 Feb 1859 in Detroit, Me.
+2500    iii. Charles[8] E. Eaton, b. 22 Feb 1869, Exeter, Me.; m. Florence.
2501    iv. Louise[8] E. Eaton, b. 5 Nov 1871; res. with her father.


**1124. Charles[7] M. Eaton** (Charles[6], Benjamin[5], Jacob[4], Joseph[3], John[2-1]) was born 28 Apr 1818 in Topsham, Me.; mar. a Topsham girl, **Deborah C. Wade**, certificate granted 28 Nov 1847. Charles was a surveyor of lumber, and the couple resided variously at Topsham, West Bath and Phippsburg , Me. He was living with son Zina at Bath in 1900.

Children:

2502    i. Zina[8] Burgess Eaton (male), b. 22 Feb 1849 in Topsham, Me.; a bachelor farmer who was farming at Bath, Me., in 1900, with his father, then 82, the only other occupant of the household.

+ **2503**   ii.  George[8] Milford Eaton, b. 10 Aug 1851; mar. Lena.

   **2504**   iii.  Harriet[8] Augusta Eaton, b. 24 Jan 1856 in Phippsburg, Me.; mar. John W. Norton, a letter carrier, 3 Oct 1878.

+ **2505**   iv.  Charles[8] Frederick Eaton, b. 2 Mar 1859; mar. Fanny W.

   **2506**   v.  Katie[8] Emma Eaton, b. 3 Aug 1861 in Phippsburg, Me.; mar. George Franklin Wallace, 1 Feb 1882, who ran a grocery store.

**1125. Joseph[7] Eaton** (Charles[6], Benjamin[5], Jacob[4], Joseph[3], John[2-1]) was born 17 Aug 1820 in Georgetown, Me., a twin of Benjamin P. Eaton; mar. 1st, **Margaret D. Clifford** (she born 6 Oct 1827 in Phippsburg) on 17 Sep 1848. They were res. in Phippsburg in 1850, when he was a "millman," on the way to becoming a lumber merchant based in Bath, Me. He mar. 2d, **Emily J. Lowell** (she born 16 Aug 1833) on 12 Sep 1858. And he mar. 3d, **Henrietta Todd** (she born 30 Oct 1841) on 17 Apr 1872.

Child with Margaret in Phippsburg, Me.:

   **2507**   i.  Charles[8] E. Eaton, b. 30 Jun 1849; was a mariner in his earlier years, but later became a lumber merchant at Bath.

Children with Emily, prob. all in Bath, Me.:

   **2508**   ii.  Helen[8] M. Eaton, b. 18 Jul 1859; mar. Edgar M. Potter, 19 Oct 1883. He was a pattern maker, res. in Bath.

   **2509**   iii.  Margaret[8] C. Eaton, b. 19 Aug 1861.

   **2510**   iv.  Frank[8] M. Eaton, b. 16 Apr 1869; died 1870.

**1133. Emery[7] W. Eaton** (Jotham[6], Benjamin[5], Jacob[4], Joseph[3], John[2-1]) was born 13 Oct 1823 in Topsham, Me.; mar. **Emily H. Tarr** on 14 Jun 1848 at Georgetown, Me. In 1850 they res. in Phippsburg where Emery, like some of his cousins, was working as a young millman. By 1860 he had moved to a farm in the Arrowsic section of Georgetown, Me., a more permanent residence.

Children:

   **2511**   i.  Charles[8] Langdon Eaton, b. 15 Oct 1851, Phippsburg, Me. He was still unmar. and living in parental home in 1900.

   **2512**   ii.  Child[8] Eaton, b. ca. 1854; died young.

   **2513**   iii.  Child[8] Eaton, b. ca. 1857; died young.

   **2514**   iv.  Sarah[8] Eaton, b. ca.1859. Alive in 1870.

+ **2515**   v.  William[8] Clay Eaton, b. 21 Sep 1861, Georgetown.

   **2516**   vi.  Carrie[8] P. Eaton, b. Jun 1865.

**1140. Jotham⁷ Edwin Eaton** (Jotham⁶, Benjamin⁵, Jacob⁴, Joseph³, John²⁻¹) was born 20 Nov 1846 in Topsham, Me.; mar. **Amelia Miller** on 25 Nov 1873, and they resided in Waldoborough, Me.

Children born in Waldoborough, Me.:

2517    i. Mattie⁸ Eaton, b. Sep 1877.
2518    ii. Seba⁸ Marble Eaton, b. Nov 1886.


**1147. Benjamin⁷ F. Eaton** (Stephen⁶, Benjamin⁵, Jacob⁴, Joseph³, John²⁻¹) was born 1 Mar 1836 in Clinton, Me.; mar. **Sarah L. Tottman** in May 1859, and after residing for a time at Clinton, became a station agent at Skowhegan, Me.

Children, born in Clinton, Me.:

2519    i. Kathleen⁸ Louisa Eaton, b. 1 Jan 1860; mar. Joseph Prescott
              Oak, 8 Jun 1889.  He was an undertaker at Skowhegan.
+2520    ii. Frederick⁸ Maurice Eaton, b. 23 Dec 1861; mar. Madeleine.


**1149. Stephen⁷ P. Eaton** (Stephen⁶, Benjamin⁵, Jacob⁴, Joseph³, John²⁻¹) was born 10 Nov 1839 in Clinton, Me.; mar. **Jennie E. Libby** of Augusta, Me. in Skowhegan on 14 Jun 1871.  They res. for a while in Augusta, but then moved to Bangor, Me., where he was conductor on the railroads until his health proved inadequate for that work.  At this point they returned to Augusta, where he went into the grocery business, and he died there 5 May 1890.

Children:

2521    i. Annie⁸ Mildred Eaton, b. 7 Oct 1875 in Bangor, Me.
2522    ii. Charles⁸ Stephen Eaton, b. 20 Nov 1878 in Bangor.
2523    iii. Philip⁸ Libby Eaton, b. 1 Mar 1886 in Augusta, Me.


**1155. George⁷ Collins Eaton** (James⁶, Benjamin⁵, Jacob⁴, Joseph³, John²⁻¹) was born 4 Mar 1840 in Fairfield, Me.; mar. **Mrs. Emily Marie (Heard) Russell** of Solon, Me. on 30 Apr 1871 at Fairfield.  The couple settled in Fairfield.

Children at Fairfield, Me.:

2524    i. George⁸ Leslie Eaton, b. 26 Jan 1874.  A solo boarder in
              Fairfield, 1900.  May have mar. later.
2525    ii. Harry⁸ Chandler Eaton, b. 10 Apr 1875.  Not with family in
              1880.

**2526** iii. Mae[9] (Mary?) Estella Eaton, b. 14 Oct 1877.

**1159. Hiram[7] Alfred Eaton** (Hiram[6], Benjamin[5], Jacob[4], Joseph[3], John[2-1]) was born in 1841 at New Limerick, Me. He mar. twice: 1st, **Hattie Morrill**, having four children; and 2d, **Sarah M. Sanders**, with whom he had another four. Hiram farmed at New Limerick.

Children with Hattie in New Limerick, Me.:

**2527** i. George[8] Eaton, b. ca. 1869.
**2528** ii. Cora[8] Eaton, b. 12 Apr 1871.
**2529** iii. Nancy[8] Eaton, b. ca. 1876.
**2530** iv. Harriet[8] M. Eaton, b. Mar 1881; mar. Theodore Hatfield.

Children with Sarah in New Limerick:

**2531** v. Nellie[8] Eaton, b. Mar 1885.
**2532** vi. Hiram[8] W. Eaton, b. Sep 1886.
**2533** vii. Lester[8] Eaton, b. Jul 1891.
**2534** viii. Fay[8] Eaton, b. Jul 1899.

**1162. Charles[7] H. Eaton** (Hiram[6], Benjamin[5], Jacob[4], Joseph[3], John[2-1]) was born Apr 1847 in New Limerick, Me.; mar. **Miranda Bragg** in 1872, and res. on a farm in Houlton, Me.

Children born in Houlton, Me.:

**2535** i. Charles[8] Leonard Eaton, b. 1874.
**2536** ii. George[8] Franklin Eaton, b. Jan 1876; later called "Frank G."
**2537** iii. Lizzie[8] May Eaton, b. May 1878; mar. a Sherwood.

**1163. Abial[7] Washburne Eaton** (Horace[6], Benjamin[5], Jacob[4], Joseph[3], John[2-1]) was born 20 Jan 1851 in Topsham, Me; mar. **Georgiana Knight** (she born Jun 1852) on 29 Dec 1871. The couple resided on the old homestead of his forebears in Topsham.

Children born in Topsham, Me.:

+**2538** i. Frank[8] W. Eaton, b. 1 Jan 1874; mar. Nellie B. Thibbets.
 **2539** ii. Stanley B. Eaton, b. 9 Sep 1879.

**1165. Henry[7] Moore Eaton** (Henry[6], Ephraim[5], Henry[4], Ephraim[3], John[2-1]) was born 6 June 1806 in Candia, N.H.; mar. 1st, **Eliza Alden Parker** (she born ca. 1803) and res. on the old homestead farm which his grandfather, Ephraim[5] Eaton had purchased of Benjamin

Batchelder (No. 113, 2d Range, 2d Division) when the former first came
from Salisbury, Mass., to Candia in 1778.   Henry ran the prosperous
farm but listed himself as a   merchant in 1850.  "Like his father and
grandfather, (Henry[7]) was a leading man in town and was much engaged
in town business.  He was selectman a number of years, town clerk, a representative to the state legislature two years and town agent for a considerable period.  He was also Captain of the Candia Light Infantry...and for
many years a member of the Congregational Church" (Moore, 1893).
After wife Eliza died of tuberculosis at Derry, N.H., 17 Jan 1860, Henry[7]
mar. 2d, **Hannah Godfrey Lane**, 26 May 1863.  He himself died 21 Mar
1886, in Candia.  Hannah died 3 Apr 1892.

Children with Eliza in Candia:

**2540**      i. Frederick[8] Parker Eaton, b. ca. 1836.  He died
              23 May 1850.
**2541**     ii. Ellen[8] Susan Eaton, b. 18 Nov 1844.  Apparently never
              mar., she d. 30 Dec 1925 at Candia.
**2542**    iii. Leonard[8] Eaton, b. 1849; mar. Ella F. Peavey, 2 Apr 1860
              in Derry, N.H., but then the trail is lost.

     **1166. Ephraim[7] Eaton** (Henry[6], Ephraim[5], Henry[4], Ephraim[3],
John[2-1]) was born 13 Sep 1808 in Candia, N.H.; mar. **Mary Jane Cilley**
of Deerfield, N.H., 5 Oct 1842.  The *History of Concord, N.H.* (1903) has
the following item: "Ephraim Eaton, a native of Candia, N.H., graduated
at Dartmouth College in 1833, studied law with Samuel Fletcher, Esq.,
and opened an office in Concord, N.H. in 1837 and continued in business till 1853, when he relinquished the practice of law and moved to
Troy, N.Y."  Ephraim had either invented or acquired possession of a
patent for the construction of anvils and moved to Troy, where there were
facilities for their manufacture not readily found elsewhere.  In the 1860
Census at Troy he lists himself as a "rivet-maker."  He died in Troy, 3
Mar 1863, leaving a widow and two children, but is bur. in Concord, N.H.

Children, with Mary Jane in Concord, N.H.:

**2543**      i. Mary[8] Jane Eaton, b. 1843.  She was a teacher for a number
              of years in the National Soldiers Home at Dayton, Ohio.
              She mar. an officer at the home, William Bayard, who in
              his last years was in the corresponding hospital in New
              Jersey.  Mary Jane was living with her mother in Deer-
              field, N.H. in the 1890s.
**2544**     ii. Henry[8] Eaton, b. 13 Aug 1847; mar. Ella Jenkins (she born
              8 Jul 1849 in East Boston, Mass.) on 22 Feb 1870 and res.
              in Chelsea, Mass at 11 Matthews St.  Henry was an invalid,
              and Ella was a compositor.  They had a daughter, Mary[8]
              Ella Eaton, b. 14 Sep 1871.  She later became a 1st assis-
              tant in the Fitz Public Library in Chelsea.

**1167. Charles[7] Edwin Eaton** (Henry[6], Ephraim[5], Henry[4], Ephraim[3], John[2-1]) was born 10 Dec 1811 in Candia, N.H. As a young man, Charles took over his uncle Peter's store in Candia when the latter moved to Concord in 1835. After three or four years in this harness, however, Charles decided to remove to Ohio. Although the timing of his marriage is unknown, it is likely that it occurred in this general period, since his wife **Elizabeth McReady**, later called "Eliza," was a N.H. native, born ca. 1814, when she was listed in his Ohio household in 1850. Or he may have found her en route, accounting for our lack of a marriage record, since in the next two Censuses her birthplace is given as N.Y. State. It is very likely that this couple had arrived in Ohio in time for the less informative 1840 Census, although the Charles E. Eaton heading a two-person household at Dresden, Muskingum Co., Ohio, in that year is checked off as age 15-19, rather than as being in his 20s, like his female companion. That this is error is signalled further by the fact that the only Charles E. Eaton in the 1850 Census for Ohio is also found in Muskingum Co., although now in Jefferson Twp, where he remains through 1870. Charles is listed as a rather prosperous "merchant" in the 1860 Census, carrying on his skills from youth; and by 1870 he is a very prosperous banker (e.g, $12,000 in real estate).

Children (at least those surviving early childhood), born in Muskingum Co., Ohio, but without further trail we can find:

2545    i. Charles[8] H. Eaton, b. ca. 1844.
2546    ii. William[8] C. (or E.) Eaton, b. ca. 1846.


**1174.    Ephraim[7] Kelley Eaton** (Peter[6], Ephraim[5], Henry[4], Ephraim[3], John[2-1]) was born 1 Aug 1814 in Candia, N.H. That Ephraim was from the outset a clever lad is enshrined in the town history (Moore, 1893). A local notable, Joseph Carr, finding himself bedeviled by squirrels demolishing his cornfield (how times change!) baited a box trap to catch one. When he found the trap sprung, he carried the box to his home, inviting in the neighbors, including Ephraim, age 14, to watch its final moments. He put an outsized tom cat at one end of the room, and then opened the box. A large bullfrog leaped out. Mr. Carr was enraged, and fingered Ephraim as the only bystander clever enough to have designed the prank. He demanded that Ephraim's father thrash him for it; but Peter[6] refused, being no little amused and impressed by his son's design. Ephraim[7] mar. **Hannah Augusta Kendall**, a native of Boston, 15 Feb 1851. Ephraim was a composer of music, and after his children were all born, removed to Gloversville, N.Y., where he died.

Children born in Candia, N.H.:

2547    i. Francis[8] Edward Eaton, b. 5 Dec 1852; died 29 Jun 1853.
2548    ii. Emily[8] Jane Eaton, b. 8 Apr 1854; died 21 Aug 1855.

**2549**    iii. Florence[8] Nightingale Eaton, b. 27 Aug 1856; mar. George
            Sparhawk, having at least one son. [The given names
            here have an unmistakable source; what is fascinating is
            the speed of transmission to the little N.H. village. The
            famed "Lady with the Lamp" had not gone to the Crimea
            with her nurses until late in 1854, and then accomplished
            little for six months or more till complaints to London
            had brought more adequate resources and a quelling of
            officer corps resistance to her efforts. Thus her opera-
            tion did not get into high gear until the summer of 1855.
            Within twelve months she had compiled a track record
            which filtered back to London sufficiently to make her
            a celebrity there; and word of this had gotten to Candia
            with enough force and luster that Ephraim and Hannah
            wanted to commemorate this angel of mercy.]

**2550**    iv. Edward[8] Kendall Eaton, b. 5 Dec 1862; died in infancy.

**2551**    v. Frederick[8] Herbert Eaton, b. 8 Jun 1864.

**1177.   Francis[7]  Brown  Eaton**  (Peter[6],  Ephraim[5],  Henry[4],
Ephraim[3], John[2-1]) was born 26 Feb 1825 in Candia, N.H. He received his
education past eighth grade at the Pembroke and New Boston Acade-
mies. In 1852 he wrote and published "History of Candia, once known
as Charmingfare, with Notices of Some of the Early Families." He was at
this time the assistant editor and Washington correspondent of the *Manchester (N.H.) Daily American.* He married **Lucretia Lane**, daughter of
John Lane, Esq., 1 Jan 1854. In 1855 he began ten years as Librarian at
the Manchester City Library, writing on the side for the *Daily Mirror,* and
acting as correspondent for the *Boston Traveller.* From Dec 1861 thru
1862 he was editor and proprietor of the *N.H. Journal of Agriculture.* In
1864 he replaced a *Boston Daily Advertiser* staff member who had been
sent to the war front in the South. After the War he became an assistant
editor of the *Boston* Journal. From 1866 to 1869 he was stationed in
Montreal and Portland, Me., for the Customs Department. He then returned to Manchester and was a bookseller for 11 years. He later compiled sketches of the life and public services of ex-Gov. Smyth, printed
for private circulation in 1885. In this period he was a director of the
First National Bank of Manchester and vice-president of the Merrimac
River Savings Bank. He was also the clerk of his church. (Adapted from
Moore, 1893). He died 26 Jul 1904 in Manchester, followed by wife
Lucretia, 18 Nov 1907. There is no report of any issue.

**1181.  Henry[7] Eaton**  (Henry[6], Peter[5A], Henry[4], Ephraim[3], John[2-1])
was born ca. May 1807, prob. in Corinth, Vt. before his parents returned
to Salisbury, Mass. He mar. **Jemima[7] Eaton (#1004)**, oldest child of
Tristram Eaton of Salisbury, int. entered 17 Aug 1829. They may have
gone briefly back to Corinth, Vt., but settled permanently in Salisbury,

Mass. Henry was a mariner when he died there of yellow fever, 17 Jul 1845. Wife Jemima survived him until 4 Aug 1869.

Children born in Salisbury, Mass.:

2552    i. Sarah[8] Ann Eaton, b. 20 Oct 1829; mar. Rev. Moses T. Cilley, a Methodist minister.
2553    ii. Abigail[8] G. Eaton, b. 4 Jul 1833; mar. Ephraim B. Wadleigh, 9 Mar 1853.
2554    iii. Adaline[8] J. Eaton, b. 2 Nov 1836; mar. Benjamin T. Carr, 12 Mar 1855.
+2555    iv. Samuel[8] Eaton, b. 12 Oct 1844; mar. Lizzie T. Dow, 1870.


**1186. Frederick[7] Plummer Eaton** (Stephen[6], Peter[5A], Henry[4], Ephraim[3], John[2-1]) was born 18 Oct 1822 in Corinth, Vt.; mar. 1st, **Julia A. Dearborn** (she born 23 June 1823 in Corinth) on 8 Nov 1842. They res. in Corinth, where he was an intelligent and enterprising farmer for many years. Wife Julia died 5 Dec 1889, and he mar. 2d, **Wid. Rebecca M.** Hansen, 15 Mar 1894. He died 23 Jan 1899 in Corinth.

Children born in Corinth, Vt.:

+2556    i. Clinton[8] Dewitt Eaton, b. 17 May 1844; mar. Belinda..
+2557    ii. Olin[8] Stanley Eaton, b. 28 Apr 1846; mar. Mary Wright.
+2558    iii. Frederic[8] Albion Eaton, b. 27 Dec 1849; mar. Julia Wright.
+2559    iv. Frank[8] Julien Eaton, twin of Fannie, b. 21 Jul 1854.
2560    v. Fannie[8] Julia Eaton, twin of Frank, b. 21 Jul 1854; mar. a Spear; taught school in Corinth when a young lady.


**1194. Peter[7] Eaton** (Peter[6-5A], Henry[4], Ephraim[3], John[2-1]) was born 19 Feb 1819 in Corinth, Vt.; mar. **Harriet Cabot** of Hartland, Vt., ca. 1844, and settled on a farm in Corinth. Wife Harriet died 9 May 1856, from complications of childbirth; Peter died 4 Jul 1873.

Children born in Corinth, Vt.:

2561    i. Cynthia[8] Ann Eaton, b. 7 Dec 1845; mar. Henry F. Porter, a carpenter, 4 Jan 1870. She soon died, 6 Nov 1872.
2562    ii. Emily[8] J. Eaton, b. 12 Feb 1848; mar. Hiram Moore, 4 Dec 1877, and they res. in Plainfield, Vt.
2563    iii. George[8] C. Eaton, b. 4 Feb 1850; died 15 Feb 1854.
+2564    iv. George[8A] C. Eaton, b. 5 May 1856; mar. Emma Burgen.


**1195. Joshua[7] French Eaton** (Samuel[6], Peter[5A], Henry[4], Ephraim[3], John[2-1]) was born 16 Aug 1808 in Salisbury, Mass.; mar. 1st, **Mary Stevens**, also of Salisbury, daughter of Samuel and Dolly Stevens, on 18 Jan

1844.   They settled in Salisbury where he inherited the prosperous homestead farm of his father and grandfather.   Days after bearing her third child, Mary died, 10 Aug 1855.   Joshua mar. 2d, **Abbie A. Fittz** (she born 4 Jun 1840 in Salisbury), on 16 Mar 1859.   They had further children; and Joshua died 29 Jul 1886.

Children with Mary in Salisbury, Mass.:

| | |
|---|---|
| **2565** | i. Emily[8] Stevens Eaton, b. 9 Jul 1846; res. Salisbury, unmar. |
| **2566** | ii. Eliza[8] Ann Eaton, b. 19 Oct 1848; died 7 Apr 1863. |
| **2567** | iii. Samuel[8] Warren Eaton, b. 7 Apr 1855; was a bachelor farmer in Salisbury. |

Children with Abbie in Salisbury, Mass.:

| | |
|---|---|
| **2568** | iv. Willard[8] French Eaton, b. 13 Dec 1861; died 11 Apr 1863. |
| **2569** | v. Herbert[8] Stacy Eaton, b. 4 Dec 1866. |
| **2570** | vi. Son[8] Eaton, b. 24 Sep 1868; died 30 Sep 1868. |
| **2571** | vii. Frederic[8] Fittz Eaton, b. 20 Oct 1870. |

**1203.  Richard**[7] **Eaton** (Henry[6], Paul[5], Jabez[4], Ephraim[3], John[2-1]) was born 12 Dec 1797 in Candia, N.H.   Tradition says that he was a fifer at Fort Constitution in Newcastle, N.H., in the War of 1812.   After the death of his mother he travelled somewhat in the Middle Atlantic states, but finally settled for a while in Fredericksburg, Va., where he mar. **Catherine C. Hughlett**, a native of that city, about 1837, and had his first child there.   He then returned to Candia for a spell, but after two more children there he went south again to res. on Capitol Hill in Washington, D. C.   He died there in 1859.   The widow died in 1875.

Children (not listed are some infant deaths between 1844 and 1858):

| | |
|---|---|
| **+2572** | i. Henry[8] True Eaton, b. Aug 1838, in Fredericksburg, Va. |
| **2573** | ii. Albert[8] Herman Eaton, b. ca. 1841 in Candia, N.H.; removed to Colorado, leaving no trail. |
| **2574** | iii. James[8] K. Polk Eaton, b. ca. 1844 in Candia. N.H.  Not visible in the area in subsequent Censuses. |
| **2575** | iv. Emma[8] Hughlett Eaton, twin of Josephine, b. ca. 1858 at Washington, D. C.  Engaged with her sister in millinery enterprises in that city. |
| **2576** | v. Josephine[8] Alice Eaton, twin of Emma, b. ca. 1858 at Washington, D.C.; a milliner with her sister. |

**1206.  Henry**[7] **S. Eaton** (Henry[6], Paul[5], Jabez[4], Ephraim[3], John[2-1]) was born 22 Oct 1802, in Candia, N.H.   He mar. 1st, **Lavina Colburn**

**Woodbury** of Acworth, N.H., who was born ca. 1802, with whom he probably had no children before her death at Candia, 22 Mar 1850; 2d, **Mary Ann Smith** of Barrington, N.H. (she born ca. 24 May 1819) on 26 Nov 1850 at Newmarket, N.H., who then died 8 May 1855; and 3d, **Alamanza Eaton** of Candia, 19 Aug 1855. He was a carpenter and lived in Candia well into the 1850s, but then took his small family north to Piermont, N.H. in Grafton Co., where he died after 1860.

Child with Mary Ann in Candia, N.H.:

2577     i. Walter[8] Henry Eaton, b. 25 Apr 1852; died 7 Feb 1894 in Andover, Mass. No sign of marriage.

**1209. True[7] Eaton** (Henry[6], Paul[5], Jabez[4], Ephraim[3], John[2-1]) was born 17 Oct 1809 in Candia, N.H.; mar. **Susan G. York** of Deerfield, N.H. ca. 1837. They res. on a farm in Candia. He was at one time Captain of a militia Company in Candia of the 17th Regt. of the 3d Brigade of the 1st N.H. Division. Wife Susan died 10 Apr 1884; True died 10 May 1886.

Children in Candia, N.H.:

+2578     i. Henry[8] True Eaton, b. 21 Sep 1838; mar. Julia Doe, 1871.
  2579    ii. Martin[8] V. B. Eaton, b. 8 May 1841; in 1880 he was at Cranston, R.I., where he was an instructor in the shoe shop of the State Prison. He brought the manufacture of shoes back to Candia, N.H., when he returned to mar. Ella J. Barker, daughter of Abraham L. Barker in Candia, on 6 Sep 1881. He continued in this line during residences in Haverhill and Lynn for the next thirty years. In 1891 he began the manufacture of antique furniture at Lynn, an industry he brought back to Concord, N.H. He then res. next to his brother Henry in Pembroke, N.H. (Stearns, 1908). No mention of children.
  2580   iii. Frank[8] Waldo Eaton, b. ca. 1843; probably never married. He was living with his parents and sister Elizabeth on the Candia homestead when age 35 in 1880, as a "shoe bottomer"; and living with sister Elizabeth there in 1900. He died in Candia in 1929.
  2581    iv. Elizabeth[8] J. Eaton, b. ca. 1845.
  2582     v. Sarah[8] True Eaton, b. 8 May 1847; mar. Charles O. Merrill in 1865 and had at least two children.,
  2583    vi. Susan[8] Ella Eaton, b. 12 Jan 1850; died 22 Feb 1852.

**1215. Ira[7] Eaton** (Azel[6], Joshua[5], Jabez[4], Ephraim[3], John[2-1]) was born in 1801, probably in Onondaga Co., N.Y., although starting at this point, and following this twig out to thru the ninth generation, our senior author provides no geography at all. He reports that Ira[7] mar. **Almira Hall**, Dec 1822, and that these six children were born to them somewhere:

+ **2584**   i. Joel[8] Hall Eaton, b. 1827; mar. Margaret Gloyd.
  **2585**  ii. Laura[8] Eaton, b. 1829; mar. John C. Stevens 21 Nov 1855 and had one child.
+ **2586**  iii. Emery[8] Eaton, b. 1833; mar. Frances Delano, 1852.
+ **2587**  iv. Galutia[8] Eaton, b. 1837; mar. Ursula Rose, 1861.
+ **2588**   v. William[8] L. Eaton, b. 1842; mar. Rebecca Jackson, 1866.
+ **2589**  vi. Hiram[8] Eaton, b. 1847; mar. Emily Day, Nov 1867.

**1218. Oliver**[7] **Eaton** (Jabez[6], Joshua[5], Jabez[4], Ephraim[3], John[2-1]) was born 29 Sep 1803 in Seabrook, N.H.. He became known throughout Rockingham Co. as "Squire Oliver." He was a careful observer of things around him, and knew more of the Eatons of his native county than any man of his day. He had a remarkable memory and could relate the incidents in the life of his grandfather with as much vividness as if they had been scenes in his own life. He was the attorney for most of the people in the towns surrounding his home. He said to the writer in his own home at Hampton Falls that he had settled over 50 estates as executor or administrator. His children having died previous to his own death, he left his homestead to his housekeeper, and the balance of his property to three trustees instructed to invest the same until it reached $20,000, whereupon they were to erect a suitable building for a high school in Seabrook.

In his genealogical manuscripts loaned to the writer [i.e., our senior author] after his death by one of his trustees, I found the following description of the scenes of his birth which is a fair sample of his style of writing:

> "On Michaelmas day of this century in the year three, I was born near the borders of the great marshes, through and over which the tide waters of the feeders of the Winacunnet River ebb and flow, in a lone cot, on a rocky glade, in the wild woods of Webbacowett, just before the gray light of the morning was mellowed by the refracted rays of the rising sun, when all nature was hushed in silence save only the distant roaring of the wavy Atlantic and the low rustling of the forest foliage in the autumnal wind. On the northeasterly part of these premises was an Indian hamlet protected on three sides by the walnut tree groves through which the Indian had filled the echoes of this wild retreat with their sweet vocal lullabies and melodies."

**Oliver**[7] **Eaton** was twice married: 1st to **Caroline Hull**, daughter of Rev. Elias Hull of Seabrook, 15 Dec 1831. She had been born 2 Nov 1806; and she died 1 Mar 1835, without issue. He mar. 2d, **Mrs. Miriam**

**(Brown) Dow** (she born 8 Feb 1810 to Jonathan and Judith Brown, and the widow of Benjamin Dow) on 15 Jan 1840. She died 3 Nov 1857. In the period into the 1860s, Oliver lived on the north side of Walton Road, on the first property west of the railroad track. Before 1870, however, he had moved a few miles north to Hampton Falls, where he died in Jan 1892.

Children with Miriam, prob. in Seabrook:

2590    i. Sarah⁸ Eaton, b. ca. late 1842; mar. John Locke, by whom she had one son, Clarence Locke. She died soon after, 21 Jan 1872.

2591    ii. Franklin⁸ T., b. ca. 1844; he can be seen as a young man, 1870, single and working in the shoe factory; d. unmar.

**1222. Edwin⁷ Eaton** (Jabez⁶, Joshua⁵, Jabez⁴, Ephraim³, John²⁻¹) was born 15 Jan 1813 in Seabrook, N.H.; mar. **Mary J. George** (b. 1819 to John George) 30 Aug 1839. It seems likely that Edwin spent some of his salad days in Pennsylvania, since his wife was a native of that state and their first child was born there. Soon thereafter, however, the couple were back in Seabrook where Edwin tended a medium-sized farm on the north side of Walton Rd. near the head of Washington St., and devoted himself primarily to teaching in the local schools. By the 1870 Census this couple had an empty nest. They both died in Seabrook: Mary in 1883; Edwin in 1891.

Children:

2592    i. Susan⁸ C. Eaton, b. 2 Jun 1840 in Philadelphia, Pa.; mar. William Moody, a carpenter, and at least in later years resided at 280 Prospect St. in Cambridge, Mass.

2593    ii. Margaret⁸ R. Eaton, b. 29 Aug 1843 in Seabrook; mar. Benjamin F. Moody, a sea captain.

2594    iii. (Edwin) Morris⁸ Eaton, b. 26 Jan 1846 in Seabrook; died 17 Apr 1870.

2595    iv. Mary⁸ Emily Eaton, b. 7 Jan 1849 in Seabrook; mar. Jeremiah F. Boyd, a soldier returned from the Civil War, 11 Nov 1867. They had five sons before Jeremiah died 12 May 1878.

**1224. Charles⁷ᴬ A. Eaton** (Jabez⁶, Joshua⁵, Jabez⁴, Ephraim³, John²⁻¹) was born 6 Nov 1827 in Seabrook, N.H.; mar. **Abby⁷ March Eaton** (#1021) (dau. of James⁶ Eaton of Salisbury) on 30 Oct 1850. Abby was one of the seven sisters who grew up on the site of the original homestead of the immigrant, John¹ Eaton, on Beach Rd. in East Salisbury, and who were co-owners of the property during their adulthood. The couple res. in Seabrook on Walton Rd. near the other brothers,

where Charles was a shoemaker and farmer.   Wife Abby died 23 Jun
1893.

Children in Seabrook, N.H.:

2596      i. Lauriston[8] M. Eaton, b. ca. Feb 1851; never mar., he died
             13 Apr 1911 at Salisbury.
2597     ii. Mary[8] Balch Eaton, a twin that survived birth, ca. 1854;
             mar. Manfred Dow, 5 Sep 1876 (Seabrook record).  This
             couple were the last of the Eatons to own the Beach Rd.
             homestead.  She died Nov 1930.
+2598    iii. LaRoy[8] A. Eaton, b. ca. 1856; mar. Josephine Wilson, 1877.
+2599    iv. James[8] Austin Eaton, b. 24 Dec 1858; mar. Alma Minard.
+2600     v. Charles[8] Eaton, b. ca. 14 Nov 1859; mar. Abbie Beckman.
+2601    vi. Edwin[8] M. Eaton, b. 11 Mar 1873; mar. Ethel May Welch.


     **1225. Giles[7] Eaton** (Joshua[6-5], Jabez[4], Ephraim[3], John[2-1]) was born
31 Jan 1802 in Seabrook, N.H.; mar. **Waity Collins** of Hampton Falls, 1
Jul 1824, at Hampton Falls.  The marriage was an unhappy one, and the
couple was soon estranged, although they had had by that time two children.  By 1830 Giles was back living in his natal home and working on
his father's farm on Walton Rd. or others in the vicinity in Seabrook,
through the death of the father in 1853 and until his own death of lung
problems, 2 Jun 1865 (Seabrook *VR* in Concord, N.H.).

Children with Waity:

2602      i. Angeline[8] Eaton, b. in 1825; mar. George W. Wetherell; res.
             in Exeter, N.H. and had one daughter, Mary, who d. at 16.
2603     ii. George[8] C. Eaton, b. 28 Jun 1827; mar. 1st, Elizabeth Ann
             Emerson of Kennebunk, Me., Jan 1850, with no issue
             from this union.  He mar. 2d, Melissa Bolley of Lebanon,
             Me., Dec 1871, and had one daughter Lizzie A. Eaton, b.
             31 Jul 1874.  The couple resided on a small farm in Exe-
             ter, N.H., where George was also a shoemaker.

                          * * * * * * *

**B.** *The Haverhill Branch*

**1236. Peter**[7] **Sidney Eaton** (Peter[6], Joseph[5], Thomas[4-2], John[1]) was born 7 Oct 1798 in Boxford, Mass.; mar. **Elizabeth Ann Leman** (she born 4 Dec 1804 in Charlestown, Mass.) on 4 Dec 1828. Peter[7] Jr. early decided to follow his father into the ministry, and he studied with this in view. He graduated at Harvard in 1818, and at Andover Theological in 1822. He was first settled into a pastorate at West Amesbury (later Merrimack, Mass.) in 1826, and remained there until 1837. He undoubtedly was a pastor at other churches as well, since he also resided at Worcester for a period. As of 1850, the family was ensconced at Chelsea, Mass., and he reported that he was a publisher there. He died at Chelsea, 13 Mar 1863.

Children:

**2604**    i. Sidney[8] Payson Eaton, b. 16 Sep 1829 in West Amesbury, Mass.; married Abigail Dunham of Bridgewater, Mass., Dec 1861, and settled in Chelsea, Mass. as an upholsterer. This marriage and career was very short-lived, with no issue reported, as less than 15 months later Sidney died in a hospital in New Orleans (17 Mar 1863), presumably a demise linked in some way to Civil War service.

**2605**   ii. Henry[8] Martyn Eaton. b. 28 Jun 1835 in West Amesbury. He was a wood engraver, and res. unmar. in West Somerville, Mass.

**2606**  iii. Elizabeth[8] Ann Eaton, b. 16 May 1841 in Worcester, Mass.; mar. Moses Foster Haskell (he b. 25 Jul 1841) in Rockport, Mass., 5 Nov 1868. He was a lithographer, and they resided in Boston.

**1242. Obadiah**[7] **Page Eaton** (Thomas[6], Moses[5], Thomas[4-2], John[1]) was born 13 Sep 1800 in Francestown, N.H. His early wanderings carried him to a church membership initiated Sep 1825 in New Ipswich, N.H., and to his bride, **Clarissa Farley** of Hollis, N.H., whom he mar. 9 Aug 1829. The couple res. New Ipswich with no issue of their own at least through the 1830 Census, but in due time Obadiah decided both to go west and to follow his father into the medical profession. He graduated from a medical college in Cincinnati, O., and then settled as a doctor in Smithland, Livingston Co., Ky., on the Ohio River well downstream from Cincinnati. He died at some time before Sep 1854.

Child (supposedly the only son):

**2607**    i. George[8] F. Eaton, b. ?  ; although family lore says that he res. as an adult in St. Louis, Mo., we have not found him there in a modest search. It is possible that he is the

George F. Eaton in the 1880 Census at Burrows, Carroll Co., Ind., age 37, reporting that he and both of his parents were born in N.H.

**1243. Moses[7] Webster Eaton** (Thomas[6], Moses[5], Thomas[4-2], John[1]) was born 14 Apr 1803 in Francestown, N.H.; mar. **Louisa Shephard Lawrence** of Alstead, N.H., 17 Sep 1828, and the couple res. on the stock farm in Francestown originally purchased by his grandfather and run by his father as well. Wife Louisa died 19 Dec 1879 in Nashua, N.H.; where Moses W. also died on 29 Dec 1883.

Children in Francestown, N.H.:

+2608    i. Thomas[8] Hutchinson Eaton, b. 1829; mar. Mary Goss, 1863.
2609    ii. Betsey[8] Susanna Eaton, b. ca. Mar 1833; mar. William Tucker Hall of No. Chelsea (now Revere), Mass. and res. there. After five children, Betsey died 24 Feb 1868 and Mr. Hall mar. 2d, Fanny Jane Goss of Henniker, N.H. Her Goss family had been connected with the Obadiah Eaton family in Weare, N.H.
2610    iii. James[8] Harvey Dudley Eaton, b. about 1835; res. in Boston, Mass., unmarried.
2611    iv. Louisa[8] Frances Eaton, b. 19 Sep 1837; mar. Cornelius V. Dearborn (b. 1832 in Corinth, Vt.), 18 Jun 1857. He held many municipal and state offices with honor to himself and to the government. They had six children. He died 18 Apr 1886.
+2612    v. Moses[8] Harvey Eaton, b. 8 Jun 1840; mar. Ann Fulton, 1867.

**1254. True[7] Eaton** (Thomas[6-2], John[1]) was born 16 Feb 1805 in Hopkinton, N.H.; mar. **Betsey Marshall** (born 13 Dec 1803 to John and Lucy Marshall in Bradford, N.H.) on 7 Jan 1838. They res. on a farm in Bradford, where True farmed and worked part-time as a cooper, while his wife busied herself with the tailor's trade. He died 6 Oct 1871, and she on 15 Dec 1872, both at Bradford.

Children in Bradford, N.H.:

+2613    i. Marshall[8] Eaton, b. 1 Apr 1840; mar. Angie Johnson, 1865.
2614    ii. John[8] Eaton, b. 11 Aug 1842; was a member of Co. H, 6th Regt., N.H. Volunteers, and died of sickness in Port Hudson, La. 24 Jul 1862; never married.
+2615    iii. Ira[8] K. Eaton, b. 21 Dec 1844; mar. Addie Barney, 1873.

**1257. Rufus[7] P. Eaton** (Thomas[6-2], John[1]) was born 6 Feb 1809 in Hopkinton, N.H.; mar. 1st, **Sophalia Gibson** of Newbury, N.H., 1 Sep

1835, and res. initially at Bradford, N.H., where they had one daughter.
The couple left Bradford in 1838 for the West, where Rufus continued
practicing law. Sophalia died in Aug 1855 at Two Rivers, Wisconsin.
Rufus then mar. 2d, **Mrs. Marietta R. Bailey** of Calumet, Wisc. She died
in Calumet, Oct. 1865, leaving no issue. He then mar. 3d, **Mrs. Rachel
Hill** of Manitowoc, Wisc., and they had one son. Rufus died 13 Apr
1883 in Manitowoc.

Child with Sophalia:

**2616**    i. Elvira[8] Eaton, b. 18 Mar 1836 in Bradford, N.H.; mar. James
            A. Loomis and lived in Kansas.

Child with Rachel:

**2617**    ii. George[8] R. Eaton, b. 19 Mar 1868 in Fond du Lac, Wisc.;
            mar. Eleanor Barnett Karns of Butler Co., Pa. 3 Jul 1889,
            and res. at 6209 Princeton Ave. in Chicago. Ill. In 1896
            he was a city employee, working as paymaster for the
            Dep't of Public Works in City Hall. In 1900 he was living
            at 6138 Wentworth Ave. in Chicago, in a dwelling unit
            with a boarder only.

**1261. Jasper[7] Hazen Eaton** (Moses[6], Thomas[5-2], John[1]) was born
16 Sep 1811 in Hopkinton, N.H.; mar. **Elizabeth Tuttle** (she born 11
Nov 1815 in Milton, N.H.) on 7 May 1837. The new couple settled in
So. Boston, Mass., where Jasper carried on a flour and grain business for
some years. For many years thereafter, he served as the "public weigher"
(verifier of weights and measures used in commerce), a tribute to his con-
scientiousness in all business transactions. Wife Elizabeth died at the So.
Boston homestead 22 Mar 1883; Jasper followed on 10 Sep 1888.

Children in So. Boston, Mass.:

**2618**    i. Albert[8] Theodore Eaton, b. 16 Feb 1839; died 3 Jun 1842.
**2619**    ii. Maria[8] Elizabeth Eaton, b. 14 Mar 1843. Never married.
**2620**    iii. Ellen[8] Augusta Eaton, b. 20 Jun 1845; an official in the
            Boston Public Library.
**2621**    iv. Emma[8] Louise Eaton, b. 24 Dec 1849; a school teacher.

**1262. Moses[7] French Eaton** (Joseph[6], Thomas[5-2], John[1]) was born
25 Dec 1810 in Groton, N.H. In early life he went to Lowell, Mass., and
from there to Pittsburgh, Pa. in 1836 where he was engaged as teacher in
the Western University (later the "University of Pittsburgh") on Third
Avenue. He mar. **Sarah E. Gregg** of the "South Side" of Pittsburgh (and
related to the prominent Ormsby family) on 16 Apr 1839. In 1868 he
removed to Philadelphia, where he spent 17 years as a teacher of elocu-

tion, after which he returned to Pittsburgh, although in the impaired health of old age. For many years he was an active member of the Trinity Episcopal Church, and for some time Superintendent of its Sunday School. The couple had no children, and wife Sarah had died in Philadelphia about 1878. Moses F. died in Pittsburgh 31 Mar 1888.

**1265. Leonard**[7] **Hobart Eaton.** (Joseph[6], Thomas[5-2], John[1]) was born 20 Apr 1817 in Groton, N.H. In 1833 he left the farm to go to Lowell, Mass., where he studied for four years to become a teacher, working as an aid in a physician's office to support himself. After teaching in Lowell, 1837-39, he removed to Pittsburgh to join his brother, Moses, in teaching at a private school. It was in this period that he met **Mary Ann Berford**, a Pittsburgh native born 17 Sep 1825, and they were mar. 26 Dec 1843. Then for nearly a half century he taught in Pittsburgh public schools, serving several lengthy stints as Principal of various Pittsburgh schools, including those in Third Ward in Allegheny City. In 1890 he retired to devote his energies to the Western Pennsylvania Humane Society of which he was President and Superintendent at the time of his death on 11 Feb 1893.

Children with Mary Ann in Pittsburgh:

2622    i. Joseph[8] Berford Eaton, b. 1 Nov 1844; mar. Emma Grace Andrews 21 May 1875 and res. in the East End, Pittsburgh, having no children.
2623    ii. Mary[8] George Eaton, b. 4 Nov 1846; in 1896 was residing with her mother in Allegheny City, Pa., unmarried.
2624    iii. Eliza[8] French Eaton, b. 4 Jun 1849; died Mar 1852, Allegheny City, Pa.
2625    iv. Sarah[8] Gregg Eaton, b. 16 Aug 1853; residing with her mother and sister in Allegheny City, unmarried.

**1272. Jerome**[7] **B. Eaton** (Moses[6], Moses[5], Moses[4], John[3], Thomas[2], John[1]) was born May 1832 in Harrington, Me.; mar. **Eliza Ann Grace** (she dau. of Tristram and Elizabeth (Jordan) Grace) on 10 Oct 1859 in Harrington. They res. at Harrington, where he died 17 Sep 1913; wife Eliza went to live with her daughter Grace in Mass., and died 26 Mar 1917 in Watertown, Mass. in an automobile accident.

Children in Harrington, Me.:

2626    i. Lena[8] Estelle Eaton, b. 1860; d. 27 Aug 1862, Harrington.
2627    ii. Rena[8] A. Eaton, b. ca. 1863; died 17 Sep 1887, marital status unknown.
2628    iii. Grace[8] Eaton, b. ca. 1865; mar. Thomas J. Perkins of Boston, 12 Oct 1892 at Harrington; she was alive in 1905.

**1273. William⁷ A. C. Eaton** (*Moses⁶, Moses⁵,* Moses⁴, John³, Thomas², John¹) was born 1833 in Harrington, Me.; mar. 1st, **Violetta M. Mitchell** (she born ca. 1838 to Jeremiah and Ruth (Cushing) Mitchell) on 7 Feb 1856. This couple res. in Harrington for the most part, although they sometimes lived in nearby Machiasport. William was a sailor by trade. Violetta died on 6 Apr 1867. William mar. 2d, **Etta J. Sylvia Cole** (she born 12 Sep 1851 in Harrington to Benjamin and Rebecca (Ramsdell) Cole) on 7 Jul 1869. William died in Harrington in 1888; Etta died there 5 Sep 1926.

Children with Violetta, in Harrison or Machiasport, Me.:

| | | |
|---|---|---|
| 2629 | i. | Rowena⁸ M. Eaton, b. Jan. 1857; died 6 May 1873. |
| 2630 | ii. | Corris⁸ B. Eaton, dau. b. ca. 1858; died ca. 1871. |
| 2631 | iii. | Caswell⁸ F. Eaton, b. 1861; lost at sea, 1890. |
| +2632 | iv. | Harvey⁸ B. Eaton, b. Oct 1863; mar. Phebe W. Colson, 1892. |

Children with Etta:

| | | |
|---|---|---|
| 2633 | v. | Hamlin⁸ Eaton, b. 1871 in Harrington; lost at sea, 1895. |
| 2634 | vi. | Lillie⁸ M. Eaton, b. Apr 1880 in Machiasport; she died 1897 in Harrington, Me. |

**1274. Moses⁷ Warren Eaton** (*Asa⁶, Moses⁵,* Moses⁴, John³, Thomas², John¹, called "Warren" as often as "Moses," was born Oct 1836 at Harrington, Me.; mar. **Sarah E. Morrison** (his first cousin born 1840 in Harrington to James and Patience (Eaton) Morrison), on 4 Nov 1859 in Milbridge, Me. This couple resided in Milbridge during their child-rearing days, but perhaps moved to Eden town on Mt. Desert Island in their later years. Moses Warren was a sailor. Sarah prob. died in the 1880-1900 period; Moses Warren prob. survived until after 1910.

Children born in Milbridge, Me.:

| | | |
|---|---|---|
| +2635 | i. | Frederick⁸ Rich Eaton, b. Apr 1866; mar. Mary Roberts. |
| 2636 | ii. | Lettie⁸ Wallace Eaton, b. 21 Mar 1869; mar. 1st, William J. Robbins, 4 Aug 1888 at Milbridge. He was a master mariner who drowned in Rockport harbor, 13 Jun 1895; and mar. 2d, James Beal, 26 Sep 1896 at Beal's Island, Jonesport, Me. Lettie died 25 Oct 1921 at Harrington, Me. |
| 2637 | iii. | Edmund⁸ Warren Eaton, b. 3 Dec 1871; mar. 1st, __?__ in 1890; mar. 2d, Mary Katherine Torrey, 15 Nov 1902 at Rockland, Me., her 2d marriage. Edmund was a teamster in this period, and they res. in Rockland, Me. She had two children from her first mar., but apparently no issue from the second. Edmund died at Rockland, 8 Jun 1932. Katherine died there 24 Dec 1945. |

**1276. Elijah⁷ Eaton** (*Asa⁶, Moses⁵*, Moses⁴, John³, Thomas², John¹) was born Dec 1841 in Harrington, Me.; mar. **Henrietta W. Whitney** (she born Jun 1845 in Whitneyville, Me. to John and Clarissa (Meserve) Whitney) on 10 Dec 1863 in Machiasport, Me. They res. in Harrington, Me., where he died 25 Feb 1916. Henrietta died soon thereafter, 31 Jul 1916, at Cherryfield, Me.

Children at Harrison, Me.:

2638    i. Winslow⁸ N. Eaton, b. Jun 1870; mar. Maria A. _?_, 1890. Resided at Harrington and Mt. Desert Island. He died 17 Jan 1962, Hampton, N.H. Apparently no issue.
+2639    ii. Charles⁸ H. Eaton, b. 18 Dec 1872; mar. Melona Cole, 1892.
2640    iii. Corris⁸ E. Eaton, b. 14 Mar 1875; mar. Arnold W. Higgins. They resided in Lawrence, Mass. and Lakewood, Ohio.
2641    iv. Sarah⁸ E. Eaton, b. 19 Jun 1877; mar. a Casey and res. at Boston, Mass.

++++++++++++++++++++++++++++++++++++++++++++++++++++++++++++++++++

## B(1). *The Nova Scotia Branch*

(Skeletal form; for details, see Arthur W. H. Eaton (1929)).

**1282. Jacob⁷ Eaton** (Stephen⁶, David⁵).

+2642    i. Thomas⁸ W. Eaton, b. 1803.
2643    ii. Ann⁸ Eliza Eaton, b. 1805.
2644    iii. Phebe⁸ Eaton, b. 1808.
+2645    iv. Stephen⁸ Eaton, b. 1810.
2646    v. Elizabeth⁸ Eaton, b. 1813.
2647    vi. Eunice⁸ Eaton, b. 1815.
2648    vii. Mary⁸ Eaton, b. 1818.
2649    viii. Jacob⁸ V. Eaton, b. 1820.
+2650    ix. Oliver⁸ Eaton, b. 1823.

**1287. Amos⁷ Eaton** (Stephen⁶, David⁵).

+2651    i. Levi⁸ W. Eaton, b. 1811. Emigrated to New Zealand.
+2652    ii. Nathan⁸ H. Eaton, b. 1814.
+2653    iii. Amos⁸ Eaton, b. 1815. Settled in No. Attleboro, Mass.
2654    iv. Margaret⁸ Lucilla Eaton, b. 1817.
+2655    v. Stephen⁸ Eaton, 1819.
2656    vi. Caroline⁸ S. Eaton, b. 1821.
2657    vii. Sarah⁸ Eliza Eaton, b. 1824.
2658    viii. James⁸ E. Eaton, b. 1826.
2659    ix. Rebecca⁸ Eaton, b. 1828.
2660    x. Alpheus⁸ Eaton, b. 1831. To California; New Zealand.

**1288.** <u>Nathan</u>[7] **Eaton** (Stephen[6], David[5]).

| | | |
|---|---|---|
| **2661** | i. | Maria[8] Eaton, b. 1810. |
| **2662** | ii. | Eliza[8] Eaton, b. 1812. |
| **2663** | iii. | Sarah[8] Ann Eaton, b. 1813. |
| **+2664** | iv. | Jacob[8] Eaton, b. 1815. |
| **2665** | v. | Rebecca[8] Eaton, b. 1817. |
| **+2666** | vi. | Levi[8] Eaton, b. 1820. |
| **2667** | vii. | Phebe[8] Eaton, b. 1822. |
| **2668** | viii. | Mary[8] Lois Eaton, b. 1824. |
| **2669** | ix. | Olivia[8] Eaton b. 1827. |
| **2670** | x. | Hannah[8] Eaton, b. 1831. |
| **2671** | xi. | Prudence[8] Eaton, b. 1833. |

**1290.** <u>Stephen</u>[7] **Eaton** (Stephen[6], David[5]).

| | | |
|---|---|---|
| **+2672** | i. | Douglas[8] W. Eaton, b. 1816. Removed to N.Y. State. |
| **+2673** | ii. | Asael[8] B. Eaton, b. 1818. In N.Y. State; then Michigan. |
| **+2674** | iii. | Ingraham[8] E. Eaton, b. 1821, New York City. N.Y.; Mich. |
| **+2675** | iv. | Stephen[8] R. Eaton, b. 1823, Porter, N.Y.; Californa. |
| **2676** | v. | Jacob[8] Eaton, b. 1826, Porter, N.Y. |
| **2677** | vi. | Mary[8] E. Eaton, b. 1829, Porter, N.Y. |
| **+2678** | vii. | Edward[8] M., b.1831, Porter, N.Y. Res. Michigan. |
| **+2679** | viii. | Adoniram[8] J. Eaton, b. 1835, Porter, N.Y. |
| **2680** | ix. | Cordelia[8] Eaton b. 1844, Porter, N.Y. |

**1292.** <u>Dan</u>[7] **Eaton** (Elisha[6], David[5]).

| | | |
|---|---|---|
| **+2681** | i. | Henry[8] K. Eaton, b. 1805. |
| **2682** | ii. | Martha[8] Eaton, b. 1807. |
| **+2683** | iii. | George[8] Eaton, b. 1809. |
| **+2684** | iv. | William[8] W. Eaton, b. 1811. Res. in Chicago, Ill. |
| **2685** | v. | Mary[8] Ann Eaton, b. 1813. |
| **2686** | vi. | Irene[8] D. Eaton, b. 1819. |
| **2687** | vii. | Clarissa[8] M. Eaton, b. 1822. |
| **+2688** | viii. | Daniel[8] L. Eaton, b. 1824. Res. Washington, D.C. |
| **2689** | ix. | Sarah[8] Eaton, b. 1830, Maine. |

**1293.** <u>Enoch</u>[7] **Eaton** (Elisha[6], David[5]).

| | | |
|---|---|---|
| **2690** | i. | Lydia[8] Ann Eaton, b. 1812. |
| **2691** | ii. | Eunice[8] M. Eaton, b. 1814. |
| **+2692** | iii. | Enoch[8], Eaton, Jr., b. 1816. |
| **+2693** | iv. | Henry[8] A. Eaton, b. 1817. |
| **+2694** | v. | Watson[8] Eaton, b. 1820. |

+**2695**  vi. Benjamin[8] Eaton, b. 1822.
 **2696**  vii. James[8] M. Eaton, b. 1824.
 **2697**  viii. Eliza[8] I. Eaton, b. 1826
 **2698**  ix. Mary[8] P. Eaton, b. 1830.
+**2699**  x. George[8] W. Eaton, b. 1834.

**1294. Elisha[7] Eaton** (Elisha[6], David[5]).

 **2700**  i. David[8] O. Eaton, b. 1822.

**1295. William[7] Eaton** (Elisha[6], David[5]).

+**2701**  i. Leonard[8] Eaton, b. 1810.
 **2702**  ii. Eliza[8] J. Eaton, b. 1812.
 **2703**  iii. Susannah[8] Eaton, b. 1814.
 **2704**  iv. Anna[8] Eaton, b. 1819.
 **2705**  v. Clement[8] B. Eaton, b. 1824.
+**2706**  vi. George[8] W. Eaton, b. 1826. Res. Melrose, Mass.
+**2707**  vii. Joseph[8] H. Eaton, b. 1828.

**1297. George[7] Eaton** (Elisha[6], David[5]).

 **2708**  i. Frances[8] T. Eaton, b. 1814.
 **2709**  ii. George[8] Eaton, b. 1816.
 **2710**  iii. Edward[8] W. Eaton, b. 1818. Left descendants at Ft. Kent, Me.
 **2711**  iv. Susan[8] A. Eaton, b. 1820.
 **2712**  v. Alexander[8] Eaton, b. ca. 1823. Died at Van Buren, Me.

**1298. David[7] Eaton** (Elisha[6], David[5]).

 **2713**  i. Rachel[8] Eaton, b. 1815.
 **2714**  ii. Lydia[8] A. Eaton, b. 1816.
 **2715**  iii. James[8] M. Eaton, b. 1818.
 **2716**  iv. Margaret[8] M. Eaton, b. 1820.
 **2717**  v. Sophia[8] A. Eaton, b. 1823.
+**2718**  vi. David[8] R. Eaton, b. 1827.
+**2719**  vii. Charles[8] F. Eaton, b. 1830.
 **2720**  viii. Susannah[8] M. Eaton, b. 1832.
 **2721**  ix. May[8] A. Eaton, b. 1834.
 **2722**  x. Emeline[8] A. Eaton, b. 1836.

**1301. James[7] Eaton** (Elisha[6], David[5]).

 **2723**  i. Armanilla[8] Eaton, b. 1823.

2724   ii. Mary[8] J. Eaton, b. 1825.
2725   iii. James[8] E. Eaton, b. 1828.
2726   iv. Irene[8] Eaton, b. 1831.
+2727   v. Levi[8] Eaton, b. 1832.
2728   vi. Amelia[8] Eaton, b. 1835.
+2729   vii. Brenton[8] H. Eaton, b. 1837.
2730   viii. Martha[8] E. Eaton, b. 1840.
2731   ix. Caroline[8] A. Eaton, b. 1842.
2732   x. Anna[8] M. Eaton, b. 1845.

**1305. Gideon[7] Eaton** (Timothy[6], David[5]).

2733   i. Prudence[8] C. Eaton, b. 1817.

**1307. Timothy[7] Eaton** (Timothy[6], David[5]).

+2734   i. Gideon[8] Eaton, b. 1822.
2735   ii. Sarah[8] A. Eaton, b.  ? .
+2736   iii. William[8] H. Eaton, b. 1826.
2737   iv. Nancy[8] Eaton, b.  ? .
2738   v. Edwin[8] Eaton, b. 1828.
+2739   vi. Otho[8] Eaton, b. 1830.
+2740   vii. Robert[8] A. Eaton, b. 1836. Res. So. Boston, Mass.

**1309. Ebenezer[7] Eaton** (Elijah[6A], David[5]).

2741   i. William[8] Eaton, b. 1810.
2742   ii. Marsden[8] Eaton, b. 1814. Killed by Indians in California.
2743   iii. James[8] Eaton, b. 1816.
2744   iv. Elijah[8] Eaton, b. 1819.
2745   v. Abraham[8] Eaton, b. 1821.
2746   vi. Isaac[8] Eaton, b.  ? .
2747   vii. Jacob[8] Eaton, b.  ? .

**1310. Caleb[7] Eaton** (Elijah[6A], David[5]).

2748   i. Mary[8] A. Eaton, b. 1811.
+2749   ii. Jonathan[8] R. Eaton, b. 1812.
2750   iii. Naomi[8] Eaton, b. 1814. Res. Bangor, Me. & St. Louis.
2751   iv. Elijah[8] Eaton, b. 1816. Res. Baltimore, Md. and California.
2752   v. Ruth[8] Eaton, b. 1817.
2753   vi. Mary[8] J. Eaton, b. 1821.
2754   vii. Caleb[8] Eaton, b. 1824 at Deer Isle, Me.
2755   viii. Eunice[8] Eaton, b. 1828, res. Deer Isle, Me.
2756   ix. Elizabeth[8] Eaton, b. 1830.

+ **2757**    x. Abel[8] B. Eaton, b. 1833.
  **2758**   xi. Joanna[8] C. Eaton, b. 1835. Died, Deer Isle, Me.
  **2759**  xii. Feynetty[8] C. Eaton, b. 1838 at Deer Isle, Me.
  **2760** xiii. Eliza[8] A. Eaton b. 1840 at Deer Isle.

### 1320. Elisha[7] Eaton (Elijah[6A], David[6]).

  **2761**    i. Eliza[8] J. Eaton, b. 1830.
  **2762**   ii. Thomas[8] W. Eaton, b. 1832.
  **2763**  iii. James[8] E. Eaton, b. 1834.
+ **2764**   iv. James[8A] E. Eaton, b. 1835.
  **2765**    v. Mary[8] L. Eaton, b. 1838.
+ **2766**   vi. Mayhew[8] E. Eaton, b. 1840.
+ **2767**  vii. Joseph[8] H. Eaton, b. 1842.
+ **2768** viii. George[8] W. Eaton, b. 1845.
  **2769**   ix. Julia[8] E. Eaton, b. 1847.
  **2770**    x. Rebecca[8] Eaton, b. 1850.
  **2771**   xi. Albert[8] R. Eaton, b. 1852. Lived in Massachusetts.

### 1322. Guy[7] Eaton (David[6-5]).

+ **2772**    i. Asael[8] Eaton, b. 1813. Removed to Iowa.
  **2773**   ii. James[8] N. Eaton, b. 1814.
  **2774**  iii. Mary[8] A. Eaton, b. 1816. Went to California..
  **2775**   iv. Eunice[8] Eaton, b. 1818. Went to California.
  **2776**    v. Benjamin[8] Eaton, b. ? .
+ **2777**   vi. Guy[8] Eaton, b. 1821.
  **2778**  vii. Ruth[8] Eaton, b. 1824. Mar. in Maine, rem. to Minnesota.
+ **2779** viii. John[8] W. Eaton, b. 1827. Removed to Minneapolis.

### 1324. Judah[7] Eaton (David[6-5]).

  **2780**    i. Amanda[8] Eaton, b. 1818.
  **2781**   ii. Ann[8] E. Eaton, b. 1820.
+ **2782**  iii. Wells[8] Eaton, b. 1822. Removed to Wisconsin, Iowa.
  **2783**   iv. Judah[8] Eaton, b. 1824.
  **2784**    v. Eunice[8] Eaton, b. 1832.

### 1325. David[7] Eaton (David[6-5]).

  **2785**    i. Emily[8] Eaton, b. 1813.
+ **2786**   ii. Gurdon[8] Eaton b. 1816.
  **2787**  iii. Lavinia[8] Eaton, b. 1818.
  **2788**   iv. Susan[8] A. Eaton, b. 1820.
+ **2789**    v. George[8] E. Eaton, b. 1822.

**2790**    vi. Jerusha[8] A. Eaton, b. 1824.
**2791**    vii. David[8] H. Eaton, b. 1827.
**2792**    viii. Eunice[8] Eaton, b. 1829.
**2793**    ix. Mary[8] A. Eaton, b. 1831.
**2794**    x. Lydia[8] E. Eaton, b. 1833.
**2795**    xi. Rebecca[8] Eaton, b. 1835.
**2796**    xii. Hannah[8] J. Eaton, b. 1839. Resided Boston, Mass.


**1331. Levi[7] Wells Eaton** (David[6-5]).

+ **2797**    i. Joseph[8] E. Eaton, b. 1838.
**2798**    ii. Charles[8] F. Eaton, b. 1840.
**2799**    iii. John[8] L. Eaton, b. 1846.
**2800**    iv. Mary[8] E. Eaton, b. 1852.
**2801**    v. Annie[8] M. Eaton, b. 1858.
+ **2802**    vi. Nathan[8] W. Eaton, b. 1860.


**1336. Edward[7] Eaton** (James[6], David[5]).

**2803**    i. James[8] H. Eaton, b. 1842.
**2804**    ii. William[8] P. Eaton, b. 1844. At Stockton, Cal., 1885.
**2805**    iii. Julia[8] E. Eaton, b. 1846.
**2806**    iv. Edward[8] M. Eaton, b. 6 Aug 1849.
**2807**    v. George[8] N. Eaton, b. 31 Jul 1851.
**2808**    vi. Anna[8] M. Eaton, b. 7 Dec 1853.
**2809**    vii. Theresa[8] F. Eaton. b. 24 Jan 1856.
**2810**    viii. Bessie[8] M. Eaton, b. 23 Jan 1858.


**1342. Ward[7] Eaton** (John[6], David[5])

**2811**    i. Ann[8] I. Eaton, b. 30 Aug 1820.
+ **2812**    ii. Leander[8] Eaton, b. 25 Dec 1821.
+ **2813**    iii. William[8] Eaton, b. 30 Sep 1823.
+ **2814**    iv. John[8] R. Eaton, b. 3 Jul 1826.
**2815**    v. Martha[8] Eaton, b. 9 Mar 1828.
+ **2816**    vi. James[8] S. Eaton, b. 4 Feb 1836.


**1343. Abijah[7] A. Eaton** (John[6], David[5])

**2817**    i. Andrew[8] Eaton, b. 17 Oct 1822.
**2818**    ii. Sarah[8] J. Eaton, b. 2 Jul 1824.
**2819**    iii. Ward[8] Eaton, b. 23 Jan 1829.
**2820**    iv. Abraham[8] Eaton, b. 29 Apr 1835.
**2821**    v. Rebecca[8] A. Eaton, b. 3 Aug 1838.

**1345. Charles$^7$ Eaton** (John$^6$, David$^5$)

2822      i. Samuel$^8$ N. Eaton, b. 8 Nov 1825.
2823     ii. Prudence$^8$ E. Eaton, b. 16 Apr 1827.
2824    iii. Sarah$^8$ A. Eaton, b. 3 May 1829.
2825     iv. Prudence$^8$ O. Eaton, b. 19 Aug 1831.
2826      v. Charles$^8$ E. Eaton, b. 28 Jun 1833.
2827     vi. Son$^8$ Eaton, b., d., 22 Mar 1835.
2828    vii. William$^8$ A. Eaton, b. 5 Jun 1836.
2829   viii. Marietta$^8$ Eaton, b. 28 Nov 1838.
2830     ix. Rebecca$^8$ Eaton, b. 17 Jul 1841.

**1352. John$^7$ White Eaton** (John$^6$, David$^5$)

2831      i. Frederick$^8$ E. Eaton, b. 16 Feb 1845.
2832     ii. Anne$^8$ S. Eaton, b. 14 Nov 1848. Res. Iowa.
2833    iii. William$^8$ P. Eaton, b. 7 Aug 1854.
2834     iv. Sarah$^8$ J. Eaton, b. 22 Jun 1856.
2835      v. Maria$^8$ L. Eaton, b. 11 Dec 1858. Res. Framingham, Mass.

(End Generation VII for Nova Scotia Branch)
++++++++++++++++++++++++++++++++++++++++++++++++++++++++++++++++++

**1361. Daniel$^7$ Poor Eaton** (Abijah$^6$, Timothy$^5$, James$^4$, Jonathan$^3$, Thomas$^2$, John$^1$) was born 24 Feb 1792 in Haverhill, Mass.; mar. **Sarah Webster** (she born 10 Jun 1794 at Salem, N.H. to Samuel and Lydia (Bradley) Webster) in 1813. Early on this couple moved to Bradford, Vt., on the Connecticut River in Orange Co. By 1816 or so, they had pushed on to establish themselves in Montreal, Quebec, and Daniel P. died there 15 Jul 1837. Wife Sarah came back to her natal region and mar. 2d, Moses Foot in 1859. She died 31 Oct 1872 at Groveland, Mass., just across the Merrimack River from Haverhill.

Children:

+ 2836      i. Samuel$^8$ Webster Eaton, b. 2 Jun 1814 in Bradford, Vt.
+ 2837     ii. Daniel$^8$ Poore Eaton, b. 2 Sep 1816 in Montreal.

**1365. Edwin$^7$ Eaton** (Abijah$^6$, Timothy$^5$, James$^4$, Jonathan$^3$, Thomas$^2$, John$^1$) was born 10 Nov 1800 in Atkinson, N.H.; mar. **Abigail Partridge** (she born 29 Apr 1810 to Ellery and Experience Partridge) on 27 Jul 1831. Edwin was a silver-plater, and early on removed Montreal, presumably to join brother Daniel. After Daniel's death the family moved to Le Roy in Genessee Co., N.Y. By 1850, Edwin was a silver-plater in Providence, R.I. with his family. He died 22 Jul 1874.

Children with Abigail:

2838     i. William[8] Jefferson Eaton, b. 7 Oct 1835, in Montreal. He
            died 2 Feb 1869.
2839     ii. Edwin[8] Herman Eaton, b. 10 May 1838 in Le Roy, N.Y.
2840     iii. Louisa[8] Allen Eaton, b. 6 Aug 1840 in Le Roy, N.Y.; mar.
            Darius Whitford, 13 Oct 1857.


**1366. Thomas[7] Jefferson Eaton** (Abijah[6], Timothy[5], James[4], Jonathan[3], Thomas[2], John[1]) was born 6 Feb 1805 in Atkinson, N.H. He mar. **Amy __?__** , she born Vt., presumably after he removed to Holland, Vt. in Orleans Co. about 1828. In 1830 Thomas J. has a female companion of the same age in Holland without sign of children as yet. In the latter half of the 1830s they moved onward to Stanstead, Quebec, just over the Vt. border; but returned to Irasburgh in Orleans Co. permanently about 1842. Thomas worked a moderate-sized farm, and died 4 Nov 1885 at Irasburgh.

Children with Amy:

2841     i. Abigail[8] Eaton, b. ca. 1834, prob. in Holland, Vt.
+2842    ii. Solomon[8] W. Eaton, b. 1836, in Stanstead, Que.; mar. Anne.
2843     iii. Philena[8] Eaton, b. 1840, in Stanstead; mar. Lyman W.
            Kinney, 24 Dec 1861, Irasburgh.
2844     iv. Benjamin[8] F. Eaton, b. 1843, Irasburgh; died of diphtheria
            11 Mar 1864, Irasburgh.
2845     v. Mary[8] Etta Eaton, b. 1846, Irasburgh.
2846     vi. Martha[8] Eaton, b. Fall, 1849; died 9 Feb 1863.


**1367. Timothy[7] Eaton** (Timothy[6-5], James[4], Jonathan[3], Thomas[2], John[1]) was born 10 Jun 1782 in Haverhill, Mass.; mar. **Mary F. Gleason** of Worcester, Mass., who was at least two decades his junior. The couple settled in the Boston area, possibly first at West Cambridge. There is no doubt, however, that they were in Ward #9 in Boston as of 1850, and Ward #8 in 1860, since in the latter year the household includes two Gleasons, one being a 23-year-old lawyer. Timothy[7] came from a wealthy family in Haverhill, and reports no occupation at age 68 to the Census-taker in 1850, while reporting himself a "Gentleman" in 1860. He was probably involved in some Boston commerce as a younger man. We only have Census inferences for two daughters, although given the lateness of the marriage for him, this may be a full roster. He apparently died in the 1860s, as we find his widow Mary in Ward #6 in 1870.

Children:

**2847**     i. Mary[8] E. Eaton, b. ca. 1827.
**2848**     ii. Josephine[8] Eaton, b. ca. 1829.


**1370. Francis[7] Eaton** (Timothy[6-5], James[4], Jonathan[3], Thomas[2], John[1]) was born 7 Sep 1787 at Haverhill, Mass.; was listed "Esq." when he mar. **Mary Hildreth**, Dec ? 1814, Haverhill. They settled in Haverhill, Mass., but this marriage was short-lived: Mary died from complications in her second birthing, 15 Feb 1817; Francis himself died at sea, 16 Mar 1822.

Children born in Haverhill, Mass.:

**2849**     i. Francis[8] Eaton, b. Mar 1815; almost surely the Francis the
              shoemaker who appears to be unmar. at Haverhill in the
              Censuses of 1850 and 1860. In the latter year he is age
              45, living in a household headed by a "shoebinder." He
              does not appear again in Haverhill.
**2850**     ii. Mary[8] Eaton, b. 6 Feb 1817.


**1373. Cyrus[7] Eaton** (Timothy[6-5], James[4], Jonathan[3], Thomas[2], John[1]) was born 30 Aug 1794 in Haverhill; he removed to Pennsylvania and there mar. **Mary Eva Kuhn** of Harrisburg, Pa. in the 1830s. We find the couple upstream from Harrisburg in 1840, at Liverpool in Perry Co., on the west bank of the Susquehanna.. In 1860 Cyrus is a rather prosperous merchant 30 miles farther north at Mifflinburg in Union Co.

Child (clearly one member of a larger brood):

**2851**     i. "Aloecis[8]" (Aloysius?) Eaton, a son b. ca. 1847.


**1381. William[7] Cater Eaton** (Daniel[6], Timothy[5], James[4], Jonathan[3], Thomas[2], John[1]) was born 9 Oct 1792 in Onslow, Nova Scotia, after his doctor father (cf. **#516**) had come to the area to visit his Uncle David[6] (who had ensconced his family there a generation earlier), and quickly fallen in love not only with the region but with William C.'s mother Esther as well. [Although this next-generation Eaton migration is acknowledged by Arthur W. H. Eaton (1929. pp. 28-29), he did not formally include this twig in his genealogy of Nova Scotia Eatons; therefore we handle it in its proper place here.] William[7] C. mar. **Lucy Smith** (she born 26 Mar 1800 to John Smith of Hartland) on 27 Sep 1820. He was an Anglican churchman and one of the first vestrymen of St. John's Church in Truro, where they settled. Lucy was a Presbyterian, but baptisms of their children were recorded at St. John's. William died in Truro, 16 Apr 1874; Lucy died there 29 Jan 1881.

Children in Truro, Nova Scotia:

2852   i. Sarah[8] Berry Eaton, b. 5 Jun 1821.
2853   ii. Eleanor[8] Smith Eaton, b. 15 Nov 1822; d. unm. 22 Jul 1838.
2854   iii. Augusta[8] Ann Eaton, b. 13 Sep 1824; mar. Lemuel McNutt in Truro on 18 Jul 1855, and had three sons.
2855   iv. Robert[8] Berry Eaton, b. 17 Jul 1826; mar. Abigail Smith on 20 Dec 1849 and res. in Hartland, Hants Co., Nova Scotia.
2856   v. John[8] Townsend Smith Eaton, b. 7 Jul 1828; mar. Catherine Dill, 17 Dec 1850, and res. in Truro. He died there 5 Jun 1865, wife Catherine having died 22 Feb 1856.
+2857   vi. Simon[8] Kollock Eaton, b. 25 Apr 1831; m. Sophia Stewart.
2858   vii. Isaac[8] Smith Eaton, b. 11 Jan 1833; died 22 Jul 1856.
+2859   viii. George[8] McDonald Eaton, b. 31 Aug 1835; mar. Martha.
+2860   ix. James[8] Hiller Eaton, b. 15 Feb 1838; mar. Anna Pitblado.
+2861   x. Hiram[8] Hyde Eaton, b. 4 Nov 1842; mar. Isabella Carlyle. It was Hiram's provision of a family Bible that gave us the above roster of children.

**1383. Daniel[7] Eaton** (Daniel[6], Timothy[5], James[4], Jonathan[3], Thomas[2], John[1]) was born 19 Sep 1797; mar. **Mary Ann Clark** of Onslow, Nova Scotia. on 26 Dec 1822. They appear to have res. at Truro, N.S., where Daniel died 1 Dec 1876. Wife Mary lived with her son Cyrus after his death. Both Daniel and Mary are buried in Onslow.

Children:

2862   i. John[8] Wheaton Eaton, b. 14 Oct 1823; died unmar. at Truro, 11 Jan 1862.
2863   ii. Elizabeth[8] Clark Eaton, b. 17 Apr 1825; mar. James Rogers of Hopewell, N.B. on 20 Jul 1864, but she died 16 Mar 1875, leaving no children.
2864   iii. James[8] Eaton, b 1 Jun 1827; died 19 Dec 1828.
+2865   iv. David[8] Hamilton Eaton, b. 13 Jun 1829; m. Caroline Eaton.
2866   v. Hannah[8] C. Eaton, b. 6 Jun 1831; d. unmar. 18 Aug 1854.
2867   vi. Lemuel[8] C. Eaton, b. 18 Jan 1834; d. unmar. 23 May 1860.
+2868   vii. Cyrus[8] Eaton, b. 19 Apr 1836; mar. Margaret Miller, 1871.

**1386. Elbridge[7] Gerry Eaton** (Phineas[6], Timothy[5], James[4], Jonathan[3], Thomas[2], John[1]) was born 29 Mar 1802 in Haverhill, Mass.; mar. **Nancy Gage** of Georgetown, Mass., 7 Dec 1841 at Georgetown. They resided mainly in Haverhill, where he was a painter, paperhanger and glazier, with a shop in 1860 at #8 Winter St. He died in 1861 in Haverhill.

Children:

**2869**  i. Eugene[8] Gerry Eaton, b. 1842; enlisted early in the Civil
and was sent South. His father had died in 1861, leaving
the family's hardware business in Haverhill unmanaged.
Eugene had become head of the family, but became
enamoured of the South during his tour of duty, and
hence was uninterested in returning to Haverhill to save
the business. His other brothers were equally disinclined
to do the business, so Eugene invited the whole family to
join him in Chattanooga, Tenn., where he was involved in
the iron ore business. His widowed mother and virtually
all of his siblings completed this migration ca. 1870
and remained there for some period of time.   Years
later when Eugene was 40 or older, he mar. a girl from
Tuscaloosa, Ala. They left issue, but unknown to us.
**+2870**  ii. Albert[8] Claude Eaton, b. 24 Nov 1843, Haverhill.
**2871**  iii. Elbridge[8] Miner Eaton, b. 30 Dec 1845, Haverhill.
**2872**  iv. James[8] Edward Eaton, b. 9 Jan 1848, Haverhill; died there 12
Feb 1848.
**+2873**  v. Frank[8] Howard Eaton, b. 14 Jul 1849, Bradford, Mass.
**2874**  vi. Mary[8] E. Eaton, b. 1854, Haverhill, Mass. In 1870 she was
living at the Lookout Mtn. Educational Institution near
Chattanooga, Tenn., taking lessons there.

**1388. Jeremiah[7A] Bodwell Eaton** (Phineas[6], Timothy[5], James[4],
Jonathan[3], Thomas[2], John[1]) was born 12 Jul 1807 in Haverhill, Mass.;
mar. **Martha J. Rollins** of Stratham, N.H., 24 May 1833.   The couple
disappears for a period; but in 1860 and 1870 they can be found in the
burgeoning factory town of Lowell, up the Merrimack River, where
Jeremiah has a well-capitalized trade in carriage-making.

Children (inferred from Censuses, with birthplaces not clear):

**2875**  i. Elizabeth[8] J. Eaton, b. ca. 1836, Mass.; was teaching school
as of 1860.
**2876**  ii. Martha[8] A. Eaton, b. ca. 1838.
**2877**  iii. Lucy[8] Eaton, b. ca. 1841.
**2878**  iv. Arvilla[8] Eaton, b. ca. 1846.

**1389. James[7] Madison Eaton** (Phineas[6], Timothy[5], James[4], Jonathan[3], Thomas[2], John[1]) was born 23 Oct 1809 at Haverhill, Mass.; mar.
**Hannah Pettengill** in 1842.   They res. in the 1840s in Nashua, N.H.,
where they began their family, but had returned to Haverhill by 1850.
They were said to have removed later to Dubois, Washington Co., Ill.,
where he died 17 Oct 1872, but we have found no Illinois records.

Children (probably very incomplete):

**2879**  i. Charles[8] Maynard Eaton, b. 9 Apr 1844 at Nashua, N.H.
**2880**  ii. Fanny[8] Elizabeth Eaton, b. 13 Dec 1847 at Nashua, N.H.


**1391. Daniel[7] Whittier Eaton** (Phineas[6], Timothy[5], James[4], Jonathan[3], Thomas[2], John[1]) was born 4 Jun 1814 at Haverhill, Mass.; mar. **Sarah L. Smith** of West Newbury, Mass. (dau. of Joseph and Sarah Smith) on 13 Nov 1845, at West Newbury. Daniel was by trade a carriage body builder, or chaise maker. The couple settled in Lowell, and then for two Censuses in West Newbury. Wife Sarah died 31 Jan 1860, and Daniel has moved to Amesbury, where he worked in a carriage shop joined by son Edward, a "carriage trimmer."

Children, all save the first b. in West Newbury, Mass:

**2881**  i. Sarah[8] Addie Eaton, b. 24 Jul 1847 in Lowell, Mass.; mar. Joseph Edmund Bailey, a merchant of Georgetown, Mass, 16 Nov 1866.
**+2882**  ii. Daniel[8] Herbert Eaton, b. 29 Jun 1849; mar. Emma Chase.
**2883**  iii. Lizzie[8] Whittier Eaton, b. 14 Jan 1851.
**2884**  iv. Edward[8] Smith Eaton, b. 25 Jul 1852; never mar., was a cook res. in Salisbury, Mass. He died of apoplexy, 6 Nov 1916.
**2885**  v. Annie[8] Little Eaton, b. 6 Aug 1854.
**2886**  vi. Ernest[8] B. Eaton, b. 12 Jan 1856; in 1880 was a clerk in a Pleasant St. store in Haverhill, apparently unmar.
**+2887**  vii. Roswell[8] Jameson Eaton, b. 6 Nov 1857; mar. Mary Allison.
**2888**  viii. Mary[8] Johnson Eaton, b. 20 Jul 1859.


**1395. Ward[7] Eaton, Jr.** (Ward[6], Timothy[5], James[4], Jonathan[3], Thomas[2], John[1]) was born 10 May 1808 in Haverhill, Mass. We know from family sources that he left Haverhill and wound up in Carbondale, Pa. We do not find him there, however, until 1850, with a substantial family. However, since his first wife **Elizabeth McNair**, whom he married 5 Aug 1831, was born in New York State about 1811 and most of their children were born there, Ward must have lived for a considerable spell, although out of Census view, in that state. The couple apparently proceeded into Pennsylvania in the mid-1840s, and in 1850 Ward was operating a farm in Carbondale, Luzerne Co., although his main interest in farming was as veterinarian. Wife Elizabeth died 10 Jul 1852; and Ward mar. 2d, **Harriet Armstrong** (born 1819), on 27 Oct 1853. About 1861 he moved to Manhattan, N. Y. C.; and from 1867 until his death he was in New York City directories as a veterinary surgeon and manufacturer of horse medicines. He died there 29 Oct 1871.

Children with Elizabeth:

+ **2889**    i. Alonzo[8] Ward Eaton, b. 10 Mar 1832, N. Y.; mar. Abigail.
  **2890**   ii. William[8] Wallace Eaton, b. 14 Feb 1834, N.Y.; mar. Evelyn
             E. Morp, 29 Apr 1854; died 2 Apr 1863.
  **2891**  iii. Roderick[8] Delevan Eaton, b. 20 Dec 1837, N.Y.; mar.
             Caroline "Carrie" Gridley, 31 Mar 1861. In 1880, this
             couple is at Jonesville, Hillsdale Co., Michigan, a few
             miles east of his older brother Alonzo in Branch Co. No
             sign of children.
  **2892**   iv. Harriet[8] Elizabeth Eaton, b. 25 Aug 1844, N.Y.
  **2843**    v. Julia[8] Frances Eaton, b. 22 Aug 1846, N.Y.
  **2894**   vi. George[8] Taylor Eaton, b. 16 Nov 1848, N.Y.
+ **2895**  vii. Edward[8] L. Eaton, b. 11 Feb 1850, N.Y.; mar. Hattie.


   **1399. James[7] Jackson Eaton** (Ward[6], Timothy[5], James[4], Jonathan[3], Thomas[2], John[1]) was born 4 Feb 1819 in Haverhill, Mass.; he mar.
**Ellen T. Fielding**, a native of England then residing in Andover, Mass.,
29 Sep 1844. The couple settled in Bradford, Mass. on the south side of
the Merrimack across from Haverhill. James was a shoe cutter, who died
13 Oct 1864. Widow Ellen died 1893.

Children at Bradford, Mass.:

  **2896**    i. George[8] Ward Eaton, b. 22 Mar 1846; prob. mar. the
             Catherine __?__ with whom he is bur. in Bradford. He
             was a shoemaker and salesman in Bradford and Haver-
             hill, who died 1899. Issue, if any, unknown.
  **2897**   ii. Harriet[8] Eaton, b. 11 Apr 1849; died young.
  **2898**  iii. Abby[8] F. Eaton, b. ca. 1850.
  **2899**   iv. Mary[8] A. Eaton, b. ca. 1852.


   **1410. Joseph[7] Eaton** (Samuel[6], James[5-4], Jonathan[3], Thomas[2],
John[1]) was born 24 Apr 1802, and removed with his family when age 15
to Reading, Vt.   He mar. **Elizabeth Day** of neighboring Plymouth, Vt.,
12 Sep 1827. The couple settled in Bridgewater, Vt., to raise their family. Joseph died there rather early, on 16 Mar 1849, before the children
were up and out.

Children at Bridgewater, Vt.:

  **2900**    i. Eliza[8] Leotina Eaton, b. 1829; died 13 Feb 1848.
  **2901**   ii. Julia[8] D. Eaton, b. ca. 1833.
  **2902**  iii. Joseph[8] Henry Eaton, b. 1845; he died in the Civil War,
             7 May 1864.

**1415. David**[7] **Eaton** (*James*[6], *James*[5], James[4], Jonathan[3], Thomas[2], John[1]) was born 7 Apr 1784 at the remote farm on Hedgehog Mountain in the township of Deering, N.H. He mar. **Susanna Rob(er)son**, dau. of William and also a Deering native, 30 Aug 1804. The couple initially settled in Deering and were there in 1810. One of their middle children was born in 1815 in Wendell (now Sunapee, N.H.), and there is a David Eaton, otherwise unaccounted for and with just the right complex family composition, next door to Wendell in Newport, N.H. for the 1820 Census. There is a David back in Deering in 1830 who again has an appropriate family composition, now dwindling in numbers of course as earlier children are up and out, who is very likely to be our current subject. Then the record fades out. The child roster below fits the apparent family structure with place markers if birth records can be found.

Children:

| | | |
|---|---|---|
| 2903 | i. | Son[8] Eaton, b. 1805-09, prob. in Deering, N.H. |
| 2904 | ii. | Daughter[8] Eaton, b. 1805-09, prob. in Deering, N.H. |
| 2905 | iii. | Son[8] Eaton, b. 1805-09, prob. in Deering, N.H. |
| 2906 | iv. | Son[8] Eaton, b. 1810-14. |
| 2907 | v. | Daughter[8] Eaton, b. 1810-14. |
| +2908 | vi. | James[8] Bradford Eaton, b. 15 Aug 1815, Wendell, N.H. |
| 2909 | vii. | Daughter[8] Eaton, b. 1820-24. |
| 2910 | viii. | Son[8] Eaton, b. 1820-24. |

**1416. John**[7] **Eaton** (*James*[6], *James*[5], James[4], Jonathan[3], Thomas[2], John[1]) was born 30 Mar 1786 at the remote farm on Hedgehog Mountain in the township of Deering, N.H. He mar. **Elizabeth "Betsey" Moor** of Francestown, N.H. on 4 Nov 1807, at Londonderry, N.H. They took up residence in Hillsboro Lower Village, N.H., and appear in Censuses there, 1810-30. John died 5 Dec 1839 at Hillsboro. His widow remained there with the large brood of children, heading the household in 1840 and 1850 Censuses. She died 24 Feb 1863.

Children in Hillsboro, N. H.:

| | | |
|---|---|---|
| 2911 | i. | Mary[8] Eaton, b. 6 Nov 1808; mar. 1st, Luther Smith of Deering and res. in Manchester; mar. 2d, Jacob Trussell of Canaan, N.H. She died 27 Jan 1879 in Hillsboro. |
| +2912 | ii. | John[8] L. Eaton, b. 16 Feb 1811; mar. Susan Gibson. |
| +2913 | iii. | Horace[8] Eaton, b. 9 Mar 1813; mar. Eliza Colby, 1836. |
| +2914 | iv. | William[8] Eaton, b. 6 Aug 1815; mar. Abigail Burtt. |
| +2915 | v. | Harrison[8] Eaton, b. 9 Dec 1817; mar. 1st, Lucy Hartshorn. |
| 2916 | vi. | Elizabeth[8] Eaton, b. 27 Apr 1820; drowned, 1826. |
| 2917 | vii. | Lucina[8] Eaton, b. 19 Apr 1823; mar. Charles Everett. She died 26 May 1852. |
| +2918 | viii. | Samuel[8] Eaton, b. 25 Sep 1825; mar. Eliza Kinson, 1846. |
| +2919 | ix. | James[8] Eaton, twin of Luther, b. 10 Jun 1828; mar. Adeline. |

+2920    x. Luther[8] S. Eaton, twin of James, b. 10 Jun 1828; m. Eleanor.
 2921    xi. Caroline[8] Eaton, b. 24 Jan 1831; mar. Charles Barker of
          Antrim. She died 14 Dec 1875 in Hillsboro.
 2922   xii. Susan[8] Eaton, b. 18 Feb 1834; mar. Henry Watson of Weare
          and resided Hillsboro, N.H. She died 8 Feb 1908.


**1417. James[7] Eaton** (*James[6], James[5]*, James[4], Jonathan[3], Thomas[2],
John) was born 7 Mar 1788 at the remote farm on Hedgehog Mountain,
Deering Township, N.H.; mar. in Deering ca. 1810, **Olive Wilson**, who
had been born 1792 in Deering to Thomas Wilson. Early on, this couple
made the difficult trek (nearly 100 miles north by a direct route over
rugged terrain on paths and primitive roads, or by easier but much
longer "water-level" routes in the Merrimack or Connecticut River valleys) to settle at the unlikely village of Bethlehem, N.H. in the western
reaches of the White Mountains. (The significance attached to this migration is made clear in Appendix C.) They had their first four children
there before moving into the nearest "market town" of Littleton about
1820. Later in the empty-nest period, they returned to Antrim, N.H., one
of the two market towns closest to James's birthplace on Hedgehog
Mountain. James died in 1860, and is buried in the downtown cemetery
at Bennington, N.H., across the river from Antrim, where his father had
spent the last years of his life and had been buried in the same cemetery
a dozen years earlier.

    Children (some crucial dates with "*" are from Bennington, N.H.
tombstones):

 2923    i. Hiram[8] Eaton, b. *1813 in Bethlehem, N.H.; d. unmar.
          *1853.
 2924   ii. Rebecca[8] Eaton, b. ca. 1815, Bethlehem; mar. Amos
          Hemphill of Medford, Mass. She died 1872.
 2925  iii. Lucinda[8] Eaton, b. ca. 1817, Bethlehem; mar. Clinton
          French of Lyndeborough, N.H. She died 1848.
 2926   iv. Roxanna[8] Eaton, b. 1818-20 (the latter date making her a
          twin of v. below), in Bethlehem. She mar. Sewall Skinner
          of Laconia, N.H., but she died, 1840.
 2927    v. Joseph[8] Eaton, b. *1820 in Littleton, N.H.; d. unmar. *1853.
+2928   vi. James[8] W. Eaton, b. ca. 15 Oct 1823 in Littleton; mar. Mary.
 2929  vii. Lucetta[8] Eaton, b. ca. 1824; mar. Henry Delano of Duxbury,
          Mass.; she died 1871.
 2930 viii. Melissa[8] Eaton, b. ca. 1827; mar. John Sampson of Charles-
          town, Mass., where they resided. She died there childless,
          1871.


    **1419. Samuel[7] Eaton** (*James[6], James[5]*, James[4], Jonathan[3], Tho-
mas[2], John[1]) was born 13 Feb 1792 at the remote farm on Hedgehog
Mountain, Deering Township, N.H.; mar. **Betsey White** (she born 12 Mar

1796 to Benjamin White of neighboring Francestown, N.H.) on 4 Dec 1817. The couple settled on Betsey's father's farm in Francestown, where Samuel was a shoe-maker by trade. He died 4 Feb 1837 in Francestown.

Children, all born in Francestown, N.H.:

2931    i. Roxana[8] Eaton, b. 23 Mar 1818; she died unmar., 13
         Nov 1839 in Francestown.
+2932   ii. Samuel[8] Willard Eaton, b. 2 Nov 1819; mar. 1st, Sarah Carr.
2933    iii. Sarah[8] Jane Eaton, b. 19 May 1823; mar. Walter Comstock
         of Newport, N.H., 26 Aug 1844. She died 17 Apr 1850
         in Newport.
2934    iv. Caroline[8] Eaton, b. 7 Jul 1828; died 5 Aug 1831.
2935    v. Emily[8] Elizabeth Eaton, b. 4 Aug 1834; died unmar. at
         Francestown, 12 Jan 1852.

**1424. Isaac[7] Eaton** (*James[6], James[5]*, James[4], Jonathan[3], Thomas[2], John[1]) was born 5 Mar 1801 at the remote farm on Hedgehog Mountain, Deering Township, N.H.; mar. **Betsey Atwood** (she born 1804), and the couple had taken up residence in Deering not long before the 1830 Census. Later in the 1830s, however, the couple moved to join brother Samuel in nearby Francestown, where they resided in 1840 and 1850. Isaac earned his living in this period as a farm laborer; and he was solo in this role back in Deering in 1860, working on the farm of an Asa Goodnough, husband of an Elizabeth (Eaton). He died by his own hand, 4 Feb 1866. Wife Betsey died 2 Apr 1880. They are buried in Maplewood Cemetery in Antrim.

Children:

2936    i. Lorinda[8] Eaton, b. ca. 1834; is not with the family in 1850,
         but she died 15 Sep 1855 and is bur. with her parents.
+2937   ii. George[8] W. Eaton, b. 30 Nov 1840; mar. Mary J. Dow.
2938    iii. John[8] H. Eaton, b. ca. 1842 in Francestown, N.H.; was in
         Co. K of a N.H. Regt. in the Civil War; died 9 Sep 1862
         in Newark, New Jersey.
2939    iv. Ruth[8] Eaton, b. ca. 1844, probably at Francestown.

**1427. Hiram[7] Eaton** (*James[6], James[5]*, James[4], Jonathan[3], Thomas[2], John[1]) was born to father James's second wife, widow Sarah White, on 11 Dec 1817 at the remote farm on Hedgehog Mountain, Deering Township, N.H. Hiram learned the blacksmith trade, and moved down across the Contoocook River into the town of Antrim in 1841 to sell his services. He soon mar. **Edna C. Sweetser** (born 1817) of Deering, 28 Mar 1844, and brought her to Antrim. Hiram teamed up with the Antrim blacksmith Jonathan White, his mother's son by her first marriage, in inventing the "Antrim shovel," the first welded steel implement of its kind,

which became a great economic success at least in the northeastern U. S.,
and perhaps more broadly. Hiram and Edna lived out their lives in Antrim, with Edna dying there in 1896 and Hiram in 1908.

Children born in Antrim, N.H.:

2940    i. Charles[8] H. Eaton, b. 22 May 1845; mar. Addie Ellms of
        Scituate, Mass., 1871.
2941    ii. Lura[8] Eaton, b. 1847; died 1853 and bur. with her parents.
2942    iii. Walter[8] S. Eaton, b. 22 Feb 1855. He appears twice in the
        1880 Census at age 25: as a machine shop worker living
        with his parents at Antrim; and working in the Globe
        Nail factory in Boston and living in a rooming-house.

**1432. James[7] Eaton** (David[6], James[5-4], Jonathan[3], Thomas[2], John[1])
was born 19 Mar 1798 at Goffstown, N.H.; mar. **Rebecca Gould** of Watertown, Mass. on 22 Jul 1826 at Newton, Mass.  The couple settled in
Goffstown, where James was a reasonably prosperous farmer.  He died
there 20 Sep 1857.  Widow Rebecca continued to reside on the farm
which was then taken over by their eldest surviving son, George, and did
not die until 27 Jun 1883.

Children born in Goffstown, N.H.:

2943    i. James[8] Eaton, b. 1827, died 1830.
2944    ii. Lucy[8] G. Eaton, b. 1831; died 1832.
+2945   iii. George[8] M. Eaton, b. 19 May 1834; mar. Mary Greer, 1861.
2946    iv. Herman[8] J. Eaton, b. 20 Jul 1839; mar. Cynthia Crombie, b.
        in N.H., 1850.  This couple was at Geneseo, Henry Co.,
        Ill., in 1880, where Herman was a hardware merchant.
        There is no sign of children.  Herman died 20 Dec 1914,
        but where?
2947    v. Frances[8] G. Eaton, b. 22 May 1845; mar. Jewett Sweetser of
        Danvers, Mass., 1868.  She died 8 May 1922.
2948    vi. Mary[8] A. Eaton, b. 17 May 1847; mar. Charles Sherman of
        Liberty (Waldo Co.), Me., in 1869.

**1436. David[7] Eaton** (David[6], James[5-4], Jonathan[3], Thomas[2], John[1])
was born 26 Sep 1804 at Goffstown, N.H.  David went west early, and he
may be the unmar. David Eaton in Clark Co., Ill., Census for 1840, although the age is slightly off.  It is clear however that by 1850 he was
farming at what would become Tremont Twp. in Tazewell Co., Illinois
(the Peoria area).  There, or somewhere on the way, he met and mar.
**Sarah __?__**, born in Kentucky ca. 1821.  The couple appears at Tremont Twp., Ill. in the Censuses from 1850 at least thru 1870.  Wife Sarah
presumably died in the 1870s, but David[7] is a "retired farmer" in 1880,
with eldest son Otis[8] running the farm.

Children:

+ **2949**    i. Otis[8] Eaton, b. 1844, Ill.; removed to Sioux City, Iowa?
  **2950**   ii. Benjamin[8] Eaton, b. 1847; apparently died young.
  **2951**  iii. William[8] Eaton, b. 1849; at home, 1860, but then disappears.
+ **2952**  iv. David[8] Eaton, b. Dec 1850; mar. Harriet.
  **2953**   v. James[8] B. Eaton, b. ca. 1855; attending college, 1880, but not found thereafter.
  **2954**  vi. Robert[8] Eaton, b. ca. 1866.


**1440. (Rev.) Horace[7] Eaton** (David[6], James[5-4], Jonathan[3], Thomas[2], John[1]) was born 5 Oct 1811 at Goffstown, N.H., near the Bedford line. He studied for the Baptist ministry at the New Hampton Institution in 1841, and he was ordained as pastor at Bradford, N.H., where he preached, 1842-45. In this period he mar. 1st, **Sarah Chandler** of Bedford, daughter of Dea. William Chandler and a friend from his youth, 18 Apr 1843. In 1845-46 he did a tour of duty as a missionary in Iowa, and then returned to become the pastor at Chester, N.H. from 1846 to 1850. He next preached at Wilton, N.H., 1850-55, and at Dunbarton, N.H., 1855-59. He was serving 1859-62 as Agent of the N.H. Baptist Convention, when wife Sarah died 9 Mar 1861 in New London, N.H. He soon mar. 2d, **Mrs. Ann Elizabeth (Hawkes) Wiley**, widow of Edmund Eaton Wiley, and daughter of Adam and Elizabeth (Hull) Hawkes of Wakefield, Mass., on 22 Oct 1861. He then was briefly acting pastor at No. Reading, Mass. in 1862-63, the family settled on his new wife's territory at Wakefield, Mass., where they remained until his death. In this period he preached at Salem, Mass. 1871-73; Richmond 1875-76; and Chester 1876-77. He died at Wakefield 15 Jun 1878 (Carter, 1906).

Children with Sarah:

  **2955**    i. William[8] Chandler Eaton, b. Feb 1844; mar. in 1866 Mary E. Burlingame, b. Jun 1845 in N.H., but whose parents were of Rhode Island. They res. in 1880 in Nashua, N.H., where he was a photographer, but in due time removed to Auburn, R.I. Later they res. in Cranston, R.I., where he was a fruit merchant. They had no issue.
  **2956**   ii. Clara[8] A. Eaton, b. 21 Mar 1847 at Chester, N.H.; mar. a Bradley, and died at Bridgeport, Conn.
  **2957**  iii. Mary[8] Eaton, b. ca. 1849 and died rapidly.

Child with Ann Elizabeth:

  **2958**   iv. Grace[8] Eaton, b. ca. 1864, Wakefield, Mass.

## #9. Broader Migrations of Our Eatons

In Sidebar #6 we summarized some of the main migration destinations of our Eatons up to 1820, as they spread out, usually northward, from their original homesteads in the Salisbury/Seabrook and
Haverhill areas. Here we take a broader look at movements of these
Eatons, both beyond 1820 and beyond the New England states.

Within New England. As we have seen, Seabrook and Deer Isle
remained well populated with our Eatons throughout the 19th century and indeed to present days. In fact, our Map #5 does not need a
lot of revision to represent the situation a generation later in 1850.
Of the eleven towns where Eaton migrants had settled most success-
fully only one, Sanbornton, has fallen below our 20-Eaton cutpoint
by 1850. A second clear loser, however, is Weare, the largest N.H.
destination for our Eaton migrants as of 1820. While there were 10
of our Eaton families in Weare in 1820 and 10 again in 1850, the
1820 families averaged 5 persons per family, while they had only 2.7
persons per family in 1850, or a collapse of nearly 50%. Beyond
these losers, the other nine clusters of Map #5 are largely holding
their own, save for the fact that if we separate Sedgwick, Me. from
Deer Isle, we find that its Eaton population in 1850 has dropped too,
by 40%. This is well hidden by a doubling of Eatons on Deer Isle in
the same period. It is also true that one of the two or three new additions to our list in Maine would be Brooklin township, which abuts
Sedgwick to the east, and probably has drawn population from it in
intervening 30 years.

However, to say that most of the other Eaton plantations of Map
#5 were "holding their own" in 1850 needs some elaboration. Actual-
ly, almost every one of them had lost population slightly in the interim, but by less than 10%, such that they had not lost much of their
numerical dominance. But in the 1820-50 interval, the New England
population had grown very significantly, so that in a relative sense
these towns had lost ground visibly. When we turn to new winners on
our migration list, it is easy to see that our Eatons were just participating in a national trend: the two main winners in N.H. were the two
big new mill towns of Manchester and Nashua. There had been no
Eatons in either area even in 1830; but by 1850 there were 55 Eatons
in the two towns. Of course the lion's share of this increase was in
Manchester, and amusingly, the decline of Sanbornton was in part
due to two of its families removing to Manchester. The big new winner of Eatons in Maine was Portland, with 33 of them in 1850. The
first stirrings of urbanization were underway.

Remarkably few of our Eatons were enticed to other New England states in any numbers, save to Boston in the later 19th Century,
and even then many of them stayed a while but later returned home.
A few families in both our Salisbury and Haverhill branches migrated

to Vermont after 1759, but to scattered sites. (The large and enduring clusters of Eatons in Vermont, such as at Castleton or Rochester, were of the Reading and Dedham branches, respectively.)

Beyond New England. This is a large and risky subject. Large for obvious reasons and risky because we have only a weak fix on the actual contingent of our Eatons who left New England. We do know a lot about some of these migrants. The problem is that there are also numerous Eaton children of Generations VI-VIII who appear to have grown up but who then vanish. Some fraction of these undoubtedly went West, but by definition we know nothing about where or when. Therefore generalizations we might make are risky.

At least two things can be said with confidence. One is that once out of New England, our Eatons scattered very widely. Over all migrants of both Salisbury and Haverhill branches, there are signs of at least some residence in 36 of the 42 non-New England contiguous states (as well as the District of Columbia), missing only Delaware in the east, the Dakotas in the Plains, and Idaho, Utah and New Mexico in the mountains. There were also at least residential stops in four Canadian provinces, the West Indies, Cuba, Mexico and Tahiti. With one great exception, we know of no large congregations of our Eatons at any of their destinations outside New England. The exception is, of course, the major Nova Scotia "plantation" founded by David[5] Eaton (#202) of the Haverhill branch as early as 1761.

A second observation is that the Haverhill Branch was considerably more "migratory" than the Salisbury one, both in rates of migration, and in distances covered around the New World. Indeed, Nova Scotia was our Eatons' first move beyond New England; and this "twig" was extremely prolific, representing in later generations a third or more of the known Haverhill Eatons. But even apart from Nova Scotia, Haverhill Eatons in the Generation VI-VIII were leaving New England at rates two to three times those of the Salisbury branch.

There is one other amusing contrast between our two branches. The normal path out of New England by land lies thru New York State. The majority of Eaton emigrants have gone on to further destinations, but we have 11 Salisbury and 12 Haverhill adults who removed specifically to New York State. All of the Haverhill migrants located in upstate New York; but only three of the Salisbury ones did, and all three, like the 12 Haverhill migrants, were departing to the west from southern New Hampshire (or Haverhill, Mass.). The remaining eight Salisbury-branch migrants settled instead in New York City (or Brooklyn). Seven of these eight were Eatons from the Maine coast. The pattern suggests that the Maine coast was in closer communication (by the sea lanes, of course) to New York City than was the interior. And indeed, in a case or two, the Eaton migrant was a ship captain of Maine changing permanently to NYC as his home port!

## ** The Senior Author of this Volume **

**1443. (Rev.) William[7] Hadley Eaton** (David[6], James[5-4], Jonathan[3], Thomas[2], John[1]) was born 4 Sep 1818 at Goffstown, N.H. He began study for the Baptist ministry with preparatory work at the New Hampton Institution. He then graduated from Brown University in 1845, and the Newton (Mass.) Theological Institution, 1848. Just before starting his first ministry at Salem, Mass. (1849-54), he mar. **Caroline Bartlett**, daughter of Abner H. and Sally (Fisher) Bartlett of Milford, N.H., on 26 Aug 1849. After Salem, Mass., he served in 1855-6 as financial agent for the New London (N.H.) Academy, and then began a lengthy pastorate at the First Baptist Church in Nashua, N.H., 1856-70, during which he raised $100,000 for the New London Academy. In 1861 he received his Doctorate of Divinity from Brown University, and served as a Trustee for Brown, 1876-79. In 1870-71 he left his Nashua post to serve as financial agent of his alma mater, Newton Theological, raising $200,000 for it. Then he took a pastorate at Keene, N.H., which he held 1872-89. He then returned and preached without charge at his Nashua Church, 1889-96. In addition to genealogical work for the first incarnation of the Eaton Family Association, where he was the reigning expert on the descendants from John[1]/Anne of Salisbury, he published a history of the Baptists of New Hampshire and some of his sermons (Carter, 1906). He died at Nashua on 10 Jun 1896, with the current volume about two-thirds complete). As there is no report to the contrary, we assume this couple was childless.

**1452. Nathaniel[7] D. Eaton** (Cotton[6], James[5-4], Jonathan[3], Thomas[2], John[1]) was born ca. 1816 in Maine, prob. at Madison or Greene; mar. **Ann B. Clark** (she born 26 Dec 1819 in New Hampshire), 20 Apr 1846, at Hermon (Penobscot Co.), Me. They settled in Hermon permanently, and Nathaniel kept a modest farm there. Nathaniel was drowned off Gay Head (Martha's Vineyard, Mass.) in the wreck of the ship The City of Columbus", 18 Jan 1884. He is buried at Snow's Corner cemetery in Hermon.

Children born in Hermon, Me.:

2959    i. Sarah[8] Augusta Eaton, b. Apr 1847; d. 3 Nov 1851, Hermon.
2960    ii. Charles[8] G. Eaton, b. 1848.
+ 2961    iii. West[8] D. Eaton, b. 1851; mar. Annie M.
2962    iv. Leanna[8] Eaton, b. 28 Sep 1852; died 8 May 1899.

**1454. Josiah[7] G. Eaton** (Cotton[6], James[5-4], Jonathan[3], Thomas[2], John[1]) born ca. 1819 in Turner, Me.; mar. 1st, **Nancy B. Snow,** 7 Nov 1848 at Brewer, Me. They settled in Hermon where he had grown up, and he was a merchant there. Nancy died early in 1858, and Josiah mar.

2d, **Aurelia E. Snow**, prob. Nancy's sister, 30 Aug 1858, also at Brewer. He died in 1899.

Children with Nancy at Hermon:

2963   i. George[8] F. Eaton, b. 21 Apr 1850; died 13 Apr 1863.
2964   ii. Charles[8] Fremont Eaton, b. 18 Nov 1853; died 10 Jan 1859.
2965   iii. Benjamin[8] G. Eaton, b. ca. 1858.

Children with Aurelia at Hermon:

+2966   iv. Fred[8] G. Eaton, b. 1859; mar. Alice Gibson.


**1460. John[7] Eaton** (John[6], Nathaniel[5], James[4], Jonathan[3], Thomas[2], John[1]) was born 7 Nov 1798 in Sutton, N.H. He was for a time apprenticed as a currier at Croydon, N.H., but then Caleb Kimball, his maternal grandfather, offered to turn his own homestead on Kimball Hill over to him if he would support him and his wife for life. John accepted the offer gratefully. He mar. **Janet Collins Andrews** 5 Jun 1829, and they settled on that homestead, beginning a large family. Janet died early, on 7 Feb 1846, but not before she had borne nine children. The farm was already handsome, and John's own energy meant that he added farm after farm to the original property, until he was the largest landholder in the section. This homestead was in time was labelled the "Eaton Grange," becoming the focal point for celebrated summer reunions of this large clan that had spread so far and wide around the country (see Sidebar #12). Father John[7] died 9 May 1873 in Sutton (cf. Worthen, 1890).

Children at Sutton, N.H.:

+2967   i. (Gen.) John[8] Eaton, b. 5 Dec 1829; mar. Alice Shirley, 1864.
2968   ii. Caroline[8] Eaton, b. 10 Jul 1831; mar. Samuel McMaster Pennock, 27 May 1869, in Toledo, Ohio. They res. in Somerville, Mass.
2969   iii. Nathan[8] Andrew Eaton, b. 11 Apr 1833. He left home at 16 to search for gold in California, and was enough of a success to be able to help his oldest brother John complete college. After a return visit to New Hampshire in 1859, he became a merchant in Waterloo, Iowa and then Chicago. In 1873 he returned to California, locating near Merle in San Diego Co., pre-empting government land and developing it into a salt works and honey industry.
+2970   iv. Frederick[8] Eaton, b. 10 Feb 1835; mar. 1st, Mary Shirley.
+2971   v. Lucien[8] Bonaparte Eaton, b. 8 Mar 1837; mar. Clara.
2972   vi. Christina[8] Landon Eaton, b. 23 Aug 1840; became the cashier for brother Fred's department store in Toledo, Ohio.
+2973   vii. James[8] Andrew Eaton, b. 30 Sep 1841; mar. Fanny Newell.

+**2974** viii. Charles[8] Eaton, b. 28 Aug 1843; mar. Marion Blanchard.
**2975** ix. Mary[8] Janet Eaton, b. 12 Jul 1845; died 10 Nov 1845.


**1464. (Dr.) Jacob[7] Sawyer Eaton** (John[6], Nathaniel[5], James[4], Jonathan[3], Thomas[2], John[1]) was born 4 Jan 1805 in Warner, N.H. He began a medical career without collegiate studies, thru an apprenticeship with a local doctor, and then began his own practice at Alexandria, N.H. He soon was to practice in Bristol, N.H. He mar. 1st, **Mrs. Harriet (Bean) Kimball** on 20 Sep 1830, but she died at Bristol 5 Dec 1837 in birthing complications. While still at Bristol he mar. 2d, **Alma Ellery Tyler** of Harvard, Mass., 20 Sep 1849. After 24 years of service to an admiring public in Bristol, Jacob moved to his new wife's territory in Massachusetts in 1855. He practiced at Stowe and So. Deerfield (there in 1860) before retiring to Harvard, Mass. where he died 5 Sep 1888.

Children with Harriet, prob. at Bristol, N. H.:

+**2976** i. John[8] Marshall Eaton, b. 12 May 1832; m. Maria Wetherbee.
**2977** ii. Frances[8] Amelia Eaton, b. 1835; died 1838.
**2978** iii. Horace[8] Augustus Eaton, b. 1837 at Bristol; died 1839.

Children with Alma:

**2979** iv. Lucien[8] Kimball Eaton, b. 7 Nov 1850 in Bristol, N.H. A natural mechanic, he went west early, working as a machinist in the railroad shops of Elkhart and Ft. Wayne, Ind. from 1876 to his death. He mar. Mary E. Titus, daughter of John Titus of Elkhart, and was active in his Presbyterian Church in Ft. Wayne, engaging in political activity as well. Although a powerfully built man in perfect health, he died after a week's illness, 16 Mar 1888. Widow Mary was back in Elkhart in 1900, living with her mother and sister, reporting no children born to her.
**2980** v. Harriet[8] Frances Eaton, b. 1853; died 1863.
+**2981** vi. James[8] Ellery Eaton, b. 10 Jul 1855, Stowe, Mass; mar. Flora.
**2982** viii. Alma[8] Tyler Eaton, b. 12 Nov 1857; taught in Harvard, Mass., schools; mar. Dr. Benjamin Royal of Garland, Me., 24 Sep 1863, and they res. Harvard, Mass.


**1466. Lucien[7] Bonaparte Eaton** (John[6], Nathaniel[5], James[4], Jonathan[3], Thomas[2], John[1]) was born in Hartley, Canada, 17 Dec 1808, although he was carried back to Sutton when still an infant, and grew up there. As a young man he struck out westward, like some of his brothers, arriving in the northeast corner of Indiana (Steuben Co.) at some time in the 1840s. For three years there he served as an itinerant minister from the Methodist Church. He continued to preach occasionally after he turned his attention to farming. On 3 Jul 1853 he mar. **Melinda Phelps**

(she born 20 Nov 1815 in Brookfield, Franklin Co. Ind., to Reuben and Ruth (Corson) Phelps). The couple settled down in Fremont Twp. His farming enterprise thrived, mirrored in explosive growth of his real estate valuations from $1,600 in 1850 to $8,000 in 1860 and $20,000 in 1870. Lucien died 27 Feb 1889, leaving 800 acres and over $5,000 to establish and maintain a home for indigent women in Steuben Co. He left the rest of his estate, 120 acres, to his son Isaac, the sole child born to this late-marrying couple (from Worthen, 1890).

Child, born in Fremont, Ind.:

**2983**    i. Isaac[8] Eaton, b. 12 Jan 1855. He apparently never married, as he lived alone in 1900, a decade after his father's death. He may also have fallen on hard times in spite of his legacy, since he lists himself in 1910 as a "general farm employee."

**1467. (Rev.) Horace[7] Eaton** (John[6], Nathaniel[5], James[4], Jonathan[3], Thomas[2], John[1]) was born 7 Oct 1810 in Sutton, N.H. As an adolescent he served as an apprentice to his silversmith and watch-making brother Hiram in St. Albans, Vt., 1824-30. He later attended Dartmouth College (1835-39) and then completed study for the ministry at Union Theological Seminary in New York City in 1842. He was ordained pastor of the 6th St. Presbyterian Church in New York City, Jun 1843. He subsequently mar. **Anna Ruth Webster**, born in Boscawen, N.H. and a graduate of Mt. Holyoke Female Seminary, on 13 Aug 1845. The couple then took a pastorate in western N.Y. State near Rochester, at Palmyra, where they would spend the rest of their lives. However, Rev. Horace travelled through Europe and the Holy Land on two occasions. He wrote a great deal for the press, and published many of his sermons. He received an honorary Doctorate of Divinity from his alma mater, Dartmouth College. He died in Palmyra, N.Y., 21 Oct 1883.

Children born in Palmyra:

**2984**    i. Horace[8] Webster Eaton, b. 28 Jun 1846. A Yale graduate, 1870; in 1880, res. with parents in Palmyra, N.Y. and was a clerk in a broker's office; later clerked in the government service in Washington, D.C.

**2985**    ii. John[8] Spaulding Eaton, b. 27 Aug 1848; died 4 Jul 1869.

**2986**    iii. Anna[8] Sawyer Eaton, b. 1851; died 1853.

**2987**    iv. Mary[8] Sawyer Eaton, b. 19 Dec 1853; taught school in New York, Michigan and Ontario.

**2988**    v. Elizabeth[8] Webster Eaton, b. 25 Mar 1857; a graduate of Mt. Holyoke, she taught school in various places in the states of Iowa and Colorado.

**1468.  Jubal[7] Harrington  Eaton** (Elijah[6], Nathaniel[5], James[4], Jonathan[3], Thomas[2], John[1]) was born 1 Aug 1798 at Haverhill, Mass., but was taken to Sutton, N.H. when he was two.  In 1813 he went to live with his uncle and aunt, James and Pamelia (Eaton) Messer.  When his father died in 1818, he returned home to help with the farm.  Jubal went South for a period, but returned to mar. 1st, **Pluma Putney**, dau. of Stephen and Sarah of Boscawen, N.H., Oct 1827.  They settled on the "Kendrick farm" in Sutton; but Pluma died there, Feb 1833.  Jubal then mar. 2d, **Mrs. Sarah (Dresser) Brown**, dau. of Samuel and Rachel (Story) Dresser, on 5 Mar 1835 in Sutton (also recorded in Hopkinton, N.H.). The couple soon removed to Warner, where Jubal was in the business of brick-making for a period, but then concentrated on farming.  He died at Warner, 2 Nov 1878 (see Worthen, 1890).

Children with Pluma in Sutton:

2989    i. Sumner[8] Eaton, b. 2 Sep 1828; died Jun 1843 at Warner.
2990    ii. Sarah[8] Elizabeth Eaton, b. 11 Nov 1830; mar. James Morrill
            of Concord, Sep 1852.

Children with Sarah in Warner:

2991    iii. Pluma[8] Eaton, b. 16 Jan 1836; mar. Sullivan Marston of
            Deerfield, N.H.; they res. at Newport, N.H.
+2992   iv. Jubal[8] Harrington Eaton, b. 1 Nov 1839; m. Martha Bryant.
2993    v. Jacob[8] Eaton, b. 14 Feb 1843; died 2 Oct 1847.


**1470.  Elijah[7] Eaton** (Elijah[6], Nathaniel[5], James[4], Jonathan[3], Thomas[2], John[1]) was born 24 Mar 1803 in Sutton, N.H.; mar. **Fanny Sawyer** (born 25 Jun 1804 to Joshua and Sarah (George) Sawyer), on 16 Apr 1835, in Warner.  He was a trader and merchant. They res. in Warner, although Elijah died early, on 24 Mar 1843.

Children born in Warner, N.H.:

2994    i. Frances[8] A. Eaton, b. 29 Jun 1836; mar. Lucius H. Tyler of
            Hopkinton, N.H., 26 Jun 1883.
2995    ii. Mary[8] S. Eaton, b. 1837; died 1853.
2996    iii. Roxanna[8] Eaton, b. 1840; died 1843.
2997    iv. Sarah[8] Eaton, b. 1842; died 1843.


**1471.  Nathaniel[7A] Eaton** (Elijah[6], Nathaniel[5], James[4], Jonathan[3], Thomas[2], John[1]) was born 27 Apr 1805 at Sutton, N.H.  He went west to seek his wife and a fortune, and mar. a N. Y. native, **Martha __?__** born ca. 1806, settling in Alabama Twp., Genessee Co., near Batavia, N.Y. Like his brother Elijah back home, he died there early, on 26 Mar 1844.

Children, prob. all but the first born in Alabama, N.Y.:

**2998**    i. Sumner[8] J. Eaton, b. ca. 1832; mar. Harriett S. __?__, a
        Vt. native; res. in Newstead (Erie Co.), N.Y., where he
        was farming in 1870 and 1880 with no sign of issue.
**2999**    ii. Martha[8] Eaton, b. ca. 1836; died before 1850.
**3000**    iii. Ruth[8] A. Eaton, b. ca. 1839.
**3001**    iv. Nathaniel[8] J. Eaton, b. 1844; died in the Civil War.


**1475. Ariel[7] Kendrick Eaton** (Elijah[6], Nathaniel[5], James[4], Jonathan[3], Thomas[2], John[1]) was born 1 Dec 1813 in Sutton, N.H., and was
named for a charismatic young preacher of the period in west central
New Hampshire. He set out in 1832 in search of a better education than
he could get at home. He alternated teaching school with study for a
number of years, first at various towns in New Hampshire, and later at a
select school at Chelmsford, Mass. In 1836 he removed to Ohio to study
law while teaching, mostly at Washington Court House, Fayette County
(south of Columbus). In this period he mar. 1st, **Sarah McArthur** of
nearby Ross Co., on 3 Jun 1839. After the first child, wife Sarah M. died
15 Jun 1840. Ariel then removed to Indiana, where he served as county
auditor for Randolph Co., 1841-44, and in the process was admitted to
the bar in 1842. He moved to Iowa in 1844, participating actively in the
development of the state. He returned to Randolph Co., Ind., to mar. 2d,
**Sarah Jarnagin** (she born 24 Apr 1827 in Highland Co., Ohio) on 7
Dec 1845. From 1846 to 1855 the couple lived in Delhi, Delaware Co.
just west of Dubuque, Iowa, where he practiced law, held county offices
and served in the state legislature for four years. From 1855 to 1858 he
presided over the sale for more than two million acres of public land in
the Turkey River district. By this time he had removed his family to
Osage, Mitchell Co., near the Minnesota state line.

Child with Sarah McArthur in Ohio:

**3002**    i. Byron[8] Eaton, b. 29 May 1840; died in infancy.

Children with Sarah Jarnagin in various states:

**3003**    ii. Marshall[8] S. Eaton, b. 1846; died 1848.
**+3004**    iii. Willard[8] Lee Eaton, b. 13 Oct 1848 in Delhi, Iowa.
**+3005**    iv. Sumner[8] Franklin Eaton, b. 5 Dec 1851 in Delhi, Iowa.
**3006**    v. Jones[8] Eaton, b. 1858 in Osage, Iowa; died 1861.


**1477. Carlos[7] Smith Eaton** (Elijah[6], Nathaniel[5], James[4], Jonathan[3],
Thomas[2], John[1]) was born 4 May 1818 at Sutton, N.H., and brought up
by his widowed mother there. He mar. **Laura Warner Dimond** of Warner (she born 11 Dec 1822 to Ezekiel and Lydia (Hardy) Dimond of
Warner) on 14 May 1850. The family homestead in Sutton, which fell to

Carlos after all of his siblings were up and out, usually to a wider world, was not originally a large one.  But this is where he and Laura spent the rest of their days, and through frugality and efficiency managed to double the size of the estate.  Carlos died there 18 Nov 1886.  His widow removed to Charlestown, Mass.

Children born in Sutton, N.H.:

**3007**   i. Martha[8] A. Eaton, b. 17 Mar 1851; mar. Charles A. Bemis of Dublin, N.H. 17 Oct 1872; they res. at Boston Highlands.
**3008**   ii. Ellen[8] Maria Eaton, b. 29 Mar 1853; mar. Austin Calvin Stearnes of Hopkinton, Mass., 23 Sep 1880; they res. in Peterborough, N.H.
**3009**   iii. Mary[8] Elizabeth Eaton, b. 6 Apr 1855; mar. Benning M. Bean, 14 Sep 1889.  Mr. Bean was a stock-raiser; they res. Grass Range, Montana.


**1478. Nathaniel[7] Eaton** (Ebenezer[6], Nathaniel[5], James[4], Jonathan[3], Thomas[2], John[1]) was born ca. 1795, perhaps at Sutton, N.H.; mar. **Susan Philbrick** (born ca. 1797 to John and Dorothy (Coburn) Philbrick), on 24 Feb 1820 in Sutton.  The couple settled permanently at Lempster, N.H., where they appear in consecutive Censuses, 1830-70.  Nathaniel worked a small farm there.  He died before 1880; wife Susan died 8 May, 1886.

Children, all but perhaps the first in Lempster, N.H.:

**+3010**   i. Sumner[8] Eaton, b. ca. 1821; mar. Emily Booth, 1845.
**3011**   ii. Daughter[8] Eaton, b. ca. 1822-25.
**3012**   iii. Minerva[8] Eaton, b. ca. 1831.
**3013**   iv. Mary[8] Eaton, b. ca. 1833.
**3014**   v. Daughter[8] Eaton, b. ca. 1835; died young.


**1487. (Hon.) Leonard[7] Eaton** (Nathaniel[6-5], James[4], Jonathan[3], Thomas[2], John[1]) was born 10 Jun 1800 in Hopkinton, N.H.; mar. at Warner, 2 Feb 1829, **Susan(na) Evans**, b. 25 Jan 1801 to Hon. Benjamin and Susan (Wadleigh) Evans.  Before marriage he had graduated from the medical school of Dartmouth College in 1826, and practised a few years at Hampstead, N.H.  About the time of his marriage, however, he bought the practice of his original mentor in Warner, and the couple settled there for life.  He was a skilled physician with a large practice well beyond Warner.  He actively supported the local Baptist Church and led its choir.  He was a representative in the state legislature in 1851-52, and a State Senator, 1853-54.  He died 22 Nov 1868; and wife Susan died in Jul 1874 (Worthen, 1890).

Children at Warner, N.H.:

**3015**    i. Susan[8] Evans Eaton, b. 24 Feb 1833; completed her studies at New Hampton, and was recognized as one of the most successful teachers in the region over the course of her life. She d. 11 Dec 1889 at her sister's in Concord, N.H.

**3016**    ii. Maria[8] George Eaton, b. 22 Aug 1835; mar. Hon. John Y. Mugridge, 31 Dec 1857. He was one of the most eminent lawyers in New Hampshire. He served in the state senate, and presided over it in 1868-69. He d. 14 Apr 1884, after which his widow and sister Susan spent a year of touring in Europe.

**3017**    iii. Sophronia[8] Badger Eaton, b. 19 Feb 1837; mar. Hilliard Davis of Davisville, Warner. She d. 28 Feb 1864.

**1489. Alvin[7] Eaton** (Nathaniel[6-5], James[4], Jonathan[3], Thomas[2], John[1]) was born 18 Dec 1805 in Sutton, N.H. In 1829-30 he removed to Woodstock, Md., where as a stoneworker he owned and managed the Fox Rock granite quarry operation there. He was very energetic and built a large contracting business, providing the stone for many municipal buildings in Baltimore including the city hall and the B&O R.R. depot, as well as for the extension of the post office building in Washington, D.C. He mar. 1st, **Hannah W. Hardy** (she born 21 Dec 1820) on 3 Mar 1845. She died 11 Jun 1857, and Alvin mar. 2d, **Sylvia Hazeltine** (she born 25 Dec 1823 in Rockingham, Vt., to James and Fanny Hazeltine) on 3 Jan 1859. Alvin died Mar 1878 (Worthen, 1890).

Children with Hannah at Woodstock, Md.:

**3018**    i. Alvin[8] Eaton, b. 10 Dec 1847; died 1847.

**3019**    ii. Ellen[8] Maria Eaton, b. 3 Mar 1849; mar. John J. Evans of Wales, England, and settled in Woodstock, Md.

**3020**    iii. George[8] S. Eaton, b. 7 Oct 1852; died May 1857.

**1490. Nathaniel[7] Eaton** (Nathaniel[6-5], James[4], Jonathan[3], Thomas[2], John[1]) was born 22 Jan 1808 in Sutton, N.H. He studied medicine in some degree through his brother, Leonard, but also followed lectures at Dartmouth and at Bowdoin. He practiced in Mississippi and Texas. He mar. late, to a Kentucky native, **Harriet Augustine Ricketts** (she born ca. 1824) on 18 Feb 1855. He made one trip home, and then retired to Mountain View, Cal., where he died April, 1874. No apparent issue.

**1492. (Hon.) George[7] Clinton Eaton** (Nathaniel[6-5], James[4], Jonathan[3], Thomas[2], John[1]) was born 28 Jul 1814 at Sutton, N.H.; mar. 1st, **Lorinda Rowell** (she born Oct 1821 to Silas and Susan (Pettee) Rowell) in Oct 1842. George C. never lived anywhere but at his father's old homestead. Since his father was well-to-do and lived five days beyond his 100th birthday, he remained the head of household for Census purposes for much of George's life. George took a good farm and made it one of the very best in town. He was also able to travel through many parts of the country. He was greatly trusted in local affairs, being a selectman of the town for many years, and represented Sutton in the state legislature. Wife Lorinda died 15 Jul 1851, and George mar. 2d, **Betsey Jane Pressey** (b. 12 Apr 1837 to Winthrop and Hannah (Bean) Pressey), on 19 Mar 1863.

Child with Lorinda in Sutton, N.H.:

**3021**   i. Georgiana[8] Eaton, b. 31 Dec 1849; died 7 Jul 1865.


**1496. Ichabod[7] Eaton** (Ichabod[6], Nathaniel[5], James[4], Jonathan[3], Thomas[2], John[1]) was born 28 Aug 1803 at Haverhill, Mass.; mar. 1st, **Louisa M. Jones** (of Canaan, N.H., she born 1812) about 1836. The couple settled in Hopkinton, N.H. near father Ichabod[6]'s homestead. Louisa died in 1857; and Ichabod mar. 2d, **Mrs. Mary J. George** (she born 1816), on 19 Apr 1858 in Salem, N.H. Ichabod[7] remained a farmer of quite limited means, and died 2 Jan 1867 in Hopkinton.

Children born to Louisa in Hopkinton, N.H.:

**3022**   i. Dana[8] Bradford Eaton, b. 23 Dec 1838; died 15 Feb 1845.
**3023**   ii. Helen[8] Maria Eaton, b. 15 Oct 1842; died 15 Oct 1842.
**3024**   iii. Ellen[8] Louisa Eaton, b. 1 Sep 1844; died 23 Dec 1928 at
              Hopkinton.
**3025**   iv. (Moses) Kimball[8] Eaton, b. 27 1846. He served in Co. E,
              14th Regt. of the N.H. Volunteers, and died 20 Sep 1863.


**1497. Nathaniel[7] Clarks Eaton** (Ichabod[6], Nathaniel[5], James[4], Jonathan[3], Thomas[2], John[1]) was born 1 Sep 1805 at Haverhill, Mass.; mar. **Harriet Wetherill**, also born ca. 1805 (both then of Hopkinton) on 29 May 1834 in Hopkinton, N.H. This couple settled first in Hopkinton, but about 1842 they bought land in Hillsborough, N.H., and resided there for a period spanning the 1850 Census, when we can see the family composition. Nathaniel was a mason by trade, and we cannot find him after 1850.

Apparent children as of 1850:

**3026**   i. Charles[8] W. Eaton, b. ca. 1836 in Hopkinton, N.H.?
**3027**   ii. George[8] H. Eaton, b. ca. 1840 in Hopkinton, N.H
**3028**   iii. Franklin[8] T. Eaton, b. ca. 1842, prob. in Hopkinton, N.H.
**3029**   iv. Mary[8] E. Eaton, b. ca. 1849 in Hillsborough, N.H.

**1515. James[7] W. Eaton** (Josiah[6], Ebenezer[5], James[4], Jonathan[3], Thomas[2], John[1]) was born 22 Aug 1817 in Somerville, N.J., but grew up in the Albany, N.Y. area. He mar. **Elizabeth Brenner**, ca. 1840. He began as a stone mason, but rapidly developed into a major contractor and builder in the Albany area. In 1874 James W. was appointed by Gov. Dix as Superintendent of Construction of the State Capitol, a role he performed with distinction until 1883. The family res. in Albany in the early days, but later moved to nearby Watervliet. James W. died in 1891.

Children born in Albany, N.Y.:

3030 i. Mary[8] Eaton, b. ca. 1841.
+3031 ii. Calvin[8] W. Eaton, b. Jul 1842; mar. Anna __?__ in 1865.
+3032 iii. James[8] Webster Eaton, b. 14 May 1857; mar. Hortense.


**1521. Kimball[7] Eaton** (Kimball[6], Enoch[5], James[4], Jonathan[3], Thomas[2], John[1]) was born 16 Feb 1806 at Cavendish, Vt. He probably accompanied his parents westward in N.Y. State as an adolescent. Somewhere he met and mar. **Margaret __?__** and the couple had an early child in Buffalo, N.Y. In due time, however, they returned to Bennington Co., Vt., settling in Arlington there, where he was a stone cutter and dealer in marble.

Children (perhaps others not surviving infancy or childhood):

3033 i. Charles[8] J. Eaton, b. 2 Apr 1836 at Buffalo, N.Y. He served in the Civil War in Co. D of the 22d Regiment of Volunteers, and died of typhoid, 18 May 1862, at Washington, D.C.
3034 ii. William[8] P. Eaton, b. ca. 1838, Middletown, Vt.; mar. M. Jenks; res. Arlington, Vt.


**1522. Ryland[7] Fletcher Eaton** (Kimball[6], Enoch[5], James[4], Jonathan[3], Thomas[2], John[1]) was born 18 Mar 1808 in Cavendish, Vt. It is not clear how much of his father's move into New York State during the 1820s the young Ryland participated in. In any event, he mar. on 11 Aug 1833, **Clarissa Cook Clark**, who was of Middletown Springs in Rutland Co., Vt., which would have been a halfway station from Cavendish to the west side of the mountains and the New York line. The couple later res. just over the line in Salem, N.Y. (1850); and in Adams, Jefferson Co., N.Y. near Lake Ontario (1860), both sites having some rough proximity to places where father Kimball had taken the family in later years in northern N.Y. State. Like his brother Kimball, Ryland lists his occupation as stone cutter.

Children with Clarissa:

**3035**  i. Emmett[8] D. Eaton, b. 1 Mar 1835 in Vt.; was in the Confederate service in the Civil War.
**3036**  ii. Augusta[8] E. Eaton, b. 1 Mar 1837.
**+3037**  iii. Frank[8] T. Eaton, b. 8 Jan 1840; removed to Iowa, and died in Cedar Rapids, 1884.
**3038**  iv. Frances[8] Eaton, b. 1842; d. 23 Feb 1861, Washington, D.C.
**3039**  v. Barton[8] C. Eaton, b. 10 Sep 1843.
**3040**  vi. Fannie[8] A. Eaton, b. 13 Jan 1845 in Arlington, Vt.
**+3041**  vii. John[8] R. Eaton, b. 5 Apr 1849; mar. Sophia E. Vail.
**+3042**  viii. Charles[9] A. Eaton, b. 22 Feb 1852 in Woodville, N.Y.

**1528. Warren[7] Eaton** (Enoch[6-5], James[4], Jonathan[3], Thomas[2], John[1]) was born 2 Apr 1814 presumably in Bowdoinham, Me.; but also prob. went west with his family to Oxford, Chenango Co., N.Y. early enough to have done some growing up there; mar. **Eliza Penston** on 12 Aug 1838. Warren died 1889. (Molyneux, 1911 (p. 439), whose N.Y. sources were often reasonable, given that the work was written in Syracuse, N.Y.)

Children:

**3043**  i. George[8] A. Eaton, b. ca. 1840; died young.
**3044**  ii. James[8] Warren Eaton, b. ca. 1843; fought in Civil War, and died in a No. Carolina prison, 3 Jan 1865.
**3045**  iii. Mary[8] Elizabeth Eaton, b. ca. 1845; died young?
**3046**  iv. Amanda[8] C. Eaton, b. ca. 1848; mar. George B. Fletcher, 12 Mar 1873.
**3047**  v. Emma[8] Eaton, b. May 1850; mar. Charles Brown and res. in Waverley, N.Y.
**3048**  vi. Lizzie[8] Eaton, b. 185?
**+3049**  vii. George[8A] P. Eaton, b. 1855; mar. Emma Kennear.
**+3050**  viii. Charles[8] B. Eaton, b. Jul 1861; mar. 1st, Ida Sherwood.

**1532. (Capt.) Edmund[7] Eaton** (Warren[6], Enoch[5], James[4], Jonathan[3], Thomas[2], John[1]) was born 6 Mar 1799 in Topsham, Me.; mar. **Ann Fisher** (she born 1797) on 24 May 1834 in Bowdoinham, Me. They settled first in Topsham, Me. But by 1840, however, they had moved to nearby Bowdoinham, and spent most of the rest of their lives there. Edmund was a sea captain. Wife Ann died in 1884; he died at nearby Topsham, 1892.

Children:

**+3051**  i. Edmund[8] A. Eaton, b. ca. 1836 in Topsham; mar. Harriet.
**3052**  ii. Isaac[8] F. Eaton, b. ca. 1839 in Topsham.

**3053**   iii. Mary[8] Ellen Eaton, b. ca. 1847.


**1540. Benjamin[7] Eaton** (Jonathan[6-3], Thomas[2], John[1]) was born in N.H. according to his later Census report in New York State, and prob. at Plaistow, ca. 1794. He mar. and settled in Bath, Steuben Co., where he had spent at least his adolescent years. His wife apparently died at a fairly early age, prob. by 1840 or so. In 1850 at Bath he had a very small farm, and the house was run by one of his daughters. In the 1850s he moved to Cameron, N.Y., a dozen miles southwest of Bath., and appears there in 1860-70 with a woman named "Morey" twenty-plus years his junior, who is either a housekeeper or a second wife.

Children with first wife in Bath, N.Y. (reconstructed from Census entries):

**3054**   i. Henry[8] Eaton, b. ca. 1827.
**3055**   ii. Daughter[8] Eaton, b. ca. 1829.
**3056**   iii. Sarah[8] E. Eaton, b. ca. 1831.


**1550. John[7] G. Eaton** (Jonathan[6], Amos[5], Jonathan[4-3], Thomas[2], John[1]) was b. ca. 1816 at Haverhill, Mass. or Plaistow, N.H.; he mar. **Mehitable Emerson** (she born 1823 to George P. Emerson) 8 May 1845. They res. early in Plaistow, but by 1860 they had crossed over into Haverhill. John G. was a shoemaker by trade.

Children, in Plaistow, N.H. or Haverhill, Mass.:

**3057**   i. Ann[8] F. Eaton, b. ca. 1846.
**3058**   ii. John[8] G. Eaton, b. ca. 1847; still lives with parents in 1880, and works in the shoe shop.
**3059**   iii. Maria[8] S. Eaton, b. 1850.
**3060**   iv. Charles S. Eaton, b. 1859.


**1552. Albert[7] W. Eaton** (Jonathan[6], Amos[5], Jonathan[4-3], Thomas[2], John[1]) was born ca. 1828 in Plaistow, N.H.; he mar. **Mary Burley** (she born 1835) at Plaistow. He was a shoemaker, and they res. in the No. Parish of Haverhill, Mass. and Plaistow at various times.

Children, in Plaistow, N.H. or Haverhill, Mass.

**3061**   i. Willard[8] Winslow Eaton, b. ca. 21 May 1856; d. 4 Sep 1866.
**3062**   ii. Mary[8] E. Eaton, b. ca. 1862.
**3063**   iii. Lewis[8] Albert Eaton, b. ca. 7 Apr 1864; d. 2 Nov 1870.
**3064**   iv. Anna[8] B. Eaton, b. ca. 1867.
**+3065**   v. Albert[8] W. Eaton, b. Feb 1870, Haverhill, Mass.; mar. Ethel.

**1564. John**[7A] **L. Eaton** (Samuel[6], Job[5], Samuel[4], Job[3], Thomas[2], John[1]) was born 27 Jul 1798, prob. in Salisbury, N.H. after his family had recently moved there from Plaistow, N.H; mar., 1st **Mary Morgan** of Plainfield, N.H. on 22 May, 1825. They settled in Salisbury, N.H. After bearing three children, Mary died 20 Apr 1834 at Salisbury, and the two younger of her three children died three months later. In due time John L. mar. 2d, **Lovey Bickford** of Maine in Mar. 1837 in Lowell, Mass. John L. was very active in real estate transactions in Salisbury and was a prospering farmer there. Around 1844, however, he decided to move westward to the rich soil of the Illinois frontier. By 1850 he was established in Bureau Co., at a township that would soon become Princeton, Illinois. The value of his real estate rapidly increased in the new setting, and he became very well-to-do. He died 7 Sep 1870 in Princeton.

Children with Mary in Salisbury, N.H.:

3066    i. Mary[8] Ann Eaton, b. 17 Apr 1826; mar. Rev. Ira Case,
            15 Nov 1849, and res. in No. Scituate, R.I.
3067    ii. Betsey[8] Eaton, b. Jul 1828; died 18 Jul 1834.
3068    iii. Andrew[8] J. Eaton, b. Oct 1830, died 20 Jul 1834.

Children with Lovey (first three in Salisbury; the last in Illinois):

3069    iv. Andrew[8A] J. Eaton, b. ca. 1838; in 1880 at age 42 he was
            living with his mother on the farm left by his father in
            Princeton, Ill. Prob. never married.
3070    v. Sarah[8] E. Eaton, b. ca. 1840; mar. D. K. Warren, a lumber
            dealer in Oregon and a State Senator. They resided in
            Astoria, Ore.
3071    vi. Truman[8] Eaton, b. ca. 1843; a lumber dealer at Astoria, Ore.
3072    vii. Lewis[8] M. Eaton, b. ca. 1845.

**1566. Jesse**[7] **Eaton** (Samuel[6], Job[5], Samuel[4], Job[3], Thomas[2], John[1]) was born 13 May 1803 at Salisbury, N.H.; mar. **Susan Hemphill Rogers** of Lempster, N.H. (she born 1814) on 10 Jun 1832. After older brother John L. departed for Illinois, Jesse inherited the family homestead in Salisbury, N.H., and spent his life there. He died 20 Aug 1861; wife Susan died in 1872.

Children at Salisbury, N.H.:

+3073    i. Samuel[8] Eaton, b. 5 May 1833; mar. 1st, Sarah Wormin.
3074    ii. Mary[8] R. Eaton, b. 17 Oct 1835; she died 4 Jul 1860.
3075    iii. (Ella) Harriet[8] Eaton, b. 26 Feb 1846; mar. W. A. Brown
            and res. Manchester, N.H.

**1569. Job[7] Eaton, Jr.** (Job[6-5], Samuel[4], Job[3], Thomas[2], John[1]) is inferred to have been born to Job[6] ca. 1788, prob. to his first wife Sarah, either at Plaistow or at some way station as the family moved northward from Plaistow, arriving in Wentworth, Grafton Co., N.H., in time to be registered for the 1790 Census. There certainly was a "Job Eaton, Jr." in the Wentworth area in the 1810-50 period, as we report below. The only plausible question is whether this Job, Jr. was an early unrecorded son of Job[6] (**#577**), or of his younger brother Moses[6] (**#581**), since the tag "Jr." in this period simply means that there are two people with the same given name in an area---not necessarily father and son, which is the meaning now---that need to be distinguished since they are of different ages. Here the record assures us multiply that Job[7], Jr., was indeed an early son of Job[6] and not Moses[6]. For example, in Apr 1810 Job Sr. arranges a mortgage transwer of the family farm in Wentworth (Lot #3, 2d Range, 2d Division) to Job, Jr. for a nominal sum (Grafton Deeds 70-460/61). Not only is it unlikely Job Sr. would make such a transfer to a Job who was only his nephew; but in addition, while we lack a marriage date for the younger Moses[6], it is almost certain for several reasons that he had no unrecorded son earlier than 1793, and hence such a transfer to a "nephew" who himself was still a minor is again unlikely in the extreme. Thus our Job, Jr. here is clearly an unrecorded eldest son of Job[6]. Moreover, after Job[6] died intestate in 1830, three of his four younger sons join together to buy a quitclaim of this Job, Jr. (by then living in Vermont) to a piece of land in their father's estate (Grafton Deed 127-235). The conveyance is not explicit about the fraternal relationships here, but it is rather obvious what they must be.

Job, Jr. mar. a **Sarah "Sally" Brown** (she born ca. 1788), date unknown. He came on the tax stream in Wentworth in 1810 and remained there through 1822, although he did not appear in current Censuses as a household head. He was active in trading real estate in neighboring Piermont as well as Wentworth. He then removed across the Connecticut River to reside for a while in nearby Bradford, Vt., where he appears in the 1830 Census. By 1850 he is solo as head of a dwelling unit in Warren, N.H., where several households of his generation of Eatons have congregated (the lands of the original Eaton plantation straddled the town line between Wentworth and Warren). He had a very small farm. Next door was a household of Jewells which contains a Sally Eaton, now age 62 to Job's 60, who is almost surely his original wife, Sally (Brown). This Jewell family is headed by a Levi age 30 who may well be a son of Job's older sister Hannah (Eaton) Jewell.

Children (we have birth records of no children from Job[7]/Sally although they had a normal complement of children under their wings when they headed the household in Bradford, Vt. in 1830. From this we show the likely if anonymous and possibly misleading child roster, in order to leave place markers for future discoveries):

**3076**    i. Daughter[8] Eaton, b. 1810-14.
**3077**    ii. Daughter[8] Eaton, b, 1810-14.

**3078**    iii. Daughter[8] Eaton, b. 1815-19.
**3079**    iv. Daughter[8] Eaton, b. 1815-19.
**3080**    v. Daughter[8] Eaton, b. 1820-24.
**3081**    vi. Daughter[8] Eaton, b. 1820-24.
**3082**    viii. Son[8] Eaton, b. 1825-29.


**1570. Moses[7] Eaton** (Job[6-5], Samuel[4], Job[3], Thomas[2], John[1]) was born ca . 1791 in Wentworth, N.H., to Job[6] and his second wife Phebe. Moses mar. **Abigail Blood** (she born 1791) on 29 Jan 1816 at Orford, N.H. The couple resided on a reasonably prosperous farm near the northern edge of Wentworth where Moses died, 18 Aug 1841.

Children at Wentworth, N.H.:

**3083**    i. Mary[8] A. Eaton, b. ca. 1817.
**+3084**    ii. Augustus[8] K. Eaton, b. 20 Feb 1825; mar. Ruth Noyes, 1850.
**3085**    iii. Merrill[8] Eaton, b. ca. 1827; apparently died before 1830.


**1571. Jonathan[7] Merrill Eaton** (Job[6-5], Samuel[4], Job[3], Thomas[2], John[1]) was born ca. 11 Jun 1794 (from age at death) in Wentworth, N.H.; mar **Betsey Merrill** (she born 1791, the daughter of Jonathan Merrill, a popular inn-keeper in adjacent Warren, N.H). The couple settled in Warren, where Jonathan ran a prosperous farm. He died there 5 Aug 1888.

Children born in Warren, N.H.:

**3086**    i. Son[8] Eaton, b. ca. 1820; prob. died young.
**3087**    ii. Susannah[8] M. Eaton, b. 1823; died 1825.
**3088**    iii. Jonathan[8] Merrill Eaton, Jr., b. 1827; he was still living with his parents and farming in 1870; he died in 1877, apparently never married and without issue.
**3089**    iv. Benjamin[8] F. Eaton, b. 1829; died 1831.
**3090**    v. Hannah[8] Eaton, b. and died, 1833.
**3091**    vi. William[8] F. Eaton, b. 1834; he was still without sign of wife and working his parents' farm at age 45 in 1880.


**1573. Ezra[7] Bartlett Eaton** (Job[6-5], Samuel[4], Job[3], Thomas[2], John[1]) was born 24 Aug 1799 in Wentworth, N.H.; mar. 1st, **Mary Eaton Currier** (she born ca. 1801). They settled for a while in Plymouth, N.H., where they were living in 1830. But they had returned to Wentworth by 1840, and wife Mary died there, 19 Dec 1845. At some time before 1850, Ezra had mar. 2d, **Emily __?__**, born N.H. ca. 1815. She died 1 Dec 1854, and later he mar. 3d, **Mrs. Mary J. W. (Emerson) Webster**, born ca. 1820. Ezra died testate, 13 Apr 1873 at Wentworth.

Children with Mary, mainly in Plymouth, N.H.:

+ **3092**    i. Samuel[8] C. Eaton, b. ca. 1823; mar. Lydia, rem. to Lowell.
  **3093**    ii. Malinda[8] Eaton, b. ca. 1825; mar. Leavitt.
  **3094**    iii. Amanda[8] Eaton, b. ca. 1827; mar. Keazer.
+ **3095**    iv. Ezra[8] B. Eaton, b. 1829; mar. Melissa Pillsbury, 1856.
  **3096**    v. Emily[8] F. Eaton, b. 9 May 1832; mar. John H. Pearson, and they res. in California.
  **3097**    vi. Mary[8] E. Eaton, b. 1838; mar. Stockman.

**1574. Worcester[7] Eaton** (Job[6-5], Samuel[4], Job[3,] Thomas[2], John[1]) was born 1803 in Wentworth, N.H.; mar. **Maria M. __?__**, a native of New York State. This may explain why he cannot be found in any New England Census before 1850: he may have gone west for a while in early adulthood. And indeed we find a record for a "Wooster Eaton" of the right decade of age in the 1830 Census for Perrysburg, N.Y., in Cattaraugus Co., a dozen miles or so from the Lake Erie shore. He did return to New England, however, arriving at Lowell, Mass. in the mid-1840s. Two sons of his brother Ezra[7] B. resided there, Ezra[8] B., Jr. briefly around 1850; and Samuel[8] C. for a much longer time, making a fortune in popcorn. Worcester was first a grocer, and later probably in wholesale food distribution. His wife in 1870 is listed as Margaret, not Maria; but her age and N.Y. birth fit Maria perfectly, and it may be her middle name.

Children (the first three listed as born in N.H., although some should have been in New York State):

  **3098**    i. James[8] W. Eaton, b. ca. 1825.
  **3099**    ii. Eliza[8] A. Eaton, b. ca. 1828.
  **3100**    iii. Sarah[8] M. Eaton, b. ca. 1841.
  **3101**    iv. Georgiana[8] Eaton, b. 4 Apr 1844 at Lowell, Mass.

**1579. Samuel[7A] Eaton** (Jesse[6], Job[5], Samuel[4], Job[3], Thomas[2], John[1]) was born 6 Aug 1805 in Plaistow, N.H.; and spent the rest of his life in Plaistow. He mar. 1st, **Emeline M. Colby**; and 2d **Elizabeth J. Mills**. We lack details about either marriage; and while there are other young people in their Plaistow household in 1830 and 1840, there is no consistent sign of any children being raised. Samuel died 6 Aug 1850, and the Census-taker arrived three days later to find that widow Elizabeth had sought haven with her in-laws, once again with no children present. Elizabeth later became the second wife of Albert Heath, 22 Apr 1852.

**1585. Jesse[7] Eaton** (Moses[6], Job[5], Samuel[4], Job[3], Thomas[2], John[1]) was born 28 Aug 1796 in Wentworth, N.H.; mar. **Elinor Page** (she born 1800 to John Page of Wentworth). He farmed the family homestead for all of his lengthy life. He was a Democrat in politics until the election of native son Franklin Pierce; thereafter he voted Republican. He was active politically himself, being a selectman in the town, and tax collector for many years. He also represented the district in the State Legislature. He died 28 Feb 1771. Widow Elinor survived until 1884.

Children born in Wentworth, N.H.:

3102　　i. Abigail[8] H. Eaton, b. 22 Aug 1826; mar. William H. Bailey. She died 25 Nov 1880.
3103　　ii. Susan[8] M. Eaton, b. 27 Sep 1827; mar. Parker Wright. She died 11 Feb 1879.
+3104　　iii. John[8] P. Eaton, b. 9 Sep 1829; m. Harriet Burroughs, 1859.
3105　　iv. Hannah[8] Eaton, b. 9 Sep 1831; mar. Francis Goodell.
3106　　v. Louisa[8] J. Eaton, b. 24 Sep 1834; became 2d wife of Parker Wright after her sister's death.
3107　　vi. Martha[8] J. Eaton, b. 1836; mar. H. E. Carr.
+3108　　vii. (Dr.) Moses[8] C. Eaton, b. 26 Sep 1838; mar. Nellie Ward.

**1592. Job[7] Eaton** (James[6], Job[5], Samuel[4], Job[3], Thomas[2], John[1]) was born 9 Jan 1795 in Plaistow, N.H.; mar. **Ruth P. Sawyer**, 28 May 1818 at neighboring Hampstead, N.H. They settled across the state line in Haverhill, Mass. Job died there in 1847.

Children in Haverhill, Mass.:

+3109　　i. William[8] B. Eaton, b. 17 May 1819; mar. Abiah Sargent.
3110　　ii. Mary[8] Hazen Eaton, b. 12 Jan 1822.
3111　　iii. James[8] Augustus Eaton, b. 23 Sep 1824. He was a tin-plate worker who died of typhus young and unmar., 27 Oct 1845, in Haverhill.
+3112　　iv. Charles[8] Otis Eaton, b. 6 Jan 1828; mar. Charlotte Stickney.
3113　　v. George[8] Francis Eaton, b. 20 May 1836. Lived with his widowed mother Ruth in 1850, but cannot find further.

**1594. Daniel[7] Eaton** (James[6], Job[5], Samuel[4], Job[3], Thomas[2], John[1]) was born 27 Jan 1815 in Plaistow, N.H.; mar. **Louisa Hadley**. They res. on a small farm in Plaistow, and they were both long-lived. Louisa died 3 Aug 1891; Daniel followed on 10 May 1894.

Children in Plaistow, N.H.:

3114　　i. Sylvester[8] B. Eaton, b. 1 Mar 1840; died 4 Dec 1843.
3115　　ii. Almira[8] Josephine Eaton, b. 7 May 1842; she died 31 Jan 1917 at Plaistow.
3116　　iii. Fred[8] Perley Eaton, b. 11 May 1845; d. 1 Jun 1862, Plaistow.
+3117　　iv. Albert[8] Eugene Eaton, b. 17 Mar 1854; m. Carrie Lancaster.

**1595. Alonzo[7] Willis Eaton** (James[6], Job[5], Samuel[4], Job[3], Thomas[2], John[1]) was born ca. 1817 in Plaistow, N.H.; mar. **Louisa Noyes** of neighboring Atkinson, N.H., 3 Jun 1835 at Plaistow. This household managed to evade the Census-taker and other officialdom for many years. Finally in 1870 we find Alonzo and wife (called here "Eliza," but an appropriate age and N.H. birthplace) in Boston's 3d Ward. Alonzo is at this time a "Ticket Master" for the railroad and quite well-to-do indeed. He died in Dec 1875 in Boston. His widow retreated to Atkinson, N.H., dying there on 19 Oct 1897.

Child (prob. more unknown):

3118    i. Mary[8] E. Eaton, b. 1845 in N.H.


**1598. Timothy[7] Eaton** (Samuel[6], Ebenezer[5], Samuel[4], Job[3], Thomas[2], John[1]) was born 29 Aug 1789 at Landaff, N.H.; mar. **Martha "Patty" J. Northy** (she born ca. 7 Nov 1786) on 28 Jul 1812. The couple settled in Landaff, where Timothy bought in 1816 a 57-acre tract which was the east part of Lot #3, 4th Range, 1st Division, abutting the school lot. Timothy died 19 Apr 1867; Patty died 19 Dec 1876.

Children at Landaff, N.H.:

+3119    i. John[8] Eaton, b. 28 Mar 1813; mar. Mahala Wells, 1837.
 3120   ii. Elizabeth[8] "Betsey" Eaton, b. 30 Nov 1814; m. Archimedes Young, 8 Feb 1838. She died 10 May 1871 at Landaff.
+3121  iii. James[8] K. Eaton, b. 26 Mar 1817; mar. 1st, Drusilla Priest.
 3122   iv. Timothy[8] A. Eaton, b. 15 Jun 1821; died 1826.
 3123    v. Ebenezer[8] Eaton, b. 13 Mar 1824; died 1826.
+3124   vi. Samuel[8] Eaton, b. 5 Aug 1826; m. Sarah McConnell, 1856.


**1599. Ebenezer[7] Eaton** (Samuel[6], Ebenezer[5], Samuel[4], Job[3], Thomas[2], John[1]) was born 9 Oct 1791, Landaff, N.H.; mar. **Betsey Chandler** (daughter of Ezra and Fanny (Allard) Chandler) on 2 Dec 1819 at Landaff. In 1816 Ebenezer had joined with Seth Chandler, a later in-law, to buy the 60-acre Percy farm in Landaff, and this is where the couple settled and had their family. Ebenezer died 6 Dec 1856; widow Betsey died 27 Mar 1859, also in Landaff.

Children in Landaff, N.H.:

3125    i. Mary[8] C. Eaton, b. 29 Oct 1820; mar. James Clough.
3126   ii. Eliza[8] Prudence Eaton, b. 16 Aug 1822; mar. 1st, William L. Hunt; 2d, a Bowles. She died 1862.
3127  iii. Infant[8] Eaton, b. 25 Nov 1824; died quickly.
3128   iv. Moses[8] Eaton, b. 1826; died 1832.

**3129**   v. John[8] C. Eaton, b. 1828; died 1832.

**1607. Ira[7] Eaton** (Ebenezer[6-5], Samuel[4], Job[3], Thomas[2], John[1]) was born 6 Jul 1798 in Landaff, N.H.; mar. **Priscilla Reading McKean** (she born ca. 1806 to father James) on 24 Jan 1822 in Landaff. This couple settled for much of their child-bearing years in Landaff. But around 1830 they decided remove westward. We next find the family in Westminster, Windham Co., Vt. in the 1840 Census. By 1850 they have proceeded to Colden, not far from Lake Erie in N. Y. State. where Ira was a farmer on a small tract. In 1870, with their nest emptied save for unmarried daughter Hattie, the couple has moved to Aurora, N.Y., one township north. By 1880, widower Ira[7] was still surviving at 82, living in his son Ira[8A]'s household back in Colden.

Children (roster made up largely by combining a Bath, N.H. doctor's record of birthing dates for this family while in Landaff which lacks any given names---LDS Film #0870592---with other age information):

**3130**   i. Ira[8] Eaton, b. 9 Dec 1823 in Landaff; died 18 Sep 1830 in Westminster, Vt.
+**3131**   ii. James[8] McKean Eaton, b. 11 Apr 1828 in Landaff.
**3132**   iii. John[8] Eaton, b. 11 Mar 1830 in Landaff.
+**3133**   iv. Ira[8A] Eaton, b. ca. 1831 in Vermont; mar. Mary.
**3134**   v. Harriet[8] Eaton, b. 7 Aug 1837; prob. died young.
**3135**   vi. Thankful[8] Eaton, b. ca 1839, Westminster, Vt.
**3136**   vii. Franklin[8] Eaton, b. ca. 1844, N.Y. State.

**1608. Mitchell[7] Hutchins Eaton** (Ebenezer[6-5], Samuel[4], Job[3], Thomas[2], John[1]) was born 19 Apr 1800 in Landaff, N.H.; mar. a native of Canada, **Sarah Eastman** (she born 22 Jan 1798 to Ebenezer Eastman) on 21 Mar. 1833. This couple settled first at Landaff during the period their children were born, but in the 1840s they moved north into the adjoining town of Lisbon, where Mitchell continued farming. For their elderly years they moved north again into the town of Littleton, N.H., in 1868. In the later period Mitchell was a Republican. He died back in Lisbon, 1 Jun 1886; and Sarah died at Littleton three weeks later.

Children born in Landaff, N.H.:

+**3137**   i. Charles[8] Eaton, b. 9 Jun 1834; mar. Sarah Jane Green, 1863.
**3138**   ii. Ann[8] Eaton, b. 14 Jul 1837; does not appear with the family in the 1850 Census.
**3139**   iii. Julia[8] Ann Eaton, b. 11 Jan 1839; d. 2 May 1862 in Lisbon.

**1612. Peter**[7] **Eaton** (David[6], Ebenezer[5], Samuel[4], Job[3], Thomas[2], John[1]) was born 17 Apr 1800 in Landaff, N.H.; mar. **Elizabeth C.** __?__, about whom little is known. Being a "machinist" by trade, Peter was not tied to the land: the couple removed from the northwestern part of the state to Dover, N.H., in the southeast soon after they were married, for the 1830 Census. In 1840 they had moved on to Barnstead, N.H., and by 1850 they moved again, to spend their last years at Gilmanton, N.H. Peter died there in 1862.

Children (times and places not always clear):

3140    i. James[8] A. Eaton, b. ca. 1830, prob. at Dover; died in 1839.
3141   ii. Sarah[8] A. Eaton, b. ca. 1833.
3142  iii. George[8] W. Eaton, b. ca. 1837.
3143   iv. Abba[8] A. Eaton, a dau. b. ca. 1839.
3144    v. John[8] P. Eaton, b. ca. 1843.
3145   vi. Martha[8] Eaton, b. ca. 1848.


**1614. David**[7] **Fox Eaton** (David[6], Ebenezer[5], Samuel[4], Job[3], Thomas[2], John[1]) was born 21 Dec 1805 in Landaff, N.H. His mar. record is somewhat uncertain: it seems likely that he mar. 1st, an **Eleanor** __?__, with whom he began his family, and then mar. 2d, a **Sarah Lord**. While it is possible this is just one wife, we shall assume it is two. David F. was a wheelwright, and as mobile as his older brother Peter above, and he was residing in Barnstead, N.H. by 1829, where Peter would join him for a period. After 1850, David and Sarah removed to Berwick, Me., only 25 miles away. He died there 7 Feb 1855.

Children (presumably with Eleanor, and prob. incomplete):

3146    i. Elizabeth[8] A. Eaton, b. ca. 1832 in Barnstead, N.H..
3147   ii. Eleanor[8] Frances Eaton, b. 4 May 1836 in Barnstead; died 18 Mar 1853 at Berwick, Me.

Children with Sarah:

3148  iii. Rosanna[8] F. Eaton, b. ca. 1849 in Barnstead, N.H.
3149   iv. David[8] Fox Eaton, Jr., b. 25 Aug 1855 in Berwick, Me., some months after his father's death; he himself died 8 Jun 1856 at Berwick.


**1617. Nathan**[7] **Eaton** (Peter[6], Ithamar[5], Samuel[4], Job[3], Thomas[2], John[1]) was born 1797 in Weare, N.H.; mar. **Dorcas Marshall** (she born ca. 1804) on 26 Sep 1826 in Weare. They remained in Weare for the next 50 years, where Nathan farmed a tract of medium proportions. He died 21 Oct 1885 in Goshen, N.H.

Children at Weare, N.H.:

**3150**    i. Daughter[8] Eaton, b. 1829, prob. died young.
**3151**    ii. George[8] W. Eaton, b. ca. 1833; mar. Lydia Marshall, 1857.
**3152**    iii. May[8] Eaton, b. ca. 1836.
**3153**    iv. William[8] Eaton, b. ca. 1841.


**1622. Ithamar[7] Eaton** (Samuel[6], Ithamar[5], Samuel[4], Job[3], Thomas[2], John[1]) was born ca. 1805 in Weare, N.H.; mar. **Anna R. Bartlett**, dau. of John, Jr. and Mary (Morrill) Bartlett, on 9 Apr 1839 in Derry, N.H. They settled in Hampstead, N.H. where Ithamar as of 1850 was working as a laborer. He died in the 1850s; wife Anna died 2 Apr 1887, also at Hampstead.

Children born in Hampstead, N.H.:

**3154**    i. Child[8] Eaton, b. and died, 11 Oct 1841.
**3155**    ii. Edwina[8] M. Eaton, b. Apr 1848; mar. Charles W. Peasley. She died 26 Apr 1869.


**1623. Nathan[7] Ordway Eaton** (Jacob[6], Ithamar[5], Samuel[4], Job[3], Thomas[2], John[1]) was born 14 Nov 1799 in East Kingston, N. H.; he mar. 1st, **Mrs. Ruth Martain**, 12 Sep 1819 at Kingston. The couple settled in East Kingston, where Nathan was a farmer. His wife Ruth died there, 29 Jan 1863; and he mar. 2d, **Ruth Bagley**. This latter union was brief, as Nathan himself died 14 Jul 1865 in East Kingston.

Children with Ruth (Martain) in East Kingston, N.H.:

**+3156**    i. James[8] Cleaves Eaton, b. 19 Feb 1821; m. Josephine Stevens.
**3157**    ii. Jacob[8] Ordway Eaton, b. 27 Sep 1822; died 21 Dec 1843.
**3158**    iii. Jonathan[8] Alpha Eaton, b. 19 Sep 1824; died 12 Dec 1843.
**+3159**    iv. Stephen[8] B. Eaton, b. 1 Nov 1826; mar. Patience Blaisdell.
**+3160**    v. Nathan[8] Eaton, b. Jan 1830; mar. Sarah, 1849.
**3161**    vi. Joseph[8] Eaton, b. ca. 1832.


**1626. Merchant[7] Cleaves Eaton** (Jacob[6], Ithamar[5], Samuel[4], Job[3], Thomas[2], John[1]) was born 15 Mar 1806 in East Kingston, N.H.; mar. **Mary A. Lawrence** ca. 1830. The couple settled in East Kingston, where Merchant was a rather prosperous farmer. The development of their family was disrupted, however, when wife Mary died, 15 Mar 1839; and Merchant did not remarry. He himself died 27 May 1862 in East Kingston.

Children born in East Kingston, N.H.:

+**3162**    i. Ithamar[8] Eaton, b. 24 Aug 1832; mar. 1st, Phebe Pillsbury.
**3163**    ii. Sally[8] Eaton, b. 1837.


**1632. Andrew[7] Leach Eaton** (Ithamar[6-5], Samuel[4], Job[3], Thomas[2], John[1]) was born 9 Jun 1807 in Weare, N.H., but before he was 13 the family removed to his mother's native turf on Cape Anne, Essex Co., Mass., so he spent his adolescent years in Manchester-by-the-Sea. He mar. **Caroline E. Allen** 1 Dec 1833 in Beverly, Mass., and established himself as a "cordwainer," or shoemaker there, where they appear in Censuses from 1840 through at least 1870.

Children in Beverly, Mass.:

**3164**    i. John[8] A. Eaton, b. 18 Apr 1834; may have d. young.
+**3165**   ii. Andrew[8] L. Eaton, b. 6 Jun 1835.
**3166**   iii. Harriet[8] Ordway Eaton, b. 17 Apr 1839.


**1634. John[7] Lee Eaton** (Ithamar[6-5], Samuel[4], Job[3], Thomas[2], John[1]) was born 24 Jan 1813 in Weare, N.H., near the time when his family removed to his mother's native turf on Cape Anne, Essex Co., Mass., where John L. mainly grew up in Manchester-by-the-Sea.. He mar. there **Mary Abigail Trask** on 6 Jan 1836. They remained in Manchester where he was a cabinetmaker, until he died of consumption 3 Sep 1845. His widow later mar. Capt. Samuel Crowell, int. 11 Sep 1848, Manchester.

Children in Manchester, Mass.:

**3167**    i. Mary[8] Abby Eaton, b. 1 Nov 1836.
+**3168**   ii. John[8] Leach Eaton, b. 8 Nov 1837.
**3169**   iii. Richard[8] Trask Eaton, b. 29 Apr 1841; we lack further traces unless he is the Richard Eaton , a carpenter age 31 b. Mass., who is listed in the 1870 Census in Ward #2 of Springfield, Mass., with an apparent wife Lizzie, b. ca. 1844 in Pennsylvania. The occupation of carpenter cannot be truly diagnostic; but the John[7] Lee Eaton family is like a numerous other Eaton families, being saturated with workers in wood, including the father and a brother or two (cf. Sidebar #15).
+**3170**   iv. Edward[8] Payson Eaton, b. 12 May 1843.


**1636. (Rev.) William[7] Lowe Eaton** (George[6], Ithamar[5], Samuel[4], Job[3], Thomas[2], John[1]) was born 21 Mar 1814 in Weare, N.H. He graduated from Dartmouth College in 1837. He took up teaching as a profession initially, serving as Principal at Jaffrey (N.H.) Academy, 1837-39, and then becoming Professor of Mathematics and Natural Philosophy at the New Hampton (N.H.) Institution, 1839-43. In this period he mar. **Hannah Shurtleff Maine,** dau. of Stephen Maine of Hartland, Vt., on 20 Aug 1841 at Windsor, Vt. And he decided to broaden out professionally as well by establishing credentials for the Baptist ministry. He was first licensed to preach in his home church at Weare, and then formally ordained as an evangelist, New Hampton, 20 Apr 1842. He then removed to Michigan, teaching and preaching at Schoolcraft, 1843-45; and Ypsilanti, also Mich., 1845-48. Then he became Professor at the Theological Institute in Kalamazoo, Mich., while also active at the Marshall (Mich.) Academy. He died 25 Dec 1853 in Kalamazoo (Carter, 1906).

Children:

| 3171 | i. Adaline[8] Maine Eaton, b. 25 Jan 1843 in New Hampton, N.H. |
| 3172 | ii. William[8] Low Eaton, b. 15 Dec 1850, Kalamazoo, Mich. His father died when he was still a toddler. We find him in 1870, age 20, living with his mother in Kalamazoo, and working as an attendant in the State Asylum for the Insane in that town. In 1880 he is still living with his mother there, but by now is an "editor" by occupation. He may have gone westward. |

**1637. Peter[7] Eaton** (George[6], Ithamar[5], Samuel[4], Job[3], Thomas[2], John[1]) was born 9 Nov 1815 in Weare, N.H.; mar. **Eliza A. Pillsbury** of Henniker, N.H., on 15 Dec 1840 in Henniker. They settled for a while at Weare and then were in Henniker in 1850 (Peter a mechanic) and 1860 (Peter a harness-maker). Peter died 23 Jun 1867.

Only known child:

| 3173 | i. Alice[8] Lou Eaton, b. 6 Mar 1849 in Weare, N.H. |

NOTE. Since "Peter" was not a common given name for Eatons; and since only three Eaton heads of household are recorded at Henniker in all the Censuses from 1790 thru 1850, with only one of them---Paige[6] Eaton (see **#604**)---sighted there more than once, it would seem likely that the Peter Eaton joining Paige as a household head in 1850 would of course be his son Peter, b. ca. 1826 at Henniker. That the 1850 Peter at Henniker cannot not be Paige's son is attested to most directly by the fact that his 1850 Census age is 34, whereas Paige's son was only 24 at the time. Of course ages can be dissembled, as well as misunderstood by the Census-taker. But the 1840 date of marriage with Eliza of the 1850 Peter is a solid one; and hence to insist that the 1850 Peter is nonetheless Paige's son runs into the problem that Paige's son would, under this construction, have married Eliza when he was only age 14. Happily, the young Peter from Weare above was born late in

1815, which fits the 1850 Census age report perfectly; and Henniker not only abuts Weare but does so on the northern edge, near to which the Weare Peter was born.

**1646. Benjamin[7] P. Eaton** (Samuel[6], Obadiah[5], Samuel[4], Job[3], Thomas[2], John[1]) was born ca. 1815 in Weare, N.H., but as a youngster removed with his family to Barnstead, N.H., where he grew up. He mar. **Abigail Ayers**, and they res. in Barnstead, including in their household there in 1850 Benjamin's widowed mother Betsey and his older brother Obadiah[7]. Benjamin himself died in 1854 in Barnstead.

Children in Barnstead, N.H.:

3174   i. Louisa[8] Eaton, b. ca. 1841.
3175   ii. Samuel[8] P. Eaton, b. ca. 1846. By 1870 he has moved to Strafford, N.H. and worked at the shoe factory there. Before 1880 he began to farm, and mar. Eveline (Gray) Eaton, living with her and her mother that year, without sign of children. In 1900 he was living without relatives in Strafford, with a housekeeper and boarders.
3176   iii. William[8] Eaton, b. 1849.


**1647. Thomas[7] Eaton** (Benjamin[6], Obadiah[5], Samuel[4], Job[3], Thomas[2], John[1]) was born 12 Mar 1802 in Hopkinton, N.H. He removed to Maine as a young man, and mar. **Elizabeth M. Henley** of Portland, Me. (she born there 24 Jul 1804) on 12 Jun 1825 in Portland. The couple settled in Bath, Me., where he listed himself in 1850 as a Postmaster. He was still residing in Bath as of 1870.

Children born in Bath, Me.:

3177    i. Francis[8] Douglas Eaton, b. 10 Apr 1826; died 26 Jan 1827.
+3178    ii. James[8] Henley Eaton, b. 23 Jun 1828; mar. Clara.
+3179    iii. Albert[8] Green Eaton, b. 28 Nov 1831; mar. Martha.
3180    iv. Mary[8] Elizabeth Eaton, b. 23 Apr 1834; died 30 Aug 183?.
3181    v. Francis[8A] Edward Eaton, b. 24 Mar 1836.
3182    vii. Thomas[8] Gilman Eaton, b. 23 Oct 1838; died 1 Sep 1839.
3183    viii. Gilman[8] Stockbridge Eaton, b. 15 Aug 1840; died young.
3184    ix. George[8] Thomas Eaton, b. 20 Nov 1843.
3185    x. Charles[8] Howard Eaton, twin of Frederick, b. 16 Oct 1846; died 14 Jul 1847.
3186    xi. Frederick[8] Augustus Eaton, twin of Charles, b. 16 Oct 1846; died 17 Sep 1847.


**1656. Samuel[7] Eaton** (Ebenezer[6], John[5], Thomas[4], Job[3], Thomas[2], John[1]) was born 1 Jun 1785 in Bradford, N.H.; mar. **Margaret Aiken**, on 26 Aug 1810 in Bradford. The couple res. in Bradford for their brief life together before Samuel died there 1 Aug 1824, leaving the widow and four children.

Children at Bradford, N.H.:

3187    i. Louisa[8] Eaton, b. ca. 1812; died 6 Jan 1879 in Bradford.
3188    ii. Amanda[8] Eaton, b. ca. 1814.
3189    iii. Margaret[8] J. Eaton, b. May 1816; mar. William H. Miller.
            They res. in Bradford, where she died 11 Mar 1895.
3190    iv. Elman[8] Eaton, b. 1820; died 15 Jan 1840 in Bradford.


**1657. Elisha[7] Eaton** (Ebenezer[6], John[5], Thomas[4], Job[3], Thomas[2], John[1]) was born 11 Apr 1788 in Bradford, N.H.; mar. **Eliza Jackman** of Boscawen, 20 Oct 1811. They settled for life in Bradford, where Elisha ran a rather prosperous farm. He died 24 Mar 1862 in Bradford.

Children born in Bradford, N.H.:

3191    i. Ebenezer[8] Ozmyn Eaton, b. 27 Aug 1812.
3192    ii. Eliza[8] Pettengill Eaton, b. 4 Dec 1814. She d. 15 Jul 1837.
+3193   iii. Elisha[8] Harrison Eaton, b. 22 Sept 1816; mar. 1st, Roena.
3194    iv. Philippa[8] Harriet Eaton, b. 1822; died 1837.
3195    v. Robert[8] Page Eaton, b. 18 Jul 1825; mar. Ann  Elizabeth
            Goodhue, 20 Oct 1851. He was prob. a physician in
            Vershire, Orange Co., Vt. in the early 1850s, then
            removing to New Hampton, N.H. He died 20 Sep 1855,
            and we have no record of children.
3196    vi. Hannah[8] Augusta Eaton, b. 24 Jul 1834.


**1659. Moses[7] Eaton** (Nathaniel[6], John[5], Thomas[4], Job[3], Thomas[2], John[1]) was born ca. 1788, perhaps in Bradford, N.H., although his father moved permanently to Hopkinton, N.H. in 1804 when he was in early adolescence. He mar. **Judith Merrill**, dau. of Deac. David Merrill, 4 Sep 1813 in Hopkinton where the couple settled. In 1818 Moses bought two tracts of land totalling 21 acres from his father-in-law on the west side of Hopkinton where he died, 7 Feb 1840.

Children born in Hopkinton:

+3197   i. (Dr.) Harrison[8] Eaton, b. 13 Dec 1813; mar. 1st, Charlotte.
+3198   ii. David[8] Merrill Eaton, b. ca. Mar 1815; mar. Mary.


**1663. Thomas[7] Eaton** (Nathaniel[6], John[5], Thomas[4], Job[3], Thomas[2], John[1]) was born ca. 1797, prob. in Bradford, N.H., but went to Hopkinton, N.H., as a young child with his family. He mar. **Anna B . Cressey** (also of Hopkinton although born ca. 1797 in Conn.) on 15 Jan 1818 in

Hopkinton. He was a farmer in Hopkinton, but the circumstances of his
tenure are unclear, since in 1850, when he was in the conventional prime
of his life at age 53, he, his wife and his sister Betsey are living within the
household headed by their son-in-law Thomas Piper, age 35, husband of
their daughter Louisa, now age 29; and by the real estate report Piper
owns the farm. Thomas[7] may have been ailing by this time, since he died
27 Jan 1851 at age 54; and wife Anna lived on in Louisa's household
until she died, 8 Apr 1863.

Children born in Hopkinton:

**3199**    i. Son[8] Eaton, b. ca. 1818-19.
**3200**    ii. Louisa[8] Eaton, b. 30 Dec 1820; mar. Thomas C. Piper then
of Manchester, N.H., on 13 Feb 1842. Louisa had several
children with him, and she died 5 Mar 1888, Hopkinton.

**1665. Timothy[7] P. Eaton** (Daniel[6], John[5], Thomas[4], Job[3], Thomas[2], John[1]) was born 11 Jun 1790 in Tunbridge, Vt.; mar. **Sarah Forest**
on 7 Oct 1816 at Tunbridge in Orange Co. The couple settled first in the
adjoining township of Royalton, Vt. in Windsor Co., where they res. in
1820. By 1830 they have moved north again into Orange Co. at Thetford, Vt.. Then they disappear from New England, but we feel we have
plausibly found them in 1840 in Arrieta Twp., Hamilton Co., N.Y., since
the family head is Timothy "B." with both parents in the right age brackets and, most diagnostically, the 1840 version of their complex family
composition of 1830 is just what one would expect. We do not, however,
find them again in 1850, where we might learn some child names.

Children, none of whom died very young:

**3201**    i. Son[8] Eaton, b. ca. 1818.
**3202**    ii. Daughter[8] Eaton, b. 1820-24.
**3203**    iii. Son[8] Eaton, b. 1820-24.
**3204**    iv. Son[8] Eaton, b. 1825-29.
**3205**    v. Son[8] Eaton, b. 1830-34.

**1666. Joshua[7] Eaton** (Daniel[6], John[5], Thomas[4], Job[3], Thomas[2],
John[1]) was born 30 Apr 1792 in Tunbridge, Vt.. He served in the War of
1812, and then mar. **Susan Cleveland** on 23 Sep 1814. They res. in
Tunbridge, where Joshua was a stone cutter as of 1850. On 20 Aug 1868
he died of leprosy in Tunbridge.

Children in Tunbridge, Vt.:

**+3206**    i. Daniel[8] Clement Eaton, b. 31 Jul 1815; mar. Augusta Cilley.
**3207**    ii. Martha[8] Porter Eaton, b. 16 Jul 1817.
**3208**    iii. Son[8] Eaton, b. ca. 1819.

**3209**     iv. Son[8] Eaton, b. 1820-24.
**3210**     v. Daughter[8] Eaton, b. 1820-24.
**+3211**     vi. (Henry) Porter[8] Eaton, b. 14 Dec 1831; mar. Isabel.


**1669. James[7] Eaton** (John[6-5], Thomas[4], Job[3], Thomas[2], John[1]) was born 28 May 1805 in Bradford, N.H.; mar. **Lydia __?__** (b. 1805, N.H.) ca. 1831. In 1840 he was running the farm in Newbury for his aging parents; but he himself died ca. 1849, leaving his widow with five children still at home for the 1850 Census at Newbury.

Children in Newbury, N.H.:

**3212**     i. William[8] Eaton, b. ca. 1833; in 1850 is laboring on the nearby Bailey farm, but cannot find thereafter.
**3213**     ii. Elizabeth[8] Eaton, b. ca. 1837.
**3214**     iii. Levi[8] H. Eaton, b. ca. 1841; mar. Eliza J. Tandy of Goshen, N.H. (she b. Jul 1842), prob. in the 1870s. They settled in Bradford, N.H., where he was a farmer. In 1880 the couple lived with Eliza's mother Submit and her brother, Austin Tandy, without any sign of children of their own. In 1900 Eliza lives alone in Bradford, prob. widowed.
**+3215**     iv. George[8] W. Eaton, b. Jul 1843; mar. Alice M. Currier.
**3216**     v. Lydia[8] A. Eaton, b. ca. 1846.
**+3217**     vi. James[8] Eaton, b. Dec 1848; mar. 1st, Rosina.


**1671. Ebenezer[7] Eaton** (John[6-5], Thomas[4], Job[3], Thomas[2], John[1]) was born 7 Feb 1809 in Bradford, N.H.; mar. **Hannah B. Cross** of Salem, Mass., 7 Jan 1836. This couple moved into neighboring Newbury, N.H. to settle, as had his older brother John. Ebenezer identified himself as a "laborer" in 1850, and had rather limited means. He died 4 Feb 1872 back in Bradford, N.H.

Children in Newbury, N.H.:

**3218**     i. Phineas[8] Eaton, b. 1836; died in the 1850s.
**3219**     ii. John[8] G. (or A.?) Eaton, b. 11 Mar 1838. In 1860 he is farming with his family at Newbury, but then disappears.
**+3220**     iii. Albert[8] S. Eaton, twin of Alfred, b. 13 Aug 1841; m. Emma.
**3221**     iv. Alfred[8] S. Eaton, twin of Albert, b. 13 Aug 1841; d. young?
**+3222**     v. Jesse[8] W. F. Eaton, b. 8 Apr 1843; mar. Nellie Maxfield.
**3223**     vi. Edwin[8] A. Eaton, b. 16 Apr 1846; no sign after 1860.
**3224**     vii. Phineas[8A] A. Eaton, b. 3 Nov 1856; not listed with family at Newbury even in 1860, and presumably died young.


**1672. Moses[7] Eaton** (Joshua[6], John[5], Thomas[4], Job[3], Thomas[2], John[1]) was born 9 Apr 1793 in Hopkinton, N.H.; mar. **Polly Whittemore**

(she born 1 Aug 1793 to popular local teacher Peter Whittemore) about 1815. This couple settled first in Bradford, where they appear in 1820, but had moved to neighboring Newbury by 1830, where he had a substantial farm into the 1850s, when Moses prob. dies. In the child-rearing years there are diverse children reported in their home by Censuses, but viewed as a development over time they are quite incoherent. There was a first son who ages stably, and is without much doubt the George Eaton who lives next door to them in 1850, and hosts his widowed mother Polly in 1860, with a large entourage of grandchildren. Polly died 16 Jan 1871 and was bur. at Salisbury, N.H.

Child (one of probably several):

+ **3225**   i. George[8] Eaton, b. ca. 1816; mar. Mary A. __?__.


**1674. Joshua[7] Eaton** (Joshua[6], John[5], Thomas[4], Job[3], Thomas[2], John[1]) was born 22 Dec 1817 in Bradford, N.H.; on 20 Mar 1840 he mar. 1st, **Alzina E. Gillingham** at Newbury, N.H. They settled on his farm in Bradford, but Alzina died early, on 6 Oct 1851. Soon thereafter he mar. 2d, **Louisa A. McNeal** (b. ca. 17 Nov 1823 at Weare, N.H., to John and Louise (Clark) McNeal) and had at least one further child with her. Joshua was a prosperous farmer. He died 21 Sep 1900 in Bradford.

Children with Alzina in Bradford, N.H.:

**3226**   i. Alzina[8] Eaton, b. 5 Jan 1841. A school teacher in 1860.
**3227**   ii. Al(v)(b?)erton[8] Eaton, b. Aug 1843; died 2 Feb 1846.
**3228**   iii. (Ella) Alzina[8A] Eaton, b. Jan 1848. In 1860 was living with her family in Newbury and teaching school. In 1900 an Alzina Eaton born in this year, apparently unmarried, was a nurse at a children's Home in Dover, N.H.

Child with Louisa (perhaps were more):

+**3229**   iv. (Joshua) Willis[8] Eaton, b. Dec 1856; mar. Nellie Boyce.


**1675. John[7] Hill Eaton** (Joshua[6], John[5], Thomas[4], Job[3], Thomas[2], John[1]) was born 22 Nov 1819 in Bradford, N.H.; mar. 1st, **Hannah Twiss** on 9 Apr 1841. They settled in Bradford where John developed a substantial farm. Wife Hannah died early, in Sep 1850; and he mar. 2d, **Mary J. Lawrence** of Alstead, N.H., in Bradford in 1852. John died 2 Jul 1893 in Bradford.

Children with Hannah in Bradford:

**3230**   i. Hannah[8] M. Eaton, b. ca. 1843; died young.
**3231**   ii. Roxanna[8] B. Eaton, b. ca. 27 May 1846.

**3232**   iii. Mary[8] Eaton, b. 1848.

Children with Mary J. in Bradford:

**3233**   iv. Martha[8] J. Eaton, b. 11 Mar 1853; mar. Lawrence E. Davis of Warner, 1878.  She died 23 Jun 1923.
**3234**   v. Louisa Eaton, b. ca. 1855.
**3235**   iv. John[8] Eaton, b. ca. 1858; d. unm., 20 Nov 1890, Bradford.

# Generation Eight

## A. *The Salisbury Branch*

**1681. Caleb**[8] **Eaton** (William[7], Ebenezer[6], John[5-1]) was born 30 Jan 1778 in Seabrook, N.H., but as a young lad his family removed to Sanbornton, N.H.  He mar. **Sarah Cass**, daughter of Jonathan, on 28 June 1799 (Seabrook *VR* at Concord), and the couple settled on a farm "just above his father's place" in Sanbornton (Runnels, 1881).  He was to some extent a dealer in real estate, before dying of consumption, 22 Dec 1829, age 51; widow Sarah died 8 Jan 1855, age 73.

Children with Sarah at Sanbornton, N.H.:

3236    i. Betsey[9] Eaton, b. 2 May 1801; mar. William Plumer, 1827, and settled in Meredith, N.H., where she had five children.

3237    ii. Fanny[9] Eaton, b. 11 Jan 1803; died of consumption, 20 Sep 1824.

3238    iii. Elmira[9] Eaton, b. 5 Feb 1805; mar Deacon Daniel Huse of Sanbornton in 1831 and had three children.

+3239    iv. Caleb[9] Eaton, b. 25 Apr 1809; mar. Irena Davis, 1833.

+3240    v. William[9] Eaton, b. 28 Mar 1811; mar. 1st, Mary A. Gordon.

3241    vi. Child[9] Eaton, a twin b. 13 May 1822; died at birth.

3242    vii. James[9] Eaton, a twin b. 13 May 1822; died 22 Jun 1822.

**1683. Jonathan**[8] **Eaton** (William[7], Ebenezer[6], John[5-1]) was born 25 May 1783 in Seabrook, N.H., but moved with his family to Sanbornton, N.H. as a child.  He mar. **Molly Prescott**, daugher of Joseph, on 21 Jan 1808, and also settled on a farm there.  This family appears to have removed to Manchester, N.H., about 1839, just as the mills there began to attract migrants at a great rate, and prob. appear there in the 1840 Census.  On 7 Dec 1843, Jonathan left home on a trip to New York City, with a stopover in Rhode Island, presumably to visit his younger brothers or other friends from his earlier stay there with his parents.  After this visit of a few days, however, he set off for New York City and was never heard from again.

The children of Jonathan and Molly were the subjects of a sampler at an antique shop in Franklin reported in *NEHGR*, Vol. 85.  Presumably born at Sanbornton:

3243    i. Eliza[9] Eaton, b. 9 Dec 1810; mar. William Henry Lawrence

of Lexington, Mass., 9 May 1838 at Boston, and then
resided at Jamaica Plain, Mass. They res. in East Lexington, Mass., where she had five children.

**3244**   ii. Joseph[9] P. Eaton, b. 20 Oct 1812, Sanbornton; mar. 1st Mary
Ann Mason, dau. of Benjamin Mason, 31 Jan 1833. They
had a daughter Eliza Jane, b. 18 Jan 1834, Sanbornton,
who mar. George H. Flagg of Boston on 3 Jul 1858. Wife
Mary Ann died 7 Aug 1841, age 29. Joseph[9] P. then mar.
2d, Betsey F. Cass, daughter of Simeon Cass, although
without issue. He was a farmer of limited means, a har-
nessmaker, and called himself a peddler in 1850. He died
10 Aug 1858.

**3245**   iii. Mary[9] Prescott Eaton, b. 1 Jul 1816; mar. Stephen Gordon,
farmer of New Hampton, Apr 1841; she had five children.

**3246**   iv. Susan[9] Prescott Eaton, b. 11 Oct 1818; mar. Joseph Mason.

**3247**   v. Marcia[9] B. Eaton, b. 23 Jul 1820; died 9 Nov 1834.

**3248**   vi. Charles[9] Woodman Eaton, b. 1 May 1822, Sanbornton; mar,
Abigail M. Swain, 1843. They res. in Manchester, N.H.,
where Charles was a carder in a textile mill and later an
overseer. They had three children but two died very
young. The survivor, Mary[10] A. Eaton, b. 1847, later resided in California. Charles died 25 Aug 1856.

**3249**   vii. Sarah[9] Bartlett Eaton, b. 13 Apr 1824, Sanbornton; mar.
David M. Cass of Rindge, N.H., 4 Dec 1843. They were
first on a farm in New Hampton, but later moved to
Methuen, Mass. They had six children.

**1684. William[8] Eaton** (William[7], Ebenezer[6], John[5-1]) was born 25
May 1785 at Seabrook, but moved with his family to Sanbornton as a
child. He mar. **Judith Burleigh**, daughter of Joseph, 16 Nov 1806.
They resided first at Sanbornton, and he was prob. the William 3d of that
town who served as an ensign in Capt. Perkins's camp in 1814. After
four children were born to them at Sanbornton, they removed to St. Armand, Quebec, where he was a farmer. He died in Philipsburg, Que., 29
Aug 1858; his widow died there as well 21 Feb 1862.

Children at Sanbornton:

+**3250**   i. Joseph[9] Eaton, b. 11 Apr 1807; mar. Almira Simpson.

**3251**   ii. Eliza[9] Eaton, b. 9 Dec 1810; mar. James R. Smith of Stan-
bridge, Quebec Province, in 1828. He was a farmer in
Stanbridge and died in 1876. She died in St. Armand,
Quebec, in 1888.

**3252**   iii. Melinda[9] Holt Eaton, b. 15 Jan 1815; mar. Charles Derrick,
a farmer of Armand West, 18 Mar 1845, and lived on
a farm in Noyan, Quebec, having three children. She
died in Noyan 28 Oct 1861.

+**3253**   iv. Jonathan[9] Wyatt Eaton, b. 19 Nov 1820; mar. Mary Smith.

**1688. Reuben⁸ B. Eaton** (William⁷, Ebenezer⁶, John⁵⁻¹) was born 4 Sep 1794 in Sanbornton, N.H. Being well into his twenties when his parents went back to Sanbornton after more than a decade in Rhode Island, it is likely that he simply decided to stay on with his younger brother Joseph, as he appears at So. Kingston, R.I. in the 1820 Census. He mar. **Elizabeth Peckham** early in 1821 and had seven children with her at So. Kingston, where he was an overseer in a factory, before he died prematurely in the 1830s. Widow Elizabeth was the family head, still in So. Kingston, in the 1840 Census.

Children, all born with Elizabeth in So. Kingston, R.I.:

| | | |
|---|---|---|
| +3254 | i. | Edgar⁹ R. Eaton, b. Oct 1821; mar. Mary Ann Smith, 1842. |
| 3255 | ii. | Girl⁹ Eaton, b. 1823-25. |
| 3256 | iii. | Boy⁹ Eaton, b. 1823-25. |
| 3257 | iv. | Benjamin⁹ P. Eaton, b. 1828; mar Sarah __?__. Unknown if any issue; but he and wife Sally still flourish in So. Kingston, R.I. in the 1900 Census. |
| +3258 | v. | Reuben⁹ B., Jr., b. 1830; mar. (2d) Lydia T. Sweet. |
| 3259 | vi. | Boy⁹ Eaton, b. 1831-35. |
| 3260 | vii. | Boy⁹ Eaton, b. 1831-35. |

**1690. Joseph⁸ Eaton** (William⁷, Ebenezer⁶, John⁵⁻¹) was born 28 Feb 1799 in Sanbornton, N.H., but removed as a young child with his family to Rhode Island, where his father had served for a year during the Revolution. It is not clear whether he stayed on with his older brother Reuben after his parents returned to Sanbornton, or came back later from Sanbornton. But he mar. **Abby __?__**, born in Rhode Island ca. 1806, probably about 1830. They resided in So. Kingston where he worked in a factory with brother Reuben. As of 1850, Joseph records his occupation as a "manufacturer," but he is a farmer without much property in 1860, and at age 78 in 1870, he considers carpentry as his trade.

Children, all born Rhode Island, and prob. at So. Kingston:

| | | |
|---|---|---|
| +3261 | i. | Joseph⁹ P. Eaton, b. ca. 1832; mar. Celia Brown, 1850. |
| 3262 | ii. | Abby Ann⁹ Eaton, b. ca. 1834; mar. __?__, 1854. |
| 3263 | iii. | Mary⁹ J. Eaton, b. ca. 1836. |
| 3264 | iv. | Sarah⁹ E. Eaton, b. 1 Feb 1837; mar. Mr. Gardiner. She died 18 Mar 1892. |
| 3265 | v. | Martha⁹ Eaton, b. ca. 1840. |
| 3266 | vi. | Benjamin⁹ Eaton, b. ca. 1842. |
| 3267 | vii. | James⁹ Eaton, b. ca. 1844. |
| 3268 | viii. | William⁹ Eaton, b. 29 Aug 1846. He died 16 Jul 1932. |
| 3269 | ix. | Jane⁹ M. Eaton, b. Apr 1850. |

### #10. Eaton "Twigs" that Populated 1857 Seabrook

Map 7 was drawn from a Seabrook map showing residences of household heads as of 1857. Our version only shows detail for the southern part of Seabrook, where all of our Eatons resided. The reader with a good magnifying glass may note that most family heads listed on that map are accompanied by a pair of three-digit numbers (e. g., "145-123)." These numbers cross-reference to the numbering of the households in the 1850 and 1860 Censuses which bracket the 1857 residential map. The second number is the actual household number for 1860, which list started with #1. The first number gives the same information for 1850 if one adds 350 to it (since the 1850 listing started the town at #351).

Of course all Seabrook Eatons were of the Salisbury Branch, which means that they all were sired by way of John[1] and his elder son John[2]. But a whole new array of twigs began to ramify in subsequent generations, and it is interesting to ask which of these twigs was most represented in the Seabrook of 1857, and how these twigs distributed themselves from neighborhood to neighborhood in that year.

John[2] had five sons, but one was lost at sea and a second left the Salisbury area soon after marriage. A third, Capt. Joseph[3], stayed in Salisbury but never lived in Seabrook, nor did any of his sons, most whom went to Maine. Thus only John[3] and Ephraim[3] contributed to Eatons in 1857 Seabrook. Of the 31 Eaton households we can follow in that year, 28 stem from John[3], and only three from Ephraim[3]. The latter are all from the twig (Jabez[4], Joshua[5-6]), and reside on the north side of Walton Rd., near patriarch Ephraim's original stake between Collins and Walton Rd., west of Washington St.

John[3] had four sons living in Seabrook. But of the 28 households tracing to John[3], a full 15 stem from one path out thru Generation 6. They are all eldest sons of eldest sons, who tend to inherit the the family place: John[4-5] to Ebenezer[6]. Ebenezer's many 1857 scions are about half and half, seventh and eight generation; and they reside all over southern Seabrook, from South Main St. at the southeast extreme to Walton Rd. in the northwest. They are represented in Map 9 by a centroid with rays to many points.

The final 13 Eaton households trace to 7 different sixth-generation twigs out of John[3]. The largest, with four households, is made up in 1857 of two sons of Jonathan[6] (Joseph[5], John[4-i]) with a grandson each, three of them in adjacent houses on Washington St., and the fourth a few doors away on So. Main St. Three more twigs have two members, each also living close together (see Map 9).

All told, it is clear that the eldest sons of John[3] and their descendants dominate the 1857 Seabrook scene, and have scattered widely. The other twigs of any size seem to be found in fairly compact clusters, usually reflecting the original land stakes of their forebears.

## Map 9. Diverse Eaton "Twigs" in 1857 Seabrook
(Based on Map 7, but limited to Eaton dwellings;
see discussion in Sidebar #10 opposite.)

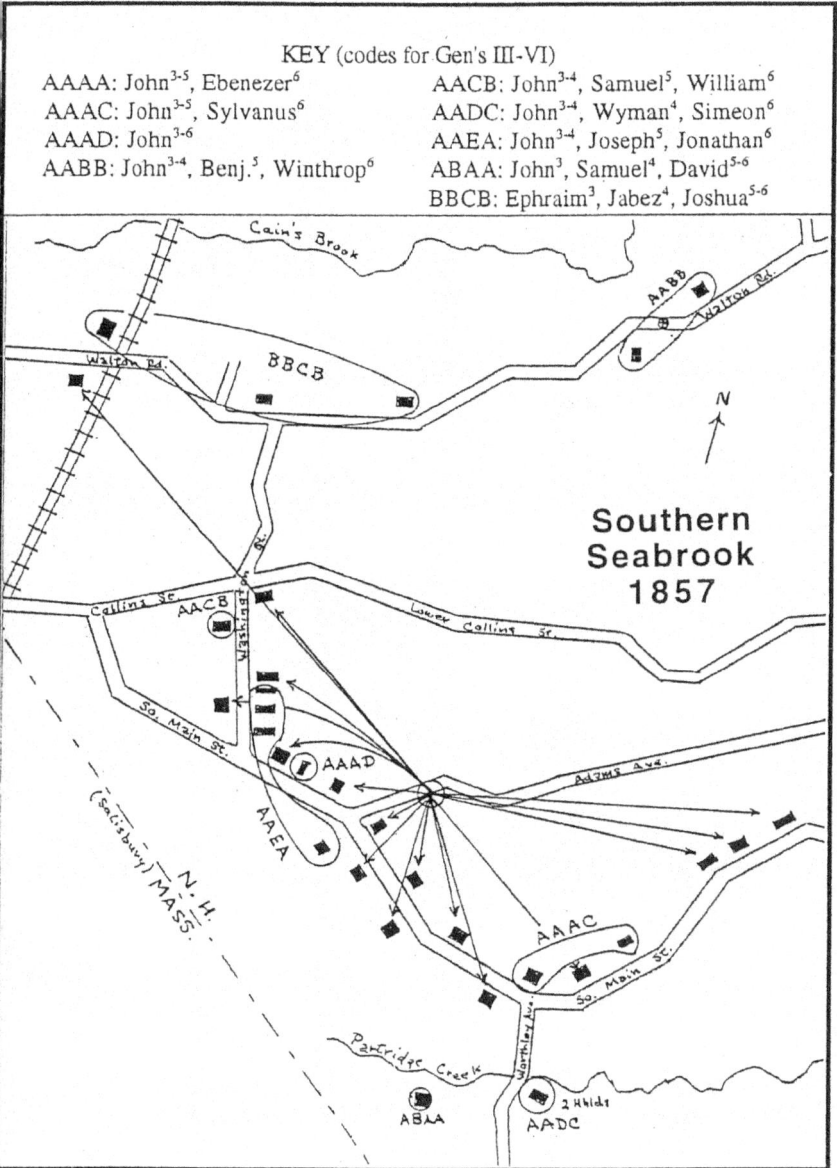

KEY (codes for Gen's III-VI)

AAAA: John[3-5], Ebenezer[6]          AACB: John[3-4], Samuel[5], William[6]
AAAC: John[3-5], Sylvanus[6]          AADC: John[3-4], Wyman[4], Simeon[6]
AAAD: John[3-6]                       AAEA: John[3-4], Joseph[5], Jonathan[6]
AABB: John[3-4], Benj.[5], Winthrop[6]   ABAA: John[3], Samuel[4], David[5-6]
                                      BBCB: Ephraim[3], Jabez[4], Joshua[5-6]

**1693. Henry**[8] **Eaton** (Henry[7], Ebenezer[6], John[5-1]) was born 30 Nov 1792 (Seabrook *VR* at Concord) in Seabrook, N.H.; mar. on 3 Jan 1812, **Hannah**[7] **Eaton (#640)**, b. 1789 in Seabrook. They resided in Seabrook where Henry was a mariner and fisherman by trade and was lost at sea off Newfoundland on 28 Aug 1841 after siring a substantial family. Widow Hannah died 11 Nov 1857 at Seabrook.

Children, all born Seabrook:

|        |                                                                              |
|--------|------------------------------------------------------------------------------|
| +3270  | i. Robert[9] Eaton, b. 12 Mar 1812; mar. 1st, Dolly Beckman.                 |
| +3271  | ii. Henry[9] Eaton, b. 8 Nov 1814; mar. Abigail Perry.                       |
| 3272   | iii. Daniel[9] Eaton, b. 31 Aug 1817; he died unmar. 16 Feb 1854 in Seabrook. |
| 3273   | iv. Sarah[9] Eaton, b. 17 Aug 1820; died 10 Dec 1820.                        |
| +3274  | v. Lewis[9] C. Eaton, b. 19 Apr 1822; mar. Louisa Felch, 1842.              |
| +3275  | vi. Moses[9] D. Eaton, b. 1 Dec 1824; mar. Almira Worthley.                 |
| 3276   | vii. Sally[9] Eaton, b. 27 Aug 1830; died 25 Feb 1836.                      |

**1696. True**[8]**(worthy) Eaton** (Henry[7], Ebenezer[6], John[5-1]) was born ca. 1800 in Seabrook, N.H.; mar. **Betsey Brown**, daughter of Benjamin. They settled on a small farm in Seabrook on the south side of Adams Ave. at the corner with So. Main St. True engaged in fishing in the proper seasons. He was still a seaman in 1850, but in later years managed a precarious existence on the farm. He died 25 Nov 1875; Betsey died 10 Aug 1889.

Their children were poorly recorded at Seabrook, but have been largely reconstructed from other records and personal testimonies:

|        |                                                                                       |
|--------|---------------------------------------------------------------------------------------|
| 3277   | i. Sarah[9] Eaton, b. ca. 1822; mar. Jacob B. Collins. She died 19 Sep 1897.          |
| 3278   | ii. Ann[9] Eaton, b. ca. 1824; mar. Joseph Bartlett, 6 Oct 1846 at Newburyport, Mass. |
| +3279  | iii. Caleb[9] Eaton, b. 11 Nov 1826; mar. Louisa Marshall, 1851.                      |
| +3280  | iv. Moses[9] B. Eaton, b. 10 Dec 1831; mar. Betsey Follansbee.                         |
| 3281   | v. Rebecca[9] Bartlett Eaton, b. Nov 1833; mar. Jacob[8] Eaton (**#1747**), as his 2d wife. |
| 3282   | vi. Nancy[9] B. Eaton, b. 28 Feb 1836; mar. Daniel E. Janvrin, 31 Dec 1854, and res. in Seabrook. She died 26 Nov 1898. |
| +3283  | vii. William[9] T. Eaton, b. ca. 1840; mar. Sarah J. Dow, 1861.                       |

**1699. Edward**[8] **Dearborn Eaton** (Henry[7], Ebenezer[6], John[5-1]) was born 4 Aug 1807; mar. **Elizabeth**[8] **Eaton (#1981)**, dau. of Wyman[7], 8 Feb 1832 at Seabrook. The couple lived on a small lot on the north side of Adams Ave., across from brother True[8]. Edward may have been at sea some in early adulthood, but by 1850 he lists his occupation as "none," and in the next two Censuses is a farm laborer.  Wife Elizabeth died in 1864; he died 14 Mar 1884 at Seabrook.

Children at Seabrook:

**3284**    i. Lydia[9] Ann Eaton, b. Mar 1833; mar. John M. Dow, 6 Jul 1851; she died 27 Dec 1910.

+**3285**   ii. Wyman[9] Eaton, b. 21 Jan 1833; mar. Mary J. Wright, 1852.

+**3286**   iii. William[9] Q. Eaton, b. 21 Aug 1836; mar. Lucretia Souther.

**3287**   iv. Margaret[9] Eaton, b. ca. 1843; she became the 2d wife of Christopher[8] Eaton (**#1738**) in 1883, but they had no children achieving adulthood, and Margaret died, 1926.

+**3288**   v. Almon[9] S. Eaton, b. 10 Mar 1846; mar. Mary Wright, 1867.

**3289**   vi. Hial[9] Eaton, b. ca. 1848; may have died in the Civil War.

**3290**  vii. Fanny[9] Eaton, b. 22 Sep 1850; mar. 1st, Henry Felch, 1867; 2d. Hiram Gove, 1870. She died 7 Feb 1914.

**3291** viii. (Miriam) Jane[9] Eaton, b. ca. 1854; mar. Joseph Lewis Boyd, 14 Jul 1880 (he born 1840). She died, 1926.

**3292**   ix. Alvado[9] Eaton, b. Apr 1858; mar. or had a liaison with widow Cynthia Ann (Eaton) Robinson, producing at least one son, Willie[10] A., b. 6 Mar 1881 and d. 29 Feb 1892. Cynthia died soon after the birth.  Alvado was a mariner and cobbler who died 12 Jul 1938 in Seabrook.

**1700. Moses**[8] **Eaton** (Henry[7], Ebenezer[6], John[5-1]) was born 2 Dec 1808 in Seabrook; mar. **Rebecca**[8] **Eaton** (**#1980**) on 29 Dec 1829, Salisbury, Mass.  The couple resided in Seabrook, where Moses had a 12-acre farm, and he worked as a shoemaker on the side.  He died 16 Jan 1868, and with wife Rebecca is bur. at Longhill Cemetery, Salisbury.

Children at Seabrook:

**3293**    i. Sarah[9] Ann Eaton, b. 1834; mar. David Flanders of Wilmot Flat, N.H.

**3294**   ii. Martha[9] Ellen Eaton, b. 20 Mar 1842; mar. Edward R. Cunningham of Belfast, Me. and res. in Washington, D.C., altho after her death 13 Feb 1824 she was bur. with her parents in Salisbury, Mass.

**1701. Lowell**[8] **Eaton** (Henry[7], Ebenezer[6], John[5-1]) was born ca. 1812 in Seabrook, N.H.; mar. **Pauline Hunt**, 13 Nov 1838 (Seabrook *VR* at Concord).  In 1857 they resided on the north side of So. Main St. about halfway to the point from the Worthley Ave. intersection.  Following a familiar Seabrook career line, Lowell was mainly a mariner and fisherman owning no real estate until he was age 50 or so; later he took a job in the shoe factory.  He died in 1880; Pauline died 1 Sep 1882.

Children in Seabrook (wife Pauline reported 13 births, but not all have been identified and we leave placeholders):

**3295**    i. Clarissa[9] R. Eaton, b. Dec 1840; first wife of Christopher[8] Eaton (#1738), mar. 9 Oct 1859; she died 3 Mar 1875.

**3296**   ii. Abner[9] L. Eaton, b. 2 Aug 1842; mar. Philena R. Fowler, ca. 1862. He was prob. a shoemaker res. in Seabrook, where their children were born: Sarah[10] M. Eaton, b. 5 Oct 1863, and mar. Abram Dow;  Celia[10] A. Eaton, b. 12 Dec 1866 but d. 17 Feb 1869; Elmer[10] E. Eaton, b. 11 Jun 1868; James[10] S. Eaton, b. 22 Mar 1871 but d. infancy; Ellis[10] J. Eaton, b. 31 Mar 1876 but d. infancy; and Celia[10] Eaton, b. 17 Mar 1880.

**3297**  iii. Jacob[9] D. Eaton, b. 12 May 1845; possibly mar. Mrs. Mary A. (Perkins) Stackpole of Beverly, Mass; but in any event he adopted her daughter Almira, born in 1863/64 with her husband Edwin Stackpole, as an Eaton. Thus Jacob D. is listed as her father when she (Almira "Eaton") mar David Fowler, as well as on her death record. Jacob D. worked in the shoe factory; died 28 Oct 1923.

**3298**   iv. Charles[9] Henry Eaton, b. 1847; mar. Mrs. Rhoda  (Hook) Fowler 5 Dec 1871, but there was prob. no issue before Charles, a shoemaker, died 29 Jan 1875.

**3299**    v. John[9] H. Eaton, b. 1849; mar. Susan Souther, 26 Oct 1868. Their first child, Willie[10], was born 5 Dec 1868, but father John drowned 19 Aug 1869.

**3300**   vi. Sarah[9] A. Eaton, b. 1851; mar. William H. Randall, 15 May 1870; died 27 Feb 1887.

**3301**  vii. Mary[9] Jane Eaton, b. ca. 1854; mar. Abel Souther, 7 Nov 1875. She died 13 Oct 1897.

**3302** viii. Joanna[9] Eaton, b. 12 Jul 1857; mar. Reese Owen of Seabrook, 7  Mar 1877. She died 13 Nov 1946.

**3303**   ix. Susan[9] H. Eaton, b. 1861; mar. James A. Beckman, 3 July 1889. She died 7 Apr 1926.

**3304**    x. John[9A] H. Eaton, b. 16 Aug 1864; died 7 Jun 1931 (death record at Concord lists as son of Lowell and Pauline at Seabrook: could he have been renamed at five to honor his departed elder brother of the same given names?).

**3305**   xi. Boy[9] Eaton, b. in year ending 31 Mar 1866.

**3306**  xii. Probable earlier stillbirth.

**3307** xiii. Probable earlier stillbirth.

**1709. Thomas[8] Eaton** (Thomas[7], Ebenezer[6], John[5-1]) was born 1798 in Seabrook, N.H.; mar. his first cousin **Rhoda[8] Eaton** (#1695), ca. 1818. We know very little about Thomas and Rhoda. In fact, this is one of the more frustrating Seabrook families to reconstruct, in that the couple appears to have had at least seven children before both of them died prior to 1850, but only three of these have names and visible life histories. In the ten years after 1836, Thomas executes seven land deeds, in each case selling small pieces of land to relatives and neighbors. In an 1842 deed he sells his eldest son Isaiah[9] half of his own home, plus an undivided tenth of another two acres with buildings. Throughout, Thomas is described as a "Seabrook mariner." He signed the final deed of the series in June, 1846.

Children born in Seabrook:

+ **3308**     i. Isaiah[9] D. Eaton, b. 16 Aug 1819; int., Hannah Hunt, 1841.
  **3309**    ii. Boy[9] Eaton, b. 1820-24. Possibly a Joshua?
+ **3310**    iii. Thomas[9], Jr., Eaton, b. 5 Nov 1826; m. Betsey Brown, 1847.
  **3311**    iv. Girl[9] Eaton, b. 1825-29. An Almiretta?
  **3312**     v. Girl[9] Eaton, b. 1830-34.
  **3313**    vi. Boy[9] Eaton, b. 1830-34. A Dudley?
  **3314**   vii. Betsey[9] D. Eaton, b. 1840; mar. 1st, Levi Collins, Jr., 1857; 2d, Horace Moreland, 1863.

NOTE. There is a competing hypothesis as to which Thomas Eaton mar. "cousin" Rhoda. In fact, the senior author's manuscript is apparently faulty at a crucial point involving just this question. In his Generation VII he lists the first-born son of Thomas[7]/Sally (cf. **#627**) as the Thomas[8] above, saying that this son "mar. Rhoda Eaton, Dau. of Henry Eaton," but giving no continuation or other sign of issue. On the very next page he lists another Thomas[7] Eaton, also a Thomas, Jr. (Thomas[6], John[5-1]), saying that he was born "about 1795" in Seabrook, and that he "m. Rhoda Eaton, dau. of Henry and Sarah Eaton." Now there were eight or nine little Rhoda Eatons growing up in Seabrook and Salisbury around the turn of the century; but only one of these was a daughter of Henry Eaton. So the senior author has these two Thomas, Jr., Eatons marrying the same Rhoda Eaton. This is not absolutely impossible: in a time and place where young men were often lost at sea, one of these Thomases might have died early with his widow marrying the other one. It is, however, suspiciously coincidental. Most importantly, however, the two known children in the roster above were in the senior author's account attributed to the second Thomas, grandson of John[5] (**#85**), rather than to the above Thomas, grandson of Ebenezer[6]. Hard records surrounding both of these Thomases are on toward non-existent. Of the two, the sheer existence of the Thomas[6], Sr., putative father of the second Thomas, is also a matter of dispute, as we have noted while saving him a place as **#246** (cf. discussion there). Therefore we have selected Ebenezer's grandson as the true wife of Rhoda and father of her children, although it would take but a small jot of hard evidence to reverse this decision. (A twist which would leave us wondering whatever happened to the slightly more substantial Thomas[8], Jr., our subject above.)

**1710. Caleb[8] Eaton** (Thomas[7], Ebenezer[6], John[5-1]) was born 1 Aug 1800 in Seabrook, N.H.; mar. 1st, a **Hannah Eaton**, otherwise unidentified, on 14 Sep 1824, "both of Seabrook." They prob. had a first

child Caleb, Jr., who died in 1827 (Mrs. Locke's List), a few months after
his mother Hannah died 7 Jan 1827 (also Mrs. Locke). Caleb mar. 2d, a
**Mary Eaton**, not clearly identified either, but prob. the daughter of
Moses and Rhoda Eaton (cf. **#1705**), on 4 May 1828, again "both of
Seabrook." On his two sole land deeds in 1833, Caleb was called a mariner in one and a husbandman in the other, the most common local mix
of trades. And almost certainly, he was the "Caleb Eaton, supposed of or
near Newburyport, lost from a vessel and found on the beach, bur. 22
Oct 1835." (Gloucester, Mass. *VR*).

Child with Hannah at Seabrook:

**3315**    i. Caleb[9], Jr. Eaton, b. ca. 1825; died 3 Jun 1827.

Possible child with Mary at Seabrook, among others:

**3316**    ii. Ruth[9] Eaton, b. ca. 1831.

A later illegitimate birth commonly ascribed to Caleb's widow
Mary:

**3317**    ?. Joshua[9] Eaton, b. ca. 8 Aug 1844; mar. Sarah Louise
            Fowler, dau. of David/Sarah Fowler, 31 Dec 1877. Joshua
            died 29 Sep 1910, with parents listed as "Caleb & Mary."


**1711. Joshua[8] Eaton** (Thomas[7], Ebenezer[6], John[5-1]) was born 7
Sep 1802 in Seabrook, N.H.; mar. **Cynthia Collins**, 16 Jan 1825, and
they resided in Seabrook on "South Road," presumably later So. Main
St., a bit west of the Worthley intersection. According to several of his
land deeds, Joshua farmed and was a mariner. Wife Cynthia died 17
May 1850. In Oct 1851, Joshua and other Seabrook Eatons were caught
in the infamous gale that smashed the fishing fleet at Bay Chaleur in the
Gulf of St. Lawrence. Joshua, his son Enoch, his brother Chase, along
with Winthrop Eaton and his son, all were drowned. Joshua and Cynthia
have a common gravestone at the Methodist Cemetery, Seabrook.

Children are not all well recorded, but the child roster apparent in
the 1840 Census, of five sons and one daughter, fits our reconstruction,
with a single later addition;

+ **3318**    i. Reuben[9] Eaton, b. 10 Aug 1826; m. Cynthia[9] Eaton (**#3329**).
+ **3319**    ii. Joshua[9] Jr., Eaton, b. Jul 1828; mar. Eleanor Dow, 1848.
+ **3320**    iii. Samuel[9] Collins Eaton, b. 15 Aug 1830; mar. Achsah, 1849.
  **3321**    iv. Enoch[9] Hoit Eaton, b. ca. Oct 1832; died 20 Feb 1853, and
            is buried in the Methodist Cemetery.
  **3322**    v. Jabez[9] T. Eaton, b. ca. 1836; res. Seabrook, never married.
  **3323**    vi. Mary[9] C. Eaton, b. ca. 1838; is most prob. the Mary who
            mar. 1st, 3 Oct 1854, John[8] Curtis Eaton (**#2008**). He

divorced her for abandonment, 28 Oct 1874, with no issue. She then mar. 2d, Charles[8] Colby Eaton (his first wife) (#3381, q. v.).

3324    vii. Abigail[9] B. Eaton, b. 1840, post-Census; she prob. mar. Samuel[8] A. Eaton (#2010). She died 5 Dec 1893.

**1713. Chase[8] Eaton** (Thomas[7], Ebenezer[6], John[5-1]) was born ca. 1806 in Seabrook, N.H.; mar. **Miriam[7] Eaton (#646)**, dau. of John[6-1], on 28 Nov 1825. They settled in Seabrook, where he was a mariner and husbandman. This family was missed by the 1850 Census, but in Oct 1851, Chase was lost with his brother Joshua and at least three other Seabrook Eatons in the great gale that smashed the fishing fleet at Bay Chaleur in the Gulf of St. Lawrence. In all, eleven Seabrook citizens failed to return.

Children at Seabrook:

3325    i. Luther[9] C. Eaton, b. 1829, mar. Amanda Pike, 29 Nov 1855 at Newburyport, where they appear also in 1860 with two children, a daughter Amanda[10] b. ca. 1858; and a son Luther[10] b. early 1860.

+3326    ii. Leonard[9] William Eaton, b. 1838; mar. Mercy Wells, 1854.

3327    iii. Angeline[9] Eaton, b. 1840; mar. James A. Wright (b. ca. 1838), son of James and Mary (Souther) Wright.

**1714. William[8] Eaton** (Thomas[7], Ebenezer[6], John[5-1]) was born 11 Sep 1809 in Seabrook, N.H.; mar. **Nancy Brown**, 24 May 1827 (from divorce records, Concord, N.H.). She was the daughter of Henry and Eleanor[7] (Eaton: #634) Brown. They resided in Seabrook adjacent to his wife's family of origin on So. Main St. near Worthley Ave, and had a large family, of whom eight survived to be married. They were not prosperous (in 1850 William reported no real estate), but he made a living as a fisherman, shoemaker and hired hand. Wife Nancy divorced William, Oct 1874, for abandonment. He died 30 Dec 1887; ex-wife Nancy died 25 Aug 1908.

Children in Seabrook (four infant deaths not included):

3328    i. Hannah[9] Eaton, b. 13 Sep 1827; mar. 1st, Samuel F. Fowler, Jr., 1844; and 2d, Sewell B. Fowler. She died 1 Aug 1907.

3329    ii. Cynthia[9] Eaton, b. 19 Sep 1829; mar. her first cousin Reuben[9] Eaton (#3318, q.v. for children). She died 12 May, 1912.

3330    iii. Soviah[9] (spelling from gravestone: variants abound!) Eaton, b. 1833; mar. Christopher D. Brown, 29 Dec 1851. She died 28 Jul 1890.

**3331**    iv. Nancy[9] Eaton, b. 19 Nov 1835; mar. John Boyd in 1852 at
Salisbury. She died 26 May 1921.
**3332**    v. George[9] P. Eaton, b. 9 Feb 1841; mar. Ellen[10] Jane Eaton
(**#5016**), daughter of Isaiah[9] D. Eaton, int. 4 Oct 1861.
Their children were Amanda[10] P. Eaton, b. 27 Feb 1862,
who mar. William E. Randall; Clara[10] E. Eaton, b. 28 Jan
1867, who mar. A. J. Gynan; (Infant death, unnamed);
George[10] P. Eaton, Jr., b. 21 Mar 1869; Anda[10] Eaton, b.
9 Oct 1874.
**3333**    vi. William[9] Alfred Eaton, Jr., b. Oct 1843; died in the hospital
of wounds in the Civil War, 14 Dec 1864.
**3334**    vii. Alice[9A] Jane Eaton, b. 15 Oct 1851; mar. Dennis D.
Knowles. She was res. on Washington St., Seabrook, when
she died 7 Jan 1924.
**3335**    viii. Alvado[9] F. Eaton, b. 5 Feb 1855; mar. Charlotte M. Janvrin,
ca. 1874, and res. in Seabrook. Charlotte died 6 Apr
1883. Their children were Wallace[10] M. Eaton, b. 23 Nov
1874; Minnie[10] A. Eaton, b. 10 Jan 1877, d. infancy; and
Minnie[10A] Eaton, b. 19 May 1878.
**3336**    ix. Jabez[9] William Eaton, b. 18 Jun 1860; may have married a
Maggie Eaton, unidentified, although he was solo in the
1900 Census. He died 28 May 1939 at Brentwood, N.H.

**1716. Reuben[8] D. Eaton** (Thomas[7], Ebenezer[6], John[5-1]) was born
ca. Jun 1813 in Seabrook, N.H.; mar. **Sarah "Sally" Brown**, daughter of
Moses Brown and Olive (Eaton), 31 Mar 1833 in Seabrook. In the Censuses of 1850-70 he is listed respectively as a seaman, a shoemaker and a
farmer, or the common mix of occupations for this period in Seabrook.
He died 12 Apr 1876; widow Sally died 9 May 1899, age 75 yrs, 3 mos.

Children in Seabrook, N.H.:

**3337**     i. Elvira[9] P. Eaton, b. 29 Apr 1833; she d. unm., 2 Feb 1911.
**+3338**    ii. Reuben[9] Amos Eaton, b. 19 Sep 1834; mar. Annie Gynan.
**3339**    iii. Julia[9] F. Eaton, b. Oct 1836; she died unmar., 30 May 1913.
**3340**    iv. Ellen[9] Eaton, b. ca. 1839; mar. George H. French, 18 Oct
1862, and died 23 Feb 1824.
**3341**    v. Martha[9] Eaton, b. Jun 1843; mar. Lowell Boyd, (int.) 23
Aug 1862. She died 1925.
**3342**    vi. Gustavus[9] A. Eaton, b. 5 Jan 1846; res. unmar. in Seabrook,
and died 24 Jun 1914.
**3343**    vii. John[9] Webster Eaton, b. 30 Jan 1849; mar. Julia Bryant.
They res. first in Seabrook, but later moved to Salisbury,
Mass., res. on the Lafayette Rd. there. They had at least
seven children. He died 12 Sep 1929.
**3344**    viii. Emma[9] E. Eaton, b. 1852; mar. Henry P. Upham, 4 Oct
1873.
**3345**    ix. Alvah[9] F. Eaton, b. 25 Dec 1855; res. unmar. in Seabrook,

and died 22 Feb 1915.


**1720. John⁸ A. "Brown" Eaton** (Israel⁷, Benjamin⁶, John⁵⁻¹) was born in 1858 in Vermont, prob. at Winooski. He was already a young man by the time his family returned to Seabrook in the later 1870s. He later mar. **Sarah L. Brown** (then age 20) on 27 Jul 1885 at Seabrook. They were the parents of some six children, three of whom died soon after birth. John A. died 6 Apr 1927; wife Sarah died 14 Mar 1928.

Children (partial):

**3346**    i. Willis⁹ B. Eaton, b. of mother Sarah, 9 Feb 1883, premari-
                tally; mar. Nettie Elizabeth Eaton, daughter of William H.
                and Eliza A. (Bagley) Eaton, Nov 1905, with Willis
                identifying John A. Eaton as his father. He died 1945.
**3347**   ii. George⁹ B. Eaton, b. 22 Mar 1888; died of diphtheria on
                7 Jan 1891.


**1728. Ezekiel⁸ Collins Eaton** (Abel⁷, Silvanus⁶, John⁵⁻¹) was born ca. 1813 in Seabrook. Having lost his father at sea as a little child, Ezekiel prob. was raised in the household of David Fowler, who became his mother Polly (Collins) Eaton's second husband, 10 Sep 1818 at Seabrook. Ezekiel mar. **Nancy Souther**, 22 Nov 1836 at Seabrook. They resided in Seabrook, where Ezekiel was a seaman. He died 9 Feb 1861; Nancy died 9 Mar 1878, age 62.

Known children at Seabrook, N.H. (perhaps partial):

**+3348**    i. Abel⁹ Eaton, b. 1838; mar. Zelphia A. Bragg, 1856.
**3349**   ii. Sally⁹ Augusta Eaton, b. ca. 1841; mar. 1st, Charles¹⁰ W.
                Eaton (**#4952**) son of Henry⁹ , 11 Nov 1859; Charles was
                "killed by the cars" (RR), 4 Jul 1868 (N.H. record). Sally
                mar. 2d, Owen Perley Sargent, 2 Nov 1869. She died
                29 Apr 1893, Newburyport, Mass.


**1730. Cyrus⁸ Eaton** (Christopher⁷, Silvanus⁶, John⁵⁻¹) was born ca. 1814 in Seabrook, N.H.; mar. **Sally E. Collins** 30 Oct 1837. They resided in Salisbury, Mass. They are said to have had two children, both of them dying very young. Cyrus was prob. a seaman, and was lost at sea or died of other causes in the early 1840s, since his widow Sally became the second wife of Jacob⁸ Eaton (**#1979**) on 17 Nov 1844. Within a few years, Jacob died childless, and widow Sally mar. Elihu Dow, and a daughter Florence was born with whom Sally spent her last years in Malden, Mass.

**1731. True⁸ Eaton** (Christopher⁷, Silvanus⁶, John⁵⁻¹) was born 11 Jan 1819 in Seabrook, N.H.; mar **Jane Moody** of Salisbury, Mass. on 16 May 1841 in Salisbury. They settled on the north side of Beach Road in Salisbury, by the brook which forms the beginning of the Little River, two doors east of John French Eaton on the 1884 map of that village. True was a mariner in the first half of his adulthood and shoemaker in his later years. He died 21 Jun 1901 at Salisbury; Jane died 29 Jun 1890.

Children, all born Salisbury, Mass.:

3350    i. Mary⁹ Emeline Eaton, b. 1841; mar. Calvin D. Blaisdell in
            1866 at Salisbury. They resided with two sons in Salis-
            bury. She died 13 Dec 1917.
3351    ii. Eunice⁹ Merrill Eaton, b. 11 Jun 1845; died of dysentery
            13 Sep 1847.
3352    iii. Josephine⁹ Merrill Eaton, b. 13 Dec 1849; mar. J. Edwin
            True in 1868 and resided in Salisbury. She died, however,
            24 Apr 1871.
3353    iv. Lydia⁹ Ann Eaton, b. 18 Sep 1853; died 21 Dec 1856.

**1733. Andrew⁸ Eaton** (Christopher⁷, Silvanus⁶, John⁵⁻¹) was born ca. 1823 in Seabrook, N.H.; on 24 Oct 1844 he mar. **Lois Dow** of Salisbury, daughter of Levi and Nancy (Eaton). They resided in Salisbury, and he was mainly a mariner early in adulthood and a shoemaker thereafter. He died 30 Jun 1888; Lois died 8 Jan 1911, both Salisbury.

Children in Salisbury, Mass.:

3354    i. Charles⁹ Henry Eaton, b. 5 Jan 1845; died in 1846.
3355    ii. Charles⁹ᴬ Henry Eaton, b. 22 Aug 1847; mar. Ruth A.
            Moody, 3 Apr 1866 and they res. in Salisbury. He was a
            conductor on the electric car on Beach Rd., a busy job in
            summer carrying bathers to Salisbury Beach. They had
            at least a daughter, Sarah¹⁰ Emily Eaton, b. 27 Oct 1866.

**1736. Lowell⁸ Eaton** (Christopher⁷, Silvanus⁶, John⁵⁻¹) was born ca. Aug 1832 in Seabrook, N.H.; mar. **Mrs. Hannah (Brown) Eaton** on 22 Feb 1855 in Salisbury, Mass. She was widow of Emery⁸ B. Eaton (**#1745**), who had died 24 Jul 1854 (gravestone, Longhill Cemetery), and seven years the senior of the groom. She brought to the marriage a daughter Mary Ednah, b. 1849. Lowell settled with her in Salisbury, where he was mainly a shoemaker, but did some sea fishing as well. Hannah died 15 Feb 1889; Lowell died 8 Sep 1900 in Salisbury.

Child at Salisbury, Mass.:

**3356** i. Lowell[9] Emery Eaton, b. 14 Jul 1860, and often listed as "Emery L." With that name, he mar. Hattie F. Towle, 23 Dec 1884 in Salisbury. No children are known. He died a widower 21 Jun 1916, Salisbury.

**1738. Christopher[8] Eaton** (Christopher[7], Silvanus[6], John[5-1]) was born 5 Sep 1839 in Seabrook; mar. 1st, **Clarissa[9] R. Eaton (#3295)** in Seabrook on 9 Oct 1859. They resided in Seabrook, much of the time living under the same roof as his parents, but as a separate household. Christopher, like many of his associates, followed the sea in season but also made shoes and was a farm laborer. Clarissa died before 1880; and Christopher mar. 2d, **Margaret[9] Eaton (#3287)**, on 12 Mar 1883, although this marriage had but one child who died young. Christopher died 30 Mar 1910; Margaret followed, 1926.

Children (about ten were born to Clarissa in Seabrook, although quite a number of them died young; our imperfect list was supplied by a relative):

**3357** i. Sarah[9] Eaton, b. ca. Apr 1860; died 22 May 1865.
**3358** ii. Andrew[9] J. Eaton, b. Dec 1861; died 13 Apr 1869 of whooping cough.
**3359** iii. William[9] H. Eaton, b. 11 Feb 1864; mar. Eliza Bagley, 20 Nov 1886. He died Aug 1917.
**3360** iv. Ednah[9] Eaton, b. 9 Jul 1866; died in the 1870s.
**3361** v. Helen[9] "Nellie" B. Eaton, a twin b. 20 Aug 1868; mar. John E. Souther on 15 Sep 1890. She died 1903.
**3362** vi. Twin[9] Eaton, b. 20 Aug 1868; died unnamed.
**3363** vii. Ruth[9] Ann Eaton, b. 22 Nov 1870; mar. Sewell B. Fowler, Jr., 25 Nov 1892. She died 21 Feb 1938.
**3364** viii. Mary[9] Lydia Eaton, b. 13 Jul 1874; died in the year ending 31 Mar 1876.

**1740. Winthrop[8] Dow Eaton** (Samuel[7], John[6-1]) was born ca. 1811 in Seabrook, N.H., and presumably named after his maternal grandfather; mar. **Hannah Brown**, (int.) 21 Sep 1835 at Seabrook. In 1840 they were living in Seabrook, prob. on So. Main St. Winthrop was listed as a mariner in his few deeds in this period (1837 and 1842). This was apparently the death of him, for he and an unnamed elder son were lost in the fishing fleet in the gale at Bay Chaleur, Gulf of St. Lawrence, in Oct. 1851. His widow is probably the Hannah Eaton dying in 1856, leaving the children orphans. One of these, Joshua W., lived in a household on Seabrook Rd. in Salisbury in the 1860 Census headed by Daniel Eaton, 75, and a subfamily headed by Edward Brown, 42.

Children, all but the last at Seabrook (Winthrop and Hannah had
two children under five living with them as of 1840, but their names are
not certain. The last three children are well known.)

3365    i. Boy[9] (William?) Eaton, b. ca. 1835/6; presumed to be the
           unnamed son lost with father Winthrop at Bay Chaleur,
           1851.
3366   ii. Girl[9] Eaton. b. ca. 1838/9.
3367  iii. Eunice[9] Eaton, b. 7 Jul 1841 (tombstone and death record at
           Hampton, N.H.); mar. John Sherburne Locke of Hampton
           on 9 Jul 1865. She died 10 Oct 1910, age 69.
+3368  iv. Joshua[9] Winthrop Eaton, b. late 1844; mar. Ann Dyer, 1866.
3369    v. Mary[9] Frances Eaton, b. ca. 28 Oct 1846 at Salisbury; mar.
           David P. Goodwin, 1866, and resided at Salisbury. She
           died 4 Dec 1918.

**1745. Emery[8] B. Eaton** (Jacob[7], John[6-1]) was born ca. Feb 1824
in Seabrook, N.H. He was of Newburyport when mar. **Hannah Brown**
ca. 1845 and the couple settled in Salisbury, Mass. Emery died at a
young age on 24 Jul 1854 and is buried at Longhill Cemetery, Salisbury.
His widow Hannah then mar. Lowell Eaton (**#1736**), bringing to the marriage her sole surviving child Mary[9].

Children at Salisbury, Mass.:

3370    i. Edwin[9] Eaton, b. 14 Jan 1846; died 10 Sep 1848, Salisbury.
3371   ii. Mary[9] Edna Eaton, b. 3 Oct 1849; mar. Orson Daniels, 1871.
           She died 1888.

**1747. Jacob[8] Eaton** (Jacob[7], John[6-1]) was born 14 Jan 1830 in
Seabrook, N.H. There is some controversy as to whether this Jacob[8] mar.
1st, **Belinda Fowler**, 13 Jul 1848 at Seabrook. She was a daughter of
Jacob Fowler and Sarah[7] J. Eaton (**#763**). If this marriage occurred, Belinda must have disappeared from the scene, apparently childless, in advance of the time five years later when this particular Jacob[8] (Jacob[7])
joined in mar. intentions with 2d (or 1st, as the case may be!) **Rebecca[9]
Eaton** (**#3281**). These intentions were registered at Newburyport, Mass.
on 13 Jul 1853. Once past the possibility of the first marriage, which
includes for its limited support the given name of the first Jacob/Rebecca
daughter, the remaining history of this second couple has fewer points of
dispute. Jacob was by vocation a shoemaker, although "for thirty-five
years he passed his life on the sea as a fisherman" (Hazlett, 1915). Jacob
died 13 Jan 1894 at Seabrook. Wife Rebecca lived into the 20th century,
reporting in the 1900 Census that she had borne seven children to Jacob,
rather than the six commonly reported for this couple, the difference
probably being accounted for by something approaching a stillbirth.

Children at Seabrook with Rebecca:

3372   i. Belinda[9] J. Eaton, b. 1854; mar. William[8] S. Eaton (**#2379**).
3373   ii. Caroline[9] A. Eaton, b. 1856; died 1873, age 17.
3374   iii. Jacob[9] F. Eaton, b. Jul 1857; died 1 Aug 1867.
3375   iv. Emery[9] Newell Eaton, b. 20 Jan 1859; mar. Alberta Janvrin.
3376   v. Jacob[9] Lawrence Eaton, b. ca. 1867; died 24 Jan 1873.
3377   vi. Boy[9] Eaton, b. 2 Mar 1872.
3378   vii. Caddie[9] J. Eaton, b. ?

**1750. Enoch[8] Hoyt Eaton** (John[7-1]) was born 9 Mar 1824 in Salisbury, Mass.; mar. 1st, **Mary[8] L. Eaton (#1912)** on 13 Jun 1853 in Salisbury. The couple settled in Salisbury, and while Enoch is listed early (1850) as a fisherman when still living in his parental household, he soon leaves the sea for a mix of farming and shoemaking. Wife Mary died after bearing two children, on 24 Aug 1856 at age 22. Enoch mar. 2d, **Clara C. Patten** of Amesbury (born ca. 1822), on 25 Nov 1859. This second marriage was without issue. Enoch died a widower for the second time, on 20 Feb 1900 in Salisbury.

Children in Salisbury with Mary L.:

3379   i. Israel[9] B. Eaton, b. ca. Dec. 7, 1854 (from age at death); mar. Susan[10] Jeanette Eaton (**#4975**), daughter of Moses[9] B. and Betsey, on 3 Oct 1876. They had three children, two dying young. He died 27 Apr 1929.
3380   ii. Mary[9] F. Eaton, b. ca. 31 Jan 1856; mar. Cyrus L. Fowler, (int.) 12 Sep 1873, and had eight children, one named Enoch Hoyt Fowler. She died 27 Feb 1888.

**1752. John[8] Colby Eaton** (John[7-1]) was born 28 Jul 1827 in Salisbury, Mass.; mar. **Mary Jane Eaton (#2013)** 7 Aug 1850 at Salisbury. They resided in Seabrook, where John was a shoemaker by trade. Mary Jane died 12 Jan 1877. John C. died 8 Jan 1883.

Children at Seabrook:

3381   i. Charles[9] Colby Eaton, b. 1850; mar. 1st, Mary C. Eaton (**#3323**) (her 2d marriage). They adopted a Charles Blanchard in Boston, 1879, making him "Charles Blanchard Eaton." But Mary C. died 16 Jan 1884, Charles[9] mar. 2d, Mary R. Moreland, having children of his own and losing interest in the Blanchard child, who resumed the surname Blanchard.
3382   ii. John[9] Curtis Eaton, b. 14 Oct 1853; mar. Eunice[10] A. Eaton, (**#4985**) daughter of Wyman[9], 16 Feb 1878. He died 22 Jul 1921, Newburyport, Mass. Eunice died 26 Feb 1932.

3383    iii. Frederick⁹ Eaton, b. 1858; mar. 1st, Lizzie Bragg, 8 Apr
        1878 and 2d, Emma Fowler, 23 Nov 1890, having several
        children from each union. He died 21 Jan 1935.
3384    iv. Albert⁹ Merrill Eaton, b. 26 Jun 1859; mar. Phebe⁹ K. Eaton,
        (#3730), 15 Oct 1881. He died of tuberculosis 9 Mar
        1919 (Newburyport record); Phebe died 2 Sep 1936.
3385    v. Sylvester⁹ Eaton, b. 1862; mar. 1st, Frances M. (or Florence)
        Pike, 9 Jun 1881. They had a large family, and Frances
        died, 1900. He mar. 2d, Laura F. (Hoyt) Coffin, 17 Aug
        1902; and 3d, Hannah A. Fowler, 26 Aug 1905. He died
        1950; bur. at Wildwood with Hannah who died in 1962.

**1760. Samuel⁸ Perley Eaton** (Moody⁷, Ephraim⁶, Benjamin⁵,
John⁴⁻¹) was born ca. 1801-02 in "N.H.," and therefore, presumably in
Seabrook, before the parents removed to Maine. On 8 Sep 1833, he
mar. **Love(y) Huckins**, a Maine native born ca. 1805, and the couple
settled in Lubec, Maine. Samuel P. farmed a small parcel of land there.
Lovey died 12 Aug 1853.

Children at Lubec, Me.:

3386    i. Margery⁹ Ann Eaton, b. 2 Apr 1834.
3387    ii. Sarah⁹ Eaton, b. 23 Aug 1835.
3388    iii. Martha⁹ H. Eaton, b. 28 Jun 1837.
3389    iv. John⁹ A. Eaton, b. 10 Mar 1839.
3390    v. Jemima⁹ Eaton, b. Jul 1841.

**1762. James⁸ Moody Eaton** (Moody⁷, Ephraim⁶, Benjamin⁵,
John⁴⁻¹) was born 18 Jul 1808 in Eastport, Me.; mar. **Eliza Ann Ramsdell**
in Lubec, Me., where they resided. He farmed a small parcel of land.
Wife Eliza died on 10 Mar 1883; James died five days later, both of them
at Lubec.

Children at Lubec, Me.:

3391    i. Elvira⁹ Eaton, b. 1 Jul 1832.
3392    ii. Henry⁹ Moody Eaton, b. 27 Sep 1834.
3393    iii. Lucetta⁹ Eaton, b. 19 Sep 1836.
3394    iv. Emeline⁹ Eaton, b. 14 Mar 1839.
3395    v. Belinda⁹ Eaton, b. Apr 1842; mar. James A. Rice, Aug 1861.
3396    vi. James⁹ P. Eaton, b. Apr 1843; mar. Lucretia Huddleston,
        26 Nov 1865 at Lubec. Their first children were daugh-
        ters Elvia¹⁰ Eaton (b. 29 Jan 1867) and Bertha¹⁰ Eaton
        (b. 1868). Then wife Lucretia died 11 Jul 1869.
3397    vii. George⁹ W. Eaton, b. Nov 1847; mar. (Mary) Ellen Brad-
        bury, 21 Oct 1865 at Lubec. Their first child, George¹⁰
        Burnham Eaton was b. 6 Apr 1866 at Lubec. Other

children, if any, not known. George[9] W. died 18 Nov
1877 at Portland, Me. from second leg amputation
(septicemia), and is bur. at Lubec. Widow Ellen mar. 2d,
William H. Jones, 24 Sep 1881 at Lubec.
**3398**   viii. Albertina[9] Eaton, b. 1852.


**1776. Washington[8] Eaton** (Winthrop[7-6], Benjamin[5], John[4-1]) was
born 18 Sep 1825 in Seabrook; mar. **Clarissa Boyd**, also of Seabrook,
on 2 Dec 1850. Washington reports his occupation as a shoemaker just
before his marriage, but they settled on the corner of Washington St. and
Walton Rd. in Seabrook. For some period they ran a store from their
house, although Washington typically styled himself a farmer, and it was
a relatively prosperous household. Washington died of consumption, 25
Nov 1889, and Clarissa died 20 Jan 1899.

Children in Seabrook:

**3399**   i. Nelson[9] Eaton, b. 7 Nov 1852; died 29 May 1874.
**3400**   ii. Sevilla[9] Eaton, b. 31 Jan 1856; mar. George L. Fellows,
             1883. She died 5 Apr 1930.
**3401**   iii. Adeline[9] Eaton, b. 25 May 1860; mar. John D. McAllister.
             She died 23 Dec 1929.
**3402**   iv. Newell[9] Eaton, b. 6 Apr 1863; died 29 Nov 1863 (Bible).


**1789. George[8] Levi Eaton** (Stephen[7], Levi[6], Benjamin[5], John[4-1])
was born 29 Jul 1836 in Boston, Mass; grew up with his family in So.
Hampton, N.H., mar. **Elizabeth "Lizzie" A. Delaware** on 1 Jan 1860
(So. Hampton *VR* at Concord). This extended family had major interest
in removing to Iowa, and there is reason to believe that there was some
shuttling back and forth of parts of the family, but the chronology of all
this is dim. George L. and his bride were said to have settled first in So.
Hampton for a few years and then in Kingston, N.H. George was a carpenter. Then the couple removed to Melrose (Monroe Co.) Iowa around
1866, and his father Stephen[7] J.and perhaps his mother removed there as
well, although since father Stephen died in Oct 1867, things were hap-
pening at a rapid clip. If children's birthplaces of record are not too ambiguous, George and Lizzie were indeed in Iowa in 1867, but then returned to South Hampton until about 1873, when they removed permanently to Iowa. They were variously at sites in the three adjacent counties of Monroe (Melrose and Jackson), Appanoose, and Wapello
(Ottumwa) over the next four decades until George L. died 30 Oct 1913.

Children, with apparent birthplaces:

**3403**   i. Eliza[9] Ann Eaton, b. 18 May 1861, at So. Hampton, N.H.
**3404**   ii. Francis[9] Eaton, b. 7 Jan 1863, So. Hampton; d. 10 Feb 1863.
**3405**   iii. George[9] Frank Eaton, b. 15 Jun 1864, So. Hampton; mar.

Martha Dora Smith, 17 Jan 1886.  He died 17 Feb 1899.

**3406**    iv. Eddie[9] Lowell Eaton, b. 7 Feb 1866, So. Hampton; mar.
Jennie Myrtle Argyle, 8 Jan 1891.  He died 8 Mar 1940.

**3407**    v. Nettie[9] Jones Eaton, b. 3 Dec 1867, Iowa.; mar. Harvey O.
Bowman, 10 Feb 1886.  She died 1 Mar 1927.

**3408**    vi. Joseph[9] Sumner Eaton, b. 26 Mar 1870, So. Hampton; mar.
Carrie Linden Manly, 24 Dec 1891.

**3409**    vii. William[9] Clarence Eaton, b. 5 Apr 1872, So. Hampton; mar.
Auria Belle Honnold, 13 Mr 1894.  He died 20 Oct 1940.

**3410**    viii. Grace[9] Melvina Eaton, b. 18 Jun 1874, Iowa; d. 11 Jan
1887.

**3411**    ix. Fred[9] Lermont Eaton, b. 13 Aug 1876, Melrose, Iowa; mar.
Ina Blanche Olney, 26 Nov 1905; died 19 Sep 1955.

**3412**    x. Alice[9] May Eaton, b. 11 Sep 1879, Melrose, Iowa; died 20
Oct 1879.

**3413**    xi. Levi[9] Delaware Eaton, b. 20 Sep 1880, Appanoose Co.,
Iowa ; mar. Henrietta Parthena Wagner, 23 Nov 1904.

**3414**    xii. Hattie[9] Ethel Eaton, b. 13 Apr, 1883, Melrose, Iowa; died
5 Sep 1884.

**3415**    xiii. Elizabeth[9] Adele Eaton, b. 5 Mar 1885, Melrose, Iowa; mar.
Albert Louis Mitchell, 22 May 1906; she d.14 Feb 1937.

**3416**    xiv. Caroline[9] Prescott Eaton, b. 22 May 1888, Melrose, Iowa;
mar. John E. Johnson, 23 Mar 1919; died 24 Sep 1944.


**1796.  Lowell[8] Dennett Eaton** (Samuel P.[7-6] Benjamin[5], John[4-1])
was born 1 Feb 1852 in So. Hampton, N.H.  On 27 Nov 1878 he mar. in
Amesbury, Mass., **Wilhelmina Morris**, then 25 and a native of Stratham,
N.H.

Children in So. Hampton:

**3417**    i. Perley[9] D. Eaton. b. 17 Mar 1879.
**3418**    ii. Girl[9] Eaton, b. 17 Aug 1882.


**1798.  Solomon[8] Eaton, Jr.** (Solomon[7], Eliakim[6], William[5], John[4],
John[3-1] was born 27 Nov 1802 on Little Deer Isle, Me.; in Feb 1828, he
mar. **Sophia L. Hendrick**, who was born to James and Hannah (Gray)
Hendrick.  Her father was English by birth and had enlisted in the War of
1812, presumably on the British side, and never returned.  His wife Hannah remar. a Samuel Blastow in 1817.  Solomon and Sophia had eight
children, and he died 12 Jun 1849 (Noyes, 1943).

Children on Little Deer Isle:

**3419**    i. Susannah[9] Eaton, b. 8 Aug 1828; mar. John Holland of
Buck's Harbor, 1 Dec 1866.  They lived at first in the old
Jeremiah Eaton house at No. Deer Isle, but then moved to

the James Eaton place on Little Deer Isle. There was
much consumption in Susannah's family and she rapidly
fell prey to it, dying childless before 1870. Her husband
John mar. 2d, Lydia⁹ Jane Eaton (#3436), 8 Nov 1870.
3420   ii. Isaiah⁹ Valentine Eaton, b. 27 Nov 1830; m. Susan Haskell,
also of Deer Isle, 1 Feb 1850; they res. on Deer Isle,
where he was a mariner who was lost at sea in 1865 in
Civil War-related sailing. They had eight children in the
1851-64 period, with six surviving infancy.
3421   iii. Eunice⁹ Catherine Eaton, b. 27 Jul 1833; died 9 Jan 1838.
3422   iv. Hannah⁹ Catherine Eaton, b. 15 May 1838; d. 21 Jan 1838.
3423   v. Sophia⁹ F. Eaton, b. 27 Feb 1840; mar. John Soper of
Brooksville, 29 Jun 1865.
3424   vi. David⁹ Hill Eaton, b. 16 Nov 1843; died 7 Nov 1838.
3425   vii. George⁹ D. Eaton, b. 29 Jul 1845; died as a young man of
a fever contracted on a vessel on the southern seaboard.
3426   viii. Lydia⁹ P. Eaton, b. ca 1850; mar. Horatio W. Bowden,
int. 7 Nov 1870.

**1799. Benjamin⁸ H. Eaton** (Solomon⁷, Eliakim⁶, William⁵, John⁴,
John³⁻¹) was born ca. 1803-04 on Little Deer Isle, Me.; mar. on 22 Oct
1804, **Maria C. Weed**, also Deer Isle, born ca. 1806 to Jeremiah and
Alethia (Joyce) Weed. They res. on Deer Isle, and Benjamin was a mari-
ner. Late in life he and Maria took up residence on Stave Island, a tiny
islet south of Deer Isle, where his grandfather Eliakim had once settled.
Maria died there 13 Sep 1878; and Benjamin followed 25 Oct 1887.
They both are buried there.

Children on Deer Isle:

3427   i. Hezekiah⁹ Colby Eaton, b. 11 Jan 1825; died in boyhood.
3428   ii. Joan⁹ Weed Eaton, b. 7 Feb 1826; mar. Abijah Wheeler
Hardy of Little Deer Isle. They had several children and
later removed to Winterport, Me.
3429   iii. John⁹ C. Eaton, b. 29 Feb 1827; died in infancy.
3430   iv. John⁹ᴬ C. Eaton, b. 4 May 1828; mar. Hannah Harvey, 21
Oct 1857. He died rather rapidly thereafter: he had at
most a son who died young. His widow mar. 2d, John⁹ B.
Eaton (#3440), son of James Eaton of Little Deer Isle.
3431   v. Nathan⁹ B. Eaton, b. 4 Apr 1830; mar. Martha Ann Eaton
(#3541), int. 21 Jan 1860. They had a large family.
3432   vi. Sophia⁹ Eleanor Eaton, b. ca. 1833; mar. Alfred⁸ Eaton of
Little Deer Isle (see #1848 for children).
3433   vii. Mary⁹ Elizabeth Eaton, b. Nov 1834; mar. 1st, Antonio de
Silva , a Portuguese sailor who died or was lost at sea after
they had had three children; and 2d to George Gray, int.
8 Feb 1866, but separated from him within days; and 3d,
to Isaac Noyes, 9 Sep 1866. She had no children by

Noyes and they lived under depressed circumstances in a
little hut on Stave Island.
3434   viii. James⁹ B. Eaton, b. ca. 1837; mar. 1st, Lucy⁹ Jane Eaton
(#3451), dau of Mark⁸/Lydia (Benson); mar 2d. Eme-
line Weed, 16 Dec 1863. Had six children.
3435   ix. (Warren) Merrill⁹ Eaton, b. 22 Jul 1843; mar. 1st, Nancy
Helen Spinney, 11 Apr 1862; mar. 2d, Nancy T. Holland
of Brooksville, Me., int. 6 Mar 1868; and mar. 3d, Orilla
Eaton (#3537), dau. of William and Elizabeth (Weed).
3436   x. Lucy⁹ Ann Eaton, b. ca. 1845; mar. Alfred E. Weed, also of
Deer Isle, 12 May 1866. They had no children and removed to Winterport, where they separated. She mar. 2d,
a Portuguese sailor.

**1800. James⁸ Eaton** (Solomon⁷, Eliakim⁶, William⁵, John⁴⁻¹) was
born ca. 1805 on Deer Isle. He pub. int. with Lucinda Jordan, 9 May
1825 at Brooksville, on the mainland across the Reach from Deer Isle,
but this marriage apparently did not take place. He subsequently mar.
another Brooksville girl, **Sarah Blake** in 1829 (27 Aug in D.I. records; 8
Oct at Brooksville). This couple was peripatetic, residing for a while at
Bucksport, Me. as well as Deer Isle during their child-raising. They also
were at Little Deer Isle and perhaps on other islands in Penobscot Bay.
James was a fisherman. Late in life after he was widowed he became
quite incapacitated and was on the pauper rolls. He died 29 Jan 1890 at
the house of his grandson, Peter H. Haskell, son of his daughter Nancy.

Children (poorly recorded, and mainly deduced from his household composition in 1850):

3437   i. Nancy⁹ Eaton, b. ca. 1830; mar. Peter Haskell, son of Peter
H. Haskell and Susan (Eaton). This couple had five children, and took care of her father James in old age.
3438   ii. Margaret⁹ A. Eaton, b. ca. 1832; mar. Solomon Eaton Haskell, 23 Sep 1849.
3439   iii. Charlotte⁹ Eaton, b. ca. 1834; mar. 3 Oct 1853, Orrace R.
Haskell, brother to Solomon just above.
3440   iv. John⁹ Blake Eaton, b. ca. 1836; mar. 1st, Hannah (Harvey)
Eaton, widow of John C. Eaton (#3430); he had a large
family with Hannah, but after she died, he mar. 2d,
Elmira (Conary) Pickering.
3441   v. Sarah⁹ Jeanette Eaton, b. ca. 1838; she mar. 1st, Jeremiah
Weed of Deer Isle, with whom she had four children;
mar. 2d, John Webber at Bar Harbor, having two more
children with him; and finally mar. 3d, John Lawford,
also at Bar Harbor, and she died there, 2 Dec 1915.
3442   vi. James⁹ Blake Eaton, Jr., b. ca. 1842; he was mustered into
the service in the Civil War 18 Jun 1861. He returned
from desertion on 26 May 1864, and was permitted to

re-enlist. At some time after the War, James died instantly when he fell off the coal stage. He was a fisherman,
and prob. never married.

3443   vii. William⁹ Blake Eaton, b. ca. 1845; he mar. 1st an Irish
woman from Boston; and mar. 2d, a Mrs. Barbara
Robbins, widow of Lewis, left with a large family to
support. He later mar. 3d a Mary E. __?__, and had several children with her. He ultimately died of heart
trouble at Rockland, Me., 1 Mar 1907.

3444   viii. (Lydia) Jane⁹ Eaton, b. ca. 1847; mar. 1st, John Holland,
int. 8 Nov 1870, his 2d wife after the death of Susannah
Eaton (#3419). After four children, John Holland died
27 Oct 1888 at Deer Isle, and Lydia mar. 2d, Jeremiah
Pressey Eaton (#3540).

**1801. John⁸ Calhoun Eaton** (Solomon⁷, Eliakim⁶, William⁵,
John⁴⁻¹) was born 14 Feb 1807 on Little Deer Isle, Me.; on 2 Sep 1833 he
pub. int. with **Phebe Billings**, daughter of Samuel and Patience Billings
of Sedgwick, Me. across the Reach from Deer Isle. They settled in
Sedgwick, where John was a farmer and a mariner. He died, however, in
Sep 1842. Widow Phebe mar. 2d, Johnson Grindle and had three children by him.

Children (all born in Sedgwick, Me.):

3445   i. William⁹ Nelson Eaton, b. 1 Aug 1834; died 16 Jan 1843.
3446   ii. Otis⁹ Roberts Eaton, b. 9 Jul 1836; died of yellow fever
and buried in the West Indies when still 19 years old.
3447   iii. Eben⁹ Eaton, b. 13 Apr 1838; mar. Elizabeth Billings,
dau. of Nathan. Eben was a ship carpenter, and died in
Burlington, Me., where the couple had lived some years.
Widow Elizabeth had him buried in Brewer, Me., where
she had gone to live with their children.
3448   iv. Susan⁹ Mary Eaton, b. 25 Oct 1840; mar. William Anson
Hooper of Sedgwick. He was a carpenter in Sargentville, and died there one day before he would have
turned 80, 28 Jun 1917. Susan was for years a widow
and removed to Stonington, Me., in 1922 about, to live
with her daughter.

**1804. Mark⁸ Haskell Eaton** (Solomon⁷, Eliakim⁶, William⁵,
John⁴⁻¹) was born 11 Dec 1814 on Little Deer Isle (D.I. Town Records),
and named in honor of Capt. Mark Haskell of Deer Isle village, admired
by his father for his leadership in town affairs. On 11 Feb 1835 he mar.
**Lydia A. Benson** (b. 16 Jul 1814), prob. in Brooksville, Me. They settled on the south side of Swain's Cove on Little Deer Isle. Mark was
mainly a mariner. He died 24 Jan 1900.

Children on Little Deer Isle:

3449    i. Mark[9] Haskell Eaton, Jr., b. 5 Jul 1836; died 6 Sep 1837.
3450    ii. Otis[9] Little Eaton, b. 13 Apr 1837; mar. Joanna Hardy
          Eaton (#1823), 14 Sep 1856. He died 26 Jan 1913.
          They had seven children.
3451    iii. Lucy[9] Jane Eaton, b. 18 Jul 1840; mar. James B. Eaton
          (#3484); she died early, 23 Nov 1862.
3452    iv. Rhoda[9] Ann McIntire Eaton, 11 Mar 1842, and named for
          the Camden McIntires; mar. John J. Billings, 7 Oct 1860.
3453    v. Eliakim[9] Harlan Eaton, b. 3 Jun 1845; mar. Electa Gray of
          Deer Isle, 8 Feb 1866. They res. at Sunset, Deer Isle, and
          and had three children. He died 22 Aug 1906.
3454    vi. Martha[9] Howard Eaton, b. 19 Mar 1848; mar. John Davis of
          Deer Isle, 21 Feb 1867.
3455    vii. Joseph[9] Hewett Eaton, b. 26 Mar 1850; mar. Lauretta
          Knowlton of Deer Isle, 6 Dec 1874. They resided at
          Stonington, Me. He died 26 Mar 1931 in Burlington, Vt.
3456    viii. Lydia[9] Margaret Eaton, b. 10 Jan 1852.
3457    ix. (William) Haskell[9] Eaton, b. 18 May 1854; died 6 Apr 1879.


**1807.   Isaac[8] Billings Eaton**  (Solomon[7], Eliakim[6], William[5],
John[4-1]) was born 24 Jul 1824 on Little Deer Isle; on 2 Nov 1844 he pub.
int. to mar. 1st, **Barbara Robbins Smith**, who had been born 28 Sep
1827, at Isle au Haut to George and Sally (Knowlton) Smith.  Isaac[8] and
Barbara lived for about two years on a small farm on the east side of
Verona Island in the Penobscot River.  Then when Barbara's mother
needed care, the couple went to Isle au Haut, with the parents giving them
the homestead.  After Barbara died there, Isaac mar. 2d, **Elizabeth E.
"Lizzie" Gross**, 16 Jan 1868.  They stayed on at Isle au Haut, and Isaac
died there 7 Dec 1879.  Widow Lizzie then mar. 2d, Joshua Hart of St.
George, Me., 1 Jun 1880.  After his death she mar. 3d, George Duke, 7
Mar 1901 at Stonington, Me.  She died of consumption, 3 Sep 1920.

Children with Barbara at Isle au Haut, Me.:

3458    i. Harriet[9] Coffin Eaton, b. 14 Apr 1845; mar. 1st, Sylvester
          Arey of Vinalhaven, Me., 24 Oct 1860. They separated
          after they had two children, and Sylvester died in Vinal-
          haven. Harriet then mar. 2d, a Sanborn in N.H., and
          she died in Laconia, N.H.
3459    ii. Joseph[9] Smith Eaton, b. 27 Jun 1847; mar. on 29 Jul 1868,
          Sarah Knowlton Colby. They settled in Stonington, Me.,
          where he was a carpenter and a builder of rowboats.
          They had no children.
3460    iii. Jonathan[9] R. Eaton, b. 28 Jul 1850; died as an infant.

**3461** iv. (William) Elwell[9] Eaton, b. ca. 1851-52; as a young unmar.
mariner, he died in a gale at sea.

**3462** v. Inez[9] Roxanna Eaton, ca. 1854; mar. 1st, Frederick Small,
int. 16 Dec 1860. He died in Rockland, Me. 6 Dec
1879, after Inez had borne two daughters. She mar. 2d,
Fred's brother, Albert Small, int. 21 Mar 1884.

**3463** vi. Violette[9] Sarah "Lettie" Eaton, b. ca. 1856; mar. 1st,
Americus Merithew in Vinalhaven, Me. 9 Mar 1873.
She divorced him and mar. again, but had no children
from either union.

**3464** vii. Sarah[9] Ellen Eaton, b. 1859; mar. Roscoe Brown, b. in
Vinalhaven "and a shiftless fellow whose chief ambi-
tions were to play the fiddle and ramble around with
a gun" (Noyes, 1942). He died ca. 1882, after two
children. Sarah, or "Nellie", mar. 2d, in California.

Children with Elizabeth at Isle au Haut:

**3465** viii. Sylvia[9] Eaton, b. ca. 1868; died in infancy.

**3466** ix. Amos[9] Eaton, b. 2 Feb 1869; he drowned 8 Feb 1890
when traversing to Stonington from Isle au Haut in
a small row boat.

**3467** x. Maggie[9] T. Eaton, b. 27 Dec 1871; mar. elsewhere and
moved to California.

**3468** xi. Samuel[9] Holden Eaton, b. 18 Apr 1874; he drowned
off Scott's Island (Stonington) 4 Jul 1904, unmarried.

**3469** xii. Cora[9] Alwilda Eaton, b. 28 Mar 1876; mar. a cousin,
George Edward Gross, and they res. in Stonington, Me.

**3470** xiii. Boy[9] Eaton, died at birth. May have been earlier in order.

**1809. Daniel[8] Billings Eaton** (Solomon[7], Eliakim[6], William[5],
John[4-1]) was born 21 Jul 1827 on Little Deer Isle; mar. on 20 Apr 1846,
**Philena Harvey**, born 17 Sep 1828 to George and Sarah (Stone) Harvey. They resided for a while on Isle au Haut after marriage, but Daniel
was a mariner of the "nomadic type," shifting around among the islands
that speckled Penobscot Bay, and after 1850 removed to Bear Island
principally. Daniel died about 1855, and widow Philena mar. 2d, Thomas Buckminster Gross, 25 May 1857, becoming his second wife.

Children with Philena (all but first prob. at Bear Island):

**3471** i. Peter[9] Harvey Eaton, b. 22 Jan 1847; mar. 1st, Rebecca
Robbins, 27 Apr 1871; and 2d, Minnie Etta Knowlton,
28 Jan 1890, with children by both wives. Peter died
11 Oct 1912.

**3472** ii. Sarah[9] Harvey Eaton, b. 25 Apr 1851; mar. 1st, Peter H.
Billings, but the union ended in divorce as Peter became

deranged; mar. 2d, Jeremiah Greenlaw, 3 Nov 1887, as
his second wife.

**3473**   iii. George[9] Harvey Eaton, b. 15 Aug 1853; mar. Mrs. Maggie
A. Morey 16 Aug 1875. (She was born Margaret Gross
of Oceanville on Deer Isle.) They lived for a while on
Crotch Island, where George was a quarryman and
Maggie, a fine cook, ran a boarding house. George had
begun to organize his own company in quarrying, but he
had a severe accident in a premature blast and the firm
collapsed. They moved to Moose Island for another
boarding house operation. George finally died, largely
incapacitated, 18 Aug 1927.

**3474**   iv. Israel[9] Eaton, b. 10 Apr 1855; mar. on 14 Apr 1876, Ida
W. Gross, sister of brother George's wife Maggie. They
had several children.

**1810. Amos[8] Allen Eaton** (Solomon[7], Eliakim[6], William[5], John[4-1])
was born 3 May 1831 on Little Deer Isle; mar. **Sarah Dow Stinson** of
Deer Isle, (int.) 2 Jan 1853. Amos was a carpenter, and after living some
time in Mountainville, he built the family a house in So. Deer Isle.
However, this was a family racked with consumption (tuberculosis), and
Amos died of this affliction in So. Deer Isle, 6 Aug 1871. Widow Sarah
became the 2d wife of Mark Sawyer, who died ca. 1893 in Mountainville; whereupon Sarah mar 3d, William Robbins of Sedgwick.

Children of Amos and Sarah on Deer Isle:

**3475**   i. Laura[9] Etta Eaton, b. 12 Oct 1853; she died of consumption
at the So. Deer Isle house, early 1871.

**3476**   ii. John[9] Kempton Turner Eaton, b. 25 Oct 1855; mar. Lydia
Helen Simpson, 3 Oct 1880, and had one child who died
young, but adopted two others. Resided Stonington on
Deer Isle, Me.

**3477**   iii. Elizabeth[9] "Lizzie" Lampher Eaton, b. 17 Apr 1857; mar.
Andrew Small 2 Sep 1873 on Deer Isle. She died child-
less of consumption in the Mountainville house.

**3478**   iv. Helen[9] Knight Eaton, b. 22 Nov 1863; called "Nellie", she
died of consumption, 16 Feb 1879.

**3479**   v. Son[9] Eaton, stillborn and unnamed.

**1811. (Peter) Hardy[8] Eaton** (Solomon[7], Eliakim[6], William[5],
John[4-1]) was born 3 Jun 1835 on Little Deer Isle, Me.; mar. 1st, **Mary J.
C. Haskell**, 11 Feb 1861. Mary apparently died early, childless. Hardy[8]
mar. 2d, **Rebecca Robbins**, also of Deer Isle, 27 Apr 1871, for whom
there is record of one child:

**3480**    i. Newell[9] Eaton, b. 23 Nov 1872; mar. a Morey girl and in the 1900 Census is found on Deer Isle living with his father-in-law, Roland H. Morey.

**1813. Isaac[8] Eaton, Jr.** (Peter[7] H., Eliakim[6]. William[5], John[4-1]) was born ca. Nov 1802 on (Little?) Deer Isle. His father Isaac[7] had married Lucy Hardy in Feb 1802, and his father had died of consumption four months thereafter, or five months before his own birth. His life is somewhat obscure, although we glimpse him in the 1850 Census. He is age 48, a laborer, living in Township #6, Penobscot Co., Me. (prob. the northern reaches of that county), with an apparent wife **Lucy __?__**, age 24, and three children (below); and without any stated financial resources. In 1860 we find a likely sequel, i.e., an Isaac head (ae 56) and Lucy wife (ae 37), with the notation that Isaac has died in June, just before the Census is taken, so Lucy by then is actually widowed. This couple was now living in Greenbush, somewhat downstream on the Penobscot River relative to Twp. #6. The child roster has changed, with additional births in the 1850s and two of three older children missing. But if we accept that the "Ellen" age 6 in 1850 is the "Eleanor" age 16 in 1860, then the fit is complete.

Children, prob. b. in northern Penobscot Co:

**3481**    i. Eleanor[9] ("Ellen"?) Eaton, b. ca. 1844.
**3482**   ii. Melville[9] Eaton, b. ca. 1846.
**3483**  iii. Ann[9] Eaton, b. 1848.
**3484**   iv. Martha[9] P. Eaton, b. 1851.
**3485**    v. Flora[9] E. Eaton, b. 1867.

**1815. Jonathan[8A] Haskell Eaton** (Peter[7] H., Eliakim[6], William[5], John[4-1]) was born 10 Oct 1821 on Deer Isle, Me.; mar. on 30 Apr 1846 **Martha Harvey**, daughter of George and Sarah (Stone) Harvey and sister of his brother's (cf. **#1817**) wife Louise. Jonathan was a fisherman and prob. missed by the 1850 Census because he was elsewhere in the Penobscot Bay islands. In 1860 and 1870 he is on Bear Island, owning a moderate tract of land. His extended family lived "in good circumstances" (Noyes, 1942) because they owned or controlled a number of the tiny islands where they could breed and feed stock, and the like. Jonathan died 18 May 1886; widow Martha died 29 Mar 1897. Both are buried on Bear Island.

Children (most or all at Bear Island, Me.):

**3486**    i. James[9] Stone Eaton, b. ca. 1850; mar. Flora Emeline Parsons, 5 Jul 1868 at Deer Isle. In 1870 this couple was living on Bear Island with his parents. They soon moved to Stockton Springs and res. there the rest of their lives. James[9] used several islets for sheep pasturage, and later purchased a lobster smack to make runs to Castine, Me.

**3487**    ii. Benjamin[9] F. Eaton, b. 12 Aug 1854; died 18 Dec 1856.
**3488**    iii. John[9] Winfield Eaton, b. 15 Feb 1856; died 16 Dec 1858.


**1817. Peter[8A] Hardy Eaton** (Peter[7] H., Eliakim[6], William[5], John[4-1]) was born 25 Aug 1826 on Little Deer Isle; mar. on 30 Jan 1844, the sister of his older brother's wife: **Louisa Harvey**. daughter of George and Sarah (Stone) Harvey. They lived on Bear Island, and for at least some of the time had John C. Eaton (**#3430**) with another Harvey sister, Hannah, living in a portion of their house. Peter H. was a rather prosperous fisherman, and the couple were members of the Latter Day Saints church in Mountainville. This couple removed from Bear Island in 1885, and Peter died in Mountainville, 3 Jul 1904.

Children:

**3489**    i. Daniel[9] Harvey Eaton, b. 4 Oct 1845 on Deer Isle, but baptized on Bear Island; mar. 1st, Lucy Ann Blastow, 1 Jan 1877. Lucy died 3 Aug 1881; Daniel mar. 2d, Lydia A. West, 15 Apr 1884. This couple removed from Blastow's Cove on Bear Island to Sedgwick on the mainland, where he died, 1927. There were no children by Lucy, and one son, Cecil[10] Eaton, from the 2d mar. to Lydia.
**3490**    ii. Thomas[9] Harvey Eaton, b. 1 Mar 1847 (record of local LDS church, Deer Isle); mar. Charity Ames, 5 Jul 1868. Children: Henry[10] R.; Emery[10] F., Calvin[10] A.; and Cornelia[10].
**3491**    iii. Jonathan[9] E. Eaton, b. 22 May 1853 (LDS record for Bear Island; mar. Hattie A. Billings 15 Nov 1884. They had children: William[10] Thomas, Herbert[10], Vesta[10] M. and Russell[10], all Eatons. After Jonathan's death, Hattie mar. 2d, Charles Smith.


**1819. Samuel[8] S. Eaton** (Peter[7] H., Eliakim[6], William[5] John[4-1]) was born 19 Mar 1831 on Deer Isle; mar. 1st,  like his two older brothers, to another Harvey sister, this being **Margaret T. Harvey**, daughter of George and Sarah (Stone) Harvey, on 21 Feb 1850. The couple lived on islands between Deer Isle and Isle au Haut, mainly McGlathery Island, although Samuel served as an Elder of the L.D.S. branch church at Mountainville on Deer Isle. Margaret died, and Samuel S. mar. 2d, **Mary[9] Ellen Eaton** (**#3543**), int. 21 Jul 1868, Deer Isle. Later this couple moved to Campbell Island closer to Mountainville, and here Samuel died 21 Feb 1907. Widow Mary died of breast cancer 2 Apr 1914.

Children with 1st, Margaret, in the islands:

**3492**     i. Susan[9] Eaton, b. 1850-51; mar. 1st, Frank Hassel of Isles-
                boro; 2d, George Monroe, who disappeared westward;
                and 3d, an unidentified Eaton of Boston, Mass.
**3493**     ii. Levi[9] Eaton, b. ?   ; died 28 Mar 1873 in the deadly diph-
                theria epidemic of that year; bur. McGlathery Island.
**3494**     iii. Lois[9] Eaton, b.  ? ; died at two years of age.

Children with 2d, Mary (Eaton):

**3495**     iv. Freeman[9] C. "Alma" Eaton, b. 20 May 1869; died 18 Oct
                1892 of consumption.
**3496**     v. Moody[9] Princeton Eaton, b. 11 May 1874; mar. 31 Jan
                1895, (Carrie) Belle Morey of Campbell's Neck, a center
                of the tuberculosis infection, to which she succumbed,
                childless. Moody then mar. 2d, Rose Anna Dunbar (her
                2d husband), 5 Dec 1804 at Rockland, Me.. Moody was
                a rather well-to-do fisherman who resided some years in
                Stonington, before retiring near his father's on Oak Point,
                Campbell's Neck, Deer Isle. He was an L.D.S. Elder. He
                lived past 1911.
**3497**     vi. Clara[9] Louise Eaton, b. 25 Jul 1875 on Deer Isle; she died
                after bearing one child, 22 Aug 1890.
**3498**     vii. Herman[9] E. Eaton, b. 29 Dec 1883; died 26 Jan 1891.
**3499**     viii. Frederick[9] Delmont Eaton, b. 27 Sep 1886; mar. Ethel Mar-
                shall, 13 Feb 1906.
**3500**     ix. Parker[9] Leon Eaton, b. 17 Dec 1895; mar. Helen Louise
                Beam, 7 May 1916.

**1820. George[8] Washington Eaton** (Peter[7] H., Eliakim[6], William[5],
John[4-1]) was born 25 Oct 1833 on Little Deer Isle; mar. on 2 Dec 1855,
**Hannah[9] Etta Eaton (#3529)**. When the Civil War broke out, George
took his family north to the islands just into New Brunswick, Canada
(Grand Manan and Campobello) on his vessel <u>Lovinia</u>, part of a broader
movement that "stayers" referred to as the "skedaddlers".   On Grand
Manan Island there was a major revival meeting in progress. and George
converted to the Mormon faith.   He became an important prosyletizer
for that faith in ensuing years, returning in the <u>Lovinia</u> for example to
McGlathery Island, then owned by Samuel Eaton **(#1819)** to establish
branch L.D.S. churches there and at Stonington.   When he returned
more permanently in 1869, he resided a while at North Deer Isle, and
then removed to Green's Landing by Stonington.   Then he took the
family east again to Addison (Washington Co.), Me., where they stayed
until about 1876. He then returned to Stonington and spent some years
erecting a large house there. He later had a long siege of physical difficulties, including gall stones, phlebitis, the complications of which led to
his death on 22 Oct 1900.   George was noted as an excellent mechanic
and builder, and was a major influence in the Latter-Day Saints organization.

Children with Hannah:

**3501**     i. Lovinia[9] Bragg Eaton, b. 29 Aug 1856 on Little Deer Isle;
           she was the only child of this family surviving the huge
           diptheria epidemic on Campobello Island in 1865, but
           then succumbed to tuberculosis when the family was at
           Green's Landing, 5 Nov 1872.

**3502**    ii. Emma[9] Frances Eaton, b. 3 Aug 1858 on McGlathery
           Island; died on Campobello Island, N.B., 7 Jan 1865 of
           diphtheria.

**3503**   iii. Angeline[9] Eaton, b. 8 Oct 1860, McGlathery Island; died
           of diphtheria, 8 Jan 1865, at Campobello Island.

**3504**   iv. Freeland[9] Zelotus Eaton, b. 11 Jan 1862, McGlathery
           Island; died of diphtheria on Campobello Island.

**3505**    v. Etta[9] Eaton, b. 3 Apr 1864, McGlathery Island; died 5 Jan
           1865 of diphtheria on Campbello.

**3506**   vi. George[9] Freeland Eaton, b. 15 Apr 1865, Campobello Is
           land; perished 12 Dec 1895 on Wreck Island.

**3507**  vii. Sarah[9] Eaton, b. 10 Sep 1867 on Bear Island in Penobscot
           Bay; mar. William Merrill Powers of Sunset (Deer Isle).

**3508** viii. Joseph[9] Emaron Eaton, b. 10 Sep 1869 at No. Deer Isle;
           mar. in Stonington (Deer Isle ) Me., 9 Dec 1901, Sadie
           Frances Eaton (b. 1880, Deer Isle, to Henry[9] and Hannah
           M. (Barbour) Eaton).  He was a steam yachtsman, and
           they had three children.

**3509**   ix. Rosaline[9] Eaton, b. 12 Feb 1874; mar. 1st, Edward Hardy,
           but were divorced "without issue"; and 2d, to Eben Currier
           Candage.

**1821. Otis[8] Convers Eaton** (Peter[7] H., Eliakim[6], William[5], John[4-1])
was born 16 Aug 1834 on Little Deer Isle; mar. **Zemira A. Billings**, 3 1
Mar 1856.  She was the daughter of Edward C. and Abigail (Gray) Billings.  The couple settled for nearly twenty years on Little Deer Isle, and
then about 1875 moved to Winterport up the Penobscot River, where the
rest of his children were born, and where wife Zemira died of pneumonia, 22 Mar 1885.  Otis was a mariner for these four decades, but just before 1895 he returned to Stonington (D.I.) and built a house on the
south side of Main St. where he lived out his days.  In the last decade he
was active trading in hay, grain and other wares, doing general freighting
with his large sloop <u>Passport</u>.  He was a faithful member of the Latter-
Day Saints after his baptism by his brother George W. in 1866.  He died
25 Dec 1905 of spinal paralysis at Stonington.

Children:

**3510**    i. Israel[9] C. Eaton, an apparent twin b. 28 Jun 1856; died 27
           Mar 1865 at Deer Isle.

**3511**  ii. Isabelle[9] Eaton, twin of Israel b. 28 Jun 1856; infant death.
**3512**  iii. Abigail[9] "Abbie" B. Eaton, b. 9 Apr 1858; she died of tuber-
          culosis after her family moved to Winterport in 1875.
**3513**  iv. Henry[9] Eaton, b. ca. 1860; died 15 May 1860.
**3514**  v. Catherine[9] "Kate" Etta Eaton, b. 15 Jul 1861; mar. Daniel
          Theodore Haskell and had five children with him at
          Winterport, b. 1883-92. Kate died of stroke, 3 May 1928.
**3515**  vi. Albert[9] "Bert" Henry Eaton, b. 19 Feb 1864; mar. Ora A.
          Small of Camden, Me., 2 Feb 1889. Bert was baptized
          in the L.D.S. Church, and the couple had one child. Bert
          was committed to the hospital for the insane in Augusta,
          and was later moved to Bangor.
**3516**  vii. Lewis[9] Alma Eaton, b. 25 Nov 1866 (D.I. record); never mar.
          but was long a mariner. Then he clerked in a clothing
          store in Bangor for a few years till rheumatism and spinal
          troubles made such work difficult. Later he bought a
          vessel, the <u>Robert W.</u>, and carried freight, while overseeing
          the construction of wharfs and piers in Isleboro and
          North Haven, Me. He died 26 Oct 1928 from an acute
          cardial attack while rowing a boat off Little Deer Isle.
**3517**  viii. Nancy[9] Jane Eaton, b. 3 Aug 1870 on Little Deer Isle;
          mar. George W. Nelson, a paving cutter of Winterport,
          Me.. They lived at "Winkhole" in Winterport, but spent
          the years from 1899 to 1907 at Stonington (Deer Isle)
          where four of their seven children were born, before re-
          turning to Winterport for their last years.
**3518**  ix. Susie[9] Eaton, b. ? ; mar. Fred Smith of Bucksport, Me.,
          a bank cashier. They had two children at Bucksport,
          were still living there, 1933.
**3519**  x. Charles[9] Babson Eaton, b. ca. 1875; was taken into a
          wealthy family with his brother Wallace (who did not
          stay with this family), and received a strong education,
          especially in music, at which he excelled. He mar. Pearl
          Jones in Independence, Mo., although he suffered in
          later years from shaking palsy.
**3520**  xi. Bertha[9] May Eaton, b. 1 Aug 1878 in Winterport, Me.
          She worked for some years for a Belledue family
          in Massachusetts, but returned to Stonington to work
          the cotton mills. She soon died, still single, from pul-
          monary tuberculosis, 9 Oct 1910.
**3521**  xii. Edward[9] Mansfield Eaton, b. 29 Dec 1879 in Winterport, Me.
          He was a fisherman residing on School St. in Stonington
          in 1910. He mar. Gertrude Louise Thompson at North
          Deer Isle, 26 Jan 1913. They had two children.
**3522**  xiii. Wallace F. Eaton, b. ca. 1883-84. Placed in a wealthy home
          with brother Charles at a young age, he soon left these
          benefactors to steer his own course. He enlisted in the
          army and served his stint at Ft. Wright, N.Y. well before
          World War I. He then mar. in New Haven, Conn. and was

last heard from in Springfield, Mass., exercising his talent for the manufacture of small articles such as engraved key rings.

**1834. (Capt.) William⁸ R. Eaton** (Asa⁷ B., Jeremiah⁶, William⁵, John⁴⁻¹) was born 2 Feb 1827 on Deer Isle; mar. **Ann B. Saunders**, 1851. This couple settled for some years on Deer Isle, but then removed to Wakefield, Mass. in 1867. In 1880, Capt. William took his family to Newburyport, Mass., and resided there until 1883, when he established a final home in Reading, Mass. He was an enterprising master mariner, with a very interesting family.

Children: (i-iv at Deer Isle, Me.); v at Wakefield, Mass.)

3523    i. Edward⁹ R. Eaton, b. 27 Oct 1855; mar. Isabella Byers of
             Nova Scotia, 4 Oct 1879, in Wakefield, Mass. He was a
             clerk, residing in Reading, Mass.
3524    ii. Frank⁹ W. Eaton, b. 5 May 1857; mar. Helen Byers of Nova
             Scotia, 15 Sep 1880; later res. Newburyport, Mass.
3525    iii. Arthur⁹ Eaton, b. 22 Dec 1858; mar. Alice E. Blood of
             Reading, Mass., 20 Sep 1879. He was a carpenter, and
             died in Cuba, 7 Jul 1885.
3526    iv. Helen⁹ H. Eaton, b. 8 May 1865; died 11 Jul 1879 in
             Wakefield, Mass.
3527    v. Bessie⁹ L. Eaton, b. 22 Aug 1873; at home, unmar., 1895.

**1835. Nathan⁸ H. Eaton** (Asa⁷ B., Jeremiah⁶, William⁵, John⁴⁻¹) was born 3 Apr 1829 on Deer Isle; mar. **Clara W. Stinson**, of Rockport, 15 Jun 1853. As of 1860 he was a mariner. This couple res. on Deer Isle. Nathan died at sea on a passage from Cuba to New York City, 4 Aug 1880.

Children born on Deer Isle:

3528    i. Marion⁹ F. Eaton, b. 4 Jun 1854.
3529    ii. George⁹ W. Eaton, b. 17 Sep 1856.
3529a  iii. Sarah⁹ J. Eaton, b. 1859.
3530    iv. Lawrence⁹ Eaton, b. 7 Oct 1861.

**1840. (Capt.) William⁸ᴬ Augustus Eaton** (William⁷⁻⁵, John⁴⁻¹) was born 29 Apr 1814 on Deer Isle, Me.; mar. 1st, 24 Jan 1836, **Susan Noyes Webster**, born at Castine, Me. on 8 Feb 1817 to Jonathan and Elcy (Haskell) Webster. They res. first on Deer Isle, but then moved to Castine, where they had their later children. William was a pilot in the revenue service, and later in his career was given the captaincy of a U.S. cutter. Wife Susan died in Castine, 21 Oct 1879, and in due time, William mar. 2d, **Sarah Nash** of Windham, Me. William was still serving as Captain when he died in 1897 at the St. Julian Hotel, Portland, where he and his wife were boarding.  His body was returned to Castine to be buried with his first wife.

Children (i-iv supposedly born Deer Isle; v-vii at Castine, Me.):

3531    i. Pauline[9] Eaton, b. 26 Jun 1837; died 6 Mar 1858, Deer Isle.
3532    ii. Caroline[9] W. Eaton, b. 29 Oct 1840; called "Carrie" and "Cad." She mar. Edwin F. Davis, a Civil War veteran, postmaster and undertaker at Castine, Me., 7 May 1856.
3533    iii. William[9] Leverrett Eaton, b. 6 Jul 1842; he drowned in Apr 1850 near Castine.
3534    iv. James[9] W. Eaton, b. 23 Apr 1844; mar. a Brophy of Castine who died there of consumption, along with their daughter.
3535    v. Charles[9] Noyes Eaton, b. 2 Oct 1846; "Charlie" served in the War and received an honorable discharge.  But soon after his return he shipped with Capt. Sylvester in the Josephine Tilton, and all were lost in Bay Chaleur, 30 Oct 1867.
3536    vi. Lucretia[9] S. Eaton, b. 1 Oct 1848; mar. Frank D. Wardwell of Penobscot, Me. She had only one child, who died young; and Lucretia died of cancer, Apr 1886.
3537    vii. William[9A] Leverett Eaton, b. 3 Nov 1851; died unmar. ca. 1889 at Castine.

**1845. Jeremiah[8] Eaton, Jr.** (Jeremiah[7], William[6-5], John[4-1]) was born 3 Mar 1813 on Deer Isle; mar. on 15 Sep 1836, **Angeline Blastow**, who was born 14 Apr 1817 to Samuel and Hannah (Gray) Blastow.  The couple resided on Deer Isle, where Jeremiah is listed as a sailor and fisherman. He died of a cancer of the eye 15 Mar 1880 at Little Deer Isle. Widow Angeline, usually known as "Aunt Adeline," survived him by many years.

Children at Deer Isle:

3538    i. Samuel[9] Newell Eaton, b. 22 Mar 1837; mar. Abigail Dunbar, daughter of Elijah, (int.) 4 Jul 1884.
3539    ii. Hannah[9] Etta Eaton, b. 13 Mar 1839; mar. George[8] W. Eaton (**#1820** q.v.), 2 Dec 1855.
3540    iii. (Jeremiah) Pressey[9] Eaton, b. 13 Mar 1841; mar. 1st, Eliza Clapp Spaulding, (int.) 10 Sep 1860; and after she died of tuberculosis, mar. 2d, Lydia Jane (Eaton) Holland (see **#3444**), widow of John Holland of Brooksville on 24 May 1894 at Sargentville.  There were nine children from the first marriage.
3541    iv. Martha[9] Ann Eaton, b. 2 May 1845; mar. Nathan[9] B. Eaton (**#3431**, q.v.) 4 Feb 1861, and they had a large family. She later mar. 2d, Asa O. Candage.

3542    v. Zelotus[9] Freeman Eaton, b. ca. 1848; mar. 20 Mar 1871,
        Diantha Blastow, dau. of William and Mary Blastow.

3543    vi. Mary[9] Ellen Eaton, b. 27 Apr 1851; became the 2d wife of
        Samuel S. Eaton (#1819), int. 21 Jul 1868, and they had
        six children (q.v.).

3544    vii. George[9] Adelbert Eaton, b. 13 Feb 1854; mar. Frances[9]
        "Fanny" Maria Eaton (#3565) on 6 May 1877.
        He was a fisherman, yachtsman and farmer on Little Deer
        Isle, and they had four children. He died 1918.

3545    viii. Thomas[9] Elwell Eaton, b. 10 Oct 1856; mar. Caroline S.
        Hendrick, also of Deer Isle, 1 Jan 1877; they had a large
        family on Little Deer Isle.

3546    ix. Sylvanus[9] "Vene" P. Eaton, b. 18 May 1858 at Deer Isle;
        mar. 1st, Mary[9] Abigail Eaton (#3560), daughter of
        William Eaton, on 9 May 1879, and had three children.
        Sylvanus had a general grocery store at Little Deer Isle,
        along with a fishery business at the shore. When wife
        Mary died, he mar. 2d, the widow Ann (Hutchinson)
        Titus, and there were no children.

3547    x. Hosea[9] Billings Eaton, b. 30 Aug 1862; mar. Rose Shephard,
        also of Deer Isle, 4 Mar 1883, and had a large family on
        Little Deer Isle.

**1846. Samuel[8] Eaton** (Jeremiah[7], William[6-5], John[4-1]) was born ca.
1815 on Little Deer Isle; mar. on 24 Apr 1834, **Olive Joyce Weed**,
daughter of Jeremiah and Elethea (Joyce) Weed. He was a sailor, and
after a period elsewhere, they resided on Little Deer Isle.

Children on Little Deer Isle:

3548    i. Jeremiah[9] Weed Eaton, a twin of Eleanor, b. 7 Nov 1834;
        mar. Sarah C. Hardy, also Deer Isle, 15 Dec 1859. They
        had several children in Deer Isle and then moved to
        Winterport, Me., where she had considerable family. Jere-
        miah was Captain of the Couston. He died 1899.

3549    ii. Eleanor[9] Eaton, twin of Jeremiah W., born 7 Nov 1834; mar.
        1st, Charles B. Weed, also of Deer Isle, 12 Oct 1852. They
        had three children before Charles died, 25 Feb 1874. She
        mar. 2d, Jesse Bray, 21 Dec 1880, as his fourth wife.

3550    iii. (Davis) Haskell[9] Eaton, b. 12 Oct 1836; mar. Susan Gray
        Hendrick 19 Dec 1860. They had six children, and he
        died in 1907.

3551    iv. Ebenezer[9] ("Eben") Weed Eaton, b. ca. 1838-39; mar.
        Rosella H. Hardy, int. 2 Mar 1860. They had five child-
        ren, although he died 25 Feb 1874.

3552    v. Olive[9] J. Eaton, b. 17 Sep 1845; mar. Hezekiah Tilton Weed,
        29 Jun 1863. They lived near George Eaton's store, and
        had eight children before Hezekiah died in 1888.

**3553** vi. Samuel[9] Newall Eaton, b. 26 Jun 1847; mar. Joanna G. Weed, 16 Oct 1870. Samuel was a mariner, and they had several children, but moved to Boston and died there.

**3554** vii. Esther[9] Eaton, b. Sep 1849, but died in infancy.

**3555** viii. Susan[9] Mary Eaton, b. 9 Aug 1851; mar. John McKenney, also of Deer Isle, 11 Jan 1874. He was a mariner and they long resided at Little Deer Isle, but then moved to Rockland, Me.

**1847. William[8] Eaton** (Jeremiah[7], William[6-5], John[4-1]), was born ca. 1818 on Little Deer Isle; mar. **Elizabeth Weed**, sister of the Olive who mar. his brother Samuel, on 29 Oct 1844. They res. at his father Jeremiah[7]'s family homestead on Little Deer Isle, where William farmed more than most of his sea-faring friends.

Children on Little Deer Isle:

**3556** i. Lydia[9] Ellen Eaton, b. 22 Mar 1846; mar. Otis Gray of Brooksville, Me., 28 Apr 1867.

**3557** ii. Orilla[9] Eaton, b. 4 Oct 1848; became the 3d wife of (Warren) Merrill[9] Eaton (**#3435**), whose mother was her aunt.

**3558** iii. Asenath[9] Eaton, b. 16 Apr 1852; mar. Horatio Gates Hardy, int. 14 Feb 1873. After Horatio's death, she mar. his brother, Silas Hardy, Jr., but had no children by either marriage. Husband Silas died, 1931, leaving widow Asenath in poor health, cared for by their adopted son, Melvin Everett Bray.

**3559** iv. Obadiah[9] Eaton, b. 26 Feb 1863; mar. Flora[10] E. (Florette) Eaton, daughter of Samuel[9] N. (**#3538**), on 8 Dec 1878. They had a large family while residing on Little Deer Isle at Sally Cove toward Stave Island. Obadiah died 21 Nov 1916.

**3560** v. Mary[9] Abigail ("Abbie") Eaton, b. 16 May 1856; mar. Sylvanus P. Eaton (**#3546**, q.v.) 9 May 1879.

**3561** vi. Charlotte[9] Curtis Eaton, b. 12 Oct 1857; mar. Orrin[10] Eaton, son of Samuel[9] N. (**#3538**) Eaton, 5 mar 1878, and had three children.

**3562** vii. Frederick[9] P. Eaton, b. 15 May 1860; mar. Lizzie H. Parker, 15 Apr 1883. They had their nine or so children on Little Deer Isle, but later moved to New London, Conn., where he was also a ship's captain. He died there in Feb. 1925. Widow Lizzie returned to live with a daughter in Rockland, Me.

**3563** viii. Clarissa[9] H. Eaton, b. 29 Nov 1822; mar. Everett Bray, 22 Jan 1882; their daughter Clarissa ("Caddie") was only a few days old when mother Clarissa died, and her husband Everett died six months later, leaving the little daughter to be raised by her aunt Mary[9] at the Sylvanus

Eaton house.

**1848. Alfred**[8] **Eaton** (Jeremiah[7], William[6-5], John[4-1]) was born 5 May 1820 at Deer Isle, Me.; mar. **Sophia**[9] **Eleanor Eaton (#3432)** about 1850, prob. at Winterport, Me. Alfred was sailing out of Winterport in this period, and farming when on Little Deer Isle. The couple settled at Joe's Point on that Isle, and raised their large family there. Alfred died, 22 Jan 1904. "Aunt Sophia" survived as a "most kind and generous-hearted woman, who helped feed and clothe many of the poorer children on the island" (Noyes, 1942). She died of pneumonia 17 Feb 1915, by then a great, great grandmother to a new baby girl.

Children born on Little Deer Isle, Me.:

**3564**   i. Georgiana[9] Eaton, b. 30 Dec 1852; died at age 10 or 12.
**3565**   ii. Frances[9] "Fannie" Maria Eaton, twin b. 7 Dec 1854; mar. George[9] Adelbert Eaton (**#3544**, q.v.).
**3566**   iii. Esther[9] W. Eaton, twin of Frances b. 7 Dec 1854; mar. Isaiah[10] Valentine Eaton, son of Samuel[9] N. Eaton (**#3538**) 22 Aug 1884. They had three children.
**3567**   iv. Harriet[9] J. "Hattie" Eaton, b. 8 Oct 1856; died age 16-17.
**3568**   v. Susan[9] Elizabeth "Lizzie" Eaton, b. 8 Nov 1858; mar. Capt. George A. Hendrick, also of Deer Isle, 2 Aug 1886. They had no children. She died early 1890s; he died 13 Oct 1931 in Rockland, Me.
**3569**   vi. Luella[9] Jane Eaton, b. 29 Apr 1860; mar. 1st, Freeman Charles Haskell, 14 Mar 1878. After two daughters, they were divorced, and Luella mar. 2d, John Meredith Ellis, Jr., from Wales, England.
**3570**   vii. Frank[9] Benjamin Eaton, b. 16 Jun 1864; mar. Nancy[11] May Eaton, daughter of Rodney[10] B. Eaton and granddaughter of Jeremiah[9A] P. Eaton (**#3540**). Frank was a mariner who had his own vessel. Frank and Nancy were at Vinalhaven for a short period and then removed to Camden, Me., where they had a substantial family.
**3571**   viii. Jasper[9] Hardy Eaton, b. 10 Sep 1866; m. Rebecca Clara Shepard, also of Deer Isle. They res. on Little Deer Isle and had a large family.
**3572**   ix. Henry[9] Blaisdell Eaton, b. 6 Apr. 1868; mar. Mary Ellen Weed, and res. on Little Deer Isle. About five children.
**3573**   x. Nina[9] May Eaton, b. ca. 1872; mar. Sherman Ellis Thompson. They had a son, and then Sherman died at Fish Creek. Nina first moved to Rockland, Me., and prob. later to Boston.
**3574**   xi. William[9] Freeman Eaton, b. 19 Feb 1876; mar. Laura Jane Haskell, 27 Apr 1902, at Deer Isle. He was a fisherman on Little Deer Isle, and they had one son.

**1859. Samuel**[8] **Warren Eaton** (Jeremiah[7], Samuel[6] W., William[5], John[4-1]) was born 14 Aug 1809 at Chesterville, Me.; mar. **Mary "Polly" Hanson** (b. Mar 1808 in Lebanon, York Co.. Me.) about 1829. They res. first at Chesterville, later removed to Jay, Me. and then, by 1850, to Wilton, Me., all in Franklin Co. He was a reasonably prosperous farmer through the 1860 Census in Wilton, and presumably died in the 1860s.

Children (i-iv. at Chesterville, v. at Wilton)

| | |
|---|---|
| **3575** | i. Charles[9] Warren Eaton, b. 1 Sep 1830. |
| **3576** | ii. David[9] Hanson Eaton, b. 26 Jan 1832. |
| **3577** | iii. Mary[9] Augusta Eaton, b. 24 Dec 1833. |
| **3578** | iv. Livonia[9] Parker Eaton, b. 30 Apr 1838. |
| **3579** | v. Anna[9] A. Eaton, b. 1849. |

**1864. Sewall**[8] **Eaton** (Isaac[7], Samuel[6] W., William[5], John[4-1]) was born 8 Jul 1814 in Chesterville, Me.; mar. 1st, **Elizabeth K. Porter** of Mt. Vernon, Me., on 15 Jun 1845. They settled briefly in Chesterville, although by 1846 they had removed to Vienna, Me., the next township east, but in Kennebec Co., where Sewall was a fairly prosperous farmer in 1850 through 1870. After wife Elizabeth died, Sewall mar. 2d, **Hattie Sanderson.**

Children with Elizabeth at Vienna, Me.:

| | |
|---|---|
| **3580** | i. (Mary) Camilla[9] Eaton, b. 12 Mar 1846; she became an editor in New York City. |
| **3581** | ii. Olive[9] Violette, b. 8 Jun 1851; mar. George Stevens of the firm of Stevens and Son, scythemakers at Oakland, Me. They had two sons and a daughter. |
| **3582** | iii. Crosby[9] Gordon Eaton, b. 3 Mar 1858; mar. Fanny Jordan and had a daughter. He was a physician in Oakland, Me. |

**1868. Crosby**[8] **Eaton** (Isaac[7], Samuel[6] W., William[5], John[4-1]) was born 3 Jun 1823 in Chesterville, Me.; mar. 1st, **Ellen Maria Woodman** (born 20 Mar 1829 in Leeds, Me.) on 9 Jul 1851. Ellen died in Leeds, probably of complications ensuing from her first childbirth, 13 Mar 1853. Then Crosby mar. 2d, **Sarah Jane Wilson** of Calais, Me. about 2 Nov 1855. The couple headed westward, settling at South Haven, Mich., where Crosby took an active role in schools, at one time serving as County School Supervisor. He was also active politically. He died 14 Jan 1886.

Child with Ellen Maria in Leeds, Me.:

**3583**    i. Fred[9] Woodman Eaton, b. 6 Dec 1852 died 18 Jul 1853.

Children with Sarah Jane, prob. at So. Haven, Mich.:

**3584**    ii. Ellen[9] Maria Eaton, b. 26 Jan 1857; she mar. Willis Halleck
of So. Haven, Mich. in Nov 1882, and had two children.

**3585**    iii. Jessie[9] Belle Eaton, b. 6 Mar 1862; became a teacher.

**3586**    iv. Abby[9] Jane Eaton, b. 30 Jul 1864; mar. Charles Sellars and
removed to San Diego, Cal. They had two children.

**3587**    v. Fred[9] Wilson Eaton, b. Mar 1866; unmar. as of early 1890s,
working as a newspaper correspondent, res. So. Haven.


**1871. John[8] Calvin Eaton** (Isaac[7]. Samuel[6] W., William[5], John[4-1])
was born 22 Feb 1832 in Chesterville, Me.; mar. **Lucy A. Sanderson**,
(also a Chesterville native, she born 21 Oct 1834) on 14 Nov 1861. With
the older brothers up and out, John C. and his wife were able to reside at
the old family homestead in So. Chesterville. He died there 8 Nov 1890.

Children in Chesterville:

**3588**    i. Lillian[9] O. Eaton, b. 23 Nov 1864.

**3589**    ii. Archie[9] Calvin Eaton, b. 3 Mar 1872. In 1900 both children
were still unmar. at the ancestral home.


**1881. George[8] Eaton** (Thomas[7], Josiah[6], Thomas[5], John[4-1]) was
born 1 Apr 1797 in Kennebunk, Me.; mar. **Elizabeth Wiswell Trowbridge** on 5 Oct 1819. They settled in Portland, where he was a housewright, and also traded in real estate. They had a large family, but
George died 11 Feb 1852. Widow Elizabeth died 27 Feb 1875.

Children, all prob. born in Portland, Me.:

**3590**    i. Ellen[9] Augusta Eaton, b. 1 Jul 1820; mar. William Chase, 2
Mar 1843 at Portland, and had eight sons, two daughters.

**3591**    ii. George[9] Bradbury Eaton, b. 16 Jun 1822, mar. Helena
Virginia de Eau, 23 Jan 1845; settled in Cambridgeport,
Mass. They later returned to Maine: wife Helena died
9 Jan 1876; and George died in Paris, Maine, 1877. They
had four children: Clifford[10] Chase Eaton, b. 6 May 1847;
George[10] Lewis Eaton, b. 20 Mar 1849; Newell[10] Hayes
Eaton, b. 20 Dec 1852; and Helena[10] Virginia Eaton.

**3592**    iii. Julia[9] Ann Trowbridge Eaton, b. 2 May 1824; mar. Lewis B.
Smith, 28 Oct 1847.

**3593**    iv. Eunice[9] Stone Eaton, b. 31 Oct 1826.

**3594**    v. Benjamin[9] Webster Eaton, b. 14 Dec 1828; d. 13 Sep 1838.

**3595**    vi. Charles[9] Carroll Eaton, b. 7 Mar 1832; mar. Julia A.
Osgood of Chelsea, Mass, 24 Mar 1858. He died 14 Jan

1860, and widow Julia died 5 Jul 1860.

**3596** vii. Maria[9] Miller Eaton, b. 27 Oct 1834.

**3597** viii. Mary[9] Elizabeth F. Eaton, b. 12 Aug 1836; d. 16 Oct 1838.

**3598** ix. Daniel[9] Webster Eaton, b. 8 Mar. 1838; mar. 1st, Ellen Montgomery Packard, 29 Nov 1860, in Portland, Me.; she died 20 Jul 1872. He mar. 2d, Susie M. Packard, 15 Feb 1876 in Portland. They had two daughters: Charlotte[10] Elizabeth Eaton, b. 23 Apr 1864; and Ellen[10] Chase Eaton, b. 13 Feb 1866. Daniel died 20 Oct 1890 of consumption.

**3599** x. (Mary) Elizabeth[9] Eaton, b. 28 Aug 1840; d. 9 May 1868.

**1884. John[8] Eaton** (Thomas[7], Josiah[6], Thomas[5], John[4-1]) was born 19 Jul 1803 in Kennebunk, Me.; mar. **Susan Emerson** of New York (but born in Amherst, N.H.) on 9 Dec 1833. John was a printer, and they resided in Cambridge, Mass. He died there, 5 Feb 1873.

Children, born in Cambridge, Mass.:

**3600** i. Susan[9] Emerson Eaton, b. 19 Sep 1834; died 19 Jun 1839.

**3601** ii. Phebe[9] Louise Eaton, b. 1838.

**3602** iii. Frances[9] Tenney Eaton, b. 16 Nov 1840; died 10 Jul 1852.

**3603** iv. Catherine[9] Doran Eaton, b. 18 Aug 1843; mar. William Jason Gold, a native of Washington, D.C., in 1868. He was a grandson of the Hon. Amos Kendall who was Postmaster General in the Andrew Jackson administration. He became a professor in the Episcopal Divinity School in Chicago, Ill.

**3604** v. Elizabeth[9] Young Eaton, b. 15 1846; died 1 Apr 1847.

**3605** vi. William[9] Henry Dexter, b. 14 1849.

**1893. Horace[8] Perkins Eaton** (Wheeler[7], William[6], Thomas[5], John[4-1]) was born 30 Aug 1811 in Weare, N.H.; mar. on 1 Apr 1837, **Ismenie S. Merrill**, born 23 Dec 1816 at Franklin, N.H. to Ezekiel Merrill subsequently of Plymouth, N.H. Horace farmed with his father Wheeler at Franklin for years, but after the latter died in 1871, Horace moved into the village of Hill, N.H. He represented the town in the legislature in 1881, and died 26 Aug 1886 at Hill.

Children born at Franklin, N.H.:

**3606** i. Frank[9] Wheeler Eaton, b. 13 Aug 1838; mar. Frances S. Young, 23 Nov 1875, having three sons and a daughter.

**3607** ii. Abbie[9] Perkins Eaton, b. 12 May 1840; mar. John P. Sanborn of Franklin. They res. on a farm in Hebron, N.H. Abbie died 29 Mar 1883; bur., Tilton, N.H.

**3608** iii. Lilla[9] Mary Eaton, a twin b. 3 Oct 1849; mar. Charles F.

Young, a carriage painter of Hill.

**3609**    iv. Nancy[9] Jane Eaton, twin of Lilla, b. 3 Oct 1849; mar. Edwin W. Lane, 3 Aug 1869, and resided in Sanbornton.

**1894. Cyrus[8] Wheeler Eaton** (Wheeler[7], William[6], Thomas[5], John[4-1]) was born in May 1813 at Weare, N.H.; mar. **Phebe W. Goodwin** of Weare ca. 1837. Cyrus had learned the carpenter's trade, and decided to establish himself in Bristol, N.H. He died in Bristol, Aug 1849.

Children, all with the possible exception of (i.) born in Bristol:

**3610**    i. Cyrus[9] Perkins Eaton, b. Jan 1839; mar. Etta Vanderwoerd of Holland; worked in a watch factory at Waltham, Mass.
**3611**    ii. Emily[9] Jane Eaton, b. ca. 1842; mar. 1st, Charles Spencer; and 2d, Gilbert Dollof. Resided at Bridgewater, N.H.
**3612**    iii. George[9] W. Eaton, b. ca. 1844; served in the 9th Regt., N.H. in the Civil War.
**3613**    iv. Clara[9] J. Eaton, b. 30 May 1848; mar. Jonathan Hoag, Jan 1866. They resided at Cambridgeport, Mass.

**1895. Gorham[8] Eaton** (Wheeler[7], William[6], Thomas[5], John[4-1]) was born 6 Jan 1816 in Weare, N.H.. He went as a young man to Illinois and taught school in the district where the famous Rev. Peter Carthwright resided. He mar. the Rev.'s daughter, **Weltha Mary Jane Cartwright**, on 27 Mar 1840. He thus came into possession of a fine farm in Richland, Sangamon Co., Ill. He died there early, however, on 26 Aug 1845, leaving three children.

Children born at Richland, Ill.:

**3614**    i. Emily[9] F. Eaton, b. 27 May 1841.
**3615**    ii. Mary[9] A. Eaton, b. 11 Sep 1842.
**3616**    iii. Horace[9] Gorham Eaton, b. 31 Oct 1844, and served in the Civil War. He mar. 1st, Mary E. Allen, 27 Jun 1868, but she rapidly died, 5 Nov 1869, from complications in the birth of their daughter Ella[10] Jane. He mar. 2d, Mary Jones, 14 Jan 1875, and had a a daughter Grace[10] and a son Herbert with her. The couple removed to North Lawrence, Kansas in 1880.

**1899. Warren[8] Eaton** (Thomas[7], William[6], Thomas[5], John[4-1]) was born 18 Nov 1820 in Sanbornton, N.H.; mar. **Zilpha Hancock** of Franklin, N.H. in Mar 1845. Warren was a machinist, and began adulthood in the period when the young from N.H. farms were flocking to the new mills in Manchester, N.H. So he brought his skills there as well.

He is still in Manchester, Ward #2, in 1870. But he died 16 Aug 1882 back in Sanbornton.

Children, all but perhaps the first, born in Manchester, N.H.:

**3617**    i. Charles[9] Eaton, b. May 1847; mar. Ella Powell and res. in Manchester, a machinist like his father.
**3618**   ii. Augusta[9] Eaton, b. 8 Aug 1855.
**3619**  iii. Cora[9] Eaton, b. 28 Aug 1863.

**1901. John[8] Wiggin Eaton** (Thomas[7], William[6], Thomas[5], John[4-1]) was born 15 Dec 1825 in Sanbornton, N.H.; mar. **Climena Davis** of Concord, N.H., ca. 1851. They resided in the Fisherville neighborhood of Hill, N.H., and John W. worked in a match factory in Hill. In fact, he died on 31 Oct 1864, allegedly *in consequence* of that employment.

Children born at Hill, N.H.:

**3620**    i. Ella[9] Orill Eaton, b. 14 Jan 1853; mar. Folsom C. Lang of Strafford, N.H., 24 Dec 1871.
**3621**   ii. Addie[9] Viola Eaton, b. 18 Dec 1854; mar. George Edward Hanaford of Fisherville, 30 May 1872, and res. at Tilton.
**3622**  iii. Frances[9] Arvilla Eaton, b. May 1857; mar. Frank Davis of Fisherville, Sep 1875. She was a tailoress in town.

**1902. Joshua[8] Eaton** (Thomas[7], William[6], Thomas[5], John[4-1]) was born 15 May 1829 in Sanbornton, N.H.; mar. **Rachel T. Mason**, (b. 1830 to Benjamin Mason) on 11 Nov 1852. Joshua was a merchant in the firm of Mason and Eaton at Hill, N.H., presumably involving his in-laws. Rachel died of consumption 8 Jul 1873, leaving one child.

Child:

**3623**    i. Ida[9] May Eaton, b. 28 Feb 1867.

**1903. Ira[8] Blake Eaton** (Thomas[7], William[6], Thomas[5], John[4-1]) was born 11 Nov 1832 at Sanbornton, N.H.; mar. 1st, **Elizabeth Sargent** of Goffstown, N.H., Jan 1854 at Fisherville. They had a daughter, but Elizabeth died early, and Ira mar. 2d, **Roanna Farley** of Hollis, N.H., 24 Nov 1859 at Hollis. By 1876, Ira was a photographer in Boston, Mass.

Child with Elizabeth, birthplace uncertain:

**3624**    i. Ardella[9] Eaton, b. ca. 1856.

Children with Roanna, birthplace uncertain:

**3625**    ii. Alfred[9] Farley, a twin b. 8 Nov 1860.
**3626**    iii. Lillie[9] Roanna, a twin b. 8 Nov 1860.


**1904. Horace[8] Eaton** (Thomas[7], William[6], Thomas[5], John[4-1]) was born 24 Sep 1834 in Sanbornton, N.H.; mar. **Esther Ann Burleigh**, daughter of Thomas Burleigh, 25 Apr 1858. Horace farmed a small parcel east of the family homestead and worked in a mill in Tilton, N.H.

Child, Sanbornton or Tilton, N.H.

**3627**    i. Odin[9] B. Eaton, b. 11 May 1864.


**1909. George[8] Folsom Eaton** (Joshua[7], William[6], Thomas[5], John[4-1]) was born in Salisbury, N.H., 27 Jan 1824; mar. **Eunice Dow** of Salisbury, 10 Dec 1854. They resided in Haverhill, Mass., where in 1865 George was listed as a carriage smith. Wife Eunice died 28 Jul 1880; and he died 15 Jun 1888.

Child, born Haverhill?:

**3628**    i. Sarah[9] E. Eaton, b. 27 Aug 1856; died 9 Jul 1911.


**1910. (Manual) Bryant[8] Eaton** (Joshua[7], William[6], Thomas[5], John[4-1]) was born 8 Sep 1826 in Salisbury, N.H; mar. **Ann Bagley** of Clinton, Me., Jul 1862. Bryant was a rather prosperous retail grocer in Seabrook, N.H. He died 21 Mar 1892. Ann died 6 Mar 1913.

Children, b. Seabrook:

**3629**    i. Child[9] Eaton, b. 1862-63; died in infancy.
**3630**    ii. Clinton[9] Joshua Eaton, b. 9 Jan 1867; he was a teacher when he mar. Isabella T. Charles of East Greenwich, R.I., 26 Mar 1890, at Greenwich. He was in forestry. She died 30 Nov 1936 at Newburyport, Mass. and is bur. in the Methodist Cemetery, Seabrook. They had a boy and a girl.


**1917. Jeremiah[8] Wilson Eaton** (Moses[7], Aaron[6], Thomas[5], John[4-1]) was born 29 Dec 1821 in So Hampton, N.H.; mar **Polly Jane Currier** on 24 Dec 1846. Jeremiah was a carpenter by trade, and in the 1860 Census he describes himself as a "manufacturer," with quite substantial personal and real estate for his age and station. Soon, however, this couple removed from So. Hampton, N.H., to Lawrence, Mass., one of the burgeoning new mill towns harnessing the energy of the Merrimack River. Jeremiah died 10 Sep 1895.

They appear to have had only one child:

3631    i. Clara[9] Janette Eaton, b. 25 Jan 1851; mar. Amos Willard
        Towle, 5 Jul 1881, and resided in Lawrence, Mass, having
        two sons.


**1918. Jacob[8] Eaton** (Moses[7], Aaron[6], Thomas[5], John[4-1]) was born
21 Nov 1823 in So. Hampton, N.H.; mar. on 27 Jun 1860, **Elizabeth
"Lizzie" Paige**, also of So. Hampton, the daughter of Samuel and Rebecca B. Paige. For some years after completing his education, Jacob
had been involved in various business enterprises. He ran a "carriage
manufactory" for about 20 years, and was both a manufacturer and
dealer in wood and lumber. At the time they were married, however,
they settled on a 58-acre farm in So. Hampton which he diligently developed, specializing in fruit growing: his six-acre orchard produced ap-
ples, pears, peaches and other fruits which sold for good prices. In politics, Jacob, once a Whig, had been a Republican since the formation of
that party. He was active in public affairs in So. Hampton, a Selectman
for 13 years and Chair of that body for nine, Town Clerk for three years,
Treasurer for seven, and Moderator of town meetings for fifteen. He was
a representative in the state legislature for two widely spaced terms, 1866-
68 and 1889-90 (*Biographical Review*, 1896). Lizzie died in 1907; Jacob died in 1908, both So. Hampton.

Children, born So. Hampton, N.H.:

3632    i. Fannie[9] Bayard Eaton, b. 22 Jul 1861, who was a school
        teacher; died 18 Jul 1902.
3633    ii. Lizzie[9] Paige Eaton, b. 22 Jun 1863; mar. Fred M. Jewell of
        So. Hampton, and had one daughter.
3634    iii. Ella[9] "Abbie" Whittier Eaton, b. 15 Oct 1864; she was a
        nurse, who died 2 Nov 1936 at Newburyport, Mass.
3635    iv. Rebecca[9] Lewis Eaton, b. 28 May 1866; died 24 Aug 1866.
3636    v. Arthur[9] Beck Eaton, b. 8 Dec 1867; died 24 Aug 1868.


**1919. Thomas[8] Eaton** (Moses[7], Aaron[6], Thomas[5], John[4-1]) was
born 8 Jul 1826 in So. Hampton, N.H.; mar. 1st, **Mary J. Morrill** of
Salisbury, Mass, 3 Jul 1855. They settled early in Amesbury, Mass.,
where he was a master builder. Wife Mary, who gave him two children,
died in Feb 1859. He mar. 2d, **Mary A. Bailey** of Andover, Mass., 13
Nov 1862. In 1865 the family moved to a farm in Warrensburg Twp.,
Ill., in Macon Co. near Decatur.

Children with Mary J. (Morrill) in Amesbury, Mass.:

3637    i. Abbie[9] E. Eaton, b. Oct 1857; died Nov 1857, age 4 weeks.

**3638**    ii. William[9] Thomas Eaton, b. 6 Feb 1859; mar. Augusta
            Bachelder of Pittsfield, N.H.; removed to Kansas, Arkansas
            and Texas; res. in Texarkana, Tex. He died 23 Jul 1939.

Children with Mary (Bailey) in Illinois:

**3639**    iii. Frank[9] B. Eaton, b. 22 Jan 1868.
**3640**    iv. Fred[9] Henry Eaton, b. 17 Nov 1870.
**3641**    v. Joseph[9] Moses Eaton, b. 23 Feb 1873.
**3642**    vi. Abbie[9A] Morrill Eaton, b. 11 Aug 1874.
**3643**    vii. John[9] Bailey Eaton, b. 8 Mar 1877.
**3644**    viii. Nellie[9] Elizabeth Eaton, b. 6 Jul 1879.

**1921. Moses[8] J. Eaton** (Moses[7], Aaron[6], Thomas[5], John[4-1]) was
born 26 Apr 1834 in So. Hampton, N.H.; mar. **Mary Jane Follansbee**,
daughter of Joseph and Mary J. (Woodman) Follansbee of Amesbury, on
13 Apr 1865. His father, Moses, Sr., owned one of the finest farms in
So. Hampton, and worked closely with his father in his younger years.
In due time his father turned the homestead farm over to him, and Moses
Jr. showed great enterprise in its further development, especially its fruit
orchard. Moses was also active in politics as a Republican, served in all
the town offices, a was a Representative in the state legislature in 1877-8.

Children in So. Hampton:

**3645**    i. William[9] Sherman Eaton, b. 5 Sep 1865. He was a carriage-
            builder, and mar. 1st Susan B. Manson. She died in 1892,
            and he mar. 2d, 1899, Olive Lang. Had six children.
**3646**    ii. Adelaide[9] Frances Eaton, b. 10 May 1867; taught school
            and then mar. S. Walter Stevens.
**3647**    iii. Mary[9] Bessie Eaton, b. 19 Nov 1868; taught school.
**3648**    iv. Joseph[9] Derby Eaton, b. 11 Jun 1877; stayed on and farmed
            the homestead. He died 12 May 1907 at So. Hampton.

**1922. (Rev.) Benjamin[8] Franklin Eaton** (Moses[7], Aaron[6],
Thomas[5], John[4-1]) was born 16 Sep 1836 in So. Hampton, N. H; mar.
**Helen N. Kennard** of Dover, 5 May 1867. He was a Universalist minis-
ter, and they settled in Worcester, Mass. after their children were born.

Children:

**3649**    i. Clarence[9] L. Eaton, b. 14 May 1868 in Dayton, Ohio.
**3650**    ii. Minnie[9] L. Eaton, b. 23 Dec 1869 in Zanesville, Ohio.

**1935. (Rev.) Jeremiah[8] Sewall Eaton** (Jacob[7], Humphrey[6]. Wyman[5], John[4-1]) was born 19 Jun 1810 in East Weare, N.H. He graduated

at Union College, Schenectady 1835; and Newton Theological Institution, (Mass.) 1839. He mar. **Harriet Hope Agnes Bacon**, daughter of Josiah and Agnes (Ramsay) Bacon of Boston, Mass. He was ordained at the First Baptist Church in Hartford, Conn, 13 Nov 1839, and was its pastor, 1839-44. He then was Pastor at the Free Street Baptist Church, 1844-54, in Portland, Me., resigning after ten years due to declining health. He died there 27 Sep 1857 (Carter, 1906). Widow Harriet died 10 Jun 1885 at Hartford, Conn.

Children with Harriet:

3651    i. Franklin[9] H. Eaton, b. 14 Jul 1843 in Hartford, Conn.; mar. Adaline M. Dickson of Darlington Court House, N.C., 1 Oct 1866. He had enlisted in Maine's 20th Infantry Regt. 10 Sep 1862. He re-enlisted in the Maine 29th and was discharged 12 May 1866, not long before the marriage. Their three children were born at Columbia, S.C.: Mary[10] A. Eaton, b. 16 Aug 1871; Frances[10] H. Eaton, b. 12 Nov 1873; and Sarah[10] J. Eaton, b. 6 Sep 1877. Prob. by 1880 they had removed to Philadelphia, Pa., where he was a bookkeeper and died 2 Aug 1887.

3652    ii. Agnes[9] Ramsay Eaton, b. May 24, 1849 in Portland, Me. died 24 Jun 1887 at Hartford.

3653    iii. Harriet[9] J. Eaton, b. 4 Jan 1855 in Portland, Me.; returned to reside in Hartford, Conn.

**1939. Humphrey[8] F. Eaton** (Tristram[7], Humphrey[6], Wyman[5], John[4-1]) was born ca. 1814 in Weare, N.H.; he went south when his family moved to Gainsville, Ala.. He mar. 1st there, **Elisa __?__** ca. 1839, and had four children with her. She died ca. 1849, and he mar. 2d, **Amanda Mobley**, 23 May 1850 in Gainesville, Ala. Humphrey was a merchant. He died 2 May 1859 at Gainesville.

Children with Elisa at Gainesville, Ala.:

3654    i. Joel[9] B. Eaton, b. ca. 1841.
3655    ii. Mary A. Eaton, b. ca. 1843.
3656    iii. Jasper[9] W. Eaton, b. ca. 1845.
3657    iv. Hannah[9] E. Eaton, b. ca. 1849.

Child with Amanda at Gainesville, Ala.

3658    v. Alice[9] M. Eaton, b. 21 Oct 1852; mar. H. D. Long of Gainesville, 1 Sep 1879. She died there 2 Oct 1880, without issue.

**1940. Jacob$^8$ Eaton** (John$^{7-6}$, Wyman$^5$, John$^{4-1}$) was born 10 Apr 1793 in Buxton, Me.; he mar. **Dorcas Edgecomb**, ca. 1816. They resided in Buxton through the 1840 Census, but disappear subsequently.

Children in Buxton, Me. (birth order partially based on will):

3659    i. Eliza$^9$ Ann Eaton.
3660    ii. John$^9$ Eaton.
3661    iii. Robert$^9$ E. Eaton, b. ca. 1823; mar. Frances C. Lowell of Biddeford, Me., 14 Jun 1849. He was a house carpenter and they res. in Saco, Me. He died 21 May 1884. They had three children: Mary$^{10}$ A. Eaton, b. 12 Apr 1850 and mar. Frank Foss of Portland, Me. 26 Nov 1873; Eliza$^{10}$ A. Eaton, b. 3 Oct 1861 and died 15 Oct 1893, unmar.; and Allan$^{10}$ A. Eaton, b. 15 Apr 1864; died 14 Aug 1867.
3662    iv. Albert$^9$ E. Eaton, b. 5 Feb 1829; mar. 1st, Susan M. Perry of So. Boston, Mass. in Jul 1856. She died 3 Mar 1863, without issue. He mar. 2d, Harriet E. Jordan, 3 Mar 1865, and she had O. K.$^{10}$ Eaton, b. 8 Apr 1866; Ralph$^{10}$ H. Eaton, b. 11 May 1867; and Fanny$^{10}$ Eaton, b. 31 Jul 1868. Albert was a trader and res. in Portland, Me., where he died 27 Aug 1889.
3663    v. Edward$^9$ Eaton, b. ca. 1832; a carpenter's apprentice at Hollis, Me., in 1850.
3664    vi. Moses$^9$ E. Eaton, b. 8 May 1834; mar. 1st, Mary A. Colton of Palestine Grove, Ill.; and 2d, Louisa Clark of Bromley, Ala., with the couple residing at Bromley. He was a farmer and fisherman. He served in the Civil War in the 19th Mich. Regt.; was taken prisoner, and spent six days in the Libby Prison.
3665    vii. Noah$^9$ N. Eaton, b. 11 Nov 1835; mar. 1st, Lydia Bradbury of Buxton, 19 Nov 1856, with whom he had three sons and two daughters; and 2d, Emma Davis of Orono, Me. about 1869, with whom he had six more children, residing in Buxton, Me.
3666    viii. Humphrey$^9$ W. Eaton, b. 5 Sep 1837; mar. 1st, Hattie A. Bradeen, 31 Mar 1861, who died the following Sept. Humphrey then enlisted in the Civil War in Co. H of the 12th Maine Regt. on 14 Oct 1861, and re-enlisted in Co. D. of the same Regt. on 1 Jan 1864 at Madisonville, La. After a total of four years, six months service, he was discharged 18 Apr 1866 at Savannah, Georgia. In the late stages of his service, he had mar. 2d, a local Savannah girl, Bertha M. Harris, on 8 Jan 1866. The couple had no children, but res. in Dixon, Ill., where he was a cabinet-maker and upholsterer.

**1941. Simeon[8] Eaton** (John[7-6], Wyman[5], John[4-1]) was born 23 Aug 1795 in Buxton, Me.; mar. **Betsey Paine** (born 16 June 1796 in Parsons-field, Me.) in 1816. They removed to Conway, N.H. where their children were born and where Simeon became a well-to-do farmer. He died 28 Jul 1862. Betsey died there 28 Sep 1877.

Children, born in Conway, N.H.:

3667   i. John[9] B. Eaton, b. 17 Mar 1817; mar. 1st, Mary J. Brooks of Washington, D.C., 4 Mar 1843, with whom he had a daughter. He practiced law at Cincinnati, Ohio, where he mar. 2d, Elizabeth R. Allen of that city, 1 Apr 1847. After 20 years or so, and six more children, he returned to New England in 1866, and res. at Fryeburg, Me., where he died 23 Oct 1880. His wife Elizabeth died 10 Oct 1878 at Washburn, Ill.

3668   ii. William[9] P. Eaton, b. 5 Jan 1819; died 25 Dec 1839 in Thomaston, Me., where he was a teacher.

3669   iii. Lorenzo[9] Dow Eaton, b. 30 Dec 1821; mar. Maria Moore of North Bend, Ohio in 1851, and they res. on a farm in Dustin, Holt Co., Neb. His three sons went on to become ranchers in Wyoming. These were Charles[10] L. Eaton, b. 4 Oct 1853, mar. Mary Simmons of Ill. in 1876; Washington[10] L., b. 12 Oct 1855; and Samuel[10] A. Eaton, b. 11 Aug 1857, They also had a final daughter, Sarah[10] A. Eaton, b. 8 Jan 1859.

3670   iv. Hannah[9] P. Eaton, b. 15 Dec 1823; mar. Asa L. Brown of Quincy, Ill; later removed to Plattesville, Wisc. They had no children.

3671   v. Eliza[9] J. Eaton, b. 12 Dec 1825; mar. Jeremiah B. Lord of So. Boston, Mass., 27 Apr 1846. They had two sons and a daughter. She died 12 May 1890.

3672   vi. Alpheus[9] R. Eaton, b. 27 Jun 1827; mar. Phebe A. Storer of Brownfield, Me., 23 Jun 1852. He was a lawyer in Brownfield, and after nine children with Phebe, he died there 10 Oct 1888.

3673   vii. Joseph[9] Perry Eaton, b. 12 Sep 1829; mar. 1st, Joanna Chadbourne, 1857; and mar. 2d, Mary Elizabeth Chadbourne, 10 Sep 1868 in Brownfield, Oxford Co., Me. They res. on a farm in Brownfield, and Joanna left two sons: Jesse[10] W. Eaton, b. 27 Oct 1858 and mar. Eva. Wentworth 29 Sep 1888; and Russell[10] C. Eaton, b. 15 Jul 1859.

3674   viii. James[9] S. Eaton, b. 8 Oct 1831; mar. Joanna Leavitt, also of Conway, N.H., 26 Jul 1857. He was a mechanic, and they res. in Conway Center. They had three children: Perley[10] L. Eaton, b. 27 Apr 1858; Annie[10] B. Eaton, b. 31 Jul 1860; and John Burnham Eaton, b. 27 Jul 1881.

3675   ix. Abel[9] E. Eaton, 20 May 1834; mar. Mary E. Baird of

Union, Ore. 6 Nov 1867. He was a farmer and dealer
in livestock. They had no children.

**3676**    x. Annie[9] L. Eaton, b. 10 Jul 1837; mar. William A. Bowden
of So. Boston, Mass, 15 Mar 1857. She died 9 Dec 1858,
childless.

**3677**    xi. William[9] F. Eaton, b. 22 Mar 1839; mar. Adaline A. Perry
of Roxbury, Mass., 6 May 1863, and they settled on a
farm in Conway where they had four sons, six daughters.


**1944. John[8] Green Eaton** (John[7-6], Wyman[5], John[4-1]) was born 10
Aug 1802 in Buxton, Me.; mar. **Hannah Boulter,** 19 Nov 1837 of Stan-
dish, Me. They resided on a farm in New Gloucester, Cumberland Co.,
Me. He died there, 31 Mar 1853.

Children, born in New Gloucester:

**3678**    i. Josiah[9] J. Eaton, b. 23 Oct 1838; mar. Susan E. Hambly, of
Tiverton, R. I., 27 Sep 1860. They res. in Fall River,
Mass., where he was a carpenter. Their three children
were John[10] G., Jr. Eaton, b. 17 Sep 1862 and d. before
six months; Fred[10] S. Eaton, b. 7 Jan 1867; and Mattie[10]
M. Eaton, b. 13 Jan 1874.

**3679**    ii. Mary[9] F. Eaton, b. 19 Jun 1843; mar. Robert H. Starbird of
Poland, Me., 2 Mar 1862. They had a son and daughter.


**1950. Stephen[8] Woodman Eaton** (Tristram[7], John[6], Wyman[5],
John[4-1]) was born 2 Mar 1806 in Buxton, Me. He studied civil engineer-
ing, and was in the party first surveying the line of the Atlantic and St.
Lawrence Railroad. He subsequently mar. **Miranda B. Knox** of Port-
land, a descendant of the famed General Henry Knox of the Revolution.
They settled in Gorham, Me., and he had a business office in Portland.
He died 5 Mar 1877, leaving an enterprising family (Stearns, 1908).

Children in Gorham and Portland, Me. save where otherwise
noted:

**3680**    i. Stephen[9] Marks Eaton, b. 7 Oct 1833; mar. Elizabeth B.
Deane of Portland, 23 Nov 1858. Attended Bowdoin in
the Class of 1855; served as a 2d Lt. in Co. K of the
Maine Regt. in 1861 and as Civil War proceeded he advanced to a captaincy in the U.S. Signal Corps, then to
Brevet Major, 1864, and Lt. Col. in 1865. He became
Post Master at New Orleans under the Harrison Administration and res. there at least through 1893. The couple
had three children: May[10], Stephen[10] Jr., and Belle[10].

**3681**    ii. Samuel[9] Knox Eaton, b. 1 Oct 1835; mar. Sarah R. Lord,
14 May 1866, and came to reside in New Berne, N. C.,

a dealer in watches, jewelry, etc.

**3682**    iii. George[9] Roscoe Eaton, b. 16 Nov 1837; mar. Sarah J.
Parker, (b. Saco, Me.) 11 Jun 1861. He was a major
figure in the development of railroads, lumbering and
banking in the northern reaches of New Hampshire in the
latter half of the century, being based chiefly in Berlin
and Stratford, N.H. He represented Berlin in the state
legislature, 1872-73. He and Sarah had three children.
(for more, see Stearns, 1908).

**3683**    iv. Minnie[9] E. Eaton, b. 9 Apr 1840; mar. Myron Hovey of
Boston, 2 Jun 1869. She died 11 Apr 1878, childless.

**3684**    v. Charles[9] P. Eaton, b. 9 Apr 1843; mar. Mattie R. Wentworth, Aug 1869. He was involved in sowing machines
in the farmlands of Kansas, and died in Carbondale in
that state, 13 Apr. 1881, without issue.

**3685**    vi. Woodman[9] S. Eaton, b. 15 Oct 1846; mar. Nettie C. Colby,
of Gorham, 16 Oct 1867. He became General Freight
Agent of the Maine Central Railroad and res. Portland.
Two children: William[10] C., b. 1869; Stephen[10] E., 1870.

**3686**    vii. Howard[9] B. Eaton, b. 14 Nov 1850 at Cape Elizabeth, Me.;
mar. Ida F. Tewksbury of Conway, N.H. 8 Oct 1884. He
was a hotel clerk in Lyndon, Vt., and they had a daughter Lydia[10] L. Eaton, b. 26 Jun 1887.

**3687**    viii. Edward[9] Eaton, b. 21 Jan 1853; died 17 Sep 1870,
Gorham, Me.


**1952. Isaac[8] W. Eaton** (Tristram[7], John[6], Wyman[5], John[4-1]) was
born 11 Jan 1811 in Buxton, Me.; mar. **Phebe Hazeltine** of Buxton in
1834. Isaac worked a rather prosperous farm in Buxton, where all of
their children were born. He died 12 Jan 1891.

Children in Buxton, Me.:

**3688**    i. Eliza[9] G. Eaton, b. 3 Oct 1834; died Jun 1850.
**3689**    ii. Sarah[9] B. Eaton, b. 16 Jun 1836; died 14 May 1865.
**3690**    iii. Miranda[9] Knox Eaton, b. 1 Jun 1838; mar. 1st, Thomas
Witham of Portland, 1862, and had two daughters. She
later mar., 2d, William Meserve of Buxton. She died
7 Aug 1886 at Buxton.
**3691**    iv. Phebe[9] A. Eaton, b. 19 Mar 1840; died 27 Jun 1842.
**3692**    v. Isaac[9] T. Eaton, b. 7 Mar 1842; mar. 1st, Abby Whitehouse
of Hollis Center, Me., 1864; she died in 1876. He mar.
2d, Delia Whitehouse, 14 Nov 1877, also of Hollis. They
resided at Buxton, where Isaac was a farmer and shoemaker. One child with Abby, a Woodman[10] Eaton; and
three more with Delia: twins Frank[10] and Fred[10] Eaton,
b. Jul 1879; and Dora[10] G. Eaton, b. 27 Sep 1889.
**3693**    vi. William[9] H. Eaton, b. 5 Sep 1844; died 25 Aug 1848.

**3694**    vii. James[9] O. Eaton, b. 30 Sep 1847; mar. Lelia A. Babb, Jul
1871, Buxton.    James was a shoemaker who resided in
Portland, Me., a son Arthur[10] Eaton, b. 17 Jan 1873.
**3695**    viii. Harriet[9] E. Eaton, b. 25 Apr 1851; mar. John Miles of
Limerick, Me., 2 Jun 1876.    They had a son.
**3696**    ix. William[9A] H. Eaton, a twin b. 10 Feb 1854; mar. Sarah
Meserve of Buxton, 3 May 1877.    He was a teamster in
Alfred, Me.    They had daughters Mabel[10] A. Eaton, b.
24 Oct 1880; and Ethel[10] P. Eaton, b. 6 Jun 1889.
**3697**    x. Wyman[9] H. Eaton, a twin b. 10 Feb 1854; mar. Eldora
Clark of Hollis Center, Me. 1 Jan 1885 and res. in
Hollis.    A farmer who also worked in saw mills.    No
issue as of 1895.

**1953. Humphrey[8] W. Eaton** (Tristram[7], John[6], Wyman[5], John[4-1])
was born 1 Nov 1812 in Buxton, Me.; mar. **Annorill C. Pray** of Livermore, Me. in 1845.    They resided in Portland, where Humphrey was the
General Freight Agent for the Portland, Saco and Portsmouth Railroad.
He died 2 Nov 1851.

Children, born Portland, Me.:

**3698**    i. Wyman[9] H. Eaton, b. 15 Dec 1845; died 19 Jul 1848.
**3699**    ii. Emma[9] L. Eaton, b. 10 Jul 1848; died 25 Dec 1883.
**3700**    iii. Ann[9] H. Eaton, b. 1 Jul 1851; died 7 Jul 1852.

**1955. Charles[8] Coffin Eaton** (Tristram[7], John[6] Wyman[5], John[4-1])
was born 14 May 1817.    Early in life Charles res. in Portland, working
with his brother Humphrey, as of the 1850 Census.    But then he returned
to the farm in Buxton and mar. **Esther Jane Frost** of nearby Limington,
Me., 15 Jun 1851.    They settled finally on a substantial farm in Limington, perhaps an inheritance of Esther's.    Charles died 12 Mar 1898 in
Portland, Me.

Children, at Buxton or Limington:

**3701**    i. Ella[9] Eaton, b. 19 May 1852; died 7 Jul 1853.
**3702**    ii. Hattie[9] R. Eaton, b. 15 Jun 1854; died 9 Aug 1870.
**3703**    iii. Helen[9] H. Eaton, b. 5 Mar 1858.

**1960. Samuel[8] T. Eaton** (Nathan[7], John[6], Wyman[5], John[4-1]) was
born 10 Nov 1826 in Buxton, Me.; mar. **Lucy A. Johnston** of Buxton,
25 Dec 1851.    Samuel owned and occupied the original Eaton farm
homestead in Buxton, first purchased by his great grandfather Wyman[5]
Eaton for his son John[6] on 1 Apr 1774.    It was a well-appointed and
prosperous farm.    Samuel died 16 Oct 1889.

Children at Buxton:

**3704**    i. Annie$^9$ E. Eaton, b. 18 Nov 1853; mar. Clarence E. Bangs of Gorham, Me., 30 Sep 1878.
**3705**    ii. Mary$^9$ H. Eaton, b. 12 Jan 1846; died 26 Aug 1876.
**3706**    iii. Amanda$^9$ S. Eaton, b. 30 Mar 1859; died 22 Apr 1862.
**3707**    iv. Margaret$^9$ B. Eaton, b. 18 Dec 1861.
**3708**    v. Willie$^9$ E. Eaton, b. 15 Nov 1864.
**3709**    vi. Emily$^9$ Eaton, b. 1 Oct 1868; died 22 Nov 1876.

**1962. Joshua$^8$ T. Eaton** (Abel$^7$, John$^6$, Wyman$^5$, John$^{4-1}$) was born 12 Feb 1811 in Buxton, Me.; mar. **Cordelia Bean** of So. Boston, Mass., in 1843. He was a trader in So. Boston. He died young, on 16 Jun 1847, leaving one daughter:

**3710**    i. Annie$^9$ Eaton, b. 21 Jan 1844; mar. Robert Bell of Roxbury, Mass., 30 Apr 1862.

**1965. John$^8$ W. Eaton** (Abel$^7$, John$^6$, Wyman$^5$, John$^{4-1}$) was born 4 Mar 1817 in Buxton, Me.; mar. **Harriet N. Noyes**, of Jay, Me., 31 Dec 1841. He was a well-to-do merchant in East Livermore, Me., in Androscoggin Co., Me. They had but a single son:

**3711**    i. John$^9$ C. Eaton, b. 18 Dec 1843; mar. 1st, Verna Bryant of Fayette, Me., 26 Dec 1870, yielding one son. Verna died 28 Aug 1883, and John mar. 2d, Margie W. Hunter of Farmington, Me., 22 Oct 1884. John was a commission merchant, and res. in East Boston, Mass.

**1978. Simeon$^8$ Eaton** (Wyman$^7$, Simeon$^6$, Wyman$^5$, John$^{4-1}$) was born ca. 1810 in Seabrook, N.H.; he mar. **Martha Jackman** of Salisbury, 12 Dec 1833, and res. in Salisbury. Simeon died early of consumption, 9 May 1845. His widow Martha mar. 2d, William Dyer.

Children at Salisbury, Mass.:

**3712**    i. Joseph$^9$ M. Eaton, b. 3 Dec 1834; mar. Martha A. Martin of Amesbury, Mass., 4 Sep 1859. They lived on a farm in Salisbury bequeathed by his father. He spent much of his time in town affairs, especially as Town Clerk, and Chair of the Board of Selectmen. They had three children.
**3713**    ii. Almond$^9$ Stuart, b. 22 Jan 1842; died, 16 Jul 1844.

**1987. Jeremiah⁸ Merrill Eaton** (Jeremiah⁷ P., Simeon⁶, Wyman⁵, John⁴⁻¹) was born 18 Sep 1828 in Seabrook, N.H.; mar. **Georgiana A. Parson (Pearson**?) of Salisbury, Mass., 2 Jul 1852, and they res. in Seabrook, next door to the old Wyman⁵ Eaton homestead on Worthley Ave. by Partridge Brook, where grandfather Simeon had died in 1851. Jeremiah died 1872, and his widow died 6 May 1906.

Children at Seabrook, N.H.:

3714    i. Isabella⁹ Eaton, b. 21 Dec 1852; mar. Rev. William Rand of Seabrook, 24 Dec 1874. He was born in Portsmouth, N.H., and died, 27 Jan 1921. She died 30 Apr 1945.

3715    ii. Georgia⁹ P. Eaton, b. 25 Jun 1855; mar. Charles C. Lunt of Newburyport, Mass., 24 Nov 1881; had one son, d. age 6.

3716    iii. Sarah⁹ Eaton, b. 26 Jan 1857; mar. 1st, Fred E. Harmon of Newburyport, Mass., 6 Jun 1874; mar. 2d, James¹⁰ B. Eaton (#5036), son of Reuben⁹, 15 Feb 1879.

3717    iv. Mary⁹ Frances Eaton, b. 16 Oct 1861; mar. Ephraim T. Chase of Hampton Falls, N.H., 20 Jun 1878 at Salisbury. She died 13 Oct 1942 (Salisbury). Ephraim died 22 May, 1943.

3718    v. Charles⁹ William Eaton, b. 16 Jul 1862; mar. Lizzie G. Dow of Seabrook, 24 Nov 1882. They had three children: Jeremiah¹⁰ M. Eaton, b. 24 Nov 1882; Charles¹⁰ A. Eaton, b. 16 Sep 1884; and Maggie¹⁰ M., b. 7 Apr 1889. He died Jan 1956.

3719    vi. Margaret⁹ Martin Eaton, b. 16 Sep 1864; mar. William Montague, 1892, Salisbury, Mass. She died 1952.

3720    vii. Jeremiah⁹ Eaton, b. 17 May 1872; died unmar. 1893.

**1990. Alvah⁸ Eaton** (Jeremiah⁷ P., Simeon⁶, Wyman⁵, John⁴⁻¹) was born 25 Apr 1836 in Seabrook, N.H.; mar. **Lydia C. Walton** of Seabrook (born 23 Jul 1839), on 24 Apr 1858. They settled on a farm in Seabrook, and Alvah worked on shoemaking in the winter. Alvah died 14 Nov 1901; Lydia died 7 Jul 1911.

Children in Seabrook:

3721    i. Florence⁹ Ella Eaton, b. 22 Sep 1858; mar. Charles H. Lord of Newburyport, Mass., 2 Jun 1877.

3722    ii. Lucy⁹ Jane Eaton, b. 24 Jan 1860; mar. Josiah Felch of Seabrook, 13 May 1877. She died 26 May 1933.

3723    iii. Sarah⁹ M. Eaton, b. 18 Nov 1861; mar. William E. Vennard of Seabrook, 25 Dec 1879. She died 13 Jul 1932.

3724    iv. Jeremiah⁹ P. Eaton, b. 22 Sep 1863; mar. Annie Kennedy of Seabrook, 5 Aug 1884; they removed to Fresno, Cal. where he raised grapes and produced raisins. They had at least three children: Florence¹⁰ Eaton, b. 5 Aug 1885;

Alvah[10] D. Eaton, b. 10 Aug 1887; and Harry[10] P.
Eaton, b. 12 Apr 1890.
3725    v. Alvah[9] A. Eaton, b. 20 Nov 1865; a teacher in Dunlap, Cal.
who mar. widow Constance Wilkins.  He died 1908 and
is buried at Hillside Cemetery, Seabrook.
3726    vi. Harry[9] P. Eaton, b. 2 Jun 1875; died 26 Oct 1889.
3727    vii. Lydia[9] Bernice Eaton, b. 5 Feb 1877; mar. 1st, Guy W.
Chase, 24 Nov 1898; was a school teacher and had two
daughters.  Mar. 2d, Albert Tuxbury.  She compiled one
of the major genealogies of the local Eatons.
3728    viii. Annie[9] M. Eaton, b. 15 Jul 1879; mar. 1st, Fred Jackman;
2d, George Garland.
3729    ix. Julia[9] Eaton, b. 10 Jun 1884; mar. Thomas Irving.


**1991. Henry[8] Eaton** (Jeremiah[7] P., Simeon[6], Wyman[5], John[4-1])
was born 25 Jul 1838 in Seabrook, N.H; mar. **Elizabeth Souther** of Seabrook, 28 Aug 1861.  They resided in Seabrook, where he farmed in the
summer and made shoes in the winter.  Henry died 22 Dec 1906; widow
Elizabeth died 5 Dec 1918.

Children in Seabrook, N.H.:

3730    i. Phebe[9] Knight Eaton, b. Nov 1862; mar. Albert[9] M. Eaton
of Seabrook (**#3384**), 15 Oct 1881.  She died 2 Sep
1936.
3731    ii. Frank[9] Ashley Eaton, b. 20 Sep 1865; drowned 10 Aug
1891 at Pettengill's Dock in Salisbury.
3732    iii. Nettie[9] D. Eaton, b. 3 Jan 1870; mar. Frank Merrill of
Seabrook, 17 Apr 1888.  He died Jan 1925, Salisbury; she
died 14 Feb 1941.
3733    iv. Fannie[9] S. Eaton, b. 15 May 1876; died 27 Mar 1878.
3734    v. Bertha[9] Russell Eaton, b. 10 Apr 1883; died 13 Nov 1923
at Newburyport, Mass.


**1992. Albert[8] Eaton** (Jeremiah[7] P., John[6], Wyman[5], John[4-1]) was
born 12 Oct 1844, and was generally known as "Prince Albert."  He mar.
**Matilda Adams Wright** of Seabrook (she born 29 Nov 1844), on 14 Oct
1861.  They settled on a farm in Salisbury, Mass., where Albert occupied
himself with shoemaking when free of farm chores.  According to his
notebook, the family moved across the Merrimack to Newburyport,
Mass, in 1886. but moved back to Salisbury again in 1892.  Albert died
30 Apr 1905; Matilda died 5 Sep 1925.

Children in Salisbury (Matilda reported 12 births as of 1900):

3735    i. Simeon[9] L. Eaton, b. 18 Dec 1863; died 25 Aug 1865.
3736    ii. Luannah[9] L. Eaton, b. 11 Feb 1865; mar. Albert Janvrin,

18 Apr 1881. She died 21 May 1805.

**3737**   iii. Albert[9] Willie Eaton, b. 18 Apr 1867; mar. Emma (Palmer) Austin of Newburyport, 2 Jun 1887. They res. at Newburyport, and had at least two children: William[10] Eaton, b. 23 Apr 1888; and Bertie[10] Eaton, 29 Mar 1892.

**3738**   iv. George[9] Nelson Eaton, b. 4 Jul 1869; mar. Sarah Ann (Souther) Fowler, 30 Dec 1965.

**3739**   v. Jane[9] Morrill Eaton, b. 31 May 1871; mar. Jacob Brown of Seabrook, 8 Apr 1890; had two sons before d. young.

**3740**   vi. Nicholas[9] Tracy Eaton, b. 19 Jan 1873; mar. 1st, Eliza[8] A. (Eaton) Souther (**#1721**, b. Vt., her 2d mar.), 1894; mar. 2d, 27 Oct 1909, Anna T. Cardigan. He died 1950 (Newburyport record).

**3741**   vii. Mabel[9] Eaton, b. 23 Sep 1876; mar. John F. Muldoon. She died 1903; bur. with parents at Wildwood Cemetery.

**3742**   viii. Lester[9] David Eaton, b. 21 Feb 1879; mar. Grace Austin, 21 Feb 1902, Newburyport, Mass; died there, 1969.

**3743**   ix. Mary[9] Arvilla Eaton, b. 18 Feb 1881; mar. Frank E. Cole, 20 Jun 1901. She died 2 Jun 1945.

**3744**   x. Matilda[9] Adams Eaton, b. ca. 1885; died 1886-87.

**3745**   xi. Child[9] Eaton, perhaps earlier stillbirth.

**3746**   xii. Child[9] Eaton, perhaps earlier stillbirth.


**1995. Azor[8] Webster Eaton** (Archelaus[7], Jonathan[6], Joseph[5], John[4-1]) was born 25 Jan 1820 in Salisbury, Mass. He removed to Vienna, Me., and mar. **Adaline Brown** of Vienna, 22 Oct 1843. They resided in Vienna, on a prosperous farm. Azor died 22 Jun 1874, Vienna.

Children born Vienna, Me.:

**3747**   i. (Marion) Freeman[9] Eaton, b. 7 Oct 1844; mar. Marietta Leighton of Mt. Vernon, Me. and had two daughters.

**3748**   ii. Sarah Elizabeth[9] Eaton, b. 22 Oct 1846; mar. Samuel Hinkson and resided in Haverhill, Mass. No issue.

**3749**   iii. Ella[9] Samantha Eaton, b. 16 Jul 1852; mar. Corey Leighton of Mt. Vernon, Me., and had twin daughters.

**3750**   iv. Fred[9] Carrol Eaton, b. 12 Jan 1856; late mar. if any.


**1996. Jabez[8] Eaton** (Archelaus[7], Jonathan[6], Joseph[5], John[4-1]) was born 18 Jun 1823 in Salisbury, Mass.; mar. 1st, **Charlotte Barker** a bit before 1850, and they res. in Salisbury. Jabez was a carpenter there, and did some shoe-making as well, like most of his peers. The couple had three children, but the marriage was an unhappy one and a separation took place sometime after 1860. Then Jabez mar. 2d, **Emma Farrar** They removed at some point to Springfield, Mass., where Jabez's sister Martha and her husband resided, and had a son born there who was named after her husband.  As a carpenter, Jabez was mobile, and at last word, in 1888, he was living in Charlestown, Mass.

Children at Salisbury with Charlotte:

**3751**    i. Austin⁹ Newell Eaton, b. 28 Jun 1851; died young.
**3752**   ii. Gustavus⁹ Eaton, b. ca. 1854; mar __?__, with two children.
**3753**  iii. Prentice⁹ Banks Eaton, b. 13 Feb 1857; mar., without issue.

Child with Emma at Springfield, Mass.:

**3754**   iv. Tilly⁹ Haynes Eaton, b. 22 Jul 1872; named for his uncle.


**1999. Samuel⁸ D. Eaton** (Archelaus⁷, Jonathan⁶, Joseph⁵, John⁴⁻¹) was born Aug 1829 in Salisbury, Mass.; and grew up alternately in Salisbury and Seabrook, N.H.  He went to see his brother Azor in Vienna, Me., and ended up marrying **Mary Mehitable Brown** (b. 1830, Vienna) there, 23 Jan 1856.  The couple at least visited back in Salisbury, and were there for the 1860 Census, where Samuel lists himself as a shoemaker.  But they seem to have resided mainly at Vienna.  Samuel D. died 11 Feb 1866 and was buried in Vienna.

Children:

**3755**    i. Harry⁹ W. Eaton, b. 25 Nov 1857, prob. in Vienna; mar.
             Effie Jaques of Lowell, Mass and had at least two children.
**3756**   ii. Lawrence⁹ B. Eaton, b. 10 Aug 1860 in Salisbury, Mass.  He
             died Feb 1931 in Moretown, Washington Co., Vt., having
             had four children.


**2004. Jabez⁸ Merrill Eaton** (Jabez⁷, Jonathan⁶, Joseph⁵, John⁴⁻¹) was born ca. 1835; mar. **Ann Downing Pierce** (daughter of Philip and Eliza Ann (Cole) Pierce) on 29 Jan 1857.  As of the 1860 Census, Jabez was a mariner sailing out of Newburyport, and they resided in Ward #1 of Newburyport, Mass. in 1880.  Jabez died in Newburyport, 1909.

Children, all born Newburyport:

**3757**    i. William⁹ Wallace Eaton, b. ca. 1859; was a fisherman at
             Newburyport in 1880.  He mar. Sadie¹⁰ Belle Eaton, dau.
             of Almon⁹ (**#3288**), 27 Jun 1888; and died 1924 at
             Newburyport.
**3758**   ii. Albert⁹ Nelson Eaton, b. ca. 1861; worked in a shoe factory
             in 1880; mar. Nellie S. Russell, 20 Oct 1881 at Newbury-
             port, and died in that city in 1945.
**3759**  iii. Helen⁹ Marian Eaton, b. ca. 1864.
**3760**   iv. James⁹ M. Eaton, b. ca. 1867; mar. Barbara Ross (born in

England), 20 Jun 1888, Newburyport.

3761      v. Lorin[9] F. Eaton, b. ca. 1869; mar. Marjorie King ca. 1897;
          and died 1928 at Newburyport.


**2008. John[8] Curtis Eaton** (Samuel[7], Jonathan[6], Joseph[5], John[4-1])
was born 20 Dec 1834 in Seabrook; mar 1st, **Mary[9] C. Eaton** (#3323)
and res. in Seabrook, with John C. a shoemaker in 1860, and both of
them working in the shoe factory as of 1870. He divorced her for abandonment, 28 Oct 1874, with no children from the union. John C. mar.
2d, **Rachel[8] Jane Eaton** (#1719), then of Winooski Falls, Vt., on 15 Oct
1877 (Seabrook *VR* at Concord).

Children with Rachel at Seabrook, N.H.:

3762      i. Samuel[9] John Tilden Eaton, b. 28 Aug 1878; mar. Lydia
          Jane Knowles of Seabrook, 2 Jan 1909.
3763      ii. Helen[9] Eaton, b. ca. 1880 and died young.
3764      iii. Mary[9] C. Eaton, b. 7 Jan 1883; mar. Andrew J. Fowler,
          2 Oct 1899. She died 27 May 1901.


**2009. Robert[8] Collins Eaton** (Samuel[7], Jonathan[6], Joseph[5],
John[4-1]) was born 7 Mar 1836 in Seabrook, N.H.; mar. **Mary Abbie
Fowler**, 24 Nov 1859. They res. in Seabrook, and in 1870 Robert was
working in the shoe factory. Robert died 4 Jan 1906 at Seabrook.

Children at Seabrook, N.H.:

3765      i. Vianna[9] Eaton, b. 2 Dec 1862; mar. Frank Merrill, 9 Dec
          1881; she died 6 Aug 1946 at Newburyport, Mass.
3766      ii. William[9] N. Eaton, b. 10 May 1866; mar. Ida E. Bragg, 27
          Feb 1886; died 3 Sep 1929, Seabrook.
3767      iii. Addie[9] M. Eaton, b. 9 Feb 1868; mar. Samuel Beckman,
          4 Dec 1884; she died 21 Jan 1950.
3768      iv. Emma[9] F. Eaton, b. 18 Dec 1869; mar. 1st, Newell[10] Eaton,
          (#5031), son of Thomas[9], 9 Feb 1885; and 2d, 20 Dec
          1913, Joshua Janvrin.
3769      v. Almena[9] P. Eaton, b. 10 May 1873; died 11 Oct 1891 of
          typhoid fever.
3770      vi. Huldah[9] D. Eaton, b. 6 Feb 1876; mar. 1st, Alick A. Brown,
          25 Jan 1891; 2d, Arthur H. Fowler, 19 Sep 1903. She
          died 30 Nov 1909.
3771      vii. Florence[9] B. Eaton, 8 Jul 1880; mar. James F. Fowler
          14 Feb 1898.


**2010. Samuel[8] A. Eaton** (Samuel[7], Jonathan[6], Joseph[5], John[4-1])
was born 5 Jul 1840 in Seabrook, N.H.; mar. **Abigail[9] B. Eaton** (#3324),

21 Jun 1858. They res. in Seabrook, where he was early (1860) a shoe-maker, and later (1870) worked in the shoe factory. He died 25 Jul 1914 in Seabrook.

Children in Seabrook:

3772    i. Adna[9] C. Eaton, b. 27 Mar 1858; died 26 Mar 1863.
3773    ii. Laura[9] M. Eaton, b. 31 Mar 1863; mar. a Taylor of Salem, N.H.
3774    iii. Adna[9] Preston Eaton, b. 25 Oct 1867; mar. Harriet Newhall Locke, 25 Dec 1894, while residing in Lynn, Mass. He died 13 Sep 1910 in Seabrook.

**2014. Frederick[8] A. Eaton** (John[7] M., Jonathan[6], Joseph[5], John[4-1]) was born 5 Sep 1836 in Seabrook, N.H.; mar. 1st, **Mary D. Fowler**, 23 Feb 1859. They res. in Seabrook and had four children before Mary died in the latter 1860s. In this earlier period, Frederick describes him-self as a fisherman; but like his peers, he probably was into shoemaking on the side. By 1870, he is working in the local shoe factory. He mar. 2d, **Eliza J. Fowler** on 2 Dec 1872, by whom he had further children. He died 16 Dec 1909. Widow Eliza died 1926.

Children with Mary at Seabrook, N.H.:

3775    i. Chestina[9] Eaton, b. 13 Aug 1858; mar. Lowell Fowler, 10 Jan 1875.
3776    ii. George[9] B. Eaton, b. ca. 21 Jun 1862?
3777    iii. Child[9] Eaton, b. ca. 24 Dec 1863; d. 6 Mar 1864.
3778    iv. Charles[9] H. Eaton, b. 30 Aug 1866; mar. Anne R. Fowler, 11 Nov 1890 (her 2d mar.); died ca. 12 Jun 1914.

Children with Eliza at Seabrook, N.H.:

3779    v. Mary[9] L. Eaton, b. 29 Jan 1874; mar. 1st, Thomas W. Charles, 1890; 2d, Albert Dunbrack, 26 Feb 1896. She died 28 Feb 1911.
3780    vi. Eunice[9] Ann Eaton, b. 8 Sep 1876; mar. Freeman Fowler, 1892. He died 1932; she died 5 Aug 1950.
3781    vii. Olive[9] C. Eaton, b. 26 Aug 1878; mar. 1st, Levi D. Collins, 18 Jun 1904; 2d, 2 Feb 1910, Charles E. Fowler. She died 18 Jan 1961.
3782    viii. Anna[9] Evelyn Eaton, b. 30 Mar 1880; mar. Daniel M. Brown, 25 Jul 1902. She died 14 Apr 1943.

**2022. Forrest[8] Eaton** (Forrest[7], Joshua[6-5], William[4], John[3-1]) was born 6 Oct 1802 at Wells, Me. on the seaward slope of Mt. Agamenticus; mar. 1st, **Harriet Porter Gordon** (born 4 Aug 1804 in Newbury, Mass.,

but then of Dover, N.H.), 28 Sep 1828.  Forrest became a cotton manufacturer at Dover, and ended up leading a rather peripatetic life.  After
two children with Harriet she died, and he mar. 2d, **Shuah Blake** of Exeter, N.H., 1 Jun 1839.  She died almost immediately, and he mar. 3d, an
**Olive Blake**, quite probably related to Shuah, 31 Aug 1840.  They
moved to Lowell, Mass., and later he at least was based in Newmarket,
N.H. and then Laurel, Md., before removing to Alfred, Me.  He mar. 4th,
**Harriet Chadbourne** of Alfred, Me., 10 Jan 1862.  Forrest had been a
member of the Common Council while at Lowell, and at Alfred he was a
selectman and town treasurer.  He was a Free Mason and a member of
the Congregational Church there.  He died in Maine, 29 Jul 1880.

Children with (1) Harriet, perhaps at Dover, N.H.:

3783    i. Edward[9] Forrest Eaton, b. 22 Nov 1830; mar. Kate Overdiez,
            Chicago, Ill., where he spent his career as a merchant.
3784    ii. Harriet[9] Ann Eaton, b. 23 Sep 1833; mar. a Benjamin Tread-
            well Bo_?_ne of Providence, R. I. 13 Jan 1855.

Child with (2) Shuah, at Lowell, Mass.:

3785    iii. Sherburne[9] Blake Eaton, b. 23 Feb 1840; mar. Anna
            McClevey, 9 Apr 1868, Chicago, Ill.  She had been born
            25 Apr 1846 at Buffalo, N. Y., and died 5 Dec 1878 in
            New York City.  Sherburne was an eminent lawyer in
            the firm of Eaton, Lewis and Hodgkins at 44 Broad St.
            in New York City.  They had no children.


**2025. (Rev.) Eben[8] Goodwin Eaton** (Forrest[7], Joshua[6-5], William[4],
John[3-1]) was born 6 Sep 1807 in Wells, Me.; mar., 1st, **Mehitable Farnum
Barker**, 6 Dec 1835 at Bridgton, Me.  He began his career succeeding to
the proprietorship of the long-established central merchandise store at
Greene Corner.  He became a minister in the local Freewill Baptist
Church for the period 1841-44, leading a powerful revival which pro-
duced 58 baptisms (Mower, 1938).  He subsequently served in diverse
other churches in the state, and also preached for several years on Cape
Sable Island, Nova Scotia.  After wife Mehitable died 17 Feb 1856, he
had mar. 2d, **Mrs. Mary Jane Frye**, ca. 1859.  He died 13 Aug 1883 in
Lewiston, Me.

Children with Mehitable:

3786    i. Catherine[9] A. Eaton, b. 7 Apr 1837 Saco, Me; mar. John H.
            Stinson, 25 Oct 1860, and resided in Sullivan, Me., where
            her husband, in the granite business, died 18 Mar 1889.
3787    ii. Austin[9] F. Eaton, b. 27 May 1838 in Saco, Me.  He became
            a teacher at Cape Sable Island, Nova Scotia, where he
            died unmar. 27 Jul 1864.

**3788** iii. William⁹ B. Eaton, b. 1 Jan 1840 in Danville, Me.; mar. Ella M. Phillips (b. 1854 in Walesville, N.Y.), on 20 Oct 1869. He was in the granite business res. in Sullivan, Me, where he died 13 Apr 1890. Child: Phillip¹⁰, b. 13 Apr 1890.

**3789** iv. Mehitable⁹ A. Eaton, b. 6 Apr 1841 in Lisbon, Me.; in 1864 at Lisbon, mar. Horatio Hovey, Jr., of East Cambridge, Mass., where she died 11 Jan 1873.

**3790** v. Clara⁹ M. Eaton, b. 20 Mar 1843 in Greene, Me.; mar. 1st, George E. Lee, 22 Oct 1865; and 2d, W. H. West, 9 Apr 1873. She res. in Cambridge, Mass.

**3791** vi. Charles⁹ B. Eaton, b. 18 Jan 1845, in Brunswick, Me.; mar. Elizabeth "Lizzie" Smith (of Bangor, but b. 29 Apr 1845 in Houlton, Me.) on 9 Oct 1872 in Greene, Me. They resided in Auburn, Me., where he was an overseer in a weave room. They had two sons, William¹⁰ Smith Eaton, b. 23 Nov 1873; and Hal¹⁰ R. Eaton, b. 16 Feb 1877, before Charles died 1 Jan 1881 in Auburn.

**3792** vii. Louise⁹ Eaton, b. 4 Aug 1847 in Saco, Me.; mar. Edwin R. Foster and resided in Cambridgeport, Mass. She died there, 11 Apr 1867.

**3793** viii. Sophia⁹ G. Eaton, b. 28 Oct 1851 in Greene, Me.; mar. Oliver H. Durrell of East Cambridge, Mass., a Boston merchant, 18 Oct 1871. They resided in Cambridge.

**2031. (Rev.) Rufus⁸ G. Eaton** (Forrest⁷, Joshua⁶⁻⁵, William⁴, John³⁻¹) was born 20 Dec 1819 at Wells, Me., but removed early with his family to Greene, Me. In part under the influence of his older brother, Rev. Eben, Rufus was recommended on 25 Dec 1841 to the Freewill Baptist Quarterly Conference for licensing as a minister of that church. He subsequently mar. **Eliza M. Trussell** of Camden, Me., and by 1848 the couple had moved to Manchester, N.H. We find them with an infant son there in the 1850 Census, but then lose their trail.

Only known child:

**3794** i. Willie⁹ Eaton, b. ca. 1848, New Hampshire.

**2042. Joshua⁸ Eaton** (Joshua⁷⁻⁵, William⁴, John³⁻¹) was born in 1822 in Kennebunkport, Me.; mar. **Elizabeth __?__**, about five years his junior. This couple settled in Kennebunkport, where Joshua was a blacksmith of modest means and where their children were raised.

Children, presumably born at Kennebunkport, Me.:

**3795** i. Ann⁹ M. Eaton, b. ca. 1851-2.
**3796** ii. Edward⁹ Eaton, b. Mar 1855; mar. Eliza and was living at Kennebunkport in 1900.

3797    iii. Henry[9] Eaton, b. 1856.
3798    iv. Marietta[9] Eaton, b. 1867.


**2046. Horace[8] Eaton** (Jabez[7], Joshua[6-5], William[4], John[3-1]) was born 4 Oct 1813 in Wells, Me.; mar. **Hannah J. Morrill**, 22 Feb 1843 at her birthplace in Wilmington, Mass.. They lived in Wilmington for a few years, but then returned to settle on a modest farm in Wells. Wife Hannah died soon after, on 6 Feb 1852. Horace died, still in middle age, 18 May 1858 at Wells

Children (the first four born Wilmington, the last two at Wells):

3799    i. Horace[9] Morrill Eaton, b. 31 Mar 1843; mar. Susan E. Jenkins of York, Me. in 1864 at Wells. They had one son, Horace[10] M. Eaton, Jr., who res. Lynn, Mass.
3800    ii. Sarah[9] Frances Eaton, b. 6 May 1844; mar. Isaiah Chadbourne of Wells, and they res. Wells; she died 6 Jan 1877.
3801    iii. Elsie[9] A. Eaton, b. 31 Aug 1845; died 30 Oct 1845.
3802    iv. Ann[9] Maria Eaton, b. 1847; prob. died before 1850.
3803    v. Mary[9] Elsie Eaton, b. 25 Nov 1849; mar. George Barnes of Plymouth, Mass., 1 Jul 1893, and res. in Lynn, Mass.
3804    vi. Charles[9] Oren Eaton, b. 5 Feb 1850; mar. 1st, Abby F. Jenkins; and 2d, Olive J. Shaw. Resided at Kittery Depot, York, Me.


**2048. John[8A] Eaton** (Jabez[7], Joshua[6-5], William[4], John[3-1]) was born 11 Aug 1819 in Wells, Me. In Boston on 3 Nov 1850, John mar. **Elizabeth Maxwell Kimball**, she having been born 25 Aug 1816 in Wells. They removed to Taunton, Mass., where John was employed as a cutter in a clothing house. Wife Elizabeth died there suddenly 29 Aug 1894.

Children born at Taunton, Mass.:

3805    i. Zuella[9] Eaton, b. 11 Apr 1852; mar. William R. Waldron of New Bedford, Mass., 13 May 1878.
3806    ii. Walter[9] Storer Eaton, b. 19 Mar 1854; mar. Lucy Ann Winfield (b. 2 Dec 1856), on 3 Nov 1879. They later res. in Fairhaven, Mass., where he was a printer in New Bedford next door. Their children were Lucy[10] Sophia Eaton, b. 19 Nov 1881, d. young; Walter[10] Eaton, b. 9 Aug 1883, d. young; Walter[10A] Winfield Eaton, b. 16 Feb 1885; Charles[10] Kimball Eaton, b. 28 Dec 1893; and John[10] Merrill Eaton, b. 28 Feb 1895 (the first three children b. Taunton, Mass.; the latter two in Fairhaven).

**2049. Walter**[8] **Eaton** (Jabez[7], Joshua[6-5], William[4], John[3-1]) was born 29 Jan 1821 in Wells, Me.; mar. **Susanna Chadbourne** of Vassalboro, Me. ca. 1851. They settled on a small farm in Wells and had a fine young family when Walter went off to the Civil War. Subsequently, Susanna became insane and died at No. Berwick, Me., while he was gone. (One date given for her death is 8 Jan 1864, but something is wrong either with this date or with the birthdate of her last child in May, 1864.) Walter himself was captured in the South and died at Salisbury Prison, 8 Dec 1864.

Children born at Wells, Me.:

3807    i. Marcia[9] F. Eaton, b. 24 Mar 1853; mar. 1st, Rufus O. Swett, 12 Nov 1870. He died in Portland, Me., 1 Feb 1872. She mar. 2d, Joseph H. Sterling, but was divorced 19 Jan 1882. She then mar. 3d, Victor S. Paige, a Lowell, Mass., jeweler, 20 Sep 1887. He died 28 Mar 1895.

3808    ii. Walter[9] F. Eaton, b. 29 May 1855; mar. Angela Proctor (b. 24 Jun 1860, in Stanbridge, P. Que.) on 3 Jun 1881. He worked for the Boston & Maine R.R. and res. in East Billerica, Mass.

3809    iii. John[9] O. Eaton, b. 24 Dec 1856; mar. Cora D. Sleeper (b. 23 Sep 1856 in Rutland, Vt.) on 26 Dec 1876. He was a railroad brakeman and they res. in Lowell, Mass. They had one son, George[10] H. Eaton, b. 16 Dec 1877 in Lawrence, Mass. John died 1 May 1886 in Lowell.

3810    iv. Edmond[9] A. Eaton, b. 26 Aug 1858, and never married. He worked for the B&M Railroad, res. Newmarket, N.H.

3811    v. Frank[9] Freeman Eaton, b. 19 Jul 1860; mar. Lucy Paul of Dover, N.H. They had three children on a Dover farm.

3812    vi. Charles[9] Thomas Eaton, b. 2 May 1864; mar. Agnes Jones (b. 21 Aug 1867 in Wolcott, Vt.) on 12 Dec 1888 and res. at least thru 1894 in East Billerica, Mass. He worked for the Electric Light Company of Boston. They had at least one child, Howard[10] Walter Eaton, b. 19 Jul 1892 in East Somerville, Mass.

**2055. Ira**[8] **Eaton** (Noah[7], Joshua[6-5], William[4], John[3-1]) was born 23 Jul 1816 in Wells, Me.. On 31 Aug 1837 he mar. **Nancy Hatch**, born 20 Aug 1817, also in Wells. They resided on a farm in Wells for their early years, but removed over the town line into No. Berwick, Me. just after 1850. Ira died there 30 Dec 1858, and his widow Nancy is there in 1860 with the remains of the family working as a domestic in the Welch household.

Children (i-iii born at Wells, Me. ; iv-vii in No Berwick, Me.):

3813    i. Augusta[9] Eaton, b. 28 Feb 1839; mar. Seath G. Allen of

York, 9 Jul 1871. He was a blacksmith, and they res. without issue in Rockport, Mass.

3814   ii. Amanda[9] Jane Eaton, b. 3 Aug 1841; mar. William Bedell of Wells, Me. 2 Dec 1856 and res. in No. Berwick, Me. He was a tinsmith, and they had three children of each sex.

3815   iii. Mary[9] Hatch Eaton, b. 12 Mar 1843; mar. Nicholas Weymouth, 6 Sep 1863 and res. in No. Berwick. He was a farmer who died 20 Jul 1879. They had one son.

3816   iv. Hollis[9] Perkins Eaton, b. 27 Aug 1845; mar. Lucy Ellen Ridley (b. 9 Mar 1845 in No. Berwick, Me.), on 13 Sep 1865. They res. for a period in Philadelphia, Pa., where he worked on the railroad. They had one child, Arthur[10] Everett Eaton, b. 10 Sep 1866 in Wellesley, Mass., who mar. Maria Nason of So. Acton, Mass. in 1884 and res. on a farm there. Arthur's mother reportedly died 28 May 1883 in Acton, Mass.

3817   v. William[9] Ford Eaton, b. 3 May 1852; mar. Laura Etta Jackson, 1874, and they res. in Portland with two children.

3818   vi. Ella[9] Frances Eaton, b. 2 Oct 1854; mar. George W. Keeble, 1 Jan 1876 and res. in Portland, Me. He was a hackman, and they had no children.

3819   vii. Forest[9] Eaton, b. 25 Oct 1857; mar. Nellie Gertrude Leavitt on 17 Nov 1886. He was a clerk in a grocery store in Portland, Me.


**2057. Isaac[8] Eaton** (Noah[7], Johsua[6-5], William[4], John[3-1]) was born 10 Jan 1821 at Wells, Me.; mar. **Sarah J. Perkins** (born 1818) on 26 Jun 1842 in Wells. Isaac was a house carpenter who became rather well-to-do, working first at Wells and by 1860-70 at No. Berwick. He died 20 Sep 1879.

Child born at Wells:

3820   i. Sarah[9] F. Eaton, b. ca. 1846.


**2060. Noah[8] Eaton** (Noah[7], Joshua[6-5], William[4], John[3-1]) was born 2 Jun 1829 in Wells, Me.; on 4 Apr 1852, mar. **Sarah F. Williams**, born 20 Sep 1834 at Kittery Point, Me. They resided at Kittery Point, where he was a carpenter.

Children at Kittery, Me.:

3821   i. Eunice[9] A. Eaton, b. 3 Aug 1852; mar. 1st, Francis Hussey, with whom she had one daughter; and mar. 2d, George F. Baker of England. She died 8 Jan 1894.

3822   ii. Emma[9] F. Eaton, b. 25 Sep 1854; mar. George S. Aldrich, a rubber boot maker, on 24 Oct 1879, and res. in Malden,

Mass.
**3823** iii. Ella⁹ Eaton, a twin b. 1 Nov 1856; mar. David W. Tuck, 1
May 1884, and res. in Malden, Mass.
**3824** iv. Etta⁹ Eaton, a twin b. 1 Nov 1856; res. unmar., Kittery.
**3825** v. Elsie⁹ Eaton, b. 19 Sep 1861; mar. Joseph W. Call, 24 Sep
1882.
**3826** vi. Noah⁹, Jr. Eaton, b. 18 Jan 1864 and res. unmar., Kittery.
**3827** vii. Phebe⁹ Eaton, b. 18 Nov 1866; mar. John Henry Pruett of
Kittery Point.


**2065. Adoniram⁸ Judson Eaton** (Joseph⁷⁻⁶, Joshua⁵, William⁴,
John³⁻¹) was born 16 Oct 1817 in Wells, Me.; mar. **Abbie Storer** of Wells
on 29 Dec 1839 at Wells. They resided in Wells: Adoniram, however,
died early, on 28 Mar 1847. In the 1850 Census we find no sign of
widow Abbie, but two children sheltered in the home of Adoniram's
younger brother Forrest (see **#2066**, below), too old to be part of Forrest's own incipient brood and set off from them in the listing order, appear to be surviving children of this marriage.

Probable children at Wells, Me.:

**3828** i. Sarah⁹ M. Eaton, b. 1841.
**3829** ii. Adoniram⁹ Judson Eaton, b. 1843.


**2066. Forrest⁸ W. Eaton** (Joseph⁷⁻⁶, Joshua⁵, William⁴, John³⁻¹)
was born 1 Oct 1821 in Wells, Me.; on 18 May 1842 he mar. **Betsey B.
Hobbs** (born 24 Jan 1822) in Wells. They settled at Wells Depot, where
Forrest was a prosperous merchant. He died in Wells in 1890.

Children born in Wells, Me.:

**3830** i. Joseph⁹ Eaton, b. 2 Mar 1843; died 28 Feb 1847.
**3831** ii. Wells⁹ Eaton, b. 26 Aug 1846; died 18 Feb 1847.
**3832** iii. Josephine⁹ Eaton, b. 19 Nov 1847; mar. Henry⁹ O. Eaton
of Wells (#2094, q.v.), 17 Dec 1879.
**3833** iv. Forrest⁹ W. Eaton, b. 10 Feb 1850; mar. Eliza A. Jenkins, 2
Apr 1878 and had a daughter Ethel¹⁰ B., 9 Jan 1879.
**3834** v. William⁹ H. Eaton, b. 1 Sept 1854; mar. Susie S. Chick, 18
Jan 1877. They res. in Wells, where William was a Selectman, 1892. Their children were Lillian¹⁰ M. Eaton, b.
23 Nov 1877; Albert¹⁰ J. Eaton, b. 4 Apr 1879; Ezra¹⁰ M.
Eaton, b. 27 Sep 1880; Joseph¹⁰ W. Eaton, b. 16 Aug
1882 but d. in two months; Agnes¹⁰ G., b. 5 Dec 1883.


**2068. Jeremiah⁸ Moulton Eaton** (John⁷, Jeremiah⁶ M., Joseph⁵,
William⁴, John³⁻¹) was born 5 Feb 1804 in Wells, Me.; mar. 1st. **Nancy**

**Ann Donnell** of Wells about 1830 and res. in Wells as had four generations of his Eatons before him. He was a prosperous lumberman, often
addressed as "Moulton," and farmed on the side. In 1868 he mar. 2d,
**Anna M. Winn** (born ca. 1830). He died in Wells, prob. soon thereafter.

Children at Wells:

**3835**   i. William[9] Gooch Eaton, b. 26 Oct 1832; after an apparent
           first marriage, he mar. Abba M. Kaler, 1873.
**3836**   ii. John[9] E. Eaton, b. 27 Mar 1834. Still living at home,
           with no stated occupation, 1870.
**3837**   iii. Luella[9] Eaton, b. 30 Nov 1835.
**3838**   iv. Joseph[9] D. Eaton, b. ca. Apr 1838; mar. Laura Littlefield,
           1868.
**3839**   v. Benjamin[9] B. Eaton, b. 11 May 1842; was a confirmed
           bachelor who was a railroad contractor in St. Paul, Minn.
**3840**   vi. Nancy[9] Ann Eaton, b. ca. Oct 1845; mar. a Perkins.

**2069. John[8] E. Eaton** (Samuel[7], Jeremiah[6] M., Joseph[5], William[4],
John[3-1]) was born 7 Dec 1807 in Wells, Me.; mar. 1st, **Almeda Hatch**
about 1830 and they resided on a small farm in Wells. Late in life he
mar. 2d, **Jane Parker** in 1881.

Children with Almeda, all born at Wells, Me.:

**3841**   i. John[9] E. Eaton, Jr., b. 15 Oct 1832; mar. Clarissa Holton.
           He was a mariner.
**3842**   ii. Samuel[9] Eaton, b. ca. 1839; a mariner who mar. Mary Ann
           Hatch, 29 Jul 1864 at Wells.
**3843**   iii. Frank[9] C. Eaton, b. 9 Jul 1842; mar. Annie Williams (b.
           Apr 1844, also in Wells) in 1865 and res. in Kittery, Me,
           where he was a driver for the U.S. Fire Department.
           They later (1894) res. in Kennebunk, Me. Their chil-
           dren were Fanny[10] A. Eaton, b. 16 Jun 1867; Addie[10] M.
           Eaton, b. 25 Jan 1873; and Mamie[10] A. Eaton, b. 6 Sep
           1876, all in Kittery, Me.
**3844**   iv. Lucinda[9] P. Eaton, b. ca. 1847; mar. William Hilton, Jr.
**3845**   v. Charles[9] W. Eaton, b. 1 Mar 1853; mar. Sarah M.
           Pettigrew (b. 25 Jul 1860 in Kittery, Me.) on 22 Sep
           1881. They res. first in Lynn, Mass., and later in Cam-
           bridge, Mass., where he was a plumber. They had two
           children, John[10] Earl Eaton, b. 8 Nov 1884; and Ralph[10]
           William Eaton, b. 1 Feb 1893.

**2070. Stephen[8] Eaton** (Samuel[7], Jeremiah[6] M., Joseph[5], William[4],
John[3-1]) was born 16 Apr 1809 in Wells, Me.; mar. **Almira __?__**, some

seven years his senior. They settled on a moderate-sized farm in Wells where they raised their daughters.

Children born in Wells, Me.:

**3846**    i. Hannah⁹ E. Eaton, b. ca. 1834. In 1870 she was still living with her parents and working in the cotton mill.
**3847**    ii. Mary⁹ Ann Eaton, b. ca. 1840; still at home, 1860, but elsewhere by 1870.
**3848**    iii. Lydia⁹ C. Eaton, b. ca. 1857. In 1870 she was still living with her parents and working in the cotton mill.

**2073. William⁸ Eaton** (Rufus⁷, William⁶, Joseph⁵, William⁴, John³, John²⁻¹) was born 23 Oct 1808 in Provincetown, Mass; mar. **Hannah Augusta Patten** (born 8 Jun 1818 in Boston), on 4 Nov 1845. He was a merchant in Boston, where they resided on Chester Square (now Massachusetts Ave.). He died 6 Nov 1875, and Hannah followed in May 1888.

Children, all born in "South End," Boston, Mass.:

**3849**    i. Leonie⁹ Jacob Eaton, b. 5 Oct 1852; died Brookline, 1930.
**3850**    ii. Julia⁹ Fraser Eaton, b. 1 Jan 1855; died Brookline, 1917.
**3851**    iii. Fannie⁹ Stavers Eaton, b. 5 Jan 1857; died, 1920.
**3852**    iv. William⁹ Eaton, b. 23 May 1859; a clerk in a Boston store at the time, he mar. Lydia Atherton Wright of Philadelphia and Riverton, N.J., 18 Jun 1898.
**3853**    v. Augusta⁹ Patten Eaton, b. 2 Feb 1862; died 1935.

**2074. Solomon⁸ Lombard Eaton** (Rufus⁷, William⁶, Joseph⁵, William⁴, John³⁻¹) was born 23 Jun 1811 in Newton, Mass.; mar. **Susan Springs Chandler** (she born 27 Apr 1814 in Roxbury, Mass) on 10 Oct 1833. They res. in Boston's 3d Ward where Solomon was a brass founder; but he died young, on 28 Apr 1843 in Boston. His widow Susan died 11 Jun 1873 in Somerville, Mass.

Children (all born in Boston):

**3854**    i. Edward⁹ Harper Eaton, b. Mar 1835; died in 1835, Boston.
**3855**    ii. Eliza⁹ Houston Eaton, b. 16 Jan 1837; mar. Wesley C. Crane, 13 Jan 1856 and res. in Boston, having four children.
**3856**    iii. Charles⁹ Frederic Eaton, b. 28 Aug 1838 and res. first in Boston, but died Oct 1859 in Iowa.
**3857**    iv. Rufus⁹ Eaton, b. 8 Mar 1840; he was a jewelry manufacturer in Boston who died unmar. 12 May 1890.
**3858**    v. Walter⁹ Watkins Eaton, b. Nov 1841; died 14 Jun 1842, Boston.
**3859**    vi. Edward⁹ Lombard Eaton, b. 21 Aug 1843; died 1863 at Port Hudson.

**2081. Cyrus⁸ James Eaton** (Rufus⁷, William⁶, Joseph⁵, William⁴, John³⁻¹) was born Jun 1830 in Boston, Mass.; mar. 1st, **Mary Brady** and had one daughter. He was a machinist and res. in Brooklyn, N.Y. on Colyer St. and Dupont St. where in 1900 he was household head for his daughter's family, an apparent widower. Probably after 1900, but perhaps before, he mar. 2d **Catherine Mulligan** of Jersey City, N.J.

Child with Mary:

**3860**    i. Mary⁹ Eaton, b. Nov 1869, perhaps Brooklyn, N.Y.; mar. James Britt and had a daughter before 1900.

**2094. Henry⁸ Oliver Eaton** (Daniel⁷, Jacob⁶, Joseph⁵, William⁴, John³⁻¹) was born 14 Feb 1850 in Wells, Me.; mar. **Josephine⁹ Eaton** (**#3832**, born Nov 1847), on 17 Dec 1879. They res. in Wells.

Children born in Wells, Me.:

**3861**    i. Daniel⁹ W. Eaton, b. Oct 1887.
**3862**    ii. Nathaniel⁹ Eaton, b. Sep 1892.

**2096. Charles⁸ Augustus Eaton** (Hophni⁷, Jacob⁶, Joseph⁵, William⁴, John³⁻¹) was born 14 Aug 1850 in Portland, Me.; mar. on 28 Sep 1875 at Portland, **Annie C. Millett**, she born 21 Apr 1854 in Portland. He was an accountant who was mainly located in Portland, although the 1900 Census finds this family res. in Houlton, in far northern Aroostook Co., Me.

Children:

**3863**    i. Florence⁹ F. Eaton, b. 24 Jun 1876 in Portland, Me. In 1900 she was living with her family of origin in Houlton, Me.
**3864**    ii. Maurice⁹ B. Eaton, b. 17 Apr 1883 in Portland; in Houlton, Me., 1900 with family.
**3865**    iii. Bessie⁹ M. Eaton, b. 6 Aug 1886 in Deering, Me.; with family in Houlton, Me. 1900.
**3866**    iv. Philip⁹ A. Eaton, b. 25 Nov 1892 in Portland, Me. Is age seven in Houlton, Me., 1900.

**2102. Charles⁸ Eaton** (John⁷⁻⁶, Joseph⁵, William⁴, John³⁻¹) was born 25 Jun 1834 in Wells, Me.; mar. **Mary Buzzell** of Wells, 30 Jun 1875 and they res. in Wells. Mary died there 2 Sep 1891.

Children born in Wells, Me.:

| 3867 | i. Emma[9] Eaton, b. 29 Aug 1875. |
| 3868 | ii. George[9] Eaton, b. 5 Mar 1877. |
| 3869 | iii. Orren[9] Eaton, b. 8 Aug 1878. |
| 3870 | iv. John[9] D. Eaton, twin b. 11 Jun 1880. |
| 3871 | v. William[9] Eaton, twin b. 11 Jun 1880. |

**2105. Christopher[8] Eaton** (John[7-6], Joseph[5], William[4], John[3-1]) was born 3 Jan 1840 in Wells, Me.; mar. **Mrs. Helen (Doves) Smith** of Boston, 3 Jan 1884. He was a sailor by trade, and res. in Wells, Me. In the 1900 Census there he is living under the same roof as his older sister, Mrs. Sarah E. Smith, with the fate of his wife Helen not clear.

Child born in Wells, Me.:

3872     i. Gladys[9] Eaton, b. 20 Oct 1884.

**2107. Elisha[8] Eaton** (Elisha[7], John[6], Elisha[5], Samuel[4], John[3-1]) was born 26 Dec 1794 in Pittfield, N.H., and was raised by his grandparents when his father died a few months after his birth, and his mother remarried and removed to Vermont. Elisha went with his grandfather's family to a new farm on the flank of Gunstock Mtn. in Gilford, N.H., in the winter of 1817-18 when he turned 23. He soon mar. **Betsey Brown** (b. 19 Nov 1799 in Gilford), on 28 Nov 1819 and they settled on the grandfather John's farm acreage in Gilford. A year or two later, Elisha took bride Betsey on a pilgrimage to Salisbury, Mass., to visit the area from which his grandfather had emigrated "up country" nearly 50 years before. (To the initial surprise of the junior author of this volume, whose line this is, the young couple were hosted in Salisbury by Samuel[5] Eaton (**#107**) on Forest Rd, rather than at the old homestead on Beach Road. In retrospect, we can see there is no surprise here. While they undoubtedly made a ritual visit to the homestead itself, it was by this time a shrinking subsistence farm, whereas host Samuel[5] was both the most prosperous Eaton "gentleman" in town and, most importantly, the uncle of young Elisha's grandfather, who no doubt helped plan the trip.) Elisha and Betsey raised their children on the Gilford farm and spent their lives there. Betsey died 7 Jul 1853. Elisha died at 74, apparently by drowning in Lake Winnipesaukee, which their mountain farm overlooked, at Alton, N.H., 14 Jun 1872.

Children born at Gilford, N.H.:

| +3873 | i. Daniel[9] Brown Eaton, b. 23 Oct 1820; mar. Susan L. Smith. |
| 3874 | ii. Sarah[9] Jane Eaton, b. 2 Feb 1823; died unm. 26 Dec 1845. |
| 3875 | iii. Miriam[9] Brown Eaton, b. 27 Jan 1825; mar. Isaiah Clough Morrill of Gilford, 27 Aug 1843. She died 23 Sep 1906. |
| 3876 | iv. Reuhamah[9] Chastina Greene Eaton, b. 17 Mar 1827; mar. |

Isaac Morrill of Gilford, 29 May 1847.  She died 24 Aug 1904.

**3877**     v. Emmeline[9] Tucker Eaton, b. 4 Aug 1829; mar. Calvin T. Rollins of Alton, N.H., 4 Jul 1857. She d. 26 Dec 1878.

**+3878**  vi. John[9] Dolby Eaton, b. 28 Jun 1831; mar. Judith P. Smith.

**3879**  vii. Mary[9] Taylor Eaton, b. 6 Jul 1833; mar. Henry J. McDuffee of Alton, N.H., 14 May 1859.

**+3880** viii. Martin[9] Van Buren Eaton, b. 22 Dec 1835; mar. Melissa.

**+3881**  ix. Joseph[9] Warren Eaton, b. 22 Apr 1840; mar. Maria Bunker.

**3882**    x. Laura[9] Ann Eaton, b. 5 Feb 1845; mar. William H. Downes of Salem, Mass, 24 Dec 1867. She died 20 Nov 1933 in Laconia, N.H.


**2109. Nathan[8] Eaton** (John[7-6], Elisha[5], Samuel[4], John[3-1]) was born 1 Jan 1803 in Pittsfield, N.H.; mar. in Nov 1827, **Mary Bowman**, born at Shapleigh, Me., 19 Dec 1802.  They res. for a while in Pittsfield, where most of their children were born; but they had removed to Concord, N.H. by 1840, then to Tilton, N.H., and to Lowell, Mass. by 1850.   By 1853 they had returned, now to Ward 6, Nashua, N.H., where Nathan is listed as a day laborer.   Nathan died 22 Oct 1865; and in 1867, widow Mary moved to Francestown, N.H., dying there at the home of her daughter, Eliza Jane, 15 Feb 1893 (Cochrane, W. and G. Wood, 1895).

Children:

**3883**    i. Mary[9] A. Eaton, b. 1828 in Pittsfield, N.H.; died 1 Apr 1853.

**3884**   ii. Frank[9] A. Eaton, b. 23 Nov 1831, Pittsfield; he removed with his mother to Francestown, 1867, a day laborer like his father. After his mother's death he was living with his sister, Eliza Jane, and apparently never married, in 1900.

**3885**  iii. John[9] W. Eaton, b. 1 Apr 1833, Pittsfield. He served in the 9th N.H. Regiment in the Civil War, and he lived with his his mother in Francestown, apparently unmar., in 1870. He died there, 26 Sep 1890.

**3886**   iv. Child[9] Eaton, b. ca. 1834, Pittsfield; died unnamed.

**3887**    v. Eliza[9] Jane Eaton, b. 3 Jul 1836, Pittsfield; mar. Joseph E. Presby of Nashua, 20 Oct 1859, and res. in Francestown.

**3888**   vi. Charles[9] Henry Eaton, b. 6 Mar 1840, Concord, N.H.; served in the 8th N.H. Regiment in the Civil War, and was a pensioner in Nashua, N.H., in the 1890s.

**3889**  vii. Lizzie[9] H. Eaton, b. 16 Nov 1842, Concord, N.H.; mar. 1st, Joseph P. Marden of Nashua, N.H., 4 Jul 1859; 2d, Benjamin Pratt of Nashua; and 3d, Charles H. Smith, also of Nashua.


**2111. Perkins[8] T. Eaton** (John[7-6], Elisha[5], Samuel[4], John[3-1]) was born 22 Dec 1806 in Pittsfield, N.H.; mar. **Phebe B. Hilton** of Maine in

1836. They settled first in Penobscot Co., Me., in the town of Orono and in Corinth Township. In 1844, however, Perkins brought his young family back to Pittsfield, N.H., to operate another farm. Perkins probably died in the 1860s.

Children:

3890    i. (Asahel) Green[9] Eaton, b. ca. 1837 in Orono, Me.; mar. Lucretia Hildred of Pittsfield, 23 Jan 1857. They res. in Pittsfield, and had one daughter. He died ca. 1879.

3891    ii. John[9] Eaton, b. 17 Sep 1840; mar. Ada Sackett of Barnstead, N.H., 1 Jan 1877. They res. in Manchester, N.H., where he ran a cigar store. He died 22 Mar 1897. They had one son, William[10] H. Eaton, b. at his grandmother's in Barnstead, 6 Nov 1877.

3892    iii. Monroe[9] Eaton, b. ca. 1843 in Orono, Me.; mar. Sarah Woods of Boston, Mass. They went west and settled on a farm in Macomb, Ill. He later brought the family back to Pittsfield, N.H. They had seven children.

3893    iv. Albert[9] Eaton, b. 1848, in Pittsfield, N.H.; mar., but who and where?, since he removed also to a farm in Macomb, Ill.

3894    v. Emma[9] Eaton, b. 1849, Pittsfield; mar. John A. Walker and res. in Pittsfield, with two sons and a daughter.

3895    vi. George[9] Eaton, b. 1851, Pittsfield, but died young.

**2116. John[8] (S.?) Eaton** (John[7-6], Elisha[5], Samuel[4], John[3-1]) was born 18 Dec 1818 in Pittsfield, N.H.; mar. **Olive True** ca. 1840, and res. on a farm in the general neighborhood of Eaton Pond near the SE corner of Pittsfield where his grandfather John[6] had first settled upon arrival from Seabrook. The deployment of this family in the 1850 Census is curious, as they seem in part "double-counted." That is, in Pittsfield there is a John Eaton age 32 with a wife Olive age 31, with two children under 10, one of whom is independently known to be theirs. In Epping, 20 miles to the southeast, we find a John Eaton age 33 (not otherwise identifiable) with a wife Olive age 31, also with two children under ten, but of different names, and ages which are perfectly complementary in timing to the two Pittsfield children, as suggested by the child roster below where we risk combining the two rosters. The Pittsfield John is listed as a horse dealer, and the Epping one as a wheelwright, two distinct but cognate trades. In any event, wife Olive died Oct 1855 at Pittsfield. John enlisted in the Civil War in 1861, and died of consumption on a ship off the Carolinas that was bringing him toward home, being buried at sea 2 Nov 1862.

Likely children (with first and third at Pittsfield, 1850, while the second and fourth are at Epping with seemingly the same parents):

3896    i. Sarah[9] A. Eaton, b. ca. 1841.

3897   ii. Francis[9] Eaton, b. ca. 1843.
3898   iii. Charles[9] F. Eaton, b. 1845; served in the Civil War from
            Pittsfield, N.H., from 14 Sep 1864 to its end. He then
            returned to res. in Pittsfield, but died there 12 Nov 1874.
3899   iv. Harriet[9] Eaton, b. 1848.


**2117. Trueworthy[8] Eaton** (John[7-6], Elisha[5], Samuel[4], John[3-1]) was
born 9 Mar 1821 in Pittsfield, N.H.; mar. **Margaret Page**. The couple
res. in Pittsfield, although "True" (as he was generally called), travelled a
good deal in his trade as a clock repair man.

Their only child, born Pittsfield:

3900       i. George[9] A. Eaton, b. 29 Sep 1847; mar. Nellie A. Meserve,
              12 Jul 1869 at Pittsfield, where they settled. Nellie died
              26 Feb 1873 after bearing their only son, Louis[10] on 30
              Jan 1873. George himself died 24 Feb 1895.


**2118. John[8] Eaton** (Joseph[7], John[6], Elisha[5], Samuel[4], John[3-1]) was
born 9 Nov 1804, prob. in the part of the Gilmanton grant that became
Gilford, N.H. in 1812. He grew up, however, at Wolfeboro and Moultonborough, N.H. as his family moved eastward along the north shore of
Lake Winnipesaukee. He mar. 1st, **Judith Caswell**, 9 Jan 1827 at Moultonborough, where the couple first resided and where all their children
were born. In the later 1840s, John moved onto the Neck (into Lake
Winnipesaukee) at Meredith, N.H. where he worked a moderate-sized
farm. Wife Judith died in the 1860s in Meredith; and John mar. 2d, **Mrs.
Dolly Johnson**, returning by himself to res. with her in Moultonborough. He was fatally injured by a cartload of hay striking against him,
and died 11 Aug 1874 in Moultonborough.

Children with Judith, all at Moultonborough, N.H.:

3901       i. Zephaniah[9] Pope Eaton, b. 9 Dec 1827; m. Hannah Almira
              Blood (b. 2 Oct 1822 in Westford, Mass.) on 15 Oct 1850.
              They continued to res. at Meredith, having three children
              there. Zephaniah died 25 Jan 1879, Meredith.
3902      ii. Andrew[9] Jackson Eaton, b. 1829; died of cancer at 8 years.
3903     iii. John[9] Mears Eaton, b. 27 May 1831; mar. Elizabeth A.
              "Lizzie" Cram, 1 Jan 1859 and res. at Meredith Neck,
              having a son and daughter there. John died 14 Nov 1910.
3904      iv. Judith[9] Ann Eaton, b. 1833; mar. Hosea D. Barney in 1855
              and died leaving two daughters, 6 Apr 1860.
3905       v. Jane[9] Wilson Eaton, b. 31 Aug 1834; died unmar. ca. 1861
              of consumption at Meredith.
3906      vi. Almira[9] Eaton, b. 13 Apr 1836; mar. Orlando Proctor in
              1856, and res. in Nashua, N.H., where he was a pattern

maker. He died of consumption in 1892. They had
three children.

**3907**   vii. Eliza[9] Ann Eaton, b. 20 Apr 1838; mar. Andrew J. Philbrick
of Manchester, N.H., and res. in Woodland, Maine.
**3908**   viii. Ella[9] Eaton, b. 1842; died 16 Sep 1845, Meredith.
**3909**   ix. Eleanor[9] Eaton, b. 1843; died 13 Sep 1857 of "consumption of blood" (?) at Newmarket, N.H.


**2125. William[8] B. Eaton** (Jonathan[7], John[6], Elisha[5], Samuel[4],
John[3-1]) was born ca. 1808 in Epsom, N.H.; mar. **Mary J. Morrill**, ca.
1833. He was a blacksmith, and during his foreshortened life, they res.
at "Meredith Bridge," now the Weirs, N.H. on Lake Winnipesaukee. William died there 30 Aug 1839.

Children at Meredith Bridge, N.H.:

**3910**   i. Ellen[9] J. Eaton, b. ca. 1835; mar. John F. Merrill. She died
at Laconia, N.H.
**3911**   ii. Sarah[9] Eaton, b. ca. 1837; mar. George A. Sanborn, 24 Nov
1860. She died at Lake Village (Lakeport?) N.H.


**2127. Abram[8] Eaton** (Jonathan[7], John[6], Elisha[5], Samuel[4], John[3-1])
was born ca. 1811 in Epsom, N.H.; mar 1st, **Asenath Parsons** (poss.
**Page**) of Kensington, N.H. on 15 May 1830. He was a wheelwright and
later, carriage-maker at Kensington. After his wife's death he mar. 2d,
**Mary Elizabeth Dodge** in the early 1870s. Abram died 6 Mar 1886 at
Kensington.

Children with Asenath at Kensington, N.H.:

**3912**   i. Hannah[9] P. Eaton, b. ca. 1831; mar. Daniel Reynolds.
**3913**   ii. Mary[9] Anne Eaton, b. ca. 1832; mar. David Brewer.
**3914**   iii. Laura[9] P. Eaton, b. ca. 1835; mar. Baxter Austin.
**3915**   iv. John[9] L. Eaton, b. ca. 1838; mar. Lois F. Bastow, 21 Sep
1862. He was a farmer at Kensington and worked in the
shoe factory. They had at least three children.
**3916**   v. Sarah[9] J. Eaton, b. ca. 1839; mar. George O. Rollins.
**3917**   vi. Abra(ha)m[9] Frank Eaton, b. ca. 1842; served in the Civil
War; mar. Hannah and res. at Lynn, Mass.
**3918**   vii. Helen[9] A. Eaton, b. ca. 1846; mar. Vernon Pevear.

Children with Mary Elizabeth at Kensington, N.H.

**3919**   viii. Samuel[9] Dodge Eaton, b. 14 Nov 1876; mar. Millie
Gilman of Rome, Me.; res. Belgrade Lakes, Me.
**3920**   ix. James[9] Perley Eaton, b. 7 Dec 1878; mar. Blanche
Higgins. He was an engineer and his wife ran a

nursing home in Salem, Mass. He died of cancer.
Apr 1946. They had no children.
**3921**   x. William[9] Eaton, b. ca. 1880; died young.
**3922**   xi. Leverett[9] Lincoln Eaton, b. 29 Jul 1882; mar. Nellie
Josephine Perley (b. Boxford, Mass.). He was an
engineer at Danvers, Mass., for over 40 years, and
the couple had four sons and a daughter.


**2129. John[8] Eaton** (Jonathan[7], John[6], Elisha[5], Samuel[4], John[3-1])
was born ca. 1814 in Epsom, N.H., and mar. a **Widow Armstrong**. He
was a railroad contractor by trade, and went west to California, where he
died.

Children:

**3923**   i. Sarah[9] Eaton, b. ? ; died young.
**3924**   ii. Raymond[9] Eaton.
**3925**   iii. Charles[9] Eaton.
**3926**   iv. Lillian[9] Eaton.


**2132. John[8] M. Eaton** (Jacob[7], John[6], Elisha[5], Samuel[4], John[3-1])
was born 29 Feb 1822 in Pittsfield, N.H., after his parents had returned
from a brief sojourn at Gilford, N.H. He mar. ca. 1840, **Julia A. Sargent**, who had been born in Loudon, N.H., 18 May 1816, to John and
Betsey (Ring) Sargent. He had a very modest farm, and depended heavily for income on shoemaking. He died 17 Mar 1886 in Pittsfield, and
Julia died the same year.

Children, all born Pittsfield, N.H.:

**3927**   i. Martha[9] A. Eaton, b. ca. 1841; mar. Charles A. Swett, a
native of Boscawen, N.H.
**3928**   ii. Julia[9] M. Eaton, b. ca. 1843; died young.
**3929**   iii. John[9] Calvin Eaton, b. 18 Aug 1845; mar, 1st, Abbie Emerson (b. 1849, Barnstead, N.H.), on 30 Jan 1867 in Pittsfield. This couple res. first in Pittsfield, where they had
two children: Amy[10] G. Eaton, b. 27 Nov 1869, who mar.
Charles Davis, a shoemaker of Epping, N.H., 1 Jan 1889
and res. in Barnstead; and Frank[10] Eaton, b. 9 Apr 1872
and also res. Barnstead. Father John was also a shoemaker, and later took the family to Somersworth, N.H. to
ply his trade. After wife Abbie's death he mar. 2d, Helen
Brackett, 18 Jul 1885, and at some time removed to Great
Falls, N.Y.
**3930**   iv. George[9] F. Eaton, b. ca. 1848; mar. Henrietta Willey, also of
Pittsfield N.H., 11 May 1873, but they had no children.
George was a shoemaker. He died, 1914.

**3931**    v. Julia[9A] M. Eaton, b. 22 Mar 1850; mar. Alanson ("Lance")
             D. Avery (born Strafford, N.H.), 1874.
**3932**    vi. Mary[9] Ellen Eaton, b. 10 Jan 1853; died 19 Jun 1853.
**3933**    vii. Charles[9] H. Eaton, b. 5 May 1855; mar. Clara Berry of
             Meredith, N.H., 12 Oct 1874 in Pittsfield. He was a shoe-
             maker, and they later resided in Lynn, Mass.
**3934**    viii. Frederick[9] B. Eaton, b. 1 Nov 1858; mar. Isabel "Belle"
             Hersom, 15 Sep 1879 in Pittsfield. He was a shoemaker,
             and died 19 Apr 1892.
**3935**    ix. Walter[9] M. Eaton, b. 23 Dec 1860; mar. 1st, Lillian Carter,
             a native of Boston, 30 Apr 1881. He was a shoemaker
             and they res. in Somersworth, N.H. He mar. 2d, Maggie
             T. Mahoney, 19 Aug 1893.
**3936**    x. Arthur[9] Thornton Eaton, b. 6 Jul 1879; died 10 Aug 1891.


**2139. John[8] L. Eaton** (Samuel[7] S., John[6], Elisha[5], Samuel[4],
John[3-1]) was born 16 Dec 1843, in Gilford, N.H.; on 5 Aug 1866 in Gilford he mar. **Amanda Charlton Emerson** (born 28 Jun 1845) of Alton,
N.H. The couple res. on a farm in Gilford Village. John L. "was engaged in agricultural pursuits all his life. In religious faith he was a Baptist; in politics a Republican" (Stearns, 1908, p. 1490). The couple was
still there in Gilford for the 1900 Census; but John L. died 30 Dec 1900.

Children in Gilford, N.H.:

**3937**    i. Arthur[9] A. Eaton, b. 28 Mar 1867; mar. Addie Hendricks,
             21 Sep 1891. They were residing in Gilford, 1900,
             unaccompanied by children.
**3938**    ii. Emma[9] B. Eaton, b. 10 Jan 1870; mar. Daniel Heath, a
             native of Haverhill, Mass., in 1888. He owned a 40-acre
             farm and developed veterinary skills to relieve animals
             from their suffering.
**3939**    iii. Mary[9] Susie Eaton, b. 20 Mar 1872 and res. in Gilford.
**3940**    iv. Samuel[9] B. Eaton, b. 14 Oct 1875; died 17 Feb 1880.
**3941**    v. (Samuel[9A]) Merton Eaton, b. 22 Oct 1882. Still at home,
             and listed as "Merton," in the 1900 Census, but later
             removed to Templeton, Mass.


**2141. Samuel[8] Eaton** (Stephen[7], Elisha[6-5], Samuel[4], John[3-1]) was
born 31 Aug 1816 in Pittsfield, N.H.; mar. **Julia Chase**, 24 Apr 1836.
He was a shoemaker and farmer, and they res. on his favorite "little
place" on the Berry Road on Catamount Mtn. in Pittsfield. He was a firm
believer in the Christian religion. He died there rather early on 6 Sep
1848. Widow Julia survived until 4 Sep 1877.

Children born at Pittsfield, N.H.:

**3942**    i. George[9] W. Eaton, b. 8 Mar 1838; when his father died early,
            George had to be put out for adoption and renamed
            "George W. McCrillis." He lived later in Knoxville, Napa
            Co., Cal., where he mar. and had at least three children.
**3943**    ii. Sarah[9] Eaton, b. 20 Jul 1839; mar. Samuel Paige of Gilman-
            ton, N.H., 1862. They res. in Lynn, Mass, without issue.
**3944**    iii. Almira[9] E. Eaton, b. 31 Mar 1841; mar. Joseph M. Cum-
            mings, also of Pittsfield, 28 Nov 1860. They res. in
            Pittsfield and had six children.
**3945**    iv. Josephine[9] Eaton, b. Jan 1843; mar. 1st. Abel Reynolds; 2d,
            Benjamin P. Sanborn. She died 9 Oct 1875, Candia, N.H.

**2143. Mark[8] Fernald Eaton** (Stephen[7], Elisha[6-5], Samuel[4], John[3-1])
was born 8 Jun 1823 in Gilford, N.H.; mar. **Eliza J. Tasker** (born 20
Aug 1823 in Barnstead, N.H.) on 23 Jan 1849 in Pittsfield. As of 1850,
Mark was residing in Pittsfield, N.H., listed as a shoemaker with a very
small farm plot to his name. After all of his children were born in
Pittsfield, with the last child given the name Horace Greeley Eaton, Mark
decided it was time to take the family westward. Family wisdom says
they settled in Genoa, Neb. However, they are not in Genoa in 1870, nor
can we locate them elsewhere at that time. In 1880, however, "Mark F."
with Eliza is a farmer on the eastern edge of Iowa, at Farmington, Cedar
Co., between Cedar Rapids and the Mississippi. Two of their three children were at that time up and out, residing independently in the Cedar
Co. area. The youngest one, Horace, then 20, is still "at home"; and he
apparently later proceeded to Genoa, Neb.; hence the family lore.

            Children, all born Pittsfield, N.H.:

**3946**    i. Frank[9] Herbert Eaton, b. 14 Jan 1851; died 1 Sep 1852.
**3947**    ii. Milton[9] Herbert Eaton, b. 3 Aug 1852; mar. Marian Rosalie
            Reed (she b. Oswego, N.Y. on 17 Jan 1855, but of New
            Liberty, Iowa at the time of marriage). He was a contrac-
            tor and they resided in Wilton, Iowa, having nine children.
**3948**    iii. Almira[9] Adelaide Eaton, b. 16 Mar 1855; mar. Oscar Shaw
            of Iowa, 8 Aug 1881, and they settled on a farm in
            Genoa, Neb., and had at least one daughter.
**3949**    iv. Horace[9] Greeley Eaton, b. 30 Jul 1859; mar. Etta M.
            Cook-Tasker (b. 17 Jun 1866 at Norwich, N.Y.), on
            28 Mar 1893 at Genoa, Neb., and they had three sons.

**2152. James[8] W. Eaton** (Reuben[7], Samuel[6], David[5], Samuel[4],
John[3-1]) was born ca. 1816 at Weare, N.H.; mar. **Mary E. Williams** (she
born 1824). They had quite a small farm in a Weare neighborhood
where several of James's uncles had adjacent lots, presumably a subdivision of grandfather Samuel[6]'s original large homestead. James is, how-

ever, only listed as a farmer. He died 5 Jul 1870; widow Mary survived until 1891, apparently living with her daughter's family.

Child at Weare:

3950    i. Lovilla[9] (or Zillah[9]) J. Eaton, b. ca. 1852; mar. her first cousin, Walter[8] S. Eaton (#2167) before the 1870 Census, where the four-person household includes the newlyweds and her parents, with Walter, as a farmer and shoemaker, adding useful land and other resources to the household.

**2155. Daniel[8A] B. Eaton** (Reuben[7], Samuel[6], David[5], Samuel[4], John[3-1]) was born 5 July 1822, Weare, N.H.; mar. **Lucretia Gould** in the mid-1840s. They res. in Weare, where Daniel was a farmer with above average acreage. He died there 7 Mar 1900; wife Lucretia died 20 Apr 1908 in Manchester, N.H. They are buried in the East Weare Cemetery.

Children at Weare:

3951    i. George[9] H. Eaton, b. ca. 1847; died 1863.
3952   ii. Thomas[9] H. Eaton, b. ca. 1856; mar. Frances I. Favor, and res. at Weare, having at least two sons and a daughter.

**2158. Pillsbury[8] R. Eaton** (Reuben[7], Samuel[6], David[5], Samuel[4], John[3-1]) was born ca. 1832 at Weare; mar. 1st, **Julia A. Felch**, ca. 1853. They res. in Weare on a medium-sized farm; and by 1870 Pillsbury added to his income by working in a cabinet shop. After bearing three children, wife Julia had died 17 May 1863 in Weare, and he mar. 2d, **Elvira J. Marshall**, on 15 Dec 1864, with whom he had three more. He was by this time a section hand on the Concord R.R. He died 21 Nov 1885; widow Elvira died 17 Nov 1893.

Children with Julia at Weare:

3953    i. Henry[9] E. Eaton, b. 25 Oct 1854; mar. Nellie M. Willard 15 Feb 1881, and res. at Sugar Hill in East Weare.
3954   ii. A. Sidney[9] Eaton, b. 7 Nov 1855; for a time he was a cabinet maker in New York, unmar. In 1900 he was living still solo in Hopkinton, N.H.
3955  iii. Catherine[9] Eaton, b. 26 May 1861; mar. Edgar C. Breed, 12 Dec 1883 and they res. on a farm in Bedford. But she died 25 Oct 1886 without issue. Her widower then mar. her cousin Nellie (#3960).

Children with Elvira at Weare:

3956   iv. Charles[9] Edwin Eaton, b. 3 Jun 1866; mar. Hattie W. Mer-

riam (b. Feb 1865). In 1900 this couple was at Weare
with two sons, and Charles's brother in the household.
**3957**    v. Archie[9] B. Eaton, b. 20 Feb 1869; educated at the Deaf &
Dumb Asylum at Hartford, Conn; he worked as a shoe-
maker, unmar. as of 1900, and res. at No. Weare.
**3958**    vi. Erminnie[9] J. Eaton, b. 26 May 1872; mar. Mason S. Colby
24 Dec 1890, who ran on a milk train from No. Weare
to Boston for D. Whitney & Son; res. Weare, no issue.


**2159. William[8] S. Eaton** (Reuben[7], Samuel[6], David[5], Samuel[4],
John[3-1]) was born ca. 1835; mar. **Eliza A. Hoyt** (b. Aug 1844) in the
mid-1850s. They res. in Weare, where he became a house painter, and
was for a time a school commissioner. At some time after 1870 they removed to neighboring Goffstown, N.H. Eliza died 19 Jan 1891; William
died 15 Apr 1906. They are bur. in East Weare.

Children:

**3959**    i. (Judith) Annie[9] Eaton, b. 15 Feb 1859; was ultimately in the
State Asylum, Concord, N.H., died unmar. 5 Dec 1898.
**3960**    ii. Nellie[9] S. Eaton, b. 21 Apr 1864; mar. Edgar C. Breed, her
cousin Catherine's (**#3955**) first husband, 3 Oct 1889, and
res. near Weare Centre on a farm.
**3961**    iii. Frank[9] Eaton, b. 3 Aug 1873. In Feb 1893 was not (yet)
mar. and working in a store at No. Weare.
**3962**    iv. Mary[9] E. Eaton, b. 6 Jan 1880; died 28 Aug 1882.


**2163. William[8A] Eaton** (Moses[7], Samuel[6], David[5], Sam'l[4], John[3-1])
was born Nov 1829 in Weare, N.H.; mar. **Celestia A. Swett** (b. Sep 1832,
Me.) on 27 Nov 1852. They res. in East Weare, where he had a farm and
was a shoemaker as well. He died there 18 Nov 1902. Widow Celestia
died 5 Oct 1917.

Children at Weare, N.H.:

**3963**    i. Frederick[9] Eaton, b. Apr 1854; still unmar. in 1900, he lived
with his mother Celestia and a niece in Weare, while father
William lived alone. Frederick worked in a sash and blind
shop.
**3964**    ii. Willie[9] Eaton, a twin b. 16 Feb 1858; mar. Melita Frazier,
Sep 1877. Was a merchant in Fitchburg, Mass; no issue.
**3965**    iii. Willis[9] Eaton, a twin b. 16 Feb 1858; died 6 Dec 1863.
**3966**    iv. Elsie[9] J. Eaton, b. 1861; died 15 Jun 1888.


**2171. Luther[8] Eaton** (Samuel[7-6], David[5], Samuel[4], John[3-1]) was
born 22 Aug 1831 in Seabrook, N.H.; mar. 1st, **Julia Ann Walton** of

Seabrook, their int. pub. 27 Jul 1851 in Seabrook. After one child from this union, Julia died 19 Jan 1857, and he mar. 2d, **Susan**[8] **Olive Eaton** (cf. **#2011**) also of Seabrook, int. 28 Dec 1859 filed in Seabrook, although the wedding was in Salisbury. He farmed a small plot of land in Seabrook, but rather early began work at the shoe factory, as did his children at early ages as well. His much later death record in Seabrook, however, lists his occupation as grocer. He died there 13 May 1908. Widow Susan died 28 Apr 1910, Salisbury.

Child with Julia in Seabrook, N.H.:

3967    i. (Julia) Climena[9] Eaton, b. 31 Aug 1854; mar. George French and res. at Salisbury. She died there 2 Jun 1942.

Children with Susan in Seabrook:

3968    ii. Helen[9] Eaton, b. 27 Jul 1862; mar. Frank A. Sanborn, 28 Aug 1884, and res. Salisbury. She died there, 20 May 1937.

3969    iii. Ada[9] P. Eaton, b. ca. 1864; mar. Hadley V. Jones. She died 28 Jun 1905.

3970    iv. Annie[9] Cora Eaton, b. ca. 10 Apr 1871; mar. Thomas E. Chase, 23 Nov 1891; died 15 May 1929, Salisbury.

3971    v. Luther[9] S. Eaton, b. 22 Feb 1874; mar. Annie Warren Hardy (b. ca. Oct 1881 to William H. and Sally A. (Eaton) Hardy) on 26 Dec 1897. They lived at the lower end of Washington St. near So. Main, and Luther was called "Old Sir" by neighboring youth. Luther died 3 Jun 1949.

**2175. William**[8] **Lucien Eaton** (William[7], Samuel[6], David[5], Samuel[4], John[3-1]) was born 11 Jun 1826 in Dexter, Me.; mar. 1st on 7 Jan 1851, **Charlotte Hare** of Lowell, Mass., at Lowell. She died early at Dexter. William then removed to San Francisco, Cal., where in due time he mar. 2d, **Isabella Franconette** of San Franciso, but born in Glasgow, Scotland. William was a refiner at the San Francisco mint.

Child, born to Charlotte in Bangor, Me.:

3972    i. William[9] Guard Eaton, b. in 1851. He removed with his father as a youngster to San Francisco, where he res. into the 1890s. He was a wool grader in that city.

**2177. (David) Walter**[8] **Eaton** (William[7], Samuel[6], David[5], Samuel[4], John[3-1]) was born 29 Dec 1830 in Dexter, Me.; mar. 1st, on 27 Oct 1853, **Betsey Shaw Hill**, b. 23 Aug 1833 in Exeter, Me. to Valentine Hill. This couple res. in Dexter and had four children before Betsey died there 9 Dec 1872. Walter mar. 2d, on 3 Sep 1874, **Adelaide Sophronia Quimby**, born 20 Feb 1856 in Cincinnati, Ohio, to the Rev. George W. Quimby, D.D. She had her only child in Dexter before the family removed to Boston, Mass., where Walter established the W. D. Eaton & Co. at #s 169 to 187 Congress St., doing an immense commission trade in domestic and foreign wools.

Children with Betsey, all born in Dexter:

3973    i. Blanche[9] Marcolla Eaton, b. 29 Jul 1854; mar. Walter Balfour Gunnison, 18 Jan 1876 in Dexter, Me. She had five Gunnison children with him, the first (1876) and third (1880) in Canton, N.Y., the second at Dexter (1877); and the last two (1886, 1890) after they had removed to Brooklyn, N.Y. where they res. at 77 Wilson St.

3974    ii. Lucien[9] Stanley Eaton, b. 15 Oct 1857; d. 17 Oct 1863.

3975    iii. Edith[9] Gertrude Eaton, b. 27 Aug 1861; mar. William Leonard Caten in Boston, Mass., 1 Dec 1886, and they settled in Dayton, Ohio, where she had two sons.

3976    iv. Mary[9] Sumner Eaton, b. 26 Jul 1864; mar. John Gurley Quimby, 19 Apr 1892 in Boston, and had one son.

Child with Adelaide, also in Dexter, Me.:

3977    v. Harriet[9] Fancher Eaton, b. 9 Aug 1876.


**2181. Perry[8] A. Eaton** (David[7], Samuel[6], David[5], Samuel[4], John[3], John[2-1]) was born 27 May 1837, Weare, N.H.; mar. **Letitia L. Williams** (b. 1839) in the later 1850s. Perry was a repairman of railroad tracks, an important specialty in this half-century, and by 1880 he had risen to the rank of "Roadmaster" for the Concord R.R., a designation he maintained for at least another twenty years. This trade made for a lot of travel, and a rather curious record of residences. The young couple settled first in Manchester, N.H., which is where his initial railroad ties began. They had removed to Keene, N.H. in connection with his job by 1870. By 1880, the family itself seemed to have returned to a base in Weare, although it is listed as the Town Alms House, which can hardly mean that the family was indigent, but was somehow involved in almshouse administration. Perry A. himself, however, is triple-listed in that Census: (1) with the family in Weare; (2) as head of a Manchester household that includes only a Mass. girl, age 32, named Emma Hawkes; and (3) also at Manchester, in what may be a lodging- or boarding-house, headed by a Harriet Hebard, age 45. In 1900, Perry and Letitia are back in Weare with their son, but Perry is also listed in that Census as a boarder at Lydia Dow's in Manchester. It helps in making sense of all this to know that this family's Weare neighborhood was about 16 miles from downtown Manchester, and unlikely to have a railroad commute linking the two.

Known children, perhaps a partial list, with birthplaces unclear, but these were all the children "at home" in 1880:

**3978**   i. Nellie[9] A. Eaton, b. 11 Jan 1864 in Walpole, N.H.; mar. C. Frank Bennett, 18 May 1880. He was a R.R. employee and they res. in Hooksett, N.H.
**3979**   ii. Clara[9] M. Eaton, b. 23 Mar 1872 in Keene, N.H.
**3980**   iii. Perry[9] A., Jr., Eaton, b. 6 Mar 1880 in Weare; he was living with his parents in Weare in 1900, and working as a farm laborer, but this was presumably a temporary adolescent occupation.

**2197. Amasa[8] Eaton** (Theophilus[7], Moses[6], Theophilus[5], Jonathan[4], John[3-1]) was born 9 Nov 1799 in Sedgwick, Me.; mar. **Roxalina** (or **Roxanna**) **Ober** of Sedgwick on 6 Sep 1823 in Sedgwick. They res. in Sedgewick, where Amasa farmed a small plot, appearing in Censuses from 1830 thru 1850. In the latter year they have two remaining children and Amasa's mother living with them. Amasa died 10 Jan 1855.

Children at Sedgwick, Me.:

**3981**   i. Nancy[9] Jane Eaton, b. 12 Jun 1824.
**3982**   ii. Susan[9] Eaton, b. 21 Apr 1826.
**3983**   iii. Jerome[9] Eaton, b. 4 Dec 1827.
**3984**   iv. Lucy[9] Ann Eaton, b. 14 Jun 1830; mar. Andrew H. Parker of Sedgwick, 22 Jan 1850. No record of issue.
**3985**   v. Hiram[9] Eaton, 7 Mar 1833; died 28 May 1837.
**3986**   vi. Lois[9] Eaton, b. 4 Sep 1835.
**3987**   vii. Hiram[9A] Eaton, b. 22 Feb 1846; mar. Harriet F. Harriman, of Brooklin, Me., 2 Apr 1869. They res. in Sedgwick and were there in 1900, with son John[10] H. born Oct 1884.

**2201. Aaron[8] Eaton** (John[7], Moses[6], Theophilus[5], Jonathan[4], John[3-1]) was born 10 Apr 1800 in Sedgwick, Me.; mar. 1st, **Eunice Neal** (possibly **Nash** instead), 26 Nov 1825 in Waldoboro, Me. They resided in Waldo thru the 1830 Census, but soon thereafter removed to nearby Belfast, Me., where he at least remains listed in Censuses through 1870, as a laborer. He mar. 2d, **Mrs. Alice Bowen**, 11 Oct 1846 in Belfast, but she does not appear with him in any of the remaining Censuses., and may have died or departed early. Aaron died 10 Mar 1878.

Children with Eunice (prob. i-iii at Waldo, Me; iv-vi at Belfast):

**3988**   i. Rebecca[9] Eaton, b. ca. 1823 (sic).
**3989**   ii. Henry[9] C. Eaton, b. ca. 1825; mar. Annie __?__. In 1850 before marriage, he was a sailor. Thereafter we cannot find him, altho his mar. was reported to be without issue.

**3990**   iii. Sarah[9] Eaton, b. 11 Oct 1829 at Waldo; mar. William D.
           Sheriffs (b. Scotland, 1812), on 10 Jun 1851. He was an
           engineer. He died in Gloucester, Mass., 22 Aug 1876.
           Widow Sarah died in East Boston, 24 Apr 1886.
**3991**   iv. Mary[9] Eaton, b. ca. 1831; mar. William Hamilton and res.
           at New York City, N.Y. She died on Long Island.
**3992**   v. Harriet[9] E. Eaton, b. ca. 1833; mar. James S. Burgin, 24
           Apr 1852. They res. Belfast, Me.
**3993**   vi. Olive[9] Jane Eaton, b. ca. 1835; never mar., res. Belfast, Me.


**2202. Joseph[8] Eaton** (John[7], Moses[6], Theophilus[5], Jonathan[4], John[3-1]) was born 19 Dec 1801 in Sedgwick, Me.; mar. **Rebecca P. Woods** of Unity, Me., 8 Oct 1828, and res. at Waldo, Me., where Joseph worked an average-sized farm. He died 20 Aug 1884; widow Rebecca died 19 Aug 1887, also at Waldo.

Children born at Waldo, Me.:

**3994**   i. Samuel[9] W. Eaton, b. 25 Jun 1830; mar. Lyceria L. French
           of Bedford, N.H., 30 Jun 1863. He was a carpenter,
           and they res. at Newport, R.I.
**3995**   ii. Benjamin[9] H. Eaton, b. 21 Sep 1831; he was a mechanic in
           in Waldo, Me., but died 10 Nov 1861.
**3996**   iii. Mary[9] Ann Eaton, b. 8 Jun 1835; mar. Richard S. Gay of
           Waldo. She died 26 May 1889.
**3997**   iv. John[9] Eaton, b. 2 Apr 1837; mar. Emeline Brier of Belfast, 4
           Sep 1859; soon thereafter he enlisted in Co. G, 6th Regt.
           of Me. Volunteers for the Civil War, and died 8 Jul 1864.
**3998**   v. George[9] W. Eaton, b. 17 Oct 1840; mar. Eliza J. Hall of
           Nobleboro, Me., 2 Sep 1865 in Waldo.
**3999**   vi. Joseph[9] H. Eaton, b. 20 Jun 1845; mar. Mrs. Emeline Brier
           Eaton, widow of his older brother John who died in the
           War, 2 Sep 1865 in Belfast, Me. He died 10 Feb 1890.
**4000**   vii. Sarah[9] E. Eaton, b. 21 Aug 1849; died 1 Mar 1850.


**2203. Pickering[8] B. Eaton** (John[7], Moses[6], Theophilus[5], Jonathan[4], John[3-1]) was born 2 Aug 1804; mar. 1st, **Barbara Marks**, 20 May 1837, and they res. on a very small farm in Sedgwick. Barbara died in Dec 1854, and Pickering mar. 2d, **Lois A. (Staples?) Closson** (born ca. 1820) of Sedgwick, on 24 Dec 1857, who brought a stepdaughter Ida Closson to the family, and then had further children with Pickering. We lack a death date for him, but he is a fixture in the Sedgwick Censuses at least thru 1870.

Children with Barbara in Sedgwick, Me.:

**4001**   i. (Sarah) Susan[9] M. Eaton, b. 15 Mar 1838.

**4002** ii. Eliza[9] J. Eaton, b. 22 Mar 1840.
**4003** iii. Maria[9] C. Eaton, b. 17 Jan 1843.
**4004** iv. Stephen[9] Marks Eaton, b. 5 Jun 1845; died 4 Sep 1865 of typhoid fever at Camp Berry, Me.
**4005** v. John[9] B. Eaton, b. 2 Mar 1849.
**4006** vi. Roselia[9] A. Eaton, b. 5 Dec 1851; mar. Daniel Hamilton of Blue Hill, Me., 23 Apr 1868.

Children with Lois in Sedgwick, Me.:

**4007** vii. Laura[9] E. Eaton, b. 16 Aug 1859; mar. John A. Grindle of Blue Hill, 3 Apr 1874.
**4008** viii. Mary[9] E. Eaton, b. 15 Feb 1862; m. Howard Cunningham.

**2205. John[8] Eaton** (John[7], Moses[6], Theophilus[5], Jonathan[4], John[3-1]) was born 16 Mar 1808 in Sedgwick, Me.; mar. **Mary K. Doten** of Frankfort, Me., (int. 3 Nov 1832), and they res. South Newburgh, Me., where he farmed a small plot. The family is listed in Censuses through 1880.

Children in South Newburgh, Me.:

**4009** i. Caroline[9] H. Eaton, b. 1835; mar. Joseph Davis.
**4010** ii. Lucinda[9] R. Eaton, b. 1837; mar. John Davis.
**4011** iii. Mary[9] H. Eaton, b. 1838; mar. Charles Abbott.
**4012** iv. Frances[9] A. Eaton, b. 1840; became the 2d wife of Joseph Davis after her sister Caroline, his wife, died.
**4013** v. Maria[9] P. Eaton, b. 1842; mar. George F. Avery; they resided in Exeter.
**4014** vi. (Harriet) Rosanna[9] (Rosella?) Eaton, b. 1848; mar. Burgess Newcomb and res. in Newburgh.

**2206. Moses[8] Eaton** (John[7], Moses[6], Theophilus[5], Jonathan[4], John[3-1]) was born 23 Apr 1810 in Sedgwick, Me. He removed to Winterport, Me., about 1830, and mar. **Abigail Lufkin**, 10 Jan 1833. They returned to Sedgwick where Moses took up a farm. Wife Abigail died 2 Jul 1853. Moses died Jun 1870.

Children in Sedgwick, Me.:

**4015** i. Mary[9] C. Eaton, b. 28 Jul 1833.
**4016** ii. Edwin[9] Horace Eaton, b. 3 Nov 1835.
**4017** iii. Sarah[9] A. Eaton, b. 24 Sep 1836.
**4018** iv. Eliza[9] Ann Eaton, b. 2 Mar 1842; mar. Benjamin R. Dyer of Brooksville, Me., int. 21 Jan 1862.
**4019** v. Lois[9] Eaton, b. 4 Mar 1846.
**4020** vi. (Alice) Abby[9] Eaton, b. 26 Apr 1848.

### #11.  Our Eatons in the Civil War

The weight of the Civil War fell on the later-borns of Generation
VIII and the earlier-borns of Generation IX Eatons in much the same
way as the Revolution had impacted on Generations V and VI nearly
a century earlier.  Because this War Between the States lay in no small
measure beyond our frame limited to Generation VIII, or to 1850,
whichever is the later, we have not invested much time in documents
surrounding individual service for this conflict.  Nonetheless, we count
some 45 of our Eatons engaged in some kind of service associated
with the Civil War.  We say "some kind of service" for several reasons.
For example, one of the 45 were sailors on Maine boats helping to
provision the Union troops in Virginia.  Another, Emmet[8] Eaton
(**#3035**) served as a Confederate soldier, despite being born in northern Vermont and growing up in northern N.Y. State.  We also count
Sidney[8] Eaton (**#2604**), who married in Dec 1861 in northern Massachusetts, but died less than 15 months later in a New Orleans hospital.
While the Civil War is not mentioned, it is hard to believe that he was
rapidly in Lousiana for some other reason.

It is almost sure that our list of 45 is a considerable undercount,
that would swell with further cases if service records were carefully examined.  An unusual number of young males of Gen. VIII disappear
from our records.  Many went west, but the Civil War is another source
of drain.

Of the 45, we know of 18 who died in connection with the War.
This need not mean "killed in action."  Two or three died in Confederate prisons; several more died, usually of typhoid fever, in encamp-
ments at points as farflung as Louisiana, Washington, D. C., Newark,
N.J., and Maine.  One died of consumption on the ship ferrying him
back to New England.  One died on return to N.H. of war wounds that
did not heal.  None of these circumstances will surprise students of
this most-lethal war.

Several of our Eatons advanced in the officer corps.  The most
dramatic case is that of Gen. John[8] Eaton (cf. **#2967**), who joined the
army as a chaplain, but was soon using other administrative skills.  But
there were at least two other Colonels (**#2971** & **#3680**) and a Captain
(**#2266**) of the USA Colored Regt.  These officers tended to be in the
oldest third of the participants, as expected.  However, the very oldest
of our Eaton soldiers was Moses[8] Eaton (**#2211**), the Brooklin, Me.
millman and farmer who, when nearly 60, left his wife and small family to go to war, dying there in 1863.

Perhaps the greatest tragedy hit the family of Jonathan[7] and wife
Judith (cf. **#998**) of Sandwich, N.H.  Four of their six sons enlisted in
the War, and two of them died in 1863 and 1864.  This loss came on
top of the death in the State Prison of their son Joshua in July, 1860,
while serving a term for a murder committed when he was fifteen.

**2207. David$^8$ Eaton** (John$^7$, Moses$^6$, Theophilus$^5$, Jonathan$^4$, John$^{3-1}$) was born 12 Nov 1812 in Sedgwick, Me.; mar. **Joanna H. Doten** in May 1839 at Frankfort, Me. They settled in Frankfort where David worked as a laborer. However, in the 1850s they acquired a small farm in Winterport, Me. near where younger brother Ebenezer lived, and were there at least through 1870.

Children born in Frankfort, Me. earlier; Winterport, Me. later:

4021    i. Thomas$^9$ D. Eaton, b. Jun 1840; prob. mar. 1st, Florence; later, ca. 1867, mar. Almena D. __?__. They resided at Winterport where Thomas was a ferryman, 1900.
4022    ii. Lydia$^9$ Augusta W. Eaton, b. 1842.
4023    iii. Clara$^9$ J. Eaton, b. 1846.
4024    iv. George$^9$ W. K. Eaton, b. 1847.
4025    v. David$^9$ Eaton, b. 1849.
4026    vi. Emma$^9$ Eaton, b. 1854.
4027    vii. Benjamin$^9$ F. Eaton, b. Jun 1859; mar. Ellen A. __?__. He was a sailor as of 1900; they had no children.


**2208. Ebenezer$^8$ J. Eaton** (John$^7$, Moses$^6$, Theophilus$^5$, Jonathan$^4$, John$^{3-1}$) was born 2 May 1816 in Sedgwick, Me.; mar. **Deborah R. Doten** ca. 1840, and resided first at Frankfort, Me., where he worked as a stevedore in 1850; and later moved on to Winterport, Me., where as of 1870 and with wife and an empty nest, he was farming a small plot near his brother David, above.

Children, perhaps partial, and only prob. born Frankfort, Me.:

4028    i. Laurianna$^9$ Eaton, b. ca. 1842.
4029    ii. James$^9$ A. Eaton, b. ca. 1845.


**2210. Amaziah$^8$ Eaton** (Benjamin$^7$, Moses$^6$, Theophilus$^5$, Jonathan$^4$, John$^{3-1}$) was born 16 Oct 1801 in Sedgwick, Me.; was commonly called "Amsie." He mar. **Roxanna "Roxie" Ober** (b. 1801), and they settled on a rather small farm in Sedgwick, where Amaziah was a mariner. He apparently died in the 1850s, perhaps lost at sea, for in 1860 Roxanna lives with her adolescent son Hiram.

Children born in Sedgwick (perhaps partial if there were early deaths):

4030    i. Lois$^9$ Eaton, b. ca. 1835.
4031    ii. Hiram$^9$ A. Eaton, b. Feb 1846; mar. Hannah F. and had at least one son, John$^{10}$ H., b. Sep 1886 (1900 Census).

**2211. Moses⁸ Eaton** (Benjamin⁷, Moses⁶, Theophilus⁵, Jonathan⁴, John³⁻¹) was born 11 Sep 1803 in Sedgwick, Me.; mar. **Hannah⁷ Webb Eaton (#969)**, and resided in Brooklin, Me., flanked by his brothers Amaziah and Ezra, where Moses was a millman but also ran a farm of some size. Rather late in life Moses joined the army in the Civil War. He died with the army on 1 Aug 1863. Widow Hannah died 9 Feb 1882.

Children:

4032     i. (Charles) Blanford⁹ Eaton, b. 6 Aug 1835 in Sedgwick; mar. 1st, Susan M. Friend of Sedgwick, 9 Sep 1857. No issue.
4033     ii. Elizabeth⁹ Eaton, b. 1852-53.

**2215. Ezra⁸ D. Eaton** (Benjamin⁷, Moses⁶, Theophilus⁵, Jonathan⁴, John³⁻¹) was born 28 Oct 1809; mar. **Lovinia Bakeman** of Brooksville, Me., 15 Nov 1843 and resided in Brooklin, Me. He was a sea captain, but also owned both a sawmill and a grist mill. He died 16 Feb 1884.

Children b. in Brooklin, Me.:

4034     i. Albert⁹ Gallatin Eaton, b. 13 Dec 1844; mar. Medora Frances Herrick (she b. 5 Oct 1846), also of Brooklin, 3 Jan 1870. They res. Brooklin where he was a Master Mariner, and they had three children.
4035     ii. Alice⁹ Augusta Eaton, b. 5 May 1847; died in Brooklin, 22 Apr 1882.
4036     iii. Annie⁹ Frank Eaton, b. 7 Jun 1850; res. in Boston, Mass.
4037     iv. Sarah⁹ May Eaton, b. 13 Feb 1853; res. in Portland, Me.
4038     v. Celia⁹ Smith Eaton, b. 7 Jun 1857; died in Brooklin, Me., 22 Aug 1860.
4039     vi. Celia⁹ Lovinia Eaton, b. 19 Apr 1861; died in Brooklin, Me., 23 May 1861.

**2219. Richard⁸ Eaton** (Moses⁷⁻⁶, Theophilus⁵, Jonathan⁴, John³⁻¹) was born 15 Aug 1812 in Sedgwick, Me.; mar. **Joanna Grant**, 23 Dec 1840. They res. in Sedgwick briefly, but then established themselves in Brooklin, where he was a sailor.

Children in Brooklin, Me.:

4040     i. Mary⁹ E. Eaton, b. 22 Oct 1841; died ca. 1869.
4041     ii. Prentiss⁹ C. Eaton, b. 20 Nov 1843; died unmar.
4042     iii. Elsie⁹ M. Eaton, b. 25 Sep 1845.
4043     iv. Elizabeth⁹ L. Eaton, b. 25 Jul 1847.

**4044**    v. Emily[9] F. Eaton, b. 17 Oct 1851.
**4045**    vi. Helen[9] A. Eaton, b. 4 Aug 1853.
**4046**    vii. Edith[9] A. Eaton, b. ca. 1856; died before 1870.
**4047**    viii. George[9] R. Eaton, b. ca. 1858.


**2222. Jesse[8] Thomas Eaton** (Moses[7-6], Theophilus[5], Jonathan[4], John[3-1]) was born 3 Nov 1819 in Sedgwick, Me.; mar. **Susan M. Grant**, 9 Oct 1844. They res. in Brooklin, Me., near his brothers, and farmed a modest plot there. They are present there at least thru 1870, but prob. Jesse died in the 1870s.

Children all born in Brooklin:

**4048**    i. Richard[9] B. Eaton, b. ca. 1845.
**4049**    ii. Susan[9] R. Eaton, b. ca. 1848.
**4050**    iii. William[9] Eaton, b. Oct 1850; mar. Martha A. Hutchins of
         Sedgwick (b. Mar 1849), on 20 Oct 1880. They were
         living with three sons in the household in 1900, Brooklin.
**4051**    iv. Anna[9] Eaton, b. ca. 1856.


**2225. Theophilus[8] Eaton** (Jonathan[7], Moses[6], Theophilus[5], Jonathan[4], John[3-1]) was born 23 Mar 1812 in Sedgwick, Me.; mar. **Mrs. Betsey Kempton** (b. 5 Sep 1810) on 19 Jan 1837. In 1850, this couple res. on Deer Isle, where Theophilus was a sailor and three of Betsey's Kempton children (b. 1832, '34 and '38) were living with them. Later he became a "sea captain of Searsport" (cf. Black, 1960, p. 87, for lists of the many schooner and barks that sailed under his commission). He died 14 Sep 1869 at Rio de Janeiro, Brazil, on his Bark <u>Robert Porter</u> on a passage from Baltimore, Md. to Sitka, Alaska. Widow Betsey died 28 Nov 1889.

Child, prob. born on Deer Isle:

**4052**    i. Joseph[9] Eaton, b. 8 Dec 1847; prob. died before 1850.


**2228. Hezekiah[8] Dodge Eaton** (Jonathan[7], Moses[6], Theophilus[5], Jonathan[4], John[3-1]) was born 11 Jan 1817 in Sedgwick, Me.; mar. 1st, **Statira Dutch**, 10 Feb 1838 in Belfast, Me. This couple removed early to a farm in the northern interior of Maine, at Sebec, Piscataquis Co., where they appear in 1840 and 1850. By 1860 Hezekiah has mar. 2d, **Hannah P. __?__**, and they are at nearby Foxcroft, Me. Then in 1870 he is farming in Charleston, not greatly removed from the earlier stops, but over the line into Penobscot Co. His stated estate grew astonishingly at each new stop, so that it was fifteenfold larger in 1870 than in 1850.

Children (all but the last few born at Sebec, Me.):

**4053**   i. Adelia[9] J. Eaton, b. ca. 1839.
**4054**   ii. Thomas[9] Eaton, b. ca. 1841.
**4055**   iii. Elmira[9] Eaton, b. ca. 1843.
**4056**   iv. Charles[9] Eaton, b. ca. 1844.
**4057**   v. Harriet[9] Eaton, b. ca. 1847.
**4058**   vi. George[9] Eaton, b. ca. 1851.
**4059**   vii. Flora[9] Eaton, b. ca. 1854.
**4060**   viii. Willard[9] R. Eaton, b. ca. 1858.

**2232. Oliver[8] Eaton** (*Jeremiah[7], Jonathan[6]*, Theophilus[5], Jonathan[4], John[3-1]) was born 15 Mar 1806 in Blue Hill, Me.; mar.1st, **Dorcas Finny** (b. 1 Apr 1800), 19 Feb 1829. They res. in Blue Hill, and she died 16 Feb 1834. Oliver mar. 2d, **Phebe M. Bartlett**, and had most of his children with her. Oliver was a farmer of average prosperity. Phebe died 24 Sep 1872, and Oliver died in the 1870s as well.

Children with Dorcas in Blue Hill, Me.:

**4061**   i. Jeremiah[9] Eaton, b. 25 Nov 1829; mar. Sarah Elizabeth Friend 1 Sep 1853 and lived on a farm in Blue Hill, where they had six children: Ida[10] Frances Eaton, b. 27 Jan 1854, who mar. George Cushing and res. in Bar Harbor, Me.; Roswell[10] Brooks Eaton, b. 26 Jul 1856; Henry[10] Willis Eaton, b. 19 Jul 1858, and mar. Cora A. Friend, 1884; Medbury[10] A. Eaton, b. 5 Apr 1861, and mar. Fanny Henderson, Dec 1882; Dorcas[10] M. Eaton, b. 23 Aug 1869 and died Aug 1874; Ulysses[10] S. Eaton, b. Dec 1872, died young.
**4062**   ii. Abner[9] Williams Eaton, b. 12 Sep 1833; died in Mar 1834.

Children with Phebe in Blue Hill, Me.:

**4063**   iii. Clarissa[9] Elizabeth Eaton, b. 26 Dec 1837.
**4064**   iv. Augustine[9] W. Eaton, mar. Sarah C. Pomeroy, 21 Dec 1864 at Tremont, Me. He was a carpenter and they res. in Blue Hill, having four children: Carrie[10] P. Eaton, b. 23 Mar 1866; Alice[10] Ursula Eaton, b. 25 Apr 1868; William[10] Preston Eaton, b. 13 Mar 1871; Georgia[10] Belle Eaton, b. 16 Jul 1881.
**4065**   v. Avery[9] W. Eaton, b. 4 Feb 1845; mar. Vianna I. Gatcomb on 22 Jun 1867 and res. in Parkville, Mo. He was a box manufacturer at 255 James St., Kansas City, Kans. in 1884. Five children: Fred[10] S. Eaton, b. Cambridge, Mass., 15 Dec 1869; George[10] A. Eaton, b. 1 May 1873, Cambridge, Mass.; Maude[10] M. Eaton, b. 24 Jul 1876 in Newton, Mass.; Mildred[10] Eaton, b. 14 Jun 1879 in Kinsley, Kans.; Annie[10] Eaton, b. 16 Oct 1882, Parkville, Mo.
**4066**   vi. William[9] M. Eaton, b. 26 May 1847; mar. Adelaide H.

Reynolds (b. Independence, N.Y.) on 9 Oct 1870 and resided in Ellisburg, Penn., where he was a contractor and builder in general merchandise. They had four children born in Allegany, Pa.: George[10] K. Eaton, b. 5 Feb 1873; Clarence[10] Eaton, b. 5 Dec 1876; Maud[10] Eaton, b. 23 Aug 1878; and William[10] Eaton, b. 24 1880.

**4067** vii. Oliver[9] Nelson Eaton, b. 18 Nov 1849.
**4068** viii. Francis[9] Marion Eaton, b. 10 Jan 1856.

**2234. Abner[8] Eaton** (*Jeremiah[7], Jonathan[6]*, Theophilus[5], Jonathan[4], John[3-1]) was born 15 May 1810 in Blue Hill, Me.; mar. 1st, **Isabel Wilson** (born 25 Dec 1814), on 27 Nov 1834. But she died rapidly, on 27 Dec 1835. Abner mar. 2d, **Martha Friend** (b. 1824), and they continued to reside at Blue Hill and had their children there. Abner was farming his father's homestead by 1860 if not sooner.

Children with Martha at Blue Hill:

**4069** i. Adelia[9] Eaton, b. 25 Jun 1842.
**4070** ii. Adelma[9] Eaton, b. 8 Apr 1846.
**4071** iii. Irena[9] Eaton, b. 17 Sep 1850.
**4072** iv. Malonet[9] (?: female) Eaton, b. ca. 1853.
**4073** v. Orlando[9] Eaton, b. Apr 1855; died young.
**4074** vi. Orlando[9A] Eaton, b. 30 Apr 1861.

**2244. Amos[8] Eaton** (Amos[7], Ebenezer[6], Theophilus[5], Jonathan[4], John[3-1]) was born 21 Mar 1809 in Sedgwick, Me.; mar. **Joanna Norris Burnham** of Tremont, Me. in 1832. This couple settled in Tremont (on Mt. Desert Island), where Amos achieved the status of master mariner at an early age. However, he drowned in trying to save his crew in 1838. Widow Joanna died 5 Jul 1873 at Tremont.

Children born in Tremont, Me.:

**4075** i. Ebenezer[9] M. E. Eaton, b. 8 Oct 1832; died as infant.
**4076** ii. Eben[9] Webster Eaton, b. 1834; he settled in Eureka, Cal., and engaged in speculation. He d. unmar. in Cal., 1878.
**4077** iii. Calvin[9] Judson Eaton, b. in 1834; he settled with his brother in Eureka, Cal., for speculation. He was mar. twice, having one son and one daughter, both dying young. He was still living, 1893.
**4078** iv. Harriet[9] Elizabeth Eaton, b. 24 Sep 1839; mar. Benjamin J. Dodge of Brooksville, Me., 15 Apr 1856 and res. in Tremont. He was a master mariner who died 19 Feb 1867 in Tremont. His widow Harriet then removed to Boston, Mass. to further the education of her son and two

daughters.

**2246. Herrick[8] Munson Eaton** (Amos[7], Ebenezer[6], Theophilus[5], Jonathan[4], John[3-1]) was born 4 Sep 1813 in Sedgwick, Me.; mar. **Joann Lankester Hopkins**, ca. 1836. They settled first with several of his siblings in Tremont (Mount Desert Island), Me. Most of his life was spent in Maine, teaching and preaching for the Methodist Episcopal denomination. Among these posts he was at Cherryfield, Washington Co., in 1840; and Trenton and Readfield, Kennebec Co. in the period up through 1850. He later labored in both Mass. and N.H., especially in Walpole, N.H. He was a strong preacher and an earnest defender of the great moral reforms of the times. He apparently left the ministry, since it is clearly he and his family at Norridgewock, Somerset Co., Me. in 1870 where he describes his occupation as a "travelling merchant." In these latter years he also was a leader in establishing and developing the Eaton Family Association which was active in the closing decades of the 18th century.

Children:

4079    i. Hamlin[9] Fairfield Eaton, b. 12 Aug 1838 in Trenton, Me.; mar. 1st, Lizzie Gardner, 4 May 1860; and 2d, Elizabeth "Lizzie" Sylvester Wheeler, also at Norridgewock, Me. He was principal of schools in Norridgewock as of 1870.

4080    ii. Amos[9] Herrick Eaton, b. 12 Jul 1843 in Trenton, Me.; mar. Alice Currier, Apr 1867, in Readfield, Me.

4081    iii. Russell[9] Williams Eaton, b. 24 Nov 1855 in ? ; mar. Grace Crosby, Sep 1882.


**2259. Moses[8] Favor Eaton** (John[7] G., Joseph[6] H., Ezekiel[5], Jonathan[4], John[3-1]) was born 19 Nov 1812 in Bennington, N.H.; mar. **Lydia Chipman Stimson Doane** of Eastham (Cape Cod), Mass., ca. 1844. We cannot find this couple in 1850, but apparently they resided in Mass., since Moses enlisted in the 50th Regt. of Mass. Volunteers early in the Civil War. He died in the winter of 1862 at the Quarantine below New Orleans.

Children (birthplaces usually unclear):

4082    i. Girl[9] Eaton, b. 1846; died unnamed.

4083    ii. Abbie[9] Elenor Eaton, b. 25 Jun 1848; mar. Alfred James Oliver, 19 Mar 1865 and had six children.

4084    iii. Arthur[9] Knowles, b. 29 May 1850; died 22 Jun 1860.

4085    iv. John[9] Henry Eaton, b. 25 Sep 1852 in Reading, Mass; mar. Clara A. Swain of Reading, and res. first at Reading. He was first a house carpenter, but after 1876 a "pyrotechnist." They res. for a while in Eastham, Mass., but re-

turned to Reading, 1879. Wife Clara died 23 May 1894.
4086      v. Moses[9] Willie Eaton, b. 27 Oct 1857; died Jul 1882.


**2260. John[8] George Eaton** (John[7] G., Joseph[6] H., Ezekiel[5], Jonathan[4], John[3-1]) was born 25 Dec 1814 in Bennington, N.H.; mar. **Martha Bullard** ca. 1835 and they res. for a while in New Boston, N.H., but soon joined the rural populations flocking to Manchester, N.H. with its great new mills. At first (i.e., as of 1850) he kept a stable in that town, but soon kept a hotel. Before 1860 he took the family west to join his brother Joseph at Maine Prairie, Stearns Co., Minn. (near St. Cloud).

Children:

4087      i.   George[9] Albert Eaton, b. 7 Sep 1841 in New Boston, N.H.;
               mar. Maria Roward Tyler at Plainfield, N.J. 30 Apr 1878.
               He was a jeweller at 12 Maiden Lane in New York City.
               They had no issue.
4088      ii.  Harry[9] Eaton. b. 20 Aug 1852 in Manchester, N.H. and
               resided in that city unmarried.


**2261. Joseph[8] Eaton** (John[7] G., Joseph[6], Ezekiel[5], Jonathan[4], John[3-1]) was born 16 Nov 1816 in Bennington, N.H.; mar. on 27 Jan 1848, **Rebekah Martin** (b. 10 Jul 1819 in Francestown, N.H.). They settled on a farm in Bennington, but as of 1850 he was working at a sawmill in Rindge, N.H. Then they returned to Bennington until the fall of 1858, when he left the family in N.H. and established a home for them in Maine Prairie, Stearns Co., Minn. (near St. Cloud). Wife Rebekah brought the rest of the family westward in the spring of 1859. For a few years hardships and dangers encompassed then. The Sioux Indians terrified and oppressed them, especially during the "Minnesota Massacre" of 1861. However, they escaped death, and after peace was restored, Joseph took 160 acres of land under the homestead law in Maine Prairie where he saw his children reach adulthood. He died there 19 Jun 1887; widow Rebekah removed to live with her daughter Mary[9] Josephine in Jamieson, Spokane Co., Washington.

Children:

4089      i.   Martin[9] Joseph Eaton, b. 1 Feb 1850 in Rindge, N.H.; died
               16 Mar 1853 in Bennington, N.H.
4090      ii.  Lydia[9] Rebekah Eaton, b. 28 Apr 1853 in Greenfield, N.H.;
               mar. on 29 Dec 1872 Napoleon B. Adley (b. Waterford,
               Me. 18 Jan 1841) in Maine Prairie, Minn. He was a
               dairyman in Melrose, Minn., and they had six children.
               Later on the family removed to Jamieson, Wash.
4091      iii. Orrin[9] Monroe Eaton, b. 23 Jun 1855 in Bennington, N.H.;
               mar. Emma L. Pike of Iowa, 16 Mar 1884.

**4092**    iv. Mary[9] Josephine Eaton, b. 1 Oct 1857 in Bennington, N.H.;
            mar. on 16 Dec 1885, Edward Fletcher of Ohio (he born
            20 Jan 1856). They settled first in Keystone, Dakota Ter-
            ritory, where they had one daughter. Later they moved
            to join with her sister's Adley family in Jamieson, Wash.
**4093**    v. Elmer[9] Martin Eaton, b. 20 Aug 1861 in Illinois, and was
            brought onward by his migrating family to Maine Prairie,
            Minn.; mar. Emma E. Swisher, also an Illinois native, Oct.
            1884, and farmed and raised stock in Maine Prairie.

**2266. Nathaniel[8] Eaton** (Nathaniel[7], Joseph[6], Ezekiel[5], Jonathan[4],
John[3-1]) born 24 Jun 1824 in Bennington, N.H.; mar. **Clara Ann Howe**
(born Mar 1820), on 16 Sep 1846. They soon removed to Nashua, N.H.,
where he was a stone mason in the Censuses 1850-70. In the Civil War
Nathaniel joined the USA Colored Regiment on 4 Mar 1864 as a 2d
Lieutenant, and was promoted to 1st Lt. that fall. Early in the Autumn of
1865 he was promoted to the rank of Captain. During the last two
months of his service he had command of Fort Fisher. He was mustered
out 4 Dec 1865, and later became a pensioner. Both Nathaniel and Clara
were still living in Nashua in 1900.

Children, all born in Nashua, N.H, save perhaps the eldest:

**4094**    i. (Orrin) Lorenzo[9] Eaton, b. 6 Jun 1847; mar. Ellen M. Gibbs,
            1870, and res. Nashua. He was a stone cutter.
**4095**    ii. John[9] Eaton, b. ca. 1852; a locksmith in 1870; mar. Laomi
            Pelkey, altho he lived with his parents in 1900.
**4096**    iii. William[9] "Willie" Eaton, b. 15 Dec 1853; an office clerk in
            1870, he mar. Arvilla Connor of Beetman, N.Y., 7 Mar
            1873, at Nashua. Overseer of a weaving room, Nashua.
**4097**    iv. Clara[9] "Carrie" Eaton, b. 23 Jun 1856; mar. George P. Gard-
            ner, a bobbin-maker, and res. in Nashua.
**4098**    v. Jennie[9] R. Eaton, b. 27 Oct 1860; mar. Charles W. Hebert,
            a machinist, and res. in Nashua.

**2267. Amos[8] W. Eaton** (Nathaniel[7], Joseph[6] H., Ezekiel[5], Jonathan[4], John[3-1]) was born 30 Aug 1826 in Bennington, N.H.; mar. **Apphia
J. Martin** (born 17 Feb 1834), 30 Oct 1857. They settled first in the
next township south, or Greenfield, N.H., where he was a shoemaker.
They later (by 1870) returned to Bennington, where Amos mainly
farmed. Amos died there 7 Mar 1898; widow Apphia died there 16 Mar
1914.

Children (early at Greenfield, N.H.; later at Bennington, N.H.):

**4099**    i. Herbert[9] A. Eaton, b. 27 Oct 1858; living with widowed
            mother and sister Ellen in Bennington, 1900. He died

20 Mar 1926, and is bur. with parents, Bennington, N.H.; presumably never married.

**4100**   ii. Mary[9] J. Eaton, b. 21 Mar 1861; died 14 Jun 1866.

**4101**   iii. George[9] Eaton, b. 21 Feb 1864; died 10 Jun 1866.

**4102**   iv. Ellen[9] C. Eaton, b. 2 Jul 1867; in 1900 was living with mother and elder brother in Bennington, age 33. May have later mar. a George M. Brown.

**4103**   v. Mary[9A] E. Eaton, b. ca. Nov 1869; died young.

**4104**   vi. Lizzie[9] M. Eaton, b. 28 Sep 1870.

**4105**   vii. John[9] A. Eaton, b. 14 Oct 1874.

**4106**   viii. Fred[9] L. Eaton, b. 2 Jul 1877

**4107**   ix. Son[9] Eaton, b. 14 Oct 1883; not named.

**2272. John[8] George Eaton** (Robert[7] W., Joseph[6] H., Ezekiel[5], Jonathan[4], John[3-1]) was born 18 Apr 1845 in Providence, Saratoga Co., N.Y.; mar. on 25 Sep 1869 **Philena Hemstreet** (born 25 Nov 1843 in Esperance, Schoharie Co., N.Y.). They resided in Gloversville (or nearby Kingsboro Twp.), Fulton Co., N. Y., where he was a sawyer in a sawmill.

Children, all listed as born in Gloversville, N.Y.:

**4108**   i. Flora[9] Margaret Eaton, b. 13 Oct 1872; in her early years at least she worked in the leading Gloversville industry of glovemaking.

**4109**   ii. Frances[9] "Fanny" Wilhelmina Eaton, b. 1 July 1877.

**4110**   iii. Bertha[9] Eaton, b. 18 Apr 1880.

**2279. George[8] Washington Eaton** (Joshua[7], James[6], Ezekiel[5], Jonathan[4], John[3-1]) was born 1 Oct 1813 in Sandown, N.H.; mar. 1st, **Mary Pevear**. This marriage was apparently without issue. George W. then mar. on 31 Mar 1844, **Sarah W. Moore** (b. ca. 1818) of Manchester, N.H. They settled first in Manchester, where George W. is listed as a farmer with substantial real estate in 1850. Allegedly they left Manchester for New Bedford, Mass.; but by 1860 they are in Ward #4, Lawrence, Mass., and in 1870 they are in Ward #5 in Lowell, Mass. He was a currier by trade in both the latter cities.

Children with Sarah in Manchester, N.H.:

**4111**   i. Willis[9] G. Eaton, b. 7 June 1845; died in Lowell, Mass., where he was a currier, on 23 Oct 1876, unmarried.

**4112**   ii. Helen[9] C. Eaton, b. 14 Mar 1848; res. New Bedford, Mass.

**2281. Harrison[8] Eaton** (Joshua[7], James[6], Ezekiel[5], Jonathan[4], John[3-1]) was born 29 Dec 1818 in Sandown, N.H.; he mar. in Jul 1844, **Martha Jane Washington Johnson**, born 12 May 1823 in Medford,

Mass. After an interval in Derry, N.H., the couple settled in Haverhill,
Mass., where Harrison was a farmer and prosperous nursery man. Before
1870 he had moved back to a farm in Sandown, N.H., his birthplace.

Children:

4113    i. Charles[9] Herbert Eaton, b. 14 Oct 1846 in Derry, N.H.; mar.
        Josephine Christy Boyd of Nashua, 25 Apr 1868. He was
        a shoe manufacturer res. in Haverhill, Mass., and the main
        source of our information about Ezekiel[5]'s descendants.
4114   ii. Byron[9] Forest Eaton, b. 5 Jul 1857 in Haverhill, Mass. He
        was a shoe manufacturer there, and mar. Annie B. Floyd
        of Boston, 1887, and had two daughters.


**2282. William[8] Henry Eaton** (Richard[7], Joseph[6-5A], Jonathan[4],
John[3-1]) was born 4 Oct 1830 in Wolfeboro, N.H.; mar. **Mary Emily
Treworgy** of Ellsworth, Me. in 1860 in Roxbury, Mass. They settled in
the Boston area, where he prematurely died of typhoid fever in 1875, at
South Boston.

Children, prob. at So. Boston:

4115    i. William[9] Perley Eaton, b. 1861; went west in 1880.
4116   ii. Edward[9] Eaton, b. 1865; died in 1867.


**2286. Richard[8] Eaton** (Richard[7], Joseph[6], Joseph[5A], Jonathan[4],
John[3-1]) was born 17 Aug 1837 in West Cambridge, Mass.; mar. 1st, **Alice
Raymond**, 1864, in Abington, Mass., but she died in 1872. He mar. 2d,
**Lizzie Emma Harris** of Lunenburg, Mass., 16 Oct 1884.

Child with Lizzie:

4117    i. Mabel[9] Frances Eaton, b. 30 Apr 1888.


**2290. Samuel[8] S. Eaton** (Chandler[7], Joseph[6-5A], Jonathan[4], John[3-1])
was born 25 Jul 1836 in Wolfeboro, N.H.; mar. **Mary E. __?__** ca.
1855. He was a farmer, and they res. in Wolfeboro thru 1860. By 1870
they were working a farm in Brookfield, N.H., instead, although since
Brookfield was across the east line of Wolfeboro township, they may
only have moved a very short distance. Samuel enlisted in the Civil War,
where he served in Co. K of the 12th Infantry with his brother. Samuel
and Mary were still in Brookfield with daughter "Lena" in the household
in 1900.

Children: earlier born Wolfeboro, N.H.: later ones in Brookfield.

**4118**    i. Albert[9] F. Eaton, b. Mar 1856; mar. Betty E. __?__, and in
1900 res. with her in Milton, Strafford Co., N.H.
**4119**    ii. Mary[9] E. Eaton, b. 1858; died before 1870.
**4120**    iii. Clare[9] E. Eaton, b. ca. Oct 1859; worked in a tailor shop
in early adulthood.
**4121**    iv. Samantha[9] B. Eaton, b. 1862.
**4122**    v. Sarah[9] M. Eaton, b. 1864.
**4123**    vi. Abby[9] M. Eaton, b. 1867.
**4124**    vii. Mary[9A] J. Eaton, b. late 1870.
**4125**    viii. Ida[9] B. Eaton, b. 1872.
**4126**    ix. Ann[9] E. Eaton, b. 1875.
**4127**    x. Silena[9] "Lena" Eaton, b. Mar 1878; mar. _?_ Perry, ca.
1896 and had two children before 1900, when she
was living in her parents' household in Brookfield.

**2293. Abial[8] Chandler Eaton** (Chandler[7], Joseph[6-5A], Jonathan[4], John[3-1]) was born 23 May 1842 in Wolfeboro, N.H. He served in Co. K of the 12th Infantry with his brother Samuel during the Civil War, and was wounded in June 1864. About 1867 he mar. **Sarah Ann Huggins** (born Jan 1834). In 1870 this couple res. under the roof of Abial's parents in Brookfield, N.H. Abial's war wounds continued to haunt him, however, and we find him next in 1880 in Concord, at the State Insane Asylum there. He died 10 Jun 1886 and was buried in Wolfeboro.

Only child:

**4128**    i. Almon[9] Wyatt Eaton, b. 7 Sep 1869; mar. Clara Jones (born
May 1869) of Wolfeboro, daughter of William H. Jones.
Almon became a general merchant in Wolfeboro, and a
more detailed notice is provided for him in *Representative Citizens* (1902).

**2294. John[8] C. Eaton** (Chandler[7], Joseph[6-5A], Jonathan[4], John[3-1]) was born 1 May 1847 in Wolfeboro, N.H.; mar. **Lois H. Martin** (born 6 Jan 1846) and settled in Brookfield, N.H., where John was a farmer. He died 12 Dec 1926 and was buried in Wolfeboro.

Only known child:

**4129**    i. Martin[9] H. Eaton, b. 20 Dec 1878; mar. Florence Elkins (she
born 6 Jan 1881 and died 29 Jan 1965). Martin died 11
Sep 1961.

**2306. Grover[8] Daniel Eaton** (Daniel[7], Joseph[6], Jonathan[5-4], John[3-1]) was born 9 Apr 1852 in Sargentville, Me.; on 28 Nov 1877 he mar. 1st, **Louisa Martha Eaton** (#2300, born 22 Dec 1855 at Sargentville). They resided in Sargentville where he was a farmer, but for some time also had charge of the ferry from Sargentville across the Reach to Deer Isle. He was gifted at "laying up money" and his household prospered. Wife Louisa died 25 Mar 1882, leaving him with one daughter. He remarried but we lack details.

Child born to Louisa in Sargentville:

4130    i. Edith[9] G. Eaton, b. 5 Sep 1880.


**2311. Charles[8] Fremont Eaton** (Daniel[7A] T., Jonathan[6-4], John[3-1]) was born 20 Oct 1856 on Deer Isle, Me.; mar. **Annie J. Johnson** (also of Deer Isle and born to Prescott and Hannah Johnson, 1 Oct 1859), on 5 Feb 1879 at Deer Isle. Charles was a farmer and they lived on the North Deer Isle Road above Carman's Rock. He was a devoted Christian and a deacon of the 2d Congregational Church, as well as a Granger and a member of the Masons. He died Aug 1925. His widow Annie survived him for some years, spending winters with their daughter Josephine in Bangor, Me. (Noyes, 1942).

Children on Deer Isle:

4131    i. Prescott[9] Johnson Eaton, b. 8 Aug 1881; mar. Ethel Small. He clerked for many years in the Johnson store at Sunset, Deer Isle, and bought the business after the owner died. They had five children (cf. Noyes, 1942).
4132    ii. Mary[9] Emma Eaton, b. 8 Nov 1883; mar. Ernest Foster.
4133    iii. Daniel[9] Torrey Eaton, b. 28 May 1886; he removed to Portland, Ore., to be a contractor and builder there, and mar. Huldah Nordstrom of Portland, Ore., 5 May 1920.
4134    iv. Josephine[9] Eaton, b. ? ; mar. Ralph Avery of Bangor, Me., where they resided.


**2317. John[8] Eaton** (Jonathan[7], John[6], Jonathan[5-4], John[3-1]) was born 28 Apr 1828 on Deer Isle, Me.; mar. on 8 Oct 1853 his cousin **Caroline Matilda Perkins**, daughter of his father's sister Olivia, born in Boston, Mass., 6 Feb 1831. John worked for about 15 years as a sea captain out of Boston, although the family resided in this period in Brooklin, Me. When age forced him to give this up in 1869, he bought a farm in Sedgwick and they lived there for the rest of their lives, with John dying about 1920 and widow Caroline dying about 1925.

Children (i-iv born in Brooklin, Me; v-viii born in Sedgwick):

4135    i. Francis[9] Wales Eaton, b. 30 Sep 1854; mar. Harriet "Hattie" Maria Billings (she b. 8 Aug 1861), 20 Dec 1878.
4136    ii. Otis[9] Redman Eaton, b. 10 Nov 1857; died 15 Nov 1858.

**4137**    iii. William[9] Leslie Eaton, b. 10 Aug 1860; died 10 Aug 1863.
**4138**    iv. Frances[9] ("Fanny") June Eaton, b. 6 Jun 1868; mar. Otis
            Hooper as his 1st wife, but died of pneumonia ca. 1900
            without issue.
**4139**    v. Addie[9] Mary Eaton, b. 24 Jan 1870; died 6 Aug 1873.
**4140**    vi. Bessie[9] Eaton, a twin b. 12 Jun 1875; died seven days later.
**4141**    vii. Carrie[9] Eaton, a twin b. 12 Jun 1875; d. in seven days also.
**4142**    viii. Mary[9] Downer Eaton, b. 24 Apr 1877; mar. Richard Bracy
            of Brooklin, son of Ernest Bracy. The couple moved to
            Ellsworth, Me., where Mary died about 1927.


**2318. Samuel[8] Jordan Eaton** (Jonathan[7], John[6], Jonathan[5-4], John[3-1]) was born 25 Sep 1829 on Deer Isle, Me.; mar. 1st on 21 Dec 1856, **Mrs. Eliza Jane (Pressey) Sylvester**, b. 11 Nov 1833 to Enoe and Abigail (Crockett) Pressey on Deer Isle. She died 20 Feb 1870, and Samuel mar. 2d, **Naomi Warren**, who had been born 11 Aug 1842 to John F. and Mary (Sylvester) Warren. Samuel built for them a house on the road from Sunset to Dunham's Point, and died there at some time after 1900. Naomi died in Jun 1915 in Rockland, Me. where she was living with a son, and was buried with Samuel in Sunset, Deer Isle.

Child with Eliza on Deer Isle, Me.:

**4143**    i. Alice[9] Jane Eaton, b. ca. 1858; mar Jesse Hamblen, son of
            Ambrose and Caroline W. Hamblen. They resided at
            West Stonington, Me., where Alice died 1 Jun 1921 of an
            apoplectic stroke.

Child with Naomi on Deer Isle:

**4144**    ii. Winfield[9] W. Eaton, b. 6 Jul 1867; lived on a farm in
            Thomaston, Me. Called "Winnie" ; was quite eccentric.


**2321. (Jasper) Stillphen[8] Eaton** (Jonathan[7], John[6], Jonathan[5-4], John[3-1]) was born 24 Jan 1835 on Deer Isle; mar. **Susan C. Pressey**, sister of two other Pressey girls married to his brothers, on 23 Jun 1853. "Stilf" was a sailor by trade, and during the Civil War helped to man a small sailing vessel which was used for government transport, carrying supplies to the armies in Virginia. He raised his family in a house in Sunset, Deer Isle, labelled "J.S. Eaton" on the Colby Atlas map of Deer Isle in 1881. Wife Susan died 25 May 1891. Stilf lived until 6 Sep 1916.

Children on Deer Isle:

**4145**    i. (Jasper Newton) Fletcher[9] Eaton, b. 24 Sep 1853; mar.Clara
            Barber, and in 1910 was listed as a "general worker" in a
            Deer Isle in Lawton's Register of inhabitants. They had

five children.

**4146**    ii. (George) Courtney[9] Eaton, b. 22 Mar 1862; mar. Abbie
            Ada Dunham, 7 Jan 1886, and had five children.

**4147**    iii. Florence[9] B. Eaton, b. 23 Dec 1875; mar. John Allen, a
            blacksmith of Sedgwick, and resided on the River Rd. in
            in that town.

**4148**    iv. Gracie[9] Lee Eaton, b. ? ; apparently died young.


**2324. Henry[8] Eaton** (Charles[7], Nathan[6], Jonathan[5-4], John[3-1]) was
born 10 Oct 1840 on Deer Isle, Me.: mar. **Tryphosa B. Raynes** on 30
Jul 1864. For some years they res. on a farm on Deer Isle. In 1871,
however, with land conveyances made that year, he was said to have made
the trek to Henry Co., in western Missouri, not far from Kansas City. In
1874 he had settled his family more permanently in Springfield, the
largest town in southwestern Missouri. We can see much of his family
there at its peak size in the 1880 Census. Henry and his brother John
were salesmen of lightning rods. Henry died 23 Mar 1913.

Children with Tryphosa:

**4149**    i. (Florence) Anna[9] "Annie" Eaton, b. Mar 1, 1865, on
           Deer Isle.

**4150**    ii. Charles[9] Eaton, b. 24 May 1867 on Deer Isle, but dis-
           appears before 1880.

**4151**    iii. Ethel[9] Eaton, b. 1873 in Missouri.

**4152**    iv. Henry[9] Eaton, b. 1877 in Missouri.

**4153**    v. Kate[9] Eaton, b. 1879 in Missouri.

**4154**    vi. Karl[9] R. Eaton, b. Jul 1880, Missouri.


**2328. (Charles) Frederick[8] Eaton** (Charles[7], Nathan[6], Jonathan[5-4], John[3-1]) was born 17 Mar 1850 on Deer Isle. "Fred" mar. on 5
Nov 1874, **Lois Imogene Sargent**, born in Sedgwick, Me., 9 Jul 1850, to
John O. and Syrena (Dority) of Ellsworth, Me. When his elder brother
Henry removed to Missouri, Fred took over his home lot and dwelling
house. He also inherited the primary role in the clamming export firm
founded by his father, called Eaton & Co., at Stonington on the south tip
of Deer Isle. Both Fred and Lois were very active in their church and
community. He died 23 Jan 1933, of coronary occlusion.

Children at Stonington, Deer Isle:

**4155**    i. Raymond[9] Eugene Eaton, b. 7 Jun 1877; removed early to
           Rockland, Me., where he mar. 1st, Mary Richardson, 3
           Oct 1898. First he was a travelling salesman in the Rock-
           land area, but later became treasurer of the new "Rock-
           land Wholesale Grocery Co." His wife died and he mar.
           2d, Maud Grant of Rockland. There was no issue from

either union.

**4156**    ii. Nellie[9] Fulton Eaton, b. 31 Mar 1882; called "Kit," she taught school for some years, being at Somerville, Mass., in 1910. She mar. P. Stewart Jolly, the manager of a steamboat company, 31 Apr 1917, in Jacksonville, Fla.


**2332. (Capt.) Oscar[8] Gilman Eaton** (Eliphalet[7], Nathan[6], Jonathan[5-4], John[3-1]) was born 6 Nov 1841 in Newburgh, Me.; mar. 1st, **Adelaide "Addie" Augusta Nichols** in 1866. He was a "Sea Captain of Searsport" (cf. Black, 1960, for several of his adventures) where he lived when on land. On one trip in 1875 he went to South America to acquire a shipload at the famous guano deposit there. Upon arrival he found 169 ships ahead of him, and he was obliged to wait over six months to get his cargo. Wife Addie died 31 Oct 1881 on his bark <u>Penobscot</u> at Singapore. He mar. 2d, **Mrs. Marietta (Lanpher) McGilvery**, born 6 Aug 1854 and who died 3 Sep 1909. Oscar retired from the sea in 1889, to serve as superintendent of the East Boston Dry Dock Co. until 1807. He then was a Marine Surveyor in Boston until 1929. Over his career he amassed a substantial fortune, but outlived his only child. He died 5 May 1935 at East Boston, Mass.

Child with Addie:

**4157**    i. Oscar[9] Edward Eaton, b. 29 Jun 1874; mar. Jennie[9] B. Eaton (**#4160**, just below). He owned dry docks in East Boston where vessels were cleaned, after he retired from seafaring. After the birth of one daughter, Adelaide[10] Martha on 29 Jun 1899, he died prematurely on 21 Sep 1905, of appendicitis, in East Boston.


**2333. Park[8] J. Eaton** (Eliphalet[7], Nathan[6], Jonathan[5-4], John[3-1]) was born 22 Jul 1843 in Searsport, Me.; mar. **Matilda M. Turner** of Deer Isle, 30 May 1868. He was a trader and they res. in Chelsea, Mass.

Only child, born at Chelsea, Mass.:

**4158**    i. Ralph[9] E. Eaton, b. 30 Aug 1873.


**2340. John[8] Sylvanus Eaton** (Frederick[7], Nathan[6], Jonathan[5-4], John[3-1]) was born 25 Jan 1845 on Deer Isle, Me.; mar. on 14 Aug 1869, **Martha G. Pickering**, dau. of Isaiah and Maria (Haskell) Pickering of Deer Isle. After residing for a time on Deer Isle, they seem to have sold their homestead on 6 Sep 1873 and thereafter were not much in the public records, leading to a guess that they had left the area. They may have done so: John was a carpenter by trade and not tied to the land. Nonetheless, they were certainly back on Deer Isle for the latter part of their lives. Death records show that John S. died "where he was born," 6 Jul 1907, probably of cancer. Widow Martha died 24 May 1932, and was buried with her husband in Mt. Adams Cemetery on Deer Isle.

Children whose births were recorded on Deer Isle:

4159    i. Rose[9] W. Eaton, b. 18 Dec 1870; mar. a sea captain, Caleb A. Haskell, with whom she had six children.
4160    ii. Jennie[9] B. Eaton, b. 23 Dec 1872; mar. 1st, Oscar[9] Edward Eaton (#4157, just above), called "Ed." She mar. 2d, Ernest C. Osborne from the Boston area, and they had no children. Later on in the 1920s and beyond, she was back in Deer Isle, a dressmaker.
4161    iii. Fred[9] P. Eaton, b. 31 Mar 1877, was known as "Little Fred" because of his very small stature, relative to the other Fred Eaton (#2328). He was a painter and carpenter who never married.

**2346. Herman[8] Eaton** (Davis[7], Nathan[6], Jonathan[5-4], John[3-1]) was born 25 Sep 1850 in Sunset, Deer Isle, Me. He was the oldest of six children and was twelve years old when a diphtheria epidemic broke out in 1862 which killed all five of his siblings. He survived by living apart in the barn from whence he could do errands for the family (Noyes, 1942). He mar. on 24 Dec 1883, **Ella Frances Thurlow**, also of Deer Isle, and born 19 Jan 1866 to Stephen B. and Rosanna (Pendecost) Thurlow. Herman was a stone mason by trade, operating a quarry on the east end of Scott's Island. The family lived on Thurlow's Hill near Stonington, Deer Isle. Wife Ella died 15 Oct 1890. Herman died 12 Sep 1921 in Brunswick, Me., where he had resided for the preceding four years.

Children on Deer Isle, Me.:

4162    i. Ada[9] Frink Eaton, b. 21 Dec 1885; mar. Thurlow Ernest Weed, 24 Dec 1908 and res. on a farm near Bangor, Me.
4163    ii. Mary[9] Thurlow Weed Eaton, b. 26 Feb 1888; mar. at Sunset, Deer Isle, 28 Sep 1915, Paul Whittier Scott and res. at Deer Isle.

**2356. Goodwin[8] Pressey Eaton** (Davis[7], Nathan[6], Jonathan[5-4], John[3-1]) was born 11 Jul 1868, Deer Isle, Me.; mar. 1st, 1 Aug 1890 at Stonington (Deer Isle), **Abbie[10] Angeline Eaton**, the daughter of Nathan[9] Eaton (#3431) born 2 May 1872. After few years, this couple was divorced, and Goodwin mar. 2d, **Mrs. Elizabeth (Snyder) Mackanellar**, a woman who had come to the area from Philadelphia, int. 12 Nov 1910. This couple lived near Dunham's Point by the town of Sunset. In 1925 or so, wife Elizabeth went back to Michigan for some years, taking daughter Lillian with her. She later returned, however.

Child on Deer Isle with Abbie:

4164    i. Sherman[9] Lee Eaton, b. ca. 1890; mar. Ethel Mae Butler on 12 Apr 1914, at Searsmont, Me. He was a fisherman, and they res. at Northwest Harbor on Deer Isle. They were later divorced, and he removed to Rockland, Me.

Children on Deer Isle with Elizabeth:

4165    ii. Child[9] Eaton, died without being named.
4166    iii. Lillian[9] Eaton, b. ? ; mar. George Weir of Detroit, Mich., but left him to return with an infant daughter to Deer Isle.

**2358. Oscar[8] Davis Eaton** (Davis[7], Nathan[6], Jonathan[5-4], John[3-1]) was born 8 Oct 1872 Sunset, Deer Isle, Me.; mar. Laura Dow, and they res. in the Pressey Village, Deer Isle, where Oscar was a "yachtsman."

Children on Deer Isle:

4167    i. (Laura) Beatrice[9] Eaton, b. 9 Sep 1893; mar. Karl Kent Knowlton, res. at Deer Isle, having six children.
4168    ii. William[9] O. Eaton, b. 1895; mar. Georgette who died in 1928, before her husband.
4169    iii. Gladys[9] S. Eaton, b. 28 Sep 1900.
4170    iv. Reginald[9] G. Eaton.
4171    v. Thelma[9] Ethelyn Eaton, b. 20 Jul 1904 in Pressey Village Deer Isle. She mar. Gardner Wilmont Hutchinson, 21 Nov 1928 at Bath, Me.

**2362. Hiram[8] Otis Eaton** (Otis[7], James[6], Jonathan[5-4], John[3-1]) was born Sep 1856, prob. in Searsport, Me.; mar. 1st, **Clara "Carrie" N. Danforth**, 5 Jul 1880. He is listed in Black (1960) as one of the "Searsport Sea Captains," and he sailed the schooner Sea Flower. He mar. 2d, **Mrs. Vesta Edna (Wiswell) Smith** on 4 Jul 1891 at Brewer, Me. In 1900 this latter couple res. at Brewer with his children ii and iii below.

Children with Clara in Searsport, Me:

4172    i. Clifford[9] Eaton, b. 28 Aug 1881.
4173    ii. Edwin[9] Eaton, b. 10 Jul 1884.

Child with Vesta in Brewer, Me.:

4174    iii. Frances[9] W. Eaton, b. May 1893.

**2363. William[8] M. Eaton** (Hiram[7], James[6], Jonathan[5-4], John[3-1]) was born ca. 1845 in Searsport, Me.; mar. **Anna E. Harriman**, born also 1845 but in Arkansas, in the late 1860s.  He is listed as a "Searsport Sea Captain" (Black, 1960).  He died 15 Jan 1890 in Tampico Bay, Mexico, on his schooner W.W. Hungerford, under circumstances unknown to us.

Children with Anna, prob. at Searsport, Me.:

**4175**    i. Abbie[9] Eaton, b. ca. 1870.
**4176**    ii. Margaret[9] M. Eaton, b. ca. 1873.
**4177**    iii. William[9], Jr., Eaton, b. ca. 1875.

**2369. James[8] S. Eaton** (Hiram[7], James[6], Jonathan[5-4], John[3-1]) was born 3 Mar 1861 in Searsport, Me.; mar. **Mary E. __?__** (she born Sep 1861).  He was a farmer at Searsport as of 1900, with his tract of land adjacent to his brother Lester's farm.  He died 14 Apr 1939.

Only known child:

**4178**    i. Lillian[9] Eaton, b. ca. 1885 in Searsport, Me.

**2374. William[8] Henry Eaton** (Jonathan[7], Joshua[6], Daniel[5-4A], John[3-1]) was born 16 Jun 1837 in Sandwich, N.H.  As a young adult he decided to seek greener pastures in more populated areas to the south.  On 23 Dec 1856, he mar. **Philean W. Hoyt** (b. 1830) of Hampstead, N.H., a town near the southern border of the state, and in the orbit of Haverhill, Mass.  The couple res. first in Peabody, Mass. near Salem, where three of their children were born.  This residence was interrupted in part when William enlisted in the Civil War, 24 Aug 1864.  He served about ten months in Co. M, 4th Regt. of Mass. Heavy Artillery, being discharged 17 June 1865.  It was in this period that the family removed to Haverhill, Mass. to have the rest of their children.  They lived on a farm located, probably coincidentally, in the same west part of Haverhill that was the predominant original birthing ground for the Haverhill branch.  This seems coincidental because William H. was of the Salisbury branch, and separated from the Haverhill branch by six or more generations of independent growth.

Children (i-iii born in Peabody, Mass., iv-vii in Haverhill):

**4179**    i. Isabelle[9] Williams Eaton, b. 25 Nov 1857; mar. Frank
             Withington Emerson, 14 Nov 1878 and res. on a farm in
             Nottingham, N.H.
**4180**    ii. Mary[9] Lizzie Eaton, b. 23 Jun 1859; mar. Calvin Howe
             Bradford (a carpenter b. 23 Aug 1859 in Derry, N.H.)

on 23 Jun 1881. They resided in Milford, N.H.

4181    iii. William[9] Frederick Eaton, b. 4 Feb 1862; a carpenter who
res. at Derry Depot, N.H.
4182    iv. Jamie[9] Lincoln Eaton, b. 18 Apr 1865; died 20 Sep 1869.
4183    v. Hannah[9] Gertrude Eaton, b. 18 Jul 1867; mar. late if ever.
4184    vi. Walter[9] Hoyt Eaton, b. 2 Jul 1869; a shoe-cutter, Haverhill.
4185    vii. Charles[9] Leroy Eaton, b. 3 Jul 1872; shoe-cutter, Haverhill.


**2379. William[8] Sherburne Eaton** (William[7], Benjamin[6], James[5], Daniel[4A], John[3-1]) was born 16 Nov 1847 in Salisbury, Mass.; mar. 1st, **Belinda[9] J. Eaton** (#3372) on 22 Feb 1873 (Seabrook *VR* at Concord, N.H.), when William was a shoemaker living with his parents in Salisbury. Belinda, however, died within the year, and he mar. 2d, **Rachel Eva Jackman** of Salisbury, Mass., 25 Jan 1882. In 1884 he built the house at 120 Beach Rd., in the triangle formed where Dock Lane forks southeast of the main street, and added the barn a year later. A rather ample 160 acres surrounded the homestead, including a fair portion of Dock Lane, marsh land for salt haying, tillage land for vegetables and upland hay with a large woodlot as well. In addition, the family had its own dock on Allen Creek at the foot of Dock Lane, with access to Black Rock Creek and the Merrimack River a mile away. This well-appointed farm was on land donated by William[8] S.'s father William[7], and was once part of the founder John[1]'s planting lot or its subsequent extensions, although a bit east of the original homestead itself. William and Rachel had their children there, and William died in 1918. Widow Rachel died 16 Dec 1929.

Child with Rachel in Salisbury:

4186    i. Emma[9] Jane "Jennie" Eaton, b. 1883; mar. Clifford True.
She died 1928.
4187    ii. Rhoda[9] Amelia Eaton, b. 1889; died 11 May 1892.
4188    iii. Rhoda[9A] Amelia Eaton, b. 1894; mar. Wilfred Tetreault
(more recently spelled "Tatro".)
4189    iv. Louisa[9] Frances Eaton, b. 1898; died 1913, Salisbury.
4190    v. (William) Sherburne[9] Eaton, Jr., b. 1900. His life and times
were the subject for an article by Woodman (1983, q.v.).
He died 1982.


**2385. George[8] Wilson Eaton** (Benjamin[7-6], James[5], Daniel[4A], John[3-1]) was born 18 Apr 1866 in Salisbury, Mass; mar. on 1 Jan 1889, **Caroline W. Fernald**, born in 1871 to Albert and Caroline B. Fernald. They res. on Ferry Rd. in Salisbury.

Children at Salisbury:

4191    i. Florence[9] Eveline Eaton, b. ca. 1889; mar. James W.

Bamford, 1907.
**4192** ii. Angela[9] Louise Eaton, b. ca. 1897; mar. Eugene A.
Sheehan, 1916.

**2389. Freedom[8] Eaton** (Moses[7], Joseph[6] T., Joseph[5A], John[4A], Joseph[3], John[2-1]) was born 19 Jan 1816 and recorded in Marshfield and Corinth, Vt. He mar. 1st, **Irene G. Pierce** (b. ca. 1818) in the fall of 1838, and was a farmer when he was having children with her in Sutton, Caledonia Co., Vt. about 1840, but was not discovered by the Census at that time. As of 1850, Irene has removed to neighboring Lyndon, also Caledonia Co. and is a single-parent household head, leading to the conclusion that the marriage has functionally dissolved one way or another. Freedom mar. (or was allied with) 2d, **Mrs. Zilphia Burlingame** by 1857 or so, as they had a child early in 1858 (interestingly enough, in Lyndon, Vt. also). Vermont *Vital Records* also show that Freedom died 28 Aug 1897 in Lyndon as well, although his invisibility to the Census continued through the rest of the century.

Children with Irene all born Lyndon, Vt.:

**4193** i. Irena[9] Ann Eaton, b. 1840; mar. Hezekiah Carpenter, 1860. They removed to Arizona.
**4194** ii. Sarah[9] Maria Eaton, b. 1842; mar. Lorenzo K. Quimby of Lyndon in 1858; had two children.
**4195** iii. Albanus[9] M. Eaton, b. 1844; mar. Clara Bartlett in Minnesota and had three children.
**4196** iv. Julius[9] C. (or F.?) Eaton, b. 1846; mar. Addie Hoyt of St. Johnsbury, Vt. in 1867 and had two children.
**4197** v. Caroline[9] W. Eaton, b. 1848; mar. Charles Allen in 1867 and removed to Minnesota.

Child with Zilphia, also in Lyndon, Vt.:

**4198** vi. Charles[9] F. Eaton, b. 12 May 1858; died 25 Jul 1862.

**2402. David[8] N. Eaton** (Samuel[7-6], Daniel[5], Samuel[4], Joseph[3], John[2-1]) was born 18 Sep 1809 in that part of Minot, Me. that later became Auburn; mar. 24 Mar 1835, **Hannah N. Merrow**, born 8 Oct 1804 to Reuben and Alice (Downing) Merrow. Although he has been listed in some family records as "Captain" David, he was a mechanic in the 1850 Census (age 41) and a farm laborer in 1860 (age 51). He died 28 Feb 1876; widow Hannah died 18 Feb 1879.

Children in Auburn, Me.:

**4199** i. Mary[9] Ann Eaton, b. 17 Jun 1837; mar. Francis T. Faulkner. She died 19 Aug 1919.

**4200**  ii. Daniel[9] Pride Eaton, b. 3 Aug 1841; mar. Lydia F. Holt.
He died 15 Feb 1898.


**2415. George[8] L. Eaton** (Daniel[7-5], Samuel[4], Joseph[3], John[2-1]) was born 20 Jun 1816 in Brunswick, Me.; mar. **Frances A. McDonald**, 31 Mar 1839, in Brunswick, where they spent their lives. George's occupational history shows him a laborer in 1850 at 44; a millman in 1860 at 54; and a watchman in 1870 at 64. Wife Frances died 14 Aug 1882, but George was still living in 1893.

Children in Brunswick, Me.:

**4201**  i. Mary[9] F. Eaton, b. 4 Mar 1842; prob. died young.
**4202**  ii. George[9] A. Eaton, b. 10 Apr 1843; mar. Lorania B. Dunning, 27 May 1871 in Brunswick.
**4203**  iii. Emily[9] A. Eaton, b. 4 May 1846.
**4204**  iv. Charles[9] E. Eaton, b. 7 Nov 1857; not with family in 1860, and prob. died young.


**2416. Ensign[8] B. Eaton** (Daniel[7-5], Samuel[4], Joseph[3], John[2-1]) was born 11 Sep 1823 in Brunswick, Me.; mar. 1st, **Rachel P. Ross**, 17 Jul 1851 in Brunswick. The couple resided early in Brunswick, where Ensign was a barber and hair dresser as of 1860, with Rachel on the scene. She died or left soon thereafter, since Ensign mar. 2d, **Caroline H. Ratliff**, 29 Sep 1864. They were said to reside also in Brunswick; but there is no sign of them there as of 1870. Ensign is solo in Brunswick in 1880, a barber listed among members of a substantial boarding house.

Child with Rachel in Brunswick:

**4205**  i. Robert[9] H. Eaton, b. 27 Dec 1852.


**2423. Charles[8] E. Eaton** (Asa[7], Moses[6], Daniel[5], Samuel[4], Joseph[3], John[2-1]) was born 22 Mar 1845 in Rome, Me.; mar. on 15 Nov 1873, **Mary M. Scarborough** who was born Mar 1852 in Ireland. They res. at 14 Lexington Ave., Charlestown, Mass., where he was a fireman and later a shipper of iron.

Children:

**4206**  i. Anna[9] Margaret Eaton, b. in Boston, 9 Sep 1874; worked as a housekeeper when young.
**4207**  ii. Sarah[9] Elizabeth Eaton, b. in Boston, 17 Jun 1876; worked as a sales-woman when young.
**4208**  iii. Lucy[9] May Eaton, b. in Abbott, Me., 10 Sep 1877; worked as a saleswoman when young.

**4209**    iv. Edna[9] Harris Eaton, b. in Charlestown, 6 Jul 1891.


   **2424. Moses[8] W. Eaton** (Asa[7], Moses[6], Daniel[5], Samuel[4], Joseph[3], John[2-1]) was born 29 Dec 1846 in Rome, Me.; on 28 Nov 1868 he mar. **Catherine "Kate" Mullaly**, who was born of Irish parents in 1849 in Massachusetts. As of 1880 they res. in Boston, where he was a cooper.

   Child (others are quite possible):

**4210**    i. Joseph[9] Eaton, b. 1879 in Massachusetts.


   **2429. Anson[8] True Eaton** (Asa[7], Moses[6], Daniel[5], Samuel[4], Joseph[3], John[2-1]) was born 4 Oct 1855 in Shirley, Me.; mar. **Ella Jane Brownlow** (born May 1860 in New Brunswick of English/Irish extraction), on 2 Oct 1880. They removed to Lowell, Mass., where Anson was a mill operative for some years but listed his occupation as iceman in 1900.

   Children, all born in Lowell, Massachusetts:

**4211**    i. Hattie[9] Bernice Eaton, b. 26 Aug 1881; died 22 Feb 1882 in Lowell, Mass.
**4212**    ii. Percival[9] "Persey" Anson Eaton, b. 6 Apr 1884.
**4213**    iii. Gertrude[9] Esther Eaton, b. 23 Aug 1889.
**4214**    iv. Inez[9] Eaton, b. Apr 1897.


   **2432. (Dr.) William[8] Winslow Eaton** (Martin[7], John[6], Daniel[5], Samuel[4], Joseph[3], John[2-1]) was born 20 May 1836, as recorded in both Brunswick and Webster, Me.; mar. **Agnes Hirst Magoun** of Carlisle, Eng., 12 Jul 1865 at Brunswick. William studied medicine and practiced both in Webster and in Danvers, Mass., where he was highly regarded as a physician and surgeon, but died at the height of his career, before 1895.

   Children:

**4215**    i. Elbert[9] Carpenter Eaton, b. 8 Aug 1866 in Wakefield, Mass.; died 31 May 1880 in Danvers, Mass.
**4216**    ii. Susan[9] Wilhelmina Eaton, b. 2 Apr 1880 in Danvers, Mass.
**4217**    iii. Harold[9] Poslet Eaton, b. 2 Jan 1882, died young.
**4218**    iv. Marion[9] Agnes Eaton, b. 19 Jun 1884.


   **2436. Alonzo[8] James Eaton** (Martin[7], John[6], Daniel[5], Samuel[4], Joseph[3], John[2-1]) was born 10 Jan 1841 in Brunswick, Me; mar. **Elizabeth A. Lyon** on 2 Mar 1861 in Brunswick. He soon thereafter went off to

serve in the Civil War. They later settled in Brunswick and dealt somewhat in real estate, especially wife Elizabeth.

Children, all prob. born in Brunswick, Me. :

4219    i. Charles$^9$ L. Eaton, b. 27 Jun 1861.
4220    ii. Benjamin$^9$ Eaton, b. 13 Oct 1866.
4221    iii. Emily$^9$ Eaton, b. 8 Dec 1867.
4222    iv. Alonzo$^9$ Eaton, b. Mar 1870.
4223    v. Henrietta$^9$ Eaton, b. Apr 1872.
4224    vi. Harry$^9$ Eaton, b. Apr 1874.

**2441.   George$^8$ W. Eaton** (John$^{7-6}$, Daniel$^5$, Samuel$^4$, Joseph$^3$,
John$^{2-1}$) was born 6 Nov 1826 in Brunswick, Me.; mar. **Diana Deane**
(born Jun 1826, Lisbon, Me.) on 21 Jan 1848. They resided in Brunswick, where George was a blacksmith, and both were still surviving in
Brunswick in 1900.

Children in Brunswick, Me. (perhaps partial):

4225    i. Child$^9$ Eaton, b. 15 Sep 1849; died 28 Sep 1849
4226    ii. George$^9$ H. Eaton, b. 14 Oct 1850; was a mariner with his
        home in Brunswick, who did not marry,
4227    iii. Abby$^9$ Halener Eaton, b. 28 Oct 1852; died 14 Jun 1854.
4228    iv. Child$^9$ Eaton, b. 9 Feb 1854; died 12 Feb 1854.

**2442.   Dexter$^8$ W. Eaton** (John$^{7-6}$, Daniel$^5$, Samuel$^4$, Joseph$^3$,
John$^{2-1}$) was born 3 Apr 1831 in Brunswick, Me.; mar. 1st, **Hannah Remick**, 18 Feb 1852 at Bath, Me. They were residing at Bath in 1860 with
Dexter's brother Alfred, with no children in the household. The two
young men were "caulkers" by trade. In 1870 a Dexter W. Eaton of the
right age and a caulker, is by then living in Kennebunkport, Me., almost
surely the subject of this notice altho he has a different wife. He apparently mar. 2d, **Laura J. Stevens**, and they were with a boy age 6 in the
household.

Child (unknown which wife is the mother):

4229    i. Charles$^9$ S. Eaton, b. ca. 1864.

**2444.   Alfred$^8$ J. Eaton** (John$^{7-6}$, Daniel$^5$, Samuel$^4$, Joseph$^3$, John$^2$,
John$^1$), was born 9 Oct 1837 in Brunswick, Me.; mar. **Mary F. Remick**,
11 Aug 1860 in Bath, Me. In 1860 he was a caulker by trade, living with
his older brother Dexter and his wife. The new couple remained at
Brunswick for some years, but then disappear from the scene.

Children born in Brunswick, Me.:

**4230**   i. Ellen⁹ Eaton, b. 11 Oct 1860.
**4231**   ii. Alphonzo⁹ A. Eaton, b. 12 Dec 1861.
**4232**   iii. Martha⁹ A. Eaton, b. 27 Dec 1865.


**2446. John⁸ Eaton** (David⁷, John⁶, Daniel⁵, Samuel⁴, Joseph³, John²⁻¹) was born 2 Jun 1822, prob. before his family removed from Brunswick, Me., to Lisbon, Me.; mar. **Ann (Pierce?)** (born 9 Feb 1815 at Lisbon) ca. 1845 and the couple settled in Brunswick for a time, but have moved on to Bath, Me. by 1860, where John was a millman and there had been no new children in the preceding decade. In 1870 they have an empty nest at Greene, Me.

Children born in Brunswick, Me.:

**4233**   i. Lucy⁹ Ann Eaton, b. 15 Jan 1847; died 15 Jul 1853.
**4234**   ii. Daniel⁹ P. Eaton, b. 12 Jul 1848; mar. Etta J. _?_ (b. 3 Apr 1846), and they res. in Greene, Kennebec Co.


**2456. John⁸ W. Eaton** (Shepard⁷, Robert⁶, Jacob⁵⁻⁴, Joseph³, John²⁻¹) was born ca. 1834, prob. in Ravenna, Ohio; mar. **Emily __?__**, and res. in Franklin Twp., Ohio., where he worked in a tobacco house.

Children, presumably born in Franklin Twp., Ohio:

**4235**   i. William⁹ E. Eaton, b. ca. 1859.
**4236**   ii. Mary⁹ A. Eaton, b. ca. 1861.
**4237**   iii. Samuel⁹ Clark Eaton, b. 1862.


**2463. Greenwood⁸ P. Eaton** (Eliab⁷, Isaac⁶, Jacob⁵⁻⁴, Joseph³, John²⁻¹) was born 22 May 1858, prob. in Manchester, Me.; mar. **Ada B. Rankin** of Hallowell, Me., 1 Feb 1886 in Manchester. He was an engineer, and they settled in Quincy, Mass.

Child:

**4238**   i. Merle⁹ (or Mark?) Laroy Eaton, b. 22 Oct 1887.


**2465. Charles⁸ G. Eaton** (Eliab⁷, Isaac⁶, Jacob⁵⁻⁴, Joseph³, John²⁻¹) was born 2 Feb 1866 in Manchester, Me.; mar. **Georgie Cummings** of Whitman, Mass., 14 May 1886. Like his brother, he was an engineer and they resided in Whitman, Mass., outside Brockton.

Children (born in Mass.):

**4239**    i. Earle[9] Laforest Eaton, b. 25 Nov 1887.
**4240**    ii. Adella[9] M. Eaton, b. 28 Feb 1889.


**2473. Lyman[8] Eaton** (Lyman[7], Jacob[6-4], Joseph[3], John[2-1]) was born Nov 1845, prob. in Orono, Me.; he mar. ca. 1866, **Catherine "Katie" __?__**, b. Feb 1844 in New Brunswick, Can. They settled at Old Town, Me., just north of Orono, where he was a railroad engineer. They were still there in 1900 with children not yet up and out.

Children born in Old Town, Me.:

**4241**    i. George[9] A. Eaton, b. ca. 1867.
**4242**    ii. Frank[9] L. Eaton, b. ca. 1870.
**4243**    iii. Davis[9] W. Eaton, b. Mar 1879.
**4244**    iv. Harold[9] Eaton, b. Oct 1882.
**4245**    v. Martha[9] E. Eaton, b. Jul 1884.


**2475. Oliver[8] Davis Eaton** (Wendell[7], Jacob[6-4]. Joseph[3], John[2-1]) was born 11 Jan 1844 in Farmington, Me. He enlisted in the Civil War, and after his discharge he went into business in New York City, where he spent his life. He mar. **Emilie Felicia Bulkley** of Brooklyn, N.Y.

Children born in New York City:

**4246**    i. Florence[9] Emily Eaton, b. 2 Jan 1866.
**4247**    ii. Elsie[9] Bulkley Eaton, b. 10 Jan 1869.
**4248**    iii. John[9] Oliver Eaton, b. 24 Feb 1871.


**2476. Jacob[8] Elihu Eaton** (Wendell[7], Jacob[6-4], Joseph[3], John[2-1]) was born 23 Jul 1845 in Farmington, Me.; while res. on the family homestead he mar. **Ella M. Fales** on 6 Apr 1876. They stayed in Farmington for a while, but then removed first to New Vineyard, and later to Jay, all within Franklin Co., Me.

Children:

**4249**    i. Lester[9] Davis Eaton, b. 28 Jul 1877.
**4250**    ii. Clarence[9] Ellery Eaton, b. 20 Apr 1879.
**4251**    iii. Arthur[9] Garfield Eaton, b. 8 Jan 1881.
**4252**    iv. Kenneth[9] Fales Eaton, b. 24 Dec 1882.


**2496. Joseph[8] Prescott Eaton** (Charles[7], Isaac[6], Benjamin[5], Jacob[4], Joseph[3], John[2-1]) was born 15 Nov 1859 in Exeter, Me.; mar. **Evie __?__**, born May 1857. They res. in Exeter, where Joseph ran a general farm in partnership with an older man, Elbridge A. Chandler.

Children, born in Exeter, Me.:

**4253**    i. Lois[9] L. Eaton, b. Oct 1888; teaching school in 1910.
**4254**    ii. Richard[9] C. Eaton, b. Nov 1891; farm laborer in 1910.


**2498. Isaac[8] Arthur Eaton** (Benjamin[7], Isaac[6], Benjamin[5], Jacob[4] Joseph[3], John[2-1]) was born 14 May 1857 in Detroit, Me.; mar. on 11 Mar 1885, **Hattie M. Quimby** (born 26 Mar 1866 in Exeter, Me.). They res. in Exeter, where Isaac was a farmer and school teacher.

Children at Exeter, Me.:

**4255**    i. Blanche[9] L. Eaton, b. Feb. 1887.
**4256**    ii. Ruby[9] Eaton, b. Aug 1893.
**4257**    iii. Orrin[9] C. Eaton, b. Nov 1896.


**2499. Howard[8] A. Eaton** (Benjamin[7], Isaac[6], Benjamin[5], Jacob[4], Joseph[3], John[2-1]) was born 15 Feb 1859 in Detroit, Me. He lived on a general farm in Exeter, and did not marry until 1894, when he took the vows with **Melvina J. __?__**.

Children born in Exeter, Me.:

**4258**    i. Benjamin[9] E. Eaton, b. May 1895.
**4259**    ii. Howard[9] A. Eaton, Jr., b. Jun 1896.
**4260**    iii. Frances[9] M. Eaton, b. May 1898.
**4261**    iv. Etha[9] M. Eaton, b. 1903.
**4262**    v. Leroy[9] F. Eaton, b. 1909.


**2500. Charles[8] E. Eaton** (Benjamin[7], Isaac[6], Benjamin[5], Jacob[4], Joseph[3], John[2-1]) was born 22 Feb 1869 in Exeter, Me. With his older brothers up and out, Charles res. for a time on the family homestead. He mar. **Florence E. __?__**, ca. 1896, and by the 1900 Census this couple had settled in Kenduskeag, Penobscot Co., Me., where they were running a boarding house. We lack later information on them.

Child (later children likely but unknown):

**4263**    i. Donald[9] E. Eaton, b. Oct 1898.


**2503. George[8] Milford Eaton** (Charles[7-6], Benjamin[5], Jacob[4], Joseph[3], John[2-1]) was born 10 Aug 1851 in Phippsburg, Me. In 1880 he was still living with his parents and three siblings, but he finally mar. **Lena A. Morse**, ca. 1894. By 1900, they were res. in Bath, Me., where George was a planer in a lumber mill.

Children (perhaps partial):

**4264**    i. Jennie[9] May Eaton, b. Sep 1895.
**4265**   ii. Zina[9] Eaton, b. Jan 1897. Prob. a son named after uncle.


**2505. Charles[8] Frederick Eaton** (Charles[7-6], Benjamin[5], Jacob[4], Joseph[3], John[2-1]) was born 2 Mar 1859 in Phippsburg, Me. He was a carpenter who migrated early to Massachusetts. He mar. on 25 Dec 1884, **Fanny Webber** of Brockton, Mass. (she born Jun 1858). This couple was living in Brockton with one child in 1900, and Charles was by then in the serving machine business.

Child born in Brockton, Mass. (more are quite possible):

**4266**    i. Mildred[9] Eaton, b. Nov 1895.


**2515. William[8] Clay Eaton** (Emery[7], Jotham[6], Benjamin[5], Jacob[4], Joseph[3], John[2-1]) was born 21 Sep 1861 in Georgetown, Me.; mar. **Nellie T. __?__** (born Nov 1867). They were living at Topsham, Me. in 1900, where William was a papermaker.

Child (may well have been others):

**4267**    i. Ernest[9] R. Eaton, b. Apr 1899.


**2520. Frederick[8] Maurice Eaton** (Benjamin[7], Stephen[6], Benjamin[5], Jacob[4], Joseph[3], John[2-1]) was born 23 Dec 1861 in Clinton, Me.; mar. **Madeleine Job Pullen** of Camden, N.J. on 26 Feb 1890. They settled in Camden, where he was a physician.

Child (others may have followed):

**4268**    i. Paul[9] Rodney Eaton, b. 26 Dec 1891.


**2538. Frank[8] W. Eaton** (Abial[7], Horace[6], Benjamin[5], Jacob[4], Joseph[3], John[2-1]) was born 1 Jan 1873 in Topsham, Me.; mar. **Nellie B. Thibbets** of Woolwich, Me. ca. 1891. The couple res. in Brunwick, where Frank was a day laborer.

Child (others may have followed):

**4269**    i. Ernest[9] C. Eaton, b. 8 May 1893.


**2555. Samuel[8] Eaton** (Henry[7-6], Peter[5A], Henry[4], Ephraim[3], John[2], John[1]) was born 12 Oct 1844 in Salisbury, Mass.; mar. **Elizabeth "Lizzie" T. Dow** (born 1849 to Andrew and Louise (Pike) Dow), on 2 Jan 1870. They res. in Amesbury, Mass., where the town meeting named him Collector of Taxes. In 1900 he was living alone in Amesbury.

Children:

**4270**    i. Henry[9] Sumner Eaton, b. 14 Feb 1875.
**4271**    ii. Charles[9] Andrew, b. 12 Jul 1878.


**2556. Clinton[8] Dewitt Eaton** (Frederick[7], Stephen[6], Peter[5A], Henry[4], Ephraim[3], John[2-1]) was born 17 May 1844 in Corinth, Vt., and was originally named "Dewitt Clinton" but preferred "Clinton" as his daily name. At a young age he went west, and on 22 Jul 1869 he mar. **Belinda J. "Binnie" Michaels**, who had been born Aug 1849 in N.Y. State to a N.Y. native father and a mother born New Jersey. In both 1880 and 1900 this family is found Wilton Twp., Muscatine Co., Iowa.

Children, all born in Iowa:

**4272**    i. Anna[9] C. Eaton, b. Mar 1875. She was a Census clerk, 1900.
**4273**    ii. John[9] O. Eaton, b. 1877.
**4274**    iii. Robert[9] J. Eaton, b. late 1879.
**4275**    iv. Ruth[9] A. Eaton, b. Jul 1882.


**2557. Olin[8] Stanley Eaton** (Frederick[7], Stephen[6], Peter[5A], Henry[4], Ephraim[3], John[2-1]) was born 28 Apr 1846 in Corinth, Vt.. Like his older brother, he went west, first to central Ohio where he mar. on 30 Dec 1869 **Mary Jane Wright** (born 12 Jan 1851 in Ohio). They soon moved west again to Iowa, and res. for a time in Centerville, near the Missouri border and well over 100 miles southwest of his brother's new homestead. Olin was a carpenter and joiner there. At some time after 1875, he decided to bring the family back to Vermont, where they res. first in White River Junction, and later removed to Island Pond (Brighton Twp.) in the far northeast corner of the state. where we find him in 1900. In addition to his carpentry, Olin served in later years as a customs house officer. He also developed skills as an electrician, but was electrocuted in a work accident.

Children:

**4276**    i. Clyde[9] V. Albion Eaton, b. 9 Nov 1873 in Centerville, Iowa; was a telegrapher.

**4277**    ii. Leta[9] Julia Eaton, b. 13 May 1875 in Centerville, Iowa; was a school teacher, at least in her early days.

**4278**    iii. Van[9] Olin Eaton, b. 18 Aug 1883 in White River Junction, Vt.; died 6 Oct 1883.

**2558. Frederick[8] Albion Eaton** (Frederick[7], Stephen[6], Peter[5A], Henry[4], Ephraim[3], John[2-1]) was born 27 Dec 1849 in Corinth, Vt. Like his older brothers, he left the family nest for greener pastures elsewhere, choosing to settle in the burgeoning mill town of Nashua, N.H. He mar. there on 16 Jul 1874, **Julia M. Wilson**, born 26 Mar 1845 in Nashua, to Joseph and Minerva Wilson. Frederick was cashier of the Second National Bank, and served the city of Nashua in many official stations, including Alderman. Their residence in 1900 was at 55 Franklin St.

Children, all born in Nashua, N.H.:

**4279**    i. Frederic[9] W. Eaton, b. 13 Apr 1875.
**4280**    ii. Eloise[9] Eaton, b. 17 May 1877.
**4281**    iii. Arthur[9] L. Eaton, b. 10 Sep 1879.
**4282**    iv. Charles[9] L. Eaton, b. 9 Oct 1882.
**4283**    v. Helen[9] Eaton, b. 13 Jun 1885.

**2559. Frank[8] Julien Eaton** (Frederick[7], Stephen[6], Peter[5A], Henry[4], Ephraim[3], John[2-1]) was a twin born 21 Jul 1854 in Corinth, Vt. On 8 Jan 1878 he mar. **Cyrene E. Spear** (born 7 Jul 1855 in Vershire, Vt.). They res. on a farm in Vershire, and then took over his family's homestead in neighboring Corinth, Vt.

Child (other later ones possible):

**4284**    i. Julian[9] Dearborn Eaton, b. 9 May 1891 in Vershire, Vt.

**2564. George[8A] C. Eaton** (Peter[7-5A], Henry[4], Ephraim[3], John[2-1]) was born May 1856 in Corinth, Vt.; mar. 5 Mar 1884, **Emma A. Burgen** (born Aug 1863 in Mass.). They res. at Vershire, Vt. where George was a farmer. He died 5 May 1901 in neighboring Corinth.

Children born in Vershire, Vt.:

**4285**    i. Edith[9] F. Eaton, b. May 1891.
**4286**    ii. Ethel[9] Eaton, b. May 1894.

**2572. Henry[8] True Eaton** (Richard[7], Henry[6] T., Paul[5A], Jabez[4], Ephraim[3], John[2-1]) was born ca. Aug 1838 in Fredericksburg, Va. As he was growing up his father brought the family back to Candia, his birthplace, for some years, but before 1850 had returned to res. in Washington, D.C. About 1870, young Henry T. mar. **Ann R. __?__**, herself a native of Washington, D.C., born Oct 1842. They resided in Washington where Henry was both a merchant and a contractor specializing in bricklaying.

Children, all born in Washington, D.C.:

**4287**    i. Henry⁹ True Eaton, Jr., b. Dec 1873. A musician in 1900.
**4288**    ii. George⁹ Eaton, b. ca. 1875. Perhaps died before age 15.
**4289**    iii. Corinne⁹ Eaton, b. Jan 1877.
**4290**    iv. Ann⁹ Eaton, b. Jun 1879.
**4291**    v. Clarence⁹ Eaton, b. Mar 1881. A plumber, 1900.
**4292**    vi. Lily⁹ B. Eaton, b. Feb 1884.


**2578. Henry⁸ True Eaton** (True⁷, Henry⁶ T., Paul⁵ᴬ, Jabez⁴ Ephraim³, John²⁻¹) was born 21 Sep 1838 in Candia, N.H.; mar. **Julia A. Doe** (born May, 1850) of Pembroke, N.H. ca. 1871. They resided first in Candia, where he was a "shoe bottomer" in 1880; later they removed to Pembroke, N.H., where he called himself a carpenter in 1900. He died, 1902, and is buried in Pembroke.

Only known child:

**4293**    i. Frederick⁹ B. Eaton, b. 30 Aug 1872.


**2584. Joel⁸ Hall Eaton** (Ira⁷, Azel⁶, Joshua⁵, Jabez⁴, Ephraim³, John²⁻¹) was born ca. 1827, prob. in Onodaga Co., N.Y., where his father had migrated, but the timing is not clear. He mar. **Margaret Gloyd**, and they lived as of 1880 in Ontario, Wayne Co., N.Y. He was a farmer there.

Children:

**4294**    i. Margaret⁹ Eaton, b. ? .
**4295**    ii. Estella⁹ Eaton, b. 1873.


**2586. Emery⁸ Eaton** (Ira⁷, Azel⁶, Joshua⁵, Jabez⁴, Ephraim³, John²⁻¹) was born ca. 1833, presumably in Onondaga Co., N.Y. whence his father had migrated, although the geography has not been confirmed. He mar. **Frances Delano** in 1852, and in 1870 this family was in Williamson, Wayne Co., N.Y., a bit over 20 miles east of Rochester, N.Y.

Children, born N.Y., prob. at Williamson:

**4296**   i. Dwight[9] Eaton, b. 5 May 1858.
**4297**   ii. Elizabeth[9] "Libbie" Eaton, b. ca. 1866.
**4298**   iii. Edith[9] Eaton, b. ca. 1871.
**4299**   iv. Cushing[9] Eaton, b. 1874.


**2587.   Galutia[8] Eaton** (Ira[7], Azel[6], Joshua[5], Jabez[4], Ephraim[3] John[2-1]) was born ca. 1837, presumably in Onondaga Co., N.Y. whence his father had migrated, altho the geography has not been confirmed. He mar. **Ursula Rose** in 1861.

Children (place of birth unclear):

**4300**   i. Franklin[9] Eaton, b. 1866.
**4301**   ii. Laura[9] Stevens Eaton, b. 1880.


**2588.   William[8] Lacy Eaton** (Ira[7], Azel[6], Joshua[5], Jabez[4], Ephraim[3], John[2-1]) was born ca. 1842 in N. Y. State; mar. **Rebecca Jackson**, 21 Mar 1866. They res. first in Ontario, Wayne Co., N.Y. (1870), but then removed to Williamson, also Wayne Co., where his older brother Emery was established. William L. was a merchant miller by trade. He kindly furnished the senior author with the memoranda in his direct line for three generations beginning with his grandfather Azel (**#457**), the latter prob. born in Seabrook, but unknown to modern scholars there.

Children born Williamson, N.Y.:

**4302**   i. Mary[9] Almira Eaton, b. 2 Jun 1869.
**4303**   ii. Clarence[9] William Eaton, b. 21 Jun 1878.


**2589.   Hiram[8] Eaton** (Ira[7], Azel[6], Joshua[5], Jabez[4], Ephraim[3], John[2-1]) was born ca. 1847 in N.Y. State; mar. **Emily Day**, Nov. 1867 and they res. early in Ontario, Wayne Co., N.Y.

Children (certainly born NY, prob. at Ontario):

**4304**   i. Daisy[9] Eaton, b. ca. 1872.
**4305**   ii. Arthur[9] Eaton, b. ca. 1875.
**4306**   iii. Royal[9] Roscoe Eaton, b. ca. 1877.
**4307**   iv. Claude[9] Eaton, b. 1879.


**2598.   LaRoy[8] Addison Eaton** (Charles[7A], Jabez[6], Joshua[5], Jabez[4], Ephraim[3], John[2-1]) was born ca. 1856 in Seabrook, N.H.; mar. **Josephine Blatchford Wilson**, 19 Mar 1877. They res. in Newburyport, Mass., where he died 1924.

Children:

**4308**    i. Alice[9] Gertrude Eaton, b. 8 Mar 1879 in Hampton Falls, N.H.
**4309**    ii. LaRoy[9] Addison, Jr., b. 1894; mar. Lulu Doyle, 17 Sep 1913 in Newburyport, Mass. He died in 1947, Newburyport.


**2599. James[8] Austin Eaton** (Charles[7A], Jabez[6], Joshua[5], Jabez[4], Ephraim[3], John[2-1]) was born 24 Dec 1858 in Seabrook, N.H.; mar. ca. 1880 **Alma E. Minard**, born 16 Jun 1860 to George and Mary Minard. They resided on what was probably his family homestead at the corner of Walton Road and Washington St. in Seabrook.    Wife Alma died 21 Oct 1907; James died 8 Oct 1940.

Children born in Seabrook, N.H.:

**4310**    i. Georgia[9] May Eaton, b. 3 Mar 1882; mar. Stephen Whitney Watts (b. 1 Nov 1882 in Swampscott, Mass.) and res. in Seabrook.
**4311**    ii. Cora[9] Eaton, b.  ?  ; mar. a Walker and they res. in New Ipswich, N.H. as of 1940.


**2600. Charles[8] F. Eaton** (Charles[7A], Jabez[6], Joshua[5], Jabez[4], Ephraim[3], John[2-1]) was born 14 Nov 1859; mar. **Abbie Adelaide Beckman**, born 20 Sep 1862 to Jacob and Mary (Eaton) Beckman, on 27 Nov 1881, and they res. in Newburyport, Mass. Charles died 8 Feb 1933 in Newburyport; widow Abbie died 15 Sep 1938.

Children, born in Newburyport:

**4312**    i. Opal[9] May Eaton, b. Dec 1882; mar. Robert Little.
**4313**    ii. Bertie[9] Eaton, b. Jul 1884; died 19 Aug 1884.
**4314**    iii. Ethel[9] E. Eaton, b. Nov 1886.


**2601. Edwin[8] M. Eaton** (Charles[7A], Jabez[6], Joshua[5], Jabez[4], Ephraim[3], John[2-1]) was born 11 Mar 1873 in Seabrook, N.H.; mar. in Salisbury in 1910, **Ethel May Welch**, born 1891 in Exeter to George and Martha Welch. They resided in Salisbury, Mass. Ethel died there 8 Dec 1948; Edwin died 20 Jun 1954.

Children born Salisbury:

**4315**    i. Edwin[9] Morris Eaton, b. 1911; mar. Judith S. True, 1935. He died 1978.
**4316**    ii. Ethel[9] May Eaton, b. 1912; mar. a Michaud.
**4317**    iii. Ellsworth[9] M. Eaton, b. 1914; mar. Doris E. Fowler, 1935.
**4318**    iv. Eben[9] Eaton, b. 1916.

\* \* \* \* \* \* \*

## B. *The Haverhill Branch*

**2608. Thomas[8] Hutchinson Eaton** (Moses[7], Thomas[6], Moses[5], Thomas[4-2], John[1]) was born in 1829 in Francestown, N.H.; mar. **Mary Catherine Goss**, 29 Apr 1863, and resided at first in Francestown, later removing to Revere, Mass. and finally to Boston, Mass., where he died 24 Nov 1878. Widow Mary later moved to Galveston, Texas, to be with her sons.

Children:

4319    i. Thomas[9] Edward Eaton, b. Apr 1865 in Francestown, N.H. In the 1890s he was chief clerk in the auditing section of the G. C. & S. F. Railway Co., and resided in Galveston, Texas.

4320    ii. Paul[9] Revere Eaton, b. Apr 1871 in Revere, Mass. In the 1890s he was a clerk for the Pierce Oil Co. in Monroe, La., but resided in Galveston, Texas.

**2612. Moses[8] Harvey Eaton** (Moses[7], Thomas[6], Moses[5], Thomas[4-2], John[1]) was born 8 Jun 1840 in Francestown, N.H.; mar. on 15 Jul 1867, **Anna Jane Fulton** (born 31 Jan 1841 in Philadelphia, Pa.). They res. in Philadelphia, where his business was centered in a warehouse for paper and envelopes. They were divorced, 6 Jul 1895.

Children born in Philadelphia, Pa.:

4321    i. William[9] Steel Eaton, b. 23 Jun 1868; died 5 Apr 1878.

4322    ii. Harvey[9] Eldridge Eaton, b. 5 May 1873. Was a painter in Philadelphia.

4323    iii. Hannah[9] Elizabeth Eaton, b. 12 Jun 1876.

**2613. Marshall[8] Eaton** (True[7], Thomas[6-2], John[1]) was born 1 Apr 1840 in Bradford, N.H.; mar. on 21 Nov 1865, **Angie J. Johnson**, she born Dec 1838. They res. in Bradford, N.H., where he was a painter. He aided the senior author greatly in preparing this genealogy. They were still at Bradford in 1900.

Child:

4324    i. Bertha[9] F. Eaton, b. 1867 in Bradford, N.H. She died of consumption 23 Aug 1881.

**2615. Ira⁸ K. Eaton** (True⁷, Thomas⁶⁻², John¹) was born 21 Dec 1844 in Bradford, N.H.; mar. 24 Dec 1873, **Adeline "Addie" M. Barney**, born Jan 1855 in Marlboro, Mass., to Lyman and Maria Barney, but then res. at Washington, N.H. They settled on a farm in Bradford. Ira died in 1910.

Sole child, b. Bradford:

4325     i. Ida⁹ May Eaton, b. 7 Oct 1877; at home with parents, 1900.

**2632. Harvey⁸ B. Eaton** (William⁷ A. C., *Moses⁶*, *Moses⁵*, Moses⁴, John³, Thomas², John¹) was born Oct 1863 in Harrington, Me.; mar. on 28 Jun 1892 at Addison, Me., **Phebe W. Colson**, b. July 1874 at Addison to John and Eunice Colson They res. at Harrington, where Harvey was a sea captain, and one of the ships that sailed under his command was the barkentine <u>Geneva</u>, which sailed to ports as far away as Africa. He died in 1902 at Harrington. Widow Phebe mar. 2d Frank L. Allen, ca. 1904. She died 30 May 1942, also at Harrington.

Children born in Harrington, Me.:

4326     i. Caswell⁹ C. Eaton, b. Jun 1894; mar. Harriet B. DeCosta;
            he died 1918.
4327    ii. Earl⁹ Clayton Eaton, b. 1897; mar. 1st. Winnie May Moon;
            2d, Adeline R. (Dow) Grass; 3d, Estella Jepson Toby. He
            died 1969.

**2635. Frederick⁸ Rich Eaton** (Moses⁷, *Asa⁶*, *Moses⁵*, Moses⁴, John³, Thomas², John¹) was born Apr 1866 in Milbridge, Me.; mar. on 21 Dec 1884 in Milbridge, **Mary Elizabeth "Lizzie" Roberts** (born 25 Aug 1865 at Jonesboro or Columbia, Me.). He was a mariner, and about 1913 he moved his family down to Portland after his ship began to stop in Boston instead of Maine. In Sep 1919, he and his son Harry were on a ship going from Boston to Cuba, that was caught in a gale and both were lost at sea. His widow died 12 May 1941 at West Bridgewater, Mass.

Children in Milbridge, Me.:

4328     i. George⁹ Edward Eaton, b. Jun 1885; m. 1st, May McLellon;
            mar. 2d, Ethel M. Dill. He died 1969.
4329    ii. Vivian⁹ Victoria Eaton, b. Apr 1887; mar. 1st, Phleman
            Cavanaugh; 2d, George Grayson Perry. She died 1955.
4330   iii. Harry⁹ Howard Eaton, b. Jul 1888; mar. Gertrude Wallace.
4331    iv. Frederick⁹ Rich Eaton Jr., b. Mar 1892; died 1912.

**4332**    v. Warren[9] Asa Eaton, b. Nov 1894; mar. 1st, Mary Jane McLean; and 2d, Ruth O'Brien.
**4333**    vi. Lillian[9] Jeannette Eaton, b. Jan 1897; mar. Gustave E. West; she died 1989.
**4334**    vii. Dorothy[9] Drucilla Eaton, b. 1898; died 1899.
**4335**    viii. Ronald[9] Maxwell Eaton, b. 1900; mar. Avis Leavitt. He died 1985.
**4336**    ix. Neil[9] James Eaton, b. 1902; mar. Mamie Adelade Couture. He died 1993.
**4337**    x. Alton[9] Spencer Eaton, b. 1905; mar. Florence Papeneau; he died 2002.
**4338**    xi. Sara[9] Elizabeth Eaton, b. 1908; mar. Russell Oldrieve Prouty; she died 2001.

**2639. Charles[8] H. Eaton** (Elijah[7], *Asa[6]*, *Moses[5]*, Moses[4], John[3], Thomas[2], John[1]) was born 18 Dec 1872 in Harrison, Me.; mar. on 12 Oct 1892 in Harrison, **Melona Etta Cole** (born Harrington 20 Apr 1873). In 1910, they were still res. in Harrison, where he was peddler of dry goods. He died 9 Dec 1931, Cherryfield, Me.; his widow died 1953, Bangor, Me.

Children, all born in Harrison:

**4339**    i. Winslow[9] Nelson Eaton, b. Apr 1893; mar. Caroline Sheppard; he died 1962.
**4340**    ii. Hazel[9] Elizabeth Eaton, b. Apr 1895; mar. John L. Taylor; she died 1968.
**4341**    iii. Susie[9] Etta Eaton, Nov. 1897; mar. James Mahaney; she died 1975.
+++++++++++++++++++++++++++++++++++++++++++++++++++++++++++++++++++

## B(1). *The Nova Scotia Branch*

(Skeletal form; for details, see Arthur W. H. Eaton (1929). In this generation, the continuation markers below (+) refer to continuations in the 1929 genealogy.)

### 2642. Thomas[8] W. Eaton (Jacob[7], Stephen[6], David[5])

**4342**    i. Mary[9] Eliza Eaton, b. 1834.
**4343**    ii. Jacob[9] Valentine Eaton, b. 1836.
**4344**    iii. Annie[9] Maria Eaton, b. 1838.
**4345**    iv. Emma[9] Jane Eaton, b. 1840.
**4346**    v. William[9] Thomas Eaton, b. 1843.
**4347**    vi. Francis[9] Eugene Eaton, b. 1845.
**4348**    vii. Burton[9] Chase Eaton, b. 1848.
+**4349**    viii. Adoniram[9] Judson Eaton, b. 1850.

### 2645. Stephen[8] Eaton (Jacob[7], Stephen[6], David[5])

4350    i. Weston[9] Hall Eaton, b. 1845.
4351    ii. Charlotte[9] Elizabeth Eaton, b. 1846.
4352    iii. Anna[9] Maria Eaton, b. 1848.
4353    iv. Jacob[9] Eaton, b. 1849.
4354    v. Leonard[9] Eaton, b. 1851.  Owned Florida orange grove.
4355    vi. Edward[9] Eaton, b. 1853.
4356    vii. Mary[9] Ella Eaton, b. 1854.
4357    viii. Edward[9A] Hall Eaton, b. 1855.
4358    ix. Melbourne[9] Eaton, b. 1857.
4359    x. James[9] Delap Eaton, b. 1859.
4360    xi. Lamont[9] Eaton, b. 1861.
4361    xii. Sarah[9] Alberta Eaton, b. 1863.
4362    xiii. Harry[9] Burkett Eaton, b. 1879.

### 2650. Oliver[8] Eaton (Jacob[7], Stephen[6], David[5])

4363      i. George[9] Thomas Eaton, b. 1848.
+4364     ii. Charles[9] Rupert Eaton, b. 1852.
4365      iii. Emma[9] Day Eaton, b. 1857.

### 2651. Levi[8] Woodworth Eaton (Amos[7], Stephen[6], David[5])

4366    i. Sarah[9] Jane Eaton, b. 1835.  Res. New Zealand.
4367    ii. Lydia[9] Ann Eaton, b. ? .  Res. New Zealand.
4368    iii. George[9] Woodworth Eaton, b. ? .  Res. Nova Scotia.
4369    iv. Albert[9] Eaton, b. ? .  Res. New Zealand.

### 2652. Nathan[8] H. Eaton (Amos[7], Stephen[6], David[5]).

4370    i. John[9] Wellington Eaton, b. 1837.
4371    ii. Amos[9] Blucher Eaton, b. 1840.
4372    iii. Judson[9] Harris Eaton, b. 1841.
4373    iv. Rebecca[9] E. Eaton, b. 1843.
4374    v. Seraphine[9] Eaton, b. 1846.
4375    vi. Annie[9] Pamelia Eaton, b. 1854.

### 2653. Amos[8] Eaton (Amos[7], Stephen[6], David[5])

4376    i. David[9] Harris Eaton, b. 1837.
4377    ii. Edward[9] Higgins Eaton, b. 1838.
4378    iii. Evan[9] McPherson Eaton, b. 1840.  Res. New York City.
4379    iv. Margaret[9] Lucilla Eaton, b. 1842.
4380    v. Isaac[9] Bigelow Eaton, b. 1845.  Res. No. Attleboro, Mass.

**4381**   vi. Ruth[9] Roach Eaton, b. 1847.
**4382**   vii. Mary[9] Jane Eaton, b. 1849.
**4383**   viii. Levi[9] Woodworth Eaton, b. 1851. Res. Newark, N.J.
**4384**   ix. Sarah[9] Elizabeth Eaton, b. 1853.
**4385**   x. Rachel[9] Adelia Eaton, b. 1855.
**4386**   xi. Annie[9] Eaton, b. 1857.
**4387**   xii. William[9] Hobbs Eaton, b. 1857.


**2655. Stephen[8] Eaton** (Amos[7], Stephen[6], David[5])

**4388**   i. Caroline[9] Matilda Eaton, b. 1842.
**4389**   ii. Robert[9] F. Eaton, b. 1844.
**4390**   iii. Howe[9] Eaton, b. 1847.
**+4391**   iv. Joseph[9] Howe Eaton, b. 1849.
**4392**   v. Emma[9] Sarah Eaton, b. 1851.
**+4393**   vi. John[9] Russell Eaton, b. 1853.
**4394**   vii. Harriet[9] S. Eaton, b. 1855.
**+4395**   viii. Cyrus[9] Black Eaton, b. 1857.
**+4396**   ix. Frederick[9] Lane Eaton, b. 1864.
**+4397**   x. Charles[9] Aubrey Eaton, b. 1868.


**2664. Jacob[8] Eaton** (Nathan[7], Stephen[6], David[5])

**4398**   i. Eunice[9] Ann Eaton, b. 1845.
**4399**   ii. Harriet[9] Maria Eaton, b. 1848.
**4400**   iii. Amos[9] Richmond Eaton, b. 1850. Res. Auburndale, Mass.
**4401**   iv. Mary[9] Eveline Eaton, b. 1853.
**4402**   v. Phebe[9] Loomer Eaton, b. 1856.
**4403**   vi. Emma[9] Jane Eaton, b. 1858.


**2666. Levi[8] Eaton** (Nathan[7], Stephen[6], David[5])

**4404**   i. Stephen[9] Eaton, b. 1847.
**4405**   ii. Charlotte[9] Eaton, b. 1849.
**4406**   iii. Prudence[9] Eaton, b. 1851.
**4407**   iv. James[9] Eaton, b. 1853.
**4408**   v. Manson[9] Henry Eaton, b. 1855.
**4409**   vi. Ida[9] Eaton, b. 1857.
**4410**   vii. Alfaretta[9] Eaton, b. 1860.
**4411**   viii. Annie[9] Eaton, b. 1862.
**4412**   ix. Levi[9], Jr., Eaton, b. 1864.


**2672. Douglas[8] W. Eaton** (Stephen[7-6], David[5])

**4413**   i. Ingraham[9] D. Eaton, b. 1843, Wilson, N.Y.

**4414**    ii. James[9] E. Eaton, b. 1849, Wilson, N.Y.
**4415**    iii. George[9] Moss Eaton, b. 1851, Porter, N.Y.
**4416**    iv. Elmer[9] William Eaton, b. 1852, Ransomville, N.Y.
**4417**    v. Charles[9] H. Eaton, b. 1862, Porter, N.Y. Later, Detroit.
**4418**    vi. Mary[9] Lillian Eaton, b. 1867, Porter, N.Y.


**2673. Asael[8] Bill Eaton** (Stephen[7-6], David[5])

**4419**    i. Oreletus[9] Palmer Eaton, b. 1845, Wilson, N.Y.
**4420**    ii. Mary[9] Elizabeth Eaton, b. 1846, Wilson, N.Y.
**4421**    iii. Washington[9] Irving Eaton, b. 1847, N.Y.; res. Michigan.


**2674. Ingraham[8] Ebenezer Eaton** (Stephen[7-6], David[5])

**4422**    i. Frances[9] A. Eaton, b. 1848.
**4423**    ii. Alice[9] J. Eaton, b. 1850.
**4424**    iii. Ida[9] M. Eaton, b. 1853.
**4425**    iv. Emma[9] Sarah Eaton, b. 1856.
**4426**    v. Grace[9] A. Eaton, b. 1858.
**4427**    vi. Stephen[9] Homer Eaton, b. 1862; prob. res. Michigan.


**2675. Stephen[8] Rand Eaton** (Stephen[7-6], David[5])

**4428**    i. Ida[9] Eaton, b. 1853.
**4429**    ii. Edward[9] Alma Eaton, b. 1855, Marysville, Calif.
**4430**    iii. Mary[9] Eleanor Eaton, b. 1856.
**4431**    iv. Frances[9] Helen Eaton, b. 1858.
**4432**    v. Charles[9] Stephen Eaton, b. 1861. Res. Oakland, Cal.
**4433**    vi. Harry[9] Eaton, b. 1863. Res. San Francisco.


**2678. Edward[8] Manning Eaton** (Stephen[7-6], David[5])

**4434**    i. Cora[9] Lovina Eaton, b. 1859, Wilson, N.Y.
**4435**    ii. George[9] Edward Eaton, b. 1869, Bloomingdale, Mich.


**2679. Adoniram[8] Judson Eaton** (Stephen[7-6], David[5])

**4436**    i. Wilbur[9] C. Eaton, b. 1863, Porter, N.Y.
**4437**    ii. Herbert[9] B. Eaton, b. 1869, Porter, N.Y.
**4438**    iii. Benjamin[9] Eaton, b. 1879.


**2681. Henry[8] Knowles Eaton** (Dan[7], Elisha[6], David[5])

4439  i. Girl[9] Eaton, b. 1831; d. young.
4440  ii. Judson[9] Eaton, b. 1832.
4441  iii. Otis[9] Eaton, b. 1835.
4442  iv. Margaret[9] Ann Eaton, b. 1837.
4443  v. Joshua[9] Tinson Eaton, b. 1840.
4444  vi. Daniel[9] Eaton, b. 1842.
4445  vii. Martha[9] Laleah Eaton, b. 1845.
4446  viii. Sarah[9] Julia Eaton, b. 1847.
4447  ix. Edward[9] Henry, b. 1850.
4448  x. Clara[9] J. S. Dewolf Eaton, b. 1852.

### 2683. George[8] Eaton (Dan[7], Elisha[6], David[5])

4449  i. Maria[9] Chapman Eaton, b. 1838.
4450  ii. Harriet[9] Elvira Eaton, b. 1840.
4451  iii. Mary[9] Anne Eaton, b. 1843.

### 2684. William[8] Wentworth Eaton (Dan[7], Elisha[6], David[5])

4452  i. Brewer[9] D. Moore Eaton, b. 1835. Grew up, Chicago, Ill.
4453  ii. Sophia[9] Eaton, b. 1838. Res. Chicago, Ill.
4454  iii. Charles[9] Peavey Eaton, b. 1842.
4455  iv. Frederic[9] Oberlin Eaton, b. 1847.

### 2688. Daniel[8] Lewis Eaton (Dan[7], Elisha[6], David[5])

4456  i. Frank[9] Eaton, b. 1859, Pittsburgh, Pa.
4457  ii. Paul[9] Eaton, b. 1861, Washington, D.C.
4458  iii. Isabel[9] Eaton, b. 1863.

### 2692. Enoch[8] Eaton (Enoch[7], Elisha[6], David[5])

4459  i. Arthur[9] Crawley Eaton, b. 1854.
4460  ii. Edgar[9] Primrose Eaton, b. 1856.

### 2693. Henry[8] Allen Eaton (Enoch[7], Elisha[6] David[5])

4461  i. Charles[9] Edwin Eaton, b. 1846.
4462  ii. Emma[9] Irene Eaton, b. 1850.
4463  iii. Flora[9] Jane Eaton, b. 1852.
4464  iv. Grace[9] Lillian Eaton, b. 1855.
+4465  v. Freeman[9] Allen Eaton, b. 1858.
+4466  vi. Albert[9] Edward Eaton, b. 1860.
4467  vii. Frank[9] Mailman Eaton, b. 1863.

**4468** viii. Bessie[9] Maria Eaton, b. 1867.

**2694. Watson[8] Eaton** (Enoch[7], Elisha[6], David[5])

**4469**   i. Hanna[9] Rebecca Eaton, b. 1848.
**4470**   ii. John[9] Shaftner Eaton, b. 1849.
**4471**   iii. Clara[9] Maria Eaton, b. 1851.
**4472**   iv. George[9] Cunnabell Eaton, b. 1853.
**4473**   v. William[9] Lloyd Garrison Eaton, b. 1856.
**4474**   vi. Charles[9] Lewis Eaton, b . 1858.
**4475**   vii. Estella[9] Eaton, b. 1860.
**4476**   viii. Watson[9], Jr., Eaton, b. 1865.
**4477**   ix. Margaret[9] Stewart Eaton, b. 1869.

**2695. Benjamin[8] Eaton** (Enoch[7], Elisha[6], David[5])

**4478**   i. James[9] Everett Eaton, b. 1848.
**4479**   ii. William[9] Edwin Eaton, b. 1849.
**4480**   iii. Eliza[9] Irene Eaton, b. 1851.
**+4481**   iv. Arthur[9] Watson Eaton, b. 1852.
**4482**   v. Eunice[9] Marie Eaton, b. 1855.
**4483**   vi. David[9] Owen Eaton, b. 1859.

**2699. George[8] Wiswell Eaton** (Enoch[7], Elisha[6], David[5])

**4484**   i. Ralph[9] Ellington Eaton, b. 1859.
**4485**   ii. Lavinia[9] Olivia Eaton, b. 1862.
**4486**   iii. Fanny[9] Adelia Eaton, b. 1864.
**4487**   iv. Burpee[9] Eaton, b. 1866.
**4488**   v. Frank[9] George Eaton, b. 1868.
**4489**   vi. Martha[9] Lorena Eaton, b. 1872.
**4490**   vii. Lillian[9] May Eaton, b. 1876.
**4491**   viii. Howard[9] Eaton, b. 1878.

**2701. Leonard[8] Eaton** (William[7], Elisha[6], David[5])

**+4492**   i. Stephen[9] Woodworth Eaton, b. 1841.
**+4493**   ii. Everard[9] Doe Eaton, b. 1844.
**+4494**   iii. Lawrence[9] Hall Eaton, b. 1846.
**4495**   iv. Anna[9] Elizabeth Eaton, b. 1849.
**4496**   v. Mary[9] Eliza Eaton, b. 1851.
**4497**   vi. Nancy[9] Adelia Eaton, b. 1854.
**+4498**   vii. Newton[9] Alfred Eaton, b. 1857.

**2706. George⁸ William Eaton** (William⁷, Elisha⁶, David⁵)

4499     i. Emma⁹ Eaton, b. 1855.
4500    ii. George⁹ Radford Eaton, b. 1857.
4501   iii. Clement⁹ Levi Eaton, b. 1859.
4502   iv. Minorah⁹ Eaton, twin b. 1862.
4503    v. Evorah⁹ Eaton, twin, b. 1862.


**2707. Joseph⁸ Henry Eaton** (William⁷, Elisha⁶, David⁵)

4504     i. Arthur⁹ William Eaton, b. 1852.
4505    ii. Aubrey⁹ Eaton, b. 1855.


**2718. David⁸ Rupert Eaton** (David⁷, Elisha⁶, David⁵)

4506      i. Laura⁹ Augusta Eaton, b. 1854.
4507     ii. Ada⁹ Theodate Eaton, b. 1855.
4508    iii. Edgar⁹ Emerson Eaton, b. 1858.
4509    iv. Horace⁹ Eugene Eaton, b. 1860.
4510     v. Frederic⁹ Rupert Eaton, b. 1862.
+4511    vi. Foster⁹ Fitch Eaton, b. 1863.
4512   vii. Aubrey⁹ William Eaton, b. 1867.
4513 viii. Harriet⁹ Maria Eaton, b. 1868.
4514    ix. Percy⁹ Havelock Eaton, twin b. 1870.
4515     x. William⁹ Bernard Eaton, twin b. 1870.


**2719. Charles⁸ Frederic Eaton** (David⁷, Elisha⁶, David⁵)

4516     i. Frederick⁹ Edmund Eaton, b. 1856.
4517    ii. Edwin⁹ Sheffield Eaton, b. 1859.
4518   iii. Charles⁹ William Eaton, b. 1867. Res. Vancouver, B.C.
4519   iv. Lewis⁹ Frederick Eaton, b. 1869.
4520    v. Edith⁹ Irene Eaton, b. 1872.


**2727. Levi⁸ Eaton** (James⁷, Elisha⁶, David⁵)

4521     i. Leverett⁹ Eugene Eaton, b. 1856. Res. Milton, Mass.
4522    ii. Agnes⁹ Lillian Eaton, b. 1859.
4523   iii. Ernest⁹ Linwood Eaton, b. 1862.
4524   iv. James⁹ Edwin Eaton, b. 1864.
4525    v. Walter⁹ Eaton, b. 1866.
4526   vi. Mabel⁹ Irene Eaton, b. 1875.
4527   vii. Caroline⁹ Maria Eaton, b. 1878.

## 2729. <u>Brenton</u>[8] <u>Halliburton Eaton</u> (James[7], Elisha[6], David[5])

**4528**    i. Llewellyn[9] Eaton, b. 1871.
**4529**   ii. James[9] Edwin Eaton, b. 1873.
**4530**  iii. Isobel[9] Jean Eaton, b. 1876.
**4531**   iv. Stella[9] Jean Eaton, twin b. 1880.
**4532**    v. Blanche[9] Mary Eaton, twin b. 1880.
**4533**   vi. Brenton[9] Halliburton Eaton, Jr., b. 1884.

## 2734. <u>Gideon</u>[8] <u>Eaton</u> (Timothy[7-6], David[5])

**4534**     i. James[9] Edwin Eaton, b. 1844. Res. Dorchester, Mass.
**4535**    ii. Nancy[9] Sophia Eaton, b. 1846.
**4536**   iii. Gideon[9] Eaton, Jr., b. 1848.
**4537**    iv. Otho[9] Eaton, b. 1849.
**4538**     v. Anne[9] Eaton, b. 1851.
**4539**    vi. William[9] Webster Eaton, b. 1852.
**4540**   vii. George[9] Frederic Eaton, b. 1854.
**4541**  viii. John[9] Chipman Eaton, b. 1855.
**4542**    ix. Sarah[9] Ellen Eaton, b. 1858.
**4543**     x. Wallace[9] Stephen Dexter Eaton, b. 1860. Lived in Boston.
**4544**    xi. Walter[9] Stuart Eaton, b. 1862.
**4545**   xii. Norman[9] Bond Eaton, b. 1863.
**4546**  xiii. Eliza[9] Katherine Eaton, b. 1865.
**4547**   xiv. Martha[9] Jane Eaton, b. 1868.

## 2736. <u>William</u>[8] <u>Henry Eaton</u> (Timothy[7-6], David[5])

**4548**     i. Enos[9] Eldridge Eaton, b. 1854.
**4549**    ii. Mary[9] Eliza Eaton, b. 1856.
**4550**   iii. Arthur[9] Stanley Eaton, b. 1857.
**4551**    iv. Josephine[9] Elizabeth Eaton, b. 1858.
**4552**     v. Anna[9] Maria Eaton, b. 1859.
**4553**    vi. Susannah[9] Selina, b. 1861.
**4554**   vii. Jacob[9] Ellsworth Eaton, b. 1863.
**4555**  viii. Sarah[9] Alice Eaton, b. 1866.
**4556**    ix. Loretta[9] May Eaton, b. 1868.
**4557**     x. Caroline[9] Lavinia Eaton, b. 1871.

## 2739. <u>Otho</u>[8] <u>Eaton</u> (Timothy[7-6], David[5])

**4558**     i. Caroline[9] Grace Eaton, b. 1866.
**4559**    ii. Rufus[9] Edmund Eaton, b. 1873.

## 2740. <u>Robert</u>[8] <u>Albert Eaton</u> (Timothy[7-6], David[5])

**4560**   i. Arthur[9] Stanley Eaton, b. 1859.
**4561**   ii. Elma[9] Euana Eaton, b. 1862.
**4562**   iii. Norman[9] Albert Eaton, b. 1863.
**4563**   iv. Nancy[9] Sophia Eaton, b. 1865.
**4564**   v. Perry[9] Wilbur Eaton, b. 1870.
**4565**   vi. Harriet[9] Belle Eaton, b. 1873.
**4566**   vii. Charles[9] Rupert Eaton, b. 1876.


### 2749. Jonathan[8] Rand Eaton (Caleb[7], Elijah[6A], David[5])

**4567**   i. Elizabeth[9] Jane Eaton, b. 1839.
**4568**   ii. Naomi[9] Caroline Eaton, b. 1841.
**4569**   iii. Asa[9] Caleb Eaton, b. 1843.
**4570**   iv. Charles[9] Alfred Eaton, b. 1845.
**4571**   v. Jonathan[9] Rand Eaton, Jr., b. 1847. Res. Gloucester, Mass.


### 2757. Abel[8] Benjamin Eaton (Caleb[7], Elijah[6A], David[5])

**4572**   i. Annie[9] Eaton, b. 1857.
**4573**   ii. Elizabeth[9] Eaton, b. 1859.
**4574**   iii. Orinda[9] Eaton, b. 1861.
**4575**   iv. Catherine[9] Eaton, b. 1864.
**4576**   v. Gertrude[9] Eaton, b. 1867.
**4577**   vi. Ada[9] May Eaton, b. 1871.
**4578**   vii. Melbourne[9] Eaton, b. 1874.


### 2764. James[8A] Edward Eaton (Elisha[7-6A], David[5])

**4579**   i. Frederick[9] Stanley Eaton, b. 1858.
**4580**   ii. William[9] Nelson Eaton, b. 1859.
**4581**   iii. Charles[9] Edward Eaton, b. 1862.
**4582**   iv. Flora[9] Blanche Eaton, b. 1866.
**4583**   v. Mary[9] Eliza Eaton, b. 1868.
**4584**   vi. Rebecca[9] Adelia, Eaton, b. 1871.
**4585**   vii. Seffie[9] Inez Eaton, b. 1875.


### 2766. Mayhew[8] Emerson Eaton (Elisha[7-6A], David[5])

**4586**   i. Bertha[9] Maria Lavinia Eaton, b. 1883.


### 2767. Joseph[8] Henry Eaton (Elisha[7-6A], David[5])

**4587**   i. Myrtle[9] Eudora Eaton, b. 1871.

**4588**    ii. Jessie[9] Blanche Sutherland Eaton, b. 1875.


**2768. George[8] William Eaton** (Elisha[7-6A], David[5])

**4589**    i. Ethel[9] Maude Eaton, b. 1876.
**4590**    ii. Ernest[9] Scott Magee Eaton, b. 1883.


**2772. Asael[8] Eaton** (Guy[7], David[6-5])

**4591**    i. Lydia[9] Ann Eaton, b. 1843.
**4592**    ii. Mary[9] Elizabeth Eaton, b. 1845.
**4593**    iii. Mayhew[9] Wells Eaton, b. 1849, in Wisconsin.
**4594**    iv. Davenport[9] Chipman Eaton, b. 1852, in Wisconsin.
**4595**    v. Ruth[9] Maria Eaton, b. 1854, in Illinois.
**4596**    vi. Rupert[9] Asael Eaton, b. 1856, in Wisconsin.
**4597**    vii. David[9] J. Eaton, b. 1850; res. Iowa.


**2777. Guy[8] Eaton** (Guy[7], David[6-5])

+**4598**    i. Charles[9] Henry Eaton, b. 1845.
**4599**    ii. Margaret[9] Ann Eaton, b. 1850.
**4600**    iii. Margaret[9A] Elizabeth Eaton, twin b. 1852.
+**4601**    iv. Frederick[9] William Eaton, twin b. 1852.
**4602**    v. James[9] Edward Eaton, b. 1854.
**4603**    vi. Alfred[9] Eaton, b. 1863.


**2779. John[8] Wells Eaton** (Guy[7], David[6-5])

**4604**    i. John[9] Franklin Eaton, b. 1852, in Oldtown, Maine.
**4605**    ii. Frederic[9] Follett, b. 1865.


**2782. Wells[8] Eaton** (Judah[7], David[6-5])

**4606**    i. William[9] Albert Eaton, b. 1846, Iowa.
**4607**    ii. George[9] Edwin Eaton, b. 1849.
**4608**    iii. Maria[9] Ellen Eaton, b. 1851.
**4609**    iv. Wells[9] Wentworth Eaton, b. 1853.
**4610**    v. Marietta[9] Eaton, b. 1855, Iowa.
**4611**    vi. Margaret[9] Eunice Eaton, b. 1857, Iowa.
**4612**    vii. Amanda[9] Jane Eaton, b. 1859, Iowa.
**4613**    viii. Eliza[9] Ann Eaton, b. 1861, Iowa.
**4614**    ix. Frank[9]L. Eaton, b. 1864.
**4615**    x. Alfred[9] Watson Eaton, b. 1866.
**4616**    xi. Scott[9] Willis Eaton, b. 1868.

## 2786. Gurdon[8] Eaton (David[7-5])

4617   i. Mary[9] Jerusha Eaton, b. 1841.
4618   ii. Eunice[9] Ann Eaton, b. 1844.
4619   iii. Asael[9] Emerson Eaton, b. 1853.
4620   iv. Edgar[9] Burton Eaton, b. 1855.
4621   v. Ella[9] Elizabeth Eaton, b. 1859.
4622   vi. Laura[9] Jeanette Eaton, b. 1862.
4623   vii. Gurdon[9] Noble Eaton, b. 1865.
4624   viii. Oressa[9] May Eaton, b. 1869.
4625   ix. Bessie[9] Leona Eaton, b. 1872.

## 2789. George[8] Edward Eaton (David[7-5])

4626   i. Abigail[9] Eaton, b. 1842.
4627   ii. Emily[9] Eddany Eaton, b. 1843.
4628   iii. David[9] Henry Eaton, b. 1845.
4629   iv. Gurdon[9] Sturtley Eaton, b. 1847; res. Los Angeles, Tucson.
4630   v. Abigail[9] Jerusha Eaton, b. 1849.
4631   vi. Nancy[9] Lavinia Eaton, b. 1851.
4632   vii. Hannah[9] Charlotte Eaton, b. 1853.
4633   viii. Charlotte[9] Anne Eaton, b. 1855.
4634   ix. George[9] Edward Eaton, b. 1857.
+4635   x. Marshall[9] Starr Eaton, b. 1859.
4636   xi. Lewis[9] Eaton, b. 1862.

## 2797. Joseph[8] Edwin Eaton (Levi[7], David[6-5])

4637   i. Harry[9] Northrup Eaton, b. 1869.
4638   ii. Mary[9] Eliza Eaton, b. 1871.
4639   iii. Nellie[9] Woodworth Eaton, b. 1874.
4640   iv. Douglas[9] Brenton Eaton, b. 1876.
4641   v. Prudence[9] Emily Eaton, b. 1877.
4642   vi. Joseph[9] Levi Eaton, b. 1881.

## 2802. Nathan[8] Woodworth Eaton (Levi[7], David[6-5])

4643   i. Victor[9] Bigelow Eaton, b. 1883.
4644   ii. Stella[9] Ellis Eaton, b. 1887.
4645   iii. Annie[9] Louise Eaton, b. 1889.
4646   iv. Levi[9] Erle Eaton, b. 1892.
4647   v. Emily[9] Woodworth Eaton, b. 1894.
4648   vi. Cedric[9] Eaton, b. 1897.
4649   vii. Nathan[9] Sheldon Eaton, b. 1900.

**4650**  viii. Ruby[9] Beatrice Eaton, b. 1902.
**4651**  ix. Hartley[9] Emerson Eaton, b. 1906.

### 2812. Leander[8] Eaton (Ward[7], John[6], David[5])

+**4652**   i. Alfred[9] Starr Eaton, b. 1851.
 **4653**  ii. Frances[9] Susan Eaton, b. 1853.
 **4654**  iii. Mary[9] Sophia Eaton, b. 1855.
 **4655**  iv. Florence[9] Jane Eaton, b. 1856.
 **4656**   v. Ralph[9] Samuel Eaton, b. 1858.
 **4657**  vi. Sarah[9] Elizabeth Eaton, b. 1860.
+**4658**  vii. Charles[9] Cottnam Eaton, b. 1863.
 **4659**  viii. Alice[9] Maude Eaton, b. 1866.

### 2813. William[8] Eaton (Ward[7], John[6], David[5])

+**4660**   i. **Arthur[9] Wentworth Hamilton Eaton**, author of this
               *Eaton Family of Nova Scotia (1929)*.
+**4661**  ii. Frank[9] Herbert Eaton, b.  ? .
 **4662**  iii. Anna[9] Morton Eaton, b.  ? .
+**4663**  iv. Rufus[9] William Eaton, b.  ? .
+**4664**   v. Harry[9] Havelock Eaton, b.  ? .
+**4665**  vi. Leslie[9] Seymour Eaton, b.  ? .
 **4666**  vii. Emily[9] Maria Hamilton Eaton, b. 1871.

### 2814. John[8] Rufus Eaton (Ward[7], John[6], David[5])

**4667**   i. Emma[9] Maria Eaton, b. 1851.  Grew up Chelsea, Mass.
**4668**  ii. Grace[9] Hunnewell, b. 1852.  Grew up Chelsea, Mass.

### 2816. James[8] Stanley Eaton (Ward[7], John[6], David[5])

 **4669**   i. Clarence[9] Ward Eaton, b. 1861.
 **4670**  ii. Agnes[9] Lillian Eaton, b. 1862.
+**4671**  iii. Walter[9] Ernest Eaton, b. 1868.
+**4672**  iv. John[9] Nicholson Eaton, b. 1874.

(End Generation VIII for Nova Scotia Branch)
++++++++++++++++++++++++++++++++++++++++++++++++++++++++++++++

**2836. Samuel[8] Webster Eaton** (Daniel[7] P., Abijah[6], Timothy[5],
James[4], Jonathan[3], Thomas[2], John[1]) was born 2 Jun 1814 in Bradford, Vt.
Moving westward as a young man he mar. 1st, **Susan Van Allen Wells**,

(she born 22 Sep 1825 at Ogdensburgh, N.Y. to William and Mary (Haskins) Wells), on 13 Mar 1841. They settled in Three Rivers and then Cleveland, both Ohio. Wife Susan died 2 Dec 1869, and Samuel mar. 2d, **Vashti P. Haskins**. He died 25 Dec 1872 in Denmark, Ohio (Poore, 1881).

Children with Susan (i-ii in Three Rivers; iii-vii in Cleveland):

4673    i. George[9] Webster Eaton, b. 25 Dec 1841; mar. Carrie Emily Pempin, 15 Sep 1863.
4674    ii. Olive[9] Eaton, b. 20 Apr 1844; mar. Charles Aaron Hitchcock, 25 Dec 1865.
4675    iii. Anna[9] Marian Eaton, b. 30 Sep 1846; mar. 1st, Martin Van Tassel, 12 Dec 1863. Also remarried, spouse unknown.
4676    iv. Sarah[9] Elizabeth Eaton, b. 9 Jan 1848; mar. Richard Parsons, 11 Oct 1866.
4677    v. Lydia[9] Adelaide Eaton, b. 14 May, 1854; mar. Charles Tory Dunn, 24 Oct 1870.
4678    vi. Mary[9] Ellen Eaton, b. 1 Jan 1858; mar. Winfield Scott, Hall, 31 Oct 1872.

**2837. Daniel[8] Poore Eaton** (Daniel[7] P., Abijah[6], Timothy[5], James[4], Jonathan[3], Thomas[2], John[1]) was born 2 Sep 1816 in Montreal, Quebec; mar. on 16 Feb 1840 **Lydia Drew**, born 9 Jun 1813 in Brookfield, N.H., to Joseph and Susan (Hill) Drew. They settled back in his family's territory of origin in Methuen, Mass., but soon removed to Williamstown, Mass.

Children (perhaps partial):

4679    i. Daniel[9] Webster Eaton, b. 23 Dec. 1841 in Methuen, Mass.
4680    ii. Olive[9] Hill Eaton, b. 1 Feb 1844 in Williamstown, Mass.

**2842. Solomon[8] W. Eaton** (Thomas[7] J., Abijah[6], Timothy[5], James[4], Jonathan[3], Thomas[2], John[1]) was born ca. 1836 in Stanstead, Quebec, just over the Canadian border from Vermont; mar. **Anne D. Kinney**, 13 Feb 1864 in Irasburgh, Vt., where this couple settled at least for a time, although they probably removed elsewhere before long.

Child in Irasburgh, Vt. (prob. others elsewhere):

4681    i. Joseph[9] Eaton, b. Sep 1868.

**2857. Simon[8] Kollock Eaton** (William[7] C., Daniel[6], Timothy[5], James[4], Jonathan[3], Thomas[2], John[1]) was born 25 Apr 1831 in Truro, Nova Scotia.; mar. **Sophia Emily Stewart**, a native of Halifax Co., N. S., on 10

Oct 1854. They resided for some years in Nova Scotia, first in Truro, then in Pictou, and finally in New Glasgow. About 1870, the family permanently removed to Natick, Mass.

Children:

4682    i. Sarah[9] Ellen Eaton, b. in Truro, N.S.; mar. Archibald McKenzie, 1873.
4683    ii. Charles[9] Owen Eaton, b. in Truro, N.S.; mar. Josephine Rhem, 1880.
4684    iii. William[9] Ward Eaton, b. in Pictou, N.S.; died young in Natick, Mass. 1875.
4685    iv. Lucy[9] Auguster Eaton, b. in Pictou, N.S.; mar. Charles Flagg of Natick, Mass.
4686    v. George[9] Alexander Eaton, b. in Pictou, N.S.
4687    vi. John[9] Robert Eaton, b. in Pictou, N.S.
4688    vii. Elizabeth[9] Jane Eaton, b. in New Glasgow, N.S.
4689    viii. Frank[9] Warren Eaton, b. 5 Nov 1871, Natick, Mass.
4690    ix. Lilla[9] Sophia Eaton, b. 22 May 1877, Natick, Mass.


**2859. George[8] McDonald Eaton** (William[7] C., Daniel[6], Timothy[5], James[4], Jonathan[3], Thomas[2], John[1]) was born 31 Aug 1835 in Truro, Nova Scotia; mar. on 7 Mar 1866, **Martha Pudsey** of Horton, King's Co., Nova Scotia, who was born 13 Feb 1842.

Children, born apparently in Nova Scotia:

4691    i. Kate[9] Evelyn Eaton, b. 15 Jan 1867.
4692    ii. Caroline[9] Maude Eaton, b. 21 Mar 1869.
4693    iii. Georgiana[9] Loretta Eaton, b. 22 Sep 1873.


**2860. James[8] Hiller Eaton** (William[7] C., Daniel[6], Timothy[5], James[4], Jonathan[3], Thomas[2], John[1]) was born 15 Feb 1838 in Truro, Nova Scotia; mar. on 2 Jan 1862, **Anna King Pitblado**, born in Dumferline, Scotland, 2 Aug 1844. They res. in Truro, N.S., where James was a civil engineer.

Children born in Truro, N.S.:

4694    i. Anna[9] Cora Eaton, b. 17 Oct 1862.
4695    ii. James[9] Pitblado Eaton, b. 29 Apr 1864; died 19 Aug 1865.
4696    iii. James[9A] Bruce Eaton, b. 10 Mar 1866; died 10 Feb 1867.
4697    iv. Lucy[9] Catherine Eaton, b. 14 May 1867.
4698    v. (Daniel Isaac) Vernon[9] Eaton, b. 19 Sep 1869; mar. in Fredericton, New Brunswick. He was a major in the Canadian Army at a precocious age, and died before

1896 in London.
**4699**   vi. Robert[9] Berry Eaton, b. 5 Aug 1871; also an officer in the Canadian Army.
**4700**   vii. Colin[9] Eaton, a twin b. 22 Jun 1873; died in infancy.
**4701**   viii. Jenny[9] Isabell Eaton, a twin b. 22 Jun 1873; died young?
**4702**   ix. Grace[9] Edith Irene Eaton. b. 25 Oct 1875.
**4703**   x. William[9] Cater Eaton, a triplet b. 31 Jan 1876; d. young?
**4704**   xi. John[9] S. Eaton, a triplet b. 31 Jan 1876; died young?
**4705**   xii. Sophia[9] A. Eaton, a triplet b. 31 Jan 1876; died young?
**4706**   xiii. Simon[9] Edwin Eaton, b. 11 May 1878; also in the Canadian Army.

**2861. Hiram[8] Hyde Eaton** (William[7] C., Daniel[6], Timothy[5], James[4], Jonathan[3], Thomas[2], John[1]) was born 4 Nov 1842 in Truro, Nova Scotia; mar. on 27 Oct 1870, **Isabella Carlyle** who was born in Truro on 29 Jul 1850. Information is lacking to us as to where this couple settled, although in context this likely means that they stayed in Truro.

Children:

**4707**   i. Frances[9] Alice Eaton, b. 24 Jul 1872.
**4708**   ii. Harry[9] Franklin Eaton, b. 4 May 1875.
**4709**   iii. Lawrence[9] Chester Eaton, b. 21 Jan 1877.
**4710**   iv. Roy[9] Wendell Eaton, b. 8 Sep 1881.
**4711**   v. Augusta[9] Ida Eaton, b. 14 Jan 1886.

**2865. David[8] Hamilton Eaton** (Daniel[7-6], Timothy[5], James[4], Jonathan[3], Thomas[2], John[1]) was born 13 Jun 1829 in Truro, Nova Scotia; mar. on 16 Sep 1866, **Caroline Matilda Eaton (#4388)**, born to Stephen[8] and Mary D. (Parker) Eaton on 22 Oct 1842 in Cornwallis, N.S. They had only one child. David died 22 Sep 1879, and his widow Mary mar. 2d, J. S. Johnson, a merchant in Truro.

Child born in Truro, N.S.:

**4712**   i. John[9] Edgar Eaton, b. 26 Feb 1871.

**2868. Cyrus[8] Eaton** (Daniel[7-6], Timothy[5], James[4], Jonathan[3], Thomas[2], John[1]) was born 10 Apr 1836 in Truro, Nova Scotia; mar. on 16 Nov 1871, **Margaret Augusta Miller**. She was the daughter of William Miller, a hardware merchant in Truro and one of the town's wealthiest men, and at one time Mayor of the town.

Children born in Truro, Nova Scotia:

**4713**   i. Alva[9] Edwin Eaton, b. 19 Dec. 1872.

**4714**    ii. William[9] Daniel Eaton, b. 21 Dec 1874.

**2870. Albert[8] Claude Eaton** (Elbridge[7], Phineas[6], Timothy[5], James[4], Jonathan[3], Thomas[2], John[1]) was born 24 Nov 1843 in Haverhill, Mass. He apparently responded to his older brother Eugene's invitation for the family to join him in Chattanooga, Tenn. after the Civil War, for he is the head of an 1880 household in Chattanooga which includes not only brother Eugene, then in the iron ore business and still unmarried; but also his widowed mother Nancy. The house is completed by his wife **Amanda**, born in N.H. in 1844, and their daughter.

Child, b. in Mass. (presumably Haverhill):

**4715**    i. Katie[9] Eaton, b. ca. 1868; taken by family to Chattanooga.

**2873. Frank[8] Howard Eaton** (Elbridge[7], Phineas[6], Timothy[5], James[4], Jonathan[3], Thomas[2], John[1]) was born 14 Jul 1849 in Bradford, Mass. He was a clerk with Hastings & Co. in Haverhill in 1869, boarding with his widowed mother. But then the family decided to accept the invitation of Frank's oldest brother Eugene to join him in Chattanooga, which had seized Eugene's fancy during his Civil War service there. So as of 1870 we find Frank clerking in a store in Whitesides Twp. outside Chattanooga, and lodging not with his family but in the household of a native of England who was a superintendent of some local coal mines. We cannot find him in 1880, but in 1900 he is a dealer in marble living on College St. in Chattanooga. He had been married in 1875 to **Susie __?__**, b. Dec. 1850 in Ohio, and they had had two children reach maturity.

Children, probably born in Chattanooga, Tenn:

**4716**    i. Fannie[9] Eaton, b. Feb 1877; is living with her parents, 1900.
**4717**    ii. Child[9] Eaton, born later.

**2882. (Daniel) Herbert[8] Eaton** (Daniel[7], Phineas[6], Timothy[5], James[4], Jonathan[3], Thomas[2], John[1]) was born 29 Jun 1849 in West Newbury, Mass.; mar. **Emma Rebecca Chase**, who was born in 1851. This couple res. first in Georgetown, Mass. where they are found in 1880; but soon thereafter removed Haverhill for most of their remaining lives. D. Herbert was a bookkeeper there in the early years, and in a grocery business for a while, but by 1890 settled in as a "shoe cutter" in the Haverhill factories until his retirement. In 1920, he and Emma lived at 53 Arlington St. in Haverhill. Later they moved to Boston, probably to be near their daughter, but he returned "home" to spend his last two years at the River Rest Home in Haverhill. He died 12 Mar 1932 at Haverhill; wife Emma died in 1938.

Children (perhaps partial):

**4718**    i. Ernest[9] Whittier Eaton, b. 1873; worked with his father as a shoe cutter in his early years, but by 1897 became a plant foreman, first in Haverhill and later at the Grover factory, Stoneham, Mass. He died 4 Jul 1916 in Stoneham, marital status unknown to us.

**4719**    ii. Edith[9] K. Eaton, b. 1877; mar. Dudley T. Fitts and resided in Boston, having at least three children there.

**2887. Roswell[8] Jameson Eaton** (Daniel[7], Phineas[6], Timothy[5], James[4], Jonathan[3], Thomas[2] John[1]) was born 6 Nov 1857 in West Newbury, Mass.; mar. **Mary E. Allison**. They resided at Merrimac, Mass., where he was a silver plater at the J.H. Murphy Plating Works for many years; and later performed the same trade in auto factories in Amesbury and even Newton, N.H. He was a clarinet player in a number of local bands and orchestras. He died at Merrimac, Mass. in Oct 1925. His widow Mary died in 1931.

Children in Merrimac, Mass.:

**4720**    i. Daughter[9] Eaton, b. ? ; mar. Charles E. Colman.

**4721**    ii. George[9] M. Eaton, b. ? .

**4722**    iii. Daughter[9] Eaton, b. ? ; mar. Warren N. Howe and resided in Haverhill.

**2889. Alonzo[8] Ward Eaton** (Ward[7-6], Timothy[5], James[4], Jonathan[3], Thomas[2], John[1]) was born 10 Mar 1832, presumably in New York State; mar. **Abigail Knickerbocker** (she born N.Y., 1829), on 19 Aug 1854. The history of this couple is somewhat murky, but we pick them up unequivocally in Butler Twp., Branch Co., Michigan, in 1860 and 1870; and at Whitewater Twp., Grand Traverse Co., Michigan in 1880. Alonzo, at least later in life, was a sawyer by trade, and attracted to places and times where a lot of lumber was being cut.

Children:

**4723**    i. George[9] Eaton, b. 2 Dec 1855, N.Y. State.

**4724**    ii. Elizabeth[9] A. Eaton, b. ca. 1859 in Butler Twp., Michigan; mar. Kasuth(?) S. Stites (b. Ohio, 1852).

**4725**    iii. Emma[9] A. Eaton, b. ca. 1866 in Butler Twp., Mich.

**4726**    iv. Charles[9] A. Eaton, b. ca. 1873.

**2895. Edward[8] L. Eaton** (Ward[7-6]. Timothy[5], James[4], Jonathan[3], Thomas[2], John[1]) was born 11 Feb 1850 in New York State, just before his family removed to Carbondale, Pa. He mar. **Hattie __?__**, b. 1860, also a N.Y. native, ca. 1876. In 1880, this young couple is found at Oakfield Twp. in Kent Co., Michigan, near Grand Rapids, where Edward is listed as a farmer.

Child:

4727    i. Edna⁹ May Eaton, b. ca. 1877.

**2908. James⁸ Bradford Eaton** (James⁷, *James⁶, James⁵*, James⁴, Jonathan³, Thomas², John¹) was born 15 Aug 1815 in "Wendell" (later the town of Sunapee), N.H.; mar. **Sarah R. Hobson** of Deering, N.H., 29 Sep 1836. They resided for a few years in Hillsborough (Bridge), N.H., but in 1841 removed to the burgeoning river town of Nashua, N.H. Although his life was cut short in middle age, he was a prominent citizen in Nashua, being a high-degree Mason and a committed member of the Methodist Episcopal Church. He was associated with railroading in Nashua, and by 1850 had become road master of the Nashua & Lowell and Boston & Lowell road. On 10 Oct 1867 he slipped on the platform of a car at the Woburn watering place and fell beneath the wheels of the the train.

Children (i-ii born at Hillsboro Bridge; iii-iv born at Nashua, N.H.):

4728    i. George⁹ F. Eaton, b. ca. 1838; mar. Arabelle M. Harding, 14 Mar 1860 in Nashua, N.H. He took advanced religious studies, becoming a Reverend and a Doctor of Divinity and later the presiding elder of the Boston North District New England Conference (for more, cf. Parker, 1897).

4729    ii. Alvin⁹ Sumner Eaton, b. 4 Dec 1840; mar. 1st, Emily J. Shaw, 5 Jul 1857. He served in the Civil War, 1861-65, and was a prisoner of war, Nov 1864 to Mar 1865. He then res. in Nashua, and mar. there 2d, Rebecca H. Sawyer of West Buxton, Me., 16 Oct 1868. He ran a market for some years, and was also in the concrete business. He was for many years a deputy sheriff in Hillsborough and Rockingham Cos., and in 1890 was named city marshal for Nashua (for more, cf. Parker, 1897).

4730    iii. Charles⁹ F. G. Eaton, b. ca. 1854; was a locomotive engineer.

4731    iv. Etta⁹ Eaton, b. 30 Oct 1856; mar. John F. Burnham.

**2912. John⁸ L. Eaton** (John⁷, *James⁶, James⁵*, James⁴, Jonathan³, Thomas², John¹) was born 16 Feb 1811 in Hillsborough, N.H.; mar. **Susan E. Gibson** (born 1818 in Mass.) ca. 1835, or several years before John's father died. The couple did settle in Hillsborough, but apparently did not take over the family's homestead farm, since John L. is listed as a farm (or "day") laborer in both 1850 and 1860; and while he is a farmer in 1870, his real estate is negligible. He died 21 Feb 1888; his widow Susan died 1894.

Children, born Hillsborough, N.H.:

4732   i. Elizabeth⁹ Eaton, b. ca. 1837; died later in Manchester, N.H.
4733   ii. John⁹ G. Eaton, b. ca. 1839; mar. Helen Weston of Amherst, N.H. He died later in Waltham, Mass.
4734   iii. Eliza⁹ J. Eaton, b. ca. 1842; res. in Manchester, N.H.
4735   iv. Leander⁹ Eaton, b. ca. 13 Aug 1846; he went off to the Civil War, but returned to Hillsborough and died there, 24 Sep 1863, prob. never married.

**2913. (Col.) Horace⁸ Eaton** (John⁷, *James⁶, James⁵*, James⁴, Jonathan³, Thomas², John¹) was born 9 Mar 1813 in Hillsborough, N.H.; mar. on 4 Nov 1836 at Peterborough, N.H., **Eliza Colby**, daughter of Daniel and Betsey (Emery) Colby of Deering, N.H. They resided in Hillsborough. Why Horace was addressed as "Col." is not clear. He was a prosperous farmer and also a moulder by trade, but very active in community affairs, holding many civic offices. He died 28 Aug 1900.

Children (all born Hillsborough, N.H .):

4736   i. Stillman⁹ S(ilvester?) Eaton, b. 8 Feb 1838; m. 1 Feb 1872, Josephine M. Gage, daughter of George W. and Nancy E. (Crane) Gage. Stillman worked in a sawmill in Hillsborough and died there 20 Sep 1878.
4737   ii. Harrison⁹ H. Eaton, b. 17 Jul 1840; d. 17 Aug 1845.
4738   iii. Warren⁹ C. Eaton, b. 27 Nov 1843; d. unmar. 9 Nov 1898.

**2914. William⁸ Eaton** (John⁷, *James⁶, James⁵*, James⁴, Jonathan³, Thomas², John¹) was born 6 Aug 1815 in Hillsborough, N.H.; mar. **Abigail "Orthana" Burtt** (b. 1821) of Bennington, N.H. They res. in Bennington where William was a carpenter. He died there, 30 May 1891.

Children (all born Bennington, N.H.):

4739   i. Mariah⁹ Louisa Eaton, b. 13 Nov 1842; d. 30 Nov 1877.
4740   ii. Charles⁹ E. Eaton, b. 16 Feb 1848; mar. Ann Cochran of Antrim, N.H. and resided in Bennington, N.H. He died there, 16 Feb 1918.

**2915. (Hon.) Harrison⁸ Eaton** (John⁷, *James⁶, James⁵*, James⁴, Jonathan³, Thomas², John¹) was born 9 Dec 1817 in Hillsborough, N.H. At 18 he went to Peterborough, N.H., to learn the foundry business, and

later settled in Amherst, N.H., with the Hartshorn & Eaton Stove Manu-
facturers. He mar 1st, **Lucy P. Hartshorn**, 4 Aug 1840 in Amherst, but
she died there 26 Nov 1843 with childbirth complications. He mar. 2d,
on 13 Dec 1846, **Laura A. Wheeler**, born 4 Mar 1822 at Merrimack,
N.H. Harrison died 9 Mar 1889 at Amherst.

Children with Lucy, b. Amherst, N.H.:

**4741**   i. Mary[9] A. Eaton, b. Oct 1840; d. 7 Mar 1844.
**4742**   ii. Henry[9] H. Eaton, b. Nov 1843; d. 17 Feb 1844.

Children with Laura:

**4743**   iii. George[9] Harry Eaton, b. 16 Sep 1849, Amherst; mar. Susie
           A. Few, 26 Jan 1871 and had three sons: Eddie[10] Eaton,
           b. 27 May 1871; Harry[10] B. Eaton, b. 18 Dec 1873; and
           Charles[10] Eaton, b. 2 Mar 1879. Harry B. d. 14 Jan 1879.
**4744**   iv. Emma[9] L. Eaton, b. 25 May 1857 in Nashua, N.H.; mar.
           Herbert Belden. She died 11 Dec 1898.

**2918. Samuel[8] Eaton** (John[7], *James[6]*, *James[5]*, James[4], Jonathan[3],
Thomas[2], John[1]) was born 25 Sep 1825 in Hillsborough, N.H. At a
young age he went to Amherst, N.H. to work as a moulder in his brother
Harrison's foundry there. He mar. **Eliza Ann Kinson** in 1846. They
spent their life in Amherst, where Samuel died 8 Dec 1892.

Children, all born Amherst, N.H.:

**4745**   i. George[9] S. Eaton, b. 19 Nov 1848; mar. Georgianna Weston,
           23 Sep 1867 in Brookline, N.H., she being the daughter
           of Isaac P. and Mary J. (Howard) Weston. He learned the
           moulder's trade in Amherst, Nashua, N.H., and Gardner,
           Mass. The couple removed to Antrim after 1870. In May
           1883 they settled on a farm four miles from Milford, N.H.
           Son Clarence[10] W. Eaton b. ca. 17 Feb 1871; died of bone
           cancer, 16 Feb 1887 in Amherst.
**4746**   ii. Infant[9] Eaton, b., d. 1850.
**4747**   iii. Elizabeth[9] "Lizzie" Eaton, b. 14 Nov 1852; mar. 1st, Frank
           Lovejoy; and 2d, Edgar Danforth. She d. 8 Mar 1817 in
           Wilton, N.H.
**4748**   iv. Nellie[9] M. Eaton, b. 23 Oct 1857; mar. Frank Taylor and res.
           in Amherst.

**2919. James[8] L. Eaton** (John[7], *James[6]*, *James[5]*, James[4], Jonathan[3],
Thomas[2], John[1]) was born a twin of Luther S. Eaton on 10 Jun 1828 in
Hillsborough, N.H., but removed early to Amherst to join his brothers.

He mar. **Adeline A. Noyes,** 12 Jan 1850, and after 1857 they removed to Mont Vernon, N.H., where he was a farmer. He died there 21 Jan 1862.

Children, both born Amherst, N.H.:

4749    i. James[9] Edwin Eaton, b. ca. 1853; removed to Pennsylvania.
4750    ii. Emma[9] E. Eaton, b. ca. 1857; mar. Edward Belden and they removed to Massachusetts.

**2920. Luther[8] S. Eaton** (John[7], *James[6], James[5]*, James[4], Jonathan[3], Thomas[2], John[1]) was born a twin of James L. Eaton on 10 Jun 1828 in Hillsborough, N.H.; mar. 1st, **Eleanor** (or **"Ellen"**) **A. Smiley** on 27 Dec 1849, and they res. in Hillsborough Bridge where Luther was a merchant tailor for many years. Wife Ellen died in the early or mid-1860s, and he mar. 2d, on 1 Sep 1868, **Abbie Hemphill** of Henniker, N.H., daughter of Stephen and Eunice (Newton) Hemphill, altho in another rendition the name was **Mercy Newhall** instead (*VR* at Concord, N.H.). This second wife died, however, on 4 Jul 1869, apparently as a result of bearing twins. Luther then mar. on 14 Nov 1871 at Hancock, N.H., **Jennie A. Boutelle/Boutwell**, born to David and Almeda (Pratt) Boutelle of that town on 18 Jul 1839, her first marriage. Luther S. died 13 Apr 1905 and was buried at Antrim, N.H. Widow Jennie died 27 Sep 1924.

Children with Ellen at Hillsborough, N.H.:

4751    i. James[9] H. Eaton, b. 30 May 1851; d. 11 Aug 1851.
4752    ii. Henry[9] B. Eaton, b. 12 Jul 1853; mar. Mary Beard Whittle, 17 Feb 1874 in Hillsborough. They had at least one son, Herbert[10] Henry Eaton, b. 27 Sep 1877, Hillsborough.
4753    iii. Estella[9] Mary Eaton, b. 2 Nov 1855.

Twins with Abbie at Hillsborough, N.H.

4754    iv. Arthur[9] N. Eaton, twin of Abbie, b. 4 Jun 1869; d. young.
4755    v. Abbie[9] Eaton, twin of Arthur, b. 4 Jun 1869; mar. Forest Morse.

Child with Jennie at Hillsborough, N.H.:

4756    vi. Bertha[9] P. Eaton, b. 12 Apr 1874; mar. Walter Prescott of Concord, N.H., a railroad engineer.

**2928. James[8] W. Eaton** (James[7], *James[6], James[5]*, James[4], Jonathan[3], Thomas[2], John[1]) was born ca. 15 Oct 1823 in Littleton, N.H. As a young man he migrated back to Antrim, N.H. in 1841, where he was a blacksmith much of his life. In 1845 he mar. **Mary Caroline Caldwell**, then of Medford, Mass., but born ca. 1822 in N.H. After their children were raised they removed in 1878 to Bennington, N.H., where he died 17 Nov 1800.

Children, all born in Antrim, N.H.:

4757    i. (Francelia) Alcesta[9] Eaton, b. 1846; mar. Amos Wyman of Hillsborough Bridge.
4758   ii. Martha[9] J. Eaton, b. ca. 1848; mar. Albert Baldwin and removed to Brattleboro, Vt.
4759  iii. Edwin[9] L. Eaton, b. ca 1853; mar. Frances ("Fannie") J. Dodge, 28 Oct 1875 in Antrim; he died of a gunshot wound, 21 Jul 1885, Antrim.
4760   iv. Ida[9] E. Eaton, b. ca. 15 Mar 1858; d. 20 Jul 1862.


**2932. Samuel[8] Willard Eaton** (Samuel[7], *James[6]*, *James[5]*, James[4], Jonathan[3], Thomas[2], John[1]) was born 2 Nov 1819 in Francestown, N.H.; mar. 1st, on 19 Jan 1843, **Sarah Ann Carr**, born 20 Feb 1820 at Antrim, N.H. They resided first in Francestown where they began their family; but before the 1850 Census they had moved to a medium-sized farm in Deering. They were back in Francestown, however, when wife Sarah died 6 Mar 1857. Samuel mar. 2d, **Hannah Lewis**, 2 Feb 1860. They remained in Francestown the rest of their lives, with Hannah dying there 18 Mar 1900, and Samuel following on 1 Oct 1902.

Children with Sarah (all but iv born in Francestown):

4761    i. Mary[9] Jane Eaton, b. 22 Nov 1843; d. 15 Dec 1868.
4762   ii. Alton[9] W. Eaton, b. 17 Apr 1846; died 24 Oct 1848, Francestown.
4763  iii. Alton[9A] W. Eaton, b. 13 Aug 1848; mar. Maria Gould of Deering, N.H. on 29 Nov 1871 in Manchester, N.H. They res. Francestown and had three children: Willard[10] Clifton Eaton, b. 10 Nov 1873; Carleton[10] Clement Eaton, b. 1 May 1876; and Anna[10] Belle Eaton, b. 9 Jun 1878. Alton[9A] died 11 Jan 1893 in Hillsborough, N.H.
4764   iv. William[9] C. Eaton, b. 12 Jul 1852 in Deering, N.H.; mar. Nancy A. Hoyt of Francestown, 7 Oct 1877. Nancy died rapidly, 3 Oct 1879; and William followed on 3 Dec 1880.

Child with Hannah in Francestown:

4765    v. Child[9] Eaton, b. May 1862; d. in infancy.


**2937. George[8] W. Eaton** (Isaac[7], James[6], James[5]. James[4], Jonathan[3], Thomas[2], John[1]) was born 30 Nov 1840 and grew up in Francestown, N.H.; before he was 20 he moved to Antrim, N.H., and mar. a local girl there, **Mary Jeannette Dow** on 4 Nov 1860. They removed to Suncook, N.H., in 1868, and then on to Woonsocket, R.I. George died in 1903 and was buried back in Antrim.

Children (all but v. born in Antrim, N.H.):

4766　i. Annie[9] J. Eaton, b. 20 Feb 1862; mar. Charles Carter. She died in 1926.
4767　ii. Hattie[9] W. Eaton, b. 17 Mar 1864.
4768　iii. Sarah[9] Eaton, b. 29 Jul 1865.
4769　iv. Charles[9] L. Eaton, b. 1 Oct 1867; died 1927.
4770　v. Nellie[9] M. Eaton, b. 30 Sep 1870 in Suncook, N.H.

**2945. George[8] M. Eaton** (James[7], David[6], James[5-4], Jonathan[3], Thomas[2], John[1]) was born 19 May 1834 in Watertown, Mass., but grew up in Goffstown, N.H.; mar. **Mary A. Greer** of Goffstown, 28 Apr 1861. They res. in Goffstown, where George was occupied with farming and lumbering for a decade or so after marriage, but removed to Grasmere, N.H. in 1873, returning by 1880 to Goffstown. He was a Baptist and a Republican in politics, and served the town as a Selectman. He died 19 Oct 1914.

Children with Mary:

4771　i. Adonelle[9] "Nellie" M. Eaton, b. 10 Jun 1863; mar. George E. Whitney. She died 1924.
4772　ii. George[9] Leon Eaton, b. 18 Apr 1867; mar. Nettie J. Robertson (she born Aug 1866); had at least one son, William[10] R. Eaton, b. 1897.
4773　iii. Elizabeth[9] M. Eaton, b. 11 Feb 1874, who graduated from the Normal School in Framingham, Mass., teaching for several years in the public schools of that state until she matriculated at Brown University for further education.

**2949. Otis[8] Eaton** (David[7-6], James[5-4], Jonathan[3], Thomas[2], John[1]) was born Sep 1844 in Tremont Twp., Ill.; mar. **Lucy Josephine __?__** (she born May 1843 in Illinois) ca. 1869. Otis took over his father's highly prosperous farm homesetead in Tremont, although by 1900 he had moved to Champaign Twp., Ill.

Children in Tremont, Ill.:

4774　i. Anna[9] Eaton, b. May 1870.
4775　ii. William[9] (H.?) Eaton, b. Sep 1872 and was a farmer.
4776　iii. Horace[9] Eaton, b. 1875.
4777　iv. Lewis[9] H. Eaton, b. Sep 1877.

**2952. David⁸ Eaton** (David⁷⁻⁶, James⁵⁻⁴, Jonathan³, Thomas², John¹) was born Dec 1850 in Tremont Twp., Ill.; mar. **Harriet E. __?__** in 1876. She had been born in Mar 1852 in Illinois. David was a farmer, and they res. for a time in Tremont, but later removed to Normal, McLean Co., Ill.

All children with Harriet (all surviving in 1990):

4778    i. Charles⁹ D. Eaton, b. May 1878.
4779    ii. H. May⁹ (fem.) Eaton, b. Jul 1880.
4780    iii. William⁹ B. Eaton, b. Mar 1892.
4781    iv. Alice⁹ C. Eaton, b. Jan 1896.


**2961. West⁸ D. Eaton** (Nathaniel⁷, Cotton⁶, James⁵⁻⁴, Jonathan³, Thomas², John¹) was born Sep 1850 in Hermon, Me.; mar. **Annie M. __?__**, b. Jul 1849 in Me., in 1875. By 1900, they res. in Bangor, where West was a miller. Annie bore him two children, but one probably died young.

Known child:

4782    i. Herbert⁹ D. Eaton, b. Feb 1880.


**2966. Fred⁸ G. Eaton** (Josiah⁷, Cotton⁶, James⁵⁻⁴, Jonathan³, Thomas², John¹) was born Aug 1859 in Hermon, Me.; mar. **Alice Louise Gibson**, born Jan 1864. In 1900 they were res. in Bangor, Me. with their four sons. Fred died in 1919 in Foxcroft, Me.

Children with Alice:

4783    i. Harold⁹ G. Eaton, b. Apr 1884.
4784    ii. Arthur⁹ G. Eaton, b. Oct 1890 in Hermon, Me.; mar. Esther
          C. Swanson. He died 1966, Bangor, Me.
4785    iii. George⁹ P. Eaton, b. Mar 1892.
4786    iv. Fred⁹ G., Jr., b. Apr 1898.


**2967. (Gen.) John⁸ Eaton** (John⁷⁻⁶, Nathaniel⁵, James⁴, Jonathan³, Thomas², John¹) was born 5 Dec 1829 in Sutton, N.H.; a graduate of Dartmouth Coll., 1854; removed to Cleveland, Ohio, to teach, 1854. He was ordained for the ministry just before the Civil War, and became chaplain of the 27th Ohio Volunteer Infantry. He was twice a prisoner of war early in the conflict. An impressive aide to higher officers, he rose rapidly through the ranks. Blacks who made their way by the thousands over the Union lines under Gen. Grant's command in western Tennessee, Mississippi and northern Alabama had to be welcomed and cared for. Since they needed employment, and crops were in risk of perishing on large plantations whose owners had fled, the notion of a "Freedman's Bureau" to organize the liberated blacks to harvest these crops took root. Gen. Grant selected Chaplain John Eaton to administer the effort. He was a great success in this role. He became a colonel of the 63rd colored infantry, and brigadier general by brevet. After the war's close, in 1866, he founded the Memphis Post as a Republican newspaper in that Tennessee City. He was also elected Tennessee superintendent of public instruction, and arranged for the instruction of 185,000 pupils in the new schools. The Grant Administration soon named him U.S. Commissioner of Education, a position he took in March 1870. He held this role until 1885, and was responsible for the growth of the Bureau of Education from a small office to an organization with significant impact on the development of schooling in the United States. He left the Bureau to become president of Marietta College in Ohio. After this stint he returned to Washington, D.C., essentially for the rest of his career, although he travelled widely abroad, and received honors in France, Brazil and Japan for his tireless efforts in the cause of broad-based public education systems. He was twice elected president of the American Social Science Assocation, and was one of the vice presidents of the American Association for the Advancement of Science. (Worthen, 1890; Wilson, 1887-89; Columbia Encyclopedia, 2002; and many articles on facets of his career.)

On 29 Sep 1864, John had mar. **Alice Eugenia Shirley** of Vicksburg, Miss., and had four children with her. He was a not-too-distant cousin of the Rev. William Hadley Eaton, senior author of this genealogy, as the Reverend's great grandfather was the General's great, great grandfather. Equally to the point, their respective branches had removed northward from Haverhill, Mass. in the same general period, the one to Goffstown, N.H., and the other to Sutton, N.H.; and these towns they each grew up in were less than 30 miles apart. Although a generation displaced on the family tree, they were nearly contemporaries, with the General being only 11 years the younger. Since they were both eminent and well-travelled, they certainly knew *of* one another, and probably had met numerous times. When the Reverend died with our genealogy here unfinished, his research materials worked their way into the custody of General John in Washington, D.C.; and it was he who deposited these precious documents with the New England Historical Genealogical Society in 1904, two years before his own death. So we are nearly as indebted to the General as to the Reverend for the wise preservation of this genealogy.

Children with Alice:

4787 i. James[9] Shirley Eaton, b. 1 Aug 1868 in Nashville, Tenn.; he entered Dartmouth College but moved to Marietta College when his father became president there, and graduated in 1889. He then became an auditor for the Tennessee, Virginia and Georgia system of railroads. He mar. Ethel Osgood Mason.

**4788**     ii. Elsie[9] Janet Eaton, b. 6 Feb 1871 in Washington, D.C.;
                  studied at the Lake Erie Seminary in Painesville, Ohio.
**4789**    iii. John[9] Quincy Eaton, b. 14 Jul 1873 in Washington, D.C.
                  He graduated from Marietta, College, 1893.
**4790**    iv. Frederick[9] Charles, b. 9 Aug 1877; d. 15 Jun 1878.


   **2970.  Frederick[8] Eaton** (John[7-6], Nathaniel[5], James[4], Jonathan[3],
Thomas[2], John[1]) was born 10 Feb 1835 in Sutton, N.H.  Early in life he
began clerking at stores, first in neighboring Bradford, N.H., and then in
a bigger establishment in Manchester, N.H.  About 1856 he went to Ohio
to visit his older brother John (above), who was at that time Superintendent of schools in Toledo, Ohio.  In the course of that visit John agreed
to use both his own good name locally and some capital, to help Fred
start something of a department store in Toledo.  The store opened the
same month as the financial crash of 1857 occurred, but after some
struggle the venture flourished, and thirty years later the enterprise was
making a million dollars annually in sales.  Fred became an influential
figure in Toledo, becoming director in several banks and manufacturing
institutions.  He was even mentioned as a Republican candidate for Governor in Ohio, but refused to let his name be put forward.
   On 8 Mar 1860, Fred mar. 1st, **Mary Helen Shirley**.  She was not
apparently of the same family as brother John's Vicksburg, Miss., wife of
the same surname, since Mary Helen was the daughter of Robert M. and
Sophia (McCutcheon) Shirley, the father being associated with the
wholesale merchandising firm of Lawrence & Shirley in Boston, but residing on Shirley Hill in Goffstown, N.H.  Presumably Fred met her in
connection with visits to his native New Hampshire.  She died 2 Jan 1887,
and Fred mar. 2d, on 23 Jan 1889, **Laura Helen Baldwin**, born 10 Jul
1852 to De Witt Clinton and Laura May (Wheeler) Baldwin.  Her grandparents held the first prayer meeting in the Western Reserve; and their
son De Witt was a central figure in the financial and railroad affairs of
Cleveland and Toledo.  Fred's second marriage was short-lived, as he
died 4 Feb 1890 after a short illness.  His widow Laura was carrying his
child at the time, and she died 2 Jun 1890, a few days after the son's
birth.

         Child with Mary in Toledo, Ohio:

**4791**     i. Helen[9] Shirley Eaton, b. 5 Aug 1866; d. 13 Apr 1876.

         Posthumous child with Laura in Toledo, Ohio:

**4792**    ii. Frederick[9] Eaton, b. 31 May 1890.


   **2971.  Lucien[8] Bonaparte Eaton** (John[7-6], Nathaniel[5], James[4],
Jonathan[3], Thomas[2], John[1]) was born 8 Mar 1837 in Sutton, N.H., named
after his father's brother (cf. **#1466**); graduated from Dartmouth, 1859,

having taught school and studied law on the side. He followed his older brothers westward to Ohio, and in Dec. 1859, became principal of a grammar school in Cleveland. After the Civil War broke, he became a second lieutenant in the 65th Ohio Volunteer Infantry, Oct. 1861. His regiment was part of "the Army of the Cumberland," and he participated in a long series of famous battles (Shiloh, Perryville, Stone River, Chickamauga, Missionary Ridge, Rocky Face Ridge, Resaca, and New Hope Church, with countless lesser skirmishes). He rose rapidly in the ranks and in 1864, just before the battle of Kenesaw Mtn. became a Lt. Col. and was dispatched to Arkansas to oversee the Freedman's Bureau there, as his older brother John was doing in Tennessee.

After the war he settled in Memphis, Tenn., and returned to the study of law. In 1866 he joined his brother in the Memphis *Daily Post*, becoming editorial and business manager. He later was appointed U. S. Marshall for the western district of Tennessee, serving from 1870 to 1877, after which he began legal practice. His interests lay in real estate, however, and he accumulated thousands of acres of cotton lands in Shelby Co., as well as hundreds of houses in Memphis that were emptied in the wake of the savage yellow fever epidemics of 1878 and 1879. He headed a firm dealing in lumber and another land title abstracts. He served as a Memphis representative in the state legislature.

On 26 Dec 1867, Lucien had mar. **Clara Winters**, daughter of Valentine and Catherine (Harshman) Winters, a banking family in Dayton, Ohio. She died 23 Aug 1885.

Children (i-ii born in Dayton, Ohio; iii-iv in Memphis, Tenn.):

**4793**    i. Valentine⁹ Winters Eaton, b. 1 Nov 1870.
**4794**    ii. Katie⁹ Eaton, b. 28 Jul 1872; d. 27 Jul 1873.
**4795**    iii. Lucien⁹ Eaton, b. 19 Oct 1877; d. 24 Nov 1877.
**4796**    iv. Clara⁹ Eaton, b. 13 Jun 1879; died 2 Jul 1879.


**2973. James⁸ Andrew Eaton** (John⁷⁻⁶, Nathaniel⁵, James⁴, Jonathan³, Thomas², John¹) was born 30 Sep 1841 in Sutton, N.H. After his studies at Phillips Academy, Andover, Mass., he went to work in the store of his brother Frederick in Toledo, Ohio. He subsequently went into business for himself in Ft. Wayne, Ind., and Memphis, Tenn. He finally went to Michigan and was in business for 17 years in Adrian, and soon after his arrival there mar. on 10 Jan 1872, **Fannie Josephine Newell**. born 24 Dec 1847 to James and Joanna Wight (Needham) Newell of Adrian, her father noted as one of the organizers of the Republican Party in that area.

Child:

**4797**    i. Mary⁹ Eaton, b. 24 Mar 1877 in Adrian, Mich.

### #12. The Eaton Grange, Sutton, N.H.

For at least the quarter century from 1865 to 1890 (and perhaps for longer, since our last information about it comes from Worthen (1890)), the "Eaton Grange" in Sutton, N.H. was the site of a remarkable and large-scale annual Eaton family reunion within the Haverhill branch. Two twigs of this branch, stemming from John[5] (#235) who had settled for a while in Bradford, N.H., before the Revolution, and from Lt. Nathaniel[5] (#208) who had helped locate his three eldest sons near the southeast corner of neighboring Sutton in the 1790s, provided the beginnings of a large Eaton community in the Bradford/Warner/Sutton area before 1800. This community was fed also to some degree by the Haverhill Eatons in Hopkinton, N.H., some 15 miles further to the southeast (see Map 5, p. 139).

The key site for these reunions lay near the brow of what was then called Kimball's hill, a local prominence some 1100 feet in altitude. One of the earliest Sutton settlers, Caleb Kimball had developed a very large and prosperous farm here, and when John[6] Eaton (#531) arrived in the area just after 1790, he married Caleb's daughter Polly, building their own house next door, where he farmed, pursued his trade as a brazier, and opened a store. This couple raised 12 children of considerable accomplishment as adults there on the hill; and as two of John's brothers and then a third came in to settle down the road, they added another 17 Eaton children of the seventh generation who reached adulthood in the neighborhood.

One of these, John[7], Jr., when recently married, was invited by his grandfather Caleb Kimball to take over the Kimball farm if he would care for his grandparents for their lives. He was an extremely energetic and wise manager, who extended the estate in all directions, such that it encompassed some 2,000 acres at its peak; and refurbished the Kimball homestead into the prepossessing dwelling that came to be called "the Eaton Grange." In this setting, six sons and two daughters were raised. These children were an extremely talented lot: they all left New Hampshire for fame and fortune all over the country, including such abodes as Washington, D. C., Toledo, Ohio,, Chicago, Memphis, Tenn., and San Diego, Cal. (cf. bios #2967-2974).

These scattered children began a habit of leaving their hot cities in the summertime to reconvene in the pleasant breezes of the Eaton Grange. In so doing, they were the core of the party, but only that, since Eaton cousins, along with Kimball, Andrews and other cousins are numerous in the general region, sharing in the hospitality of the Grange. The earlier gatherings, under the pleased eye of their father John, were somewhat limited in attendance; but after his death in 1873 the Grange became shared property of the children under the administration of the eldest son, Gen. John Eaton, with the hostessly help of his sister Christina, and was turned into a summer place for as many of the extended family as could visit it during those months.

When these groups congregated, "all mere formal restraint is laid aside. The mansion resounds with laughter and frolic, song, music and the dance, and in turn come earnest discussions and tearful memories."   On Sundays there might be a sermon from the core group's uncle, the Rev. Horace[7] Eaton (**#1467**) of Palmyra, N.Y., or a humorous performance from their uncle Jacob S. Eaton (**#1464**), the Dr. from Harvard, Mass.   And both generations were delighted to wander over the hills and fields that made up the estate, recreating the scenes of their childhood.

Although the father and the most faithful uncles died away in the 1870s and 1880s, and although life's routine demands had meant not all of the core group of six brothers and two sisters could attend the annual reunion in any given summer, this happy band of siblings had remained intact until brother Frederick died in Feb 1890. A few month earlier in September 1889, all of these siblings had been together at once at the old homestead for the first time in 40 years! For more, see Worthen (1890), pp. 1025-1034.

**2974.  Charles[8] Eaton** (John[7-6], Nathaniel[5], James[4], Jonathan[3], Thomas[2], John[1]) was born 28 Aug 1843.   After local education paid for by his brother Frederick, Charles studied law at the University of Michigan in 1865 and 1866. He then went to Memphis to join his brothers on the Memphis *Daily Post*, 1866-68.   He stayed in journalism for some years, both with the Boston *Times* and the *Toledo Blade*, and also clerked in his brother John's Bureau of Education in Washington, D.C.   He then turned to law, graduating from Columbia Law School, practicing for a while in Toledo and later joining brother Lucien's real estate operation in Memphis, Tenn.

He had mar. on 25 May 1865, **Marion Emma Blanchard**, born in Cornish, N.H., 9 Nov 1847, to Dr. John S. and Louisa (Jackson) Blanchard, later the primary physician at Meriden (later, Grantham), N.H.

Child:

**4798**     i. Charles[9] Linsley Eaton, b. 25 Nov 1866; died 23 Nov 1874 at the Eaton Grange in Sutton due to an accidental fall that severed his spine.

**2976.  (Dr.) John[8] Marshall Eaton** (Jacob[7], John[6], Nathaniel[5], James[4], Jonathan[3], Thomas[2], John[1]) was born 12 May 1832 in Bristol, N.H.; graduated from Harvard Medical College in 1856.   He mar. on 27

Oct 1858 at Waltham, Mass., **Maria Wetherbee**, born in Concord, Mass., 9 Mar 1837 to Lewis and Lucy Wetherbee. He served as an assistant surgeon in the Civil War from 1862 to 1864. He settled in Milford, Mass., where he was highly esteemed as a physician, and was state medical examiner for the county.

Sole child borne by Maria:

4799      i. Emma[9] Eaton, b. ca. 1878 in Milford, Mass.


**2981. James[8] Ellery Eaton** (Jacob[7], John[6], Nathaniel[5], James[4], Jonathan[3], Thomas[2], John[1]) was born 10 Jul 1855, in Stowe, Mass. His education was limited to public schools in So. Deerfield and Harvard, both Mass. While still in his teens he worked in a grocery store in Loudonville, N.Y. (outside Albany), showing a flair for business. He then proceeded to Toledo, Ohio, and the employ of his cousin Frederick[8] Eaton (**#2970** above), where he did so well he was finally established in partnership with him. He mar. **Flora Timpany** (born Oct 1858, who had been teaching for some years in the Toledo public schools), 27 Jul 1889.

Children as of 1900 (perhaps partial list):

4800      i. Ellery[9] T. Eaton, son b. Dec 1894.
4801     ii. P. Tyler[9] Eaton, b. Nov 1897.


**2992. Jubal[8] Harrington Eaton** (Jubal[7], Elijah[6], Nathaniel[5], James[4], Jonathan[3], Thomas[2], John[1]), born 1 Nov 1839 in Warner, N.H.; mar. **Martha P. Bryant** of Lewiston, Me., born 1846, on 25 Dec 1864. They res. in Hillsborough Bridge, where Jubal was a prosperous blacksmith. Jubal died 27 Apr 1897 in Deering, N.H. Widow Martha died in 1918.

Children:

4802      i. Jennie[9] Eaton, b. Oct 1865; d. 1866.
4803     ii. Edward[9] A. Eaton, b. 24 Mar 1870; mar. Addie C. Wood Jones (b. 10 Feb 1870). He d. 15 Sep 1920; she d. 12 Sep 1951.


**3004. Willard[8] Lee Eaton** (Ariel[7], Elijah[6], Nathaniel[5], James[4], Jonathan[3], Thomas[2], John[1]) was born 13 Oct 1848 in Delhi, Iowa; mar. **Laura R. Annis** (b. 24 Nov 1848 in Vt.) in 1874. They resided in Osage Twp., Mitchell Co., Iowa, where he was a lawyer.

Children born in Osage, Iowa (perhaps incomplete):

**4804** i. Allen[9] March Eaton, b. 15 Mar 1877.
**4805** ii. Ivan[9] Willard Eaton, b. 18 Feb 1882.


**3005. Sumner[8] Franklin Eaton** (Ariel[7], Elijah[6], Nathaniel[5], James[4], Jonathan[3], Thomas[2], John[1]) was born 5 Dec 1851 in Delhi, Iowa; mar. in 1876 **Lucy Stewart**, born in Canada, Jan 1854. They res. in Osage Twp., Iowa, where he was a farmer.

Children born in Osage, Iowa:

**4806** i. Fred[9] Eaton, b. Jul 1877.
**4807** ii. Lee[9] Eaton, b. Sep 1879.
**4808** iii. Jessie[9] Eaton, daughter b. Feb 1884.
**4809** iv. Harry[9] Eaton, b. Feb 1886.
**4810** v. Linwood[9] Eaton, b. Nov 1888.
**4811** vi. Clarence[9] Eaton, b. Jul 1893.
**4812** vii. Willard[9] Eaton, b. Feb 1895.


**3010. Sumner[8] Eaton** (Nathaniel[7], Ebenezer[6], Nathaniel[5], James[4], Jonathan[3], Thomas[2], John[1]) was born ca. 1821 in Lempster, N.H.; mar. **Emily Booth** (born 1822) on 15 Oct 1845 in Lempster. They resided in Lempster, where he worked a small farm.

Children born in Lempster, N.H.:

**4813** i. Marietta[9] Eaton, b. ca. 1848.
**4814** ii. Lucina[9] Eaton, b. ca. Mar 1850.


**3031. Calvin[8] W. Eaton** (James[7], Josiah[6], Ebenezer[5], James[4], Jonathan[3], Thomas[2], John[1]) was born in Albany, N.Y., Jul 1842; mar. in 1865, **Anna F. __?__**, born Jun 1844. In 1880 he was a lumber merchant residing in the 16th Ward in Albany. In 1900, he was a real estate agent living with his wife and elder son under the same roof as younger brother James[8] W. in Albany's 14th Ward.

Children in Albany, N.Y. (four of five surviving to 1900):

**4815** i. Mary[9] Eaton, b. 1866.
**4816** ii. Alice[9] Eaton, b. 1868.
**4817** iii. James[9] P. Eaton, b. May 1874. In 1900 was a clerk living with his parents.
**4818** iv. Edward[9] Eaton, b. 1876.


**3032. James[8] Webster Eaton** (James[7], Josiah[6], Ebenezer[5], James[4],

Jonathan³, Thomas² John¹) was born in Albany, N.Y., 14 May 1857; mar.
in 1894 **Hortense W. __?__**, b. Nov. 1862, prob. her second marriage,
as a daughter later called Levanchia V. Eaton had been born to her in
Dec 1889. They res. in Albany where James was a lawyer.

Children of James and Hortense in Albany as of 1900:

**4819**    i. Elizabeth⁹ Eaton, b. Jul 1897.
**4820**    ii. Louisa⁹ Eaton, b. Aug 1898.


**3037. Frank⁸ T. Eaton** (Ryland⁷, Kimball⁶, Enoch⁵, James⁴, Jonathan³, Thomas², John¹) was born 8 Jan 1840 in Vt., prob. in Middleton,
Rutland Co., but grew up in N.Y. State. He mar. **Carrie B. __?__**, a N.Y.
native, but later went west to settle in Cedar Rapids, Iowa., where he was a
marble cutter. He died there in 1884.

Child born in N.Y. State:

**4821**    i. Maude⁹ A. Eaton, b. ca. 1864.


**3041. John⁸ R. Eaton** (Ryland⁷, Kimball⁶, Enoch⁵, James⁴, Jonathan³, Thomas², John¹) was born 5 Apr 1849 in Arlington (Bennington
Co.), Vt.; mar. **Sophia E. Vail** of Syracuse, N.Y., 26 Jun 1872.   He
graduated from the Syracuse University College of Medicine in 1875,
and became a physician in Chittenango, N.Y. for his career (Molyneux,
1911).

Children born in Chittenango, N.Y.:

**4822**    i. Maurice⁹ Van Duyn Eaton, b. 19 Jul 1877; d. Feb. 21 1882.
**4823**    ii. Charles⁹ Emmett Eaton, b. 16 Nov 1880; d. 21 Mar 1898.
**4824**    iii. Chester⁹ Ryland Eaton, b. 21 Mar 1888.


**3042. Charles⁸ A. Eaton** (Ryland⁷, Kimball⁶, Enoch⁵, James⁴,
Jonathan³, Thomas², John¹) was born 22 Feb 1852 in Woodville, N.Y.;
mar. **Anna __?__**, also a N.Y. native. They resided in Pawlet, Rutland
Co., Vt. as of 1880, where he was a blacksmith.

Child (perhaps others after 1880):

**4825.**    i. Nelly⁹ Eaton, b. ca. 1878.


**3049. George⁸ P. Eaton** (Warren⁷, Enoch⁶⁻⁵, James⁴, Jonathan³,
Thomas², John¹) was born Feb 1854, prob. in Oxford, N.Y.; went west
and mar. **Emma Kennear** of Waitsburg, Wash. They resided at Granger,

Yakima Co., Wash. (Molyneux, 1911). Wife Emma died before 1900, when George and two of the children (Emma and Edith) are living in Tacoma, Washington.

Children:

**4826**    i. Emma⁹ A. Eaton, b. Apr 1883 in Oregon.
**4827**    ii. Warren⁹ Eaton, b. ca. 1886.
**4828**    iii. Edith⁹ M. Eaton, b. Feb 1890 in Washington.
**4829**    iv. Clara⁹ Eaton, b. early 1890s.


**3050. Charles⁸ B. Eaton** (Warren⁷, Enoch⁶⁻⁵, James⁴, Jonathan³, Thomas², John¹) was born Jul 1861, prob. in Oxford, N.Y.; studied for the law in Oxford, N.Y., at least through 1880. He mar. 1st, a N.Y. native, **Ida Sherwood**, and the couple settled in the State of Washington. Wife Ida died 17 Mar 1899. In 1900 Charles was living in Tacoma, Wash., with all four children and his sister-in-law Abigail Sherwood helping to manage the family. He later mar. 2d, **Anna Tremble**. They resided in Seattle (Molyneux, 1911).

Children (all born in Washington State):

**4830**    i. James⁹ Eaton, b. Apr 1881.
**4831**    ii. Alice⁹ Eaton, b. Mar 1892.
**4832**    iii. Ruth⁹ Eaton, b. Feb 1894.
**4833**    iv. Philip⁹ Eaton, May 1895.


**3051. Edmund⁸ A. Eaton** (Edmund⁷, Warren⁶, Enoch⁵, James⁴, Jonathan³, Thomas², John¹) was born ca. 1836 at Topsham, Me.; mar. 1st, on 12 Feb 1873 at Portland, Me., **Harriet L. Roberts**, she born 1846 to N. D. Roberts of Portland. They res. at Topsham, where Edmund was a merchant. Harriet died 13 Aug 1873, in connection with the birth of their first child. He then mar. 2d, **Mary Augusta __?__** (born 1849), but he himself died prematurely in 1881 in Topsham. His widow Mary then died of consumption at age 37, on 7 Mar 1887.

Child with Harriet, born at Topsham, Me:

**4834**    i. Annie⁹ L. Eaton, b. 10 Aug 1873; d. 26 Aug 1873.


**3065. Albert⁸ W. Eaton** (Albert⁷, Jonathan⁶, Amos⁵, Jonathan⁴⁻³, Thomas², John¹) was born Feb 1870 in Haverhill, Mass.; mar. in early 1899, **Ethel B. __?__** , born Aug 1877, also in Mass. This couple settled in Salem, Mass., where he was a bank clerk.

Child (prob. more after 1900):

**4835**    i. Hilda[9] Eaton, b. Sep 1899.


**3073. Samuel[8] Eaton** (Jesse[7], Samuel[6], Job[5], Samuel[4], Job[3], Thomas[2], John[1]) was born 5 May 1833 in Salisbury, N.H.; went west early, and mar. 1st, **Sarah J. Wormin** of Wheeling, West Va., on 10 Dec 1857. She died soon thereafter, on 20 Sep 1858, apparently without surviving issue. He then mar. 2d, **Adello Fisher** of Princeton, Ill., 11 Oct 1860. He was a merchant in Chicago, Ill., but disappears from that scene before 1880.

Children with Adello, prob. born in Chicago, Ill.:

**4836**    i. Jesse[9] Eaton, son b. 27 Nov 1865.
**4837**    ii. Annie[9] L. Eaton, b. 12 Dec 1867.
**4838**    iii. Mary[9] Eaton, b. 1 Apr 1870.


**3084. Augustus[8] K. Eaton** (Moses[7], Job[6-5], Samuel[4], Job[3], Thomas[2], John[1]) was born 20 Feb 1825 in Wentworth, N.H.; mar. **Ruth H. Noyes** early in 1850. They resided for nearly 20 years in the north end of Wentworth where Augustus ran a prosperous farm, but after 1860 they moved over the town line into Warren, N.H. Augustus died there, 19 Oct 1872.

Children (i-ii born in Wentworth, N.H.; iii in Warren, N.H.):

**4839**    i. Henry[9] A. Eaton, b. 11 Sep 1850; mar. Nelo Haines, a native of Ashland, N.H. He d. 5 Sep 1920 in Watertown, Mass.
**4840**    ii. Wilber[9] K. Eaton, b. ca. 1856-57.
**4841**    iii. Albert[9] C. Eaton, b. 8 Jan 1862; d. 11 Mar 1862.


**3092. Samuel[8] C. Eaton** (Ezra[7], Job[6-5], Samuel[4], Job[3], Thomas[2], John[1]) was born ca. 1823 in Wentworth, N.H.; mar. **Lydia __?__** ca. 1846. At some time before 1870, this couple had removed with their family to Lowell, Mass., where Samuel was to begin making a small fortune as a dealer in popcorn, a business that he soon transported to Lynn, Mass.

Children:

**4842**    i. Mary[9] E. Eaton, b. ca. 1848.
**4843**    ii. Emma[9] Eaton, b. ca. 1852.
**4844**    iii. Ella[9] Eaton, b. ca. 1854.
**4845**    iv. Charles[9] S. Eaton, b. ca. 1856.

**3095. Ezra[8] Bartlett Eaton, Jr.** (Ezra[7], Job[6-5], Samuel[4], Job[3], Thomas[2], John[1]) was born 9 Feb 1829 in Plymouth, N.H.; by 1850 he had removed to Lowell, Mass., where as "E. Bartlett" he was a young laborer lodging in the household of John Wright there. In this period he mar. **Melissa Pillsbury**, 22 Jun 1856. This couple was back in his native haunts at Warren, N.H., by 1860, where Ezra was then employed as a miller, but by 1870 was quite a prosperous merchant there, and called himself a trader by 1880.

Only a single child is visible in their household, 1860-80:

4846    i. William[9] "Willie" C. Eaton, b. ca. 1857. A store clerk living with his parents, 1880.

**3104. John[8] P. Eaton** (Jesse[7], Moses[6], Job[5], Samuel[4], Job[3], Thomas[2], John[1]) was born 9 Sep 1829 in Wentworth, N.H.; mar. **Harriet C. Burroughs** (born Sep 1834 in Vermont, probably at Newbury) on 2 Feb 1859. John took over a share of his grandfather's handsome farm, and like him lived on the Atwell Hill place all of his life, adjacent to his father Jesse who had a share of the homestead as well. Although both John and Harriet are registered with an empty nest in Wentworth in the 1900 Census, Harriet died 15 Oct 1900 in Newbury, Vt.

Harriet bore five children, but only two survived to 1900:

4847    i. Clarence[9] A. Eaton, b. 29 Jan 1860; moved off the family homestead on Atwell Hill, buying the former town farm near the ledges and the Beech Hill Rd., where he lived out his life. He mar. 1st, Emma L. Hobbs, 12 Oct 1886, and had one son, Lewis[10] C. Eaton, born Jul 1887 but died at age 15; and a daughter, Maud[10] L. Eaton, b. 8 May 1892. Wife Emma died young in 1902, the same year as her son; and Clarence mar. 2d, Harriet Walls (Bixby, 1986).
4848   ii?. Child[9] Eaton, b. ? ; died young.
4849  iii?. Child[9] Eaton, b. ? ; died young.
4850   iv?. Child[9] Eaton, b. ? ; died young.
4851    v?. Child[9] Eaton, surviving at least till 1900.

**3108. (Dr.) Moses[8] Currier Eaton** (Jesse[7], Moses[6], Job[5], Samuel[4], Job[3], Thomas[2], John[1]) was born 26 Sep 1838 in Wentworth, N.H. He graduated from Dartmouth Medical School in 1864, and then mar. **Ellen "Nellie" Louise Ward**, 15 Feb 1865 in Wentworth. He established a practice in nearby Plymouth, N.H., although he died early, 29 Mar 1872.

Child born in Wentworth, N.H.:

4852    i. Arthur[9] Ward Eaton, b. 8 Oct 1867; res. in Boston, Mass., and was early a clerk at C. F. Hovey's.


**3109. William⁸ B. Eaton** (Job⁷, James⁶, Job⁵, Samuel⁴, Job³, Thomas², John¹) was born 17 May 1819 in Haverhill, Mass.; mar. **Abiah W. Sargent** (born 1827). The couple settled in Haverhill, where William is listed as a "trader," and obviously a prosperous one over several Censuses. In 1880 he is a bookkeeper. He died in 1888, Haverhill.

Children born in Haverhill, Mass.:

4853    i. Edward⁹ Eaton, b. ca. 1857; d. young, bur. Linwood Cemetery, Haverhill.
4854    ii. Edward⁹ᴬ O. Eaton, b. ca. 1859; a bookkeeper like his father, he was living with his parents in 1880.
4855    iii. Charles⁹ Willis Eaton, b. ca. 1863;


**3112. Charles⁸ Otis Eaton** (Job⁷, James⁶, Job⁵, Samuel⁴, Job³, Thomas², John¹) was born 6 Jan 1828, in Haverhill. As a youngster in 1850 he was already living in Ward #1, Boston, Mass., and was listed as a "fancy painter." On 6 Jun 1853 he mar. 1st **Charlotte Everett Stickney**, born to William and Margaret (Nowell) Stickney on 24 Aug 1832 in Charlestown, Mass. However, she died barely a year later, on 25 Aug 1854. In 1870 he is in Ward 39, Boston, still at "fancy painting," but has at some earlier time mar. 2d, **Levina Isabelle Tewksbury**, born 1837. Her brother Charles is a grocer living with them at that time. By 1880 his trade is listed as "standard painter".

Child with Levina Isabelle in Boston, Mass.:

4856    i. L(illian) Isabelle⁹ Eaton, b. ca. 1869.


**3117. Albert⁸ Eugene Eaton** (Daniel⁷, James⁶, Job⁵, Samuel⁴, Job³, Thomas², John¹) was born 17 Mar 1854; mar. **Carrie F. Lancaster** (born Jan 1856) ca. summer, 1876. Albert began his married life in Plaistow, and the couple was there in 1880, when Albert was a shoe contractor. However, they are in Fremont, N.H. in 1900, and he was engaged in farming. Nonetheless he died in Plaistow in 1927.

Carrie bore five children, but three died young:

4857    i. Len(n)ie⁹ J. Eaton, dau. b. Apr 1877. She still lived with her parents in 1900.
4858    ii?. Child⁹ Eaton, b. ? ; died young.
4859    iii?. Child⁹ Eaton, b. ? ; died young.
4860    iv?. Child⁹ Eaton, b. ? ; died young.
4861    v. Dorothy⁹ L. Eaton, b. Jun 1894.

**3119. John⁸ Eaton** (Timothy⁷, Samuel⁶. Ebenezer⁵, Samuel⁴, Job³, Thomas², John¹) was born 28 Mar 1813 in Landaff, N.H. On 3 Mar 1837 at Benton, N.H. he mar. **Mahala Wells**, born ca. 6 Jan 1806. They res. in Landaff, where he was a farmer. He died there, 30 Apr 1867. Widow Mahala died 11 Apr 1872.

Children with Mahala in Landaff, N.H.:

4862    i. Martha⁹ Jane Eaton, b. ca. 1838; mar. a Merrill.
4863    ii. Henry⁹ Eaton, b. ca. 1845.

**3121. James⁸ K. Eaton** (Timothy⁷, Samuel⁶, Ebenezer⁵, Samuel⁴, Job³, Thomas², John¹) was born 26 Mar 1817 in Landaff, N.H.; mar. 1st, **Drusilla M. Priest**, 15 Feb 1838 in Lisbon, N.H. This couple removed across the Connecticut River to settle on a small farm in Sutton, in the north end of Caledonia Co., Vt. They appear in Censuses there from 1840 thru 1860 while they were raising their children. In the 1860s they returned to a farm in Landaff, N.H., once again, where wife Drusilla died on 23 Nov 1888. James mar. 2d, **Susan Noyes** of Lancaster, N.H. (she born 1828), on 21 Mar 1889. They both survived at Landaff in the 1900 Census. James died there 29 Aug 1908.

Children with Drusilla, most or all born in Sutton, Vt.:

4864    i. Phoebe⁹ A. Eaton, b. ca. 1839.
4865    ii. Timothy⁹ Eaton, b. ca. 1841; mar. Mary J. Bartlett on 22 Sep 1861 in Sutton, Vt. He was a farmer in Sutton, but in the later 1860s removed to Barton, Orleans Co., Vt. They had at least four children: Herbert¹⁰ Scott Eaton, b. 11 May 1862, Sutton; Ellen¹⁰ Hannah Eaton, b. 13 Jun 1864, Sutton; and twins Amos¹⁰ Joseph and Anson¹⁰ James Eaton, b. 3 May 1869 in Barton.
4866    iii. (Henry) Martin⁹ Eaton, b. ca. 1848; mar. Abbie Jane Ellis, 18 Jul 1868 in Landaff, N.H. He died there soon thereafter, 23 Mar 1873.

**3124. Samuel⁸ A. Eaton** (Timothy⁷, Samuel⁶, Ebenezer⁵, Samuel⁴, Job³, Thomas², John¹) was born 5 Aug 1826 in Landaff, N.H.; mar. **Sarah McConnell** 1 Jan 1856 in Landaff. They settled there, where Samuel was a farmer. He died 19 Jun 1894 in Landaff.

Children born in Landaff, N.H.:

4867    i. Ella⁹ Eaton, b. 19 Jul 1861; d. in 1863.

**4868**    ii. Sidney[9] W. Eaton, b. 12 Jun 1867; mar. Alice M. McKean
              on 30 Sep 1890 in Landaff, and they were farming there
              in 1900, without children in the household.
**4869**    iii. Eddie[9] Eaton, b. and d. 9 Jul 1875.
**4870**    iv. Anna[9] Dell Eaton, b. ca. 1876.


      **3131. James[8] McKean Eaton** (Ira[7], Ebenezer[6-5], Samuel[4], Job[3],
Thomas[2], John[1]) was born 11 Apr 1828 in Landaff, N.H.; mar. **Harriet
__?__** (born 1831 in N.Y. State), in the early 1850s.    James was a
farmer.

      Children born in Colden, N.Y.:

**4871**    i. John[9] Eaton, b. ca. 1854.
**4872**    ii. Jennie[9] Eaton, b. ca. 1857.  Still with parents, 1880.


      **3133. Ira[8A] Eaton** (Ira[7], Ebenezer[6-5], Samuel[4], Job[3], Thomas[2],
John[1]) was born ca. 1831 in Westminster, Vt.; mar. **Mary __?__** (born
ca. 1837 in Vt.) in the late 1850s.  They settled in Colden, N.Y., where he
had grown up, and where he was a farmer.  The 1870 Census found this
couple in neighboring Concord township; but in 1880 they are listed
again at Colden and his father Ira, Sr., now age 82, was living with them.

      Children born in Colden, N.Y.:

**4873**    i. Charles[9] Eaton, b. ca. 1861.
**4874**    ii. Rose[9] Eaton, b. ca. 1863.
**4875**    iii. Eliza[9] Eaton, b. ca. 1866.
**4876**    iv. George[9] Eaton, b. ca. 1868.
**4877**    v. William[9] Eaton, b. ca. 1876.


      **3137.   Charles[8] Eaton** (Mitchell[7], Ebenezer[6-5], Samuel[4], Job[3],
Thomas[2], John[1]) was born 9 Jun 1834 in Landaff, N.H.; on 1 Jan 1863
he mar. **Sarah Jane Green**, who had been born 16 Dec 1837 to Harry
and Marilla (Smith) Green in Lyndon, Vt.  The couple settled first in
Lisbon, N.H., where they had their first children, and where Charles was
in the general merchandise business while carrying on a meat business
sporadically as well.  In 1868 he removed to Littleton, N.H., continuing
in a merchandise business there with various partners, and took a leading
role in the Kilkenny Lumber Co., in So. Littleton, Zealand, Bethlehem
Junction, Stark and Milan.  He and his partners won a charter for the
Kilkenny Railroad and in 1887 built the road from Lancaster to Kilkenny which turned a handsome profit in due time.  His business acu-
men put him among the " 'leading men' of the North Country" (Stearns,
1908), although he was too busy to seek any major public office.  In

politics he was a Republican, and from 1899 to 1905 served as postmaster at Littleon.

Children (i-ii born in Lisbon N.H.; iii-iv in Littleton, N.H.):

**4878**    i. Julia[9] Ann Eaton, b. 19 Apr 1864.
**4879**   ii. Myra[9] Green Eaton, b., 16 Mar 1866.
**4880**  iii. Harry[9] Mitchell Eaton, b. 20 Feb 1869; graduated from Dartmouth College in 1890, and mar. Cora Bell Hopkins, 21 Feb 1898. He was for a period his father's partner in the lumber business, and later succeeded his father as postmaster in Littleton.
**4881**   iv. Charles[9] Francis Eaton, b. 17 Jul 1874.


**3156.   James[8] Cleaves Eaton** (Nathan[7] O., Jacob[6], Ithamar[5], Samuel[4], Job[3], Thomas[2], John[1]) was born 19 Feb 1821 in East Kingston, N.H.; mar. **Josephine Stevens** (born in Maine ca. 1837) around 1860. James was not obvious in N.H. records in the 1850-60 period, and probably found work and in due time a wife in Maine; but in 1870 they had just returned to East Kingston, where James was a farm laborer. They were also there with their children in 1880, and James prob. died in the 1880s.

Children:

**4882**    i. (Ruth) Anna[9] Eaton, b. ca. 1862 in Maine.
**4883**   ii. (Rosa) Adelaide[9] Eaton, b. ca. 1863, Maine.
**4884**  iii. Fred[9] Eaton, b. ca. 1867, Maine.
**4885**   iv. Joseph[9] A. Eaton, b. Nov 1871, N.H. May be the Joseph and Elizabeth A. residing in Exeter, N.H., with a daughter Alice[10] M. b. Feb 1899.

**3159. Stephen[8] B. Eaton** (Nathan[7] O., Jacob[6], Ithamar[5], Samuel[4], Job[3], Thomas[2], John[1]) was born 1 Nov 1826 in East Kingston, N.H.; mar. **Patience W. Blaisdell** (born ca. 1828 in Me.) on 18 Jun 1848 in Milton, Strafford Co., N.H. They res. until the 1860s in Milton, where Stephen was initially a shoemaker. By 1870, however, they have removed to Concord, N.H., where Stephen became a steward in the State Prison.

Child born in Milton, N.H.:

**4886**    i. (Tillie) Sarah[9] "Sally" Eaton, b. ca. 1851.


**3160. Nathan[8] S. Eaton** (Nathan[7] O., Jacob[6], Ithamar[5], Samuel[4], Job[3], Thomas[2], John[1]) was born Jan 1830 in East Kingston, N.H.; mar. **Sarah H. __?__**, a native of Massachusetts, 14 Jun 1849. They resided

in East Kingston, where Nathan worked in the shoe factory.  He died
there, 6 Jul 1879.

Child born in East Kingston, N.H.:

**4887**    i. Charles[9] P. Eaton, b. ca. 1858.  He died in 1879, the same
            year as his father.


**3162. Ithamar[8] Eaton** (Merchant[7], Jacob[6], Ithamar[5], Samuel[4],
Job[3], Thomas[2], John[1]) was born 24 Aug 1832 in East Kingston, N.H.;
mar. 1st, **Phebe A. Pillsbury** in the later 1850s, and had one child with
her.  Phebe died, however, 24 May 1861, and he mar. 2d, **Lavina __?__**
(born 1835 in Massachusetts) about 1865.  He and wife "Vina" have an
empty nest in East Kingston, 1900.  Ithamar died there 21 Apr 1916.

Child with Phebe in East Kingson, N.H.:

**4888**    i. Hannah[9] A. Eaton, b. 1858; d. 1859.

Child with Lavina in East Kingston, N.H.

**4889**    ii. Mary[9] Alice Eaton, b. 9 Sep 1865; d. 28 Sep 1879.


**3168. John[8] Leach Eaton** (John[7] L., Ithamar[6-5], Samuel[4], Job[3],
Thomas[2], John[1]) was born 8 Nov 1837 in Manchester, Mass.; was a mariner early, heading an 1860 household in Manchester with his two
younger brothers.  But within a few years he mar. **Lottie B. __?__**, some
ten years his junior, and made a living as a wood carver.

Child born Manchester, Mass.:

**4890**    i. Richard[9] Trask Eaton, b. 1866 and named after his uncle.


**3170. Edward[8] Payson Eaton** (John[7] L., Ithamar[6-5], Samuel[4],
Job[3], Thomas[2], John[1]) was born 12 May 1843 in Manchester, Mass.  By
family lore he ended up a furniture dealer, but we have not verified this
account.  He may be the Edward Eaton who is age 26 in the 1870 Census
at Wakefield, Mass., not many miles from his native town.  If so, he appears mar. to an **Eleanor __?__**, born in New Hampshire in 1846.  The
same pair is at Wakefield again in 1880.  This Edward was a shoemaker
in 1860; and a station agent in 1870.  We have not added further to this
history.

Children born to these parents in Wakefield (at least up to 1880):

**4891**   i. Grace⁹ E. Eaton, b. spring of 1870.
**4892**   ii. George⁹ E. Eaton, b. ca. 1876.

**3178. James⁸ Henley Eaton** (Thomas⁷, Benjamin⁶, Obadiah⁵, Samuel⁴, Job³, Thomas², John¹) was born 23 Jun 1828 in Bath, Me. In 1860 he was still living with his parents in Bath and working as a book-keeper. Later in the 1860s he mar. **Clara C __?__**, who was born ca. 1839 in Maine. The couple resided in Ward #6, Portland, Me. in 1870 when James was working as a bookkeeper. By 1880 he had become a wholesale grocer there. He died, however, 28 Sep 1882 at Wiscasset, Me.

Children born in Portland, Me.:

**4893**   i. Clarence⁹ Eaton, b. Mar 1870.
**4894**   ii. Weston⁹ Eaton, b. ca. 1776.

**3179. Albert⁸ Green Eaton** (Thomas⁷, Benjamin⁶, Obadiah⁵, Samuel⁴, Job³, Thomas², John¹) was born 28 Nov 1831 in Bath Me. As a youth in 1850 he was listed as a carver; in 1860 he was still living with his parents and working in Bath as an accountant. In the early 1860s he mar. **Martha A__?__** (born Jul 1831 in Me.) and they res. in Ward #2, Bath. They were still in Bath with an empty nest as of 1900.

Child born in Bath, Me.:

**4895**   i. Clara⁹ C. Eaton, b. ca. 1865. With her parents in 1880.

**3193. Elisha⁸ Harrison Eaton** (Thomas⁷, Benjamin⁶, Obadiah⁵, Samuel⁴, Job³, Thomas², John¹) was born 22 Sep 1816 in Bradford, N.H., and spent his life on his farm there. He mar. 1st, **Mrs. Roena (French) Ayer** of Bradford, on 17 Mar 1840. They apparently had but one child, and she died after a long marriage on 20 Dec 1882. He later mar. 2d, **Mary E. Smith**, 5 May 1887 in Bradford. Elisha died 19 Jan 1894 in Bradford.

Child with Roena in Bradford, N.H.:

**4896**   i. Charles⁹ Page Eaton, b. 29 Nov 1856.

Child with Mary in Bradford, N.H.:

**4897**   ii. Roy⁹ Harrison Eaton, b. 10 Jun 1889.

**3197. (Dr.) Harrison⁸ Eaton** (Moses⁷, Nathaniel⁶, John⁵, Thomas⁴, Job³, Thomas², John¹) was born 13 Dec 1813 in Hopkinton, N.H.;

mar. 1st, **Charlotte Mariah Eaton**, also of Hopkinton, on 25 Dec 1838.
They settled in Merrimack, N.H., where he practiced as a physician for
his career. Charlotte died 21 Dec 1866, and Dr. Eaton mar. 2d, **Harriet
N. Lane** of Candia, 26 Nov 1868. He died 19 Nov 1881.

Child with Charlotte in Merrimack, N.H.:

**4898**	i. Henry[9] Harrison Eaton, b. 24 Oct 1839.

NOTE. We are unable to identify Dr. Eaton's first wife. Suffice it to say
that there are several Eaton families in the Hopkinton/Weare/Concord neighborhood
in this period where child names, and especially those of daughters, are missing.

**3198. David[8] Merrill Eaton** (Moses[7], Nathaniel[6], John[5], Thomas[4],
Job[3], Thomas[2], John[1]) was born ca. Mar 1815 in Hopkinton, N.H.; mar. a
**Mary H__?__** (born 1816) in the late 1830s, and they resided in
Hopkinton, where he worked a farm of average size. He died there 6 Oct
1878; widow Mary survived until 1898.

Child with birth registered in both Andover and Henniker, N.H.:

**4899**	i. William[9] H. Eaton, b. ca. 1840. In 1860 he lived with his
		parents and taught grade school. He mar. Mary Jane
		Fuller, 24 Feb 1861 in Hopkinton, N.H.

**3206. Daniel[8] Clement Eaton** (Joshua[7], Daniel[6], John[5], Thomas[4],
Job[3], Thomas[2], John[1]) was born 31 Jul 1815 in Tunbridge, Vt.; was of
Royalton, Vt. when he mar. **Augusta M. Cilley,** 7 Oct 1840 in Tunbridge. They were residing in Tunbridge for at least a period, during
which time he was a farmer, but then disappear.

Children born in Tunbridge, Vt.:

**4900**	i. Edwin[9] R. Eaton, b. ? ; d. 12 Aug 1843 in Tunbridge.
**4901**	ii. Ellen[9] Augusta Eaton, b. 20 Nov 1845.

**3211. (Henry) Porter[8] Eaton** (Joshua[7], Daniel[6], John[5], Thomas[4],
Job[3], Thomas[2], John[1]) was born 14 Dec 1831 in Tunbridge, Vt.; mar.
**Isabel __?__** and res. Tunbridge. They had two children, both of whom
died young, and Henry himself died very early, on 18 Dec 1860 in Tunbridge.

Children born in Tunbridge:

**4902**	i. Lizzie[9] B. Eaton, b. 28 Jul 1858; d. 10 Apr 1861, Tunbridge.
**4903**	ii. Freddie[9] Eaton, b. ? ; d. 30 Sep 1864 in Tunbridge.

**3215. George⁸ W. Eaton** (James⁷, John⁶⁻⁵, Thomas⁴, Job³, Thomas², John¹) was born Jul 1843 in Bradford, N.H.; mar. **Alice M. Currier** (born Jan 1848 in Sunapee, N.H. and residing there) in the mid-1860s. They settled in Bradford where George was a farmer. They remain there in the 1900 Census.

Children born in Bradford, N.H.:

| | |
|---|---|
| 4904 | i. John⁹ A. Eaton, b. ca. 1868; mar. Grace Osgood, 1890. |
| 4905 | ii. Leland⁹ L. Eaton, b. Aug 1872. |
| 4906 | iii. Florette⁹ A. Eaton, b. 7 Jun 1874; d. 21 May 1896. |

**3217. James⁸ N. Eaton** (James⁷, John⁶⁻⁵, Thomas⁴, Job³, Thomas², John¹) was born Dec 1848 in Bradford, N.H.; mar. **Rosina A__?__** (born ca. 1852) in the early 1870s. This couple settled in Newbury, N.H., where James was a farmer.

Children in Newbury, N.H.:

| | |
|---|---|
| 4907 | i. Fred⁹ A. Eaton, a twin born 1875. |
| 4908 | ii. Frank⁹ D. Eaton, a twin born 1875. |

**3220. Albert⁸ S. Eaton** (Ebenezer⁷, John⁶⁻⁵, Thomas⁴, Job³, Thomas², John¹) was a twin of Alfred S. born 13 Aug 1841 in Newbury, N.H.; mar. 1st, **Emma C. Brown** (born Jul 1845 in N.H.) on 26 Nov 1867 in Newbury, where he was a farmer as of 1870-80. Later on they removed to Warner, where he was a hotel keeper. At some time after 1900, Emma died and he mar. 2d, **Jennie E. Kimball**. Albert died 13 Dec 1930 in Hopkinton, N.H.; and Jennie died 1 Jan 194?

Children borne by Emma in Newbury, N.H.:

| | |
|---|---|
| 4909 | i. Lula⁹ N. Eaton, b. ca. 1869. |
| 4910 | ii. Gertie⁹ L. Eaton, b. ca. 1872. |
| 4911 | iii. Mande⁹ (or Maude?) B. Eaton, b. ca. 1875. |
| 4912 | iv. Blanche⁹ B. Eaton, a twin b. Jul 1880. |
| 4913 | v. Bertha⁹ E. Eaton, a twin b. Jul 1880. She and her sister were still living with their parents in Warner in 1900 at age 19. |

**3222. Jesse⁸ Wilbur F. Eaton** (Ebenezer⁷, John⁶⁻⁵, Thomas⁴, Job³, Thomas², John¹) was born 8 Apr 1843 in Newbury, N.H. He was a farm laborer living with his parents in 1870, and still a bachelor "lumberman" living on the Charles Messer farm in Newbury in 1880. Thus it was quite late in life when he mar. **Nellie Maxfield** (born Oct 1856 in N.H.), ca. 1885. The couple was still residing in Newbury for the 1900 Census.

Child born in Newbury, N.H.:

**4914**    i. Maurice[9] E. Eaton, b. Sep 1890.


**3225. George[8] Eaton** (Moses[7], Joshua[6], John[5], Thomas[4], Job[3], Thomas[2], John[1]) was born ca. 1816 in Newbury, N.H.; mar. (possibly 2d) **Mary A__?__** (born ca. 1818) and resided in Newbury, where he was a farmer. Probably he died in the 1860s.

Children born in Newbury, N.H. (deduced from Census data):

**4915**    i. Roxana[9] Eaton, b. ca. 1842.
**4916**    ii. Louisa[9] Francella, b. ca. 1846.
**4917**    iii. Augusta[9] C. Eaton, b. ca. 1848.
**4918**    iv. Moses[9] Eaton, b. ca. 1850.
**4919**    v. Martha[9] Eaton, b. ca. 1852.
**4920**    vi. Osgood[9] P. Eaton, b. ca. 1854.
**4921**    vii. Charles[9] W. Eaton, b. ca. 1858.

NOTE. It appears that father Moses[7] and Polly had a number of children in Newbury between 1815 and 1840, but we lack records identifying who any of these children were. We are not sure that the children living with Moses and Polly in the Censuses from 1820 thru 1840 were all theirs, in part because they do not form a consistent sequence over time. However, we feel that George must have been an eldest son of theirs born in the 1815-19 period, even though he himself is not visible in the family composition in 1820. We reach this conclusion because this George[8] and Mary appear to be raising their large family next door to Moses[7]/Polly (then with an empty nest) in 1850; and in 1860, after Polly has been widowed, she lives under the same roof with George[8]/Mary, a classic pattern for a widowed mother. One other complication in these deductions is posed by the local marriage record that "George Eaton of Newbury mar. Letitia S. Colby of Warner, 29 Dec 1840." Since there are not other appropriate George Eatons of Newbury to which this record can be referred, it is quite likely that Letitia was a first wife of the subject of this notice, who died perhaps in connection with the birth of this George's oldest child.


**3229. Joshua[8] Willis Eaton** (Joshua[7-6], John[5], Thomas[4], Job[3], Thomas[2], John[1]) was born Dec 1856 in Bradford, N.H. to his father's second wife Louisa; mar. 1st, by 1877, **Nellie E. Boyce**, she born 1858 to John and Julietta Boyce of Newbury, N.H. They resided in Bradford where Joshua (often called Willis) was a farmer. In 1900 he is still there, with his aged parents in the household, but with a 2d wife, **Judith __?__**, born Nov 1858. In both 1880 and 1900 the same daughter is the only child in the household. It is of course possible that other children may have come along after the 1880 Census, who have died or left home in the interim.

Only known child, with Nellie in Bradford, N.H.:

**4922**    i. Ethel[9] L. Eaton, b. ca. 1878.

# Generation Nine

(Although this volume is an "eight-generation" genealogy, we include here some notices for those of our ninth-generations born so early that their marriages and some of their childbearing had taken place by 1850, the rough chronological limit for this work; and for a few others slightly later, where full data were at hand without special effort.)

## A. *The Salisbury Branch*

**3239. Caleb[9] Eaton** (Caleb[8], William[7], Ebenezer[6], John[5-1]) was born 25 Apr 1809 in Sanbornton, N.H.; mar. **Irena Davis**, daughter of Samuel Davis, 27 Jun 1833. In their marriage shortened by Caleb's early death, this couple resided first in Bristol, N.H., then in Plymouth, N.H., and finally in Meredith, N.H., where he joined up briefly with his brother William before he died, Jul 1843.

Children:

4923    i. Elizabeth[10] Eaton, b. 20 Oct 1834 in Bristol, N.H.; died 25 Mar 1852 in Lowell, Mass.

4924    ii. Edward[10] Kendall Eaton, b. 4 Oct 1836 in Plymouth, N.H.; res. in New York City, and mar. on 3 Sep 1862 to Maria Louise Smith (born NYC, 24 Jan 1840, to Oliver Jackson Smith). They resided in New York City, where Edward died in May 1874 after siring two children: Lizzie[11] Dell Eaton, b. 5 Dec 1865; and Edward[11] K. Eaton, Jr., b. 2 Sep 1868, both in New York City.

**3240. William[9] L. Eaton** (Caleb[8], William[7], Ebenezer[6], John[5-1]) was born 28 Mar 1811 in Sanbornton, N.H.; he removed to Meredith, N.H. as a young man and established himself there as a carpenter. Early on he had the wherewithal to buy land in Alexandria in Grafton Co., but never lived there. He mar. 1st, **Mary Ann Gordon** of neighboring New Hampton, N.H., on 19 Apr 1839, and within the year they sold out their land in Meredith and he became a teacher in New Hampton. He continued to be active in real estate dealings there, styled as a "Gentleman," working with lands associated with the New Hampton Institute, where he taught. By Oct 1844 he had taken a teaching position in the town of Schoolcraft, near Kalamazoo, Mich., but was being pursued by litigation concerning a New Hampton land deal. The couple soon returned to New Hampton by Oct 1846, living on land purchased from a relative of his wife there. In the spring of 1848, however, they removed to Bristol, N.H., where William[9], listed as a joiner, purchased land from his very distant cousin, Jacob Sawyer Eaton (**#1464**) of the Haverhill branch, who at that time was a doctor in Bristol. They resided there into the 1850s, but soon returned to New Hampton, where wife Mary Ann, with whom he had had his children, died 6 Jun 1855. William then mar. 2d, **Susan Smith** of Meredith on 19 May 1856, and the family lived in Meredith in 1860 with William a farmer. By 1870 they were back again in New Hampton--their property in the area was on the Meredith/New Hampton road--but wife Susan died, 6 Apr 1877 at Franklin, N.H. William then mar. 3d, **Mrs. Mary Edgerly**, 8 Oct 1878. He lived into the 1890s, and the senior author credits him for most of the information about the two William Eatons who removed from Seabrook to Sanbornton, N.H. around the end of the 18th century.

Children with Mary Ann:

**4925**    i. Mary[10] Melissa Eaton, b. Oct 1842 in Meredith, N.H.; mar. James Curtis of Bristol, N.H., a farmer and meat dealer.

**4926**    ii. Sarah[10] Ann Eaton, b. 14 Jan 1845; died Nov 1854 in New Hampton.

**4927**    iii. Emma[10] Harriet Eaton, b. 29 Apr 1854 in New Hampton, and died there 18 Jun 1872.

**3250. Joseph[9] Eaton** (William[8-7], Ebenezer[6], John[5-1]) was born 11 Apr 1807 in Sanbornton, N.H., but grew up with his family in Quebec near the Vermont line. He mar. **Almira Simpson** (she born 25 Apr 1814 in St. Albans, Vt., a few miles from the Quebec border) on 28 Dec 1834. The couple settled on a farm in Fairfield, Vt., nor far east of Almira's birthplace, raising their children there and remaining for the rest of their lives. Joseph died 24 Jan 1885, and widow Almira followed on 24 Jan 1889.

Children born in Fairfield, Vt.:

**4928**    i. William[10] S. Eaton, b. 4 Sep 1836; mar. Lucy C. Payne.
**4929**    ii. Samantha[10] J. Eaton, b. 11 Jan 1841; m. Julian H. Northrop.
**4930**    iii. Eunice[10] E. Eaton, b. 12 Nov 1845; never married.

**3253. Jonathan[9] Wyatt Eaton** (William[8-7], Ebenezer[6], John[5-1]) was born 19 Nov 1820 in Sanbornton, N.H., but grew up with his family in St. Armand Parish, Que. He mar. **Mary Smith**, born in this parish 13 Feb 1827, on 22 Feb 1847. The couple resided first in Philipsburg, Que., where his family had moved; but later lived for a time in Greenfield, Mass., before returning to spend the rest of their lives in Philipsburg, Que. Jonathan was a merchant and manufacturer, and died 28 May 1879.

Children, all born in Philipsburg, Que.:

4931    i. Mary[10] Helen Eaton, b. 7 Jan 1848 and died 28 Jan 1852.
4932    ii. Wyatt[10] Eaton, b. 6 May 1849; mar. 1st, Laura Constance
            Papelard, and later took a 2d wife.
4933    iii. Martha[10] Eliza Eaton, b. 27 Aug 1854; mar. Charles R.
            Wheeler.

**3254. Edgar[9] R. Eaton** (Reuben[8], William[7], Ebenezer[6], John[5-1])
was born Oct 1821 in So. Kingston, R.I.; mar. **Mary Ann Smith** on 4
Dec 1842 in So. Kingston. As of 1850, Edgar was the keeper of the St.
Judith lighthouse in So. Kingston. He died 7 Jun 1882.

Children, all born in So. Kingston, R.I.:

4934    i. Eliza[10] Eaton, b. Jun 1845; mar. Benoni Sweet, 4 Feb 1864;
            she died 20 Jan 1918.
4935    ii. Edgar[10] Eaton, b. ca. 1849; was working in the local woolen
            mill as of 1870.
4936    iii. Olive[10] Eaton, b. ca. 1853.
4937    iv. Reuben[10] Eaton, b. 1856; was working in the woolen mill as
            of 1870.

**3258. Reuben[9] B. Eaton, Jr.** (Reuben[8], William[7], Ebenezer[6],
John[5-1]) was born ca. 1830 in So. Kingston, R. I.; mar. 1st, **Sarah __?__**,
like her husband a spinner in the local woolen mill. She died soon after,
and he mar. 2d, **Lydia T. Sweet**. They resided in So. Kingston.

Children with Lydia, born in So. Kingston, R.I.:

4938    i. George[10] Sweet Eaton, b. ca. 1854-55; mar. Lydia A.
            Northrup. George died 21 Mar 1929.
4939    ii. Charles[10] E. Eaton, b. ca. 1856-57. No marriage or issue
            known, but he died 14 Nov 1929 in So. Kingston.
4940    iii. Lillian[10] Louisa Eaton, b. ca. 1859.
4941    iv. Lizzie[10] E. Eaton, b. 7 Jan 1860; died 16 May 1772.

**3261. Joseph[9] P. Eaton** (Joseph[8], William[7], Ebenezer[6], John[5-1])
was born ca. 1832 in So. Kingston, R. I.; mar. **Celia Augusta Brown**, 9
Sep 1850 at Providence, R.I. They resided in So. Kingston for more
than 15 years, but then removed to Smithfield, where Joseph, a merchant,
died 29 Aug 1881.

Children:

4942    i. Joseph[10] Lester Eaton, b. 17 Oct 1859 in So. Kingston, R. I.;

mar. Clara Lavinia Tayler, 24 Dec 1876.

4943   ii. Benjamin[10] F. Eaton, b. 27 Jul 1860 in So. Kingston.
4944   iii. Annie[10] A. Eaton, b. 7 Aug 1862 in So. Kingston, R.I.
4945   iv. Celia[10] R. Eaton, b. 19 May 1865 in So. Kingston.
4946   v. Mary[10] J. Eaton, b. 28 May 1869 in Smithfield.

**3270. Robert**[9] **Eaton** (Henry[8-7], Ebenezer[6], John[5-1]) was born 12 Mar 1812 in Seabrook, N.H.; mar. 1st, **Dorothy "Dolly" Beckman** on 3 Feb 1833 (Seabrook *Town Records*, p. 180). They settled in Seabrook, where he is listed as a shoemaker and living in the John Smith household on Walton Rd. without real estate as of 1850. He did two stints of service in the Civil War, one before and one after wife Dolly died of fever, Jan 1863. Robert later removed to the Manchester, N.H., area, and mar. 2d, widow Francis (Harris) Ferris of Methuen, Mass., 6 Apr 1865. She was the daughter of Dr. and Sarah (Ayers) Harris. He finally mar. 3d, Amanda Dickey (then age 60), 3 Aug 1881. He died 23 Apr 1899 in Auburn, N.H., just east of Manchester.

Children with Dolly in Seabrook, N.H.:

4947   i. Nancy[10] B. Eaton, b. ca. 1834; mar. Charles A. Smith in Salisbury, Mass. She died 18 Dec 1870.
4948   ii. Sally[10] Eaton, b. ca. 1837; possibly the Sarah Eaton who mar. David Joshua Chase, 4 Dec 1856. The latter died soon, and his widow Sally was a seamstress with one son.
4949   iii. Phebe[10] K. Eaton, b. Aug 1842; died 19 Oct 1844.
4950   iv. Cecilia[10] Ann Eaton, b. ca. 1849; mar. Philip Beckman; they had at least six children. A widow, she died 12 Mar 1914.
4951   v. Dolly[10] Eaton, b. ca. 1856.

**3271. Henry**[9] **Eaton** (Henry[8-7], Ebenezer[6], John[5-1]) was born 8 Nov 1814 in Seabrook, N.H.; in Nov 1833 he mar. **Abigail M. Perry** of Newburyport, born there to Charles and Abigail (Stanwood) Perry on 13 Jan 1818. The couple settled on the east side of Washington St. between Collins and So. Main Sts. in Seabrook, where Henry was a mariner and a shoemaker. He died 22 Aug 1865; widow Abigail died 7 Apr 1878.

Children born in Seabrook, N.H.:

4952   i. Mary[10] Adaline Eaton, b. 15 Jan 1835; mar. Jacob Beckman, son of James and Mary (Boyd) Beckman, 30 Mar 1851.
4953   ii. Charles[10] W. Eaton, b. ca. 1836; m. Augusta Eaton (#3349), 14 Nov 1859. A fisherman, he was "killed by the cars" (RR), 4 Jul 1868, Seabrook.
4954   iii. Hannah[10] Eaton, b. 6 Nov 1839; mar. David E. Randall, born 1836 to Edward/Abigail (Eaton) Randall. He was a Seabrook shoemaker who died in 1915. Widow Hannah died

21 May 1829, also in Seabrook.

**4955**   iv. Almira[10] Eaton, b. 12 Jun 1845; mar. John Felch (son of Samuel and Susan (Dow) Felch), int. 13 Mar 1865. They resided in Salem, Mass.

**4956**   v. Robert[10] Wallace Eaton, b. ca. Oct 1847; died 7 Oct 1851.

**4957**   vi. Robert[10A] Calvin Eaton, b. 3 Sep 1852; mar. 1st, Mary Aurila Eaton or Cummings (b. in Salisbury, 1854, to Mary Morgan who was mar. first to a William Eaton; but whose father was given as James Cummings on her marriage record) on 27 Jun 1872; and 2d, Mrs. Sarah[10] (Eaton) Fitts (**#5039**), 3 Jan 1894.

**3274. Lewis[9] C. Eaton** (Henry[8-7], Ebenezer[6], John[5-1]) was born 19 Apr 1822 in Seabrook, N.H.; mar. **Louisa Felch**, also of Seabrook, on 19 Oct 1842. They resided in Seabrook, where Lewis was a mariner who was lost at sea in 1848 or '49.

Children born in Seabrook, N.H.:

**4958**   i. Sarah[10] Elizabeth Eaton, b. 2 Jan 1843; mar. Stephen F. Knowles, born to Stephen and Sallie (Walton) Knowles in 1839, on 22 Oct 1862. He died in 1906; widow Sarah died 29 Apr 1819.

**4959**   ii. Henry[10] Eaton, b. 4 Sep 1844; a fisherman who never married. He died 22 Feb 1915.

**4960**   iii. Eliza[10] C. Eaton, b. Sep 1846; prob. mar. a Brackett (David? George?) in 1864.

**4961**   iv. Lewis[10] Dearborn Eaton, b. Nov 1847; mar. Harriet Bragg, b. 1851 to John L. and Rhoda A. (Dow) Bragg, 1 Jun 1867. They resided in Seabrook, where Harriet died in 1917 and Lewis died 6 Jul 1920.

**3275. Moses[9] D. Eaton** (Henry[8-7], Ebenezer[6], John[5-1]) was born 1 Dec 1824 in Seabrook, N.H.; on 13 Jun 1847 in Newburyport, Mass., he mar. 1st, **Almira S. Worthley**, born 19 Jun 1824 in Weare, N.H., to James/Sarah Worthley. The couple settled first in Seabrook where Moses was early a seaman and later mainly a shoemaker. In 1871, however, they removed to Salem, Mass., where Moses was employed as a foreman on a R.R. section crew. Almira died there in 1888, and Moses mar. 2d, **Marion Wayne** of St. John's, New Brunswick, on 10 Jan 1889.

Children with Almira born in Seabrook, N.H.:

**4962**   i. Otis[10] T. Eaton, b. 18 Jun 1848; mar. Mary A. Walton, 1 Dec 1865, and res. in Warsaw, "Canada West."

**4963**   ii. William[10] H. Eaton, b. 12 Jul 1850. He was a stone mason residing in Wareham, Mass.; mar. __?__ but no issue.

**4964**   iii. Samuel[10] Eaton, b. 13 Dec 1853; died 1879.
**4965**   iv. Lewis[10] Anson Eaton, b. 4 Jun 1855; mar. 1st, Anna Cheek
         of Mebane, N.C.; and later mar. 2d, Sallie Cheek, also of
         Mebane and presumably a sister.

**3279. Caleb[9] Eaton** (True[8], Henry[7], Ebenezer[6], John[5-1]) was born
11 Nov 1826 in Seabrook, N.H.; mar. **Louisa Jane Marshall**, 19 Jul
1851. She had been born 24 Dec 1828 to Joseph and Betty (Collins)
Marshall. They resided in Seabrook, where he started as a seaman but
later turned to shoemaking, working in a local factory for many years.
He died 22 May 1910; widow Louisa followed on 11 Jul 1911.

Children born in Seabrook:

**4966**   i. Helen[10] M. Eaton, b. 3 Nov 1851; mar. Charles Mace Pike,
         son of True and Mary (Smith) Pike, on 27 Nov 1872.
         They resided in Salisbury, Mass., where he was a farmer,
         having six children there. Helen died in Salisbury, 1924.
**4967**   ii. Nancy[10] E. Eaton, b. 27 Jan 1854; died 23 Dec 1871, unmar.
**4968**   iii. Abbie[10] Villa Eaton, b. 3 Nov 1856; mar. Jacob Frank Dow,
         son of Albert M. Dow, 28 Aug 1875, and had two sons.
         Abbie died 8 Mar 1941.
**4969**   iv. Louisa[10] A. Eaton, b. 28 Jan 1858; died 31 Mar 1866.
**4970**   v. Alexander[10] M. Eaton, b. 1 Nov 1859; drowned 3 Jul 1876.
**4971**   vi. Mary[10] Asenath Eaton, b. 24 Feb 1862; mar. Sidney Fowler,
         son of Newell and Caroline Fowler, 11 Apr 1880, and
         had two sons.
**4972**   vii. Betsey[10] A. Eaton, b. 22 Nov 1864; mar. Charles E. Dow,
         son of Albert M. and Keziah (Collins) Dow, 29 Apr 1886.
         They had one daughter, and Betsey died 19 Sep 1927.

**3280. Moses[9] B. Eaton** (True[8], Henry[7], Ebenezer[6], John[5-1]) was
born 10 Dec 1831 in Seabrook, N.H.; mar. **Betsey B. Follansbee** of
Weare, N.H., daughter of John and Martha (Brown) Follansbee. They
settled first in Weare, remaining there a few years while some of their
children were born, and then returning to Seabrook in time for the 1860
Census, when they shared a dwelling unit with his sister Rebecca's family
(cf. **#1747**). Moses had already been listed as a shoemaker at age 18,
and after their return spent his working life in the local shoe factories.
He died 10 May 1895 at Alton, N.H.; widow Betsey died 4 May 1903,
age 65.

Children (the earliest born in Weare, N.H.; later in Seabrook):

**4973**   i. Sarah[10] Ella Eaton, b. 16 Apr 1855; mar. Dennis Alonzo
         Fowler, son of Dennis and Emily Fowler, 6 Sep 1875,
         having three children. She died 7 Jan 1923.

**4974**    ii. Martha[10] A. Eaton, b. 5 Mar 1860; mar. Thomas Wilson of
             Salisbury, Mass., son of John and Wilhelmina Wilson, in
             1880. She died 19 Jan 1925.
**4975**    iii. Susan[10] Jeanette Eaton, b. 9 Oct 1858; mar. Israel[9] B. Eaton
             (**#3379**) on 3 Oct 1876. They had three children, two
             dying young. Susan died 1941.
**4976**    iv. Elbridge[10] B. Eaton, b. 15 Sep 1863; died single 24 Mar
             1924 in Salisbury.
**4977**    v. Annie[10] C. Eaton, b. 25 Oct 1867; never mar., died 1931.
**4978**    vi. Hattie[10] Linwood Eaton, b. 5 Oct 1872; mar. William T.
             Chase, son of Ivory W. and Lucy (Dow) Chase, 1901
             in Salisbury, Mass. She died 4 Jan 1944.
**4979**    vii. Frederick[10] Eaton, b. 13 Sep 1876; died 1 Apr 1879.


**3283. William[9] True Eaton** (True[8], Henry[7], Ebenezer[6], John[5-1])
was born ca. 1840 at Seabrook, N.H.; mar. **Sarah J. Dow** of Seabrook,
10 Feb 1861 in Salisbury, Mass. They resided in Seabrook, where he was
a shoemaker from an early age and later worked in the shoe factories. A
widower when he died 26 Sep 1902 at Salisbury, Mass.

Children born in Seabrook, N.H.:

**4980**    i. Melissa[10] T. Eaton, b. 1861; mar. Nathaniel Brown.
**4981**    ii. William[10]B Eaton, b. 1864; mar. Lena A. Moreland, dau. of
             Horace D. and Betsey (Eaton) Moreland., 17 Dec 1882.
**4982**    iii. Linna[10] C. Eaton, b. 6 Oct 1866; died 23 Mar 1868.


**3285. Wyman[9] Eaton** (Edward[8] D., Henry[7], Ebenezer[6], John[5-1])
was born 21 Jan 1833 in Seabrook, N.H.; mar. **Mary Jane Wright** on 10
Jul 1852 and they resided in Seabrook, where he was a shoemaker and
later in the shoe factories, which in 1870 were also providing employment for son Jacob (18) and daughter Eunice (14). Wife Mary J. died in
1890; Wyman died 2 Oct 1911.

Children born in Seabrook:

**4983**    i. Jacob[10] Eaton, b. 16 Oct 1852; mar. Sarah Fowler, dau. of
             John and Mercy Fowler, 13 Apr 1875. He died, 1914, in
             Newburyport, Mass.
**4984**    ii. Nancy[10] Jane Eaton, b. 1855; mar. Bonavista Brown, son of
             Jacob D. and Abigail Brown, on 2 May 1870. She died
             19 Jul 1908.
**4985**    iii. Eunice[10] Anne Eaton, b. 1857; mar. John Curtis Eaton
             (**#3382**) 16 Feb 1878. She died 26 Feb 1932.
**4986**    iv. Wyman[10] Eaton, b. ca. 1860; mar. Margaret A. Follansbee
             (dau. of Daniel B. and Emeline Follansbee), 25 Jun 1883.
             He died 13 Oct 1912.

**4987** v. Lucinda[10] Eaton, b. ca. 1861; mar. Joseph E. Janvrin, son of Joseph and Margaret (England) Janvrin, 29 Nov 1879. Lucinda died in 1924.
**4988** vi. Charles[10] H. Eaton, b. 7 Nov 1864; died young.
**4989** vii. Martha (or Maggie?)[10] Eaton, b. 19 Jul 1867.
**4990** viii. Eva[10] May Eaton, b. 24 Aug 1871.
**4991** ix. Ada[10] Eaton, b. Jul 1873; died young.
**4992** x. Ada[10A] Eaton, b. Jul 1876; mar. Wallace Eaton, son of Alvado and Charlotte (Janvrin) Eaton, 2 Jun 1893. She died 20 Jun 1897.
**4993** xi. Son[10] Eaton, b. 13 Jul 1877; infant death.
**4994** xii. John[10] Curtis Eaton, b. ca. 13 Aug 1879; mar. Marie Alice Henry, dau. of Thomas F. and Annie (Banner) Henry, 5 Dec 1905. He died 5 May 1906, ae 26y, 8mos, 22days.

**3286. William[9] Q. Eaton** (Edward[8] D., Henry[7], Ebenezer[6], John[5], John[4-1]) was born 21 Aug 1836 in Seabrook, N.H.; mar. **Lucretia (Fowler) Souther** (born Aug 1822 to Abraham and Martha Fowler), on 5 Apr 1856. They resided in Seabrook, where William was a shoemaker and worked in the shoe factories. Wife Lucretia died 19 Jan 1886; William died 24 May 1919.

Children born in Seabrook:

**4995** i. William[10] E. Eaton, b. 22 Apr 1856; he died single, 1921.
**4996** ii. John[10] Samuel Eaton, b. 27 Apr 1858; mar. 1st, Carrie[8] M. Eaton (**#1723**), dau. of Israel and Miriam (Wright) Eaton; and 2d, Emily Chase.
**4997** iii. Laura[10] Eaton, b. ca. 1861; mar. Elbridge N. Brown, son of Jacob and Abigail Brown, 18 Mar 1877.
**4998** iv. Jane[10] Hilton Eaton, b. ca. 1863; mar. Israel Frank Fowler, son of Israel E. and Nancy S. (Wright) Fowler, 15 Nov 1880. She died 31 Jan 1947.

**3288. Almon[9] S. Eaton** (Edward[8] D., Henry[7], Ebenezer[6], John[5-1]) was born 10 Mar 1846 in Seabrook, N.H.; mar. **Mary E. Wright** on 4 Jan 1867, and they resided in Seabrook, where Almon worked in a shoe factory and sired a large family which, however, suffered numerous infant deaths. He died 27 Nov 1930; widow Mary died in 1937.

Children all but last born in Seabrook:

**4999** i. Nicholas[10] Eaton, b. 30 Jan 1867; died 30 Sep 1868.
**5000** ii. Mary[10] E. Eaton, b. 16 Dec 1868.
**5001** iii. Sadie[10] Belle Eaton, b. 1869; mar. 1st, William Eaton, 27 Jun 1888; 2d, William Collins, 1 Apr 1902; 3d, Napoleon Gagnon, 15 Apr 1917.

**5002**    iv. Twin daughter[10] Eaton, b. 20 Mar 1870; died 3 Apr 1870.
**5003**    v. Twin daughter[10] Eaton, b. 20 Mar 1870; died 8 Apr 1870.
**5004**    vi. Rhoda[10] B. Eaton, b. May 1872; died in infancy.
**5005**    vii. Rhoda[10A] I. Eaton, b. 31 Mar 1873.
**5006**    viii. Hial[10] F. Eaton, b. 31 Mar 1876; died 20 Jan 1878.
**5007**    ix. Hial[10A] F. Eaton, b. 25 Mar 1878; died. 11 Jul 1879.
**5008**    x. Louise[10] P. Eaton, b. 10 May 1880; mar. Albion S. Greene. She died 1926.
**5009**    xi. Grace[10] Eaton, b. ca. 1882.
**5010**    xii. Son[10] Eaton, b. 8 Jan 1883; died in infancy.
**5011**    xiii. Mary[10] Lucy Eaton, b. ca. 1885; mar. Abbott C. Dow, 8 Mar 1902.
**5012**    xiv. Infant[10] Eaton, b. 2 Feb 1886; stillborn.
**5013**    xv. Charlotte[10] L. Eaton, b. 11 Apr 1887; mar. Arthur N. Wing, 24 Nov 1906.
**5014**    xvi. Infant[10] Eaton, b. 21 Jun 1890; stillborn.
**5015**    xvii. Elizabeth[10] Eaton, b. 1891 at Salisbury; mar. Henry F. Souther, b. 15 Apr 1906.


**3308. Isaiah**[9] **D. Eaton** (Thomas[8-7], Ebenezer[6], John[5-1]) was born 16 Aug 1819 in Seabrook, N.H.; mar. **Hannah Hunt** ca. 1841 and they resided in Seabrook, where they had a large family although five children failed to survive to adulthood, not all of whom we can list below. Isaiah followed the work pattern of most of his Seabrook generation: a seaman for some years, and then a shoemaker and worker in the shoe factories. Isaiah[9] died 4 Aug 1899.

Children born in Seabrook:

**5016**    i. Ellen[10] Jane Eaton, b. ca. 1842; mar. George[9] P. Eaton (#3332), int. 4 Oct 1861, Seabrook.
**5017**    ii. Jacob[10] F. Eaton, a twin born 12 Nov 1844; mar. Eliza Souther, daughter b. 2 Mar 1849 to Jacob and Nancy (Starr) Souther, on 14 Oct 1863. They res. in Seabrook and had nine children: William[11] Alonzo Eaton, b. 26 Oct 1864; George[11] Eaton, b. 17 Mar 1867; Leroy[11] Eaton, b. 22 Oct 1869; Margaret[11] C. Eaton, b. 29 Jul 1872; Nancy[11] Eaton, b. 16 Feb 1875; Jacob[11] F., Jr., b. 18 May 1878; Lillian[11] May, b. 18 Jun 1880; Arthur[11] H. Eaton, b. 27 Mar 1885; Ronnie[11] Ernest, b. 18 Mar 1889.
**5018**    iii. Thomas[10] F. Eaton, twin b. 12 Nov 1844; died young.
**5019**    iv. Samuel[10] F. Eaton, b. 1848; unmar.
**5020**    v. Isaiah[10] P. Eaton, b. ca. 1849; unmar.
**5021**    vi. Thomas[10A] F. Eaton, b. ca. 1851; mar. Laura E. Souther, 17 Jun 1874. They had at least one son: Samuel[11] Eaton, b. 8 Oct 1873. Thomas died 14 Nov 1907.
**5022**    vii. Chase[10] S. Eaton, b. 1854; unmar.
**5023**    viii. Hannah[10] A. Eaton, b. 1857; mar. Leonidas Souther, 9 Jul

1876.

**3310. Thomas[9] Eaton, Jr.** (Thomas[8-7], Ebenezer[6], John[5-1]) was born 5 Nov 1826 in Seabrook, N.H.; mar. **Betsey Jane Brown** (b. 15 Oct 1830) in Mar 1847, and settled in Seabrook, where he was a fisherman and a shoemaker, although he is listed as a farm laborer in 1870. He died 7 Nov 1871 in Seabrook.

Children born in Seabrook:

5024   i. Isaac[10] L. Eaton, b. 29 Sep 1848; mar. Ann Rebecca Fowler, 8 Feb 1868. Their children included Thomas[11] H. Eaton (b. 1868) and Ida[11] L. Eaton (b. 1875).
5025   ii. Adaletta[10] Eaton, b. ca. 1850; prob. died young.
5026   iii. Sadie[10] Ann Eaton, b. 23 Feb 1854; mar. Samuel F. Fowler, 20 Jun 1870.
5027   iv. Pluma[10] Ann Eaton, b. 20 Jun 1858; mar. Abner Fowler. She died 1892.
5028   v. Liona[10] B. Eaton, b. 1 Mar 1860; mar. 1st, Frank Fuller, 1877; 2d, Henry Dow, 1881.
5029   vi. Elwilda[10] Eaton, b. 1861; mar. Alvin Locke, 1881. She died in 1913.
5030   vii. Abbie[10] J. Eaton, b. 13 Feb 1864; mar. John Lewis Fowler. She died, 1894.
5031   viii. Newell[10] M. Eaton, b. 20 Jun 1866; mar. Emma[8] F. Eaton (#3768), dau. b. to Robert C. and Mary A. Eaton on 21 Dec 1869. He died 21 Jan 1910.
5032   ix. Charles[10] F. Eaton, b. 13 Jul 1869; mar. Annie M. Brown, 6 Sep 1890. He died in 1934 in Newburyport, Mass.

**3318. Reuben[9] Eaton** (Joshua[8], Thomas[7], Ebenezer[6], John[5-1]) was born 10 Aug 1826 in Seabrook, N.H.; mar. **Cynthia[9] Eaton** (#3329) about 1850. They resided mainly in Seabrook, although at times in Salisbury as well. Reuben was a fisherman who also worked for the shoe factory and in later years worked for the railroad. He died 21 Dec 1907; widow Cynthia died 12 May 1912.

Children born in Seabrook:

5033   i. Baby[10] Eaton, b. ca. 1851; died in infancy.
5034   ii. Baby[10] Eaton, b. ca. 1853; died in infancy.
5035   iii. Cynthia[10] Eaton, b. Oct 1855; mar. William C. Robinson, son of William Robinson, on 15 Jul 1872, He had died before the 1880 Census, when Cynthia was a widow.
5036   iv. James[10] Buchanan Eaton, b. 9 Jul 1857; became the second husband of Mrs. Sarah L. (Eaton) Harmon (#3716), the widow of Fred, 15 Feb 1879. He died in a fire at Cross

Beach, 15 Sep 1935.

**3319. Joshua[9] Eaton, Jr.** (Joshua[8], Thomas[7], Ebenezer[6], John[5-1]) was born Jul 1828 in Seabrook, N.H.; mar. **Eleanor M. Dow**, b. ca. 1830 to William and Sarah Dow, on 1 Feb 1848. They resided in Seabrook, where Joshua was a seaman, shoemaker and worker in a shoe factory, in that decennial sequence, starting in 1850. He died 26 Aug 1882; widow Eleanor died 10 Dec 1907.

Children, mostly born in Seabrook, N.H.:

5037　　i. William[10] Wesley Eaton, b. 12 Jul 1849; mar. Margaret A. Walton, dau. of Sewell B. and Almira (Beal) Walton. He was a shoemaker, and the marriage ended in divorce. He died 18 Jun 1918.

5038　　ii. Eliza[10] Ann Eaton, b. Oct 1851; mar. Daniel Boyd, son of Aaron and Harriet[7] (Eaton) (**#889**), on 17 Mar 1866. She died 28 Nov 1923.

5039　　iii. Sarah[10] Eaton, b. Jan 1853; mar. 1st, John P. Fitts, widower of her younger sister, Ada[10] Ellen (**#5040**), on 20 Jun 1872; and 2d, (Robert) Calvin[10] Eaton (**#4957**), 3 Jan 1894. She died 5 Aug 1911.

5040　　iv. Ada[10] Ellen Eaton, b. Jun 1855; mar. John P. Fitts, son of Joseph and Mary E. Fitts, on 28 Oct 1871, but died 20 days later, 17 Nov 1871, still age 16.

5041　　v. Elmira[10] Eaton, b. ca. 18 Jan 1859; mar. Joseph Hook Marshall, son of Joseph and Betsey Marshall, on 19 Feb 1875.

5042　　vi. Enoch[10] Eaton, b. early 1860; mar. Clarie E. Gynan, dau. of Nicholas and Miriam R. (Fowler) Gynan on 25 Jun 1878. He died a month later, 27 Jul 1878.

5043　　vii. Lester[10] Eaton, b. 31 Jul 1862; died 1868.

5044　　viii. Susan[10] Jane Eaton, b. 23 Aug 1866; mar. Rev. Arthur E. Walton, son of Benjamin and Anna E. (Felch) Walton. She died 17 May 1926.

5045　　ix. Lester[10A] Howard Eaton, b. 1868; mar. a Dolly A. Eaton; he died 19 Apr 1905.

5046　　x. Ada[10A] Ellen Eaton, a twin b. 3 Aug 1871 in Salisbury, Mass.; mar. Tristram L. Souther, son of Abram and Sarah (Eaton) Souther. She died in 1933.

5047　　xi. Joshua[10] Eaton, a twin b. 3 Aug 1871 in Salisbury, Mass.; prob. died young, before 1880.

5048　　xii. Nellie[10] Maria Eaton, b. 1873; mar. 1st, Edward P. Randall, son of George W. and Jemima (Fowler) Randall, 11 Mar 1891; and 2d, Melchior Tantaro. She died 1951.

**3320. Samuel[9] Collins Eaton** (Joshua[8], Thomas[7], Ebenezer[6], John[5-1]) was born 15 Aug 1830 in Seabrook, N.H.; mar. on 25 Oct 1849,

**Achsah Ann Brown**, born to Isaac and Mary (Dow) Brown, 24 Jun 1833. They settled in Seabrook, living initially with Samuel's cousin Thomas[9] (#**3310**), who had married his wife's sister. Samuel was progressively a seaman, then a shoemaker, then a worker in a shoe factory over the decades, and they had a large family. He died 20 Aug 1888; wife Achsah died 30 Apr 1918.

Children born in Seabrook, N.H.:

**5049**   i. Charles[10] T. Eaton, b. early 1850, but apparently d. young.

**5050**   ii. Charles[10A] E. Eaton, b. 1852; mar. Lucy A. Perkins, b. 1856 to Abram and Martha (Wright) Perkins, on 8 Jul 1874. He died 1 June 1934.

**5051**   iii. Climena[10] Eaton, b. 13 Apr 1855; mar. Valentine Bagley, Jr., son of Valentine and Elizabeth (Fowler) Bagley, on 29 Oct 1873. She died 28 Oct 1887.

**5052**   iv. Lola[10] Montez Eaton, b. 29 Jul 1857; mar. 1st, Henry N. Caswell, b. on the Isles of Shoals; and 2d, David Perkins. She died 25 Feb 1921.

**5053**   v. Sally[10] A. Eaton, b. 12 Feb 1862; mar. 1st, William H. Hardy, son of Henry M. and Lydia A. (Beckman) Hardy, on 5 Mar 1878; 2d, Enoch Knowles, son of Augustus and Hannah Ellen (Felch) Knowles. Sally died 28 Oct 1924.

**5054**   vi. Frank(lin)[10] B. Eaton, b. 9 Jul 1863; mar. Hannah Francis Collins, dau. of Robert F. and Emily A. (Fowler) Collins, 26 Oct 1885. Frank[10] died 12 Mar 1910.

**5055**   vii. Dolly[10] A. Eaton, b. 29 Oct 1865; mar. 1st, Frank Hall, son of William and Margaret Hall, 19 Jun 1886; 2d, Lester Eaton, for whom she is "wife" on her gravestone. She died 12 Dec 1922.

**5056**   viii. William[10] Q. Eaton, b. 24 Jul 1870; mar. Clara A. Collins, sister of his brother Frank's wife, 31 Oct 1892. He died 18 Jan 1926.

**5057**   ix. Susan[10] May Eaton, b. 5 Jun 1873; mar. Alvah H. Dow, son of Tristram L. and Sarah A. Dow, 15 Sep 1893. She died 5 Dec 1928.

**5058**   x. Seneca[10] Eaton, b. 1876; mar. Mary Fowler, dau. of Lowell D. and Chastina (Eaton) Fowler, 6 Nov 1899. He died 18 Nov 1956.

**5059**   xi. Carrie[10] Emma Hoyt, b. 9 Oct 1879; mar. Harry Perkins, son of Joseph and Lillian (Beckman) Perkins, 5 May 1901. She died 12 Jun 1964.

**3326. Leonard[9] William Eaton** (Chase[8], Thomas[7·], Ebenezer[6], John[5·1]) was born ca. 1838; mar. 1st, **Mercy R. Wells**, (native of Ipswich, Mass.) on 10 May 1854 in Newburyport, Mass., where they resided in the first ward and had seven children. Mercy died, and Leonard mar. 2d,

**Mrs. Sarah (Dodge) Pingree**, widow of Hial Pingree, also of Ipswich, on 31 May 1877, and had four more children with her. Leonard died 10 Oct 1890.

Children with Mercy, all born Newburyport, Mass.:

**5060**   i. John[10] Albert Eaton, b. 20 May 1855; mar. Amanda Dollof but was divorced from her.
**5061**   ii. John[10] Wells Eaton, b. 20 May 1857.
**5062**   iii. Maynard[10] Eaton, b. ca. 1858; died young.
**5063**   iv. Maynard[10A] Eaton, b. 1860; died young.
**5064**   v. Maynard[10B] Eaton, b. (30 Jul?) 1862; mar. Alice Perkins, 30 Apr 1885.
**5065**   vi. Forrest[10] Lynwood Eaton, b. 10 May 1864; died unmarried, 6 Dec 1896.
**5066**   vii. Eleanor[10] Maria Eaton, b. 28 Apr 1867; mar. Nehemiah Robbins.

Children with Sarah in Newburyport, Mass.

**5067**   viii. James[10] Eaton, b. 1877; mar. Mabel Knight (1880-1981) on 10 Apr 1899. He died 19 Aug 1969.
**5068**   ix. "Georgie"[10] Eaton, a daughter b. 18 Feb 1881.
**5069**   x. Henry[10] H. Eaton, b. ca. 7 Sep 1883; suffered a hydro-cephalic condition and died 13 May 1884.
**5070**   xi. Herbert[10] Eaton, b. 21 Apr 1887; mar. Sarah E. Souther (1884-1938) 3 Dec 1910 in Newburyport, Mass. He died, 1950.

**3338. Reuben[9] Eaton, Jr.** (Reuben[8], Thomas[7], Ebenezer[6], John[5-1]) was born 19 Sep 1834 in Seabrook, N.H.; mar. **Annie C. Gynan** (born to Patrick and Elizabeth Gynan, 11 Dec 1840 in Arichet, Nova Scotia) on 20 Dec 1857. They resided in Seabrook where Reuben was first a fisherman and later worked in a shoe factory. He died 12 Nov 1896.

Children, all born in Seabrook, N.H.:

**5071**   i. Frank[10] Eaton, b. 24 Jun 1859; died 11 Apr 1866.
**5072**   ii. Clarence[10] Lambert Eaton, b. 13 Dec 1862; m. Adelia Litch, 30 Jan 1891 in Milwaukee, Wisc. They res. in Lynn, Mass., where he was an agent for Goodyear machines. They had no children, and Clarence divorced Adelia on grounds of abandonment, 16 Nov 1917. He died on 20 Oct 1948.
**5073**   iii. William[10] D. Eaton, b. 20 Jul 1864; mar. Annie M.. Knowles, dau. of Charles and Ardesira (Eaton) Knowles, 30 Dec 1890. They res. in Seabrook, where he was a R.R. station agent in the 1890s. They had one son, Douglas[10] Lambert

Eaton, b. 1903 in Salisbury, Mass. William died 22 Jan
1932.
**5074**   iv. Andrew[10] J. Eaton, b. 30 Dec (?) 1866; mar. Lucy A. Beckman, dau. of John R. and Mary E. (Marsh) Beckman, on
15 Jun 1884. He died 15 Jul 1910.

**3348. Abel**[9] **Eaton** (Ezekiel[8], Abel[7], Silvanus[6], John[5-1]) was born
ca. 1838 in Seabrook, N.H.; mar. **Zelphia A. Bragg** on 8 Jul 1856 (Seabrook *VR* in Concord). They resided in Seabrook. He was in the Civil
War as a corporal in Co. C., the 6th Regt. He was a shoemaker and later
worked in the shoe factory. He died of tuberculosis, 31 Mar 1876.

Children born in Seabrook:

**5075**   i. Gilman[10] B. Eaton, b. 1857; mar. Abbie J. Dow, dau. of John
M. and Lydia Ann (Eaton) (**#3284**) Dow, 28 Feb 1878.
He died soon thereafter, 1881/2.
**5076**   ii. Ezekiel[10] C. Eaton, b. Jul 1859; apparently never married;
d. 15 May 1939 and bur. Methodist Cemetery, Seabrook.
**5077**   iii. Clara[10] Belle Eaton, b. 1862; mar. Asa Beckman (son of
Hiram and Adeline (Eaton) Beckman, 7 Jun 1884.
**5078**   iv. Emma[10] Eaton, b. 29 Sep 1866; mar. John Janvrin, Jr., son of
John and Mary Ann Janvrin, 30 Jun 1883.
**5079**   v. Robert[10] L. Eaton, b. 29 Oct 1868; mar. Alice F. Rowe, dau.
of William and Mary (Gove) Rowe, 21 Feb 1891; he died
27 Nov 1931 in Newburyport, Mass.
**5080**   vi. Minnie[10] (Mary) F. Eaton, b. Aug 1875; mar. 1st, John N.
Beckman, (int.) 16 Dec 1892; 2d, Samuel[11] Eaton, son of
Thomas[10A] F. Eaton (**#5021**), 7 Nov 1903. She died 14
Jan 1928.

**3368. Joshua**[9] **Winthrop Eaton** (Winthrop[8] D., Samuel[7], John[6-1])
was born late in 1844 in Salisbury, Mass. His father Winthrop was lost in
the Chaleur Bay storm when he was only 7 or 8. He served in the Civil
War with Cos. C and D of the First Battalion of Mass. Heavy Artillery,
after which he mar. **Ann Dyer** of Salisbury, Mass., in 1866, and they settled in Salisbury prob. living from the start on Beach Road. Early on he
was a shoemaker, but later became the town undertaker, as well as the superintendent of Longhill Cemetery and sexton of the Methodist church.
He died after a long illness on 30 May 1920.

Children, prob. all born in Salisbury:

**5081**   i. William[10] Carlton Eaton, b. ca. 1867; mar. Janet McLennon,
and res. in Salisbury. He was killed by a truck in Boston,
23 Sep 1923.

in Newburyport, Mass.

**5083**    iii. Roy[10] Lawrence Eaton, b. early 1880; resided in Salisbury, Mass.

**3873. Daniel[9] Brown Eaton** (Elisha[8-7], John[6], Elisha[5], Samuel[4], John[3-1]) was born in Gilford, N.H., on 23 Oct 1820; mar. 1st, on 9 Aug 1849, **Susan Lee Smith**, born 25 Feb 1828 at Alton, N.H. to Joseph Parsons and Rebekah (Glidden) Smith. They lived on a farm in Gilford, although Daniel[9] reported his occupation as carpenter in the 1850 Census and had a lifelong interest in astronomy, surveying and making woodwind musical instruments, as well as maintaining the farm. Shortly after the Civil War, he bought a new farm on Keyser Rd. just north of the village of Meredith, N.H., at the west end of Lake Winnipesaukee. Wife Susan died there 1 Feb 1876. Daniel[9] mar. 2d, **Mrs. Emily A. Corliss** of Portsmouth, N.H., 12 Oct 1882. He served Meredith on the Board of Education and other town offices. He died 18 Feb 1909 in Meredith.

Children with Susan (i-vii born, Gilford; viii-ix, Meredith, N.H.):

**5084**    i. Mary[10] Susan Eaton, b. 4 Jun 1851; mar. Rev. Charles W. Taylor, a Methodist minister, son of James Badger and Polly Taylor, 21 Mar 1873 in Meredith Village. They had one son, Karl Trafton Taylor, b. 1874 in Manchester, N.H. Mary S. died 4 Sep 1874 in Meredith. For her husband's career and second wife, see Carter (1906), p. 262.

**5085**    ii. Julia[10] Ann Eaton, b. 3 May 1853; a teacher, she died unmar. 6 Jun 1932.

**5086**    iii. Sarah[10] Jane Eaton, b. 23 Apr 1855; she died unmar. 21 Jan 1892.

**5087**    iv. John[10] Smith Eaton, b. 2 Jun 1857; died unmar., 31 Jan 1876, his mother dying of the same ailment the next day.

+**5088**    v. Daniel[10] Emery Eaton, b. 18 Jun 1859; mar. Ella Everett.

**5089**    vi. Rebecca[10] Eaton, a twin b. 1864; died 1864.

**5090**    vii. Elizabeth[10] Eaton, a twin, b. 1864; died 1864.

**5091** viii. Joseph[10] Smith Eaton, b. 1 Jun 1868; mar. Martha Evans of Freetown, Mass. on 23 Sep 1896 in New Bedford, Mass. They settled in Taunton, Mass., where Joseph was a draftsman in an engineering firm. They had three children: Marion[11] Eaton, b. 3 Jun 1898, and mar. Duncan Dunbar, 12 Sep 1925 in Taunton, removing to White Plains, N.Y.; Spencer[11] Evans Eaton, b. 1 Jan 1901 and mar. Eleanor Way, 1 Jul 1930 in Worcester, Mass., teaching at Keene State College in Keene, N.H., where he d. May 1986; and Helen[11] Eaton, who never mar. and was a librarian in Taunton.

**5092**    ix. Wallace[10] Eaton, b. and d., 1870.

**3878.   John⁹ Dolby Eaton** (Elisha⁸⁻⁷, John⁶, Elisha⁵, Samuel⁴, John³⁻¹) was born 28 Jun 1831 in Gilford, N.H.; mar. 1st, **Judith P. Smith** (she born in Gilford, 24 Oct 1833) on 6 Aug 1858.   He owned a store selling stoves at retail in Salem, Mass.  Judith died 2 Mar 1886 after two children were born, and he mar. 2d, Mrs. Lucy A. Ward, 24 Dec 1887. He later mar. 3d, Mrs. Dora Rose (Remick) Ware.  He died 27 Oct 1907.

Children with Judith, born in Salem, Mass.:

5093    i. Arthur¹⁰ Smith Eaton, b. 22 May 1863; mar. Nancy L. Brown of Somerville, Mass., 10 Jan 1918.  He died 1 Oct 1921, without issue.
5094   ii. Mary¹⁰ Jane Eaton, b. 9 Feb 1866; died of diptheria, 15 Jan 1877, in Salem.

**3880. Martin⁹ Van Buren Eaton** (Elisha⁸⁻⁷, John⁶, Elisha⁵, Samuel⁴, John³⁻¹) was born 22 Dec 1835 in Gilford, N.H.; mar. **Melissa P. Rollins** of Alton, N.H (she b. 21 Aug 1837), on 15 Nov 1859.  They resided on a farm in Gilford at first, but at some time between 1870 and 1900 moved halfway around Lake Winnipesaukee to Moultonborough. Martin died 6 Oct 1929 at Tuftonborough, N.H.

Children born at Gilford, N.H.:

5095    i. Laura¹⁰ Eaton, b. 18 Nov 1867; mar. 1st, Fred Osgood, 1890; and 2d, Lewis Goodhue, 1921.  She died 30 Jan 1946.
5096   ii. Charles¹⁰ Martin Eaton, b. 7 Nov 1869; mar. Agnes Mooney, 1895, without issue.  He d. 12 Nov 1936 at Tuftonborough, N.H.

**3881. Joseph⁹ Warren Eaton** (Elisha⁸⁻⁷, John⁶. Elisha⁵, Samuel⁴, John³⁻¹) was born 22 Apr 1840.  He early removed to Salem, Mass. to join with his brother John in the stove dealership.  There he met **Maria H. Bunker**, born in Salem 9 June 1844, and they were mar. 7 Jan 1869.

Children born at Gilford, N.H.:

5097    i. Albert¹⁰ Warren Eaton, b. 11 Feb 1870, Salem, Mass.; mar. Ethel Dearborn.  He died 8 Aug 1901, after a single child.
5098   ii. Lillian¹⁰ Frances Eaton, b. 7 May 1871; mar. Harry M. Vent of Salem.

# Generation Ten

(This brief final chapter is an indulgence of the junior author. After the lengthy labor of completing this book, it is only fair to extend its scope late enough in time to show where he fits into this Eaton tribe. Therefore this chapter will provide a notice for his grandfather as the only representative of Generation Ten.)

## A. *The Salisbury Branch*

**5088. Daniel[10] Emery Eaton** (Daniel[9], Elisha[8-7], John[6], Elisha[5], Samuel[4], John[3-1]) was born 18 June 1859 in Gilford, N.H., but removed as a youngster with his family to Meredith, N.H., where he grew up. After completing study at local public schools, he went to Boston, Mass. and took a job as a clerk in a major drygoods store, where he picked up the taste for fine textiles and natty dressing which he displayed throughout life. On returning home, he met the daughter of the Baptist minister in Meredith for the 1885-89 period, Rev. Samuel P. Everett and his first wife, Alcesta (Goodnow), who had died in 1871. On 14 Dec 1889, he mar. **Ella Alcesta Everett** (born 31 May 1858 in Rowe, Mass.) at Ayer, Mass., the pastorate to which the Everett family had removed after the Meredith stint. Ironically, in the years before the Meredith pastorate, Rev. Samuel had been the Baptist minister at So. Hampton, N.H., next door to Seabrook, N.H.; and daughter Ella was teaching at Barnard Institute in that town before her marriage. So the Everett family knew several of the Salisbury/Seabrook Eaton families that had spilled over into So. Hampton, before they arrived in Meredith to encounter yet another branch of the same family. Ella had been enrolled for a year or two at Mt. Holyoke before family illness suspended her formal study. In adult years she was very active in the church, missionary activities, and attended state and national W.C.T.U. conventions.

Daniel was musically inclined, and upon return home, he had become the organist for Rev. Everett's Baptist Church, a role he continued for over 50 years. He began work in Meredith as the teller in the one-man Meredith Village Savings bank in 1886, and in 1888 he was promoted to Treasurer, a post he occupied in the same one-man bank for 50 years as well. His family lived at #6 Waukewan St. while the children were born, but then removed to a new home on Terrace Ave. on Ladd Hill, which had a commanding view of Meredith Bay and the White Mountains. Daniel was something of a charming eccentric, who had a number of other passions, including the cultivation of a large and elegant flower garden from which he supplied the church with huge and ornate floral displays. He also liked to dress in costume and give theatrical shows, along with puckish songs, some of his own composition. He was intensely interested in family history, and was a member of the first Eaton Family Association in the 1880s, signing up again when that Association was reincarnated in the 1930s and '40s, being feted as the oldest Eaton to attend one of their later meetings at Salisbury, Mass.

Most of all he liked to travel, locally, regionally and nationally. Given this yen, it is surprising that he never learned to drive an automobile and hence never owned one (a shortcoming that his wife associated with the fact that he was mechanically challenged and had never gotten the hang of riding a bicycle either). But the B & M train station at Meredith was only a few hundred yards from his residence, giving access to much of New England; and he was among the earliest to seize upon commercial air travel as it developed during his later years. He also was an inveterate walker over the hills and dales of the Lake Region of New Hampshire, thinking nothing of tramping 20 miles to settle an estate for the bank or, for that matter, for sheer pleasure. Since no railroad ran that way, he once walked 90 miles one way to visit a cousin in Paris, Maine. He became a familiar figure to motorists of the area, and was often invited to hitch a ride with them, which occasionally he accepted, but for the most part he would respond with pride and joy: "No thanks, I'm *walking!*" After wife Ella died, 11 Jan 1938, he would often disappear to warmer climes for the winter with minimal notice to his relatives. For the winter of 1944, when he was 85, he went to San Diego, and on a whim decided to help with the manpower shortage of that war year by lying about his age and waiting on tables at an elegant seaside restaurant. When he was 90 and walking toward Meredith from a neighboring town having just missed the last train late of a wintry afternoon, he accepted a ride from an acquaintance midway. The car skidded off the road and he was in the hospital for the first time in his life. His bones were mended so that he lived tolerably for over a year after the experience, but he could no longer take long walks, and died 18 Apr 1952 in Meredith. Other accounts of his life and ways appear in Pillsbury (1927, pp. 97-98) and Converse (1960, p. 28).

Children with Ella in Meredith, N.H.:

**5099** i. Everett[11] Jewell Eaton, b. 4 Nov 1890; spent his career in the First National Bank of White River Junction, Vt. He mar. Mrs. Vivienne Hill, June 11, 1928. They had two sons: Everett[12] Daniel Eaton, b. May 1929; and Ernest[12] George Eaton, b. 8 Jul 1932, both in White River Jct.

**5100** ii. Evelyn[11] Eaton, b. 1 Dec 1895; m. Rev. Ernest L. Converse (b. 20 Aug 1883 in Amherst, N.H.), who was minister of the Meredith Baptist Church, 1912-1919, on 11 Aug 1920, a year after her graduation from Mt. Holyoke. They had three children: Paul[12] Everett Converse, b. 25 Aug 1921, Bangor, Me.; Elizabeth[12] Eaton Converse, b.

4 Aug 1924 in Laconia, N.H.; and **Philip[12] Ernest Converse, the junior author of this genealogy**, b. 17 Nov 1928 in Concord, N.H. Mother Evelyn died 7 Sep 1991 in Menlo Park, Cal. where Philip's family was at the time.

**5101**   iii. Blythe[11] Meredith Eaton, b. 29 Jun 1900; mar. 1st, Dorothy P. Scrimgeour of Lewiston, Me., 1920, and they had two daughters: Frances[12] Eleanor Eaton, b. 26 Mar 1923; and Priscilla[12] Louise Eaton, b. 22 Nov 1924. Blythe mar. 2d, Mrs. Antoinette (Cisson) Finn. He died 9 Oct 1966.

# APPENDIX

# APPENDIX A: More Sidebars

**#13.** The Original Eaton Homestead, East Salisbury, Mass.

**#14.** The Original Haverhill, Mass., Homesteads

**#15.** Our New World Eatons: Workers in Wood

### #13. The Original Eaton Homestead, East Salisbury, Mass.

In the 17th century Europe from which our New England fore-
fathers emigrated, there were two distinct styles of land tenure popular in various regions. In one, farmers lived together in small villages
and walked or rode some distance to outlying fields where they actually cultivated their land. The other style, more familiar in later rural
America, dispersed the farmhouses themselves around these outlying
fields, so that farmers worked right where they lived. When in 1639
and 1640 the Original Proprietors of the new grant of Salisbury, Mass.
began the divisions of common land into private holdings, they followed the first style. Each Proprietor received two lots: one from a set
of small house lots, most of which ringed the area set off as the village
green; and the second a larger "planting lot" somewhere in the outlying area. As we have seen, John[1] Eaton was the only maverick who, in
1640, accepted his two-acre village house lot, but decided to build his
actual dwelling on the six-acre planting lot he was assigned by the
lottery, which lay nearly two-thirds of a mile east of the village green,
on the "Great Neck" of cultivatable upland that jutted out between the
huge salt marshes inside of the lengthy outer barrier strand famous in
New England as Salisbury Beach.

The original homesteads of founding patriarchs just off the boat
are of keen interest to family historians, and our purpose here is to
review what we have succeeded in learning about the long-term history of the first land stake in the New World of our John[1] in Salisbury, Mass. There is much that is not clear in this specific case. Obviously, after 360 years we would not expect to find an original structure. Probably the homestead dwelling unit has been replaced three
or four times at least, and also not always rebuilt on exactly the same
spot. It is not even entirely clear just where the initial planting lot lay,
altho we know the location within a hundred yards or so. Actually,
that first planting lot was rather tiny, even for a small jurisdiction like
East Salisbury. Since it was by the Great Neck Bridge, it was just a
little west of the point where Dock Lane diverges from Beach Road
if we are heading east (see Map #10, opposite). But we can appreci-
ate just how small an area this planting lot was in the Beach Road
context when we are told that it was barely larger (10% at most) than
the area boxed in ("CEM.") to represent the Longhill Cemetery just
east of the Dock Lane fork. Unlike that cemetery, however, it almost
surely lay on the south Side of Beach Rd., in the general area where
Map 10 shows some four dwelling units in rather close proximity as
of 1884.

While it is true that the first dwelling must have been raised within the small planting lot, land came easily for the Original Proprietors
of new towns like Salisbury, Mass.: further divisions of meadow and

## Map 10. The 1640 Homestead Area, Beach Rd., Salisbury
(detail from a map showing residences as of 1884)

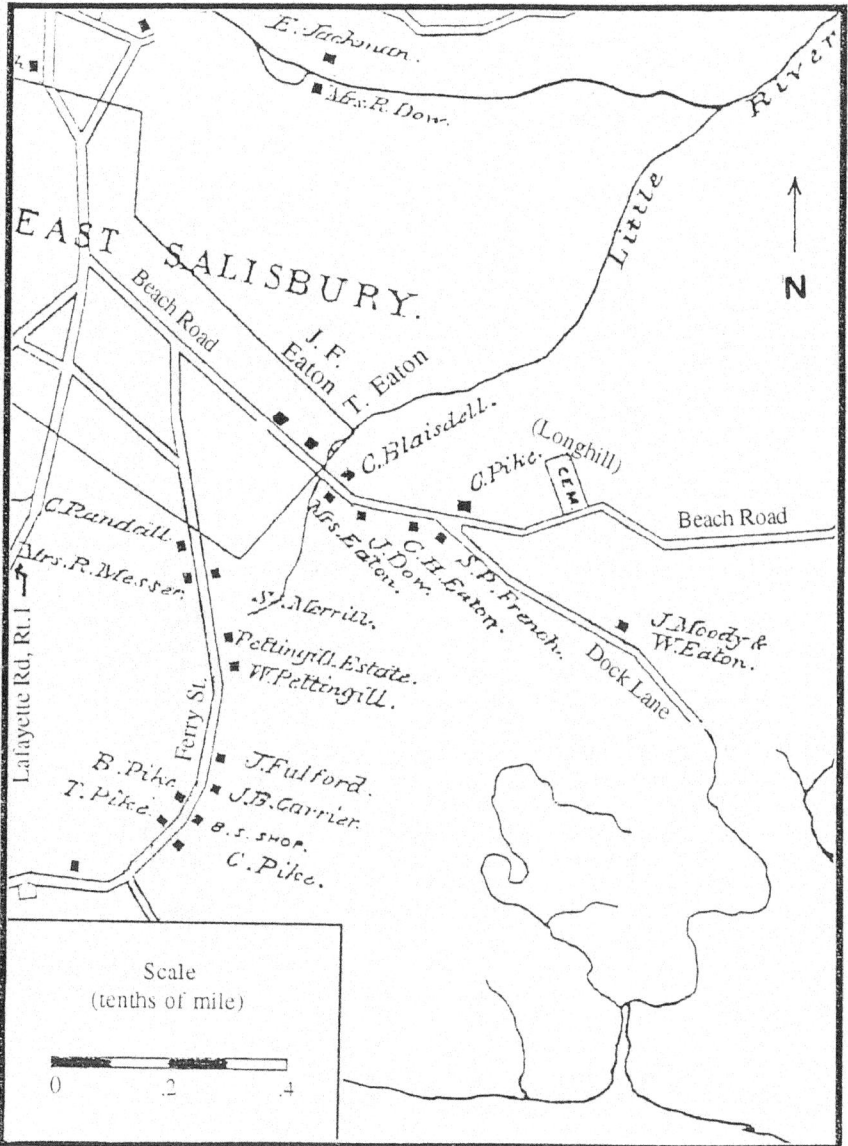

EAST SALISBURY.

Beach Road

E. Jackman.

Mrs. R. Dow.

Little River

N

J. F. Eaton

T. Eaton

C. Blaisdell.

C. Pike.

(Longhill)

C.E.M

Beach Road

C. Randall.

Mrs. R. Messer.

Mrs. Eaton.

J. Dow.

C. H. Eaton.

S. P. French.

J. Moody &
W. Eaton.

Lafayette Rd., Rt. 1

W. Merrill.

Pettingill Estate.

W. Pettingill.

Ferry St.

Dock Lane

B. Pike.

T. Pike.

J. Fulford.

J. B. Carrier.

B. S. shop.

C. Pike.

Scale
(tenths of mile)

0          .2          .4

marsh land came pell-mell even before John[1] removed to Haverhill in 1646, Given their assignment by lottery, such lands were rarely contiguous to an owner's prior parcels; but in time one could buy adjoining lands from others, especially with other family heads keeping homes in the village in the early decades. The Great Neck being a peninsula, there were some limitations to the cultivatable upland to the north, east and south. But even the marshlands were of great commercial value for their coveted salt hay. So the Eatons expanded opportunistically to the south into the marshes and a "meadow" area called "the barberries." Such acquisitions were also helpful to the family economy, as the lane to the south led to a dock on a creek system giving access in turn to the Merrimack River estuary near its mouth to the sea, all most helpful in providing a variety of types of fishing. Also over the decades, Eatons added lands on the north side of the way to the beach as well as both eastward and westward along the Neck. We lack any very clear picture of how large the Eaton holdintgs in the area were at their peak. But it is also true that while land was added, it was also being hived off for the succession of those offsprings who decided not to seek their fortunes elsewhere.

Despite this waxing and waning over the centuries, we can be sure that there was indeed some "core" throughout that reflected the the location of the original homestead. We know this in part because when the citizens of Salisbury celebrated the town's 250th birthday in 1890, they made note of the fact that Brookside Farm on Beach Rd., then co-owned equally by the seven daughters of James[6] Eaton (**#367**), had been in Eaton possession continuously since 1640. It is this core that we have tried to follow down through the years. The latter-day name "Brookside" already betrays location in some degree. We note on Map 10 that the Little River, becoming a rivulet just south of Beach Rd. where a "Mrs. Eaton" lived in in 1884, might serve as the brook being referred to, although there is another rivulet requiring a culvert to pass under Beach Rd. nearer to Dock Lane.

As we have seen, when John[1] moved on to Haverhill with the rest of his family in 1646, the Beach Rd. homestead was deeded to eldest son John[2], who undoubtedly added considerably to the domain before his death in 1682. He certainly was able in his will to distribute a number of choice pieces of upland, marsh, and orchard lots at a variety of non-adjacent locations across the large Salisbury grant to deal abundantly with all of his sons save Thomas[3], who had left the area. His youngest son Ephraim[3], for example, was given 60 acres of upland "above the mill," being presumably the mill north of the village, owned and operated by the True family. Ephraim soon thereafter married a True daughter, and this connection with this wealthy familiy put him and their progeny in enviable economic circumstances. Nonetheless, he willed his third son Samuel[3] all of his homestead, plus the land and meadow surrounding it, to be fully possessed after the death of his widowed mother. This kind of succession was not uncommon practice in this time and place. While older sons normally had priority claim on the family homestead, this rule was waived when such older sons had already been given substantial land stakes elsewhere which they had developed with their new families. By this logic, the homestead fell to Samuel[3], now 23 but unmarried and still living at home.

As we learned in Samuel's sketch (**#16**) however, he was very soon to be lost at sea. Since his mother long outlived him, not dying until 1712, she was the matron of the homestead for three further decades. It is probable that during all or much of this time, her eldest son John[3] was the man of the house on Beach Road, and hence was in charge of the property after her death. He was, however, approaching 70 himself when his mother died; and he soon passed on as well, in the winter of 1717/8. The three surviving older sons of John[3]/Mary were by this time married and living elsewhere (William[4] in Maine), so again the homestead passed to the oldest son still at home, Jonathan[4], then 19, who would soon marry Judith Ash (1720) and start a family that would ultimately number 13 children. His two younger brothers, Thomas[4] and Daniel[4A], presumably finished their adolescence on the homestead and then moved elsewhere.

Jonathan (**#35**) in turn died in 1745. He had seven surviving sons at the time, but he gave cash bequests to most of them, deeding his eldest son Theophilus[5] (**#108**), already married and with a baby daughter, two-thirds of all his residual personal and real estate to pass fully to him upon the death of his widow Judith. The other one-third went not to his second son, Abel[5], who had removed early to Maine, but to the third son Thomas[5], age 16 and still living on the homestead. Theophilus in this general period moved for a time to Haverhill, perhaps in connection with land parcels there which John[1] had deeded to his grandsons out of the Salisbury John[2]. Apparently liking what he saw on the "frontier," he had established himself by 1751 or before in the nearby west end of the large Kingston grant (soon to be set off as Sandown, N.H., in part thanks to vigorous politicking by Theophilus). Clearly he had little interest in going home to Salisbury: before the end of the 1750s he left Sandown to join his younger brother Abel in Maine, and soon thereafter went on to join his Maj. William[5] Eaton on Deer Isle. With this future yet ahead of him, in 1750 he and his mother Judith sold his younger brother Thomas[5] (**#112**), the other residual legatee and still on Beach Road, the homestead, now some 30 acres in size. For whatever reason--perhaps Thomas's greater devotion to a maritime life than to farming--Thomas soon sold the property back to mother Judith and Theophilus. Whereupon the latter sold the homestead again to their father Jonathan's youngest brother, Daniel[4A], (**#38**), who had of course grown up there but was now a man age 40 with a wife Nancy and six surviving children (and more to come).

For the next 125 years, the Beach Rd. homestead was owned and

operated by a simple sequence of fathers and sons, and we can summarize this transition swiftly. Daniel[4A] and Nancy ultimately had some
14 children, all but three of them surviving well into adulthood. In
1794, Daniel, now 84, deeded the homestead on to his youngest son
James[5], who by that point was age 35 with a wife Sarah and five children already. James was already no doubt running the farm as of this
bequest, and took care of father Daniel[4A] there until he died late in
1798. James[5] in turn died in Aug 1825, leaving widow Sarah in control of the homestead. Their two eldest sons had been married for 20
years or more with children, both mariners who were not thriving but
may not have been interested in farming either. So in 1826 the estate
sold the homestead and supplementary wood, tillage and marsh land
totalling some 31 acres, to be held in common by the two youngest
heirs, sons James[6] (#377) and Jonathan[6] (#378), then ages 27 and 25,
respectively. As time wore on, it became clear that James lived in the
actual homestead of that era, with Jonathan living elsewhere on the inherited property. Jonathan died in Oct 1873, leaving widow Betsey
and their only two children, son John French Eaton and daughter Miriam who had married almost 20 years before and was settled in Derry,
N.H. Brother James[6] died of tuberculosis the next May, leaving widow
Hannah and the seven sisters surviving from an original eight.

We now can return with profit to Map 10, to review the neighborhood of the homestead ten years later, in 1884. (The reader should
note that the residential atlas shows first, high detail for East Salisbury
Village, but just includes the west edge of the maximum for the Eaton
area; and then gives a larger-scale map including the Eaton core area,
with the prior area of detail reduced to a bloc of streets. We of course
need the broader map as a base; although we have added two Eaton
residences that actually appear at the east edge of the first map.)

The seven sisters are nowhere in sight on this map, of course:
while their mother Hannah had just died the year before, leaving the
estate to them to be held in common, all seven of the sisters had long
since married and were ensconced elsewhere with their husbands. The
elder four all lived in Seabrook, the fifth in Haverhill, Mass., the sixth
in Epping, N.H., and the seventh was the sole sister living in Salisbury,
but elsewhere in that village (cf. #1018-1025). The "Mrs. Eaton" of
our map, who appears to be residing "brookside" and closest to the
original heart of the Eaton lands is, in light of the 1880 Census, almost
surely Widow Betsey (Morrill), relict of the Jonathan[6] who shared with
James[6] the bequest of the Beach Rd. property. The sole son of Jona-
than/Betsey, John[7] French Eaton (#1026), lives on the north side of
Beach Rd. a bit west of his mother, in quarters that look quite palatial
on the detailed map. Perhaps his father Jonathan[6] won the better
house when uncle James[6] won the old homestead.

Further to the west, the "W. Eaton" sharing a dwelling unit with
J(oshua) Moody) is William[8] Sherburne Eaton (#2379), whose grand-

father, Benjamin[6] (**#371**), was an older brother of the James[6] and Jonathan[6] who shared the bequest of the old homestead. This William[8], at the time of the Map about 36 and with a young family, was only a few months away from occupying a large new house of his own in the triangle formed by Dock Lane's forking off from Beach Rd. This new house was essentially under construction at the time the 1884 map was being prepared. This house would in 1900 become the birthplace of Sherburne[9] Eaton (**#4190**), whose fascinating life is chronicled by Woodman (1983), perhaps the last leaf on the Eaton tree in this ancient Eaton domain.

The other two Eatons in Map 10 are in a sense interlopers, if cousinly ones. They are True[8] Eaton (**#1731**) and his nephew by his brother Andrew[8] (**#1733**), Charles[9A] H. EAton (**#3355**). True himself was son of Christopher[7] and Sylvanus[6], a twig of the family that had resided in Seabrook for several generations. True had come back to Salisbury and the Eaton homestead area upon his marriage in 1841. Charles[9A] would find employ as a conductor on the electric cars that brought summer bathers from the railroad station out to the Beach.

Soon after the 1890 celebration as Salisbury, the seven sisters began to die off. Abby[7], the only one to have married an Eaton, Charles[7] of Seabrook (**#1224**), was the first to go in 1893 at the age of 62. But at least two more died by 1905. In this general period, Manfred D. Dow and his wife Mary Balch (Eaton), daughter of Abby and Charles, bought up the main Beach Rd. property, thereby keeping it in the family for some years longer, although in an attenuated way. (It is possible that Manfred was a son or relative of the J(oseph F.?). Dow abutting Mrs. Eaton on Beach Rd.) On 23 Apr 1924, Manfred and Mary, in three Essex Co. Deeds 2594-534/536) sold for $1 each "and other valuable considerations" three parcels of land, including principally an 11-acre lot with the buildings, on the south side of Beach Rd.; but also three acres of cove and tillage land abutting Wm.[8] S. Eaton property by Dock Lane; and 5 acres of meadow in "the Barberries" south of the homestead. The buyer was a Lillian F. Wadlin, wife of Charles M. Wadlin of Lawrence, Mass. This may well be the moment when the old homestead land passed out of Eaton hands, although it remains possible that Lillian was herself in some sense an Eaton. In any event, after taking out a mortgage on the 11-acre lot with buildings from a Newburyport Institution for Savings in 1927, the Wadlins defaulted on payments during 1941 and the bank foreclosed, selling the property at public auction in April 1942 to Charles F. and Helen E. True for the sum of $1752.28. In June 1943 the Trues sold the same 11 acres to a Lillian E. Tripp, wife of Edward N. Tripp of Salem, Mas.s. In Jan 1947, the same Lillian Tripp, but now described as unmarried, sold the 11 acres onward to a Joseph S. Garfi, Sr., of Newburyport. By this time there seems no doubt that possession by any Eatons had been terminated.

### #14. The Original Haverhill Homesteads

The story on original homesteads in Haverhill is at least somewhat more obscure than it Salisbury counterpart . We know that John[1]
resided at some time in what became the West Parish, but we do not
know if he lived in Haverhill village for some years before moving
there, or repeated his Salisbury performance by spurning a house lot
in town in favor of a larger planting lot site two or three miles away.
It is almost certain that once he was an adult, son Thomas[2] lived a fair
distance from his parents' home. But Thomas's six sons--the third
generation--lived all over the area of Haverhill township, from the
village itself to its eastern, western and northern extremities.

With this said, there remain at least two sites in Haverhill where
early generations of Eatons did reside for an extended period of time,
thereby resembling the notion of "the old family homestead." Let us
start perversely with Thomas[2], the clearest case; and then move to his
father John[1]'s residential situation.

When Thomas arrived in Haverhill with his parents in 1646, he
was approaching age 21. He did not, however, marry his first wife for
another ten years, and undoubtedly he spent some of that time living
with his natal family. Well before his father died in 1668, however, he
had superb economic prospects. His only brother John[2] had received
control over all of his father's land claims in Salisbury, leaving Thomas the sole obvious heir to the still larger array of proprietorial divi-
divisions in Haverhill due his father. At some time he chose to set up
his own homestead on the high bluff overlooking the Merrimack River about a mile east of the village center at the junction of Groveland
and Water Streets. After Thomas died in 1715, his bachelor son Ebenezer[3] (#26) occupied the place until his own death in 1737. At this
point, his enterprising nephew, John[4] (#69), who was beginning to follow his father's footsteps as Town Clerk and Treasurer, used his inheri-
tances from his own father, just deceased, along with quitclaims purchased from some of uncle Ebenezer's beneficiaries, to acquire this
homestead, which he occupied some 50 years (see discussions under
#26 and #69), until his death in 1788. Perhaps one of his sons occu-
pied it for an additional period of time. But he had only three sons,
and the eldest, John[5] Jr,, was killed before marriage at Bunker Hill in
1775. His second son is not mentioned in his father John[4]'s will; and
the third was a confirmed bachelor. So even if one or both of these
further sons occupied the house "under the buttonwoods" for a spell
after 1788, it is very doubtful that there were heirs of John[4] in the sixth
generation. Nonetheless, we have here an "original homestead" which
was not established until the second generation, yet which was probably a home for some of our Eatons for a century or more.

Now let us return to John[1]. Over later generations of our Haverhill branch, we know these Eatons had something of a center of gravi-

ty in the West Parish, especially after that third generation which was so scattered east, west and north. On the other hand, we would not know that John[1] himself had colonized the West Parish area, save for the annotation on the homestead father Thomas[2] deeded to the third of his six sons, Jonathan[3] (**#23**). It was marked "..formerly my father John Eaton's." So this was indeed John[1]'s personal colonization of the West Parish!

Moreover, we know fairly well where this truly "original" homestead stood. We entertained the thought that John[1] might have been less concerned about huddling in the village with his colleagues in Salisbury--a form of land tenure where collective security was a worry-- and hence free to live away from others on his planting lot, because any Indian menace would arrive from the interior, or the west, and not from the ocean to the east or the tidal marshes north and south. But he located in Haverhill to the northwest of town, or just the direction from which Indian attacks would come. And so it did, after his death, in the famous Dustin episode, killing his grandson Thomas[3] and gravely threatening his grandson Jonathan[3] and family who had inherited his homestead (see Sidebar #1, p. 36). These grandsons, Thomas and Jonathan, surely had abutting properties, reflecting a division of a larger planting lot given John[1]. And Jonathan's at least, abutted the south line of the unfortunate Dustin family's lot. Given the Hannah Dustin fame, that lot is easy to find.

Markers that clarify more exactly where Jonathan's homestead was are harder to come by. But there are some further clues. Jonathan[3] resided on the old homestead for another 26 years after the Indian attack. Just before his death in 1723, he had set about building a new house on his inherited lot, without demolishing the old house, which had probably built for his grandfather John[1] in the middle of the preceding century. Jonathan's estate inventory prepared in May 1724 speaks of the "homestead 38 acres with old house, with new house with boards, nails and bricks and all other materials ready to finish it." Jonathan[3] had two sons surviving him, being James[4] by his first wife, born a week before the Indian raid and hidden in the swamp with his mother to escape the hostilities; and Jonathan[3], Jr. Eaton, born in 1705. By family lore, James[4] got the new house by virtue of being the elder. Perhaps Jonathan, Jr., was to have received the old house; but after his marriage in 1733 he and his wife Jane (Page) established themselves nearer the north edge of Haverhill, a farm that after 1741 lay partly in Atkinson, N.H. (see Sidebar #3). As far as we know, son James lived out his life in the new house, dying there in 1773. He and wife Rachel had 11 children, including six noteworthy sons, such as David[5] who went to Nova Scotia, Timothy[5] the Revolutionary firebrand, and the James[5] whose grandson began this genealogy.

## #15.  Our New World Eatons: Workers in Wood

A substantial number of the English household heads coming to
to the New England during the Great Migration, if not educated members of the liberal professions, brought with them one or another artisan skill to complement their experience as "planters" or farmers.  Our
John[1] was no exception.  He was a cooper, or barrel-maker, a trade in
high demand on the New England coast because of the importance of
barrels for storage on ships.

Moreover, in this period long before the development of voca-
tional education institutions, such skills were frequently transmitted
as a matter of course from a father to his sons.  This was not the only
way a trade could be learned, of course: parents could seek to apprentice their children to artisans outside the family.  But the family offered a "natural apprenticeship."  John[1]'s case is a good example.  The
elder of his two sons, John[2], was also a cooper; and of the five male
grandsons by John[2] in the third generation, two were coopers, and the
third was a carpenter who built houses.  (The other two may have had
such skills as well, but the record does not tell us what they did.)
Thus for nearly a century, our Eatons of the Salisbury/Seabrook
branch were distinctively involved in work with wood.

This was not true of the Haverhill branch.  There is no sign of
a woodworking skill on the part of John[1]'s younger son Thomas[2].
To be sure, over subsequent generations we find a Haverhill scion
or two who were coopers, as well as a few stray artisans in other
woodworking specialties of the period such as carpenters, "housewrights," boatrights, chairmakers, "joiners" (cabinetmakers), and
carvers.  But they turn up in isolated instances, and probably not at
any rate higher than other members of the population.  Indeed, since
Thomas[2] does not appear to have been a cooper like his older brother at Salisbury, it is quite possible that father John[1] had himself
drifted away from coopering after his move up the Merrimack River
to Haverhill.  This is plausible in part because of his copious land
acquisitions in Haverhill, and in part because a sandbar blocked
most maritime shipping from advancing some miles up that large
river, thereby leaving John[1] at greater remove from the largest demand for barrels.  The Haverhill branch did in time achieve a new
"signature" skill that affected members of several subsequent generations.  Capt. Timothy[5] Eaton (1731-1811, **#203**) became a wealthy man from a major foundry that he launched in Haverhill, and a
number of scions became workers in metal, especially in fine metals,
as witnessed by several silversmiths, verging off into such specialties
watchmaking and jewelry.  Indeed, this tradition may even have
radiated in one line to blacksmithing, and in another to the use of

mercury in feltmaking as part of the hatter's trade.

But as we have seen, the woodworking skills remained entirely prominent in the Salisbury branch through three generations. They also remain clear in the fourth generation, where among those six Eaton scions with any known skills beyond farming or fishing, we find two housewrights, a cooper and in addition, the delightful case of Benjamin[4] (**#46**), who is styled variously as a cooper *and* a carpenter *and* a housewright, all learned at his father's knee. This brings us well into the eighteenth century.

As we have pursued subsequent scions, it has seemed that while the incidence of workers in wood is declining somewhat by the fifth generation, there remain enough instances in the Salisbury branch to distinguish them from most other New England families of their time. However, this was just a casual judgment, and we were interested checking whether it was true.

There is little way to gauge the incidence of woodworking skills in the general population before the 1850 Census asked citizens to describe their occupations. We have done some sleuthing with that Census, to see whether our impressions of some remnant distinctiveness of this Eaton occupational preference can be corroborated as late as 1850. Of course it is true that geography matters enormously in local occupational structures. Farmers are more likely to work on flood plains than mountaintops; sailors on shorelines rather than in interior; and carpenters in towns where population is increasing rather than declining.

Our first comparison produced a shocking result. In the Seabrook of 1850, where the most common surname is Eaton, thirteen males identify themselves as carpenters (7) or boatwrights (6), out of some 245 occupational mentions clear enough to make sense of. But not one of these 13 is an Eaton! And this despite the fact that the original Eaton pioneers in Seabrook included a distinctive number of workers in wood.

Reconnoitering further, we discovered that our impressions of woodworking distinctiveness came heavily from the large population of our Eatons in Maine, at places like Deer Isle, Sedgwick and Wells. But in the days when populations were still growing on those shores and needing new housing, and boats were still being made of wood, carpenters, boatwrights, joiners and allied trades were fairly swarming in all these locales. So it is true that many of our Eatons were keeping up the woodworking tradition; but that tradition had faded in enough degree as of 1850 along the Maine shore that the Eaton contingent had lost much special distinctiveness in this regard. The same may be said of the new cities like Manchester, N.H. and Portland, Me.

# APPENDIX B

## EATONS IN NORTHERN NEW ENGLAND FEDERAL CENSUSES, 1790-1850

## INTRODUCTION TO THE 7-CENSUS EATON PROJECT
## FOR MAINE, NEW HAMPSHIRE AND VERMONT

In preparing this patrilineal genealogy of the descendants of John[1] Eaton of Salisbury and Haverhill, Mass., we made heavy use of Federal Censuses, along with all the other common sources: vital records, land deeds, town records, etc. In particular, we laid out a matrix of *all* Eaton heads of households (*not* just those out of John/Anne) listed in New England Census Indexes for 1790-1850 (with further adult Eatons for 1850). We then tried to identify as many of these sightings as possible. ("Identification" here means establishing the list of numbered ancestors for the Eaton sighted, all the way "back to the boat.")

We did this labor to improve our understanding of what Eatons were where when. After 1760 or so, the New England population began to move from the safer coastal areas toward the interior, in search of more arable land. But Eatons from the other Massachusetts lines mingled with our Salisbury Eatons in this flow into northern New England, captured by these Censuses. We had to study the trees of these other major lines, so that when unexpected Eatons turned up in the Census record, we could sort these sightings into their proper Eaton branches.

We actually assembled these Census data for all six New England states, and did some identifications for all of them. But since our major focus was on the Salisbury line, and since (as noted in the Introduction) few of the Salisbury line migrated southward, we had little reason to work intensively on the Census Eatons in Massachusetts (with the exception of Essex County), Rhode Island or Connecticut. Thus the data we present here cover only the seven Censuses for the northern tier of states.

Each row in these tables reflects the history of the specific Eaton named, in the town listed, whether sighted there just once or in multiple Censuses. The genealogical identification inferred for that individual, if known, appears in the lefthand margin of the table. The same individual can appear in more than one row of the table, by moving from town to town over a sequence of Censuses. Our own master matrix is annotated to show where each Eaton mover arrived from and will depart to, but we lack space to add this information here. Readers may have fun "connecting the dots" for Eaton movers of special interest to them.

Of course, some level of inference is required to make any of these identifications, even though most of the time we have other kinds of records which verify that the families identified were in the area when the sighting was made. In instances where we lack such contextual verification, our surest identifications naturally come in 1850, when we have names of spouses, more exact ages, and even lists of children. For earlier Censuses we have only the name and an approximate age of the household head, although often the family composition, despite its anonymity, helps verify the assignment. Now and again, for example, two Eaton heads turn up unexpectedly in a town for a certain Census, but the likelihood that they are brothers helps establish who they are.

562       APPENDIX B

All things considered, while we are comfortable with most of these assignments, mistakes can happen. We would expect that (Truth be known), some of them are wrong, but probably not more than five per hundred. We do, however, include some few assignments where the inferential leap is longer. We try to tag these clearly with smaller type and question marks. Perhaps (Truth be known) these could be wrong as often as three times in ten or more. It is also important to note that since the 1850 Census names more than Household Heads, some Eatons who are minors, either boarding out or at the top of a Census sheet. may appear in that Census index. We have usually ignored such listings.

We naturally have kept track of our "success rate": the fraction of all sightings that we feel we have genealogically identified. These percentages are remarkably similar by state: for Maine, 88.8, New Hampshire, 88.7, and Vermont, 87.2. While these numbers include the more tentative assignments at the margin, the number of the latter is few, so that all three states would be well over 80% without them. *Nota bene*, however, these are percentages of <u>sightings</u>, rather than of unique <u>individuals</u> identified. Thus an Eaton present in a town for four consecutive sightings counts as four identifications. Since long-term residents of communities are much more likely to have left independent traces of their presence in other records than are those "birds of passage" listed only once at a given place, the metric of sightings is more charitable than one of individuals would be. We choose it, however, because it is more calculable: if we have an unidentified John Eaton sighted in three different towns over a span of years, whose rough age brackets are congruent with the same birth year, we have no way of knowing whether this is one, two or three unidentified John Eatons. But it is clearly three different sightings.

\* \* \* \* \* \* \*

This project has provided a splendid lesson in types of error in the Census-taking process. We could write a long essay on this subject, but will limit ourselves here to some colorful examples. Take, for example, the question of the accuracy of age reports as captured in the early manuscript Censuses. This is a juicy subject since we have reviewed a large number of cases where because of successive appearances in the Census, we can note how consistent or inconsistent the age reports are internally; and very often we know from vital records for that person what the actual age report should be. (Provided, of course, that the birth records are accurate, which they occasionally are not!) We must say out front that for the most part, reported ages are pretty reliable to within a year or two, when a precise age is reported after 1840. This is harder to assess for earlier Censuses, where ages are located in broad brackets only. But even here, when a person's age should advance a bracket between a certain pair of Censuses, it usually does; and at least a few of the times when it does not, differences in timing of the two Census interviews (May vs. August?) can produce a discrepancy which is only apparent.

Nonetheless, there is a small but steady rate of larger errors, which upon rare occasion become quite grotesque, such as off by more than 15 years.  Even the large errors, however, are not astonishing, given the numerous ways in which age elicitation can go wrong in some degree.  For example, readers of the pre-1850 Censuses who have struggled with tick marks in the age bracket columns that are half a foot away from the headings, to decide just what column they are actually in, should have patience with the same problem facing enumerators as they received age reports and put the ticks down in the first place.  We also have to recognize that even where age was captured as stated, there are other reasons why a stated age may still be unreliable.  In earlier periods, precise ages were simply less salient even for persons reporting own age.  We are reminded of this by the phenomenon of "heaping" in Census age reports (a surplus of reports in rounder numbers, such as age 50 or even 55, relative to reports of individual years in between).  This phenomenon was more dramatic in the 19th century than more recently.  In addition, a large proportion of all age reports gathered in the Census situation are not self-reports, but are submitted by persons other than the "owner".  This is obviusly true for children.  But some are guessed at by spouses, and even occasionally--altho forbidden practice--by neighbors.

Finally, this exercise has reminded us that the Census indexes themselves, not surprisingly, fall short of perfection.  Careful readers may detect that the Census sightings we publish are not fully identical with what Eatons they see in the indexes.  This is because our finer examination has revealed overcounts, undercounts, and other mysteries, which we have tried to correct.  In one case, the index had (e.g.) two Moses and two John Eatons, all on the same page of the Census.  That page, nicely legible, had but one Moses and one John.  Upon occasion there is simply no such Eaton as listed by the Index on the page given.  Obviously there is some typo in the page number, and if the town is a small enough, we might forage through its pages looking for the Eaton listed.  Now and again, we found it.  But with modest frequency, we would in the process find some further Eaton family (beyond the misaddressed one), sitting there plain as day but for some reason like attention lapse by the indexer, not appearing in that year's index at all.  Often these "discovered" Eatons were in a sequence of Censuses at the town site, but were missing one Census in the middle somewhere.  Thus the discovery helped make the Census record more coherent than the index-based one had implied.

We should warn about a couple other rare but simple sources of discrepancy between the Census index and the tables below.  One of these arises when the film for the Census page for an Eaton is so under- or overexposed as to be totally unreadable.  We have simply discarded these index cases from our field of view, since we have no way to verify the addressees are even present, much less learn any contextual information about them.  Another departure from the index, or for that matter from our initial manscript tabulation, needs mention as well.  The space for the printed version of this tabulation is very limited.  Generally we like to keep returns from particular counties on the same two opposing pages.  Now and again, however, the Eaton presence in a county is so slight that it takes up less than half a page, when the next county in the alphabet requires roughly a page and a half.  This kind of county split-

ting we have done.  A more diabolical formatting problem was posed by
counties needing one or two lines more than a fully-stuffed single page.
This is diabolical because such "orphan" rows risk propagating over a
whole succession of counties.   For about four counties of three dozen
presented we solved the problem by discarding an Eaton name or two.
We did so on a "least-damage" principle: in every case, there was but a
single sighting in the row discarded, and usually involved in other senses
a marginal participant.  Thus for example, we chose to fend off one over-
flow by dropping a Mary Eaton who, in 1850, reported her birthplace as
Scotland.  We also dropped a solo male head under 21; and a single-
appearance widow or two of patriarchs with lengthy records of their own.
        Let us close with a favorite example of a Census index problem,
although one discovered years before we undertook this project.   The
native Seabrook Eatons who colonized Pittsfield, N.H., just before the
Revolution are easy to find as four young household heads signing a petition there in 1780.   Much the same list of Eatons turns up in the index
for the 1800 Census there as well.  In 1790, however, there are no Eatons
listed for the index at all.  This was hard to write off as a lapse of indexer
attention; and how could a Census-taker manage to miss  three to five
likely Eaton households altogether, when the overall size of the Pittsfield
population was about right?  We stumbled on the answer by accident
years later.  We had naturally looked for Eatons under "E" in the index.
But for 1790, our missing persons had been listed far away in the index,
under "Y": for that year they all were dubbed "Yeatons," a kind of error
that had not occurred to us.  Two of the 1790 Yeatons were unfamiliar,
and were, upon further search, actual Yeatons from an unrelated family
which had been plentiful early on the Isles of Shoals off Portsmouth,
N.H., and later in the wider Portsmouth area itself.  Perhaps the 1790
enumerator had first encountered the real Yeatons and, being coached in
how the name was spelled, merely thought he was hearing the same surname when he approached our true Eatons later in his rounds.

                                * * * * * * *

        One convention we adopt to save space and speed the reading
comprehension of our genealogical identifications is as follows.

        **FranPly**  refers to the founder Francis[1] Eaton of Plymouth.
        **JohnDed** refers to the founder John[1] Eaton of Dedham.
        **WmRed** refers to the founder William[1] Eaton of Reading, Mass.
        **JonaRed** refers to the founder Jonas[1] Eaton of Reading, Mass.

        **JohnSal** refers to the Salisbury branch through John[2-1].
        **ThoHav** refers to the Salisbury branch through Thomas[2], John[1],
                        which we have called the Haverhill branch.

## MAINE

| | 1790 | 1800 |
|---|---|---|

**Cumberland Co.**

Auburn (see earlier, Minot)
David[8] N. (Saml[7-6], Danl[5], Saml[4], Jos[3], **JohnSal**)
?? John, b. 1814, Me.
Samuel[7] (Saml[6], Dan[5], Sam[4], Jos[3], **JohnSal**)
?? William[7] S., b. ca. 1790, N.H.

Bakerstown (later, Moscow, Poland)
Ziba[5] (Barnabas[4], Saml[3-2], **FranPly**)                    Ziba[5]

Brunswick
Daniel[5]     (Saml[4], Jos[3], **JohnSal**)              Daniel[5]
Daniel[6] (Danl[5], Saml[4], Jos[3], **JohnSal**)        Daniel[6]        Daniel[5]
Moses[6] ( "        "        "        "      )          Moses[6]         Moses[6]
Samuel[6] ( "        "        "        "      )         Samuel[6]        Samuel[6]
John[6]  ( "        "        "        "      )                          John[8]
?? Moses, b. 1756-1774.                                                  Moses
Jane (Grant), relict of John[6], above.
?? Obadiah, b. < 1765.
Abner[7] (Saml[6], Danl[5], Saml[4], Jos[3], **JohnSal**)
Daniel[7]  (Danl[6-5], Saml[4], Jos[3], **JohnSal**)
Betsey[6] ? (Danl[5], Saml[4], Jos[3], **JohnSal**)
?? Hannah, b. 1776-94.
?? Elizabeth, b. 1750-59.
?? James, b. 1810-14?
Abigail[6] (Danl[5], Saml[4], Jos[3], **JohnSal**)
David[7] (John[6], Danl[5], Saml[4], Jos[3], **JohnSal**)
George[8] L. (Danl[7-5],    "        "        "      )
John[7] (John[6],   "        "        "        "      )
Moses[7] ( "        "        "        "        "      )
Jane[7]  ( "        "        "        "        "      )
Martin[7] ( "        "        "        "        "      )
John[8] (Dav[7], John[6], Danl[5],   "        "      )
??Rhoda, b. 1797, Me.
??Sarah, b. 1832, Me.
??Sarah, b. 1832, Me.
??Sewaill, b. 1826, Me.

Cape Elizabeth
??Henry A., b. 1825, Me.

Cumberland
??Abigail, b. 1780, Me.
??Hezekiah, b. 1819, Me.
??Cyrus, b. 1844, Me. (Hezekiah, ???)

## MAINE

| 1810 | 1820 | 1830 | 1840 | 1850 |
|------|------|------|------|------|

**Cumberland Co.**

| | | | | David[8] N. |
| | | | | John |
| | | | | Samuel[7] |
| | | | | William S. |

Bakerstown

Brunswick

| Daniel[6] | Daniel[6] | | | |
| Moses[6] | | | | |
| Samuel[6] | Samuel[6] | Samuel[6] | | |
| | | | | |
| Jane[w6] | Jane[w6] | | | |
| Obadiah | | | | |
| | Abner[7] | Abner[7] | | |
| | Daniel[7] | | Daniel[7] | Daniel[7] |
| | Betsey[6] | | | |
| | Hannah | | | |
| | | Elizabeth | | |
| | | James | | |
| | | | Abigail[6] | |
| | | | David[7] | David[7] |
| | | | George[8] L. | George[8] L. |
| | | | John[7] | John[7] |
| | | | Moses[7] | |
| | | | Jane[7] | Jane[7] |
| | | | | Martin[7] |
| | | | | John[8] |
| | | | | Rhoda |
| | | | | Sarah |
| | | | | Sarah |
| | | | | Sewaill |

Cape Elizabeth

| | | | | Henry A. |

Cumberland

| | | | | Abigail |
| | | | Hezekiah | Hezekiah |
| | | | | Cyrus |

## MAINE

|                                                                 | 1790      | 1800      |
|-----------------------------------------------------------------|-----------|-----------|

**Cumberland Co.** (cont.)

Durham
?? John, b. <1756                                                            John

Falmouth
?? Osborn, b. 1800-10.
?? John O., b. 1830, Me.

Harpswell
(Rev.) Samuel[5] (Elisha[4], Benj[3-2], **FranPly**)        Samuel[5]    Samuel[5]
Joseph[6] (Saml[5],  "  ,  "  "  )
William[7] (Jos[6], Saml[5], Elish[4], Benj[3-2], **FranPly**)
Stockbridge[6] (Benj[5], Jacob[4], Jos[3], **JohnSal**)

Minot  (see also Auburn)
Samuel[7] (Saml[6], Danl[5], Saml[4], Jos[3], **JohnSal**)
??William S., b. ca, 1790, N.H.
David[8] N. (Saml[7-6], Danl[5], Saml[4], Jos[3], **JohnSal**)
?? John, b. 1814, Me.

New Gloucester
John Greene[8] (John[7-6], Wyman[5], John[4-1]**Sal**)

No. Yarmouth
??Obadiah, a pauper, d. 1808.                              Obadiah

Poland  (was Bakerstown, above)
?? William

Portland
??Ebenezer H., b. 1776-94.
George[8] (Thos[7], Josiah[6], Thos[5], **John[4-1]Sal**)
??Joseph, b. 1776-94.
Thomas[7] (Josiah[6], Thos[5], **John[4-1]Sal**)
??John R., b. 1800-1810.
Stephen[8] W. (Tris[7], John[6], Wyman[5], **John[4-1]Sal**)
Humphrey[8] W. ("       "       "       "       " )
Charles[9] C. (Geo[8], Thos[7], Josi[6], Thos[5], **John[4-1]Sal**)
Eunice[9] S. ( "       "       "       "       "       " )
??Hannah, b. 1804, Me.
Hopni[7] (Jacob[6], Jos[5], Wm[4], **John[3-1]Sal**)
??James D. (Edward C.,....) b. 1823, Me.
Jeremiah[8] Sewall (Jac[7], Hum[6], Wym[5], **John[4-1]Sal**)

## MAINE

| 1810 | 1820 | 1830 | 1840 | 1850 |
|---|---|---|---|---|

**Cumberland Co.** (cont.)

| | | Osborn | | |
|---|---|---|---|---|
| | | | | John O. |

| | | | | |
|---|---|---|---|---|
| Samuel[5] | Samuel[5] | | | |
| | Joseph[6] | Joseph[6] | Joseph[6] | Joseph[6] |
| | | | | William[7] C. |
| | | | | Stockbridge[6] |

| | | | | |
|---|---|---|---|---|
| | Samuel[7] | Samuel[7] | Samuel[7] | ( <--- ) |
| | | William | William S. | ( *see* ) |
| | | | David[8] N. | (*Auburn,*) |
| | | | John | ( *CUMB.*) |

| | | | | |
|---|---|---|---|---|
| | | | | Greene[8] |

| | | | | |
|---|---|---|---|---|
| William | | | | |

| | | | | |
|---|---|---|---|---|
| | Ebenezer H. | | | |
| | George[8] | George[8] | George[8] | George[8] |
| | Joseph | | | |
| | Thomas[7] | | | |
| | | | John R. | |
| | | | Stephen[8] W. | Stephen[8] W. |
| | | | | Charles[9] C. |
| | | | | Eunice[9] S. |
| | | | | "H.[8] W." |
| | | | | Hannah |
| | | | | Hopni[7] |
| | | | | James D. |
| | | | | Jeremiah[8] S. |

# MAINE

| | 1790 | 1800 |
|---|---|---|

**Cumberland Co.** (concl.)

Scarborough
??Nathaniel B., b.1812, Mass.  Wife Ruth.

......................................................................................................

Standish
Israel[5] (Israel[4A], Benj[3], John[2], **JonaRed**)          Israel[5]          Israel[5]
?? Josiah, b. < 1766

......................................................................................................

Yarmouth
?? Moses, b. <1766


=========================================================

**Aroostook Co.**

Houlton
Jonas[7] (Jonas[6-5], Benj[4], Jonas[3], John[2], **JonaRed**)

......................................................................................................

New Limerick
Hiram[6] Moody (Benj[5], Jacob[4], Jos[3], **JohnSal**)


=========================================================

**Franklin Co.**

......................................................................................................

Chesterville (earlier, Kennebec Co.)
Jeremiah[7]          (Saml[6], Wm[5], **John[4i]Sal**)
Samuel[8] W. (Jerem[7],  "       "        "       "   )
Isaac[7]          (     "       "        "       "   )
Lowell[7]          (     "       "        "       "   )
Sarah[W7], relict of Jeremiah[7] above.
John[7] (Saml[6], Wm[5], **John[4-1]Sal**)
Sabrina[W7]. relict of Lowell[7] above.

# MAINE

| 1810 | 1820 | 1830 | 1840 | 1850 |
|------|------|------|------|------|

**Cumberland Co.**

| | | | | Nathaniel B. |
|------|------|------|------|------|

| | Israel[5] | | | |
| Josiah | | | | |

| Moses | | | | |

===================================================

**Aroostook Co.**

| | | | Jonas[7] | Jonas[7] |
|------|------|------|------|------|

| | | | Hiram[6] | Hiram[6] |

===================================================

**Franklin Co.**

| Jeremiah[7] | Jeremiah[7] | | | |
|------|------|------|------|------|
| Samuel[8] W. | Samuel[8] | Samuel[8] W. | Samuel[8] W. | |
| | Isaac[7] | Isaac[7] | Isaac[7] | Isaac[7] |
| | Lowell[7] | Lowell[7] | Lowell[7] | Lowell[7] |
| | | Sarah[W7] | | |
| | | | John[7] | John[7] |
| | | | | Sabrina[W7] |

# MAINE

|  | 1790 | 1800 |
|---|---|---|

**Franklin Co.** (cont.)

Farmington (was Sandy River, Kenn. Co.)
Betsey$^{w3}$, relict of Jacob$^5$ (Jac$^4$, Jos$^3$, **JohnSal**)                    Betsey$^{w5}$
Robert$^6$ (Jacob$^{5-4}$, Jos$^3$, **JohnSal**)                    Robert$^6$
Isaac$^6$  (    "          "          "    )
Jacob$^6$  (    "          "          "    )
Osgood$^6$ (Jerem$^{5A-4}$, Wm$^3$, John$^2$, **WmRed**)
Mary$^{w6}$, relict of Jacob$^6$ above.
Eliab$^7$ (Osg$^6$, Jerem$^{5A-4}$, Wm$^3$, John$^2$, **WmRed**)
Thomas$^8$ (Tho$^7$, Eliab$^6$, Jere$^{5-4A}$, Wm$^3$, John$^2$, **WmRed**)
Wendell$^7$ D. (Jacob$^{6-4}$, Jos$^3$, **JohnSal**)
......................................................................
Jay
John$^7$ Rowell (Eben$^6$, Jas$^5$, Benj$^4$, Wm$^3$, John$^2$, **WmRed**)
John$^8$ W. (Abel$^7$, John$^6$, Wyman$^5$, **John$^{4-1}$Sal**)
......................................................................
Strong (was Somerset Co.)
Eliab$^6$              (Jere$^{5-4}$, Wm$^3$, John$^2$, **WmRed**)
Thomas$^7$ F. (Eliab$^6$, "      "      "      "  "  )
Joshua$^7$ T. (    "      "      "      "      "  "  )
Jeremiah$^7$ (    "      "      "      "      "  "  )
Thomas$^8$ C.F. (Jere$^7$, Eliab$^6$ Jer$^{5-4}$, Wm$^3$, John$^2$, **WmRed**)
......................................................................
Temple
Beersheba$^{w6}$, relict of James$^6$ (Jas$^5$, Ben$^4$, Wm$^3$, John$^2$, **WmRed**)
......................................................................
Wilton  (was Kennebec Co.)
Ebenezer$^6$ (Jas$^5$, Benj$^4$, Wm$^3$, John$^2$, **WmRed**)
James$^6$ (James$^5$,   "      "      "      "  "  )
Beersheba$^{w6}$, relict of James$^6$ above.
Rosanna$^{w6}$, wife of Benj$^6$ (Jas$^5$, Ben$^4$, Wm$^3$, John$^2$, **WmRed**)
Daniel$^7$ (Eben$^6$, Jas$^5$, Benj$^4$, Wm$^3$, John$^2$, **WmRed**)
Elias$^7$ (Jas$^{6-5}$, Benj$^4$, Wm$^3$, John$^2$, **WmRed**)
Osgood$^7$ (Osg$^6$, Jere$^{5A-4}$, Wm$^3$, John$^2$, **WmRed**)
Tappan$^7$  (Eben$^6$, Jas$^5$, Benj$^4$, Wm$^3$, John$^2$, **WmRed**)
David$^7$ Perley (   "      "      "      "      "      "  )
Jacob$^8$ O., (Nathan$^7$, Jacob$^6$, Itha$^5$, Saml$^4$, Job$^3$, **ThoHav**)
Mary$^8$ Anne (Osg$^{7-6}$, Jerem$^{5A-4}$, Wm$^3$, John$^2$, **WmRed**
Samuel$^8$ Warren (Jerem$^7$, Saml$^6$, Wm$^5$, **John$^{4-1}$Sal**
......................................................................
Weld (was in Oxford Co.: see there for one sighting.)

# MAINE

| 1810 | 1820 | 1830 | 1840 | 1850 |
|---|---|---|---|---|

**Franklin Co.** (cont.)

| 1810 | 1820 | 1830 | 1840 | 1850 |
|---|---|---|---|---|
| Isaac[6] | Isaac[6] | Isaac[6] | Isaac[6] | Isaac[6] |
| Jacob[6] | Jacob[6] | | | |
| Osgood[6] | Osgood[6] | Osgood[6] | | |
| | | Mary[W6] | Mary[W6] | Mary[W6] |
| | | | Eliab[7] | Eliab[7] |
| | | | | Thomas[8] |
| | | | | Wendell[7] |
| | | | John[7] R. | |
| | | | John[8] W. | |
| Eliab[6] | Eliab[6] | Eliab[6] | | |
| | | Thomas[7] | Thomas[7] F. | |
| | | | Joshua[7] T. | Joshua[7] T. |
| | | Jeremiah[7] | | |
| | | | | Thomas[8] CF |
| | | | | Beersheba[W6] |
| Ebenezer[6] | Ebenezer[6] | Ebenezer[6] | | |
| James[6] | | | | |
| | Beersheba[W6] | | | |
| | Rosanna[W6] | | | |
| | | Daniel[7] | | |
| | | Elias[7] | Elias[7] | |
| | | Osgood[7] | Osgood[7] | Osgood[7] |
| | | Tappan[7] | Tappan[7] | Tappan[7] |
| | | | | David[7] P. |
| | | | | Jacob[8] O. |
| | | | | Mary[8] A. |
| | | | | Samuel[8] W. |

# MAINE

|  | 1790 | 1800 |
|---|---|---|

**Hancock Co.**
<u>Bear Island</u>
Peter[7] H. (Eliak[6], Wm[5], **John[4-1]Sal**)

..................................................

<u>Bease Island</u>
Jonathan[8A] H. (Peter[7], Eliak[6], Wm[5], **John[4-1]Sal**)

..................................................

<u>Blue Hill</u>
Jeremiah[7] (*Jonath[6]*, Theo[5], Jonath[4], **John[3-1]Sal**)
Oliver[8] (*Jere[7], Jona[6]*, "      "      "      " )
Abner[8] ( "      "      "      "      "      " )
?? Samuel, b. 1810s.

..................................................

<u>Brooklin</u>
Ezra[8] D. (Ben[7], Mose[6], Theo[5], Jona[4], **John[4-1]Sal**)
Moses[8] ( "      "      "      "      "      " )
Richard[8] (Moses[7-6], "      "      "      " )
Jesse[8] W. ( "      "      "      "      " )
Ruth[W8] (Grant), relict of Alfred[8], Richd.'s bro)

..................................................

<u>Brooksville</u>
James[8] (Solo[7], Eliak[6], Wm[5], **John[4-1]Sal**)

..................................................

<u>Castine</u>
William[8A] (Wm[7-5], **John[4-1]Sal**)

..................................................

<u>Deer Isle</u>

| | 1790 | 1800 |
|---|---|---|
| Theophilus[5] (Jonathan[4], **John[3-1]Sal**) | Theophilus[5] | |
| Jonathan[5] ( "      "      " ) | Jonathan[5] | Jonathan[5] |
| Eliakim[6] (Wm[5], **John[4-1]Sal**) | Eliakim[6] | |
| Jeremiah[6] ( "      "      " ) | Jeremiah[6] | |
| William[6] ( "      "      " ) | William[6] | William[6] |
| James[6] (Theo[5], Jona[4], **John[3-1]Sal**) | | James[6] |
| John[6] (Jona[5-4], **John[2-1]Sal**) | | John[6] |
| Jonathan[6] ( "      "      " ) | | Jonathan[6] |
| Mary[W6], relict of Eliakim[6], above | | "Widow" |
| Solomon[7] (Eliak[6], Wm[5], **John[4-1]Sal**) | | Solomon[7] |
| James[6] (Jona[5-4], **John[3-1]Sal**) | | |
| Nathan[6] ( "      "      " ) | | |
| Mary[7] (Eliak[6], Wm[5], **John[4-1]Sal**) | | |
| Wiliam[7] (Wm[6-5], **John[4-1]Sal**) | | |
| William[8] (Jere[7], "      "      " ) | | |
| Asa[7] B. (adopt Jere[6], Wm[5], **John[4-1]Sal**) | | |
| Edward[7] B. ( "      "      "      "      " ) | | |
| Jeremiah[7] (Wm[6-5], **John[4-1]Sal**) | | |

# MAINE

| 1810 | 1820 | 1830 | 1840 | 1850 |
|------|------|------|------|------|
| **Hancock Co.** | | | | |
| | | | Peter[7] | |
| .......... | .......... | .......... | .......... | .......... |
| | | | | Jonathan[8A] H. |
| .......... | .......... | .......... | .......... | .......... |
| Jeremiah[7] | Jeremiah[7] | Jeremiah[7] Oliver[8] | Jeremiah[7] Oliver[8] Abner[8] Samuel | Jeremiah[7] Oliver[8] |
| .......... | .......... | .......... | .......... | .......... |
| | | | | Ezra[8] Moses[8] Richard[8] Jesse[8] W. Ruth[W8] |
| .......... | .......... | .......... | .......... | .......... |
| | | James[8] | James[8] | |
| .......... | .......... | .......... | .......... | .......... |
| | | | | William[8A] |
| .......... | .......... | .......... | .......... | .......... |
| William[6] James[6] John[6] Jonathan[6] | William[6] Jonathan[6] | William[6] Jonathan[6] | Jonathan[6] | Jonathan[6] |
| Solomon[7] James[6] Nathan[6] Mary[7] William[7] | Solomon[7] Nathan[6] Mary[7] William[7] Asa[7] Edward[7] B. Jeremiah[7] | Solomon[7] Nathan[6] William[7] Asa[7] B. Jeremiah[7] | Solomon[7] Nathan[6] William[8] Asa[7] B. | Nathan[6] William[8] Asa[7] |

# MAINE

| | 1790 | 1800 |
|---|---|---|

**Hancock Co.** (cont.)

Deer Isle (concl.)

Jeremiah$^8$ (Jere$^7$, Wm$^{6-5}$, **John$^{4-1}$Sal**)

Benjamin$^8$ H. (Solo$^7$, Eliak$^6$, Wm$^5$, **John$^{4-1}$Sal**)

Jonathan$^7$ (John$^6$, Jonath$^{5-4}$, **John$^{3-1}$Sal**)

Solomon$^8$ (Solo$^7$, Eliak$^6$, Wm$^5$, **John$^{4-1}$Sal**)

Charles$^7$ (Nathan$^6$, Jonath$^{5-4}$, **John$^{3-1}$Sal**)

Mark$^8$ H. (Solo$^7$, Eliak$^6$, Wm$^5$, **John$^{4-1}$Sal**)

Rachel$^7$ (Eliak$^6$, Wm$^5$, **John$^{4-1}$Sal**)

Theophilus$^8$ (Jonat$^7$, Moses$^6$, Theo$^5$, Jona$^4$, **John$^{3-1}$Sal**)

Amos$^8$ A. (Solo$^7$, Eliak$^6$, Wm$^5$, **John$^{4-1}$Sal**)

Daniel$^8$ B. ( "      "      "      "      " )

David$^7$ J. (John$^6$, Jonathan$^{5-4}$, **John$^{3-1}$Sal**)

Davis$^7$ (Nathan$^6$,    "        "      " )

Frederick$^7$ ( "        "        "      " )

Isaac$^8$ B. (Solo$^7$, Eliak$^6$, Wm$^5$, **John$^{4-1}$Sal**)

James$^8$ ( "      "      "      "      " )

Olive$^8$ (Jerem$^7$, Wm$^{6-5}$, **John$^{4-1}$Sal**)

Peter$^7$ H. (Eliak$^6$, Wm$^{6-5}$, **John$^{4-1}$**)

Polly$^{W6}$ (Webb) relict of John$^6$ (Jona$^{5-4}$, **John$^{3-1}$Sal**)

Samuel$^8$ S. (Peter$^7$, Eliak$^6$, Wm$^5$, **John$^{4-1}$Sal**)

Samuel$^8$ (Jerem$^7$, Wm$^{6-5}$, **John$^{4-1}$Sal**)

Sophia$^{W8}$ (Hendrick), relict of Solomon$^8$, above.

Mt. Desert

| | 1790 | 1800 |
|---|---|---|
| David$^1$ Eaton, b. Glasgow, Scotland | David$^1$ | |

Ebenezer$^6$ (Theo$^5$, Jona$^4$, **John$^{3-1}$Sal**)

Amos$^7$ (Eben$^6$, "      "      " )

Esther$^{w7}$ Moore ? relict, Joshua$^7$ (Eben$^6$, above)

Joanna$^{W8}$ (Burnham), relict of Amos$^8$ (Amos$^7$)

Joshua$^8$ (Amos$^7$, Eben$^6$, Theo$^5$, Jona$^4$, **John$^{3-1}$Sal**)

?? Thomas, b. 1812, N.H.; wife Lucy

Orrington

Luther$^6$ (Isaac$^5$, **John$^{4-1}$Ded**)

Penobscot

| | 1790 | 1800 |
|---|---|---|
| ?? Thirza (female) | | Thirza |

Sedgwick

| | 1790 | 1800 |
|---|---|---|
| Ebenezer$^6$ (Theo$^5$, Jona$^4$, **John$^{3-1}$Sal**) | Ebenezer$^6$ | Ebenezer$^6$ |
| Jonathan$^6$ ( "      "      "      " ) | Jonathan$^6$ | Jonathan$^6$ |
| Moses$^6$ ( "      "      "      " ) | Moses$^6$ | |
| Moses$^7$ (Mose$^6$ "      "      "      " ) | | Moses$^7$ |
| Benjamin$^7$ ( "      "      "      "      " ) | | Benjamin$^7$ |
| John$^7$ ( "      "      "      "      " ) | | John$^7$ |

# MAINE

| 1810 | 1820 | 1830 | 1840 | 1850 |
|------|------|------|------|------|

**Hancock Co.**
 Deer Isle (concl.)

| 1810 | 1820 | 1830 | 1840 | 1850 |
|------|------|------|------|------|
| | | | Jeremiah$^8$ | Jeremiah$^8$ |
| | | Benjamin$^8$ | Benjamin$^8$ | Benjamin$^8$ |
| | | Jonathan$^7$ | Jonathan$^7$ | Jonathan$^7$ |
| | | Solomon$^8$ | Solomon$^8$ | |
| | | | Charles$^7$ | Charles$^7$ |
| | | | Mark$^8$ | Mark$^9$ |
| | | | Rachel$^7$ | |
| | | | Theophilus$^8$ | Theophilus$^8$ |
| | | | | Amos$^8$ |
| | | | | Daniel$^8$ |
| | | | | David$^7$ |
| | | | | Davis$^7$ |
| | | | | Frederick$^7$ |
| | | | | Isaac$^8$ B. |
| | | | | James$^8$ |
| | | | | Olive$^8$ |
| | | | | Peter$^7$ H. |
| | | | | Polly$^{W6}$ |
| | | | | Samuel$^8$ |
| | | | | Samuel$^8$ |
| | | | | Sophia$^{W8}$ |

........................................................................................................

| 1810 | 1820 | 1830 | 1840 | 1850 |
|------|------|------|------|------|
| Ebenezer$^6$ | Ebenezer$^6$ | Eben$^6$ | | |
| | | Amos$^7$ | Amos$^7$ | |
| | | | Esther$^{W7}$ | |
| | | | Joanna$^{W8}$ | |
| | | | Joshua$^8$ | |
| | | | | Thomas |

........................................................................................................

| 1810 | 1820 | 1830 | 1840 | 1850 |
|------|------|------|------|------|
| Luther$^6$ | | | | |

........................................................................................................

........................................................................................................

| 1810 | 1820 | 1830 | 1840 | 1850 |
|------|------|------|------|------|
| Jonathan$^6$ | | | | |
| Moses$^7$ | Moses$^7$ | | | |
| Benjamin$^7$ | Benjamin$^7$ | Benjamin$^7$ | | |
| John$^7$ | John$^7$ | | | |

# MAINE

|  | 1790 | 1800 |
|---|---|---|

**Hancock Co.** (concl)
 Sedgwick (concl.)
Amos$^7$ (Eben$^6$, Theo$^5$, Jona$^4$, **John$^{3\text{-}1}$Sal**)          Amos$^7$
Joseph$^6$   (Jona$^{5\text{-}4}$, **Jona$^{3\text{-}1}$Sal**)          Joseph$^6$
Joseph$^7$ (Jos$^6$, "      "      "   )
Theophilus$^7$ (Mose$^6$, Theo$^5$, Jona$^4$, **John$^{3\text{-}1}$Sal**)      Theophilus$^7$
Jonathan$^7$ (   "      "      "      "      "   )
?? James, b. <1786.
James$^2$ (David$^1$ Eaton, b. Glasgow, Scotland)
Moses$^7$   (Mose$^6$ Theo$^5$, Jona$^4$, **John$^{3\text{-}1}$Sal**)
Moses$^8$ (John$^7$,  "      "      "      "      "   )
Amasa$^8$ (Theo$^7$, "      "      "      "      "   )
John$^8$   (John$^7$,  "      "      "      "      "   )
Pickering$^8$ ( "      "      "      "      "      "   )
Daniel$^7$ (Jos$^6$, Jonathan$^{5\text{-}4}$, **John$^{3\text{-}1}$Sal**)
John$^8$ C. (Solo$^7$, Eliak$^6$, Wm$^5$, **John$^{4\text{-}1}$Sal**)
Moses$^8$ (Ben$^7$, Mose$^6$, Theo$^5$, Jona$^4$, **John$^{3\text{-}1}$Sal**)
Susan$^{W7}$ (Dodge), relict of Benj$^7$ (Mose$^6$, " )
Joann$^{W7}$, relict of Theo$^7$ (Mose$^6$, Theo$^5$....)
Harriet$^{W3}$, relict, David$^1$ of Glasgow's grandson)
?? Lewis
?? Roxanna, b. 1801.
John$^7$ (Jos$^6$, Jona$^{5\text{-}4}$, **John$^{3\text{-}1}$Sal**)

  Spruce Hill
Peter$^7$ H. (Eliak$^6$, Wm$^5$, **John$^{41}$Sal**)

  Surry
James$^2$ (David$^1$, b. in Glasgow, Scotland)
David$^3$ G. (David$^{2\text{-}1}$): a Scotch line of Eatons.

  Tremont (on Mt. Desert Island)
Amos$^7$     (Eben$^6$, Theo$^5$, Jona$^4$, **John$^{3\text{-}1}$Sal**)
Joshua$^8$ (Amos$^7$. "      "      "      "      "   )
Daniel$^8$ (   "      "      "      "      "      "   )
Joanna$^{w8}$ (Burnham), relict of Amos$^{8\text{-}7}$, Eben$^6$)

  Trenton
?? Samuel, b. 1781, Me.; wife Mary.

  Vinalhaven
Peter$^7$ H. (Eliak$^6$, Wm$^5$, **John$^{4\text{-}1}$Sal**)

## MAINE

| 1810 | 1820 | 1830 | 1840 | 1850 |
|---|---|---|---|---|
| **Hancock Co.** (concl.) | | | | |
| Sedgwick (concl.) | | | | |
| Amos[7] | Amos[7] | | | |
| Joseph[6] | | | | |
| | | Joseph[7] | Joseph[7] | Joseph[7] |
| Theophilus[7] | Theophilus[7] | Theophilus[7] | Theophilus[7] | |
| Jonathan[7] | Jonathan[7] | | | |
| | James | | | |
| | James[2] | James[2] | James[2] | James[2] |
| | Moses[7] | Moses[7] | | |
| | | | Moses[8] | Moses[8] |
| | | Amasa[8] | Amasa[8] | Amasa[8] |
| | | John[8] | | |
| | | Pickering[8] | Pickering[8] | Pickering[8] |
| | | | Daniel[7] | Daniel[7] |
| | | | John[8] C. | |
| | | | Moses[8] | |
| | | | Susan[W7] | |
| | | | | Joann[W7] |
| | | | | Harriet[W3] |
| | | | | Lewis |
| | | | | Roxanna |
| | | | | John[7] |
| | | Peter[7] | | |
| James[2] | | | | |
| | | | | Davy[3] G. |
| | | | | Amos[7] |
| | | | | Joshua[8] |
| | | | | Daniel[8] |
| | | | | Joanna[w8] |
| Samuel | Samuel | Samuel | Samuel | Samuel |
| | | Peter[7] | | |

# MAINE

|  | 1790 | 1800 |
|---|---|---|

## Kennebec Co.

### Augusta
Russell[6] (Amherst[5], Thos[4], Saml[3A], Jona[2], **JomaRed**)
Daniel[7] ? (Eben[6], Jas[5], Benj[4], Wm[3], John[2], **WmRed**)
Caroline[7] (Jotham[6], Benj[5], Jac[4], Jos[3], **John[2-1]Sal**)
?? Charles M., b. 1820, Me.

### Belgrade
?? John, b. 1756-74.                                                John

### Clinton
William[6] (Benj[5], Jacob[4], Jos[3], **John[2-1]Sal**)
Caroline[W6], relict of Stephen[6] (Ben[5], Jac[4], Jos[3], **John[2-1]**)
Rachel[W6] (Parsons), relict of William[6] just above.

### Fayette
Jeremiah[7] (Eliab[6], Jerem[5-4], Wm[3], John[2], **WmRed**)

### Gardiner
?? Edward C., b. 1800, mar. Sarah.

### Greene (now Androscoggin Co.)
Cotton[6] (Jas[5-4], Jonathan[3], **ThoHav**)
William[7]      (Jess[6], Wm[5]. Benj[4], Wm[3], John[2], **WmRed**)
William[8]
Jesse[8] N. (Wm[7], "      "      "      "      "      "      )
Philenia[W7], relict of William[7], above.

### Hallowell
?? William, b. 1776-94.
?? Sarah, b. 1783, Me.

### "Million Acres"
Barnabas[6] (Tim[5], Israel[4], John[3-2], **WmRed**)                Barnabas[6]

### Monmouth
?? Joseph, b. <1766.

### New Sharon
?? John, b. <1776

### Pittston
Barnabas[6] (Tim[5], Israel[4], John[3-2], **WmRed**)
?? Samuel, b. 1800-1809.

# MAINE

**Kennebec Co.**

| 1810 | 1820 | 1830 | 1840 | 1850 |
|------|------|------|------|------|
| | | Russell[6] | | Russell[6] |
| | | | Daniel[7] | Caroline[7] |
| | | | | Charles M. |
| | | William[6] | | |
| | | | | Caroline[W6] |
| | | | | Rachel[W6] |
| | Jeremiah[7] | | | |
| | Edward C. | | | |
| | Cotton[6] | William[7] | | |
| | | | | William[8] F. |
| | | | | Jesse[8] |
| | | | | Philenia[W7] |
| | William | | | |
| | | | | Sarah |
| Joseph | | | | |
| | John | | | |
| Barnabas[6] | | | | |
| | | Samuel | | |

# MAINE

| | 1790 | 1800 |
|---|---|---|

**Kennebec Co**. (concl.)

Readfield
Sophia[8] Ann (Tapp[7], Eben[6], Jas[5], Ben[4], Wm[3], John[2], **WmRed**)
Herrick[8] M.  (Amos[7],   "    "    "    "    "    "  )

..................................................................................................................

Read's Town
Eliab[6] (Jerem[3-4], Wm[3], John[2], **WmRed**)                                  Eliab[6]

..................................................................................................................

Rome
Moses[6] (Danl[5], Saml[4], Jos[3] **JohnSal**)
Asa[7] (Mose[6],  "    "    "    "    "  )

..................................................................................................................

Ting's Town
Ebenezer[6] (Jas[5], Benj[4], Wm[3], John[2], **WmRed**)                Ebenezer[6]

..................................................................................................................

Vassalboro
Russell[6] (Amher[5], Thos[4], Saml[3A], Jona[2], **JonaRed**)

..................................................................................................................

Vienna
Daniel[6] (Danl[5-4A], **John[3-1]Sal**)
Azor[8] (Archel[7], Jona[6], Jos[5], **John[4-1]Sal**)
Sewall[8] (Isaac[7], Saml[6], Wm[5], **John[4-1]Sal**)

..................................................................................................................

Waterville
Reuben[6] (Thos[5], **John[4-1]Ded**)

..................................................................................................................

Winslow
Benjamin[5] (Pearson[4], John[2], **JonaRed**)
Leonard[6]     (Ziba[5], Barn[4], Saml[3A-2], **FranPly**)
Clement[6] (Clemons)("     "       "  )
Joseph[7] (Solomon[6].  "  "       "       "  )

# MAINE

| 1810 | 1820 | 1830 | 1840 | 1850 |
|------|------|------|------|------|

**Kennebec Co.** (concl.)

Readfield

| 1810 | 1820 | 1830 | 1840 | 1850 |
|------|------|------|------|------|
| | | | | Sophia[8] |
| | | | | H.M.[8] |
| | Moses[6] | Moses[6] | | |
| | | | | Asa[7] |
| | | | Russell[6] | |
| Daniel[6] | Daniel[6] | Daniel[6] | Daniel[6] | |
| | | | | Azor[8] |
| | | | | Sewall[8] |
| | | Reuben[6] | Reuben[6] | Reuben[6] |
| | Benjamin[5] | | | |
| | | Leonard[6] | Leonard[6] | Leonard[6] |
| | | | Clement[6] | Clement[6] |
| | | Joseph[7] | Joseph[7] | Joseph[7] |

# MAINE

| | 1790 | 1800 |
|---|---|---|

**Lincoln Co.**
### Bath
Abel$^5$ (Jonathan$^4$, **John$^{3\text{-}1}$Sal**)                    Abel$^5$                    Abel$^5$
Thomas$^6$ ? (Eben$^5$, Saml$^4$, Jos$^3$, **ThoHav**)
Thomas$^1$, b. England; arr Bath, 1805
Thomas$^2$, (Thomas$^1$ just above)

........................................................................................

### Bowdoin
Solomon$^6$     (Ziba$^5$, Barn$^4$, Saml$^{3\text{-}2}$, **FranPly**)                    Solomon$^6$
Nathan$^7$ (Nathan$^6$, "          "          "          " )
?? Sarah? b. 1780s.

........................................................................................

### Bowdoinham
Warren$^6$ (Enoch$^5$, Jas$^4$, Jona$^3$, **ThoHav**)                    Warren$^6$
Enoch$^6$ (     "          "          "          " )
Ziba$^5$          (Barn$^4$, Saml$^{3\text{-}2}$, **FranPly**)                    Ziba$^5$
Nathan$^6$ (Ziba$^5$, "          "          " )
Ruth$^{W5}$ (Leonard), relict of Ziba$^5$ above.
Clement$^6$ (Ziba$^5$, Barn$^4$, Saml$^{3\text{-}2}$, **FranPly**)
Leonard$^6$ (     "          "          "          " )
Edmund$^7$ (Warr$^6$, Enoc$^5$, Jas$^4$, Jona$^3$, **ThoHav**)
?? Mary W., b. 1809.

........................................................................................

### Bristol
Benjamin$^6$ (Jas$^5$, Benj$^4$, Wm$^3$, John$^2$, **WmRed**)
Jeremiah$^7$ (Eliab$^6$, Jerem$^{5\text{-}4}$, "          "          " )

........................................................................................

### Damariscotta
Jeremiah$^7$     (Eliab$^6$, Jerem$^{5\text{-}4}$, Wm$^3$, John$^2$, **WmRed**)
Jeremiah$^8$ (Jere$^7$. "          "          "          "          " )

........................................................................................

### Lisbon
William$^7$ (Jess$^6$, Wm$^5$, Benj$^4$, Wm$^3$, John$^2$, **WmRed**)
David$^7$ (John$^6$, Danl$^5$, Saml$^4$, Jos$^3$, **JohnSal**)
John$^7$ (     "          "          "          "          " )
Martin$^7$ ( "          "          "          "          " )
Abner$^7$ (Saml$^6$, "          "          "          " )

........................................................................................

### Litchfield
Bradbury$^7$ (Josiah$^6$, Thos$^5$, **John$^{4\text{-}1}$Sal**)                    Bradbury$^7$

........................................................................................

### Nobleboro
?? Joseph, b. 1822, Mass.

# MAINE

| 1810 | 1820 | 1830 | 1840 | 1850 |
|---|---|---|---|---|
| **Lincoln Co.** | | | | |
| | Thomas[1] | Thomas[6] Thomas[1] | Thomas[6] | Thomas[6] Thomas[2] |
| Solomon[6] | Solomon[6] | Solomon[6] Sarah | Solomon[6] Nathan[7] | Solomon[6] Nathan[7] |
| Warren[6] Enoch[6] Nathan[6] Ruth[w5] | Warren[6] Enoch[6] Clement[6] Leonard[6] | Warren[6] | Warren[6] Edmund[7] | Warren[6] Edmund[7] Mary W. |
| Benjamin[6] | | | Jeremiah[7] | |
| | | | | Jeremiah[7] Jeremiah[8] |
| | William[7] | David[7] John[7] Martin[7] | Abner[7] | |
| Bradbury[7] | | | | |
| | | | | Joseph |

# MAINE

|  | 1790 | 1800 |
|---|---|---|

**Lincoln Co.** (cont.)
Phipsburg
Benjamin[7] (Chas[6], Ben[5], Jac[4], Jos[3], **JohnSal**)
Joseph[7] ( "    "    "    "    "    )
Emery[7] W. (Jothm[6], "    "    "    "    )

Pownalboro
Moses[6] Dalton (Tim[5], Thos[4], Job[3], **ThoHav**)      Moses[6] D.

Sandy River (later, W. Farmington)
Jacob[5] (Jacob[4], Joseph[3], **JohnSal**)      Jacob[5]
Eliab[6] (Jere[5-4], Wm[3], John[2], **WmRed**)      Eliab[5]

Thomaston
?? Mary, b. 1766-74.
?? James? b. 1776-94 to Jas. of Monmouth.
?? Hannah, b. 1880s, relict, "    "    "    .

Topsham
Benjamin[5] (Jacob[4], Jos[3], **JohnSal**)      Benjamin[5]      Benjamin[5]
Charles[6] (Benj[5], "    "    "    )
Jotham[6] ( "    "    "    "    )
Lucy, relict of Benj[5] above.
Stockbridge[6] (Ben[5], Jac[4], Jos[3], "    )
Horace[6] M. ( "    "    "    "    )
?? George? b. 1829.

Warren
Cyrus[6] (Benj[5-4], Jonas[3], John[2], **JonaRed**)
Oscar[7] (Cyr[6], "    "    "    "    )

Washington (later, Belgrade + Mt Vernon)
Jesse[6] (Wm[5], Benj[4], Wm[3]. John[2], **WmRed**)      Jesse[6]

Webster
Martin[7] (John[6], Danl[5], Saml[4], Jos[3], **JohnSal**)

Wiscasset
Charles[7] J. (Wm[6-5], Ben[4] Wm[3], John[2], **WmRed**)

Woolwich
Cotton[6] (Jas[5-4], Jonathan[3], **ThoHav**)
?? George W., b. 1800, Me.; mar. Susan.
?? Samuel G., b. 1805, Me.; mar. Mercy.

## MAINE

| 1810 | 1820 | 1830 | 1840 | 1850 |
|------|------|------|------|------|

**Lincoln Co.**

| 1810 | 1820 | 1830 | 1840 | 1850 |
|------|------|------|------|------|
| | | | | Benjamin[7] |
| | | | | Joseph[7] |
| | | | | Emery[7] W. |
| | | | | |
| | | | | |
| | | | | |
| Mary | Mary | | | |
| | James | | | |
| | | Hannah | | |
| Benjamin[5] | Benjamin[5] | | | |
| | Charles[6] | Charles[6] | Charles[6] | Charles[6] |
| | | Jotham[6] | Jotham[6] | Jotham[6] |
| | | Lucy[W5] | Lucy[W5] | |
| | | | Stockbridge[6] | |
| | | | | Horace[6] M. |
| | | | | George |
| Cyrus[6] | Cyrus[6] | Cyrus[6] | Cyrus[6] | Cyrus[6] |
| | | | | Oscar[7] |
| | | | | |
| | | | Martin[7] | |
| | | | Charles[7] J. | Charles[7] J. |
| | | Cotton[6] | | |
| | | George W. | George W. | George W. |
| | | | Samuel | Samuel |

## MAINE

|  | 1790 | 1800 |
|---|---|---|

### Oxford Co.

Buckfield
William$^7$ ? (Osg$^{6-5}$, Jere$^4$, Wm$^3$, John$^2$ **WmRed**)

........................................................................................................

Dixfield
Humphrey$^6$ M. (Ben$^5$, Jac$^4$, Jos$^3$, **JohnSal**)

........................................................................................................

Fryeburg
Sarah$^{w3}$ (Farnham), relict of Osgood$^5$.          Sarah$^{W6}$          Sarah$^{W6}$
William$^6$  (Osg$^5$, Jere$^4$, Wm$^3$ John$^2$, **WmRed**)                          William$^6$
Philip$^7$ (Wm$^6$,  "    "      "      "        "   )
William$^7$ (  "    "     "      "      "        "   )
Charlotte$^7$, dau. of Philip$^7$, above.

........................................................................................................

Lovell
Philip$^7$ (Wm$^6$, Osg$^5$, Jere$^4$, Wm$^3$, John$^2$, **WmRed**)

........................................................................................................

Rumford
Osgood$^6$ (Osg$^5$, Jere$^4$, Wm$^3$, John$^2$, **WmRed**)
Osgood$^7$ (Osg$^{6-5}$,  "      "      "        "   )
Abiel$^7$  (  "      "     "      "        "   )
Mehitable$^7$ ("     "     "      "        "   )

........................................................................................................

Weld  (more recently in Franklin, Co.)
Joshua$^7$ T. (Eliab$^6$, Jere$^{5-4}$, Wm$^3$, John$^2$ **WmRed**)

====================================================================

### Piscataquis Co.

Sebec
?? William P., b. 1790s.
Hezekiah$^8$ D. (Jona$^7$, Mose$^6$, Theo$^5$, Jona$^4$, **John$^{3-1}$Sal**)

........................................................................................................

Williams / Brownville
Thomas$^8$ F. (Jerem$^7$, Eliab$^6$, Jerem$^{5-4}$, Wm$^3$, John$^2$, **WmRed**)

# MAINE

| 1810 | 1820 | 1830 | 1840 | 1850 |
|---|---|---|---|---|

**Oxford Co.**

|  |  |  | William[7] | William[7] |
|---|---|---|---|---|
|  |  |  | Humphrey[6] |  |
| William[6] |  |  | Philip[7] | William[7] Charlotte[7] |
|  |  | Philip[7] |  |  |
| Osgood[6] | Osgood[6] | Osgood[6] | Osgood[7] Abiel[7] | Osgood[7] Mehitable[7] |
|  |  | Joshua[7] T. |  |  |

==================================================================

**Piscataquis Co.**

|  |  | William P. Hezekiah[8] | Hezekiah[8] |
|---|---|---|---|
|  |  |  | Thomas[8] F. |

# MAINE

| | 1790 | 1800 |
|---|---|---|

**Penobscot Co.**

### Bangor
Enoch[6] Abbot? (Osg[5], Jere[4], Wm[3], John[2], **WmRed**)
Joshua[7] P. (Eben[6], Jas[5], Ben[4], Wm[3], "       "    )
Lucy[W6] S., relict of Luther[6] of Eddington.

......................................................................

### Corinth
Perkins[8] T. (John[7-6], Elish[5], Saml[4], **John[3-1]Sal**)
True[7] (Jos[6-5A], John[4A], Jos[3], **Johnsal**)
Abigail[W7], wife of True[7].

......................................................................

### Dexter
William[7] (Saml[6], Dav[5], Saml[4], **John[3-1]Sal**)
William[7]? (Osg[6], Jere[5-4A], Wm[3], John[2], **WmRed**)

......................................................................

### Eddington
Luther[6] (Isaac[5], John[4-2], **JohnDed**)
Lucy[W6] S. (Holland), relict of Luther[6]

......................................................................

### Exeter
Charles[7] (Isaac[6], Ben[5], Jacob[4], Jos[3], **JohnSal**)

......................................................................

### Hermon
Cotton[6]      (Jas[5-4], Jona[3], **ThoHav**)
Josiah[7] G. (Cot[6], "      "         "      )
Nath'l[7] D. (  "    "       "          "      )

......................................................................

### Lee, (later Monroe)
?? Andrew M., b. 1810s.
?? William, b. 1800s.

......................................................................

### Newburgh
John[8] (John[7], Moses[6], Theo[5], Jona[4], **John[3-1]Sal**)

......................................................................

### Orono & Old Town
?? Obidiah M., b. 1810s.
?? Eunice, b. 1822 in Nova Scotia.
Lyman[7] (Jacob[6-4], Jos[3], **JohnSal**)

......................................................................

### Plymouth
Parker[6]      (Aaron[5-4A], Thos[3], Danl[2], **WmRed**)
Joseph[7] W. (Parker, "      "        "        "    )
Moses[7] M. (    "        "        "        "        "    )

......................................................................

### Township #6
Isaac[8] (Isaac[7], Eliak[6], Wm[5], **John[4-1]Sal**)

# MAINE

| 1810 | 1820 | 1830 | 1840 | 1850 |
|---|---|---|---|---|
| | Enoch$^6$ | Enoch$^6$ | Enoch$^6$ | Enoch$^6$<br>Joshua$^7$<br>Lucy$^{W6}$ |
| | | | Perkins$^8$ T. | True$^7$<br>Abigail$^{W7}$ |
| | | William$^7$ | William$^7$ | William$^7$<br>William$^7$ |
| | Luther$^6$ | Luther$^6$ | Lucy$^{W6}$ S. | |
| | | | | Charles$^7$ |
| | | Cotton$^6$ | | Josiah$^7$ G.<br>Nathaniel$^7$ |
| | | | Andrew M.<br>William | |
| | | | | John$^8$ |
| | | | Obidiah M. | Eunice<br>Lyman$^7$ |
| | | Parker$^6$ | Parker$^6$<br>Joseph$^7$ W.<br>Moses$^7$ M. | Joseph$^7$ W.<br>Moses$^7$ M. |
| | | | | Isaac$^8$ |

# MAINE

| | 1790 | 1800 |
|---|---|---|

**Somerset Co.**

Abbot
Daniel[7] (Danl[6-5],Saml[4], Jos[3], **JohnSal**)

...........................................................................................................................

Athens
Timothy[7] (Barn[6], Tim[5]. Isra[4], John[3-2], **WmRed**)

...........................................................................................................................

Canaan (later, Lincolnville)
Benjamin[6] (Ben[5], Pearson[4], Jos[3A], John[2], **JonaRed**)

...........................................................................................................................

Chandler
Isaac[6] (Ben[5], Jacob[4], Jos[3], **JohnSal**)

Detroit
Isaac[6] (Ben[5], Jacob[4], Jos[3], **JohnSal**)

...........................................................................................................................

East Pond Plantation (later, Smithfield + Norridgewock)
Henry[7] M. (Ephraim[6], Ben[5], **John[4-1]Sal**)
Barnabas[6]    (Tim[5], Isra[4], John[3-2], **WmRed**)
Timothy[7] (Barn[6], "    "    "        "  )
Rebecca[W6], relict of Barnabas[6]

...........................................................................................................................

Fairfield
James[6] (Ben[5], Jacob[4], Jos[3], **JohnSal**)

...........................................................................................................................

Madison
Cotton[6] (Jas[5-4], Jonathan[3], **ThoHav**

Milburn, became Skowhegan
Benjamin[6] (Benj[5], Pearson[4], Jos[3], John[2], **JonaRed**)

...........................................................................................................................

Palmyra
Parker[6] (Aaron[5A-4A], Thos[3], Danl[2], **WmRed**)
?? Isaac, b. 1800-09.
?? Angeline, b. 1822.

...........................................................................................................................

Ripley
William[7] J. ? (Osg[6], Jere[5A-4], Wm[3], John[2],**WmRed**)

...........................................................................................................................

St. Albans
?? Lydia, b. 1800-09.

...........................................................................................................................

Solon
Samuel[6]  (Samuel[5-4], **John[3-1]Sal**)
Moses[6]  ( "           "     )
Jonathan[7] (Samuel[6-4],       )
Bernet[7] (Barn[6], Tim[5], Isra[4], John[3-2], **WmRed**)

# MAINE

| 1810 | 1820 | 1830 | 1840 | 1850 |
|---|---|---|---|---|
| **Somerset Co.** | | | | |
| | | Daniel[7] | | |
| | | | Timothy[7] | Timothy[7] |
| | Benjamin[6] | | | |
| | | | Isaac[6] | |
| | | | | Isaac[6] |
| Henry[7] M. | Barnabas[6] | Timothy[7] | Rebecca[W6] | Rebecca[W6] |
| | | | James[6] | James[6] |
| Cotton[6] | | | | |
| | | Benjamin[6] | Benjamin[6] | |
| | Parker[6] | Isaac | | Angeline |
| | | | | William[7] |
| | | Lydia | | |
| Samuel[6] | Samuel[6] | Samuel[6] | | |
| | Moses[6] | Moses[6] | | Moses[6] |
| | | | | Jonathan[7] |
| | | | | Bernet[7] |

# MAINE

|  | 1790 | 1800 |
|---|---|---|

**Waldo Co.**

Belfast
Jonathan[7] (Moses[6], Theo[5], Jona[4], **John[3-1]Sal**)
Aaron[8] (John[7],  "          "          "          "    )

..................................................................................

Brooks
Sylvanus[7] (Jas[6], Theo[5], Jona[4], **John[3-1]Sal**)
Sally[7] ?  (   "          "          "          "          "    )

..................................................................................

Camden
Joseph[3]      (Jacob[4], Jos[3], **JohnSal**)                    Joseph[5]        Joseph[5]
William[6] (Jos[5],  "          "          "    )                   William[6]       William[6]
Joseph[6]  (   " ,     "          "          "    )
Joseph[7] (Wm[6], Jos[5], Jac[4], Jos[3], **JohnSal**)
Lucy[W6], relict of Wm[6] just above.
?? James W. , b. 1826, Nova Scotia.

..................................................................................

Frankfort
?? Jonathan, b. ca. 1770-74.                                                        Jonathan
David[8] (John[7], Mose[6], Theo[5], Jona[4], **John[3-1]Sal**)
John[8]   (   "          "          "          "          "    )
Ebenezer[8] (   "          "          "          "          "    )

..................................................................................

Prospect  (was Hancock Co.; later, Searsport)
James[6] (Theo[5], Jona[4], **John[3-1]Sal**)
James[6] (Jona[5-4], **John[3-1]Sal**)
Otis[7] (Jas[6],  "          "    )
Parker[7A] G. (Parker[6], Aaron[5A-4A], Thos[3], Danl[2], **WmRed**)
?? William L., b. 1811, Me.; mar. Abigail.

..................................................................................

Searsport
James[6]      (Jona[5-4], **Jona[3-1]Sal**)
Hiram[7] (Jas[6],  "          "    )
Otis[7]  (   "          "          "    )
Eliphalet[7] (Nath[6], Jona[5-4], **John[3-1]Sal**)

..................................................................................

Waldo
Joseph[8] (John[7], Mose[6], Theo[5], Jona[4], **John[3-1]Sal**)
Aaron[8]  (   "          "          "          "          "    )
Samuel[9] (Aar[8],  "          "          "          "    )

# MAINE

| 1810 | 1820 | 1830 | 1840 | 1850 |
|------|------|------|------|------|

**Waldo Co.**

| 1810 | 1820 | 1830 | 1840 | 1850 |
|------|------|------|------|------|
| | | Jonathan[7] | "Aron[8]" | Aaron[8] |
| | | Sylvanus[7] | Silvenus[7] | Sally[7] |
| Joseph[5] William[6] | William[6] Joseph[6] | William[6] Joseph[6] | William[6] | Joseph[7] Lucy[w6] James W. |
| | | | David[8] John[8] | David[8] Ebenezer[8] |
| | James[6] James[6] Jr. | James[6] | James[6] Otis[7] | Parker[7A] William L. |
| | | | | James[6] Hiram[7] Otis[7] Eliphalet[7] |
| | | Joseph[8] Aaron[8] | Joseph[8] | Joseph[8] Samuel[9] |

# MAINE

|  | 1790 | 1800 |
|---|---|---|

**Washington Co.**

Calais
??Josiah, b. 1787, Mass.

...........................................................................................................

Cherryfield
?? H.M., b. 1810s, Me.; mar. Dorcas.

...........................................................................................................

Dennysville
??Josiah, b. 1780s.

...........................................................................................................

East Machias
Joseph⁸ E. (Jos⁷, Jonas⁶⁻³, John², **JonaRed**)

...........................................................................................................

Eastport
Josiah⁶ (Jos⁵, **John⁴⁻¹Sal**)                                        Josiah⁶
Daniel⁷, (Elisha⁶, Dav⁵, Jas⁴, Jona³, **ThoHav**)
?? Caleb, b. 1824. N. B. Can.; mar. Emily.

...........................................................................................................

Harrington
*Moses⁵* (*Moses⁴*, John³, **ThoHav**)
Moses⁶ (*Moses⁵*, Moses⁴, John³, **ThoHav**)
Asa⁶    (    "          "          "          "     )

...........................................................................................................

Lubec
Henry⁷ M.    (Ephr⁶, Ben⁵, **John⁴⁻¹Sal**)
James⁸ M. (H⁷.M., "          "          "     )
Sam'l⁷ Perley ( "    "          "          "     )

...........................................................................................................

Perry
Daniel⁷ (Elish⁶, Dav⁵, Jas⁴, Jona³, **ThoHav**)

# MAINE

| 1810 | 1820 | 1830 | 1840 | 1850 |
|------|------|------|------|------|

**Washington Co.**

| 1810 | 1820 | 1830 | 1840 | 1850 |
|------|------|------|------|------|
| | | Josiah | | Josiah |
| | | | H.M. | |
| | | | Josiah | |
| | | | Joseph$^8$ E. | |
| | | Daniel$^7$ | | Caleb |
| | | Moses$^5$ | Moses$^5$<br>Moses$^6$ Jr | Asa$^6$ |
| Henry$^7$ M. | Moody$^7$ | | James$^8$ M.<br>Perly$^8$ | James$^8$ M.<br>Samuel$^8$ P. |
| | | | Daniel$^7$ | Daniel$^7$ |

# MAINE

|  | 1790 | 1800 |
|---|---|---|

## York Co.

### Alfred
Forest[7]      (Josh[6-5], Wm[4], **John[3-1]Sal**)
Joshua[8] (For[7],   "        "        "     )
Elizabeth[7] (Wm[6], Josh[5], "        "     )

................................................................

### Arundel
Joshua[7] (Joshua[6-5], Wm[4], **John[3-1]Sal**)

................................................................

### Biddeford
Humphrey[7] W. (John[6], Wym[5], **John[4-1]Sal**)

................................................................

### Buxton
| | | |
|---|---|---|
| John[6]   (Wyman[5], **John[4-1]Sal**) | John[6] | John[6] |
| John[7] (John[6], "          "    ) | | John[7] Jr. |

Abel[7] (    "        "          "     )
Tristram[7] (    "        "          "     )
Keziah[W7], relict of John[7], Jr. above.
William[6] (Wm[5], Benj[4], Wm[3], John[2], **WmRed**)
Nathn[7] (John[6,] **John[5-1]Sal**)
Jacob[8] (John[7-6], Wyman[5], **John[4-1]Sal**)
Betsey[W7], wife of Tristram[7] above.
Isaac[8] W. (Tris[7], John[6], Wym[5], **John[4-1]Sal**)
Sally[W7] (Frathy), wife of Abel[7] above.
William[8] H. (Nath[7], John[6], Wym[5], **John[4-1]Sal**)

................................................................

### Hollis
Robert[9] E. (Jacob[8], John[7-6], Wym[5], **John[4-1]Sal**)

................................................................

### Kennebunk(port)
Joshua[7] (Joshua[6-5], Wm[4], **John[3-1]Sal**)
Joshua[8] J. (Josh[7-5],    "          "     )
?? Charles, b. 1809, Me.; mar. Almira.

................................................................

### Limerick
William[6] (Wm[5], Benj[4], Wm[3], John[2], **WmRed**)

................................................................

### Sanford
Forest[7] (Josh[6-5], Wm[4], **John[3-1]Sal**)

# MAINE

| 1810 | 1820 | 1830 | 1840 | 1850 |
|------|------|------|------|------|
| **York Co.** | | | | |
| | Forest$^7$ | Forest$^7$<br>Joshua$^8$ | Forest$^7$<br><br>Elizabeth$^7$ | Forest$^7$<br>Joshua$^8$ |
| Joshua$^7$ | Joshua$^7$ | | | |
| | H.$^7$ W. | | | |
| John$^6$ | John$^6$ | | | |
| Abel$^7$<br>Tristram$^7$<br>Keziah$^{W7}$<br>William$^6$ | Abel$^7$<br>Tristram$^7$ | Abel$^7$ | Abel$^7$<br>Truston$^7$ | Abel$^7$<br>"Lustrun$^7$" |
| | Nathan$^7$<br>Jacob$^8$ | Nathan$^7$<br>Jacob$^8$<br>Betsey$^{w7}$ | Nathan$^7$<br>Jacob$^8$<br><br>Isaac$^8$ W. | Nathan$^7$<br><br><br>Isaac$^8$ W.<br>Sally$^{W7}$<br>William$^8$ H. |
| | | | Robert$^9$ E. | |
| | | Joshua$^7$ | Joshua$^7$ | Joshua$^7$<br>Joshua$^8$ J.<br>Charles |
| | William$^6$ | William$^6$ | | William$^6$ |
| Forrest$^7$ | | | | |

# MAINE

| | 1790 | 1800 |
|---|---|---|

## York Co.

### Waterboro
Isaac$^6$ (Benj$^5$, Jac$^4$, Jos$^3$, **JohnSal**)

. . . . . . . . . . . . . . . . . . . . . . . . . . . . . . . . . . . . . . . . . . . . . . . . . . . . . . . . . . . . . . . . . . . . . . . . . . . . . . . .

### Wells

| | 1790 | 1800 |
|---|---|---|
| Joseph$^5$   (Wm$^4$, **John**$^{3\text{-}1}$**Sal**) | Joseph$^5$ | Joseph$^5$ |
| Joshua$^5$   (Wm$^4$,      "      ) | Joshua$^5$ | Joshua$^5$ |
| Joshua$^6$ (Josh$^5$,  "      "      ) | Joshua$^6$ | Joshua$^6$ |
| Joseph$^6$ (  "      "      "      ) | Joseph$^6$ | Joseph$^6$ Jr. |
| Jeremiah$^6$ M. (Jos$^5$, Wm$^4$, **John**$^{3\text{-}1}$**Sal**) | Jeremiah$^6$ | |
| William$^6$ (  "      "      "      ) | William$^6$ | William$^6$ |
| Jacob$^6$ (  "      "      "      ) | | Jacob$^6$ |
| John$^6$ (  "      "      "      ) | | John$^6$ |
| Thomas$^7$ (Josiah$^6$, Thos$^5$, **John**$^{4\text{-}1}$**Sal**) | | Thomas$^7$ |

Joseph$^7$ (Jos$^6$, Josh$^5$, Wm$^4$, **John**$^{3\text{-}1}$**Sal**)
Samuel$^7$ (Jerem$^6$, Jos$^5$,  "      "      )
Jabez$^7$ (Josh$^{6\text{-}5}$, Wm$^4$, **John**$^{3\text{-}1}$**Sal**)
Noah$^7$ (  "      "      "      )
Sally$^{W6}$ (Cole), relict of John$^6$, above.
William$^7$ (Wm$^6$, Jos$^5$, Wm$^4$, **John**$^{3\text{-}1}$**Sal**)
John$^7$ C. (John$^6$, Jos$^5$, Wm$^4$, **John**$^{3\text{-}1}$**Sal**)
Daniel$^7$ (Jacob$^6$,  "      "      "      )
Ira$^8$  (Noah$^7$, Josh$^{6\text{-}5}$,  "      "      )
?? Jim M., b. 1800-09.
Stephen$^8$ (Saml$^7$, Jerem$^6$, Jos$^5$, Wm$^4$, **John**$^{3\text{-}1}$**Sal**)
John$^8$ E. (  "      "      "      "      "      )
Forest$^8$ (Jos$^{7\text{-}6}$, Josh$^5$, Wm$^4$, **John**$^{3\text{-}1}$**Sal**)
Horace$^8$ (Jabez$^7$, Josh$^{6\text{-}5}$,  "      "      )
Isaac$^8$ (Noah$^7$.  "      "      "      )

. . . . . . . . . . . . . . . . . . . . . . . . . . . . . . . . . . . . . . . . . . . . . . . . . . . . . . . . . . . . . . . . . . . . . . . . . . . . . . . .

### York
?? Jacob, b. Me.

# MAINE

| 1810 | 1820 | 1830 | 1840 | 1850 |
|------|------|------|------|------|

**York Co.**

| | Isaac[6] | Isaac[6] | | |
|---|---|---|---|---|

................................................................................................................

| 1810 | 1820 | 1830 | 1840 | 1850 |
|------|------|------|------|------|
| Joshua[6] | Joshua[6] | | | |
| Joseph[6] | Joseph[6] | Joseph[6] | | |
| William[6] | William[6] | William[6] | William[6] | |
| Jacob[6] | Jacob[6] | Jacob[6] | Jacob[6] | |
| John[6] | | | | |
| Joseph[7] | Joseph[7] | Joseph[7] | Joseph[7] | Joseph[7] |
| Samuel[7] | Samuel[7] | Samuel[7] | | |
| | Jabez[7] | Jabez[7] | Jabez[7] | Jabez[7] |
| | Noah[7] | Noah[7] | | |
| | Sally[W6] | | | |
| | William[7] | William[7] | William[7] | William[7] |
| | | John[7] C. | John[7] C. | John[7] C. |
| | | | Daniel[7] | Daniel[7] |
| | | | Ira[8] | |
| | | | Jim M. | |
| | | | Stephen[8] | Stephen[8] |
| | | | John[8] E. | |
| | | | | Forest[8] |
| | | | | Horace[8] |
| | | | | Isaac[8] |

................................................................................................................

| | | | | Jacob |

# NEW HAMPSHIRE

|  | 1790 | 1800 |
|---|---|---|

**Belknap Co.**
　Barnstead (was Strafford Co. pre-1840) | | * * * * * *
Samuel$^6$ (Obad$^5$, Saml$^4$, Job$^3$, **ThoHav**) | | * Sche- *
David$^7$ Fox (Dav$^6$. Eben$^5$, Saml$^4$, Job$^3$, **ThoHav**) | | * dules *
Peter$^7$ ( " " " " ) | | *　　　 *
Darius$^7$ (Aar$^6$, Thos$^5$, **John$^{4-1}$Sal**) | | * Lost *
Benjamin$^7$ P. (Saml$^6$, Obad$^5$, Sam'l$^4$, Job$^3$, **ThoHav**) | | *　　　 *
Esther$^7$ C. (Dav$^6$, Eben$^5$, " " " ) | | *******

　Gilford (N.B.: set off from Gilmanton, 1812)
Joshua$^6$ (Daniel$^{5-4A}$, **John$^{3-1}$Sal**)
Stephen$^7$ (Elisha$^{6-5}$, Saml$^4$, **John$^{3-1}$Sal**)
Samuel$^7$ S. (John$^6$, Elisha$^5$, Saml$^4$, **John$^{3-1}$Sal**)
Elisha$^8$ (Elish$^7$, " " " " )
Daniel$^9$ B. (Elish$^{8-7}$, " " " " )

　Gilmanton
Elias$^6$ (Jacob$^{5-4}$, Wm$^3$, John$^2$, **WmRed**) | | * * * * * * *
Benjamin$^7$ (Jacob$^{6-4}$, " " " ) | | *　　　 *
Joshua$^6$ (Danl$^{5-4A}$, **John$^{3-1}$Sal**) | | * Sche- *
Jonathan$^6$ W. (Josh$^6$, Danl$^{5-4A}$, **John$^{3-1}$Sal**) | | * dules *
Joseph$^7$ (John$^6$, Elish$^5$, Saml$^4$, **John$^{3-1}$Sal**) | | *　　　 *
Samuel$^7$ S. ( " " " " ) | | * Lost *
Abial$^7$ (Osg$^{6-5}$, Jerem$^4$, Wm$^3$, John$^2$, **WmRed**) | | *　　　 *
Peter$^7$ (Dav$^6$, Eben$^5$, Saml$^4$, Job$^3$, **ThoHav**) | | * * * * * * *

　Meredith
Jacob$^5$ (Jacob$^4$, Wm$^3$, John$^2$, **WmRed**) | Jacob$^5$ | Jacob$^5$
Jacob$^6$ (Jacob$^{5-4}$, " " " ) | Jacob$^6$ | Jacob$^6$, Jr.
Joseph$^6$ ( " " " " ) | Joseph$^6$ |
Humphrey$^6$ ( " " " " ) | | Humphrey$^6$
Caleb$^9$ (Caleb$^8$, Wm$^7$, Eben$^6$, **John$^{5-1}$Sal**)
William$^9$ ( " " " " )
John$^8$ (Jos$^7$, John$^6$, Elish$^5$, Saml$^4$, **John$^{3-1}$Sal**)

　Sanbornton
William$^6$ (Thos$^5$, **John$^{4-1}$Sal**) | | William$^6$
William$^7$ (Eben$^6$, **John$^{5-1}$Sal**) | | William$^7$
Reuben$^7$ ( " " ) | | Reuben$^7$
Caleb$^8$ (Wm$^7$, " " ) | | Caleb$^8$
Jonathan$^8$ ( " " " )
Thomas$^7$ (Wm$^6$, Thos$^5$, **John$^{4-1}$**)
Joseph$^9$ P. (Jona$^8$, Wm$^7$, Eben$^6$, **John$^{5-1}$Sal**)
Martha$^{W7}$, relict of Reuben$^7$ above.
Asa$^8$ B. (Thos$^7$, Wm$^6$, Thos$^5$, **John$^{4-1}$Sal**)
Molly$^{W8}$ (Prescott), relict of Jonathan$^8$, above.

## NEW HAMPSHIRE

| 1810 | 1820 | 1830 | 1840 | 1850 |
|---|---|---|---|---|
| **Belknap Co.** | | | | |
| | | Samuel$^6$ | Samuel$^6$ | |
| | | David$^7$ F. | David$^7$ F. | David$^7$ F. |
| | | | Peter$^7$ | |
| | | | Darius$^7$ | |
| | | | | Benjamin$^7$ P. |
| | | | | Esther$^7$ C. |
| | Joshua$^6$ | | | |
| | Stephen$^7$ | | | |
| | Samuel$^7$ S. | Samuel$^7$ | | Samuel$^7$ S. |
| | Elisha$^8$ | Elisha$^8$ | Elisha$^8$ | Elisha$^8$ |
| | | | | Daniel$^9$ B. |
| Elias$^6$ | | | | |
| Benjamin$^7$ | | | | |
| Joshua$^6$ | | | | |
| | Jonathan$^7$ W. | | | |
| Joseph$^7$ | | | | |
| | | | Samuel$^7$ S. | |
| | | | | Abial$^7$ |
| | | | | Peter$^7$ |
| | | | Caleb$^9$ | |
| | | | William$^9$ | |
| | | | | John$^8$ |
| William$^6$ | William$^6$ | William$^6$ | | |
| | William$^7$ | | | |
| | Reuben$^7$ | | | |
| Caleb$^8$ | Caleb$^8$ | | | |
| Jonathan$^8$ | Jonathan$^8$ | Jonathan$^8$ | | |
| | Thomas$^7$ | Thomas$^7$ | Thomas$^7$ | |
| | | | Joseph$^9$ P. | Joseph$^9$ P. |
| | | | Martha$^{W7}$ | |
| | | | | Asa$^8$ B. |
| | | | | Molly$^{W8}$ |

# NEW HAMPSHIRE

|  | 1790 | 1800 |
|---|---|---|

**Carroll Co.** (created 1840 from Strafford Co.)

Chatham
William[6]  (Osg[5], Jere[4], Wm[3], John[2], **WmRed**)
William[7] (Wm[6]. "    "    "    "    "    )
?? William, b. 1800-09.
James[7] V. (Wm[6], Osg[5], Jere[5], Wm[3], John[2], **WmRed**)
Jeremiah[7] (  "        "        "        "        "        "        )

..................................................................................

Conway
Simeon[8] (John[7-6], Wyman[5], **John[4-1]Sal**)
?? Sarah, b. 1815, N.H.

..................................................................................

Moultonboro
Joseph[7] (John[6], Elish[5], Saml[4], **John[3-1]Sal**)
John[8] (Jos[7], "        "        "        "        )

..................................................................................

Sandwich
Joshua[6]        (Danl[5A-4], **John[3-1]Sal**)
Jonathan[7] W. (Josh[6] , "        "        )

..................................................................................

Wolfeboro                                              * * * * * * *
?? George.                          George        * Sche-  *
Joseph[6]  (Joseph[5A], Jona[4], **John[3-1]Sal**)        * dules   *
Richard[7] (Joseph[6-5A], "        "        )        * Lost    *
Chandler[7] (  "        "        "        )        * * * * * * *

================================================================

**Coos Co.** (created 1803 from Grafton Co.)

Bartlett
?? Charles, b. 1810-20.

..................................................................................

Carroll
?? Phebe, b. 1772, Me.

..................................................................................

Indian Springs
?? David, b. 1790s.

..................................................................................

Lancaster
Joseph[7] C. (Wm[6], Osg[5], Jerem[4], Wm[3], John[2], **WmRed**)
Alfred[7]    (  "        "        "        "        "        "        )

# NEW HAMPSHIRE

| 1810 | 1820 | 1830 | 1840 | 1850 |
|---|---|---|---|---|

**Carroll Co.**

| 1810 | 1820 | 1830 | 1840 | 1850 |
|---|---|---|---|---|
| | | William[6] | William[6] | William[6] |
| | | William[7], Jr | William[7], Jr | |
| | | | William | |
| | | | James[7] | |
| | | | | Jeremiah[7] |
| | | Simeon[8] | Simeon[8] | Simeon[8] |
| | | | | Sarah |
| | | Joseph[7] | | |
| | | John[8] | John[8] | |
| | | Joshua[6] | Joshua[6] | Joshua[6] |
| | | | Jonathan[7] W. | Jonathan[7] |
| | | Joseph[6] | Joseph[6] | Joseph[6] |
| | | Richard[7] | | |
| | | | | Chandler[7] |

===================================================

**Coos Co.**

| 1810 | 1820 | 1830 | 1840 | 1850 |
|---|---|---|---|---|
| | | | Charles | |
| | | | | Phebe |
| | | David | | |
| | | | Alfred[7] | Joseph[7] C. |

# NEW HAMPSHIRE

|  | 1790 | 1800 |
|---|---|---|

**Cheshire Co.**

<u>Alstead</u>
Abraham$^5$ (John$^{4-3}$ Jona$^2$, **JonaRed**)        Abraham$^5$

<u>Chesterfield</u>
Abel$^5$   (Saml$^{4-3}$, Jona$^2$, **JonaRed**)
Abel$^6$ (Abel$^5$, "      "      "      )

<u>Dublin</u>
Moses$^5$   (Jere$^4$, Wm$^3$, **JohnDed**)
Moses$^6$ (Mose$^5$, "     "      "     )
Esther$^{W5}$, relict of Moses$^5$ above.

<u>Fitzwilliam</u>
?? John C., b. <1786.
?? Eunice$^{W7}$, relict of John C., b. Mass.
?? Charles Lincoln, b. 1822, res. solo.

<u>Hinsdale</u>
Ephraim$^5$ (Dav$^4$, Thos$^3$, **John$^{2-1}$Ded**)     Ephraim$^5$

<u>Jaffrey</u>
John$^5$      (Isra$^4$, John$^{3-2}$, **WmRed**)    John$^5$
David$^6$   (John$^5$, "    "      "    )    David$^6$     David$^6$
David$^7$ (Dav$^6$, "   "    "     )

<u>Keene</u>
?? Seth                   Seth
?? Samuel                                Samuel
?? R. C. b. 1820 in Vt.

<u>Nelson</u> (was Packersfield)
?? Luther, b. <1746.                   Luther
Benjamin$^5$ (Nathl$^{4-3}$, Jona$^2$, **JonaRed**)    Benjamin$^5$

<u>Stoddard</u>
William$^5$ (Wm$^4$ Nathl$^3$. Jona$^2$, **JonaRed**)      William$^5$

<u>Sullivan</u>
?? Jonathan                Jonathan
Benjamin$^5$   (Nathl$^{4-3}$, Jona$^2$, **JonaRed**)
Stillman$^6$ (Benj$^5$, "     "      "     )

# NEW HAMPSHIRE

| 1810 | 1820 | 1830 | 1840 | 1850 |
|------|------|------|------|------|

**Cheshire Co.**

| Abel[5] | Abel[5] | Abel[5] Abel[6] | | |
| | | Moses[5] | Moses[6] | Moses[6] Esther[W5] |
| | | John C. | Eunice | Eunice Charles |
| David[6] David[7] | | | | |
| Samuel | | | | R. C. |
| Benjamin[5] | Benjamin[5] | Stillman[6] | | |

# NEW HAMPSHIRE

|                | 1790 | 1800 |
|----------------|------|------|

**Cheshire Co.** (concl.)

Rindge
?? Charles, b. 1800-09.
?? Joseph, b. 1790-99.
?? Joseph, b. 1817.

................................................................................

Swanzey
Joel[6]  (Abel[5], Saml[4-3], Jona[2], **JonaRed**)
James[6] T. ( "          "          "          "       )
Jonathan[6A] (Jona[5], Josiah[4], Wm[3], **John[2-1]Ded**)

................................................................................

Walpole
Ebenezer[5]  (Jas[4], Jona[3], **ThoHav**)          Ebenezer[5]          Ebenezer[5]
Isaiah[6]  (Tim[5], "          "          )          Isaiah[6]          Isaiah[6]
Timothy[6] ( "    "    "          "       )          Timothy[6]
Josiah[6] (Eben[5], "       "          "   )
Zerviah[W6], relict of Josiah[6].

................................................................................

Winchester
Abel[5]  (Saml[4-3], Jona[2], **JonaRed**)                               Abel[5]
Jeduthan[5] ( "          "          "       )                           Jeduthan[5]
Abel[6] (Abel[5], "          "          "       )
Loren[6] ( "          "          "          "       )
Phebe[w5] (Turtelot), relict of Jeduthan[5].
Avery[6] (Mattiah[5], Noah[4], Jonas[3], John[2], **JonaRed**)
Ames[7] C. (Loren[6], Abel[5], Saml[4-3], Jona[2],      "       )
Loren[7]      ( "          "          "          "          "       )
John[1], b. 1795, Ireland; RR worker.
Robert[1], b. 1831, "          "          "          .

# NEW HAMPSHIRE

| 1810 | 1820 | 1830 | 1840 | 1850 |
|------|------|------|------|------|

**Cheshire Co.** (concl.)

| | | | Charles Joseph | |
| | | | | Joseph |

.....................................................................................................................

| | | | Joel[6] | |
| | | | | James[6] T. |
| | | | | Jonathan[6A] |

.....................................................................................................................

| Josiah[6] | | | | |
| | | | Zervah[W6] | |

.....................................................................................................................

| Jeduthan[5] | Jeduthan[5] | | | |
| | Abel[6] | | | |
| | | Loren[6] | Loren[6] | |
| | | | | Phebe[W5] |
| | | | | Avery[6] |
| | | | | Ames[7] C. |
| | | | | Loring[7] |
| | | | | John |
| | | | | Robert |

# NEW HAMPSHIRE

|  | 1790 | 1800 |
|---|---|---|

**Grafton Co.**

Benton
William[6] ? (William[5-4], Nathl[3], Jona[2], **JonaRed**)

....................................................................

Bethlehem
Ebenezer[6] (Nathl[5], Jas[4], Jona[3], **ThoHav**)
Elias[6] (Jacob[5-4], Wm[3], John[2]. **WmRed**)
?? Deborah, b. 1800-09.
??Horatio, b. 1803, N.H.
?? Jabez W., b. 1805, N.H.
?? Bryant, b. 1811, Me.
Philip[7] F. (Wm[6], Osg[5], Jere[4], Wm[3], John[2], **WmRed**)

....................................................................

Bristol
David[6] (Eben[5], Benj[4], Wm[3], John[2], **WmRed**)
Cyrus[8] (Wheel[7], Wm[6], Thos[5], **John[41]Sal**)
Jacob[7] S. (John[6], Nathl[5], Jas[4], Jona[3], **ThoHav**)
Ebenezer[7] (Dav[6], Eben[5], Ben[4], Wm[3], John[2]. **WmRed**)
Rufus[7]     (   "     "     "     "     "     "   )
William[9] (Caleb[8], Wm[7], Eben[6], **John[5-1]Sal**)

....................................................................

Campton
David[7] (Dav[6], Jona[5], Ben[4], Wm[3], John[2], **WmRed**)
?? Robert Y., b. 1818, N.H.
Elias[6] (Jacob[5-4], Wm[3], John[2], **WmRed**)
?? Sally, b. 1781, N.H.

....................................................................

Canaan
Moses[5]    (Mose[4], John[3], **ThoHav**)                       Moses[5]
Ebenezer[5] (   "      "      "   )
Nathaniel[6] (Eben[5], Mose[4], John[3], **ThoHav**)

....................................................................

Enfield
James[7] P.? (Jas[6-5], Benj[4], Wm[3], John[2], **WmRed**)
Edward[7] Preston    (Jas[6-5], Ben[4], Wm[3], John[2], **WmRed**)
Edward[8] Pollard (Edw[7],  "    "     "     "     "   )
Ebenezer[8] C.   (    "     "    "     "     "     "   )
?? Louisa, b. 1818, N.H.
?? Judith, b. 1795, N.H.

# NEW HAMPSHIRE

| 1810 | 1820 | 1830 | 1840 | 1850 |
|------|------|------|------|------|

**Grafton Co.**

| 1810 | 1820 | 1830 | 1840 | 1850 |
|------|------|------|------|------|
| | * * * * * * | | | |
| | *              * | | | William[6] |
| | * | | | |
| | *              * | Ebenezer[6] | | |
| | *              * | Elias[6] | | |
| | *              * | Deborah | | |
| | *              * | Horatio | Horatio | Horatio |
| | *              * | | Jabez | Jabez W. |
| | *              * | | | Bryant |
| | *              * | | | Philip F. |
| | *              * | | | |
| | *              * | David[6] | David[6] | David[6] |
| | *              * | | Cyrus[8] W. | |
| | * Sche-      * | | Jacob[7] S. | |
| | *              * | | | Ebenezer[7] |
| | * dules       * | | | Rufus[7] |
| | *              * | | | William[9] |
| | *              * | | | |
| | *              * | | David[7] | |
| | *              * | | | Robert Y. |
| | * Lost        * | | | Elias[6] |
| | *              * | | | Sally |
| | *              * | | | |
| | *              * | Ebenezer[5] | Ebenezer[5] | Ebenezer[5] |
| | *              * | Nathaniel[6] | Nathaniel[6] | Nathaniel[6] |
| | *              * | | | |
| | *              * | | James[7] P. | |
| | *              * | | Edward[7] | |
| | *              * | | | Edward[7] |
| | *              * | | | Edward[8] |
| | *              * | | | Ebenezer[8] C. |
| | *              * | | | Louisa |
| | * * * * * * | | | Judith |

## NEW HAMPSHIRE

|  | 1790 | 1800 |
|---|---|---|

**Grafton Co.** (cont.)

Groton
Joseph[6] (Tho[5-2]**Hav**)

........................................................................................................

Hanover
David[7A] (Dav[4], Tho[2], John[2A], **JohnDed**)          David[5A]
David[6] (Dav[5-4],    "        "       "    )            David[6]          David[6]
Jacob[6] (   "        "        "       "    )             Jacob[6]          Jacob6
Ebenezer[5] (Moses[4], John[3], **ThoHav**)                                 Ebenezer[5]
Calvin[6A] (Dav[5A-4], Thos[3], John[2A], **JohnDed**)
Jerusha[W6] (Hall), relict of David[6].
David[7] (Dav[6-4], Tho[3], John[2A], **JohnDed**)
Horace[7] (  "       "       "        "    )
Jonathan[6] (Dav[5A-4],  "      "        "    )
J. Frederick[7] (Cal[6A], Dav[5A-4], Tho[3], **John[2A--1]Ded**)
George[8] W. (Hor[7], Dav[6-4],    "       "    )
?? Samuel, b. 1816, Mass.

........................................................................................................

Holderness
Joseph[6] (Jacob[5-4], Wm[3], John[2], **WmRed**)

........................................................................................................

Landaff
David[6] (Eben[5], Saml[4], Job[3], **ThoHav**)          David[6]          David[6]
Ebenezer[6] ("      "      "       "    )                Ebenezer[6]       Ebenezer[6]
Samuel[6] (  "      "      "       "    )                Samuel[6]         Samuel[6]
Ebenezer[7] (Eben[6-5],  "       "       "    )
Esther[7] (Dav[6], Eben[5], "       "       "    )
Ira[7]      (Eben[6-5],    "       "       "    )
Mitchell[7] (  "         "       "       "    )
Timothy[7] (Saml[6], Eben[5], "    "       "    )
John[8] (Tim[7],  "        "       "       "    )

........................................................................................................

Lebanon
John[6] (Jas[5], Benj[4], Wm[3], John[2], **WmRed**)

........................................................................................................

Lisbon
Mitchell[7] H. (Eben[6-5], Saml[4], Job[3], **ThoHav**)
Ruth[W6] (Hutchins), relict of Ebenezer[6], Landaff.

........................................................................................................

Lyme
?? Joseph, b. 1790s.

# NEW HAMPSHIRE

| 1810 | 1820 | 1830 | 1840 | 1850 |
|---|---|---|---|---|

**Grafton Co.** (cont.)

| 1810 | 1820 | 1830 | 1840 | 1850 |
|---|---|---|---|---|
| | * * * * * * | | | |
| Joseph[6] | *       * | | | |
| | *       * | | | |
| | *       * | | | |
| | *       * | | | |
| | *       * | | | |
| Ebenezer[5] | *       * | | | |
| Calvin[6A] | *       * | Calvin[6A] | Calvin[6A] | Calvin[6A] |
| Jerusha[W6] | *       * | | | |
| | *       * | David[7] | David[7] | David[7] |
| | *       * | Horace[7] | Horace[7] | Horace[7] |
| | *       * | Jonathan[6] | | |
| | * Sche- * | | | Frederick[7] |
| | *       * | | | George[8] W. |
| | * dules * | | | Samuel |
| | *       * | | | |
| Joseph[6] | * Lost * | | | |
| | *       * | | | |
| David[6] | *       * | | | |
| Ebenezer[6] | *       * | Ebenezer[6] | | |
| Samuel[6] | *       * | | Samuel[6] | |
| | *       * | Ebenezer[7] 2d | Ebenezer[7] | Ebenezer[7] |
| | *       * | Esther[7] | | |
| | *       * | Ira[7] | | |
| | *       * | Mitchell[7] H. | Mitchell H. | |
| | *       * | Timothy[7] | Timothy[7] | Timothy[7] |
| | *       * | | John[8] | John[8] |
| | *       * | | | |
| John[6] | *       * | | | |
| | *       * | | | |
| | *       * | | | Mitchell[7] H. |
| | *       * | | | Ruth[W6] |
| | *       * | | | |
| | *       * | Joseph | | |
| | * * * * * * | | | |

# NEW HAMPSHIRE

|  | 1790 | 1800 |
|---|---|---|

**Grafton Co.**  (concl.)

Plymouth
Daniel[6]  (Jona[5], Benj[4], Wm[3], John[2], **WmRed**)
Jonathan[7A] (Dav[6], Jona[5], Ben[4], Wm[3], John[2] " )
Ezra[7] B. (Job[6-5], Saml[4], Job[3], **ThoHav**)

.....................................................................................................................

Rumney
Daniel[6] (Jona[5], Benj[4], Wm[3], John[2], **WmRed**)                                 Daniel[6]
?? Susan, b. 1828, N.H.

.....................................................................................................................

Warren
Jonathan[7] M. (Job[6-5], Saml[4], Job[3], **ThoHav**)
Job[7]           ( "      "      "       " )
Sally[W7] (Brown), wife of Job[7].
Merrill[8] (Moses[7], Job[6-5], Saml[4], Job[3], **ThoHav**)
Augustus[8] B. ( "      "      "      "       " )
Amanda[8]  (Ezra[7],  "      "      "       " )

.....................................................................................................................

Wentworth
Job[6]      (Job[5], Saml[4], Job[3], **ThoHav**)                   Job[6]              Job[6]
James[6]   ( "      "      "      " )                                         James[6]
Moses[6]   ( "      "      "      " )                                         Moses[6]
Jesse[7] (Mose[6], "      "      " )
Moses[7] (Job[6-5],  "      "      " )
Ezra[7] B. ( "      "      "      " )
Worcester[7] ( "      "      "      " )
Abigail[W6], relict of Moses[6] above.

# NEW HAMPSHIRE

| 1810 | 1820 | 1830 | 1840 | 1850 |
|---|---|---|---|---|

**Grafton Co.** (Concl.)

| 1810 | 1820 | 1830 | 1840 | 1850 |
|---|---|---|---|---|
| | * * * * * * | | | |
| Daniel[6] | *     * | Daniel[6] | | |
| | *     * | | Jonathan[7] | |
| | *     * | Ezra[7] | | |
| | *     * | | | |
| | *     * | | | |
| | *     * | | | Susan |
| | *     * | | | |
| | * Sche- * | Jonathan[7] M. | | Jonathan[7] M. |
| | *     * | | | Job[7] |
| | * dules * | | | Sally[W7] |
| | *     * | | | Merrill[8] |
| | *     * | | | Augustus[8] |
| | * Lost * | | | Amanda[8] |
| | *     * | | | |
| Job[6] | *     * | Job[6] | | |
| | *     * | | | |
| Moses[6] | *     * | Moses[6] | | |
| | *     * | Jesse[7] | Jesse[7] | Jesse[7] |
| | *     * | Moses[7] Jr. | Moses[7] | |
| | *     * | | Ezra[7] B. | Ezra[7] B. |
| | *     * | Worcester[7] | Worcester[7] | |
| | *     * | | | Abigail[W6] |
| | * * * * * * | | | |

# NEW HAMPSHIRE

|  | 1790 | 1800 |
|---|---|---|

**Hillsborough Co.**

### Amherst
John$^{5A}$ (John$^{4-3}$, Jona$^2$, **JonaRed**)   John$^{5A}$   John$^{5A}$
Philip$^6$ (John$^{5A-3}$, Jona$^2$.   "   )
Edmund$^7$ (Edm$^{6-5}$, Jona$^4$, Tho$^3$, Josh$^2$, **JonaRed**)
Loammi$^6$ (Thos$^{5-4}$, John$^3$, Jona$^2$, **JonaRed**)
Harrison$^8$ (John$^7$, *Jas$^6$*, *Jas$^5$*, Jas$^4$, Jona$^3$, **ThoHav**)
Samuel$^8$ (   "   "   "   "   "   "   )

### Antrim
Hiram$^7$ (*Jas$^6$*, *Jas$^5$*, Jas$^4$, Jona$^3$, **ThoHav**)
James$^7$ (   "   "   "   "   "   )

### Bedford
Samuel$^6$ ? (James$^{5-4}$, Jona$^3$, **ThoHav**)   Samuel$^6$
?? Calvin, b. 1790s.
?? Jesse, b. 1800-09.

### Bennington
Nathaniel$^7$ (Jos$^6$, Ezek$^5$, Jona$^4$, **John$^{3-1}$Sal**)
William$^8$ (John$^7$, *Jas$^6$*, *Jas$^5$*, Jas$^4$, Jona$^3$, **ThoHav**)
?? Joseph, b. 1828, N.H.

### Deering
*James$^6$* (*Jas$^5$*, Jas$^4$, Jona$^3$, **ThoHav**)   James$^6$   James$^6$
David$^7$ (*Jas$^6$*, *Jas$^5$*, Jas$^4$, Jona$^3$, **ThoHav**)
?? David, b. 1790s.
Isaac$^7$ (*Jas$^6$*, *Jas$^5$*, Jas$^4$, Jona$^3$, **ThoHav**)
James$^7$ (   "   "   "   "   "   )
Samuel$^8$ W. (Saml$^7$, *Jas$^6$*, *Jas$^5$*, Jas$^4$, Jona$^3$, **ThoHav**)

### Dunstable
?? Ebenezer, b. 1795-1804.

### Francestown
Moses$^5$ (**Tho$^{4-2}$Hav**)   Moses$^5$   Moses$^5$
Thos$^6$ (Mose$^5$,   "   )   Thomas$^6$
Moses$^7$ W. (Thos$^6$, Mose$^5$, **Tho$^{4-2}$Hav**)
Samuel$^7$ (*Jas$^6$*, *Jas$^5$*. Jas$^4$, Jona$^3$, **ThoHav**)
Isaac$^7$ (   "   "   "   "   "   )
?? Betsey.
James$^7$ (*Jas$^6$*, *Jas$^5$* Jas$^4$, Jona$^3$, **ThoHav**)

# NEW HAMPSHIRE

| 1810 | 1820 | 1830 | 1840 | 1850 |
|------|------|------|------|------|

## Hillsborough Co.

| 1810 | 1820 | 1830 | 1840 | 1850 |
|------|------|------|------|------|
| John$^{5A}$<br>Philip$^6$ | John$^{5A}$ | | Edmund$^7$<br>Loammi$^6$ | Loammi$^6$<br>Harrison$^8$<br>Samuel$^8$ |
| | | | | Hiram$^7$<br>James$^7$ |
| | | Calvin | Jesse | |
| | | | | Nathaniel$^7$<br>William$^8$<br>Joseph |
| James$^6$<br>David$^7$ | James$^6$ | David<br>Isaac$^7$ | James$^7$. Jr | Samuel$^8$ W. |
| | Ebenezer | | | |
| Moses$^5$<br>Thomas$^6$ | Thomas$^6$ | Thomas$^6$<br>Moses$^7$ W.<br>Samuel$^7$ | Thomas$^6$<br>Moses$^7$ W.<br><br>Mrs. Betsey | Thomas$^6$<br>Moses$^7$ W.<br><br>Isaac$^7$<br><br>James$^7$ |

# NEW HAMPSHIRE

|  | 1790 | 1800 |
|---|---|---|

**Hillsborough Co.** (cont.)

Goffstown
Enoch[5] (Jas[4], Jona[3], **ThoHav**)                    Enoch[5]
James[5] ( "        "        "     )                    James[5]              James[5]
Samuel[6] (Jas[5-4], "        "     )                    Samuel[6]
David[6] ( "        "        "     )                                          David[6]
?? James, "Jr." b. 1756-74.                                                    James, Jr.
Jonathan[6] (Enoc[5], Jas[4], Jona[3], **ThoHav**)                            Jonathan[6]
Betsy[W6] (Hadley), relict of David[6] above.
?? James, b. 1790s.
James[7] (Dav[6], Jas[5-4], Jona[3], **ThoHav**)
?? John, b. 1810.
..................................................................................

Greenfield
Joseph[6] H.   (Ezek[5], Jona[4], **John[3-1]Sal**)       Joseph[6] H.         Joseph[6]
Nathaniel[7]  (Jos[6], "      "        "     )
Amos[8] (Nathl[7], "      "      "        "     )
..................................................................................

Hancock
Lemuel[5] (Jerem[4], Wm[3], **John[2-1]Ded**)            Lemuel[5]
Moses[5] ( "        "        "     )                    Moses[5]
Samuel[5] ( "        "        "     )                    Samuel[5]
Lucy[W5], relict of Samuel[5] above.
Lemuel[6] (Lem[5], Jere[4], Wm[3], **John[2-1]Ded**)
John[6] (Saml[5],   "        "        "     )
Betsey[6] ( "      "        "        "     )
Rebecca[6] ( "      "        "        "     )
..................................................................................

Hillsborough
Abram[5] ? (John[4-3], Jona[2], **JonaRed**)             Abraham[5]
James[6] (Timo[5], Jas[4], Jona[3], **ThoHav**)          James[6]             James[6]
John[7] (*Jas[6], Jas[5]*, Jas[4], Jona[3], **ThoHav**)
?? James, b. 1790s.
Horace[8] (John[7], *Jas[6], Jas[5]*, Jona[3], **ThoHav**)
??Nathaniel, b. 1805, Mass.
Elizabeth[W7] "Betsey" (Moore). relict of John[7] above.
John[8] L. (John[7], *Jas[6], Jas[5]*, Jas[4], Jona[3], **ThoHav**)
Susan[W6]? Relict of David[7] (Jas[6] of Deering)?
..................................................................................

Hollis
?? Clarissa.

# NEW HAMPSHIRE

| 1810 | 1820 | 1830 | 1840 | 1850 |
|------|------|------|------|------|

**Hillsborough Co.** (cont.)

| 1810 | 1820 | 1830 | 1840 | 1850 |
|------|------|------|------|------|
| David$^6$ | David$^5$ | David$^5$ | | |
| | | | Betsey$^{W6}$ | |
| | | | James | |
| | | | James$^7$ | James$^7$ |
| | | | | John |

| 1810 | 1820 | 1830 | 1840 | 1850 |
|------|------|------|------|------|
| Joseph$^6$ | Joseph$^6$ | Joseph | | |
| | Nathaniel$^7$ | Nathaniel$^7$ | Nathaniel$^7$ | |
| | | | | Amos$^8$ |

| 1810 | 1820 | 1830 | 1840 | 1850 |
|------|------|------|------|------|
| | Lemuel$^5$ | Lemuel$^5$ | | |
| Samuel$^5$ | Samuel$^5$ | | | |
| | | Lucy$^{W5}$ | | |
| | | | Lemuel$^6$ | Lemuel$^6$ |
| | | | | John$^6$ |
| | | | | Betsey$^6$ |
| | | | | Rebecca$^6$ |

| 1810 | 1820 | 1830 | 1840 | 1850 |
|------|------|------|------|------|
| James$^6$ | James$^6$ | | | |
| John$^6$ | John$^6$ | John$^6$ | | |
| | | James | | |
| | | | Horace$^8$ | Horace$^8$ |
| | | | | Nathaniel |
| | | | Mrs. Elizabeth$^{W7}$ | Elizabeth$^{W7}$ |
| | | | | John$^8$ L. |
| | | | Mrs. Susannah$^{W6}$ | Susan$^{W6}$ |

Clarissa

# NEW HAMPSHIRE

|        | 1790 | 1800 |
|--------|------|------|

**Hillsborough Co.** (cont.)

Hudson
Alfred[8] (Geo[7], Thos[6-4], John[3-2], **WmRed**)
Edwin[8] (    "         "         "         "    )

......................................................................................................................

Lyndeborough
?? Mary J., b. 1825, N.H.

......................................................................................................................

Manchester
?? Calvin, b. 1790s.
George[8] W. (Josh[7], Jas[6], Ezekiel[5], Jona[4], **John[3-1]Sal**)
?? James, b. 1800-09.
Jonathan[8] (Wm[7], Eben[6], **John[5-1]Sal**)
?? Samuel, b. 1770s.
Rufus[8] G. (Forest[7], Josh[6-5], Wm[4], **John[3-1]Sal**)
?? Arabella, b. 1813, N.H.
?? Amanda, b. 1822, N.H.
?? Leonard, b. 1826, Vt.
?? Nancy, b. 1810, Vt.
 Charles[9] W. (Jona[8], Wm[7], Eben[6], **John[5-1]Sal**)
?? John S., b. 1824, N.H.; wife Eliza A.
John[8] W. (Thos[7], Wm[6], Thos[5], **John[4-1]Sal**)
Warren[8] (    "         "         "         "    )
John[8] G. (John[7] G, Jos[6], Ezek[5], Jona[4], **John[3-1]Sal**)
Peter[6]        (Ephr[5], Hen[4], Ephr[3], **John[2-1]Sal**)
Caroline[7] (Hen[6], "      "        "        "    )
?? Frances, b. 1789, N.H.
?? Jesse, b. 1801, N.H.
?? William, b. 1828, N.H.

......................................................................................................................

Mason
Abijah[7] (Aaron[4A], Thos[3]. Dan[2], **WmRed**)        Abijah[5]        Abijah[5]
Abijah[6] (Abij[5], "        "         "         "    )
?? Abigail, b. 1790s.
Josiah[7] (Josi[6], John[5], Josi[4], Wm[3], **John[2-1]Ded**)
Otis[7] W. ( "        "         "         "         "    )

......................................................................................................................

Merrimack
?? Jesse, b. 1801, N.H.
Harrison[8] (Mose[7], Nathl[6], John[5], Thos[4], Job[3], **ThoHav**)
??Daniel, b. 1822, N.H.; mar. Lucretia.

# NEW HAMPSHIRE

| 1810 | 1820 | 1830 | 1840 | 1850 |
|------|------|------|------|------|

**Hillsborough Co.**

| 1810 | 1820 | 1830 | 1840 | 1850 |
|------|------|------|------|------|
| | | | | Alfred[8] |
| | | | | Edwin[8] |
| | | | | Mary J. |
| | | | Calvin G.[8] W. | George[8] W. |
| | | | James | |
| | | | Jonathan[8] | |
| | | | Samuel | |
| | | | | Rufus[8] G. |
| | | | | Arabella |
| | | | | Amanda |
| | | | | Leonard |
| | | | | Nancy |
| | | | | Charles[9] W. |
| | | | | John S. |
| | | | | John[8] W. |
| | | | | Warren[8] |
| | | | | John[8] G. |
| | | | | Peter[6] |
| | | | | Caroline[7] |
| | | | | Frances |
| | | | | Jesse |
| | | | | William |
| | Abijah[6] | Abijah[6] | | Abijah[6] |
| | | | Abigail | |
| | | | | Josiah[7] |
| | | | | Otis[7] W. |
| | | Jesse | | |
| | | | Harrison[8] | Harrison[8] |
| | | | | Daniel |

# NEW HAMPSHIRE

|  | 1790 | 1800 |
|---|---|---|

**Hillsborough Co.** (cont.)

Milford
?? Sarah D., b. 1803, Me.

Nashua
Philip[7] F. (Wm[6], Osg[5], Jerem[4], Wm[3], John[2], **WmRed**)
?? Rebecca, b. 1780s.
Edmund[7] (Edm[6-5], Jona[4], Thos[3], Josh[2], **JonaRed**)
?? James, b. 1799, N.H. mar. Nancy.
?? Isaac, b. 1825, N.H., Mar. Harriet.
?? Abby, b. 1825, Me.
Nathaniel[8] (Nathl[7], Jos[6], Ezek[5], Jona[4], **John[3-1]Sal**)
?? Lorenzo D., b. 1826, N.H.

Nashville
Philip[7] F. (Wm[6], Osg[5], Jerem[4], Wm[3]. John[2], **WmRed**)
James[8] B. (Dav[7], Jas[6], Jas[5], Jas., Jona[3] (**ThoHav**)

New Ipswich
Joseph[5] (Pearson[4], Jos[3A], John[2], **JonaRed**)                    Joseph[5]
Benjamin[5](    "    "    "    "    )
Obadiah[7] P. (Thos[6], Mose[5], **Tho[4-2]Hav**)
?? William, b. 1775-84.                    William
Merrick[7] (Josi[6], John[5], Josi[4], Wm[3], **John[2-1]Ded**)
Hosea[7] (    "    "    "    "    "    )

Peterborough
Moses[5] (Jerem[4], Wm[3], **John[2-1]Ded**)
?? Charles, b. 1809, Mass.; mar. Theresa.

"Society Land"
John[7] G. (Jos[6], Ezek[5], Jona[4], **John[3-1]Sal**)
James[6] (Jas[5], Jas[4], Jona[3], **ThoHav**)
Joseph[8] (John[7], Jos[6], Ezek[5], Jona[4], **John[3-1]Sal**)

Temple
Benjamin[5] (Nathl[4-3], Jona[2] (**JonaRed**)

Weare  (begun)
Humphrey[6] (Wyman[5], **John[4-1]Sal**)                    Humphrey[6]    Humphrey[6]
Ithamar[5] (Saml[4], Job[3], **ThoHav**)                    Ithamar[5]     Ithamar[5]
Obadiah[5] (    "    "    "    )                    Obadiah[5]
Betsey[W5] (Paige), relict of Obadiah[5].                                   Betsey[W5]

# NEW HAMPSHIRE

| 1810 | 1820 | 1830 | 1840 | 1850 |
|------|------|------|------|------|

**Hillsborough Co.**

| 1810 | 1820 | 1830 | 1840 | 1850 |
|------|------|------|------|------|
| | | | | Sarah D. |
| | | | Philip[7] F, Rebecca | |
| | | | | Edmund[7] James Isaac Abby Nathaniel[8] Lorenzo D. |
| | | | | Philip[7] F. James[8] B. |
| Joseph[5] Benjamin[5] | | | | |
| | | | O.[7] P. | |
| | | | | Merrick[7] Hosea[7] |
| Moses[5] | Moses[5] | Moses[5] | | |
| | | | | Charles |
| | John[7] G. | John[7] G. James[6] | James[6] Joseph[8] | |
| | | | | Benjamin[5] |
| Humphrey[6] | Humphrey[6] | | | |

# NEW HAMPSHIRE

|  | 1790 | 1800 |
|---|---|---|

**Hillsborough Co.** (concl.)

Weare  (concl.)
Samuel[6] (Dav[5] Saml[4], **John[3-1]Sal**)                          Samuel[6]
Jacob[7] (Hump[6], Wyman[5], **John[4-1]Sal**)
Joseph[6] (Itha[5], Saml[4], Job[3], **ThoHav**)
Peter[6] ( "          "          "          "          )
Samuel[6] (Obad[5], "          "          "          )
?? Luther, b. <1766.
?? Luther, b. 1766-84.
Tristram[7] (Hump[6], Wym[5], **John[4-1]Sal**)
Elizabeth[W6], relict of Peter[6] above.
Mary[W6], relict of Samuel[6] (Dav[5]) above.
Moses[7] (Saml[6], Dav[5], Saml[4], **John[3-1]Sal**)
Reuben[7] ( "          "          "          "          )
(Geo.) Washington[6] (Itha[5], Saml[4], Job[3], **ThoHav**)
Wheeler[7] (Wm[6], Thos[5], **John[4-1]Sal**)
Nathan[7] (Peter[6], Itha[5], Saml[4], Job[3], **ThoHav**)
David[7] (Saml[6], Dav[5], Saml[4], **John[3-1]Sal**)
John[8] Q. (Jacob[7]. Hump[6], Wym[5], **John[4-1]Sal**)
Jane[W7] (Goodwin), relict of Jacob[7] (Hump[6])
James[7] (G. Wash'ton[6], Itha[5],Saml[4], Job[3], **ThoHav**)
Willis[7] ( "          "          "          "          "          )
Thomas[8] (Reub[7], Saml[6], Dav[5], Saml[4], **John[3-1]Sal**)
Pillsbury[8] ( "          "          "          "          "          )
James[8] ( "          "          "          "          "          )
Thomas[6] (Thos[5A], **Tho[4-2]Hav**)

...................................................................................................................

Wilton
Thomas[5] (Thos[4], John[3], Jona[2-], **JonaRed**)     Thomas[5]     Thomas[5]
Amos[5-] ( "          "          "          "          )                          Amos[5]
Thomas[6] (Thos[5-4], "          "          "          )
Loammi[6] ( "          "          "          "          )
Amos[6] (Amos[5], Thos[4], John, Jona[2], **JonaRed**)
Abel[6] ( "          '''          "          "          "          )
Charles[7] (Amos[6-5], "          "          "          "          )
Samuel[7] ( "          "          "          "          "          )
Horace[7] (Dav[6], Jas[5-4], Jona[3], **ThoHav**)

# NEW HAMPSHIRE

| 1810 | 1820 | 1830 | 1840 | 1850 |
|------|------|------|------|------|

**Hillsborough Co.** (concl.)

| 1810 | 1820 | 1830 | 1840 | 1850 |
|------|------|------|------|------|
| Samuel[6] | | | | |
| Jacob[7] | Jacob[7] | Jacob[7] | | |
| Joseph[6] | | | | |
| Peter[6] | | | | |
| Samuel[6-] | Samuel[6] | | | |
| Luther | | | | |
| Luther | | | | |
| Tristram[7] | Tristram[7] | Tristram[7] | | |
| | Elizabeth[W6] | | | |
| | Mary[W6] | Mary[w6] | | |
| | Moses[7] | Moses[7] | Moses[7] | Moses[7] |
| | Reuben[7] | Reuben[7] | Reuben[7] | |
| | Washington[6] | Washington[6] | Washington[6] | |
| | Wheeler[7] | Wheeler[7] | | |
| | | Nathan[7] | Nathan[7] | Nathan[7] |
| | | | David[7] | David[7] |
| | | | J.Q.[8] | |
| | | | | Jane[W7] |
| | | | | James[7] L. |
| | | | | Willis[7] |
| | | | | Thomas[8] |
| | | | | Pillsbury[8] |
| | | | | James[8] |
| | | | | Thomas[6] |

| 1810 | 1820 | 1830 | 1840 | 1850 |
|------|------|------|------|------|
| Amos[5] | Amos[5] | Amos[5] | | |
| Thomas[6] | | | | |
| Loammi[6] | | | | |
| | | Amos[6] | Amos[6] | Amos[6] |
| | | | Abel[6] | Abel[6] |
| | | | | Charles[7] |
| | | | | Samuel[7] |
| | | | | Horace[7] |

# NEW HAMPSHIRE

|  | 1790 | 1800 |
|---|---|---|

**Merrimack Co.**

Boscawen
?? Moses, b. 1750s.
Asa[7] (Danl[6], Jona[5], Benj[4], Wm[3], John[2], **WmRed**)

........................................................................................

Bradford
Ebenezer[6] (John[5], Thos[4], Job[3], **ThoHav**)    Ebenezer[6]    Ebenezer[6]
John[6]   (    "     "     "     "    )                                 John[6]
Joshua[6]  (    "     "     "     "    )                               Joshua[6]
Nathaniel[6] ( "     "     "     "    )                          Nathaniel[6]
Samuel[7] (Eben[6], "    "     "     "    )
Elisha[7] (   "    "    "    "     "    )
Nathaniel[7] (Eben[6], Nathl[5], Jas[4], Jona[3], **ThoHav**)
Hannah[W6], relict of Ebenezer[6], above.
Moses[7] (Josh[6], John[5], Thos[4], Job[3], **ThoHav**)
Margaret[W7] (Aiken), relict of Saml[7] above.
True[7] (**Tho[6-2]Hav**)
Phebe[W6] (Brockway). relict of John[6], above.
Anna[W6], relict of Joshua[6] above.
Joshua[7] (Josh[6], John[5], Thos[4], Job[3], **ThoHav**)
John[7] H. (   "    "    "    "     "    )

........................................................................................

Chichester
Samuel[5] (Jabez[4], Ephr[3], **JohnSal**)                               Samuel[5]
Benjamin[6] (Jonathan[5-3], **ThoHav**)

........................................................................................

Concord
Thomas[5A] (**Tho[4-2]Hav**)                         Thomas[5A]
Moses[6] (**Tho[5A-2]Hav**)                                    Moses[6]
Mary[W5] (Molly) (Swain), relict of Thos[5A].
??Sally, b. 1766-84.
Calvin[7] (Cal[6A], Dar[5A-4], Thos[2], **JohnDed**)
John[7] (Dav[6], Eben[5], Benj[4], Wm[3], John[2], **WmRed**)
Nathan[8] (John[7-6], Elisha[5], Saml[4], **John[3-1]Sal**)
P. R., b. 1825, N.H.
Ephraim[7] (Hen[6], Ephr[5], Hen[4], Ephr[3] **John[2-1]Sal**)
?? Harriet, b. 1805, N.H.
?? Catharine J. b.1812, N.H.

........................................................................................

Dunbarton
Samuel[6] (Itha[5], Saml[4], Job[3], **ThoHav**)                         Samuel[6]
?? Elizabeth J., b. 1822.

# NEW HAMPSHIRE

| 1810 | 1820 | 1830 | 1840 | 1850 |
|------|------|------|------|------|

**Merrimack Co.**

| 1810 | 1820 | 1830 | 1840 | 1850 |
|------|------|------|------|------|
| | | Moses<br>Asa[7] | Asa[7] | |

| 1810 | 1820 | 1830 | 1840 | 1850 |
|------|------|------|------|------|
| John[6]<br>Joshua[6] | John[6]<br>Joshua[6] | Joshua[6] | Joshua[6] | |
| Samuel[7] | Samuel[7]<br>Elisha[7]<br>Nathaniel[7]<br>Hannah[w6]<br>Moses[7] | Elisha[7] | Elisha[7] | Elisha[7] |
| | | Widow M.[w7] | Margaret[w7]<br>True[7] | Margaret[w7]<br>Truman[7]<br>Phebe[w6]<br>Anna[w6]<br>Joshua[7]<br>John[7] H. |

Benjamin[6]

| 1810 | 1820 | 1830 | 1840 | 1850 |
|------|------|------|------|------|
| Moses[6]<br>Mary[w5]<br>Sally | | | Calvin[7]<br>John[7]<br>Nathan[8] | Calvin[7]<br>John[7]<br><br>P.R.<br>Ephraim[7]<br>Harriet<br>Catherine J. |

| 1810 | 1820 | 1830 | 1840 | 1850 |
|------|------|------|------|------|
| | | | | Elizabeth J. |

# NEW HAMPSHIRE

|  | 1790 | 1800 |
|---|---|---|

**Merrimack Co.** (cont.)

### Franklin
Wheeler$^7$ (Wm$^6$, Thos$^5$, **John$^{4-1}$Sal**)
Horace$^8$ P. (Wheel$^7$. "　　　"　　　"　　　)

..........................................................................................

### Henniker
?? John　　　　　　　　　　　　John
Page$^6$ (Obad$^5$, Saml$^4$, Job$^3$ **ThoHav**)
Peter$^7$ (Page$^6$, "　　"　　　"　　　"　　)

..........................................................................................

### Hopkinton
John$^5$ (Thos$^4$, Job$^3$, **ThoHav**)　　　　John$^5$　　　John$^5$
Nathaniel$^6$ (Nathl$^5$, Jas$^4$, Jona$^3$, **ThoHav**)　　　　Nathaniel$^6$
Thomas$^6$ (**Tho$^{5-2}$Hav**)　　　　　　　　Thomas$^6$
Benjamin$^6$ (Obad$^5$, Saml$^4$, Job$^3$, **ThoHav**)　　Benjamin$^6$
Phebe$^{W6}$, relict of Benj$^6$ above.
Nathaniel$^6$ (John$^5$, Thos$^4$, Job$^3$, **ThoHav**)
Phebe$^7$? (John$^{6-5}$, Thos$^4$, Job$^3$, **ThoHav**)
Ichabod$^6$, (Nathl$^5$, Jas$^4$, Jona$^3$, **ThoHav**)
Joseph$^6$ (Itha$^5$, Saml$^4$, Job$^3$, **ThoHav**)
Moses$^6$ (**Tho$^{5-2}$Hav**)
Moses$^7$ (Nathl$^6$, John$^5$, Thos$^4$, Job$^3$, **ThoHav**)
Peter$^6$ (**ThoHav**)
Thomas$^7$ (Nathl$^6$, John$^5$, Thos$^4$, Job$^3$, **ThoHav**)
David$^8$ M. (Mose$^7$, Nathl$^6$, John$^5$, Tho$^4$, Job$^3$, **ThoHav**)
Jubal$^7$ (Elij$^6$, Nathl$^5$, Jas$^4$, Jona$^3$, **ThoHav**)
Nathaniel$^7$ (Icha$^6$, "　　"　　"　　　"　　)
Richard$^7$ (　"　　"　　"　　"　　　"　　)
Ichabod$^7$ (　"　　"　　"　　"　　　"　　)
Molly/Polly$^7$ (**Tho$^{6-2}$Hav**)

..........................................................................................

### Newbury (once Fisherfield)
John$^7$ (John$^{6-5}$, Thos$^4$, Job$^3$, **ThoHav**)
Moses$^7$ (Josh$^6$, John$^5$, Thos$^4$, Job$^3$, **ThoHav**)
?? William A., b. 1790s.
Eben$^7$ (John$^{6-5}$, Thos$^4$, Job$^3$, **ThoHav**)
George$^8$? (Mose$^7$, Josh$^6$, John$^5$. Tho$^4$, Job$^3$, **ThoHav**)
Lydia$^{W7}$, relict of James$^7$ (John$^{6-5}$, "　　"　　　"　)

..........................................................................................

### Pembroke
Joseph$^7$ C. (Nathl$^{6-5}$, Wm$^4$, Nathl$^3$, Jona$^{2-}$, **JonaRed**)
?? Cynthia, b. 1805, N.H.

# NEW HAMPSHIRE

| 1810 | 1820 | 1830 | 1840 | 1850 |
|---|---|---|---|---|

**Merrimack Co.** (cont.)

| 1810 | 1820 | 1830 | 1840 | 1850 |
|---|---|---|---|---|
|  |  |  | Wheeler[7] | Wheeler[7] Horace[8] P. |

....................................................................................................

| 1810 | 1820 | 1830 | 1840 | 1850 |
|---|---|---|---|---|
|  | Page[6] |  |  | Page[6] Peter[7] |

....................................................................................................

| 1810 | 1820 | 1830 | 1840 | 1850 |
|---|---|---|---|---|
| John[5] |  |  |  |  |
| Thomas[6] | Thomas[6] | Thomas[6] | Thomas[6] |  |
| Benjamin[6] |  |  |  |  |
| Phebe[W6] | Phebe[W6] | Phebe[W6] | Phebe[W6] | Phebe[W6] |
| Nathaniel[6] | Nathaniel[6] |  |  |  |
| Phebe[7] |  |  |  |  |
|  | Ichabod[6] | Ichabod[6] |  | Ichabod[6] |
|  | Joseph[6] |  |  |  |
|  | Moses[6] | Moses[6] | Moses[6] | Moses[6] |
|  | Moses[7] | Moses[7] |  |  |
|  | Peter[6] |  |  |  |
|  | Thomas[7] | Thomas[7] | Thomas[7] | Thomas[7] |
|  |  |  | David[8] M. | David[8] M. |
|  |  |  | Jubal[7] |  |
|  |  |  | Nathaniel[7] |  |
|  |  |  | Richard[7] |  |
|  |  |  | Ichabod[7] | Ichabod[7] |
|  |  |  |  | Polly[7] |

....................................................................................................

| 1810 | 1820 | 1830 | 1840 | 1850 |
|---|---|---|---|---|
|  |  | John[7] | John[7] |  |
|  |  | Moses[7] | Moses[7] | Moses[7] |
|  |  | William A. | William A. |  |
|  |  |  | Eben[7] | Ebenezer[7] |
|  |  |  |  | George[8] |
|  |  |  |  | Lydia[W7] |

....................................................................................................

| 1810 | 1820 | 1830 | 1840 | 1850 |
|---|---|---|---|---|
|  |  |  |  | Joseph[7] C. Cynthia |

# NEW HAMPSHIRE

|  | 1790 | 1800 |
|---|---|---|

**Merrimack Co.** (cont.)

Pittsfield
John$^6$ (Elish$^5$, Saml$^4$, **John$^{3\text{-}1}$Sal**) — John$^6$ — John$^6$
Jonathan$^5$ ( "        "        ) — Jonathan$^5$ — Jonathan$^5$
Daniel$^5$    (Danl$^{4A}$,        "        ) — Daniel$^5$ — Daniel$^5$
John$^7$ (John$^6$, Elish$^5$, Saml$^4$, **John$^{3\text{-}1}$Sal**) — — John$^7$, Jr.
Thomas$^6$ (Jona$^5$, Saml$^4$, **John$^{3\text{-}1}$Sal**) — — Thomas$^6$
Anna$^{W5}$, relict of Jonathan$^5$.
Hannah$^{W6}$, widow of Elisha$^{6\text{-}5}$, Sam$^4$, **John$^{3\text{-}1}$Sal**)
Jonathan$^7$ (John$^6$ Elish$^5$, Saml$^4$, **John$^{3\text{-}1}$Sal**)
Daniel$^6$ (Danl$^{5\text{-}4A}$, **John$^{3\text{-}1}$Sal**)
?? Betsey, b. 1780s.
Jonathan$^7$ (Thos$^6$, Jona$^5$, Saml$^4$, **John$^{3\text{-}1}$Sal**)
Nathan$^8$ (John$^{7\text{-}6}$, Elisha$^5$, Saml$^4$, **John$^{3\text{-}1}$Sal**)
Stephen$^7$ (Elish$^{6\text{-}5}$, Saml$^4$, **John$^{3\text{-}1}$Sal**)
Jacob$^7$ (John$^6$, Elish$^5$, Saml$^4$, **John$^{3\text{-}1}$Sal**)
?? Elisha, b. 1810s.
Perkins$^8$ (John$^{7\text{-}6}$, Elish$^5$, Saml$^4$. **John$^{3\text{-}1}$Sal**)
Darius$^7$ (Aaron$^6$, Thos$^5$, **John$^{4\text{-}1}$**)
John$^8$ S. (John$^{7\text{-}6}$, Elish$^5$, Sam$^4$, **John$^{3\text{-}1}$Sal**)
Trueworthy$^8$ ( "        "        "        "        )
John$^8$ (Jacb$^7$, John$^6$,    "        "        "        )
Mark$^8$ F. (Steph$^7$, Elish$^{6\text{-}5}$,    "        "        )

..............................................................................

Salisbury
Levi$^6$ (Benj$^5$, **John$^{4\text{-}1}$Sal**) — Levi$^6$
Samuel$^6$    (Job$^5$, Saml$^4$, Job$^3$, **ThoHav**) — — Samuel$^6$
Jesse$^7$ (Saml$^6$, "        "        "        "        )
John$^7$ L. ( $^6$    "        "        "        "        )
Jubal$^7$ (Elij$^6$, Nathl$^5$, Jas$^4$, Jona$^3$,    "    )
?? Moses, b. 1791, N.H.

..............................................................................

Sutton
David$^5$    (Benj$^4$, Wm$^3$, John$^2$, **WmRed**) — David$^5$ — David$^5$
Jonathan$^6$ (Dav$^5$, " ,    "        "        "    ) — — Jonathan$^6$
John$^6$ (Nathl$^5$, Jas$^4$, Jona$^3$, **ThoHav**) — — John$^5$
Ebenezer$^6$ (Nathl$^5$, Jas$^4$, Jona$^3$, **ThoHav**)
Elijah$^6$ (    "        "        "        "        )
Nathaniel$^6$ (    "        "        "        "        )
Elizabeth$^{W6}$ (Vose), relict of Elijah.
John$^7$ (John$^6$, Nathl$^5$, Jas$^4$, Jona$^3$, **ThoHav**)
Carlos$^7$ (Elij$^6$,    "        "        "        "        )

# NEW HAMPSHIRE

| 1810 | 1820 | 1830 | 1840 | 1850 |
|---|---|---|---|---|

**Merrimack Co.**

| 1810 | 1820 | 1830 | 1840 | 1850 |
|---|---|---|---|---|
| John[6] | | | | |
| Daniel[5] | | | | |
| John[7], Jr. | John[7], Jr. | John[7], Jr. | John[7] | John[7] Jr. |
| Thomas[6] | Thomas[6] | Thomas[6] | Thomas[6] | Thomas[6] |
| Anna[w5] | | | | |
| "Widow" | | | | |
| Jonathan[7] | | | | |
| | Daniel[6] | | | |
| | | Betsey | Betsey | Betsey |
| | | Jonathan[7] | Jonathan[7] | Jonathan[7] |
| | | Nathan[8] | | |
| | | Stephen[7] | Stephen[7] | |
| | | | Jacob[7] | |
| | | | Elisha | |
| | | | | Perkins[8] |
| | | | | Darius[7] |
| | | | | John[8] |
| | | | | Trueworthy[8] |
| | | | | John[8] M. |
| | | | | Mark[8] F. |

| 1810 | 1820 | 1830 | 1840 | 1850 |
|---|---|---|---|---|
| Samuel | Samuel[6] | | | |
| | | Jesse[7] | Jesse[7] | Jesse[7] |
| | | John[7] L. | John[7] L. | |
| | | Jubal[7] | | |
| | | | | Moses |

| 1810 | 1820 | 1830 | 1840 | 1850 |
|---|---|---|---|---|
| Ebenezer[6] | | | | |
| Elijah[6] | | | | |
| Nathaniel[6] | Nathaniel[6] | Nathaniel[6] | Nathaniel[6] | Nathaniel[6] |
| | Elizabeth[W6] | Elizabeth[W6] | | |
| | | John[7] | John[7] | John[7] |
| | | | Carlos[7] | Carlos[7] |

# NEW HAMPSHIRE

| | 1790 | 1800 |
|---|---|---|

**Merrimack Co.** (concl.)

Warner

Ebenezer[6] ? Cf. adjoining Bradford.　　　　　　　　　　Ebenezer[6]
Thomas[6] (**Tho[5A-2]Hav**)　　　　　　　　　　　　　　Thomas[6]
Frederick[7] (John[6], Nathl[5], Jas[4], Jona[3], **ThoHav**)
Leonard[7]　(Nathl[6],　　"　　　"　　　"　　　　"　　)
Elijah[7]　　(Elijah[6],　"　　　"　　　"　　　　"　　)
Jubal[7]　　(　　"　　　"　　　"　　　"　　　　"　　)
Fanny[W7] (Sawyer), relict of Elijah[7] above.

===========================================================

**Rockingham Co.** (Begin)

　　　　　　　　　　　　　　　　　　　　　　　　　* * * * * * *
Atkinson　　　　　　　　　　　　　　　　　　　　　* Lost *
Abijah[6] (Tim[5], Jas[4] Jona[3], **ThoHav**)　　　　　* * * * * * *

...........................................................

Auburn (set off from Chester)
Edward[7] (Ben[6], Wm[5], Ben[4], Wm[3], John[2], **WmRed**)
Lyman[7] (　"　　"　　"　　"　　"　　　　"　　)
Sarah[7] (　"　　"　　"　　"　　"　　　　"　　)

...........................................................

Candia
Abigail[W4], relict of Rev. Benj[4].　　　　　　Abigail[W4]
Benjamin[6] (Wm[5], Ben[4], Wm[3], John[2], **WmRed**) Benjamin[6]
Jesse[5] (Ben[4], Wm[3], John[2], **WmRed**)　　　Jesse[5]　　　Jesse[5]
?? John　　　　　　　　　　　　　　　　　　John
Ephraim[5] (Ephr[4-3], **JohnSal**)　　　　　　Ephraim[5]　　Ephraim[5]
Paul[5A] (Jabez[4A], Ephr[3],　"　)　　　　　Paul[5A]　　　Paul[5A]
Henry[6] T. (Paul[5A], Jab[4A], Ephr[3], **JohnSal**)　　　　H.[6] True
Henry[6] (Eph[5], Hen[4], Eph[3], **JohnSal**)
Peter[6] (　"　　"　　"　　"　)
Jesse[6] (Jess[5], Ben[4], Wm[3], John[2], **WmRed**)
Eben[6] (　"　　"　　"　　"　　"　)
Henry[7] M. (Hen[6], Eph[5], Hen[4], Eph[3], **JohnSal**)
Henry[7] S. (H.T.[6], Paul[5A], Jab[4],　"　　"　)
True[7] (　"　　"　　"　　"　　"　)
Sarah[W6], relict of Ebenezer[6], above.

# NEW HAMPSHIRE

| 1810 | 1820 | 1830 | 1840 | 1850 |
|------|------|------|------|------|

**Merrimack Co.** (concl.)

|  |  | Frederick[7] | Frederick[7] | Frederick[7] |
|  |  | Leonard[7] | Leonard[7] | Leonard[7] |
|  |  |  | Elijah[7] |  |
|  |  |  |  | Jubal[7] |
|  |  |  |  | Fanny[w7] |

=============================================================

**Rockingham Co.** (Begin)

Abijah[6]
...........................................................................................................

|  |  | Edward[7] D. | Edward[7] D. | Edward[7] D. |
|  |  |  |  | Lyman[7] |
|  |  |  |  | Sarah[7] |

...........................................................................................................

| Ephraim[5] | Ephraim[5] |  |  |  |
| Paul[5A] |  |  |  |  |
| H[6]. True | Henry[6] T. | Henry[6] T. | Henry[6] T. | Henry[6] T. |
| Henry[6] | Henry[6] | Henry[6] | Henry[6] | Henry[6] |
|  | Peter[6] | Peter[6] | Peter[6] |  |
| Jesse[6] | Jesse[6] | Jesse[6] | Jesse[6] | Jesse[6] |
|  |  | Ebenezer[6] | Eben[6] |  |
|  |  |  | Henry[7] M. | Henry[7] M. |
|  |  |  | Henry[7] S. | Henry[7] S. |
|  |  |  | True[7] | True[7] |
|  |  |  |  | Sarah[W6] |

# NEW HAMPSHIRE

|  | 1790 | 1800 |
|---|---|---|

**Rockingham Co.** (cont.)

Chester
Alexander[6] (Jas[5], Ben[4], Wm[3], John[2], **WmRed**) Alexander[6]   Alexander[6]
Benjamin[6] (Jona[5], " " " " )
Benjamin[6] (Wm[5], " " " " )
William[6] (Jona[5], " " " " )
Cyrus[7] (Jona[6], Dav[5], " " " " )

Danville (formerly "Hawke")
Jabez[6] (Jos[5A], John[4A], Jos[3], **JohnSal**) Jabez[6] Jabez[6]
Joseph[6] T. ( " " " " ) Joseph[6] T. Joseph[6] T.
Samuel[7] (Jab[6], " " " " )

Derry
Alexander[6] (Jas[5], Ben[4], Wm[3], John[2], **WmRed**)

East Kingston
Jacob[6] (Itha[3], Saml[4], Job[3], **ThoHav**)
Nathan[7] (Jac[6], " " " " )
Merchant[7] ( " " " " " )
Ruth[W7] (Martain), wife of Nathan[7].

Epping
John[8] S. ? (John[7-6], Elish[5], Sam[4], **John[3-1]Sal**)

Exeter
Jeremiah[6] ? (Jerem[5A-4], Wm[3], John[2], **WmRed**) Jeremiah[6]

Hampstead
James[6] (Jona[5], Ben[4], Wm[3], John[2], **WmRed**)
?? Sarah.
Ithamar[7] (Saml[6], Ith[5], Saml[4], Job[3], **ThoHav**)

Kensington
Abraham[8] (Jona[7], John[6], Elish[5], Saml[4], **John[3-1]Sal**)
?? Mary, b. 1830, N.H.

Kingston
Abraham[8] (Jona[7], John[6], Elish[5], Saml[4], **John[3-1]Sal**)

Londonderry         \* \* \* \* \* \* \*
Alexander[6] (Jas[5], Ben[4], Wm[3], John[2], **WmRed**) \* Scheds\*
Joseph[7] (Alex[6], " " " " " ) \* lost \*
Abigail[W7], relict of Joseph[7], just above. \* \* \* \* \* \* \*

# NEW HAMPSHIRE

| 1810 | 1820 | 1830 | 1840 | 1850 |
|------|------|------|------|------|

**Rockingham Co.** (cont.)

| 1810 | 1820 | 1830 | 1840 | 1850 |
|------|------|------|------|------|
| Benjamin[6] | Benjamin[6] Benjamin[6] | Benjamin[6] Benjamin[6] William[6] | Benjamin[6] | |
| | | | Cyrus[6] | |
| Jabez[6] | Jabez[6] | Jabez[6] | | |
| | | | | Samuel[7] |
| | | Alexander[6] | | |
| Jacob[6] | Jacob[6] Nathan[7] | Jacob[6] Nathan[7] Merchant[7] | Jacob[6] Nathan[7] Merchant[7] | Nathan[7] Merchant[7] Ruth[W7] |
| | | | | John[8] B. |
| Jeremiah[6] | Jeremiah[6] | | | |
| James[6] Sarah | | | | |
| | | | Ithamar[7] | Ithamar[7] |
| | | | Abraham[8] | Abraham[8] Mary |
| | | Abraham[8] | | |
| Alexander[6] | Alexander[6] Joseph[7] | Joseph[7] | Joseph[7] | |
| | | | | Abigail[W7] |

# NEW HAMPSHIRE

|                | 1790 | 1800 |
|----------------|------|------|

**Rockingham Co.** (cont.)

### Newton
?? Diana, b. 1810, Mass.

### Plaistow

| | 1790 | 1800 |
|---|---|---|
| Daniel[6] (Jona[5], Ben[4], Wm[3], John[2], **WmRed**) | Daniel[6] | * * * * * * |
| Jesse[6] (Job[5], Saml[4], Job[3], **ThoHav**) | Jesse[6] | *        * |
| Job[6]   (    "      "      "        "      ) | Job[6] | *        * |
| James[6]  (    "      "      "        "      ) |  | *  Sche-  * |
| Daniel[7] (Jas[6],  "      "      "      ) |  | *        * |
| Alonzo[7] (    "      "      "      "      "      ) |  | *  dules  * |
| Samuel[7A] (Jess[6],  "      "      "      ) |  | *        * |
| Jonathan[6] (Amos[5], Jona[4-3], **ThoHav**) |  | *        * |
| Elizabeth[W7A], 2d wife of Saml[7A] above. |  | *  Lost  * |
| John[7] G. (Jona[6], Amos[5], Jona[4-3], **ThoHav**) |  | *        * |
| Sarah[W6] (Dow), relict of James[6] above. |  | *        * |
| Susan[W6], relict of Jona[6] above. |  | * * * * * * |

### Poplin
?? Joseph, b. 1760s or 1810s.

### Portsmouth

| | 1790 | 1800 |
|---|---|---|
| Daniel[6] (Jos[5], Wm[4], **John[3-1]Sal**) |  | Daniel[6] |

### Sandown

| | 1790 | 1800 |
|---|---|---|
| Ezekiel[5]    (Jona[4], **John[3-1]Sal**) | Ezekiel[5] | Ezekiel[5] |
| James[6]   (Ezek[5],  "       " ) | James[6] | James[6] |
| Joshua[7] (Jas[6],  "       "       " ) |  |  |
| Hannah[W6], relict of James[6] above. |  |  |
| James[8] (Josh[7], Jas[6], Ezek[5], Jona[4], **John[3-1]Sal**) |  |  |

### Seabrook

| | 1790 | 1800 |
|---|---|---|
| John[5] (**John[4-1]Sal**) | John[5] | * * * * * * |
| William[5] (  "  ) | William[5] | *        * |
| Thomas[5] (  "  ) | Thomas[5] | *        * |
| Wyman[5] (  "  ) | Wyman[5] | *  Sche-  * |
| Joseph[5] (  "  ) | Joseph[5] | *        * |
| David[5] (Saml[4], **John[3-1]Sal**) | David[5] | *  dules  * |
| Samuel[5] (Jabez[4A], Ephr[3], **JohnSal**) | Samuel[5] | *        * |
| Ebenezer[6] (**John[5-1]Sal**) | Ebenezer[6] | *        * |
| Jane[W5], wife of William[5]. | Jane[W5] | *  Lost  * |
| Jabez[5] (Jab[4A], Eph[3], **JohnSal**) | Jabez[5] | *        * |
| Ephraim[6] (Benj[5], **John[4-1]Sal**) | Ephraim[6] | *        * |
| Joshua[5] (Jab[4A], Eph[3], **JohnSal**) | Joshua[5] | *        * |

# NEW HAMPSHIRE

| 1810 | 1820 | 1830 | 1840 | 1850 |
|------|------|------|------|------|

**Rockingham Co.** (cont.)

| 1810 | 1820 | 1830 | 1840 | 1850 |
|------|------|------|------|------|
|  |  |  |  | Diana |
| ............ | ............ | ............ | ............ | ............ |
| Jesse[6] |  | Jesse[6] |  |  |
|  | James[6] | James[6] | James[6] | Daniel[7] |
|  |  |  | Daniel[7] |  |
|  |  |  | Alonzo[7] |  |
|  |  | Samuel[7A] | Samuel[7A] |  |
|  |  |  | Jonathan[6] |  |
|  |  |  |  | Elizabeth[W7A] |
|  |  |  |  | John[7] G. |
|  |  |  |  | Sarah[W6] |
|  |  |  |  | Susan[W6] |
| ............ | ............ | ............ | ............ | ............ |
|  |  |  | Joseph |  |
| ............ | ............ | ............ | ............ | ............ |
| Daniel[6] |  |  |  |  |
| ............ | ............ | ............ | ............ | ............ |
| Ezekiel[5] |  |  |  |  |
| James[6] | James[6] | James[6] |  |  |
| Joshua[7] | Joshua[7] | Joshua[7] | Joshua[7] | Joshua[7] |
|  |  |  | Hannah[W6] |  |
|  |  |  |  | James[8] |
| ............ | ............ | ............ | ............ | ............ |
| Ebenezer[6] |  |  |  |  |
| Ephraim[6] | Ephraim[6] |  |  |  |
| Joshua[5] | Joshua[5] | Joshua[5] |  |  |

# NEW HAMPSHIRE

|  | 1790 | 1800 |
|---|---|---|

**Rockingham Co.** (cont.)

  Seabrook  (cont.)                                 * * * * * *

Winthrop$^6$ (Benj$^5$, **John$^{4\text{-}1}$Sal**)        Winthrop$^6$     *          *

David$^6$ (Dav$^5$, Saml$^4$, **John$^{3\text{-}1}$Sal**)  David$^6$       *          *

Silvanus$^6$ (**John$^{5\text{-}1}$Sal**)           Silvanus$^6$    *          *

William$^6$ (Thos$^5$, **John$^{4\text{-}1}$Sal**)    William$^6$     *          *

William$^6$ (Dav$^5$, Saml$^4$, **John$^{3\text{-}1}$**)  William$^6$ 3d  *  Sche-  *

Bryant$^6$ (Thos$^5$, **John$^{4\text{-}1}$Sal**)     Bryant$^6$      *          *

Reuben$^7$ (Eben$^6$, **John$^{5\text{-}1}$Sal**)    Reuben$^7$     *  dules *

Samuel$^6$ W. (Wm$^5$, **John$^{4\text{-}1}$Sal**)  Samuel$^6$ W.  *         *

John$^6$ (**John$^{5\text{-}1}$Sal**)             John$^6$, Jr.   *         *

Samuel$^6$ Perley (Benj$^5$, **John$^{4\text{-}1}$Sal**) Samuel$^6$ P.  *         *

Benjamin$^6$ (**John$^{5\text{-}1}$Sal**)                          *         *

Jonathan$^6$ (Joseph$^5$, **John$^{4\text{-}1}$Sal**)                *         *

Henry$^7$ (Eben$^6$, **John$^{5\text{-}1}$Sal**)                  *         *

Moses$^7$ (     "        "       )               *  Lost  *

Simeon$^6$ (Wyman$^5$, **John$^{4\text{-}1}$Sal**)              *         *

Thomas$^7$ (Eben$^6$, **John$^{5\text{-}1}$Sal**)                  *         *

Jabez$^6$ (Josh$^5$, Jab$^{4A}$, Eph$^3$, **JohnSal**)    *

Jonathan$^8$ ? (Wm$^7$, Eben$^6$, **John$^{5\text{-}1}$Sal**)  *         *

Abraham$^7$ (Dav$^{6\text{-}5}$, Saml$^4$, **John$^{3\text{-}1}$Sal**)  *         *

Samuel$^7$ (**John$^{6\text{-}1}$Sal**)                       *         *

Wyman$^7$ (Simeon$^6$, Wym$^5$, **John$^{4\text{-}1}$Sal**)  *         *

Hannah$^{W6}$ (Fowler)(Souther), relict of John$^6$, above.  *    *

Jonathan$^7$, Jr. (Winth$^6$, Benj$^5$, **John$^{4\text{-}1}$**)     *

Joshua$^6$ (Josh$^5$, Jabez$^{4A}$, Eph$^3$, **JohnSal**)

Ephraim$^7$ (Eph$^6$, Ben$^5$, **John$^{4\text{-}1}$Sal**)

Polly$^{W7}$, relict of Sam$^7$ (**John$^{6\text{-}1}$Sal**)

Joseph$^7$ R. (Dav$^{6\text{-}5}$, Saml$^4$, **John$^{3\text{-}1}$Sal**)

Daniel$^7$   (     "      "      "       )

Henry$^8$ (Hen$^7$, Eben$^6$, **John$^{5\text{-}1}$Sal**)

Christopher$^7$ (Silv$^6$, **John$^{5\text{-}1}$Sal**)

Jacob$^7$ (**John$^{6\text{-}1}$Sal**)

Grace$^{W6}$ (Beckman), relict of Benj$^6$, above.

Sally$^{W6}$ (Bagley), relict of Bryant$^6$, above.

Winthrop$^7$ (Winth$^6$, Benj$^5$, **John$^{4\text{-}1}$Sal**)

Thomas$^8$ (Tho$^7$, Eben$^6$, **John$^{5\text{-}1}$Sal**)

Trueworthy$^8$ (Hen$^7$, "      "       )

Caleb$^8$    (Thos$^7$,    "      "       )

Joshua$^8$ (    "      "      "       )

Samuel$^7$ (Saml$^6$, Dav$^5$, Saml$^4$, **John$^{3\text{-}1}$Sal**)

Jeremiah$^7$ (Simeon$^6$, Wym$^5$, **John$^{4\text{-}1}$Sal**)

Israel$^7$ (Benj$^6$, **John$^{5\text{-}1}$Sal**)

Chase$^8$ (Thos$^7$, Eben$^6$, **John$^{5\text{-}1}$Sal**)

# NEW HAMPSHIRE

| 1810 | 1820 | 1830 | 1840 | 1850 |
|------|------|------|------|------|

**Rockingham Co.** (cont.)

| 1810 | 1820 | 1830 | 1840 | 1850 |
|------|------|------|------|------|
| Winthrop$^6$ | Winthrop$^6$ | Winthrop$^6$ | Winthrop$^6$ | |
| David$^6$ | David$^6$ | David$^6$ | | |
| Silvanus$^6$ | Silvanus$^6$ | Venus$^6$ | | |
| | | | | |
| Bryant$^6$ | Bryant$^6$ | | | |
| | | | | |
| John$^6$ | | | | |
| | | Perley$^6$ | | |
| Benjamin$^6$ | Benjamin$^6$ | | | |
| Jonathan$^6$ | Jonathan$^6$ | Jonathan$^6$ | | |
| Henry$^7$ | Henry$^7$ | Henry$^7$ | | |
| Moses$^7$ | Moses$^7$ | Moses$^7$ | Moses$^7$ | Moses$^7$ |
| Simeon$^6$ | Simeon$^6$ | Simeon$^6$ | Simeon$^6$ | Simeon$^6$ |
| Thomas$^7$ | Thomas$^7$ | | | |
| Jabez$^6$ | Jabez$^6$ | Jabez$^6$ | | |
| Jonathan$^8$ | | | | |
| Abraham$^7$ | Abraham$^7$ | Abraham$^7$ | Abraham$^7$ | Abraham$^7$ |
| Samuel$^7$ | | | | |
| Wyman$^7$ | Wyman$^7$ | | | |
| | Hannah$^{W6}$ | | | |
| | Jonathan$^7$ | Jonathan$^7$ | | |
| | Joshua$^6$ | Joshua$^6$ | Joshua$^6$ | Joshua$^6$ |
| | Ephraim$^7$ | Ephraim$^7$ | | |
| | Polly$^{W7}$ | Polly$^{W7}$ | | |
| | Joseph$^7$ | Joseph$^7$ | Joseph$^7$ R. | Joseph$^7$ R. |
| | Daniel$^7$ | Daniel$^7$ | Daniel$^7$ | Daniel$^7$ |
| | Henry$^8$ | Henry$^8$ | Henry$^8$ | |
| | Christopher$^7$ | Christopher$^7$ | Christopher$^7$ | Christopher$^7$ |
| | Jacob$^7$ | Jacob$^7$ | | |
| | | Gracey$^{W6}$ | Grace$^{W6}$ W. | |
| | | Sally$^{w6}$ | | |
| | | Winthrop$^7$ | | |
| | | Thomas$^8$ | Thomas$^8$ | |
| | | Trueworthy$^8$ | True$^8$ | True$^8$ |
| | | Caleb$^8$ | | |
| | | Joshua$^8$ | Joshua$^8$ | Joshua$^8$ |
| | | Samuel$^7$ | Samuel$^7$ | Samuel$^7$ |
| | | Jeremiah$^7$ | | |
| | | Israel$^7$ | Israel$^7$ | Israel$^7$ |
| | | Chase$^8$ | Chase$^8$ | |

# NEW HAMPSHIRE

|  | 1790 | 1800 |
|--|------|------|

**Rockingham Co**. (cont.)

Seabrook (concl.)
?? James, Jr.
Moses[8] (Hen[7], Eben[6], **John[5-1]Sal**)
William[8] (Thos[7], "          "          )
Oliver[7] (Jab[6], Josh[5], Jab[4], Eph[3], **JohnSal**)
Mary[W8], relict of Caleb[8] above.
Mehitable[W7] (Dow), relict of Winth[7], above.
Cyrus[8] (Chris[7], Silv[6], **John[5-1]Sal**)
?? Gilbert, b. 1770s.
Archelaus[7] (Jona[6], Jos[5], **John[4-1]**)
??William 3d, b. 1810s.
?? Widow Betsey, b. 1800-09.
Joshua[7] (Wm[6], Thos[5], **John[4-1]Sal**)
Sarah[6+W7] (Dav[5], Sam[4], **John[3-1]Sal**), wife of Henry[7].
Jabez[7] (Jona[6], Jos[5], **John[4-1]Sal**)
John[7] M. ( "          "          "          )
Samuel[7], Jr. (" "          "          )
Ezekiel[8] (Abel[7], Silv[6],          "          )
Henry[9] (Hen[8-7], Eben[6], **John[5-1]Sal**)
Thomas[6] (Jona[5], Saml[7], **John[3-1]Sal**)
Winthrop[8]? (Saml[7], **John[6-1]Sal**)
Lowell[8] (Hen[7], Eben[6], **John[5-1]Sal**)
Reuben[8] (Thos[7],          "          "          )
Dearborn[8] (Hen[7], "          "          )
Edwin[7] (Jab[6], Josh[5], Jab[4], Eph[3], **JohnSal**)
Louisa[W9] (Felch), relict of Lewis[9] C.
Elizabeth[7] S. (Benj[6], **John[5-1]Sal**)
Jonathan[8] G. (Jona[7], Wm[6], Ben[5], **John[41]Sal**)
Phebe[7] ( Winth[6], Benj[5], **John[4-1]Sal**)
Washington[8] (Win[7-6], ",          "          )
Susanna[W6] (Beckman), relict of Jabez[6].
Robert[9] (Hen[8-7], Eben[6], **John[5-1]Sal**)
Polly[W7] (Dow), relict of Samuel[7].
Thomas[9] (Thos[8-7], Eben[6]. **John[5-1]Sal**)
?? Sarah, b. 1779, N.H.
Jacob[8] (Jacob[7], **John[6-1]Sal**)
Moses[9] D. (Henry[8-7], Eben[6], **John[5-1]**)
Reuben[9] (Josh[8], Thos[7], "          " )
Henry[9]          (Henry[8-7], "          " )
Jacob[8] (Wym[7], Sim[6], Wym[5], **John[4-1]**)
Isaiah[9] (Thos[8-7], Eben[6], **John[5-1]Sal**)
Nancy[7] A. ? (Thos[6], Jona[5], Saml[4], **John[3-1]Sal**)

# NEW HAMPSHIRE

| 1810 | 1820 | 1830 | 1840 | 1850 |
|------|------|------|------|------|

**Rockingham Co.**

|  |  |  |  |  |
|--|--|--|--|--|
|  |  | James, Jr. |  |  |
|  |  | Moses, Jr. | Moses, Jr. | Moses, Jr. |
|  |  | William[8] | William[2] | William[8] |
|  |  |  | Oliver[7] | Oliver[7] |
|  |  |  | Mary[W8] |  |
|  |  |  | Mehitable[7] |  |
|  |  |  | Cyrus[8] |  |
|  |  |  | Gilbert |  |
|  |  |  | Archelaus[7] |  |
|  |  |  | William 3d |  |
|  |  |  | Widow Betsey |  |
|  |  |  | Joshua[7] 2d | Joshua[7] Jr. |
|  |  |  | Sarah[6] |  |
|  |  |  | Jabez[7] |  |
|  |  |  | John[7] M. | John[7] M. |
|  |  |  | Samuel[7] Jr. |  |
|  |  |  | Ezekiel[8] | Ezekiel[9] |
|  |  |  | Henry[9] Jr. |  |
|  |  |  | Thomas[6] |  |
|  |  |  | Winthrop[8] |  |
|  |  |  | Lowell[8] | Lowell[8] |
|  |  |  | Reuben[8] D. | Reuben[8] D. |
|  |  |  | Dearborn[8] | Edward[8] D. |
|  |  |  |  | Edwin[7] |
|  |  |  |  | Louisa[W9] |
|  |  |  |  | Elizabeth[7] |
|  |  |  |  | Jonathan[9] G. |
|  |  |  |  | Phebe[7] |
|  |  |  |  | Washingon[8] |
|  |  |  |  | Susanna[W8] |
|  |  |  |  | Robert[9] |
|  |  |  |  | Polly[W7] |
|  |  |  |  | Thomas[9] |
|  |  |  |  | Sarah |
|  |  |  |  | Jacob[8] |
|  |  |  |  | Moses[9] D. |
|  |  |  |  | Reuben[9] |
|  |  |  |  | Henry[9] |
|  |  |  |  | Jacob[8] |
|  |  |  |  | Isaiah[9] |
|  |  |  |  | Nancy[7] |

# NEW HAMPSHIRE

|   | 1790 | 1800 |
|---|---|---|

**Rockingham Co.** (concl.)

South Hampton
Aaron[6] (Thos[5], **John[4-1]Sal**)
Levi[6] (Benj[5],          "      )
Moses[7] (Aar[6], Thos[5], "   )
Moses[7] (Benj[6], Wm[5], Benj[4], Wm[3], John[2], **WmRed**)
Mary[W6], relict of Levi[6], above.
Stephen[7A] J. (Levi[6], Benj[5], **John[4-1]Sal**)
Aaron[7] (Aar[6], Thos[5], **John[4-1]Sal**)
?? Betsey, b. 1777, N.H.
Jeremiah[8] W. (Mose[7], Aar[6], Thos[5], **John[4-1]Sal**)
S. Perley[7] (Levi[6], Benj[5], **John[4-1]Sal**)

====================================================================

**Strafford Co.**

Dover

Peter[7] (Dav[6], Eben[5], Saml[4], Job[3], **ThoHav**
William[6] ? (Lot[5], Noah[4-3], Jona[2], **JonaRed**)
?? Mary, b. 1828, N.H.

Farmington

Philander[7] (Silas[6-5], Noah[4], Jonas[3], John[2], **JonaRed**)

Lee

Dexter[7] (Luther[6], Noah[5-4], Jonas[3], John[2], **JonaRed**)

Milton

Stephen[8] B. (Nathn[7], Jacob[6], Itha[5], Saml[4], Job[3]. **ThoHav**)

Somersworth

| Francis | ) | |
|---|---|---|
| Moses | ) | These four household heads are listed as "Eatons" in 1790; |
| Samuel | ) | however., Francis is clearly a "Yeaton" from the Isles of |
| Trestin | ) | Shoals, and we believe the other three here are as well. |

# NEW HAMPSHIRE

| 1810 | 1820 | 1830 | 1840 | 1850 |
|------|------|------|------|------|

**Rockingham Co.**

| 1810 | 1820 | 1830 | 1840 | 1850 |
|------|------|------|------|------|
| Aaron[6] | Aaron[6] | Aaron[6] | Aaron[6] | Aaron[6] |
|  | Levi[6] | Levi[6] |  |  |
|  |  | Moses[7] | Moses[7] | Moses[7] |
|  |  | Moses[7] | Moses[7] | Moses[7] |
|  |  |  | Mary[w6] |  |
|  |  |  | Stephen[7A] A. | Stephen[7A] J. |
|  |  |  |  | Aaron[7] Jr. |
|  |  |  |  | Betsey |
|  |  |  |  | Jeremiah[8] W. |
|  |  |  |  | Perley[7] |

==================================================================

**Strafford Co.**

| 1810 | 1820 | 1830 | 1840 | 1850 |
|------|------|------|------|------|
|  |  | Peter[7] |  |  |
|  |  |  | William[6] | William[6] |
|  |  |  |  | Mary |
|  |  |  |  | Philander[7] |
|  |  |  | Dexter[7] | Dexter[7] |
|  |  |  |  | Stephen[8] B. |

# NEW HAMPSHIRE

|  | 1790 | 1800 |
|---|---|---|

**Sullivan Co.**

### Acworth

Darius$^7$ J. (Asa$^6$, Ben$^5$, Pearson$^4$, Jos$^{3A}$, John$^2$, **JonaRed**)

### Goshen

??David C., b. 1776-94.

### Grantham

Edward$^7$ P. (Alex$^6$, Jas$^5$, Ben$^4$, Wm$^3$, John$^2$, **WmRed**)
John$^6$　　(James$^5$, Benj$^4$, Wm$^3$, John$^2$, **WmRed**)
Moses$^7$　　(John$^6$,　　"　　"　　"　　　"　　)
John$^7$　　(　　"　　"　　"　　"　　　"　　)
Jacob$^7$　　(　　　"　　"　　"　　"　　　"　　)
Byron$^8$ G. (Jacob$^7$,　"　　"　　"　　　"　　)
Orville$^8$ T. (Mose$^7$,　"　　"　　"　　　"　　)

### Lempster

Nathaniel$^7$　(Eben$^6$, Nathl$^5$, Jas$^4$, Jona$^3$, **ThoHav**)
Sumner$^8$ (Nathl$^7$, "　,　"　　"　　"　　　"　　)

### Newport

David$^7$ (James$^{6-4}$, Jona$^3$, **ThoHav**)

### Plainfield

John$^6$ (Jas$^5$, Benj$^4$, Wm$^3$, John$^2$, **WmRed**)　　　　　　John$^6$

### Unity

Loammi$^6$ (Thos$^{5-4}$, John$^3$, Jona$^2$, **JonaRed**)

### Washington

?? Mary, b. 1776-94.
?? Hiram, b. 1804 in Hillsborough, N.H.

# NEW HAMPSHIRE

| 1810 | 1820 | 1830 | 1840 | 1850 |
| --- | --- | --- | --- | --- |
| **Sullivan Co.** | | | | |
| | | | | Darius[7] |
| | David C. | | | |
| | Edward[7] | Edward[7] | | |
| | John[6] | John[6] | | |
| | | Moses[7] | Moses[7] | |
| | | John[7] Jr. | John[7] | John[7] |
| | | | Jacob[7] | Jacob[7] |
| | | | | Byron[8] G. |
| | | | | Orville[8] T. |
| | | Nathaniel[7] | Nathaniel[7] | Nathaniel[7] |
| | | | | Sumner[8] |
| | David[7] | | | |
| | | Loammi[6] | | |
| Mary | | | | |
| | Hiram | Hiram | Hiram | |

# VERMONT

|  | 1790 | 1800 |
|---|---|---|

**Addison Co.**

### Addison

Reuben[7] W. (Luth[6], Nathl[5-4], Tho[3], **John[2A-1]Ded**)

### Granville

David[7] (Dav[6], Asa[5], Dav[4], Thos[3], **John[2A-1]Ded**)
James[7] (Jas[6],   "      "      "      "    )
Amasa[7] ( "      "      "      "      "    )

### Middlebury

Horace[7] (Eliphaz[6], John[5], Francis[4], Benj[3-2], **FranPly**)

### Monkton

Luther[6]        (Nathl[5A-4], Thos[3], **John[2A-1]Ded**)
Luther[7] R. (Luth[6],  "          "          "      )
William[7] (  "      "          "          "      )
Jeduthan[7] (  "      "          "          "      )

### New Haven

Luther[6] (Nath[5A-4], Thos[3], **John[2A-1]Ded**)                    Luther[6] A.

### Salisbury

?? William, b. 1829, Vt.

# VERMONT

| 1810 | 1820 | 1830 | 1840 | 1850 |
|------|------|------|------|------|
| **Addison Co.** | | | | |
| | | | Reuben$^7$ W. | Reuben$^7$ W. |
| | | | David$^7$ | |
| | | | | James$^7$<br>Amasa$^7$ |
| | | | | Horace$^7$ |
| Luther$^6$ | Luther$^6$ | Luther$^7$ R. | | |
| | William$^7$ | Jeduthan$^7$ | William$^7$<br>Jeduthan$^7$ | William$^7$<br>Jeduthan$^7$ |
| | | | | William |

# VERMONT

|  | 1790 | 1800 |
|---|---|---|

**Bennington Co.**

<u>Arlington</u>

Kimball[7] (Kimb[6], Enoc[5], Jas[4], Jona[3], **ThoHav**)

........................................................................................

<u>Dorset</u>

Luther[6] (Nathl[5-4A], Thos[3], **John[2A-1]Ded**)          Luther[6]

........................................................................................

<u>Manchester</u>

Ebenezer[6]  (Eben[5], Thos[4-3], **John[2A-1]Ded**)     Ebenezer[6]
Nathan[6]      ( "          "              "     )          Nathan[6]
Gurdeon[7] (Nathn[6], "         "              "     )
Orville[7] B.  ( "          "         "          "     )

........................................................................................

<u>Pownal</u>

Benjamin[5] (Fran[4], Benj[3-2], **FranPly**)       Benjamin[5]
?? William                                                        William

........................................................................................

<u>Reedsboro</u>

Comfort[5] (John[4], Jona[3], **John[2A-1]Ded**)

........................................................................................

<u>Shaftsbury</u>

?? Richard, b. 1756-74.                                         Richard
?? Solomon, b. 1766-84.

........................................................................................

<u>Stamford</u>

Comfort[5] (John[4], Jona[3], **John[2A--1]Ded**)       Comfort[5]
?? Liskuer? b. 1766-84.
?? William, b. 1776-94.
Noadiah[6] (Comf[5], John[4], Jona[3], **John[2A--1]Ded**)

........................................................................................

<u>Winhall</u>

Ebenezer[6] (Eben[5], Thos[4-3], **John[2A--1]Ded**)     Ebenezer[6]
Nathan[6]   ( "          "          "         )            Nathan[6]
?? John, b. 1821, Vt.

# VERMONT

| 1810 | 1820 | 1830 | 1840 | 1850 |
|---|---|---|---|---|
| **Bennington Co.** | | | | |
| | | | Kimball[7] | Kimball[7] |
| | | | | |
| | | | | |
| Nathan[6] | Nathan[6] | | | |
| | Gurden[7] | Gurden[7] | Gurdon[7] | Gurdeon[7] |
| | | | Orville[7] B. | |
| | | | | |
| | | Comfort[5] | | |
| Solomon | | | | |
| Comfort[5] | Comfort[5] | | | |
| Liskuer | | | | |
| | William | | | |
| | | Noadiah[6] | | |
| | | | | John |

# VERMONT

|  | 1790 | 1800 |
|---|---|---|

**Caledonia Co.**

Danville

Ebenezer$^6$ (Nathl$^{5\text{-}4}$, Tho$^3$ **John$^{2A\text{-}1}$Ded**)
Moses$^7$ (Jos$^6$ T., Jos$^5$, John$^4$, Jos$^3$, **JohnSal**)
Benjamin$^7$ (Eben$^6$, Nathl$^{5\text{-}4}$, Tho$^3$ **John$^{2A\text{-}1}$Ded**)
William$^7$ (    "          "          "          "          )
Nathaniel$^7$ (    "          "          "          "          )

Hardwick

Jacob$^6$  (Dav$^{5A\text{-}4}$, Tho$^3$, **John$^{2A\text{-}1}$Ded**)
Jeduthan$^6$ ( "          "          "          )
Nathaniel$^7$ (Jacob$^6$, Dav$^{5\text{--}4}$, Tho$^3$, **John$^{2A\text{-}1}$Ded**)
Phebe$^{W7}$, relict of Isaac$^7$, son of Jacob$^6$.

Lyndon

Irene$^{W8}$ (Pierce), wife of Freedom$^8$ (**#2389**)

Peacham

?? Solomon.                                    Solomon

St. Johnsbury

Samuel$^6$ (Saml$^5$, Jab$^{4A}$, Ephr$^3$, **JohnSal**)

Sutton

Stephen$^6$? (Simeon$^5$, Dav$^4$, Tho$^3$, **John$^{2A\text{-}1}$Ded**)
James$^8$ (Tim$^7$, Saml$^6$, Eben$^5$, Saml$^4$, Job$^3$, **ThoHav**)
Samuel$^7$ N. (Saml$^{6\text{-}A}$, Dav$^5$, Benj$^4$, Wm$^3$, John$^2$, **WmRed**)
Charles$^7$ L. (Stephen$^6$, Simeon$^5$, Dav$^4$, Tho$^3$, **John$^{2A\text{-}1}$Ded**)

Waterford

Eliphalet$^6$ (Eben$^5$, Jas$^4$, Jona$^3$, **ThoHav**)                    Eliphalet$^6$
Samuel$^6$ (Saml$^5$, Jab$^4$, Eph$^3$, **JohnSal**)

# VERMONT

| 1810 | 1820 | 1830 | 1840 | 1850 |
|---|---|---|---|---|

**Caledonia Co.**

| 1810 | 1820 | 1830 | 1840 | 1850 |
|---|---|---|---|---|
| Ebenezer$^6$ | Ebenezer$^6$ Moses$^7$ | Ebenezer$^6$ | Ebenezer$^6$ Benjamin$^7$ William$^7$ | Ebenezer$^6$ William$^7$ Nathaniel$^7$ H. |

| 1810 | 1820 | 1830 | 1840 | 1850 |
|---|---|---|---|---|
| Jacob$^6$ Jeduthan$^6$ | Nathaniel$^7$ Phebe$^{W7}$ | | | |

| 1810 | 1820 | 1830 | 1840 | 1850 |
|---|---|---|---|---|
| | | | | Irene$^{W8}$ |

| 1810 | 1820 | 1830 | 1840 | 1850 |
|---|---|---|---|---|
| Samuel$^6$ | | | | |

| 1810 | 1820 | 1830 | 1840 | 1850 |
|---|---|---|---|---|
| | | Stephen$^6$ | Stephen$^6$ James$^8$ Samuel$^7$ N. | James$^8$ Samuel$^7$ N. Charles$^7$ L. |

| 1810 | 1820 | 1830 | 1840 | 1850 |
|---|---|---|---|---|
| | Samuel$^6$ | | | |

# VERMONT

|  | 1790 | 1800 |
|---|---|---|

**Chittenden Co.**

### Burlington

?? Jesse, b. 1756-74.                                                 Jesse
?? William, b. 1756-74.                                      William
?? Ralph, b. 1830, Pa.
?? John, b. 1820. Me.
?? Katherine, b. 1830, Me.
James[7] P. (Jas[6-5], Benj[4], Wm[3], John[2], **WmRed**)

### Charlotte

?? John, b. 1775-84.                                         John
Luther[7] R. (Luth[6], Nathl[5A-4]. Tho[3], **John[2A-1]Ded**)
?? Henry (otherwise illegible).

### Colchester

?? Joseph A., b. 1832, Mass.

### Duxbury (later, in Wash. Co.)

?? Moses, b. <1756.                                       Moses

### Essex

Luther[7] R. (Luth[6], Nathl[5A-4], Tho[3], **John[2A-1]Ded**)

### Richmond

?? Alvin B., b. 1801, Vt.; mar. Elizabeth b. Ireland.
?? Ebenezer   (nearly illegible)

### Underhill

Abner[5]     (Jona[4-3], **John[2A-1]Ded**)         Abner[5]      Abner[5]
Alpheus[6] (Abn[5], "             "   )
Jonathan[6] (  "     "            "   )
Huldah, relict of Abner[6] (Abner[5]...)
?? Martin.
Abner[7] E. (Abner[6-5], Jona[4-3], **John[2A-1]Ded**

### Waitsfield

?? James, b. <1756,                                         James

# VERMONT

| 1810 | 1820 | 1830 | 1840 | 1850 |
|------|------|------|------|------|

**Chittenden Co.**

| | | | | |
|---|---|---|---|---|
| | | | Ralph | |
| | | | John | |
| | | | Katherine | |
| | | | James[7] P. | |

| | | | Luther[7] R. | |
|---|---|---|---|---|
| | | | Henry | |

| | | | Joseph A. | |
|---|---|---|---|---|

| | | | Luther[7] R. | |
|---|---|---|---|---|

| | | | Alvin B. | Alvin B. |
|---|---|---|---|---|
| | | | | Ebenezer |

| Abner[5] | | | | |
|---|---|---|---|---|
| | Alpheus[6] | | Alpheus[6] | Alpheus[6] |
| | Jonathan[6] J. | Jonathan[6] J. | | |
| | | Huldah[W6] | | |
| | | Martin | | |
| | | | Abner[7] E. | |

# VERMONT

|      | 1790 | 1800 |
|------|------|------|

## Essex Co.

### Lunenburgh

Jesse[5] Moore (Saml[4-3A], Jona[2], **JonaRed**)

.........................................................................................

### Minehead

Jonathan[6] (Reuben[5A], Jona[4], Saml[3A], Jona[2], **JonaRed**)

.........................................................................................

### Westmore (later in Orleans Co.)

Samuel[6A] (Dav[5], Benj[4], Wm[3], John[2], **WmRed**)
David[6]  (  "      "      "      "       "   )

===============================================================

## Franklin Co.

### Coit's Gore (later, Waterville)

Sylvanus[5]  (Jona[4-3], **John[2A-1]Ded**)
Sylvanus[6] (Syl[5], "        "        )

.........................................................................................

### Enosburg

Eliphaz[6]   (John[5], Fran[4], Benj[3-2], **FranPly**)
Jairus[6]    (  "        "        "         "     )
Bennett[7] (Jair[6],  "        "        "     )
Horace[7] (Eliphz[6], "        "        "     )
Jairus[7]   (Jair[6],   "        "        "        "     )
Rollin[7] ( Eliphz[6],  "        "        "     )
Maro[7] (    "        "        "        "        "     )
Polly[W6], relict of Eliphaz[6]

.........................................................................................

### Fairfield

Joseph[9] (Jona[8], Wm[7], Eben[6], **John[5-1]Sal**)

.........................................................................................

### Georgia

?? John, b. 1800, Vt.

# VERMONT

| 1810 | 1820 | 1830 | 1840 | 1850 |
|------|------|------|------|------|

**Essex Co.**

Jesse[5]     Jesse[5]     Jesse[5] M.     Jesse[5] M.     Jesse[5] M.

Jonathan[6]

Samuel[6A]
David[6]

===============================================================

**Franklin Co.**

Silvenus[5]
            Silvenus[6]

| Eliphaz[6] | Eliphaz[6] | Eliphaz[6] | Oliphas[6] | |
| Jairus[6] | Jairus[6] | Jairus[6] | Jairus[6] | Jairus[6] |
| | | | Bennett[7] | Bennett[7] |
| | | | Horace[7] | |
| | | | Jairus[7] Jr. | Jairus[7] |
| | | | | Rollin[7] |
| | | | | Maro[7] |
| | | | | Polly[W6] |

Joseph[9]     Joseph[9]

John

# VERMONT

|                | 1790 | 1800 |
|----------------|------|------|

**Franklin Co.** (concl.)

St. Albans

?? Sally
Hiram[7] (John[6], Nathl[5], Jas[4], Jona[3], **ThoHav**)
Silas[7] W. (Josi[6] Silas[5], Noah[4], Jonas[3], John[2] **JonaRed**)
?? John, b. 1795, Vt.
?? William, b. 1797, Vt.; wife Sabra.

Waterville  (see Lamoille Co.)

Sylvanus[6] (Sylvanus[5], Jona[4-3], **John[2A-1]Ded**)

===========================================================

**Grand Isle Co.**

North Hero

Jacob[7] (Jacob[6-4], Wm[3], John[2], **WmRed**)

# VERMONT

| 1810 | 1820 | 1830 | 1840 | 1850 |
|------|------|------|------|------|

**Franklin Co.** (concl.)

| 1810 | 1820 | 1830 | 1840 | 1850 |
|------|------|------|------|------|
| Sally | Sarah | | | |
| | | Hiram[7] | | |
| | | Silas[7] | | |
| | | | | John |
| | | | | William[7] |

Sylvanus[6]

===========================================================

**Grand Isle Co.**

Jacob[7]

# VERMONT

|  | 1790 | 1800 |
|---|---|---|

**Lamoille Co.**

<u>Cambridge</u>  (earlier, in Chitt. & Frank. Cos.)

Samuel$^6$ (Sam$^5$, Jacb$^4$, Wm$^3$, John$^2$, **WmRed**)    Samuel$^6$
Sylvanus$^5$ (Jona$^{4-3}$, **John$^{2A-1}$Ded**)                             Sylvanus$^5$
?? Orlando, b. 1830, Vt.
?? Olivia, b. 1796, Vt.

<u>Johnson</u>

Samuel$^5$    (Jacob$^4$. Wm$^3$, John$^2$, **WmRed**)    Samuel$^5$    Samuel$^5$
Samuel$^6$ (Saml$^5$, "   "   "     " )                        Samuel$^6$
Henry$^6$ (  "   "   "   "     " )                        Henry$^6$
Sylvanus$^6$ (Sylv$^5$, Jona$^{4-3}$, **John$^{2A-1}$Ded**)

<u>Morristown</u>

Abial$^6$ (Ephr$^5$, Dav$^4$, Tho$^3$, **John$^{2A-1}$Ded**)
Erastus$^6$ ("     "     "      " )
Judith$^{W7}$, relict of Abial$^7$, Jr.
?? Erastus, b. 1829, Vt.; son or neph of Eras$^6$?
Lathrop$^7$ (Abial$^6$, Eph$^5$, Dav$^4$, Tho$^3$, **John$^{2A-1}$Ded**)
Hartwell$^7$ (  "     "     "      " )
?? Abial, b. 1800-09.
?? Ephraim, b. 1790s.

<u>Sterling</u>  (in Franklin Co, pre-1840)

Henry$^6$ (Saml$^5$, Jacob$^4$, Wm$^3$, John$^2$, **WmRed**)
Moses$^6$ (  "     "     "    "     " )
?? Ephraim, b. 1800, Vt.; grandson of Eph$^5$?
Hartwell$^7$ (Abial$^6$, Ephr$^5$, Dav$^4$, Tho$^3$, **John$^{2A-1}$Ded**)
Henry$^7$ (Henry$^6$, Saml$^5$, Jacob$^4$, Wm$^3$, John$^2$, **WmRed**)
?? Lucy, b. 1782, Conn.

<u>Stowe</u>

?? Amos, b. 1790s.

<u>Wolcott</u>

Jonathan$^6$ (Dav$^{5A-4}$. Thos$^3$, **John$^{2A-1}$Ded**)
Bennett$^7$ (Jairus$^6$, John$^5$, Fran$^4$, Benj$^{3-2}$, **FranPly**)

# VERMONT

| 1810 | 1820 | 1830 | 1840 | 1850 |
|---|---|---|---|---|

**Lamoille Co.**

| | | | Orlando | |
| | | | Olivia | |

| Samuel$^5$ | Samuel$^5$ | | | |
| | | | Sylvanus$^6$ | |

| Abial$^6$ | Abial$^6$ | "Beal$^{6}$" | Erastus$^6$ | Erastus$^6$ |
| Erastus$^6$ | Erastus$^6$ | Erastus$^6$ | Judith$^{W7}$ | |
| | | | | Erastus |
| | | Lathrop$^7$ | | Lathrop$^7$ |
| | | Artwell$^7$ | | |
| | | Abial | | |
| | | Ephraim | | |

| Henry$^6$ | Henry$^6$ | Henry$^6$ | Henry$^6$ | Henry$^6$ |
| | Moses$^6$ | Moses$^6$ | Moses$^6$ | |
| | | | Ephraim | Ephraim |
| | | | Hartwell$^7$ | |
| | | | Henry$^7$ Jr. | Henry$^7$ Jr. |
| | | | | Lucy |

| | | | Amos | |

| | | | Jonathan$^6$ | Jonathan$^6$ |
| | | | | Bennett$^7$ |

# VERMONT

|  | 1790 | 1800 |
|---|---|---|

**Orange Co.**

<u>Bradford</u>
Jonathan[6] (Dav[5], Ben[4], Wm[3], John[2], **WmRed**) Jonathan[6]
Job[7] Jr. (Job[6-5], Saml[4], Job[3], **ThoHav**)

...............................................................................

<u>Braintree</u>
Jason[7]  (Jacb[6], Dav[5A-4], Thos[3], **John[2A-1]Ded**)
Hiram[7] (Sime[6], Asa[5], Dav[4],  "        "    )

<u>Chelsea</u>
Levi[6] (Benj[5], **John[4-1]Sal**)                                        Levi[6]

<u>Corinth</u>
Peter[6] (Pete[5A], Hen[4], Eph[3], **John[2-1]Sal**)
Stephen[6] (  "      "     "          "    )
Frederick[7] (Step[6], Pet[5A], Hen[4] Eph[3],  " )

...............................................................................

<u>Newbury</u>
Jonathan[6] (Dav[5], Benj[4], Wm[3], John[2], **WmRed**)

...............................................................................

<u>Randolph</u>
Daniel[6]   (Saml[5], Barn[4], Saml[3A-22], **FranPly**)             Daniel[6]
Daniel[7] (Dan[6], "       "       "         "    )

...............................................................................

<u>Thetford</u>
?? Orange.                                          Orange
William[6] (Nathl[5A-4], Thos[3], **John[2A-1]Ded**)  William[6]
?? John, b. 1828, N.H.
Timothy[7] (Danl[6], John[5], Thos[4], Job[3], **ThoHav**)

...............................................................................

<u>Topsham</u>
Peter[6]  (Peter[5A], Hen[4], Eph[3], **John[2-1]Sal**)
Stephen[6] (  "      "      "        "    )

...............................................................................

<u>Tunbridge</u>
Daniel[6] (John[5], Thos[4], Job[3], **ThoHav**)          Daniel[6]          Daniel[6]
Samuel[6A] (Dav[5], Benj[4], Wm[3], John[2], **WmRed**)  Samuel[6A]      Samuel[6A]
James[6]  (  "       "       "      "       "    )      James[6]
Joshua[7] (Danl[6], John[5], Thos[4], Job[3], **ThoHav**)
Lyman[7] E. (Jas[6], Dav[5], Ben[4], Wm[3], John[2], **WmRed**)
?? J.C.

...............................................................................

<u>Vershire</u>
Joseph[6] T. (Jos[5A], John[4A], Jos[3], **John[2-1]Sal**)

# VERMONT

| 1810 | 1820 | 1830 | 1840 | 1850 |
|------|------|------|------|------|

**Orange Co.**

Job[7] Jr.

.................................................................................................................

Jason[6]

Hiram[7]

.................................................................................................................

Levi[6]

.................................................................................................................

| | Peter[6] | Peter[6] | Peter[6] | Peter[6] |
| | Stephen[6] | Stephen[6] | Stephen[6] | Stephen[6] |
| | | | | Frederick[7] P. |

.................................................................................................................

Jonathan[6]                    Jonathan[6]

.................................................................................................................

| Daniel[fl] | Daniel[6] | Daniel[6] | Daniel[6] | Daniel[6] |
| | | | | Daniel[7] Jr. |

.................................................................................................................

John

Timothy[7]

.................................................................................................................

Peter[6]
Stephen[6]

.................................................................................................................

| | Joshua[7] | Joshua[7] | Joshua[7] | Joshua[7] |
| | Lyman[7] | | | |
| | | | J.C. | |

.................................................................................................................

Joseph[6] T.

# VERMONT

|  | 1790 | 1800 |
|---|---|---|

**Orleans Co.**

Barton

Cyrus[7] (Jona[6], Dav[5], Benj[4], Wm[3], John[2], **WmRed**)
?? Albert S., b. 1823, Nova Scotia.
.........................................................................................................................

Brownington

Cyrus[7] (Jona[6], Dav[5], Benj[4], Wm[3], John[2], **WmRed**)
.........................................................................................................................

Charleston

Cyrus[7] (Jona[6], Dav[5], Benj[4], Wm[3], John[2], **WmRed**)
.........................................................................................................................

Coventry

Thomas[6] (Jona[5-4], Thos[3], Josh[2], **JonaRed**)
John[7] (Thos[6], "          "          "          "     )
.........................................................................................................................

Craftsbury

Samuel[6] (Asa[5], Dav[4], Thos[3], **John[2A-1]Ded**)
.........................................................................................................................

Derby

?? Stephen, b. 1776-94.      (One of these to Sutton,
?? Stephen, Jr., b. 1776-94. ( Caledonia; but which?
.........................................................................................................................

Holland

Thomas[7] J. (Abij[6], Tim[5], Jas[4], Jona[3], **ThoHav**)
.........................................................................................................................

Irasburgh

Thomas[7] J. (Abij[6], Tim[5], Jas[4], Jona[3], **ThoHav**)
.........................................................................................................................

Morgan

Thomas[6]    (Jona[5-4], Thos[3], Josh[2], **JonaRed**)
Samuel[7] (Thos[6], "          "          "          "     )
.........................................................................................................................

Westfield
Calvin[5] (Pearsn[4], Jos[3A]. John[2], **JonaRed**
Charles[7] (Jas[6], Asa[5], Dav[4], Thos[3], **John[2A-1]Ded**)

# VERMONT

| 1810 | 1820 | 1830 | 1840 | 1850 |
|------|------|------|------|------|

**Orleans Co.**

|  |  |  |  | Cyrus[7]<br>Albert S. |
|--|--|--|--|--|

|  | Cyrus[7] | Cyrus[7] |  |  |
|--|--|--|--|--|

|  |  |  | Cyrus[7] |  |
|--|--|--|--|--|

|  |  | Thomas[6] | Thomas[6]<br>John[7] |  |
|--|--|--|--|--|

|  |  |  | Samuel[6] |  |
|--|--|--|--|--|

|  | Stephen<br>Stephen, Jr. |  |  |  |
|--|--|--|--|--|

|  |  | Thomas[7] J. |  |  |
|--|--|--|--|--|

|  |  |  |  | Thomas[7] J. |
|--|--|--|--|--|

|  |  |  |  | Thomas[6]<br>Samuel[7] |
|--|--|--|--|--|

| Calvin[5] |  |  |  |  |
|--|--|--|--|--|

|  |  |  |  | Charles[7] |
|--|--|--|--|--|

# VERMONT

|  | 1790 | 1800 |
|---|---|---|

**Rutland Co.**

Castleton

| | | |
|---|---|---|
| Daniel[6] (Danl[5A-2], **WmRed**) | Daniel[6] | Daniel[6] |
| Enoch[6] (    "          "    ) | Enoch[6] | Enoch[6] |
| John[5] (Danl[4-2],        "        ) | John[5] | |
| Rebekah[W5A], relict of Danl[5A] | Rebekah[W5A] | Rebecca[W5A] |
| Elihu[6A] (Danl[5A-2], **WmRed**) | | Elihu[6A] |
| Jonathan[6] (    "        "    ) | | Jonathan[6] |
| Stephen[6] D. (  "        "    ) | | Stephen[6] |
| Ardon[6]  (      "        "    ) | | |
| Enoch[7] (Enoc[6], "      "    ) | | |
| Edward[7] (  "      "      "    ) | | |

Oliver[7]  (Danl[6-2], **WmRed**)
Anson[7] (Elihu[6A], Danl[5A-2], **Wm Red**)
?? Oliver, b. 1800-09.
Philo[7] (Jona[6], Danl[5A-2], **WmRed**)
Gilbert[7] (  "      "        "    )
?? Horace, b. 1790s.
Milo[7] (Steph[6], Danl[5A-2], **WmRed**)
?? Andrew, Jr., b. 1810s.
Elihu[7] (Elih[6A], Danl[5A-2], **WmRed**)
George[7] R. (Jona[6], "      "    )
Leander[7] (    "      "      "    )
John[8] F. (Milo[7], Steph[6], Dan[5A-2], **WmRed**)
Jonathan[7]  (Jona[8],      "        "    )
Nancy[W6] (Charter), relict of Danl[6] above.
Marcus[8] (Edw[7], Enoc[6], Danl[5A-2], **WmRed**)
Ardon[7]    (Ardon[6],        "        "    )
?? Cullen C., b. 1820, Vt.
Zilpha[7] (Elih[6A], Danl[5A-2], **WmRed**)

...................................................................................

Middleton
Ryland[7] (Kimb[6], Enoc[5], Jas[4], Jona[3], **ThoHav**)

...................................................................................

Pawlet
Rice[6], (Eben[5], Josh[4], Jonas[3], John[2], **JonaRed**)          Rice[6]

...................................................................................

Shrewsbury
Abraham[3] (John[4-3], Jona[2], **JonaRed**)

...................................................................................

Wallingford
Gardner[6] (William[5-4], Nathl[3], Jona[2], **JonaRed**)

# VERMONT

| 1810 | 1820 | 1830 | 1840 | 1850 |
|------|------|------|------|------|

**Rutland Co.**

| 1810 | 1820 | 1830 | 1840 | 1850 |
|------|------|------|------|------|
| Daniel[6] | Daniel[6] | Daniel[6] | Daniel[6] | |
| Enoch[6] | Enoch[6] | Enoch[6] | | |
| | | | | |
| Elihu[6A] | Elihu[6A] | Elihu[6A] | Elihu[6A] | Elihu[6A] |
| Jonathan[6] | Jonathan[6] | Jonathan[6] | Jonathan[6] | Jonathan[6] |
| Stephen[6] D. | Stephen[6] D. | Stephen[6] | Stephen[6] | |
| Cordon | | Ardon[6] | Ardon[6] | Ardon[6] |
| | Enoch[7] Jr. | | | |
| | Edward[7] | Edward[7] | Edward[7] | Edward[7] |
| | Oliver[7] | Oliver[7] | | |
| | | Anson[7] | | |
| | | | Oliver | |
| | | Filow[7] | Philo[7] | |
| | | Gilbert[7] | | |
| | | Horace | | |
| | | Milow[7] | Milo[7] | Milo[7] |
| | | | Andrew Jr. | |
| | | | Elihu[7], Jr | |
| | | | George[7] R. | |
| | | | | Leander[7] |
| | | | | John[8] F. |
| | | | | Jonathan[7] |
| | | | | Nancy[W6] |
| | | | | Marcus[8] |
| | | | | Ardon[7] |
| | | | | Cullen C. |
| | | | | Zilpha[7] |

Ryan[7]

Abraham[5]

Gardner[6]

# VERMONT

|                                                                                  | 1790 | 1800 |
|---|---|---|

**Windham Co.**

<u>Brattleboro</u>
Simeon[5A] ?  (Dav[4], Thos[3], **John[2A-1]Ded**)              Simeon[5A]          Simeon[5A]
Simeon[6]  (Sim[5A], "    "        "    )

...............................................................................

<u>Grafton</u>
Stillman[6] (Benj[5], Nathl[4-3], Jona[2], **JonaRed**)

...............................................................................

<u>Jamaica</u>
Humphrey[6] (Eben[5], Josi[4], Wm[3], **John[2A-1]Ded**)
Mary[W6], relict of Humphrey[6].

...............................................................................

<u>Londonderry</u>
Abijah[5] (Aaron[4A], Thos[3], Danl[2], **WmRed**)
Susannah[W6], relict of Josh[6](Tho[5-4], John[3], Jona[2], **JonaRed**)
Gardner[6] (Wm[5-4], Nathl[3], Jona[2], **JonaRed**)

...............................................................................

<u>Rockingham</u>
James[6] (Asa[5], Dav[4], Thos[3], **John[2A-1]Ded**)
Ellis[7] (Asa[6], Ben[5], Pearsn[4], Jos[3A], John[2], **JonaRed**)

...............................................................................

<u>Springfield</u>
Asa[6] (Benj[5], Pearsn[4], Jos[3A], John[2], **JonaRed**)
Joshua[6] (Thos[5-4], John[3], Jona[2], **JonaRed**)

...............................................................................

<u>Wardsboro</u>
Abiel[6] (Eph[5], Dav[4], Thos[3], **John[2A-1]Ded**)                        Abiel[6]
Ebenezer[6] (Eben[5], Josi[4], Wm[3], **John[2A-1]Ded**)
Alfred[7] (Eben[6-5], Josi[4], Wm[3], **John[2A-1]Ded**)

...............................................................................

<u>Westminster</u>
Asa[5]     (Dav[4], Tho[3], **John[2A-1]Ded**)                Asa[5]          Asa[5]
David[5A]  ( "      "        "     )              David[5A]
Asa[6]     (Asa[5], "    "        "     )         Asa[6]
Maverick[6] (Josi[5], "    "        "    )        Marvelick[6]    Maverick[6]
?? Maverick, Jr.                                  Marvelick, Jr.
Isaiah[6] (Tim[5], Jas[4], Jona[3], **ThoHav**)
James[6] (Asa[5], Dav[4], Thos[3], **John[2A-1]Ded**)
Samuel[6] ( "      "       "        "     )
?? Thomas, b. <1776.
David[6] (Dav[5A-4], Tho[3], **John[2A-1]Ded**)
Jere[7] (Maverk[6], Josi[5], Dav[4], Tho[3], **John[2A-1]Ded**)
Ira[7 or 8] (Eben[6-5], Saml[4], Job[3], **ThoHav**)
Josiah[6] (Josi[5], Dav[4], Thos[3], **John[2A-1]Ded**)
John[7] West (Isai[6], Tim[5], Jas[4], Jona[3], **ThoHav**)

# VERMONT

| 1810 | 1820 | 1830 | 1840 | 1850 |
|---|---|---|---|---|
| **Windham Co.** | | | | |
| Simeon$^{5A}$ | | | | |
| Simeon$^{6}$ Jr. | | | Simeon$^{6}$ | |
| | | | Stilman$^{6}$ | Stilman$^{6}$ |
| Humphrey$^{6}$ | Humphrey$^{6}$ | Humphrey$^{6}$ | Humphrey$^{6}$ | |
| | | | | Mary$^{w6}$ |
| | Abijah$^{5}$ | | | |
| | Susannah$^{w6}$ | | | |
| | | | Gardner$^{6}$ | |
| James$^{6}$ | | | | |
| | | Elias$^{7}$ | Ellis$^{7}$ | |
| Asa$^{6}$ | | | | |
| Joshua$^{6}$ | | | | |
| Ebenezer$^{6}$ | Ebenezer$^{6}$ | Ebenezer$^{6}$ | | |
| | | | Alfred$^{7}$ | |
| Asa$^{5}$ | | | | |
| Maboruk$^{6}$ | Manurink$^{6}$ | Marvorit$^{6}$ | | |
| Isaiah$^{6}$ | Isaiah$^{6}$ | | | |
| | James$^{6}$ | | | |
| | Samuel$^{6}$ | Samuel$^{6}$ | | |
| | Thomas | | | |
| | | David$^{6}$ | | |
| | | Jery$^{7}$ | Jere$^{7}$ | |
| | | | Ira$^{7}$ | |
| | | | Josiah$^{6}$ | |
| | | | | John$^{7}$ W. |

# VERMONT

|  | 1790 | 1800 |
|---|---|---|

### Windsor Co.

Andover
Joseph$^5$ (Pearson$^4$, Jos$^{3A}$, John$^2$, **JonaRed**)

..................................................................................................

Barnard
Zebina$^6$ (Elij$^5$, Fran$^4$, Benj$^{3-2}$, **FranPly**)                    Zebina$^6$
Edwin$^8$ W. (Adna$^7$, Zebi$^6$, Elij$^5$, Fran$^4$, Ben$^{3-2}$, **FranPly**)

..................................................................................................

Bethel
Lyman$^7$ E. (Jas$^6$, Dav$^5$, Ben$^4$, Wm$^3$, John$^2$, **WmRed**)

..................................................................................................

Bridgewater
Adna$^7$ (Zebi$^6$, Elij$^5$, Fran$^4$, Ben$^{3-2}$, **FranPly**)

..................................................................................................

Cavendish
Enoch$^5$     (Jas$^4$, Jona$^3$, **ThoHav**)                          Enoch$^5$
Frazier$^6$ (Enoc$^5$, "      "        "    )                          Frazier$^6$
Kimball$^6$ ( "      "     "        "    )                          Kimball$^6$
Joseph$^7$ P. (Jos$^{6-5}$, Pearsn$^4$, Jos$^{3A}$, John$^2$, **JonaRed**)

..................................................................................................

Chester
Abraham$^5$ (John$^{4-3}$, Jona$^2$, **JonaRed**)            Abraham$^5$      Abraham$^5$
Joseph$^6$ (Jos$^5$, Pearsn$^4$, Jos$^3$, John$^2$, **JonaRed**)
Kendall$^7$ (Loam$^6$, Tho$^{5-4}$, John$^3$, Jona$^2$, "   )
Charles$^7$ W. (Jos$^{6-5}$, Pearsn$^4$, Jos$^{3A}$, John$^2$, "   )

..................................................................................................

Hartford
Brigham$^5$ (Josh$^4$, Jona$^3$, John$^2$, **JonaRed**)      Brigham$^5$      Brigham$^5$

..................................................................................................

Ludlow
William$^5$   (Wm$^4$, Nathl$^3$, Jona$^2$, **JonaRed**)
Jeremiah$^7$ (Jos$^{6-5}$, Pearsn$^4$, Jos$^{3A}$, John$^2$, "   )
Joseph$^5$      (          "         "         "        "   )
Joseph$^6$      (Jos$^5$,         "         "         "         "   )
Gardner$^6$ (Wm$^{5-4}$, Nathl$^3$, Jona$^2$,         "         "   )
Nathan$^7$   (Jos$^{6-5}$, Pearsn$^4$, Jos$^{3A}$,         "         "   )

..................................................................................................

Plymouth
Samuel$^6$     (Jas$^{5-4}$, Jona$^3$, **ThoHav**)
Joseph$^7$ (Saml$^6$, "        "        "        )
Elizabeth$^{W7}$ (Day). relict of Jos$^7$ above.

..................................................................................................

Reading
Samuel$^6$ (Jas$^{5-4}$, Jona$^3$, **ThoHav**)

# VERMONT

| 1810 | 1820 | 1830 | 1840 | 1850 |
|------|------|------|------|------|

**Windsor Co.**

|  |  |  | Joseph[5] |  |
|--|--|--|--|--|

| Zebina[6] | Zebina[6] | Zebina[6] | Zebina[6] | Zebina[6]<br>Edmund[8] W. |

|  |  |  |  | Lyman[7] E. |

|  | Adna[7] | Adna[7] | Adna[7] |  |

Enoch[5]

|  |  |  |  | Joseph[7] P. |

| Abraham[5] | Abram[5] |  |  | Joseph[6]<br>Kendall[7]<br>Charles[7] W. |

William[5]

|  | Jeremiah[7]<br>Joseph[5]<br>Joseph[6] Jr. | Jeremiah[7]<br>Joseph[6] Jr.<br>Gordner[6]<br>Nathan[7] |  |  |

|  |  |  | Samuel[6]<br>Joseph[7] |  |
|  |  |  |  | Elizabeth[W7] |

|  | Samuel[6] | Samuel[6] |  |  |

# VERMONT

|  | 1790 | 1800 |
|---|---|---|

**Windsor Co.**  (concl.)

<u>Rochester</u>

Asa$^6$  (Asa$^5$, Dav$^4$, Tho$^3$, **John$^{2-1}$Ded**)
Simeon$^6$ ( "        "        "        "      )                    Simeon$^6$
David$^6$ (   "       "        "        "      )                    David$^6$
James$^6$ (   "       "        "        "      )
?? Amos, b. 1790s.
Hiram$^7$ (Sime$^6$, Asa$^5$, Dav$^4$, Tho$^3$, **John$^{2-1}$Ded**)
Asa$^7$   (   "        "        "        "        "      )
Caleb$^7$ (   "        "        "        "        "      )
Amasa$^7$ (Jas$^6$,     "        "        "        "      )
David$^7$ (David$^6$,    "        "        "        "      )

<u>Royalton</u>

Timothy$^7$ ? (Danl$^6$, John$^5$, Tho$^4$, Job$^3$, **ThoHav**)
?? Alvah, b. 1800-09.

<u>Springfield</u>

Asa$^6$ (Benj$^5$, Pearsn$^4$, Jos$^{3A}$, John$^2$, **JonaRed**)
Loammi$^6$ (Thos$^{5-4}$, John$^3$. Jona$^2$,      "      )
Joshua$^6$ (    "          "          "          "      )
Kendall$^7$ (Loam$^6$, Thos$^{5-4}$, John$^3$, Jona$^2$, **JonaRed**)
?? Betsey, b. 1801, Vt.; perh. eldest ch, David$^6$, above.
?? John, b. 1820, Vt.
Livermore$^7$ K. (Peter$^6$, **Tho$^{5-2}$Hav**)
Calvin$^8$ M. (Ellis$^7$, Asa$^6$, Ben$^5$, Pearsn$^4$, Jos$^{3A}$, John$^2$, **JonaRed**)

<u>Stockbridge</u>

Samuel$^6$ (Asa$^5$, Dav$^4$, Thos$^3$, **John$^{2A-1}$Ded**)

<u>Windsor Town</u>

?? Levi, b. 1829, Vt.
?? Hezekiah, b. 1827, Mass.

<u>Woodstock</u>

Joel$^6$  (Abel$^5$, Saml$^{4-3}$, Jona$^2$, **JonaRed**)
Jacob$^6$ (  "          "        "        "      )

# VERMONT

| 1810 | 1820 | 1830 | 1840 | 1850 |
|------|------|------|------|------|

**Windsor Co.** (concl.)

| 1810 | 1820 | 1830 | 1840 | 1850 |
|------|------|------|------|------|
| Asa[6] | Asa[6] | Asa[6] | Asa[6] | Asa[6] |
| Simeon[6] | Simeon[6] | Simeon[6] | Simeon[6] | Simeon[6] |
| | David[6] | | | |
| | | James[6] | James[6] | |
| | | Amos | | |
| | | Hiram[7] | Hiram[7] | |
| | | | Asa[7] 2d | |
| | | | Caleb[7] | Caleb[7] |
| | | | Amasa[7] | |
| | | | | David[7] |

| | Timothy[7] | | | |
| | | | Alvah | |

| Asa[6] | Asa[6] | Asa[6] | Asa[6] | Asa[6] |
| | Loammi[6] | | | |
| Joshua[6] | Joshua[6] | | | |
| | | | Kendall[7] B. | |
| | | | | Betsey |
| | | | | John |
| | | | | Livermore[7] |
| | | | | Calvin[8] M. |

| | | | Samuel[6] | Samuel[6] |

| | | | | Levi |
| | | | | Hezekiah |

| | | Joel[6] | | Joel[6] |
| | | | Jacob[6] | |

# APPENDIX C

### DEAD MAN WALKING?

### The mysterious James Eaton of Deering, N.H.

There is litttle room in a genealogy like this to recount the endless twists and turns of the sleuthing that has generated the bare facts for the thousands of Eatons we have covered. This misses part of the joy of the hunt, and we have tried to give brief note in our main text to examples of the unexpected but crucial discoveries that have clinched this or that identification (or, now and then, demolished an identification we presumed was sterling). But there should be room here at last for one rollicking detective story with space to enumerate a lot of particulars.

We have no trouble knowing which of our thousands of cases to choose. It is the case with three important characteristics. First, this James of Deering represents by some margin the most consequential identification we have been unable to clinch. "Consequential" here means that he had many children, who themselves went on to have many further children about which we have a lot of records. Knowing who this James was is thus important because the branch of our Eatons we think he founded is not just a "branch": it is about the largest "bough" in our Eaton tree around the sixth generation. Secondly, we have devoted more research time to this single case than to any other in this volume. We cannot claim that we know more about this James than any other Eaton treated here, for some few Eatons like Gen. John[8] Eaton (#2967) were nationally famous enough to have hundreds of pages of biographical information extant. But given that there is next to no "canned" information about this James at all, and that the one paragraph exception proves upon even cursory examination to be about two-thirds wrong, we have painstakingly assembled over a period of many years a remarkable number of stray pieces of the jigsaw puzzle of his life. These go far beyond his vital statistics or those of his family of origin or the names of his own children. They extend to a great searching of the context in which he

lived:  such as who his neighbors were, who his children interacted with as
adults, etc.  This mass of information about the James who lived for
many years in Deering and died in 1849 at neighboring Antrim, N.H.,
seems, moreover, to be remarkably coherent.  That is to say, even though
numerous pieces of the puzzle are indeed missing, and probably irretrievably so, his detailed adult life history has few if any internal contra-
dictions.  Thirdly, and most to the point, our broader knowledge of the
Haverhill branch of the Eatons seems to make it entirely "obvious" just
where he had to be born, and to which parents.  So it is almost "case
closed," save for the one "ugly little fact" mentioned in our main text: the
James Eaton out of Goffstown, N.H. who he (almost) "has to be," is reported in the reigning Goffstown history (Hadley, 1924) as having died
in Feb 1785.  This is indeed the stuff of a good detective story.

We could write many scores of pages about James of Deering,
and the step-by-step details of our hunt over the years.  With an intrigu-
ing exception or two, we shall skip over the many false leads and dry
wells encountered, to focus on the most central facts that seem fruitful.
And we shall finish with an extended hypothesis based on all we know,
which could plausibly explain a report of his death in 1785 that might be
"greatly exaggerated."

### BACKGROUND: THE "TWO-JAMES PROBLEM"

Our difficulties with James of Deering first surfaced as one half
of a two-James mystery.  One James was solved definitively in due time,
but since the two cases are somewhat related, we review them both.

As we tackled the unexpected problem of the Haverhill branch
that our senior author died before finishing, we encountered an initial
perplexity.  Census records for Hillsborough Co., N.H., show two James
Eatons, nearly contemporary and nearly neighbors, each of whom appears in several consecutive Censuses.  One is at Hillsborough Lower
Village, and is listed in five Censuses from 1790 through 1830.  He was
buried there in 1832, with his wife Mary, who had predeceased him in
1825.  The other James is listed in six straight Censuses, first at Deering,
1790-1820, and in 1830-40 at the next township south, then called
"Society Land" but later "Bennington, N.H."  He was buried there in
1849, although actually he lived his his last few years with his son Hiram
just across the river in Antrim, N.H.

The important point here is that Hillsborough township abuts
Deering to the latter's north.  Better yet, these two Jameses lived for several decades about four miles apart as the crow flies, although at a somewhat greater distance (five miles? six?) by a more water-level route.  Here
a moment of geography is useful.  As the Contoocook River descends
from its headwaters on Monadnock Mtn. by Peterborough, N.H., it first
runs nearly due north, and forms the town line between Deering to the
east and Antrim to the west.  Shortly after passing Antrim village, it flows
below the brow of Hedgehog Mtn. (more latterly and more properly,
"Hedgehog Hill"), on the south flank of which James of Deering had his

farm. It then runs north a couple more miles to the Hillsborough township line, where it bends to the northeast. The original settlement of Hillsborough was a village near the geographic centroid of the township. However, the population center soon moved to the southeast corner of the township, to take advantage of the water power of the Contoocook, by far the largest stream in the immediate region. This center on the north bank of the River just after that stream enters the township was first called "Atherton's Mills" or "Hillsboro Mills" and later "Hillsborough Lower Village", to distinguish it from the dwindling original Hillsborough village. More recently, it has become the town of "Hillsborough", and the other village demoted to "Hillsborough Center." The land bought by the Hillsborough James in 1789 was a mile or two from the burgeoning new mill village, straddling the main road to neighboring Henniker. It was soon added to, so that it straddled the river as well. Thus it was a most prosperous farm in the alluvial plain of the Contoocook.

These two initially unexplained James Eatons were, by Census and other accounts, nearly of an age, although the Deering James appears to have been slightly older (see below). The fact that they had the same names and lived in considerable proximity for many years does not, of course, mean that they had any blood relationship or even, for that matter, ever met each other, although Hillsborough would have been one of the only two "market towns" available to the Deering James, the other being Antrim, at this period a less preposessing village. (Deering village remains to this day even less prepossessing, and is as close to the east boundary of the township as the Deering James Eaton was to its west boundary, with rugged terrain in between.) However, migrations depended in this era on familial and neighborly communications, so the proximity is at the very least congruent with a likelihood that these two Eatons were connected in some way. Our hypothesis is of course that they were first cousins.

Despite their residential proximity, these two Jameses were direct opposites in their life styles, residences, prosperity and progeny. The Hillsborough James had a low tax valuation in his first year, 1790, barely above the bottom quartile for the village (28th percentile), although this was not unusual for a male in his mid-twenties. He rocketed upward, however, as he improved his property, being in the 46th percentile in 1791 and the 72nd percentile in 1792. This position was entirely unusual for a young man still not yet 30, and bespeaks the likelihood of affluent backing from elsewhere. From the outset, he immersed himself in town affairs. He had at most a child or two, and probably none.

The Deering James settled on a steep and forested hillside remote from civilization. When we tried to visit the site in 1996 we found a primitive two-track through a meadow. Sixty yards from the corner was a farmhouse at the edge of a woods, too near to be our target. As we approached the woods the trail was deteriorating at a fair rate, and a kindly elderly lady from the house emerged to warn that it was a distance to the next farm, where the tracks ended, and the access was such that it really required four-wheel drive. (Given time problems, we gave up on this inspection.) This remote James had 17 children. The contrast with the Hillsborough James in these regards could hardly be more dramatic. **The Hillsborough James Solved.** So here we had two mystery James Eatons. And suggestively, at least, our senior author, whose writing up of his own Haverhill Eatons had not yet become very serious after the fifth generation, had one otherwise unexplained James Eaton listed for the sixth generation, with one very promising scrap of information attached. After reviewing the Revolutionary exploits of the affluent Haverhill Capt. Timothy[5] Eaton, we find listed as his fifth child:

"James[6], b. Aug. 6: 1763 [at Haverhill]; died Jan. 29: 1832 at Hillsborough, N.H. No account of his marriage."

It is of interest that this is the only one of Capt. Timothy's seven sons for which our senior author wrote no continuation sketch. The death date of course matches the death of the Hillsborough James, and indeed, it is not difficult to substantiate this identification through several other channels. At this point the interested reader would do well to go back and read the notice for this James (#513, p. 193), containing details we shall not repeat here that clinch the linkage of Capt. Timothy's son and the Hillsborough James.

The further wonder here is that our senior author specifies that he knows of no marriage for this James. This is wondrous from several points of view. One is that the marriage is listed in the *VR* for Haverhill, Mass., a source he must have consulted often in the 1890s. It is also wondrous given a whole cascade of other facts. First, our senior author's father David[6], who was born and spent his own life in Goffstown, was a first cousin of the Hillsborough James. The latter was a Goffstown resident with his bride Polly when in 1789 he bought the Hillsborough land, and although they would have lived near the northwest corner of the township while David lived near the south edge of it, one would think that kin of this proximity in a new land would have gotten together. But even after James and Polly had soon removed to Hillsborough, this was less than twenty miles from Goffstown; and the two cousins lived for over forty subsequent years at this small remove from one another. Our senior author himself was seven when Polly died in Hillsborough; and thirteen before James of Hillsborough died himself. But our aging senior author, at least, professed to know nothing of any marital status, and lacked enough information to write a further sketch for them!

In any event, however, it is beyond question that the Hillsborough James was the son of Capt. Timothy[5] of Haverhill.


## SO WHO WAS JAMES OF DEERING?

James of Deering remains a much more recalcitrant puzzle. Our senior author, who himself was born and grew up in Goffstown, grandson of the original Goffstown migrant, James[5], mentions no such person, but this seems to be due to the simple fact that he died before he began to carry his own Eaton branch beyond the fifth generation: he had not yet done a biographical note for his grandfather, much less made any mention of his own father or his paternal uncles. However, this sixth generation is known to us from the family Bible kept by migrant James[5], a listing which later became enshrined in the main Goffstown history. A James[6] Eaton was born to the Goffstown-bound migrant James[5] in Haverhill, Mass., 17 Dec 1760, or 40 months older than his cousin James of Hillsborough. A second Bible entry notes James[6]'s 1785 death.

Since this James[6] is the obvious candidate to be the later James of Deering, let us make very clear the background of his birth. His father, James[5] Sr., born in Haverhill in 1738, was the younger brother of Capt. Timothy by some seven years. This father James[5] married when he was about twenty, and apparently settled first with his bride in Hampstead, N.H. By this time his older brother Timothy was immersed in land speculation, and probably his first target, along with colleague Samuel White, was the new town of Goffstown being developed on the west bank of the Merrimack River. Therefore it is not surprising that kid brother James[5], with his bride Abigail and a child or two in hand, moved about 1762 from Hampstead to the southern part of Goffstown near Bedford. While this was a land stake much more modest than what Timothy would arrange for his own children a half-generation later, it was where James[5] raised his family and spent the rest of his life. For nearly 20 years during and after the Revolution he was joined in Goffstown by his (and Capt. Timothy's) youngest brother, Enoch, who would move on to Vermont after his own children were born (cf. **#210**).

We know that newlyweds James[5] and Abigail lived at least briefly in Hampstead before settling in Goffstown, since they were members of the Hampstead church for a spell; and even after they came to reside in Goffstown, they returned a good 15 miles to the Hampstead Church to have their second and third children baptized there, possibly because a new church was not yet conveniently available to them in southern Goffstown, or they had not yet transferred membership. In any event, these Hampstead records report that a child "James, son of James Eaton of Goffstown," was baptized there in Sept., 1761 (LDS Film #870156).

At this point the reader would do well to read our sketch of this James, Jr, (**#522**, p. 197). It is to be kept in mind that this sketch treats James of Deering as though he were indeed the James[5], Jr., who grew up in Goffstown, whereas for sleuthing purposes our text here has not yet covered enough ground to form any such conclusion. In fact, if the report of the death of this Goffstown James[6] in 1785 is correct, there is no way he could have been James of Deering, the very nub of our mystery.

We also mentioned earlier that one brief account of the life of James of Deering exists, and this is the moment to introduce it. It appears in the magisterial history of the town of Hillsborough published by G. Waldo Browne in 1922, in his section for local genealogy::

> "James [Eaton], b. in Chester, in 1753, was a soldier in the Revolution, serving most of the time during the war. He was in the Bennington campaign, in Peter Clark's Company under Gen. John

Stark.  He m.  Martha McClure of Goffstown, and settled in Deering at the south side of Hedgehog Mountain, on what is now
known as the Shepherd of Gingras place.  Here they lived many
years, and reared a large family.  After her death he went to Antrim, where he died at the age of 96 years." [Vol. II, p, 189]

Before considering errors in this account, we must note how bizarre it seems that it was written for publication in the town history at all.
Browne surely steeped himself in the town records in preparing his book;
and one of the names most frequently found in those records, in the crucial early period of 1790-1804, was indeed our Hillsborough James Eaton, frequent Selectman, co-founder of the Hillsborough Public Library
and for forty years a pillar of the community.  But Browne gives no
sketch of this James Eaton at all, choosing instead to write about the
mountain James Eaton, a man not even a Hillsborough resident.  (He
then finishes his Eatons with only a sketch of John Eaton[7], born to James[6]
in Deering but who did at least reside in Hillsborough as an adult.)
In any event, if Browne's account were generally true, it would
clearly rule out the possibility that James of Deering could have been the
James[6] of Goffstown, and do so on several counts independent of the report of his death in 1785.  But while some of his facts are true, such as
the report that the Deering James's tombstone in Bennington, N.H. says
that he was age 96 when he died in Jan. 1849 (implying he was born in
the last 360 days of 1752 or the first five days of 1753), he was in a more
general way barking up the wrong tree.
He is correct that a James Eaton born in Chester, N.H., was one of
the fairly prominent Eaton soldiers in the Revolution.  In fact, if we only
had some few original sources available, we might well conclude that this
Chester native was the only James Eaton born in N.H. in the Revolutionary service at all.  But this is not true; and as a matter of fact, enough is
known about this Eaton of Chester that there is no possible way to con-
found him with the Deering James.  For one thing, he was born in 1735,
not 1753.  He was a sergeant in the Massachusetts militia fighting of
1775, a rank not likely to have been attained by a 22-year-old.  He is
listed in the N.H. State Papers (Appendix to Vol. XV) among a variety of
N.H. soldiers not otherwise catalogued in those volumes, because he
fought under Mass. command.  It is very unlikely that he fought at Bennington.  He was a son of that Rev. Benjamin[4] Eaton of the William of
Reading line, who early took up pastorates in the southern tier of New
Hampshire townships such as Dunstable and Chester.  Sgt. James himself
spent his life in the Candia area that was carved out of the old Chester
grant in 1763.  He married Abigail Wood, and had nine children by her,
More detail of his life is provided in Stearns (1908), p 1487.
Thus the Sgt. James Eaton of Chester has no bearing on the ori-
gins of James of Deering.  But the Browne account for him raises other
issues we shall address one by one.
**Age as Diagnostic.**  We have only a single precise age report for
James of Deering, the one giving his age at death (96) mentioned by
Browne.  On the other hand, a less precise bracket age is given for him in

the five Censuses from 1800 to 1840.  These reports suffer no point of
inconsistency;  and if every one of those five reports were exactly true,
then we would conclude that James of Deering must have been born not
earlier than 1756 nor later than 1759.  Of course the 1752 date mainly
implied by his gravestone is out of this range.  The range also falls short
of the birthdate for the Goffstown James[6], but this deviation is hardly
worrisome.  It is well known that where the truth lies close to a bracket
cutpoint for age, the report may wander to either side.  More particularly
here, we must be sensitive to the phenomenon of "heaping", so obvious in
19th-century Censuses.  When the details of age were less salient to re-
spondents than today, ages were given with considerable frequency by
the nearest round number.  The only two reports that do not include the
Goffstown James's actual birth date in mid-December, 1760, are the last
ones in 1830 and 1840.  We obviously do not know what James did say
for these Censuses.  But if James were actually aged 69 years and five to
nine months when the Census Enumerator came in 1830, it would not be
surprising for the age to be reported more simply as " seventy", thereby
putting his birth in the 1750s rather than the 1760s, and repeating the
same "heaping" by rounding his age to 80 when the Census returned 10
years later.  Or perhaps in his dotage he was beginning to exaggerate his
longevity, not an unfamiliar phenomenon either, a matter which could
have led in due time to an extreme exaggeration on his gravestone.  His
midlife reports seem to say more clearly that he was not born anywhere
nearly as early as 1752.  His life stages seem to testify in the same direction.  That is, he was apparently a lusty fellow who sired 17 children, and
one who had departed his original home for the maturing independence
of war service at a very precocious age.  If asked whether such a fellow
would be more likely to have first married a month short of age 22 or a
month short of age 30, most would answer the former.  Or if the question
were put as to whether he was more likely to have sired his last child with
his second and much younger wife when he was roughly 65 or 73, the
former number seems more likely although of course the latter number
is not impossible.  In short, we do not have age data for this James which
strongly verfies the Dec 1760 birthdate for him.  On the other hand, the
weight of the evidence in front of us is more congruent with a 1760 birth
than with a 1752 one, in spite of the gravestone "age at death."

   **Given Name as Diagnostic.**  In one sense we regret disposing of
two other James Eatons--of Hillsborough and Chester--before getting
down to brass tacks about what James Eaton was really at Bennington and
later in Deering.  (The James of Hillsborough is obviously disqualified
from Bennington service because he had just turned 14 a few days before
the battle and was residing in Haverhill at the time.)  This introduction
may build an impression in the casual reader that Revolutionary New
England in general, or certainly the woods of southern New Hampshire,
were fairly jumping with a great plethora of James Eatons including
some we have no clue about, any one of whom could have played this
role, leaving us the hopeless task of finding the James of Deering needle
in a large haystack.  This is very far from the case.

Actually, the number of James Eatons who could have been at
Bennington and later lived their lives in Deering is very small, and the
odds are substantial that we must know nearly every one of them. We
can demonstrate this with the data base we built in connection with the
Census identification project of Appendix B, because it covers not just
the Eatons descending from John and Anne of Salisbury, but from all of
the lines who arrived in New England during the Great Migration.

It would be nice if our coverage of all these descendants were
complete, and of course it is not. There actually are two threats to our
coverage. One is the loss of viable Eaton twigs who permanently disappear from our field of view at each generation. Since this "leakage" cumulates, by the time we arrive at the eighth generation, our coverage
probably has become quite marginal indeed, although it is hard to estimate whether we still have 80% coverage of the actual patrilineal descendants extant in the eighth generation, or only 50%. In the analysis of
given names we have made from our big Eaton database to apply here to
our James of Deering mystery, we have only examined Eaton children
named before 1780. These naming decisions were thus made almost
completely by parents who themselves were born before 1760 (and usually well before!) which means they are largely of parents of the fifth
generation or earlier, with a small admixture of the earliest parents of the
sixth generation. Hence coverage has remained much closer to complete
than if we had used later generations as well. Indeed, one cause of serious leakage is a population in far-ranging geographic motion. The New
England population remained in a relative sense, at least, remarkably sta-
tionary until 1760, when the northern New England interior "wilderness"
was opened for settlement. This development was followed after the
Revolution by a still larger mass movement out of New England westward. Since we use no births after 1779, our given names are very little
impacted by the first of these migrations, and not at all by the second.

The preceding paragraph refers to "coverage" of descendants
from the original Great Migration Eatons. The second threat to our inferences would be the entry of additional Eaton lines to New England in
the period after 1650. There is no question from our own researches that
by 1850, the original population of Great Migration Eatons in New
England was being notably modified by Eaton newcomers from England, Scotland and Ireland. On the other hand, it is well known that after
the Great Migration, immigration to New England fell to a very small
trickle prior to the Revolution. With our outer limit of 1780, our data
have no need for more than trivial adjustment for any new arrivals.

Before we apply our given-name data to the James of Deering
problem, let us describe a few more general findings from it. These are,
in particular, findings suggesting that given names are at least somewhat
rarer than casual genealogists understand. And with this rarity comes
heightened diagnostic value that should not be ignored. If we find a
"John Eaton" (or any other surname of interest) out of context in some
document or other, we are very unlikely to waste effort pursuing a firmer
identification, because after all, "John" is such a common name that there
must be dozens of them lurking at this time and place. How could we

ever sort them all out? Well, it is true that of the 823 names bestowed by Eaton parents descending from Great Migration Eatons before 1780, far and away the most popular given name is indeed "John." It is well out in front of the second thru the sixth places on the popularity list, the latter five names finishing in just about a dead heat (Thomas, Joseph, Benjamin, Samuel and William). Nonetheless, there is in the repertoire such a staggering number of given-name possibilities that even John Eatons are not overwhelmingly numerous. Over the time frame covered, only about eight out of every 100 Eaton sons were christened "John." For second-place "Thomas," the number is already down to five per hundred.

The reader should be cautioned at this point that while the more abstract facts of given-name structure we cite here probably have fair generality for New England in this period, the hierarchy of specific names is based on Eaton practices, and may well generalize very poorly to lines of other surnames. This is because given-name choices are very "lumpy" by lineage, a fact vivid even within all these Eatons. While "John" might well win a comparable popularity contest run within many New England surnames, its strong performance for these Eaton lineages is clearly helped along by the fact that two of the five original migrants were themselves christened "John." Within those two lines, 9.3 sons per 100 are christened John, or nearly half again the rate of Johns in the other three lines (6.7 per 100), Similarly, in the line descended from William Eaton of Reading, nearly 12 sons per hundred were also Williams, whereas in the three Eaton lines rooted elsewhere than Reading, only 3.7 sons per 100 were named William. (For the other Reading line out of Jonas, Williams were 4.6 per 100.) None of these comparisons should imply that Eaton parents in 1750 were necessarily trying to name their children after their first ancestor off the boat. The fact of having a grandfather and a favorite uncle named William--relatively common in the William line and very uncommon elsewhere--would of course suffice to continue the tradition.

The rarity of most given names even in colonial times, when the palette of name possibilities was vastly smaller than it is today, is best illustrated by turning to the opposite extreme of our popularity listing. 44% of all *names* given by Eaton parents (as opposed to *babies* named) were singletons, given to only one Eaton son in the whole set of 823. And well over half (60%) of 133 names found were used twice or less.

Given this context, it is not surprising that the commonness of "James" lies between these extremes. Actually, it is in one sense fairly common, since it just misses the top ten of our popularity list. But with the numbers as they are, this does not mean it is in any absolute sense very common at all. Only about 2.8 per hundred of Eaton sons in our data set were given the name James. Furthermore, this overall average conceals some family lumpiness of great importance to us. In all but one of the lineages we trace, James is given as a name only 2.1 times per 100; but in the small Haverhill branch from John of Salisbury and son Thomas[2], "James" sons occur 7.5 times per 100. This is still not *absolutely* very common; but James is almost as popular in the Haverhill branch in this period as John is for the data set as a whole, a standard usually

thought of as very common.  Moreover, if the point is to locate the roots
of the mystery James Eaton of Deering who supposedly fought at Bennington, then the Haverhill Branch is even more relevant, since at least
80% or more of the James Eatons (i.e. of the total of 23 in our data set
from the period pre-1780) can be disqualified on *prima facie* grounds,
meaning that they patently lived either at the wrong time or too distant
from the swath of southern New Hampshire that Gen. Stark's junior officers worked for recruits to bring to Bennington.  This swath ran through
communities like Chester and Candia, Goffstown, Lyndeborough and
westward.  Apart from the William Eaton twig in Candia (its Sgt. James
not a participant as we have seen), this swath in the relevant period was
otherwise the home territory of Eaton settlers from the Haverhill.

   Before departing from the diagnoses permitted by given-name
analysis to pursue the road to Bennington, there is one more stop to
make.  We can raise the dispensing of given names to another level of
rarity, to increase our diagnostic power.  (This requires extended explanation of a mildly technical sort; uninterested readers are encouraged to
leap to the Bennington subhead below.)  We have mentioned that genealogists often get faint-hearted if given the task of identifying a John,
because Johns are just too common.  We have pointed out that yes, they
are relatively common; but absolutely, they are rare enough to be worth
some search.  Now we want to up this ante.  A genealogist who is interested in a married *couple* named John and Mary may feel equally faint-
hearted, because after all, "Mary," in addition to being a grand old name,
may also be just as common for girls (let's say) as John is for boys.  But
there is a logical fallacy here.  Assume for purposes of argument that
John and Mary did not get married in part or whole because of some felt
attraction to commonness of given names.  In other words, either could
as easily have married somebody with a totally different name, which is
another way of saying that the two married for reasons "independent" of
the specific given names involved.  Then a probability rule of great importance governing such chance *joint* occurrences comes into play.  If
the probability of a John occurring in a given male population is 8 per
100; and if (let's say) the probability of a Mary in the female population
is 8 per 100 as well, the probability of a John/Mary marriage is not also 8
times per 100 as some might guess, but rather the product of the two
probabilities ($.08 \times .08 = .0064$), or 64 times in 10,000, or 6.4 times per
1000, or roughly two-thirds of one time in 100.  Thus a John/Mary tan-
dem is much, much rarer than either taken alone.  More practically
speaking, this means that if you find a John/Mary couple in a lineage of
interest, at a time and place that are reasonably appropriate, you need not
fret that there might be lots of other John/Mary couples to be confused
with them, merely because the two names are so common.

   With parents of colonial times having large child litters and be-
stowing multiple given names, we have a chance to look for joint occurrences of names among siblings that might be very sharply diagnostic.
(We shall not formally pursue the multiplication of probabilities rule for
sibling names in this settting because it would require a messy adjustment
to take account of the fact that a family with a dozen sons would have

much greater opportunity to use a given pair of male names than a family with only two sons; and a family with but a single son would unable to do any pairing at all.  But the high improbability of any given pairing, if names were picked by chance, remains a useful machine to harness.)  We have already pointed out that parents of the Haverhill branch of Eatons were fond of the given name James, using it much more than any other Eatons in our net.  They were not quite as fond of the name David overall; but they showed a strong tendency to produce brothers who were named David as well as James, as a sort of a package.

We have assembled the data from all of the New England lines, to see where in all of these family branches the package of James and David sons might have been most noteworthy.  A family that might like to have both James and David sons has to start with one or the other, so we limit our attention to those litters of children with at least one of these names. Each row in our tabulation below represents one of these Eaton lineages, using the tags for each that are explained in the preceding Appendix B (p. 564).  Since it is illuminating here as elsewhere for us to keep the descendants of John[1] and Anne of Salisbury divided  into the Salisbury and Haverhill branches, we display six lineages rather than the customary five.  And given that some of these lineages are considerably larger than others, we show in parentheses after the lineage name the number of child names given out by parents in the colonial period covered.

The first two number columns show how many sons overall were given the names James and David in the lineage noted, during the period to 1780.  The third column shows the number of times that parents actually gave these two names to a pair of their sons; and the fourth column shows the number of times they could have completed a James-David pair by adding the missing name to any one of their other newborn sons. The fifth column is simply the percent of these potential pairs in the fourth column that were actually completed.  This percent would not have much meaning in situations where there was only one son born to the couple (by definition, bearing either the name James or David), but there is only one such instance in the whole table (one case of the six for JohnDed).  The final column shows a composite birth year for each pair,

### Brothers Named James & David, pre-1780
(Diagnostic Eaton Given Names, by Lineage.)

| Lineage | #Jas | #Dav | J-D Pairs | Other PossPrs | % Prs Comp | Pair Timing |
|---|---|---|---|---|---|---|
| FranPly (79) | 2 | 3 | 0 | 5 | 0 | ---- |
| JohnSal (186) | 3 | 2 | 0 | 5 | 0 | ---- |
| JohnDed(147) | 3 | 3 | 1 | 6 | 17 | 1748 |
| JonaRed (175) | 2 | 3 | 1 | 3 | 33 | 1777 |
| WmRed (130) | 4+ | 3+ | 1/3 | 5/3 | 50 | 1738 ('74, '78) |
| ThoHav (106) | 7 | 5 | 4 | 4 | 50 | 1702, '34, '66, '68 |

being simply the average year of birth of the two brothers. The one irregularity in the table concerns the row for the William of Reading line, where alternate numbers are entered. This is because our field of view for these christenings stops at 1780. However, in the William line there was one David born in the 1770s who received a James brother in 1782, and one James born in the 1770s winning a David brother in 1782 as well. Obviously the completion of these additional James/David "packages" should be recognized in the table, despite technically being beyond our time window. And taking these tardy births into account means that the William line shows 5 Jameses and 4 Davids.

If we were to bundle together all the data above for the first four lineages, then the low incidence of James/David pairs we see would be reasonably close to the chance expectation for adding the second name, given that we have limited these data to cases where one name is already present. The situation is totally different in the final two rows. For both of these rows, the frequency of James/David brother is vastly beyond any chance expectation on the basis of joint occurrence. This is obviously because of traditions in both lineages which look favorably on both James and David as given names. This tradition is a bit stronger in the Haverhill branch than for the William line of Reading. And it seems to have been there longer as well, since most signs of the special package of James and David for the William line do not begin to register until the late 1770s. These results suggest that we would most likely find the Deering James within the Haverhill branch, but if we fail there, it could be worth our time to examine the William line from Reading. We are not in the least sanguine about looking at the latter, however, because of what we already know, i.e., that the early James/David pair featured Sgt. James of Chester, who seems disqualified; and the other three Jameses out of William's line are way too late in time to qualify for Bennington service. The earliest one is in fact a son of Sgt. James, not born until 1770.

At very long last, the reader is now prepared for the real punch line of this analysis of given names. It is obvious that the Goffstown James[6], named in the last days of 1760, is merely one symptom of the strong James (and secondarily, David) tradition in the Haverhill branch. On the other hand, none of the given names dispensed by mystery James of Deering to his sons has been included in the data presented so far, For one thing, the jury is still out on which lineage James of Deering belongs to, so we would not have known where to put his choices. But in addition we had intentionally put a deadline of 1780 on these data, or just before the Deering James began to have his children. We set the analysis up in this way precisely because we wanted to understand the family traditions about naming which had accumulated up to the time when the Deering James and his wife Martha began to have their own children in the early 1780s.

Now we shall unveil these later given names. The young Deering couple, James and Martha Eaton, chose to name their firstborn son David in 1784; and after a John in 1786, their thirdborn son was named James. So they delivered their James/David package in short order. These family decisions heighten our sense that the Deering James must have come out of the Haverhill branch, since there are no Jameses of the William line available. But six of the seven known Haverhill Jameses born before 1780 have other preemptive life histories. Four in fact, starting with James of Hillsborough in 1763, were born too late to be at the Battle of Bennington. Only the Goffstown James[6] has no competing adult history and was in exactly the right place at the right time for the Bennington battle. But he could not have been James of Deering we are told, because death kept him from having much of an adult history anyway.

The Bennington Connection. Although our sketch for James[6] of Goffstown cum James of Deering (#522) has summarized away some details about the march to Bennington, none of those seem diagnostically valuable in this quest, so we shall not add much firm fact here. But we shall try to poke a few holes in what we think we know.

On the broadest cynical note, it is possible that neither of these two James Eatons (if two there are, instead being of one and the same) fought at Bennington; or if they are two, that one did and the other did not. Surely the Battle of Bennington was in its time the most glorious moment of the Revolution for the population of northern New England; and this means that the number of persons of the appropriate age cohorts who later believed, or at least claimed, that they were there, would have filled a second battle-field or more. (Reports from less romantic tours of duty that never faced actual military engagement are probably more trustworthy.) Beyond the officer corps, knowledge of who was where when rests on long lists of privates, in this case lists printed in the *N.H. State Papers* volumes of Revolutionary Rolls. Here is a point when the commonness of some given names and the rarity of others is of extreme importance. While there are not a lot of John Eatons in an absolute sense, identifying a John Eaton in an unannotated list of 40 other privates is a bit daunting. Occasionally such lists are identified by community of residence, an enormous help, even where common names are involved. Propinquity on one of these long lists is also worth putting some weight upon; and sometimes one can infer the community of origin of a common name by seeing if it is imbedded in a series of more unusual names that can be found to have had a common residence.

The military record of James of Deering is about as robust as one can normally expect for privates, although it is prey to some ambiguities. The saving grace here is that in 1855, six years after her husband's death, James's widow Sarah, a good 35 years his junior and surviving until 1883, filed for a land bounty warrant on the basis of her husband's Revolutionary service. This is a document we have not seen; but it is referred to when she applied for a Revolutionary War Pension at the late date of 1878. In both documents, apparently, she described three Revolutionary service stints performed by husband James. While it is not important for this story, it is interesting that the second application in 1878 was challenged by screening authorities in Concord, N.H., because in 1855 she had supposedly signed her name, but in 1878 she had just made her "mark," because of inability to sign. She responded that for the first application, one of her sons had guided her hand through a signature; she had not had this assistance for the second application.

What is important for our cynical account here is that Sarah's statement of the three service stints of James of Deering, leading off with the Battle of Bennington, mirrors very nicely a sequence of records in the *N.H State Papers* (Vol XV) attributed to a Private James Eaton, not otherwise identified or individuated. Indeed, it is this fit that gives us some assurance that it was not the James Eaton of Chester who is the referent for some or all of the records. (There are independent assurances as well, such as the fact that James of Chester had been a sergeant earlier in Massachusetts, and was an older man, born 1735, long married and with at least six children to feed and more on the way at the time of Bennington. Hence he was unlikely to have signed up again, now as a private in a N.H. muster.)

Nonetheless, to a cynical eye, the fit can seem a little too nice for a second-hand account from a widow on toward a century later than the actual events. This can raise several questions, foremost of which is why we find no record that James of Deering himself applied for a War pension in either 1818 or 1832, dates at which he was apparently still very *compos mentis.* Had he done so, he would have laid out the three service stints firsthand, and then the widow's copy of them years later would be less wondrous, since there are citations of chains of command that are not things memorable to mere listeners many years later. But perhaps he had drafted such a statement with an eye to earlier application; or perhaps some of his children had captured information of this kind. The big worry, of course, is that the widow's applications were ginned up from some clever reading of the State Papers, looking for a plausible sequence of service stints attributed to an otherwise unidentified and unidentifiable James Eaton. The fact that she herself was illiterate is some mild assurance that this is unlikely; but she might have had help. On the other hand, the fact that James of Deering took up residence in Deering in a quadrant of town which is laden with distinctive names of co-resident men on the lists of fellow privates marching on to Bennington, seems to offer objective and unfalsiable information that allays a lot of worries about the possible ambiguity of the record. All told, therefore, we have been willing to accord a good deal of face validity to this service record, and have seen it as a considerable reassurance that James of Deering, whoever he may otherwise be, was in fact at Bennington and had two other service stints, terminating in a discharge on 4 Jan 1779.

If James[6] of Goffstown died in 1785 without morphing into James of Deering, the record is largely credible that he too went off to fight at Bennington, raising questions as to why there are not more unidentifiable James Eatons at that battle. Also, if we take the matter from the front-side Goffstown point of view, rather than the backside Deering point of view, we can still find a nagging doubt or two. In the run-up to the Battle of Bennington, the crucial mustering point was at Lyndeborough, N.H., a minor township, the second southwest of Goffstown, N.H., and the second to the south of Deering itself. Of course Lyndeborough itself had little population, and was merely the geographic center of a

catchment basin where the mobilization of troops had been highly publicized.  (In military payrolls for this period and area, one help in localiz-
ing recruits is whether or not they are paid for the ferry charges across
the Merrimack River, necessary for those originating east of it, but not
for Goffstown or most of the other recruits at Lyndeborough.)   The
muster here was most generally into Capt. Peter Clark's Co., of Col.
Stickney's Regt., of Gen. Stark's Brigade.  This muster occurred in the
last week of July 1777; the actual Battle of Bennington took place Aug.
16, 1777.  Clark's Co. went on to reinforce the Continental Army at Stillwater, N.Y. after the Bennington victory, and James Eaton is on the pay-
roll with it.

   Among recruits from Goffstown, we have an Enoch[5] Eaton, unquestionably the youngest brother of Capt. Timothy Eaton in Haverhill
(#210), 28 years of age at the time, who had married in 1769 and had
recently removed to Goffstown, with four children already in hand.  With
him supposedly are two nephews, sons of his brother James[5], the one who
had removed to Goffstown 15 years earlier to raise his family.  The elder
is Samuel[6], at this moment just turned 18; the younger is our famous
James[6], who had only turned 16 the preceding December.  All were privates.  We find Enoch and Samuel listed as a separate pair on p. 174 of
the *New Hampshire Papers*, Vol. XV.  They are a good example of an
easy identification once we are presented with a combination of two
names, even if only one of the two names is unusual: we know beyond
little doubt that they are our Haverhill branch residing in Goffstown, and
are the young Eatons in that town of ages most likely to go off to war.
We would be happier if they were listed as a trio with James, and we do
not understand why they are not.  But there is a James Eaton, also in the
pay of Peter Clark's Co., in a fairly short list of names which are unfamiliar, but some of whom figure as later Deering residents and neighbors
of James of Deering there.  It occurs to us to mention that if this James
Eaton were somehow not actually James[6], but some other James Eaton,
there is in context only one other candidate even faintly plausible, and
this would be father James[5], brother of Enoch and the original Eaton migrant to Goffstown.  This is not a very likely possibility however.  James[5]
Sr. at this time was 39 years old, having sired eight children.  The three
youngest had died in rapid succesion the preceding year, presumably of
some contagious disease, and his wife was expecting their ninth child six
weeks after the moment of the Lyndeborough muster.  James[5] is thus a
vastly less likely candidate to be bound for Bennington than his son
James[6].  But even if it could be proved that it was the father and not the
son who was the Bennington James, it would do very little to resolve our
identification problems: there is no way that Father James[5] could be
transmogrified into the later James of Deering, in the way that his son
James[6] is on all counts (save the little one of early death) neatly fitted for.

   After the James who did the three service stints ending in Jan.
1779 (be he somehow only the James of Deering and not also James[6] of
Goffstown) was discharged, it seems likely that he would return home,
wherever that might be.  It could also be presumed that having turned 18
and seen the world, that he might be in a courting mood.  Actually,

courtship under conditions prevailing at the time were typically very local hometown affairs.  This was least true, of course, for young bucks who had gone off to war in foreign parts, as supposedly James[6] had.  (We have been amazed, for example, at the number of our Civil War Eatons from New England who ended up marrying Southern belles.)  But the majority do return home to start or resume local romances.

We lack useful information as to what James[6] of Goffstown did after his return from service and before his alleged death.  That period is simply a blank: for all we know he may have gone to sea and was lost there in 1785, although this would have been an unprecedented move for a Goffstown lad.  We also lack hard information about James of Deering's whereabouts before his marriage to Martha McClure at the end of November, 1782.  There is reason to imagine that he was getting his new stake organized in Deering by the time of the wedding, although he does not emerge on the public tax record in Deering until 1784.  But when we learn that his 1782 bride was "of Goffstown," it is something of a bombshell.  If we have become irretrievably convinced that the death report for Goffstown's James[6] in 1785 is true and James[6] cannot possibly be the same fellow as James of Deering, then it seems we should be struck by the remarkable coincidence that this other James of Deering at some time between 1779 and 1782 found and romanced his life-partner-to-be right there in James[6]'s own home town.  Perhaps he even stole her from him!!

* * * * * * *

To summarize, if it were not for the report of James[6]'s 1785 death, we doubt anyone would question that James of Deering must be the adult continuation of James[6] of Goffstown.  The death report aside, there is not a sour note in sight to challenge this continuation.  The age is right, the timing is right, the geography is right, the early military experience is right and the family traditions are right.  Any one of these taken alone could be written off as a minor coincidence: but it is the five-ply fit at every point of test which makes for overwhelming joint evidence.

Complementing this positive evidence is the seemingly total absence of plausible competing hypotheses as to who James of Deering might otherwise have been.  To be sure, a long genealogical tradition would give precious little weight to the latter point, on grounds that you never could know just how much you don't know; and there is always a legion of these unknown replacements lurking stage left and stage right in any of these complex situations.  Certainly, it would be argued, the lack of any rival explanation for James of Deering can't begin to compete with the news entered in the family Bible that James[6] died in 1785.

We continue to feel that our position is much stronger than usual in terms of having some sense of what we don't know, simply because we have a considerable fix on all five major lineages of Eatons in the New England of 1760, by which time the James of Deering must have been on the scene.  This coverage is certainly not complete by the time we have arrived at 1760, because there has been some progressive leakage.  However, what catches the eye at this point are the several rounds of circumstantial evidence above, to the effect that whoever James of Deering was (if not the Goffstown James), the odds are very high that he was spawned in the lineage out of Haverhill. This is because it is very likely that across our six Eaton lineages, the coverage of the Haverhill branch in 1760 should be most complete. This in turn is because our senior author, himself a member of that lineage, worked diligently to complete that line for publication through the fourth generation; and had subsequently done the fifth generation (without yet much care for their sixth-generation offspring), all with the help of inside family information, and was assembling these materials at a time when the trail was much warmer.

After all, much of what we call "leakage" is betrayed by palpable signs, and these signs are remarkably few in the first five or six generations of the Haverhill branch. In fact, we can lay our a hierarchy of what we call "palpable signs" here, from very threatening to much less so. The most threatening type of sign is represented in patrilineal genealogies by cases in which a son is born, marries, and then disappears. The odds here are very high, especially in the early period, that there will be children, and even quite a number, who will start more or less geometrical multiplications of their own twigs outside the view of the genealogist, thereby leaking away from its coverage. The incidence of such cases rises significantly in New England after 1760, as we have seen, because of increasing emigration, especially of newlyweds. But of course it exists pre-1760 in lesser degree as well. The next most serious sign is the kind of "stub" where a son's birth is listed without further information, such as assurance of death before maturity. Often when the truth can be learned, they did die young; but some may have been farmed out to other families and the like, such that the further children of these "disappeared" progeny should be numbered in the lineage but can't be. This means more leakage. Also threatening, of course, are instances where there is evidence (such as in pre-1850 Census family compositions) that a couple had more children than are known by name. And certainly one must accept the probability that some sons who survive to adulthood have left no signs at all.

We have evaluated the first six generations of the Haverhill branch for the "palpable" signs of leakage up through the sixth generation, a search which carries us well beyond 1760. For the first five generations, which by themselves bring us on balance nearly to 1760, there is not a single _palpable_ sign of leakage. That is, every male child known to have arrived at adulthood and to have married is given a continuation sketch dealing with _his_ children Furthermore, this leaves quite a set of sons whose deaths before marriage are specifically attested to; and a few further sons who had adult histories but were confirmed bachelors. There is not, in this particular set, even a married Eaton who had no issue. We do not draw the message from these counts that our coverage for the Haverhill branch is 100% out through 1760. In fact, we begin to see sixth-generation members of this line whom we know to have married and had unknown further seventh-generation children. So more serious leakage is starting by Generation VII. But that is beyond the horizon of what we need to cover to find somebody to step in as James of Deering.

Nonetheless, even within that horizon there are more hidden forms of leakage which occur at a low rate, so that our coverage of Eatons of the Haverhill branch for males born between 1750 and 1761 (the largest birth interval a "true" James of Deering can come from) may not be higher than, say, 95%.

Of course, the set of Haverhill Eaton males known to have been born between 1750 and 1761 is very small. In our data set, it is all of 14 Eatons. If we are failing to include in our count 5% of Eatons here, then given these numbers, we are most likely to be missing about .74 of an Eaton, which may be thought of--since Eatons don't come in fractions-- as meaning that in 3 of 4 trials we would find one missing Eaton and in the other there would be no missing Eatons at all. But the issue for us is not just finding missing Eatons, but missing *James* Eatons who might be available to take the role of James of Deering, since no other Jameses in the known set are available, already having adult histories of their own. And we surely should not make the mistake of assuming that all of the three missing Eatons we would expect to find in four trials would carry the name James. Quite to the contrary, even in the part of the James-loving Haverhill branch we know about, only about 8 sons in 100 were named James. Our best assumption being that missed Eatons will have about the same proportions of Jameses as Eatons we have counted, then we can see that a majority of the trials would have no missed *James* Eatons at all. Hence any illusions we might have that James of Deering can probably be explained by one of the James Eatons we have missed because of leakage are pretty ridiculous.

We have run through these steps to suggest why we do not see it as likely that if we search long enough, a James Eaton is likely to turn up elsewhere in the Haverhill branch whom we can use to account for James of Deering, thereby freeing up the Goffstown James to have died. Our more general point is even more important. While it may seem only common sense that we cannot know what we don't know in such a case, in some structured situations common in genealogy it is often very easy to make a rational assessment of *how much* we are likely not to know (as in our estimate of the leakage rate); and even to get from that to a rational assessment of what the contours of *what* we don't know are most plausibly going to look like (such as the likelihood of finding a James among the Eatons we have missed). These are powerful diagnostic tools.

Now do we think that there is practically no chance that James of Deering is not the Goffstown James, which is to say that there is practically no chance that the latter died in 1785? No, not at all. We are congenital sceptics about any extreme statements of this kind. The numbers we were using above have to do with the small (but not zero!) likelihood that some other real James of Deering could be found in the Haverhill branch of Eatons. While that is indeed a long shot, there are lots of other long shots which could equally provide for a James of Deering other than the Goffstown one. Perhaps he comes out of one of the other New England Eaton lines, who are much less likely to name a son James, but do so now and again; and who in any event, probably have significantly worse leakage rates in our data. Or perhaps he was a dissident born in

England who ventured to New England as a youngster just before the Revolution and enjoyed the chance to battle for liberation from the crown. Or perhaps his real name was Joe Finkelstein, but he liked the alias James Eaton better. None of these possibilities by itself has more than a chemical trace of being true. But the number of such possibilities we might spin out is very large indeed, and a good probability estimate has to add all of these very small possibilities together.

Our problem is that even adding together all sorts of quirky ways that we could find some other precursor for James of Deering does not bring us to a very high likelihood. One chance in five? Two? But we could not carry this very high. Which has left us with the feeling that the odds are better than 50-50 that something must be wrong with the 1785 death for James. Hence we tried for a time to find other ways of assessing the probability that such a death actually happened. One gambit here was to try to find in Goffstown a cemetery with a gravestone covering this death, which for us would have raised the probability that the acount was true.

There is no trouble accounting in this fashion for the deaths of James[6]'s three brothers. His oldest brother Samuel[6] removed to Vermont and is buried there. His second brother David[6] and his family are buried prominently in Goffstown. The third brother, Cotton[6], removed to Maine, and we have inspected his grave in Hermon. We find no grave in Goffstown for James[6] but he died almost 25 years before his parents. We find no graves for them, either, but they died decades before the other brothers. Obviously the main Goffstown cemeteries were created too late for these earlier deaths. We expected this and tried to find the kind of local antiquarian who might know of ancient and out-of-the-way burial plots on the south side of Goffstown, but were not successful.

Our second approach was to try to imagine a kind of scenario in which the Goffstown James died in one sense, but not in another. We close this detective story with the thoughts this provoked.


## DID JAMES OF GOFFSTOWN REALLY DIE IN 1785?

The most obvious way that James[6], Jr. of Goffstown might have "died" merely in the eyes of his father, James[5], Sr., was some extremely bitter falling out between father and son in 1785 which produced a rancorous estrangement and disinheritance, presumably involving threats of "never darken our door again," or such a meltdown that James, Sr., angrily decided to enshrine it in the family Bible as an actual death report.

We naturally then ask what could have touched off such a total rejection of the son by the father? This is even less answerable than most of the other questions we have been asking in this essay. Most likely it was some private family matter that could never be reconstructed, such as a belief of the father that his son had stolen from him, or had betrayed him in some way.

Nevertheless, we began to imagine a falling out that might reflect the disparate times and perspectives of this father and this son, about whom we actually know a good deal. So what we are about to recount is a "just-so" story, in the pejorative way in which that term is used, meaning that it is all made up whole cloth, and does not pretend to have any roots in intimate facts about this father and this son at all. But it does try to stay within an envelope which is faithful to important aspects of the historical context in which father and son had developed their views of the world.

Interested readers should at this point take a moment to read (or re-read) Sidebar #3 (p. 59) to refresh familiarity with certain tides that shook the middle Merrimack River in the middle decades of the 1700s, for we are about to use them quite centrally here.

* * * * * * *

Father James[5] of Goffstown (**#206**) had been born in Haverhill in 1738; and it is reasonable to imagine that he was well trained in the deep antagonisms felt by Haverhill citizens against the "Irish Party" of "papists" who had settled in force at Londonderry N.H. and made land claims that overlapped with those of Haverhill. He himself was not born until well after the peak of the bloodshed in these turf wars in 1730. On the other hand he was already three years old before the irate Haverhill citizenry managed to activate London to complete a more professional establishment of the Massachusetts-New Hampshire state line in 1741. And after Haverhill saw what London had done, by drawing the line farther south into Haverhill territory than had ever been presumed before, the outrage deepened.

It apparently mattered little to the Haverhill folks that the Londonderry adversaries were neither truly Irish nor in any way Catholic. They were instead Scotch Presbyterians who had fled to Ireland to avoid the religious persecution of King James against Protestants in Scotland. Londonderry was not only reviled in Haverhill, but for decades was treated as something of a foreign enclave on New Hampshire soil as well. The epithet "the Irish Party" as a "code" innuendo against the presumed Catholicism in Londonderry did not disappear from the formal papers of the N.H. authorities until after 1820. These hatreds ran deep.

For his part, son James[6] grew up in Goffstown in a period featuring a mood of rising resentment against British rule. He probably was politically unaware for most of his early years, although his elders were quite a divided lot. One uncle, Timothy[5] in Haverhill was a Son of Liberty and intensively active in the Revolutionary cause. Another uncle, David[5], whom he may never have seen, had gone to Connecticut before nephew James was born, and then had proceeded with others to line up for lucrative English grants to New England colonists to take over rich lands in Nova Scotia after the French "Acadians" who had developed them had been driven out, in an early bout of ethnic cleansing. David presumably was a devout Tory, and it is probably as well that he lived far away.

News reached Goffstown on son James's 14th birthday concerning the Boston Tea Party, In the spring following he was too young to respond to the alarm for Concord and Lexington or the later battle at Bunker Hill. But by the summer of 1777, then 16, he was able set off for the muster at Lyndeborough with his uncle Enoch and his older brother Samuel. This was undoubtedly an exciting new world for James, and he would re-up for two further stints in the army, probably more on his own, since his Uncle Enoch and perhaps his brother as well had returned to Goffstown. On the march to Bennington he was immersed in a group of buddies whose Scotch-Irish families were still in, or had recently spread outward from, the town of Londonderry. If he had ever shared his father's antagonism to Londonderry people, it certainly did not keep him from warming to his new friends. And the charismatic leader of the Bennington force was Gen. John Stark, another Londonderry man who had already played an outstanding role managing the N.H. forces at Bunker Hill. Stark had had some political snubs from the Continental Congress in the interim, but he was masterful in his direction of his forces at Bennington, becoming widely renowned and New Hampshire's favorite Conquering Hero despite his "Irish" background. It was reputedly Stark who gave N.H. its motto "Live free or die!" (Holden, 1958). Under these circumstances the Irish Party could not be all bad; and probably James was free of any libellous belief that tried to hint that these folks were crypto-papists. Indeed, from his closer familiarity with Londonderry people he may have felt some contempt that his father could hold such ignorant or contrarian beliefs.

By the fall of 1778, the hostilities had drifted southward out of New England for the most part, and son James[6] was discharged from the Army. Presumably he went home to Goffstown. By this time he had had two years out from under the family wing, and if he had any adolescent rebelliousness at all it was probably insufferable by the time of his return. We do not know of course whether father and son tangled at this point over their differences in tolerance of the Scotch-Irish. Certainly Stark's fame at that point may have left father James subdued about his own antagonisms. But son James's close relations with his war buddies, and his plan to rejoin them for a farming career in Deering, may well have produced a growing friction on the subject between the two. This would have come to a head, of course, as son James began courting Martha McClure, whose early Londonderry family had more recently moved to Goffstown. A David McClure, who was either Martha's father or brother, had also been on the Bennington march, and we can presume that this is how the young couple met.

By the fall of 1782, with marriage such a marriage in view, son James's uncomfortable relationship with his father may have been deteriorating further. In fact, this could be the reason why the couple chose to be married in Hillsborough rather than on their home turf. Or perhaps the rancor was so extreme that the fact of marriage was even to be kept secret for a time. And it would not be impossible that the final straw in the relationship involved a latter-day revelation of this secret. Whatever touched off the final explosion 27 months later remains unknown, but one can imagine an enraged son James[6] returning to Deering, never to darken his father's door again.

* * * * * * *

All made up of course, but a not-implausible story that saves the death report and leaves son James[5] a long life with his family in Deering. If there is single case in this volume where further spadework into original sources could be helpful, this is surely it.

# BIBLIOGRAPHY

(This bibliography is somewhat incomplete, and for several reasons. First, the senior author's original manuscript, in the style of the time, had no citations at all. He used both interviews of elderly informants and correspondence with farflung Eatons for a lot of his material, and these sources are somewhat difficult to subject to standard citations in any event. But he no doubt used more formal sources, and we have no way of reconstructing them. Second, the junior author spent the first half of his time on this project with no plans for publication at all, collecting information simply out of private curiosity. In this period he kept rather casual tabs on sources, and there are surely some references that belong below but have been lost sight of. Third, some of the resources that we have worked most heavily find no useful place in this bibliography. We have, for example, reviewed some thousands of land deeds, most of them routine or otherwise uninformative, but some dozens of considerable interest. Many of the most crucial of these we cite in the standard county, volume and page format where relevant in the text; and it would be nonsense even to list these crucial references again here, much less provide the parent list of a thousand or two. The same can be said of Census data, since the time and place is typically obvious when relevant data are mentioned; so rather than cite all the Census Index books we have used and the vastly larger number of reels of film we have run, we assume readers can find their way easily to the source. We also have used tax lists where available, and in communities where lots of our Eatons have congregated, we have done some community-wide statistical analyses, the better to locate our Eatons within the local social structure. Such tax lists tend to be more fugitive, but if we cite tax data for a community, it means they definitely exist for the time period mentioned, and should not take great magic to find.)

Allen, Mildred S. (1982). *Deer Isle's History: comprising that territory now the towns of Deer Isle, Stonington, and Isle au Haut, Maine.* Salt Lake City: FHL US/CAN #1033802, item 7.

Annett, A. & Alice E. E. Lehtinen (1934). *History of Jaffrey, N.H.* Pub. by the Town of Jaffrey.

Banks, Charles Edward (1929). *The English Ancestry and Homes of the Pilgrim Fathers.* New York City.

Banks, Charles Edward (1935). *History of York, Maine.* Boston: Calkins Press.

Beaman, Alden (1978). *Rhode Island Vital Records, New Series: Vol. 4, Washington County.* Princeton, Mass.: published by the compiler.

Bedford Historical Society (c. 1972). *History of Bedford, N.H., 1737-1791*. Published by the Society.

Bell, Charles (1851). *History of Chester, N.H., 1720-1784*. Concord: G. Parker Lyon.

Bittinger, J. Q. (1888). *History of Haverhill, N.H.* Pub. Haverhill, N.H.

Bixby [Ed.] (1897). *Biographical Sketches of Leading Citizens of Grafton County, New Hampshire.* Buffalo, New York: Biographical Publishing Co.

Bixby, Roland (1986). *History of Warren [N.H.]*. Typescript.

Black, Col. Frederick F. (1960). *Searsport Sea Captains.* Searsport, Me.: Penobscot Marine Museum.

Blood, Grace H. (c1948). *Manchester on the Merrimack: the story of a City.* Manchester, N.H.: Lew A. Cummings.

Brooks, Thelma Eye (1983). *Inscriptions of Cemeteries in Hermon, Me.* LDS Archive, Salt Lake City.

Brown, Warren (1900). *History of Hampton Falls, N.H.* Concord, N.H.: Rumford Press.

Browne, G. Waldo (1922). *History of Hillsborough, N.H.* Manchester, N.H.: Town Clarke Co.

Bundy, David A. (c1975). *100 Ares More or Less: the History of the Land and People of Bow, N.H.* Canaan, N.H.: Phoenix Pub.

Burgess, Walter H. (1920). *John Robinson, the Pastor of the Pilgrims.* London, England.

Burnham, Henry (1880). *Brattleboro, Windham Co., Vermont: Early History.* Brattleboro: D. Leonard.

Butler, F. G. (1885). *History of Farmington, Franklin Co., Me., 1776-1885.* Farmington, Me.: Knowlton, McCleary & Co.

Carter, Rev. N. F. (1906). *The Native Ministry of New Hampshire.* Concord, N.H.: Rumford Printing Co.

Chase, Benjamin (1869). *History of Old Chester from 1719 to 1869.* Auburn, N.H.: Benjamin Chase.

Chase, George W. (1861). *History of Haverhill, Mass.* Published by the author at Haverhill.

Chase, Lydia Bernice (Eaton) (undated). *Genealogy of the Eatons of Salisbury, Mass. and Seabrook, N.H.* Manuscript at the Seabrook Historical Society.

Chelsea [Vt.] Historical Society (1984). *A History of Chelsea, Vermont.*

Chipman, Scott Lee (1993). *New England Vital Records from the Essex Newsletter, 1831-40.* Special Publication #2 of the N.H. Genealogical Society.

Clifford, Susannah (c1995). *Village in the Hills: a History of Danville, Vermont, 1786-1995.* West Kennebunk, Me.: Phoenix Publishing.

Coburn, Louise H., *et al.* (1941). *Skowhegan on the Kennebec.* Skowhegan, Me.: Independent Reporter Press.

Cochrane, Rev. W. R. (1880). *History of Antrim, N.H.* Manchester, N.H.: Mirror Steam Printing Press.

Cochrane, Rev. W. R. & George K. Wood (1895). *History of Francestown, N.H.* Nashua, N.H.: published by the Town.

Coffin, Charles C. (1878). *History of Boscawen and Webster [N.H.]. from 1733 to 1878.* Concord, N.H.: Republican Press Assn.

Cogswell, Leander W. (c1973). *History of the Town of Henniker, Merrimack Co., N. H.* Somersworth, N.H.: the New Hampshire Publishing Co.

*Columbia Encyclopedia* (2002). New York: Columbia University Press.

Committee (1886). *History of Washington, N.H.* Pub. Claremont, N.H.

Converse, Evelyn Eaton (1960). "The Obsolete Art of Walking," *New Hampshire Profiles* (May 1960), p.28ff.

Copeley, William N. (1994). New Hampshire family records. Bowie, Md.: Heritage Books.

Corinth, Vt., Town History Committee (1984). *The History of Corinth, Vt., 1764-1964.*

Corliss, Augustus W. (1956). *Historical and Genealogical Memoranda for a History of the Towns of North Yarmouth and Yarmouth, Maine. Salt Lake City: Film FHL US/CAN #11593 -94. -95.*

Cronan, Francis W. (1965). *Red Sunday: the Saltonstalls, the Dustons & the Fighting Ayers.* Haverhill, Mass.: Record Publishing Co.

Cudworth, Addison E. (1936). *The History of Londonderry, Vt. with Genealogical Sketches.* Montpelier, Vt.: Vermont Historical Society.

Cutter, Daniel B. (1881). *History of the Town of Jaffrey, New Hampshire.* Concord, N.H.: Republican Press Association.

Cutter, William R. *Genealogical and personal memoirs relating to the families of the State of Massachusetts.*

Davis, Isaac F., Jr. (1962). *A History of Solon, Maine.* Orono, Me.: University of Maine.

Dearborn, Jeremiah W. (1995). *History of Parsonsfield, Maine, 1771 to 1885.* Hampton, N.H.: Peter E. Randall.

Dearborn, John H. (1890). *History of Salisbury, N.H.* Manchester, N.H.: W. E. Moore.

De Wolfe, Edith (1953). *The History of Putney, Vermont, 1753-1953.* Putney, Vt.: Fortnightly Club of Putney.

Donovan, Rev. D. & Jacob A. Woodward (1906). *History of Lyndeborough.* Lyndeborough, N.H.: H. W. Whittemore.

Dow, Robert Piercy (1929). *The Book of Dow.* Claremont, N.H.: Private printing.

Dunbar, Robert E. & George F. Dow (1988). *Nobleboro, Maine, a History.* Nobleboro: Nobleboro Historical Society.

**Eaton, Arthur Wentworh Hamilton (1929).** *The Eaton Families of Nova Scotia. 1760-1929.* **Cambridge, Mass.: The Murray Printing Company: private printing.**

Eaton, Francis B. (1852). *History of Candia, N.H., once known as Charmingfare.* Manchester, N.H., J.O. Adams.

Elder, Janus G. (1989). *A History of Lewiston, Me.: with a genealogical register of early families.* Bowie, Md.: Heritage Books.

Emery, Edwin (1901). *The History of Sanford, Maine, 1661-1900.* Fall River, Mass.: W. M. Emery.

Erwin, Charles H. (1917). *An Early History of Painted Post and the
    Town of Erwin.* Painted Post, New York: Automatic Press.
*Etonian News.* Published by the Eaton Families Association, active
    1882-1899; re-estabished May 4, 1933. Sporadic Issues, starting
    with Vol. 1, No. 1 (Jan 1933), with at least 22 issues following,
    running well into the 1950s.
Felch, Wm. F. (1881). *Memorial History of the Felch Family.*
Ferriss, Rachel (Eaton) (1878). *Interesting Sketch of Captain Robert
    Eaton.* The Painesville (Ohio) Telegraph, 31 Oct 1878.
Fipphen, John (1993). *Cemetery Inscriptions, Wolfeboro, N.H.* Bowie,
    Md.: Heritage Books.
Fisher, Carleton E. (1970). *History of Clinton, Me.* Augusta, Me.:
    KJ Printing.
Fisher, Carleton E. & Sue G. Fisher (c 1982). *Soldiers, Sailors and
    Patriots of the Revolutionary War: Maine.* Louisville, Ky.:
    National Society of the Sons of the American Revolution.
Fisher, Carleton E. & Sue G. Fisher (1992). *Soldiers, Sailors and
    Patriots of the Revolutionary War: Vermont.* Camden, Me.:
    Picton Press.
Folsom, George (1830). *History of Saco and Biddeford, Me.* Saco:
    Alexander Putnam.
Frizzell, Martha M. (1963). *A History of Walpole New Hampshire.*
    Walpole, N.H.: Walpole Historical Society.
Fullonton, Joseph (1875). *The History of Raymond, N.H.* Dover, N.H.:
    Morning Star Job Printing House.
General Society of Colonial Wars (1941). *Supplement to the 1922
    Index of Ancestors.* Hartford, Conn.
Gilbert, Edgar (1903). *History of Salem, New Hampshire.* Concord,
    N.H.: Rumford Printing Co.
Goss, K. David & David Zarowin (1985). *Massachusetts Officers and
    Soldiers in the French and Indian Wars, 1755-1756.* Boston,
    Mass.: Society of Colonial Wars in the Commonwealth of Massa-
    chusetts.
Grant, Stephen A. (1956). *Limerick, Maine: History, Town and Vital
    Records.* Salt Lake City: Genealogical Society of Utah: FHL
    US/CAN Film #11542.
Gray, Ruth (1990). *Abstract of Penobscot (Me.) Wills.* Camden, Me.:
    Picton Press.
Griffin, Simon G. (1980). *The History of Keene, N.H.* Bowie, Md.:
    Heritage Books.
Greene, David L. (1997). "Notes on Francis[1] Eaton of Plymouth," *The
    American Genealogist* (Jul-Oct 1997), pp. 305-309.
Gunscheon, Mildred et al. (197?). *Two Hundred Plus: Bradford, N.H.,
    in Retrospect.* Canaan, N.H.: Phoenix Publishing.
Hadley, George P. (1924). *The History of Goffstown, N.H., 1733-
    1920.* Published by the Town.
Hanaford, Mary E. (1932). *Meredith, N.H., annals and genealogies.*
    Concord, N.H.: Rumford Press.

Harriman, Walter (1879). *The History of Warner, N.H. for one hundred and forty-four years, 1735 to 1879.* Concord, N.H.: Republican Press Association.

Harrison, Henry (1969), *Surnames of the United Kingdom: a Concise Etymological Dictionary.* Baltimore: Genealogical Publishing Company.

Hatch, William Collins (1893). *A History of the Town of Industry, Franklin Co. Maine.* Farmington, Me.: Knowlton, McLeary.

Hay, Cecile B. & Mildred B. (1967). *History of Derby [Vt.].* Littleton, N.H.: Courier Printing.

Hayward, Silvanus (1881). *History of Gilsum, N.H.* Pub. Manchester, N.H.

Hazlett, Charles A. (1915). *History of Rockingham County (N.H.) and Representative Citizens.* Chicago, Ill.: Richmond-Arnold Pub.

Hill, Mary P. [Ed.] (1929). *VR of Topsham, Me. to 1892.* Maine Historical Society.

Hill, Mary P. [Ed.] (1935). *VR of Phippsburg, Me. to 1892.* Maine Historical Society.

*Historical New Hampshire (1964), Colonial Innkeepers,* Volume XIX, No. 1, pp. 14, 29 and 45.

Hoiland, Doris R. (1975). *Pioneers of the Southern Tier: Steuben Co. (N.Y.).* Elmira, N.Y.

Holden, Raymond P. (1958). *The Merrimack.* (One of the *Rivers of America* Books). New York City: Rinehart & Co.

Holmes, Richard (c1988). *A View from Meeting-House Hill: a History of Sandown, N.H.* Portsmouth, N.H.: Peter E. Randall.

Horton, Louise S., *et al.* (1900?). *Piermont, New Hampshire, 1764-1947.* Bradford, Vt.: Green Mountain Press.

Hosmer, George L. (1905). *An Historical Sketch of the Town of Deer Isle, Maine.* Boston, Mass: the Fort Hill Press.

Hoyt, David W. (1871). *Genealogical History of the Hoyt, Haight, and Hight Families.* Providence, R.I.: The Providence Press Co.

Hoyt, David W. (1982). *The Old Families of Salisbury and Amesbury, Massachusetts.* Original Three Volumes & Supplement in One Volume. Baltimore: Genealogical Publishing Co. [Original volumes published at Providence, Rhode Island, Vol. I: 1897-99; Vol. II: 1902-05; Vol. III: 1916; Additions, Corrections, 1919.]

Hoyt, Peter L. (1976). *Hoyt's History of Wentworth, New Hampshire.* Littleton, N.H.: Courier Publishing Company,

Hubbard, C. Horace & Justus Dartt (1895). *History of Springfield, Vermont, with a genealogical record, 1752-1895.* Boston: G. H. Walker.

Jackson, James R. & Ezra S. Stearns (1905). *History of Littleton, N.H.* Cambridge: Published for the Town by the University Press.

Jackson, Mary S. & Edward F. (1998). *Marriage Notices from Steuben County, New York, Newspapers, 1797-1884.* Heritage Books.

Janvrin, Lance K. (1???). *Janvrin Genealogy.* Seabrook, N.H. Historical Society.

Jewett, Jeremiah P. (1872). *History of Barnstead, N.H.* Lowell, Mass.:
    Marden & Rowell.
Jewett, Martin H. (1976). *A History of Hollis, Me., formerly Little Falls,
    later Phillipsburg.* Farmington, Me.: Knowlton & McLeary.
Johnston, John (1873). *A History of the towns of Bristol and Bremen in
    the State of Maine.* Albany: Joel Munsell.
Jones, Erasmus (1897). *History of the Town of Frankfort [Me.].*
    Winterport: C. R. Lougee.
Jones, William H. (1998). *Vital Statistics of Seabrook, N.H., 1768-1903.*
    Bowie, Md.: Heritage Books.
Kernoul, Helen W. (198?). *Georgetown, Maine, Records.*
Kidder, Frederic (1852). *History of New Ipswich, N.H.* Boston: Gould
    & Lincoln.
Kingsbury, F. B. (1932). *History of Langdon, N.H.* Pub. White River
    Junction, Vt.
Lancaster, Daniel (1845). *History of Gilmanton, N.H.* Gilmanton, N.H.:
    Alfred Prescott.
Leonard, L. W. & J. L. Seward. (1920). *History of Dublin, N.H.*
Little, George Thomas [Ed.] (1909). *Genealogical & Family History of
    the State of Maine.* New York: Lewis Historical Publishing Co.
Little, William (1870). *The History of Warren, a Mountain Hamlet
    Located among the White Hills of New Hampshire.* Manchester,
    N.H.: William E. Moore.
Little, William (1888). *History of Weare, N.H.* Lowell, Mass.: S. W.
    Huse.
Livermore, A. A. & S. Putnam. (1888). *History of the Town of Wilton,
    N.H.* Lowell, Mass.: Marden & Rowell.
Locke, Mrs. Samuel (1881). *Record of Deaths in Seabrook, N.H.,
    between 1806 and 1865.* Xerox of Manuscript at N.H. Histori-
    cal Society, Concord, N.H.
Long, Alice MacD. (1992). *Marriage Records of Hancock Co., Me.*
    Camden, Me.: Picton Press.
Lord, C. C. (1890). *Life and Times in Hopkinton, N.H.* Concord:
    Republican Press Association.
Lyford, James O. [Ed.] (1903). *History of Concord, N.H.* Concord,
    N.H.: Rumford Press.
MacKay, Robert E. (c1978). *Massachusetts Soldiers in the French and
    Indian wars, 1744-1755.* Boston, Mass.: Society of Colonial
    Wars.
Maraspin, Davis G. [compiler] (1930). *Eaton, Fox, Newcomb and
    Seward Ancestry of George B. & Edward E. Wendell.* Type-
    script at New England Historical and Genealogical Society
    (NEHGS).
Martin, Yvonne E. (1988). *Marriages & Deaths from Steuben County,
    N. Y., Newspapers, 1797-1868.* Bowie, Md.: Heritage Books.
*Massachusetts Soldiers and Sailors in the War of the Revolution* (1896-
    1908). Boston, Mass.: Wright & Potter Printing.
McClellan, Hugh D. (1903). *History of Gorham, Me.* Portland, Me.:
    Smith & Sale.

McKeen, Silas (1875). *A History of Bradford, Vermont.* Montpelier, Vt.: J. D. Clark & Sons.

Merrill, Rev. J. L. (1869). *History of Acworth, N.H.* Pub. by Town of Acworth.

Merrill, Stuart (1979). *History and Genealogy of the Barnstead Early Families from 1727 to 1770. Typescript "2d edition."*

Merrimack Historical Society (c1976). *The History of Merrimack, N.H., Vol. 1.* Merrimack, N.H.

Miller, Samuel L. (1910). *History of the Town of Waldoboro, Maine.* Wiscasset, Me.: Emerson.

**Molyneux, Nellie Z. R. (1911). *History of the Eaton Families.* Syracuse, N.Y.: C. W. Bardeen.**

Minard, M. Elizabeth (c1983). *History of Westminster [Vt.], 1791-1981.* Westminster, Vt.: Town of Westminster.

Moore, J. Bailey (1893). *History of the Town of Candia, Rockingham County, N.H.* Manchester, N.H.: Geo. W. Browne.

Moses, John M. (1951). *Early Settlers of Northwood, N.H.* Typescript, filmed on FHL US/CAN 15551, item 5.

Moulton, Virginia P. (1995). *A History of Jay, Maine.* Penobscot Press.

Mower, Walter L. (1938), *Sesquicentennial History of the Town of Greene, Me., 1775 to 1900.* Bowie, Md.: Heritage Books, Inc.

Mulligan, Adair D. (1995). *The Gunstock Parish: a History of Gilford, N.H.* West Kennebunk, Me.: Phoenix Publishing.

Musgrove, Richard W. (1904). *History of Bristol, N.H.* Bristol, N.H.: R. W. Musgrove.

North, James W. (1870). *The History of Augusta from the earliest settlement to the present time.* Augusta, Me.: Clapp & North.

Noyes, Benjamin Lake (ca.. 1942?). *Genealogical History of Deer Isle Families. Series 2, Vol. 10: Eaton.* L.D.S. Film #0 896 712. [N.B.: this item contains much local color about Eaton families on Deer Isle and its environs. It is, however, somewhat erratic on detailed facts, and certainly was never proofread with care. My favorite passage is the introduction of James[6] Eaton, the youngest son of Theophilus[5]: "b. abt. 1754; d. abt 1760, so last son named James & he succeeded to his father's estate at "Dow Town," on the north shore of North West Harbor, D. Isle, and sold it about 1913 & moved to Prospect, Me. Prospect records have "Deacon James Eaton d. Mar. 13, 1825."]

Noyes, Harriet E. (1899, 1903). *A Memorial History of Hampstead, N.H.*, Vols. I and II. Boston, Mass.: George B. Reed.

Oak, Lyndon (1912). *History of Garland, Me.* Dover, Me.: Observer Publishing Co.

Oesterlin, Pauline Johnson (1998). *Hopkinton, N.H., Vital Records, Vol. I.* Bowie Md.: Heritage Books, Inc.

Oread Literary Club (1907). *History of the Town of Johnson, Vermont.* Burlington, Vt.: Free Press Printing.

*Papers of the New Haven Colony Historical Society* (1888), Vols. IV & VII. New Haven: Printed for the Society.

Parker, Benjamin F. (1901), *History of the Town of Wolfeborough, N.H.*
    Published by the Town.
Parker, Edward L. (1851). *The History of Londonderry, comprising the
    Towns of Derry and Londonderry, N.H.* Boston, Mass.: Perkins
    and Whipple.
Parker, Judge E. E. (1897). *History of the City of Nashua, N.H.* Nashua
    Telegraph publication.
Parsons, Usher (1872). *A Centennial History of Alfred, York Co., Me.*
    Sanford: Everts and Co.
Perkins, Esselyn G. (1971). *Wells; the Frontier Town of Maine.* Ogun-
    quit, Me,: E. G. Perkins.
Perley, Rev. Samuel (1897). "Marriages by Rev. Samuel Perley, While
    Minister at Hampton, N.H. and Other Places, 1767-1782." Com-
    municated by Rev. Henry Thayer. *New England Historic Gene-
    alogical Register, Vol. 51* (Oct. 1897), pp. 460-466.
Perley, Sidney (1880). *The History of Boxford, Essex Co., Mass., from
    the earliest settlement.* Boxford, Mass.: Sidney Perley.
Philbrick, John (undated). *Journal of Seabrook, N.H. Vital Records*
    (mostly deaths in the middle 19th century). Hand manuscript,
    Seabrook Historical Society.
Pickwick, Hazel A. (1963). *Lisbon's 10 Score Years, 1763-1963.*
    Lisbon, N.H.
Pillsbury, Hobart (1927). *New Hampshire: Resources, Attractions and
    Its People.* New York: the Lewis Historical Publishing Co.
Pitkin, Ozias C. & Fred E. Pitkin (1941). *History of Marshfield, Vermont.*
    Pub. at No. Andover, Mass.
Poling, Evangeline K. (c. 1977). *Welcome Home to Deering, N.H.*
    Canaan, N.H.:Phoenix Publishing.
Poore, Alfred (1881). *A Memoir and Genealogy of John Poore.* FHL
    US/CAN Film #1435473, item 15.
Putnam, Cora (c1958). *The Story of Houlton [Me.].* Portland, Me.:
    House of Falmouth.
Ramsdell, George A. (1901). *History of Milford, N.H.* Concord, N.H.:
    Rumford Press.
Randall, Oran Edward (1882). *History of Chesterfield, N.H.* Pub.
    Brattleboro, Vt.
*Representative Citizens of the State of New Hampshire* (1902). A volume
    of *The American Series of Popular Biographies.* Boston, Mass.:
    New England Historical Publishing Company.
Read, Benjamin (1892). *The History of Swanzey, N.H.* Salem, Mass:
    Salem Press.
Reed, Parker M. (1893). *History of Bath [Me.] and Environs.* Salem,
    Mass.: Higginson Book Co.
Remich, Daniel (1911). *History of Kennebunk from its earliest settle-
    ment to 1890.*
Richardson, Douglas (1993). "The English Origin of John[1] Eaton
    (1590-1668) of Salisbury and Haverhill, Massachusetts,"
    *The American Genealogist* (Jan. 1993), pp. 48-54.

Roberts, Millard F. (1891). *Historical Gazeteer of Steuben County, New York.* Syracuse, New York.

Robinson, Reuel (1907). *History of Camden & Rockport, Me.* Camden, Me.: Camden Pub. Co.

Rollins, Alden M. (1997). *Vermont Warnings Out.* Camden, Me.: Picton Press.

Runnels, Rev. M. T. (1881). *History of Sanbornton, N.H.* Boston, Mass.: Mudge & Son.

Sanborn, Melinda Lutz (2002). "Vital Records from the Argus and Spectator of Newport, N.H.," *The New Hampshire Genealogical Record* (Vol. 19, No. 1, p. 23).

Saunderson, Rev. Henry H. (1876). *History of Charlestown, N.H.* Pub. Claremont, N.H.

Sawyer, Rev. Roland D. (1946). *History of Kensington, N.H., 1663 to 1945.* Farmington, Me.: Knowlton & McLeary.

Scales, John (1923). *History of Dover, N.H.* Manchester, N.H.: J. B. Clarke.

Secomb, Daniel F. (1883). *History of the Town of Amherst, N.H.* Concord, N.H.: Evans, Sleeper & Woodbury.

Sewall, Oliver (1875). *History of Chesterville, Me.* Farmington, Me.: J. Swift, Publisher.

Seward, Josiah L. (1921). *History of Sullivan, N.H.,* Vol. II.

Shores, Venila L. & Ruth H. McCarty (1986). *Lyndon [Vt.]. Gem in the Green.* Lyndonville, Vt.: Town of Lyndon.

Smith, Etta (1954). *History of Peterborough, N.H.,* Vol. II. Pub. Rindge, N.H.

*Society of Colonial Wars, 1892-1967: 75th Anniversary* (1967).

Stackpole, Everett S. (1899). *History of Durham, Me.; with genealogical notes.* Lewiston, Me.: Press of Lewiston Journal Co.

Stackpole, Everett S. (1903). *Old Kittery and her Families.* Lewiston, Me.: Press of Lewiston Journal Co.

Stark, Caleb (1860). *History of the Town of Dunbarton, Merrimack Co., New Hampshire, 1751-1860.* Concord, N.H.: G. P. Lyon.

Stearns, Ezra S. (1906). *History of Plymouth, N.H.,* Vol. II. Cambridge, Mass.: University Press.

Stearns, Ezra S. (Ed.) (1908). *Genealogical and Family History of the State of New Hampshire.* Vol. I. New York: The Lewis Publishing Co.

Stinchfield, John C. (1901). *History of the Town of Leeds, Androscoggin Co.* Lewiston, Me.: Press of Lewiston Journal Co.

Tenney, Jonathan (1883). *New England in Albany (New York).* Boston: Crocker & Co.

Thayer, Mildred N. & Mrs. E. W. Ames (1962). *Brewer, Orrington, Holden and Eddington: History and Families.* Brewer, Me.: Press of L.H. Thompson.

Thompson, Daniel P. (1860). *History of the Town of Montpelier [Vt], 1781-1860, with biographical sketches.* Montpelier, Vt.: E. P. Walton.

Thompson, Neil D. (1997). "The Origin and Parentage of Francis Eaton
    of the *Mayflower*." *The American Genealogist* (Jul-Oct 1997),
    pp. 301-304.
Townsend, Patricia McCurdy (1996). *Vital Records of Lubec, Maine,
    prior to 1882.* Rockport, Me.: Picton Press.
Van Antwerp (1996) (with R. S. Wakefield). *Family of Francis Eaton.*
    Vol. 9 of *Mayflower Families through Five Generations.* Ply-
    mouth, Mass.: General Society of Mayflower Descendants.
Van Attan, Laurence J. (1875). *History of the Town of Rindge, N.H.
    from 1736 to 1874.* Boston, Mass.: Press of Geo. H. Ellis.
Vickery, James B. (1954). *A History of the Town of Unity, Maine.*
    Manchester, Me.: Falmouth Pub. House.
Vose, Ellen F. (1932). *Robert Vose and his Descendants.* Boston, Mass.:
    Private printing.
Voye, Nancy S. [Ed.] (c. 1975) *Massachusetts Officers in the French
    and Indian Wars, 1748-1763.* Boston, Mass: Society of Colo-
    nial Wars in Massachusetts.
Walker, George H. & Co. (1982) provided the maps first published in
    the late nineteenth century, which have since been reprinted in
    several volumes, including *The Old Maps of Northeastern Essex
    County, Mass. in 1884,* by the Saco Valley Printing Co.,
    Fryeburg, Me., the latter being published in 1982.
Wallace, R. Stuart (1994). "The "Irish Party" and the New Hampshire/
    Massachusetts Boundary Controversy, 1719-1741." *Historical
    New Hampshire,* Vol. 49, No. 2.
Wallace, William Allen (1910). *History of Canaan, N.H.* Concord, N.H.:
    Rumford Press.
Warren, Henry P. (1879). *The History of Waterford, Oxford Co., Maine.*
    Portland, Me.: Hoyt, Fogg & Danham.
Watts, J.Y. & Maresh, I.M. (1985). *Camden-Rockport, Me. Births-
    Deaths-Marriages.* Typescript.
Welch, Linda, Carmine Guica & Barbara Kingsbury (1995). *Families
    of Cavendish [Vt.], Early settlers in the Black River Valley,
    Windsor Co., Vt.* Cavendish: Cavendish Historical Scoiety.
Wells, Frederic P. (1902). *History of Newbury, Vermont: from the
    discovery of the Coos country to the present.* St. Johnsbury, Vt.:
    Caledonian Co.
Wheeler, Edmund (1879). *History of Newport, N.H.* Concord, N.H.
Wheeler, George A. (1873). *History of Castine, Penobscot and Brooks-
    ville, Me.* Bangor, Me.: Burr and Robinson.
Wheeler, George A. & Henry W. Wheeler (1878). *History of Brunswick,
    Topsham and Harpswell, Me.* Boston, Mass.: Alfred Mudget.
Whitcher, William F. (1905). *Some Things About Coventry-Benton, New
    Hampshire.* Woodsville, N.H.: News Print.
Whitcher, William F. (1919). *History of the Town of Haverhill, N.H.*
    Concord, N.H.: Rumford Press.
Whittemore, Joel (1888). *History of Fitzwilliam, N.H.* New York: Burr.
Williamson, Joseph (1887). *History of the City of Belfast in the State of
    Maine, Vol. I.* Portland, Me.: Loring, Short and Harmon.

Wilson, James G. and John Fiske (1887-9), *Appleton's Cyclopedia of American Biography.* D. Appleton and Co.

Woodman, Betsey H. (1983). "Salt Haying, Farming and Fishing in Salisbury, Massachusetts: The Life of Sherb Eaton (1900-1982). *Eseex Institute Historical Collections*: July 1983.

Worcester, Samuel T. (1879). *History of the Town of Hollis, N.H.* Boston, Mass.: A. Williams.

Worthen, Augusta H. W. (1890). *History of Sutton, N.H.* Concord, N.H.: Republican Press Association

Young, E. Harold (1953). *History of Pittsfield, New Hampshire.*

# INDEX OF COGNATE FAMILIES

This index is dedicated to surnames other than Eaton. For the most part, this means surnames referring to families who have intermarried with our Eatons. Other types of cognate relationships, such as the adoption of children into or from non-Eaton families, are also included here, although such cases are few. Added as well are page references to a few other non-Eaton surnames important to our Eatons, such as "Molyneux," one of the main authors of Eaton genealogies.

**Abbot:** Charles 445 Thomas 99 197
**Ackerman:** Sally 78 147
**Adams:** Catherine 290 Joshua 43
**Adley:** Napoleon 453
**Aiken:** Margaret 359-60
**Aldrich:** George 426
**Alexander:** Ezekiel 124
**Allen:** Caleb 35 Caroline 357 Elizabeth 411 John 460 Mary 404 Seath 425 Truman 168 William 204
**Allenwood:** Joseph 297
**Allison:** Mary 327 497
**Ames:** Charity 392
**Anderson:** Thomas 177
**Andrews:** Emma 314 Janet 201 337
**Annis:** Laura 510
**Anson:** Theresa 240
**Arey:** Sylvester 388
**Argyle:** Jennie 384

**Armstrong:** Harriet 327 Widow 267 436
**Arnold:** Mrs Anna 48 76-7 Thomas 51
**Ash:** Judith 31 45 48
**Atwood:** Betsey 199 331
**Austin:** Baxter 435 Mrs Emma 418 George 148 Grace 418
**Avery:** Alanson 437 David 297 George 445 John 84
**Ayer(s):** Abigail 219 359 Peter 104 Mrs Rachel 39 58 Mrs Roena 521

**Babb:** Lelia 414
**Babson:** 277
**Bacon:** Harriet 251 409
**Badger:** Mary 164 292 Polly 201
**Bagley:** Ann 406 Eben 56 Eliza 377 379 Elizabeth 129-30 Mary 122 Sarah 129-30 Ruth 356 Valentine 537
**Bailey:** Alfred 265

Ebenezer 61 John 148 Joseph 327 Marietta 185 313 Mary 407 Ruth 114 225 William 352
**Baird:** Mary 411
**Bakeman:** Lovinia 275 448
**Baker:** George 426 Sarah A. 288
**Baldwin:** Albert 502
**Bamford:** James 465
**Bangs:** Clarence 415
**Barber:** Clara 459
**Barker:** Charles 330 Charlotte 257 418 Ella 307 Levi 242 Mehitable 422 Nathaniel 263
**Barnard:** Edmund 120 Edward 271 Reuben 146
**Barney:** Addie 312 480 Hosea 434
**Barnes:** George 153 424
**Barr:** John 199
**Barrett:** Orlando 166
**Bartlett:** Anna 218 356 Caroline 200 336 Jacob 236 Josseph 370 Mary 34

708

517 Nicholas 269
Phebe 450 Stephen
227
**Barton:** Mary 247
**Bass:** David 199
**Ba(t)chelder:** Au-
gusta 408 Freeman
217 William 114
**Battles:** James 280
**Beal:** Henry 262
James 315
**Beam:** Helen 393
**Bean:** Benning 342
Cordelia 254 415
Harriet 202 338
Vernon 197
**Beckman:** Abbie
310 478 Asa 539
David 161 Dolly
370 529 Grace 66
115 Hiram 271
Israel 228 Jacob 529
James 372 John 539
Lucy 539 Philip
529 Samuel 235
420 Susan 96 182
William 96
**Bedell:** William 426
**Beetle:** Henry 168
**Beigle:** Hiram 291
**Belden:** Edward 501
Herbert 500
**Bell:** Robert 415
**Bemis:** Charles 342
Lewis 290
**Bennett:** Frank 443
**Benson:** Lydia 241
387 Rufus 124
**Berford:** Mary 186
314
**Berry:** Clara 437
Frances (Mrs.) 225
Levi 174
**Bickford:** Jacob 251
Lovey 348 Mehit-

able 137 259
**Bidwell:**
George 269
**Billings:** Caroline
193 Catherine 242
Elizabeth 387 Grace
(Mrs.) 191 Harriet
458 Hattie 392 Jere-
miah 245 John 388
Mary 240 Peter 389
Phebe 241 387 Sol-
omon 81 Vesta 282
Zemira 242 394
**Blaisdell:**
Anna: 224 Calvin
378 John 257
Patience 356 519
**Blake:** Betsey 129
248 Elizabeth 44
74 Hezekiah 92
Olive 422 Sarah
241 386 Shuah 422
**Blakeslee:** Lucinda
107  209
**Blanchard:** Charles
381 David 99 Mar-
ion 338 509
**Blast-er** or **-ow:**
Angelina 244 397
Diantha 398 Lois
435 Lucy Ann 392
William 241
**Bliss:** Irene 102
**Blood:** Abigail 214
350 Alice 396
Hannah 434
**Bolley:** Melissa 310
**Bond:** Daniel 199
**Booth:** Emily 342
511
**Boston:** Mary 72
**Boulter:** Hannah
252 412
**Bourne** Abigail 73
140

**Boutwell** (-elle)
Jennie A. 501
**Bowan:** Elizabeth
113 222
**Bowdeleau:** John
156
**Bowden**: Horatio
385 William 412
**Bowen:** Alice 443
**Bowles:** 353
**Bowman:** Harvey
384 Mary 265 432
**Boyce:** Nellie 363
524
**Boyd:** Aaron 148
Clarissa 238 383
Daniel 536 David
161 Enoch? 74
Jeremiah 309 John
376 Joseph 371 Jo-
sephine 456 Lowell
376 Thomas 256
William 225
**Boyington:** Hartley
165
**Brackenbury:**
Elizabeth 112 217
**Brackett:** David?
530 George? 530
Helen 436
**Bracy:** Richard 459
**Bradbury:** Benjamin
132 Lydia 410 Mary
Ellen 382 Jacob 49
**Bradeen:** Hattie 410
**Bradford:** Abigail
90 168 Moses 98
Robert 98 Roxanna
113 220
**Bradley:** 333 Sally
109, 215
**Brady:** Mary 262
430
**Bragdon:** Abner 140
Sarah A. 140 263

538 Gilbert 404
**Donnell:** James
140 Nancy 427-8
**Dority:** Herbert
281 Lucius 281
**Doten:** Deborah
274 447 Joanna
274, 447 Mary
274 445
**Douglas(s):** Hannah 164 291-2
Moses 164 Sarah
193
**Doves:** Helen 430
**Dow:** Aaron 129
Abbie 539 Abbott
534 Adeline 480
Alvah 537 Betsey
146 270 Charles
531 Daniel 159
Diana 47 83-84
Eleanor 374, 536
Elihu 47 147 Eunice 406 Ezra 251
George 162 Henry
535 Jacob 147 531
Jane 256 Jeremiah
121 John 371 Joseph 51 Joshua 128
Laura 286 463 Levi
85 Lizzie 305 416
474 Lois 234 378
Lovilla 234 Manfred
310 Margaret 238
Mary J 331 503 Mehitable 121 238
Miriam, Mrs 308-9
Phebe, Mrs. 22
Philip 256 Polly
119 234 Sally 135
215 Samuel 128 Sarah 241 257 370
532 William 135
Zophar 115
**Downer:** Robert 28

**Downes:** William
432
**Drake:** Abraham 44
**Drande:** Aaron 123
**Draper:** Isaac 293
**Dresser:** Ambrose
186 Samuel 201
Sarah 202 340
**Drew:** John 252
Lydia 493 O. 276
**Drown:** Elsie
(Davis) 72 135-6
Mr. 136
**Dudley:** Alonzo 291
James 185
**Dunbar:** Rose 393
Samuel 397
**Dunham:** Abbie
460 Abigail 311
**Dunlap:** Jane 50 86
Lucy 165 294 Mary
87 164-5
**Dunn:** Charles 493
**Dunning:** Lorania
467
**Durgin:** Betsey 149
272
**Durrell:** Oliver 423
**Dustin:** Hannah 37
555 Thomas 36-7
**Dutch:** Ebenezer 104
Statira 276 449
**Dyer:** Ann 539 Benjamin 445
**Dykeman:** George
264

**Ealot:** Jonathan 49
**Earl:** Mr. 165
**Eastman:** Ammi
278 Elizabeth 212
Ezra 98 George 278
Mary 163 Mehitable
86 163 Sarah: 98
185 216 354

**Eau, de:** Helena 402
**Edes:** Edward 137
**Edgecomb:** Dorcas
252 410
**Edgerly:** Mary 527
**Edmunds:** Betsey 99
219 Polly 153 279
**Edwards:** Mercy 170
**Ela:** Betsey (Swain)
227
**Eldridge:** Nancy
253
**Elkins:** Florence
457
**Ellinwood:** Joseph
268
**Ellis:** Abbie J. 517
John 400 Ralph 287
**Ellms:** Addie 332
**Emerson:** Abbie
436 Abigail 58 104
Abraham 56 Alice
108 211 Amanda
268 437 Comfort
106 Elizabeth 95
181 195 310 Frank
464 Hannah 61-2
95-6 Marden 146
Mary J. W. 350-1
Mehitable 212 347
Oliver 62 Phineas
104 Sarah 57-58
105 204 Susan 247
403 Stephen 86
**Em(m)erton:** Lucy
151 Sally 81 150-51
**Emery:** Hannah 169
297 Mary 73 137
Philip 197 Stephen
261
**English:** Alice 101
**Evans:** George 257
Joanna 149 273
John 343 Martha
540 Sarah 295 Susa-

nna 204 342
**Everett:** Charles
329 Ella 540 542

**Fabyan:** Horace 247
Samuel 260
**Fairbanks:** Joseph
90 168
**Fales:** Ella 296, 471
**Farley:** Clarissa 185
311 Roanna 405
**Farnham:** Esther
292
**Farnsworth:** Lucy
102
**Farrar:** Emma 418
Randall 268
**Farrington:** Patty
112
**Faulkner:** Francis
466
**Favor:** Frances 439
Polly 153 278
**Felch:** Elias 160
Henry 371 Jane
(Page) 68 John 530
Josiah 416 Julia 270
439 Louisa 370 530
Reuben D. 183
**Fellows:** Abigail 45
79 George 383 Hub-
bard 178 Lucy 136
258
**Fenley:** William
263
**Fernald:** Carrie 289
465
**Ferrin:** Ebenezer
197 Francis 197
**Ferriss:** E. J.: 167
**Few:** Susie 500
**Fielding:** Ellen 196
328
**Fifield:** Peter 213
**Finn:** Antoinette

544
**Finny:** Dorcas 276
450
**Fisher:** Adello 514
Ann 208 346
**Fittz(s):** Abby 180
306 Dudley 497
John 536 (2) Sarah
(Eaton) 530
**Flagg:** Charles 494
**Flanders:** 144 And-
rew 142 David 371
Ezekiel 266 Philip
28
**Fletcher:** Edward
454 George 346
John K. 156
**Flint:** Adams 153
Daniel 184
**Flood:** David 129
Samuel 171
**Floyd:** Annie 456
**Follansbee:** Betsey
370 531 Mary 250
408 Margaret 532
William 257
**Folsom:** Abigail 58
106
**Foote:** Lucien 229
**Forest:** Sarah 223
361
**Foster:** Edwin 423
Ernest 458 Henry
124 241 Joseph 219
Polly: 96 181-2
**Fought:** Columbus
170
**Fowler:** Abner 535
Andrew 420 Anne
421 535 Arthur 420
Belinda 380 Charles
421 Cyrus 381 Den-
nis 531 Eliza J. 421
Elizabeth 115 232
Emma 382 Freeman

421 Hannah 42 63
Israel F. 533 Jacob
133 229 James 118
420 Jesse 203 John
535 Lowell 421 Lu-
cretia: 533 Lydia 44
74-75 Mary 258 (2)
420-1 537 Miriam
133 Philena 372
Rhoda (Hook) 372
Samuel 375 535
Sarah 374 535 418
Sewell 375 379
Sidney: 531
**Franconette:** Isa-
bella: 441
**Frathy**: Sally 254
**Frazier:** Melita 440
**French:** Abigail 70
Benjamin 165 Bet-
sey 85 160 Clinton
330 David 246 Ebe-
nezer 199 George
376 441 Hannah 99
113 186 222 Josiah
79 96 Josiah, Jr 67
Lycertia 444 Mary
28 32 33 50-51 Mo-
ses(?) 178 Phineas
163 Roena 521
Ruth 93 179-80
Sally: 79 141-3
149 Sarah 74
**Friend:** Cora 450
Elisha 277 Jeremi-
ah 274 Martha 276
451 Sarah 450 Su-
san 448
**Frost:** Esther 253
414 John D. 257
Joseph M. 171
**Frye:** Elizabeth 104
192 Mary Jane: 422
**Fuller:** Frank 535
Mary J. 522

714

**Fulton:** Ann 312
479
**Furbush:** Aphia 137
260
**Furlong:** Frank 172

**Gage:** 227 Josephine
499 Mary 61 108
Nancy 195 325
Pearse 60
**Gale:** Levi B 185
**Gard(i)ner:** Almon
246 George 454 Liz-
zie 452 Mr. 367
William 170
**Garfi:** Joseph 553
**Garland:** Eudoxy
253 George 417
**Gatcomb:** Vianna
450
**Gay:** Jabez 90
Richard 444
**George:** Elizabeth
82 152-3 Ezekiel
153 Jemima 82 153
Mary 182 309 344
Nathan 146 Sarah
198 William 153
**Gerrish:** Franklin
130
**Getchell:** Isaac 261
**Gibbs:** Ellen 454
**Gibson:** Alice 337
504 Sophalia 185
312 Susan 329 498
**Gile:** John K. 107
**Gillingham:** Alzina
224 363
**Gilman:** Hope 143
267 Millie 435
**Gleason:** Mary 192
**Glines:** Lavinia 148
Susan 148
**Glover:** Thomas
170

**Gloyd:** Margaret 308
476
**Godkin:** Elizabeth
196
**Gold:** William 403
**Goodell** Francis 352
**Goodhue:** Ann 360
Lewis 541
**Goodridge:** Eliza-
beth 205 Nathaniel
168
**Goodwin:** Jane 131
251 Judith 70 130
Louise 137 259
Phebe 248 404
**Gordon:** Harriet 259
421-2 Mary 365 526
Sally 105 Samuel
141 164 Stephen
366
**Goss:** Fanny J 312
Mary C. 312 479
**Gould:** Daniel 439
Lucretia 270 Mary
289 Maria 501
Nathaniel 191
Rebecca 199 332
**Gove:** Hiram 371
Judith 163 290
Mary (Stickney) 68
**Grace:** Eliza Ann
187 314
**Graham:** John 191
**Grant:** Jane 87 165
Joanna 275 448
Maud 460 Ruth 275
Simeon 155 Susan
275 448
**Grass:** Adaline, Mrs.
480
**Gray:** Amaziah 245
Christopher 124
Electa 388 Eveline
359 George 385
John 244 Otis 399

Robert 282 William
241
**Greeley:** Abigail 54
93 Edward 112
Hannah 85 161 Mo-
ses 213 Rachel 44
78 95
**Green:** Abigail 265
Albion 534 Jacob
34 41 70 Jemima
71 132 Nathan 54
Phebe 67 120-1
Sarah J 518 Sulli-
van 157
**Greenlaw:** Jeremi-
ah 390 Lillian 284
Sarah J. 354 Susan
157, 285-6 William
126
**Greenleaf:** Philip
85
**Greer:** Mary 332
503
**Gregg:** Sarah 186
313-4
**Gridley:** Caroline
328
**Griffin:** S.P. 172
**Griffing:** Daniel 58
**Grindle:** Johnson
387 Joshua 277
**Gross:** Elizabeth
388 George 389
Ida W. 390 Marga-
ret 390
**Groth:** John 28
**Grout:** Azubah 103
190
**Gunner:** Jennie 260
**Gunnison:** Walter
442
**Gutterson:** James
108
**Gynan:** A. J. 376
Annie 376 538

Clarie E. 536

**Hackett:** Betsey 135
256 Julia 168 295
**Hadley:** Alice 104
196 Betsey 104 199
Louisa 215 352
**Hagar:** Solon 156
**Hale:** Judith 38 56
**Haley:** Alonzo 172
John 91
**Hall:** Almira 182
308 Eliza J. 444
Frank 537 William
312 Winfield 493
**Halleck:** Willis 402
**Hamblen:** Jesse 459
**Hambly:** Susan 412
**Hamilton:** Daniel
445 William 444
**Hanaford:** Lucy 169
296-7 George 405
**Hancock:** Zilpha
248 404-5
**Hansen:** Rebecca
(Mrs.) 305
**Hanson:** Polly 245
401
**Harding:** Arabelle
498 Josiah 81
**Hardy:** Abijah 385
Annie 441 Edward
394 Hannah 204
343 Horatio 399
Jacob 29 Joanna
388 Lucy 124 241
391 Rosella 398
Sarah C. 398
William H.: 537
**Hare:** Charlotte 441
**Harmon:** Fred 416
Sarah (Eaton) 535
**Harriman:** Anna
464 Harriet 443
Joseph 38 Mehitable

39 61 William 287
**Harris:** Bertha 410
Jerome 290 Emma
456
**Hartshorn:** Lucy
329 500
**Harvey:** Hannah 153
385-6 Joseph 242
Louisa 242 392
Margaret 242 392
Martha 391 Philena
389
**Haskell:** Abigail
124 Barbara 157 285
Caleb 462 Daniel
395 Everett S 285
Freeman 400 Han-
nah 125-6 Ignatius
125 Laura Jane 400
Mary 241, 285 390
Moses 311 Orrace
386 Peter 241 386
Solomon 386 Susan
385
**Haskins:** Vashti
493
**Hassel:** Frank 393
**Hatch:** Almeda 262
428 Benjamin 72
Betsey 137 261
Dorcas 137 261
Eben 260 261 James
137 Mary Ann 428
Nancy: 261 425
Sarah 137 261
**Hatfield:** Theodore
301
**Hathorne:** Warren
171
**Hawkes:** Ann 333
**Hayes:** Edward 174
John 141
**Haynes:** Augustus
227 J.C. 217 Julia
146 271 Tilly 257

**Hayward:** Rebecca
196
**Hazeltine:** Joseph
35 Lucy 99 186
Moses 103 Phebe
253 413 Rebecca
105 204-5 Sylvia
343
**Heald:** Nancy 169
297
**Heard:** Emily 300
**Heath:** Abiah 201
Daniel 437 Nehe-
miah 61
**Hebert:** Charles 454
**Hemmenway:** 278
**Hemphill:** Abbie
501 Amos 330
**Hemstreet:** Philena
279 455
**Henderson:** Fanny
450 George 233
**Hendrick(s):** Addie
437 Caroline 398
George 400 Sophia
241 384 Susan G.
398
**Henley:** Elizabeth
220 359
**Henry:** Mary 533
**Herrick:** Abigail 81
151 Medora 448 Mr.
276 Susanna 151
276
**Hersom:** Isabel 437
**Higgins:** Arnold
316 Blanche 435
**Hildred:** Lucretia
433
**Hildreth:** Mary 192
324
**Hill(s):** Anna
(Blaisdell) 224
Betsey 441 Rachel
185 313 Samuel 73

716

Stephen 247 Vivi-
enne (Mrs.) 543
William 123
**Hilliard:** Daniel
227
**Hilton:** Jane 114
225 Phebe 265 432
William 428
**Hinkson:** Benjamin
257 Hebor 257 John
49 Samuel 418
**Hislid:** David 246
**Hitchcock:** Charles
493
**Hoag:** Jonathan 404
**Hobbs:** Betsey 261
427 Emma 515
**Hobson:** Sarah 498
**Holden:** Amasa 125
**Holland:** John 384
387 Lydia (Eaton)
397 Nancy 386
**Holt:** Lydia 467
**Holton:** Clarissa
428 Elias 216
**Honnold:** Auria 384
**Hook:** Elizabeth 49
Rhoda 79 147 372
Sally 93 179
**Hooper:** Otis 459
William A. 387
**Hopkins:** 134 Allen
151 Joanna 277 452
**Horne:** Richard 154
William 199
**Hosmer:** Asa 91
Harriet 170 297
**Houston:** Mr. 152
**Hovey:** Horatio 423
Myron 413
**How(e):** 172 Calvin
464 Clara 278 454
Henry 286 Joseph
97 Warren 497
**Howard:** Abigail

125 243 Betsey 84
158 Catherine 124
240 Edward 80
George 243 244
Martha 240 Thomas
240 William 170
**Hoyt:** Eben 136
Eliza 270 440
Enoch 249 Laura
382 Nancy 502
Pelatiah 75 Philean
287 464 Sarah 113
224
**Hubbard:** Hannah
27 33 Thankful 51
87
**Huckins:** Love(y)
236
**Huddleston:** Lucre-
tia 382
**Huggins:** Sarah 457
**Hughlett:** Catherine
181 306
**Hull:** Caroline 182
308-9
**Hunkins:** Edna 61
Lovey 382
**Hunnewell:** Louisa
149 272-3
**Hunt:** Hannah 373
534 Pauline 228
371-2 William 353
**Huntoon:** Philip
101 Joseph 213
**Huse:** Daniel 365
Moody 270 (2)
**Hussey:** Francis 426
**Hutchins:** Jane 42
66-7 Jeremiah 105
Martha 449 Ruth
109 216 Stilson
105, 205
**Hutchinson:** Ann
398 Charles 285
Gardner 463 Isaac

254

**Ingalls:**
Judith 104 196
Ruth 25
**Irving:** Thomas 417

**Jackman:** Abigail
66 117-8 Eliza 360
Ezra 160 Francis
288 Fred 417 Levi
93 Martha 255 415
Rachel 465 Rebecca
477 William 213
**Jackson:** Laura
425 Rebecca 308
**Jacobs:** Abigail
262 Bela 90 Dorcas
141 264 William
140
**Jameson:** 260
**Janvrin:** Albert 417
Alberta 381 Char-
lotte 376 Daniel
370 Joanna 258
John 255 639
Joseph E. 533
**Jaques:** Effie 419
**Jaquith:** Parker
245
**Jarnagin:** Sarah
341
**Jarvis:** Charles 291
**Jenkins:** Abby 424
Eliza 427 Ella 302
Susan E. 424
**Jenks:** M. 345
**Jewell:** Aaron 213
Fred M. 407 Benja-
min R.: 250
**Jewett:** Abner 295
George 132
**Johnson:** Angie 312
479 Annie 282 458
Dolly (Mrs.) 434

**Meeder:** Abigail 54
93 142 265
**Merithew**: Americus 389
**Merriam:** Hattie
439-40
**Merrick:** Hezekiah
245
**Merrill:** 286 517
Abither 74 Andrew
235 Betsey 350
Charles O. 307
Cynthia Ann 259
Frank 417 420
Ismenie 248 403
John 71 192 435
Judith 222 360
Lovilla (Dow) 234
Mary 50 Molly 55
94-95 Nancy 66 115
Parker 131 Ruth 42
70-71 96 182-3
Samuel 39 71 (2)
Sarah 71 135
William 149
**Merrow:** Abigail
276 Hannah 291
466
**Meserve:** Nellie 434
Sarah 414
**Messer:** James 105
Robert 144
**Michaels:** Belinda
474
**Miers:** William 294
**Miles:** John 414
**Miller:** Amelia 172
300 Margaret 325
495 William 360
**Millet:**Annie 87
164 264 430
**Mills:** Elizabeth J.
351
**Minard:** Alma: 310
478

**Mitchell:** Albert
384 Lydia 100 187
Sarah 100 187
Violetta 187 315
**Mobley:** Amanda
409
**Molyneux:** Nellie
Z. R. ix-xi 44 52
58 106 296 346
**Monahan:** John
153
**Monroe:** George
393
**Montague:** William 416
**Moody:** Benjamin
309 Jane 234 378
Joseph 160 Joshua
255 Lucy 91 Ruth
378 Sarah 67 119
William 309
**Moon:** Winnie May
480
**Mooney:** Agnes
541
**Moor(e):** Betsy
94 180 198 329
Esther 151 Hiram
305 Jacob B. 92
Maria 411 Sarah
455
**Moreland:** Lena
532 Mary 381
**Morey:** 391 Belle
393 Maggie (Gross)
390 William 282
**Morgan:** Mary 213
348 Patty: 83, 154
Robert 259
**Morp:** Evelyn 328
**Morrill:** 236 Betsy
85 162 Hannah 260
424 Hattie 174 300
Isaac 432 Isaiah 431
James 340 Lucy 119

235 Mary 250 267
407 435 Moses 234
Sarah 33 51 William 160
**Morris:** Wilhelmina
384
**Morrison:** James
100 Nancy 92 174
Sarah E. 187 315
**Morse:** Caleb 104
Charity 247 Harris
267 John 247 Lena
473 Timothy 95
**Moulton:** Eunice
47 82 Jeremiah 261
Lydia 43 73 Moses
101
**Mountford:** Margaret: 208
**Mudgett:** Moses
159
**Mugridge:** John
343
**Muldoon:** John 418
**Mullaly:** Catherine
293 468
**Mulligan:** Catherine 430
**Murray:** Abigail
132 252

**Nash:** Henry 136
Sarah: 397
**Nason:** Maria 426
Nancy 164 Nathaniel 164
**Neal:** Eunice 274
443
**Nelson:** George 395
**Newcomb:** Burgess
445
**Newell:** Fanny 337
507
**Newhall:** Edward
262 Mercy 501

Mary 372 Mr. 156
Nancy: 272 Sarah
131 261 426 Tho-
mas J. 314
**Perley:** Joshua: 90
Samuel 65
**Perry:** 457 Abigail
370 529 Adaline
412 George 480
Nellie 436 Samuel
252 Susan M. 410
**Pettengill:** Hannah
195 326 John 192
**Pettigrew:**
Sarah M.: 428
**Pevear:** Mary 455
Vernon 435
**Phelps:** John 270
Melinda 339
**Philbrick:** Andrew
435 Sarah 120 236
Susan 203 342
**Phillips:** Ella 423
**Pickering:** Martha
285 461 Sally 150
**Pierce:** Ann 257
419 470 Irene 466
William S. 136
**Pike:** 271 Albert
268 Amanda 375
Caleb 49 Charles
531 Emma 453
Florence 382 Fran-
ces M.: 382 John J
288 Joshua 51 Nan-
cy 31 47 True 160
William: 47
**Pillsbury:** Eliza
219 358 Lyman 279
Melissa 351 515
Phebe 520
**Pingree:**
Sarah (Dodge): 538
**Piper:** Thomas 361
**Pitblado:** Anna 325

494
**Plum(m)er:** Betsey
57 99-100 Sarah 33
52-53 William 365
**Pollard:** Eunice 153
278
**Pomeroy:** Sarah
450
**Poor:** Elizabeth 104
191
**Porter:** Elizabeth
245 401 Henry 305
**Pottle:** A.W. 173
**Powell:** Ella 405
**Powers:** Levi 191
Moody 125 Will-
am 394
**Pratt:** Benjamin 432
**Pray:** Annorill 253
414
**Preble:** Thomas 251
**Presby:** Joseph 432
**Prescott:** Eliza Ann
179 Molly 365 Sal-
ly 227 Sarah 142
265 Walter 501
**Pressey:** Betsey 344
Clementine 283 Do-
rothy 84 157 Eliza J
283 459 Harriet 285
Polly 125 Susan C.
283 459
**Preston:** E. M. 296
**Price:** Florence 196
**Priest** David H. 193
Drusilla 353 517
Sylvester 192
**Prince:** Belle 174
Jane 112 218
Joel: 247
**Pritchard:** Mr. 47
**Proctor:** Hugh 82
Orlando 434
**Proudfit:** (Rev.)
148

**Prouty:** Russell 481
**Pruce:** 291
**Pruett:** John H. 427
**Pudsey:** Martha 494
**Pullen:** Madeleine J.
473
**Pulsifer:** C. K. 173
**Purrington:** Robert
82
**Putney:** Pluma 202
340

**Quimby:** Adelaide
442 Hattie 472
James 153 John 442
Lorenzo K. 466

**Ramsdell:** Eliza
236 382
**Rand:** Abigail 102
Elizabeth 102 Tabi-
tha 102 William
416
**Randall:** David 529
Edward 119 536
Isaac 172 William
372, 376
**Rankin:** Ada 295
470
**Ratliff:** Caroline
467
**Raymond:** Alice
456
**Raynes:** John 81
Mercy 125 Tryphosa
284 460
**Redlow:** Hannah
253
**Reed:** M. P. 172
Marion 438
William 168
**Remick:** Hannah
294 469 Mary 294
469-70
**Reynolds:** Abel

# INDEX OF EATONS

This index lists Eatons, alphabetized by given names, and ordered by generation within given names, to facilitate searches by era. The index does not cover the Appendix materials. We do, however, include wives who were Eatons by marriage, giving the their husband's generation plus a "W" suffix. (These same wives should also show up under their maiden names in the cognate family index.) Page citations in **bold** signal the person's most extensive reference, being usually the page(s) for their biographical note. Readers should know other conventions used as well. Like any other populations, Eatons often have multiple given names, and nicknames to boot. We have indexed mainly by relatively formal first given names (by "Sarah" even though the received designation is "Sarah 'Sally' Eaton"). But when our only reference is to "Sally Eaton," we list her as Sally, although formally she may indeed have been Sarah. In cases where the first given name is put in parentheses to show that the owner preferred the middle name, however, we have typically listed under both names. Also in some few cases where the record shows different spellings for a name pronounced the same way (Margery/Marjorie, or Alan/Allan/Allen), we have put all mentions in a single bin. These primary names are spelled out for the earliest generation presented, but shortened tags are entered for later generations in each bin. Finally, our page references do not indicte how many persons of the same name appear on this one page. The best rule is to study the whole page, even if you think you have already found your quarry on the first line.

379 434 Andr[10] 539
Angela[9] 466 Ang[9W] 425
Angeline[8] 283 310 Ange[8W] **397-8**
 Ange[9] 375 394
Angie[8W] **479**
Ann[3] 28 Ann[7] 132 169 173 189
 Ann[7W] **333 336 346-7** Ann[8] 297
 316 320 321 347 354 Ann[8W] **396
 419-20 470 475-6** Ann[9] 370
 391 414 423 424 457 476 Ann[9W]
 398 499 **539** Ann[10W] 535
Anna[5] 51 Anna[5W] **72-3 76-78 96
 97-8 108 224** Anna[6] 71 73 95
 108 Anna[7] 137 185 Anna[7W] **295
 316 339 356 360** Anna[8] 227 280
 288 291 318 319 321 339 347 Anna[8W] **427-8 464 479 494 511
 512 513** Anna[9] 401 421 449 460
 467 474 482 486 488 492 493 494
 503 518 519 Anna[9W] 418 422 Anna[10] 502 Anna[10W] 531
Anne[1W] **20-22** Anne[2W] 25 Anne[4]
 38 Anne[8] 322 Anne[8W] **493** Anne[9]
 488 Anne[9W] 421
Annie[7] 164 Anni[8] 263 293 300 321
 327 Anni[8W] **430 458 504** Anni[9]
 412 415 417 440 441 448 481 482
 483 489 491 503 513 514 Anni[9W]
 416 428 441 456 **538** Anni[10] 411
 450 529 532 Anni[10W] 538
Annoril[8W] **414**
Anson[8] 293 298 **468** Anson[10] 517
Antoinette[11W] 544
Apphia[7] 153 Aphi[7W] **260-61** Aphi[8]
 262
Aprandy[7] 174
Arabelle[9W] 498
Archelaus[7] 135 **256-7**
Archie[9] 402 440
Ardella[9] 405
Ardesira[8] 235 258
Ariel[7] 123 203 **341**
Armanilla[8] 318
Aroline[8] 251 288
Arthur[9] vii-ix 102-3 396 407 414

437 452 471 475 477 485 486
 487 488 489 492 501 504 515
 Art[10] 426 541
Arvilla[7] 183 Arv[8] 246 248 326 Arv[9W]
 454
Asa[6] 100 **187** Asa[7] 125 165 **243
 292-3** Asa[9] 489
Asa(h)el[8] 317 320 **484** 490 Asah[9]
 433 491
Asenath[7] 189 Asen[7W] **282** Asen[8] 249
 276 Asen[8W] **435-6** Asen[9] 399
Aubrey[9] 487
Augusta[7] 171 Aug[8] 325 346 Aug[8W]
 **522** Aug[9] 405 425 429 495 524
 529 Aug[9W] 408
Augustine[9] 450
Augustus[8] 258 284 350 **514**
Aura[8] 296
Aurelia[7] 134 225 Aurel[7W] **337**
Auria[9W] 384
Austin[9] 419 422
Avery[9] 450
Avis[9W] 481
Azel[6] 96 **181-2**
Azor[8] 257 **418**
Azuba[6W] **190-1**

Barbara[7W] **285** Barb[8W] **388-9 444-5**
 Barb[9W] 387 419
Barton[8] **346**
Beatrice[9] 463
Belinda[7] 133 Beli[7W] **269** Beli[8] 257
 Beli[8W] **380-1 465 474** Beli[9] 381
 382
Belle[9W] 393 Bel[10] 412
Benjamin[4] 33 **51** Benj[5] 42 49 51 53
 60 63 **66-7 84 91-2** Benj[6] 63 66
 79 84 85 87 91 94 107 113 **116-7
 160-1 209-10 220** Benj[7] 120
 140 150 161 170 171 173 193 211
 219 **272 274-5 288 298 300
 347 359** Benj[8] 233 241 249 250
 275 278 288 298 318 320 323 333
 337 350 **385-6 408 486** Benj[9]
 367 392 402 428 444 447 469 472

97 98 108 112 113 Mary⁶ᵂ **122-3
124 137 162 164-5 167-8 207**
Mary⁷ 116 119 142 146 147 148
151 152 155 156-7 159 160 161
167 168 169 170 171 174 177 178
183 184 186 188 189 193 195 197
199 205 208 211 212 217 218 253
Mary⁷ᵂ **240-1 253-4 268 270
271 275 276 280 281-2 292
302 305-6 307 309 314 323
324 325 344 347 348 350
356-7 357 363-4** Mary⁸ 227 229
233 238 239 240 241 243 244 247
249 250 254 255 258 260 261 262
263 265 266 268 271 273 274 275
277 279 280 284 285 287 291 292
294 296 302 309 310 314 316 317
318 319 320 321 323 324 326 327
328 329 332 333 338 339 340 342
344 345 346 347 348 350 351 352
353 357 359 364 **373-4 381
392-3** Mary⁸ᵂ **390-1 401 407-
8 408 419 420 421 430 430-1
432 435 435-6 438-9 445 455
456 456-7 467-8 469-70 474-
5 479 480-1 497 501-2 502-3
503 506 513 518 521 522 524**
Mary⁹ 366 367 372 374 378 379
380 381 385 398 399 401 403 404
408 409 412 415 416 418 420 421
424 426 429 430 432 435 437 440
442 444 445 448 454 455 457 458
459 462 464 466 467 470 477 481
482 483 484 485 486 488 489 490
491 492 493 500 502 507 511 514
520 Mary⁹ᵂ 366 372 381 382 387
400 404 410 411 428 460 481 501
517 522 **526 527 528 530 532
533** Mary¹⁰ 366 409 410 527 528
529 531 533 534 540 541 Mary¹⁰ᵂ
411 530
Matilda⁶ 105 205 246 Matil⁸ᵂ **417-
8 461** Matil⁹ 418
Mattie⁸ 300 Mat⁹ᵂ 413 Mat¹⁰ 412
Maude⁹ 512 523 Mau⁹ᵂ 460 Mau¹⁰

450 515
Maurice⁹ 430 512 524
May⁸ 318 356 May⁹ 504 May⁹ᵂ 480
May¹⁰ 412
Maynard¹⁰ 538
Mayhew⁸ 320 **489** 490
Medbury¹⁰ 450
Medora⁹ᵂ 448
Mehitable⁴ᵂ **47 61 62** Mehit⁵ 56
61 62 Mehit⁶ 109 113 Mehit⁶ᵂ
**163 172** Mehit⁷ 136 213 214
215 Mehit⁷ᵂ **238 259-60 347**
Mehit⁸ 259 260 275 Mehit⁸ᵂ **422-
3** Mehit⁹ 423
Melbourne⁹ 482 489
Melinda⁷ 189 Melin⁷ᵂ **338-9** Melin⁸
351 Melin⁹ 366
Melissa⁶ᵂ **172** Melis⁷ 172 Melis⁸
330 Melis⁸ᵂ **515 541** Melis¹⁰ 532
Melita⁹ᵂ 440
Melona⁸ᵂ **481**
Melville⁹ 391
Melvina⁸ᵂ **472**
Merchant⁷ 218 **356-7**
Mercy⁵ᵂ **52** Mercy⁶ 96 Mercy⁶ᵂ
**170** Mercy⁷ᵂ **243 289-90**
Mercy⁹ᵂ **501 537**
Meribah⁵ᵂ **67-9** Merib⁶ᵂ **133**
Merib⁸ 255 256
Merrill⁷ 183 350 Merr⁹ 386
Merle⁹ 470
Merton⁹ 437
Meshellum⁷ 204
Mildred⁹ 473 Mild¹⁰ 450
Millie⁹ᵂ 435
Milton⁹ 438
Mindwell⁸ 292
Minerva⁸ 342
Minnie⁹ 408 413 Min⁹ 389 Min¹⁰
376 539
Minora⁹
Minot⁷ 196
Miranda⁷ᵂ **301** Miran⁸ᵂ **412-3** Mi-
ran⁹ 413
Miriam⁶ 66 Miri⁶ᵂ **127-8** Miri⁷

www.ingramcontent.com/pod-product-compliance
Lightning Source LLC
Chambersburg PA
CBHW072036020426
42334CB00017B/1288